AA
The 2007
Golf Course
Guide

21st edition published 2006
Published by AA Publishing, which is a trading name of Automobile Association Developments Limited, whose registered office is:
Fanum House, Basingstoke, Hampshire RG21 4EA
Registered number 1878835

Advertisement Sales: advertisingsales@theAA.com
Editorial: lifestyleguides@theAA.com

Picture credits: Corbis cover, 3, 4, 5, 6, 10, 13, 15, 16, 17, 20, 318, 392, 421; AA 7; AA/P Bennett 8; AA/M Birkitt 12; AA/R Strange 9; Photodisc 11.

Typeset/repro by Servis Filmsetting Ltd, Manchester
Printed and bound in Italy by Printer Trento S.r.l

A CIP catalogue record for this book is available from the British Library
ISBN-10: 074954 9173
ISBN-13: 978 074954 9173
A02827

Maps prepared by the Cartography Department of The Automobile Association.

Contents

Using the guide 4

AA hotel & guest accommodation 6

Driving ranges 8

Golf courses

England 20

Channel Islands 314

Isle of Man 316

Scotland 318

Wales 392

Ireland 421

Atlas of golf course locations 480

Index of locations 497

Classified advertising 510

Using the guide

The golf courses in the AA Golf Course Guide are selected by the AA and their entry is free of charge. The guide is updated every year for new courses, changes, closures and new features, and an AA recommended accommodation follows most entries. To avoid disappointment we recommend that you phone before visiting a golf course; please mention the guide when you make an enquiry.

The country directories are arranged alphabetically by county, then by town or village name. The town or village locations are shown on the atlas and listed in the index at the end of the guide. The details of a sample entry are explained below.

Sample Entry

1 **OXFORD** Map 04 SP50

2 **North Oxford** Banbury Rd OX2 8EZ

☎ 01865 554924 🖷 01865 515921

3 **Gently undulating parkland course.**

4 ***18 holes, 5736yds, Par 67, SSS 67, Course record 62. Club membership 700.***

5 **Visitors** Mon-Sun & BHs. 6 **Societies** Booking required.

7 **Green Fees** not confirmed. 8 **Prof** Robert Harris

9 **Facilities** 10 **Conf** Facilities Available 11 **Location** 3m N of city centre on A423

12 **Hotel** ★★★ 66% The Oxford Hotel, Godstow Rd, Wolvercote Roundabout, OXFORD

☎ 01865 489988 173 en suite

1. **Town name and map reference** The atlas at the end of the guide shows the locations of the courses. The map reference includes the atlas page number and the National Grid reference. The grid references for the Republic of Ireland are unique to this atlas.
2. **Club name and contact details** Where the club name appears in italic we have been unable to verify current course details with the club. You should check any details with the club before your visit.
3. **Description** The description highlights the significant features of the course or courses.
4. **Course statistics** The number of holes, distance, par, Standard Scratch Score, Course Record, and the number of club members.
5. **Visitor information** Playing days, booking requirements or restrictions are noted. A small number of courses in the guide are not open to visitors and we have included their details for information only.
6. **Society information** Booking requirements or restrictions for societies.
7. **Green fees** The most up-to-date green fees are given, including any variations or restrictions. Where green fees are not confirmed you should contact the club for current rates. An asterisk * denotes 2006 fees.
8. **Professional** The name of the club professional(s).
9. **Facilities** See the key to symbols on page 5.

KEY TO SYMBOLS

☎ Phone number
Fax number
€ Euro (Republic of Ireland only)
No credit card
Lunch
Dinner
Bar snacks
Tea/coffee
Bar open midday and evenings
Accommodation at club
Changing rooms
Well-stocked shop
Clubs for hire
Motorised cart/trolley for hire
Buggies for hire
Trolley for hire
Driving range
★ AA Star hotel
♦ AA Diamond guest house
Town House Hotel
Country House Hotel
Restaurant with Rooms
U Hotel not yet rated by the AA
Travel Accommodation: AA Travel Accommodation

⑩ **Conference facilities** The available conference facilities are noted, and corporate hospitality days.

⑪ **Location** The location of the club is given in relation to the nearest town or motorway junction. Many golf courses are in rural locations and we do not provide detailed directions in the guide. You should contact the club for further details, or use the club's postcode on the **Route Planner** at **www.theAA.com**.

⑫ **Accommodation** An AA recognised hotel is provided for most entries. This does not imply that the hotel offers special terms for the golf club, though in some cases the golf course is in the grounds of the hotel. The Star or Diamond rating, Quality Assessment (%) score and AA Rosette restaurant award appear as applicable. Contact details and the number of rooms are given. Where there is no nearby AA recognised hotel, an AA guest accommodation is recommended. See pages 6-7 for details of AA ratings. Where golf courses offer club accommodation the bed symbol appears under Facilities. Unless the club accommodation has an AA Star or Diamond classification, the only AA recognised accommodation is the hotel or guest house that follows the entry.

Golf courses and hotels in the guide can illustrate their entry with a photograph or an advertisement.

To recommend a new course for the guide, please write to:
The Editor, AA Golf Course Guide
Fanum House Floor 14
Basingstoke, Hampshire RG21 4EA

Championship courses

Major championship courses have a full-page entry in the guide with a more extensive description. A selection of AA recognised hotels is given for these courses in the main directory.

Selected courses

Green boxes in the guide highlight selected courses considered to be of particular merit or interest. These may include historic clubs, particularly testing or enjoyable courses, or those in holiday areas popular with visiting golfers. The selection is not exhaustive nor totally objective, but it is independent - courses cannot pay to have an entry in the guide, nor can they pay to have a highlighted entry. Highlighted courses do not represent any formal category on quality or other grounds.

AA hotel & guest accommodation

AA hotel classification

★

In a one-Star hotel you should expect relatively informal yet competent service and an adequate range of facilities, including a television in the lounge or bedroom, and a reasonable choice of hot and cold dishes. The majority of bedrooms are en suite with a bath or shower room always available.

Run by professionally presented staff and offers at least one restaurant or dining room for breakfast and dinner.

★★★

Three-Star hotels have direct-dial phones, a wide selection of drinks in the bar, and last orders for dinner no earlier than 8pm.

★★★★

A four-Star hotel is characterised by uniformed, well-trained staff, additional services, a night porter and a serious approach to cuisine.

Finally, and most luxurious of all, five-Star hotels offer many extra facilities, attentive staff, top-quality rooms and a full concierge service. A wide selection of drinks, including cocktails, are available in the bar, and the impressive menu reflects the hotel's own style of cooking.

The Quality Assessment score appears after the Star rating for hotels in this guide. This is an additional assessment made by AA hotel inspectors, covering everything the hotel has to offer, including hospitality. The Quality Assessment score allows a quick comparison between hotels with the same Star rating: the higher the score the better the hotel.

Red stars highlight the very best hotels in Britain and Ireland across all ratings. Such hotels offer outstanding levels of quality, comfort, cleanliness and customer care, and serve food of at least one-Rosette standard. No Quality Assessment score is shown for hotels with red Stars.

The AA inspects and classifies hotels and guest accommodation under common quality standards agreed among the AA, VisitBritain, VisitScotland and VisitWales. Hotels receive a classification from one to five Stars, and guest houses receive from one to five Diamonds. AA recognised establishments pay an annual fee that varies according to the classification and the number of bedrooms. The establishments receive an unannounced inspection from a qualified AA inspector who recommends the appropriate classification. Return visits check that standards are maintained; the classification is not transferable if an establishment changes hands. These ratings show that your accommodation meets the AA's highest standards of cleanliness with the emphasis on professionalism, proper booking procedures, and a prompt and efficient service. The annual AA Hotel Guide and AA Bed & Breakfast Guide give further details of AA recognised establishments and the classification schemes. Details of AA recognised hotels, guest accommodation, restaurants and pubs are also available at www.theAA.com, along with a useful Route Planner and Map Finder.

AA guest house classification

♦

The AA's Diamond awards cover bed and breakfast establishments, reflecting guest accommodation at five grades of quality, with one Diamond indicating the simplest and five Diamonds the top end. The criteria for eligibility are guest care and quality rather than extra facilities. Guests should receive a prompt professional check in and check out, comfortable accommodation equipped to modern standards, regularly changed bedding and towels, a sufficient hot water supply at all times, good well-prepared meals, and a full English or continental breakfast.

Red Diamonds indicate the best places among three, four and five-Diamond ratings.

AA restaurant awards

Out of the many thousands of restaurants in the UK and Ireland, the AA recognises some 1800 as the best. The following is an outline of what to expect from restaurants with AA Rosette awards. To find your nearest restaurant, go to www.theAA.com.

Excellent local restaurants serving food prepared with care, understanding and skill, using good quality ingredients.

The best local restaurants, which aim for and achieve higher standards, better consistency and where a greater precision is apparent in the cooking. There will be obvious attention to the selection of quality ingredients.

Outstanding restaurants that demand recognition well beyond their local area.

Among the very best restaurants in the UK and Ireland, where the cooking demands national recognition.

The finest restaurants in the UK and Ireland, where the cooking stands comparison with the best in the world.

Driving ranges

ENGLAND

Bedfordshire

BEDFORD
The Bedford GC 21
Bedfordshire GC 21
Mowsbury GC 21
COLMWORTH
Colmworth & North Bedfordshire Golf Course 22
LUTON
Stockwood Park GC 23
SHEFFORD
Beadlow Manor Hotel & Golf & Country Club 23
TILSWORTH
Tilsworth Golf Centre 23
WYBOSTON
Wyboston Lakes 24

Berkshire

ASCOT
The Berkshire GC 24
Lavender Park Golf Centre 24
Mill Ride GC 24
BINFIELD
Blue Mountain Golf Centre 25
CHADDLEWORTH
West Berkshire Golf Course 25
MAIDENHEAD
Bird Hills Golf Centre 26
MORTIMER
Wokefield Park GC 26
READING
Hennerton GC 27
SINDLESHAM
Bearwood GC 27
SUNNINGDALE
Sunningdale GC 28
WOKINGHAM
Downshire Golf Complex 28
Sand Martins GC 28

Bristol

BRISTOL
Bristol & Clifton GC 28

Buckinghamshire

AYLESBURY
Aylesbury Golf Centre 31
BEACONSFIELD
Beaconsfield GC 31
BLETCHLEY
Windmill Hill Golf Centre 31
BURNHAM
Burnham Beeches GC 32
The Lambourne Club 32
CHALFONT ST GILES
Oakland Park GC 32
DAGNALL
Whipsnade Park 33
DENHAM
Buckinghamshire GC 33
IVER
Iver GC 33
Richings Park GC 34
LITTLE BRICKHILL
Woburn Golf & Country Club 35
LOUDWATER
Wycombe Heights Golf Centre 34
MARLOW
Harleyford GC 36
MENTMORE
Mentmore Golf & Country Club 36
MILTON KEYNES
Abbey Hill GC 36
STOKE POGES
Stoke Park Club 37
STOWE
Silverstone Golf Course 37
WAVENDON
Wavendon Golf Centre 37
WEXHAM STREET
Wexham Park GC 37
WING
Aylesbury Vale GC 38

Cambridgeshire

BOURN
Bourn Golf Course 38
BRAMPTON
Brampton Park GC 38
CAMBRIDGE
The Gog Magog GC 38
HEMINGFORD ABBOTS
Hemingford Abbots Golf Course 39
LONGSTANTON
Cambridge GC 39
MELDRETH
Malton Golf Course 39
PETERBOROUGH
Elton Furze GC 39
Peterborough Milton GC 40
PIDLEY
Lakeside Lodge GC 40
RAMSEY
Old Nene Golf & Country Club 40
ST NEOTS
Abbotsley Golf & Squash Club 40
THORNEY
Thorney Golf Centre 41

Cheshire

ANTROBUS
Antrobus GC 42
CHESTER
De Vere Carden Park Hotel Golf Resort & Spa 42
Eaton GC 42
Vicars Cross GC 42
DELAMERE
Delamere Forest GC 43
KNUTSFORD
Heyrose GC 44
Mere Golf & Country Club 44
MACCLESFIELD
The Tytherington Club 45
TARPORLEY
Portal Golf & Country Club 47
WILMSLOW
De Vere Mottram Hall 48
Styal GC 48
WINWICK
Alder Root GC 49

Cornwall & Isles of Scilly

BODMIN
Lanhydrock GC 49
CAMELFORD
Bowood Park Hotel & Golf Course 50
CONSTANTINE BAY
Trevose GC 51
FALMOUTH
Falmouth GC 51
LAUNCESTON
Trethorne GC 52
LOSTWITHIEL
Lostwithiel Hotel, Golf & Country Club 53
MAWGAN PORTH
Merlin Golf Course 54
ROCK
St Enodoc GC 55
ST AUSTELL
Porthpean GC 55

St Austell GC 55
ST MELLION
St Mellion Hotel, Golf & Country Club 56
ST MINVER
Roserrow Golf & Country Club 56
SALTASH
China Fleet Country Club 56
TRURO
Killiow GC 58
WADEBRIDGE
St Kew Golf Course 58

Cumbria

BRAMPTON
Brampton GC 59
CARLISLE
Stony Holme Municipal GC 60
CROSBY-ON-EDEN
Eden Golf Course 61
KENDAL
Carus Green Golf Course & Driving Range 61
PENRITH
Penrith GC 62
SEASCALE
Seascale GC 62

Derbyshire

BREADSALL
Marriott Breadsall Priory Hotel & Country Club 64
BUXTON
Cavendish GC 64
CHESTERFIELD
Grassmoor Golf Centre 65
HORSLEY
Horsley Lodge GC 66
LONG EATON
Trent Lock Golf Centre 67
MORLEY
Morley Hayes Golf Course 67
NEW MILLS
New Mills GC 67
STANTON BY DALE
Erewash Valley 68

Devon

BLACKAWTON
Dartmouth Golf & Country Club 68
CULLOMPTON
Padbrook Park GC 70
EXETER
Woodbury Park Hotel, Golf & Country Club 71
HIGH BICKINGTON
Libbaton GC 71
HOLSWORTHY
Holsworthy GC 72
ILFRACOMBE
Ilfracombe GC 72
IVYBRIDGE
Dinnaton GC 72
MORETONHAMPSTEAD
Bovey Castle 72
NEWTON ABBOT
Dainton Park GC 73
OKEHAMPTON
Ashbury Hotel 73
SAUNTON
Saunton GC 75
TEDBURN ST MARY
Fingle Glen Golf Hotel 75

Dorset

BELCHALWELL
Dorset Heights GC 77
BERE REGIS
The Dorset Golf & Country Club 78
BOURNEMOUTH
Open Golf Centres 78
Solent Meads Golf Centre 79
BRIDPORT
Bridport & West Dorset GC 79
FERNDOWN
Dudsbury GC 79
Ferndown Forest GC 80
HALSTOCK
Halstock Golf Enterprises 80
HURN
Parley Golf Course 80
POOLE
Parkstone GC 81
VERWOOD
Crane Valley GC 82
WEYMOUTH
Weymouth GC 82
WIMBORNE
Canford Magna GC 82

Durham, County

BILLINGHAM
Wynyard GC 83
CHESTER-LE-STREET
Roseberry Grange Golf Course 84
DARLINGTON
Headlam Hall Hotel 84
Stressholme GC 85
DURHAM
Mount Oswald Manor & Golf Course 85
DURHAM
Ramside Hall GC 85
NEWTON AYCLIFFE
Oakleaf Golf Complex 86
SEDGEFIELD
Knotty Hill Golf Centre 87

Essex

ABRIDGE
Abridge Golf & Country Club 87
BILLERICAY
Stock Brook Golf & Country Club 88
BRENTWOOD
Warley Park GC 88
BULPHAN
Langdon Hills GC 89
CANVEY ISLAND
Castle Point GC 89
CHELMSFORD
Channels GC 89
Regiment Way Golf Centre 90
CHIGWELL
Hainault Forest Golf Complex 90
COLCHESTER
Colchester GC 91
Lexden Wood GC 91
Stoke by Nayland GC 91
EARLS COLNE
The Essex Golf & Country Club 92
EPPING
The Epping Golf Course 92
Nazeing GC 92
HARLOW
North Weald GC 93
MALDON
Forrester Park GC 94
SAFFRON WALDEN
Saffron Walden GC 94
SOUTH OCKENDON
Belhus Park Golf Course 95
SOUTH OCKENDON
Top Meadow Golf Course 95
STANFORD-LE-HOPE
St Clere's Hall GC 95
STOCK
Crondon Park GC 95
TOLLESHUNT KNIGHTS
Five Lakes Resort 96
TOOT HILL
Toot Hill GC 96
WOODHAM WALTER
Warren GC 97

Gloucestershire

ALMONDSBURY
Bristol GC 97
CIRENCESTER
Cirencester GC 98
COALPIT HEATH
The Kendleshire Golf Course 98
CODRINGTON
The Players Club 98

- Driving ranges -

COLEFORD
Forest Hills GC 98
DYMOCK
Dymock Grange GC 99
GLOUCESTER
Brickhampton Court GC 99
Ramada Hotel & Resort Gloucester 99
Rodway Hill Golf Course 99
MINCHINHAMPTON
Minchinhampton GC 100
TEWKESBURY
Tewkesbury Park Hotel Golf & Country Club 101
THORNBURY
Thornbury Golf Centre 102
WESTONBIRT
Westonbirt Golf Course 102

Greater London

ADDINGTON
Addington Court 102
BIGGIN HILL
Cherry Lodge GC 104
CARSHALTON
Oaks Sports Centre Ltd 104
CHESSINGTON
Chessington Golf Centre 104
CROYDON
Selsdon Park Hotel & GC 105
GREENFORD
Lime Trees Park GC 107
HADLEY WOOD
Hadley Wood GC 107
HAMPTON WICK
Hampton Court Palace GC 107
HOUNSLOW
Airlinks GC 108
NORTHWOOD
Sandy Lodge GC 109
ORPINGTON
Chelsfield Lakes Golf Centre 109
Cray Valley GC 109
Ruxley Park Golf Centre 109
RICHMOND UPON THAMES
The Richmond GC 110
ROMFORD
Maylands GC 110
Risebridge Golf Centre 111
RUISLIP
Ruislip GC 111

Greater Manchester

ALTRINCHAM
Altrincham GC 113
BOLTON
Regent Park Golf Course 115
MANCHESTER
Blackley GC 117
Marriott Worsley Park Hotel& Country Club 118
MIDDLETON
Manchester GC 118
PRESTWICH
Heaton Park Golf Centre 119
ROCHDALE
Castle Hawk GC 119
WESTHOUGHTON
Hart Common GC 122
WIGAN
Haigh Hall Golf Complex 122

Hampshire

ALTON
Worldham Golf Course 123
ANDOVER
Hampshire GC 123
BASINGSTOKE
Dummer GC 124
Weybrook Park GC 124
BOTLEY
Botley Park Hotel, Golf & Country Club 124
CRONDALL
Oak Park GC 125
DIBDEN
Dibden Golf Centre 126
EASTLEIGH
East Horton Golf Centre 126
KINGSCLERE
Sandford Springs 127
LIPHOOK
Old Thorns Golf & Country Estate 128
OVERTON
Test Valley GC 129
OWER
Paultons Golf Centre 129
PORTSMOUTH
Great Salterns Public Course 130
SHEDFIELD
Marriott Meon Valley Hotel & Country Club 130
SOUTHAMPTON
Chilworth GC 131
TADLEY
Bishopswood Golf Course 131
WICKHAM
Wickham Park GC 132
WINCHESTER
Hockley GC 132
South Winchester GC 132

Herefordshire

KINGTON
Kington GC 133
ROSS-ON-WYE
Ross-on-Wye GC 134
South Herefordshire GC 134

Hertfordshire

BISHOP'S STORTFORD
Bishop's Stortford GC 135
Great Hadham Golf & Country Club 135
BROXBOURNE
Hertfordshire Golf & Country Club 136
BUSHEY
Bushey Golf & Country Club 136
Hartsbourne Golf & Country Club 136
ELSTREE
Elstree Golf and Country Club 137
GRAVELEY
Chesfield Downs GC 137
HARPENDEN
Harpenden GC 137
HEMEL HEMPSTEAD
Little Hay Golf Complex 138
LETCHWORTH
Letchworth GC 138
LITTLE GADDESDEN
Ashridge GC 138
RADLETT
Porters Park GC 139
REDBOURN
Redbourn GC 139
RICKMANSWORTH
The Grove 139
Moor Park GC 139
ROYSTON
Heydon Grange Golf & Country Club 140
Kingsway Golf Centre 140
ST ALBANS
Verulam GC 140
STEVENAGE
Stevenage Golf Centre 142
WARE
Marriott Hanbury Manor Golf & Country Club 141
Whitehill Golf Course 142
WELWYN GARDEN CITY
Mill Green GC 143

Isle of Wight

NEWPORT
Newport GC 279

Kent

ADDINGTON
West Malling GC 143
ASH
The London GC 143
ASHFORD
Homelands Bettergolf Centre 144
BARHAM
Broome Park GC 144
BIDDENDEN
Chart Hills GC 144
BRENCHLEY
Kent National Golf & Country Club 144
CHART SUTTON
The Ridge GC 145
DARTFORD
Birchwood Park Golf Centre Ltd 145
DEAL
Royal Cinque Ports GC 146
EDENBRIDGE
Sweetwoods Park 146
EYNSFORD
Austin Lodge GC 146
FAVERSHAM
Boughton Golf 146
FOLKESTONE
Etchinghill Golf Course 146
HALSTEAD
Broke Hill GC 147

- Driving ranges -

HEADCORN
Weald of Kent Golf Course 147
HEVER
Hever Castle GC 148
HOO
Deangate Ridge GC 148
LITTLESTONE
Littlestone GC 149
Romney Warren GC 149
LYDD
Lydd GC 149
MAIDSTONE
Marriott Tudor Park Hotel & Country Club 150
NEW ASH GREEN
Redlibbets GC 150
ROCHESTER
Rochester & Cobham Park GC 150
SANDWICH
Prince's GC 152
Royal St George's GC 151
SITTINGBOURNE
The Oast Golf Centre 153
Upchurch River Valley Golf Centre 153
SNODLAND
Oastpark Golf Course 153
TENTERDEN
London Beach Hotel & GC 154
WEST KINGSDOWN
Woodlands Manor GC 155
WESTERHAM
Westerham GC 155
WEST MALLING
Kings Hill GC 155

Lancashire

BLACKPOOL
De Vere Herons Reach 157
CLITHEROE
Clitheroe GC 158
GARSTANG
Garstang Country Hotel & GC 159
HEYSHAM
Heysham GC 159
LEYLAND
Leyland GC 160
LONGRIDGE
Longridge GC 160
LYTHAM ST ANNES
Royal Lytham & St Annes GC 161
ORMSKIRK
Hurlston Hall GC 163
PLEASINGTON
Pleasington GC 163
POULTON-LE-FYLDE
Poulton Le Fylde GC 163
PRESTON
Preston GC 164
UPHOLLAND
Beacon Park Golf & Country Club 165

Leicestershire

BOTCHESTON
Forest Hill GC 166
EAST GOSCOTE
Beedles Lake Golf Centre 166
KIBWORTH
Kibworth GC 166
KIRBY MUXLOE
Kirby Muxloe GC 166
LEICESTER
Humberstone Heights GC 167
Western Golf Course 167
LUTTERWORTH
Kilworth Springs GC 167
MELTON MOWBRAY
Melton Mowbray GC 168
Stapleford Park 168
SEAGRAVE
Park Hill GC 169
SIX HILLS
Six Hills GC 169
WHETSTONE
Whetstone GC 169
WILSON
Breedon Priory Golf Centre 169

Lincolnshire

BELTON
De Vere Belton Woods Hotel 170
BOSTON
Boston GC 170
Boston West Golf Centre 170
BOURNE
Toft Hotel GC 171
CLEETHORPES
Tetney GC 171
GAINSBOROUGH
Gainsborough GC 172
GEDNEY HILL
Gedney Hill Golf Course 172
GRANTHAM
Sudbrook Moor GC 172
GRIMSBY
Waltham Windmill GC 172
HORNCASTLE
Horncastle GC 172
LOUTH
Kenwick Park GC 173
SCUNTHORPE
Forest Pines GC 174
Grange Park GC 175
SPALDING
Spalding GC 176
SUTTON BRIDGE
Sutton Bridge GC 176
TORKSEY
Millfield Golf Complex 178
WOODHALL SPA
The National Golf Centre 177

London

E4
West Essex GC 179
N14
Trent Park GC 180
N20
South Herts GC 180
NW4
The Metro Golf Centre 181
NW7
Mill Hill GC 181
SE28
Thamesview Golf Centre 182
SW15
Richmond Park Golf Course 182
SW17
Central London Golf Centre 182
SW19
Royal Wimbledon GC 183

Merseyside

BLUNDELLSANDS
West Lancashire GC 184
FORMBY
Formby Hall Golf & Country Club 186
HOYLAKE
Royal Liverpool GC 185
RAINHILL
Blundells Hill GC 188
ST HELENS
Sherdley Park Golf Course 188
SOUTHPORT
Hillside GC 190
The Royal Birkdale GC 189

Norfolk

BARNHAM BROOM
Barnham Broom Hotel & GC 191
BAWBURGH
Bawburgh GC 191
DEREHAM
The Norfolk Golf & Country Club 192
FRITTON
Caldecott Hall Golf & Leisure 192
HUNSTANTON
Searles Leisure Resort 193
KING'S LYNN
Eagles Golf Centre 193
King's Lynn GC 194

MIDDLETON
Middleton Hall GC 194
MUNDESLEY
Mundesley GC Ltd 194
NORWICH
De Vere Dunston Hall Hotel 194
Marriott Sprowston Manor Hotel & Country Club 195
Wensum Valley Hotel, Golf & Country Club 195
WATTON
Richmond Park GC 196

Northamptonshire

CHACOMBE
Cherwell Edge GC 197
COLD ASHBY
Cold Ashby GC 197
COLLINGTREE
Collingtree Park Golf Course 197
KETTERING
Pytchley Golf Lodge 198
NORTHAMPTON
Brampton Heath Golf Centre 198
Delapre Golf Centre 199
Northamptonshire County GC 199
STAVERTON
Staverton Park GC 200
WHITTLEBURY
Whittlebury Park Golf & Country Club 200

Northumberland

BELFORD
The Belford GC 202
BELLINGHAM
Bellingham GC 202
BERWICK-UPON-TWEED
Berwick-upon-Tweed (Goswick) GC 202
FELTON
Burgham Park Golf & Leisure Club 203
HEXHAM
De Vere Slaley Hall Hotel, Golf Resort & Spa 203
LONGHORSLEY
Linden Hall 203
MATFEN
Matfen Hall Country House Hotel & GC 204
SWARLAND
Swarland Hall 205

Nottinghamshire

CALVERTON
Ramsdale Park Golf Centre 205
Springwater GC 000
HUCKNALL
Hucknall Golf Centre 206
KIRKBY IN ASHFIELD
Notts GC 206
NEWARK-ON-TRENT
Newark GC 206
NOTTINGHAM
Edwalton Municipal Golf Course 207
OLLERTON
Rufford Park Golf & Country Club 207
OXTON
Oakmere Park 208
RADCLIFFE ON TRENT
Cotgrave Place GC 208
SOUTHWELL
Norwood Park Golf Course 209
WORKSOP
Bondhay Golf & Fishing Club 209
College Pines Golf Course 209

Oxfordshire

ABINGDON
Drayton Park Golf Course 210
CHIPPING NORTON
The Wychwood GC 211
DIDCOT
Hadden Hill GC 211
FARINGDON
Carswell Golf & Country Club 211
HENLEY-ON-THAMES
Henley GC 212
HORTON-CUM-STUDLEY
Studley Wood GC 212
KIRTLINGTON
Kirtlington GC 212
MILTON COMMON
The Oxfordshire GC 212
NUFFIELD
Huntercombe GC 213
OXFORD
Hinksey Heights Golf Course 213
WATERSTOCK
Waterstock Golf Course 214
WITNEY
Witney Lakes Golf Course 215

Rutland

GREAT CASTERTON
Rutland County GC 215
GREETHAM
Greetham Valley GC 215

Shropshire

CLEOBURY MORTIMER
Cleobury Mortimer GC 216
NEWPORT
Aqualate Golf Centre 217
OSWESTRY
Mile End Golf Course 217
SHREWSBURY
Shrewsbury GC 218
TELFORD
The Shropshire Golf Centre 218
Telford Golf & Country Club 218
WESTON-UNDER-REDCASTLE
Hawkstone Park Hotel & Golf Centre 219
WHITCHURCH
Hill Valley Golf & Country Club 219

Somerset

BATH
Bath GC 219
BRIDGWATER
Cannington Golf Course 220
CHARD
Windwhistle GC 221
CONGRESBURY
Mendip Spring GC 221
FARRINGTON GURNEY
Farrington Golf & Country Club 222
FROME
Frome GC 222
Orchardleigh GC 222
GURNEY SLADE
Mendip GC 222
KEYNSHAM
Stockwood Vale GC 222
LONG ASHTON
Woodspring Golf & Country Club 223
SOMERTON
Long Sutton Golf Course 223
TAUNTON
Oake Manor GC 224
Taunton Vale GC 224
WELLS
Wells (Somerset) GC 225
WESTON-SUPER-MARE
Weston-Super-Mare GC 225
YEOVIL
Yeovil GC 226

Staffordshire

BURTON UPON TRENT
Belmont Driving Range & Golf Course 226
Branston Golf & Country Club 226
The Craythorne 226
Hoar Cross Hall Health Spa Resort 227
CANNOCK
Beau Desert GC 227
GOLDENHILL
Goldenhill Golf Centre 227
LICHFIELD
Seedy Mill GC 228
NEWCASTLE-UNDER-LYME
Jack Barkers Keele Golf Centre 228
PENKRIDGE
The Chase GC 229
PERTON
Perton Park GC 229
STOKE-ON-TRENT
Trentham GC 230
STONE
Barlaston GC 230
Izaak Walton GC 231
UTTOXETER
Manor GC 231

Suffolk

CRETINGHAM
Cretingham GC 233
HALESWORTH
Halesworth GC 233
IPSWICH
Fynn Valley GC 234
MILDENHALL
West Suffolk Golf Centre 235
RAYDON
Brett Vale GC 235
STOWMARKET
Stowmarket GC 236

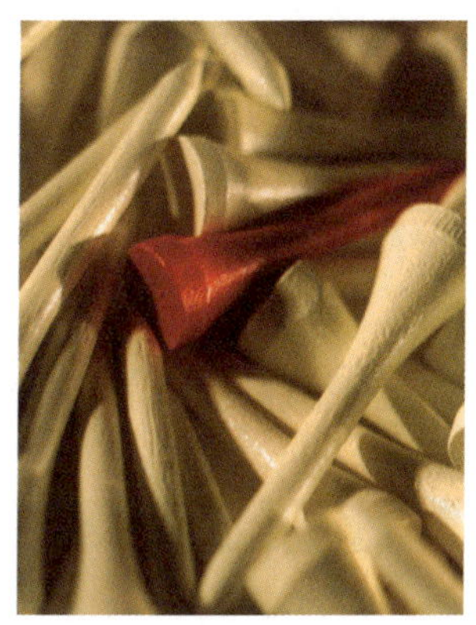

STUSTON
Diss GC 236
WOODBRIDGE
Best Western Ufford Park Hotel Golf & Leisure 236
Seckford Golf Centre 237

Surrey

BAGSHOT
Windlesham Golf Course 238
BRAMLEY
Bramley GC 239
CAMBERLEY
Pine Ridge GC 239
CATERHAM
Surrey National GC 239
CHIDDINGFOLD
Chiddingfold Golf Course 240
COBHAM
Silvermere GC 240
CRANLEIGH
Cranleigh Golf & Leisure Club 241
Wildwood Country Club 241
EAST HORSLEY
Drift GC 241
EFFINGHAM
Effingham GC 241
ENTON GREEN
West Surrey GC 242
EPSOM
Horton Park Golf & Country Club 242
FARLEIGH
Farleigh Court GC 242
FARNHAM
Blacknest GC 242
GODALMING
Broadwater Park GC & Driving Range 243
GUILDFORD
Merrist Wood GC 243
Roker Park Golf Course 244
HINDHEAD
The Hindhead GC 244
KINGSWOOD
Kingswood Golf & Country Club 244
Surrey Downs GC 244
LEATHERHEAD
Pachesham Park Golf Centre 244
LINGFIELD
Lingfield Park GC 245
NEWDIGATE
Rusper Golf Course 245
OCKLEY
Gatton Manor Hotel Golf & Country Club 245
OTTERSHAW
Foxhills Club and Resort 245
PUTTENHAM
Puttenham GC 256
REIGATE
Reigate Hill GC 246
SHEPPERTON
Sunbury Golf Centre 248
SOUTH GODSTONE
Home Park GC 248
VIRGINIA WATER
Wentworth Club 247
WALTON-ON-THAMES
Burhill GC 249
WEST BYFLEET
West Byfleet GC 249
WEST CLANDON
Clandon Regis GC 249
WEST END
Windlemere GC 249
WOKING
Hoebridge Golf Centre 250
Pyrford GC 250
WOLDINGHAM
Woldingham GC 252

Sussex, East

BEXHILL
Cooden Beach GC 252
BRIGHTON & HOVE
West Hove GC Ltd 253
DITCHLING
Mid Sussex GC 253
HAILSHAM
Wellshurst Golf & Country Club 255
HASTINGS & ST LEONARDS
TEN66 GC 255
HEATHFIELD
Horam Park Golf Course 255
SEAFORD
Seaford GC 256
SEDLESCOMBE
Sedlescombe GC 256
TICEHURST
Dale Hill Hotel & GC 256
UCKFIELD
East Sussex National Resort Hotel & Spa 257
Piltdown GC 256

Sussex, West

BURGESS HILL
Burgess Hill Golf Centre 258
CHICHESTER
Chichester GC 258
CRAWLEY
Tilgate Forest Golf Centre 259
GOODWOOD
Marriott Goodwood Park Hotel & Country Club 260
HASSOCKS
Hassocks GC 260
HAYWARDS HEATH
Haywards Heath GC 260
Paxhill Park GC 260
HORSHAM
Horsham Golf & Fitness 260
HURSTPIERPOINT
Singing Hills Golf Course 260
MANNINGS HEATH
Mannings Heath GC 261
MIDHURST
Cowdray Park GC 261
PULBOROUGH
West Sussex GC 261
SLINFOLD
Slinfold Park Golf & Country Club 262
WEST CHILTINGTON
West Chiltington GC 262
WORTHING
Worthing GC 262

Tyne & Wear

BOLDON
Boldon GC 263
GOSFORTH
Parklands 263
RYTON
Tyneside GC Ltd 264
WALLSEND
Wallsend GC 265
WASHINGTON
George Washington Golf & Country Club 265

Warwickshire

BIDFORD-ON-AVON
Bidford Grange GC 266
BRANDON
City of Coventry-Brandon Wood GC 266
HENLEY-IN-ARDEN
Henley Golf & Country Club 266
LEA MARSTON
Lea Marston Hotel & Leisure Complex 267
LEEK WOOTTON
The Warwickshire 267
LOWER BRAILES
Brailes GC 267
RUGBY
Whitefields Golf Course 268
STRATFORD-UPON-AVON
Ingon Manor Golf & Country 268
Menzies Welcombe Hotel & Golf Course 270
Stratford Oaks 270
WARWICK
Warwick GC 270
WISHAW
The De Vere Belfry 269

West Midlands

BIRMINGHAM
Alison Nicholas Golf Academy 271
COVENTRY
Ansty Golf Centre 272

DUDLEY
Swindon GC 273
MERIDEN
Marriott Forest of Arden Golf & Country Club 275
Stonebridge GC 274
SEDGLEY
Sedgley Golf Centre 274
SOLIHULL
Olton GC 274
Widney Manor GC 276
SUTTON COLDFIELD
Little Aston GC 276
Moor Hall GC 276
WALSALL
Calderfields Golf Academy 277
WOLVERHAMPTON
South Staffordshire GC 278
Three Hammers Short Course 278

Wiltshire

BRADFORD-ON-AVON
Cumberwell Park GC 280
CALNE
Bowood Golf & Country Club 280
CASTLE COMBE
The Manor House Hotel & GC 280
CHIPPENHAM
Chippenham GC 280
ERLESTOKE
Erlestoke Sands Golf Course 281
GREAT DURNFORD
High Post GC 281
HIGHWORTH
Wrag Barn Golf & Country Club 281
KINGSDOWN
Kingsdown GC 282
LANDFORD
Hamptworth Golf & Country Club 282
OGBOURNE ST GEORGE
Ogbourne Downs GC 282
SALISBURY
Salisbury & South Wilts GC 282
SWINDON
Broome Manor Golf Complex 282
TOLLARD ROYAL
Rushmore GC 283
WOOTTON BASSETT
The Wiltshire Golf & Country Club 283

Worcestershire

BEWDLEY
Wharton Park GC 284
BISHAMPTON
Vale GC 284
BROADWAY
Broadway GC 284
BROMSGROVE
Bromsgrove Golf Centre 285
DROITWICH
Ombersley GC 285
KIDDERMINSTER
Wyre Forest GC 286
REDDITCH
Abbey Hotel Golf & Country Club 287
WORCESTER
Bank House Hotel Golf & Country Club 288

Yorkshire, East Riding of

AUGHTON
The Oaks GC 289
BRIDLINGTON
Bridlington Links 289
COTTINGHAM
Cottingham Parks Golf & Country Club 290
DRIFFIELD (GREAT)
Driffield GC 290
HOWDEN
Boothferry GC 290

Yorkshire, North

COPMANTHORPE
Pike Hills GC 292
EASINGWOLD
Easingwold GC 292
HARROGATE
Rudding Park Hotel & Golf 293
MALTON
Malton & Norton GC 294
MIDDLESBROUGH
Middlesbrough Municipal Golf Centre 295
NORTHALLERTON
Romanby Golf & Country Club 295
PANNAL
Pannal GC 295
SALTBURN-BY-THE-SEA
Hunley Hall GC & Hotel 296
SELBY
Selby GC 297
YORK
Forest of Galtres GC 298
Forest Park GC 298
Swallow Hall Golf Course 298

Yorkshire, South

BARNSLEY
Sandhill GC 299
BAWTRY
Bawtry GC 299
ROTHERHAM
Grange Park GC 301
Phoenix GC 301
SHEFFIELD
Concord Park GC 301
Hillsborough GC 302
Rother Valley Golf Centre 302

Yorkshire, West

ADDINGHAM
Bracken Ghyll GC 303
BINGLEY
Bingley St Ives GC Ltd 304
BRIGHOUSE
Willow Valley GC 305
HUDDERSFIELD
Bradley Park Golf Course 307
Huddersfield GC Ltd 307
LEEDS
Cookridge Hall GC 308
De Vere Oulton Hall Golf Course 308
Leeds Golf Centre 309
Moor Allerton GC 309
Moortown GC 310
OTLEY
Otley GC 311
PONTEFRACT
Mid Yorkshire Golf Course 311
SHIPLEY
Marriott Hollins Hall Hotel & Country Club 312
WETHERBY
Wetherby GC 314

ISLANDS

Guernsey

L'ANCRESSE VALE
Royal Guernsey GC 314
CASTEL
La Grande Mare Golf & Country Club 315
ST PETER PORT
St Pierre Park GC 315

Jersey

LA MOYE
La Moye GC 315
ST CLEMENT
St Clement Golf & Sports Centre 315
ST OUEN
Les Mielles Golf & Country Club 315

Isle of Man

CASTLETOWN
Castletown Golf Links 316
DOUGLAS
Mount Murray Hotel & Country Club 316

SCOTLAND

Aberdeen City

ABERDEEN
Murcar Links GC 319

Aberdeenshire

BALMEDIE
East Aberdeenshire Golf Centre 321
BANCHORY
Inchmarlo GC 321
CRUDEN BAY
Cruden Bay GC 322
HUNTLY
Huntly GC 322
NEWBURGH
Newburgh on Ythan GC 323
NEWMACHAR
Newmachar GC 323
PORTLETHEN
Portlethen GC 324

Angus

BARRY
Panmure GC 326

CARNOUSTIE
Carnoustie Golf Links 325
EDZELL
Edzell GC 326
FORFAR
Forfar GC 326

Argyll & Bute
ERISKA
Isle of Eriska 328

City of Edinburgh
EDINBURGH
Bruntsfield Links Golfing Society 330
Marriott Dalmahoy Hotel Golf & Country Club 331

City of Glasgow
GLASGOW
Cowglen GC 334

Dumfries & Galloway
DUMFRIES
Pines Golf Centre 337
GRETNA
Gretna GC 338
KIRKCUDBRIGHT
Brighouse Bay Golf Course & Driving Range 338
PORTPATRICK
Lagganmore Hotel 339

Dundee City
DUNDEE
Ballumbie Castle Golf Course 340

East Lothian
GIFFORD
Castle Park GC 344
GULLANE
Gullane GC 344
NORTH BERWICK
Whitekirk Golf & Country Club 347
PRESTONPANS
Royal Musselburgh GC 347

Fife
BURNTISLAND
Burntisland Golf House Club 349
COLINSBURGH
Charleton Golf Course 350
CRAIL
Crail Golfing Society 350
DUNFERMLINE
Forrester Park Golf Course 351
ELIE
Golf House Club 351
LADYBANK
Ladybank GC 352
LEUCHARS
Drumoig Hotel & Golf Course 352
ST ANDREWS
Duke's Course 354
St Andrews Bay Golf Resort & Spa 354
St Andrews Links Trust 355
SALINE
Saline GC 356

Highland
AVIEMORE
Spey Valley Golf Course 356
INVERNESS
Loch Ness Golf Course 359
NAIRN
The Nairn GC 360
THURSO
Thurso GC 362

Midlothian
LASSWADE
Kings Acre Golf Course & Academy 363

Moray
BALLINDALLOCH
Ballindalloch Castle Golf Course 363
BUCKIE
Strathlene Buckie GC 364
ELGIN
Elgin GC 364
SPEY BAY
Spey Bay Golf Course 365

Perth & Kinross
ALYTH
The Alyth GC 1894 369
Strathmore Golf Centre 369
AUCHTERARDER
The Gleneagles Hotel 371
CRIEFF
Crieff GC 370
PERTH
Murrayshall Country House Hotel & Golf Course 374

Scottish Borders
KELSO
The Roxburghe Golf Course 378
PEEBLES
Macdonald Cardrona Hotel, Golf & Country Club 379

South Ayrshire
GIRVAN
Brunston Castle Golf Course 380
TROON
Royal Troon GC 381
TURNBERRY
The Westin Turnberry Resort 383

South Lanarkshire
HAMILTON
Strathclyde Park GC 384

Stirling
BANNOCKBURN
Brucefields Family Golfing Centre 385
CALLANDER
Callander GC 385

West Lothian
LIVINGSTON
Deer Park Golf & Country Club 388
WHITBURN
Polkemmet Country Park 388

WALES

Blaenau Gwent
NANTYGLO
West Monmouthshire GC 393

Bridgend
BRIDGEND
Southerndown GC 394
PENCOED
St Mary's Hotel Golf & Country Club 394
PORTHCAWL
Royal Porthcawl GC 394
PYLE
Pyle & Kenfig GC 394

Caerphilly
CAERPHILLY
Mountain Lakes & Castell Heights 395
MAESYCWMMER
Bryn Meadows Golf & Country Hotel 395
OAKDALE
Oakdale Golf Course 395

Cardiff
CARDIFF
Cottrell Park GC 396
Radyr GC 396

Carmarthenshire
GARNANT
Garnant Park GC 397
KIDWELLY
Glyn Abbey GC 398

LLANELLI
Machynys Peninsula Golf & Country Club 398

Ceredigion
LLANRHYSTUD
Penrhos Golf & Country Club 399

Denbighshire
BODELWYDDAN
Kimnel Park GC & Driving Range 401
ST ASAPH
Llannerch Park Golf Course 402

Flintshire
MOLD
Padeswood & Buckley GC 403
NORTHOP
Northop Golf & Country Club 403
WHITFORD
Pennant Park GC 404

Gwynedd
ABERSOCH
Abersoch GC 404
DOLGELLAU
Dolgellau GC 406
PORTHMADOG
Porthmadog GC 407

Monmouthshire
ABERGAVENNY
Wernddu Golf Centre 408
BETTWS NEWYDD
Alice Springs GC 408
CAERWENT
Dewstow GC 408
CHEPSTOW
Marriott St Pierre Hotel & Country Club 409

Neath Port Talbot
MARGAM
Lakeside Golf Course 410

Newport
CAERLEON
Caerleon Golf Course 412
LLANWERN
Llanwern GC 412
NEWPORT
The Celtic Manor Resort 413
Parc Golf Course 412

Pembrokeshire
NEWPORT
Newport (Pemb) GC Ltd 414

Powys
BRECON
Cradoc GC 414
LLANDRINDOD WELLS
Llandrindod Wells GC 415

Rhondda Cynon Taff
PENRHYS
Rhondda GC 416

Swansea
SOUTHGATE
Pennard GC 417
SWANSEA
Clyne GC 417
THREE CROSSES
Gower GC 418
UPPER KILLAY
Fairwood Park GC 418

Torfaen
CWMBRAN
Green Meadow Golf & Country Club 418

Vale of Glamorgan
BARRY
St Andrews Major Golf Course 419
HENSOL
Vale Hotel Golf & Spa Resort 419

Wrexham
CHIRK
Chirk GC 420
WREXHAM
Clays Golf Centre 420

NORTHERN IRELAND

Antrim
BALLYCLARE
Ballyclare GC 422
Greenacres Golf Course 422
BALLYGALLY
Cairndhu GC 422
BALLYMENA
Galgorm Castle Golf & Country Club 422
BALLYMONEY
Gracehill Golf Course 423
MAZE
Down Royal Park Golf Course 424
NEWTOWNABBEY
Ballyearl Golf & Leisure Centre 424
PORTRUSH
Royal Portrush GC 425
WHITEHEAD
Bentra Municipal Golf Course 424

Armagh
ARMAGH
County Armagh GC 424
CULLYHANNA
Ashfield GC 424
LURGAN
Craigavon Golf & Ski Centre 424

Belfast
BELFAST
Fortwilliam GC 426
Mount Ober Golf & Country Club 427

Down
BANBRIDGE
Banbridge GC 428
BANGOR
Blackwood Golf Centre 428
HOLYWOOD
Holywood GC 429
KILLYLEAGH
Ringdufferin Golf Course 430

Fermanagh
ENNISKILLEN
Ashwoods Golf Centre 430
Castle Hume Golf Course 430

Londonderry
LIMAVADY
Benone Tourist Complex 433
Radisson SAS Roe Park Hotel & Golf Resort 433
LONDONDERRY
Foyle International Golf Centre 433

REPUBLIC OF IRELAND

Carlow
TULLOW
Mount Wolseley Hilton, Spa, Golf & Country Club 435

Cavan
BALLYCONNELL
Slieve Russell Hotel Golf & Country Club 435
CAVAN
County Cavan Golf Course 436

Cork
CHARLEVILLE
Charleville GC 438
CORK
Cork GC 438
Fota Island 439

DOUGLAS
Douglas GC 440
KINSALE
Old Head Golf Links 440
LITTLE ISLAND
Harbour Point GC 440
MIDLETON
East Cork GC 441
MONKSTOWN
Monkstown GC 441
OVENS
Lee Valley Golf & Country Club 442

Donegal

BALLYLIFFIN
Ballyliffin GC 442
ROSAPENNA (MACHAIR LOISCTHE)
Rosapenna GC 444

Dublin

BALLYBOUGHAL
Hollywood Lakes GC 444
CASTLEKNOCK
Elm Green Golf Course 445
Luttrellstown Castle Golf & Country Club 445
DUBLIN
Elm Park Golf & Sports Club 447
Hollystown Golf Course 447
The Open Golf Centre 448
Rathfarnham GC 448
The Royal Dublin GC 448
St Margaret's Golf & Country Club 448
SAGGART
City West Hotel & Golf Resort 450

Galway

BALLINASLOE
Ballinasloe GC 452
BALLYCONNEELY
Connemara Championship Links 452
GALWAY
Glenlo Abbey Golf Course 453
MOUNTBELLEW
Mountbellew Golf Course 453
ORANMORE
Athenry GC 453
Galway Bay Golf Resort 454
OUGHTERARD
Oughterard GC 454

Kerry

BALLYBUNION
Ballybunion GC 455
KENMARE
Ring of Kerry Golf & Country Club 456
KILLARNEY
Killarney Golf & Fishing Club 456
WATERVILLE (AN COIREÁN)
Waterville House & Golf Links 457

Kildare

CARBURY
Highfield Golf Course 458
MAYNOOTH
Carton House GC 458
STRAFFAN
The K Club 459

Kilkenny

KILKENNY
Kilkenny GC 460
THOMASTOWN
Mount Juliet Hotel & GC 461

Laois

PORTLAOISE
The Heath GC 462

Limerick

LIMERICK
Limerick County Golf & Country Club 463
NEWCASTLE WEST
Newcastle West GC 463

Louth

ARDEE
Ardee GC 463
DUNDALK
Ballymascanlon House Hotel GC 464
Dundalk GC 464
GREENORE
Greenore GC 464
TERMONFECKIN
Seapoint GC 464

Mayo

BALLINROBE
Ballinrobe GC 465
BALLYHAUNIS
Ballyhaunis GC 465
WESTPORT
Westport GC 466

Meath

DUNSHAUGHLIN
Black Bush GC 466

Monaghan

CLONES
Clones GC 468
MONAGHAN
Rossmore GC 468

Offaly

BIRR
Birr GC 468

Sligo

INISHCRONE (ENNISCRONE)
Enniscrone GC 470

Tipperary

CAHIR
Cahir Park GC 470
MONARD
Ramada Hotel & Suites 471
THURLES
Thurles GC 471
TIPPERARY
Tipperary Golf Course 472

Waterford

DUNGARVAN
Gold Coast GC 472
LISMORE
Lismore GC 472
WATERFORD
Waterford Castle GC 473

Westmeath

MOATE
Mount Temple Golf Course 474
MULLINGAR
Mullingar GC 474

Wexford

ENNISCORTHY
Enniscorthy GC 474
ROSSLARE
St Helen's Bay Golf & Country Club 475

Wicklow

ARKLOW
Arklow GC 475
BLESSINGTON
Tulfarris Hotel & Golf Resort 475
BRAY
Bray GC 475
DUNLAVIN
Rathsallagh House Golf & Country Club 476
ENNISKERRY
Powerscourt GC 478
GREYSTONES
Charlesland Golf & Country Club Hotel 478
KILCOOLE
Druids Glen GC 477

Find it with...

www.theAA.com

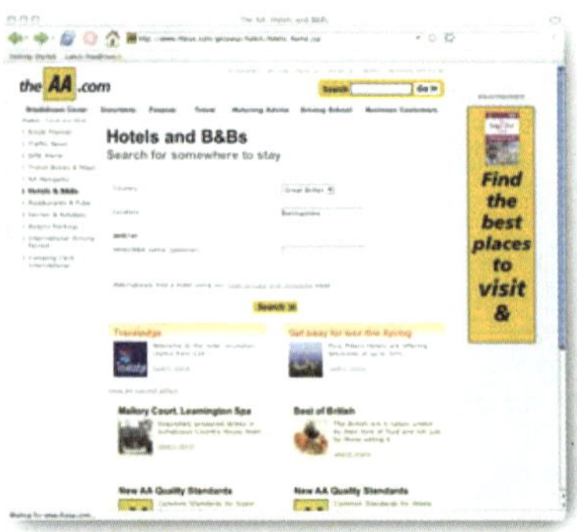

Go to **theAA.com** for maps and the **Route Planner** to help you find AA listed guest houses, hotels, pubs and restaurants – more than 12,000 establishments.

Click on the home page, then simply enter your postcode and the establishment postcode given in this guide and click Get route. Check your details and you are on your way. Or, search on the home page for a Hotel/B&B or a Pub/Restaurant by location or establishment name. Scroll down the list of finds for the interactive map and local routes.

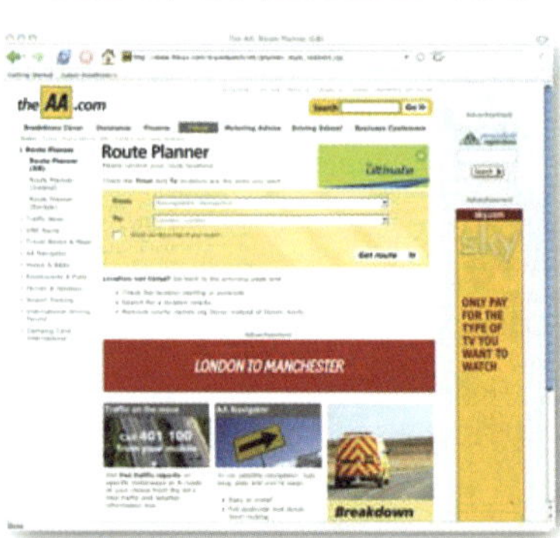

Postcode searches can also be done on www.ordnancesurvey.co.uk and www.multimap.com, and the latter provides useful aerial views of your destination.

Discover new horizons with
Britain's largest travel publisher

England

BEDFORDSHIRE

ASPLEY GUISE Map 04 SP93

Aspley Guise & Woburn Sands West Hill MK17 8DX
☎ 01908 583596 ▤ 01908 583596 (secretary)
A fine undulating course in expansive heathland interspersed with attractive clumps of gorse, broom and bracken. Some well-established silver birch is a feature. The really tough 7th, 8th and 9th holes complete the first half.
18 holes, 6079yds, Par 71, SSS 70, Course record 65. Club membership 590.
Visitors Mon-Sun except BHs. Booking required Sat & Sun. Handicap certificate. Dress code. **Societies** Booking required. **Green Fees** £33 per round, £50 Sat & Sun. **Prof** Colin Clingan **Course Designer** Sandy Herd **Facilities** ⊗ Ⅲ ⛳ ☕ 🍸 ⛰ 🚗 ⛳ 🚜 ✓ **Conf** Corporate Hospitality Days **Location** M1 junct 13, 2m W

Hotel ★★★ 69% Moore Place Hotel, The Square, ASPLEY GUISE ☎ 01908 282000 37 en suite 27 annexe en suite

BEDFORD Map 04 TL04

Bedford Great Denham Golf Village, Carnoustie Dr, Biddenham MK40 4FF
☎ 01234 320022 ▤ 01234 320023
e-mail: thebedford@btopenworld.com
web: www.kolvengolf.com
American-style course with 89 bunkers, eight large water features and large contoured USPGA specification greens. Built on sand and gravel the course is open all year round.
18 holes, 6471yds, Par 72, SSS 72, Course record 63. Club membership 500.
Visitors Mon-Sun & BHs. Booking required. Dress code. **Societies** Booking required. **Green Fees** £30 per 18 holes, £40 Sat & Sun. **Prof** Zac Thompson **Course Designer** David Pottage **Facilities** ⊗ Ⅲ ⛳ ☕ 🍸 ⛰ 🚗 ⛳ ✎ 🚜 ✓ ⛳ **Conf** facs Corporate Hospitality Days **Location** 2.5m W of Bedford off A428

Hotel ⌂ Innkeeper's Lodge Bedford, 403 Goldington Rd, BEDFORD ☎ 0870 243 0500 & 01234 272707 ▤ 01234 343926 47 en suite

Bedford & County Green Ln, Clapham MK41 6ET
☎ 01234 352617 ▤ 01234 357195
web: www.bedfordandcountrygolfclub.co.uk
A mature, undulating parkland course established in 1912 with views over Bedford and surrounding countryside. Beware of the brook that discreetly meanders through the 7th, 10th, 11th and 15th holes. The testing par 4 15th is one of the most challenging holes in the area.
18 holes, 6420yds, Par 70, SSS 70, Course record 66. Club membership 600.
Visitors Mon-Fri except BHs. Handicap certificate. Dress code. **Societies** Booking required. **Green Fees** £32 per day, £26 per round. ⊘ **Prof** R Tattersall **Facilities** ⊗ Ⅲ ⛳ ☕ 🍸 ⛰ 🚗 ✓ **Conf** Corporate Hospitality Days **Location** 2m N off A6 in Clapham

Hotel ⌂ Premier Travel Inn Bedford, Priory Country Park, Barkers Ln, BEDFORD ☎ 08701 977030 32 en suite

Bedfordshire Spring Ln, Stagsden MK43 8SR
☎ 01234 822555 ▤ 01234 825052
e-mail: office@bedfordshiregolf.com
web: www.bedfordshiregolf.com
A challenging 18-hole course on undulating terrain with established trees and woods and water hazards. Magnificent views.
18 holes, 6565yds, Par 70, SSS 72, Course record 65. Academy Course: 9 holes, 1354yds, Par 28, SSS 28. Club membership 700.
Visitors Mon-Fri. Booking required. **Societies** Booking required. **Green Fees** phone. **Prof** David Armor **Course Designer** Cameron Sinclair **Facilities** ⊗ Ⅲ by arrangement ⛳ ☕ 🍸 ⛰ 🚗 ⛳ 🚜 ✓ ⛳ **Conf** facs Corporate Hospitality Days **Location** 3m W of Bedford on A422 at Stagsden

Hotel ⌂ Travelodge Bedford Marston Morstaine, Beancroft Rd Junction, MARSTON MORETAINE ☎ 08700 850 950 54 en suite

Mowsbury Cleat Hill, Kimbolton Rd, Ravensden MK41 8DQ
☎ 01234 771041 & 216374 (pro) ▤ 01234 771041
e-mail: mgc@freenet.co.uk
18 holes, 6451yds, Par 72, SSS 71, Course record 66.
Course Designer Hawtree **Location** 2m N of town centre on B660
Phone for further details

Hotel ⌂ Innkeeper's Lodge Bedford, 403 Goldington Rd, BEDFORD ☎ 0870 243 0500 & 01234 272707 ▤ 01234 343926 47 en suite

CHALGRAVE Map 04 TL02

Chalgrave Manor Dunstable Rd LU5 6JN
☎ 01525 876556 & 876554
e-mail: steve@chalgravegolf.co.uk
web: www.chalgravegolf.co.uk
Undulating parkland course set in 150 acres of Bedfordshire countryside. No two consecutive holes play in the same direction. Four holes have water hazards including the signature tenth hole, playing 130yds across water to a sloping green. The par 5 9th, at 621yds, is one of the longest holes in the country.
18 holes, 6382yds, Par 72, SSS 70, Course record 69. Club membership 550.
Visitors Mon-Fri. Booking required Sat, Sun & BHs. Dress code. **Societies** Booking required. **Green Fees** £20 per round Sat, Sun & BHs £30. **Prof** Geoff Swain **Course Designer** M Palmer **Facilities** ⊗ Ⅲ by arrangement ⛳ ☕ 🍸 ⛰ 🚗 🚜 ✓ **Conf** facs Corporate Hospitality Days **Location** M1 junct 12, A5120 through Toddington, signed 1m

Hotel ★★★ 63% Old Palace Lodge, Church St, DUNSTABLE ☎ 01582 662201 68 en suite

If the name of the club appears in italics, details have not been confirmed for this edition of the guide

COLMWORTH Map 04 TL15

Colmworth & North Bedfordshire New Rd
MK44 2NN
☎ 01234 378181 🖹 01234 376678
e-mail: colmworth@btopenworld.com
web: www.colmworthgolfclub.co.uk

18 holes, 6435yds, Par 72, SSS 71, Course record 69.
Course Designer John Glasgow **Location** Off A1 between Bedford Neots
Phone for further details

Hotel ★★★ 65% Corus hotel Bedford, Cardington Rd, BEDFORD ☎ 0870 609 6108 48 en suite

DUNSTABLE Map 04 TL02

Dunstable Downs Whipsnade Rd LU6 2NB
☎ 01582 604472 🖹 01582 478700
e-mail: dunstabledownsgc@btconnect.com
web: www.dunstable-golf.co.uk
A fine downland course set on two levels with far-reaching views and frequent sightings of graceful gliders. The 9th hole is one of the best short holes in the country.
18 holes, 6320yds, Par 70, SSS 70, Course record 64.
Club membership 600.
Visitors Mon-Fri. Dress code. **Societies** Booking required. **Green Fees** £30 per round. **Prof** Michael Weldon **Course Designer** James Braid **Facilities** **Conf** Corporate Hospitality Days **Location** 2m S off B4541

Hotel ★★★ 63% Old Palace Lodge, Church St, DUNSTABLE ☎ 01582 662201 68 en suite

Griffin Chaul End Rd, Caddington LU1 4AX
☎ 01582 415573 🖹 01582 415314
e-mail: griffin@griffingolfclub.fsbusiness.co.uk
web: www.vauxhallrecreation.co.uk

Continued

18 holes, 6240yds, Par 71, SSS 70.
Location M1 junct 11, after 0.5m exit left at Tesco rdbt, towards Dunstable
Phone for further details

Hotel ★★★ 63% Old Palace Lodge, Church St, DUNSTABLE ☎ 01582 662201 68 en suite

LEIGHTON BUZZARD Map 04 SP92

Leighton Buzzard Plantation Rd LU7 3JF
☎ 01525 244800 (office) 🖹 01525 244801
e-mail: lbgc.secretary1@btopenworld.com
web: www.leightonbuzzardgolf.net
Mature parkland and heathland with easy walking. The 17th and 18th holes are challenging tree-lined finishing holes with tight fairways. The par 3 11th is signature hole.

18 holes, 6101yds, Par 71, SSS 70, Course record 63.
Club membership 700.
Visitors Mon-Fri. Handicap certificate. Dress code. **Societies** Booking required. **Green Fees** phone. **Prof** Maurice Campbell **Facilities** **Conf** facs **Location** 1.5m N of town centre off A4146

Hotel ★★★ 63% Old Palace Lodge, Church St, DUNSTABLE ☎ 01582 662201 68 en suite

LOWER STONDON Map 04 TL13

Mount Pleasant Station Rd SG16 6JL
☎ 01462 850999
e-mail: manager@mountpleasantgolfclub
web: www.mountpleasantgolfclub.co.uk
Undulating meadowland course with three ponds in play and many tree plantations. A deep ditch, sometimes with water, runs through the middle of the course and is crossed four times per nine holes. The main feature of the course is its presentation and superb greens. The course is seldom closed by bad weather.
9 holes, 6185yds, Par 70, SSS 70, Course record 68.
Club membership 300.
Visitors Mon-Sun & BHs. Booking required. Dress code. **Societies** Booking required. **Green Fees** £16 per 18 holes, £9 per 9 holes, £20/£11.50 Sat & Sun. **Prof** Glen Kemble **Course Designer** Derek Young **Facilities** by arrangement **Leisure** undercover driving nets. **Conf** Corporate Hospitality Days **Location** 0.75m W of A600, 4m N of Hitchin

Hotel ★★★ Menzies Flitwick Manor, Church Rd, FLITWICK ☎ 01525 712242 17 en suite

LUTON Map 04 TL02

South Beds Warden Hill Rd LU2 7AE
☎ 01582 591500 🖹 01582 495381
e-mail: office@southbedsgolfclub.co.uk
web: www.southbedsgolfclub.co.uk
An 18-hole and a nine-hole chalk downland course, slightly undulating.
Galley Hill Course: 18 holes, 6438yds, Par 71, SSS 71, Course record 64.
Warden Hill Course: 9 holes, 2425yds, Par 32, SSS 32.
Club membership 1000.
Visitors Booking required. Handicap certificate for Galley Hill. Dress code. **Societies** Booking required. **Green Fees** phone. **Prof** Eddie Cogle **Facilities** **Conf** Corporate Hospitality Days **Location** 3m N of Luton on A6

Stockwood Park London Rd LU1 4LX
☎ 01582 413704 (pro shop)
18 holes, 6049yds, Par 69, SSS 69, Course record 67.
Location 1m S
Phone for further details

MILLBROOK Map 04 TL03

Millbrook Millbrook Village MK45 2JB
☎ 01525 840252 🖹 01525 406249
e-mail: info@themillbrook.com
web: www.themillbrook.com
Long parkland course on rolling countryside high above the Bedfordshire plains. Laid out on well-drained sandy soil with many fairways lined with silver birch, pine and larch. The course provides a continuous test of the tee where length and accuracy pay a huge premium.
18 holes, 7021yds, Par 74, SSS 73, Course record 68.
Club membership 560.
Visitors Mon-Sun & BHs. Handicap certificate. Dress code. **Societies** Booking required. **Green Fees** £25 per 18 holes, £30 Fri pm, £35 Sat, Sun & BHs pm. **Prof** Geraint Dixon **Course Designer** William Sutherland **Facilities** **Conf** facs Corporate Hospitality Days **Location** M1 junct 12/13, A507 Woburn-Ampthill road

Hotel ★★★ Menzies Flitwick Manor, Church Rd, FLITWICK ☎ 01525 712242 17 en suite

PAVENHAM Map 04 SP95

Pavenham Park MK43 7PE
☎ 01234 822202 🖹 01234 826602
e-mail: kolvengolf@ukonline.co.uk
web: www.kolvengolf.com
18 holes, 6400yds, Par 72, SSS 71, Course record 63.
Course Designer Zac Thompson **Location** 1.5m from A6, N of Bedford
Phone for further details

Hotel Travelodge Bedford Marston Morstaine, Beancroft Rd Junction, MARSTON MORETAINE
☎ 08700 850 950 54 en suite

SANDY Map 04 TL14

John O'Gaunt Sutton Park SG19 2LY
☎ 01767 260360 🖹 01767 262834
e-mail: admin@johnogauntgolfclub.co.uk
web: www.johnogauntgolfclub.co.uk
Two magnificent parkland courses - John O'Gaunt and Carthagena - covering a gently undulating and tree-lined terrain. The John O'Gaunt course makes the most of numerous natural features, notably a river which crosses the fairways of four holes. The Carthagena course has larger greens, longer tees and from the back tees is a challenging course.
John O'Gaunt Course: 18 holes, 6513yds, Par 71, SSS 71, Course record 64.
Carthagena Course: 18 holes, 5869yds, Par 69, SSS 69.
Club membership 1500.
Visitors Mon-Fri. Handicap certificate. Dress code. **Societies** Booking required. **Green Fees** £50 per day, £35 per round, £60 per day/round Sat, Sun & BHs. **Prof** Lee Scarbrow **Course Designer** Hawtree **Facilities** **Conf** Corporate Hospitality Days **Location** 3m NE of Biggleswade on B1040

SHEFFORD Map 04 TL13

Beadlow Manor Hotel & Golf & Country Club SG17 5PH
☎ 01525 860800 🖹 01525 861345
e-mail: beadlowmanor@talk21 co.uk
web: www.beadlowmanor.co.uk
A 36-hole golf and leisure complex. The Baroness Manhattan and the Baron Manhattan courses are undulating with water hazards on numerous holes. These are good challenging courses for both the beginner and low handicap player.
Baroness Course: 18 holes, 6072yds, Par 71, SSS 69, Course record 67.
Baron Course: 18 holes, 6619yds, Par 73, SSS 72, Course record 67.
Club membership 850.
Visitors Booking required. **Societies** Booking required. **Green Fees** Baroness £15 per round, £20 Sat & Sun. Baron £15 per round, £20 Sat & Sun. **Prof** Gordon Morrison **Facilities** **Conf** facs Corporate Hospitality Days **Location** On A507

Hotel ★★★ Menzies Flitwick Manor, Church Rd, FLITWICK ☎ 01525 712242 17 en suite

TILSWORTH Map 04 SP92

Tilsworth Dunstable Rd LU7 9PU
☎ 01525 210721/2 🖹 01525 210465
e-mail: nick@tilsworthgolf.co.uk
web: www.tilsworthgolf.co.uk
The course is in first-class condition and, although not a long course, is particularly demanding and challenging where the key is straight driving. The course has its own Amen Corner between the 14th and 16th holes, which will challenge all golfers. Panoramic views of three counties from the 6th tee.
18 holes, 5306yds, Par 69, SSS 66, Course record 61.
Club membership 400.
Visitors Mon-Fri. Booking required Sat, Sun & BHs. Dress code. **Societies** Booking required. **Green Fees** £17 per 18 holes, £19.50 Sat, Sun & BHs. **Prof** Nick Webb **Facilities** **Conf** facs Corporate Hospitality Days **Location** 0.5m NE off A5, N of Dunstable

Hotel ★★★ 63% Old Palace Lodge, Church St, DUNSTABLE ☎ 01582 662201 68 en suite

Continued

WYBOSTON Map 04 TL15

Wyboston Lakes MK44 3AL
☎ 01480 212625 Fax 01480 223000
e-mail: venue@wybostonlakes.co.uk
web: www.wybostonlakes.co.uk
Parkland with narrow fairways and small greens, set around four lakes and a river, which provide the biggest challenge on this very scenic course.

18 holes, 5955yds, Par 70, SSS 69, Course record 65. Club membership 375.
Visitors Mon-Fri. Booking required Sat, Sun & BHs. **Societies** Booking required. **Green Fees** phone. **Prof** Paul Ashwell **Course Designer** N Oakden **Facilities** **Leisure** heated indoor swimming pool, fishing, sauna, solarium, gymnasium, watersports. **Conf** facs Corporate Hospitality Days **Location** 1m S of St Neots off A1/A428

Hotel ★★★ 65% Corus hotel Bedford, Cardington Rd, BEDFORD ☎ 0870 609 6108 48 en suite

BERKSHIRE

ASCOT Map 04 SU96

Berkshire Swinley Rd SL5 8AY
☎ 01344 621495 Fax 01344 623328
Two classic heathland courses, with splendid tree-lined fairways, that have remained the same since they were constructed in 1928. The Red Course, on slightly higher ground, is a little longer than the Blue. It has an unusual assortment of holes, six par 3s, six par 4s and six par 5s, the short holes, particularly the 10th and 16th, being the most intimidating. The Blue Course starts with a par 3 and shares with the 16th the reputation of being the finest holes of the 18.
Red Course: 18 holes, 6379yds, Par 72, SSS 71.
Blue Course: 18 holes, 6260yds, Par 71, SSS 71.
Visitors Mon-Fri. Booking required. Dress code. **Societies** Booking required. **Green Fees** £115 per day, £85 per round. **Prof** P Anderson **Course Designer** H Fowler **Facilities** **Conf** Corporate Hospitality Days **Location** M3 junct 3, 2.5m NW on A332

Hotel ★★★★ 70% Macdonald Berystede Hotel & Spa, Bagshot Rd, Sunninghill, ASCOT ☎ 0870 400 8111 125 en suite

Lavender Park Swinley Rd SL5 8BD
☎ 01344 893344
e-mail: lavenderpark@yahoo.com
web: www.lavenderparkgolf.co.uk
Public parkland course, ideal for the short game featuring challenging narrow fairways. Driving range with nine-hole par 3 course, floodlit until 10pm.
9 holes, 1102yds, Par 27, SSS 28.
Visitors Mon-Sun & BHs. **Societies** Booking required. **Green Fees** phone. **Prof** David Johnson **Facilities** **Leisure** snooker. **Location** 1.5m W of Ascot, off the A329 on the B3017

Hotel ★★★★ 70% Macdonald Berystede Hotel & Spa, Bagshot Rd, Sunninghill, ASCOT ☎ 0870 400 8111 125 en suite

Mill Ride Mill Ride SL5 8LT
☎ 01344 886777 Fax 01344 886820
e-mail: c.sheffield@mill-ride.com
web: www.mill-ride.com
Formerly a prestigious polo club and stud of King George V, this 18-hole course combines links and parkland styles. The manicured and cross cut fairways intermingle with lakes and the mounding and hollows which gives the course a unique parkland design coupled with an inland links feel to the starting and closing holes.

18 holes, 6807yds, Par 72, SSS 72, Course record 64. Club membership 350.
Visitors Booking required. **Societies** Booking required. **Green Fees** phone. **Prof** Terry Wild **Course Designer** Donald Steel **Facilities** **Leisure** sauna. **Conf** facs Corporate Hospitality Days **Location** 2m W of Ascot

Hotel ★★★★ 70% Macdonald Berystede Hotel & Spa, Bagshot Rd, Sunninghill, ASCOT ☎ 0870 400 8111 125 en suite

Royal Ascot Winkfield Rd SL5 7LJ
☎ 01344 625175 Fax 01344 872330
e-mail: golf@royalascotgc.fsnet.co.uk
web: www.royalascotgolfclub.co.uk
Heathland course inside Ascot racecourse and exposed to weather.
18 holes, 5716yds, Par 68, SSS 68, Course record 65. Club membership 620.
Visitors With member. **Societies** Booking required. **Green Fees** phone. **Prof** Alistair White **Course Designer** JH Taylor **Facilities** **Location** 0.5m N on A330

Hotel ★★★★ 70% Macdonald Berystede Hotel & Spa, Bagshot Rd, Sunninghill, ASCOT ☎ 0870 400 8111 125 en suite

Swinley Forest Coronation Rd SL5 9LE
☎ 01344 874979 (secretary) 🖷 01344 874733
e-mail: swinleyfgc@aol.com
An attractive and immaculate course of heather and pine situated in the heart of Swinley Forest. The 17th is as good a short hole as can be found, with a bunkered plateau green, and the 12th is one of the most challenging par 4s.
18 holes, 6100yds, Par 69, SSS 70, Course record 62.
Club membership 350.
Visitors Mon-Fri except BHs. With member. **Societies** Booking required. **Green Fees** £125 per day. **Prof** Stuart Hill **Course Designer** Harry Colt **Facilities** **Leisure** Video studeo. **Conf** Corporate Hospitality Days **Location** 2m S of Ascot, off A30

Hotel ★★★★ 70% Macdonald Berystede Hotel & Spa, Bagshot Rd, Sunninghill, ASCOT ☎ 0870 400 8111 125 en suite

BINFIELD — Map 04 SU87

Blue Mountain Golf Centre Wood Ln RG42 4EX
☎ 01344 300200 🖷 01344 360960
e-mail: bluemountain@americangolf.uk.com
web: www.bluemountain-golf.co.uk
18 holes, 6097yds, Par 70, SSS 70, Course record 63.
Location A329(M)/A322 onto B3408, 2nd rdbt onto Temple Way, 1st left
Phone for further details

Hotel ★★★★ 73% Coppid Beech, John Nike Way, BRACKNELL ☎ 01344 303333 205 en suite

CHADDLEWORTH — Map 04 SU47

West Berkshire RG20 7DU
☎ 01488 638574 🖷 01488 638781
e-mail: info@thewbgc.co.uk
web: www.thewbgc.co.uk
Challenging and interesting downland course with views of the Berkshire Downs. The course is bordered by ancient woodland and golfers will find manicured fairways with well-constructed greens and strategically placed hazards. The testing 627yd 5th hole is one of the longest par 5s in southern England. Bunkers are well placed from tees and around the greens to catch any wayward shots.
18 holes, 7001yds, Par 73, SSS 74.
Club membership 650.
Visitors Mon-Fri. Booking required Sat, Sun & BHs. Dress code. **Societies** Booking required. **Green Fees** £27 per round, Sat, Sun & BHs £35 per round. **Prof** Paul Simpson **Facilities** **Conf** Corporate Hospitality Days **Location** 1m S of village off A338

COOKHAM — Map 04 SU88

Winter Hill Grange Ln SL6 9RP
☎ 01628 527613 (secretary) 🖷 01628 527479

18 holes, 6408yds, Par 72, SSS 71, Course record 63.
Course Designer Charles Lawrie **Location** 1m NW off B4447
Phone for further details

Hotel ★★★★ 71% Macdonald Compleat Angler, Marlow Bridge, MARLOW ☎ 0870 400 8100 64 en suite

CROWTHORNE — Map 04 SU86

East Berkshire Ravenswood Ave RG45 6BD
☎ 01344 772041 🖷 01344 777378
e-mail: thesecretary@eastberksgc.fsnet.co.uk
An attractive heathland course with an abundance of heather and pine trees. Walking is easy and the greens are exceptionally good. Some fairways become tight where the heather encroaches on the line of play. The course is testing and demands great accuracy.
18 holes, 6236yds, Par 69, SSS 70.
Club membership 766.
Visitors Mon-Fri. Booking required. Handicap certificate. Dress code. **Societies** Booking required. **Green Fees** £50 per day. **Prof** Jason Brant **Course Designer** P Paxton **Facilities** **Location** W side of town centre off B3348

Hotel ★★★★★ Pennyhill Park Hotel & The Spa, London Rd, BAGSHOT ☎ 01276 471774 26 en suite 97 annexe en suite

DATCHET — Map 04 SU97

Datchet Buccleuch Rd SL3 9BP
☎ 01753 543887 & 541872 🖷 01753 541872
e-mail: secretary@datchetgolfclub.co.uk
web: www.datchetgolfclub.co.uk
Meadowland course, easy walking.
9 holes, 6087yds, Par 70, SSS 69, Course record 63.
Club membership 430.
Visitors Mon-Sun & BHs. Dress code. **Societies** Booking required. **Green Fees** £25 per 18 holes, Sat, Sun & BHs £30. **Prof** Ian Godelman **Course Designer** JH Taylor **Facilities** **Location** NW side of Datchet off B470

Hotel ★★★ 74% Macdonald Castle Hotel, 18 High St, WINDSOR ☎ 0870 400 8300 38 en suite 70 annexe en suite

MAIDENHEAD Map 04 SU88

Bird Hills Drift Rd, Hawthorn Hill SL6 3ST
☎ 01628 771030 🖷 01628 631023
e-mail: info@birdhills.co.uk
web: www.birdhills.co.uk

A gently undulating course with easy walking and many water hazards. Some challenging holes are the par 5 6th dog-leg, par 3 9th surrounded by water and bunkers, and the 16th which is a long uphill par 4 and a two-tier green.

18 holes, 6176yds, Par 72, SSS 69, Course record 65. Club membership 400.

Visitors Mon-Sun & BHs. Booking required. Dress code. **Societies** Booking required. **Green Fees** phone. **Prof** Nick Slimming **Facilities** **Leisure** pool tables. **Conf** facs **Location** M4 junct 8/9, 4m S on A330

Hotel ★★★ 71% Stirrups Country House, Maidens Green, BRACKNELL ☎ 01344 882284 30 en suite

Maidenhead Shoppenhangers Rd SL6 2PZ
☎ 01628 624693 🖷 01628 780758
e-mail: manager@maidenheadgolf.co.uk
web: www.maidenheadgolf.co.uk

Pleasant parkland with excellent greens and some challenging holes. The long par 4 4th and short par 3 13th are only two of the many outstanding aspects of this course.

18 holes, 6364yds, Par 70, SSS 70. Club membership 750.

Visitors Booking required. Handicap certificate. Dress code. **Societies** Booking required. **Green Fees** £45 per day, £30 per round, £40 per round Sat & Sun. **Prof** Steve Geary **Course Designer** Alex Simpson **Facilities** **Conf** facs **Location** S side of town centre off A308

Hotel ★★★★ Fredrick's Hotel, Restaurant & Spa, Shoppenhangers Rd, MAIDENHEAD ☎ 01628 581000 34 en suite

Temple Henley Rd, Hurley SL6 5LH
☎ 01628 824795 🖷 01628 828119
e-mail: templegolfclub@btconnect.com

Open parkland with extensive views over the Thames Valley. Firm, relatively fast greens, natural slopes and subtle contours provide a challenging test to golfers of all abilities. Excellent drainage assures play during inclement weather.

18 holes, 6266yds, Par 70, SSS 70. Club membership 480.

Continued

Visitors Booking required. Handicap certificate. Dress code. **Societies** Booking required. **Green Fees** £55 per day, £42 per round, £60/£50 Sat & Sun. **Prof** James Whiteley **Course Designer** Willie Park (Jnr) **Facilities** by arrangement **Conf** Corporate Hospitality Days **Location** M4 junct 8/9, A404M then A4130, signed Henley

Hotel ★★★★ 71% Macdonald Compleat Angler, Marlow Bridge, MARLOW ☎ 0870 400 8100 64 en suite

MORTIMER Map 04 SU66

Wokefield Park Wokefield Park RG7 3AE
☎ 0118 933 4029 🖷 0118 933 4031
e-mail: wokefieldgolf@initialstyle.co.uk
web: www.golf-isc.co.uk

Set in a prime location amid the peaceful and picturesque Berkshire countryside. The course architect has retained the numerous mature trees, and these, together with the winding streams, nine lakes and large bunkers, contribute to the beauty and challenge of this championship course.

18 holes, 6579yds, Par 72, SSS 72, Course record 65. Club membership 350.

Visitors Booking required. **Societies** Booking required. **Green Fees** phone. **Prof** Gary Smith **Course Designer** Jonathan Gaunt **Facilities** **Leisure** hard tennis courts, heated indoor swimming pool, fishing, sauna, gymnasium, jacuzzi. **Conf** facs Corporate Hospitality Days **Location** M4 junct 11, A33 towards Basingstoke. 1st rdbt, 3rd exit towards Grazeley After 2.5m right bend club on right

Hotel ★★★ 72% Romans Country House Hotel, Little London Rd, SILCHESTER ☎ 0118 970 0421 11 en suite 14 annexe en suite

NEWBURY Map 04 SU46

Donnington Valley Snelsmore House, Snelsmore Common RG14 3BG
☎ 01635 568140 🖷 01635 568141
e-mail: golf@donningtonvalley.co.uk
web: www.donningtonvalleygolfclub.co.uk

18 holes, 6353yds, Par 71, SSS 71, Course record 71.
Course Designer Mike Smith **Location** 2m N of Newbury
Phone for further details

Hotel ★★★★ 77% Donnington Valley Hotel & Golf Course, Old Oxford Rd, Donnington, NEWBURY ☎ 01635 551199 58 en suite

Newbury & Crookham Bury's Bank Rd, Greenham RG19 8BZ
☎ 01635 40035 🖹 01635 40045
e-mail: steve.myers@newburygolf.co.uk
web: www.newburygolf.co.uk
A traditional English parkland course, whose tree-lined fairways provide a challenge of consistency and accuracy.
18 holes, 5969yds, Par 69, SSS 68, Course record 63. Club membership 800.
Visitors Mon-Fri. Handicap certificate. Dress code. **Societies** Booking required. **Green Fees** £40 per day, £35 per round. **Prof** David Harris **Course Designer** JH Taylor **Facilities** **Conf** Corporate Hospitality Days **Location** 4m S of M4 off A339

READING Map 04 SU77

Calcot Park Bath Rd, Calcot RG31 7RN
☎ 0118 942 7124 🖹 0118 945 3373
e-mail: info@calcotpark.com
web: www.calcotpark.com
A delightfully picturesque, slightly undulating parkland course just outside the town, which celebrated its 75th anniversary in 2005. The subtle borrows on the greens challenge all categories of golfer. Hazards include streams, a lake and many trees. The 6th is a 503yd par 5, with the tee-shot hit downhill over cross-bunkers to a well-guarded green; the 7th (156yds) is played over the lake to an elevated green and the 13th (also 156yds) requires a carry across a valley to a plateau green.
18 holes, 6216yds, Par 70, SSS 70, Course record 63. Club membership 730.
Visitors Mon-Fri. Booking required. Handicap certificate. Dress code. **Societies** Booking required. **Green Fees** £50 per day/round. Off-peak rates. **Prof** Mark Grieve **Course Designer** H Colt **Facilities** **Leisure** fishing. **Conf** facs Corporate Hospitality Days **Location** 1.5m from M4 junct 12 on A4 towards Reading

Hotel ★★★ 67% The Copper Inn Hotel & Restaurant, PANGBOURNE ☎ 0118 984 2244 14 en suite 8 annexe en suite

Hennerton Crazies Hill Rd, Wargrave RG10 8LT
☎ 0118 940 1000 🖹 0118 940 1042
web: www.hennertongolfclub.co.uk
Overlooking the Thames Valley, this course has many existing natural features and a good number of hazards such as bunkers, mature trees and two small lakes. An extended 18-hole course opened in 2005.
9 holes, 5460yds, Par 68, SSS 67, Course record 62. Club membership 450.
Visitors Booking required. **Societies** Booking required. **Green Fees** phone. **Prof** William Farrow **Course Designer** Col D Beard **Facilities** **Conf** Corporate Hospitality Days **Location** Signed from A321 Wargrave High St

Mapledurham Chazey Heath, Mapledurham RG4 7UD
☎ 0118 946 3353 🖹 0118 946 3363
web: www.theclubcompany.com
An 18-hole parkland and woodland course designed by Bob Sandow. Flanked by hedgerows and mature woods, it is testing for players of all levels.
18 holes, 5700yds, Par 69, SSS 67, Course record 65. Club membership 750.
Visitors Mon-Sun & BHs. Booking required. Dress code. **Societies** Booking required. **Green Fees** £20 per round, £26 Sat & Sun. **Prof** Tim Gilpin **Course Designer** Robert Sandow **Facilities** **Leisure** heated indoor swimming pool, sauna, solarium, gymnasium. **Conf** Corporate Hospitality Days **Location** On A4074 to Oxford

Hotel ★★★ 78% The French Horn, SONNING ON THAMES ☎ 0118 969 2204 13 en suite 8 annexe en suite

Reading 17 Kidmore End Rd, Emmer Green RG4 8SG
☎ 0118 947 2909 (secretary) 🖹 0118 946 4468
e-mail: secretary@readinggolfclub.com
web: www.readinggolfclub.com
Pleasant parkland, part hilly and part flat with interesting views and several challenging par 3s. After the opening holes the course moves across the valley. The par 4 5th is played from an elevated tee and although relatively short, the well-placed bunkers and trees come into play. The 470yd par 4 12th is a great hole. It has a slight dog-leg and requires an accurate second shot to hit a well-guarded green. The finishing hole requires two great shots to have any chance of reaching par.
18 holes, 6212yds, Par 70, SSS 70, Course record 65. Club membership 600.
Visitors Mon-Thu. Dress code. **Societies** Booking required. **Green Fees** £48 per day, £32 per round. **Prof** Scott Fotheringham **Course Designer** James Braid **Facilities** **Leisure** indoor nets. **Conf** Corporate Hospitality Days **Location** 2m N off B481

Hotel ★★★ 78% The French Horn, SONNING ON THAMES ☎ 0118 969 2204 13 en suite 8 annexe en suite

SINDLESHAM Map 04 SU76

Bearwood Mole Rd RG41 5DB
☎ 0118 976 0060
e-mail: barrytustin@btconnect.com
Flat parkland with one water hazard, the 40-acre lake that features on the challenging 6th and 7th holes.
9 holes, 5610yds, Par 70, SSS 68, Course record 66. Club membership 500.
Visitors Mon-Sun & BHs. Handicap certificate. Dress code. **Societies** Booking required. **Green Fees** phone. **Prof** Bayley Tustin **Course Designer** Barry Tustin **Facilities** **Location** 1m SW on B3030

Hotel ★★★★ 75% Millennium Madejski Hotel Reading, Madejski Stadium, READING ☎ 0118 925 3500 140 en suite

SONNING Map 04 SU77

Sonning Duffield Rd RG4 6GJ
☎ 0118 969 3332 0118 944 8409
e-mail: secretary@sonning-golf-club.co.uk
web: www.sonning-golf-club.co.uk
A quality parkland course and the scene of many county championships. Wide fairways, not over-bunkered, and very good greens. Holes of changing character through wooded belts. Four challenging par 4s over 450yds.
18 holes, 6366yds, Par 70, SSS 70, Course record 65.
Club membership 750.
Visitors Mon-Fri. Booking required. Handicap certificate. Dress code. **Societies** Wed. Booking required. **Green Fees** £40.50 before 10.30am, £30.50 after 10.30am. **Prof** R McDougall **Course Designer** JH Taylor **Facilities** **Conf** facs Corporate Hospitality Days
Location 1m S off A4

Hotel ★★★ 78% The French Horn, SONNING ON THAMES ☎ 0118 969 2204 13 en suite 8 annexe en suite

STREATLEY Map 04 SU58

Goring & Streatley RG8 9QA
☎ 01491 873229 01491 875224
e-mail: secretary@goringgc.org
web: www.goringgc.org
18 holes, 6355yds, Par 71, SSS 70, Course record 65.
Course Designer Tom Morris **Location** N of village off A417
Phone for further details

Hotel ★★★★ 69% The Swan at Streatley, High St, STREATLEY ☎ 01491 878800 46 en suite

SUNNINGDALE Map 04 SU96

Sunningdale **see page 29**

Hotel ★★★★★ Pennyhill Park Hotel & The Spa, London Rd, BAGSHOT ☎ 01276 471774 26 en suite 97 annexe en suite

Hotel ★★★★ 70% Macdonald Berystede Hotel & Spa, Bagshot Rd, Sunninghill, ASCOT ☎ 0870 400 8111 01344 872301 125 en suite

Hotel ★★★★ The Royal Berkshire Ramada Plaza, London Rd, Sunninghill, ASCOT ☎ 01344 623322 01344 627100 63 en suite

Hotel ★★ 66% Brockenhurst Hotel, Brockenhurst Rd, SOUTH ASCOT ☎ 01344 621912 01344 873252 12 en suite 5 annexe en suite

Sunningdale Ladies Cross Rd SL5 9RX
☎ 01344 620507
e-mail: ladiesgolf@lineone.net
18 holes, 3616yds, Par 60, SSS 60, Course record 51.
Location 1m S off A30
Phone for further details

Hotel ★★★★ 70% Macdonald Berystede Hotel & Spa, Bagshot Rd, Sunninghill, ASCOT ☎ 0870 400 8111 125 en suite

WOKINGHAM Map 04 SU86

Downshire Easthampstead Park RG40 3DH
☎ 01344 302030 01344 301020
e-mail: paul.stanwick@bracknell-forest.gov.uk
Beautiful municipal parkland course with mature trees. Water hazards come into play on the 14th & 18th holes, & especially on the short 7th, a testing downhill 169yds over the lake. Pleasant easy walking. Challenging holes: 7th (par 4), 15th (par 4), 16th (par 3).
18 holes, 6416yds, Par 73, SSS 71.
Club membership 1000.
Visitors Booking required up to 10 days in advance. **Societies** Booking required. **Green Fees** phone. **Prof** Wayne Owers **Facilities** **Leisure** 9 hole pitch & putt. **Location** 3m SW of Bracknell. M4 junct 10, signs for Crowthorne

Hotel ★★★★ 73% Coppid Beech, John Nike Way, BRACKNELL ☎ 01344 303333 205 en suite

Sand Martins Finchampstead Rd RG40 3RQ
☎ 0118 979 2711 0118 977 0282
e-mail: info@sandmartins.com
web: www.sandmartins.com
Two different nine-hole loops: the front nine is mostly tree lined with ponds and the back nine is similar to a links course.

18 holes, 6212yds, Par 70, SSS 70, Course record 65.
Club membership 800.
Visitors Booking required. **Societies** Booking required. **Green Fees** phone. **Prof** Andrew Hall, Stephen Cox **Course Designer** Edward Fox **Facilities** **Conf** facs **Location** 1m S of Wokingham

Hotel ★★★ 69% Corus hotel Bracknell, Duke's Ride, CROWTHORNE ☎ 0870 609 6111 79 en suite

BRISTOL

BRISTOL Map 03 ST57

Bristol and Clifton Beggar Bush Ln, Failand BS8 3TH
☎ 01275 393474 01275 394611
e-mail: mansec@bristolgolf.co.uk
web: www.bristolgolf.co.uk
Utilising the aesthetics and hazards of a former quarry, a valley, stone walls and spinneys of trees, the course is a stern challenge but one always in tip top condition, due in summer to the irrigation and in winter to the natural draining land upon which it is situated. Par 3s

Continued

Championship Course

Sunningdale

Berkshire

Sunningdale

Map 04 SU96

The club has two championship courses, laid out on the most glorious piece of heathland and both courses have their own individual characteristics. The Old Course, founded in 1900, was designed by Willie Park. It is a classic course at just 6308yds long, with gorse and pines, silver birch, heather and immaculate turf. The New Course was created by Harry Colt in 1922 at 6443yds and is a mixture of wood and open heath with long carries and tight fairways.

Ridgemount Rd SL5 9RR
☎ 01344 621681 Fax 01344 624154
web: www.sunningdalegolfclub.co.uk

Old Course: 18 holes, 6308yds, Par 70, SSS 70.
New Course: 18 holes, 6443yds, Par 71, SSS 72.
Club membership 1000.

Visitors Mon-Thu. Booking required. Handicap certificate. Dress code. **Societies** Booking required. **Green Fees** Old Course £165 per round. New Course £125 per round. 36 holes £225. **Prof** Keith Maxwell **Course Designer** W Park **Facilities** **Conf** Corporate Hospitality Days **Location** 1m S off A30

from 120 to 220yds, dog-legs which range from the gentle to the brutal and a collection of natural obstacles and hazards add to the charm of the layout.

Bristol and Clifton

18 holes, 6387yds, Par 70, SSS 71, Course record 63. Club membership 850.

Visitors Mon-Fri except BHs. Booking required Sat & Sun. Handicap certificate. Dress code. **Societies** Booking required. **Green Fees** £40 per day, £45 Sat & Sun. **Prof** Paul Mitchell **Facilities** ⊗ 🍴 🍽 ☕ 🍷 🛍 🏌 🚗 ⛳ 🏌 **Leisure** chipping green, practice bunkers. **Conf** facs Corporate Hospitality Days **Location** M5 junct 19, A369 for 4m, onto B3129, club 1m on right

Hotel ★★★ 68% Corus hotel Bristol, Beggar Bush Ln, Failand, BRISTOL ☎ 0870 609 6144 112 en suite

Filton Golf Course Ln, Filton BS34 7QS
☎ 0117 969 4169 🖷 0117 931 4359
e-mail: thesecretary@filtongolfclub.co.uk
web: www.filtongolfclub.co.uk

Interesting and challenging mature parkland course situated on high ground north of the city. Extensive views can be enjoyed from the course to the Concorde and Severn bridges.

18 holes, 6173yds, Par 70, SSS 70, Course record 61. Club membership 750.

Visitors Mon-Fri. Handicap certificate. Dress code. **Societies** Booking required. **Green Fees** £28 per round. **Prof** D Kelley **Facilities** ⊗ 🍴 🍽 ☕ 🍷 🛍 🏌 **Conf** Corporate Hospitality Days **Location** M5 junct 15, off A38

Hotel ⌂ Premier Travel Inn Bristol (Filton), Shield Retail Park, Gloucester Rd North, Filton, BRISTOL ☎ 0870 9906456 60 en suite

Henbury Henbury Hill, Westbury-on-Trym BS10 7QB
☎ 0117 950 0044 & 950 2121 (pro) 🖷 0117 959 1928
e-mail: thesecretary@henburygolfclub.co.uk
web: www.henburygolfclub.co.uk

18 holes, 6007yds, Par 69, SSS 70, Course record 65.

Location 3m NW of city centre on B4055 off A4018

Phone for further details

Hotel ★★★ 66% Henbury Lodge Hotel, Station Rd, Henbury, BRISTOL ☎ 0117 950 2615 12 en suite 9 annexe en suite

Knowle West Town Ln, Brislington BS4 5DF
☎ 0117 977 0660 🖷 0117 972 0615
e-mail: mike@knowlegolfclub.co.uk
web: www.knowlegolfclub.co.uk

Parkland with nice turf. The first five holes climb up and down hill but the remainder are on a more even plane.

18 holes, 6006yds, Par 69, SSS 69, Course record 61. Club membership 700.

Visitors Mon-Sun & BHs. Booking required. Handicap certificate. Dress code. **Societies** Booking required. **Green Fees** £35 per day, £28 per round, £40/£33 Sat & Sun. **Prof** Robert Hayward **Course Designer** Hawtree, JH Taylor **Facilities** ⊗ 🍴 🍽 ☕ 🍷 🛍 🏌 🚗 ⛳ **Location** 3m SE of city centre off A37

Hotel ★★★ 79% Hunstrete House Hotel, HUNSTRETE ☎ 01761 490490 25 en suite

Mangotsfield Carsons Rd, Mangotsfield BS17 3LW
☎ 0117 956 5501

18 holes, 5337yds, Par 68, SSS 66, Course record 61.

Course Designer John Day **Location** 6m NE of city centre off B4465

Phone for further details

Hotel ⌂ Premier Travel Inn Bristol East, 200-202 Westerleigh Rd, Emersons Green, BRISTOL ☎ 08701 977042 40 en suite

Shirehampton Park Park Hill, Shirehampton BS11 0UL
☎ 0117 982 2083 🖷 0117 982 5280
e-mail: info@shirehamptonparkgolfclub.co.uk
web: www.shirehamptonparkgolfclub.co.uk

Lovely parkland course with views across the Avon Gorge.

18 holes, 5430yds, Par 67, SSS 66, Course record 63. Club membership 600.

Visitors Mon-Fri. Booking required. Handicap certificate. Dress code. **Societies** Booking required. **Green Fees** phone. **Prof** Brent Ellis **Facilities** ⊗ 🍽 ☕ 🍷 🛍 🏌 ⛳ **Location** M5 junct 18, 2m E on B4054

Hotel ★★★ 68% Corus hotel Bristol, Beggar Bush Ln, Failand, BRISTOL ☎ 0870 609 6144 112 en suite

Woodlands Trench Ln, Almondsbury BS32 4JZ
☎ 01454 619319 🖷 01454 619397
e-mail: info@woodlands-golf.com
web: www.woodlands-golf.com

Situated on the edge of the Severn Valley, bordered by Hortham Brook and Shepherds Wood, this interesting parkland course features five testing par 3s set around the course's five lakes, notably the 206yd 5th hole which extends over water.

18 holes, 6068yds, Par 70, SSS 69. Club membership 45.

Visitors Mon-Sun & BHs. **Societies** welcome. **Green Fees** £14 per round, £16 Sat, Sun & BHs. **Prof** L Riddiford **Facilities** ⊗ 🍴 🍽 ☕ 🍷 🛍 🏌 🚗 ⛳ **Leisure** fishing. **Conf** facs Corporate Hospitality Days **Location** M5 junct 16, A38 towards Bradley Store

Hotel ★★ 68% The Bowl Inn, 16 Church Rd, Lower Almondsbury, BRISTOL ☎ 01454 612757 11 rms (2 en suite) 2 annexe en suite

BUCKINGHAMSHIRE

AYLESBURY Map 04 SP81

Aylesbury Golf Centre Hulcott Ln, Bierton HP22 5GA
☎ 01296 393644
Parkland with magnificent views to the Chiltern Hills. A good test of golf with out of bounds coming into play on nine of the holes, plus a number of water hazards and bunkers.
18 holes, 5965yds, Par 71, SSS 69.
Club membership 200.
Visitors Mon-Sun & BHs. Booking required. Dress code. **Societies** Booking required. **Green Fees** phone. **Prof** Richard Wooster **Course Designer** TS Benwell **Facilities** **Conf** Corporate Hospitality Days **Location** 1m N of Aylesbury on A418

Hotel Premier Travel Inn Aylesbury, Buckingham Rd, AYLESBURY ☎ 08701 977019 64 en suite

Aylesbury Park Andrews Way, Off Coldharbour Way, Oxford Rd HP17 8QQ
☎ 01296 399196 01296 336830
e-mail: info@aylesburyparkgolf.com
web: www.aylesburyparkgolf.com
Parkland with mature trees, located just south-west of Aylesbury.
18 holes, 6166yds, Par 70, SSS 69, Course record 66.
Club membership 379.
Visitors Mon-Sun & BHs. **Societies** Booking required. **Green Fees** £16.50, £22 Sat & Sun. **Course Designer** M Hawtree **Facilities** **Leisure** 9 hole par 3 course. **Location** 0.5m SW of Aylesbury, on A418

Hotel ★★★★ Hartwell House Hotel Restaurant & Spa, Oxford Rd, AYLESBURY ☎ 01296 747444 30 en suite 16 annexe en suite

Chiltern Forest Aston Hill, Halton HP22 5NQ
☎ 01296 631267 01296 632709
e-mail: secretary@chilternforest.co.uk
web: www.chilternforest.co.uk
The course nestles in the Chiltern Hills above Aylesbury with stunning views of the surrounding countryside and meanders around challenging wooded terrain. Although not a long course the tightly wooded holes and smallish greens present a challenge to all standards of golfer.
18 holes, 5765yds, Par 70, SSS 69, Course record 65.
Club membership 650.
Visitors Mon-Fri. Handicap certificate. Dress code. **Societies** Booking required. **Green Fees** £40 per day, £34 per round. **Prof** A Lavers **Facilities** **Conf** Corporate Hospitality Days **Location** off A41 between Tring and Aylesbury

Hotel Innkeeper's Lodge Aylesbury East, London Rd, ASTON CLINTON ☎ 01296 632777 11 en suite

Ellesborough Wendover Rd, Butlers Cross HP17 0TZ
☎ 01296 622114 01296 622114
e-mail: admin@ellesboroughgolf.co.uk
web: www.ellesboroughgolf.co.uk
Once part of the property of Chequers, and under the shadow of the famous Coombe monument at the

Continued

Wendover end of the Chilterns. A downland course, it is rather hilly with most holes enhanced by far-ranging views over the Aylesbury countryside.
18 holes, 6360yds, Par 71, SSS 71, Course record 64.
Club membership 700.
Visitors Mon-Fri. Handicap certificate. Dress code. **Societies** Booking required. **Green Fees** £50 per day, £30 per round. **Prof** Mark Squire **Course Designer** James Braid **Facilities** **Conf** Corporate Hospitality Days **Location** 1m W of Wendover on B4010 towards Princes Risborough

Hotel Innkeeper's Lodge Aylesbury South, 40 Main St, Weston Turville, AYLESBURY
☎ 01296 613131 & 0870 243 0500 01296 616902
16 en suite

BEACONSFIELD Map 04 SU99

Beaconsfield Seer Green HP9 2UR
☎ 01494 676545 01494 681148
e-mail: secretary@beaconsfieldgolfclub.co.uk
web: www.beaconsfieldgolfclub.co.uk
An interesting and, at times, testing tree-lined and parkland course which frequently plays longer than appears on the card. Each hole differs to a considerable degree and here lies the charm. Walking is easy, except perhaps to the 6th and 8th. Well bunkered.
18 holes, 6506yds, Par 72, SSS 71, Course record 63.
Club membership 900.
Visitors Mon-Fri except BHs. Booking required. Handicap certificate. Dress code. **Societies** Phone for details **Green Fees** £60 per day. £50 per round. **Prof** Michael Brothers **Course Designer** H Colt **Facilities** **Conf** Corporate Hospitality Days **Location** M40 junct 2, next to Seer Green railway station

Hotel Innkeeper's Lodge Beaconsfield, Aylesbury End, BEACONSFIELD ☎ 01494 671211 32 en suite

BLETCHLEY Map 04 SP83

Windmill Hill Tattenhoe Ln MK3 7RB
☎ 01908 631113 & 366457 (sec) 01908 630034

Windmill Hill Golf Course: 18 holes, 6720yds, Par 73, SSS 72, Course record 68.
Course Designer Henry Cotton **Location** W side of town centre on A421
Phone for further details

Hotel Campanile, 40 Penn Rd, Fenny Stratford, Bletchley, MILTON KEYNES ☎ 01908 649819
80 en suite

BUCKINGHAM Map 04 SP63

Buckingham Tingewick Rd MK18 4AE
☎ 01280 815566 01280 821812
e-mail: admin@buckinghamgolfclub.co.uk
web: www.buckinghamgolfclub.co.uk
Undulating parkland with a stream and river affecting eight holes.
18 holes, 6162yds, Par 71, SSS 70, Course record 66.
Club membership 740.
Visitors Mon-Fri. Dress code. **Societies** Booking required. **Green Fees** £45 per day, £35 per 18 holes. **Prof** Greg Hannah **Course Designer** Peter Jones **Facilities** **Leisure** snooker room. **Location** 1.5m W on A421

Hotel ★★★ 67% Best Western Buckingham Beales Hotel, Buckingham Ring Rd, BUCKINGHAM ☎ 01280 822622 70 en suite

BURNHAM Map 04 SU98

Burnham Beeches Green Ln SL1 8EG
☎ 01628 661448 01628 668968
e-mail: enquiries@bbgc.co.uk
web: www.bbgc.co.uk
Wooded parkland on the edge of the historic Burnham Beeches Forest with a good variety of holes.
18 holes, 6449yds, Par 70, SSS 71, Course record 66.
Club membership 670.
Visitors Mon, Tue pm, Wed-Sun except BHs. Handicap certificate. Dress code. **Societies** Booking required. **Green Fees** £40 per round. **Prof** Ronnie Bolton **Course Designer** JH Taylor **Facilities** **Location** 0.5m NE of Burnham

Hotel ★★★ 64% Burnham Beeches Hotel, Grove Rd, BURNHAM ☎ 0870 609 6124 82 en suite

Lambourne Dropmore Rd SL1 8NF
☎ 01628 666755 01628 663301
A championship standard 18-hole parkland course. Undulating terrain with many trees and several lakes, notably on the tricky 7th hole which has a tightly guarded green reached via a shot over a lake. Seven par 4s over 400yds with six picturesque lakes, excellent drainage and full irrigation.
18 holes, 6771yds, Par 72, SSS 73, Course record 67.
Club membership 650.
Visitors Mon-Fri. Booking required. Dress code. **Societies** Booking required. **Green Fees** £60 per round. **Prof** David Hart **Course Designer** Donald Steel **Facilities** **Leisure** sauna. **Location** M4 junct 7 or M40 junct 2, towards Burnham

Hotel ★★★ 64% Burnham Beeches Hotel, Grove Rd, BURNHAM ☎ 0870 609 6124 82 en suite

CHALFONT ST GILES Map 04 SU99

Harewood Downs Cokes Ln HP8 4TA
☎ 01494 762184 01494 766869
e-mail: secretary@hdgc.co.uk
web: www.hdgc.co.uk
A testing undulating parkland course with sloping greens and plenty of trees.
18 holes, 5958yds, Par 69, SSS 69, Course record 63.
Club membership 600.
Visitors Booking required. Handicap certificate. Dress code. **Societies** Booking required. **Green Fees** £33 per round, £38 Sat & Sun. **Prof** GC Morris **Course Designer** JH Taylor **Facilities** by arrangement **Conf** Corporate Hospitality Days **Location** 2m E of Amersham on A413

Hotel ★★★ 67% The Crown, High St, AMERSHAM ☎ 0870 400 8103 19 en suite 18 annexe en suite

Oakland Park Threehouseholds HP8 4LW
☎ 01494 871277 & 877333 (pro) 01494 874692
e-mail: info@oaklandparkgolf.co.uk
web: www.oaklandparkgolf.co.uk
Parkland with mature trees, hedgerows and water features, designed to respect the natural features of the land and lakes while providing a good challenge for players at all levels.
18 holes, 5246yds, Par 67, SSS 66, Course record 66.
Club membership 650.
Visitors Mon-Sun & BHs. Booking required. Dress code. **Societies** Booking required. **Green Fees** £25 per 18 holes, £30 Sat, Sun & BHs. **Prof** Alistair Thatcher **Course Designer** Jonathan Gaunt **Facilities** **Conf** Corporate Hospitality Days **Location** M40 junct 2, 3m N

Hotel ★★★ 67% The Crown, High St, AMERSHAM ☎ 0870 400 8103 19 en suite 18 annexe en suite

CHARTRIDGE Map 04 SP90

Chartridge Park HP5 2TF
☎ 01494 791772 01494 786462
e-mail: ian@cpgc.co.uk
web: www.cpgc.co.uk
A family run, easy walking parkland course set high in the beautiful Chiltern Hills, affording breathtaking views.
18 holes, 5516yds, Par 69, SSS 67, Course record 65.
Club membership 700.
Visitors Mon-Sun except BHs. Booking required. Handicap certificate. Dress code. **Societies** Booking required. **Green Fees** phone. **Course Designer** John Jacobs **Facilities** **Conf** facs Corporate Hospitality Days **Location** 3m NW of Chesham

Hotel ★★★ 67% The Crown, High St, AMERSHAM ☎ 0870 400 8103 19 en suite 18 annexe en suite

CHESHAM Map 04 SP90

Chesham & Ley Hill Ley Hill Common HP5 1UZ
☎ 01494 784541 01494 785506
e-mail: secretary@cheshamgolf.co.uk
web: www.cheshamgolf.co.uk
Wooded parkland on hilltop with easy walking.
9 holes, 5296yds, Par 67, SSS 65, Course record 62.
Club membership 350.
Visitors Mon-Fri. Dress code. **Societies** Booking required. **Green Fees** £15. **Prof** James Short **Facilities** **Leisure** practice net. **Conf** facs **Location** 2m E of Chesham, off A41 on B4504 to Ley Hill

Hotel ★★★ 67% The Crown, High St, AMERSHAM ☎ 0870 400 8103 19 en suite 18 annexe en suite

Continued

DAGNALL Map 04 SP91

Whipsnade Park Studham Ln HP4 1RH
☎ 01442 842330 🗎 01442 842090
e-mail: whipsnadeparkgolfc@btopenworld.com
web: www.whipsnadeparkgolf.co.uk
Parkland on downs adjoining Whipsnade Zoo. Easy walking, good views.
18 holes, 6800yds, Par 73, SSS 72, Course record 66. Club membership 600.
Visitors Mon-Sun & BHs. Booking required. Dress code. **Societies** Booking required. **Green Fees** £40 per day, £29 per round (after 1pm Sat, Sun & BHs). **Prof** Mark Day **Facilities** by arrangement **Location** 1m E off B4506 between Dagnall

Hotel ★★★ 63% Old Palace Lodge, Church St, DUNSTABLE ☎ 01582 662201 68 en suite

DENHAM Map 04 TQ08

Buckinghamshire Denham Court Dr UB9 5PG
☎ 01895 835777 🗎 01895 835210
e-mail: enquiries@buckinghamshiregc.co.uk
web: www.buckinghamshiregc.com
The course runs in two loops of nine starting and finishing at the clubhouse. The fairways wander through three distinct areas incorporating woodland, lakes and rivers and undulating links style land, providing a variety of golfing terrain calling for careful thought on every shot. The greens are constructed to USGA specification with excellent drainage and smooth true putting surfaces.
18 holes, 6880yds, Par 72, SSS 73, Course record 62. Club membership 600.
Visitors Mon-Sun & BHs. Booking required. Dress code. **Societies** Booking required. **Green Fees** £90 per 18 holes, £100 Fri-Sun & BHs. **Prof** Paul Schunter **Course Designer** John Jacobs **Facilities** **Conf** facs Corporate Hospitality Days **Location** M25 junct 16, signed Uxbridge

Hotel ★★★ 71% Barn Hotel, West End Rd, RUISLIP ☎ 01895 636057 59 en suite

Denham Tilehouse Ln UB9 5DE
☎ 01895 832022 🗎 01895 835340
e-mail: club.secretary@denhamgolfclub.co.uk
web: www.denhamgolfclub.co.uk
A beautifully maintained parkland and heathland course, home of many county champions. Slightly hilly and calling for good judgement of distance in the wooded areas.
18 holes, 6462yds, Par 70, SSS 71, Course record 66. Club membership 790.
Visitors Booking required. Handicap certificate. **Societies** Tue-Thu. Booking required. **Green Fees** phone. **Prof** Stuart Campbell **Course Designer** H Colt **Facilities** **Conf** Corporate Hospitality Days **Location** 0.5m N of North Orbital Road, 2m from Uxbridge

Hotel ★★★ 71% Barn Hotel, West End Rd, RUISLIP ☎ 01895 636057 59 en suite

FLACKWELL HEATH Map 04 SU89

Flackwell Heath Treadaway Rd, High Wycombe HP10 9PE
☎ 01628 520929 🗎 01628 530040
e-mail: secretary@flackwellheathgolfclub.co.uk
web: www.flackwellheathgolfclub.co.uk
Open sloping heath and tree-lined course on hills overlooking the Chilterns. Some good challenging par 3s and several testing small greens.
18 holes, 6211yds, Par 71, SSS 70, Course record 63. Club membership 700.
Visitors Wed & Thu. Booking required. Handicap certificate. Dress code. **Societies** Wed & Thu. Booking required. **Green Fees** £30 per round. **Prof** Paul Watson **Course Designer** JH Taylor **Facilities** **Conf** facs Corporate Hospitality Days **Location** E side of High Wycombe, NE side of town centre

Hotel Premier Travel Inn High Wycombe, Thanestead Farm, London Rd, Loudwater, HIGH WYCOMBE ☎ 08701 977135 81 en suite

GERRARDS CROSS Map 04 TQ08

Gerrards Cross Chalfont Park SL9 0QA
☎ 01753 883263 (sec) & 885300 (pro) 🗎 01753 883593
e-mail: secretary@gxgolf.co.uk
A wooded parkland course that has been modernised in recent years and is now a very pleasant circuit with infinite variety. The best part lies on the plateau above the clubhouse where there are some testing holes.
18 holes, 6212yds, Par 69, SSS 70, Course record 64. Club membership 700.
Visitors Mon-Fri. Booking required. Handicap certificate. Dress code. **Societies** Booking required. **Green Fees** £53 per day, £40 per round. **Prof** Matthew Barr **Course Designer** Bill Pedlar **Facilities** **Location** NE side of town centre off A413

HIGH WYCOMBE Map 04 SU89

Hazlemere Penn Rd, Hazlemere HP15 7LR
☎ 01494 719300 🗎 01494 713914
e-mail: enquiries@hazlemeregolfclub.co.uk
web: www.hazlemeregolfclub.co.uk
Undulating parkland course located in the Chiltern Hills in an area of outstanding natural beauty. Deceiving in its yardage and a challenge to golfers of all standards.
18 holes, 5810yds, Par 70, SSS 67, Course record 61. Club membership 600.
Visitors Mon-Sun & BHs. Booking required. Dress code. **Societies** Booking required. **Green Fees** phone. **Prof** Gavin Cousins, Paul Harrison **Course Designer** Terry Murray **Facilities** **Conf** facs **Location** On B474 between Beaconsfield , 2m NE of High Wycombe

Hotel ★★★ 67% The Crown, High St, AMERSHAM ☎ 0870 400 8103 19 en suite 18 annexe en suite

IVER Map 04 TQ08

Iver Hollow Hill Ln, Langley Park Rd SL0 0JJ
☎ 01753 655615 🗎 01753 654225
Fairly flat, pay and play parkland course with challenging par 5s, plenty of hazards - water and ditches - and strong crosswinds to contend with. Most

Continued

greens are elevated with plenty of slopes. The short par 3 course is challenging with very small greens.
9 holes, 6288yds, Par 72, SSS 72, Course record 66.
Club membership 200.
Visitors Mon-Fri. Booking required. **Societies** Booking required. **Green Fees** phone. **Prof** Jim Lynch **Facilities** **Leisure** bunker & chipping area, par 3 course. **Location** M4 junct 5, 1.5m SW off B470

Hotel ★★★★ 70% Slough/Windsor Marriott Hotel, Ditton Rd, Langley, SLOUGH ☎ 0870 400 7244 382 en suite

Richings Park Golf & Country Club North Park SL0 9DL

☎ 01753 655370 & 655352 (pro shop) 01753 655409
e-mail: info@richingspark.co.uk
web: www.richingspark.co.uk
Set among mature trees and attractive lakes, this testing par 70 parkland course provides a suitable challenge to golfers of all abilities. Well-irrigated greens and abundant wildlife.
18 holes, 6144yds, Par 70, SSS 69, Course record 63.
Club membership 500.
Visitors Mon-Thu. Booking required Fri-Sun & BHs. Handicap certificate. Dress code. **Societies** Booking required. **Green Fees** £25 per round, £32 Sat, Sun & BHs. **Prof** Ben Tarry **Course Designer** Alan Higgins **Facilities** **Conf** facs Corporate Hospitality Days **Location** M4 junct 5, A4 towards Colnbrook, left at lights, Sutton Lane, right at next lights North Park

Hotel ★★★ 69% Courtyard by Marriott Slough/Windsor, Church St, SLOUGH ☎ 0870 400 7215 & 07153 551551 0870 400 7315 150 en suite

Thorney Park Thorney Mill Rd SL0 9AL

☎ 01895 422095 01895 431307
e-mail: sales@thorneypark.com
web: www.thorneypark.com
An 18-hole parkland course which will test both the beginner and established golfer. Fairway irrigation ensures lush green fairways and smooth putting surfaces. Many interesting holes including the testing par 4 9th which needs a long drive to the water's edge and a well-hit iron onto the bunker-guarded green. The back nine finishes with two water holes, the 17th, a near island green and the shot of 150yds makes this a picturesque hole. The 18th has more water than grass.
18 holes, 5765yds, Par 69, SSS 68, Course record 69.
Club membership 350.
Visitors Mon-Sun & BHs. Dress code. **Societies** Booking required. **Green Fees** £22 per 18 holes, £28 per round Sat & Sun. **Prof** Andrew Killing **Course Designer** David Walker **Facilities** **Conf** facs Corporate Hospitality Days **Location** M4 junct 5, left onto A4, left onto Sutton Ln, right for Thorney Mill Rd

Hotel ★★★★ 70% Slough/Windsor Marriott Hotel, Ditton Rd, Langley, SLOUGH ☎ 0870 400 7244 382 en suite

LITTLE BRICKHILL Map 04 SP93

Woburn Golf & Country Club see page 35

Hotel ★★★ Menzies Flitwick Manor, Church Rd, FLITWICK ☎ 01525 712242 17 en suite

Hotel ★★★ 74% The Inn at Woburn, George St, WOBURN ☎ 01525 290441 01525 290432 50 en suite 7 annexe en suite

Hotel ★★★ 69% Moore Place Hotel, The Square, ASPLEY GUISE ☎ 01908 282000 01908 281888 37 en suite 27 annexe en suite

LITTLE CHALFONT Map 04 SU99

Little Chalfont Lodge Ln HP8 4AJ

☎ 01494 764877 01494 762860
Gently undulating parkland surrounded by mature trees.
9 holes, 5752yds, Par 70, SSS 68, Course record 66.
Club membership 300.
Visitors Mon-Sun. Booking required. **Societies** Booking required. **Green Fees** phone. **Prof** M Dunne **Course Designer** JM Dunne **Facilities** **Leisure** one motorised cart for hire by arrangement. **Conf** facs Corporate Hospitality Days **Location** M25 junct 18, on A404 between Little Chalfont & Chorleywood

Hotel ★★★ 67% The Crown, High St, AMERSHAM ☎ 0870 400 8103 19 en suite 18 annexe en suite

LOUDWATER Map 04 SU89

Wycombe Heights Golf Centre Rayners Ave HP10 9SZ

☎ 01494 816686 01494 816728
An impressive tree-lined parkland course with panoramic views of the Chilterns. The final four holes are particularly challenging. A delightful 18 hole par 3 course and floodlit driving range complement the High Course.

High Course: 18 holes, 6265yds, Par 70, SSS 71, Course record 64.
Club membership 600.
Visitors Booking required. Dress code. **Societies** Booking required. **Green Fees** £17 per round, £25 Sat, Sun & BHs. **Prof** Joe McKie **Course Designer** John Jacobs **Facilities** **Leisure** par 3 course. **Conf** facs Corporate Hospitality Days **Location** M40 junct 3, A40 towards High Wycombe. 0.5m right onto Rayners Ave at lights

Hotel Premier Travel Inn High Wycombe, Thanestead Farm, London Rd, Loudwater, HIGH WYCOMBE ☎ 08701 977135 81 en suite

Continued

Woburn

Buckinghamshire

Little Brickhill

Map 04 SP93

Easily accessible from the M1, Woburn is famed not only for its golf courses but also for the magnificent stately home and wildlife park, which are both well worth a visit. Charles Lawrie of Cotton Pennink designed two great courses here among trees and beautiful countryside. From the back tees they are rather long for the weekend amateur golfer. The Duke's Course is a tough challenge for golfers at all levels. The Duchess Course, although relatively easier, still demands a high level of skills to negotiate the fairways guarded by towering pines. The Duke's has become the home of the increasingly popular Weetabix Women's British Open, held here since 1990. The town of Woburn and the abbey are in Bedfordshire, while the golf and country club are over the border in Buckinghamshire.

MK17 9LJ
☎ 01908 370756 🖹 01908 378436
e-mail: enquiries@woburngolf.com
web: www.woburngolf.com

Duke's Course: 18 holes, 6973yds, Par 72, SSS 74, Course record 62.
Duchess Course: 18 holes, 6651yds, Par 72, SSS 72.
Marquess Course: 18 holes, 7214yds, Par 72, SSS 74.

Visitors Mon-Fri. Booking required. Handicap certificate. **Societies** Booking required. **Green Fees** May-Oct £140-£150 per day including lunch. Nov-Feb £75, Mar £95, Apr £115. Aug & Oct £100-£115 per round including lunch.. **Prof** Luther Blacklock **Course Designer** Charles Lawrie **Facilities** ⊗ **Leisure** heated outdoor swimming pool. **Conf** Corporate Hospitality Days **Location** M1 junct 13, 4m W off A5130

Marlow Map 04 SU88

Harleyford Harleyford Estate, Henley Rd SL7 2SP
☎ 01628 816164 01628 816160
e-mail: info@harleyfordgolf.co.uk
web: www.harleyfordgolf.co.uk
Set in 160 acres, this Donald Steel designed course, founded in 1996, makes the most of the natural rolling contours of the beautiful parkland of the historic Harleyford Estate. A challenging course to golfers of all handicaps. Stunning views of the Thames Valley.

18 holes, 6708yds, Par 72, SSS 72, Course record 68. Club membership 750.
Visitors Mon-Fri after 10am. Sat & Sun after 11.30am. Booking required. Dress code. **Societies** Booking required. **Green Fees** phone. **Prof** Darren Brewer **Course Designer** Donald Steel **Facilities** **Conf** facs Corporate Hospitality Days **Location** S side A4156 Marlow-Henley road

Hotel ★★★★ 85% Danesfield House Hotel & Spa, Henley Rd, MARLOW-ON-THAMES ☎ 01628 891010 87 en suite

Mentmore Map 04 SP91

Mentmore Golf & Country Club LU7 0UA
☎ 01296 662020 01296 662592
Rosebery Course: 18 holes, 6777yds, Par 72, SSS 72, Course record 68.
Rothschild Course: 18 holes, 6700yds, Par 72, SSS 72.
Course Designer Bob Sandow **Location** 4m S of Leighton Buzzard
Phone for further details

Hotel ★★★ 63% Old Palace Lodge, Church St, DUNSTABLE ☎ 01582 662201 68 en suite

Milton Keynes Map 04 SP83

Abbey Hill Monks Way, Two Mile Ash MK8 8AA
☎ 01908 562408
e-mail: steve.tompkins@ukonline.co.uk

18 holes, 6122yds, Par 71, SSS 69, Course record 71.
Location 2m W of town centre off A5
Phone for further details

Hotel ★★★ 66% Quality Hotel & Suites Milton Keynes, Monks Way, Two Mile Ash, MILTON KEYNES
☎ 01908 561666 88 en suite

Three Locks Great Brickhill MK17 9BH
☎ 01525 270050 01525 270470
e-mail: info@threelocksgolfclub.co.uk
web: www.threelocksgolfclub.co.uk
Parkland course offering a challenge to beginners and experienced golfers, with water coming into play on ten holes. Magnificent views.
18 holes, 6036yds, Par 70, SSS 69, Course record 60. Club membership 300.
Visitors Mon-Sun & BHs. Dress code. **Societies** Booking required. **Green Fees** £28 per day, £19 per round, £35/£25 Sat, Sun & BHs. **Prof** G Harding **Course Designer** MRM Sandown **Facilities** **Leisure** fishing. **Location** A4146 between Leighton Buzzard & Bletchley

Hotel Campanile, 40 Penn Rd, Fenny Stratford, Bletchley, MILTON KEYNES ☎ 01908 649819 80 en suite

Princes Risborough Map 04 SP80

Whiteleaf Upper Icknield Way, Whiteleaf HP27 0LY
☎ 01844 274058 01844 275551
e-mail: whiteleafgc@tiscali.co.uk
A picturesque nine-hole course on the edge of the Chilterns. Good views over the Vale of Aylesbury. A short challenging course requiring great accuracy.
9 holes, 5391yds, Par 66, SSS 66, Course record 64. Club membership 300.
Visitors Mon, Wed-Fri. Booking required Thu. Handicap certificate. Dress code. **Societies** Booking required. **Green Fees** £17.50 per 18 holes, £12 per 9 holes. **Prof** Ken Ward **Facilities** **Location** 1m NE off A4010

STOKE POGES Map 04 SU98

Farnham Park Park Rd SL2 4PJ
☎ 01753 643332 & 647065 Fax 01753 643332 & 647065
e-mail: farnhamparkgolfclub@btopenworld.com
web: www.farnhampark.co.uk
18 holes, 6172yds, Par 71, SSS 70, Course record 68.
Course Designer Hawtree **Location** W side of village off B416
Phone for further details

Hotel ★★★★ 70% Slough/Windsor Marriott Hotel, Ditton Rd, Langley, SLOUGH ☎ 0870 400 7244 382 en suite

Stoke Park Stoke Park, Park Rd SL2 4PG
☎ 01753 717171 Fax 01753 717181
e-mail: info@stokeparkclub.com
web: www.stokeparkclub.com
Judgement of the distance from the tee is all important on this classic parkland course. Fairways are wide and the challenge seemingly innocuous - testing par 4s, superb bunkering and fast putting surfaces. The 7th hole is the model for the well-known 12th hole at Augusta.
Course 1: 18 holes, 6721yds, Par 71, SSS 72, Course record 65.
Course 2: 18 holes, 6551yds, Par 72, SSS 73.
Course 3: 18 holes, 6318yds, Par 71, SSS 70.
Club membership 2500.
Visitors Booking required. **Societies** Booking required. **Green Fees** phone. **Prof** Stuart Collier **Course Designer** H Colt **Facilities** **Leisure** hard and grass tennis courts, heated indoor swimming pool, fishing, sauna, gymnasium, indoor tennis courts. treatment room spa. **Conf** facs Corporate Hospitality Days **Location** Off A4 at Slough onto B416 Stoke Poges Ln, club 1.5m on left

Hotel ★★★★ 70% Slough/Windsor Marriott Hotel, Ditton Rd, Langley, SLOUGH ☎ 0870 400 7244 382 en suite

STOWE Map 04 SP63

Silverstone Silverstone Rd MK18 5LH
☎ 01280 850005 Fax 01280 850156
e-mail: proshop@silverstonegolfclub.co.uk
Set in the rolling north Buckinghamshire countryside, the course offers an interesting challenge for both experienced players and those with a higher handicap. Fairly flat parkland with water features on nine holes.
18 holes, 6472yards, Par 72, SSS 71, Course record 65.
Club membership 432.
Visitors Mon-Sun. **Societies** Booking required. **Green Fees** phone. **Prof** Rodney Holt **Course Designer** David Snell **Facilities** **Conf** facs Corporate Hospitality Days **Location** From Silverstone signs to Grand Prix track. Club 1m past entrance on right

Hotel ★★★★ 65% Villiers Hotel, 3 Castle St, BUCKINGHAM ☎ 01280 822444 46 en suite

WAVENDON Map 04 SP93

Wavendon Golf Centre Lower End Rd MK17 8DA
☎ 01908 281811 Fax 01908 281257
e-mail: wavendon@jack-barker.co.uk
web: www.jack-barker.co.uk
Pleasant parkland course set within mature oak and lime trees and incorporating several small lakes as water hazards. Easy walking.

18 holes, 5570yds, Par 69, SSS 68.
Club membership 300.
Visitors Mon-Sun & BHs. **Societies** Booking required. **Green Fees** phone. **Prof** Greg Iron **Course Designer** J Drake, N Elmer **Facilities** **Leisure** 9 hole par 3 course. **Conf** facs **Location** M1 junct 13, off A421

Hotel ★★★ 69% Moore Place Hotel, The Square, ASPLEY GUISE ☎ 01908 282000 37 en suite 27 annexe en suite

WESTON TURVILLE Map 04 SP81

Weston Turville Golf New Rd HP22 5QT
☎ 01296 424084 Fax 01296 395376
e-mail: westonturvillegc@btconnect.com
web: www.westonturvillegolfclub.co.uk
18 holes, 6008yds, Par 69, SSS 69, Course record 68.
Location 2m SE of Aylesbury, off A41
Phone for further details

Hotel Innkeeper's Lodge Aylesbury South, 40 Main St, Weston Turville, AYLESBURY
☎ 01296 613131 & 0870 243 0500 Fax 01296 616902
16 en suite

WEXHAM STREET Map 04 SU98

Wexham Park SL3 6ND
☎ 01753 663271 Fax 01753 663318
e-mail: wexhamgolf@freenetname.co.uk
web: www.wexhamparkgolfcourse.co.uk
Gently undulating parkland. Three courses, an 18 hole, a challenging nine hole, and another nine hole suitable for beginners.
Blue: 18 holes, 5346yds, Par 68, SSS 66.
Red: 9 holes, 2822yds, Par 34.
Green: 9 holes, 2233yds, Par 32.
Club membership 850.
Visitors Mon-Sat except BHs. Booking required. **Societies** Booking required. **Green Fees** £15 per 18 holes, £8.50 per 9 holes, £19.50/£11 Sat & Sun. **Prof** John Kennedy **Course Designer** E Lawrence, D Morgan **Facilities** **Conf** Corporate Hospitality Days **Location** 0.5m S

Hotel ★★★★ 70% Slough/Windsor Marriott Hotel, Ditton Rd, Langley, SLOUGH ☎ 0870 400 7244 382 en suite

WING Map 04 SP82

Aylesbury Vale Stewkley Rd LU7 0UJ
☎ 01525 240196 🖹 01525 240848
e-mail: info@avgc.co.uk
web: avgc.co.uk
This gently undulating course is set amid tranquil countryside. There are five ponds to pose the golfer problems, notably on the par 4 420yd 13th - unlucky for some - where the second shot is all downhill with an inviting pond spanning the approach to the green. In addition there is a practice putting green.
18 holes, 6612yds, Par 72, SSS 72, Course record 67.
Club membership 515.
Visitors Mon-Sun & BHs. Booking required. Dress code. **Societies** Booking required. **Green Fees** £25 per day, £20 per round, £10 per 9 holes. £29 per day, £25 per round, £20 after 11am Sat & Sun. **Prof** Terry Bunyan **Course Designer** D Wright **Facilities** **Conf** facs Corporate Hospitality Days **Location** 2m NW of Leighton Buzzard on unclassified Stewkley road, between Wing & Stewkley

Hotel ★★★ 63% Old Palace Lodge, Church St, DUNSTABLE ☎ 01582 662201 68 en suite

CAMBRIDGESHIRE

BAR HILL Map 05 TL36

Menzies Cambridge Hotel Bar Hill CB3 8EU
☎ 01954 780098 & 249971 🖹 01954 780010
web: www.cambridgeshiregolf.co.uk
18 holes, 6734yds, Par 72, SSS 73, Course record 68.
Location M11/A14, then B1050 (Bar Hill)
Phone for further details

Hotel ★★★★ 75% Hotel Felix, Whitehouse Ln, CAMBRIDGE ☎ 01223 277977 52 en suite

BOURN Map 05 TL35

Bourn Toft Rd CB3 7TT
☎ 01954 718958 🖹 01954 718908
e-mail: proshop@bourn-golf-club.co.uk
web: www.club-noticeboard.com/bourn
Meadow and parkland with many water features and some very challenging holes.
18 holes, 6417yards, Par 72, SSS 71.
Club membership 600.
Visitors Mon-Sun & BHs. Dress code. **Societies** welcome. **Green Fees** £18, £25 Sat & Sun after 1pm & BHs. **Prof** Craig Watson **Course Designer** J Hull **Facilities** **Leisure** heated indoor swimming pool, sauna, solarium, gymnasium. **Conf** facs Corporate Hospitality Days

Hotel Travelodge Cambridge Lolworth, Huntingdon Rd, LOLWORTH ☎ 08700 850 950 36 en suite

BRAMPTON Map 04 TL27

Brampton Park Buckden Rd PE28 4NF
☎ 01480 434700 🖹 01480 411145
e-mail: admin@bramptonparkgc.co.uk
web: www.bramptonparkgc.co.uk
Set in truly attractive countryside, bounded by the River Great Ouse and bisected by the River Lane.

Continued

Great variety with mature trees, lakes and water hazards. One of the most difficult holes is the 4th, a par 3 island green, 175yds in length.
18 holes, 6300yds, Par 71, SSS 72, Course record 62.
Club membership 650.
Visitors contact club for details. **Societies** welcome. **Green Fees** phone. **Prof** Alisdair Currie **Course Designer** Simon Gidman **Facilities** **Conf** facs Corporate Hospitality Days **Location** Signs from A1 or A14 to RAF Brampton

Hotel ★★★★ 70% Huntingdon Marriott Hotel, Kingfisher Way, Hinchingbrooke Business Park, HUNTINGDON ☎ 01480 446000 150 en suite

CAMBRIDGE Map 05 TL45

Gog Magog Shelford Bottom CB2 4AB
☎ 01223 247626 🖹 01223 414990
e-mail: secretary@gogmagog.co.uk
web: www.gogmagog.co.uk
Situated just outside the centre of the university town, Gog Magog, established in 1901, is known as the nursery of Cambridge undergraduate golf. The chalk downland courses are on high ground, and it is said that if you stand on the highest point and could see far enough to the east the next highest ground would be the Ural Mountains. The courses are open but there are enough trees and other hazards to provide plenty of problems. Views from the high parts are superb. The nature of the ground ensures good winter golf. The area has been designated a Site of Special Scientific Interest.
Old Course: 18 holes, 6398yds, Par 70, SSS 70, Course record 62.
Wandlebury: 18 holes, 6735yds, Par 72, SSS 72, Course record 67.
Club membership 1400.
Visitors Mon-Fri except BHs. Booking required. Handicap certificate. Dress code. **Societies** Booking required. **Green Fees** £45 per day, £38 per round. **Prof** Ian Bamborough **Course Designer** Hawtree Ltd **Facilities** **Conf** Corporate Hospitality Days **Location** 3m SE on A1307

Hotel ★★★ 71% Gonville Hotel, Gonville Place, CAMBRIDGE ☎ 01223 366611 & 221111 🖹 01223 315470 103 en suite

ELY Map 05 TL58

Ely City 107 Cambridge Rd CB7 4HX
☎ 01353 662751 (Office) 🖹 01353 668636
e-mail: elygolf@lineone.net
web: www.elygolf.co.uk.
Slightly undulating parkland with water hazards formed by lakes and natural dykes. Demanding par 4 5th hole (467yds), often into a headwind, and a testing par 3 2nd hole (160yds) played over two ponds. Magnificent views of the cathedral.
18 holes, 6627yds, Par 72, SSS 72, Course record 65.
Club membership 750.
Visitors Mon-Sun & BHs. Handicap certificate. Dress code. **Societies** Booking required. **Green Fees** £34 per day, £40 Sat & Sun. **Prof** Andrew George **Course Designer** Sir Henry Cotton **Facilities** **Conf** Corporate Hospitality Days **Location** S of city on A10

Hotel ★★★ 67% Lamb Hotel, 2 Lynn Rd, ELY ☎ 01353 663574 31 en suite

GIRTON Map 05 TL46

Girton Dodford Ln CB3 0QE
☎ 01223 276169 🖹 01223 277150
e-mail: secretary@girtongolfclub.sagehost.co.uk
web: www.club-noticeboard.co.uk
Flat, open, easy walking parkland with many trees and ditches.
18 holes, 6012yds, Par 69, SSS 69, Course record 66.
Club membership 800.
Visitors Mon-Fri. Booking required. **Societies** Booking required in writing. **Green Fees** phone. **Prof** Scott Thomson **Course Designer** Allan Gow **Facilities** **Location** 3m from Cambridge. Just off A14 junct 31

Hotel ★★★★ 75% Hotel Felix, Whitehouse Ln, CAMBRIDGE ☎ 01223 277977 52 en suite

HEMINGFORD ABBOTS Map 04 TL27

Hemingford Abbots Cambridge Rd PE28 9HQ
☎ 01480 495000 & 493900 🖹 01480 4960000
9 holes, 5468yds, Par 68, SSS 68, Course record 69.
Course Designer Ray Paton **Location** A14 Hemingford Abbots turn, between St Ives & Huntingdon
Phone for further details

Hotel ★★★ 78% The Old Bridge Hotel, 1 High St, HUNTINGDON ☎ 01480 424300 24 en suite

LONGSTANTON Map 05 TL36

Cambridge Station Rd CB4 5DR
☎ 01954 789388
Undulating parkland with bunkers and ponds.
18 holes, 6736yds, Par 72, SSS 73.
Club membership 300.
Visitors contact club for details. **Societies** Booking required. **Green Fees** £12 per 18 holes, £8 per 9 holes, £15/£10 Sat & Sun. **Prof** Geoff Huggett, A Engelman **Facilities** **Leisure** fishing, hot air ballons. **Conf** facs

Hotel Travelodge Cambridge Swavesey, Cambridge Rd, SWAVESEY ☎ 08700 850 950 36 en suite

MARCH Map 05 TL49

March Frogs Abbey, Grange Rd PE15 0YH
☎ 01354 652364 🖹 01354 658142
e-mail: secretary@marchgolfclub.co.uk
web: www.marchgolfclub.co.uk
A nine-hole parkland course with a particularly challenging par 3 9th hole, with out of bounds on the right and high hedges to the left.
9 holes, 6204yds, Par 70, SSS 70, Course record 65.
Club membership 367.
Visitors contact club for details. Dress code. **Societies** Booking required. **Green Fees** phone. **Prof** Alex Oldham **Facilities** **Location** 0.5m off A141, March bypass

Hotel ★★ 61% Olde Griffin Hotel, High St, MARCH ☎ 01354 652517 21 rms (20 en suite)

MELDRETH Map 05 TL34

Malton Malton Rd, Malton SG8 6PE
☎ 01763 262200 🖹 01763 262209
e-mail: desk@maltongolf.co.uk
web: www.maltongolf.co.uk
Set among 230 acres of beautiful undulating countryside. The River Cam bisects part of the course which is surrounded by woodlands and wetlands.
18 holes, 6708yards, Par 72, SSS 72, Course record 67.
Visitors Mon-Sun & BHs. Booking required. Dress code. **Societies** Booking required. **Green Fees** £10 per 18 holes, £16 Sat, Sun & BHs. Twilight after 4pm £7, Sat, Sun & BHs £10. **Prof** Bill Lyon **Facilities** **Location** Between Orwell

Hotel ★★★ 74% Duxford Lodge Hotel, Ickleton Rd, DUXFORD ☎ 01223 836444 11 en suite 4 annexe en suite

PETERBOROUGH Map 04 TL19

Elton Furze Bullock Rd, Haddon PE7 3TT
☎ 01832 280189 & 280614 (pro shop) 🖹 01832 280299
e-mail: secretary@eltonfurzegolfclub.co.uk
web: www.eltonfurzegolfclub.co.uk
Elton Furze Golf Club is set in the picturesque surroundings of the Cambridgeshire countryside. The course has been designed in and around mature woodland with ponds and slopes, which provides the golfer with an interesting and enjoyable round of golf.
18 holes, 6279yds, Par 70, SSS 71, Course record 66.
Club membership 620.
Visitors Mon-Fri. Sat & Sun booking required. **Societies** welcome. **Green Fees** £49 per day, £31 per round, £55/£35 Sat & Sun. **Prof** Glyn Krause **Course Designer** Roger Fitton **Facilities** by arrangement **Conf** facs Corporate Hospitality Days **Location** 4m SW of Peterborough, off A605/A1

Hotel ★★★★ 65% Peterborough Marriott Hotel, Peterborough Business Park, Lynchwood, PETERBOROUGH ☎ 01733 371111 163 en suite

Orton Meadows Ham Ln, Orton Waterville PE2 5UU
☎ 01733 237478 🖹 01733 332774
e-mail: enquiries@ortonmeadowsgolfcourse.co.uk
web: www.ortonmeadowsgolfcourse.co.uk
Picturesque course with trees, lakes and an abundance of water fowl, providing some challenges with water featuring on 10 holes.
18 holes, 5269yds, Par 67, SSS 68, Course record 64.
Club membership 650.
Visitors Booking required 7 days in advance. **Societies** Booking required. **Green Fees** phone. **Prof** Ashley Howard **Course Designer** D & R Fitton **Facilities** **Leisure** 12 hole pitch & putt. **Location** 3m W of town on A605

Hotel ★★★ 70% Best Western Orton Hall Hotel, Orton Longueville, PETERBOROUGH ☎ 01733 391111 65 en suite

Peterborough Milton Milton Ferry PE6 7AG
☎ 01733 380489 & 380793 (pro) 🖹 01733 380489
e-mail: miltongolfclub@aol.com
web: www.peterboroughmiltongolfclub.co.uk
Designed by James Braid, this well-bunkered parkland course is set in the grounds of the Milton Estate, many of the holes being played in full view of Milton Hall. Challenging holes are the difficult dog-leg 10th and 15th. Easy walking.
18 holes, 6541yds, Par 71, SSS 72, Course record 69. Club membership 800.
Visitors Mon-Sun & BHs. Booking required. Handicap certificate. Dress code. **Societies** Booking required. **Green Fees** £50 per 36 holes, £40 per 18 holes. **Prof** Jason Barker **Course Designer** James Braid **Facilities** **Conf** facs Corporate Hospitality Days **Location** 2m W of Peterborough on A47

Hotel Travelodge Peterborough Eye Green, Crowlands Rd, PETERBOROUGH ☎ 08700 850 950 42 en suite

Thorpe Wood Thorpe Wood, Nene Parkway PE3 6SE
☎ 01733 267701 🖹 01733 332774
e-mail: enquiries@thorpewoodgolfcourse.co.uk
web: www.thorpewoodgolfcourse.co.uk
Gently undulating, parkland course designed by Peter Alliss and Dave Thomas. Challenging holes include the 5th, the longest hole, usually played with prevailing wind, and the 14th, which has a difficult approach shot over water to a two-tier green.
18 holes, 7086yds, Par 73, SSS 74, Course record 68. Club membership 750.
Visitors Booking required 7 days in advance. **Societies** Booking required. **Green Fees** phone. **Prof** Roger Fitton **Course Designer** Peter Allis, Dave Thomas **Facilities** **Location** 3m W of city centre on A47

Hotel ★★★ 70% Best Western Orton Hall Hotel, Orton Longueville, PETERBOROUGH ☎ 01733 391111 65 en suite

PIDLEY Map 05 TL37

Lakeside Lodge Fen Rd PE28 3DF
☎ 01487 740540 🖹 01487 740852
e-mail: info@lakeside-lodge.co.uk
web: www.lakeside-lodge.co.uk
A well-designed, spacious course incorporating eight lakes, 12,000 trees and a modern clubhouse. The 9th and 18th holes both finish dramatically alongside a lake in front of the clubhouse. Also nine-hole par 3, and 25-bay driving range. The Manor provides an interesting contrast with its undulating fairways and angular greens.
Lodge Course: 18 holes, 6885yds, Par 72, SSS 73. The Manor: 9 holes, 2601yds, Par 34, SSS 33. The Church: 12 holes, 3290yds, Par 44. Club membership 1200.
Visitors Mon-Sun & BHs. Booking required. Dress code. **Societies** Booking required. **Green Fees** £17 per 18 holes, £26 Sat, Sun & BHs, £9 per 9/12 holes, £13 Sat, Sun & BHs. **Prof** Scott Waterman **Course Designer** AW Headley **Facilities** **Leisure** solarium, ten pin bowling. **Conf** facs Corporate Hospitality Days **Location** A141 from Huntingdon

Hotel ★★★ 70% Slepe Hall Hotel, Ramsey Rd, ST IVES ☎ 01480 463122 16 en suite

RAMSEY Map 04 TL28

Old Nene Golf & Country Club Muchwood Ln, Bodsey PE26 2XQ
☎ 01487 815622 🖹 01487 813610
e-mail: info@oldnene.freeserve.co.uk
9 holes, 5605yds, Par 68, SSS 68, Course record 64.
Course Designer R Edrich **Location** 0.75m N of Ramsey towards Ramsey Mereside
Phone for further details

Hotel ★★★ 78% The Old Bridge Hotel, 1 High St, HUNTINGDON ☎ 01480 424300 24 en suite

Ramsey 4 Abbey Ter PE26 1DD
☎ 01487 812600 🖹 01487 815746
e-mail: admin@ramseyclub.co.uk
web: www.ramseyclub.co.uk
Flat parkland with water hazards and well-irrigated greens, mature tees and fairways - a good surface whatever the conditions. The impression of wide-open spaces soon punishes the wayward shot.
18 holes, 6163yds, Par 71, SSS 68, Course record 64. Club membership 600.
Visitors Mon-Thu except BHs. Booking required. Handicap certificate. Dress code. **Societies** Booking required. **Green Fees** £25 per 18 holes. **Prof** Stuart Scott **Course Designer** J Hamilton Stutt **Facilities** **Leisure** snooker tables, bowls rinks. **Location** 12m SE of Peterborough on B1040

Hotel ★★★ 78% The Old Bridge Hotel, 1 High St, HUNTINGDON ☎ 01480 424300 24 en suite

ST IVES Map 04 TL37

St Ives (Cambs) Westwood Rd PE27 6DH
☎ 01480 468392 🖹 01480 468392
e-mail: stivesgolfclub@zoom.co.uk
Picturesque parkland course.
9 holes, 6180yds, Par 70, SSS 70, Course record 68. Club membership 500.
Visitors Mon-Sun & BHs. Booking required. Handicap certificate. Dress code. **Societies** Booking required. **Green Fees** £26 per day, £13 winter. **Prof** Mark Pond **Facilities** **Conf** facs Corporate Hospitality Days **Location** W side of town centre off A1123

Hotel ★★★ 70% Slepe Hall Hotel, Ramsey Rd, ST IVES ☎ 01480 463122 16 en suite

ST NEOTS Map 04 TL16

Abbotsley Golf & Squash Club Eynesbury Hardwicke PE19 6XN
☎ 01480 474000 🖹 01480 403280
e-mail: abbotsley@crown-golf.co.uk
Set in 250 acres of idyllic countryside, with two 18-hole courses and a nine-hole par 3. The Cromwell course is the less challenging of the two, offering a contrast to the renowned Abbotsley course with its holes meandering through woods and streams. One of the most memorable holes is the Abbotsley 2nd hole known as the Mousehole, which requires an accurate tee shot to a green that is protected by a stream and shaded by the many trees that surround it.

Continued

Abbotsley Course: 18 holes, 6311yds, Par 73, SSS 72, Course record 69.
Cromwell Course: 18 holes, 6087yds, Par 70, SSS 69, Course record 66.
Club membership 550.
Visitors Mon-Sun & BHs. Dress code. **Societies** Booking required. **Green Fees** Abbotsley £26 per 18 holes, £42.50 Sat, Sun & BHs. Cromwell £17 per 18 holes, £23 Sat, Sun & BHs. Winter reduced rates. **Prof** Denise Hastings, Steve Connolly **Course Designer** D Young, V Saunders **Facilities** **Leisure** squash, solarium, gymnasium. **Conf** facs Corporate Hospitality Days **Location** Off A1 & A428

St Neots Crosshall Rd PE19 7GE
☎ 01480 472363 🖷 01480 472363
e-mail: office@stneots-golfclub.co.uk
web: www.stneots-golfclub.co.uk
Set in picturesque rolling parkland and divided by the river Kym, the course offers a challenge to all standards of golfer with tree-lined fairways, water hazards and outstanding greens.
18 holes, 6033yds, Par 69, SSS 69, Course record 64.
Club membership 630.
Visitors Mon-Fri. Booking required. Handicap certificate. Dress code. **Societies** Booking required. **Green Fees** £40 per day, £30 per round. **Prof** Paul Toyer **Course Designer** H Vardon **Facilities** **Conf** Corporate Hospitality Days **Location** A1 onto B1048 into St Neots

THORNEY Map 04 TF20

Thorney English Drove, Thorney PE6 0TJ
☎ 01733 270570 🖷 01733 270842
The 18-hole Fen course is ideal for the beginner, while the Lakes Course has a challenging links-style layout with eight holes around water.
Fen Course: 18 holes, 6104yds, Par 70, SSS 69, Course record 66.
Lakes Course: 18 holes, 6402yds, Par 71, SSS 70, Course record 65.
Club membership 500.
Visitors Booking required for Fen course. Lakes course booking required Sat & Sun. **Societies** Booking required. **Green Fees** phone. **Prof** Mark Templeman **Course Designer** A Dow **Facilities** **Leisure** par 3 course. **Location** Off A47, 7m NE of Peterborough

Hotel Travelodge Peterborough Eye Green, Crowlands Rd, PETERBOROUGH ☎ 08700 850 950 42 en suite

TOFT Map 05 TL35

Cambridge National Comberton Rd CB3 7RY
☎ 01223 264700 🖷 01223 264701
e-mail: meridian@golfsocieties.com
web: www.golfsocieties.com
Set in 207 acres to a Peter Allis and Clive Clark design with sweeping fairways, lakes and well-bunkered greens. The 4th hole has bunker complexes, a sharp dog-leg and a river with the green heavily guarded by bunkers. The 9th and 10th holes challenge the golfer with river crossings.
18 holes, 6651yds, Par 73, SSS 72, Course record 72.
Club membership 400.

Continued

Cambridge National

Visitors Mon-Sun & BHs. Booking required. Dress code. **Societies** Booking required. **Green Fees** £16 per 18 holes, £25 Sat & Sun. **Prof** Jamie Donaldson **Course Designer** Peter Alliss, Clive Clark **Facilities** by arrangement **Conf** facs Corporate Hospitality Days **Location** 3m W of Cambridge, on B1046

CHESHIRE

ALDERLEY EDGE Map 07 SJ87

Alderley Edge Brook Ln SK9 7RU
☎ 01625 586200
e-mail: honsecretary@aegc.co.uk
web: www.aegc.co.uk
Well-wooded, undulating pastureland course. A stream crosses seven of the nine holes. A challenging course even for the low handicap player.
9 holes, 5823yds, Par 68, SSS 68, Course record 62.
Club membership 400.
Visitors Mon, Wed-Fri & Sun. Booking required. Handicap certificate. Dress code. **Societies** Booking required. **Green Fees** phone. **Prof** Peter Bowring **Facilities** **Conf** facs Corporate Hospitality Days **Location** 1m NW on B5085

Hotel ★★★ 78% Alderley Edge Hotel, Macclesfield Rd, ALDERLEY EDGE ☎ 01625 583033 52 en suite

ALDERSEY GREEN Map 07 SJ45

Aldersey Green CH3 9EH
☎ 01829 782157
e-mail: bradburygolf@aol.com
web: www.alderseygreengolfclub.co.uk
18 holes, 6145, Par 70, SSS 69, Course record 72.
Location On A41 Whitchurch Rd, 6m S of Chester
Phone for further details

Hotel ★★★★ 72% De Vere Carden Park, Carden Park, BROXTON ☎ 01829 731000 113 en suite 79 annexe en suite

ALSAGER Map 07 SJ75

Alsager Golf & Country Club Audley Rd ST7 2UR
☎ 01270 875700 🖷 01270 882207
e-mail: business@alsagergolfclub.com
web: www.alsagergolfclub.com
18 holes, 6225yds, Par 70, SSS 70, Course record 67.
Location M6 junct 16, 2m NE
Phone for further details

Hotel ★★★ 69% Manor House Hotel, Audley Rd, ALSAGER ☎ 01270 884000 57 en suite

ANTROBUS Map 07 SJ68

Antrobus Foggs Ln CW9 6JQ
☎ 01925 730890 📠 01925 730100
e-mail: info@antrobusgolfclub.co.uk
web: www.antrobusgolfclub.co.uk
A challenging parkland course where water is the main feature with streams and ponds in play on most holes. Large undulating greens.
18 holes, 6220yards, Par 71, SSS 71, Course record 65. Club membership 500.
Visitors Mon-Fri, Sun & BHs. Booking required. Dress code. **Societies** Booking required. **Green Fees** £25 per day, £28 Sun & BHs. **Prof** Paul Farrance **Course Designer** Mike Slater **Facilities** **Leisure** fishing. **Conf** facs **Location** M56 junct 10, A559 towards Northwich, 2nd left after Birch pub onto Knutsford Rd, 1st left into Foggs Ln

Hotel ★★★ 64% The Floatel, Northwich, London Rd, NORTHWICH ☎ 01606 44443 60 en suite

CHESTER Map 07 SJ46

Chester Curzon Park CH4 8AR
☎ 01244 677760 📠 01244 676667
e-mail: vfcwood@chestergolfclub.co.uk
web: www.chestergolfclub.co.uk
Meadowland course on two levels contained within a loop of the River Dee. The car park overlooks the racecourse across the river.
18 holes, 6508yds, Par 72, SSS 71, Course record 66. Club membership 820.
Visitors Mon, Tue, Thu & Fri. Booking required. Handicap certificate. Dress code. **Societies** Booking required. **Green Fees** £35 per day. **Prof** Scott Booth **Facilities** **Location** 1m W of city centre

Hotel ★★★ 74% Grosvenor Pulford Hotel, Wrexham Rd, Pulford, CHESTER ☎ 01244 570560 73 en suite

De Vere Carden Park Hotel CH3 9DQ
☎ 01829 731000 📠 01829 731032
e-mail: golf.carden@devere-hotels.com
web: www.devereonline.co.uk
A superb golf resort set in 750 acres of beautiful Cheshire countryside. Facilities include the mature parkland Cheshire Course, the Nicklaus Course, the nine-hole par 3 Azalea Course, Golf School and a luxurious clubhouse.
Cheshire: 18 holes, 6891yds, Par 72, SSS 72, Course record 64.
Nicklaus: 18 holes, 7094yds, Par 72, SSS 72, Course record 64.
Club membership 250.
Visitors Mon-Sun & BHs. Booking required. Dress code. **Societies** Booking required. **Green Fees** phone. **Prof** Paul Hodgson **Course Designer** Jack Nicklaus (Nicklaus course) **Facilities** **Leisure** hard tennis courts, heated indoor swimming pool, sauna, solarium, gymnasium, residential golf school, snooker room, dance studio. **Conf** facs Corporate Hospitality Days **Location** S of city on A41, right at Broxton rdbt onto A534 signed Wrexham. Situated 1.5m on left

Hotel ★★★★ 72% De Vere Carden Park, Carden Park, BROXTON ☎ 01829 731000 113 en suite 79 annexe en suite

Eaton Guy Ln, Waverton CH3 7PH
☎ 01244 335885 📠 01244 335782
e-mail: office@eatongolfclub.co.uk
web: www.eatongolfclub.co.uk
Parkland with a liberal covering of mature trees and new planting enhanced by natural water hazards.

18 holes, 6562yds, Par 72, SSS 71, Course record 68. Club membership 550.
Visitors Mon, Tue, Thu-Sun & BHs. Booking required. Handicap certificate. Dress code. **Societies** Booking required. **Green Fees** Summer £30 per round, £35 Sat, Sun & BHs. Winter £20/£25. **Prof** William Tye **Course Designer** Donald Steel **Facilities** **Location** 3m SE of Chester off A41

Hotel ★★★★★ The Chester Grosvenor & Spa, Eastgate, CHESTER ☎ 01244 324024 80 en suite

Upton-by-Chester Upton Ln, Upton-by-Chester CH2 1EE
☎ 01244 381183 📠 01244 376955
Pleasant, tree-lined parkland. Not easy for low-handicap players to score well. Testing holes are 2nd (par 4), 14th (par 4) and 15th (par 3).
18 holes, 5807yds, Par 69, SSS 68, Course record 63. Club membership 750.
Visitors Mon-Fri. Booking required Sat, Sun & BHs. Handicap certificate. Dress code. **Societies** Booking required. **Green Fees** £35 per day, £25 per round. **Prof** Stephen Dewhurst **Course Designer** Bill Davies **Facilities** **Conf** Corporate Hospitality Days **Location** N side off A5116

Hotel ★★★★ 70% Mollington Banastre Hotel, Parkgate Rd, CHESTER ☎ 01244 851471 63 en suite

Vicars Cross Tarvin Rd, Great Barrow CH3 7HN
☎ 01244 335595 📠 01244 335686
e-mail: secretary@vcgc.fsnet.co.uk
web: www.vicarscrossgc.co.uk
18 holes, 6446yds, Par 72, SSS 71, Course record 64.
Course Designer J Richardson **Location** 4m E on A51
Phone for further details

Hotel ★★★★ 76% Rowton Hall Country House Hotel, Whitchurch Rd, Rowton, CHESTER ☎ 01244 335262 38 en suite

CONGLETON Map 07 SJ86

Astbury Peel Ln, Astbury CW12 4RE
☎ 01260 272772 🖷 01260 276420
e-mail: admin@astburygolfclub.com
web: www.astburygolfclub.com
Parkland course in open countryside, bisected by a canal. The testing 12th hole involves a long carry over a tree-filled ravine. Large practice area.
18 holes, 6296yds, Par 71, SSS 70, Course record 61.
Club membership 720.
Visitors contact club for details. Handicap certificate. Dress code. **Societies** Booking required. **Green Fees** £30 per round. **Prof** Ashley Salt **Facilities** **Location** 1.5m S between A34 a527

Inn ♦♦♦♦ Egerton Arms Hotel, Astbury Village, CONGLETON ☎ 01260 273946 6 en suite

Congleton Biddulph Rd CW12 3LZ
☎ 01260 273540
9 holes, 5103yds, Par 68, SSS 65.
Location 1.5m SE on A527
Phone for further details

Inn ♦♦♦♦ Egerton Arms Hotel, Astbury Village, CONGLETON ☎ 01260 273946 6 en suite

CREWE Map 07 SJ75

Crewe Fields Rd, Haslington CW1 5TB
☎ 01270 584099 🖷 01270 256482
e-mail: secretary@crewsgolfclub.co.uk
web: www.crewegolfclub.co.uk
Undulating parkland.
18 holes, 6424yds, Par 71, SSS 71, Course record 63.
Club membership 674.
Visitors Tue. Booking required. Handicap certificate. Dress code. **Societies** Booking required. **Green Fees** £36 per day, £16 winter. **Prof** David Wheeler **Course Designer** James Braid **Facilities** **Location** 2.25m NE off A534

Hotel ★★★ 73% Hunters Lodge Hotel, Sydney Rd, Sydney, CREWE ☎ 01270 583440 57 en suite

Queen's Park Queen's Park Dr CW2 7SB
☎ 01270 666724 🖷 01270 569902
e-mail: crewe@americangolf.co.uk
9 holes, 4920yds, Par 68, SSS 64, Course record 67.
Location Located behind Queen's Park. Well signposted
Phone for further details

Hotel ★★★ 73% Hunters Lodge Hotel, Sydney Rd, Sydney, CREWE ☎ 01270 583440 57 en suite

If the name of the club appears in italics, details have not been confirmed for this edition of the guide

DELAMERE Map 07 SJ56

Delamere Forest Station Rd CW8 2JE
☎ 01606 883264 & 883800 🖷 01606 889444
e-mail: info@delameregolf.co.uk
web: www.delameregolf.co.uk
Played mostly on undulating open heath there is great charm in the way this course drops down into the occasional pine sheltered valley. Six of the first testing nine holes are from 420 to 455yds in length.

18 holes, 6348yds, Par 72, SSS 71, Course record 65.
Club membership 500.
Visitors Tue-Fri. Dress code. **Societies** Booking required. **Green Fees** £55 per day, £40 per round. **Prof** Ellis B Jones **Course Designer** H Fowler **Facilities** by arrangement **Conf** Corporate Hospitality Days **Location** 1.5m NE, off B5152

Hotel ★★ 64% Hartford Hall, School Ln, Hartford, NORTHWICH ☎ 01606 780320 20 en suite

DISLEY Map 07 SJ98

Disley Stanley Hall Ln SK12 2JX
☎ 01663 764001 🖷 01663 762678
e-mail: secretary@disleygolfclub.co.uk
web: www.disleygolfclub.co.uk
Straddling a hilltop site above Lyme Park, this undulating parkland and moorland course affords good views and requires accuracy of approach to almost all the greens which lie on either a ledge or plateau. Testing holes are the 3rd and 4th.

18 holes, 6015yds, Par 70, SSS 69, Course record 63.
Club membership 650.
Visitors Mon-Wed & Fri except BHs. Handicap certificate. Dress code. **Societies** Booking required. **Green Fees** £28 per day, £35 Sat & Sun. **Prof** Andrew Esplin **Course Designer** James Braid **Facilities** **Conf** Corporate Hospitality Days **Location** NW side of village off A6

ELLESMERE PORT Map 07 SJ47

Ellesmere Port Chester Rd, Childer Thornton CH66 1QF
☎ 0151 339 7689 🖹 0151 339 7502
18 holes, 6432yds, Par 71, SSS 70.
Course Designer Cotton, Pennick & Lawrie **Location** NW side of town centre. M53 junct 5, A41 for Chester, club 2m on left
Phone for further details

Hotel ★★★ 69% Quality Hotel Chester, Berwick Rd, Little Sutton, ELLESMERE PORT ☎ 0151 339 5121 75 en suite

FRODSHAM Map 07 SJ57

Frodsham Simons Ln WA6 6HE
☎ 01928 732159 🖹 01928 734070
e-mail: alastair@frodshamgolf.co.uk
web: www.frodshamgolfclub.co.uk
Undulating parkland with pleasant views from all parts. Emphasis on accuracy over the whole course, the long and difficult par 5 18th necessitating a drive across water to the green. Crossed by two footpaths so extreme care needed.
18 holes, 6328yds, Par 70, SSS 70, Course record 63.
Club membership 700.
Visitors Mon-Fri except BHs. Booking required. Dress code. **Societies** Booking required. **Green Fees** £40 per round. **Prof** Graham Tonge **Course Designer** John Day **Facilities** **Leisure** snooker. **Location** M56 junct 12, 1.5m SW, signs for Forest Hills Hotel, Golf Club 1st left on Simons Ln

Hotel ★★★ 70% Forest Hills Hotel & Leisure Complex, Overton Hill, FRODSHAM ☎ 01928 735255 58 en suite

HELSBY Map 07 SJ47

Helsby Towers Ln WA6 0JB
☎ 01928 722021 🖹 01928 725384
e-mail: secathgc@aol.com
This gentle but challenging parkland course was originally designed by James Braid. With a wide variety of trees and natural water hazards interspersed throughout the course, it is an excellent test of golfing ability. The last six holes are reputed to be among the most difficult home stretch in Cheshire, with the last being a par 3 of 205yds to a narrow green guarded by bunkers. A wide variety of wildlife lives around the several ponds which are features to be noted (and hopefully avoided).
18 holes, 6221yds, Par 70, SSS 70, Course record 69.
Club membership 640.
Visitors Mon-Fri except BHs. Booking required. Dress code. **Societies** Booking required. **Green Fees** £28 per round. **Prof** Matthew Jones **Course Designer** James Braid (part) **Facilities** **Conf** Corporate Hospitality Days **Location** M56 junct 14, 1m. 6m from Chester

Hotel ★★★★★ The Chester Grosvenor & Spa, Eastgate, CHESTER ☎ 01244 324024 80 en suite

KNUTSFORD Map 07 SJ77

Heyrose Budworth Rd, Tabley WA16 0HZ
☎ 01565 733664 🖹 01565 734578
e-mail: info@heyrosegolfclub.com
web: www.heyrosegolfclub.com
An 18-hole course in wooded and gently undulating terrain. The par 3 16th (237yds), bounded by a small river in a wooded valley, is an interesting and testing hole - one of the toughest par 3s in Cheshire. Several water hazards. Both the course and the comfortable clubhouse have attractive views.
18 holes, 6499yds, Par 73, SSS 71, Course record 66.
Club membership 600.
Visitors Mon-Sun & BHs. Booking required. Dress code. **Societies** Booking required. **Green Fees** £26 per round Mon-Fri & BHs, £31 Sat & Sun. **Prof** Philip Bills **Course Designer** CN Bridge **Facilities** **Leisure** practice bunker, practice nets. **Conf** facs Corporate Hospitality Days **Location** M6 junct 19, 1m, follow tourist signs

Hotel ★★★★ 73% Cottons Hotel & Spa, Manchester Rd, KNUTSFORD ☎ 01565 650333 109 en suite

High Legh Park Warrington Rd, Mere & High Legh WA16 0WA
☎ 01565 830888 🖹 01565 830999
Championship: 18 holes, 6715yds, Par 72.
South: 18 holes, 6281yds, Par 70.
North: 18 holes, 6472yds, Par 70.
Location M6 junct 20, A50 to High Legh
Phone for further details

Hotel ★★★★ 73% Cottons Hotel & Spa, Manchester Rd, KNUTSFORD ☎ 01565 650333 109 en suite

Knutsford Mereheath Ln WA16 6HS
☎ 01565 633355
9 holes, 6288yds, Par 70, SSS 70.
Location N side of town centre off A50
Phone for further details

Hotel ★★★★ 73% Cottons Hotel & Spa, Manchester Rd, KNUTSFORD ☎ 01565 650333 109 en suite

Mere Golf & Country Club Chester Rd, Mere WA16 6LJ
☎ 01565 830155 🖹 01565 830713
e-mail: enquiries@meregolf.co.uk
web: www.meregolf.co.uk
A gracious parkland championship course designed by James Braid in the Cheshire sand belt, with several holes close to a lake. The round has a tight finish with four testing holes.

Continued

18 holes, 6817yds, Par 71, SSS 73, Course record 64.
Club membership 550.
Visitors Mon, Tue & Thu except BHs. Booking required. Handicap certificate. Dress code. **Societies** Booking required. **Green Fees** £70 per day, £50 Oct-Mar. **Prof** Peter Eyre **Course Designer** James Braid, George Duncan **Facilities** **Leisure** hard tennis courts, heated indoor swimming pool, squash, sauna, solarium, gymnasium. **Conf** facs Corporate Hospitality Days **Location** M6 junct 19, 1m E. M56 junct 7, 1m W

Hotel ★★★★ 73% Cottons Hotel & Spa, Manchester Rd, KNUTSFORD ☎ 01565 650333 109 en suite

Peover Plumley Moor Rd, Lower Peover WA16 9SE
☎ 01565 723337 ▤ 01565 723311
e-mail: mail@peovergolfclub.co.uk
web: www.peovergolfclub.co.uk
18 holes, 6702yds, Par 72, SSS 72, Course record 69.
Course Designer PA Naylor **Location** M6 junct 19, A556 onto Plumley Moor Rd
Phone for further details

Hotel ★★ 76% The Longview Hotel & Restaurant, 55 Manchester Rd, KNUTSFORD ☎ 01565 632119 13 en suite 19 annexe en suite

LYMM Map 07 SJ68

Lymm Whitbarrow Rd WA13 9AN
☎ 01925 755020 ▤ 01925 755020
e-mail: lymmgolfclub@btconnect.com
web: www.lymm-golf-club.co.uk
First ten holes are gently undulating with the Manchester Ship Canal running alongside the 6th hole. The remaining holes are comparatively flat.
18 holes, 6341yds, Par 71, SSS 70.
Club membership 800.
Visitors Mon-Fri. Booking required. Handicap certificate. Dress code. **Societies** Booking required. **Green Fees** £32 per round. **Prof** Steve McCarthy **Facilities** **Location** 0.5m N off A6144

Hotel ★★★ 68% The Lymm Hotel, Whitbarrow Rd, LYMM ☎ 0870 1942121 14 en suite 48 annexe en suite

MACCLESFIELD Map 07 SJ97

Macclesfield The Hollins SK11 7EA
☎ 01625 423227 ▤ 01625 260061
e-mail: secretary@maccgolfclub.co.uk
web: maccgolfclub.co.uk
Hillside heathland course situated on the edge of the Pennines with excellent views across the Cheshire Plain. The signature hole is the 410yd 3rd, which drops majestically to a plateau green situated above a babbling brook. The temptation is to over-club, thus bringing the out of bounds behind into play. The 7th hole is aptly named Seven Shires as seven counties can be seen on a clear day, as well as the mountains.
18 holes, 5714yds, Par 70, SSS 68, Course record 63.
Club membership 620.
Visitors Mon-Wed & Fri except BHs. Booking required. Handicap certificate. Dress code. **Societies** Booking required. **Green Fees** £30. **Prof** Tony Taylor **Course Designer** Hawtree & Son **Facilities** **Conf** Corporate Hospitality Days **Location** SE side of town centre off A523

Hotel ★★★ 70% Best Western Hollin Hall, Jackson Ln, Kerridge, Bollington, MACCLESFIELD ☎ 01625 573246 54 en suite

Shrigley Hall Hotel Shrigley Park, Pott Shrigley SK10 5SB
☎ 01625 575626 ▤ 01625 575437
e-mail: shrigleyhall@paramount-hotels.co.uk
web: www.shrigleyhall.co.uk

18 holes, 6281yds, Par 71, SSS 71, Course record 68.
Course Designer Donald Steel **Location** Off A523 Macclesfield-Stockport road
Phone for further details

Hotel ★★★★ 68% Shrigley Hall Hotel Golf & Country Club, Shrigley Park, Pott Shrigley, MACCLESFIELD ☎ 01625 575757 150 en suite

Tytherington Dorchester Way, Tytherington SK10 2JP
☎ 01625 506000 ▤ 01625 506040
e-mail: tytherington.events@clubhaus.com
web: www.clubhaus.com
18 holes, 6765yds, Par 72, SSS 74.
Course Designer Dave Thomas, Patrick Dawson **Location** 1m N of Macclesfield off A523
Phone for further details

Hotel ★★★★ 68% Shrigley Hall Hotel Golf & Country Club, Shrigley Park, Pott Shrigley, MACCLESFIELD ☎ 01625 575757 150 en suite

NANTWICH Map 07 SJ65

Reaseheath Reaseheath College CW5 6DF
☎ 01270 625131 ▤ 01270 625665
e-mail: chrisb@reaseheath.ac.uk
web: www.reaseheath.ac.uk
The course here is attached to Reaseheath College, which is one of the major centres of green-keeper training in the UK. It is a short nine-hole parkland course with challenging narrow fairways, bunkers and a water hazard, all of which make accuracy essential.
9 holes, 1882yds, Par 62, SSS 58, Course record 55.
Club membership 600.
Visitors Mon-Sun & BHs. Booking required. Dress code. **Societies** Booking required. **Green Fees** £10 per day, £8 Oct-Mar. **Course Designer** D Mortram **Facilities** **Conf** facs **Location** 1.5m NE of Nantwich, off A51

Hotel ★★★★ 74% Rookery Hall, Main Rd, Worleston, NANTWICH ☎ 01270 610016 30 en suite 16 annexe en suite

Continued

OSCROFT Map 07 SJ56

Pryors Hayes Willington Rd CH3 8NL
01829 741250 & 740140 01829 749077
e-mail: info@pryors-hayes.co.uk
web: pryors-hayes.co.uk
A picturesque 18-hole parkland course set in the heart of Cheshire. Gently undulating fairways demand accurate drives, and numerous trees and water hazards make the course a challenging test of golf.
18 holes, 6054yds, Par 69, SSS 69, Course record 65. Club membership 530.
Visitors Mon-Sun & BHs. Booking required. Dress code. **Societies** Booking required. **Green Fees** £30, £40 Sat & Sun. **Prof** Martin Redrup **Course Designer** John Day **Facilities** **Location** Between A54 , 6m E of Chester

Hotel ★★★ 66% Macdonald Blossoms Hotel, St John St, CHESTER 0870 400 8108 64 en suite

POYNTON Map 07 SJ98

Davenport Worth Hall, Middlewood Rd SK12 1TS
01625 876951 01625 877489
e-mail: elaine@davenportgolf.co.uk
web: www.davenportgolf.co.uk
Gently undulating parkland. Extensive view over the Cheshire plain from elevated 7th tee. Testing 1st hole, par 4. Several long par 3s, water hazards and tree-lined fairways make this a challenging test of golf.
18 holes, 6034yds, Par 69, SSS 69, Course record 64. Club membership 700.
Visitors Mon, Tue, Thu, Fri, Sun & BHs. Booking required. Handicap certificate. Dress code. **Societies** Booking required. **Green Fees** phone. **Prof** Gary Norcott **Facilities** by arrangement by arrangement **Leisure** snooker. **Conf** facs Corporate Hospitality Days **Location** 1m E off A523

PRESTBURY Map 07 SJ97

Prestbury Macclesfield Rd SK10 4BJ
01625 828241 01625 828241
e-mail: office@prestburygolfclub.com
web: www.prestburygolfclub.com
Undulating parkland with many plateau greens. The 9th hole has a challenging uphill three-tier green and the 17th is over a valley. Host to county and inter-county championships, including hosting an Open qualifying event annually until 2009.

18 holes, 6371yds, Par 71, SSS 71, Course record 64. Club membership 702.
Visitors Mon-Fri except BHs. Booking required Thu.

Continued

Dress code. **Societies** Booking required. **Green Fees** £45 per day. **Prof** Nick Summerfield **Course Designer** Harry S Colt **Facilities** **Conf** Corporate Hospitality Days **Location** S side of village off A538

Hotel ★★★★ 69% De Vere Mottram Hall, Wilmslow Rd, Mottram St Andrew, Prestbury, 01625 828135 132 en suite

RUNCORN Map 07 SJ58

Runcorn Clifton Rd WA7 4SU
01928 574214 01928 574214
e-mail: secretary@runcorngolfclub.ltd.uk
Easy walking parkland with tree-lined fairways. Fine views over Mersey and Weaver valleys. Testing holes: 7th par 5; 14th par 5; 17th par 4.
18 holes, 6048yds, Par 69, SSS 69, Course record 63. Club membership 570.
Visitors Mon & Wed-Fri except BHs. Booking required. Handicap certificate. Dress code. **Societies** Booking required. **Green Fees** phone. **Prof** Kevin Hartley **Facilities** by arrangement **Location** 1.25m S of Runcorn Station

Hotel ★★★ 70% Lawson House Hotel & Conference Centre, Moughland Centre, RUNCORN 01928 593300 30 en suite

SANDBACH Map 07 SJ76

Malkins Bank Betchton Rd, Malkins Bank CW11 4XN
01270 765931 01270 764730
e-mail: phil.pleasance@congleton.gov.uk
web: www.congleton.gov.uk
This parkland course has a different challenge around every corner. The four par 3s on the course are all a challenge, especially the signature hole 14th. Trees in all directions make the short par 3 a really exciting hole. In fact, holes 12, 13 and 14 are the Amen Corner of Malkins Bank. Three very tricky holes, yet for straight hitters low scores are possible.
18 holes, 6005yds, Par 70, SSS 69, Course record 65. Club membership 500.
Visitors Mon-Sun & BHs. Booking required. Dress code. **Societies** Booking required. **Green Fees** £11 per 18 holes, £8 per 9 holes, £13/£9.50 Sat & Sun. Winter reduced rates. **Prof** D Hackney **Course Designer** Hawtree **Facilities** **Location** 1.5m SE off A533

Hotel ★★★ 63% The Chimney House Hotel, Congleton Rd, SANDBACH 0870 609 6164 48 en suite

SANDIWAY Map 07 SJ67

Sandiway Chester Rd CW8 2DJ
01606 883247 (secretary) 01606 888548
e-mail: info@sandiwaygolf.fsnet.co.uk
web: www.sandiwaygolf.co.uk
Delightful undulating wood and heathland course with long hills up to the 8th, 16th and 17th holes. Many dog-leg and tree-lined holes give opportunities for the deliberate fade or draw. True championship test and one of the finest inland courses in north-west England.
18 holes, 6404yds, Par 70, SSS 71, Course record 65. Club membership 750.
Visitors Mon-Sun & BHs. Booking required. Handicap certificate. Dress code. **Societies** Booking required. **Green**

Continued

Fees £55 per day, £45 per round, £60 per round Sat & Sun. **Prof** William Laird **Course Designer** Ted Ray **Facilities** **Location** 2m W of Northwich on A556

Hotel ★★ 64% Hartford Hall, School Ln, Hartford, NORTHWICH ☎ 01606 780320 20 en suite

SUTTON WEAVER Map 07 SJ57

Sutton Hall Aston Ln WA7 3ED
☎ 01928 790747 🖷 01928 759174
Undulating parkland on south-facing slopes of the Weaver valley. A challenge to all levels of play.
18 holes, 6608yards, Par 72, SSS 72, Course record 69.
Club membership 750.
Visitors Booking required. **Societies** Booking required. **Green Fees** phone. **Prof** Jamie Hope **Course Designer** Ace Golf Associates **Facilities** **Location** M56 junct 12, follow signs for A56 to Warrington, on entering Sutton Weaver take 1st turn right

Hotel ★★★ 70% Forest Hills Hotel & Leisure Complex, Overton Hill, FRODSHAM ☎ 01928 735255 58 en suite

TARPORLEY Map 07 SJ56

Portal Golf & Country Club Cobbler's Cross Ln CW6 0DJ
☎ 01829 733933 🖷 01829 733928
e-mail: portalgolf@aol.com

Championship Course: 18 holes, 7037yds, Par 73, SSS 74, Course record 64.
Premier Course: 18 holes, 6508yds, Par 71, SSS 72, Course record 64.
Arderne Course: 9 holes, 1724yds, Par 30.
Course Designer Donald Steel **Location** Off A49
Phone for further details

Hotel ★★★ 68% The Wild Boar, Whitchurch Rd, Beeston, TARPORLEY ☎ 01829 260309 37 en suite

WARRINGTON Map 07 SJ68

Birchwood Kelvin Close, Science Park North, Birchwood WA3 7PB
☎ 01925 818819 (club) & 816574 (pro) 🖷 01925 822403
e-mail: birchwoodgolfclub.com@lineone.net
web: www.birchwoodgolfclub.org
Very testing parkland course with many natural water hazards and the prevailing wind creating a problem on each hole. The 11th hole is particularly challenging.
Pilgrims: 18 holes, 6727yds, Par 71, SSS 73, Course record 66.
Progress: 18 holes, 6359yds, Par 71, SSS 72.
Mayflower (ladies course): 18 holes, 5849yds, Par 74, SSS 74.
Club membership 745.
Visitors Booking required. **Societies** Mon, Wed & Thu. Booking required. **Green Fees** phone. **Prof** Paul McEwan **Course Designer** TJA Macauley **Facilities** **Conf** facs Corporate Hospitality Days **Location** M62 junct 11, signs for Science Park North, course 2m

Leigh Kenyon Hall, Broseley Ln, Culcheth WA3 4BG
☎ 01925 762943 (secretary) 🖷 01925 765097
e-mail: golf@leighgolf.fsnet.co.uk
web: www.leighgolf.co.uk
This compact parkland course has benefited in recent years from intensive tree planting and extra drainage. An interesting course to play with narrow fairways making accuracy from the tees essential.
18 holes, 5853yds, Par 69, SSS 69, Course record 64.
Club membership 850.
Visitors Sun-Fri & BHs. Dress code. **Societies** welcome. **Green Fees** Summer £32, £40 Sun. Winter £20, £27 Sun. **Prof** Andrew Baguley **Course Designer** Harold Hilton **Facilities** **Conf** Corporate Hospitality Days **Location** 5m NE off A579

Hotel ★★★ 72% Fir Grove Hotel, Knutsford Old Rd, WARRINGTON ☎ 01925 267471 52 en suite

Poulton Park Dig Ln, Cinnamon Brow, Padgate WA2 0SH
☎ 01925 822802 & 825220 🖷 01925 822802
e-mail: secretary@poultonparkgolfclub.com
web: www.poultonparkgolfclub.co.uk
A short but rather testing course which runs between houses and the motorway embankment. A range of varied trees have been placed precisely to catch the wayward drive. The 7th hole, in particular, is an excellent test of golf and you can easily lose a couple of shots on this par 4. The golfer needs to drive well, keep out of the trees and putt like a champion to play to their handicap.
9 holes, 5179yds, Par 68, SSS 66, Course record 66.
Club membership 350.
Visitors Tue-Thu. Booking required. **Societies** Booking required. **Green Fees** phone. **Prof** Ian Orrell **Facilities** **Conf** Corporate Hospitality Days **Location** 3m from Warrington on A574

Hotel ★★★ 72% Fir Grove Hotel, Knutsford Old Rd, WARRINGTON ☎ 01925 267471 52 en suite

Walton Hall Warrington Rd, Higher Walton WA4 5LU
☎ 01925 263061 (bookings) 🖷 01925 263061
Set in a picturesque parkland setting with fine views from the 13th tee. It has many mature trees, and a lot of water comes into play on seven of the holes. Three par 3s are over 200yds.
18 holes, 6647yds, Par 72, SSS 73, Course record 70.
Club membership 250.
Visitors Mon-Sun & BHs. Booking required. Dress code. **Societies** Booking required in writing. **Green Fees** phone. **Prof** John Jackson **Course Designer** Peter Allisss, Dave Thomas **Facilities** **Location** M56 junct 11, 2m

Continued

Hotel ★★★★ 69% De Vere Daresbury Park, Chester Rd, Daresbury, WARRINGTON ☎ 01925 267331 181 en suite

Warrington Hill Warren, London Rd, Appleton WA4 5HR
☎ 01925 261775 (secretary) 🖷 01925 265933
e-mail: secretary@warrington-golf-club.co.uk
web: www.warrington-golf-club.co.uk
Meadowland, with varied terrain and natural hazards. Major work has recently been carried out on both the clubhouse and the course to ensure high standards. The course is a constant challenge with ponds, trees and bunkers threatening the errant shot.

18 holes, 6305yds, Par 72, SSS 70, Course record 61. Club membership 840.
Visitors Booking required. **Societies** Booking required with secretary. **Green Fees** phone. **Prof** Reay Mackay **Course Designer** James Braid **Facilities** **Conf** Corporate Hospitality Days **Location** M56 junct 10, 1.5m N on A49

Hotel ★★★★ 70% The Park Royal Hotel, Stretton Rd, Stretton, WARRINGTON ☎ 01925 730706 142 en suite

WIDNES Map 07 SJ58

Mersey Valley Golf & Country Club Warrington Rd, Bold Heath WA8 3XL
☎ 0151 4246060 🖷 0151 2579097
web: www.merseyvalley golfclub.co.uk
Parkland with very easy walking.
18 holes, 6374yards, Par 72, SSS 71, Course record 70. Club membership 500.
Visitors Mon-Sun & BHs. Booking required. Dress code. **Societies** Booking required. **Green Fees** £30 per day, £22 per round, £40/£25 Sat, Sun & BHs. **Prof** Andy Stevenson **Course Designer** R Bush **Facilities** **Leisure** fishing. **Conf** facs Corporate Hospitality Days **Location** M62 junct 7, A57 towards Warrington, club 2m on left

Hotel ★★★ 62% The Hillcrest Hotel, 75 Cronton Ln, WIDNES ☎ 0870 609 6174 50 en suite

St Michael Jubilee Dundalk Rd WA8 8BS
☎ 0151 424 6230 🖷 0151 495 2124
e-mail: dchapmam@aol.com
18 holes, 5925yds, Par 69, SSS 67.
Location W side of town centre off A562
Phone for further details

Hotel Travelodge Widnes, Fiddlers Ferry Rd, WIDNES ☎ 08700 850 950 32 en suite

Widnes Highfield Rd WA8 7DT
☎ 0151 424 2440 & 424 2995 🖷 0151 495 2849
e-mail: email@widnes-golfclub.co.uk
web: www.widnes-golfclub.co.uk
An easy walking parkland course, challenging in parts.
18 holes, 5719yds, Par 69, SSS 68, Course record 64. Club membership 700.
Visitors Booking required. **Societies** Contact the secretary in writing. **Green Fees** phone. **Prof** J O'Brien **Facilities** **Conf** Corporate Hospitality Days **Location** M62 junct 7, A57 to Warrington, right at lights onto Wilmere Ln, right at T-junct. 1st left at rdbt onto Birchfield Rd, right after 3rd pelican crossing onto Highfield Rd, right before lights

Hotel Travelodge Widnes, Fiddlers Ferry Rd, WIDNES ☎ 08700 850 950 32 en suite

WILMSLOW Map 07 SJ88

De Vere Mottram Hall Wilmslow Rd, Mottram St Andrew SK10 4QT
☎ 01625 828135 🖷 01625 829312
e-mail: dmhgolf@devere-hotels.com
web: www.deveregolf.co.uk
Championship-standard course - flat meadowland on the front nine and undulating woodland on the back nine, with well-guarded greens. The course is unusual as each half opens and closes with par 5s. Good test for both professional and novice golfers alike.
18 holes, 7006yds, Par 72, SSS 74, Course record 63. Club membership 250.
Visitors Mon-Sun & BHs. Booking required. Handicap certificate. Dress code. **Societies** Booking required. **Green Fees** £60 per round summer, £30 per round winter. **Prof** Matthew Turnock **Course Designer** Dave Thomas **Facilities** **Leisure** hard tennis courts, heated indoor swimming pool, squash, sauna, solarium, gymnasium, day store & drying room, satellite navigation buggies. **Conf** facs Corporate Hospitality Days **Location** On A538 between Wilmslow and Prestbury

Hotel ★★★★ 69% De Vere Mottram Hall, Wilmslow Rd, Mottram St Andrew, Prestbury, ☎ 01625 828135 132 en suite

Styal Station Rd, Styal SK9 4JN
☎ 01625 531359 🖷 01625 416373
e-mail: gtraynor@styalgolf.co.uk
web: www.styalgolf.co.uk
Well-designed flat parkland course with USGA specification greens. Challenging and enjoyable test for all standards of golfer. The par 3 course is widely regarded as one of the finest short courses in the country.
18 holes, 6194yds, Par 70, SSS 70, Course record 63. Club membership 800.
Visitors Mon-Sun & BHs. Booking required. Dress code. **Societies** Booking required. **Green Fees** £22 per round, £26 Sat & Sun. **Prof** Simon Forrest **Course Designer** Tony Holmes **Facilities** **Leisure** par 3 9 hole course. **Conf** facs Corporate Hospitality Days **Location** M56 junct 5

Hotel ★★★ 67% Belfry House Hotel, Stanley Rd, HANDFORTH ☎ 0161 437 0511 81 en suite

Continued

Wilmslow Great Warford, Mobberley WA16 7AY
☎ 01565 872148 🖹 01565 872172
e-mail: info@wilmslowgolfclub.co.uk
web: www.wilmslowgolfclub.co.uk
Peaceful parkland in the heart of the Cheshire countryside offering golf for all levels.
18 holes, 6607yds, Par 72, SSS 72, Course record 62. Club membership 800.
Visitors contact club for details. Handicap certificate. Dress code. **Societies** Booking required. **Green Fees** £55 per day, £45 per round, £65/£55 Sat, Sun & BHs. **Prof** John Nowicki **Facilities** **Conf** Corporate Hospitality Days **Location** 2m SW off B5058

Hotel ★★★ 78% Alderley Edge Hotel, Macclesfield Rd, ALDERLEY EDGE ☎ 01625 583033 52 en suite

WINSFORD Map 07 SJ66

Knights Grange Grange Ln CW7 2PT
☎ 01606 552780
e-mail: knightsgrangewinsford@valeroyal.gov.uk
web: www.valeroyal.gov.uk/leisure
An 18-hole course set in beautiful Cheshire countryside on the town outskirts. The front nine is mainly flat but players have to negotiate water, ditches and other hazards along the way. The back nine takes the player deep into the countryside, with many of the tees offering panoramic views. A lake known as the Ocean is a feature of many holes - a particular hazard for slicers of the ball. There are also many mature woodland areas to catch the wayward drive.
18 holes, 5921yds, Par 70, SSS 68.
Visitors Mon-Sun & BHs. **Societies** Booking required. **Green Fees** £8.90 per 18 holes, £11.10 Sat & Sun. **Course Designer** Steve Dawson **Facilities** **Leisure** hard and grass tennis courts. **Location** N side of town off A54

Hotel Travelodge Middlewich, M6 Junction 18, A54, MIDDLEWICH ☎ 08700 850 950 32 en suite

WINWICK Map 07 SJ69

Alder Root Alder Root Ln WA2 8R2
☎ 01925 291919 🖹 01925 291961
e-mail: admin@alderroot.wanadoo.co.uk
web: www.alderroot.com
A woodland course, flat in nature but with many undulations. Several holes have water hazards. One of the most testing nine-hole courses in the north-west.
9 holes, 5837yds, Par 69, SSS 68, Course record 67. Club membership 400.
Visitors Mon-Fri. Booking required Sat, Sun & BHs. Dress code. **Societies** welcome. **Green Fees** phone. **Prof** C McKevitt **Course Designer** Lander, Millington **Facilities** **Location** M62 junct 9, A49 N for 800yds, left at lights right into Alder Root Ln

CORNWALL & ISLES OF SCILLY

BODMIN Map 02 SX06

Lanhydrock Lostwithiel Rd PL30 5AQ
☎ 01208 73600 🖹 01208 77325
e-mail: golfing@lanhydrock-golf.co.uk
web: wwww.lanhydrock-golf.co.uk
An acclaimed parkland and moorland course adjacent to the National Trust property of Lanhydrock House. Nestling in a picturesque wooded valley of oak and birch, this undulating course provides an exciting and enjoyable challenge.

18 holes, 6100yds, Par 70, SSS 70, Course record 66. Club membership 300.
Visitors Booking required. **Societies** Booking required. **Green Fees** phone. **Prof** Phil Brookes **Course Designer** Hamilton Stutt **Facilities** **Conf** facs Corporate Hospitality Days **Location** 1m S of Bodmin off B3268

Hotel ★★★ 69% Restormel Lodge Hotel, Castle Hill, LOSTWITHIEL ☎ 01208 872223 24 en suite 12 annexe en suite

BUDE Map 02 SS20

Bude & North Cornwall Burn View EX23 8DA
☎ 01288 352006 🖹 01288 356855
e-mail: secretary@budegolf.co.uk
web: www.budegolf.co.uk
A traditional links course established in 1891. Situated in the centre of Bude with magnificent views to the sea. A challenging course with super greens and excellent drainage enables course to be playable throughout the year off regular tees and greens.
18 holes, 6057yds, Par 71, SSS 70. Club membership 800.
Visitors Mon-Sun & BHs. Booking required. Handicap certificate. Dress code. **Societies** Booking required. **Green Fees** £27 per day, £27 per round Sat, Sun & BHs. **Prof** John Yeo **Course Designer** Tom Dunn **Facilities** **Leisure** snooker room. **Conf** facs Corporate Hospitality Days **Location** N side of town

Hotel ★★★ 68% Camelot Hotel, Downs View, BUDE ☎ 01288 352361 24 en suite

BUDOCK VEAN Map 02 SW73

Budock Vean-The Hotel on the River

Mawnan Smith TR11 5LG
☎ 01326 250288 (hotel) & 252102 (shop)
01326 250892
e-mail: relax@budockvean.co.uk
web: www.budockvean.co.uk

Set in 65 acres of mature grounds with a private foreshore to the Helford River, this 18-tee undulating parkland course has a tough par 4 5th hole (456yds) which dog-legs at halfway around an oak tree. The 16th hole measures 572yds, par 5.

9 holes, 5255yds, Par 68, SSS 65, Course record 58. Club membership 200.

Visitors Mon-Sun & BHs. Booking required. Dress code. **Societies** Booking required. **Green Fees** £22 per day, £26 Sat, Sun & BHs. **Prof** Tony Ramsden, David Short **Course Designer** James Braid **Facilities** **Leisure** hard tennis courts, heated indoor swimming pool, fishing, boating facilities, health spa. **Location** 1.5m SW of Mawnan Smith

Hotel ★★★★ 73% Budock Vean-The Hotel on the River, MAWNAN SMITH
☎ 01326 252100 & 0800 833927 01326 250892
57 en suite

CAMBORNE Map 02 SW64

Tehidy Park TR14 0HH

☎ 01209 842208 01209 842208
e-mail: secretary-manager@tehidyparkgolfclub.co.uk
web: www.tehidyparkgolfclub.co.uk

A well-maintained parkland course providing good holiday golf and a challenge for golfers of all abilities.

18 holes, 6241yds, Par 71, SSS 71, Course record 62. Club membership 850.

Visitors Mon-Sun & BHs. Booking required. Handicap certificate. Dress code. **Societies** Booking required. **Green Fees** £25.50 per day, £30.50 Sat, Sun & BHs. **Prof** James Dumbreck **Facilities** **Conf** Corporate Hospitality Days **Location** On Portreath-Pool road, 2m S of Camborne

Hotel ★★★ 70% Penventon Park Hotel, REDRUTH
☎ 01209 203000 68 en suite

Prices may change during the currency of the guide, always check when booking

CAMELFORD Map 02 SX18

Bowood Park Hotel Lanteglos PL32 9RF

☎ 01840 213017 01840 212622
e-mail: golf@bowoodpark.com
web: www.bowoodpark.com

A rolling parkland course set in 230 acres of ancient deer park once owned by the Black Prince; 27 lakes and ponds test the golfer and serve as a haven for wildlife.

18 holes, 6736yds, Par 72, SSS 72, Course record 68. Club membership 3500.

Visitors Booking required. **Societies** Booking required. **Green Fees** phone. **Prof** John Phillips **Course Designer** Sandow **Facilities** **Leisure** fishing, masseur available. **Conf** facs Corporate Hospitality Days **Location** Through Camelford, 0.5m turn right Tintagel/Boscastle B3266, 1st left at garage

CARLYON BAY Map 02 SX05

Carlyon Bay Hotel Beach Rd PL25 3RD

☎ 01726 814250 01726 814250
e-mail: golf@carlyonbay.com
web: www.carlyonbay.com

A championship-length, clifftop parkland course, running east to west and back again - and also uphill and down a fair bit. The fairways stay in excellent condition all year as they have since the course was laid down in 1925. Magnificent views from the course across St Austell Bay; particularly from the 9th green, where an approach shot remotely to the right will plummet over the cliff edge.

18 holes, 6597yds, Par 72, SSS 71, Course record 63. Club membership 500.

Visitors Mon-Sun & BHs. Booking required. Handicap certificate. Dress code. **Societies** Booking required. **Green Fees** £25-£42 per round per season. £10 per extra round. **Prof** Mark Rowe **Course Designer** Hamilton Stutt

Continued

Facilities ⊗ 〽 🅱 ☕ 🍷 ⛰ 🏠 🏌 🛏 ✈ 🚗 ✐ **Leisure** hard tennis courts, outdoor and indoor heated swimming pools, sauna, solarium, 9 hole par 3 course. **Conf** Corporate Hospitality Days **Location** 3m SE of St Austell off A390, signposted

Hotel ★★★★ 75% Carlyon Bay Hotel, Sea Rd, Carlyon Bay, ST AUSTELL ☎ 01726 812304 87 en suite

CONSTANTINE BAY Map 02 SW87

Trevose PL28 8JB

☎ 01841 520208 🖷 01841 521057
e-mail: info@trevose-gc.co.uk
web: www.trevose-gc.co.uk

Well-known links course with early holes close to the sea on excellent springy turf. A championship course affording varying degrees of difficulty appealing to both the professional and higher handicap player. It is a good test with well-positioned bunkers, and a meandering stream, and the wind playing a decisive role in preventing low scoring.

Championship Course: 18 holes, 6863yds, Par 72, SSS 73, Course record 66.
New Course: 9 holes, 3031yds, Par 35.
Short Course: 9 holes, 1360yds, Par 29.
Club membership 1650.

Visitors Mon-Sun & BHs. Booking required. Handicap certificate. Dress code. **Societies** Booking required. **Green Fees** Championship course £35-£55 per season. **Prof** Gary Lenaghan **Course Designer** H Colt **Facilities** ⊗ 〽 🅱 ☕ 🍷 ⛰ 🏠 🏌 🛏 ✈ 🚗 ✐ ⛳ **Leisure** hard tennis courts, heated outdoor swimming pool, self catering accommodation & a la carte restaurant, snooker room. **Conf** facs Corporate Hospitality Days **Location** 4m W of Padstow on B3276, to St Merryn, 500yds past x-rds turn, signed

Hotel ★★★★ 69% Treglos Hotel, CONSTANTINE BAY ☎ 01841 520727 42 en suite

If the name of the club appears in italics, details have not been confirmed for this edition of the guide

FALMOUTH Map 02 SW83

Falmouth Swanpool Rd TR11 5BQ

☎ 01326 311262 🖷 01326 317783
e-mail: falmouthgc@onetel.com
web: www.falmouthgolfclub.com

Stunning sea and coastal views. The club is under new ownership and the course has been adjusted to make it fairer, while still a good test of golf. Excellent greens and a well-drained course which rarely closes.

18 holes, 6037yds, Par 71, SSS 70.
Club membership 500.

Visitors Mon-Sun & BHs. Booking required. Dress code. **Societies** Booking required. **Green Fees** £30 per round. **Prof** Nick Rogers **Facilities** ⊗ 〽 🅱 ☕ 🍷 ⛰ 🏠 🏌 ✈ 🚗 ✐ ⛳ **Conf** Corporate Hospitality Days **Location** SW of town centre

Hotel ★★★★ 72% Royal Duchy Hotel, Cliff Rd, FALMOUTH ☎ 01326 313042 43 en suite

HOLYWELL BAY Map 02 SW75

Holywell Bay TR8 5PW
☎ 01637 830095 🖷 01637 831000
e-mail: golf@trevornick.co.uk
web: www.holywellbay.co.uk/golf

Situated beside a family fun park with many amenities. The course is an 18-hole par 3 with excellent sea views. Fresh Atlantic winds make the course hard to play and there are several tricky holes, particularly the 18th over the trout pond. The site also has an excellent 18-hole Pitch and Putt course for the whole family.

18 holes, 2784yds, Par 61, Course record 58. Club membership 100.

Visitors Mon-Sun & BHs. **Societies** welcome. **Green Fees** £11 per 18 holes, £13.50 including half set clubs. **Course Designer** Hartley **Facilities** ⊗)Ⅲ ℡ ☕ ♀ 🏠 ⛳ ✓ **Leisure** heated outdoor swimming pool, fishing, touring & camping facilities. **Location** Off A3075 Newquay-Perranporth road

Hotel ★★★ 67% Barrowfield Hotel, Hilgrove Rd, NEWQUAY ☎ 01637 878878 81 en suite

LAUNCESTON Map 02 SX38

Launceston St Stephens PL15 8HF
☎ 01566 773442 🖷 01566 777506
e-mail: secretarylgc@tiscali.co.uk
web: www.launcestongolfclub.co.uk

Highly rated course with magnificent views over the historic town and moors. Noted for superb greens and lush fairways.

18 holes, 6407yds, Par 70, SSS 71, Course record 65. Club membership 800.

Visitors Mon-Sun & BHs. Booking required. Handicap certificate. Dress code. **Societies** Booking required. **Green Fees** £30 per day, £25 per round. **Prof** John Tozer **Course Designer** Hamilton Stutt **Facilities** ⊗ ℡ ☕ ♀ ⛺ 🏠 ⛳ ✎ 🛒 ✓ **Leisure** practice nets. **Conf** facs Corporate Hospitality Days **Location** NW of town centre on B3254

Hotel ★★ 65% Eagle House Hotel, Castle St, LAUNCESTON ☎ 01566 772036 14 en suite

Trethorne Kennards House PL15 8QE
☎ 01566 86903 🖷 01566 880925
e-mail: mark@trethornegolfclub.com
web: www.trethornegolfclub.com

Rolling parkland course with well maintained fairways and computer irrigated greens. Plenty of trees and natural water hazards make this well respected course a good challenge.

Continued

Trethorne

18 holes, 6178yds, Par 71, SSS 71, Course record 69. Club membership 250.

Visitors Mon-Sun & BHs. Dress code. **Societies** Booking required. **Green Fees** £28 per round. **Prof** Chris Isaac **Course Designer** Frank Frayne **Facilities** ⊗)Ⅲ ℡ ☕ ♀ ⛺ 🏠 ⛳ 🛏 ✎ 🛒 ✓ 🚶 **Leisure** leisure farm and tenpin bowling. **Conf** facs Corporate Hospitality Days **Location** Off junct A30 & A395, 3m W of Launceston

Hotel ★★ 65% Eagle House Hotel, Castle St, LAUNCESTON ☎ 01566 772036 14 en suite

LELANT Map 02 SW53

West Cornwall TR26 3DZ
☎ 01736 753401 🖷 01736 753401
e-mail: ian@westcornwallgolfclub.fsnet.co.uk
web: www.westcornwallgolfclub.co.uk

A seaside links with sandhills and lovely turf adjacent to the Hayle estuary and St Ives Bay. A real test of the player's skill, especially Calamity Corner starting at the 5th on the lower land by the River Hayle.

18 holes, 5884yds, Par 69, SSS 69, Course record 63. Club membership 813.

Visitors Mon-Sun & BHs. Handicap certificate. Dress code. **Societies** Booking required. **Green Fees** £28 per day, £33 Sat, Sun & BHs. **Prof** Jason Broadway **Course Designer** Reverend Tyack **Facilities** ⊗)Ⅲ ℡ ☕ ♀ ⛺ 🏠 ⛳ ✓ **Location** N side of village off A3074

Hotel ★★ 72% Pedn-Olva Hotel, West Porthminster Beach, ST IVES ☎ 01736 796222 30 en suite

LOOE Map 02 SX25

Looe Bindown PL13 1PX
☎ 01503 240239 🖷 01503 240864
e-mail: enquiries@looegolfclub.co.uk
web: www.looegolfclub.co.uk

Designed by Harry Vardon in 1935, this downland and

Continued

parkland course commands panoramic views over south-east Cornwall and the coast. Easy walking.
18 holes, 5940yds, Par 70, SSS 69, Course record 64. Club membership 420.
Visitors Mon-Sun & BHs. Booking required. Dress code. **Societies** Booking required. **Green Fees** £25 per 18 holes. **Prof** Jason Bowen **Course Designer** Harry Vardon **Facilities** **Conf** Corporate Hospitality Days **Location** 3.5m NE off B3253

Hotel ★★★ 66% Hannafore Point Hotel, Marine Dr, West Looe, LOOE ☎ 01503 263273 37 en suite
See advertisement on this page

LOSTWITHIEL Map 02 SX15

Lostwithiel Hotel, Golf & Country Club

Lower Polscoe PL22 0HQ
☎ 01208 873550 01208 873479
e-mail: reception@golf-hotel.co.uk
web: www.golf-hotel.co.uk

This 18-hole course is one of the most varied in the county, designed to take full advantage of the natural features of the landscape, combining two distinct areas of hillside and valley. The challenging front nine has magnificent views of the surrounding countryside, while the picturesque back nine runs through parkland flanked by the River Fowey.

18 holes, 5984yds, Par 72, SSS 71, Course record 67. Club membership 500.
Visitors Mon-Sun & BHs. Booking required. Dress code. **Societies** Booking required. **Green Fees** phone. **Prof** Tony Nash **Course Designer** S Wood **Facilities** **Leisure** hard tennis courts, heated indoor swimming pool, fishing, gymnasium, indoor golf simulator. **Conf** facs Corporate Hospitality Days **Location** 1m from Lostwithiel off A390

Hotel ★★★ 65% Lostwithiel Hotel Golf & Country Club, Lower Polscoe, LOSTWITHIEL ☎ 01208 873550 27 en suite

MAWGAN PORTH Map 02 SW86

Merlin TR8 4DN
☎ 01841 540222 🖷 01841 541031
web: www.merlingolfcourse.co.uk

18 holes, 6210yds, Par 71, SSS 71.
Course Designer Ross Oliver **Location** On Newquay-Padstow coast road. After Mawgan Porth signs for St Eval, course on right
Phone for further details
See advertisement on page 53

MAWNAN SMITH

See **Budock Vean**

MULLION Map 02 SW61

Mullion Cury TR12 7BP
☎ 01326 240685 (sec) & 241176 (pro) 🖷 01326 241527
e-mail: secretary@mulliongolfclub.plus.com
Founded in 1895, a clifftop and links course with panoramic views over Mounts Bay. A steep downhill slope on 6th and the 10th descends to the beach with a deep ravine alongside the green. Second most southerly course in the British Isles.
18 holes, 6083yds, Par 70, SSS 70.
Club membership 800.
Visitors Mon-Sun & BHs. Handicap certificate. Dress code. **Societies** Booking required. **Green Fees** £30 per day, £25 per round, £35/£30 Sat, Sun & BHs. **Prof** Ian Harris **Course Designer** W Sich **Facilities** **Leisure** indoor computerised teaching academy. **Location** 1.5m NW of Mullion, off A3083

Hotel ★★★ 71% Polurrian Hotel, MULLION
☎ 01326 240421 39 en suite

NEWQUAY Map 02 SW86

Newquay Tower Rd TR7 1LT
☎ 01637 874354 🖷 01637 874066
e-mail: info@newquay-golf-club.co.uk
web: www.newquay-golf-club.co.uk
One of Cornwall's finest seaside links with magnificent views over the Atlantic Ocean. Open to the unpredictable nature of the elements and possessing some very demanding greenside bunkers, the prerequisite for good scoring at Newquay is accuracy.
18 holes, 6150yds, Par 69, SSS 69, Course record 63.
Club membership 600.
Visitors contact club for details. Handicap certificate. Dress code. **Societies** Booking required. **Green Fees** £30 per day, £25 per round, £30 per round Sat, Sun & BHs. **Prof** Mark Bevan **Course Designer** H Colt **Facilities** **Leisure** Snooker. **Conf** Corporate Hospitality Days **Location** W side of town

Hotel ★★★ 70% Hotel Bristol, Narrowcliff, NEWQUAY
☎ 01637 875181 74 en suite

Treloy TR8 4JN
☎ 01637 878554 🖷 01637 871710
e-mail: paull@treloy.freeserve.co.uk
9 holes, 2143yds, Par 32, SSS 31, Course record 63.
Course Designer MRM Sandow **Location** On A3059 Newquay-St Columb Major road
Phone for further details

Hotel ★★ 72% Whipsiderry Hotel, Trevelgue Rd, Porth, NEWQUAY ☎ 01637 874777 & 876066 🖷 01637 874777 20 rms (19 en suite)

PADSTOW

See **Constantine Bay**

PERRANPORTH Map 02 SW75

Perranporth Budnic Hill TR6 0AB
☎ 01872 573701
e-mail: perranporth@golfclub92.fsnet.co.uk
web: www.perranporthgolfclub.com
There are three testing par 5 holes on the links course (2nd, 5th, 11th). This seaside links course has magnificent views of the North Cornwall coastline, and excellent greens. The drainage of the course, being sand-based, is also exceptional.

18 holes, 6272yds, Par 72, SSS 72, Course record 62.
Club membership 650.
Visitors Mon-Sun & BHs. Booking required. Dress code. **Societies** Booking required. **Green Fees** £25 per round, £30 per round Sat, Sun & BHs. £5 per extra hole. **Prof** D Michell **Course Designer** James Braid **Facilities** **Conf** Corporate Hospitality Days **Location** 0.75m NE on B3285

Continued

Hotel ★★★ 68% Rosemundy House Hotel, Rosemundy Hill, ST AGNES ☎ 01872 552101 46 en suite

PORTWRINKLE Map 02 SX45

Whitsand Bay Hotel Golf & Country Club
PL11 3BU
☎ 01503 230276 🖷 01503 230329
e-mail: whitsandbayhotel@btconnect.com
web: www.whitsandbayhotel.co.uk

Testing seaside course laid out on cliffs overlooking Whitsand Bay. Easy walking after first hole. The par 3 3rd hole is acknowledged as one of the most attractive holes in Cornwall.

18 holes, 6030yds, Par 69, SSS 68, Course record 62. Club membership 400.

Visitors Mon-Sun & BHs. Booking required. Dress code. **Societies** Booking required. **Green Fees** £22 per round, £28 Sat & Sun. **Prof** Steve Dougan **Course Designer** Fernie **Facilities** ⊗ **Leisure** heated indoor swimming pool, sauna, solarium, gymnasium. **Conf** Corporate Hospitality Days **Location** 5m from Torpoint off A374

Hotel ★★★ 68% Whitsand Bay Hotel & Golf Club, PORTWRINKLE ☎ 01503 230276 32 en suite

PRAA SANDS

Praa Sands
Germoe Cross Roads TR20 9TQ
☎ 01736 763445 🖷 01736 763399
e-mail: praasandsgolf@aol.com

A beautiful parkland course, overlooking Mount's Bay with outstanding sea views from every tee and green.

9 holes, 4122yds, Par 62, SSS 60, Course record 59. Club membership 220.

Visitors contact club for details. **Societies** welcome. **Green Fees** from £10. **Course Designer** R Hamilton **Facilities** ⊗ **Leisure** pool, darts. **Location** A394 between Penzance & Helston

Inn ♦♦♦♦ Harbour Inn, Commercal Rd, PORTHLEVEN ☎ 01326 573876 10 en suite

ROCK Map 02 SW97

St Enodoc
PL27 6LD
☎ 01208 863216 🖷 01208 862976
e-mail: enquiries@st-enodoc.co.uk
web: www.st-enodoc.co.uk

Classic links course with huge sand hills and rolling fairways. James Braid laid out the original 18 holes in 1907 and changes were made in 1922 and 1935. On the Church, the 10th is the toughest par 4 on the course and

Continued

on the 6th is a truly enormous sand hill known as the Himalayas. The Holywell is not as exacting as the Church; it is less demanding on stamina but still a real test of skill for golfers of any handicap.

Church Course: 18 holes, 6243yds, Par 69, SSS 70, Course record 64.
Holywell Course: 18 holes, 4142yds, Par 63, SSS 61.
Club membership 1300.

Visitors Mon-Fri & Sun except BH. Booking required. Handicap certificate. Dress code. **Societies** Booking required. **Green Fees** Church £65 per day, £45 per round, £55 per round Sat & Sun. Holywell £25 per day, £16 per round. **Prof** Nick Williams **Course Designer** James Braid **Facilities** ⊗ **Location** W side of village

Hotel ★★ 63% The Molesworth Arms Hotel, Molesworth St, WADEBRIDGE ☎ 01208 812055 16 rms (14 en suite)

ST AUSTELL Map 02 SX05

Porthpean
Porthpean PL26 6AY
☎ 01726 64613 🖷 01726 71643
e-mail: ktuckerpgc@aol.com
web: www.porthpean-golf.co.uk

A picturesque 18-hole course, the outward holes are in a pleasant parkland setting while the return holes command spectacular views over St Austell Bay.

18 holes, 5210yds, Par 67, SSS 66. Club membership 300.

Visitors Mon-Sun. **Societies** Booking required. **Green Fees** phone. **Facilities** ⊗ **Location** 1.5m from St Austell bypass

Hotel ★★ 73% The Pier House, Harbour Front, Charlestown, ST AUSTELL ☎ 01726 67955 26 en suite

St Austell
Tregongeeves Ln PL26 7DS
☎ 01726 74756 🖷 01726 71978

18 holes, 6089yds, Par 69, SSS 69, Course record 64.

Location 1m W of St Austell on A390
Phone for further details

Hotel ★★★ 72% Porth Avallen Hotel, Sea Rd, Carlyon Bay, ST AUSTELL ☎ 01726 812802 27 en suite

Guest House ♦♦♦♦♦ 88% Wisteria Lodge, Boscundle, Tregrehan, ST AUSTELL ☎ 01726 810800 5 en suite

St Ives Map 02 SW54

Tregenna Castle Hotel, Golf & Country Club TR26 2DE

01736 797381 01736 796066
e-mail: hotel@tregenna-castle.co.uk
web: www.tregenna-castle.co.uk
Parkland course surrounding a castellated hotel and overlooking St Ives Bay and harbour.
14 holes, 1846yds, Par 42, SSS 42.
Club membership 140.
Visitors Mon-Sun & BHs. **Societies** Booking required. **Green Fees** £15 per round. **Course Designer** J Abercromby **Facilities** **Leisure** hard tennis courts, outdoor and indoor heated swimming pools, squash, sauna, solarium, gymnasium, badminton court. **Conf** facs Corporate Hospitality Days **Location** Off A30 past Hayle onto A3074

Hotel ★★★ 65% Tregenna Castle Hotel, ST IVES
01736 795254 81 en suite

St Just (near Land's End) Map 02 SW33

Cape Cornwall Golf & Country Club

Cape Cornwall TR19 7NL
01736 788611 01736 788611
e-mail: info@capecornwall.com
web: www.capecornwall.com
Coastal parkland, walled course. The walls are an integral part of its design. Britain's first and last 18-hole course overlooking the only cape in England, with views of the north Cornwall coast and fishing coves. Features a flat front nine followed by a challenging back nine. Extremely scenic views.

18 holes, 5632yds, Par 69, SSS 68, Course record 64.
Club membership 750.
Visitors Booking required. Dress code. **Societies** Booking required. **Green Fees** phone. **Prof** Jonathan Lamb **Course Designer** Bob Hamilton **Facilities** **Leisure** heated indoor swimming pool, sauna, solarium, gymnasium. **Conf** facs Corporate Hospitality Days **Location** 1m W of St Just

Hotel ★★ 66% The Old Success Inn, Sennen Cove, SENNEN 01736 871232 12 en suite

St Mellion Map 02 SX36

St Mellion Hotel, Golf & Country Club see page 57

Hotel ★★★ 68% St Mellion International, ST MELLION
01579 351351 39 annexe en suite

Hotel ★★ Well House Hotel, St Keyne, LISKEARD
01579 342001 01579 343891 9 en suite

Hotel ★★★ 67% China Fleet Country Club, SALTASH
01752 848668 01752 848456 40 en suite

St Minver Map 02 SW97

Roserrow Golf & Country Club Roserrow PL27 6QT

01208 863000 01208 863002
e-mail: mail@roserrow.co.uk
web: www.roserrow.co.uk/golf
Challenging par 72 course in an undulating wooded valley. Stunning views over the Cornish countryside and out to Hayle Bay.

18 holes, 6551yds, Par 72, SSS 72, Course record 68.
Club membership 450.
Visitors Mon-Sun & BHs. Booking required. Dress code. **Societies** Booking required. **Green Fees** £27.50, winter £20. **Prof** Guy Hovil **Facilities** **Leisure** hard tennis courts, heated indoor swimming pool, sauna, solarium, gymnasium, outdoor bowling green. **Conf** facs Corporate Hospitality Days **Location** Off B3314 between Wadebridge

Hotel ★★ 63% The Molesworth Arms Hotel, Molesworth St, WADEBRIDGE 01208 812055 16 rms (14 en suite)

Saltash Map 02 SX45

China Fleet Country Club PL12 6LJ

01752 848668 01752 848456
e-mail: golf@china-fleet.co.uk
web: www.china-fleet.co.uk
Parkland with river views. The 14th tee shot has to carry a lake of some 150yds.
18 holes, 6551yds, Par 72, SSS 72, Course record 69.
Club membership 600.
Visitors Mon-Sun & BHs. Booking required. Handicap certificate. Dress code. **Societies** Booking required. **Green Fees** phone. **Prof** Paul Kent **Course Designer** Hawtree **Facilities** **Leisure** hard tennis courts, heated indoor swimming pool, squash, sauna, solarium, gymnasium, **Conf** facs Corporate Hospitality Days **Location** 1m from the Tamar Bridge

Hotel ★★★ 67% China Fleet Country Club, SALTASH
01752 848668 40 en suite

Continued

Championship Course

Cornwall

St Mellion Hotel

St Mellion

Map 02 SX36

Set among 450 acres of glorious Cornish countryside, St Mellion with its two outstanding courses is heralded as the premier golf and country club in the south-west. The Old Course is perfect for golfers of all abilities. Complete with well-sited bunkers, strategically tiered greens and difficult water features, this is definitely not a course to be overlooked. But if you really want to test your game, then head to the renowned Nicklaus Course, designed by the great man himself. On its opening in 1998 Jack declared, 'St Mellion is potentially the finest golf course in Europe'. The spectacularly sculptured fairways and carpet greens of the Nicklaus Course are a challenge and an inspiration to all golfers.

PL12 6SD
☎ 01579 351351 🖷 01579 350537
e-mail: stmellion@crown-golf.co.uk
web: www.st-mellion.co.uk

Nicklaus Course: 18 holes, 6592yds, Par 72, SSS 74, Course record 63.
The Old Course: 18 holes, 5782yds, Par 68, SSS 68, Course record 60.
Club membership 2850.

Visitors Mon-Sun & BHs. Booking required. Dress code. **Societies** Booking required. **Green Fees** Nicklaus £85 per day, £59 per round. Old Course £70 per day, £40 per round. **Prof** David Moon **Course Designer** Old Course HJ Stutt, Jack Nicklaus **Facilities** **Leisure** hard tennis courts, heated indoor swimming pool, squash, sauna, solarium, gymnasium. **Conf facs** Corporate Hospitality Days **Location** A38 to Saltash, onto A388 to Callington

TRURO Map 02 SW84

Killiow Park Kea TR3 6AG
☎ 01872 270246 01872 240915
e-mail: killiowsec@yahoo.co.uk
A picturesque and testing parkland course in the grounds of Killiow Estate, with mature trees, water hazards, small greens and tight fairways making this a challenge for golfers of all abilities. Five holes are played across or around water. Floodlit, all-weather driving range and practice facilities.
18 holes, 6266yds, Par 72, SSS 71.
Club membership 500.
Visitors Mon-Sun & BHs. Booking required. Dress code. **Societies** Booking required. **Green Fees** £21 per 18 holes. Winter reduced rates. **Course Designer** Ross Oliver **Facilities** **Leisure** 3 hole academy course. **Location** 3m SW of Truro, off A39

Hotel ★★★ 75% Alverton Manor, Tregolls Rd, TRURO
☎ 01872 276633 32 en suite

Truro Treliske TR1 3LG
☎ 01872 278684 (manager) 01872 225972
e-mail: trurogolfclub@tiscali.co.uk
web: www.trurogolfclub.co.uk
A picturesque and gently undulating parkland course with lovely views of the cathedral city of Truro and the surrounding countryside. The 5306yd course offers a great challenge to golfers of all standards and ages. The many trees and shrubs offer open invitations for wayward balls, and with many fairways boasting out of bounds markers, play needs to be safe and sensible. Fairways are tight and the greens small and full of character, making it difficult to play to one's handicap.
18 holes, 5306yds, Par 66, SSS 66, Course record 59.
Club membership 1000.
Visitors Mon-Sun & BHs. Handicap certificate. Dress code. **Societies** Booking required. **Green Fees** £25 per day, £30 Sat, Sun & BHs. **Prof** Nigel Bicknell **Course Designer** Colt, Alison & Morrison **Facilities** **Location** 1.5m W on A390 towards Redruth, adjacent to Treliske Hospital

Hotel ★★★ 75% Alverton Manor, Tregolls Rd, TRURO
☎ 01872 276633 32 en suite

Guest House ♦♦♦ Gwel-Tek Lodge Guest House, 41 Treyew Rd, TRURO ☎ 01872 276843
01872 242574 7 en suite

WADEBRIDGE Map 02 SW97

St Kew St Kew Highway PL30 3EF
☎ 01208 841500 01208 841500
e-mail: fjb@stkewgolfclub.fsnet.co.uk
web: www.thisisnorthcornwall.com
An interesting, well-laid out nine-hole parkland course with six holes with water and 15 bunkers. In a picturesque setting there are 10 par 4s and eight par 3s. No handicap certificate required but some experience of the game is essential. Nine extra tees now allow a different teeing area for the back nine.
9 holes, 4550yds, Par 64, SSS 62, Course record 63.
Club membership 350.
Visitors Mon-Sun. Booking required. **Societies** Booking required **Green Fees** phone. **Prof** David Boyes **Course Designer** David Derry **Facilities** **Leisure** fishing, ten pin bowling from end of 2005. **Conf** Corporate Hospitality Days **Location** 2m N of Wadebridge main A39

Hotel ★★ 63% The Molesworth Arms Hotel, Molesworth St, WADEBRIDGE ☎ 01208 812055 16 rms (14 en suite)

CUMBRIA

ALSTON Map 12 NY74

Alston Moor The Hermitage, Middleton in Teesdale Rd CA9 3DB
☎ 01434 381675 & 381354 (sec) 01434 381675
10 holes, 5518yds, Par 68, SSS 66, Course record 67.
Location 1 S of Alston on B6277
Phone for further details

Hotel ★★ 76% Nent Hall Country House Hotel, ALSTON
☎ 01434 381584 18 en suite

APPLEBY-IN-WESTMORLAND Map 12 NY62

Appleby Brackenber Moor CA16 6LP
☎ 017683 51432 017683 52773
e-mail: appleby.gc@tiscali.co.uk
web: www.applebygolfclub.org.uk
This remotely situated heather and moorland course offers interesting golf with the rewarding bonus of several long par 4 holes that will be remembered and challenging par 3s. There are superb views of the Pennines and the Lakeland hills. Renowned for the excellent greens and very good drainage.
18 holes, 5901yds, Par 68, SSS 68, Course record 61.
Club membership 800.
Visitors Mon-Sun & BHs. Dress code. **Societies** Booking required. **Green Fees** £26 per day, £21 per round, £31/£25 Sat, Sun & BHs. **Prof** James Taylor **Course Designer** Willie Fernie **Facilities** **Leisure** buggy for disabled use. **Conf** Corporate Hospitality Days **Location** 2m E of Appleby 0.5m off A66

Hotel ★★★ 78% Appleby Manor Country House Hotel, Roman Rd, APPLEBY-IN-WESTMORLAND
☎ 017683 51571 23 en suite 7 annexe en suite

ASKAM-IN-FURNESS Map 07 SD27

Dunnerholme Duddon Rd LA16 7AW
☎ 01229 462675 & 467421 🖷 01229 462675
e-mail: dunnerholmegolfclub@btinternet.com
Unique 10-hole (18-tee) links course with view of the Cumbrian mountains and Morecambe Bay. Two streams run through and around the course, providing water hazards on the 1st, 2nd, 3rd and 9th holes. The par 3 6th is the feature hole on the course, playing to an elevated green on Dunnerholme Rock, an imposing limestone outcrop jutting out into the estuary.
10 holes, 6138yds, Par 72, SSS 69.
Club membership 450.
Visitors Mon & Wed-Fri. Handicap certificate. Dress code. **Societies** apply in writing to the secretary. **Green Fees** £15 per day. **Facilities** **Location** 1m N on A595

Hotel ★★ 64% Lisdoonie Hotel, 307-309 Abbey Rd, BARROW-IN-FURNESS ☎ 01229 827312 12 en suite

BARROW-IN-FURNESS Map 07 SD26

Barrow Rakesmoor Ln, Hawcoat LA14 4QB
☎ 01229 825444
e-mail: barrowgolf@supanet.com
Pleasant course laid out on two levels of meadowland, with extensive views of the nearby Lakeland fells and west to the Irish Sea. Upper level is affected by easterly winds.

18 holes, 6010yds, Par 71, SSS 70, Course record 65.
Club membership 520.
Visitors Mon-Sun & BHs. Booking required. Handicap certificate. Dress code. **Societies** Booking required. **Green Fees** £28 per day, £35 Sat, Sun & BHs. **Prof** Mike Newton **Course Designer** AM Duncan **Facilities** **Location** M6 junct 35, A590 towards Barrow. 2m to K Papermill, left to top of hill

Hotel ★★★ 71% Clarence House Country Hotel & Restaurant, Skelgate, DALTON-IN-FURNESS ☎ 01229 462508 7 en suite 12 annexe en suite

Furness Central Dr LA14 3LN
☎ 01229 471232
e-mail: enquiries@furnessgolfclub.co.uk
web: www.furnessgolfclub.co.uk
Links golf with a fairly flat first half but a much sterner second nine played across subtle sloping ground. There are good views of the Lakes, north Wales and the Isle of Man.
18 holes, 6363yds, Par 71, SSS 71, Course record 65.
Club membership 630.
Visitors Mon-Sun & BHs. Booking required Sat & Sun. Handicap certificate. Dress code. **Societies** welcome. **Green Fees** £15 per day, £25 Sat, Sun & BHs. **Facilities** **Location** 1.75 W of town centre off A590 to Walney Island

Hotel ★★ 64% Lisdoonie Hotel, 307-309 Abbey Rd, BARROW-IN-FURNESS ☎ 01229 827312 12 en suite

BOWNESS-ON-WINDERMERE Map 07 SD49

Windermere Cleabarrow LA23 3NB
☎ 015394 43123 🖷 015394 43123
e-mail: windermeregc@btconnect.com
web: www.windermeregolfclub.net
Located in the heart of the Lake District, just 2m from Windermere. The course offers some of the finest views in the country. Not a long course but makes up for its lack of distance with heather and tight undulating fairways. The 6th hole has a nerve wracking but exhilarating blind shot - 160yds over a rocky face to a humpy fairway with a lake to avoid on the second shot.
18 holes, 5122yds, Par 67, SSS 65, Course record 58.
Club membership 890.
Visitors Mon-Sun & BHs. Booking required. Handicap certificate. Dress code. **Societies** welcome. **Green Fees** £30 per round, £37 Sat, Sun & BHs. **Prof** WSM Rooke **Course Designer** G Lowe **Facilities** **Leisure** snooker. **Conf** Corporate Hospitality Days **Location** B5284 1.5m from Bowness

Hotel ★★★ 68% Famous Wild Boar Hotel, Crook, WINDERMERE ☎ 015394 45225 36 en suite

BRAMPTON Map 12 NY56

Brampton Tarn Rd CA8 1HN
☎ 016977 2255 🖷 01900 827852
e-mail: secretary@bramptongolfclub.com
web: www.bramptongolfclub.com

Undulating heathland course set in rolling fell country. A number of particularly fine holes, the pick of which may arguably be the lengthy 3rd and 11th. The

Continued

challenging nature of the course is complemented by unspoilt panoramic views of the Lake District, Pennines and southern Scotland.
18 holes, 6407yds, Par 72, SSS 71, Course record 64. Club membership 800.
Visitors Mon-Fri. Booking required Sat, Sun & BHs. Dress code. **Societies** Booking required. **Green Fees** £30 per day £26 round, £38/£32 Sat, Sun & BHs. **Prof** Stewart Wilkinson **Course Designer** James Braid **Facilities** **Leisure** games room. **Conf** Corporate Hospitality Days **Location** 1.5m SE of Brampton on B6413

Hotel ★★★ Farlam Hall Hotel, BRAMPTON ☎ 016977 46234 11 en suite 1 annexe en suite

CARLISLE Map 11 NY35

Carlisle Aglionby CA4 8AG
☎ 01228 513029 (secretary) 01228 513303
e-mail: secretary@carlislegolfclub.org
web: www.carlislegolfclub.org
Majestic, long-established parkland course with great appeal providing a secure habitat for red squirrels and deer. A complete but not too severe test of golf, with fine turf, natural hazards, a stream and many beautiful trees; no two holes are similar.
18 holes, 6263yds, Par 71, SSS 70, Course record 63. Club membership 700.
Visitors Mon, Wed, Fri & BHs. Handicap certificate. Dress code. **Societies** welcome. **Green Fees** £45 per day, £35 per round. **Prof** Graeme Lisle **Course Designer** Mackenzie Ross **Facilities** **Conf** facs Corporate Hospitality Days **Location** M6 junct 43, 0.5m E on A69

Hotel ★★★ 72% Crown Hotel, Wetheral, CARLISLE ☎ 01228 561888 49 en suite 2 annexe en suite

Stony Holme Municipal St Aidans Rd CA1 1LS
☎ 01228 625511 01228 625511
e-mail: stephenli@carlisle-city.gov.uk
web: www.4leisure.gov.uk
Municipal parkland course, bounded on three sides by the River Eden with a backdrop of the Lakeland fells. Water comes into play on 11 holes.

18 holes, 5783yds, Par 69, SSS 68, Course record 64. Club membership 350.
Visitors Sat & Sun booking required. **Societies** Booking required. **Green Fees** phone. **Prof** S Ling **Facilities** **Conf** Corporate Hospitality Days **Location** M6 junct 43, A69, 2m W

Hotel ★★★ 61% The Crown & Mitre, 4 English St, CARLISLE ☎ 01228 525491 74 en suite 20 annexe en suite

COCKERMOUTH Map 11 NY13

Cockermouth Embleton CA13 9SG
☎ 017687 76223 & 76941 017687 76941
e-mail: secretary@cockermouthgolf.co.uk
web: www.cockermouthgolf.co.uk
Fell course, fenced, with exceptional views of Lakeland hills and valleys and the Solway Firth. A hard climb on the 3rd and 11th holes. Testing holes: 10th and 16th (rearranged by James Braid).

18 holes, 5496yds, Par 69, SSS 66, Course record 62. Club membership 600.
Visitors Mon-Sun except BHs. Booking required Sat & Sun. Dress code. **Societies** Booking required. **Green Fees** £20 per day, £25 Sat, Sun & BHs. **Course Designer** J Braid **Facilities** **Conf** Corporate Hospitality Days **Location** 3m E off A66

Hotel ★★★ 76% The Trout Hotel, Crown St, COCKERMOUTH ☎ 01900 823591 43 en suite

CROSBY-ON-EDEN Map 12 NY45

Eden CA6 4RA
☎ 01228 573003 & 573013 🖷 01228 818435
e-mail: alistair.wannop@virgin.net
web: www.edengolf.co.uk

18 holes, 6410yds, Par 72, SSS 72, Course record 64.
Location M6 junct 44, 5m on A689 towards Brampton
Phone for further details

Hotel Travelodge Carlisle Todhills, A74 Southbound, Todhills, CARLISLE ☎ 08700 850 950 40 en suite

GRANGE-OVER-SANDS Map 07 SD47

Grange Fell Fell Rd LA11 6HB
☎ 015395 32536
e-mail: grangefellgc@aol.com
A fell course with no excessive climbing and dependant on how straight you hit the ball. Fine views in all directions.
9 holes, 5292yds, Par 70, SSS 66, Course record 65.
Club membership 300.
Visitors Mon-Sun & BHs. Booking required Tue, Sat & Sun. Dress code. **Green Fees** £15 per day, £20 Sat, Sun & BHs. **Course Designer** AB Davy **Facilities**
Location 1m W on Grange-Over-Sands/Cartmel

Hotel ★★★ 75% Netherwood Hotel, Lindale Rd, GRANGE-OVER-SANDS ☎ 015395 32552 32 en suite

Grange-over-Sands Meathop Rd LA11 6QX
☎ 015395 33180 or 33754 🖷 015395 33754
e-mail: dwright@ktdinternet.com
web: www.grangegolfclub.co.uk
Interesting parkland course with well-sited tree plantations, ditches and water features. The four par 3s are considered to be some of the best in the area.
18 holes, 5958yds, Par 70, SSS 69, Course record 68.
Club membership 650.
Visitors Mon-Fri, Sun & BHs. Booking required. Handicap certificate. Dress code. **Societies** Booking required. **Green Fees** £30 per day, £25 per round, £35/£30 Sun & BHs. **Prof** Andrew Pickering **Course Designer** MacKenzie (part) **Facilities**
Conf Corporate Hospitality Days **Location** NE of town centre off B5277

Hotel ★★★ 67% Graythwaite Manor Hotel, Fernhill Rd, GRANGE-OVER-SANDS ☎ 015395 32001 & 33755 🖷 015395 35549 21 en suite

KENDAL Map 07 SD59

Carus Green Burneside Rd LA9 6EB
☎ 01539 721097 🖷 01539 721097
e-mail: info@carusgreen.co.uk
web: www.carusgreen.co.uk
Flat 18-hole course surrounded by the rivers Kent and Mint with an open view of the Kentmere and Howgill fells. The course is a mixture of relatively easy and difficult holes. These rivers come into play on five holes and there are also a number of ponds and bunkers.
18 holes, 5691yds, Par 70, SSS 68, Course record 65.
Club membership 600.
Visitors Mon-Sun & BHs. Booking required. Dress code. **Societies** Booking required. **Green Fees** £18 per round, £20 Sat, Sun & BHs. **Prof** D Turner, N Barron **Course Designer** W Adamson **Facilities**
Conf Corporate Hospitality Days **Location** 1m from Kendal centre

Hotel ★★★ 60% Riverside Hotel Kendal, Beezon Rd, Stramongate Bridge, KENDAL ☎ 01539 734861 47 en suite

Kendal The Heights LA9 4PQ
☎ 01539 723499 (pro) 🖷 01539 736466
e-mail: secretary@kendalgolfclub.co.uk
web: www.kendalgolfclub.co.uk
Elevated parkland and fell course with breathtaking views of Lakeland fells and the surrounding district.
18 holes, 5737yds, Par 70, SSS 67, Course record 65.
Club membership 552.
Visitors Mon-Fri, Sun & BHs. Booking required. Handicap certificate. Dress code. **Societies** Booking required. **Green Fees** £30 per day, £23 per round, £40/£30 Sun. **Prof** Peter Scott **Facilities**
Leisure Golf clinic with computer analysis.
Location 1m W of town centre, turn left at town hall and follow signposts

Hotel ★★★ 77% The Castle Green Hotel in Kendal, KENDAL ☎ 01539 734000 100 en suite

KESWICK Map 11 NY22

Keswick Threlkeld Hall, Threlkeld CA12 4SX
☎ 017687 79324 🖷 017687 79861
e-mail: secretary@keswickgolf.com
web: www.keswickgolf.com
18 holes, 6225yds, Par 71, SSS 72, Course record 68.
Course Designer Eric Brown **Location** 4m E of Keswick, off A66
Phone for further details

Hotel ★★★ 70% Keswick Country House Hotel, Station Rd, KESWICK ☎ 0845 458 4333 74 en suite

KIRKBY LONSDALE Map 07 SD67

Kirkby Lonsdale Scaleber Ln, Barbon LA6 2LJ
☎ 015242 76365 🖷 015242 76503
e-mail: klgolf@dial.pipex.com/
web: www.klgolf.dial.pipex.com/
Parkland on the east bank of the River Lune and crossed by Barbon Beck. Mainly following the lie of the land, the gently undulating course uses the beck to provide water hazards.
18 holes, 6538yds, Par 72, SSS 71, Course record 67.
Club membership 600.

Continued

Visitors Mon-Sun & BHs. Booking required. Dress code. **Societies** Booking required. **Green Fees** £30 per day, £35 Sat, Sun & BHs. **Prof** Chris Barrett **Course Designer** Bill Squires **Facilities** **Conf** Corporate Hospitality Days **Location** 3m NE of Kirkby Lonsdale on A683

Hotel ★★ 68% The Whoop Hall, Burrow with Burrow, KIRKBY LONSDALE ☎ 015242 71284 24 rms (23 en suite)

MARYPORT Map 11 NY03

Maryport Bankend CA15 6PA
☎ 01900 812605 01900 15626
e-mail: maryportgcltd@one-tel.com

A tight seaside links course exposed to Solway breezes. Fine views across Solway Firth. Course comprises nine links holes and nine parkland holes, and small streams can be hazardous on several holes. The first three holes have the seashore on their left and an errant tee shot can land in the water. Holes 6-14 are parkland in quality, gently undulating and quite open. Holes 15-18 revert to links.

18 holes, 5982yds, Par 70, SSS 69, Course record 65. Club membership 539.

Visitors Mon-Sun & BHs. Booking required Thu, Sat, Sun & BHs. Handicap certificate. Dress code. **Societies** Booking required. **Green Fees** £23 per day, £32 Sat, Sun & BHs. **Facilities** **Location** 1m N on B5300

Hotel ★★★ 80% Washington Central Hotel, Washington St, WORKINGTON ☎ 01900 65772 46 en suite

PENRITH Map 12 NY53

Penrith Salkeld Rd CA11 8SG
☎ 01768 891919 01768 891919
e-mail: golf@penrithgolfclub.co.uk

A beautiful and well-balanced course, always changing direction, and demanding good length from the tee. It is set on rolling moorland with occasional pine trees and some fine views.

18 holes, 6047yds, Par 69, SSS 69, Course record 63. Club membership 850.

Visitors Mon-Sun & BHs. Handicap certificate. Dress code. **Societies** Booking required. **Green Fees** £31 per day, £26 per round, £36/£31 Sat & Sun. **Prof** Garry Key **Facilities** **Conf** facs **Location** M6 junct 41, A6 to Penrith, left after 30mph sign

Hotel ★★ 67% Brantwood Country Hotel, Stainton, PENRITH ☎ 01768 862748 7 en suite

ST BEES Map 11 NX91

St Bees Peckmill, Beach Rd CA27 0EJ
☎ 01946 824300

Picturesque 10-hole layout on the cliffs overlooking St Bees beach with views of the Solway Firth and the Isle of Man. Not overly long but testing for golfers of all abilities.

10 holes, 5306yds, Par 66, SSS 66, Course record 64. Club membership 400.

Visitors Mon-Sun. After 3pm Sat & Sun. Not after 4pm Wed. **Societies** Booking required. **Green Fees** phone. **Facilities** **Location** 0.5m W of village off B5345

Hotel ★★★ 70% Ennerdale Country House Hotel, CLEATOR ☎ 01946 813907 30 en suite

SEASCALE Map 06 NY00

Seascale The Banks CA20 1QL
☎ 019467 28202 019467 28202
e-mail: seascalegolfclub@aol.com
web: www.seascalegolfclub.co.uk

A tough links requiring length and control. The natural terrain is used to give a variety of holes and considerable character. Undulating greens add to the challenge. Fine views of the western fells, the Irish Sea and the Isle of Man.

18 holes, 6416yds, Par 71, SSS 71, Course record 64. Club membership 700.

Visitors Mon-Sun & BHs. Booking required. Handicap certificate. Dress code. **Societies** Booking required. **Green Fees** £30 per day, £25 per round, £35/£30 Sat, Sun & BHs. **Prof** Sean Rudd **Course Designer** Willie Campbell **Facilities** **Conf** facs **Location** NW side of village off B5344

Hotel ★★ 71% Low Wood Hall Hotel & Restaurant, NETHER WASDALE ☎ 019467 26100 6 rms (5 en suite) 6 annexe en suite

SEDBERGH Map 07 SD69

Sedbergh Dent Rd LA10 5SS
☎ 015396 21551 015396 21551
e-mail: info@sedberghgolfclub.co.uk
web: www.sedberghgolfclub.co.uk

A tree-lined parkland course with superb scenery in the Yorkshire Dales National Park. Undulating fairways cross or are adjacent to the Dee and Rawthey rivers. Well guarded greens and many water features make the course a test for golfers of all abilities.

9 holes, 5624yds, Par 70, SSS 68, Course record 66. Club membership 250.

Visitors contact club for details. Dress code. **Societies** Booking required. **Green Fees** £20 per 18 holes, £14 per 9 holes. **Course Designer** WG Squires **Facilities** **Leisure** fishing. **Conf** facs Corporate Hospitality Days **Location** 1m S off A683

Hotel Premier Travel Inn Kendal (Killington Lake), Killington Lake, Motorway Service Area, Killington, KENDAL ☎ 08701 977145 36 en suite

SILECROFT Map 06 SD18

Silecroft Silecroft, Millom LA18 4NX
☎ 01229 774250
Seaside links course parallel to the coast of the Irish Sea with spectacular views inland of Lakeland hills. Looks deceptively easy but an ever present sea breeze ensures a sporting challenge.
9 holes, 5896yds, Par 68, SSS 68, Course record 66. Club membership 240.
Visitors Mon-Sun & BHs. Dress code. **Societies** Booking required. **Green Fees** £15 per day, £20 Sat, Sun & BHs. **Facilities** **Location** 3m W of Millom

SILLOTH Map 11 NY15

Silloth on Solway The Clubhouse CA7 4BL
☎ 016973 31304 016973 31782
e-mail: sillothgolfclub@lineone.net
web: www.sillothgolfclub.co.uk
Billowing dunes, narrow fairways, heather and gorse and the constant subtle problems of tactics and judgement make these superb links on the Solway an exhilarating and searching test. The 13th is a good long hole. Superb views.
18 holes, 6041yds, Par 72, SSS 69, Course record 59. Club membership 700.
Visitors Mon-Sun & BHs. Booking required. Handicap certificate. Dress code. **Societies** Booking required. **Green Fees** £35 per day, £48 per round Sat & Sun. **Prof** J Graham **Course Designer** David Grant, Willie Park Jnr **Facilities** **Conf** facs **Location** S side of village off B5300

Hotel ★★ 67% Golf Hotel, Criffel St, SILLOTH
☎ 016973 31438 22 en suite

ULVERSTON Map 07 SD27

Ulverston Bardsea Park LA12 9QJ
☎ 01229 582824 01229 588910
e-mail: enquiries@ulverstongolf.co.uk
web: www.ulverstongolf.co.uk
Undulating parkland course overlooking Morecambe Bay with extensive views to the Lakeland Fells.
18 holes, 6201yds, Par 71, SSS 70, Course record 64. Club membership 808.
Visitors Mon-Fri. Booking required. Handicap certificate. Dress code. **Societies** Booking required. **Green Fees** phone. **Prof** PA Stoller **Course Designer** A Herd, HS Colt **Facilities** **Leisure** practice ball dispensing machine. **Conf** Corporate Hospitality Days **Location** 2m S off A5087

Hotel ★★★ 67% Whitewater Hotel, The Lakeland Village, NEWBY BRIDGE ☎ 015395 31133 35 en suite

WINDERMERE

See **Bowness-on-Windermere**

WORKINGTON Map 11 NY02

Workington Branthwaite Rd CA14 4SS
☎ 01900 67828 01900 607123
e-mail: golf@workingtongolfclub.freeserve.co.uk

18 holes, 6217yds, Par 72, SSS 70, Course record 65.
Course Designer James Braid **Location** 1.75m E off A596
Phone for further details

Hotel ★★★ 80% Washington Central Hotel, Washington St, WORKINGTON ☎ 01900 65772 46 en suite

DERBYSHIRE

ALFRETON Map 08 SK45

Alfreton Wingfield Rd, Oakerthorpe DE55 7LH
☎ 01773 832070
A small, well-established parkland course with tight fairways and many natural hazards.
11 holes, 5393yds, Par 67, SSS 66, Course record 66. Club membership 350.
Visitors Booking required. **Societies** Booking required. **Green Fees** phone. **Facilities** by arrangement by arrangement **Location** 1m W on A615

Hotel ★★★★ 68% Renaissance Derby/Nottingham Hotel, Carter Ln East, SOUTH NORMANTON
☎ 01773 812000 & 0870 4007262 158 en suite

ASHBOURNE Map 07 SK14

Ashbourne Wyaston Rd DE6 1NB
☎ 01335 347960 (pro shop) 01335 347937
e-mail: sec@ashbournegc.fsnet.co.uk
web: www.ashbournegolfclub.co.uk
With fine views over surrounding countryside, the course uses natural contours and water features.
18 holes, 6302yds, Par 71, SSS 71. Club membership 650.
Visitors Mon-Fri & BHs. Booking required. Dress code. **Societies** Booking required. **Green Fees** £45 per 36 holes, £27 per 18 holes, £33 per 18 holes Sat, Sun & BHs. Winter reduced winter. **Prof** Andrew Smith **Course Designer** D Hemstock **Facilities** **Leisure** snooker table. **Location** Off Wyaston Rd, club signed

Hotel ★★★ 75% Callow Hall, Mappleton Rd, ASHBOURNE ☎ 01335 300900 16 en suite

BAKEWELL Map 08 SK26

Bakewell Station Rd DE45 1GB
☎ 01629 812307
web: www.bakewellgolfclub.org.uk
Hilly parkland course with plenty of natural hazards to test the golfer. Magnificent views across the Wye Valley.
9 holes, 5240yds, Par 68, SSS 66, Course record 68.
Club membership 340.
Visitors Mon-Sun except BHs. Booking required Tue, Thu, Sat, Sun. Dress code. **Societies** Booking required. **Green Fees** phone. **Facilities** **Conf** Corporate Hospitality Days **Location** E side of town off A6

Hotel ★★★ 68% Rutland Arms Hotel, The Square, BAKEWELL ☎ 01629 812812 18 en suite 17 annexe en suite

BAMFORD Map 08 SK28

Sickleholme Saltergate Ln S33 0BN
☎ 01433 651306 📠 01433 659498
e-mail: sickleholme.gc@btconnect.com
web: www.sickleholme.co.uk
Undulating downland course in the lovely Peak District, with rivers and ravines and spectacular scenery.
18 holes, 6064yds, Par 69, SSS 69, Course record 62.
Club membership 700.
Visitors Mon-Sun & BHs. Booking required. Handicap certificate. Dress code. **Societies** Booking required. **Green Fees** £29 per round/day, £34 Sat & Sun. **Prof** PH Taylor **Facilities** **Conf** Corporate Hospitality Days **Location** 0.75m S on A6013

Hotel ★★ 72% Yorkshire Bridge Inn, Ashopton Rd, Hope Valley, BAMFORD ☎ 01433 651361 14 en suite

BREADSALL Map 08 SK33

Marriot Breadsall Priory Hotel & Country Club Moor Rd, Morley DE7 6DL
☎ 01332 836080 📠 01332 836036
e-mail: john.winterbottom@marriotthotels.co.uk
Set in 200 acres of mature parkland, the Priory Course is built on the site of a 13th-century priory. Full use has been made of natural features and fine old trees. In contrast the Moorland Course, designed by Donald Steel and built by Brian Piersen, features Derbyshire stone walls and open moors heavily affected by winds. Open when most other clubs are closed in winter.
Priory Course: 18 holes, 6100yds, Par 72, SSS 69, Course record 63.
Moorland Course: 18 holes, 6028yds, Par 70, SSS 69.
Club membership 900.
Visitors Mon-Sun & BHs. Booking required. Dress code. **Societies** welcome. **Green Fees** from £20. **Prof** Darren Steels **Course Designer** D Steel **Facilities** **Leisure** hard tennis courts, heated indoor swimming pool, sauna, solarium, gymnasium. **Conf** facs Corporate Hospitality Days **Location** 0.75m W

Hotel ★★★★ 67% Marriott Breadsall Priory Hotel & Country Club, Moor Rd, MORLEY ☎ 01332 832235 12 en suite 100 annexe en suite

BUXTON Map 07 SK07

Buxton & High Peak Waterswallows Rd SK17 7EN
☎ 01298 26263 & 23453 📠 01298 06333
e-mail: admin@bhpgc.co.uk
web: www.buxtonandhighpeakgolfclub.co.uk
Bracing, well-drained meadowland course, the highest in Derbyshire. Challenging course where wind direction is a major factor on some holes; others require blind shots to sloping greens.
18 holes, 5966yds, Par 69, SSS 69.
Club membership 650.
Visitors Booking required. **Societies** Booking required. **Green Fees** phone. **Prof** Gary Brown **Course Designer** J Morris **Facilities** by arrangement **Conf** facs Corporate Hospitality Days **Location** 1m NE off A6

Hotel ★★★★ 67% Palace Hotel, Palace Rd, BUXTON ☎ 01298 22001 122 en suite

Cavendish Gadley Ln SK17 6XD
☎ 01298 79708 📠 01298 79708
e-mail: admin@cavendishgolfcourse.com
web: www.@cavendishgolfcourse.com
This parkland and moorland course with its comfortable clubhouse nestles below the rising hills. Generally open to the prevailing west wind, it is noted for its excellent surfaced greens which contain many deceptive subtleties. Designed by Alister MacKenzie, good holes include the 8th, 9th and 18th.

18 holes, 5721yds, Par 68, SSS 68, Course record 61.
Club membership 650.
Visitors Mon-Sun & BHs. Booking required. Handicap certificate. Dress code. **Societies** Booking required. **Green Fees** phone. **Prof** Paul Hunstone **Course Designer** A MacKenzie **Facilities** by arrangement by arrangement **Location** 0.75m W of town centre off A53

Hotel ★★★ 77% Best Western Lee Wood Hotel, The Park, BUXTON ☎ 01298 23002 35 en suite 5 annexe en suite

CHAPEL-EN-LE-FRITH Map 07 SK08

Chapel-en-le-Frith The Cockyard, Manchester Rd SK23 9UH
☎ 01298 812118 & 813943 (sec) 📠 01298 814990
e-mail: info@chapelgolf.co.uk
web: www.chapelgolf.co.uk
Scenic parkland surrounded by spectacular mountain views. A new longer and challenging front nine, a testing short par 4 14th and possibly the best last three-

Continued

hole finish in Derbyshire.
18 holes, 6434yds, Par 72, SSS 71, Course record 71.
Club membership 690.
Visitors contact club for details. **Societies** Booking required. **Green Fees** phone. **Prof** David J Cullen **Course Designer** David Williams **Facilities** ⊗ Ⅲ ⊾ ☕ ♀ ⚲ ⌂ ⚑ ✓ **Location** On B5470

Hotel ★★★ 77% Best Western Lee Wood Hotel, The Park, BUXTON ☎ 01298 23002 35 en suite 5 annexe en suite

CHESTERFIELD Map 08 SK37

Chesterfield Walton S42 7LA

☎ 01246 279256 🖹 01246 276622
e-mail: secretary@chesterfieldgolfclub.co.uk
web: www.chesterfieldgolfclub.co.uk
A varied and interesting, undulating parkland course with trees picturesquely adding to the holes and the outlook alike. Stream hazard on the back nine.
18 holes, 6281yds, Par 71, SSS 70, Course record 65.
Club membership 600.
Visitors Mon-Fri. Booking required. Handicap certificate. Dress code. **Societies** Booking required. **Green Fees** £40 per day, £32 per round, £40 per round Sat & Sun. ⊘ **Prof** Mike McLean **Facilities** ⊗ Ⅲ ⊾ ☕ ♀ ⚲ ⌂ ✓ **Leisure** snooker/pool. **Conf** Corporate Hospitality Days **Location** 2m SW off A632

Hotel ★★★ 65% Sandpiper Hotel, Sheffield Rd, Sheepbridge, CHESTERFIELD ☎ 01246 450550 46 en suite

Grassmoor Golf Centre North Wingfield Rd, Grassmoor S42 5EA

☎ 01246 856044 🖹 01246 853486
e-mail: enquiries@grassmoorgolf.co.uk
web: www.grassmoorgolf.co.uk
An 18-hole heathland course with interesting and challenging water features, testing greens and testing par 3s.
18 holes, 5723yds, Par 69, SSS 69, Course record 67.
Club membership 450.
Visitors contact club for details. Dress code. **Societies** Booking required. **Green Fees** £12 per 18 holes, £15 Sat, Sun & BHs. **Prof** Gary Hagues **Course Designer** Hawtree **Facilities** ⊗ ⊾ ☕ ♀ ⚲ ⌂ ⚑ ⚐ 🚜 ✓ ⚐ **Conf** Corporate Hospitality Days **Location** M1 junct 29, 4m off B6038 between Chesterfield & Grassmoor

Stanedge Walton Hay Farm, Stonedge, Ashover S45 0LW

☎ 01246 566156
e-mail: chrisshaw56@tiscali.co.uk/stanedge
web: www.stanedgegolfclub.co.uk
Moorland course in hilly situation open to strong winds. Some tricky short holes with narrow fairways, so accuracy is paramount. Magnificent views over four counties. Extended course now open.
9 holes, 5786yds, Par 69, SSS 68, Course record 68.
Club membership 310.
Visitors Mon-Fri. Dress code. **Societies** Booking required. **Green Fees** £15 per round. ⊘ **Facilities** ⊾ ☕ ♀ ⚲ **Location** 5m SW off B5057 near Famous Red Lion pub

Tapton Park Tapton Park, Tapton S41 0EQ

☎ 01246 239500 & 273887 🖹 01246 558024
Municipal parkland course with some fairly hard walking. The 625yd (par 5) 5th is a testing hole.
Tapton Main: 18 holes, 6104yds, Par 71, SSS 69.
Dobbin Clough: 9 holes, 2613yds, Par 34, SSS 34.
Club membership 300.
Visitors Mon-Sun & BHs. Booking required. Dress code. **Societies** Booking required. **Green Fees** £12 per 18 holes, £7 per 9 holes, £13.50/£8 Fri-Sun & BHs. ⊘ **Prof** Andrew Carnall **Facilities** ⊗ Ⅲ ⊾ ☕ ♀ ⚲ ⌂ ⚑ 🚜 ✓ **Conf** facs Corporate Hospitality Days **Location** 0.5m E of Chesterfield station

CODNOR Map 08 SK44

Ormonde Fields Golf & Country Club

Nottingham Rd DE5 9RG
☎ 01773 570043 (secretary) 🖹 01773 742987
Parkland course with undulating fairways and natural hazards. There is a practice area.
18 holes, 6502yds, Par 71, SSS 72, Course record 68.
Club membership 500.
Visitors Booking required. Dress code. **Societies** Booking required. **Green Fees** £25 per 18 holes, £30 Sat, Sun & BHs. ⊘ **Prof** Matthew Myford **Course Designer** John Fearn **Facilities** ⊗ Ⅲ ⊾ ☕ ♀ ⚲ ⌂ 🚜 ✓ **Conf** facs Corporate Hospitality Days **Location** 1m SE on A610

Hotel ★★★ 70% Makeney Hall Hotel, Makeney, Milford, BELPER ☎ 01332 842999 27 en suite 18 annexe en suite

DERBY Map 08 SK33

Allestree Park Allestree Hall, Duffield Rd, Allestree DE22 2EU

☎ 01332 550616 🖹 01332 541195
Public course, picturesque and undulating, set in 300-acre park with views across Derbyshire.
18 holes, 5806yds, Par 68, SSS 68, Course record 61.
Club membership 220.
Visitors Mon-Sun & BHs. Booking required. **Societies** welcome. **Green Fees** £13.50 per round. **Prof** Leigh Woodward **Facilities** ⊗ ⊾ ☕ ♀ ⚲ ⌂ ⚑ ✓ **Leisure** fishing, pool table. **Conf** Corporate Hospitality Days **Location** N of Derby, A38 onto A6 N, course 1.5m on left

Hotel ★★★★ 67% Marriott Breadsall Priory Hotel & Country Club, Moor Rd, MORLEY ☎ 01332 832235 12 en suite 100 annexe en suite

Mickleover Uttoxeter Rd, Mickleover DE3 9AD

☎ 01332 518662 🖹 01332 516011
Undulating parkland course of two loops of nine holes, in a pleasant setting and affording splendid country views. There is a premium in hitting tee shots in the right place for approaches to greens, some of which are on elevated plateaux. Some attractive par 3s which are considered to be very exacting.
18 holes, 5702yds, Par 68, SSS 68, Course record 64.
Club membership 800.
Visitors Mon-Fri & Sun except BHs. Booking required. Dress code. **Societies** Booking required. **Green Fees** phone. **Prof** Tim Coxon **Course Designer** J Pennink **Facilities** ⊗ Ⅲ ⊾ ☕ ♀ ⚲ ⌂ ⚑ ⚐ 🚜 ✓ **Conf** Corporate Hospitality Days **Location** 3m W of Derby on A516/B5020

Hotel ★★★★ 74% Menzies Mickleover Court, Etwall Rd, Mickleover, DERBY ☎ 01332 521234 99 en suite

Sinfin Wilmore Rd, Sinfin DE24 9HD
☎ 01332 766462 01332 769004
web: www.sinfingolfcourse.co.uk
Municipal parkland course with tree-lined fairways; an excellent test of golf and famous for its demanding par 4s. Generally a flat course, it is suitable for golfers of all ages.
18 holes, 6163yds, Par 70, SSS 70.
Club membership 244.
Visitors Booking required. **Societies** Booking required. **Green Fees** £12.40 per round. **Prof** Daniel Delaney **Facilities** **Location** 2.5m S of city centre

Hotel ★★★ 63% International Hotel, 288 Burton Rd, DERBY ☎ 01332 369321 41 en suite 21 annexe en suite

DRONFIELD Map 08 SK37

Hallowes Hallowes Ln S18 1UR
☎ 01246 411196 01246 413753
e-mail: proshop@hallowesgolfclub.org
web: www.hallowesgolfclub.org
Attractive moorland and parkland in the Derbyshire hills. Several testing par 4s and splendid views.
18 holes, 6302yds, Par 71, SSS 71, Course record 64.
Club membership 630.
Visitors Mon-Fri except BHs. Booking required. **Societies** Booking required. **Green Fees** £40 per day, £35 per round. **Prof** Philip Dunn **Facilities** **Leisure** short game facility, snooker. **Conf** Corporate Hospitality Days **Location** S side of town, off B6057 onto Cemetery Rd & Hallowes Rise/Dr

Hotel ★★★ 65% Sandpiper Hotel, Sheffield Rd, Sheepbridge, CHESTERFIELD ☎ 01246 450550 46 en suite

DUFFIELD Map 08 SK34

Chevin Golf Ln DE56 4EE
☎ 01332 841864 01332 844028
e-mail: secretary@chevingolf.fsnet.co.uk
web: www.chevingolf.co.uk
A mixture of parkland and moorland, this course is rather hilly which makes for some hard walking, but with most rewarding views of the surrounding countryside. The 8th hole, aptly named Tribulation, requires an accurate tee shot, and is one of the most difficult holes in the county.
18 holes, 6057yds, Par 69, SSS 69, Course record 64.
Club membership 750.
Visitors Mon-Fri & Sun except BHs. Booking required Sun. Handicap certificate. Dress code. **Societies** Booking required. **Green Fees** phone. **Prof** Willie Bird **Course Designer** J Braid **Facilities** **Conf** facs Corporate Hospitality Days **Location** N side of town off A6

Hotel ★★★ 70% Makeney Hall Hotel, Makeney, Milford, BELPER ☎ 01332 842999 27 en suite 18 annexe en suite

GLOSSOP Map 07 SK09

Glossop and District Hurst Ln, off Sheffield Rd SK13 7PU
☎ 01457 865247
Moorland course in good position, excellent natural hazards. Difficult closing hole (9th & 18th).
11 holes, 5800yds, Par 68, SSS 68, Course record 64.
Club membership 350.
Visitors Mon, Tue, Thu, Fri except BHs. **Societies** Booking required. **Green Fees** phone. **Prof** Daniel Marsh **Facilities** **Conf** Corporate Hospitality Days **Location** 1m E off A57 from town centre

Continued

HORSLEY Map 08 SK34

Horsley Lodge Smalley Mill Rd DE21 5BL
☎ 01332 780838 01332 781118
e-mail: enquiries@horsleylodge.co.uk.
web: www.horsleylodge.co.uk.
This lush meadowland course set in 180 acres of Derbyshire countryside, has some challenging holes. Also floodlit driving range. Big undulating greens designed by former World Champion Peter McEvoy.

18 holes, 6400yds, Par 71, SSS 71, Course record 65.
Club membership 650.
Visitors Mon-Sun & BHs. Booking required Sat & Sun. Dress code. **Societies** Booking required. **Green Fees** £25 per 18 holes. **Prof** G Lyall **Course Designer** Bill White **Facilities** **Leisure** fishing. **Conf** facs Corporate Hospitality Days **Location** 4m NE of Derby, off A38 at Belper then follow tourist signs

Hotel ★★★★ 67% Marriott Breadsall Priory Hotel & Country Club, Moor Rd, MORLEY ☎ 01332 832235 12 en suite 100 annexe en suite

KEDLESTON Map 08 SK34

Kedleston Park DE22 5JD
☎ 01332 840035 01332 840035
e-mail: secretary@kedleston-park-golf-club.co.uk
web: www.kedlestonparkgolf.co.uk
The course is laid out in flat mature parkland with fine trees and background views of historic Kedleston Hall (National Trust). Many testing holes are included in each nine and there is an excellent modern clubhouse.
18 holes, 6675yds, Par 72, SSS 72, Course record 64.
Club membership 718.
Visitors contact club for details. Handicap certificate. Dress code. **Societies** Booking required. **Green Fees** £55 per day, £45 per round. **Prof** Paul Wesselingh **Course Designer** James Braid **Facilities** **Leisure** sauna. **Conf** Corporate Hospitality Days **Location** Signposted Kedleston Hall from A38

Hotel ★★★ 63% International Hotel, 288 Burton Rd, DERBY ☎ 01332 369321 41 en suite 21 annexe en suite

LONG EATON — Map 08 SK43

Trent Lock Golf Centre Lock Ln, Sawley NG10 2FY
☎ 0115 946 4398 Fax 0115 946 1183
e-mail: trentlockgolf@aol.com
Main course has two par 5, five par 3 and eleven par 4 holes, plus water features and three holes adjacent to the river. A challenging test of golf. A 24-bay floodlit golf range is available.
Main Course: 18 holes, 5848yds, Par 69, SSS 68, Course record 67.
9 hole: 9 holes, 2911yds, Par 36.
Club membership 500.
Visitors Mon-Sun & BHs. Booking required. Dress code. **Societies** Booking required. **Green Fees** 18 hole course £17.50 per round, £22.50 Sat & Sun. 9 hole course £6 per round, £7.50 per round Sat & Sun. **Prof** M Taylor **Course Designer** E McCausland **Facilities** **Conf** facs Corporate Hospitality Days

Hotel ★★★ 66% Novotel Nottingham/Derby, Bostock Ln, LONG EATON ☎ 0115 946 5111 108 en suite

MATLOCK — Map 08 SK36

Matlock Chesterfield Rd, Matlock Moor DE4 5LZ
☎ 01629 582191 Fax 01629 582135
web: www.matlockgolfclub.co.uk
18 holes, 5996yds, Par 70, SSS 69, Course record 63.
Course Designer Tom Williamson **Location** 1.5m NE of Matlock on A632
Phone for further details

MICKLEOVER — Map 08 SK33

Pastures Social Centre, Hospital Ln DE3 5DQ
☎ 01332 521074
9 holes, 5095yds, Par 64, SSS 65, Course record 67.
Course Designer JF Pennik **Location** 1m SW off A516
Phone for further details

Hotel ★★★ 63% International Hotel, 288 Burton Rd, DERBY ☎ 01332 369321 41 en suite 21 annexe en suite

MORLEY — Map 08 SK34

Morley Hayes Main Rd DE7 6DG
☎ 01332 780480 & 782000 (shop) Fax 01332 781094
e-mail: golf@morleyhayes.com
web: www.morleyhayes.com
Peaceful pay and play course set in a splendid valley and incorporating charming water features and woodland. Floodlit driving range. Challenging nine-hole short course (Tower Course).

Manor Course: 18 holes, 6726yds, Par 72, SSS 72, Course record 63.
Tower Course: 9 holes, 1614yds, Par 30.
Visitors welcome. **Societies** Booking required. **Green Fees** phone. **Prof** Mark Marriott **Facilities** **Conf** facs Corporate Hospitality Days **Location** On A608 4m N of Derby

Hotel ★★★★ 67% Marriott Breadsall Priory Hotel & Country Club, Moor Rd, MORLEY ☎ 01332 832235 12 en suite 100 annexe en suite

NEW MILLS — Map 07 SK08

New Mills Shaw Marsh SK22 4QE
☎ 01663 743485 Fax 01663 743485
web: www.newmillsgolfclub.com
Moorland course with panoramic views and first-class greens.
18 holes, 5604yds, Par 69, SSS 67, Course record 62.
Club membership 483.
Visitors contact club for details. **Societies** welcome. **Green Fees** phone. **Prof** Carl Cross **Course Designer** Williams **Facilities** **Conf** Corporate Hospitality Days **Location** 0.5m N off B6101

RENISHAW — Map 08 SK47

Renishaw Park Club House, Mill Ln S21 3UZ
☎ 01246 432044 & 435484 Fax 01246 432116
web: www.renishawparkgolf.co.uk
Part parkland and part meadowland with easy walking.
18 holes, 6107yds, Par 71, SSS 70, Course record 64.
Club membership 750.
Visitors Mon-Sun & BHs. Booking required BHs. Handicap certificate. Dress code. **Societies** Booking required. **Green Fees** phone. **Prof** John Oates **Course Designer** Sir George Sitwell **Facilities** **Conf** Corporate Hospitality Days **Location** M1 junct 30, 1.5m W

Hotel ★★★ 65% Sitwell Arms Hotel, Station Rd, RENISHAW ☎ 01246 435226 & 01246 437327 Fax 01246 433915 29 en suite

RISLEY — Map 08 SK43

Maywood Rushy Ln DE72 3ST
☎ 0115 939 2306 & 9490043 (pro)
18 holes, 6424yds, Par 72, SSS 71, Course record 70.
Course Designer P Moon **Location** M1 junct 25
Phone for further details

SHIRLAND — Map 08 SK45

Shirland Lower Delves DE55 6AU
☎ 01773 834935 Fax 01773 832515
Rolling parkland and tree-lined course with extensive views of Derbyshire countryside.
18 holes, 6072yds, Par 71, SSS 70, Course record 67.
Club membership 250.
Visitors Mon-Sun & BHs. Booking required Sat & Sun. Dress code. **Societies** welcome. **Green Fees** phone. **Prof** Neville Hallam **Facilities** **Conf** facs Corporate Hospitality Days **Location** S side of village off A61

Hotel ★★★★ 68% Renaissance Derby/Nottingham Hotel, Carter Ln East, SOUTH NORMANTON ☎ 01773 812000 & 0870 4007262 158 en suite

Continued

STANTON BY DALE Map 08 SK43

Erewash Valley DE7 4QR
☎ 0115 932 2984 0115 944 0061
e-mail: secretary@erewashvalley.co.uk
web: www.erewashvalley.co.uk
Parkland and meadowland course overlooking valley and M1. Unique 4th and 5th in Victorian quarry bottom; 5th testing par 3.
18 holes, 6557yds, Par 72, SSS 71, Course record 67.
Club membership 750.
Visitors Booking required. Handicap certificate. **Societies** Booking required. **Green Fees** £40 per day, £30 per round, £40 per round Sat & Sun. **Prof** MJ Ronan **Course Designer** Hawtree **Facilities** **Location** 1m W. M1 junct 25, 2m

UNSTONE Map 08 SK37

Birch Hall Sheffield Rd S18 4DB
☎ 01246 291979 01246 412912
Very testing woodland/moorland course demanding respect and a good straight game if one is to walk away with a respectable card. Sloping fairways gather wayward drives into thick gorse and deep ditches. Signature holes are the tough 6th and scenic 13th, the latter begs a big-hitter to go for a shot to the green.
18 holes, 6379yds, Par 73, SSS 71, Course record 72.
Club membership 320.
Visitors Mon-Sun & BHs. Booking required. Dress code. **Societies** Booking required. **Green Fees** £10 per round, £5 per 9 holes. **Prof** Pete Ball **Course Designer** D Tucker **Facilities** **Location** Off A61 between Sheffield , outskirts of Unstone

Hotel ★★★ 65% Sandpiper Hotel, Sheffield Rd, Sheepbridge, CHESTERFIELD ☎ 01246 450550 46 en suite

DEVON

AXMOUTH Map 03 SY29

Axe Cliff Squires Ln EX12 4AB
☎ 01297 21754 01297 24371
e-mail: davidquinn@axecliff.co.uk
web: www.axecliff.co.uk
One of the oldest courses in Devon, established in 1884. An undulating links course with spectacular coastal views over Lyme Bay. Good natural drainage.
18 holes, 6000yds, Par 70, SSS 70, Course record 64.
Club membership 327.
Visitors Mon-Sun & BHs. Dress code. **Societies** Booking required. **Green Fees** £17 per day, £22 Sat, Sun & BHs. Twilight after 4.30pm £10. Winter reduced rates. **Prof** Mark Dack **Course Designer** James Braid **Facilities** **Conf** Corporate Hospitality Days **Location** 0.75m S on B3172

Hotel ★★ 77% Swallows Eaves, COLYFORD
☎ 01297 553184 8 en suite

BIGBURY-ON-SEA Map 03 SX64

Bigbury TQ7 4BB
☎ 01548 810557 (secretary) 01548 810207
web: www.bigburygolfclub.com
Clifftop pasture and parkland with easy walking. Exposed to winds, but with fine views over the sea and River Avon. The 7th hole is particularly tricky.
18 holes, 5896yds, Par 70, SSS 69, Course record 65.
Club membership 850.
Visitors Mon-Sun & BHs. Handicap certificate. Dress code. **Societies** Booking required. **Green Fees** £30 per day, £35 Sat & Sun. **Prof** Simon Lloyd **Course Designer** JH Taylor **Facilities** by arrangement **Conf** Corporate Hospitality Days **Location** 1m S on B3392 between Bigbury -on-Sea

Hotel ★★★★ 72% Thurlestone Hotel, THURLESTONE
☎ 01548 560382 64 en suite

BLACKAWTON Map 03 SX85

Dartmouth Golf & Country Club TQ9 7DE
☎ 01803 712650 01803 712628
e-mail: info@dgcc.co.uk
web: www.dgcc.co.uk
The nine-hole course and the 18-hole Championship Course are both worth a visit and not just for the beautiful views. The Championship is one of the most challenging courses in the West Country with 12 water hazards and a daunting par 5 4th hole that visitors will always remember. The spectacular final hole, looking downhill and over a water hazard to the green, can be difficult to judge and has been described as one of the most picturesque finishing holes in the country.
Championship Course: 18 holes, 6663yds, Par 72, SSS 72, Course record 68.
Dartmouth Course: 9 holes, 4791yds, Par 66, SSS 64.
Club membership 600.
Visitors Mon-Sun & BHs. Booking required. **Societies** Booking required. **Green Fees** Championship £35, £45 Sat & Sun. Dartmouth £15, £16 Sat & Sun. **Course Designer** Jeremy Pern **Facilities** **Leisure** heated indoor swimming pool, sauna, solarium, gymnasium, Massage. **Conf** facs Corporate Hospitality Days **Location** On A3122 4m from Dartmouth

Hotel ★★★ 67% Stoke Lodge Hotel, Stoke Fleming, DARTMOUTH ☎ 01803 770523 25 en suite

BUDLEIGH SALTERTON Map 03 SY08

East Devon Links Rd EX9 6DG
☎ 01395 443370 01395 445547
e-mail: secretary@edge.co.uk
web: www.edge.co.uk
An interesting course with downland turf, much heather and gorse, and superb views over the bay. Laid out on cliffs 250 to 400 feet above sea level, the early holes climb to the cliff edge. The downhill 17th has a heather section in the fairway, leaving a good second to the green. In addition to rare orchids, the course enjoys an abundance of wildlife including deer and peregrine falcons.
18 holes, 6231yds, Par 70, SSS 70, Course record 61.
Club membership 850.
Visitors Mon-Sun & BHs. Booking required. Handicap certificate. Dress code. **Societies** Booking required. **Green Fees** £45 per 27/36 holes, £36 per 18 holes. **Prof** Trevor Underwood **Facilities** **Conf** Corporate Hospitality Days **Location** W side of town centre

Continued

CHITTLEHAMHOLT Map 03 SS62

Highbullen Hotel EX37 9HD
☎ 01769 540561 🖷 01769 540492
e-mail: info@highbullen.co.uk
web: www.highbullen.co.uk
Mature parkland with water hazards and outstanding views to Exmoor and Dartmoor. An easy walking course with some outstanding holes. Excellent greens, which will hold a well-flighted ball, invite you to shoot for the heart of the green past well-maintained bunkers that have been intelligently placed to add to the golfing challenge.
18 holes, 5755yds, Par 68, SSS 67.
Club membership 150.
Visitors Mon-Sun & BHs. Dress code. **Societies** Booking required. **Green Fees** £22, £26 Sat, Sun & BHs. **Prof** Paul Weston **Course Designer** M Neil, J Hamilton **Facilities** **Leisure** hard and grass tennis courts, outdoor and indoor heated swimming pools, fishing, sauna, gymnasium, golf simulator. **Conf** facs Corporate Hospitality Days **Location** 0.5m S of village

CHRISTOW Map 03 SX88

Teign Valley EX6 7PA
☎ 01647 253026 🖷 01647 253026
e-mail: welcome@teignvalleygolf.co.uk
web: www.teignvalleygolf.co.uk

18 holes, 5913yds, Par 70, SSS 69.
Course Designer P Nicholson **Location** A38 Teign Valley exit, Exeter/Plymouth Expressway signs on B3193
See advertisement on this page

CHULMLEIGH Map 03 SS61

Chulmleigh Leigh Rd EX18 7BL
☎ 01769 580519 🖷 01769 580519
e-mail: chulmleighgolf@aol.com
web: www.chulmleighgolf.co.uk
Situated in a scenic area with views to distant Dartmoor, this undulating meadowland course offers a good test for the most experienced golfer and is enjoyable for newcomers to the game. Short 18-hole summer course with a tricky 1st hole; in winter the course is changed to nine holes and made longer for players to extend their game.
Summer Course: 18 holes, 1407yds, Par 54, SSS 54, Course record 49.
Club membership 110.
Visitors Mon-Sun & BHs. **Societies** Booking required. **Green Fees** £8.50 per 18 holes, £7.50 before 10am. **Course Designer** John Goodban **Facilities** **Location** SW side of village just off A377

Hotel ★★★ Northcote Manor, BURRINGTON
☎ 01769 560501 11 en suite

CHURSTON FERRERS Map 03 SX95

Churston Dartmouth Rd TQ5 0LA
☎ 01803 842751 & 842218 🖷 01803 845738
e-mail: manager@churstongc.freeserve.co.uk
web: www.churstongolfclublimited.co.uk
18 holes, 6219yds, Par 70, SSS 70, Course record 64.
Location NW side of village on A379
Phone for further details

Hotel ★★★ 67% Berryhead Hotel, Berryhead Rd, BRIXHAM ☎ 01803 853225 32 en suite

CREDITON Map 03 SS80

Downes Crediton Hookway EX17 3PT
☎ 01363 773025 & 774464 🖷 01363 775060
e-mail: secretary@downescreditongc.co.uk
web: www.downescreditongc.co.uk
Parkland with water features. Flat front nine. Hilly and wooded back nine.
18 holes, 5954yds, Par 70, SSS 69.
Club membership 700.
Visitors Mon-Sun & BHs. Booking required. Handicap certificate. Dress code. **Societies** Booking required. **Green Fees** £28 per day, £32 Sat & Sun. **Prof** Barry Austin **Facilities** **Conf** Corporate Hospitality Days **Location** 1.5m SE off A377

Hotel ★★★ 71% Barton Cross Hotel & Restaurant, Huxham, Stoke Canon, EXETER ☎ 01392 841245 9 en suite

CULLOMPTON Map 03 ST00

Padbrook Park EX15 1RU

☎ 01884 836100 🖷 01884 836101
e-mail: padbrookpark@fsmail.net
web: www.padbrookpark.co.uk

A nine-hole, 18-tee parkland course with many water and woodland hazards and spectacular views. The dog-leg 2nd and pulpit 7th are particularly challenging to golfers of all standards. Greens to USPGA specification.

9 holes, 6108yds, Par 70, SSS 69, Course record 65.
Club membership 280.

Visitors Mon-Sun & BHs. Dress code. **Societies** Booking required. **Green Fees** £18 per 18 holes, £13 per 9 holes, £21/£16 Sat & Sun. **Prof** Robert Thorpe, Richard Coffin **Course Designer** Bob Sandow **Facilities** **Leisure** fishing, solarium, gymnasium, indoor bowling centre. **Conf** facs Corporate Hospitality Days **Location** M5 junct 28, 1m on S edge of town

See advertisement on page 71

Hotel ★★★ 70% Padbrook Park, CULLOMPTON ☎ 01884 38286 40 en suite

DAWLISH WARREN Map 03 SX97

Warren EX7 0NF

☎ 01626 862255 & 864002 🖷 01626 888005
e-mail: secretary@dwgc.co.uk
web: www.dwgc.co.uk

Typical flat, genuine links course lying on spit between sea and Exe estuary. Picturesque scenery, a few trees but much gorse. Testing in windy conditions. The 7th hole provides the opportunity to go for the green across a bay on the estuary.

18 holes, 5921yds, Par 69, SSS 69, Course record 65.
Club membership 600.

Visitors Mon-Sun & BHs. Handicap certificate. Dress code. **Societies** Booking required. **Green Fees** £30 per day, £35 Sat, Sun & BHs. Rates exclusive of £1 players' insurance. **Prof** Darren Prowse **Course Designer** James Braid **Facilities** **Conf** facs **Location** E side of village

Hotel ★★★ 71% Langstone Cliff Hotel, Dawlish Warren, DAWLISH ☎ 01626 868000 62 en suite 4 annexe en suite

DOWN ST MARY Map 03 SS70

Waterbridge EX17 5LG

☎ 01363 85111
web: www.waterbridgegc.co.uk

A testing course of nine holes set in a gently sloping valley. The par of 32 will not be easily gained, with one par 5, three par 4s and five par 3s, although the course record holder has par 29. The 3rd hole which is a raised green is surrounded by water and the 4th (439yds) is demanding for beginners.

9 holes, 3910yds, Par 64, SSS 64.
Club membership 120.

Visitors Mon-Sun & BHs. **Societies** Booking required. **Green Fees** £12.50 per 18 holes, £7.50 per 9 holes, £14.50/£8.50 Sat, Sun & BHs. **Prof** David Ridyard **Course Designer** D Taylor **Facilities** **Conf** Corporate Hospitality Days **Location** A377 from Exeter towards Barnstaple, 1m past Copplestone

Hotel ★★★ Northcote Manor, BURRINGTON ☎ 01769 560501 11 en suite

EXETER Map 03 SX99

Exeter Golf & Country Club Topsham Rd, Countess Wear EX2 7AE

☎ 01392 874139 🖷 01392 874914
e-mail: info@exetergcc.fsnet.co.uk
web: www.exetergcc.com

Sheltered parkland with some very old trees and known as the flattest course in Devon. Situated in the grounds of a fine mansion, which is now the clubhouse. The 15th and 17th are testing par 4 holes. Small, well-guarded greens.

18 holes, 5980yds, Par 69, SSS 69, Course record 62.
Club membership 800.

Visitors Mon-Fri. Booking required. Handicap certificate. Dress code. **Societies** Booking required. **Green Fees** £42 per day, £34 per round. **Prof** Gary Milne **Course Designer** J Braid **Facilities** **Leisure** hard tennis courts, outdoor and indoor heated swimming pools, squash, sauna, solarium, gymnasium, jacuzzi. **Conf** facs Corporate Hospitality Days **Location** SE side of city centre off A379

Hotel ★★★ 66% Buckerell Lodge Hotel, Topsham Rd, EXETER ☎ 01392 221111 53 en suite

Continued

Woodbury Park Hotel, Golf & Country Club Woodbury Castle, Woodbury EX5 1JJ
☎ 01395 233500 🖷 01395 233384
e-mail: golfbookings@woodburypark.co.uk
web: www.woodburypark.co.uk

Irrigated 18-hole Oaks championship course and excellent nine-hole Acorns course set in 500 acres of wooded parkland with stunning views.

Oaks: 18 holes, 6578yds, Par 72, SSS 72, Course record 66.
Acorn: 9 holes, 2297yds, Par 32, SSS 32.
Club membership 700.

Visitors Mon-Sun & BHs. Booking required. Handicap certificate. Dress code. **Societies** Booking required. **Green Fees** Oaks £45 per 18 holes, £55 Sat & Sun. Acorns £13 per 9 holes. **Prof** Alan Richards **Course Designer** J Hamilton-Stutt **Facilities** **Leisure** hard tennis courts, heated indoor swimming pool, squash, fishing, sauna, gymnasium, health spa. **Conf** facs Corporate Hospitality Days **Location** M5 junct 30, A3052

Continued

Hotel ★★★★ 71% Woodbury Park Hotel Golf & Country Club, Woodbury Castle, WOODBURY ☎ 01395 233382 57 en suite

HIGH BICKINGTON Map 02 SS52

Libbaton EX37 9BS
☎ 01769 560269 & 560167 🖷 01769 560342
e-mail: gerald.hemiman@tesco.net

Parkland on undulating land. Water comes into play on 11 of the 18 holes, as well as a quarry, ditches, trees and eight raised greens. Not a heavily bunkered course, but those present are well positioned and the sharp sand they contain makes them tricky. Five par 5s could easily get you thinking this course is only for big hitters but as with many good courses, sound course management is the key to success.

18 holes, 6481yds, Par 73, SSS 71, Course record 72.
Club membership 500.

Visitors Mon-Sun & BHs. Dress code. **Societies** Booking required. **Green Fees** £20 per 18 holes, £26 Sat & Sun. **Prof** Andrew Norman **Course Designer** Col Badham **Facilities** **Conf** facs Corporate Hospitality Days **Location** B3217 1m of High Bickington, off A377

HOLSWORTHY Map 02 SS30

Holsworthy Killatree EX22 6LP
☎ 01409 253177 📠 01409 253177
e-mail: hgcsecretary@aol.com
web: www.holsworthygolfclub.co.uk
Pleasant parkland with gentle slopes, numerous trees and a few strategic bunkers. Small greens offer a good test for players of all abilities.
18 holes, 6059yds, Par 70, SSS 69, Course record 64.
Club membership 500.
Visitors Mon-Sun & BHs. Dress code. **Societies** Booking required. **Green Fees** phone. **Prof** Alan Johnston **Facilities** **Conf** facs Corporate Hospitality Days **Location** 1.5m W on A3072 towards Bude

Hotel ★★★ 72% Falcon Hotel, Breakwater Rd, BUDE ☎ 01288 352005 27 en suite

HONITON Map 03 ST10

Honiton Middlehills EX14 9TR
☎ 01404 44422 & 42943 📠 01404 46383
Founded in 1896, this level parkland course is situated on a plateau 850ft above sea level. Easy walking and good views. The 4th hole is a testing par 3. The 17th and 18th provide a challenging finish. A premium is placed on accuracy especially from the tee.
18 holes, 5895yds, Par 69, SSS 68, Course record 63.
Club membership 800.
Visitors Mon-Sun & BHs. Booking required. Handicap certificate. Dress code. **Societies** Booking required. **Green Fees** £26 per day, £30 Sat, Sun & BHs. **Prof** Adrian Cave **Facilities** **Leisure** hardstanding for touring caravans with services. **Conf** Corporate Hospitality Days **Location** 1.25m SE of Honiton, turn towards Farway at Tower Cross on A35

Hotel ★★ 71% Home Farm Hotel & Restaurant, Wilmington, HONITON ☎ 01404 831278 8 en suite 5 annexe en suite

ILFRACOMBE Map 02 SS54

Ilfracombe Hele Bay EX34 9RT
☎ 01271 862176 & 863328 📠 01271 867731
e-mail: ilfracombegolfclub@btinternet.com
web: www.ilfracombegolfclub.com
A challenging clifftop, heathland course with views over the Bristol Channel and moors from every tee and green.
18 holes, 5596yds, Par 69, SSS 67, Course record 66.
Club membership 520.
Visitors Mon-Sun & BHs. Booking required. Handicap certificate. Dress code. **Societies** Booking required. **Green Fees** £25 per round, £30 Sat, Sun & BHs. **Prof** Mark Davies **Course Designer** TK Weir **Facilities** **Location** 1.5m E of Ilfracombe, off A399

Hotel ★★ 72% Elmfield Hotel, Torrs Park, ILFRACOMBE ☎ 01271 863377 11 en suite 2 annexe en suite

IPPLEPEN Map 03 SX86

Dainton Park Totnes Rd, Ipplepen TQ12 5TN
☎ 01803 815000
e-mail: dpgolf@globalnet.co.uk
web: www.daintonparkgolf.co.uk
A challenging parkland course in typical Devon countryside, with gentle contours, tree-lined fairways and raised tees. Water hazards make the two opening holes particularly testing. The 8th, a dramatic 180yd drop hole totally surrounded by sand, is one of four tough par 3s on the course.
18 holes, 6400yds, Par 71, SSS 71, Course record 69.
Club membership 700.
Visitors Mon-Sun & BHs. Booking required. Dress code. **Societies** Booking required. **Green Fees** £22 per round, £25 Sat & Sun. **Prof** Jason Fullard **Course Designer** Adrian Stiff **Facilities** **Leisure** gymnasium, fitness gym. **Conf** Corporate Hospitality Days **Location** 2m S of Newton Abbot on A381

Hotel ★★ 68% Queens Hotel, Queen St, NEWTON ABBOT ☎ 01626 363133 20 en suite

IVYBRIDGE Map 02 SX65

Dinnaton Blachford Rd PL21 9HU
☎ 01752 690020 & 892512 📠 01752 698334
e-mail: info@mccaulays.com
web: www.mccaulays.com
Challenging nine-hole moorland course overlooking the South Hams. With five par 4 and four par 3 holes, three lakes and tight fairways; excellent for improving the short game. Floodlit practice area.
9 holes, 4089yds, Par 64, SSS 60.
Club membership 130.
Visitors Mon-Sun. **Societies** Mon-Sun. **Green Fees** phone. **Prof** Richard Stephenson **Course Designer** Cotton & Pink **Facilities** **Leisure** hard tennis courts, heated indoor swimming pool, squash, sauna, solarium, gymnasium. **Conf** facs **Location** Off A38 at Ivybridge junct towards town centre, 1st rdbt brown signs for club 1m

Hotel ★★ 74% Glazebrook House Hotel & Restaurant, SOUTH BRENT ☎ 01364 73322 10 en suite

MORETONHAMPSTEAD Map 03 SX78

Bovey Castle TQ13 8RE
☎ 01647 445009 📠 01647 440961
e-mail: richard.lewis@boveycastle.com
web: www.boveycastle.com
This enjoyable parkland course has enough hazards to make any golfer think. Most hazards are natural such as the Rivers Bowden and Bovey which meander through the first eight holes.
18 holes, 6303yds, Par 70, SSS 70, Course record 63.
Club membership 130.
Visitors Mon-Sun & BHs. Booking required. Dress code. **Societies** Booking required. **Green Fees** £125 per round. **Prof** Richard Lewis **Course Designer** J Abercromby **Facilities** **Leisure** hard and grass tennis courts, outdoor and indoor heated swimming pools, fishing, sauna, solarium, gymnasium. **Conf** facs Corporate Hospitality Days **Location** 2m W of Moretonhampstead, off B3212

MORTEHOE Map 02 SS44

Mortehoe & Woolacombe EX34 7EH
☎ 01271 870667 & 870566
e-mail: malcolm_wilkinson@northdevon.gov.uk
Easewell: 9 holes, 4690yds, Par 66, SSS 63, Course record 66.
Course Designer D Hoare **Location** 0.25m before Mortehoe on station road
Phone for further details

Hotel ★★★ 81% Watersmeet Hotel, Mortehoe, WOOLACOMBE ☎ 01271 870333 25 en suite

NEWTON ABBOT Map 03 SX87

Newton Abbot (Stover) Bovey Rd TQ12 6QQ
☎ 01626 352460 (secretary) 🖷 01626 330210
e-mail: stovergolfclub@aol.com
web: www.stovergolfclub.co.uk
Mature wooded parkland with water coming into play on eight holes.
18 holes, 5764yds, Par 69, SSS 68, Course record 63.
Club membership 800.
Visitors Booking required. Handicap certificate. **Societies** Thu. Booking required. **Green Fees** phone. **Prof** Malcolm Craig **Course Designer** James Braid **Facilities** **Conf** Corporate Hospitality Days **Location** 3m N of Newton Abbot on A382. Bovey Tracey exit on A38

Hotel ★★ 68% Queens Hotel, Queen St, NEWTON ABBOT ☎ 01626 363133 20 en suite

OKEHAMPTON Map 02 SX59

Ashbury Hotel Higher Maddaford EX20 4NL
☎ 01837 55453 🖷 01837 55468
web: www.ashburygolfhotel.co.uk
The courses occupy a lightly wooded parkland setting in rolling Devon countryside on the foothills of Dartmoor National Park. Extra hazards have been added to the natural ones already present, with over 100 bunkers and 18 lakes. The courses are open throughout the year with either larger main greens or purpose built alternate ones.

Oakwood: 18 holes, 5400yds, Par 68, SSS 66, Course record 65.
Pines: 18 holes, 5628yds, Par 69, SSS 67.
Beeches: 18 holes, 5351yds, Par 68, SSS 66.
Club membership 170.
Visitors Mon-Thu. Booking required. Handicap certificate. Dress code. **Societies** Booking required. **Green Fees** £25 per round. **Course Designer** David Fensom **Facilities** **Leisure** hard tennis courts, heated indoor swimming pool, fishing, sauna, par 3 course, indoor bowls, snooker. **Location** Off A3079 Okehampton-Holsworthy
See advertisement on page 74

Hotel ★★ 66% Ashbury Hotel, Higher Maddaford, Southcott, OKEHAMPTON ☎ 01837 55453 69 en suite 30 annexe en suite

Okehampton Tors Rd EX20 1EF
☎ 01837 52113 🖷 01837 52734
e-mail: okehamptongc@btconnect.com
web: www.okehamptongc.co.uk
A good combination of moorland, woodland and river makes this one of the prettiest, yet testing courses in Devon.
18 holes, 5268yds, Par 68, SSS 66, Course record 66.
Club membership 600.
Visitors contact club for details. **Societies** welcome. **Green Fees** £25 per day, £20 per round, £25 Sat & Sun. **Prof** Ashley Moon **Course Designer** JF Taylor **Facilities** **Location** 1m S off A30, signed from town centre

Hotel ★★ 67% White Hart Hotel, Fore St, OKEHAMPTON ☎ 01837 52730 & 54514 🖷 01837 53979 19 en suite

PLYMOUTH Map 02 SX45

Elfordleigh Hotel Golf Leisure Colebrook, Plympton PL7 5EB
☎ 01752 336428 (hotel) & 348425 (golf shop)
🖷 01752 344581
e-mail: reception@elfordleigh.co.uk
web: www.elfordleigh.co.uk
Undulating, scenic parkland course set deep in the secluded Plym valley and offering a true challenge to all levels of player. The 11th hole, par 3 is one of the best in the South West area.
18 holes, 5664yds, Par 69, SSS 67, Course record 66.
Club membership 500.
Visitors Mon-Sun & BHs. Handicap certificate. Dress code. **Societies** Booking required. **Green Fees** £25 per round, £30 Sat, Sun & BHs. **Prof** Nick Cook **Course Designer** JH Taylor **Facilities** **Leisure** hard tennis courts, heated indoor swimming pool, squash, sauna, solarium, gymnasium, golf tuition breaks. **Conf** facs Corporate Hospitality Days **Location** 2m NE off A374, follow signs from Plympton town centre

Hotel ★★★ 71% Elfordleigh Hotel Golf Leisure, Colebrook, Plympton, PLYMOUTH ☎ 01752 336428 34 en suite

Staddon Heights Plymstock PL9 9SP
☎ 01752 402475 🖷 01752 401998
e-mail: roger.brown@btconnect.com
web: www.staddon-heights.co.uk
Cliff top course affording spectacular views across Plymouth Sound, Dartmoor and Bodmin Moor.
18 holes, 6164yds, Par 70, SSS 70, Course record 66.
Club membership 750.
Visitors Mon-Sun except BHs. Booking required Wed. Dress code. **Societies** Booking required. **Green Fees** £22, £26 Sat & Sun. **Prof** Ian Marshall **Course Designer** Hamilton Stutt **Facilities** **Conf** facs **Location** 5m SW of city centre

Hotel ★★ 73% Langdon Court Hotel, Down Thomas, PLYMOUTH ☎ 01752 862358 18 en suite

Continued

FREE GOLF ALL YEAR ROUND

27 Holes of Free Golf per night of stay

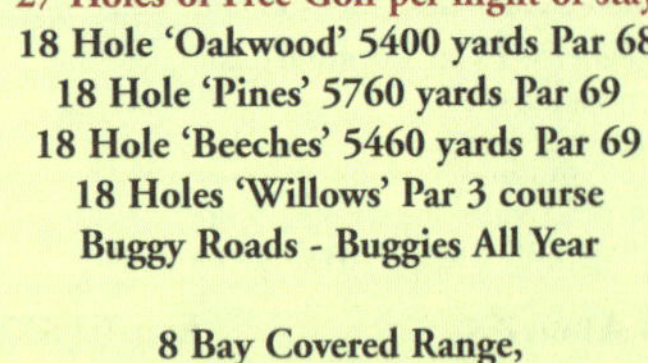

18 Hole 'Oakwood' 5400 yards Par 68
18 Hole 'Pines' 5760 yards Par 69
18 Hole 'Beeches' 5460 yards Par 69
18 Holes 'Willows' Par 3 course
Buggy Roads - Buggies All Year

8 Bay Covered Range,
Practice Area, Putting Green,
Golf Coaching

Golf Shop - Club and Trolley Hire
Club Locker and Drying Room

INDOOR SPORT - Bowls, Tennis, Badminton, Squash, Table Tennis, 10 Pin, Snooker - **FREE**

OUTDOOR SPORT - Tennis, Bowls, Pitch & Putt, Guided Walks, Crazy Golf - **FREE**

LEISURE - Pools, Spas, Saunas, Solarium, Steam Room - **FREE**

CRAFT CENTRE - Pottery + 14 Tutored Crafts, including Picture Framing, Glass Engraving, Candle Making, & Enamelling - price at cost.
Available to Residents of Both Hotels.

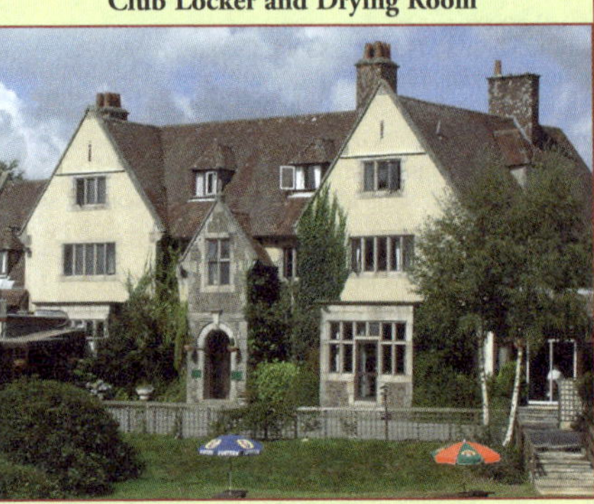

Buggy Prices £4 - £17

Spring Breaks 3 nights from £151 4 nights from £183
Summer Breaks 3 nights from £200 4 nights from £237
Autumn Breaks 3 nights from £155 4 nights from £187
Winter Breaks 3 nights from £131 4 nights from £159

Price Per Person

All Rooms Ensuite, TV/Video, Tea/Coffee facilities Safe (F.O.C.) and Telephone.

Full Board, Party Discounts, Bargain Breaks

Manor House & Ashbury Hotels Okehampton Devon EX20 4NA

FREEPHONE 0800 197 7556

www.manorhousehotel.co.uk **www.ashburygolfhotel.co.uk**

3 x 18 Hole Long Courses
18 Hole Par 3 · Range · Golf Buggies

SAUNTON Map 02 SS43

Saunton EX33 1LG
☎ 01271 812436 🖷 01271 814241
e-mail: info@sauntongolf.co.uk
web: www.sauntongolf.co.uk
Two traditional championship links courses. Windy, with natural hazards.

East Course: 18 holes, 6427yds, Par 71, SSS 71, Course record 64.
West Course: 18 holes, 6138yds, Par 71, SSS 70, Course record 63.
Club membership 1450.
Visitors Mon-Sun & BHs. Booking required. Handicap certificate. Dress code. **Societies** Booking required. **Green Fees** £80 per day, £55 per round. **Prof** AT MacKenzie **Course Designer** F Pennick, WH Fowler **Facilities** by arrangement **Conf** Corporate Hospitality Days **Location** S side of village off B3231

Hotel ★★★★ 74% Saunton Sands Hotel, SAUNTON ☎ 01271 890212 92 en suite

SIDMOUTH Map 03 SY18

Sidmouth Cotmaton Rd, Peak Hill EX10 8SX
☎ 01395 513451 & 516407 🖷 01395 514661
18 holes, 5100yds, Par 66, SSS 65, Course record 59.
Course Designer JH Taylor **Location** W side of town centre
Phone for further details

Hotel ★★★★ 77% Victoria Hotel, The Esplanade, SIDMOUTH ☎ 01395 512651 61 en suite

SOUTH BRENT Map 03 SX66

Wrangaton (S Devon) Golf Links Rd, Wrangaton TQ10 9HJ
☎ 01364 73229 🖷 01364 73229
e-mail: wrangatongc@tiscali.co.uk
web: www.wrangatongolfclub.co.uk
Unique 18-hole course with nine holes on moorland and nine holes on parkland. The course lies within Dartmoor National Park. Spectacular views towards sea and rugged terrain. Natural fairways and hazards include bracken, sheep and ponies.
18 holes, 6065yds, Par 70, SSS 69, Course record 66.
Club membership 680.
Visitors Mon-Sun & BHs. Booking required. Handicap certificate. Dress code. **Societies** Booking required. **Green Fees** phone. **Prof** Glenn Richards **Course Designer** DMA Steel **Facilities** by arrangement **Location** 2.25m SW off A38, between South Brent & Ivybridge

Continued

Hotel ★★ 74% Glazebrook House Hotel & Restaurant, SOUTH BRENT ☎ 01364 73322 10 en suite

SPARKWELL Map 02 SX55

Welbeck Manor & Sparkwell Golf Course
Blacklands PL7 5DF
☎ 01752 837219 🖷 01752 837219
9 holes, 2886yds, Par 68, SSS 68, Course record 68.
Course Designer John Gabb **Location** 1m N of A38 Plymouth-Ivybridge road
Phone for further details

Hotel ★★ 63% The Moorland Hotel, Wotter, Shaugh Prior, PLYMOUTH ☎ 01752 839228 18 en suite

TAVISTOCK Map 02 SX47

Hurdwick Tavistock Hamlets PL19 0LL
☎ 01822 612746 🖷 01822 612746
An executive parkland course with many bunkers and fine views. Executive golf originated in America and the concept is that a round should take no longer than 3 hours while offering a solid challenge.
18 holes, 5302yds, Par 68, SSS 67, Course record 67.
Club membership 110.
Visitors Mon-Sun & BHs. Dress code. **Societies** Booking required. **Green Fees** £20 per day. **Course Designer** Hawtree **Facilities** **Location** 1m N of Tavistock on the Brentor Road

Hotel ★★★ 64% Bedford Hotel, 1 Plymouth Rd, TAVISTOCK ☎ 01822 613221 30 en suite

Tavistock Down Rd PL19 9AQ
☎ 01822 612344 🖷 01822 612344
e-mail: tavygolf@hotmail.org
web: www.tavistockgolfclub.org.uk
Set on Whitchurch Down in south-west Dartmoor with easy walking and magnificent views over rolling countryside into Cornwall. Downland turf with some heather, and interesting holes on undulating ground.
18 holes, 6495yds, Par 71, SSS 71, Course record 60.
Club membership 700.
Visitors Mon-Sun & BHs. Booking required. Dress code. **Societies** Booking required. **Green Fees** £28 per day/round, £36 Sat, Sun & BHs. **Prof** D Rehaag **Course Designer** H Fowler **Facilities** **Conf** Corporate Hospitality Days **Location** 1m SE of town centre, on Whitchurch Down

Hotel ★★★ 64% Bedford Hotel, 1 Plymouth Rd, TAVISTOCK ☎ 01822 613221 30 en suite

TEDBURN ST MARY Map 03 SX89

Fingle Glen Golf Hotel EX6 6AF
☎ 01647 61817 🖷 01647 61135
e-mail: fingle.glen@btinternet.com
web: www.fingleglen.com
Fingle Glen has been extended in recent years into a fine 18 hole parkland course. Further alterations were made to two holes in 2005.
18 holes, 5878yds, Par 70, SSS 68, Course record 63.
Club membership 650.
Visitors Mon-Sun & BHs. Dress code. **Societies** welcome **Green Fees** £20 per round, £22 Sat, Sun & BHs. **Prof** Stephen Gould **Course Designer** Bill Pile **Facilities**

Continued

Conf facs Corporate Hospitality Days **Location** 5m W of Exeter, off A30

Hotel ★★★ 72% St Olaves Hotel, Mary Arches St, EXETER ☎ 01392 217736 15 en suite

TEIGNMOUTH Map 03 SX97

Teignmouth Haldon Moor TQ14 9NY
☎ 01626 777070 01626 777304
e-mail: tgc@btconnect.com
web: www.teignmouthgolfclub.co.uk
This fairly flat heathland course is high up with fine panoramic views of sea, moors and river valley. Good springy turf with some heather and an interesting layout makes for very enjoyable holiday golf. Designed by Alister MacKenzie, the world-famous architect who also designed Augusta GC USA.
18 holes, 6200yds, Par 69, SSS 69, Course record 63. Club membership 900.
Visitors Mon-Sun & BHs. Booking required Sat. Handicap certificate. Dress code. **Societies** Booking required. **Green Fees** £40 per day. **Prof** Rob Selley **Course Designer** A MacKenzie **Facilities** **Conf** facs Corporate Hospitality Days **Location** 2m NW off B3192

THURLESTONE Map 03 SX64

Thurlestone TQ7 3NZ
☎ 01548 560405 01548 562149
e-mail: info@thurlestonegc.co.uk
web: www.thurlestonegc.co.uk
Situated on the edge of the cliffs with downland turf and good greens. The course, after an interesting opening hole, rises to higher land with fine sea views, and finishes with an excellent 502yd downhill hole to the clubhouse.
18 holes, 6340yds, Par 71, SSS 70, Course record 65. Club membership 770.
Visitors Booking required.Handicap certificate. **Green Fees** phone. **Prof** Peter Laugher **Course Designer** Harry S Colt **Facilities** by arrangement **Leisure** hard and grass tennis courts. **Location** S side of village

Hotel ★★★★ 72% Thurlestone Hotel, THURLESTONE ☎ 01548 560382 64 en suite

TIVERTON Map 03 SS91

Tiverton Post Hill EX16 4NE
☎ 01884 252187 01884 251607
e-mail: tivertongolfclub@lineone.net
web: www.tivertongolfclub.co.uk
Parkland with many different species of tree, and lush pastures that ensure some of the finest fairways in the south-west. The undulating ground provides plenty of variety and there are a number of interesting holes which visitors will find a real challenge.
18 holes, 6236yds, Par 71, SSS 71, Course record 65. Club membership 750.
Visitors Thu, Sat, Sun & BHs. Booking required. Handicap certificate. Dress code. **Societies** Booking required. **Green Fees** £32 per 18 holes. **Prof** Michael Hawton **Course Designer** Braid **Facilities** **Conf** Corporate Hospitality Days **Location** 3m E of Tiverton. M5 junct 27, through Sampford Peverell & Halberton

Continued

Hotel ★★★ 70% The Tiverton Hotel, Blundells Rd, TIVERTON ☎ 01884 256120 69 en suite

TORQUAY Map 03 SX96

Torquay 30 Petitor Rd, St Marychurch TQ1 4QF
☎ 01803 314591 01803 316116
e-mail: info@torquaygolf club.org.uk
web: www.torquaygolfclub.org.uk
Unusual combination of cliff and parkland golf, with wonderful views over the sea and Dartmoor.
18 holes, 6164yds, Par 69, SSS 69, Course record 63. Club membership 725.
Visitors Mon-Sun & BHs. Booking required. Handicap certificate. Dress code. **Societies** Booking required. **Green Fees** £30, £35 Sat, Sun & BHs. **Prof** Martin Ruth **Facilities** **Location** 1.25m N

Hotel ★★ 64% Norcliffe Hotel, 7 Babbacombe Downs Rd, Babbacombe, TORQUAY ☎ 01803 328456 26 en suite

TORRINGTON (GREAT) Map 02 SS41

Torrington Weare Trees, Great Torrington EX38 7EZ
☎ 01805 622229 & 623878 01805 623878
e-mail: theoffice@torringtongolf.fsnet.co.uk
Attractive and challenging nine-hole course. Free draining to allow play all year round. Excellent greens and outstanding views.
9 holes, 4423yds, Par 64, SSS 62, Course record 58. Club membership 420.
Visitors Mon, Thu, Fri. Tue, Wed, Sat & Sun pm. Booking required. Dress code. **Societies** Booking required. **Green Fees** £20 per day, £15 per round. **Facilities** **Location** 1m W of Torringdon

Hotel ★★★ 70% Royal Hotel, Barnstaple St, BIDEFORD ☎ 01237 472005 32 en suite

WESTWARD HO! Map 02 SS42

Royal North Devon Golf Links Rd EX39 1HD
☎ 01237 473817 01237 423456
e-mail: info@royalnorthdevongolfclub.co.uk
web: www.royalnorthdevongolfclub.co.uk
Oldest links course in England with traditional links features and a museum in the clubhouse.
18 holes, 6716yds, Par 72, SSS 72, Course record 65. Club membership 1150.
Visitors Mon-Sun & BHs. Booking required. Handicap certificate. Dress code. **Societies** Booking required. **Green Fees** £44 per day, £38 per round, £50/£44 Sat, Sun & BHs. **Prof** Iain Parker **Course Designer** Old Tom Morris **Facilities** **Leisure** Museum of Golf Memorabilia, snooker. **Location** N side of village off B3236

Guest House ♦♦♦♦ Culloden House, Fosketh Hill, WESTWARD HO! ☎ 01237 479421 5 en suite

WOOLFARDISWORTHY Map 02 SS32

Hartland Forest EX39 5RA
☎ 01237 431442 01237 431734
e-mail: castleacre1@btconnect.com
web: www.hartlandforestgolf.co.uk
Exceptionally varied course with many water hazards and gentle slopes.
18 holes, 5900yds, Par 70, SSS 68.
Club membership 100.
Visitors Mon-Sun & BHs. **Societies** Booking required. **Green Fees** £20 per 18 holes, £13 per 9 holes. **Course Designer** A Cartwright **Facilities** **Leisure** hard tennis courts, heated indoor swimming pool, fishing, sauna, gymnasium. **Conf** Corporate Hospitality Days **Location** 4m S of Clovelly Cross, 1.7m E of A39

Hotel ★★★ 72% Penhaven Country House, Rectory Ln, PARKHAM ☎ 01237 451388 & 451711 01237 451878 12 en suite

YELVERTON Map 02 SX56

Yelverton Golf Links Rd PL20 6BN
☎ 01822 852824 01822 854869
e-mail: secretary@yelvertongc.co.uk
web: www.yelvertongc.co.uk
An excellent course on Dartmoor with plenty of gorse and heather. Tight lies in the fairways, fast greens and challenging hazards. Three of the best holes in Devon (12th, 13th and 16th) and outstanding views.

18 holes, 6353yds, Par 71, SSS 71, Course record 64.
Club membership 650.
Visitors Mon-Fri, Sun & BHs. Handicap certificate. Dress code. **Societies** welcome. **Green Fees** £34 per day. **Prof** Tim McSherry **Course Designer** Herbert Fowler **Facilities** **Leisure** indoor golf academy. **Conf** facs Corporate Hospitality Days **Location** 1m S of Yelverton, off A386

Hotel ★★★ 72% Moorland Links Hotel, YELVERTON ☎ 01822 852245 45 en suite

DORSET

ASHLEY HEATH Map 04 SU10

Moors Valley Horton Rd BH24 2ET
☎ 01425 479776
e-mail: golf@eastdorset.gov.uk
web: www.moors-valley.co.uk/golf
Skilfully designed by Hawtree, this mature heathland and woodland course is scenically set within a wildlife conservation area, exuding peace and tranquillity. Each hole has its own character, the back seven being in particular very special. The course is renowned for its greens.
18 holes, 6337yds, Par 72, SSS 70, Course record 67.
Visitors Mon-Sun & BHs. Booking required. Dress code. **Societies** Booking required. **Green Fees** £21 per round. **Course Designer** Hawtree & Son **Facilities** by arrangement **Leisure** fishing, 4 hole game improvement course, bike hire, aerial assault course. **Conf** facs Corporate Hospitality Days **Location** Signed from A31 Ashley Heath rdbt

Hotel Travelodge Ringwood, St Leonards, RINGWOOD ☎ 08700 850 950

BEAMINSTER Map 03 ST40

Chedington Court South Perrott DT8 3HU
☎ 01935 891413 01935 891217
e-mail: admincgc@tiscali.co.uk
web: www.chedingtongolf.co.uk
This beautiful 18-hole parkland course is set on the Dorset-Somerset borders with mature trees and interesting water hazards. A challenge from the first hole, par 5, blind drive to the elevated tee on the 15th, and the closing holes can be tricky.

18 holes, 5924yds, Par 70, SSS 70, Course record 68.
Club membership 400.
Visitors Sat & Sun booking required. **Societies** Booking required. **Green Fees** phone. **Prof** Seven Ritchie **Course Designer** David Hemstock, Donald Steel **Facilities** **Conf** Corporate Hospitality Days **Location** 5m NE of Beaminster on A356 Dorchester-Crewkerne

Hotel ★★★ 72% Bridge House Hotel, 3 Prout Bridge, BEAMINSTER ☎ 01308 862200 9 en suite 5 annexe en suite

BELCHALWELL Map 03 ST70

Dorset Heights DT11 0EG
☎ 01258 860900 01258 860900
18 holes, 6138yds, Par 70, SSS 70, Course record 74.
Course Designer David Astill
Phone for further details

Hotel ★★★ 71% Crown Hotel, West St, BLANDFORD FORUM ☎ 01258 456626 32 en suite

Continued

BERE REGIS Map 03 SY89

Dorset Golf & Country Club BH20 7NT

☎ 01929 472244 🖷 01929 471294
e-mail: admin@dorsetgolfresort.com
web: www.dorsetgolfresort.com

The Lakeland/Parkland is the longest course in Dorset. Designed by Martin Hawtree with numerous interconnected water features, carefully planned bunkers and sculptured greens. A player who completes a round within handicap has every reason to celebrate. The Woodland course, although shorter, is equally outstanding with rhododendron and tree-lined fairways.

Lakeland/Parkland Course: 18 holes, 6580yds, Par 72, SSS 73, Course record 69.
Woodland Course: 9 holes, 5032yards, Par 66, SSS 64.
Club membership 600.

Visitors Mon-Sun & BHs. Booking required. Dress code. **Societies** Booking required. **Green Fees** £38, £42 Sat, Sun & BHs. **Prof** Scott Porter **Course Designer** Martin Hawtree **Facilities** **Leisure** fishing. **Conf** facs Corporate Hospitality Days **Location** 5m from Bere Regis on Wool Road

Hotel ★★ 69% Kemps Hotel, East Stoke, WAREHAM ☎ 01929 462563 4 en suite 10 annexe en suite

BLANDFORD FORUM Map 03 ST80

Ashley Wood Wimborne Rd DT11 9HN

☎ 01258 452253 🖷 01258 450590
e-mail: generalmanager@ashleywoodgolfclub.com
web: www.ashleywoodgolfclub.com

The course is one of the oldest in the country. The first record of play on Keyneston Down was in 1896, and part of the ancient course is played over Buzbury Rings, a prehistoric hill fort with magnificent views over the Stour and Tarrant valleys. Constructed on downland, the fairways are undulating and, apart from the 3rd hole with a short sharp hill, all holes are easy walking. Four holes are played within the ancient woodland of Ashley Woods. The natural chalk provides excellent drainage.

18 holes, 6276yds, Par 70, SSS 70, Course record 66.
Club membership 600.

Visitors Mon-Sun except BHs. Dress code. **Societies** Booking required. **Green Fees** £42 per day, £26.50 per 18 holes after 10am, £31.50 per 18 holes Sat & Sun. **Prof** Jon Shimmons **Course Designer** P Tallack **Facilities** by arrangement **Conf** Corporate Hospitality Days **Location** 2m E on B3082

Hotel ★★★ 71% Crown Hotel, West St, BLANDFORD FORUM ☎ 01258 456626 32 en suite

BOURNEMOUTH Map 04 SZ09

The Club at Meyrick Park Central Dr, Meyrick Park BH2 6LH

☎ 01202 786000 🖷 01202 786020
e-mail: meyrickpark.lodge@theclubcompany.com
web: www.theclubcompany.com

Picturesque municipal parkland course founded in 1890.

18 holes, 5600yds, Par 69, SSS 69.

Visitors Mon-Sun & BHs. Booking required. Dress code. **Societies** Booking required. **Green Fees** £20 Mon-Fri per round, £23 Sat, Sun & BHs. **Prof** Andy Britton **Facilities** **Leisure** heated indoor swimming pool, sauna, solarium, gymnasium, spa and steam room. **Conf** facs

Knighton Heath Francis Av, West Howe BH11 8NX

☎ 01202 572633 🖷 01202 590774
e-mail: khgc@btinternet.com

Undulating heathland course on high ground inland from Poole.

18 holes, 6084yds, Par 70, SSS 69.
Club membership 700.

Visitors Mon-Thu. Booking required. Handicap certificate. Dress code. **Societies** Booking required. **Green Fees** £35 per day, £30 per round. **Prof** Paul Brown **Facilities** **Location** N side of Poole, junct A348 signed at rdbt

Guest House ♦♦♦♦ Ashton Lodge, 10 Oakley Hill, WIMBORNE ☎ 01202 883423 5 rms (2 en suite)

Open Golf Centres Riverside Av, off Castle Ln East BH7 7ES

☎ 01202 436436 🖷 01202 436400
e-mail: info@opengolfcentres.co.uk
web: www.opengolfcentres.co.uk

Lakes Course: 18 holes, 6277yards, Par 72, SSS 69.

Course Designer John Jacobs Golf Associates **Location** Off A338 at Cooper Dean rdbt onto A3060 for Christchurch, over minirdbt, left onto Riverside Av, 500yds on right

Phone for further details

Hotel Innkeeper's Lodge Bournemouth, Cooper Dean Roundabout, Castle Ln East, BOURNEMOUTH ☎ 01202 390837 28 en suite

Queen's Park Queens Park Dr West BH8 9BY

☎ 01202 437807 🖷 01202 302611
e-mail: queenspark@bournemouth.gov.uk
web: www.littledowncentre.co.uk/qpgolf

Mature parkland with undulating tree-lined fairways. A demanding test of golf, with each hole having a unique character.

18 holes, 6090yds, Par 71, SSS 69, Course record 69.
Club membership 370.

Visitors Mon-Sun & BHs. Booking required. Handicap certificate. Dress code. **Societies** welcome. **Green Fees** £15 per round, £19.50 Sat, Sun & BHs. Day ticket £25. Winter reduced rates. **Facilities** **Conf** facs **Location** 2m NE of Bournemouth town centre off A338

Hotel ★★★ 68% Queens Hotel, Meyrick Rd, East Cliff, BOURNEMOUTH ☎ 01202 554415 109 en suite

Solent Meads Rolls Dr, Hengistbury Head BH6 4NA
☎ 01202 420795
e-mail: solentmeads@yahoo.co.uk
web: www.solentmeads.co.uk
An 18-hole par 3 links course overlooking Hengistbury Head with fine views of Christchurch Harbour and the Isle of Wight. Expect a sea breeze.
18 holes, 2182yards, Par 54.
Visitors Mon-Sun & BHs. **Societies** welcome. **Green Fees** £7.50 per 18 holes. **Prof** Warren Butcher **Facilities** **Leisure** 9 hole pitch & putt. **Conf** Corporate Hospitality Days **Location** A35 onto B3509 signed Tuckton/Southbourne, over 2nd rdbt, 1st left (Broadway), 0.75m left onto Rolls Dr

Hotel Premier Travel Inn Christchurch West, Barrack Rd, CHRISTCHURCH ☎ 08701 977063 42 en suite

BRIDPORT Map 03 SY49

Bridport & West Dorset The Clubhouse, Burton Rd DT6 4PS
☎ 01308 421491 & 421095 🖷 01308 421095
e-mail: secretary@bridportgolfclub.org.uk
web: www.bridportgolfclub.org.uk
Seaside links course on the top of the east cliff, with fine views over Lyme Bay and surrounding countryside. The signature 6th hole, known as Port Coombe, is only 133yds but dropping from the top of the cliff to a green almost at sea level far below. Fine sea views along the Chesil Bank to Portland Bill and across Lyme Bay.
18 holes, 5875yds, Par 70, SSS 68.
Club membership 600.
Visitors Mon-Sun & BHs. Dress code. **Societies** Booking required. **Green Fees** £26 per day, £20 after 2pm, £12 after 5pm. **Prof** David Parsons **Course Designer** Hawtree **Facilities** **Leisure** pitch & putt (high season). **Conf** Corporate Hospitality Days **Location** 1m E of Bridport on B3157

Hotel ★★★ 65% Haddon House Hotel, West Bay, BRIDPORT ☎ 01308 423626 & 425323 🖷 01308 427348 12 en suite

BROADSTONE Map 03 SZ09

Broadstone (Dorset) Wentworth Dr BH18 8DQ
☎ 01202 692595 🖷 01202 642520
e-mail: admin@broadstonegolfclub.com
web: www.broadstonegolfclub.com
Undulating and demanding heathland course with the 2nd, 7th, 13th and 16th being particularly challenging holes.

18 holes, 6315yds, Par 70, SSS 70, Course record 65.
Club membership 620.

Continued

Visitors Mon-Sun except BHs. Booking required. Handicap certificate. Dress code. **Societies** Booking required. **Green Fees** £70 per 27/36 holes, £46 per round, £60 per round Sat & Sun. **Prof** Matthew Wilson **Course Designer** Colt, Dunn **Facilities** **Conf** Corporate Hospitality Days **Location** N side of village off B3074

Guest House ♦♦♦♦ Ashton Lodge, 10 Oakley Hill, WIMBORNE ☎ 01202 883423 5 rms (2 en suite)

CHRISTCHURCH Map 04 SZ19

Dudmoor Farm Dudmoor Farm Rd, Off Fairmile Rd BH23 6AQ
☎ 01202 473826 🖷 01202 480207
web: www.dudmoorfarm.co.uk
A testing par 3 and 4 woodland course in an Area of Outstanding Natural Beauty.
9 holes, 1428mtrs, Par 31.
Visitors Mon-Sun & BHs. **Societies** Booking required. **Green Fees** £8 per 9/18 holes, £9 Sat, Sun & BHs. **Facilities** **Leisure** squash, adjoining riding stables. **Location** Private road off B3073 Christchurch-Hurn road

Hotel ★★★ 75% Waterford Lodge Hotel, 87 Bure Ln, Friars Cliff, CHRISTCHURCH
☎ 01425 272948 & 278801 🖷 01425 279130 18 en suite

DORCHESTER Map 03 SY69

Came Down Came Down DT2 8NR
☎ 01305 813494 (manager) 🖷 01305 815122
e-mail: manager@camedowngolfclub.co.uk
web: www.camedowngolfclub.co.uk
Scene of the West of England championships on several occasions, this fine course lies on a high plateau commanding glorious views over Portland. Three par 5 holes add interest to a round. The turf is of the springy, downland type.
18 holes, 6255yds, Par 70, SSS 70.
Club membership 750.
Visitors Mon-Sun & BHs. Handicap certificate. Dress code. **Societies** Booking required. **Green Fees** £28 per day, £32 Sat & Sun. **Prof** Nick Rodgers **Course Designer** JH Taylor, H Colt **Facilities**
Location 2m S off A354

Guest House ♦♦♦♦♦ Yalbury Cottage Hotel & Restaurant, Lower Bockhampton, DORCHESTER
☎ 01305 262382 8 en suite

FERNDOWN Map 04 SU00

Dudsbury 64 Christchurch Rd BH22 8ST
☎ 01202 593499 🖷 01202 594555
e-mail: golf@dudsbury.demon.co.uk
web: www.thedudsbury.co.uk
Set in 160 acres of beautiful Dorset countryside rolling down to the River Stour. Wide variety of interesting and challenging hazards, notably water which comes into play on 14 holes. The well-drained greens are protected by large bunkers and water hazards. A feature hole is the 16th where the green is over two lakes; the more aggressive the drive the greater the reward.

Continued

Championship Course: 18 holes, 6904yds, Par 71, SSS 73, Course record 64.
Club membership 600.
Visitors Mon-Sun & BHs. Booking required. Handicap certificate. Dress code. **Societies** Booking required. **Green Fees** £45 per 36 holes, £35 per 18 holes, £50/£40 Sat, Sun & BHs. **Prof** Steve Pockneall **Course Designer** Donald Steel **Facilities** **Leisure** fishing, 6 Hole Par 3 short game Academy Course. **Conf** facs Corporate Hospitality Days **Location** 3m N of Bournemouth on B3073

Hotel Premier Travel Inn Bournemouth/ Ferndown, Ringwood Rd, Tricketts Cross, FERNDOWN
08701 977102 32 en suite

Ferndown 119 Golf Links Rd BH22 8BU
01202 874602 01202 873926
e-mail: ferndowngc@lineone.net
web: www.ferndown-golf-club.co.uk
Fairways are gently undulating among heather, gorse and pine trees, giving the course a most attractive appearance. There are a number of dog-leg holes.
Championship Course: 18 holes, 6505yds, Par 71, SSS 71, Course record 63.
Presidents Course: 9 holes, 5604yds, Par 70, SSS 68.
Club membership 600.
Visitors Tue & Fri. Booking required. Handicap certificate. Dress code. **Societies** Booking required. **Green Fees** Championship £80 per day, £60 per round. **Prof** Neil PIke **Course Designer** Harold Hilton **Facilities** **Conf** Corporate Hospitality Days **Location** S side of town centre off A347

Hotel Premier Travel Inn Bournemouth/ Ferndown, Ringwood Rd, Tricketts Cross, FERNDOWN
08701 977102 32 en suite

Ferndown Forest Forest Links Rd BH22 9PH
01202 876096 01202 894095
e-mail: golf@ferndownforestgolf.co.uk
web: www.ferndownforestgolf.co.uk
Flat parkland dotted with mature oaks, several interesting water features, and some tight fairways.
18 holes, 5068yds, Par 68, SSS 65, Course record 69.
Club membership 400.
Visitors Mon-Sun & BHs. Dress code. **Societies** Booking required. **Green Fees** £14 per day, £16 Sat, Sun & BHs. **Prof** Mike Dodd **Course Designer** Guy Hunt, Richard Graham **Facilities** **Conf** facs Corporate Hospitality Days **Location** Off A31 N of Ferndown, follow signs to Dorset Police Headquarters

Hotel Premier Travel Inn Bournemouth/ Ferndown, Ringwood Rd, Tricketts Cross, FERNDOWN
08701 977102 32 en suite

Booking a tee time is always advisable

HALSTOCK Map 03 ST50

Halstock Common Ln BA22 9SF
01935 891689 & 891968 (pro shop) 01935 891839
e-mail: halstock.golf@feeuk.com
18 holes, 4481yds, Par 66, SSS 63, Course record 63.
Location 6m S of Yeovil
Phone for further details

Hotel ★★★★ Summer Lodge, EVERSHOT
01935 482000 10 en suite 14 annexe en suite

HIGHCLIFFE Map 04 SZ29

Highcliffe Castle 107 Lymington Rd BH23 4LA
01425 272210 01425 272953
Picturesque parkland with easy walking.
18 holes, 4776yds, Par 64, SSS 63, Course record 58.
Club membership 450.
Visitors Mon-Sun & BHs. Handicap certificate. Dress code. **Societies** Booking required. **Green Fees** £26 per round, £36 Sat & Sun am. **Facilities** by arrangement **Conf** Corporate Hospitality Days **Location** SW side of town on A337

Hotel ★★★ 75% Waterford Lodge Hotel, 87 Bure Ln, Friars Cliff, CHRISTCHURCH
01425 272948 & 278801 01425 279130 18 en suite

HURN Map 04 SZ19

Parley Parley Green Ln BH23 6BB
01202 591600 01202 579043
e-mail: info@parleygolf.co.uk
web: www.parleygolf.uk
Flat testing parkland course with few hazards including par 5s. Renowned 5th hole, bordering the River Stour.

9 holes, 4938yds, Par 68, SSS 64, Course record 69.
Club membership 200.
Visitors Mon-Sun & BHs. Dress code. **Societies** welcome. **Green Fees** £11 per 18 holes, £8 per 9 holes, £12/£9.50 Sat & Sun. **Prof** Richard Hill **Course Designer** P Goodfellow **Facilities** by arrangement **Conf** Corporate Hospitality Days **Location** On B3073 opp Bournemouth airport

Hotel Premier Travel Inn Bournemouth/Ferndown, Ringwood Rd, Tricketts Cross, FERNDOWN
08701 977102 32 en suite

LYME REGIS Map 03 SY39

Lyme Regis Timber Hill DT7 3HQ
☎ 01297 443822
e-mail: secretary@lymeregisgolfclub.co.uk
web: www.lymeregisgolfclub.co.uk
Undulating cliff-top course with magnificent views of Golden Cap and Lyme Bay.

18 holes, 6283yds, Par 71, SSS 70, Course record 65.
Club membership 575.
Visitors Mon-Sun & BHs. Booking required Thu & Sun. Handicap certificate. Dress code. **Societies** Booking required. **Green Fees** £35 per day, £30 per 18 holes before 2pm, £25 after 2pm. **Prof** Duncan Driver **Course Designer** Donald Steel **Facilities** **Location** W end of A5 Charmouth bypass onto A3052 to Lyme Regis, 1.5m from A3052 & A35 rdbt

Hotel ★★★ 71% Hotel Alexandra, Pound St, LYME REGIS ☎ 01297 442010 25 en suite 1 annexe en suite

LYTCHETT MATRAVERS Map 03 SY99

Bulbury Woods Bulbury Ln BH16 6HR
☎ 01929 459574 🖷 01929 459000
e-mail: general@bulbury-woods.co.uk
Parkland with a mixture of American and traditional style greens and extensive views over the Purbecks and Poole harbour. A comprehensive programme of tree planting coupled with ancient woodland ensures a round that is picturesque as well as providing interest and challenge.
18 holes, 6002yds, Par 71, SSS 69.
Club membership 450.
Visitors Mon-Sun & BHs. Booking required. Dress code. **Societies** Booking required. **Green Fees** £16 Mon-Fri, £22 Sat, Sun & BHs. **Facilities** **Conf** facs Corporate Hospitality Days **Location** A35 Poole-Dorchester, 3m from Poole centre

Hotel ★★★ 68% Springfield Country Hotel & Leisure Club, Grange Rd, WAREHAM ☎ 01929 552177 48 en suite

POOLE Map 04 SZ09

Parkstone Links Rd, Parkstone BH14 9QS
☎ 01202 707138 🖷 01202 706027
e-mail: admin@parkstonegolfclub.co.uk
web: www.parkstonegolfclub.co.uk
Very scenic heathland course with views of Poole Bay. Designed in 1909 by Willie Park Jnr and enlarged in 1932 by James Braid. The result of this highly imaginative reconstruction was an intriguing and

Continued

varied test of golf set among pines and heather fringed fairways where every hole presents a different challenge.
18 holes, 6250yds, Par 72, SSS 70, Course record 63.
Club membership 700.
Visitors contact club for details. Handicap certificate. Dress code. **Societies** Booking required. **Green Fees** £75 per day, £50 per round, £85/£60 Sat, Sun & BHs. **Prof** Martyn Thompson **Course Designer** Willie Park Jnr **Facilities** **Conf** Corporate Hospitality Days **Location** E side of town centre off A35

Hotel ★★★ 66% Arndale Court Hotel, 62-66 Wimborne Rd, POOLE ☎ 01202 683746 39 en suite

SHERBORNE Map 03 ST61

Sherborne Higher Clatcombe DT9 4RN
☎ 01935 814431 🖷 01935 814218
e-mail: sherbornegc@btconnect.com
Beautiful mature parkland to the north of Sherborne on the Dorset-Somerset border, with extensive views. Recently extended to 6414yds.
18 holes, 6414yds, Par 72, SSS 71, Course record 62.
Club membership 600.
Visitors Booking required. Handicap certificate. **Societies** Tue & Wed. Booking required. **Green Fees** phone. **Prof** Alistair Tresidder **Course Designer** James Braid (part) **Facilities** **Location** 2m N off B3145

Hotel ★★★ 72% Eastbury Hotel, Long St, SHERBORNE ☎ 01935 813131 21 en suite

STURMINSTER MARSHALL Map 03 ST90

Sturminster Marshall Moor Ln BH21 4AH
☎ 01258 858444 🖷 01258 858262
web: www.scoot.co.uk/sturminster_golf_club
9 holes, 4882yds, Par 68, SSS 64.
Course Designer John Sharkey, David Holdsworth
Location On A350, signed from village
Phone for further details

Hotel ★★★ 71% Crown Hotel, West St, BLANDFORD FORUM ☎ 01258 456626 32 en suite

If the name of the club appears in italics, details have not been confirmed for this edition of the guide

SWANAGE Map 04 SZ07

Isle of Purbeck BH19 3AB
☎ 01929 450361 & 450354 Fax 01929 450501
e-mail: enquiries@purbeckgolf.co.uk
web: www.purbeckgolf.co.uk

Purbeck Course: 18 holes, 6295yds, Par 70, SSS 70, Course record 66.
Dene Course: 9 holes, 4014yds, Par 60.
Course Designer H Colt **Location** 2.5m N on B3351
Phone for further details

Hotel ★★★ 69% The Pines Hotel, Burlington Rd, SWANAGE ☎ 01929 425211 49 en suite

VERWOOD Map 04 SU00

Crane Valley The Club House BH31 7LE
☎ 01202 814088 Fax 01202 813407
e-mail: general@crane-valley.co.uk
web: www.crane-valley.co.uk
Two secluded parkland courses set amid rolling Dorset countryside and mature woodland. The 6th nestles in the bend of the River Crane and there are four long par 5s ranging from 499 to 545yds.
Valley: 18 holes, 6445yds, Par 72, SSS 71, Course record 66.
Woodland: 9 holes, 2060yds, Par 33, SSS 30.
Club membership 700.
Visitors Valley course booking required. Woodland course Mon-Sun. **Societies** Booking required. **Green Fees** phone. **Prof** Darrel Ranson **Course Designer** Donald Steel **Facilities** **Conf** facs Corporate Hospitality Days **Location** 6m W of Ringwood on B3081

WAREHAM Map 03 SY98

Wareham Sandford Rd BH20 4DH
☎ 01929 554147 Fax 01929 557993
e-mail: warehamgolf@tiscali.co.uk
web: www.warehamgolfclub.com
At the entrance to the Purbeck Hills with splendid views over Poole Harbour and Wareham Forest. A mixture of undulating parkland and heathland fairways. A challenge for all abilities.
18 holes, 5766yds, Par 69, SSS 68, Course record 66.
Club membership 500.
Visitors Mon-Sun & BHs. Handicap certificate. Dress code. **Societies** Booking required. **Green Fees** £40 per day, £28 per round, £35 per round Sat, Sun & BHs. **Facilities** **Location** 0.5m N of Wareham on A351

Continued

Hotel ★★★ 68% Springfield Country Hotel & Leisure Club, Grange Rd, WAREHAM ☎ 01929 552177 48 en suite

WEYMOUTH Map 03 SY67

Weymouth Links Rd DT4 0PF
☎ 01305 773981 (Manager) & 773997 (pro)
Fax 01305 788029
e-mail: weymouthgolfclub@aol.com
web: www.weymouthgolfclub.co.uk
A seaside parkland course, almost 100 years old, situated in the heart of the town. The 5th is played off an elevated tee over copse.
18 holes, 5996yds, Par 70, SSS 69, Course record 60.
Club membership 750.
Visitors Mon-Sun except BHs. Booking required. Handicap certificate. Dress code. **Societies** Booking required. **Green Fees** £30 per day, £35 Sat & Sun. **Prof** Des Lochrie **Course Designer** James Braid **Facilities** **Conf** Corporate Hospitality Days **Location** N side of town centre off B3157

Hotel ★★★ 64% Hotel Rex, 29 The Esplanade, WEYMOUTH ☎ 01305 760400 31 en suite

WIMBORNE Map 03 SZ09

Canford Magna Knighton Ln BH21 3AS
☎ 01202 592552 Fax 01202 592550
e-mail: admin@canfordmagnagc.co.uk
web: www.canfordmagnagc.co.uk
Lying in 350 acres of Dorset countryside, the Canford Magna Golf Club provides 45 holes of challenging golf for the discerning player. The 18-hole Parkland and Riverside courses are quite different and the new nine-hole Knighton course demands the same level of playing skill. For those wishing to improve their handicap, the Golf Academy offers a covered driving range, pitching greens, a chipping green and bunkers, together with a 6-hole par 3 academy course.
Parkland: 18 holes, 6519yds, Par 71, SSS 71, Course record 65.
Riverside: 18 holes, 6214yds, Par 70, SSS 70, Course record 68.
Knighton: 9 holes, 1377yds, Par 27, Course record 26.
Club membership 1000.
Visitors Mon-Sun & BHs. Booking required. Dress code. **Societies** Booking required. **Green Fees** Parkland £22.50 per round, £26 Sat & Sun. Riverside £18/£21. Knighton £7/£8. **Prof** Martin Cummins **Course Designer** Howard Swan **Facilities** **Conf** facs Corporate Hospitality Days **Location** On A341

Guest House ♦♦♦♦ Ashton Lodge, 10 Oakley Hill, WIMBORNE ☎ 01202 883423 5 rms (2 en suite)

CO DURHAM

BARNARD CASTLE Map 12 NZ01

Barnard Castle Harmire Rd DL12 8QN
☎ 01833 638355 Fax 01833 695551
e-mail: sec@barnardcastlegolfclub.org.uk
web: www.barnardcastlegolfclub.org.uk
Flat parkland in open countryside. Plantations and natural water add colour and interest to this classic course.

Continued

Barnard Castle

18 holes, 6406yds, Par 73, SSS 71, Course record 63.
Club membership 650.
Visitors Mon-Sun & BHs. Booking required. Handicap certificate. Dress code. **Societies** Booking required. **Green Fees** £22 per round, £32 Sat, Sun & BHs. **Prof** Darren Pearce **Course Designer** A Watson **Facilities** **Conf** Corporate Hospitality Days **Location** 1m N of town centre on B6278

Hotel ★★ Rose & Crown Hotel, ROMALDKIRK ☎ 01833 650213 7 en suite 5 annexe en suite

BEAMISH Map 12 NZ25

Beamish Park DH9 0RH

☎ 0191 370 1382 🖷 0191 370 2937
e-mail: bpgc@beamishparkgc.fsbusiness.co.uk
web: www.beamishgolfclub.co.uk
Parkland course designed by Henry Cotton and W Woodend.
18 holes, 6183yds, Par 71, SSS 70, Course record 64.
Club membership 630.
Visitors Mon-Fri except BHs. Booking required. Handicap certificate. **Societies** Booking required. **Green Fees** £28 per day, £25 per round. **Prof** Chris Cole **Course Designer** H Cotton **Facilities** **Conf** Corporate Hospitality Days **Location** 1m NW off A693

Hotel ★★★ 69% Beamish Park Hotel, Beamish Burn Rd, MARLEY HILL ☎ 01207 230666 47 en suite

BILLINGHAM Map 08 NZ42

Billingham Sandy Ln TS22 5NA

☎ 01642 533816 & 557060 (pro) 🖷 01642 533816
e-mail: billinghamgc@onetel.com
web: www.billinghamgolfclub.com
Undulating parkland with water hazards.
18 holes, 6346yds, Par 71, SSS 70, Course record 62.
Club membership 1050.
Visitors Booking required. Handicap certificate. **Societies** Booking required. **Green Fees** phone. **Prof** Michael Ure **Course Designer** F Pennick **Facilities** **Location** 1m W of town centre

Hotel ★★★ 73% Parkmore Hotel & Leisure Park, 636 Yarm Rd, Eaglescliffe, STOCKTON-ON-TEES ☎ 01642 786815 55 en suite

Wynyard Wellington Dr, Wynyard Park TS22 5QJ

☎ 01740 644399 🖷 01740 644599
e-mail: chris@wynyardgolfclub.co.uk
Built against the delightful backdrop of the Wynyard estate, the Wellington Course combines a fine blend of rolling parkland and mature woodland. It represents the ultimate in challenge and excitement for both the novice and the highly experienced player.
Wellington: 18 holes, 7063yds, Par 72, SSS 73, Course record 63.
Club membership 350.
Visitors Mon-Sun & BHs. Booking required Fri-Sun & BHs. Handicap certificate. Dress code. **Societies** Booking required. **Green Fees** £60 per 18 holes. **Prof** Chris Mounter **Course Designer** Hawtree **Facilities** **Leisure** David Leadbetter Golf Academy. **Conf** facs Corporate Hospitality Days **Location** off A689 between A19 & A1

BISHOP AUCKLAND Map 08 NZ22

Bishop Auckland High Plains, Durham Rd DL14 8DL

☎ 01388 661618 🖷 01388 607005
e-mail: enquiries@bagc.co.uk
web: www.bagc.co.uk
A rather hilly parkland course with many well-established trees offering a challenging round. A small ravine adds interest to several holes including the short 7th, from a raised tee to a green surrounded by a stream, gorse and bushes. Pleasant views down the Wear Valley and over the residence of the Bishop of Durham. Has the distinction of having three consecutive par 5 holes and two consecutive par 3s.
18 holes, 6379yds, Par 72, SSS 70, Course record 63.
Club membership 950.
Visitors Mon-Fri. Booking required Sat, Sun & BHs. Handicap certificate. Dress code. **Societies** welcome. **Green Fees** £30 per day, £25 per round. **Prof** David Skiffington **Course Designer** James Kay **Facilities** **Leisure** snooker. **Conf** facs Corporate Hospitality Days **Location** 1m NE on A689

Hotel ★★★ 74% Whitworth Hall Country Park Hotel, Mear, SPENNYMOOR ☎ 01388 811772 29 en suite

BURNOPFIELD Map 12 NZ15

Hobson Hobson NE16 6BZ

☎ 01207 270941 🖷 01207 271069
Meadowland course with very easy walking.
18 holes, 6403yds, Par 69, SSS 68, Course record 65.
Club membership 700.
Visitors contact club for details. Dress code. **Societies** Booking required. **Green Fees** £19 per round, £22 Sat & Sun. **Prof** Jack Ord **Facilities** **Location** 0.75m S on A692

CHESTER-LE-STREET Map 12 NZ25

Chester-le-Street Lumley Park DH3 4NS

☎ 0191 388 3218 (secretary)
e-mail: clsgc@ukonline.co.uk
web: www.clsgc.co.uk
Parkland course in castle grounds, good views, easy walking.
18 holes, 6437yds, Par 71, SSS 70, Course record 67.
Club membership 650.

Continued

Visitors Mon-Sun & BHs. Booking required. Dress code. **Societies** Booking required. **Green Fees** £30 per day, £25 per round, £35/£30 Sat & Sun. **Prof** David Fletcher **Course Designer** JH Taylor **Facilities** **Conf** Corporate Hospitality Days **Location** 0.5m E off B1284

Hotel ★★★ 72% Ramside Hall Hotel, Carrville, DURHAM ☎ 0191 386 5282 80 en suite

Roseberry Grange Grange Villa DH2 3NF
☎ 0191 3700670 🖹 0191 3700224
Parkland course providing a good test of golf for all abilities. Fine panoramic views of County Durham.
18 holes, 6152yds, Par 71, SSS 69.
Club membership 620.
Visitors Booking required. Dress code. **Societies** Booking required. **Green Fees** phone. **Prof** Chris Jones **Course Designer** Durham County Council **Facilities** **Location** 5m W of Chester-le-Street. Off A694 into West Pelton, signed

Hotel ★★★ 68% George Washington Golf & Country Club, Stone Cellar Rd, High Usworth, WASHINGTON ☎ 0191 402 9988 103 en suite

CONSETT Map 12 NZ15

Consett & District Elmfield Rd DH8 5NN
☎ 01207 505060 (secretary) 🖹 01207 505060
e-mail: consettgolfclub@btconnect.com
web: www.consettgolfclub.com
Undulating parkland and moorland course with views across the Derwent Valley to the Cheviot Hills.
18 holes, 6080yds, Par 71, SSS 69, Course record 63.
Club membership 650.
Visitors Mon-Sun & BHs. Booking required. Handicap certificate. Dress code. **Societies** Booking required. **Green Fees** £20 per day, £30 Sat, Sun & BHs. **Prof** Shaun Cowell **Course Designer** Harry Vardon **Facilities** **Leisure** snooker room. **Conf** Corporate Hospitality Days **Location** N side of town on A691

CROOK Map 12 NZ13

Crook Low Jobs Hill DL15 9AA
☎ 01388 762429 🖹 01388 762137
web: www.crookgolfclub.com
Meadowland and parkland on an elevated position with natural hazards and varied holes. Panoramic views over Durham and the Cleveland Hills.
18 holes, 6102yds, Par 70, SSS 69, Course record 64.
Club membership 550.
Visitors Mon-Sun & BHs. Booking required Sat & Sun. Dress code. **Societies** Booking required. **Green Fees** phone. **Prof** Gordon Cattrell **Facilities** **Conf** facs **Location** 0.5m E off A690

Hotel ★★★ 66% Helme Park Hall Hotel, FIR TREE ☎ 01388 730970 13 en suite

DARLINGTON Map 08 NZ21

Blackwell Grange Briar Close, Blackwell DL3 8QX
☎ 01325 464458 🖹 01325 464458
e-mail: secretary@blackwellgrangegolf.com
web: www.blackwellgrangegolf.com
One of the most attractive courses in north-east England. Clever use of the trees on this easy walking course gives a feeling of having the course to oneself. Three ponds add to the variety of holes on offer.
18 holes, 5621yds, Par 68, SSS 67, Course record 63.
Club membership 1000.
Visitors Mon-Sun & BHs. Booking required. Dress code. **Societies** Booking required. **Green Fees** £25 per day, £20 per round, £30 per round Sat, Sun & BHs. **Prof** Joanne Furby **Course Designer** F Pennink **Facilities** **Conf** Corporate Hospitality Days **Location** 1.5m SW off A66 into Blackwell, signed

Hotel ★★★ 64% The Blackwell Grange Hotel, Blackwell Grange, DARLINGTON
☎ 0870 609 6121 & 01325 509955 99 en suite 11 annexe en suite

Darlington Haughton Grange DL1 3JD
☎ 01325 355324 🖹 01325 488126
e-mail: darlington.golfclub@virgin.net
18 holes, 6181yds, Par 70, SSS 69, Course record 65.
Course Designer A MacKenzie **Location** N side of town centre off A1150
Phone for further details

Hotel ★★★ 75% Headlam Hall, Headlam, Gainford, DARLINGTON ☎ 01325 730238 19 en suite 15 annexe en suite

Hall Garth Golf & Country Club Hotel
Coatham Mundeville DL1 3LU
☎ 01325 320246 🖹 01325 310083
web: www.corushotels.co.uk/hallgarth

9 holes, 6621yds, Par 72, SSS 72.
Course Designer Brian Moore **Location** A1(M) junct 59, 0.5m off A167
Phone for further details

Hotel ★★★ 73% Hall Garth Golf and Country Club Hotel, Coatham Mundeville, DARLINGTON ☎ 0870 6096131 40 en suite 11 annexe en suite

Headlam Hall Headlam, Grinford DL2 3HA
☎ 01325 730238 🖹 01325 730790
e-mail: admin@headlamhall.co.uk
web: www.headlamhall.co.uk
Course set over the mature rolling pastureland of Headlam Hall. Abundance of natural features including rig and fur, woodland, streams and ponds, making the course both challenging to the player and pleasing to the eye. Each hole has its own character but the 7th Pond Hole is particularly special with a stepped green protruding into a picturesque pond with woodland lining the back.
9 holes, 2075yards, Par 31, SSS 56.
Club membership 200.

Continued

Visitors Mon-Sun & BHs. Booking required Sat & Sun. Dress Code. **Societies** Booking required. **Green Fees** Summer £18 per 18 holes, £12 per 9 holes. Winter £15/£10. **Prof** Steven Carpenter **Course Designer** Ralph Givens **Facilities** **Leisure** hard tennis courts, heated indoor swimming pool, fishing, sauna, gymnasium. **Conf** facs Corporate Hospitality Days **Location** 8m W of Darlington, off A67

Hotel ★★★ 75% Headlam Hall, Headlam, Gainford, DARLINGTON ☎ 01325 730238 19 en suite 15 annexe en suite

Stressholme Snipe Ln DL2 2SA

☎ 01325 461002 🖷 01325 461002

web: www.darlington.gov.uk

Picturesque municipal parkland course, long but wide, with 98 bunkers and a par 3 hole played over a river.

18 holes, 6431yds, Par 71, SSS 70, Course record 69.
Club membership 450.

Visitors contact club for details. **Societies** Booking required. **Green Fees** £21 per day, £13.50 per round, £26.25/£15.50 Sat & Sun. **Prof** Ralph Givens **Facilities** **Conf** facs Corporate Hospitality Days **Location** SW of town centre on A67

Hotel ★★★ 64% The Blackwell Grange Hotel, Blackwell Grange, DARLINGTON
☎ 0870 609 6121 & 01325 509955 99 en suite 11 annexe en suite

DURHAM Map 12 NZ24

Brancepeth Castle Brancepeth Village DH7 8EA

☎ 0191 378 0075 🖷 0191 378 3835

e-mail: enquiries@brancepeth-castle-golf.co.uk

web: www.brancepeth-castle-golf.co.uk

Parkland course overlooked at the 9th hole by beautiful Brancepeth Castle.

18 holes, 6400yds, Par 70, SSS 70, Course record 64.
Club membership 780.

Visitors Mon-Fri except BHs. Booking required. Handicap certificate. Dress code. **Societies** Booking required. **Green Fees** £38 per day, £33 per round. **Prof** David Howdon **Course Designer** H Colt **Facilities** **Conf** facs Corporate Hospitality Days **Location** 4m from Durham A690 towards Crook, left at x-rds in Brancepath, left at Castle Gates, 400yds

Hotel ★★★★ 72% Durham Marriott Hotel, Royal County, Old Elvet, DURHAM ☎ 0191 386 6821 142 en suite 8 annexe en suite

Durham City Littleburn, Langley Moor DH7 8HL

☎ 0191 378 0069 🖷 0191 378 4265

e-mail: durhamcitygolf@lineone.net

web: www.durhamcitygolf.co.uk

Undulating parkland course bordered on several holes by the River Browney.

18 holes, 6326yds, Par 71, SSS 70, Course record 67.
Club membership 750.

Visitors Mon-Fri. Booking required Sat, Sun & BHs. **Societies** Booking required. **Green Fees** £30, £40 Sat, Sun & BHs. **Prof** Steve Corbally **Course Designer** C Stanton **Facilities** **Conf** Corporate Hospitality Days **Location** 2m W of Durham City, turn left off A690 into Littleburn Ind Est

Hotel ★★★ 66% Bowburn Hall Hotel, Bowburn, DURHAM ☎ 0191 377 0311 19 en suite

Mount Oswald South Rd DH1 3TQ

☎ 0191 386 7527 🖷 0191 386 0975

e-mail: information@mountoswald.co.uk

web: www.mountoswald.co.uk

Picturesque parkland that gently undulates through the Durham countryside. The easy walking course attracts golfers of all levels and abilities.

18 holes, 5984yds, Par 71, SSS 69.
Club membership 200.

Visitors Mon-Fri. Booking required Sat, Sun & BHs. **Societies** Booking required. **Green Fees** £14.50 per round, £17.50 Sat, Sun & BHs. Winter reduced rates. **Prof** Chris Calder **Facilities** **Conf** facs Corporate Hospitality Days **Location** On A177, 1m SW of city centre

Hotel ★★★ 72% Ramside Hall Hotel, Carrville, DURHAM ☎ 0191 386 5282 80 en suite

Ramside Hall Carrville DH1 1TD

☎ 0191 386 9514 🖷 0191 386 9519

e-mail: golf@ramsidegolfclub.fsnet.co.uk

web: www.ramsidehallhotel.co.uk

Princes: 9 holes, 3235yds, Par 36, SSS 36.
Bishops: 9 holes, 3285yds, Par 36.
Cathedral: 9 holes, 2874yds, Par 34.

Course Designer Jonathan Gaunt **Location** 500yds from junct A1

Phone for further details

Hotel ★★★ 72% Ramside Hall Hotel, Carrville, DURHAM ☎ 0191 386 5282 80 en suite

EAGLESCLIFFE Map 08 NZ41

Eaglescliffe and District Yarm Rd TS16 0DQ
☎ 01642 780238 (office) 🖷 01642 780238
e-mail: eaglescliffegcsec@tiscali.co.uk
web: www.eaglescliffegolfclub.co.uk
Undulating wooded parkland with views over the River Tees to the Cleveland Hills. A tee on the riverbank makes for a daunting tee shot at the 14th signature hole.
18 holes, 6275yds, Par 72, SSS 70, Course record 64.
Club membership 970.
Visitors Mon, Wed-Fri & Sun except BHs. Handicap certificate. Dress code. **Societies** Booking required. **Green Fees** £40 per day, £32 per round, £55/£40 Sun. **Prof** Graeme Bell **Course Designer** J Braid, H Cotton **Facilities** **Conf** Corporate Hospitality Days **Location** On E side of A135 between Yarm -on-Tees

Hotel ★★★ 73% Parkmore Hotel & Leisure Park, 636 Yarm Rd, Eaglescliffe, STOCKTON-ON-TEES ☎ 01642 786815 55 en suite

HARTLEPOOL Map 08 NZ53

Castle Eden Castle Eden TS27 4SS
☎ 01429 836510 🖷 01429 836510
e-mail: derek.livingston@btinternet.com
web: www.ceden-golf.co.uk
18 holes, 6262yds, Par 70, SSS 70, Course record 64.
Course Designer Henry Cotton **Location** 2m S of Peterlee on B1281 off A19
Phone for further details

Hartlepool Hart Warren TS24 9QF
☎ 01429 274398 🖷 01429 274129
web: www.hartlepoolgolfclub.co.uk
A seaside course, half links, overlooking the North Sea. A good test and equally enjoyable to all handicap players. The 10th, par 4, demands a precise second shot over a ridge and between sand dunes to a green down near the edge of the beach, alongside which several holes are played.
18 holes, 6200yds, Par 70, SSS 70, Course record 62.
Club membership 700.
Visitors Mon-Fri except BHs. Booking required. Dress code. **Societies** Booking required. **Green Fees** £32 per day, £42 Sat & Sun. **Prof** Graham Laidlaw **Course Designer** Braid (part) **Facilities** **Location** N of Hartlepool, off A1086

Hotel Premier Travel Inn Hartlepool, Maritime Av, Hartlepool Marina, HARTLEPOOL ☎ 08701 977127 40 en suite

MIDDLETON ST GEORGE Map 08 NZ31

Dinsdale Spa Neasham Rd DL2 1DW
☎ 01325 332297 🖷 01325 332297
Mainly flat parkland on high land above the River Tees with views of the Cleveland Hills. Water hazards in front of the 15th tee and green; the prevailing west wind affects the later holes. There is a practice area by the clubhouse.
18 holes, 6099yds, Par 71, SSS 69, Course record 65.
Club membership 870.

Continued

Visitors Mon & Wed-Fri except BHs. Handicap certificate. Dress code. **Societies** Booking required. **Green Fees** £25 per day. **Prof** Martin Stubbings **Facilities** **Conf** Corporate Hospitality Days **Location** 1.5m SW

Hotel ★★★ 69% The Croft, Croft-on-Tees, DARLINGTON ☎ 01325 720319 20 en suite

NEWTON AYCLIFFE Map 08 NZ22

Oakleaf Golf Complex School Aycliffe Ln DL5 6QZ
☎ 01325 310820 🖷 01325 318918
A parkland course in a country setting with established trees, streams and lakes, the signature hole being the 15th. Excellent views.
18 holes, 5568yds, Par 70, SSS 67, Course record 67.
Club membership 450.
Visitors Mon-Sun & BHs. Booking required. Dress code. **Societies** Booking required. **Green Fees** phone. **Prof** Ernie Wilson **Facilities** **Leisure** squash, fishing. **Location** 6m N of Darlington, off A6072

Hotel ★★★★ 70% Redworth Hall Hotel, REDWORTH ☎ 01388 770600 100 en suite

Woodham Golf & Country Club Burnhill Way DL5 4PN
☎ 01325 320574 (office) 315257 (pro shop)
🖷 01325 315254
The course was originally opened in 1981 and the excellent design was by James Hamilton Scott. It is laid out in 229 acres of parkland with the two loops of nine holes starting and finishing at the clubhouse. Mature woodland with large trees and numerous lakes.
18 holes, 6688yds, Par 73, SSS 72, Course record 66.
Club membership 600.
Visitors Booking required. **Societies** Booking required. **Green Fees** phone. **Prof** Peter Kelly **Course Designer** James Hamilton Stutt **Facilities** **Location** A1 onto A689 towards Bishop Auckland, 0.5m from Rushford

Hotel Premier Travel Inn Durham (Newton Aycliffe), Great North Rd, NEWTON AYCLIFFE ☎ 08701 977085 44 en suite

SEAHAM Map 12 NZ44

Seaham Dawdon SR7 7RD
☎ 0191 5130837 & 5812354
e-mail: seahamgc@onetel.com
web: www.seahamgolfclub.co.uk
Heathland links course with several holes affected by strong winds.
18 holes, 6017yds, Par 70, SSS 69, Course record 64.
Club membership 600.
Visitors Mon-Fri & BHs. Dress code. **Societies** Booking required. **Green Fees** £22 per day, £27 Sat & Sun. **Prof** Andrew Blunt **Facilities** **Location** 3m E of A19, exit for Seaham

Hotel ★★★★ 69% Sunderland Marriott Hotel, Queen's Pde, Seaburn, SUNDERLAND ☎ 0191 529 2041 82 en suite

SEATON CAREW Map 08 NZ52

Seaton Carew Tees Rd TS25 1DE
☎ 01429 261040 📠 01429 267952
web: www.seatoncarewgolfclub.org.uk
A championship links course taking full advantage of its dunes, bents, whins and gorse. Renowned for its par 4 17th; just enough fairway for an accurate drive followed by another precise shot to a pear-shape sloping green that is severely trapped.
The Old Course: 18 holes, 6622yds, Par 72, SSS 72.
Brabazon Course: 18 holes, 6857yds, Par 73, SSS 73.
Club membership 700.
Visitors Mon-Sun & BHs. Booking required. Handicap certificate. Dress code. **Societies** Booking required. **Green Fees** phone. **Prof** Mark Rogers **Course Designer** A MacKenzie **Facilities** **Conf** Corporate Hospitality Days **Location** SE side of village off A178

Hotel Premier Travel Inn Hartlepool, Maritme Av, Hartlepool Marina, HARTLEPOOL ☎ 08701 977127 40 en suite

SEDGEFIELD Map 08 NZ32

Knotty Hill Golf Centre TS21 2BB
☎ 01740 620320 📠 01740 622227
e-mail: khgc21@btopenworld.com
web: www.knottyhillgolfcentre.co.uk
The 18-hole Princes Course is set in rolling parkland with many holes routed through shallow valleys. Several holes are set wholly or partially within woodland and water hazards abound. Bishops Course is a developing 18-hole course with varied water features on attractive terrain. Several holes are routed through mature woodland.
Princes Course: 18 holes, 6433yds, Par 72, SSS 71.
Bishops Course: 18 holes, 5976yds, Par 70.
Visitors Mon-Sun & BHs. **Societies** Booking required. **Green Fees** £12 per round, £14 Sat & Sun. **Course Designer** C Stanton **Facilities** **Leisure** gymnasium, tuition range. **Conf** facs Corporate Hospitality Days **Location** A1(M) junct 60, 1m N of Sedgefield on A177

Hotel ★★★ 75% Hardwick Hall Hotel, SEDGEFIELD ☎ 01740 620253 52 en suite

STANLEY Map 12 NZ15

South Moor The Middles, Craghead DH9 6AG
☎ 01207 232848 📠 01207 284616
e-mail: bryandavison@southmoorgc.freeserve.co.uk
web: www.southmoorgolfclub.com
Moorland course with natural hazards, designed by Alister MacKenzie in 1926 and still one of the most challenging of its type in north east England. Out of bounds features on 11 holes from the tee, and the testing par 5 12th hole is uphill and usually against a strong headwind.
18 holes, 6271yds, Par 72, SSS 70, Course record 66.
Club membership 500.
Visitors Mon-Sat except BHs. Booking required. Dress code. **Societies** Booking required. **Green Fees** £25 per day, £18 per round, £30/20 Sat. **Prof** Shaun Cowell **Course Designer** A MacKenzie **Facilities** **Leisure** snooker table. **Conf** Corporate Hospitality Days **Location** 1.5m SE on B6313

Continued

Hotel ★★★ 69% Beamish Park Hotel, Beamish Burn Rd, MARLEY HILL ☎ 01207 230666 47 en suite

STOCKTON-ON-TEES Map 08 NZ41

Norton Norton TS20 1SU
☎ 01642 676385 📠 01642 608467
An interesting parkland course with long drives from the 7th and 17th tees. Several water hazards.
18 holes, 5855yds, Par 70.
Visitors Mon-Sun & BHs. Dress code. **Societies** Mon-Fri. **Green Fees** £11.50 per 18 holes, £13.50 Sat, Sun & BHs. **Course Designer** T Harper **Facilities** **Leisure** bowling green. **Conf** Corporate Hospitality Days **Location** In Norton 2m N off A19

Hotel ★★★ 73% Parkmore Hotel & Leisure Park, 636 Yarm Rd, Eaglescliffe, STOCKTON-ON-TEES ☎ 01642 786815 55 en suite

Teesside Acklam Rd, Thornaby TS17 7JS
☎ 01642 616516 & 673822 (pro) 📠 01642 676252
e-mail: teessidegolfclub@btconnect.com
web: www.teessidegolfclub.com
Flat, easy walking parkland.
18 holes, 6535yds, Par 72, SSS 71, Course record 64.
Club membership 700.
Visitors Mon-Sun & BHs. Booking required. Handicap certificate. Dress code. **Societies** Booking required. **Green Fees** phone. **Prof** Ken Hall **Facilities** **Location** 1.5m SE on A1130, off A19 at Mandale interchange

Hotel ★★★ 73% Parkmore Hotel & Leisure Park, 636 Yarm Rd, Eaglescliffe, STOCKTON-ON-TEES ☎ 01642 786815 55 en suite

ESSEX

ABRIDGE Map 05 TQ49

Abridge Golf and Country Club Epping Ln, Stapleford Tawney RM4 1ST
☎ 01708 688396 📠 01708 688550
e-mail: info@abridgegolf.com
web: www.abridgegolf.com
Easy walking parkland. The quick drying course is a challenge for all levels. This has been the venue of several professional tournaments. Abridge is a golf and country club and has all the attendant facilities.
18 holes, 6704yds, Par 72, SSS 72, Course record 67.
Club membership 600.
Visitors Mon & Wed-Fri except BHs. Tue, Sat & Sun pm. Booking required. Handicap certificate. Dress code. **Societies** Booking required. **Green Fees** £35 per 18 holes, £45 Sat & Sun. **Prof** Stuart Layton **Course Designer** Henry Cotton **Facilities** **Leisure** swimming pool, 3 snooker tables. **Conf** facs Corporate Hospitality Days **Location** 1.75m NE

Hotel Premier Travel Inn Romford West, Whalebone Ln North, Chadwell Heath, ROMFORD ☎ 0870 9906450 40 en suite

BASILDON Map 05 TQ78

Basildon Clay Hill Ln, Kingswood SS16 5JP
☎ 01268 533297 🖷 01268 284163
e-mail: basildongc@onetel.net.uk
web: www.basildongolfclub.org.uk
18 holes, 6236yds, Par 72, SSS 70.
Course Designer A Cotton **Location** 1m S off A176
Phone for further details

Hotel ⌂ Innkeeper's Lodge Basildon/Wickford, Runwell Rd, WICKFORD ☎ 01268 769671 24 en suite

BENFLEET Map 05 TQ78

Boyce Hill Vicarage Hill, South Benfleet SS7 1PD
☎ 01268 793625 & 752565 🖷 01268 750497
e-mail: secretary@boycehillgolfclub.co.uk
web: www.boycehillgolfclub.co.uk
Hilly parkland with good views.
18 holes, 6003yds, Par 68, SSS 69, Course record 61.
Club membership 700.
Visitors Mon, Wed-Fri except BHs. Handicap certificate. Dress code. **Societies** Booking required. **Green Fees** £45 per 27/36 holes, £35 per 18 holes. **Prof** Graham Burroughs **Course Designer** James Braid **Facilities** **Location** 0.75m NE of Benfleet Station

Hotel ★★ 71% Balmoral Hotel, 34 Valkyrie Rd, Westcliff-on-Sea, SOUTHEND-ON-SEA
☎ 01702 342947 29 en suite

BILLERICAY Map 05 TQ69

The Burstead Tye Common Rd, Little Burstead CM12 9SS
☎ 01277 631171 🖷 01277 632766
18 holes, 6275yds, Par 71, SSS 70, Course record 69.
Course Designer Patrick Tallack **Location** M25 onto A127, off A176
Phone for further details

Hotel ★★★ 69% Chichester Hotel, Old London Rd, Wickford, BASILDON ☎ 01268 560555 2 en suite 32 annexe en suite

Stock Brook Golf & Country Club Queens Park Av, Stock CM12 0SP
☎ 01277 653616 & 650400 🖷 01277 633063
e-mail: events@stockbrook.com
web: www.stockbrook.com
Set in 250 acres of picturesque countryside the 27 holes comprise three undulating 9s, offering the challenge of water on a large number of holes. Any combination can be played, but the Stock and Brook courses make the 18-hole, 6750 yard championship course. There are extensive clubhouse facilities.
Stock & Brook Courses: 18 holes, 6728yds, Par 72, SSS 72, Course record 66.
Manor Course: 9 holes, 2997yds, Par 35.
Visitors Mon-Fri, Sat & Sun pm. Booking required. Handicap certificate. Dress code. **Societies** Booking required. **Green Fees** phone. **Prof** Craig Lawrence **Course Designer** Martin Gillet **Facilities**
Leisure hard tennis courts, heated indoor swimming pool, sauna, solarium, gymnasium, bowls. **Conf** facs Corporate Hospitality Days

Continued

Hotel ★★★★ 73% Marygreen Manor Hotel, London Rd, BRENTWOOD ☎ 01277 225252 4 en suite 40 annexe en suite

BRAINTREE Map 05 TL72

Braintree Kings Ln, Stisted CM77 8DD
☎ 01376 346079 🖷 01376 348677
e-mail: manager@braintreegolfclub.co.uk
web: www.braintreegolfclub.co.uk
Parkland with many rare mature trees. Good par 3s with the 14th - Devils Lair - regarded as one of the best in the county.
18 holes, 6228yds, Par 70, SSS 70, Course record 64.
Club membership 750.
Visitors Mon, Wed-Sat & BHs. Tue & Sun pm. Booking required. Handicap certificate. Dress code. **Societies** Booking required. **Green Fees** £45 per day, £35 per round, £60/£50 Sat, Sun & BHs. **Prof** Tony Parcell **Course Designer** Hawtree **Facilities** **Conf** Corporate Hospitality Days **Location** 1m E, off A120

Hotel ★★★ 65% White Hart Hotel, Bocking End, BRAINTREE ☎ 01376 321401 31 en suite

Unex Towerlands Panfield Rd CM7 5BJ
☎ 01376 326802 🖷 01376 552487
e-mail: info@towerlands.com
web: www.unextowerlands.com
Undulating, grassland course, nine holes with 18 tees.
9 holes, 5559yds, Par 68.
Club membership 250.
Visitors Mon-Sat & BHs. Sun pm. Booking required. Dress code. **Societies** Booking required. **Green Fees** phone. **Course Designer** G Shiels **Facilities** **Leisure** squash, gymnasium. **Location** On B1053

Hotel ★★★ 65% White Hart Hotel, Bocking End, BRAINTREE ☎ 01376 321401 31 en suite

BRENTWOOD Map 05 TQ59

Bentley Ongar Rd CM15 9SS
☎ 01277 373179 🖷 01277 375097
e-mail: info@bentleygolfclub.com
web: www.bentleygolfclub.com
Parkland with water hazards.
18 holes, 6703yds, Par 72, SSS 72.
Club membership 580.
Visitors Mon-Sun & BHs. Booking required. Handicap certificate. Dress code. **Societies** Booking required. **Green Fees** £27.50 per 18 holes, £40 Sat & Sun. **Prof** Nick Garrett **Course Designer** Howard SWann **Facilities** **Conf** Corporate Hospitality Days **Location** 3m NW on A128

Hotel ★★★ 71% Weald Park Hotel, Golf & Country Club, Coxtie Green Rd, South Weald, BRENTWOOD
☎ 01277 375101 32 annexe en suite

Hartswood King George's Playing Fields, Ingrave Rd CM14 5AE
☎ 01277 218850 🖷 01277 218850
Municipal parkland course, easy walking.
18 holes, 6192yds, Par 70, SSS 69, Course record 68.
Club membership 250.
Visitors contact club for details. Dress code. **Societies** Booking required. **Green Fees** £12.50, £17.50 Sat, Sun &

Continued

BHs. **Prof** Stephen Cole **Course Designer** H Cotton **Facilities** **Location** 0.75m SE of Brentwood town centre on A128 from A127

Hotel ★★★ 71% Weald Park Hotel, Golf & Country Club, Coxtie Green Rd, South Weald, BRENTWOOD ☎ 01277 375101 32 annexe en suite

Warley Park Magpie Ln, Little Warley CM13 3DX
☎ 01277 224891 01277 200679
e-mail: enquiries@warleyparkgc.co.uk
web: www.warleyparkgc.co.uk
Parkland with numerous water hazards, reasonable walking. There is also a golf practice ground.
1st & 2nd: 18 holes, 5985yds, Par 69, SSS 67, Course record 66.
1st & 3rd: 18 holes, 5925yds, Par 71, SSS 69, Course record 65.
2nd & 3rd: 18 holes, 5917yds, Par 70, SSS 69, Course record 65.
Club membership 800.
Visitors Mon-Wed except BHs. Booking required. Handicap certificate. Dress code. **Societies** Booking required. **Green Fees** £50 per day, £36 per round. **Prof** Kevin Smith **Course Designer** Reg Plumbridge **Facilities** by arrangement **Conf** facs Corporate Hospitality Days **Location** M25 junct 29, A127 E onto B186, 0.5m N

Hotel ★★★ 71% Weald Park Hotel, Golf & Country Club, Coxtie Green Rd, South Weald, BRENTWOOD ☎ 01277 375101 32 annexe en suite

Weald Park Hotel, Golf & Country Club Coxtie Green Rd, South Weald CM14 5RJ
☎ 01277 375101 01277 374888
e-mail: wealdpark@americangolf.uk.com
web: americangolf.com
18 holes, 6285yds, Par 71, SSS 70, Course record 65.
Course Designer Reg Plumbridge **Location** 3m from M25
Phone for further details

Hotel ★★★ 71% Weald Park Hotel, Golf & Country Club, Coxtie Green Rd, South Weald, BRENTWOOD ☎ 01277 375101 32 annexe en suite

BULPHAN Map 05 TQ68

Langdon Hills Lower Dunton Rd RM14 3TY
☎ 01268 548444 01268 490084
e-mail: info@golflangdon.co.uk
web: www.golflangdon.co.uk
Langdon & Bulphan Course: 18 holes, 6760yds, Par 72, SSS 72, Course record 67.
Bulphan & Horndon Course: 18 holes, 6537yds, Par 73, SSS 72.
Horndon & Langdon Course: 18 holes, 6279yds, Par 71, SSS 71.
Course Designer Howard Swan **Location** Off A13 onto B1007
Phone for further details

Hotel ★★★★ 73% Marygreen Manor Hotel, London Rd, BRENTWOOD ☎ 01277 225252 4 en suite 40 annexe en suite

BURNHAM-ON-CROUCH Map 05 TQ99

Burnham-on-Crouch Ferry Rd, Creeksea CM0 8PQ
☎ 01621 782282 01621 784489
e-mail: burnhamgolf@hotmail.com
Undulating meadowland riverside course, easy walking and stunning views. Challenging for all standards of player.
18 holes, 6056yds, Par 70, SSS 69, Course record 66.
Club membership 580.
Visitors Mon-Wed, Fri except BHs. Thu, Sat & Sun pm. Booking required. Handicap certificate. Dress code. **Societies** Booking required. **Green Fees** £36, £42 Sat & Sun. **Course Designer** Swan **Facilities** **Location** 1.25m W off B1010

CANEWDON Map 05 TQ99

Ballards Gore Gore Rd SS4 2DA
☎ 01702 258917 01702 258571
web: www.locallife.co.uk/ballardsgore
18 holes, 6874yds, Par 73, SSS 73, Course record 69.
Course Designer D & J J Caton **Location** 2m NE of Rochford
Phone for further details

Guest House ♦♦♦♦ Ilfracombe House Hotel, 9-13 Wilson Rd, SOUTHEND-ON-SEA ☎ 01702 351000 20 en suite

CANVEY ISLAND Map 05 TQ78

Castle Point Somnes Av SS8 9FG
☎ 01268 510830 & 511149 01268 511758
A flat seaside links and part parkland course with water hazards on 13 holes and views of the estuary and Hadleigh Castle. Always a test for any golfer when the wind starts to blow.
18 holes, 6176yds, Par 71, SSS 69, Course record 66.
Club membership 275.
Visitors Booking required Sat & Sun. **Societies** Booking required. **Green Fees** phone. **Prof** Steven Richardson **Facilities** **Conf** Corporate Hospitality Days **Location** SE of Basildon, A130 to Canvey Island

Hotel ★★★ 69% Chichester Hotel, Old London Rd, Wickford, BASILDON ☎ 01268 560555 2 en suite 32 annexe en suite

CHELMSFORD Map 05 TL70

Channels Belstead Farm Ln, Little Waltham CM3 3PT
☎ 01245 440005 01245 442032
e-mail: info@channelsgolf.co.uk
web: www.channelsgolf.co.uk
The Channels course is built on land from reclaimed gravel pits, 18 very exciting holes with plenty of lakes providing an excellent test of golf. Belsteads, a nine-hole course, is mainly flat but has three holes where water has to be negotiated.
Channels Course: 18 holes, 6402yds, Par 71, SSS 71, Course record 65.
Belsteads: 9 holes, 2467yds, Par 34, SSS 32.
Club membership 800.
Visitors Channels Course: booking required. Belsteads Course: Mon-Sun. **Societies** Booking required. **Green Fees** phone. **Prof** Ian Sinclair **Course Designer** Cotton & Swan **Facilities** **Leisure** fishing, 9 hole pitch & putt course.

Continued

Conf facs Corporate Hospitality Days **Location** 2m NE on A130

Channels

Hotel ★★★ 72% The County Hotel, Bar & Restaurant, Rainsford Rd, CHELMSFORD ☎ 01245 455700 54 en suite

Chelmsford Widford Rd CM2 9AP

☎ 01245 256483 🖹 01245 256483
e-mail: office@chelmsfordgc.co.uk
web: www.chelmsfordgc.co.uk

An undulating parkland course, hilly in parts, with three holes in woods and four difficult par 4s. From the reconstructed clubhouse there are fine views over the course and the wooded hills beyond.

18 holes, 5981yds, Par 68, SSS 69, Course record 61. Club membership 650.

Visitors Mon-Fri except BHs. Booking required. Handicap certificate. Dress code. **Societies** Booking required. **Green Fees** £40 per round. **Prof** Mark Welch **Course Designer** Tom Dunn **Facilities** **Location** 1.5m S of town centre off A12

Hotel ★★★ 72% Pontlands Park Country Hotel, West Hanningfield Rd, Great Baddow, CHELMSFORD ☎ 01245 476444 36 en suite

Regiment Way Back Ln, Little Waltham CM3 3PR

☎ 01245 362210 & 361100 🖹 01245 442032
e-mail: info@channelsgolf.co.uk
web: www.regimentway.co.uk

A nine-hole course with alternate tee positions, offering a par 64 18-hole course. Fully automatic tee and green irrigation plus excellent drainage ensure play at most times of the year. The course is challenging but at the same time can be forgiving.

9 holes, 4887yds, Par 65, SSS 64. Club membership 265.

Continued

Visitors Mon-Sun & BHs. **Societies** Booking required. **Green Fees** £15 per 18 holes, £11 per 9 holes. **Prof** David March, Mark Sharman **Course Designer** R Stubbings, R Clark **Facilities** **Conf** facs Corporate Hospitality Days **Location** off A130 N of Chelmsford

Hotel Premier Travel Inn Chelmsford (Borehamwood), Main Rd, Boreham, CHELMSFORD ☎ 0870 9906394 78 en suite

CHIGWELL Map 05 TQ49

Chigwell High Rd IG7 5BH

☎ 020 8500 2059 🖹 020 8501 3410
e-mail: info@chigwellgolfclub.co.uk
web: www.chigwellgolfclub.co.uk

A course of high quality, mixing meadowland with parkland. For those who believe 'all Essex is flat' the undulating nature of Chigwell will be a refreshing surprise. The greens are excellent and the fairways tight with mature trees.

18 holes, 6296yds, Par 71, SSS 70, Course record 66. Club membership 800.

Visitors Mon, Wed & Thu. Tue pm. Booking required. Handicap certificate. Dress code. **Societies** Booking required. **Green Fees** £45 per day, £35 per round. **Prof** James Fuller **Course Designer** Hawtree, Taylor **Facilities** **Conf** facs Corporate Hospitality Days **Location** 0.5m S on A113

Hotel Premier Travel Inn Romford Central, Mercury Gardens, ROMFORD ☎ 08701 977220 64 en suite

Woolston Manor Abridge Rd IG7 6BX

☎ 020 8500 2549 🖹 020 8501 5452
e-mail: golf@woolstonmanor.co.uk
web: www.woolstonmanor.co.uk

Woolston Manor was once owned by William the Conqueror and is mentioned in the Domesday Book. The course, in 200 acres of Essex countryside, built to USGA specifications with superb irrigation, generous teeing areas, dramatic bunker shapes and water coming into play on twelve holes.

Manor Course: 18 holes, 6510yards, Par 72, SSS 72, Course record 67. Club membership 465.

Visitors Booking required 2 days in advance. **Societies** Tue-Thu. **Green Fees** phone. **Prof** Paul Eady **Course Designer** Neil Coles **Facilities** **Leisure** outdoor and indoor heated swimming pools, sauna, solarium, gymnasium. **Conf** facs Corporate Hospitality Days **Location** M11 junct 5, 1m

Hotel Premier Travel Inn Romford West, Whalebone Ln North, Chadwell Heath, ROMFORD ☎ 0870 9906450 40 en suite

CHIGWELL ROW Map 05 TQ49

Hainault Forest Romford Rd, Chigwell Row IG7 4QW
☎ 020 8500 2131 📠 020 8501 5196
e-mail: info@essexgolfcentres.com
web: www.essexgolfcentres.com
No 1 Course: 18 holes, 5687yds, Par 70, SSS 67, Course record 65.
No 2 Course: 18 holes, 6238yds, Par 71, SSS 71.
Course Designer Taylor & Hawtree **Location** 0.5m S on A1112
Phone for further details

CLACTON-ON-SEA Map 05 TM11

Clacton West Rd CO15 1AJ
☎ 01255 421919 📠 01255 424602
e-mail: secretary@clactongolfclub.com
web: www.clactongolfclub.com
The course covers 110 acres and runs alongside the sea wall and then inland. Easy walking layout, part open and part woodland. The course is well bunkered and a unique feature is the fleets, ditches and streams that cross and border many of the fairways, demanding accuracy and good striking.
18 holes, 6448yds, Par 71, SSS 71, Course record 67.
Club membership 650.
Visitors Mon-Fri & BHs. Booking required. Handicap certificate. Dress code. **Societies** Booking required. **Green Fees** £35 per day, £25 per round, £45/£30 Sat, Sun & BHs. **Prof** SJ Levermore **Course Designer** Jack White **Facilities** **Leisure** practice nets available. **Location** 1.25m SW of town centre

Hotel ★★ 68% Esplanade Hotel, 27-29 Marine Pde East, CLACTON-ON-SEA ☎ 01255 220450 29 en suite

COLCHESTER Map 05 TL92

Birch Grove Layer Rd, Kingsford CO2 0HS
☎ 01206 734276
web: www.rosmar.demon.co.uk/index.htm
A pretty, undulating course surrounded by woodland - small but challenging with excellent greens. Challenging 6th hole cut through woodland with water hazards and out of bounds.
9 holes, 4532yds, Par 66, SSS 63, Course record 66.
Club membership 250.
Visitors Mon-Sun & BHs. Dress code. **Societies** Booking required. **Green Fees** £14 per 18 holes, £10 per 9 holes. **Course Designer** LA Marston **Facilities** **Conf** facs Corporate Hospitality Days **Location** 2.5m S on B1026

Colchester Braiswick CO4 5AU
☎ 01206 853396 📠 01206 852698
e-mail: colchester.golf@btinternet.com
web: www.colchestergolfclub.fsnet.co.uk
Fairly flat yet scenic parkland, with tree-lined fairways and small copses. Mainly level walking.
18 holes, 6347yds, Par 70, SSS 70, Course record 63.
Club membership 700.
Visitors contact club for details. **Societies** Booking required. **Green Fees** phone. **Prof** Mark Angel **Course Designer** James Braid **Facilities** **Location** 1.5m NW of town centre on B1508 (West Bergholt Rd)

Lexden Wood Bakers Ln CO3 4AU
☎ 01206 843333 📠 01206 854775
web: www.lexdenwood.com
Challenging 18-hole, parkland course with many water features. A mix of undulating and flat land with testing greens. Also a nine-hole pitch and putt course, and a floodlit driving range.
18 holes, 5500yds, Par 67, Course record 63.
Club membership 500.
Visitors Mon-Sun & BHs. Booking required. Dress code. **Societies** welcome. **Green Fees** £22, £30 Sat, Sun & BHs, £25 after 11am. **Prof** Phil Grice **Course Designer** J Johnson **Facilities** **Leisure** 9 hole par 3. **Conf** Corporate Hospitality Days **Location** A12 towards Colchester Central, follow tourist signs

Hotel ★★★ 74% The Rose and Crown Hotel, East St, COLCHESTER ☎ 01206 866677 38 en suite

Stoke-by-Nayland Keepers Ln, Leavenheath CO6 4PZ
☎ 01206 262836 📠 01206 263356
e-mail: mary.saward@stokebynayland.com
web: www.stokebynaylandclub.co.uk
Two 18-hole championship courses, the Gainsborough and the Constable. Created in the 1970s, both courses are well established and feature mature woodland, undulating fairways and picturesque water features which include 4 large natural lakes. The 18th hole on both courses presents a challenging and spectacular finish with tee-offs over the largest of the lakes to a green resting in front of the clubhouse. The courses are best between March and October but are open all year round and offer winter buggy paths on the Gainsborough course.

Gainsborough Course: 18 holes, 6498yds, Par 72, SSS 71, Course record 66.
Constable Course: 18 holes, 6544yds, Par 72, SSS 71, Course record 67.
Club membership 1200.
Visitors Mon-Sun & BHs. Booking required. Dress code. **Societies** Booking required. **Green Fees** £45 per day, £28.50 per round, £55/£38.50 Sat & Sun. **Prof** Kevin Lovelock **Course Designer** Howard Swan **Facilities** **Leisure** heated indoor swimming pool, squash, fishing, sauna, solarium, gymnasium. **Conf** facs Corporate Hospitality Days **Location** 1.5m NW of Stoke-by-Nayland on B1068

Hotel ★★★ Maison Talbooth, Stratford Rd, DEDHAM ☎ 01206 322367 10 en suite

EARLS COLNE Map 05 TL82

Colne Valley Station Rd CO6 2LT
☎ 01787 224343 & 220770 🖷 01787 224126
e-mail: info@colnevalleygolfclub.co.uk
web: www.colnevalleygolfclub.co.uk
Opened in 1991, this surprisingly mature parkland course belies its tender years. Natural water hazards, and well-defined bunkers, along with USGA standard greens offer year round playability, and a stimulating test for all abilities.
18 holes, 6301yds, Par 70, SSS 71, Course record 68.
Club membership 500.
Visitors Mon-Fri. Booking required. Dress code. **Societies** Booking required. **Green Fees** £25 per 18 holes. **Prof** Peter Garlick **Course Designer** Howard Swan **Facilities** **Leisure** fishing. **Conf** facs Corporate Hospitality Days **Location** Off A1124

Hotel ★★★ 70% White Hart Hotel, Market End, COGGESHALL ☎ 01376 561654 18 en suite

Essex Golf & Country Club CO6 2NS
☎ 01787 224466 🖷 01787 224410
e-mail: essexgolfops@theclubcompany.com
web: www.the clubcompany.com
Created on the site of a World War II airfield, this challenging course contains 10 lakes and strategically placed bunkering. Also a nine-hole course and a variety of leisure facilities.
County Course: 18 holes, 7019yds, Par 73, SSS 73, Course record 67.
Garden Course: 9 holes, 2190yds, Par 34, SSS 34.
Club membership 700.
Visitors Mon-Sun & BHs. Booking required. Dress code. **Societies** Booking required. **Green Fees** Country £26 per round, £31 Sat & Sun. Garden £15 per day. **Prof** Lee Cocker, Paul Grotier **Course Designer** Reg Plumbridge **Facilities** **Leisure** hard tennis courts, heated indoor swimming pool, fishing, sauna, solarium, gymnasium, video golf tuition studio. **Conf** facs Corporate Hospitality Days **Location** Signed off A120 onto B1024

Hotel ★★★ 70% White Hart Hotel, Market End, COGGESHALL ☎ 01376 561654 18 en suite

EPPING Map 05 TL40

Epping Fluxs Ln CM16 7PE
☎ 01992 572282 🖷 01992 575512
e-mail: neilsjoberg@hotmail.com
web: www.eppinggolfcourse.org.uk
Undulating parkland with extensive views over Essex countryside and excellent fairways. Incorporates many water features designed to use every club in the bag. Some driveable par 4s, and the spectacular 18th Happy Valley is rarely birdied. The new clubhouse has a bar and restaurant.
18 holes, 5405yds, Par 68, SSS 65, Course record 67.
Club membership 350.
Visitors Mon-Fri. Booking required Sat, Sun & BHs. Dress code. **Societies** Booking required. **Green Fees** £20 per day, £14 per round, £23/£17 Sat, Sun & BHs. **Course Designer** Sjoberg **Facilities** **Leisure** Petanque. **Conf** facs Corporate Hospitality Days **Location** M11 junct 7, 2.5m on B1393, left in Epping High Rd towards station

Continued

Hotel Travelodge Harlow North Weald, A414 Eastbound, Tylers Green, North Weald, HARLOW ☎ 08700 850 950 60 en suite

Nazeing Middle St, Nazeing EN9 2LW
☎ 01992 893798 🖷 01992 893882
e-mail: secretary@nazeinggolfclub.co.uk
Parkland course built with American sand-based greens and tees and five strategically placed lakes. One of the most notable holes is the difficult par 3 13th with out of bounds and a large lake coming into play.
18 holes, 6617yds, Par 72, SSS 72, Course record 68.
Club membership 400.
Visitors Mon-Fri. Sat, Sun & BHs pm. Booking required. Dress code. **Societies** Booking required. **Green Fees** Mon £18 per round, Tue-Thu £22, Fri £25, £30 Sat, Sun & BHs. **Prof** Robert Green **Course Designer** M Gillete **Facilities** **Conf** facs Corporate Hospitality Days **Location** M25 junct 26, near Waltham Abbey

Hotel ★★★★ 71% Waltham Abbey Marriott Hotel, Old Shire Ln, WALTHAM ABBEY ☎ 01992 717170 162 en suite

FRINTON-ON-SEA Map 05 TM22

Frinton 1 The Esplanade CO13 9EP
☎ 01255 674618 🖷 01255 682450
e-mail: frintongolf@lineone.net
web: www.frintongolfclub.com
Deceptive, flat seaside links course providing fast, firm and undulating greens that will test the best putters, and tidal ditches that cross many of the fairways, requiring careful placement of shots. Its open character means that every shot has to be evaluated with both wind strength and direction in mind. Easy walking.

Long Course: 18 holes, 6265yds, Par 71, SSS 70, Course record 63.
Short Course: 9 holes, 3062yds, Par 60, SSS 60.
Club membership 850.
Visitors contact club for details. Handicap certificate. Dress code. **Societies** Booking required. **Green Fees** Long £32, £38 Sat & Sun. Short £9.50/£15. **Prof** Peter Taggart **Course Designer** Willy Park Jnr, Harry Colt **Facilities** by arrangement by arrangement **Leisure** indoor practice nets. **Conf** facs Corporate Hospitality Days **Location** SW of town centre

Hotel Premier Travel Inn Clacton-On-Sea, Crown Green Roundabout, Colchester Rd, Weeley, CLACTON-ON-SEA ☎ 08701 977064 40 en suite

Continued

Additional hotel ★★ 68% Hotel Continental, 28-29 Marine Pde, Dovercourt, HARWICH ☎ 01255 551298 🖹 01255 551698 14 en suite

GOSFIELD Map 05 TL72

Gosfield Lake The Manor House, Hall Dr CO9 1RZ
☎ 01787 474747 🖹 01787 476044
e-mail: gosfieldlakegc@btconnect.com
web: www.gosfield-lake-golf-club.co.uk
Parkland with bunkers, lakes and water hazards. Designed by Sir Henry Cotton, Howard Swan. Also a nine-hole course; ideal for beginners and improvers.
Lakes Course: 18 holes, 6615yds, Par 72, SSS 72, Course record 68.
Meadows Course: 9 holes, 4180yds, Par 64, SSS 61.
Club membership 650.
Visitors Mon-Fri & BHs. Sat & Sun pm. Booking required. Handicap certificate for Lakes course. Dress code. **Societies** Booking required. **Green Fees** Lakes £30 per round, Meadows £15 per round. **Prof** Richard Wheeler **Course Designer** Henry Cotton, Howard Swan **Facilities** **Leisure** sauna. **Conf** Corporate Hospitality Days **Location** 1m W of Gosfield off B1017

Hotel ★★★ 65% White Hart Hotel, Bocking End, BRAINTREE ☎ 01376 321401 31 en suite

HARLOW Map 05 TL41

Canons Brook Elizabeth Way CM19 5BE
☎ 01279 421482 🖹 01279 626393
web: www.canonsbrook.com
Challenging parkland course designed by Henry Cotton. Accuracy is the key requiring straight driving from the tees, especially on the par 5 11th to fly a gap with out of bounds left and right before setting up the shot to the green.
18 holes, 6800yds, Par 73, SSS 72, Course record 65.
Club membership 650.
Visitors Mon-Fri. Dress code. **Societies** Booking required. **Green Fees** phone. **Prof** Alan McGinn **Course Designer** Henry Cotton **Facilities** **Location** M11 junct 7, 3m NW

Hotel ★★★ 60% Corus hotel Harlow, Mulberry Green, Old Harlow, HARLOW ☎ 0870 609 6146 55 annexe en suite

North Weald Rayley Ln, North Weald CM16 6AR
☎ 01992 522118 🖹 01992 522881
e-mail: info@northwealdgolfclub.co.uk
web: www.northwealdgolfclub.co.uk
Although only opened in November 1995, the blend of lakes and meadowland give this testing course an air of maturity.
18 holes, 6377yds, Par 71, SSS 71, Course record 64.
Club membership 500.
Visitors Mon-Fri. Sat, Sun & BHs pm. Dress code. **Societies** Booking required. **Green Fees** £30 per day, £20 per round, £30 per round Sat & Sun. **Prof** David Rawlings **Course Designer** David Williams **Facilities** **Leisure** fishing, gymnasium. **Conf** facs Corporate Hospitality Days **Location** M11 exit 7, A414 2m towards Chipping Ongar

Hotel Travelodge Harlow North Weald, A414 Eastbound, Tylers Green, North Weald, HARLOW ☎ 08700 850 950 60 en suite

HARWICH Map 05 TM23

Harwich & Dovercourt Station Rd, Parkeston CO12 4NZ
☎ 01255 503616 🖹 01255 503323
Flat parkland with easy walking. The 234yd par 3 9th hole to an invisible green is a real experience.
9 holes, 5900yds, Par 70, SSS 69, Course record 59.
Club membership 420.
Visitors contact club for details. Handicap certificate. Dress code. **Societies** Booking required. **Green Fees** £20 per 18 holes, £10 per 9 holes. **Facilities** by arrangement **Conf** Corporate Hospitality Days **Location** Off A120 near Ferry Terminal

Hotel ★★★ 76% The Pier at Harwich, The Quay, HARWICH ☎ 01255 241212 7 en suite 7 annexe en suite

INGRAVE Map 05 TQ69

Thorndon Park CM13 3RH
☎ 01277 810345 🖹 01277 810645
e-mail: office@thorndonpark.com
web: www.thorndonparkgolfclub.com
Course built on clay substructure and playable even at the wettest time of the year. Holes stand on their own surrounded by mature oaks, some of which are more than 700 years old. The lake in the centre of the course provides both a challenge and a sense of peace and tranquillity. The Palladian Thorndon Hall, site of the old clubhouse, is the magnificent backdrop to the closing hole.
18 holes, 6512yds, Par 71, SSS 71, Course record 68.
Club membership 600.
Visitors Mon, Tue, Thu & Fri. Booking required. Handicap certificate. Dress code. **Societies** Booking required. **Green Fees** phone. **Prof** Brian White **Course Designer** Colt, Alison **Facilities** **Conf** Corporate Hospitality Days **Location** W side of village off A128

Hotel ★★★ 71% Weald Park Hotel, Golf & Country Club, Coxtie Green Rd, South Weald, BRENTWOOD ☎ 01277 375101 32 annexe en suite

LOUGHTON Map 05 TQ49

High Beech Wellington Hill IG10 4AH
☎ 020 8508 7323
9 holes, 1477, Par 27, Course record 25.
Location M25 junct 26
Phone for further details

Continued

Loughton Clays Ln, Debden Green IG10 2RZ
☎ 020 8502 2923
Nine-hole parkland course on the edge of Epping Forest. A good test of golf.
9 holes, 4652yds, Par 66, SSS 63, Course record 69.
Club membership 150.
Visitors Mon-Sun & BHs. Booking required Sun & BHs. **Societies** Booking required. **Green Fees** £13 per 18 holes, £8 per 9 holes, £15/£9 Sat, Sun & BHs. **Facilities** **Location** 1.5m SE of Theydon Bois

Hotel ★★★★ 71% Waltham Abbey Marriott Hotel, Old Shire Ln, WALTHAM ABBEY ☎ 01992 717170 162 en suite

MALDON Map 05 TL80

Forrester Park Beckingham Rd, Great Totham CM9 8EA
☎ 01621 891406 🖹 01621 891406
Set in undulating parkland in the Essex countryside and commanding some beautiful views across the River Blackwater. Accuracy is more important than distance and judgement more important than strength on this traditional club course. There is a separate 10-acre practice ground.
18 holes, 6073yds, Par 71, SSS 69, Course record 69.
Club membership 1000.
Visitors Mon-Sun & BHs. Booking required. Dress code. **Societies** Booking required. **Green Fees** phone. **Prof** Gary Pike **Course Designer** TR Forrester-Muir **Facilities** **Leisure** hard tennis courts, indoor swimming pool. **Conf** facs Corporate Hospitality Days **Location** 3m NE of Maldon off B1022

Hotel ★★ Benbridge Hotel, Holloway Rd, The Square, Heybridge, MALDON ☎ 01621 857666 & 853667 🖹 01621 841966 13 en suite

Maldon Beeleigh, Langford CM9 6LL
☎ 01621 853212 🖹 01621 855232
e-mail: maldon.golf@virgin.net
Flat parkland in a triangle of land bounded by the River Chelmer and the Blackwater Canal. Small greens provide a test for iron shots and the short game. Testing par 3 14th (166yds) demanding particular accuracy to narrow green guarded by bunkers and large trees.
9 holes, 6253yds, Par 71, SSS 70, Course record 66.
Club membership 380.
Visitors Mon, Wed-Fri. Booking required. Handicap certificate. Dress code. **Societies** welcome. **Green Fees** £25 per day, £18 per round. **Prof** John Edgington **Course Designer** Thompson of Felixstowe **Facilities** **Location** 1m NW off B1019

Hotel ★★★ 72% Pontlands Park Country Hotel, West Hanningfield Rd, Great Baddow, CHELMSFORD ☎ 01245 476444 36 en suite

ORSETT Map 05 TQ68

Orsett Brentwood Rd RM16 3DS
☎ 01375 891352 🖹 01375 892471
e-mail: enquiries@orsettgolfclub.co.uk
web: www.club-noticeboard.co.uk/orsett
A very good test of golf - this heathland course with its sandy soil is quick drying and provides easy walking. Close to the Thames estuary it is seldom calm and the main hazards are the prevailing wind and thick gorse. Any slight deviation can be exaggerated by the wind and result in a ball lost in the gorse. The clubhouse has been modernised to very high standards.
18 holes, 6614yds, Par 72, SSS 72, Course record 65.
Club membership 770.
Visitors Mon-Fri. Booking required. Handicap certificate. **Societies** Booking required. **Green Fees** phone. **Prof** Paul Joiner **Course Designer** James Braid **Facilities** **Leisure** coaching. **Conf** Corporate Hospitality Days **Location** Junct A13 & A128, S towards Chadwell St Mary

PURLEIGH Map 05 TL80

Three Rivers Stow Rd, Cold Norton CM3 6RR
☎ 01621 828631 🖹 01621 828060
web: www.threeriversclub.com
Set in landscaped wooded parkland, Kings Course is fully matured with 18-holes, affording good valley views over the Crouch, Blackwater and Roach rivers that give the club its name. With ponds and dog-legs among the challenges it is ideal for seasoned golfers. The Jubilee Course offers an alternative in both style and challenge with all weather tees and greens built to USGA specification.
Kings Course: 18 holes, 6403yds, Par 72, SSS 71, Course record 66.
Jubilee Course: 18 holes, 4501yds, Par 64, SSS 62.
Club membership 900.
Visitors Mon-Sun & BHs. Booking required. Dress code. **Societies** Booking required. **Green Fees** Kings £22 per 18 holes, £28 Sat, Sun & BHs. Jubilee £11.50/£13.50. **Prof** Kevin Clark **Course Designer** Hawtree **Facilities** **Leisure** gymnasium, video swing analysis centre. **Conf** facs Corporate Hospitality Days **Location** 2.5m from South Woodham Ferrers

Hotel ★★★ 72% Pontlands Park Country Hotel, West Hanningfield Rd, Great Baddow, CHELMSFORD ☎ 01245 476444 36 en suite

ROCHFORD Map 05 TQ89

Rochford Hundred Hall Rd SS4 1NW
☎ 01702 544302 🖹 01702 541343
e-mail: admin@rochfordhundredgolfclub.co.uk
Parkland with ponds and ditches as natural hazards.
18 holes, 6292yds, Par 72, SSS 71, Course record 64.
Club membership 800.
Visitors Mon-Fri except BHs. Booking required. Handicap certificate. Dress code. **Societies** Booking required. **Green Fees** £45 per day, £35 per round. **Prof** Graham Hill **Course Designer** James Braid **Facilities** **Location** W on B1013

Guest House ♦♦♦♦ Ilfracombe House Hotel, 9-13 Wilson Rd, SOUTHEND-ON-SEA ☎ 01702 351000 20 en suite

SAFFRON WALDEN Map 05 TL53

Saffron Walden Windmill Hill CB10 1BX
☎ 01799 522786 🖹 01799 520313
e-mail: office@swgc.com
web: swgc.com
Undulating parkland in the former deer park of Audley End House. Fine views over rolling countryside. Two par 3 signature holes, the 5th and 18th.
18 holes, 6606yds, Par 72, SSS 72, Course record 63.
Club membership 950.
Visitors Mon-Fri except BHs. Handicap certificate. Dress

Continued

code. **Societies** welcome. **Green Fees** £50 per day, £40 per 18 holes. **Prof** Philip Davis **Facilities** ⊗ Ⅲ ⊾ ☕ ♀ ⛺ ⊟ ✎ ⛟ ✓ ⚐ **Conf** Corporate Hospitality Days **Location** N side of town centre off B184

Hotel ★★★ 69% The Crown House, GREAT CHESTERFORD ☎ 01799 530515 8 en suite 14 annexe en suite

SOUTHEND-ON-SEA Map 05 TQ88

Belfairs Eastwood Rd North, Leigh on Sea SS9 4LR
☎ 01702 525345 & 520202
web: www.southend.gov.uk
Municipal parkland course. Tight second half through thick woods, easy walking.
18 holes, 5840yds, Par 70, SSS 68, Course record 68.
Club membership 350.
Visitors Mon-Sun & BHs. Booking required. Dress code. **Societies** Booking required. **Green Fees** £12 per 18 holes, £17.60 Sat, Sun & BHs. ⊘ **Prof** Steve Spittles **Course Designer** H Colt **Facilities** ⊗ by arrangement Ⅲ by arrangement ☕ ⊟ ⚐ ✓ **Leisure** hard tennis courts. **Location** Off A127/A13

Hotel ★★ 71% Balmoral Hotel, 34 Valkyrie Rd, Westcliff-on-Sea, SOUTHEND-ON-SEA
☎ 01702 342947 29 en suite

Thorpe Hall Thorpe Hall Av, Thorpe Bay SS1 3AT
☎ 01702 582205 🖷 01702 584498
e-mail: sec@thorpehallgc.co.uk
web: www.thorpehallgc.co.uk
Tree-lined parkland with narrow fairways, where placement rather than length is essential.
18 holes, 6290yds, Par 71, SSS 70, Course record 62.
Club membership 995.
Visitors Mon-Fri except BHs. Booking required. Handicap certificate. Dress code. **Societies** Booking required. **Green Fees** £40 per day/round. ⊘ **Prof** Bill McColl **Course Designer** Various **Facilities** ⊗ Ⅲ by arrangement ⊾ ☕ ♀ ⛺ ⊟ ✎ ⛟ ✓ **Leisure** squash, sauna, snooker room. **Conf** facs **Location** 2m E off A13

Hotel ★★ 71% Balmoral Hotel, 34 Valkyrie Rd, Westcliff-on-Sea, SOUTHEND-ON-SEA
☎ 01702 342947 29 en suite

SOUTH OCKENDON Map 05 TQ58

Belhus Park Belhus Park RM15 4QR
☎ 01708 854260 🖷 01708 854260
18 holes, 5589yds, Par 69, SSS 68, Course record 67.
Course Designer Capability Brown **Location** Off B1335, brown tourist signs to course
Phone for further details

Hotel ⌂ Hotel Ibis Thurrock, Weston Av, WEST THURROCK ☎ 01708 686000 102 en suite

Top Meadow Fen Ln, North Ockendon RM14 3PR
☎ 01708 852239
e-mail: info@topmeadow.co.uk
web: www.topmeadow.co.uk
18 holes, 6348yds, Par 72, SSS 71, Course record 68.
Course Designer Burns, Stock **Location** M25 junct 29, A127 towards Southend, B186 towards Ockendon
Phone for further details

Hotel ⌂ Travelodge Brentwood East Horndon, EAST HORNDON ☎ 08700 850 950 45 en suite

STANFORD LE HOPE Map 05 TQ68

St Clere's Hall London Rd SS17 0LX
☎ 01375 361565 🖷 01375 361565
18 holes, 6474yds, Par 72, SSS 71, Course record 71.
Course Designer A Stiff **Location** 5m from M25 on A13, Stanford turn towards Linford, St Clere on left
Phone for further details

STAPLEFORD ABBOTTS Map 05 TQ59

Stapleford Abbotts Horsemanside, Tysea Hill RM4 1JU
☎ 01708 381108 🖷 01708 386345
e-mail: staplefordabbotts@americangolf.uk.com
web: www.staplefordabbotts@americangolf.co.uk
Abbotts Course: 18 holes, 6501yds, Par 72, SSS 71.
Priors Course: 18 holes, 5735yds, Par 70, SSS 69.
Course Designer Henry Cotton, Howard Swan **Location** 1m E of Stapleford Abbotts, off B175
Phone for further details

Hotel ★★★★ 73% Marygreen Manor Hotel, London Rd, BRENTWOOD ☎ 01277 225252 4 en suite 40 annexe en suite

STOCK Map 05 TQ69

Crondon Park Stock Rd CM4 9DP
☎ 01277 841115 🖷 01277 841356
e-mail: paul@crondon.com
web: www.crondon.com
Undulating parkland with many water hazards, set in the Crondon valley.
18 holes, 6585yards, Par 72, SSS 71, Course record 67.
Club membership 700.
Visitors Mon-Fri. Sat & Sun pm. Booking required. **Societies** Booking required. **Green Fees** phone. **Prof** Chris Wood, Freddie Sunderland **Course Designer** M Gillet **Facilities** ⊗ Ⅲ ⊾ ☕ ♀ ⛺ ⛟ ✓ ⚐ **Conf** facs Corporate Hospitality Days **Location** On B1007, between Stock

Hotel ★★★★ 73% Marygreen Manor Hotel, London Rd, BRENTWOOD ☎ 01277 225252 4 en suite 40 annexe en suite

THEYDON BOIS Map 05 TQ49

Theydon Bois Theydon Rd CM16 4EH
☎ 01992 812460 & 813054 🖷 01992 815602
e-mail: theydonboisgolf@btconnect.com
The original nine holes built into Epping Forest were later extended to 18 holes, which are well-bunkered. The old nine in the Forest are short and have two bunkers between them, but even so a wayward shot can be among the trees. The autumn colours here are truly magnificent.

Continued

18 holes, 5490yds, Par 68, SSS 67, Course record 64.
Club membership 600.
Visitors Mon-Wed & Fri except BHs. After 2pm Sat & Sun. Dress code. **Societies** Booking required. **Green Fees** £30 per round. **Prof** R Hall **Course Designer** James Braid **Facilities** **Location** M25 junct 26, 2m

Hotel Travelodge Harlow North Weald, A414 Eastbound, Tylers Green, North Weald, HARLOW ☎ 08700 850 950 60 en suite

TOLLESHUNT KNIGHTS Map 05 TL91

Five Lakes Hotel, Golf, Country Club & Spa Colchester Rd CM9 8HX
☎ 01621 868888 & 862426 📠 01621 869696
e-mail: golfoffice@fivelakes.co.uk
web: www.fivelakes.co.uk
Set in 320 acres, the two 18-hole courses both offer their own particular challenges. The Lakes, a PGA championship course, offers generous fairways with water features. The Links has narrow fairways and strategically placed bunkers.

Links Course: 18 holes, 6181yds, Par 71, SSS 70, Course record 67.
Lakes Course: 18 holes, 6751yds, Par 72, SSS 72, Course record 63.
Club membership 430.
Visitors Mon-Sun & BHs. Booking required. Dress code. **Societies** Booking required. **Green Fees** phone. **Prof** Gary Carter **Course Designer** Neil Coles **Facilities** **Leisure** hard tennis courts, heated indoor swimming pool, squash, sauna, solarium, gymnasium, snooker, badminton, fitness studio. **Conf** facs Corporate Hospitality Days **Location** 1.75m NE on B1026, 15 mins from A12 Kelvedon exit. Brown tourist signs

Hotel ★★★★ 73% Five Lakes Resort, Colchester Rd, TOLLESHUNT KNIGHTS ☎ 01621 868888 114 en suite 80 annexe en suite

TOOT HILL Map 05 TL50

Toot Hill School Rd CM5 9PU
☎ 01277 365523 📠 01277 364509
Pleasant course with several water hazards and sand greens.
18 holes, 6053yds, Par 70, SSS 69, Course record 65.
Club membership 400.
Visitors contact club for details. Dress code. **Societies** Booking required. **Green Fees** £25 per round, £30 Sat & Sun. **Prof** Mark Bishop **Course Designer** Martin Gillett **Facilities** **Conf** facs **Location** 7m SE of Harlow off A414

Hotel ★★★ 60% Corus hotel Harlow, Mulberry Green, Old Harlow, HARLOW ☎ 0870 609 6146 55 annexe en suite

WITHAM Map 05 TL81

Benton Hall Golf & Country Club Wickham Hill CM8 3LH
☎ 01376 502454 📠 01376 521050
e-mail: benton.retail@theclubcompany.com
web: www.theclubcompany.com
Set in rolling countryside surrounded by dense woodland, this challenging course provides a severe test even to the best golfers. The River Blackwater dominates the front nine and natural lakes come into play on five other holes. A multi-million pound refurbishment of the clubhouse in June 2006 incorporated health and fitness facilities.

18 holes, 6574yds, Par 72, SSS 72, Course record 64.
Club membership 600.
Visitors Mon-Sun & BHs. Booking required. Dress code. **Societies** Booking required. **Green Fees** phone. **Prof** Colin Fairweather **Course Designer** Alan Walker, Charles Cox **Facilities** **Leisure** heated indoor swimming pool, sauna, gymnasium, 9 hole par 3 course. **Conf** facs Corporate Hospitality Days **Location** Off A12 at Witham, signed

Hotel ★★★ 65% White Hart Hotel, Bocking End, BRAINTREE ☎ 01376 321401 31 en suite

WOODHAM WALTER Map 05 TL80

Bunsay Downs Little Baddow Rd CM9 6RU
☎ 01245 222648 📠 01245 223989
Attractive 9-hole public course, challenging for all abilities. Also undulating and lengthy par 3 course.
9 holes, 2932yds, Par 70, SSS 68.
Badgers: 9 holes, 1319yds, Par 54.
Club membership 400.
Visitors Mon-Sun & BHs. Dress code. **Societies** Booking required. **Green Fees** £13 per 18 holes, £15 Sat & Sun. **Prof** Henry Roblin **Course Designer** John Durham **Facilities** **Location** 2m from Danbury on A414, signed

Hotel ★★★ 72% The County Hotel, Bar & Restaurant, Rainsford Rd, CHELMSFORD ☎ 01245 455700 54 en suite

Continued

Warren CM9 6RW
☎ 01245 223258 🖹 01245 223989
e-mail: enquiries@thewarrengolfclub.co.uk
web: www.warrengolfclub.co.uk
Attractive parkland with natural hazards and good views.
18 holes, 6263yds, Par 70, SSS 70, Course record 62. Club membership 765.
Visitors Wed, Sat & Sun pm. Booking required. **Societies** Mon, Tue, Thu & Fri. Booking required. **Green Fees** phone. **Prof** David Brooks **Facilities** **Location** 0.5m SW

Hotel ★★★ 72% The County Hotel, Bar & Restaurant, Rainsford Rd, CHELMSFORD ☎ 01245 455700 54 en suite

GLOUCESTERSHIRE

ALMONDSBURY Map 03 ST68

Bristol St Swithins Park, Blackhorse Hill BS10 7TP
☎ 01454 620000 🖹 01454 202700
e-mail: enquiries@bristolgolfclub.co.uk
web: www.bistolgolfclub.co.uk
An undulating course set in 200 acres of parkland with magnificent views of the Severn estuary and surrounding countryside.
18 holes, 6111yds, Par 70, SSS 69, Course record 63. Club membership 800.
Visitors Mon-Sun & BHs. Booking required. Dress code. **Societies** welcome. **Green Fees** £28 per 18 holes, £32 Sat, Sun & BHs. **Prof** Jon Palmer **Course Designer** Pierson **Facilities** **Leisure** par 3 academy course. **Conf** facs Corporate Hospitality Days **Location** M5 junct 17, 100yds

Hotel ★★★ 66% Henbury Lodge Hotel, Station Rd, Henbury, BRISTOL ☎ 0117 950 2615 12 en suite 9 annexe en suite

CHELTENHAM Map 03 SO92

Cotswold Hills Ullenwood GL53 9QT
☎ 01242 515264 🖹 01242 515317
e-mail: contactus@cotswoldhills-golfclub.com
web: www.cotswoldhills-golfclub.com
A gently undulating course with open aspects and views of the Cotswolds.
18 holes, 6557yds, Par 72, SSS 71, Course record 67. Club membership 750.
Visitors contact club for details. Handicap certificate. Dress code. **Societies** Booking required. **Green Fees** £33 per day, £38 Sat, Sun & BHs. **Prof** James Latham **Course Designer** MD Little **Facilities** **Conf** Corporate Hospitality Days **Location** 3m SE on A435

Hotel ★★★★ 65% Cheltenham Park Hotel, Cirencester Rd, Charlton Kings, CHELTENHAM ☎ 01242 222021 33 en suite 110 annexe en suite

Lilley Brook Cirencester Rd, Charlton Kings GL53 8EG
☎ 01242 526785 🖹 01242 256880
e-mail: secretary@lilleybrook.co.uk
web: www.lilleybrook.co.uk
Undulating parkland with magnificent views of Cheltenham and the surrounding countryside.
18 holes, 6212yds, Par 69, SSS 70, Course record 61. Club membership 900.
Visitors Mon-Sun. Booking required. Handicap certificate. Dress code. **Societies** Booking required. **Green Fees** phone. **Prof** Karl Hayler **Course Designer** A MacKenzie **Facilities** **Conf** facs Corporate Hospitality Days **Location** 2m S of Cheltenham on A435

Hotel ★★★★ 65% Cheltenham Park Hotel, Cirencester Rd, Charlton Kings, CHELTENHAM ☎ 01242 222021 33 en suite 110 annexe en suite

Shipton Shipton Oliffe, Andoverford GL54 4HT
☎ 01242 890237 🖹 01242 820336
9 holes, 2516yds, Par 35, SSS 63, Course record 33.
Location On A436, S of A40 junct
Phone for further details

Hotel ★★★ 70% Charlton Kings Hotel, London Rd, Charlton Kings, CHELTENHAM ☎ 01242 231061 13 en suite

CHIPPING SODBURY Map 03 ST78

Chipping Sodbury Trinity Ln BS37 6PU
☎ 01454 319042 🖹 01454 320052
e-mail: info@chippingsodburygolfclub.co.uk
web: www.chippingsodburygolfclub.co.uk
Founded in 1905, a parkland course of championship proportions on the edge of the Cotswolds. The easy walking terrain, delicately interrupted by a medley of waterways and lakes, is complimented by a stylish clubhouse.
Beaufort Course: 18 holes, 6912yds, Par 73, SSS 73, Course record 65. Club membership 800.
Visitors Mon-Fri except BHs. Dress code. **Societies** welcome. **Green Fees** £32 per round. **Prof** Mike Watts **Course Designer** Hawtree **Facilities** **Leisure** 6 hole academy course. **Conf** facs Corporate Hospitality Days **Location** 0.5m N

Hotel ★★ 70% Compass Inn, TORMARTON ☎ 01454 218242 & 218577 🖹 01454 218741 26 en suite

CIRENCESTER Map 04 SP00

Cirencester Cheltenham Rd, Bagendon GL7 7BH
☎ 01285 652465 01285 650665
e-mail: info@cirencestergolfclub.co.uk
web: www.cirencestergolfclub.co.uk
Undulating open Cotswold course with excellent views.

18 holes, 6055yds, Par 70, SSS 69, Course record 65.
Club membership 800.
Visitors Mon-Sun & BHs. Handicap certificate. Dress code. **Societies** Booking required. **Green Fees** £35 per round/day, £40 Sat & Sun. **Prof** Ed Goodwin **Course Designer** J Braid **Facilities** **Leisure** 6 hole par 3 Academy course. **Conf** facs Corporate Hospitality Days **Location** 2m N of Cirencester on A435

Hotel ★★★ 70% Stratton House Hotel, Gloucester Rd, CIRENCESTER ☎ 01285 651761 41 en suite

CLEEVE HILL Map 03 SO92

Cleeve Hill GL52 3PW
☎ 01242 672025 01242 67444
e-mail: hugh.fitzsimons@btconnect.com
web: www.cleevehillgolfcourse.com
Undulating and open heathland course affected by crosswinds. Situated on the highest point of the Cotswolds with fine views over Cheltenham racecourse, the Malvern Hills and the Bristol Channel. An ideal setting to enjoy a challenging round of golf.
18 holes, 6448yds, Par 72, SSS 71, Course record 66.
Club membership 600.
Visitors Mon-Fri. Booking required Sat, Sun & BHs. Dress code. **Societies** Booking required. **Green Fees** £15 per round, £18 Sat & Sun. **Prof** Dave Finch **Facilities** **Conf** facs Corporate Hospitality Days **Location** 1m NE on B4632

Hotel ★★★ 63% The Prestbury House Hotel, The Burgage, Prestbury, CHELTENHAM ☎ 01242 529533 7 en suite 8 annexe en suite

If the name of the club appears in italics, details have not been confirmed for this edition of the guide

COALPIT HEATH Map 03 ST68

The Kendleshire Henfield Rd BS36 2TG
☎ 0117 956 7007 0117 957 3433
e-mail: info@kendleshire.com
web: www.kendleshire.com
Opened in 1997, the course has 27 holes with water coming into play on 18 holes. Notable holes are the 11th, the 16th and the 27th. The 11th is a short hole with an island green set in a 3-acre lake and the 16th has a second shot played over water. The course is never short of interest and the greens have been built to USGA specification.
18 holes, 6550, Par 71, SSS 71, Course record 63.
18 holes, 6249, Par 71, SSS 70, Course record 68.
18 holes, 6353, Par 70, SSS 70, Course record 68.
Club membership 900.
Visitors Mon-Sun & BHs. Booking required. Dress code. **Societies** Booking required. **Green Fees** £33 per round, £38 Sat & Sun. **Prof** Tony Mealing **Course Designer** A Stiff, P McEvoy **Facilities** **Conf** facs Corporate Hospitality Days **Location** M32 junct 1, on Avon Ring Road

Hotel ★★★★ 65% Jurys Bristol Hotel, Prince St, BRISTOL ☎ 0117 923 0333 192 en suite

CODRINGTON Map 03 ST78

Players Club BS37 6RX
☎ 01454 313029 01454 323446
e-mail: enquiries@theplayersgolfclub.com
web: www.theplayersgolfclub.com
This Adrian Stiff designed layout can measure up to 7607yds. Often described as an inland links, the rolling sand based fairways encounter an unusual mix of gorse and water.
Championship: 18 holes, 6847yards, Par 72, SSS 72.
Club membership 2000.
Visitors Mon-Sun & BHs. Booking required. Dress code. **Societies** Booking required. **Green Fees** £70 Mon-Thu, £90 Fri-Sun. **Prof** Paul Barrington **Course Designer** Adrian Stiff **Facilities** **Leisure** fishing, 9 hole par 3 course. **Conf** facs Corporate Hospitality Days **Location** M4 junct 18, 1m on B4465

Hotel ★★ 70% Compass Inn, TORMARTON ☎ 01454 218242 & 218577 01454 218741 26 en suite

COLEFORD Map 03 SO51

Forest Hills Mile End Rd GL16 7QD
☎ 01594 810620 01594 810823
e-mail: foresthills@btopenworld.com
web: foresthillsgolfclub.co.uk
Parkland on a plateau with panoramic views of Coleford and Forest of Dean. Some testing holes with the par 5 13th hole sitting tight on a water hazard, and the challenging 18th with second shot over large pond to a green protected by another pond and bunker - all in front of the clubhouse.
18 holes, 6740yds, Par 72, SSS 68, Course record 64.
Club membership 550.
Visitors Mon-Sun. **Societies** Booking required. **Green Fees** phone. **Prof** Richard Ballard **Course Designer** A Stiff **Facilities** **Leisure** fishing, solarium. **Conf** facs

Continued

Hotel ★★★ 68% The Speech House, COLEFORD
☎ 01594 822607 15 en suite 22 annexe en suite

Forest of Dean Golf Club & Bells Hotel

Lords Hill GL16 8BE
☎ 01594 832583 01594 832584
e-mail: enquiries@bells-hotel.co.uk
web: www.bells-hotel.co.uk

Established in 1973 and now matured into an extremely pleasant parkland course. Well bunkered with light rough, a few blind tee shots and water in play on several holes.

18 holes, 6033yds, Par 70, SSS 69, Course record 63. Club membership 375.

Visitors Mon-Sun & BHs. Dress code. **Societies** Booking required. **Green Fees** £20 per 18 holes. Winter £9.95. **Prof** Paul Davies **Course Designer** John Day **Facilities** **Leisure** hard tennis courts, gymnasium, bowling green. **Conf** facs **Location** 0.25m from Coleford town centre on B4431 Coleford-Parkend road

Hotel ★★★ 68% The Speech House, COLEFORD
☎ 01594 822607 15 en suite 22 annexe en suite

DURSLEY Map 03 ST79

Stinchcombe Hill Stinchcombe Hill GL11 6AQ

☎ 01453 542015 01453 549545
e-mail: secretary@stinchcombehill.plus.com
web: www.stinchcombehillgolfclub.com

High on the hill with splendid views of the Cotswolds, the River Severn and the Welsh hills. A downland course with good turf, some trees and an interesting variety of greens. Protected greens make this a challenging course in windy conditions.

18 holes, 5734yds, Par 68, SSS 68, Course record 63. Club membership 550.

Visitors Mon-Sun & BHs. Booking required Tue, Thu, Sat, Sun & BHs. Handicap certificate. Dress code. **Societies** Booking required. **Green Fees** £34 per day, £27 per 18 holes, £42/£36 Sat, Sun & BHs. **Prof** Paul Bushell **Course Designer** Arthur Hoare **Facilities** by arrangement **Conf** Corporate Hospitality Days **Location** 1m W off A4135

Hotel ★★★ 66% Prince of Wales Hotel, BERKELEY ROAD ☎ 01453 810474 43 en suite

DYMOCK Map 03 SO73

Dymock Grange The Old Grange, Leominster Rd GL18 2AN

☎ 01531 890840 01531 890860

A challenging course set in 75 acres of attractive parkland.

Old Course: 9 holes, 5786yards, Par 72, SSS 70, Course record 71.
New Course: 9 holes, 3390yards, Par 60, SSS 60.
Club membership 185.

Visitors Booking required. **Societies** Booking required. **Green Fees** phone. **Prof** Tim Morgan **Course Designer** Cufingham **Facilities** **Conf** Corporate Hospitality Days **Location** On B4215 Leominster road

GLOUCESTER Map 03 SO81

Brickhampton Court Cheltenham Rd, Churchdown GL2 9QF

☎ 01452 859444 01452 859333
e-mail: info@brickhampton.co.uk
web: www.brickhampton.co.uk

Rolling parkland featuring lakes, streams, strategic white-sand bunkers, plantations - but no steep hills.

Spa: 18 holes, 6449yds, Par 71, SSS 71, Course record 65.
Glevum: 9 holes, 1859yds, Par 31.
Club membership 860.

Visitors Mon-Sun & BHs. Dress code. **Societies** Booking required. **Green Fees** Spa £23 per round, £26 Fri, £30 Sat, Sun & BHs. Glevum £8.50 per 9 holes, £10.50 Sat, Sun & BHs. **Prof** Bruce Wilson **Course Designer** Simon Gidman **Facilities** **Conf** facs Corporate Hospitality Days **Location** M5 junct 11, A40 towards Gloucester, at Elmbridge Court rdbt B4063 signed Churchdown, 2m

Hotel ★★★ 70% Macdonald Hatherley Manor, Down Hatherley Ln, GLOUCESTER ☎ 0870 1942126 52 en suite

Ramada Hotel & Resort Gloucester Matson Ln, Robinswood Hill GL4 6EA

☎ 01452 525653 01452 307212
web: www.gloucestergolf.com

18 holes, 6170yds, Par 70, SSS 69, Course record 65.

Location 2.5m SE of Gloucester, off B4073
Phone for further details

Hotel U Ramada Hotel & Resort Gloucester, Matson Ln, Robinswood Hill, GLOUCESTER ☎ 01452 525653 107 en suite

Rodway Hill Newent Rd, Highnam GL2 8DN

☎ 01452 384222 01452 313814
e-mail: info@rodway-hill-golf-course.co.uk
web: www.rodway-hill-golf-course.co.uk

A challenging 18-hole course with superb panoramic views. Testing front five holes and the par 3 13th and par 5 16th affected by strong crosswinds off the River Severn.

18 holes, 6040yds, Par 70, SSS 69, Course record 71. Club membership 400.

Visitors Mon-Sun & BHs. Booking required. Dress code. **Societies** Booking required. **Green Fees** £14 per 18 holes, £8 per 9 holes, £16/£9 Sat & Sun. **Prof** Chris Murphy **Course Designer** John Gabb **Facilities** **Conf** Corporate Hospitality Days **Location** 2m outside Gloucester on B4215

Continued

Hotel ★★★ 70% Macdonald Hatherley Manor, Down Hatherley Ln, GLOUCESTER ☎ 0870 1942126
52 en suite

LYDNEY Map 03 SO60

Lydney Lakeside Av GL15 5QA
☎ 01594 841186
web: www.members.tripod.co.uk/kenfar.lgc
Flat parkland and meadowland course with prevailing wind along fairways.
9 holes, 5298yds, Par 66, SSS 66, Course record 63.
Club membership 220.
Visitors Mon-Sat except BHs. Dress code. **Societies** welcome. **Green Fees** £10 per round. **Facilities** **Location** SE side of town centre

Hotel ★★★ 68% The Speech House, COLEFORD
☎ 01594 822607 15 en suite 22 annexe en suite

MINCHINHAMPTON Map 03 SO80

Minchinhampton (New Course) New Course GL6 9BE
☎ 01453 833866 🖷 01453 837360
e-mail: alan@mgcnew.co.uk
web: www.mgcnew.co.uk
The Cherington course, a South West Regional qualifying course for the Open Championship, is set in undulating upland. Large contoured greens, pot bunkers, and, at times, a stiff breeze present a very fair test of skill. The Avening course has a variety of holes including water on the 10th and 13th.
Avening: 18 holes, 6263yds, Par 70, SSS 70, Course record 61.
Cherington: 18 holes, 6430yds, Par 71, SSS 71, Course record 64.
Club membership 1200.
Visitors Mon-Sun & BHs. Booking required. Handicap certificate. Dress code. **Societies** Booking required. **Green Fees** £50 per day, £40 per round, £60/£50 Sat, Sun & BHs. **Prof** Chris Steele **Course Designer** Hawtree & Son **Facilities** **Conf** Corporate Hospitality Days **Location** B4014 from Nailsworth into Avening, left at Cross pub towards Minchinhampton, club 0.25m on right

Hotel ★★★ 71% Hare & Hounds Hotel, Westonbirt, TETBURY ☎ 01666 880233 & 881000 🖷 01666 880241
24 en suite 7 annexe en suite

Minchinhampton (Old Course) Old Course GL6 9AQ
☎ 01453 832642 & 836382 🖷 01453 832642
e-mail: alan@mgcold.co.uk
web: www.mgcold.co.uk
An open grassland course 600 feet above sea level. The numerous humps and hollows around the greens test the golfer's ability to play a variety of shots - often in difficult windy conditions. Panoramic Cotswold views. Two of the par 3s, the 8th and the 16th, often require an accurate long iron or wood depending on the strength and direction of the wind.
18 holes, 6088yds, Par 71, SSS 69.
Club membership 550.
Visitors contact course for details. Dress code. **Societies** Booking required. **Green Fees** £15 per 18 holes, £18 Sat, Sun & BHs. **Prof** Peter Dangerfield **Facilities** **Location** 1m NW

Hotel ★★ 71% Egypt Mill Hotel, NAILSWORTH
☎ 01453 833449 10 en suite 17 annexe en suite

NAUNTON Map 04 SP12

Naunton Downs GL54 3AE
☎ 01451 850090 🖷 01451 850091
e-mail: admin@nauntondowns.co.uk
web: www.nauntondowns.co.uk
Naunton Downs course plays over beautiful Cotswold countryside. A valley running through the course is one of the main features, creating one par 3 hole that crosses over it. The prevailing wind adds extra challenge to the par 5s (which play into the wind), combined with small undulating greens.
18 holes, 6161yds, Par 71, SSS 69, Course record 67.
Club membership 750.
Visitors Mon-Sun & BHs. Booking required. Dress code. **Societies** Booking required. **Green Fees** £19 Mon, £22 Tue-Fri, £28 Sat, Sun & BHs. **Prof** Nick Ellis **Course Designer** J Pott **Facilities** **Leisure** hard tennis courts. **Conf** facs Corporate Hospitality Days **Location** B4068 Stow-Cheltenham

Hotel ★★★ Lords of the Manor, UPPER SLAUGHTER
☎ 01451 820243 27 en suite

PAINSWICK Map 03 SO80

Painswick GL6 6TL
☎ 01452 812180
e-mail: hello@painswickgolf.com
Downland course set on the Cotswolds at Painswick Beacon, with fine views. Short course more than compensated by natural hazards and tight fairways.
18 holes, 4895yds, Par 67, SSS 63, Course record 61.
Club membership 480.
Visitors Mon-Sat except BHs. Booking required. Dress code. **Societies** Booking required. **Green Fees** £12-£17.50 per 18 holes, £20 Sat. **Facilities** **Conf** Corporate Hospitality Days **Location** 1m N of Painswick, off A46 to Cheltenham

Hotel ★★★ 77% Painswick Hotel and Restaurant, Kemps Ln, PAINSWICK ☎ 01452 812160 19 en suite

TEWKESBURY Map 03 SO83

Hilton Puckrup Hall Puckrup GL20 6EL
☎ 01684 271591 🖷 01684 271550
web: www.hilton.co.uk/tewkesbury
Set in 140 acres of undulating parkland with lakes,

Continued

existing trees and marvellous views of the Malvern hills. There are water hazards at the 5th, and a cluster of bunkers on the long 14th, before the challenging tee shot across the water to the par 3 18th.

18 holes, 6219yds, Par 70, SSS 70, Course record 63. Club membership 380.

Visitors Mon-Sun & BHs. Booking required. Dress code. **Societies** Booking required. **Green Fees** £30 per round, £35 Sat & Sun. **Prof** Mark Fenning **Course Designer** Simon Gidman **Facilities** **Leisure** heated indoor swimming pool, sauna, solarium, gymnasium. **Conf** facs Corporate Hospitality Days **Location** 4m N of Tewkesbury on A38

Hotel ★★ 65% The Bell Hotel, 52 Church St, TEWKESBURY ☎ 01684 293296 24 en suite

Tewkesbury Park Hotel Golf & Country Club

Lincoln Green Ln GL20 7DN
☎ 01684 295405 🖷 01684 292386
e-mail: tewkesburypark@corushotels.com
web: www.tewkesburyparkgolfclub.co.uk

The course offers many interesting and testing holes, with wooded areas and water hazards early in the round, opening up onto spacious fairways on the back nine of the undulating course.

18 holes, 6533yds, Par 73, SSS 72, Course record 66. Club membership 550.

Visitors Mon-Sun & BHs. Booking required. Dress code. **Societies** Booking required. **Green Fees** phone. **Prof** Marc Cottrell **Course Designer** Frank Pennick **Facilities** **Leisure** hard tennis courts, heated indoor swimming pool, squash, sauna, solarium, gymnasium. **Conf** facs Corporate Hospitality Days **Location** 1m SW off A38

Hotel ★★★ 69% The Tewkesbury Park Hotel Golf & Country Club, Lincoln Green Ln, TEWKESBURY ☎ 0870 609 6101 80 en suite

THORNBURY Map 03 ST69

Thornbury Golf Centre Bristol Rd BS35 3XL
☎ 01454 281144 📠 01454 281177
e-mail: info@thornburygc.co.uk
web: www.thornburygc.co.uk
Two 18-hole pay and play courses designed by Hawtree and set in undulating terrain with views towards the Severn estuary. The Low 18 is a par 3 with holes ranging from 80 to 207yds and is ideal for beginners. The High course puts to test the more experienced golfer. Excellent 25 bay floodlit driving range.

High Course: 18 holes, 6308yds, Par 71, SSS 69.
Low Course: 18 holes, 2195yds, Par 54.
Club membership 480.
Visitors Mon-Sun & BHs. Booking required. Dress code. **Societies** Booking required. **Green Fees** phone. **Prof** Mike Smedley **Course Designer** Hawtree **Facilities** **Conf** facs Corporate Hospitality Days **Location** M5 junct 16, off A38 towards Gloucester

Hotel ★★ 66% Thornbury Golf Lodge, Bristol Rd, THORNBURY ☎ 01454 281144 11 en suite

WESTONBIRT Map 03 ST88

Westonbirt Westonbirt School GL8 8QG
☎ 01666 880242 & 881338 📠 01666 880385
e-mail: doyle@westonbirt.gloucs.sch.uk
web: www.westonbirt.gloucs.sch.uk
Parkland with good views.
9 holes, 4504yds, Par 64, SSS 64.
Club membership 287.
Visitors Mon-Sun & BHs. Dress code. **Societies** Booking required. **Green Fees** £10 per round. **Facilities** **Conf** facs **Location** E side of village off A433

Hotel ★★★ 71% Hare & Hounds Hotel, Westonbirt, TETBURY ☎ 01666 880233 & 881000 📠 01666 880241 24 en suite 7 annexe en suite

WICK Map 03 ST77

Tracy Park Tracy Park Estate, Bath Rd BS30 5RN
☎ 0117 937 2251 📠 0117 937 4288
e-mail: golf@thegloucestershire.com
web: www.thegloucestershire.com
Two 18-hole championship courses on the south-western escarpment of the Cotswolds, affording fine views. Both courses present a challenge to all levels of player, with water playing a part on a number of occasions. The elegant clubhouse dates from 1600, set in the 221-acre estate of this golf and country club.
Crown Course: 18 holes, 6252yds, Par 69, SSS 70.
Cromwell Course: 18 holes, 6246yds, Par 71, SSS 70.
Club membership 600.
Visitors Mon-Sun. Booking required. **Societies** Booking required with Robert Ford. **Green Fees** phone. **Prof** David Morgan **Facilities** **Conf** facs Corporate Hospitality Days **Location** S side of village off A420

Hotel ★★★ The Queensberry Hotel, Russel St, BATH ☎ 01225 447928 29 en suite

WOTTON-UNDER-EDGE Map 03 ST79

Cotswold Edge Upper Rushmire GL12 7PT
☎ 01453 844167 📠 01453 845120
e-mail: nnewman@cotswoldedgegolfclub.org.uk
web: www.cotswoldedgegolfclub.org.uk
Meadowland course situated in a quiet Cotswold valley with magnificent views. First half flat and open, second half more varied.
18 holes, 6170yds, Par 71, SSS 71.
Club membership 800.
Visitors Mon-Fri. Booking required. **Societies** Booking required. **Green Fees** phone. **Prof** Rod Hibbitt **Facilities** **Location** N of town on B4058 Wotton-Tetbury road

Hotel ★★ 71% Egypt Mill Hotel, NAILSWORTH ☎ 01453 833449 10 en suite 17 annexe en suite

GREATER LONDON

Those courses which fall within the confines of the London Postal District area (i.e. have London postcodes) are listed under the county heading of **London** in the gazetteer.

ADDINGTON Map 05 TQ36

The Addington 205 Shirley Church Rd CR0 5AB
☎ 020 8777 1055 📠 020 8777 6661
e-mail: info@addingtongolf.com
web: www.addingtongolf.com
This heather and woodland course is possibly one of the best laid out courses in Southern England with the world famous 13th, par 3 at 230yds. A good test of golfing ability with no two holes the same.
18 holes, 6338yds, Par 68, SSS 71, Course record 66.
Visitors Mon-Sun & BHs. Booking required. Handicap certificate. Dress code. **Societies** Booking required. **Green Fees** £75, £95 Sat & Sun after 10.30am. **Course Designer** J Abercromby **Facilities** **Conf** Corporate Hospitality Days **Location** M25 junct 7, 3m from Croydon

Continued

The Addington

Hotel ★★★★ 69% Selsdon Park Hotel & Golf Course, Addington Rd, Sanderstead, CROYDON ☎ 020 8657 8811 204 en suite

Addington Court Featherbed Ln CR0 9AA
☎ 020 8657 0281 (booking) & 8651 5270 (admin)
020 8651 0282
e-mail: addington@americangolf.uk.com
Championship Course: 18 holes, 5577yds, Par 68, SSS 67, Course record 60.
Falconwood: 18 holes, 5472yds, Par 68, SSS 67.
9 Hole: 9 holes, 1804yds, Par 31.
Course Designer Hawtree Snr **Location** 1m S off A2022
Phone for further details

Hotel ★★★★ 69% Selsdon Park Hotel & Golf Course, Addington Rd, Sanderstead, CROYDON ☎ 020 8657 8811 204 en suite

Addington Palace Addington Park, Gravel Hill CR0 5BB
☎ 020 8654 3061 020 8655 3632
e-mail: johnb@addingtonpalacegolf.co.uk
web: www.addingtonpalacegolf.co.uk
Set in the grounds of Addington Palace, which was the home of the Archbishops of Canterbury for a number of years. There are a number of tree-lined fairways and the 17th hole follows one of the original roads into the Palace and has a fine array of horse chestnut trees. The course winds its way through tree-lined fairways for the first nine holes. The second nine holes opens out and needs full concentration to achieve a good score. The 12th hole is one to remember, over a fountain and onto a green bunkered on all sides.
18 holes, 6339yds, Par 71, SSS 70, Course record 63.
Club membership 700.
Visitors Mon-Fri except BHs. Booking required. Dress code. **Societies** Booking required. **Green Fees** £45 per day, £40 per round. **Prof** Roger Williams **Course Designer** JH Taylor **Facilities** by arrangement **Leisure** snooker. **Conf** Corporate Hospitality Days **Location** 2m SE of Croydon station on A212

Hotel ★★★★ 69% Selsdon Park Hotel & Golf Course, Addington Rd, Sanderstead, CROYDON ☎ 020 8657 8811 204 en suite

BARNEHURST Map 05 TQ57

Barnehurst Mayplace Rd East DA7 6JU
☎ 01322 523746 01322 523860
e-mail: barnehurst@bexley.gov.uk
Public parkland course with well matured greens. Easy walking.
9 holes, 4796yds, Par 70, SSS 67.
Club membership 180.
Visitors Mon-Sun & BHs. Booking required. Dress code. **Societies** Booking required. **Green Fees** £11.70 per 18 holes, £8.25 per 9 holes, £15.60/£11.50 Sat, Sun & BHs. **Course Designer** James Braid **Facilities** **Conf** facs Corporate Hospitality Days **Location** 0.75m NW of Crayford off A2000

Hotel ★★★★ 67% Bexleyheath Marriott Hotel, 1 Broadway, BEXLEYHEATH ☎ 0870 400 7245 142 en suite

BARNET Map 04 TQ29

Arkley Rowley Green Rd EN5 3HL
☎ 020 8449 0394 020 8440 5214
e-mail: secretary@arkleygolfclub.co.uk
web: arkleygolfclub.co.uk
Wooded parkland on highest spot in Hertfordshire with fine views.
9 holes, 6046yds, Par 69, SSS 69.
Club membership 400.
Visitors Mon-Fri except BHs. Dress code. **Societies** Booking required. **Green Fees** £32 per day, £25 per round. **Prof** Andrew Hurley **Course Designer** Braid **Facilities** **Conf** Corporate Hospitality Days **Location** Off A1 at Arkley sign

Hotel ★★★ 69% Corus hotel Elstree, Barnet Ln, ELSTREE ☎ 0870 609 6151 47 en suite

Dyrham Park Country Club Galley Ln EN5 4RA
☎ 020 8440 3361 020 8441 9836
18 holes, 6369yds, Par 71, SSS 70, Course record 65.
Location 3m NW off A1081
Phone for further details

Hotel Innkeeper's Lodge Borehamwood, Studio Way, BOREHAM WOOD ☎ 020 8905 1455 55 en suite

Old Fold Manor Old Fold Ln, Hadley Green EN5 4QN
☎ 020 8440 9185 020 8441 4863
e-mail: manager@oldfoldmanor.co.uk
web: www.oldfoldmanor.co.uk
Superb heathland course with fine greens, breathtaking views and a challenge for all levels of golfer. Slightly undulating in parts, the course meanders around a historic battle site and gets progressively tougher as it develops.
18 holes, 6447yds, Par 71, SSS 71, Course record 66.
Club membership 560.
Visitors contact club for details. **Societies** welcome. **Green Fees** £38 per 36 holes, £34 per 27 holes, £30 per 18 holes. **Prof** Peter McEvoy **Facilities** **Conf** Corporate Hospitality Days **Location** Off A1000 between Barnet & Potters Bar

Hotel ★★★★ 73% West Lodge Park Hotel, Cockfosters Rd, HADLEY WOOD ☎ 020 8216 3900 46 en suite 13 annexe en suite

BECKENHAM Map 05 TQ36

Beckenham Place Park The Mansion, Beckenham Place Park BR3 2BP
☎ 020 8650 2292 🖹 020 8663 1201
18 holes, 5722yds, Par 68, SSS 69.
Location Off A2015
Phone for further details

Hotel ★★★ 71% Bromley Court Hotel, Bromley Hill, BROMLEY ☎ 020 8461 8600 114 en suite

Langley Park Barnfield Wood Rd BR3 6SZ
☎ 020 8658 6849 🖹 020 8658 6310
e-mail: manager@langleyparkgolf.co.uk
web: www.langleyparkgolf.co.uk
A pleasant, well-wooded but difficult parkland course. Natural hazards include a lake at the par 3 18th hole. Although most fairways are bordered by woodland, they are wide with forgiving rough and friendly bunkers.
18 holes, 6453yds, Par 69, SSS 71, Course record 65.
Club membership 700.
Visitors Mon-Fri except BHs. Booking required. Handicap certificate. Dress code. **Societies** Booking required. **Green Fees** £60 per day, £40 per round. **Prof** Colin Staff **Course Designer** JH Taylor **Facilities** **Conf** Corporate Hospitality Days **Location** 0.5 N of Beckenham on B2015

Hotel ★★★ 71% Bromley Court Hotel, Bromley Hill, BROMLEY ☎ 020 8461 8600 114 en suite

BEXLEYHEATH Map 05 TQ47

Bexleyheath Mount Rd DA6 8JS
☎ 020 8303 6951
Undulating course.
9 holes, 5162yds, Par 66, SSS 66, Course record 65.
Club membership 330.
Visitors contact club for details. **Societies** welcome. **Green Fees** phone. **Facilities** **Location** 1m SW

Hotel ★★★★ 67% Bexleyheath Marriott Hotel, 1 Broadway, BEXLEYHEATH ☎ 0870 400 7245 142 en suite

BIGGIN HILL Map 05 TQ45

Cherry Lodge Jail Ln TN16 3AX
☎ 01959 572250 🖹 01959 540672
e-mail: info@cherrylodgegc.co.uk
web: www.cherrylodgegc.co.uk
Undulating parkland 600ft above sea level with panoramic views of the surrounding countryside. An enjoyable test of golf for all standards. The 14th is 434yds across a valley and uphill, requiring two good shots to reach the green.
18 holes, 6593yds, Par 72, SSS 73, Course record 66.
Club membership 700.
Visitors Mon-Fri. Booking required. **Societies** Booking required. **Green Fees** phone. **Prof** Nigel Child **Course Designer** John Day **Facilities** **Location** 1m E

Hotel ★★★ 71% Donnington Manor, London Rd, Dunton Green, SEVENOAKS ☎ 01732 462681 60 en suite

BROMLEY Map 05 TQ46

Bromley Magpie Hall Ln BR2 8JF
☎ 020 8462 7014 🖹 020 8462 6916
9 holes, 2745yds, Par 70, SSS 67.
Location 2m SE off A21
Phone for further details

Hotel ★★★ 71% Bromley Court Hotel, Bromley Hill, BROMLEY ☎ 020 8461 8600 114 en suite

Sundridge Park Garden Rd BR1 3NE
☎ 020 8460 0278 🖹 020 8289 3050
e-mail: gm@spgc.co.uk
web: www.spgc.co.uk
The East Course is longer than the West but many think the shorter of the two courses is the more difficult. The East is surrounded by trees while the West is more hilly, with good views. Both are certainly a good test of golf. An Open qualifying course with year round irrigation of fairways.
East Course: 18 holes, 6516yds, Par 71, SSS 71, Course record 63.
West Course: 18 holes, 6019yds, Par 69, SSS 69, Course record 65.
Club membership 1200.
Visitors contact club for details. **Societies** Booking required. **Green Fees** £85 per day, £65 per round Mon-Fri. **Prof** Stuart Dowsett **Course Designer** Willie Park **Facilities** **Conf** facs Corporate Hospitality Days **Location** N side of town centre off A2212

Hotel ★★★ 71% Bromley Court Hotel, Bromley Hill, BROMLEY ☎ 020 8461 8600 114 en suite

CARSHALTON Map 04 TQ26

Oaks Sports Centre Woodmansterne Rd SM5 4AN
☎ 020 8643 8363 🖹 020 8770 7303
e-mail: golf@oaks.sagehost.co.uk
web: www.oakssportscentre.co.uk
Public parkland course with floodlit, covered driving range.
18 Holes: 18 holes, 6054yds, Par 70, SSS 69, Course record 65.
9 Holes: 9 holes, 1497yds, Par 28, SSS 28.
Club membership 432.
Visitors Mon-Sun & BHs. Booking required Sat, Sun & BHs. Dress code. **Societies** Booking required. **Green Fees** £17.40 per 18 holes, £8.70 per 9 holes, £21/£10.50 Sat & Sun. **Prof** Horley, Pilkington, Mulcahy **Facilities** **Conf** facs **Location** 0.5m S on B278

Hotel ★★★ 69% Aerodrome Hotel, Purley Way, CROYDON ☎ 020 8710 9000 & 8680 1999 🖹 020 8681 6438 84 en suite

CHESSINGTON Map 04 TQ16

Chessington Garrison Ln KT9 2LW
☎ 020 8391 0948 🖹 020 8397 2068
e-mail: info@chessingtongolf.co.uk
web: www.chessingtongolf.co.uk
Tree-lined parkland course designed by Patrick Tallack, with panoramic views over the Surrey countryside.

9 holes, 1679yds, Par 30, SSS 28.
Club membership 90.
Visitors Mon-Sat & BHs, Sun after 11am. **Societies** Booking required. **Green Fees** £9 per round, £11 Sat, Sun & BHs. **Prof** Mark Janes **Course Designer** Patrick Tallack **Facilities** **Leisure** automated ball teeing facility on driving range. **Location** M25 junct 9, 3m N on A243

Hotel Premier Travel Inn Chessington, Leatherhead Rd, CHESSINGTON ☎ 08701 977057 42 en suite

CHISLEHURST Map 05 TQ47

Chislehurst Camden Park Rd BR7 5HJ
☎ 020 8467 6798 020 8295 0874
e-mail: thesecretary@chislehurstgolfclub.co.uk
web: www.chislehurstgolfclub.co.uk
The course was established in 1894 and is dominated by an imposing 17th century building of great historical interest. The challenging parkland course has an overall area of less than 70 acres and accuracy is always more important than distance off the tee. There are trees, hills and dales and the excellent greens are neither too large or too flat. Only the 7th hole remains from the original nine-hole course.
18 holes, 5080yds, Par 66, SSS 65, Course record 61.
Club membership 760.
Visitors Mon, Tue, Thu, Fri. Booking required. Handicap certificate. Dress code. **Societies** Booking required. **Green Fees** £30 per round. **Prof** Jonathan Bird **Course Designer** Park **Facilities** by arrangement **Leisure** snooker room. **Conf** facs

Hotel ★★★ 71% Bromley Court Hotel, Bromley Hill, BROMLEY ☎ 020 8461 8600 114 en suite

COULSDON Map 04 TQ25

Coulsdon Manor Hotel Coulsdon Court Rd CR5 2LL
☎ 020 8668 0414 020 8668 3118
e-mail: reservations.coulsdon@swallowhotels.com
web: www.swallowhotels.com
Designed by Harry S Colt and set in its own 140 acres of landscaped parkland.
18 holes, 6037yds, Par 70, SSS 68.
Club membership 150.
Visitors Mon-Sun & BHs. Booking required. Dress code. **Societies** Booking required. **Green Fees** £16.50 per round, £21.50 Sat, Sun & BHs. **Prof** Matt Asbury **Course Designer** Harry Colt **Facilities** **Leisure** hard tennis courts, squash, sauna, solarium, gymnasium. **Conf** facs Corporate Hospitality Days **Location** 0.75m E off A23 on B2030

Woodcote Park Meadow Hill, Bridle Way CR5 2QQ
☎ 020 8668 2788 020 8660 0918
e-mail: info@woodcotepgc.com
web: www.woodcotepgc.com
Slightly undulating parkland.
18 holes, 6720yds, Par 71, SSS 72, Course record 66.
Club membership 700.
Visitors Mon-Fri. Booking required. Handicap certificate. Dress code. **Societies** Booking required. **Green Fees** £45 per day/round. **Prof** Wraith Grant **Course Designer** H Colt **Facilities** **Conf** facs Corporate Hospitality Days **Location** 1m N of town centre off A237

Hotel ★★★ 69% Aerodrome Hotel, Purley Way, CROYDON ☎ 020 8710 9000 & 8680 1999 020 8681 6438 84 en suite

CROYDON Map 04 TQ36

Croham Hurst Croham Rd CR2 7HJ
☎ 020 8657 5581 020 8657 3229
e-mail: secretary@chgc.co.uk
web: www.chgc.co.uk
Easy walking parkland with tree-lined fairways and bounded by wooded hills.
18 holes, 6290yds, Par 70, SSS 70.
Club membership 800.
Visitors Mon-Fri except BHs. Booking required. Handicap certificate. Dress code. **Societies** Booking required. **Green Fees** £50 per round. **Prof** Matthew Paget **Course Designer** Hawtree, Braid **Facilities** **Conf** facs Corporate Hospitality Days **Location** 1.5m SE of Croydon on B269

Hotel ★★★★ 69% Selsdon Park Hotel & Golf Course, Addington Rd, Sanderstead, CROYDON ☎ 020 8657 8811 204 en suite

Selsdon Park Hotel Addington Rd, Sanderstead CR2 8YA
☎ 020 8657 8811 020 8651 6171
e-mail: caroline.aldred@principal-hotels.com
web: www.principal-hotels.com
Parkland course. Full use of hotel's sporting facilities by residents.
18 holes, 6473yds, Par 73, SSS 71, Course record 63.
Visitors Mon-Sun & BHs. Booking required. Dress code. **Societies** Booking required. **Green Fees** £28 per 18 holes, £40 Sat, Sun & BHs. **Prof** Malcolm Churchill **Course Designer** JH Taylor **Facilities** **Leisure** hard and grass tennis courts, outdoor and indoor heated swimming pools, squash, sauna, solarium, gymnasium. **Conf** facs Corporate Hospitality Days **Location** 3m S on A2022

Hotel ★★★★ 69% Selsdon Park Hotel & Golf Course, Addington Rd, Sanderstead, CROYDON ☎ 020 8657 8811 204 en suite

Shirley Park 194 Addiscombe Rd CR0 7LB
☎ 020 8654 1143 020 8654 6733
e-mail: secretary@shirleyparkgolfclub.co.uk
web: www.shirleyparkgolfclub.co.uk
The parkland course lies amid fine woodland with good views of Shirley Hills. The more testing holes come in the middle section of the course. The remarkable 7th hole calls for a 187yd iron or wood shot diagonally across a narrow valley to a shelved green set right-handed into a ridge. The 13th hole, 160yds, is considered to be one of the finest short holes in the county.
18 holes, 6210yds, Par 71, SSS 70, Course record 64.
Club membership 600.
Visitors Mon-Fri except BHs & Sun pm. Booking required Sun. Dress code. **Societies** Booking required. **Green Fees** £40 Mon-Fri, £48 Sun. **Prof** Michael Taylor **Course Designer** Tom Simpson, Herbert Fowler **Facilities** **Leisure** snooker. **Conf** Corporate Hospitality Days **Location** E of town centre on A232

Hotel ★★★★ 69% Selsdon Park Hotel & Golf Course, Addington Rd, Sanderstead, CROYDON ☎ 020 8657 8811 204 en suite

Downe — Map 05 TQ46

High Elms High Elms Rd BR6 7JL
☎ 01689 853232 & 858175 bookings Fax 01689 856326
18 holes, 6210yds, Par 71, SSS 70, Course record 68.
Course Designer Hawthorn **Location** 2m E of A21
Phone for further details

Hotel ★★★ 71% Bromley Court Hotel, Bromley Hill, BROMLEY ☎ 020 8461 8600 114 en suite

West Kent Milking Ln BR6 7LD
☎ 01689 851323 Fax 01689 858693
e-mail: golf@wkgc.co.uk
web: www.wkgc.co.uk
Undulating woodland course close to south London but providing a quiet rural setting in three valleys.
18 holes, 6426yds, Par 71, SSS 71, Course record 68. Club membership 700.
Visitors Mon-Fri except BHs. Booking required. Handicap certificate. Dress code. **Societies** Booking required. **Green Fees** £55 per day, £40 per round. **Prof** Chris Forsyth **Course Designer** H Colt **Facilities** **Location** M25 junct 4, A21 towards Bromley, left signed Downe, through village on Luxted road 0.5m, West Hill on right

Hotel ★★★ 71% Bromley Court Hotel, Bromley Hill, BROMLEY ☎ 020 8461 8600 114 en suite

Enfield — Map 04 TQ39

Crews Hill Cattlegate Rd, Crews Hill EN2 8AZ
☎ 020 8363 6674 Fax 020 8363 2343
web: www.crewshillgolfclub.co.uk
Parkland course in countryside.
18 holes, 6281yds, Par 70, SSS 70, Course record 65. Club membership 600.
Visitors Mon, Wed-Fri except BHs. Booking required Wed-Fri. Handicap certificate. Dress code. **Societies** Booking required. **Green Fees** phone. **Prof** Neil Wichelow **Course Designer** Harry Colt **Facilities** by arrangement **Conf** facs Corporate Hospitality Days **Location** M25 junct 24, A1005 for Enfield, signed

Hotel ★★★ 75% Royal Chace Hotel, The Ridgeway, ENFIELD ☎ 020 8884 8181 92 en suite

Enfield Old Park Rd South EN2 7DA
☎ 020 8363 3970 Fax 020 8342 0381
e-mail: secretary@enfieldgolfclub.co.uk
web: www.enfieldgolfclub.co.uk
Parkland with tree-lined fairways and a meandering brook that comes into play on nine holes. There are no hidden or unfair hazards and, although not easy, the course is highly playable and always attractive.
18 holes, 6154yds, Par 72, SSS 70, Course record 61. Club membership 600.
Visitors Mon-Sun & BHs. Booking required. Handicap certificate. Dress code. **Societies** Booking required. **Green Fees** £28, £36 Sat, Sun & BHs. **Prof** Martin Porter **Course Designer** James Braid **Facilities** **Conf** facs Corporate Hospitality Days **Location** M25 jnct 24, A1005 to Enfield to rdbt with church on left, right down Slades Hill, 1st left to end

Hotel ★★★ 75% Royal Chace Hotel, The Ridgeway, ENFIELD ☎ 020 8884 8181 92 en suite

Whitewebbs Park Whitewebbs Ln EN2 9HH
☎ 020 8363 4454 Fax 020 8366 2257
This challenging parkland course was first opened for play in 1932 and is set in over 140 acres of attractive rolling countryside with mature woodland and the meandering Cuffley brook that comes into play on four holes.
18 holes, 5782yds, Par 68, SSS 68, Course record 64. Club membership 350.
Visitors Mon-Sun & BHs. Dress code. **Societies** welcome. **Green Fees** £23 per day, £14 per round, £28/£18 Sat & Sun. **Prof** Gary Sherriff **Facilities** **Location** N of town centre

Hotel ★★★ 75% Royal Chace Hotel, The Ridgeway, ENFIELD ☎ 020 8884 8181 92 en suite

Greenford — Map 04 TQ18

C & L Golf & Country Club Westend Rd, Northolt UB5 6RD
☎ 020 8845 5662 Fax 020 8841 5515
18 holes, 4458yds, Par 67, SSS 62, Course record 58.
Course Designer Patrick Tallack **Location** Junct Westend Rd
Phone for further details

Hotel ★★★ 64% The Bridge Hotel, Western Av, GREENFORD ☎ 020 8566 6246 68 en suite

Ealing Perivale Ln UB6 8SS
☎ 020 8997 0937 Fax 020 8998 0756
e-mail: ealinggolfoffice@aol.com
web: www.ealinggolfclub.com
The home of English and European champions. Inland parkland with the River Brent providing natural hazards across several holes.
18 holes, 6216yds, Par 70, SSS 70, Course record 62. Club membership 650.
Visitors Mon-Fri except BHs. Sat & Sun pm. Booking required. Handicap certificate. Dress code. **Societies** Booking required. **Green Fees** £35 Mon-Fri. **Prof** Ricky Willison **Course Designer** H Colt **Facilities** by arrangement **Conf** facs Corporate Hospitality Days **Location** Off A40

Hotel ★★★ 64% The Bridge Hotel, Western Av, GREENFORD ☎ 020 8566 6246 68 en suite

Horsenden Hill Whitton Av, Woodland Rise UB6 0RD
☎ 020 8902 4555 Fax 020 8902 4555
A distinctive picturesque course designed over hilly landscape. Very challenging comprising eight par 3s (3 over 200yds) and a par 4 of 292yds. Overlooks the London skyline to Canary Wharf and the London Eye.
9 holes, 1632yds, Par 28, SSS 28. Club membership 135.
Visitors Mon-Sun. **Societies** Booking required. **Green Fees** phone. **Prof** Jeff Quarshie **Facilities** **Conf** Corporate Hospitality Days **Location** 3m NE on A4090

Hotel ★★★ 64% The Bridge Hotel, Western Av, GREENFORD ☎ 020 8566 6246 68 en suite

Lime Trees Park Ruislip Rd, Northolt UB5 6QZ
☎ 020 8842 0442 🖹 020 8842 0542
9 holes, 5836yds, Par 71, SSS 69.
Location 300yds off A40 at Polish War Memorial, A4180 towards Hayes
Phone for further details

Hotel ★★★ 64% The Bridge Hotel, Western Av, GREENFORD ☎ 020 8566 6246 68 en suite

Perivale Park Stockdove Way UB6 8TJ
☎ 020 8575 7116
Parkland beside the River Brent.
9 holes, 2667yds, Par 68, SSS 67.
Club membership 250.
Visitors Mon-Sun. **Green Fees** phone. **Prof** Peter Bryant **Facilities** **Location** E side of town centre, off A40

Hotel ★★★ 68% Best Western Cumberland Hotel, 1 St Johns Rd, HARROW ☎ 020 8863 4111 41 en suite 43 annexe en suite

HADLEY WOOD — Map 04 TQ29

Hadley Wood Beech Hill EN4 0JJ
☎ 020 8449 4328 & 4486 🖹 020 8364 8633
e-mail: gm@hadleywoodgc.com
web: www.hadleywoodgc.com
Parkland on the north-west edge of London. The gently undulating fairways have a friendly width inviting the player to open his shoulders, though the thick rough can be very punishing to the unwary. The course is pleasantly wooded and there are some admirable views.

18 holes, 6514yds, Par 72, SSS 71, Course record 67.
Club membership 650.
Visitors Mon-Fri & Sun except BHs. Booking required. Handicap certificate. Dress code. **Societies** Booking required. **Green Fees** £50 per 18 holes. **Prof** Peter Jones **Course Designer** A MacKenzie **Facilities** **Conf** facs Corporate Hospitality Days **Location** M25 junct 24, take A111 to Cockfosters, 2m to 3rd turning right

Hotel ★★★★ 73% West Lodge Park Hotel, Cockfosters Rd, HADLEY WOOD ☎ 020 8216 3900 46 en suite 13 annexe en suite

HAMPTON — Map 04 TQ17

Fulwell Wellington Rd, Hampton Hill TW12 1JY
☎ 020 8977 3844 & 020 8977 2733 🖹 020 8977 7732
e-mail: secretary@fulwellgolfclub.co.uk
web: www.fulwellgolfclub.co.uk
Championship-length parkland course with easy walking. The 575-yd 17th and the water feature 9th are notable.

18 holes, 6544yds, Par 71, SSS 71.
Club membership 750.
Visitors contact club for details. Dress code. **Societies** Booking required. **Green Fees** £36 per round, £50 Sat & Sun. **Prof** Nigel Turner **Course Designer** John Morrison **Facilities** **Location** 1.5m N on A311

Hotel ★★★ 69% The Richmond Hill Hotel, Richmond Hill, RICHMOND UPON THAMES ☎ 020 8940 2247 138 en suite

HAMPTON WICK — Map 04 TQ16

Hampton Court Palace Home Park KT1 4AD
☎ 020 8977 2423 🖹 020 8614 4747
e-mail: hamptoncourtpalace@crown-golf.co.uk
web: www.crown-golf.co.uk
Flat course with easy walking situated in the grounds of Hampton Court Palace. Unique blend of parkland and inland links built on a base of sand and gravel, making it one of the finest winter courses in the country.
18 holes, 6513yds, Par 71, SSS 71, Course record 64.
Club membership 750.
Visitors Mon-Sun & BHs. Booking required. Dress code. **Societies** Booking required. **Green Fees** £41 Mon-Thu, £46.50 Fri-Sun & BHs. **Prof** Edward Litchfield **Course Designer** Willie Park **Facilities** **Conf** facs Corporate Hospitality Days **Location** Off A308 on W side of Kingston Bridge

Hotel ★★★ 69% The Richmond Hill Hotel, Richmond Hill, RICHMOND UPON THAMES ☎ 020 8940 2247 138 en suite

HILLINGDON — Map 04 TQ08

Hillingdon 18 Dorset Way UB10 0JR
☎ 01895 233956 & 239810 🖹 01895 233956
9 holes, 5490yds, Par 68, SSS 67.
Location W of town off A4020
Phone for further details

Hotel ★★★ 70% Novotel London Heathrow, Cherry Ln, WEST DRAYTON ☎ 01895 431431 178 en suite

HOUNSLOW Map 04 TQ17

Airlinks Southall Ln TW5 9PE
☎ 020 8561 1418 🖹 020 8813 6284
Meadowland and parkland with four water holes.
18 holes, 6000yds, Par 71, SSS 69, Course record 63. Club membership 550.
Visitors Mon-Sun. Booking required. **Societies** Booking required.. **Green Fees** phone. **Prof** Tony Martin, Greg Fenner **Course Designer** P Alliss, D Thomas **Facilities** **Leisure** hard tennis courts, outdoor and indoor heated swimming pools, squash, sauna, solarium, gymnasium. **Location** M4 junct 3, W of Hounslow

Hotel ★★★ 65% Best Western Master Robert Hotel, 366 Great West Rd, HOUNSLOW ☎ 020 8570 6261 96 annexe en suite

Hounslow Heath Municipal Staines Rd TW4 5DS
☎ 020 8570 5271 🖹 020 8570 5205
18 holes, 5901yds, Par 69, SSS 68, Course record 62.
Course Designer Fraser M Middleton **Location** On A315 towards Bedfont
Phone for further details

Hotel ★★★ 65% Best Western Master Robert Hotel, 366 Great West Rd, HOUNSLOW ☎ 020 8570 6261 96 annexe en suite

ILFORD Map 05 TQ48

Ilford Wanstead Park Rd IG1 3TR
☎ 020 8554 2930 🖹 020 8554 0822
e-mail: ilfordgolfclub@btconnect.com
web: www.ilfordgolfclub.com
Fairly flat parkland on the River Roding. The river borders four holes, and is crossed by three holes. While not a particularly long course, the small greens, and many holes requiring brains rather than brawn, provide a challenging test to all.
18 holes, 5299yds, Par 67, SSS 66, Course record 61. Club membership 500.
Visitors Booking required. **Societies** Booking required. **Green Fees** phone. **Prof** S Jackson **Course Designer** Whitehead **Facilities** **Conf** facs Corporate Hospitality Days **Location** NW of town centre off A12

ISLEWORTH Map 04 TQ17

Wyke Green Syon Ln TW7 5PT
☎ 020 8847 0685 (pro) & 8560 8777 (sec)
🖹 020 8569 8392
e-mail: office@wykegreengolfclub.co.uk
web: www.wykegreengolfclub.co.uk
Fairly flat parkland. Seven par 4 holes over 420yds.
18 holes, 6182yds, Par 69, SSS 70, Course record 64. Club membership 650.
Visitors Mon-Fri, Sat, Sun & BHs after 4pm. Dress code. **Societies** Booking required. **Green Fees** £30 per round,, £35 Sat & Sun. **Prof** Neil Smith **Course Designer** Hawtree **Facilities** **Conf** Corporate Hospitality Days **Location** 0.5m N on B454, off A4 at Gillette Corner

Hotel ★★★ 65% Best Western Master Robert Hotel, 366 Great West Rd, HOUNSLOW ☎ 020 8570 6261 96 annexe en suite

KINGSTON UPON THAMES Map 04 TQ16

Coombe Hill Golf Club Dr, Coombe Ln West KT2 7DF
☎ 020 8336 7600 🖹 020 8336 7601
e-mail: thesecretary@chgc.net
web: www.coombehillgolfclub.com
A splendid course in wooded terrain. The undulations and trees make it an especially interesting course of great charm. And there is a lovely display of rhododendrons in May and June.
18 holes, 6293yds, Par 71, SSS 71, Course record 67. Club membership 550.
Visitors Mon, Tue, Thu & Fri except BHs. Wed pm. Booking required. Handicap certificate. Dress code. **Societies** Booking required. **Green Fees** Mon-Fri £100 per 36 holes, £80 per 18 holes. **Prof** Andy Dunn **Course Designer** J Abercromby **Facilities** **Leisure** sauna. **Conf** Corporate Hospitality Days **Location** 1.75m E on A238

Hotel Travelodge London Kingston Upon Thames, 21-23 London Rd, KINGSTON UPON THAMES ☎ 08700 850 950 72 en suite

Coombe Wood George Rd, Kingston Hill KT2 7NS
☎ 020 8942 0388 🖹 020 8942 5665
e-mail: info@coombewoodgolf.com
web: www.coombewoodgolf.com
Mature parkland with seven varied and challenging par 3s.

18 holes, 5299yds, Par 66, SSS 66, Course record 59. Club membership 700.
Visitors Mon-Sun & BHs. Booking required. Dress code. **Societies** Booking required. **Green Fees** £30 per round, £35 Sat & Sun. **Prof** Phil Wright **Course Designer** Tom Williamson **Facilities** **Conf** facs Corporate Hospitality Days **Location** 1.25m NE on A308

Hotel Travelodge London Kingston Upon Thames, 21-23 London Rd, KINGSTON-UPON-THAMES ☎ 08700 850 950 72 en suite

MITCHAM Map 04 TQ26

Mitcham Carshalton Rd, Mitcham Junction CR4 4HN
☎ 020 8648 4280 🖹 020 8647 4197
e-mail: mitchamgolfclub@hotmail.com
web: www.mitchamgc.co.uk
A wooded heathland course on a gravel base, playing as an inland links course.
18 holes, 5935yds, Par 69, SSS 68, Course record 65. Club membership 500.
Visitors Mon-Fri. Booking required Sat, Sun & BHs.

Continued

Dress code. **Societies** Booking required. **Green Fees** £15, £20 Sat & Sun, £25 BHs. **Prof** Paul Burton **Course Designer** T Scott, T Morris **Facilities** **Location** 1m S

Hotel ★★★ 69% Aerodrome Hotel, Purley Way, CROYDON ☎ 020 8710 9000 & 8680 1999 020 8681 6438 84 en suite

New Malden Map 04 TQ26

Malden Traps Ln KT3 4RS
☎ 020 8942 0654 020 8336 2219
e-mail: manager@maldengolfclub.com
web: www.maldengolfclub.com
Parkland course with the hazard of the Beverley Brook which affects 4 holes (3rd, 7th, 8th and 12th).
18 holes, 6252yds, Par 71, SSS 70.
Club membership 800.
Visitors Mon-Fri except BHs. Booking required. Dress code. **Societies** Booking required. **Green Fees** phone. **Prof** Robert Hunter **Facilities** **Conf** Corporate Hospitality Days **Location** N of town centre off B283

Hotel Travelodge London Kingston Upon Thames, 21-23 London Rd, KINGSTON-UPON-THAMES ☎ 08700 850 950 72 en suite

Northwood Map 04 TQ09

Haste Hill The Drive HA6 1HN
☎ 01923 825224

18 holes, 5787yds, Par 68, SSS 68, Course record 63.
Location 0.5m S off A404
Phone for further details

Hotel ★★★ 68% Quality Harrow Hotel, 12-22 Pinner Rd, HARROW ☎ 020 8427 3435 79 en suite

Northwood Rickmansworth Rd HA6 2QW
☎ 01923 821384 01923 840150
e-mail: secretary@northwoodgolf.co.uk
web: www.northwoodgolf.co.uk
A high quality parkland course that provides a good test of golf to the experienced golfer and can hold many surprises for the unsuspecting. The par 4 10th hole, Death or Glory, has wrecked many good cards in the past, while the long par 4 5th hole requires two very good shots to make par.
18 holes, 6535yds, Par 71, SSS 71, Course record 67.
Club membership 650.
Visitors Mon, Thu, Fri. Booking required. Dress code. **Societies** Booking required. **Green Fees** £50 per day, £36 per round. **Prof** CJ Holdsworth **Course Designer** James

Continued

Braid **Facilities** **Conf** Corporate Hospitality Days **Location** On A404

Hotel ★★★ 68% Quality Harrow Hotel, 12-22 Pinner Rd, HARROW ☎ 020 8427 3435 79 en suite

Sandy Lodge Sandy Lodge Ln HA6 2JD
☎ 01923 825429 01923 824319
e-mail: info@sandylodge.co.uk
web: www.sandylodge.co.uk
A links-type, very sandy, heathland course.
18 holes, 6347yds, Par 71, SSS 71, Course record 64.
Club membership 780.
Visitors Mon-Fri. Handicap certificate. Dress code. **Societies** Booking required. **Green Fees** £45 per round. **Prof** Jeff Pinsent **Course Designer** H Vardon **Facilities** **Conf** Corporate Hospitality Days **Location** N of town centre off A4125

Hotel ★★★ 67% The White House, Upton Rd, WATFORD ☎ 01923 237316 57 en suite

Orpington Map 05 TQ46

Chelsfield Lakes Golf Centre Court Rd BR6 9BX
☎ 01689 896266 01689 824577
web: www.hannam.mcmail.com
18 holes, 6077yds, Par 71, SSS 69, Course record 64.
Warren: 9 holes, 1188yds, Par 27.
Course Designer M Sandow **Location** M25 junct 4, on A224
Phone for further details

Hotel ★★★ 71% Bromley Court Hotel, Bromley Hill, BROMLEY ☎ 020 8461 8600 114 en suite

Cray Valley Sandy Ln, St Paul's Cray BR5 3HY
☎ 01689 837909 & 871490 01689 891428
18 hole: 18 holes, 5669yds, Par 70, SSS 67.
9 holes: 9 holes, 2140yds, Par 32.
Location 1m off A20, Critley's Corner junction
Phone for further details

Hotel ★★★ 71% Bromley Court Hotel, Bromley Hill, BROMLEY ☎ 020 8461 8600 114 en suite

Ruxley Park Golf Centre Sandy Ln, St Paul's Cray BR5 3HY
☎ 01689 871490 01689 891428
18 holes, 5703yds, Par 70, SSS 68, Course record 63.
Location 2m NE on A223
Phone for further details

Hotel ★★★ 71% Bromley Court Hotel, Bromley Hill, BROMLEY ☎ 020 8461 8600 114 en suite

Prices may change during the currency of the guide, always check when booking

Pinner Map 04 TQ18

Grims Dyke Oxhey Ln, Hatch End HA5 4AL
☎ 020 8428 4539 🖹 020 8421 5494
e-mail: grimsdykegolfclub@hotmail.com
web: www.club-noticeboard.co.uk/grimsdyke

18 holes, 5596yds, Par 69, SSS 67, Course record 61.
Course Designer James Baird **Location** 3m N of Harrow on A4008
Phone for further details

Hotel ★★★ 68% Best Western Cumberland Hotel, 1 St Johns Rd, HARROW ☎ 020 8863 4111 41 en suite 43 annexe en suite

Pinner Hill Southview Rd, Pinner Hill HA5 3YA
☎ 020 8866 0963 🖹 020 8868 4817
e-mail: pinnerhillgc@uk2.net
web: www.pinnerhillgc.com
On the top of Pinner Hill surrounded by rolling parkland and mature woods, this peaceful atmosphere will make you feel a million miles from North West London's suburbia. Two nine-hole loops of mature fairways and undulating greens will lift and challenge your game.
18 holes, 6392yds, Par 71, SSS 71.
Club membership 710.
Visitors Mon-Fri except BHs. Booking required Mon, Tue & Fri. Dress code. **Societies** welcome. **Green Fees** phone. **Prof** Chris Dack **Course Designer** JH Taylor **Facilities** **Conf** facs Corporate Hospitality Days **Location** 2m NW off A404

Hotel ★★★ 68% Quality Harrow Hotel, 12-22 Pinner Rd, HARROW ☎ 020 8427 3435 79 en suite

Purley Map 05 TQ36

Purley Downs 106 Purley Downs Rd CR2 0RB
☎ 020 8657 8347 🖹 020 8651 5044
e-mail: info@purleydowns.co.uk
web: www.purleydownsgolfclub.co.uk
Hilly downland course which is a good test for golfers.
18 holes, 6262yds, Par 70, SSS 70, Course record 64.
Club membership 750.
Visitors contact club for details. **Societies** welcome. **Green Fees** phone. **Prof** Graham Wilson **Course Designer** J Taylor, HS Colt **Facilities**
Location E of town centre off A235

Hotel ★★★ 69% Aerodrome Hotel, Purley Way, CROYDON ☎ 020 8710 9000 & 8680 1999 🖹 020 8681 6438 84 en suite

Richmond (upon Thames) Map 04 TQ17

Richmond Sudbrook Park, Petersham TW10 7AS
☎ 020 8940 4351 (office) & 8940 7792 (shop)
🖹 8940 8332/7914
e-mail: admin@richmondgolfclub.co.uk
web: www.the richmondgolfclub.com
Beautiful and historic parkland on the edge of Richmond Park dating from 1891 and extensively modernised in recent years. The clubhouse is one of the most-distinguished small Georgian mansions in England.
18 holes, 6100yds, Par 70, SSS 70, Course record 65.
Club membership 650.
Visitors Mon-Fri except BHs. Booking required Wed. Handicap certificate. Dress code. **Societies** Booking required. **Green Fees** £40/£45 per 18 holes. **Prof** Steve Burridge **Course Designer** Tom Dunn **Facilities** by arrangement **Conf** facs Corporate Hospitality Days **Location** 1.5m S off A307 between Kingston & Richmond

Hotel ★★★ 69% The Richmond Hill Hotel, Richmond Hill, RICHMOND UPON THAMES ☎ 020 8940 2247 138 en suite

Royal Mid-Surrey Old Deer Park, Twickenham Rd TW9 2SB
☎ 020 8940 1894 🖹 020 8939 0150
e-mail: secretary@rmsgc.co.uk
web: www.rmsgc.co.uk
A long playing historic parkland course. The flat fairways are cleverly bunkered. The 1st hole at 245yds from the medal tees is a tough par 3 opening hole. The 18th provides an exceptionally good par 4 finish with a huge bunker before the green to catch the not quite perfect long second. The Inner Course, while shorter than the Outer, offers a fair challenge to all golfers. Again the 18th offers a strong par 4 finish with bunkers threatening from the tee. A long second to a sloping, well-bunkered green will reward the accurate player.
Outer Course: 18 holes, 6343yds, Par 69, SSS 71, Course record 62.
Inner Course: 18 holes, 5544yds, Par 68, SSS 67.
Club membership 1400.
Visitors Mon-Fri except BHs. Booking required. Handicap certificate. Dress code. **Societies** Booking required. **Green Fees** phone. **Prof** Peter Cherry **Course Designer** JH Taylor **Facilities** **Leisure** snooker. **Conf** facs Corporate Hospitality Days **Location** 0.5m N of Richmond off A316

Hotel ★★★ 69% The Richmond Hill Hotel, Richmond Hill, RICHMOND UPON THAMES ☎ 020 8940 2247 138 en suite

Romford Map 05 TQ58

Maylands Colchester Rd, Harold Park RM3 0AZ
☎ 01708 341777 🖹 01708 343777
e-mail: maylands@maylandsgolf.com
web: www.maylandsgolf.com
Picturesque undulating parkland course.
18 holes, 6361yds, Par 71, SSS 70, Course record 62.
Club membership 650.
Visitors Mon-Fri. Booking required Sat, Sun & BHs. Handicap certificate. Dress code. **Societies** Booking

Continued

required. **Green Fees** £35 per round, £45 Sat, Sun & BHs. **Prof** Darren Parker **Course Designer** H Colt **Facilities** ⊗ **Conf** Corporate Hospitality Days **Location** M25 junct 28, A12 0.5m towards London, club on right

Hotel Premier Travel Inn Romford Central, Mercury Gardens, ROMFORD ☎ 08701 977220 64 en suite

Risebridge Golf Centre Risebridge Chase, Lower Bedfords Rd RM1 4DG
☎ 01708 741429 🖷 01708 741429
e-mail: pa.jennings@virgin.net
web: www.golfersdirect.co.uk/site/pauljennings
18 holes, 6000yds, Par 71, SSS 70, Course record 66.
Course Designer Hawtree **Location** Between Collier Row Hill
Phone for further details

Hotel Premier Travel Inn Romford Central, Mercury Gardens, ROMFORD ☎ 08701 977220 64 en suite

Romford Heath Dr, Gidea Park RM2 5QB
☎ 01708 740986 🖷 01708 752157
18 holes, 6410yds, Par 72, SSS 70, Course record 64.
Course Designer H Colt **Location** 1m NE on A118
Phone for further details

Hotel Premier Travel Inn Romford Central, Mercury Gardens, ROMFORD ☎ 08701 977220 64 en suite

RUISLIP — Map 04 TQ08

Ruislip Ickenham Rd HA4 7DQ
☎ 01895 638081 & 638835 🖷 01895 635780
e-mail: ruislipgolf@btconnect.com
web: www.middlesexgolf.com
Municipal parkland course. Many trees.

18 holes, 5700yds, Par 69, SSS 68, Course record 65.
Club membership 300.
Visitors Mon-Sun & BHs. Booking required. Dress code. **Societies** Booking required. **Green Fees** £14.50 per 18 holes, £21 Sat, Sun & BHs. **Prof** Paul Glozier **Course Designer** Sand Herd **Facilities** ⊗ **Location** 0.5m SW on B466 opposite Ruislip underground station

Hotel ★★★ 68% Quality Harrow Hotel, 12-22 Pinner Rd, HARROW ☎ 020 8427 3435 79 en suite

SIDCUP — Map 05 TQ47

Sidcup 7 Hurst Rd DA15 9AE
☎ 020 8300 2150 🖷 020 8300 2150
e-mail: sidcupgolfclub@tiscali.co.uk
Easy walking parkland with two lakes and the River Shuttle running through.
9 holes, 5722yds, Par 68, SSS 68.
Club membership 370.
Visitors Mon-Thu except BHs. Booking required. Handicap certificate. Dress code. **Societies** Booking required. **Green Fees** phone. **Course Designer** James Braid **Facilities** ⊗ **Location** N of town centre off A222

Hotel ★★★★ 67% Bexleyheath Marriott Hotel, 1 Broadway, BEXLEYHEATH ☎ 0870 400 7245 142 en suite

SOUTHALL — Map 04 TQ17

West Middlesex Greenford Rd UB1 3EE
☎ 020 8574 3450 🖷 020 8574 2383
e-mail: westmid.gc@virgin.net
web: www.westmiddxgolfclub.co.uk
Gently undulating parkland course founded in 1891, the oldest private course in Middlesex designed by James Braid.
18 holes, 6119yds, Par 69, SSS 69, Course record 64.
Club membership 600.
Visitors Mon-Fri & BHs. Sat & Sun pm. Booking required. Dress code. **Societies** Booking required. **Green Fees** Mon £14 per round, Wed-Fri £16, Sat-Sun £25. **Prof** T Talbot **Course Designer** James Braid **Facilities** ⊗ **Leisure** fishing. **Conf** facs Corporate Hospitality Days **Location** W of town centre on A4127

Hotel ★★★ 65% Best Western Master Robert Hotel, 366 Great West Rd, HOUNSLOW ☎ 020 8570 6261 96 annexe en suite

STANMORE — Map 04 TQ19

Stanmore 29 Gordon Av HA7 2RL
☎ 020 8954 2599 🖷 020 8954 2599
e-mail: secretary@stanmoregolfclub.co.uk
web: www.stanmoregolfclub.co.uk
A quiet and peaceful parkland course in the suburbs of north-west London, with incredible views over the Thames basin from the 3th and 5th tees. The course is short but very challenging as all the fairways are lined with trees. Accuracy plays a major role and notable holes are the 2nd, 8th, 11th and 13th. The signature hole is the par 4 7th, played over a fir tree from an elevated tee onto the fairway.
18 holes, 5885yds, Par 68, SSS 68, Course record 61.
Club membership 500.
Visitors Booking required. **Societies** Booking required. **Green Fees** phone. **Prof** J Reynolds **Course Designer** A MacKenzie **Facilities** ⊗ **Conf** Corporate Hospitality Days **Location** S of town centre between Stanmore & Belmont

Hotel ★★★ 68% Quality Harrow Hotel, 12-22 Pinner Rd, HARROW ☎ 020 8427 3435 79 en suite

SURBITON Map 04 TQ16

Surbiton Woodstock Ln KT9 1UG
☎ 020 8398 3101 (sec) 020 8339 0992
e-mail: gill.whitelock@surbitongolfclub.com
web: www.surbitongolfclub.com
Parkland with easy walking.
18 holes, 6055yds, Par 70, SSS 69, Course record 63.
Club membership 700.
Visitors Mon-Fri except BHs. Booking required. Handicap certificate. Dress code. **Societies** Booking required. **Green Fees** £40 summer, £35 winter. **Prof** Paul Milton **Course Designer** Tom Dunn **Facilities** **Location** A3 Hook junct, A309 S 2m, left onto Woodstock Ln

Hotel Premier Travel Inn Chessington, Leatherhead Rd, CHESSINGTON ☎ 08701 977057 42 en suite

TWICKENHAM Map 04 TQ17

Amida Staines Rd TW2 5JD
☎ 0845 2309 111 020 8783 9475
e-mail: hampton.golf.shop@amidaclubs.com
web: www.amidaclubs.com
A nine-hole pay and play course situated within 70 acres of mature parkland with a water feature coming into play on the 2nd and 3rd holes. The course is mature but has undergone extensive recent improvement work, including new tees and greens and the installation of an automated irrigation system.
9 holes, 2788yds, Par 35, SSS 69.
Club membership 100.
Visitors Sat, Sun & BHs booking required. **Societies** Booking required. **Green Fees** phone. **Prof** Suzy Watt **Facilities** **Leisure** hard tennis courts, heated indoor swimming pool, squash, sauna, solarium, gymnasium, indoor virtual golf. **Conf** facs Corporate Hospitality Days **Location** 2m W on A305

Hotel ★★★ 69% The Richmond Hill Hotel, Richmond Hill, RICHMOND UPON THAMES ☎ 020 8940 2247 138 en suite

Strawberry Hill Wellesley Rd, Strawberry Hill TW2 5SD
☎ 020 8894 0165 & 8898 2082 020 8898 0786
e-mail: secretary@shgc.net
web: www.strawberryhillgolfclub.co.uk
Parkland with easy walking.
9 holes, 4762yds, Par 64, SSS 63, Course record 59.
Club membership 300.
Visitors Mon-Fri. Dress code. **Societies** welcome. **Green Fees** £25/£18 per day, £18/£11 per 18 holes, £14/£8 per 9 holes. **Prof** Peter Buchan **Course Designer** JH Taylor **Facilities** by arrangement **Location** S of town centre off A316

Hotel ★★★ 69% The Richmond Hill Hotel, Richmond Hill, RICHMOND UPON THAMES ☎ 020 8940 2247 138 en suite

If the name of the club appears in italics, details have not been confirmed for this edition of the guide

UPMINSTER Map 05 TQ58

Upminster 114 Hall Ln RM14 1AU
☎ 01708 222788 (secretary) 01708 222484
e-mail: secretary@upminstergolfclub.co.uk
web: www.upminstergolfclub.co.uk
The meandering River Ingrebourne features on several holes of this partly undulating parkland course, situated on one side of the river valley. It provides a challenge for golfers of all abilities. The clubhouse is a beautiful Grade II listed building.
18 holes, 6076yds, Par 69, SSS 69, Course record 62.
Club membership 1000.
Visitors Mon, Wed-Fri except BHs. Booking required. Handicap certificate. Dress code. **Societies** Booking required. **Green Fees** phone. **Prof** Steve Cipa **Course Designer** WG Key **Facilities** **Leisure** bowling, snooker. **Location** Junct M25 & A127, 2m W

Hotel Premier Travel Inn Romford Central, Mercury Gardens, ROMFORD ☎ 08701 977220 64 en suite

UXBRIDGE Map 04 TQ08

Stockley Park Stockley Park UB11 1AQ
☎ 020 8813 5700 020 8813 5655
e-mail: k.soper@stockleyparkgolf.com
web: www.stockleyparkgolf.com
Hilly and challenging course set in 240 acres of parkland and designed by Robert Trent Jones senior. Accessible to a complete range of golfer.
18 holes, 6548yds, Par 72, SSS 71.
Visitors Mon-Sun & BHs. Booking required. Dress code. **Societies** Booking required. **Green Fees** £25 per round, £37 Sat, Sun & BHs. **Prof** Stuart Birch **Course Designer** Robert Trent Jones Snr **Facilities** **Conf** facs Corporate Hospitality Days **Location** M4 junct 4, 1m N off A408

Hotel ★★★★ 76% Crowne Plaza London - Heathrow, Stockley Rd, WEST DRAYTON ☎ 0870 400 9140 458 en suite

Uxbridge The Drive, Harefield Place UB10 8AQ
☎ 01895 237287 01895 813539
e-mail: higolf@btinternet.com

18 holes, 5750yds, Par 68, SSS 68, Course record 66.
Location 2m N off B467
Phone for further details

Hotel ★★★★ 76% Crowne Plaza London - Heathrow, Stockley Rd, WEST DRAYTON ☎ 0870 400 9140 458 en suite

WEMBLEY Map 04 TQ18

Sudbury Bridgewater Rd HA0 1AL
☎ 020 8902 3713 🖹 020 8902 3713
e-mail: enquiries@sudburygolfclubltd.co.uk
web: www.sudburygolfclubltd.co.uk
Undulating parkland near the centre of London.

18 holes, 6282yds, Par 69, SSS 70, Course record 63.
Club membership 650.
Visitors Mon-Fri except BHs. Handicap certificate. Dress code. **Societies** Booking required. **Green Fees** £30 per 18 holes. **Prof** Neil Jordan **Course Designer** Colt **Facilities** **Conf** facs **Location** SW of town centre on A4090

Hotel ★★★ 64% The Bridge Hotel, Western Av, GREENFORD ☎ 020 8566 6246 68 en suite

WEST DRAYTON Map 04 TQ07

Heathpark Stockley Rd UB7 9NA
☎ 01895 444232 🖹 01895 444232
9 holes, 2032yds, Par 64, SSS 60, Course record 64.
Course Designer Neal Coles **Location** M4 junct 4, off A408
Phone for further details

Hotel ★★★★ 76% Crowne Plaza London - Heathrow, Stockley Rd, WEST DRAYTON ☎ 0870 400 9140 458 en suite

WOODFORD GREEN Map 05 TQ49

Woodford Sunset Av IG8 0ST
☎ 020 8504 3330 & 8504 0553 🖹 020 8559 0504
e-mail: office@woodfordgolfclub.fsnet.co.uk
web: www.woodfordgolf.co.uk
Forest land course on the edge of Epping Forest. Views over the Lea valley to the London skyline. When played as 18 holes from dual tees, the course is comprised of four par 3s, two par 5s and twelve par 4s. Although fairly short, the tree-lined fairways and subtle undulations provide and excellent test of golfing skill.
9 holes, 5806yds, Par 70, SSS 68, Course record 66.
Club membership 350.
Visitors Mon, Wed-Fri & Sun except BHs. Tue pm. Dress code. **Societies** Booking required. **Green Fees** £15 per 18 holes, £9 per 9 holes. **Prof** Jon Robson **Course Designer** Tom Dunn **Facilities** by arrangement **Conf** Corporate Hospitality Days **Location** NW of town centre off A104

GREATER MANCHESTER

ALTRINCHAM Map 07 SJ78

Altrincham Stockport Rd WA15 7LP
☎ 0161 928 0761 🖹 0161 928 8542
e-mail: scott.partington@tclt.co.uk
web: www.altringhamgolfclub.org.uk
Municipal parkland course with easy walking, water on many holes, rolling contours and many trees. Driving range in grounds.
18 holes, 6385yds, Par 71, SSS 69.
Club membership 350.
Visitors Mon-Sun & BHs. Booking required. Dress code. **Societies** Booking required. **Green Fees** £10.50 per round, £15 Sat, Sun & BHs. **Prof** Scott Partington **Facilities** **Conf** Corporate Hospitality Days **Location** 0.75m E of town ventre on A560

Hotel ★★★ 68% Cresta Court Hotel, Church St, ALTRINCHAM ☎ 0161 927 7272 136 en suite

Dunham Forest Oldfield Ln WA14 4TY
☎ 0161 928 2605 🖹 0161 929 8975
e-mail: email@dunhamforestgolfclub.com
An attractive parkland course cut through magnificent beech woods.
18 holes, 6636yds, Par 72, SSS 72.
Club membership 680.
Visitors Mon-Fri except BHs. Booking required. **Societies** Booking required. **Green Fees** phone. **Prof** Ian Wrigley **Course Designer** Dave Thomas **Facilities** by arrangement **Leisure** hard tennis courts. **Conf** Corporate Hospitality Days **Location** 1.5m W off A56

Hotel ★★★ 66% Quality Hotel Altrincham, Langham Rd, Bowdon, ALTRINCHAM ☎ 0161 928 7121 91 en suite

Ringway Hale Mount, Hale Barns WA15 8SW
☎ 0161 980 2630 🖹 0161 980 4414
e-mail: andrew@ringwaygolfclub.co.uk
web: www.ringwaygolfclub.co.uk
Parkland with interesting natural hazards. Easy walking and good views of the Pennines and the Peak District.
18 holes, 6482yds, Par 71, SSS 71, Course record 65.
Club membership 800.
Visitors Mon-Sun & BHs. Booking required. Handicap certificate. Dress code. **Societies** welcome. **Green Fees** £40, £50 Sat & Sun. **Prof** Nick Ryan **Course Designer** Colt **Facilities** **Conf** Corporate Hospitality Days **Location** M56 junct 6, A538 for 1m signed Hale, right onto Shay Ln

Hotel ★★★ 68% Cresta Court Hotel, Church St, ALTRINCHAM ☎ 0161 927 7272 136 en suite

ASHTON-IN-MAKERFIELD Map 07 SJ59

Ashton-in-Makerfield Garswood Park, Liverpool Rd WN4 0YT
☎ 01942 719330 🖹 01942 719330
18 holes, 6250yds, Par 70, SSS 70, Course record 63.
Location M6 junct 24, 5m W on A580
Phone for further details

Hotel Premier Travel Inn Wigan South, 53 Warrington Rd, Ashton-in-Makerfield, WIGAN ☎ 0870 9906582 28 en suite

ASHTON-UNDER-LYNE Map 07 SJ99

Ashton-under-Lyne Gorsey Way, Higher Hurst OL6 9HT
☎ 0161 330 1537 📠 0161 330 6673
e-mail: info@ashtongolfclub.co.uk
A testing, varied moorland course, with large greens. Easy walking.
18 holes, 5754yds, Par 69, SSS 68.
Club membership 760.
Visitors Booking required. **Societies** Booking required. **Green Fees** phone. **Prof** Colin Boyle **Facilities** **Conf** facs Corporate Hospitality Days **Location** N off B6194

Hotel ★★★★ 65% Menzies Avant Hotel, Windsor Rd, Manchester St, OLDHAM ☎ 0161 627 5500 103 en suite

Dukinfield Lyne Edge, Yew Tree Ln SK16 5DB
☎ 0161 338 2340 📠 0161 303 0205
e-mail: dgclub@tiscali.co.uk
web: www.dukinfieldgolfclub.co.uk
Recently extended, tricky hillside course with several challenging par 3s and a very long par 5.
18 holes, 5338yds, Par 67, SSS 66.
Club membership 500.
Visitors Mon-Fri. Booking required. play from yellow blocks. **Societies** Booking required. **Green Fees** phone. **Prof** David Green **Facilities** **Conf** Corporate Hospitality Days **Location** S off B6175

Hotel Premier Travel Inn Manchester (Mottram), Stockport Rd, Mottram, HYDE ☎ 0870 9906334 83 en suite

BOLTON Map 07 SD70

Bolton Lostock Park, Chorley New Rd BL6 4AJ
☎ 01204 843067 & 843278 📠 01204 843067
e-mail: boltongolf@lostockpark.fsbusiness.co.uk
This well-maintained heathland course is always a pleasure to visit. The 12th hole should be treated with respect and so too should the final four holes which have ruined many a card.
18 holes, 6237yds, Par 70, SSS 70, Course record 64.
Club membership 612.
Visitors Mon, Wed-Fri except BHs. Booking required. Dress code. **Societies** Booking required. **Green Fees** £28, winter £22.50. **Prof** R Longworth **Facilities** **Conf** facs Corporate Hospitality Days **Location** 3m W of Bolton on A673

Hotel Premier Travel Inn Bolton, 991 Chorley New Rd, Horwich, BOLTON ☎ 08701 977282 40 en suite

Breightmet Red Bridge, Ainsworth BL2 5PA
☎ 01204 527381 & 399275 📠 01204 399275
Long parkland course.
18 holes, 6351yds, Par 72, SSS 71, Course record 67.
Club membership 400.
Visitors Mon, Tue, Thu, Fri except BHs. Handicap certificate. **Societies** Booking required. **Green Fees** £20 per 18 holes. **Course Designer** D Griffiths **Facilities** **Location** E of town centre off A58

Hotel ★★★★ 71% Macdonald Last Drop Village Hotel & Spa, Bromley Cross, BOLTON ☎ 0870 1942117 118 en suite 10 annexe en suite

Deane Broadford Rd, Deane BL3 4NS
☎ 01204 61944 (professional) & 651808 (secretary) 📠 01204 652047
Undulating parkland with small ravines on the approach to some holes.
18 holes, 5652yds, Par 68, SSS 67, Course record 64.
Club membership 470.
Visitors Mon-Fri, Sun & BHs. Booking required. Handicap certificate. Dress code. **Societies** Booking required. **Green Fees** £25 per round, £30 Sun & BHs. **Prof** David Martindale **Facilities** **Conf** facs **Location** M61 junct 5, 1m towards Bolton

Hotel Premier Travel Inn Bolton, 991 Chorley New Rd, Horwich, BOLTON ☎ 08701 977282 40 en suite

Dunscar Longworth Ln, Bromley Cross BL7 9QY
☎ 01204 303321 📠 01204 303321
e-mail: secretary@dunscargolfclub.fsnet.co.uk
A scenic moorland course with panoramic views.
18 holes, 5982yds, Par 71, SSS 69, Course record 63.
Club membership 600.
Visitors Booking required. Handicap certificate. **Societies** Booking required in writing. **Green Fees** phone. **Prof** Gary Treadgold **Facilities** **Location** 2m N off A666

Hotel Travelodge Bolton West (M61 Southbound), Bolton West Service Area, Horwich, BOLTON ☎ 08700 850 950 32 en suite

Great Lever & Farnworth Plodder Ln, Farnworth BL4 0LQ
☎ 01204 656137 📠 01204 656137
Downland course with easy walking.
18 holes, 6044yds, Par 70, SSS 69, Course record 67.
Club membership 600.
Visitors Booking required. Handicap certificate. **Societies** Booking required. **Green Fees** phone. **Prof** Tony Howarth **Facilities** **Location** M61 junct 4, 1m

Hotel ★★★★ 71% Macdonald Last Drop Village Hotel & Spa, Bromley Cross, BOLTON ☎ 0870 1942117 118 en suite 10 annexe en suite

Harwood Roading Brook Rd, Harwood BL2 4JD
☎ 01204 522878 & 524233 📠 01204 524233
e-mail: secretary@harwoodgolfclub.co.uk
web: www.harwoodgolfclub.co.uk
Mainly flat parkland with several water hazards.
18 holes, 5813yds, Par 70, SSS 68, Course record 65.
Club membership 590.
Visitors Mon, Tue, Thu, Fri except BHs. Handicap certificate. Dress code. **Societies** Booking required. **Green Fees** £25 per round. **Prof** C Maroney **Course Designer** G Shuttleworth **Facilities** **Location** 2.5m NE off B6196

Hotel Premier Travel Inn Bolton, 991 Chorley New Rd, Horwich, BOLTON ☎ 08701 977282 40 en suite

Old Links Chorley Old Rd, Montserrat BL1 5SU
☎ 01204 842307 🖷 01204 842307 ext 25
e-mail: mail@boltonoldlinks.co.uk
web: www.boltonoldlinks.co.uk
Championship moorland course.
18 holes, 6469yds, Par 71, SSS 72.
Club membership 600.
Visitors Mon, Wed-Fri, Sun except BHs. Booking required. Handicap certificate. Dress code. **Societies** welcome. **Green Fees** £35 per day, £45 Sun. **Prof** Paul Horridge **Course Designer** A MacKenzie **Facilities** **Conf** facs **Location** NW of town centre on B6226

Hotel Travelodge Bolton West (M61 Southbound), Bolton West Service Area, Horwich, BOLTON
☎ 08700 850 950 32 en suite

Regent Park Links Rd, Chorley New Rd BL6 4AF
☎ 01204 495421 🖷 01204 844620
Parkland course with exceptional moorland views.
18 holes, 6130yds, Par 70, SSS 69, Course record 63.
Club membership 200.
Visitors Mon-Sun & BHs. Booking required. Dress code. **Societies** Booking required. **Green Fees** £10 per round, £12.50 Sat & Sun. **Prof** Neil Brazell **Course Designer** James Braid **Facilities** **Conf** facs Corporate Hospitality Days **Location** M61 junct 6, 1m E off A673

Hotel Travelodge Bolton West (M61 Southbound), Bolton West Service Area, Horwich, BOLTON
☎ 08700 850 950 32 en suite

Turton Wood End Farm, Chapeltown Rd, Bromley Cross BL7 9QH
☎ 01204 852235 🖷 01204 856921
e-mail: info@tgc.com
web: www.turtongolfclub.com
Moorland course with panoramic views. A wide variety of holes which challenge any golfer's technique.
18 holes, 6124yds, Par 70, SSS 69, Course record 68.
Club membership 450.
Visitors Mon, Tue, Thu, Fri, Sun & BHs. Booking required. Dress code. **Societies** Booking required. **Green Fees** £24 per round, £28 Sun & BHs. **Prof** Mark Saunders **Course Designer** Alex Herd **Facilities** **Location** 3m N off A666, follow signs for 'Last Drop Village'

Hotel ★★★★ 71% Macdonald Last Drop Village Hotel & Spa, Bromley Cross, BOLTON ☎ 0870 1942117
118 en suite 10 annexe en suite

BRAMHALL Map 07 SJ88

Bramall Park 20 Manor Rd SK7 3LY
☎ 0161 485 7101 🖷 0161 485 7101
e-mail: secretary@bramallparkgolfclub.co.uk
web: www.bramallparkgolfclub.co.uk
Attractive parkland with some testing, lengthy par 4s, especially after the recent rebunkering of the whole course.
18 holes, 6247yds, Par 70, SSS 70, Course record 63.
Club membership 829.
Visitors Mon, Tue, Thu, Fri except BHs. Booking required. Handicap certificate. Dress code. **Societies** Booking required. **Green Fees** £38 per day, £34 per round. **Prof** M Proffitt **Course Designer** James Braid **Facilities** **Conf** facs Corporate Hospitality Days **Location** NW of town centre off B5149

Bramhall Ladythorn Rd SK7 2EY
☎ 0161 439 6092 🖷 0161 439 0264
e-mail: office@bramhallgolfclub.com
web: www.bramhallgolfclub.com
Undulating parkland with easy walking.
18 holes, 6347yds, Par 70, SSS 70.
Club membership 700.
Visitors Mon-Sun & BHs. Booking required. Handicap certificate. Dress code. **Societies** Booking required. **Green Fees** phone. **Prof** Richard Green **Facilities** by arrangement **Conf** Corporate Hospitality Days **Location** E of town centre off A5102

BURY Map 07 SD81

Bury Unsworth Hall, Blackford Bridge, Manchester Rd BL9 9TJ
☎ 0161 766 4897 🖷 0161 796 3480
web: www.burygolfclub.com
Moorland course, difficult in part. Tight and good test of golf.
18 holes, 5961yds, Par 69, SSS 69, Course record 61.
Club membership 650.
Visitors Mon, Wed-Sun & BHs. Booking required Sat, Sun & BHs. Dress code. **Societies** Booking required. **Green Fees** £30, £35 Sat & Sun. **Prof** G Coope **Course Designer** A MacKenzie **Facilities** **Conf** facs Corporate Hospitality Days **Location** 2m N of M60 junct 17 on A56

Hotel ★★★ 66% Bolholt Country Park Hotel, Walshaw Rd, BURY ☎ 0161 762 4000 65 en suite

Lowes Park Hilltop, Lowes Rd BL9 6SU
☎ 0161 764 1231 🖷 0161 763 9503
e-mail: lowes@parkgc.fsnet.co.uk
web: www.lowesparkgc.co.uk
Moorland with easy walking. Exposed outlook with good views.
9 holes, 6009yds, Par 70, SSS 69, Course record 65.
Club membership 350.
Visitors Tue, Thu, Fri, Sun except BHs. Booking required. Handicap certificate. Dress code. **Societies** Booking required. **Green Fees** £15, £10 winter. **Facilities** **Conf** facs Corporate Hospitality Days **Location** N side of town centre off A56

Hotel ★★★ 66% Bolholt Country Park Hotel, Walshaw Rd, BURY ☎ 0161 762 4000 65 en suite

Walmersley Garretts Close, Walmersley BL9 6TE
☎ 0161 764 1429 & 0161 764 7770 🖷 0161 764 7770
Moorland hillside course, with wide fairways, large greens and extensive views. Testing holes: 2nd (484 yds) par 5; 5th par 4 with severe dog leg and various hazards.
18 holes, 5341yds, Par 69, SSS 67.
Club membership 475.
Visitors Mon, Wed-Fri. Sun & BHs after 10am. Booking required. Dress code. **Societies** Booking required. **Green Fees** £25 per day, £28 Sun & BHs. **Prof** P Thorpe **Course Designer** S Marnoch **Facilities** **Location** 2m N off A56

Hotel ★★★ 66% Bolholt Country Park Hotel, Walshaw Rd, BURY ☎ 0161 762 4000 65 en suite

Continued

CHEADLE Map 07 SJ88

Cheadle Cheadle Rd SK8 1HW
☎ 0161 491 4452
e-mail: cheadlegolfclub@msn.com
web: www.cheadlegolfclub.com
Parkland with hazards on every hole, from sand bunkers and copses to a stream across six of the fairways.
9 holes, 5006yds, Par 64, SSS 65.
Club membership 425.
Visitors Mon, Wed-Fri, Sun & BHs. Handicap certificate. Dress code. **Societies** Booking required. **Green Fees** £25, £28 Sun. **Prof** D Cain **Course Designer** T Renouf **Facilities** **Location** S of village off A5149

Hotel ★★ 69% The Wycliffe Hotel, 74 Edgeley Rd, Edgeley, STOCKPORT ☎ 0161 477 5395 18 en suite

DENTON Map 07 SJ99

Denton Manchester Rd M34 2GG
☎ 0161 336 3218 Fax 0161 336 4751
e-mail: dentongolfclub@btinternet.com
web: www.dentongolfclub.com
Easy walking parkland course with brook running through. One notable hole is called Death and Glory.
18 holes, 6443yds, Par 71, SSS 71, Course record 66.
Club membership 740.
Visitors Mon-Fri & BHs. Handicap certificate. Dress code. **Societies** Booking required. **Green Fees** phone. **Prof** M Hollingworth **Course Designer** R McCauley **Facilities** by arrangement **Location** M60 junct 24, 1.5m W on A57

Hotel ★★★ 65% Old Rectory Hotel, Meadow Ln, Haughton Green, Denton, MANCHESTER
☎ 0161 336 7516 30 en suite 6 annexe en suite

FAILSWORTH Map 07 SD80

Brookdale Medlock Rd M35 9WQ
☎ 0161 681 4534 Fax 0161 688 6872
e-mail: info@brookdalegolfclub.co.uk
web: www.brookdalegolfclub.co.uk
Challenging parkland course in the Medlock valley with great Pennine views, although only 5m from the centre of Manchester. The river Medlock meanders through the course and features on six of the holes.
18 holes, 5864yds, Par 68, SSS 68, Course record 64.
Club membership 700.
Visitors Mon-Fri. Booking required. Dress code. **Societies** Booking required. **Green Fees** phone. **Prof** Tony Cuppello **Facilities**
Location M60/A62 Oldham exit towards Manchester, left at NatWest bank, left at road end right, right at minirdbt, 0.5m on left

Hotel ★★★★ 65% Menzies Avant Hotel, Windsor Rd, Manchester St, OLDHAM ☎ 0161 627 5500 103 en suite

FLIXTON Map 07 SJ79

William Wroe Municipal Pennybridge Ln, Flixton Rd M41 5DX
☎ 0161 748 8680
18 holes, 4395yds, Par 64, SSS 65.
Location E of village off B5158, 3m from Manchester centre
Phone for further details

Continued

Hotel Premier Travel Inn Manchester (Sale), Carrington Ln, Ashton-Upon-Mersey, SALE
☎ 08701 977179 40 en suite

GATLEY Map 07 SJ88

Gatley Waterfall Farm, Styal Rd, Heald Green SK8 3TW
☎ 0161 437 2091
e-mail: enquiries@gatleygolfclub.com
web: www.gatleygolfclub.com
Moderately testing parkland course with a tough finish.
9 holes, 5934yds, Par 68, SSS 68, Course record 67.
Club membership 400.
Visitors Mon, Wed-Fri, Sun & BHs. Handicap certificate. Dress code. **Societies** welcome. **Green Fees** £20 per 18 holes. **Prof** James Matterson **Facilities** **Conf** Corporate Hospitality Days **Location** S of village off B5166

Hotel ★★★ 67% Belfry House Hotel, Stanley Rd, HANDFORTH ☎ 0161 437 0511 81 en suite

HAZEL GROVE Map 07 SJ98

Hazel Grove Buxton Rd SK7 6LU
☎ 0161 483 3978
Testing parkland course with tricky greens and water hazards coming into play on several holes. Year round play on the greens.
18 holes, 6310yds, Par 71, SSS 70, Course record 62.
Club membership 600.
Visitors Mon, Wed-Sun & BHs. Dress code. **Societies** Booking required. **Green Fees** phone. **Prof** J Hopley **Course Designer** A MacKenzie **Facilities** **Leisure** golf electronic teaching system (GASP). **Conf** facs Corporate Hospitality Days **Location** 1m E off A6

HINDLEY Map 07 SD60

Hindley Hall Hall Ln WN2 2SQ
☎ 01942 255131 Fax 01942 253871
18 holes, 5913yds, Par 69, SSS 68, Course record 64.
Location M61 junct 6, 3m, 1m N off A58
Phone for further details

Hotel ★★★ 65% Quality Hotel Wigan, Riverway, WIGAN ☎ 01942 826888 88 en suite

HYDE Map 07 SJ99

Werneth Low Werneth Low Rd, Gee Cross SK14 3AF
☎ 0161 368 2503 & 336 9496 (secretary) Fax 0161 320 0053
e-mail: adfwoodley@ukonline.co.uk
Hard walking but good views of six counties from this undulating moorland course, which is played in a 7-4-7 loop. Exposed to wind with small greens. A good test of golfing skill.
11 holes, 6113yds, Par 70, SSS 70, Course record 64.
Club membership 375.
Visitors Mon, Tue pm, Wed, Thu am, Fri. Sat booking required. **Societies** Booking required 14 days in advance. **Green Fees** phone. **Prof** Tony Bacchus **Facilities** **Conf** Corporate Hospitality Days
Location 2m S of town centre

Hotel ★★ 78% Wind in the Willows Hotel, Derbyshire Level, GLOSSOP ☎ 01457 868001 12 en suite

KEARSLEY Map 07 SD70

Manor Moss Ln BL4 8SF
☎ 01204 701027 🖷 01204 796914
18 holes, 5010yds, Par 66, SSS 64, Course record 65.
Course Designer Jeff Yates **Location** Off A666 Manchester Rd
Phone for further details

Hotel ★★★ 64% Novotel Manchester West, Worsley Brow, WORSLEY ☎ 0161 799 3535 119 en suite

LITTLEBOROUGH Map 07 SD91

Whittaker Whittaker Ln OL15 0LH
☎ 01706 378310
Moorland course with outstanding views of Hollingworth Lake Countryside Park and the Pennine Hills.
9 holes, 5632yds, Par 68, SSS 67, Course record 61.
Club membership 240.
Visitors Mon-Sat except BHs. Booking required. **Societies** welcome. **Green Fees** £14 per 18 holes, £18 Sat. Winter reduced rates. **Facilities** **Location** 1.5m from Littleborough off A58

Hotel ★★★★ 62% Macdonald Norton Grange Hotel, Manchester Rd, Castleton, ROCHDALE ☎ 0870 1942119 51 en suite

MANCHESTER Map 07 SJ89

Blackley Victoria Ave East, Blackley M9 7HW
☎ 0161 643 2980 & 654 7770 🖷 0161 653 8300
e-mail: office@blackleygolfclub.com
web: www.blackleygolfclub.com
Parkland course crossed by a footpath. The course has recently been redesigned giving greater challenge and interest including water features.
18 holes, 6168yds, Par 70, SSS 71.
Club membership 800.
Visitors Mon-Sun & BHs. Booking required Thu, Sat, Sun & BHs. Handicap certificate. Dress code. **Societies** Booking required. **Green Fees** phone. **Prof** Craig Gould **Course Designer** Gaunt & Marnoch **Facilities** by arrangement **Conf** Corporate Hospitality Days **Location** 4m N of city centre

Hotel ★★★ 76% Malmaison, Piccadilly, MANCHESTER ☎ 0161 278 1000 167 en suite

Chorlton-cum-Hardy Barlow Hall, Barlow Hall Rd, Chorlton-cum-Hardy M21 7JJ
☎ 0161 881 5830 🖷 0161 881 4532
e-mail: chorltongolf@hotmail.com
web: www.chorltoncumhardygolfclub.sagenet.co.uk
Set in the grounds of Barlow Hall, this challenging parkland course winds its way around the way around the banks of the Mersey. The testing opening holes lead up to the stroke 1 7th, an impressive 474yd par 4, with its elevated green. The course then meanders through parkland culminating at the par 4 18th.
18 holes, 6039yds, Par 70, SSS 69, Course record 61.
Club membership 700.
Visitors Mon-Sun & BHs. Booking required. Dress code. **Societies** Booking required. **Green Fees** phone. **Prof** David Valentine **Facilities** **Leisure** snooker. **Conf** Corporate Hospitality Days **Location** 4m S of Manchester, A5103/A5145

Chorlton-cum-Hardy

Hotel ★★★ 68% Willow Bank Hotel, 340-342 Wilmslow Rd, Fallowfield, MANCHESTER ☎ 0161 224 0461 117 en suite

Davyhulme Park Gleneagles Rd, Davyhulme M41 8SA
☎ 0161 748 2260 🖷 0161 747 4067
e-mail: davyhulmeparkgolfclub@email.com
Parkland course.
18 holes, 6237yds, Par 72, SSS 70, Course record 64.
Club membership 700.
Visitors Mon, Tue & Thu. **Societies** Booking required. **Green Fees** phone. **Prof** Dean Butler **Facilities** **Leisure** snooker. **Conf** Corporate Hospitality Days **Location** Next to Trafford General Hospital

Hotel Premier Travel Inn Manchester (Sale), Carrington Ln, Ashton-Upon-Mersey, SALE ☎ 08701 977179 40 en suite

Didsbury Ford Ln, Northenden M22 4NQ
☎ 0161 998 9278 🖷 0161 902 3060
e-mail: golf@didsburygolfclub.com
web: www.didsburygolfclub.com
Parkland course.
18 holes, 6273yds, Par 70, SSS 70, Course record 60.
Club membership 750.
Visitors Mon, Tue, Thu, Fri & Sun except BHs. Booking required. Dress code. **Societies** Booking required. **Green Fees** £29 per day, £33 Sun. **Prof** Peter Barber **Facilities** **Conf** facs Corporate Hospitality Days **Location** 6m S of city centre off A5145

Hotel Travelodge Manchester Didsbury, Kingsway, DIDSBURY ☎ 08700 850 950 62 en suite

Fairfield "Boothdale", Booth Rd, Audenshaw M34 5QA
☎ 0161 301 4528 🖷 0161 301 4254
e-mail: secretary@fairfieldgolf.co.uk
18 holes, 4956yds, Par 68, SSS 66, Course record 63.
Location 5m E of Manchester off A635
Phone for further details

Hotel ★★★ 65% Old Rectory Hotel, Meadow Ln, Haughton Green, Denton, MANCHESTER ☎ 0161 336 7516 30 en suite 6 annexe en suite

Continued

Marriott Worsley Park Hotel & Country Club Worsley Park, Worsley M28 2QT
☎ 0161 975 2043 🖹 0161 975 2058
web: www.marriott.co.uk/golf
Set in 200 acres of parkland with a range of tee positions, eight lakes and 70 strategically placed bunkers and providing an exciting challenge to golfers of all abilities, very often requiring brains rather than brawn to make a successful score.
18 holes, 6611yds, Par 71, SSS 72, Course record 61. Club membership 400.
Visitors Mon-Sun & BHs. Booking required. Dress code. **Societies** Booking required. **Green Fees** £48, £60 Sat, Sun & BHs. **Prof** David Screeton **Course Designer** Ross McMurray **Facilities** **Leisure** heated indoor swimming pool, sauna, solarium, gymnasium, Short game area. **Conf** facs **Location** M60 junct 13, A585, course 0.5m on left

Hotel ★★★★ 69% Marriott Worsley Park Hotel & Country Club, Worsley Park, Worsley, MANCHESTER ☎ 0161 975 2000 158 en suite

Northenden Palatine Rd, Northenden M22 4FR
☎ 0161 998 4738 🖹 0161 945 5592
e-mail: manager@northendengolfclub.com
web: www.northendengolfclub.com
Parkland course surrounded by the River Mersey with 18 newly rebuilt USGA specification greens.

18 holes, 6432yds, Par 72, SSS 71, Course record 64. Club membership 800.
Visitors Mon-Fri, Sun & BHs. Booking required. Handicap certificate. Dress code. **Societies** Booking required. **Green Fees** £32 per day, £35 Sat, Sun & BHs. **Prof** J Curtis **Course Designer** Renouf, S Gidman **Facilities** **Leisure** indoor teaching facility. **Conf** Corporate Hospitality Days **Location** 6.5m S of city centre on B1567

Hotel Travelodge Manchester Didsbury, Kingsway, DIDSBURY ☎ 08700 850 950 62 en suite

Withington 243 Palatine Rd, West Didsbury M20 2UE
☎ 0161 445 9544 🖹 0161 445 5210
18 holes, 6410yds, Par 71, SSS 71.
Location 4m SW of city centre off B5167
Phone for further details

Hotel Travelodge Manchester Didsbury, Kingsway, DIDSBURY ☎ 08700 850 950 62 en suite

Worsley Stableford Av, Worsley M30 8AP
☎ 0161 789 4202 🖹 0161 789 3200
Well-wooded parkland course.
18 holes, 6252yds, Par 71, SSS 70, Course record 65. Club membership 600.
Visitors contact club for details. **Societies** welcome. **Green Fees** phone. **Prof** Ceri Cousins **Course Designer** James Braid **Facilities** **Location** 6.5m NW of city centre off A572

Hotel ★★★ 64% Novotel Manchester West, Worsley Brow, WORSLEY ☎ 0161 799 3535 119 en suite

MELLOR Map 07 SJ98

Mellor & Townscliffe Gibb Ln, Tarden SK6 5NA
☎ 0161 427 2208 (secretary)
web: www.mellorgolf.co.uk
Scenic parkland and moorland course, undulating with some hard walking. Good views. Testing 200yd 9th hole, par 3.
18 holes, 5925yds, Par 70, SSS 69. Club membership 650.
Visitors Mon-Fri, Sun & BHs. Booking required. Handicap certificate. Dress code. **Societies** Booking required. **Green Fees** £24 per day, £32 Sun & BHs. **Prof** Gary R Broadley **Facilities** **Location** 7m SE of Stockport off A626

Hotel ★★★ 69% Bredbury Hall Hotel & Country Club, Goyt Valley, BREDBURY ☎ 0161 430 7421 150 en suite

MIDDLETON Map 07 SD80

Manchester Hopwood Cottage, Rochdale Rd M24 6QP
☎ 0161 643 3202 🖹 0161 643 9174
e-mail: secretary@mangc.co.uk
web: www.mangc.co.uk
Moorland golf of unique character over a spaciously laid out course with generous fairways sweeping along to large greens. A wide variety of holes will challenge the golfer's technique, particularly the testing last four holes.
18 holes, 6491yds, Par 72, SSS 72, Course record 63. Club membership 650.
Visitors Mon-Fri except BHs. Booking required. Handicap certificate. Dress code. **Societies** Booking required. **Green Fees** £40 per day, £25 per round. **Prof** Brian Connor **Course Designer** Shapland Colt **Facilities** **Leisure** snooker. **Conf** facs Corporate Hospitality Days **Location** 2.5m N off A664

Hotel ★★★★ 62% Macdonald Norton Grange Hotel, Manchester Rd, Castleton, ROCHDALE ☎ 0870 1942119 51 en suite

New North Manchester Rhodes House, Manchester Old Rd M24 4PE
☎ 0161 643 9033 🖹 0161 643 7775
e-mail: tee@nmgc.co.uk
web: www.nmgc.co.uk
Delightful moorland and parkland with several water features. Challenging but fair for the accomplished golfer.
18 holes, 6527yds, Par 71, SSS 71, Course record 66. Club membership 610.

Continued

Visitors Mon-Fri except BHs. Booking required. Handicap certificate. Dress code. **Societies** Booking required. **Green Fees** £30 per day, £28 per round. **Prof** Jason Peel **Course Designer** J Braid **Facilities** **Leisure** 2 full size snooker tables. **Location** W of town centre off A576

Hotel ★★★★ 65% Menzies Avant Hotel, Windsor Rd, Manchester St, OLDHAM ☎ 0161 627 5500 103 en suite

MILNROW Map 07 SD91

Tunshill Kiln Ln OL16 3TS
☎ 01706 342095
Testing moorland course with two demanding par 5s and out of bounds features on eight of the nine holes.
9 holes, 5743yds, Par 70, SSS 68, Course record 64. Club membership 300.
Visitors Mon-Fri. Dress code. **Societies** Booking required. **Green Fees** £16 Mon-Fri. **Facilities** by arrangement by arrangement by arrangement by arrangement **Location** 1m NE M62 exit junct 21 off B6225

Hotel ★★★★ 62% Macdonald Norton Grange Hotel, Manchester Rd, Castleton, ROCHDALE ☎ 0870 1942119 51 en suite

OLDHAM Map 07 SD90

Crompton & Royton Highbarn, Royton OL2 6RW
☎ 0161 624 0986 0161 652 4711
e-mail: secretary@cromptonandroytongolfclub.co.uk
web: www.cromptonandroytongolfclub.co.uk
18 holes, 6214yds, Par 70, SSS 70, Course record 62.
Location 0.5m NE of Royton
Phone for further details

Hotel ★★★★ 65% Menzies Avant Hotel, Windsor Rd, Manchester St, OLDHAM ☎ 0161 627 5500 103 en suite

Oldham Lees New Rd OL4 5PN
☎ 0161 624 4986
Moorland course, with hard walking.
18 holes, 5122yds, Par 66, SSS 65, Course record 62. Club membership 320.
Visitors Mon-Sun. **Societies** Booking required. **Green Fees** phone. **Prof** R Heginbotham **Facilities** **Location** 2.5m E off A669

Hotel ★★★★ 65% Menzies Avant Hotel, Windsor Rd, Manchester St, OLDHAM ☎ 0161 627 5500 103 en suite

Werneth Green Ln, Garden Suburb OL8 3AZ
☎ 0161 624 1190
e-mail: secretary@wernethgolfclub.co.uk
web: www.wernethgolfclub.co.uk
Semi-moorland course, with a deep gully and stream crossing eight fairways. Testing hole: 3rd (par 3).
18 holes, 5363yds, Par 68, SSS 66, Course record 61. Club membership 520.
Visitors Mon, Wed, Fri & BHs. Dress code. **Societies** Booking required. **Green Fees** £16 per day. **Prof** Roy Penney **Course Designer** Sandy Herd **Facilities** **Conf** Corporate Hospitality Days **Location** S of town centre off A627

Hotel ★★★★ 65% Menzies Avant Hotel, Windsor Rd, Manchester St, OLDHAM ☎ 0161 627 5500 103 en suite

PRESTWICH Map 07 SD80

Heaton Park Municipal Heaton Park, Middleton Rd M25 2SW
☎ 0161 654 9899 0161 653 2003
web: www.manchester.gov.uk/leisure/parks/heaton/golf
A parkland-style course in historic Heaton Park, with rolling hills and lakes, designed by five times Open Champion JH Taylor. It has some spectacular holes and is a good test for golfers of all abilities.
Championship: 18 holes, 5755yds, Par 70, SSS 68.
Visitors Mon-Fri. Booking required Sat, Sun & BHs. Dress code. **Societies** Booking required. **Green Fees** £10.50, £14 Sat & Sun. **Prof** Gary Dermott **Course Designer** JH Taylor **Facilities** **Leisure** fishing, 18 hole par 3 course. **Conf** facs **Location** N of Manchester near M60 junct 19

Hotel Premier Travel Inn Manchester West, East Lancs Rd, SWINTON ☎ 0870 9906480 27 en suite

Prestwich Hilton Ln M25 9XB
☎ 0161 773 1404 0161 772 0700
18 holes, 4846yds, Par 65, SSS 65, Course record 60.
Location N of town centre on A6044
Phone for further details

Hotel ★★★ 64% Novotel Manchester West, Worsley Brow, WORSLEY ☎ 0161 799 3535 119 en suite

ROCHDALE Map 07 SD81

Castle Hawk Chadwick Ln, Castleton OL11 3BY
☎ 01706 640841 01706 860587
e-mail: teeoff@castlehawk.co.uk
web: www.castlehawk.co.uk
New Course: 9 holes, 2699yds, Par 34, SSS 34, Course record 30.
Old Course: 18 holes, 3189yds, Par 55, SSS 55.
Course Designer T Wilson **Location** M62 junct 20, S of Rochdale
Phone for further details

Hotel ★★★★ 62% Macdonald Norton Grange Hotel, Manchester Rd, Castleton, ROCHDALE ☎ 0870 1942119 51 en suite

Marland Park Springfield Park, Bolton Rd OL11 4RE
☎ 01706 656401 (Sat & Sun)
18 holes, 5237yds, Par 67, SSS 66, Course record 64.
Location 1.5m SW off A58
Phone for further details

Hotel ★★★★ 62% Macdonald Norton Grange Hotel, Manchester Rd, Castleton, ROCHDALE ☎ 0870 1942119 51 en suite

Rochdale Edenfield Rd OL11 5YR
☎ 01706 643818 01706 861113
e-mail: office@rochdalegolfclub.fsnet.com
Easy walking parkland for enjoyable golf.
18 holes, 6050yds, Par 71, SSS 69, Course record 65. Club membership 750.
Visitors Booking required. **Societies** Booking required. **Green Fees** phone. **Prof** Andrew Laverty **Course Designer** George Lowe **Facilities** **Conf** facs Corporate Hospitality Days **Location** 1.75m W on A680

Continued

Hotel ★★★★ 62% Macdonald Norton Grange Hotel, Manchester Rd, Castleton, ROCHDALE ☎ 0870 1942119 51 en suite

ROMILEY Map 07 SJ99

Romiley Goose House Green SK6 4LJ
☎ 0161 430 2392 🖷 0161 430 7258
e-mail: office@romileygolfclub.org
web: www.romileygolfclub.org
Semi-parkland course on the edge of the Derbyshire Hills, providing a good test of golf with a number of outstanding holes, notably the 6th, 9th, 14th and 16th. The latter enjoys magnificent views from the tee.

18 holes, 6454yds, Par 70, SSS 71, Course record 66. Club membership 700.
Visitors contact club for details. **Societies** welcome. **Green Fees** phone. **Prof** Lee Paul Sullivan **Facilities** **Location** E of town centre off B6104

Hotel ★★ 69% The Wycliffe Hotel, 74 Edgeley Rd, Edgeley, STOCKPORT ☎ 0161 477 5395 18 en suite

SALE Map 07 SJ79

Ashton on Mersey Church Ln M33 5QQ
☎ 0161 976 4390 & 962 3727 🖷 0161 976 4390
e-mail: golf@aomgc.fsnet.co.uk
web: www.aomgc.co.uk
Parkland with easy walking alongside the River Mersey.
9 holes, 6146yds, Par 71, SSS 69, Course record 66. Club membership 485.
Visitors Mon, Wed-Fri & BHs. Handicap certificate. Dress code. **Societies** Booking required. **Green Fees** £20.50. **Prof** Mike Williams **Facilities** by arrangement **Leisure** sauna. **Conf** facs **Location** M60 junct 7, 1m W off Glebelands Rd

Hotel ★★★ 68% Cresta Court Hotel, Church St, ALTRINCHAM ☎ 0161 927 7272 136 en suite

Sale Golf Rd M33 2XU
☎ 0161 973 1638 (office) & 973 1730 (pro)
🖷 0161 962 4217
e-mail: mail@salegolfclub.com
web: www.salegolfclub.com
Tree-lined parkland course. Feature holes are the 13th - Watery Gap - and the par 3 3rd hole of 210yds over water. Four new holes in play from 2005.
18 holes, 6301yds, Par 70, SSS 69, Course record 63. Club membership 700.
Visitors Mon-Fri except BHs. Booking required. Dress code. **Societies** Booking required. **Green Fees** £28 per day, £33 Sat & Sun. **Prof** Mike Stewart **Facilities**

Continued

Conf Corporate Hospitality Days **Location** M60 junct 6, 0.5m NW of town centre off A6144

Hotel ★★★ 68% Cresta Court Hotel, Church St, ALTRINCHAM ☎ 0161 927 7272 136 en suite

SHEVINGTON Map 07 SD50

Gathurst 62 Miles Ln WN6 8EW
☎ 01257 255235 (secretary) 🖷 01257 255953
A testing parkland course, slightly hilly.
18 holes, 6016yds, Par 70, SSS 69, Course record 64. Club membership 630.
Visitors Mon, Tue, Thu & Fri. Handicap certificate. Dress code. **Societies** welcome. **Green Fees** £30 per round. **Prof** David Clarke **Course Designer** N Pearson **Facilities** **Location** M6 junct 27, 1m SW of village on B5375

Hotel ★★★★ 63% Macdonald Kilhey Court, Chorley Rd, Standish, WIGAN ☎ 0870 1942122 62 en suite

STALYBRIDGE Map 07 SJ99

Stamford Oakfield House, Huddersfield Rd SK15 3PY
☎ 01457 832126
e-mail: stamford.golfclub@totalise.co.uk
Undulating moorland course.
18 holes, 5701yds, Par 70, SSS 68, Course record 62. Club membership 600.
Visitors Mon-Sun & BHs. Dress code. **Societies** welcome. **Green Fees** £20 per day, £25 Sat & Sun after 3pm. **Prof** Brian Badger **Facilities** **Conf** facs Corporate Hospitality Days **Location** 2m NE off A635

Guest House ♦♦♦♦ Mallons Restaurant with Guest Rooms, 792-794 Huddersfield Rd, Austerlands, OLDHAM ☎ 0161 622 1234 5 rms (4 en suite)

STANDISH Map 07 SD51

Standish Court Rectory Ln WN6 0XD
☎ 01257 425777 🖷 01257 425777
e-mail: info@standishgolf.co.uk
web: www.standishgolf.co.uk
Undulating 18-hole parkland course, not overly long but provides a good test for all levels of players. The front nine is more open with room for errors, back nine very scenic through woodland, a number of tight driving holes. Greens in excellent condition.
18 holes, 4860yds, Par 68, SSS 64, Course record 63. Club membership 375.
Visitors Mon-Sun & BHs. Booking required. Dress code. **Societies** Booking required. **Green Fees** £9.50 Mon, Tue, £12 Wed-Fri, £16 Sat, Sun & BHs. **Prof** Blake Toone **Course Designer** P Dawson **Facilities** **Conf** facs Corporate Hospitality Days **Location** E of town centre on B5239

Hotel ★★★★ 63% Macdonald Kilhey Court, Chorley Rd, Standish, WIGAN ☎ 0870 1942122 62 en suite

STOCKPORT Map 07 SJ89

Heaton Moor Heaton Mersey SK4 3NX
☎ 0161 432 2134 🖷 0161 432 2134
e-mail: heatonmoorgolfclub@yahoo.co.uk
web: www.heatonmoorgolfclub.co.uk
Gently undulating parkland with two separate nine holes starting from the clubhouse. The narrow fairways are challenging.

Continued

18 holes, 5968, Par 70, SSS 69, Course record 66.
Club membership 700.
Visitors Mon-Fri, Sun & BHs. Dress code. **Societies** Booking required. **Green Fees** phone. **Prof** Simon Marsh **Facilities** ⊗ ℿ ♨ ☕ 🍸 ⛺ 🏠 🏌 **Location** N of town centre off B5169

Hotel ★★★ 69% Bredbury Hall Hotel & Country Club, Goyt Valley, BREDBURY ☎ 0161 430 7421 150 en suite

Houldsworth Houldsworth Park, Reddish SK5 6BN

☎ 0161 442 1712 🖷 0161 947 9678
e-mail: secretary@houldsworthgolfclub.co.uk
web: www.houldsworthgolfclub.co.uk
Flat, tree-lined parkland course with water hazards. Testing holes 9th (par 5) and 13th (par 5).
18 holes, 6209yds, Par 71, SSS 70, Course record 65.
Club membership 680.
Visitors Booking required. **Societies** Mon, Thu & Fri. Booking required with secretary. **Green Fees** phone. ⊛ **Prof** Steven McLean **Course Designer** Dave Thomas **Facilities** ⊗ ℿ ♨ ☕ 🍸 ⛺ 🏠 ⛳ 🏌 **Location** 4m SE of city centre off A6

Hotel ★★★ 68% Willow Bank Hotel, 340-342 Wilmslow Rd, Fallowfield, MANCHESTER ☎ 0161 224 0461 117 en suite

Marple Barnsfold Rd, Hawk Green, Marple SK6 7EL

☎ 0161 427 2311 & 427 1195 (pro) 🖷 0161 427 2311
e-mail: marple.golf.club@ukgateway-net
web: www.marplegolfclub.4t.com
Parkland with several ponds or other water hazards. Gentle slopes overlook the Cheshire plains.
18 holes, 5552yds, Par 68, SSS 67, Course record 66.
Club membership 640.
Visitors Mon, Tue pm, Wed, Thu am, Fri. Booking required Sat & Sun. **Societies** Booking required. **Green Fees** phone. ⊛ **Prof** David Myers **Facilities** ⊗ ℿ ♨ ☕ 🍸 ⛺ 🏠 🏌 **Leisure** snooker. **Conf** Corporate Hospitality Days **Location** S of town centre

Hotel ★★★ 69% Bredbury Hall Hotel & Country Club, Goyt Valley, BREDBURY ☎ 0161 430 7421 150 en suite

Reddish Vale Southcliffe Rd, Reddish SK5 7EE

☎ 0161 480 2359 🖷 0161 480 2359
e-mail: admin@rvgc.co.uk
web: www.rvgc.co.uk
Undulating heathland course in the Tame valley, designed by Alister MacKenzie.
18 holes, 6100yds, Par 69, SSS 69, Course record 64.
Club membership 550.
Visitors Mon-Fri. Dress code. **Societies** welcome. **Green Fees** £38 per day, £28 per round, £40 per round Sat, Sun & BHs. **Prof** Bob Freeman **Course Designer** A MacKenzie **Facilities** ⊗ ℿ ♨ ☕ 🍸 ⛺ 🏠 ⛳ 🏌 **Conf** Corporate Hospitality Days **Location** Off Reddish Road, M6 junct 1/27

Hotel ★★ 69% The Wycliffe Hotel, 74 Edgeley Rd, Edgeley, STOCKPORT ☎ 0161 477 5395 18 en suite

Stockport Offerton Rd, Offerton SK2 5HL

☎ 0161 427 8369 🖷 0161 427 8369
e-mail: info@stockportgolf.co.uk
web: www.stockportgolf.co.uk
A beautifully situated course in wide open countryside with views of the Cheshire and Derbyshire hills. It is not too long but requires that the player plays all the shots, to excellent greens. Demanding holes include the dog-leg 3rd, 12th and 18th and the 460yd opening hole is among the toughest in Cheshire. Regional qualifying course for Open Championship.

Continued

18 holes, 6326yds, Par 71, SSS 71, Course record 64.
Club membership 500.
Visitors Mon, Wed-Sun & BHs. Booking required Wed-Sun & BHs. Handicap certificate. Dress code. **Societies** Booking required. **Green Fees** £50 per day, £40 per 18 holes, £55/£45 Sat & Sun. ⊛ **Prof** Mike Peel **Course Designer** P Barrie, A Herd **Facilities** ⊗ ℿ ♨ ☕ 🍸 ⛺ 🏠 ⛳ 🏌 **Conf** Corporate Hospitality Days **Location** 4m SE on A627

Hotel ★★★ 69% Bredbury Hall Hotel & Country Club, Goyt Valley, BREDBURY ☎ 0161 430 7421 150 en suite

SWINTON — Map 07 SD70

Swinton Park East Lancashire Rd M27 5LX

☎ 0161 794 0861 🖷 0161 281 0698
e-mail: info@spgolf.com
web: www.spgolf.com
One of Lancashire's longest inland courses. Designed and laid out in 1926 by James Braid.

18 holes, 6472yds, Par 73, SSS 71.
Club membership 600.
Visitors Mon-Wed, Fri. Booking required. Handicap certificate. **Societies** Booking required in writing. **Green Fees** phone. ⊛ **Prof** James Wilson **Course Designer** James Braid **Facilities** ⊗ ℿ ♨ ☕ 🍸 ⛺ 🏠 🏌 **Conf** facs **Location** 1m W off A580

Hotel ★★★ 64% Novotel Manchester West, Worsley Brow, WORSLEY ☎ 0161 799 3535 119 en suite

UPPERMILL — Map 07 SD90

Saddleworth Mountain Ash OL3 6LT

☎ 01457 873653 🖷 01457 820647
e-mail: secretary@saddleworthgolfclub.org.uk
web: www.saddleworthgolfclub.org.uk
Moorland course, with superb views of Pennines.
18 holes, 6118yds, Par 71, SSS 69, Course record 61.
Club membership 800.
Visitors Mon-Fri except BHs. Booking required Wed & Fri. Handicap certificate. Dress code. **Societies** Booking required. **Green Fees** £25, £35 Sat & Sun. ⊛ **Prof** Robert Johnson **Course Designer** George Lowe, A MacKenzie **Facilities** ⊗ ℿ ♨ ☕ 🍸 ⛺ 🏠 ⛳ 🛒 🚗 🏌 **Location** E of town centre off A670

Hotel ★★★ 73% Hotel Smokies Park, Ashton Rd, Bardsley, OLDHAM ☎ 0161 785 5000 73 en suite

URMSTON Map 07 SJ79

Flixton Church Rd, Flixton M41 6EP
☎ 0161 748 2116 🖷 0161 748 2116
web: www.flixtongolfclub.co.uk
Meadowland course bounded by the River Mersey.
9 holes, 6410yds, Par 71, SSS 71.
Club membership 430.
Visitors Mon-Fri, Sun & BHs. Booking required Sun & BHs. **Societies** welcome **Green Fees** £22, £32 Sat & Sun. **Prof** Gary Coope **Facilities** ⊗ 🍴 🍽 ☕ 🍸 🛍 🏠 🏌 **Location** S of town centre on B5213

Hotel ★★★★ 68% Copthorne Hotel Manchester, Clippers Quay, Salford Quays, MANCHESTER ☎ 0161 873 7321 166 en suite

WALKDEN Map 07 SD70

Brackley Municipal M38 9TR
☎ 0161 790 6076
A mostly flat testing parkland course. The fairways are forgiving but the greens quite testing.
9 holes, 3003yds, Par 35, SSS 69, Course record 68.
Club membership 65.
Visitors Mon-Sun & BHs. **Societies** welcome. **Green Fees** phone. 🚭 **Facilities** ☕ 🛍 **Location** 2m NW on A6

Hotel ★★★ 64% Novotel Manchester West, Worsley Brow, WORSLEY ☎ 0161 799 3535 119 en suite

WESTHOUGHTON Map 07 SD60

Hart Common Wigan Rd BL5 2BX
☎ 01942 813195
A parkland course on green belt land with many water features, including the signature hole, the 7th, which has water all down the left hand side.
18 holes, 5719yards, Par 71, SSS 68.
Club membership 400.
Visitors Mon-Sun & BHs. Booking required. Dress code. **Societies** Booking required. **Green Fees** £12, £16 Sat, Sun & BHs. **Prof** Simon Reeves **Course Designer** Mike Shattock **Facilities** ⊗ 🍴 🍽 ☕ 🍸 🛍 🛒 🚗 🏌 🏌 **Leisure** par 3 Academy course. **Conf** Corporate Hospitality Days **Location** On A58 between Bolton

Hotel ★★★ 65% Quality Hotel Wigan, Riverway, WIGAN ☎ 01942 826888 88 en suite

Westhoughton Long Island, School St BL5 2BR
☎ 01942 811085 & 608958 🖷 01942 811085
e-mail: honsec@westhoughtongc.fsnet.co.uk
Compact downland course.
18 holes, 5918yds, Par 70, SSS 69, Course record 64.
Club membership 325.
Visitors Mon-Fri. **Societies** Booking required. **Green Fees** phone. 🚭 **Course Designer** Jeff Shuttleworth **Facilities** ⊗ 🍴 🍽 ☕ 🍸 🛍 🏠 **Leisure** snooker. **Location** 0.5m NW off A58

Hotel ★★★ 65% Quality Hotel Wigan, Riverway, WIGAN ☎ 01942 826888 88 en suite

WHITEFIELD Map 07 SD80

Stand The Dales, Ashbourne Grove M45 7NL
☎ 0161 766 3197 🖷 0161 796 3234
e-mail: secretary@standgolfclub.co.uk
A semi-parkland course with five moorland holes. Undulating fairways with views of five counties. A fine test of golf with a very demanding finish.
18 holes, 6411yds, Par 72, SSS 71, Course record 66.
Club membership 500.
Visitors Mon, Wed-Fri & BHs. Booking required. Handicap certificate. Dress code. **Societies** welcome. **Green Fees** £35. **Prof** Mark Dance **Course Designer** G Lowe, A Herd **Facilities** ⊗ 🍴 🍽 ☕ 🍸 🛍 🏠 🚗 🏌 **Conf** Corporate Hospitality Days **Location** 1m W off A667

Hotel ★★★ 66% Bolholt Country Park Hotel, Walshaw Rd, BURY ☎ 0161 762 4000 65 en suite

Whitefield Higher Ln M45 7EZ
☎ 0161 351 2700 🖷 0161 351 2712
e-mail: enquiries@whitefieldgolfclub.com
Fine sporting parkland course with well-watered greens.
18 holes, 6063yds, Par 69, SSS 69, Course record 64.
Club membership 540.
Visitors Mon-Sat except BHs. Booking required. Dress code. **Societies** Booking required. **Green Fees** phone. **Prof** Andrew McKenzie **Facilities** ⊗ 🍴 🍽 ☕ 🍸 🛍 🏠 🚗 🏌 **Leisure** tennis courts, snooker room. **Conf** Corporate Hospitality Days **Location** N of town centre on A665

Hotel ★★★ 76% Malmaison, Piccadilly, MANCHESTER ☎ 0161 278 1000 167 en suite

WIGAN Map 07 SD50

Haigh Hall Golf Complex Copperas Ln, Haigh WN2 1PE
☎ 01942 831107 🖷 01942 831417
e-mail: hhgen@wiganmgc.gov.uk
web: www.haighhall.net
This recently completed golf complex provides all the golfer requires for playing or practice/tuition facilities. The scenic setting provides an excellent location for the two courses, an 18 hole and a 9 hole.
Balcarres Course: 18 holes, 6300yards, Par 70, SSS 71.
Crawford Course: 9 holes, 1446yards, Par 28.
Club membership 150.
Visitors contact course for details. Dress code. **Societies** welcome. **Green Fees** 18 hole course £7.50-£16. 9 hole course £4-£5.50. **Prof** Ian Lee **Course Designer** Steve Marnoch **Facilities** ⊗ 🍽 ☕ 🍸 🛍 🏠 🚗 🏌 🏌 **Leisure** golf academy. **Conf** Corporate Hospitality Days **Location** M6 junct 27/M61 junct 5 or 6, signed Haigh Hall

Hotel ★★ 65% Bel-Air Hotel, 236 Wigan Ln, WIGAN ☎ 01942 241410 11 en suite

Wigan Arley Hall, Haigh WN1 2UH
☎ 01257 421360
e-mail: info@wigangolfclub.co.uk
web: www.wigangolfclub.co.uk
Fairly level parkland with outstanding views and magnificent trees. The fine old clubhouse is the original Arley Hall, and is surrounded by a medieval moat.
18 holes, 6009yds, Par 70, SSS 69.
Club membership 300.
Visitors Mon, Wed-Fri, Sun except BHs. Booking required Thu, Fri & Sun. Handicap certificate. Dress code. **Societies** Booking required. **Green Fees** £30 per round. 🚭 **Course Designer** Gaunt & Marnoch **Facilities** ⊗ 🍴 🍽 ☕ 🍸 🛍 **Conf** facs Corporate Hospitality Days **Location** M6 junct 27, 3m NE off B5238

Continued

Continued

Hotel ★★★ 65% Quality Hotel Wigan, Riverway, WIGAN ☎ 01942 826888 88 en suite

WORSLEY Map 07 SD70

Ellesmere Old Clough Ln M28 7HZ
☎ 0161 799 0554 (office) 🖹 0161 790 7322
e-mail: honsec@ellesmeregolf.fsnet.co.uk
web: www.ellesmeregolfclub.co.uk
Parkland with natural hazards and hard walking. Trees and two streams running through the course make shot strategy an important aspect of the round. Testing holes: 3rd (par 5), 9th (par 3), 15th (par 5).
18 holes, 6248yds, Par 70, SSS 70, Course record 67.
Club membership 700.
Visitors Mon-Fri & Sun except BHs. Booking required. Handicap certificate. Dress code. **Societies** Booking required. **Green Fees** £33 per day/round. **Prof** Simon Wakefield **Facilities** **Conf** Corporate Hospitality Days **Location** N of village off A580

Hotel ★★★ 64% Novotel Manchester West, Worsley Brow, WORSLEY ☎ 0161 799 3535 119 en suite

HAMPSHIRE

ALDERSHOT Map 04 SU85

Army Laffans Rd GU11 2HF
☎ 01252 337272 🖹 01252 337562
e-mail: secretary@armygolfclub.com
web: www.armygolfclub.co.uk
The second-oldest course in Hampshire. Picturesque heathland with three par 3s over 200yds.
18 holes, 6550yds, Par 71, SSS 71, Course record 66.
Club membership 750.
Visitors Mon-Fri. Handicap certificate. Dress code. **Societies** Booking required. **Green Fees** £40 per 36 holes, £30 per 18 holes. **Prof** Graham Cowley **Facilities** **Conf** facs Corporate Hospitality Days **Location** 1.5m N of town centre off A323/A325

Hotel ★★★ 66% Potters International Hotel, 1 Fleet Rd, ALDERSHOT ☎ 01252 344000 100 en suite

ALTON Map 04 SU73

Alton Old Odiham Rd GU34 4BU
☎ 01420 82042
web: www.altongolfclub.org.uk
9 holes, 5744yds, Par 68, SSS 68, Course record 62.
Course Designer James Braid **Location** 2m N of Alton off B3349 at Golden Pot
Phone for further details

Worldham Park Cakers Ln, East Worldham GU34 3BF
☎ 01420 543151 🖹 01420 544606
e-mail: worldhampark@virgin.net
Picturesque parkland setting with an abundance of challenging holes (dog-legs, water and sand). Suitable for all golfing standards.
18 holes, 6257yds, Par 71, SSS 70.
Club membership 400.
Visitors Mon-Sun & BHs. Booking required. Dress code. **Societies** Booking required. **Green Fees** £14 per 18 holes Mon-Thu, £16 Fri, £18 Sat, Sun & BHs. **Prof** Anthony Cook **Course Designer** FJ Whidborne **Facilities** by arrangement **Conf** Corporate Hospitality Days **Location** B3004, 2 mins from Alton

Continued

Hotel ★★★ 72% Alton Grange Hotel, London Rd, ALTON ☎ 01420 86565 26 en suite 4 annexe en suite

AMPFIELD Map 04 SU42

Ampfield Par Three Winchester Rd SO51 9BQ
☎ 01794 368480
web: www.databridge.co.uk/golf/ampfield.html
18 holes, 2478yds, Par 54, SSS 53, Course record 49.
Course Designer Henry Cotton **Location** 4m NE of Romsey on A31
Phone for further details

Hotel ★★★ 68% Corus hotel Romsey, Winchester Rd, Ampfield, ROMSEY ☎ 0870 609 6155 54 en suite

ANDOVER Map 04 SU34

Andover 51 Winchester Rd SP10 2EF
☎ 01264 358040 🖹 01264 358040
e-mail: secretary@andovergolfclub.co.uk
web: www.andovergolfclub.co.uk
Undulating downland course combining a good test of golf for all abilities with breathtaking views across Hampshire countryside. Well-guarded greens and a notable par 3 9th (225yds) with the tee perched on top of a hill, 100ft above the green. Excellent drainage on the chalk base.
9 holes, 6096yds, Par 70, SSS 69, Course record 64.
Club membership 450.
Visitors Mon-Sun & BHs. Dress code. **Societies** Booking required. **Green Fees** £21 per 18 holes, £26 Sat & Sun. **Prof** D Lawrence **Course Designer** JH Taylor **Facilities** **Conf** facs Corporate Hospitality Days **Location** 0.5m S on A3057

Hotel ★★★ 62% Quality Hotel Andover, Micheldever Rd, ANDOVER ☎ 01264 369111 13 en suite 36 annexe en suite

Hampshire Winchester Rd SP11 7TB
☎ 01264 357555 (pro shop) & 356462 (office)
🖹 01264 356606
e-mail: enquiry@thehampshiregolfclub.co.uk
web: www.thehampshiregolfclub.co.uk
Pleasant undulating parkland with fine views and a backdrop of 35,000 young trees and shrubs. The challenging Manor course has two lakes to catch the unwary. Based on chalk which provides very good drainage, with a superb finishing hole.

Manor: 18 holes, 6382yds, Par 72, SSS 71, Course record 67.

Continued

Club membership 650.
Visitors Booking required. **Societies** Booking required. **Green Fees** phone. **Prof** Iain Powell **Facilities** **Leisure** 9 hole par 3 course. **Conf** facs Corporate Hospitality Days **Location** 1.5m S of Andover on A3057

Hotel ★★★ 62% Quality Hotel Andover, Micheldever Rd, ANDOVER ☎ 01264 369111 13 en suite 36 annexe en suite

BARTON-ON-SEA Map 04 SZ29

Barton-on-Sea Milford Rd BH25 5PP
☎ 01425 615308 01425 621457
web: www.barton-on-sea-golf.co.uk
A cliff top course with three loops of nine giving a great variety and challenge to golfers of all handicaps. Fine views over the Solent to the Isle of Wight.
9 holes, 3012yds, Par 36.
Needles: 9 holes, 3078yds, Par 35.
Stroller: 9 holes, 2989yds, Par 36.
Club membership 800.
Visitors Mon-Sun & BHs. Booking required. Handicap certificate. Dress code. **Societies** Booking required. **Green Fees** £42 per day, £50 Sat, Sun & BHs. **Prof** Peter Rodgers **Course Designer** Vardon, Colt, Stutt **Facilities** by arrangement **Leisure** snooker tables. **Conf** Corporate Hospitality Days **Location** B3058 SE of town

Hotel ★★★★★ Chewton Glen Hotel, Christchurch Rd, NEW MILTON ☎ 01425 275341 58 en suite

BASINGSTOKE Map 04 SU65

Basingstoke Kempshott Park RG23 7LL
☎ 01256 465990 01256 331793
e-mail: enquiries@basingstokegolfclub.co.uk
web: www.basingstokegolfclub.co.uk
A well-maintained parkland course with wide and inviting fairways. You are inclined to expect longer drives than are actually achieved - partly on account of the trees. There are many two-hundred-year-old beech trees, since the course was built on an old deer park.
18 holes, 6350yds, Par 70, SSS 70, Course record 66.
Club membership 700.
Visitors Mon-Fri except BHs. Booking required. **Societies** Booking required. **Green Fees** phone. **Prof** Guy Shoesmith **Course Designer** James Braid **Facilities** **Conf** facs Corporate Hospitality Days **Location** M3 junct 7, 3.5m SW on A30

Hotel ★★★★ 70% Apollo Hotel, Aldermaston Roundabout, BASINGSTOKE ☎ 01256 796700 125 en suite

Dummer Dummer RG25 2AF
☎ 01256 397888 (office) & 397950 (pro) 01256 397889
e-mail: enquiries@dummergolfclub.com
web: www.dummergolfclub.com
Designed by Peter Alliss, this course is set in 165 acres of fine Hampshire countryside with panoramic views. The course meanders around lakes, mature trees and hedgerows. The course combines large, level teeing areas, undulating fairways, fast true greens and cleverly positioned bunkers to provide a challenging golf experience.

Continued

18 holes, 6500yds, Par 72, SSS 71, Course record 62.
Club membership 650.
Visitors Mon-Sun & BHs. Booking required. Dress code. **Societies** Booking required. **Green Fees** £28 per round. **Prof** Andrew Fannon **Course Designer** Pete Alliss **Facilities** **Leisure** sauna. **Conf** facs Corporate Hospitality Days **Location** M3 junct 7, towards Dummer, club 0.25m on left

Hotel Premier Travel Inn Basingstoke South, NORTH WALTHAM ☎ 0870 9906476 28 en suite

Weybrook Park Rooksdown Ln RG24 9NT
☎ 01256 320347 01256 812973
e-mail: weybrookpark@aol.com
web: www.weybrookpark.co.uk
An all year course designed to be enjoyable for all standards of player. Easy walking with fabulous views.
18 holes, 6468yds, Par 71, SSS 71.
Club membership 600.
Visitors Mon-Fri. Sat, Sun & BHs pm. Sat & Sun booking required. Dress code. **Societies** Booking required. **Green Fees** phone. **Prof** Anthony Dillon **Facilities** **Conf** facs Corporate Hospitality Days **Location** 2m W of town centre via A339

Hotel ★★★★ 70% Apollo Hotel, Aldermaston Roundabout, BASINGSTOKE ☎ 01256 796700 125 en suite

BORDON Map 04 SU73

Blackmoor Firgrove Rd, Whitehill GU35 9EH
☎ 01420 472775 01420 487666
e-mail: admin@blackmoorgolf.co.uk
web: www.blackmoorgolf.co.uk
A first-class moorland course with a great variety of holes. Fine greens and wide pine tree-lined fairways are a distinguishing feature. The ground is mainly flat and walking easy.
18 holes, 6164yds, Par 69, SSS 70, Course record 63.
Club membership 750.
Visitors Mon-Fri. Handicap certificate. Dress code. **Societies** Booking required. **Green Fees** £49 per 36 holes. £37 per 18 holes Mon-Fri. **Prof** Stephen Clay **Course Designer** H Colt **Facilities** by arrangement **Conf** Corporate Hospitality Days **Location** 6m S from Farnham on A325, through Whitehill, right at rdbt

BOTLEY Map 04 SU51

Botley Park Hotel, Golf & Country Club
Winchester Rd, Boorley Green SO32 2UA
☎ 01489 780888 01489 789242
e-mail: info@botleypark.macdonald.hotels.co.uk
18 holes, 6341yds, Par 70, SSS 70, Course record 67.
Course Designer Ewan Murray **Location** 1m NW of Botley on B3354
Phone for further details

Hotel ★★★★ 69% Macdonald Botley Park, Golf & Country Club, Winchester Rd, Boorley Green, BOTLEY ☎ 0870 1942132 100 en suite

BROCKENHURST Map 04 SU20

Brokenhurst Manor Sway Rd SO42 7SG
☎ 01590 623332 (secretary)
e-mail: secretary@brokenhurst-manor.org.uk
web: www.brokenhurst-manor.org.uk
An attractive forest course set in the New Forest, with the unusual feature of three loops of six holes each to complete the round. Fascinating holes include the short 5th and 12th, and the 4th and 17th, both dog-legs. A stream also features on seven of the holes.
18 holes, 6222yds, Par 70, SSS 70, Course record 63.
Club membership 700.
Visitors Mon-Sun & BHs. Booking required Thu. Handicap certificate. Dress code. **Societies** Booking required. **Green Fees** £65 per day, £48 per round, £58 Sat, Sun & BHs. **Prof** Bruce Parker **Course Designer** H Colt **Facilities** **Location** 1m S on B3055

Hotel ★★ 66% Watersplash Hotel, The Rise, BROCKENHURST ☎ 01590 622344 23 en suite
See advertisement on this page

BURLEY Map 04 SU20

Burley Cott Ln BH24 4BB
☎ 01425 402431 & 403737 🖷 01425 404168
e-mail: secretary@burleygolfclub.fsnet.co.uk
web: www.burleygolfclub.co.uk
Undulating heather and gorseland. The 7th requires an accurately placed tee shot to obtain par 4. Played off different tees on second nine.
9 holes, 6151yds, Par 71, SSS 69, Course record 68.
Club membership 520.
Visitors Mon-Fri. After 4pm Sat. Booking required. Handicap certificate. **Societies** Booking required. Max 14 persons. **Green Fees** phone. **Facilities** **Location** E of village

Hotel ★★★ 67% Moorhill House, BURLEY
☎ 01425 403285 31 en suite

CORHAMPTON Map 04 SU62

Corhampton Shepherds Farm Ln SO32 3GZ
☎ 01489 877279 🖷 01489 877680
e-mail: secretary@corhamptongc.co.uk
web: www.corhamptongc.co.uk
Free draining downland course situated in the heart of the picturesque Meon Valley.
18 holes, 6444yds, Par 71, SSS 71.
Club membership 800.
Visitors contact club for details. **Societies** welcome.

Continued

Green Fees £40 per 36 holes, £30 per 18 holes. **Prof** Ian Roper **Facilities** **Location** 1m W of Corhampton off B3035

Hotel ★★ 70% Old House Hotel & Restaurant, The Square, WICKHAM ☎ 01329 833049 8 en suite 4 annexe en suite

CRONDALL Map 04 SU74

Oak Park Heath Ln GU10 5PB
☎ 01252 850850 🖷 01252 850851
e-mail: oakpark@crown-golf.co.uk
Oak Park is a gently undulating parkland course overlooking a pretty village. Woodland is undulating on holes 10 to 13. Panoramic views, mature trees, very challenging; 16-bay floodlit driving range, practice green and practice bunker.
Woodland: 18 holes, 6352yds, Par 70, SSS 70.
Village: 9 holes, 3279yds, Par 36.
Club membership 730.
Visitors Mon-Fri. Sat, Sun & BHs pm. Booking required. Dress code. **Societies** Booking required. **Green Fees** phone. **Prof** Gary Murton **Course Designer** Patrick Dawson **Facilities** **Leisure** gymnasium. **Conf** facs Corporate Hospitality Days **Location** 0.5m E of village off A287 Farnham-Odiham

DENMEAD Map 04 SU61

Furzeley Furzeley Rd PO7 6TX
☎ 023 9223 1180 🖷 023 9223 0921
A well-laid parkland course with many features including several strategically placed lakes which

Continued

provide a good test set in beautiful scenery. Straight hitting and club selection on the short holes is the key to manufacturing a low score.
18 holes, 4488yds, Par 62, SSS 61, Course record 56.
Club membership 250.
Visitors contact course for details. Dress code. **Societies** Booking required. **Green Fees** £13 per 18 holes, £7.70 per 9 holes, £14.50/£8.50 Sat, Sun & BHs. **Prof** Derek Brown **Course Designer** Mark Sale, Robert Brown **Facilities** **Location** From Waterlooville NW onto Hambledon road, signed

Hotel ★★★★ 65% Portsmouth Marriott Hotel, Southampton Rd, PORTSMOUTH ☎ 0870 400 7285 174 en suite

DIBDEN Map 04 SU40

Dibden Main Rd SO45 5TB
☎ 023 8020 7508 & 8084 5596
web: www.nfdc.gov.uk/golf
Municipal parkland course with views over Southampton Water. A pond guards the green at the par 5 3rd hole. Twenty bay driving range.
Course 1: 18 holes, 5931yds, Par 70, SSS 69, Course record 64.
Course 2: 9 holes, 1520yds, Par 29.
Club membership 600.
Visitors 18 hole course booking required. 9 hole Mon-Sun. **Societies** Booking required. **Green Fees** phone. **Prof** Paul Smith & John Slade **Course Designer** Hamilton Stutt **Facilities** **Location** 2m NW of Dibden Purlieu, off A326 to Hythe

Hotel ★★★ 67% Forest Lodge Hotel, Pikes Hill, Romsey Rd, LYNDHURST ☎ 023 8028 3677 28 en suite

EASTLEIGH Map 04 SU41

East Horton Golf Centre Mortimers Ln, Fair Oak SO50 7EA
☎ 023 8060 2111 023 8069 6280
e-mail: info@easthortongolf.co.uk
web: www.easthortongolf.co.uk
Courses set out over 260 acres of Hampshire countryside with parkland fairways and mature trees in abundance. The Greenwood course sets out across a stream and around a large woodland, returning to the stream for the 18th. Fine views from the top holes and from the 16th tee, even the best golfers need to concentrate with a 160yd carry over an imposing lake. The parkland course has relatively wide fairways and the stream has to be negotiated a few times. The five par 3s may not be as easy as they appear.
Greenwood: 18 holes, 5960yds, Par 70, SSS 69.
Club membership 700.
Visitors Booking up to 1 week in advance. **Societies** Booking required. **Green Fees** phone. **Prof** Miles Harding **Course Designer** Trevor Pearce **Facilities** **Leisure** Par 3 course. **Conf** facs Corporate Hospitality Days **Location** off B3037

Hotel Premier Travel Inn Eastleigh, Leigh Rd, EASTLEIGH ☎ 08701 977090 60 en suite

Fleming Park Passfield Av SO50 9NL
☎ 023 8061 2797 023 8065 1686
e-mail: ianwarwick@flemingparkgolfcourse.co.uk
Parkland and woodland course with stream, Monks Brook, running through. Good greens.

Continued

18 holes, 4436yds, Par 65, SSS 62, Course record 62.
Club membership 390.
Visitors Mon-Sun. Booking required. **Societies** Booking required. **Green Fees** phone. **Prof** Ian Warwick **Course Designer** David Miller **Facilities** **Leisure** hard and grass tennis courts, heated indoor plus outdoor swimming pool, squash, sauna, solarium, gymnasium. **Location** E of town centre

Hotel Travelodge Southampton Eastleigh, Twyford Rd, EASTLEIGH ☎ 08700 850 950 32 en suite

FAREHAM Map 04 SU50

Cams Hall Cams Hall Estate PO16 8UP
☎ 01329 827222 01329 827111
e-mail: camshall@americangolf.uk.com
web: americangolf.com
Creek Course: 18 holes, 6244yds, Par 71, SSS 70, Course record 69.
Park Course: 9 holes, 3247yds, Par 36, SSS 36.
Course Designer Peter Alliss **Location** M27 junct 11, A27
Phone for further details

Hotel ★★★ 66% Lysses House Hotel, 51 High St, FAREHAM ☎ 01329 822622 21 en suite

FARNBOROUGH Map 04 SU85

Southwood Ively Rd, Cove GU14 0LJ
☎ 01252 548700 01252 549091
Municipal parkland golf course.
18 holes, 5738yds, Par 69, SSS 68, Course record 61.
Club membership 650.
Visitors Mon-Sun & BHs. Booking required. **Societies** Booking required. **Green Fees** £16.80 per 18 holes, £19.60 Sat, Sun & BHs. **Prof** Chris Hudson **Course Designer** Hawtree & Son **Facilities** **Conf** facs Corporate Hospitality Days **Location** 0.5m W

Hotel ★★★ 65% Falcon Hotel, 68 Farnborough Rd, FARNBOROUGH ☎ 01252 545378 30 en suite

FLEET Map 04 SU85

North Hants Minley Rd GU51 1RF
☎ 01252 616443 01252 811627
e-mail: secretary@north-hants-fleetgc.co.uk
web: www.northhantsgolf.co.uk
Picturesque tree-lined course with much heather and gorse close to the fairways. A comparatively easy par 4 first hole may lull the golfer into a false sense of security, only to be rudely awakened at the testing holes which follow. The ground is rather undulating and, though not tiring, does offer some excellent blind shots, and more than a few surprises in judging distance.

Continued

18 holes, 6472yds, Par 70, SSS 72, Course record 66.
Club membership 600.
Visitors Mon-Wed & Fri. Booking required. Handicap certificate. Dress code. **Societies** Booking required. **Green Fees** phone. **Prof** Steve Porter **Course Designer** James Braid **Facilities** **Conf** Corporate Hospitality Days **Location** 0.25m N of Fleet station on B3013

Hotel ★★★ 65% Falcon Hotel, 68 Farnborough Rd, FARNBOROUGH ☎ 01252 545378 30 en suite

GOSPORT Map 04 SZ69

Gosport & Stokes Bay Off Fort Rd, Haslar PO12 2AT
☎ 023 9252 7941 023 9252 7941
e-mail: secretary@gosportandstokesbaygolfclub.co.uk
A testing links course overlooking the Solent, with plenty of gorse and short rough. Changing winds.
9 holes, 5999yds, Par 70, SSS 69, Course record 65.
Club membership 499.
Visitors Mon-Wed, Fri & Sat except BHs. Dress code. **Societies** Booking required. **Green Fees** £17 Mon-Fri, £22 Sat. Twilight £8.50. **Facilities** **Location** A32 S from Fareham, E onto Fort Rd to Haslar

Hotel ★★★ 66% Lysses House Hotel, 51 High St, FAREHAM ☎ 01329 822622 21 en suite

HARTLEY WINTNEY Map 04 SU75

Hartley Wintney London Rd RG27 8PT
☎ 01252 844211 (sec/gen mgr) 01252 844211
e-mail: office@hartleywintneygolfclub.com
web: www.hartleywintneygolfclub.com
Easy walking parkland and partly wooded course in pleasant countryside. A challenging test for golfers of all abilities with many mature trees and water hazards.

18 holes, 6240yds, Par 71, SSS 71, Course record 63.
Club membership 750.
Visitors Mon-Sun & BHs. Booking required Wed, Sat, Sun & BHs. Dress code. **Societies** Booking required. **Green Fees** £45 per day, £30 per 18 holes, £50/£35 Sat, Sun & BHs. **Prof** Martin Smith **Facilities** **Leisure** indoor teaching studio. **Conf** facs Corporate Hospitality Days **Location** NE of village on A30

Hotel ★★★ 68% The Elvetham, HARTLEY WINTNEY ☎ 01252 844871 41 en suite 29 annexe en suite

HAYLING ISLAND Map 04 SU70

Hayling Links Ln PO11 0BX
☎ 023 9246 4446 023 9246 1119
e-mail: generaloffice@haylinggolf.co.uk
web: www.haylinggolf.co.uk
A delightful links course among the dunes offering fine seascapes and views of the Isle of Wight. Varying sea breezes and sometimes strong winds ensure that the course seldom plays the same two days running. Testing holes at the 12th and 13th, both par 4. Club selection is important.
18 holes, 6531yds, Par 71, SSS 71, Course record 65.
Club membership 1000.
Visitors contact club for details. Handicap certificate. Dress code. **Societies** Booking required. **Green Fees** £60 per day, £45 per round, £60 per round Sat & Sun. **Prof** Raymond Gadd **Course Designer** Taylor 1905, Simpson 1933 **Facilities** **Conf** facs Corporate Hospitality Days **Location** SW side of island at West Town

Hotel ★★★ 69% Brookfield Hotel, Havant Rd, EMSWORTH ☎ 01243 373363 40 en suite

KINGSCLERE Map 04 SU55

Sandford Springs Wolverton RG26 5RT
☎ 01635 296800 & 296808 (pro shop) 01635 296801
e-mail: garye@sandfordspringsgolf.co.uk
web: www.sandfordsprings.co.uk
The course has unique variety in beautiful surroundings and offers three distinctive loops of nine holes. There are water hazards, woodlands and gradients to negotiate, providing a challenge for all playing categories.

The Park: 9 holes, 2963yds, Par 34.
The Lakes: 9 holes, 3042yds, Par 35.
The Wood: 9 holes, 3180yds, Par 36.
Club membership 700.
Visitors Booking required. **Societies** Booking required. **Green Fees** phone. **Prof** Rhys ap Iolo **Course Designer** Hawtree & Son **Facilities** **Conf** facs **Location** On A339 between Basingstoke & Newbury

KINGSLEY Map 04 SU73

Dean Farm GU35 9NG
☎ 01420 489478
Undulating downland course.
9 holes, 1600yds, Par 31.
Visitors Mon-Sun & BHs. **Societies** Booking required. **Green Fees** Mon-Fri £12 per day, £5.50 per 9 holes. **Prof** Matthew Howard **Facilities** **Location** W of village off B3004

Hotel ★★★ 72% Alton Grange Hotel, London Rd, ALTON ☎ 01420 86565 26 en suite 4 annexe en suite

LECKFORD Map 04 SU33

Leckford SO20 6JF
☎ 01264 810320 01264 811122
e-mail: golf@leckfordestate.co.uk
Old Course: 9 holes, 6394yds, Par 72, SSS 71.
New Course: 9 holes, 4562yds, Par 66, SSS 62.
Location 1m SW off A3057
Phone for further details

LEE-ON-THE-SOLENT Map 04 SU50

Lee-on-the-Solent Brune Ln PO13 9PB
☎ 023 9255 1170 023 9255 4233
e-mail: enquiries@leeonthesolentgolfclub.co.uk
web: www.leeonthesolentgolfclub.co.uk
Predominately heath and oak woodland. While not long in length, still a good test of golf requiring accuracy off the tee to score well. Excellent greens.
18 holes, 5962yds, Par 69, SSS 69, Course record 63.
Club membership 725.
Visitors Booking required. Handicap certificate. **Societies** Booking required. **Green Fees** phone. **Prof** Rob Edwards **Facilities** **Conf** facs Corporate Hospitality Days **Location** 3m S of Fareham

Hotel ★★★ 66% Lysses House Hotel, 51 High St, FAREHAM ☎ 01329 822622 21 en suite

LIPHOOK Map 04 SU83

Liphook Wheatsheaf Enclosure GU30 7EH
☎ 01428 723271 & 723785 01428 724853
e-mail: liphookgolfclub@btconnect.com
web: www.liphookgolfclub.com
Heathland course with easy walking and fine views.
18 holes, 6167yds, Par 70, SSS 69, Course record 67.
Club membership 800.
Visitors Mon, Wed-Sat. Sun & BHs pm. Booking required. Handicap certificate. Dress code. **Societies** Booking required. **Green Fees** £55 per day, £44 per round, £66/£55 Sat, £66 Sun & BHs pm. **Prof** Ian Mowbray **Course Designer** AC Croome **Facilities** **Location** 1m S on B2070

Hotel ★★★★ 71% Lythe Hill Hotel & Spa, Petworth Rd, HASLEMERE ☎ 01428 651251 41 en suite

Old Thorns Golf & Country Estate Griggs Green GU30 7PE
☎ 01428 724555 01428 725036
e-mail: sales@oldthorns.com
web: www.oldthorns.com
A challenging 18-hole championship course with rolling hills, undulating greens, demanding water features and magnificent views. A challenge to any level of golfer.

18 holes, 6461yds, Par 72, SSS 72.
Club membership 200.
Visitors Mon-Sun & BHs. Booking required. **Societies** Booking required. **Green Fees** £40 per round, £60 Sat, Sun & BHs. **Prof** Steven Hall **Course Designer** Peter Alliss **Facilities** **Leisure** hard tennis courts, heated indoor swimming pool, fishing, sauna, solarium, gymnasium. **Conf** Corporate Hospitality Days **Location** Off A3 at Griggs Green, S of Liphook, signed Old Thorns

Hotel ★★★ 75% Old Thorns Golf & Country Estate, Griggs Green, LIPHOOK ☎ 01428 724555 29 en suite 4 annexe rms (3 en suite)

LYNDHURST Map 04 SU20

Bramshaw Brook SO43 7HE
☎ 023 8081 3433 023 8081 3460
e-mail: golf@bramshaw.co.uk
web: www.bramshaw.co.uk
Manor Course: 18 holes, 6527yds, Par 71, SSS 71, Course record 65.
Forest Course: 18 holes, 5774yds, Par 69, SSS 68, Course record 65.
Location M27 junct 1, 1m W on B3079
Phone for further details

Hotel ★★★ 67% Bell Inn, BROOK ☎ 023 8081 2214 25 en suite

Prices may change during the currency of the guide, always check when booking

New Forest Southampton Rd SO43 7BU
☎ 023 8028 2752 🖷 023 8028 4030
e-mail: tonyatnfgc@aol.com
web: www.newforestgolfclub.co.uk
This picturesque heathland course is laid out in a typical stretch of the New Forest on high ground a little above the village of Lyndhurst. The first two holes are somewhat teasing, as is the 485yd (par 5) 9th. Walking is easy.
18 holes, 5526yds, Par 69, SSS 67.
Club membership 500.
Visitors Mon-Sun & BHs. Booking required. Handicap certificate. Dress code. **Societies** Booking required. **Green Fees** £17 per 18 holes, £23 Sat, Sun & BHs. **Prof** Colin Murray **Facilities** **Conf** Corporate Hospitality Days **Location** 0.5m NE off A35)

Hotel ★★★ 70% Crown Hotel, High St, LYNDHURST ☎ 023 8028 2922 39 en suite

NEW ALRESFORD Map 04 SU53

Alresford Cheriton Rd, Tichborne Down SO24 0PN
☎ 01962 733746 & 733998 (pro shop) 🖷 01962 736040
e-mail: secretary@alresford-golf.demon.co.uk
web: www.alresfordgolf.co.uk
A rolling downland course on well-drained chalk. The five difficult par 3s, tree-lined fairways and well-guarded fast greens ensure that the course offers a true test of skill, even for the most experienced golfer.

18 holes, 5905yds, Par 69, SSS 69, Course record 63.
Club membership 600.
Visitors Mon-Sun except BHs. Dress code. **Societies** Booking required. **Green Fees** Summer £28 per 18 holes, £35 Sat & Sun. Winter £22, £30 Sat & Sun. **Prof** Malcolm Scott **Course Designer** Scott Webb Young **Facilities** by arrangement **Conf** Corporate Hospitality Days **Location** situated 1m S of Alresford on the B3046 with easy access from the A31 and M3

Hotel ★★ 65% Swan Hotel, 11 West St, ALRESFORD ☎ 01962 732302 & 734427 🖷 01962 735274 11 rms (10 en suite) 12 annexe en suite

NEW MILTON Map 04 SZ29

Chewton Glen Hotel Christchurch Rd BH25 5QS
☎ 01425 275341 🖷 01425 272310
e-mail: reservations@chewtonglen.com
web: www.chewtonglen.com
A nine-hole, par 3 course within the hotel grounds plus a practice area. Please note - only open to residents of the hotel or as a guest of a member of the club.
9 holes, 854yds, Par 27.
Club membership 150.
Visitors Mon-Sun & BHs. Booking required. **Societies** Booking required. **Green Fees** phone. **Facilities** **Leisure** hard tennis courts, outdoor and indoor heated swimming pools, sauna, gymnasium, Spa & health club. **Conf** facs Corporate Hospitality Days **Location** Off A337 W of town centre

Hotel ★★★★★ Chewton Glen Hotel, Christchurch Rd, NEW MILTON ☎ 01425 275341 58 en suite

OVERTON Map 04 SU54

Test Valley Micheldever Rd RG25 3DS
☎ 01256 771737 🖷 01256 771285
e-mail: info@testvalleygolf.com
web: www.testvalleygolf.com
A downland course with excellent drainage, fine year-round greens and prominent water and bunker features. On undulating terrain with lovely views over the Hampshire countryside.
18 holes, 6165yds, Par 72, SSS 69.
Club membership 500.
Visitors Booking required. Dress code. **Societies** Booking required. **Green Fees** £24 per round, £30 Sat & Sun. **Prof** Alastair Briggs **Course Designer** Don Wright **Facilities** **Conf** facs Corporate Hospitality Days **Location** 1.5m N of A303 on Overton road

Hotel ★★★★ 73% The Hampshire Centrecourt, Centre Dr, Chineham, BASINGSTOKE ☎ 01256 319700 90 en suite

OWER Map 04 SU31

Paultons Golf Centre Old Salisbury Rd SO51 6AN
☎ 023 8081 3992 🖷 023 8081 3993
e-mail: paultons@americangolf.uk.com
18 holes, 6238yds, Par 71, SSS 70, Course record 67.
Course Designer JR Smith **Location** M27 junct 2, A36 towards Salisbury, 1st rdbt 1st exit, 1st right at Vine pub
Phone for further details

Hotel ★★★ 69% Bartley Lodge, Lyndhurst Rd, CADNAM ☎ 023 8081 2248 31 en suite

PETERSFIELD Map 04 SU72

Petersfield Tankerdale Ln, Liss GU33 7QY
☎ 01730 895165 (office) 🖷 01730 894713
e-mail: richard@petersfieldgolfclub.co.uk
web: www.petersfieldgolfclub.co.uk
Gently undulating course of downland and parkland with mature trees and hedgerows. Very free drainage in an area of outstanding natural beauty.
18 holes, 6450yds, Par 72, SSS 71, Course record 68.
Club membership 725.
Visitors contact club for details. **Societies** welcome. **Green Fees** £40 per day, £28 per round, £35 per round Sat, Sun & BHs. **Prof** Greg Hughes **Course Designer** M Hawtree **Facilities** **Location** Off A3(M) southbound between Liss & Petersfield exits

Hotel ★★★ 69% Southdowns Country Hotel, Dumpford Ln, Trotton, MIDHURST ☎ 01730 821521 22 en suite

Continued

PORTSMOUTH Map 04 SU60

Great Salterns Public Course Burrfields Rd PO3 5HH
☎ 023 9266 4549 023 9265 0525
web: www.portsmouthgolfcentre.co.uk
Easy walking, seaside course with open fairways and testing shots onto well-guarded, small greens. Testing 13th hole, par 4, requiring 130yd shot across a lake.
18 holes, 5575yds, Par 70, SSS 67, Course record 64. Club membership 700.
Visitors Booking up to 1 week in advance. **Societies** Booking required. **Green Fees** phone. **Prof** Terry Healy **Facilities** **Location** NE of town centre on A2030

Hotel ★★★★ 65% Portsmouth Marriott Hotel, Southampton Rd, PORTSMOUTH ☎ 0870 400 7285 174 en suite

ROMSEY Map 04 SU32

Dunwood Manor Danes Rd, Awbridge SO51 0GF
☎ 01794 340549 01794 341215
e-mail: admin@dunwood-golf.co.uk
web: www.dunwood-golf.co.uk
18 holes, 5767yds, Par 69, SSS 68, Course record 65.
Location 4m NW of Romsey off A27
Phone for further details

Hotel ★★★ 67% Bell Inn, BROOK ☎ 023 8081 2214 25 en suite

Romsey Romsey Rd, Nursling SO16 0XW
☎ 023 8073 4637 023 8074 1036
e-mail: mike@romseygolf.co.uk
web: www.romseygolfclub.com
Parkland and woodland course with narrow tree-lined fairways. Six holes are undulating, the rest are sloping. There are superb views over the Test valley. Excellent test of golf for all standards.
18 holes, 5718yds, Par 69, SSS 68, Course record 64. Club membership 800.
Visitors Mon-Fri except BHs. Dress code. **Societies** Booking required. **Green Fees** £36 per day, £30 per round. **Prof** James Pitcher **Facilities** **Conf** facs Corporate Hospitality Days **Location** 1m N M27 junct 3 on A3057

Wellow Ryedown Ln, East Wellow SO51 6BD
☎ 01794 323833 & 322872 01794 323832
web: www.wellowgolfclub.co.uk
Three nine-hole courses set in 217 acres of parkland surrounding Embley Park, former home of Florence Nightingale.
Ryedown & Embley: 18 holes, 5966yds, Par 70, SSS 69, Course record 65.
Embley & Blackwater: 18 holes, 6295yds, Par 72, SSS 70.
Blackwater & Ryedown: 18 holes, 5819yds, Par 70, SSS 68.
Club membership 600.
Visitors Mon-Fri except BHs. Booking required. Dress code. **Societies** Booking required. **Green Fees** £19 per 18 holes. **Prof** Neil Bratley **Course Designer** W Wiltshire **Facilities** **Leisure** gymnasium. **Conf** facs Corporate Hospitality Days **Location** M27 junct 2, A36 towards Salisbury, 1m right

ROTHERWICK Map 04 SU75

Tylney Park RG27 9AY
☎ 01256 762079 01256 763079
e-mail: martinkimberley@msn.com
18 holes, 6109yds, Par 70, SSS 69, Course record 66.
Course Designer W Wiltshire **Location** M3 junct 5, 2m NW of Hook
Phone for further details

Hotel ★★★★ Tylney Hall Hotel, ROTHERWICK ☎ 01256 764881 35 en suite 77 annexe en suite

ROWLAND'S CASTLE Map 04 SU71

Rowlands Castle 31 Links Ln PO9 6AE
☎ 023 9241 2784 023 9241 3649
e-mail: manager@rowlandscastlegolfclub.co.uk
web: www.rowlandscastlegolfclub.co.uk
Reasonably dry in winter, the flat parkland course is a testing one with a number of tricky dog-legs and bunkers much in evidence. The par 4 13th is a signature hole necessitating a drive to a narrow fairway and a second shot to a two-tiered green. The 7th, at 522yds, is the longest hole on the course and leads to a well-guarded armchair green.
18 holes, 6630yds, Par 72, SSS 72, Course record 68. Club membership 800.
Visitors Sun-Fri & BHs. Booking required. Handicap certificate. Dress code. **Societies** Booking required. **Green Fees** phone. **Prof** Peter Klepacz **Course Designer** Colt **Facilities** **Conf** Corporate Hospitality Days **Location** W of village off B2149

Hotel ★★★ 69% Brookfield Hotel, Havant Rd, EMSWORTH ☎ 01243 373363 40 en suite

SHEDFIELD Map 04 SU51

Marriott Meon Valley Hotel & Country Club Sandy Ln SO32 2HQ
☎ 01329 833455 01329 834411
It has been said that a golf-course architect is as good as the ground on which he has to work. Here Hamilton Stutt had magnificent terrain at his disposal and a very good and lovely parkland course is the result. There are three holes over water. The hotel provides many sports facilities.
Meon Course: 18 holes, 6520yds, Par 71, SSS 71, Course record 66.
Valley Course: 9 holes, 2721yds, Par 35, SSS 33.
Club membership 700.
Visitors Mon-Sun & BHs. Booking required. Dress code. **Societies** Booking required. **Green Fees** £44 per round, £54 Sat, Sun & BHs. **Prof** Neal Grist **Course Designer** Hamilton Stutt **Facilities** **Leisure** hard tennis courts, heated indoor swimming pool, sauna, solarium, gymnasium. **Conf** facs Corporate Hospitality Days **Location** M27 junct 7, off A334 between Botley & Wickham

Hotel ★★★★ 66% Marriott Meon Valley Hotel & Country Club, Sandy Ln, SHEDFIELD ☎ 01329 833455 113 en suite

SOUTHAMPTON Map 04 SU41

Chilworth Main Rd, Chilworth SO16 7JP
☎ 023 8074 0544 🖷 023 8073 3166
A course with two loops of nine holes, with a booking system to allow undisturbed play. The front nine is fairly long and undulating and include water hazards. The back nine is tighter and quite a challenge.
Manor Golf Course: 18 holes, 5915yds, Par 69, SSS 69, Course record 68.
Club membership 600.
Visitors Mon-Sun & BHs. Dress code. **Societies** Booking required. **Green Fees** £12 per 18 holes, £6 per 9 holes, £15/£10 Sat, Sun & BHs. **Prof** Darren Newing **Course Designer** J Garner **Facilities** **Location** A27 between Chilworth & Romsey

Hotel ★★★ 70% Chilworth Manor, CHILWORTH
☎ 023 8076 7333 95 en suite

Southampton Golf Course Rd, Bassett SO16 7LE
☎ 023 8076 0478 & 8076 0546 (booking) 🖷 023 8076 0472
e-mail: golf.course@southampton.gov.uk
18 holes, 6103yds, Par 69, SSS 70.
9 holes, 2395yds, Par 33.
Course Designer Halmree, AP Taylor **Location** 4m N of city centre off A33
Phone for further details

Hotel ★★ 68% The Elizabeth House Hotel, 42-44 The Avenue, SOUTHAMPTON ☎ 023 8022 4327 18 en suite 7 annexe en suite

Stoneham Monks Wood Close, Bassett SO16 3TT
☎ 023 8076 9272 🖷 023 8076 6320
e-mail: richard.penley-martin@stonehamgolfclub.org.uk
web: www.stonehamgolfclub.org.uk
Undulating through an attractive parkland and heathland setting with views over the Itchen valley towards Winchester, this course rewards brains over brawn. It is unusual in having 5 par 5's and 5 par 3's and no two holes alike. The quality of the course means that temporary greens are never used and the course is rarely closed.
18 holes, 6392yds, Par 72, SSS 70, Course record 63.
Club membership 800.
Visitors Mon-Sun & BHs. Dress code. **Societies** Booking required. **Green Fees** £45 per day, £40 per round, £60/£50 Sat, Sun & BHs. **Prof** Ian Young **Course Designer** Willie Park Jnr **Facilities** **Conf** facs Corporate Hospitality Days **Location** 4m N of city centre off A27

Hotel ★★★ 70% Chilworth Manor, CHILWORTH
☎ 023 8076 7333 95 en suite

SOUTHWICK Map 04 SU60

Southwick Park Naval Recreation Centre
Pinsley Dr PO17 6EL
☎ 023 923 80131 🖷 023 9221 0289
e-mail: southwick.park@ukonline.co.uk
Set in 100 acres of parkland.
18 holes, 5884yds, Par 69, SSS 69, Course record 64.
Club membership 700.
Visitors Mon-Sun & BHs. Booking required. Dress code. **Societies** Booking required. **Green Fees** £30 per 36 holes, £23 per 18 holes, £26 per 18 holes Sat, Sun & BHs. **Prof** John Green **Course Designer** C Lawrie **Facilities** **Conf** Corporate Hospitality Days **Location** 0.5m SE off B2177

Hotel ★★ 70% Old House Hotel & Restaurant, The Square, WICKHAM ☎ 01329 833049 8 en suite 4 annexe en suite

TADLEY Map 04 SU66

Bishopswood Bishopswood Ln RG26 4AT
☎ 0118 981 2200 🖷 0118 940 8606
e-mail: david@bishopswoodgolfcourse.co.uk
web: www.bishopswoodgolfcourse.co.uk
Wooded parkland with numerous water hazards. Considered to be one of the best nine-hole courses in the UK and venue of the National 9's regional finals.
9 holes, 6474yds, Par 72, SSS 71, Course record 66.
Club membership 450.
Visitors Mon-Fri except BHs. Booking required. Dress code. **Societies** Booking required. **Green Fees** £19 per 18 holes, £13 per 9 holes. **Prof** Steve Ward **Course Designer** MW Phillips, G Blake **Facilities** **Conf** Corporate Hospitality Days **Location** 6m N of Basingstoke off A340

Hotel ★★★ 72% Romans Country House Hotel, Little London Rd, SILCHESTER ☎ 0118 970 0421 11 en suite 14 annexe en suite

WATERLOOVILLE Map 04 SU60

Portsmouth Crookhorn Ln, Purbrook PO7 5QL
☎ 023 9237 2210 🖷 023 9220 0766
e-mail: info@portsmouthgc.com
web: www.portsmouthgc.com
18 holes, 6139yds, Par 69, SSS 70, Course record 64.
Course Designer Hawtree **Location** 2m S off A3
Phone for further details

Hotel ★★★★ 65% Portsmouth Marriott Hotel, Southampton Rd, PORTSMOUTH ☎ 0870 400 7285 174 en suite

Waterlooville Cherry Tree Av, Cowplain PO8 8AP
☎ 023 9226 3388 🖷 023 9224 2980
e-mail: secretary@waterloovillegolfclub.co.uk
web: www.waterloovillegolfclub.co.uk
Easy walking but challenging parkland course, with five par 5s over 500yds and featuring four ponds and a stream running through. The 13th hole, at 556yds, has a carry over a pond for a drive and a stream crossing the fairway and ending in a very small green.
18 holes, 6602yds, Par 72, SSS 72, Course record 64.
Club membership 800.
Visitors Mon-Fri. Booking required Sat, Sun & BHs. Handicap certificate. Dress code. **Societies** Booking required. **Green Fees** £44 per day, £34 per round. **Prof** John Hay **Course Designer** Henry Cotton **Facilities** **Conf** Corporate Hospitality Days **Location** NE of town centre off A3

Hotel ★★★ 69% Brookfield Hotel, Havant Rd, EMSWORTH ☎ 01243 373363 40 en suite

Continued

WICKHAM Map 04 SU51

Wickham Park Titchfield Ln PO17 5PJ
☎ 01329 833342 01329 834798
e-mail: wickham@crown-golf.co.uk
web: www.crown-golf.co.uk
An attractive 18-hole parkland course set in the Meon Valley. Ideal for beginners and established golfers alike. The course is not overly demanding but is challenging enough to provide an enjoyable round of golf.
18 holes, 5898yards, Par 69, SSS 68, Course record 69.
Club membership 600.
Visitors Mon-Sun & BHs. Booking required. Dress code. **Societies** Booking required. **Green Fees** phone. **Prof** Scott Edwards **Facilities** **Leisure** chipping area. **Conf** facs Corporate Hospitality Days **Location** M27 junct 9/10

Hotel ★★ 70% Old House Hotel & Restaurant, The Square, WICKHAM ☎ 01329 833049 8 en suite 4 annexe en suite

WINCHESTER Map 04 SU42

Hockley Twyford SO21 1PL
☎ 01962 713165 01962 713612
e-mail: secretary@hockleygolfclub.com
web: www.hockleygolfclub.com
Downland course with good views.
18 holes, 6500yds, Par 71, SSS 70, Course record 64.
Club membership 750.
Visitors Mon-Sun & BHs. Dress code. **Societies** Booking required. **Green Fees** £45 per day, £35 per round, £50 Sat & Sun. **Prof** Gary Stubbington **Course Designer** James Braid **Facilities** **Conf** Corporate Hospitality Days **Location** M3 junct 11, signed to Twyford

Hotel ★★★★ 63% Macdonald Wessex Hotel, Paternoster Row, WINCHESTER ☎ 0870 400 8126 94 en suite

Royal Winchester Sarum Rd SO22 5QE
☎ 01962 852462 01962 865048
e-mail: manager@royalwinchestergolfclub.com
web: royalwinchestergolfclub.com
The Royal Winchester course is a sporting downland course centred on a rolling valley, so the course is hilly in places with fine views over the surrounding countryside. Built on chalk downs, the course drains extremely well and offers an excellent playing surface.
18 holes, 6216yds, Par 71, SSS 70, Course record 65.
Club membership 800.
Visitors Mon-Fri except BHs. Booking required. Handicap certificate. Dress code. **Societies** Booking required. **Green Fees** £60 per day, £36 per round. **Prof** Steven Hunter **Course Designer** JH Taylor **Facilities** by arrangement **Conf** Corporate Hospitality Days **Location** 1.5m W off A3090

Hotel ★★★★ Lainston House Hotel, Sparsholt, WINCHESTER ☎ 01962 863588 50 en suite

South Winchester Romsey Rd SO22 5QX
☎ 01962 877800 01962 877900
e-mail: swgc@crown-golf.co.uk
web: www.crown-golf.co.uk/southwinchester
This links style course in two loops of nine holes provides all golfers with a fair challenge. The course undulates between grassy slopes and beside several lakes offering easy walking and excellent views. Excellent drainage on the chalk based surface.
18 holes, 7086yds, Par 72, SSS 74, Course record 68.
Club membership 750.
Visitors Mon-Fri. After 10.30am Sat & Sun. **Societies** Booking required. **Green Fees** phone. **Prof** Richard Adams **Course Designer** Dave Thomas **Facilities** **Conf** facs Corporate Hospitality Days **Location** M3 junct 11, on A3090 Romsey road

Hotel ★★★ 73% The Winchester Royal, Saint Peter St, WINCHESTER ☎ 01962 840840 19 en suite 56 annexe en suite

HEREFORDSHIRE

BODENHAM Map 03 SO55

Brockington Hall Golf Club & Country House HR1 3HX
☎ 01568 797877 01568 797877
e-mail: info@brockingtonhall.co.uk
web: www.brockingtonhall.co.uk
A well-maintained course set in attractive countryside with fine greens and defined fairways separated by mixed plantations. A meandering brook runs through the course making it a testing but enjoyable game of golf.
9 holes, 2344yds, Par 66, SSS 63, Course record 32.
Club membership 178.
Visitors contact club for details. Dress code. **Societies** Booking required. **Green Fees** £11 per 18 holes, £7 per 9 holes, £12/£8 Sat & Sun. **Prof** Kevin Davis **Course Designer** Derek Powell **Facilities** **Conf** facs Corporate Hospitality Days **Location** on A417 on outskirts of Bodenham village.

Hotel ★★★ 66% Talbot Hotel, West St, LEOMINSTER ☎ 01568 616347 20 en suite

CLIFFORD Map 03 SO24

Summerhill HR3 5EW
☎ 01497 820451 01497 820451
Undulating parkland deep in the Wye Valley on the Welsh border.
9 holes, 2872yds, Par 70, SSS 67, Course record 71.
Club membership 240.
Visitors Mon-Sun & BHs. **Societies** Booking required. **Green Fees** phone. **Prof** Andy Gealy **Course Designer** Bob Sandow **Facilities** by arrangement **Leisure** 3 hole par 3 course. **Conf** facs Corporate Hospitality Days **Location** 0.5m N from Hay on B4350, on right

Inn ♦♦♦♦♦ The Talkhouse, Pontdolgoch, CAERSWS ☎ 01686 688919 3 en suite

HEREFORD Map 03 SO53

Belmont Lodge Belmont HR2 9SA
☎ 01432 352666 🖷 01432 358090
e-mail: info@belmont-hereford.co.uk
web: www.belmont-hereford.co.uk
Parkland course designed in two loops of nine. The first nine take the higher ground, offering magnificent views over Herefordshire. The second nine run alongside the River Wye with five holes in play against the river.The course is situated in typically beautiful Herefordshire countryside. The walking is easy on gently rolling fairways with a background of hills and woods and in the distance, the Welsh mountains. Some holes are played through mature cider orchards and there are two lakes to negotiate. A fair but interesting test for players of all abilities.

18 holes, 6511yds, Par 72, SSS 71, Course record 66. Club membership 500.
Visitors Mon-Sun & BHs. Booking required. Dress code. **Societies** Booking required. **Green Fees** £25 per 18 holes, £30 Sat, Sun & BHs. Winter reduced rates. **Prof** Mike Welsh **Course Designer** Bob Sandow **Facilities** **Leisure** hard tennis courts, fishing. **Conf** facs Corporate Hospitality Days **Location** 2m S off A465

Hotel ★★★ 69% Belmont Lodge & Golf, Belmont, HEREFORD ☎ 01432 352666 30 en suite

Burghill Valley Tillington Rd, Burghill HR4 7RW
☎ 01432 760456 🖷 01432 761654
e-mail: info@bvgc.co.uk
web: www.bvgc.co.uk
The course is situated in typically beautiful Herefordshire countryside. The walking is easy on gently rolling fairways with a background of hills and woods and in the distance, the Welsh mountains. Some holes are played through mature cider orchards and there are two lakes to negotiate. A fair but interesting test for players of all abilities.
18 holes, 6239yds, Par 71, SSS 70, Course record 66. Club membership 700.
Visitors Booking required. **Societies** Booking required. **Green Fees** phone. **Prof** Keith Preece, Andy Cameron **Course Designer** M Barnett **Facilities** **Leisure** chipping practice area. **Location** 4m NW of Hereford

Hotel Premier Travel Inn Hereford, Holmer Rd, Holmer, HEREFORD ☎ 08701 977134 60 en suite

Hereford Municipal Hereford Leisure Centre, Holmer Rd HR4 9UD
☎ 01432 344376 🖷 01432 266281
This municipal parkland course is more challenging than first appearance. The well-drained greens are open all year round with good drainage for excellent winter golf.
9 holes, 3060yds, Par 35, SSS 68. Club membership 195.
Visitors Mon-Sun & BHs. Booking required. **Societies** Booking required. **Green Fees** £8.50 per 18 holes, £5.50 per 9 holes. **Prof** Gary Morgan **Course Designer** J Leek **Facilities** **Leisure** squash, gymnasium, Leisure centre. **Location** Within racecourse on A49 Hereford-Leominster

Hotel Premier Travel Inn Hereford, Holmer Rd, Holmer, HEREFORD ☎ 08701 977134 60 en suite

KINGTON Map 03 SO25

Kington Bradnor Hill HR5 3RE
☎ 01544 230340 (club) & 231320 (pro shop)
🖷 01544 230340/231320 (pro)
The highest 18-hole course in England, with magnificent views over seven counties. A natural heathland course with easy walking on mountain turf cropped by sheep. There is bracken to catch any really bad shots but no sand traps. The greens play true and fast and are generally acknowledged as some of the best in the west Midlands.
18 holes, 5980yds, Par 70, SSS 68, Course record 63. Club membership 510.
Visitors Mon-Sun & BHs. Handicap certificate. Dress code. **Societies** welcome. **Green Fees** £26 per day, £20 per round, £32/£26 Sat, Sun & BHs. **Prof** Andy Gealy **Course Designer** Major CK Hutchison **Facilities** **Location** 0.5m N of Kington off B4355

Hotel ★★★ 66% Talbot Hotel, West St, LEOMINSTER ☎ 01568 616347 20 en suite

LEOMINSTER Map 03 SO45

Leominster Ford Bridge HR6 0LE
☎ 01568 610055 🖷 01568 610055
e-mail: contact@leominstergolfclub.co.uk
web: www.leominstergolfclub.co.uk
On undulating parkland with the lower holes running alongside the River Lugg and others on the higher part of the course affording fine panoramic views over the surrounding countryside.
18 holes, 6026yds, Par 70, SSS 69. Club membership 520.
Visitors Mon-Sun & BHs. Booking required. Dress code. **Societies** Booking required. **Green Fees** £20 per day Mon-Fri, £10 per 18 holes Mon & Fri, £15 Tue-Thu, £30 per day Sat, Sun & BHs, £25 per round. **Prof** Nigel Clarke **Course Designer** Bob Sandow **Facilities** **Leisure** fishing. **Conf** facs **Location** 3m S of Leominster on A49, signed

Hotel ★★★ 66% Talbot Hotel, West St, LEOMINSTER ☎ 01568 616347 20 en suite

ROSS-ON-WYE Map 03 SO62

Ross-on-Wye Two Park, Gorsley HR9 7UT
☎ 01989 720267 🖷 01989 720212
e-mail: secretary@therossonwyegolfclub.co.uk
web: www.therossonwyegolfclub.co.uk
This undulating, parkland course has been cut out of a silver birch forest. The fairways are well-screened from each other and tight, the greens good and the bunkers have been restructured.
18 holes, 6451yds, Par 72, SSS 71, Course record 68.
Club membership 730.
Visitors Wed-Sun & BHs. Booking required. Handicap certificate. Dress code. **Societies** Booking required. **Green Fees** £50 per 36 holes, £46 per 27 holes, £40 per round. **Prof** Paul MIddleton **Course Designer** CK Cotton **Facilities** **Leisure** snooker. **Conf** Corporate Hospitality Days **Location** M50 junct 3, on B4221 N

Hotel ★★★ 74% Pengethley Manor, Pengethley Park, ROSS-ON-WYE ☎ 01989 730211 11 en suite 14 annexe en suite

South Herefordshire Twin Lakes HR9 7UA
☎ 01989 780535 🖷 01989 740611
e-mail: shgc.golf@clara.co.uk
Impressive 6672yd parkland course fast maturing into one of Herefordshire's finest. Magnificent panoramic views of the Welsh mountains and countryside. Drains well and is playable in any weather. The landscape has enabled the architect to design 18 individual and varied holes.
Twin Lakes: 18 holes, 6672yds, Par 71, SSS 72, Course record 71.
Club membership 300.
Visitors Booking required. **Societies** Booking required. **Green Fees** phone. **Prof** Edward Litchfield **Course Designer** John Day **Facilities** **Conf** Corporate Hospitality Days **Location** M50 junct 4, to Upton Bishop, right onto B4224, 1m left

Hotel ★★★ 66% Pencraig Court Country House Hotel, Pencraig, ROSS-ON-WYE ☎ 01989 770306 11 en suite

UPPER SAPEY Map 03 SO66

Sapey WR6 6XT
☎ 01886 853288 & 853567 🖷 01886 853485
e-mail: anybody@sapeygolf.co.uk
web: www.sapeygolf.co.uk
Easy walking parkland with views of the Malvern Hills. The mixture of long or short holes, including trees, lakes and water hazards, is a demanding challenge for all golfers.
The Rowan: 18 holes, 5935yds, Par 69, SSS 68, Course record 63.
The Oaks: 9 holes, 1203, Par 27, SSS 27.
Club membership 400.
Visitors Mon-Sun & BHs. Booking required. Dress code. **Societies** Booking required. **Green Fees** Rowan £20 per round, £25 Sat & Sun. Oaks £6, £7 Sat & Sun. **Prof** Chris Knowles **Course Designer** R McMurray **Facilities** by arrangement **Conf** Corporate Hospitality Days **Location** B4203 Bromyard-Stourport road

Hotel ★★★ 66% Talbot Hotel, West St, LEOMINSTER ☎ 01568 616347 20 en suite

WORMSLEY Map 03 SO44

Herefordshire Ravens Causeway HR4 8LY
☎ 01432 830219 & 830465 (pro) 🖷 01432 830095
e-mail: herefordshire.golf@breath.com
web: www.herefordshiregolfclub.co.uk
Undulating parkland with expansive views of the Clee Hills to the east and the Black Mountains to the west. Peaceful and relaxing situation.
18 holes, 6078yds, Par 70, SSS 69, Course record 61.
Club membership 750.
Visitors Mon-Sat except BHs. Booking required. Handicap certificate. Dress code. **Societies** Booking required. **Green Fees** £25, £35 Sat. **Prof** Richard Hemming **Course Designer** James Braid **Facilities** **Conf** Corporate Hospitality Days **Location** 7m NW of Hereford on B road to Weobley

Hotel Premier Travel Inn Hereford, Holmer Rd, Holmer, HEREFORD ☎ 08701 977134 60 en suite

HERTFORDSHIRE

ALDBURY Map 04 SP91

Stocks Hotel & Golf Club Stocks Rd HP23 5RX
☎ 01442 851341 & 851491 (pro) 🖷 01442 861253
e-mail: info@stockshotel.co.uk
web: www.stockshotel.co.uk
18 holes, 6804yds, Par 72, SSS 73, Course record 66.
Course Designer Mike Billcliffe **Location** 2m from A41 at Tring, towards Tring station
Phone for further details

Hotel ★★★★ 68% Pendley Manor, Cow Ln, TRING ☎ 01442 891891 74 en suite

ALDENHAM Map 04 TQ19

Aldenham Golf and Country Club Church Ln WD25 8NN
☎ 01923 853929 🖷 01923 858472
e-mail: info@aldenhamgolfclub.co.uk
web: www.aldenhamgolfclub.co.uk
Undulating parkland with woods, water hazards and ditches. Many specimen trees and beautiful views across the countryside.
Old Course: 18 holes, 6480yds, Par 70, SSS 71.
White Course: 9 holes, 2350yds, Par 33, SSS 32.
Club membership 500.
Visitors Mon-Fri & BHs. Sat & Sun pm. Booking required Old Course. Dress code. **Societies** Booking required.

Continued

Green Fees Old Course £30 per round, £40 Sat, Sun & BHs. White Course £12, £15 Sat, Sun & BHs. **Prof** Tim Dunstan **Facilities** ⊗ ☕ 🍷 **Conf** facs Corporate Hospitality Days **Location** M1 junct 5, 0.5m W of village

Aldenham Golf and Country Club

Hotel ★★★ 67% The White House, Upton Rd, WATFORD ☎ 01923 237316 57 en suite

BERKHAMSTED Map 04 SP90

Berkhamsted The Common HP4 2QB
☎ 01442 865832 🖷 01442 863730
e-mail: barryh@berkhamstedgc.co.uk
web: www.berkhamstedgolfclub.co.uk

There are no sand bunkers on this Championship heathland course but this does not make it any easier to play. The natural hazards will test the skill of the most able players, with a particularly testing hole at the 11th, 568yds, par 5. Fine greens, long carries and heather and gorse. The clubhouse is very comfortable.

18 holes, 6605yds, Par 71, SSS 72, Course record 65. Club membership 700.

Visitors Mon-Sun & BHs. Handicap certificate. Dress code. **Societies** Booking required. **Green Fees** £55 per day, £40 per 18 holes, £50 per 18 holes Sat, Sun & BHs. **Prof** John Clarke **Course Designer** Colt, Braid **Facilities** ⊗ ☕ 🍷 **Location** 1.5m E

Hotel ★★★★ 68% Pendley Manor, Cow Ln, TRING ☎ 01442 891891 74 en suite

BISHOP'S STORTFORD Map 05 TL42

Bishop's Stortford Dunmow Rd CM23 5HP
☎ 01279 654715 🖷 01279 655215
e-mail: office@bsgc.co.uk
web: www.bsgc.co.uk

Well-established parkland course, fairly flat, but undulating, with easy walking.

18 holes, 6404yds, Par 71, SSS 71, Course record 64. Club membership 900.

Visitors Mon-Fri except BHs. Handicap certificate. Dress code. **Societies** Booking required. **Green Fees** £40 per day, £32 per 18 holes. **Prof** Simon Sheppard **Course Designer** James Braid **Facilities** ⊗ ☕ 🍷 **Leisure** snooker tables. **Conf** facs **Location** M11 junct 8, 0.5m W on A1250

Hotel ★★★ 70% Stansted Manor Hotel, Birchanger Ln, BIRCHANGER ☎ 01279 859800 70 en suite

Great Hadham Golf & Country Club
Great Hadham Rd, Much Hadham SG10 6JE
☎ 01279 843558 🖷 01279 842122
e-mail: info@ghgcc.co.uk

An undulating meadowland and links course offering excellent country views and a challenge with its ever present breeze.

18 holes, 6854yds, Par 72, SSS 73, Course record 67. Club membership 800.

Visitors Mon-Fri. Sat, Sun & BHs pm. Booking required. Dress code. **Societies** Booking required. **Green Fees** £20 per 18 holes, £12 per 9 holes, £27/£15 pm Sat & Sun. **Prof** Kevin Lunt **Course Designer** Iain Roberts **Facilities** **Leisure** sauna, solarium, gymnasium. **Conf** facs Corporate Hospitality Days **Location** On the B1004, 3m SW of Bishop's Stortford

Hotel ★★★★ 71% Down Hall Country House Hotel, Hatfield Heath, BISHOPS STORTFORD ☎ 01279 731441 99 en suite

BRICKENDON Map 05 TL30

Brickendon Grange Pembridge Ln SG13 8PD
☎ 01992 511258 🖷 01992 511411
e-mail: play@brickendongrangegc.co.uk
web: www.brickendongrangegc.co.uk

Undulating parkland with some fine par 4s. The 17th hole reputed to be best in the county.

18 holes, 6458yds, Par 71, SSS 71, Course record 67. Club membership 680.

Visitors Mon-Fri except BHs. Booking required. Dress code. **Societies** Booking required. **Green Fees** £45 per day, £38 per round. **Prof** Graham Tippett **Course Designer** CK Cotton **Facilities** ⊗ ☕ 🍷 **Conf** facs **Location** W of village

BROOKMANS PARK Map 04 TL20

Brookmans Park Golf Club Rd AL9 7AT
☎ 01707 652487 🖷 01707 661851
e-mail: info@bpgc.co.uk
web: www.bpgc.co.uk/dev

18 holes, 6473yds, Par 71, SSS 71, Course record 65.

Course Designer Hawtree, Taylor **Location** N of village off A1000

Phone for further details

Hotel ★★★ 71% Bush Hall, Mill Green, HATFIELD ☎ 01707 271251 25 en suite

Continued

BROXBOURNE Map 05 TL30

Hertfordshire Broxbournebury Mansion, White Stubbs Ln
☎ 01992 466666 & 441268 (pro shop) 🖹 01992 470326
e-mail: hertfordshire@americangolf.uk.com
web: www.americangolf.com
18 holes, 6314yds, Par 70, SSS 70, Course record 62.
Course Designer Jack Nicklaus II **Location** Off A10 for Broxbourne, signs for Paradise Wildlife Park, left at Bell Ln over A10, on right
Phone for further details

BUNTINGFORD Map 05 TL32

East Herts Hamels Park SG9 9NA
☎ 01920 821978 (office) & 821922 (pro) 🖹 01920 823700
e-mail: brian@ehgc.co.uk
web: www.ehgc.co.uk
Mature, attractive, undulating parkland course with magnificent specimen trees.
18 holes, 6456yds, Par 71, SSS 71, Course record 62.
Club membership 640.
Visitors Mon, Tue, Thu, Fri except BHs. Booking required. Handicap certificate. Dress code. **Societies** Booking required. **Green Fees** £43 per day, £32 per round. **Prof** G Culmer **Facilities** ⊗ Ⅲ ⛳ ☕ 🍷 ⛼ 🏠 ⛳ ⛳ 🚗 ⛳ **Conf** Corporate Hospitality Days **Location** 1m N of Puckeridge off A10, opposite Pearce's Farm Shop

Hotel ★★★ 66% Novotel Stevenage, Knebworth Park, STEVENAGE ☎ 01438 346100 101 en suite

BUSHEY Map 04 TQ19

Bushey Golf & Country Club High St WD23 1TT
☎ 020 8950 2215 (pro shop) & 8950 2283 (club)
🖹 020 8386 1181
e-mail: info@busheycountryclub.com
web: www.busheycountryclub.com
Undulating parkland with challenging 2nd and 9th holes. The latter has a sweeping dog-leg left, playing to a green in front of the clubhouse. For the rather too enthusiastic golfer, Bushey offers its own physiotherapist.

9 holes, 6120yds, Par 70, SSS 69, Course record 67.
Club membership 475.
Visitors Mon, Tue, Fri except BHs. After 3.30pm Sat & Sun. Dress code. **Societies** Booking required. **Green Fees** £20 per 18 holes, £12 per 9 holes, £25/£14 Sat & Sun. **Prof** Grahame Atkinson **Course Designer** Donald Steele **Facilities** ⊗ Ⅲ ⛳ ☕ 🍷 🏠 🚗 ⛳ ⛳ **Leisure** sauna, solarium, gymnasium, health & fitness club. **Conf** Corporate Hospitality Days

Hotel ★★★ 69% Corus hotel Elstree, Barnet Ln, ELSTREE ☎ 0870 609 6151 47 en suite

Bushey Hall Bushey Hall Dr WD23 2EP
☎ 01923 222253 🖹 01923 229759
e-mail: info@golfclubuk.co.uk
web: www.busheyhallgolfclub.co.uk
A tree-lined parkland course, the oldest established club in Hertfordshire.
18 holes, 6099yds, Par 69, SSS 69, Course record 62.
Club membership 500.
Visitors Mon-Sun & BHs. Booking required. Dress code. **Societies** Booking required. **Green Fees** £26 per round, £35 Sat, Sun & BHs. **Prof** Ken Wickham **Course Designer** J Braid **Facilities** ⊗ Ⅲ by arrangement ⛳ ☕ 🍷 ⛼ 🏠 ⛳ ⛳ 🚗 ⛳ **Conf** facs Corporate Hospitality Days **Location** M1 junct 5, A41 to Harrow to Bushey, 4th exit at rdbt, club 150yds on left

Hotel ★★★ 69% Corus hotel Elstree, Barnet Ln, ELSTREE ☎ 0870 609 6151 47 en suite

Hartsbourne Golf & Country Club Hartsbourne Ave WD2 1JW
☎ 020 8950 1133
18 holes, 6305yds, Par 71, SSS 70, Course record 62.
Location 5m SE of Watford
Phone for further details

Hotel ★★★ 69% Corus hotel Elstree, Barnet Ln, ELSTREE ☎ 0870 609 6151 47 en suite

CHESHUNT Map 05 TL30

Cheshunt Park Cheshunt Park, Park Ln EN7 6QD
☎ 01992 624009 🖹 01992 636403
e-mail: brox.golf@lineone.net
Municipal parkland course, well bunkered with ponds, easy walking.
18 holes, 6692yds, Par 72, SSS 71.
Club membership 350.
Visitors Mon-Sun & BHs. Booking required. **Societies** Booking required. **Green Fees** phone. **Prof** David Banks **Course Designer** P Wawtry **Facilities** ⊗ Ⅲ ⛳ ☕ 🍷 ⛼ 🏠 ⛳ 🚗 ⛳ **Leisure** Club repair service. **Conf** Corporate Hospitality Days **Location** 1.5m NW off B156. M25 junct 25, 3m N

CHORLEYWOOD Map 04 TQ09

Chorleywood Common Rd WD3 5LN
☎ 01923 282009 🖹 01923 286739
e-mail: secretary@chorleywoodgolfclub.co.uk
Very attractive mix of woodland and heathland with natural hazards and good views.
9 holes, 5686yds, Par 68, SSS 67.
Club membership 300.
Visitors contact club for details. Handicap certificate. Dress Code. **Societies** Booking required. **Green Fees** £20 per round, £15 per 9 holes, £25/15 Sat & Sun. ⛳ **Facilities** ⊗ ⛳ ☕ 🍷 ⛼ **Location** M25 junct 18, E of village off A404

Hotel ★★★ 71% The Bedford Arms Hotel, CHENIES ☎ 01923 283301 10 en suite 8 annexe en suite

Continued

ELSTREE Map 04 TQ19

Elstree Watling St WD6 3AA
☎ 020 8953 6115 or 8238 6941 020 8207 6390
e-mail: admin@elstree-golf.co.uk
web: www.elstree-golfclub.co.uk
Undulating parkland course incorporating ponds and streams.
18 holes, 6556yds, Par 73, SSS 72.
Club membership 400.
Visitors Mon-Sun & BHs. Dress code. **Societies** Booking required. **Green Fees** £37 Mon-Fri, £45 Sat & Sun. **Prof** Marc Warwick **Course Designer** Donald Steel **Facilities** **Leisure** snooker, golf academy. **Conf** Corporate Hospitality Days **Location** A5183 between Radlett & Elstree, next to Wagon & Horses pub

Hotel ★★★ 69% Corus hotel Elstree, Barnet Ln, ELSTREE ☎ 0870 609 6151 47 en suite

ESSENDON Map 04 TL20

Hatfield London Country Club Bedwell Park AL9 6HN
☎ 01707 260360 01707 278475
e-mail: info@hatfieldlondon.co.uk
web: www.hatfieldlondon.co.uk
Parkland course with many varied hazards, including ponds, a stream and a ditch. A 19th-century clubhouse.
Old Course: 18 holes, 6808yds, Par 72, SSS 72.
New Course: 18 holes, 6938yds, Par 72, SSS 73.
Club membership 350.
Visitors Mon-Sun & BHs. Booking required Fri-Sun & BHs. Dress code. **Societies** Booking required. **Green Fees** Old Course £25, £35 Sat, Sun & BHs. New Course £30, £50 Sat, Sun & BHs. **Course Designer** Fred Hawtree **Facilities** **Leisure** 9 hole pitch and putt, Japanese bath. **Conf** facs Corporate Hospitality Days **Location** 1m S on B158

Hotel ★★★ 65% Quality Hotel Hatfield, Roehyde Way, HATFIELD ☎ 01707 275701 76 en suite

GRAVELEY Map 04 TL22

Chesfield Downs Jack's Hill SG4 7EQ
☎ 01462 482929 01462 482930
e-mail: chesfielddowns-manager@crown-golf.co.uk
web: www.crown-golf.co.uk
An undulating, open downland course with an inland links feel.
18 holes, 6648yds, Par 71, SSS 72.
Club membership 500.
Visitors Mon-Sun & BHs. Booking required. Dress code. **Societies** Booking required. **Green Fees** £23 per round, £30 Sat & Sun. **Prof** Jane Fernley **Course Designer** J Gaunt **Facilities** by arrangement **Leisure** par3 9 hole course. **Conf** facs Corporate Hospitality Days **Location** A1 junct 8, B197 to Graveley

Hotel Hotel Ibis Stevenage, Danestrete, STEVENAGE ☎ 01438 779955 98 en suite

HARPENDEN Map 04 TL11

Aldwickbury Park Piggottshill Ln AL5 1AB
☎ 01582 760112 01582 760113
e-mail: enquiries@aldwickburyparkgolfclub.com
web: www.aldwickburyparkgolfclub.com
Wooded parkland with lakes and spectacular views across the Lea valley.
18 holes, 6352yds, Par 71, SSS 70, Course record 66.
Club membership 700.
Visitors Mon-Fri. Sat & Sun after 1pm. Booking up to 3 days in advance. **Societies** Booking required. **Green Fees** phone. **Prof** Robin Turley **Course Designer** Ken Brown, Martin Gillett **Facilities** **Leisure** gymnasium, 9 hole par 3 course. **Conf** facs Corporate Hospitality Days **Location** M1 junct 9, off Wheathampstead Rd between Harpenden & Wheathampstead

Hotel ★★★ 67% Corus hotel Harpenden, 18 Southdown Rd, HARPENDEN ☎ 01582 449955 17 en suite 59 annexe en suite

Harpenden Hammonds End, Redbourn Ln AL5 2AX
☎ 01582 712580 01582 712725
e-mail: office@harpendengolfclub.co.uk
web: www.harpendengolfclub.co.uk
Gently undulating parkland, easy walking.
18 holes, 6377yds, Par 70, SSS 70, Course record 65.
Club membership 800.
Visitors Mon-Wed, Fri-Sun & BHs. Booking required Sat, Sun & BHs. Handicap certificate Sat, Sun & BHs. Dress code. **Societies** Booking required. **Green Fees** £45 per day, £35 per round, Sat, Sun & BHs £40 per round. **Prof** Peter Lane **Course Designer** Hawtree & Taylor **Facilities** by arrangement **Conf** Corporate Hospitality Days **Location** 1m S on B487

Hotel ★★★ 67% Corus hotel Harpenden, 18 Southdown Rd, HARPENDEN ☎ 01582 449955 17 en suite 59 annexe en suite

Harpenden Common Cravells Rd, East Common AL5 1BL
☎ 01582 711328 (pro shop) 01582 711321
e-mail: manager@hcgc.co.uk
web: www.hcgc.co.uk
Flat, easy walking, parkland with good greens. Golf has been played on the common for well over 100 years.
18 holes, 6214yds, Par 70, SSS 70, Course record 64.
Club membership 710.
Visitors Mon-Sun. Handicap certificate. Dress code. **Societies** Booking required. **Green Fees** £45 per 36 holes, £40 per round . **Prof** Danny Fitzsimmons **Course Designer** K Brown **Facilities** **Location** On A1081 0.5m S of Harpenden

Hotel ★★★ 67% Corus hotel Harpenden, 18 Southdown Rd, HARPENDEN ☎ 01582 449955 17 en suite 59 annexe en suite

HEMEL HEMPSTEAD Map 04 TL00

Boxmoor 18 Box Ln, Boxmoor HP3 0DJ
☎ 01442 242434
web: www.boxmoorgolfclub.co.uk
The second-oldest course in Hertfordshire. Challenging, hilly, moorland course with sloping fairways divided by trees. Fine views. Testing holes: 3rd (par 3), 4th (par 4).

Continued

The 3rd has not been holed in one since the course was founded in 1890 and the par for the course has only been broken once.
9 holes, 4812yds, Par 64, SSS 63, Course record 62.
Club membership 280.
Visitors Mon-Sun & BHs. Dress code. **Societies** Booking required. **Green Fees** £10 per round. **Facilities** **Location** 2m SW on B4505

Hotel ★★ 70% The Two Brewers, The Common, CHIPPERFIELD ☎ 01923 265266 20 en suite

Little Hay Box Ln, Bovingdon HP3 0DQ
☎ 01442 833798 01442 831399
e-mail: chris.gordon@dacorum.gov.uk
Semi-parkland, inland links.
18 holes, 6300yds, Par 72, SSS 72.
Visitors Mon-Sun & BHs. Booking required. **Societies** Booking required. **Green Fees** £15 per round, £20 Sat, Sun & BHs. **Prof** N Allen, M Perry **Course Designer** Hawtree **Facilities** **Location** 1.5m SW off A41 onto B4505

Hotel ★★★ 67% The Bobsleigh Hotel, Hempstead Rd, Bovingdon, HEMEL HEMPSTEAD ☎ 0870 1942130 30 en suite 15 annexe en suite

Shendish Manor London Rd, Apsley HP3 0AA
☎ 01442 251806 01442 230683
e-mail: tconcannon@shendish.fsnet.co.uk
web: www.shendish-manor.com

18 holes, 5660yds, Par 70, SSS 67.
Course Designer D Steel **Location** Off A4251
Phone for further details

Hotel ★★★★ 68% Pendley Manor, Cow Ln, TRING
☎ 01442 891891 74 en suite

KNEBWORTH Map 04 TL22

Knebworth Deards End Ln SG3 6NL
☎ 01438 812752 01438 815216
e-mail: knebworth.golf@virgin.net
web: www.knebworthgolfclub.com
Easy walking parkland.
18 holes, 6492yds, Par 71, SSS 71, Course record 66.
Club membership 900.
Visitors Mon-Fri. Handicap certificate. **Societies** Mon, Tue & Thu. Booking required. **Green Fees** phone. **Prof** Garry Parker **Course Designer** W Park (Jun) **Facilities** **Conf** Corporate Hospitality Days **Location** N of village off B197

Hotel ★★★ 66% The Roebuck Inn, London Rd, Broadwater, STEVENAGE ☎ 0870 011 9076 54 en suite

LETCHWORTH Map 04 TL23

Letchworth Letchworth Ln SG6 3NQ
☎ 01462 683203 01462 484567
e-mail: secretary@letchworthgolfclub.com
Planned over 100 years ago by Harry Vardon, this is an adventurous parkland course. To its variety of natural and artificial hazards is added an unpredictable wind.
18 holes, 6450yds, Par 71, SSS 71, Course record 66.
Club membership 950.
Visitors Mon & Wed-Fri. Booking required. Handicap certificate. Dress code. **Societies** Booking required. **Green Fees** phone. **Prof** Karl Teschner **Course Designer** Harry Vardon **Facilities** **Leisure** 9 hole par 3 course. **Conf** Corporate Hospitality Days **Location** S side of town centre off A505

Hotel ★★★ 63% Corus hotel Stevenage, High St, Old Town, STEVENAGE ☎ 0870 6096107 76 en suite

LITTLE GADDESDEN Map 04 SP91

Ashridge HP4 1LY
☎ 01442 842244 01442 843770
e-mail: info@ashridgegolfclub.ltd.uk
web: www.ashridgegolfclub.ltd.uk
Classic wooded parkland in area of outstanding natural beauty.
18 holes, 6625yds, Par 72, SSS 71, Course record 63.
Club membership 720.
Visitors Mon-Fri except BHs. Booking required. Dress code. **Societies** Booking required. **Green Fees** phone. **Prof** Andrew Ainsworth **Course Designer** Sir G Campbell, C Hutchinson, NV Hotchkin **Facilities** **Conf** Corporate Hospitality Days **Location** 5m N of Berkhamsted on B4506

Hotel ★★★ 67% Corus hotel Harpenden, 18 Southdown Rd, HARPENDEN ☎ 01582 449955 17 en suite 59 annexe en suite

MUCH HADHAM Map 05 TL41

Ash Valley Little Hadham Rd SG10 6HD
☎ 01279 843253 01279 842389
Naturally undulating course with good views extending to Canary Wharf in London on a clear day. Tough enough for lower handicapped players but forgiving for the beginner and higher handicapped player.
18 holes, 6586yds, Par 72, SSS 71, Course record 64.
Club membership 150.
Visitors Mon-Fri. Booking required Sat, Sun & BHs. **Societies** welcome. **Green Fees** £12 per round, £17.50 Sat, Sun & BHs. **Prof** John Hamilton **Course Designer** Martin Gillett **Facilities** **Leisure** par 3 pitch and putt. **Location** 1.5m S of A120 Little Hadham lights

Hotel ★★★ 68% Roebuck Hotel, Baldock St, WARE
☎ 01920 409955 50 en suite

POTTERS BAR Map 04 TL20

Potters Bar Darkes Ln EN6 1DE
☎ 01707 652020 🖷 01707 655051
e-mail: info@pottersbargolfclub.com
web: www.pottersbargolfclub.com
Undulating parkland.
18 holes, 6279yds, Par 71, SSS 70.
Club membership 560.
Visitors Mon, Tue, Thu & Fri except BHs. Handicap certificate. Dress code. **Societies** Booking required. **Green Fees** £26 per 18 holes. **Prof** Gary A'Ris, Julian Harding **Course Designer** James Braid **Facilities** **Location** M25 junct 24, 1m N

Hotel Days Inn South Mimms, Bignells Corner, POTTERS BAR ☎ 01707 665440 74 en suite

RADLETT Map 04 TL10

Porters Park Shenley Hill WD7 7AZ
☎ 01923 854127 🖷 01923 855475
e-mail: info@porterspark.fsnet.co.uk
web: www.porterspark.com
A splendid, undulating parkland course with fine trees and lush grass. The holes are all different and interesting - on many, accuracy of shot to the green is of paramount importance.
18 holes, 6313yds, Par 70, SSS 70, Course record 64.
Club membership 700.
Visitors Mon-Fri. Booking required 1 day in advance. **Societies** Wed & Thu. Booking required in writing. **Green Fees** phone. **Prof** David Gleeson **Course Designer** Braid **Facilities** **Location** NE of village off A5183

Hotel Innkeeper's Lodge Borehamwood, Studio Way, BOREHAM WOOD ☎ 020 8905 1455 55 en suite

REDBOURN Map 04 TL11

Redbourn Kinsbourne Green Ln AL3 7QA
☎ 01582 793493 🖷 01582 794362
e-mail: enquiries@redbourngolfclub.com
web: www.redbourngolfclub.com
A mature parkland course offering a fair test of golf to all standards. Water comes into play on a number of holes.
Ver Course: 18 holes, 6506yds, Par 70, SSS 71, Course record 67.
Kingsbourne Course: 9 holes, 1361yds, Par 27.
Club membership 800.
Visitors Mon-Sun & BHs. Booking required. Dress code. **Societies** Booking required. **Green Fees** £29 per 18 holes Mon-Thu, £34 Fri-Sun. **Prof** Stephen Hunter **Facilities** **Conf** Corporate Hospitality Days **Location** M1 junct 9, 1m N off A5183

Hotel ★★★ 67% Corus hotel Harpenden, 18 Southdown Rd, HARPENDEN ☎ 01582 449955 17 en suite 59 annexe en suite

RICKMANSWORTH Map 04 TQ09

The Grove Chandler's Cross WD3 4TG
☎ 01923 294266 🖷 01923 294268
e-mail: golf@thegrove.co.uk
web: www.thegrove.co.uk
A course built to USGA specifications but following the slopes, ridges and mounds that occur naturally within the landscape. The fairway grass encourages crisp ball striking and the greens are superb. Continuous hidden cart path around all holes.
18 holes, 7152yds, Par 72, SSS 74.
Visitors Mon-Sun & BHs. **Societies** Booking required. **Green Fees** phone. **Prof** Blyth Reid **Course Designer** Kyle Phillips **Facilities** **Leisure** hard tennis courts, outdoor and indoor heated swimming pools, sauna, gymnasium. **Conf** facs Corporate Hospitality Days **Location** M25 junct 20, A411

Hotel ★★★★★ 74% The Grove, Chandler's Cross, RICKMANSWORTH ☎ 01923 807807 227 en suite

Moor Park WD3 1QN
☎ 01923 773146 🖷 01923 777109
e-mail: enquiries@moorparkgc.co.uk
web: www.moorparkgc.co.uk
Two parkland courses with rolling fairways - High Course is challenging and will test the best golfer and West Course demands a high degree of accuracy. The clubhouse is a grade 1 listed mansion.
High Golf Course: 18 holes, 6713yds, Par 72, SSS 72, Course record 63.
West Golf Course: 18 holes, 5815yds, Par 69, SSS 68, Course record 60.
Club membership 1700.
Visitors Mon-Sun & BHs. Booking required. Handicap certificate. Dress code. **Societies** Booking required. **Green Fees** High £80 per round. West £50 per round. **Prof** Lawrence Farmer **Course Designer** H Colt **Facilities** **Leisure** hard and grass tennis courts, chipping green, snooker room. **Conf** facs Corporate Hospitality Days **Location** M25 junct 17/18, off A404 to Northwood

Hotel ★★★ 71% The Bedford Arms Hotel, CHENIES ☎ 01923 283301 10 en suite 8 annexe en suite

Rickmansworth Public Course Moor Ln WD3 1QL
☎ 01923 775278
Undulating, municipal parkland course, short but tests skills to the full.
18 holes, 4656yds, Par 65, SSS 63.
Club membership 240.
Visitors Booking required, 7 day booking. **Societies** Booking required. **Green Fees** phone. **Prof** Alan Dobbins **Course Designer** Colt **Facilities** **Conf** facs Corporate Hospitality Days **Location** 2m S of town off A4145

Hotel ★★★ 71% The Bedford Arms Hotel, CHENIES ☎ 01923 283301 10 en suite 8 annexe en suite

ROYSTON Map 05 TL34

Barkway Park Nuthampstead Rd, Barkway SG8 8EN
☎ 01763 849070
18 holes, 6997yds, Par 74, SSS 74.
Course Designer Vivien Saunders **Location** A10 onto B1368
Phone for further details

Hotel ★★★ 74% Duxford Lodge Hotel, Ickleton Rd, DUXFORD ☎ 01223 836444 11 en suite 4 annexe en suite

Continued

Heydon Grange Golf & Country Club

Heydon SG8 7NS
01763 208988 01763 208926
e-mail: enquiries@heydon-grange.co.uk
web: www.heydongrange.co.uk

Three nine-hole parkland courses - the Essex, Cambridgeshire and Hertfordshire - situated in gently rolling countryside. Courses are playable all year round.

Essex: 9 holes, 2891yds, Par 36, SSS 35, Course record 64.
Cambridgeshire: 9 holes, 3057yds, Par 36, SSS 36.
Hertfordshire: 9 holes, 2937yds, Par 36, SSS 36.
Club membership 250.

Visitors Mon-Fri. Booking required Sat, Sun & BHs. Dress code. **Societies** welcome. **Green Fees** £17.50 per 18 holes, £12.50 per 9 holes, £23/£14.50 Sat, Sun & BHs. **Prof** Mike Snow **Course Designer** Cameron Sinclair **Facilities** **Conf** Corporate Hospitality Days **Location** M11 junct 10, A505 between Royston & Duxford

Hotel ★★★ 74% Duxford Lodge Hotel, Ickleton Rd, DUXFORD 01223 836444 11 en suite 4 annexe en suite

Kingsway Cambridge Rd, Melbourn SG8 6EY

01763 262727 01763 263298

The Melbourn course is short and deceptively tricky. This nine-hole course provides a good test for both beginners and experienced golfers. Out of bounds and strategically placed bunkers come into play on several holes, in particular the tough par 3 7th. The Orchard course is a cleverly designed par 3 course set among trees. Ideal for sharpening the short game or as a family introduction to golf.

Melbourn Course: 9 holes, 2455yds, Par 33, SSS 32.
Orchard Course: 9 holes, 727yds, Par 27, SSS 27.
Club membership 150.

Visitors Mon-Sun & BHs. **Societies** welcome. **Green Fees** phone. **Prof** S Brown, D Hastings, M Sturgess **Facilities** **Location** Off A10

Hotel ★★★ 74% Duxford Lodge Hotel, Ickleton Rd, DUXFORD 01223 836444 11 en suite 4 annexe en suite

Royston Baldock Rd SG8 5BG

01763 242696 01763 246910
e-mail: roystongolf@btconnect.com
web: www.roystongolfclub.co.uk

Heathland course on undulating terrain and fine fairways. The 8th, 10th and 15th are the most notable holes on this all weather course.

18 holes, 6052yds, Par 70, SSS 70, Course record 63.
Club membership 750.

Visitors Mon-Sun & BHs. Dress code. **Societies** by arrangement Mon-Fri. **Green Fees** phone. **Prof** Sean Clark **Course Designer** Harry Vardon **Facilities** **Conf** facs Corporate Hospitality Days **Location** 0.5m W of town centre

Hotel ★★★ 74% Duxford Lodge Hotel, Ickleton Rd, DUXFORD 01223 836444 11 en suite 4 annexe en suite

ST ALBANS Map 04 TL10

Abbey View Westminster Lodge Leisure Ctr, Holywell Hill AL1 2DL

01727 868227 01727 848468
e-mail: abbey.view@leisureconnection.co.uk
web: www.leisureconnection.co.uk

Abbey View is a picturesque public course in the centre of the city, suitable for beginners and those wishing to test their short game. Fine views of the cathedral.

9 holes, 1411yds, Par 29, Course record 27.
Club membership 140.

Visitors Mon-Sun & BHs. Dress code. **Societies** Booking required. **Green Fees** £6.15, £7.15 Sat, Sun & BHs. **Prof** Mark Flitton **Facilities** **Leisure** hard and grass tennis courts, heated indoor swimming pool, sauna, solarium, gymnasium, crazy golf. **Conf** Corporate Hospitality Days **Location** City centre, off Holywell Hill in Verulamium Park

Hotel ★★★ 78% St Michael's Manor, Fishpool St, ST ALBANS 01727 864444 30 en suite

Batchwood Hall Batchwood Dr AL3 5XA

01727 844250 01727 858506
e-mail: batchwood@leisureconnection.co.uk
web: www.stalbans.gov.uk

Municipal parkland course designed by JH Taylor and opened in 1935.

18 holes, 6487yds, Par 71, SSS 71.
Club membership 350.

Visitors Booking up to 7 days in advance. **Societies** Booking required. **Green Fees** phone. **Prof** Mark Flitton **Course Designer** JH Taylor **Facilities** **Leisure** hard tennis courts, squash, gymnasium, Indoor tennis courts. **Conf** Corporate Hospitality Days **Location** 1m NW off A5183

Hotel ★★★ 78% St Michael's Manor, Fishpool St, ST ALBANS 01727 864444 30 en suite

Verulam London Rd AL1 1JG

01727 853327 01727 812201
e-mail: gm@verulamgolf.co.uk
web: www.verulamgolf.co.uk

Easy walking parkland with 14 holes having out of bounds. Water affects the 12th, 13th and 14th holes. Samuel Ryder was captain here in 1927 when he began the now celebrated Ryder Cup competition.

18 holes, 6448yds, Par 72, SSS 71, Course record 67.
Club membership 720.

Visitors Mon-Sun & BHs. Booking required. Handicap certificate. Dress code. **Societies** Booking required. **Green Fees** £25 per round Mon, £35 Tue-Fri, £50 Sat & Sun. **Prof** Nick Burch **Course Designer** Braid **Facilities** by arrangement **Conf** facs Corporate Hospitality Days **Location** 0.5m from St Albans centre on A1081 London Rd, signed by railway bridge

Hotel ★★★★ 72% Sopwell House, Cottonmill Ln, Sopwell, ST ALBANS 01727 864477 113 en suite 16 annexe en suite

Championship Course

Hertfordshire Marriott Hanbury Manor

Ware Map 05 TL31

There can be few golf venues that combine so successfully the old and the new. The old is the site itself, dominated since the 19th century by Hanbury Manor, a Jacobean-style mansion; the wonderful grounds included a nine-hole parkland course designed by the legendary Harry Vardon. The new is the conversion of the estate into the golf and country club; the manor now offers a five-star country house hotel, while Jack Nicklaus II redesigned the grounds for an 18-hole course. The American-style design took the best of Vardon's original and added meadowland to produce a course that looks beautiful and plays superbly. Hanbury Manor has hosted a number of professional events, including the Women's European Open in 1996 and the Men's European Tour's English Open from 1997 to 1999, won respectively by Per Ulrik Johannson, Lee Westwood and Darren Clarke.

SG12 0SD
☎ 01920 487722 🖷 01920 487692
e-mail: golf.hanburymanor@marriotthotels.co.uk
web: www.hanbury-manor.com

18 holes, 7016yds, Par 72, SSS 74, Course record 61.
Club membership 850.

Visitors Mon-Sun & BHs. Booking required. Handicap certificate. Must be hotel resident. **Societies** Booking required. **Green Fees** phone. **Prof** Adam Goreman **Course Designer** Jack Nicklaus II **Facilities** **Leisure** hard tennis courts, heated indoor swimming pool, sauna, solarium, gymnasium. **Conf facs** Corporate Hospitality Days **Location** M25 junct 25, 12m N on A10

SAWBRIDGEWORTH Map 05 TL41

Manor of Groves Golf & Country Club
High Wych CM21 0JU
☎ 01279 603539 🖹 01279 726972
e-mail: golf@manorofgroves.com
web: www.manorofgroves.co.uk
The course is set out over 150 acres of established parkland and rolling countryside and is a true test of golf for the club golfer.

18 holes, 6228yds, Par 71, SSS 70, Course record 63. Club membership 550.
Visitors Mon-Fri & BHs. Sat & Sun pm. Dress code. **Societies** Booking required. **Green Fees** £28 per 18 holes, £32 Sat, Sun & BHs. **Prof** Christian Charlier **Course Designer** S Sharer **Facilities** **Leisure** heated indoor swimming pool, sauna, solarium, gymnasium. **Conf** Corporate Hospitality Days **Location** 1.5m west of town centre

Hotel ★★★ 72% Manor of Groves Hotel, High Wych, SAWBRIDGEWORTH ☎ 01279 600777 80 en suite

STANSTEAD ABBOTTS Map 05 TL31

Briggens House Hotel Briggens Park, Stanstead Rd SG12 8LD
☎ 01279 793742 🖹 01279 793685
web: www.corushotels.com/briggenshouse
An attractive nine-hole course set in the grounds of a hotel which was once a stately house in 80 acres of countryside.
9 holes, 2793yds, Par 36, SSS 69, Course record 31. Club membership 230.
Visitors Mon-Wed, Fri, Sat, Sun pm. Dress code. **Societies** Booking required. **Green Fees** phone. **Prof** Alan McGinn **Facilities** **Leisure** hard tennis courts, heated outdoor swimming pool, fishing. **Conf** facs Corporate Hospitality Days **Location** Off A414 Stanstead road

STEVENAGE Map 04 TL22

Stevenage Golf Centre 6 Aston Ln, Aston
SG2 7EL
☎ 01438 880223 & 880424 (pro shop) 🖹 01438 880040
Municipal course designed by John Jacobs, with natural water hazards and some wooded areas.
Bragbury Course: 18 holes, 6451yds, Par 72, SSS 71, Course record 63.
Aston Course: 9 holes, 880yds, Par 27, SSS 27.
Club membership 600.
Visitors Mon-Sun & BHs. Booking required. Dress code. **Societies** Booking required. **Green Fees** phone. **Prof** Pat Winston **Course Designer** John Jacobs **Facilities** **Leisure** Par 3 course. **Conf** Corporate Hospitality Days **Location** 4m SE off B5169

Hotel ★★★ 66% The Roebuck Inn, London Rd, Broadwater, STEVENAGE ☎ 0870 011 9076 54 en suite

WARE Map 05 TL31

Chadwell Springs Hertford Rd SG12 9LE
☎ 01920 461447 🖹 01920 466596
9 holes, 6418yds, Par 72, SSS 71, Course record 68.
Location 0.75m W on A119
Phone for further details

Hotel ★★★ 68% Roebuck Hotel, Baldock St, WARE ☎ 01920 409955 50 en suite

Marriott Hanbury Manor Golf & Country Club see page 141

Hotel ★★★★★ 71% Marriott Hanbury Manor Hotel & Country Club, WARE ☎ 01920 487722 & 0870 400 7222 🖹 01920 487692 134 en suite 27 annexe en suite

Hotel ★★★ 68% Roebuck Hotel, Baldock St, WARE ☎ 01920 409955 🖹 01920 468016 50 en suite

Whitehill Dane End SG12 0JS
☎ 01920 438495 🖹 01920 438891
e-mail: whitehillgolf@btconnect.com
web: www.whitehillgolf.co.uk
Undulating course providing a good test for both the average golfer and the low handicapper. Several lakes in challenging positions.
18 holes, 6618yds, Par 72, SSS 72. Club membership 600.

Continued

Visitors Dress code. **Societies** Booking required. **Green Fees** phone. **Prof** David Ling **Facilities** **Conf** Corporate Hospitality Days

Hotel ★★★ 68% Roebuck Hotel, Baldock St, WARE ☎ 01920 409955 50 en suite

WATFORD Map 04 TQ19

West Herts Cassiobury Park WD3 3GG
☎ 01923 236484 01923 222300

Set in parkland, the course is close to Watford but its tree-lined setting is beautiful and tranquil. Set out on a plateau the course is exceedingly dry. It also has a very severe finish with the 17th, a hole of 378yds, the toughest on the course. The last hole measures over 480yds.

18 holes, 6620yds, Par 72, SSS 72, Course record 65. Club membership 700.

Visitors Mon-Sun & BHs. Booking required. Dress code. **Societies** Booking required. **Green Fees** £40 per 18 holes, £50 Sat & Sun. **Prof** Charles Gough **Course Designer** Tom Morris **Facilities** **Leisure** indoor teaching facility. **Conf** Corporate Hospitality Days **Location** W of town centre off A412

Hotel ★★★ 67% The White House, Upton Rd, WATFORD ☎ 01923 237316 57 en suite

WELWYN GARDEN CITY Map 04 TL21

Mill Green Gypsy Ln AL7 4TY
☎ 01707 276900 & 270542 (pro shop) 01707 276898
e-mail: millgreen@crown-golf.co.uk

The course plays over the second 9 holes around the lakes and sweeps back through the woods. The first 9 holes are subject to the prevailing winds. The par 3 9-hole gives a good test for improving the short game.

18 holes, 6615yds, Par 72, SSS 72, Course record 64. Club membership 850.

Visitors Mon-Fri. Booking required. Dress code. **Societies** Booking required. **Green Fees** phone. **Prof** Ian Parker **Course Designer** Alliss & Clark **Facilities** **Leisure** 9 hole par 3 course. **Conf** facs Corporate Hospitality Days **Location** A1(M) junct 4, A414 to Mill Green

Hotel ★★★ 61% Quality Hotel Welwyn, The Link, WELWYN ☎ 01438 716911 96 en suite

Panshanger Golf & Squash Complex
Old Herns Ln AL7 2ED
☎ 01707 333350 01707 390010
e-mail: michaelcorlass@finesseleisure.com
web: www.finesseleisure.com

Picturesque and challenging mature course overlooking Mimram Valley. Excellent condition all year round.

18 holes, 6347yds, Par 72, SSS 70, Course record 65. Club membership 400.

Visitors Mon-Sun & BHs. Booking required. Dress code. **Societies** Booking required. **Green Fees** £17 per 18 holes, £21 Sat & Sun. **Prof** Bryan Lewis, Mick Corlass **Course Designer** Peter Kirkham **Facilities** **Leisure** squash, 9 hole pitch and putt. **Conf** facs Corporate Hospitality Days **Location** 1m N of town centre signed off B1000

Hotel ★★★ 61% Quality Hotel Welwyn, The Link, WELWYN ☎ 01438 716911 96 en suite

Welwyn Garden City Mannicotts, High Oaks Rd AL8 7BP
☎ 01707 325243 01707 393213
e-mail: secretary@welwyngardencitygolfclub.co.uk
web: www.welwyngardencitygolfclub.co.uk

Undulating parkland with a ravine. A former course record holder is Nick Faldo.

18 holes, 6114yds, Par 70, SSS 69, Course record 63. Club membership 930.

Visitors Mon-Fri except BHs. Dress code. **Societies** Booking required. **Green Fees** phone. **Prof** Richard May **Course Designer** Hawtree **Facilities** by arrangement **Conf** Corporate Hospitality Days **Location** A1 junct 6, W of city

Hotel ★★★ 61% Quality Hotel Welwyn, The Link, WELWYN ☎ 01438 716911 96 en suite

WHEATHAMPSTEAD Map 04 TL11

Mid Herts Lamer Ln, Gustard Wood AL4 8RS
☎ 01582 832242 01582 834834
e-mail: secretary@mid-hertsgolfclub.co.uk
web: www.mid-hertsgolfclub.co.uk

18 holes, 6060yds, Par 69, SSS 69, Course record 61.

Location 1m N on B651

Phone for further details

Hotel ★★★ 67% Corus hotel Harpenden, 18 Southdown Rd, HARPENDEN ☎ 01582 449955 17 en suite 59 annexe en suite

KENT

ADDINGTON Map 05 TQ65

West Malling London Rd ME19 5AR
☎ 01732 844785 01732 844795
e-mail: mike@westmallinggolf.com
web: www.westmallinggolf.com

Two 18-hole parkland courses.

Spitfire Course: 18 holes, 6142yds, Par 70, SSS 70, Course record 67.

Hurricane Course: 18 holes, 6281yds, Par 70, SSS 70, Course record 68.

Visitors Mon-Fri. Sat & Sun pm. Booking required. **Societies** Booking required. **Green Fees** phone. **Prof** Duncan Lambert **Course Designer** Max Falkner **Facilities** **Leisure** gymnasium, jaccuzi & steam room. **Conf** facs Corporate Hospitality Days **Location** 1m S off A20

ASH Map 05 TQ66

The London South Ash Manor Estate TN15 7EN
☎ 01474 879899 01474 879912
e-mail: golf@londongolf.co.uk
web: www.londongolf.co.uk

The two courses were designed by Jack Nicklaus: both include a number of lakes, generous fairways framed with native grasses and many challenging holes. A state-of-the-art drainage system ensures continuous play. Visitors may play the International course; the Heritage is for members and their guests.

Continued

Continued

Heritage Course: 18 holes, 7208yds, Par 72, SSS 75, Course record 67.
International Course: 18 holes, 7005yds, Par 72, SSS 74.
Club membership 500.
Visitors International Course Mon-Sun & BHs. Booking required. Handicap certificate. Dress code. **Societies** Booking required. **Green Fees** International Course £85 per round, £95 Sat, Sun & BHs. **Prof** Paul Stuart **Course Designer** Jack Nicklaus **Facilities** **Leisure** sauna, spa bath. **Conf** facs Corporate Hospitality Days **Location** A20, 2m from Brands Hatch

ASHFORD Map 05 TR04

Ashford (Kent) Sandyhurst Ln TN25 4NT
☎ 01233 622655
e-mail: secretary@ashfordgolfclub.co.uk
web: www.ashfordgolfclub.co.uk
Parkland with good views and easy walking. Narrow fairways and tightly bunkered greens ensure a challenging game for all levels of golfer.
18 holes, 6263yds, Par 71, SSS 70, Course record 65.
Club membership 672.
Visitors Mon-Sun & BHs. Booking required. Handicap certificate. Dress code. **Societies** Booking required. **Green Fees** £30, £35 Sat, Sun & BHs. Winter reduced rates. **Prof** Hugh Sherman **Course Designer** Cotton **Facilities** **Conf** facs Corporate Hospitality Days **Location** 1m NW M20 junct 9

Hotel ★★★★ 69% Ashford International, Simone Weil Av, ASHFORD ☎ 01233 219988 177 en suite

Homelands Bettergolf Centre Ashford Rd, Kingsnorth TN26 1NJ
☎ 01233 661620
e-mail: isj@bettergolf.co.uk
web: www.bettergolf.co.uk
Challenging nine-hole course designed by Donald Steel to provide a stern test for experienced golfers and for others to develop their game. With four par 3s and five par 4s it demands accuracy rather than length. Floodlit driving range.
9 holes, 2205yds, Par 32, SSS 31, Course record 32.
Club membership 400.
Visitors Mon-Sun & BHs. Booking required. Dress code. **Societies** Booking required. **Green Fees** phone. **Prof** John Masterson **Course Designer** Donald Steel **Facilities** **Location** M20 junct 10, A2070, signed from 2nd rdbt to Kingsnorth

Hotel Premier Travel Inn Ashford Central, Hall Av, Orbital Park, Sevington, ASHFORD ☎ 08701 977305 60 en suite

BARHAM Map 05 TR25

Broome Park The Broome Park Estate CT4 6QX
☎ 01227 830728 01227 832591
e-mail: golf@broomepark.co.uk
web: www.broomepark.co.uk
Championship-standard parkland course in a valley, with a 350-year-old mansion clubhouse.
18 holes, 6580yds, Par 72, SSS 71, Course record 66.
Club membership 700.
Visitors Mon-Sun & BHs. Booking required. Dress code. **Societies** Booking required. **Green Fees** £40 per round, £50 Sat & Sun. **Prof** Tienne Britz **Course Designer** Donald Steel **Facilities** **Leisure** hard tennis courts. **Conf** facs Corporate Hospitality Days **Location** 1.5m SE on A260

Continued

BEARSTED Map 05 TQ85

Bearsted Ware St ME14 4PQ
☎ 01622 738198 01622 735608
Parkland with fine views of the North Downs.
18 holes, 6437yds, Par 72, SSS 71.
Club membership 780.
Visitors Mon-Sun except BHs. Booking required. Handicap certificate. Dress code. **Societies** Booking required. **Green Fees** £42 per 36 holes, £32 per 18 holes. **Prof** Tim Simpson **Facilities** **Location** M20 junct 7, right at rdbt, left at minirdbt, left at 2nd minirdbt. Pass Bell pub on right, under bridge, on left

Hotel ★★★★ 71% Marriott Tudor Park Hotel & Country Club, Ashford Rd, Bearsted, MAIDSTONE ☎ 01622 734334 120 en suite

BIDDENDEN Map 05 TQ83

Chart Hills Weeks Ln TN27 8JX
☎ 01580 292222 01580 292233
e-mail: info@charthills.co.uk
web: www.charthills.co.uk

18 holes, 7107yds, Par 72, SSS 74, Course record 61.
Course Designer Nick Faldo **Location** 1m N of Biddenden off A274
Phone for further details

Hotel ★★★ 75% London Beach Hotel & Golf Club, Ashford Rd, TENTERDEN ☎ 01580 766279 26 en suite

BOROUGH GREEN Map 05 TQ65

Wrotham Heath Seven Mile Ln TN15 8QZ
☎ 01732 884800 01732 887370
18 holes, 5954yds, Par 70, SSS 69, Course record 66.
Course Designer Donald Steel (part) **Location** 2.25m E on B2016
Phone for further details

Hotel Premier Travel Inn Sevenoaks/Maidstone, London Rd, Wrotham Heath, WROTHAM ☎ 08701 977227 40 en suite

BRENCHLEY Map 05 TQ64

Kent National Golf & Country Club
Watermans Ln TN12 6ND
☎ 01892 724400 01892 723300
e-mail: info@kentnational.com
web: www.kentnational.com
A rolling parkland course with dramatic views over the Weald of Kent. The challenging holes are the par 4 8th

Continued

with its tough dog-leg, the 10th where there is a wooded copse with a Victorian bath-house to be avoided, and the 14th where the approach to the green is guarded by oak trees.

18 holes, 6693yds, Par 72, SSS 72, Course record 63. Club membership 620.

Visitors Mon-Sun & BHs. Booking required. Dress code. **Societies** Booking required. **Green Fees** from £20 per round. **Prof** Gary Stewart **Course Designer** T Saito **Facilities** **Leisure** hard tennis courts. **Conf** facs Corporate Hospitality Days **Location** 3m N of Brenchley off B2160

Hotel ★★ 65% Russell Hotel, 80 London Rd, TUNBRIDGE WELLS ☎ 01892 544833 21 en suite 5 annexe en suite

BROADSTAIRS — Map 05 TR36

North Foreland Convent Rd, Kingsgate CT10 3PU

☎ 01843 862140 🖹 01843 862663
e-mail: office@northforeland.co.uk
web: www.northforeland.co.uk

A picturesque cliff top course situated where the Thames Estuary widens towards the sea. One of the few courses where the sea can be seen from every hole. Walking is easy and the wind is deceptive. The 8th and 17th, both par 4, are testing holes. There is also an 18-hole approach and putting course.

18 holes, 6430yds, Par 71, SSS 71, Course record 63. Club membership 1100.

Visitors Mon-Sun except BHs. Handicap certificate. Dress code. **Societies** Booking required. **Green Fees** £50 per day, £35 per round, £75/£50 Sat & Sun. **Prof** Darren Parris **Course Designer** Fowler & Simpson **Facilities** **Leisure** hard tennis courts, 18 hole par 3 course. **Location** 1.5m N off B2052

Hotel ★★★ 68% Royal Albion Hotel, Albion St, BROADSTAIRS ☎ 01843 868071 19 en suite

CANTERBURY — Map 05 TR15

Canterbury Scotland Hills, Littlebourne Rd CT1 1TW

☎ 01227 462865 🖹 01227 784277
e-mail: cgc@freeola.com

Undulating parkland, densely wooded in places, with elevated tees and challenging drives on several holes.

18 holes, 6272yds, Par 71, SSS 70, Course record 64. Club membership 700.

Visitors Mon-Sun except BHs. Booking required. Handicap certificate. Dress code. **Societies** Booking required. **Green Fees** phone. **Prof** Paul Everard **Course Designer** Harry Colt **Facilities** **Conf** facs Corporate Hospitality Days **Location** 1.5m E on A257

CHART SUTTON — Map 05 TQ84

The Ridge Chartway St, East Sutton ME17 3DL

☎ 01622 844382

18 holes, 6254yds, Par 71, SSS 70, Course record 68.

Course Designer Tyton Design **Location** 5m S of Bearsted off A274

Phone for further details

Hotel ★★★★ 71% Marriott Tudor Park Hotel & Country Club, Ashford Rd, Bearsted, MAIDSTONE ☎ 01622 734334 120 en suite

CRANBROOK — Map 05 TQ73

Hemsted Forest Golford Rd TN17 4AL

☎ 01580 712833 🖹 01580 714274
e-mail: golf@hemstedforest.co.uk
web: www.hemstedforest.co.uk

Scenic parkland with easy terrain, backed by Hemstead Forest. The course lies in a beautiful natural setting and offers a tranquil haven. The clubhouse, a converted oast, is the only one of its kind.

18 holes, 6305yds, Par 70, SSS 71, Course record 64. Club membership 1600.

Visitors Tue-Sun & BHs. Booking required. Dress code. **Societies** Booking required. **Green Fees** £28 per round, £40 Sat & Sun. **Prof** Chris Weston **Course Designer** Commander J Harris **Facilities** **Conf** facs Corporate Hospitality Days **Location** 2m E

Hotel ★★★ 75% London Beach Hotel & Golf Club, Ashford Rd, TENTERDEN ☎ 01580 766279 26 en suite

DARTFORD — Map 05 TQ57

Birchwood Park Birchwood Rd, Wilmington DA2 7HJ

☎ 01322 662038 & 660554 🖹 01322 667283
e-mail: info@birchwoodparkgc.co.uk
web: www.birchwoodparkgc.co.uk

The main course offers highly challenging play and will test golfers of all abilities. Beginners and those requiring a quick game or golfers wishing to improve their short game will appreciate the Orchard course where holes range from 96 to 258yds.

Parkland: 18 holes, 6364yds, Par 71, SSS 70, Course record 64.
Orchard: 9 holes, 1349yds, Par 29.
Club membership 600.

Visitors Mon-Sun & BHs. Booking required 7 days in advance. Dress code. **Societies** Mon-Sun & BHs. Dress code. **Green Fees** phone. **Course Designer** Howard Swann **Facilities** **Leisure** sauna, solarium, gymnasium. **Conf** facs Corporate Hospitality Days **Location** B258 between Dartford & Swanley

Hotel ★★★★ 67% Bexleyheath Marriott Hotel, 1 Broadway, BEXLEYHEATH ☎ 0870 400 7245 142 en suite

Dartford Heath Ln (Upper), Dartford Heath DA1 2TN

☎ 01322 226455 🖹 01322 226455
e-mail: dartfordgolf@hotmail.com

Challenging parkland course with tight fairways and easy walking.

18 holes, 5909yds, Par 69, SSS 69, Course record 61. Club membership 700.

Continued

Visitors Mon-Fri. Handicap certificate. **Societies** Mon & Fri. Booking required. **Green Fees** phone. **Prof** John Gregory **Course Designer** James Braid **Facilities** **Conf** Corporate Hospitality Days **Location** 2m from town centre off A2

Hotel Campanile, 1 Clipper Boulevard West, Crossways Business Park, DARTFORD ☎ 01322 278925 125 en suite

DEAL Map 05 TR35

Royal Cinque Ports Golf Rd CT14 6RF
☎ 01304 374007 01304 379530
e-mail: rcpgcsec@aol.com
web: www.royalcinqueports.com
18 holes, 6899yds, Par 72, SSS 73.
Course Designer James Braid **Location** On seafront at N end of Deal
Phone for further details

Hotel ★★★ 75% Wallett's Court Country House Hotel & Spa, West Cliffe, St Margarets-at-Cliffe, DOVER ☎ 01304 852424 & 0800 0351628 01304 853430 3 en suite 13 annexe en suite

EDENBRIDGE Map 05 TQ44

Sweetwoods Park Cowden TN8 7JN
☎ 01342 850729 (pro shop) 01342 850866
e-mail: danhowe@sweetwoodspark.com
web: www.sweetwoodspark.com
An undulating and mature parkland course with very high quality greens, testing water hazards and fine views across the Weald from four holes. A good challenge off the back tees. Signature holes include the 2nd, 4th and 14th.
18 holes, 6617yds, Par 72, SSS 72, Course record 63. Club membership 700.
Visitors Mon-Sun & BHs. Dress code. **Societies** Booking required. **Green Fees** £30 per round, £36 Sat, Sun & BHs. **Prof** Paul Lyons **Course Designer** P Strand **Facilities** **Leisure** Sussex College of Golf. **Conf** facs Corporate Hospitality Days **Location** 4m E of East Grinstead on A264

Hotel ★★★ Gravetye Manor Hotel, EAST GRINSTEAD ☎ 01342 810567 18 en suite

EYNSFORD Map 05 TQ56

Austin Lodge Upper Austin Lodge Rd DA4 0HU
☎ 01322 863000 01322 862406
e-mail: linda@pentlandgolf.co.uk
web: www.pentlandgolf.co.uk
A well-drained course designed to lie naturally in three secluded valleys in rolling countryside. Over 7000yds from the medal tees. Practice ground, nets and a putting green add to the features.
18 holes, 7026yds, Par 73, SSS 71, Course record 68. Club membership 400.
Visitors Mon-Fri & BHs. Sat & Sun pm. Booking required. Dress code. **Societies** Booking required. **Green Fees** £19.50 per 18 holes, £27.50 Sat, Sun & BHs. **Prof** Martin Windsor **Course Designer** P Bevan **Facilities** **Location** 6m S of Dartford

Hotel ★★★★ 74% Brandshatch Place Hotel, Brands Hatch Rd, Fawkham, BRANDS HATCH ☎ 01474 875000 26 en suite 12 annexe en suite

FAVERSHAM Map 05 TR06

Boughton Brickfield Ln, Boughton ME13 9AJ
☎ 01227 752277 01227 752361
e-mail: greg@pentlandgolf.co.uk
web: www.pentlandgolf.co.uk
Rolling parkland and downland course set in 160 acres of Kent countryside, providing a good test of golf, even for the more accomplished players.
18 holes, 6469yds, Par 72, SSS 71, Course record 68. Club membership 500.
Visitors Mon-Sun & BHs. Booking required. Dress code. **Societies** Booking required. **Green Fees** £19.50 per 18 holes, £26.50 Sat, Sun & BHs. **Prof** Greg Haenen, Trevor Dungate **Course Designer** P Sparks **Facilities** **Location** M2 junct 7, Brenley Corner

Hotel ★★★★ 74% Eastwell Manor, Eastwell Park, Boughton Lees, ASHFORD ☎ 01233 213000 23 en suite 39 annexe en suite

Faversham Belmont Park ME13 0HB
☎ 01795 890561 01795 890760
e-mail: themanager@favershamgolf.co.uk
web: www.favershamgolf.co.uk
A beautiful inland course laid out over part of a large estate with pheasants walking the fairways quite tamely. Play follows two heavily wooded valleys but the trees affect only the loose shots going out of bounds. Fine views.

18 holes, 6012yds, Par 70, SSS 69, Course record 62. Club membership 800.
Visitors Mon-Fri except BHs. Booking required. Handicap certificate. Dress code. **Societies** Booking required. **Green Fees** £35 per round. **Prof** Stuart Rokes **Facilities** **Conf** Corporate Hospitality Days **Location** 3.5m S on Belmont road

Hotel ★★★★ 74% Eastwell Manor, Eastwell Park, Boughton Lees, ASHFORD ☎ 01233 213000 23 en suite 39 annexe en suite

FOLKESTONE Map 05 TR23

Etchinghill Canterbury Rd, Etchinghill CT18 8FA
☎ 01303 863863 01303 863210
e-mail: jill@pentlandgolf.co.uk
web: www.pentlandgolf.co.uk
A varied course incorporating parkland and an interesting downland landscape with many challenging holes on the back nine.
27 holes, 6101yds, Par 70, SSS 69, Course record 67. Club membership 600.

Continued

Visitors Mon-Sun & BHs. Dress code. **Societies** Booking required. **Green Fees** phone. **Prof** Roger Dowle **Course Designer** John Sturdy **Facilities** **Leisure** 9 hole par3. **Conf** facs **Location** M20 junct 11/12

Hotel ★★★ 70% Clifton Hotel, The Leas, FOLKESTONE ☎ 01303 851231 80 en suite

GILLINGHAM Map 05 TQ76

Gillingham Woodlands Rd ME7 2AP
☎ 01634 853017 (office) 01634 574749
e-mail: golf@gillinghamgolf.idps.co.uk
Mature parkland course with views of the estuary.
18 holes, 5495yds, Par 69, SSS 66, Course record 64.
Club membership 900.
Visitors Mon-Fri. Booking required. Handicap certificate. **Societies** Sat & Sun. Booking required. **Green Fees** phone. **Prof** Steven Green, Andrew Brroks **Course Designer** James Braid, Steel **Facilities** **Leisure** small practice area. **Conf** Corporate Hospitality Days **Location** 1.5m SE on A2

Hotel Premier Travel Inn Gillingham, Kent, Will Adams Way, GILLINGHAM ☎ 08701 977105 45 en suite

GRAVESEND Map 05 TQ67

Mid Kent Singlewell Rd DA11 7RB
☎ 01474 568035 01474 564218
e-mail: secretary@mkgc.co.uk
web: www.mkgc.co.uk
A well-maintained downland course with some easy walking and some excellent greens. The first hole is short, but nonetheless a real challenge. The slightest hook and the ball is out of bounds or lost.
18 holes, 6106yds, Par 70, SSS 69, Course record 60.
Club membership 900.
Visitors Mon-Fri except BHs. Handicap certificate. Dress code. **Societies** Tue. Booking required. **Green Fees** £50 per day, £35 per round. **Prof** Mark Foreman **Course Designer** Frank Pennick **Facilities** by arrangement **Leisure** snooker. **Location** S of town centre off A227

Hotel Premier Travel Inn Gravesend, Wrotham Rd, GRAVESEND ☎ 08701 977118 36 en suite

Southern Valley Thong Ln, Shorne DA12 4LF
☎ 01474 568568 01474 360366
e-mail: info@southernvalley.co.uk
web: www.southernvalley.co.uk
All year playing conditions on a course landscaped with gorse, bracken and thorn and designed to enhance the views across the Thames Estuary. The course features undulating greens, large trees and rolling fairways with the 9th and 18th holes located close to the clubhouse.
18 holes, 6200yds, Par 69, SSS 69, Course record 62.
Club membership 450.
Visitors Mon-Sun & BHs. Booking required. Dress code. **Societies** Booking required. **Green Fees** £16.50 per 18 holes, £10.50 per 9 holes, £22/£12.50 Sat, Sun & BHs. **Prof** Larry Batchelor **Course Designer** Weller, Richardson **Facilities** **Conf** facs Corporate Hospitality Days **Location** A2 junct 4, off slip-road left onto Thong Ln, continue 1m

Continued

Hotel ★★★ 72% Manor Hotel, Hever Court Rd, GRAVESEND ☎ 01474 353100 59 en suite

HALSTEAD Map 05 TQ46

Broke Hill Sevenoaks Rd TN14 7HR
☎ 01959 533225 01959 532680
e-mail: bhgc@crown-golf.co.uk
web: www.crown-golf.co.uk/brokehill
A challenging game awaits all golfers. The fairways have strategically placed bunkers, some of which come into play off the tee. Five holes have water hazards, the most significant being the 18th where a lake has to be carried to get onto the green.

18 holes, 6454yds, Par 72, SSS 71, Course record 65.
Club membership 650.
Visitors Mon-Fri except BHs. Dress code. **Societies** welcome. **Green Fees** £40 per round. **Course Designer** David Williams **Facilities** **Leisure** sauna. **Conf** facs Corporate Hospitality Days **Location** M25 junct 4, opp Knockholt station

Hotel ★★★ 71% Donnington Manor, London Rd, Dunton Green, SEVENOAKS ☎ 01732 462681 60 en suite

HAWKHURST Map 05 TQ73

Hawkhurst High St TN18 4JS
☎ 01580 754074 & 752396 01580 754074
e-mail: hawkhurstgolfclub@tiscali.co.uk
web: hawkhurstgolfclub.org.uk
Undulating parkland.
9 holes, 5751yds, Par 70, SSS 68, Course record 69.
Club membership 450.
Visitors Mon, Wed, Fri except BHs. Booking required. Dress code. **Societies** Booking required. **Green Fees** £29 per day, £22 per round. **Prof** MIke Barton **Course Designer** WA Baldock **Facilities** **Leisure** squash, squash. **Conf** facs **Location** W of village off A268

Hotel ★★★ 75% London Beach Hotel & Golf Club, Ashford Rd, TENTERDEN ☎ 01580 766279 26 en suite

HEADCORN Map 05 TQ84

Weald of Kent Maidstone Rd TN27 9PT
☎ 01622 890866 01622 890070
e-mail: info@weald-of-kent.co.uk
Enjoying delightful views over the Weald, this pay and play course features a range of natural hazards, including lakes, trees, ditches and undulating fairways. A good test to golfers of every standard.
18 holes, 6240yds, Par 70, SSS 70, Course record 67.
Club membership 350.

Continued

Visitors Mon-Sun & BHs. Booking required. Dress code. **Societies** Robin Goodway **Green Fees** phone. **Prof** Paul Fosten **Course Designer** John Millen **Facilities** **Leisure** training academy. **Conf** facs Corporate Hospitality Days **Location** M20 junct 8, through Leeds village, A274 towards Headcorn, course on left

Hotel ★★★★ 71% Marriott Tudor Park Hotel & Country Club, Ashford Rd, Bearsted, MAIDSTONE ☎ 01622 734334 120 en suite

HERNE BAY Map 05 TR16

Herne Bay Eddington CT6 7PG
☎ 01227 374727
18 holes, 5567yds, Par 68, SSS 68.
Course Designer James Braid **Location** On junct A291
Phone for further details

HEVER Map 05 TQ44

Hever Castle Hever Rd, Edenbridge TN8 7NP
☎ 01732 700771 🖹 01732 700775
e-mail: mail@hevercastlegolfclub.co.uk
web: www.hevercastlegolfclub.co.uk
Originally part of the Hever Castle estate, set in 250 acres of Kentish countryside, the Kings and Queens championship course has matured well and, with the addition of the Princes' nine holes, offers stunning holes to challenge all golfers. Water plays a prominent part in the design of the course, particularly around Amen Corner, holes 11 through 13. The golfer is then met with the lengthy stretch home, especially up the 17th, a daunting 644yd par 5, one of Europe's longest.
Kings & Queens Course: 18 holes, 6761yds, Par 72, SSS 73, Course record 69.
Princes Course: 9 holes, 2784yds, Par 35.
Club membership 450.
Visitors Mon-Sun & BHs. Booking required. Dress code. **Societies** Booking required. **Green Fees** Kings & Queens Course from £27, Princes Course from £13. **Prof** Peter Parks **Course Designer** Dr Nicholas **Facilities** **Conf** facs Corporate Hospitality Days **Location** Off B269 between Oxted & Tonbridge, 0.5m from Hever Castle

Hotel ★★★★ 71% The Spa Hotel, Mount Ephraim, TUNBRIDGE WELLS ☎ 01892 520331 69 en suite

HILDENBOROUGH Map 05 TQ54

Nizels Nizels Ln TN11 9LU
☎ 01732 838926 (Bookings) 🖹 01732 833764
e-mail: nizels.retail@clubhaus.com
18 holes, 6408yds, Par 72, SSS 71, Course record 65.
Course Designer Donaldson, Edwards Partnership
Location Off B245
Phone for further details

Hotel ★★★ 67% Rose & Crown Hotel, 125 High St, TONBRIDGE ☎ 01732 357966 54 en suite

HOO Map 05 TQ77

Deangate Ridge Dux Court Rd ME3 8RZ
☎ 01634 251180 🖹 01634 250537
Parkland, municipal course designed by Fred Hawtree. 18-hole pitch and putt.
18 holes, 6300yds, Par 71, SSS 70, Course record 65.
Club membership 500.
Visitors Mon-Sun & BHs. Booking required. Dress code.

Continued

Societies Booking required. **Green Fees** phone. **Prof** Richard Fox **Course Designer** Hawtree **Facilities** **Leisure** hard tennis courts, gymnasium. **Location** 4m NE of Rochester off A228

Hotel ★★★★ 74% Bridgewood Manor, Bridgewood Roundabout, Walderslade Woods, CHATHAM ☎ 01634 201333 100 en suite

HYTHE Map 05 TR13

Hythe Imperial Princes Pde CT21 6AE
☎ 01303 267441 🖹 01303 264610
e-mail: hytheimperial@marstonhotels.com
web: www.marstonhotels.com
9 holes, 5560yds, Par 68, SSS 66, Course record 62.
Location Exit M20 junct 11. Follow into Hythe towards the town centre. Turn right into Twiss Road. Golf course is in grounds of the Hythe Imperial
Phone for further details

Hotel ★★★★ 77% The Hythe Imperial, Princes Pde, HYTHE ☎ 01303 267441 100 en suite

Sene Valley Sene CT18 8BL
☎ 01303 268513 (Manager) 🖹 01303 237513
e-mail: senevalleygolf@bt.connect.com
web: www.senevalleygolfclub.co.uk
A two-level downland course, standing 350 feet above the town and providing interesting golf over an undulating landscape with sea views. A typical hole that challenges most players, is the par 3, 11th which combines a stunning sea view with a testing tee shot to a green surrounded by bunkers and gorse.
18 holes, 6271yds, Par 71, SSS 70, Course record 65.
Club membership 700.
Visitors Mon-Sun & BHs. Handicap certificate. Dress code. **Societies** Booking required **Green Fees** Mon-Fri £30, Sat & Sun after 11am £45. **Prof** Nick Watson **Course Designer** Henry Cotton **Facilities** **Conf** Corporate Hospitality Days **Location** M20 junct 12, A20 towards Ashford for 3m, left at rdbt, Hythe Rd for 1m

Hotel ★★★ 65% Stade Court, West Pde, HYTHE ☎ 01303 268263 42 en suite

KINGSDOWN Map 05 TR34

Walmer & Kingsdown The Leas CT14 8EP
☎ 01304 373256 🖹 01304 382336
e-mail: info@kingsdowngolf.co.uk
web: www.kingsdowngolf.co.uk
This beautiful downland site is situated near Deal and, being situated on top of the famous White Cliffs, offers breathtaking views of the Channel from every hole.

Continued

18 holes, 6471yds, Par 72, SSS 71, Course record 66. Club membership 640.
Visitors Mon-Sun except BHs. Booking required. Handicap certificate. Dress code. **Societies** Booking required. **Green Fees** £50 per day, £30 per round, Sat & Sun after 2pm £40 per round. **Prof** Jude Read **Course Designer** James Braid **Facilities** **Conf** Corporate Hospitality Days **Location** 1.5m E of Ringwould off A258 Dover-Deal road

Hotel ★★★ 71% Dunkerleys Hotel & Restaurant, 19 Beach St, DEAL ☎ 01304 375016 16 en suite

LAMBERHURST Map 05 TQ63

Lamberhurst Church Rd TN3 8DT
☎ 01892 890591 🖹 01892 891140
e-mail: secretary@lamberhurstgolfclub.com
web: www.lamberhurstgolfclub.com
Parkland course crossing the river twice. Fine views.
18 holes, 6439yds, Par 72, SSS 70, Course record 65. Club membership 650.
Visitors Mon-Fri. Sat, Sun & BHs pm. Booking required. Handicap certificate. Dress code. **Societies** Booking required. **Green Fees** £45 per day, £32 per round. **Prof** Brian Impett **Facilities** **Conf** facs Corporate Hospitality Days **Location** N of village on B2162

Hotel ★★★★ 71% The Spa Hotel, Mount Ephraim, TUNBRIDGE WELLS ☎ 01892 520331 69 en suite

LITTLESTONE Map 05 TR02

Littlestone St Andrew's Rd TN28 8RB
☎ 01797 363355 🖹 01797 362740
e-mail: secretary@littlestonegolfclub.org.uk
web: www.littlestonegolfclub.org.uk
Located in the Romney Marshes, this fairly flat seaside links course calls for every variety of shot. The 8th, 15th, 16th and 17th are regarded as classics by international golfers. Fast running fairways and faster greens.
18 holes, 6486yds, Par 71, SSS 72, Course record 66. Club membership 550.
Visitors Mon-Fri. Booking required. Handicap certificate. Dress code. **Societies** Booking required. **Green Fees** £60 per day, £40 per round. **Prof** Andrew Jones **Course Designer** Laidlaw Purves **Facilities** **Leisure** hard tennis courts. **Conf** Corporate Hospitality Days **Location** 1m from New Romney off Littlestone road B2070

Hotel ★★★★ 77% The Hythe Imperial, Princes Pde, HYTHE ☎ 01303 267441 100 en suite

Romney Warren St Andrews Rd TN28 8RB
☎ 01797 362231 🖹 01797 363511
e-mail: info@romneywarrengolfclub.org.uk
web: www.littlestonegolfclub.org.uk
A links-style course, normally very dry. Flat providing easy walking and play challenged by sea breezes. Although not overly long, narrow fairways and small greens place a premium on shot selection and placement.
18 holes, 5126yds, Par 67, SSS 65, Course record 63. Club membership 300.
Visitors Mon-Sun & BHs. Booking required. Dress code. **Societies** Booking required. **Green Fees** £30 per day, £18 per round, £34/£23 Sat & Sun. **Prof** Andrew Jones **Course Designer** Evans, Lewis **Facilities** **Location** N of Littlestone centre

Hotel ★★★★ 77% The Hythe Imperial, Princes Pde, HYTHE ☎ 01303 267441 100 en suite

LYDD Map 05 TR02

Lydd Romney Rd TN29 9LS
☎ 01797 320808 🖹 01797 321482
e-mail: info@lyddgolfclub.co.uk
web: www.lyddgolfclub.co.uk
A links-type course on marshland, offering some interesting challenges, including a number of eye-catching water hazards, wide fairways and plenty of semi-rough. A constant breeze makes club selection difficult A good test for experienced golfers and appealing to the complete novice.

18 holes, 6529yds, Par 71, SSS 71, Course record 65. Club membership 400.
Visitors Mon-Sun & BHs. Booking required. Dress code. **Societies** Booking required. **Green Fees** £21, £30 Sat & Sun. **Prof** Richard J Perkins **Course Designer** Mike Smith **Facilities** **Leisure** 6 hole Academy course. **Conf** facs Corporate Hospitality Days **Location** A259 onto B2075 by Lydd Airport

MAIDSTONE Map 05 TQ75

Cobtree Manor Park Chatham Rd, Sandling ME14 3AZ
☎ 01622 753276 🖹 01634 262003
web: www.medwaygolf.co.uk
Undulating parkland with some water hazards.
18 holes, 5611yds, Par 69, SSS 69, Course record 66. Club membership 400.
Visitors Mon-Sun & BHs. Booking required. Dress code. **Societies** Booking required. **Green Fees** phone. **Prof** Paul Foston **Facilities** **Conf** facs Corporate Hospitality Days **Location** M20 junct 6, 0.25m N on A229

Hotel ★★★ 69% Russell Hotel, 136 Boxley Rd, MAIDSTONE ☎ 01622 692221 42 en suite

Leeds Castle Ashford Rd ME17 1PL
☎ 01622 767828 & 880467 🖹 01622 735616
e-mail: stevepurves@leeds-castle.co.uk
web: www.leeds-castle.co.uk
Situated around Leeds Castle, this is one of the most picturesque courses in Britain. Redesigned in the 1980s by Neil Coles, it is a challenging nine-hole course with the added hazard of the castle moat.

Continued

Leeds Castle

9 holes, 2681yds, Par 33, SSS 33, Course record 29.
Visitors Mon-Sun & BHs. Booking required. Dress code. **Societies** Booking required. **Green Fees** phone. **Prof** Steve Purves **Course Designer** Neil Coles **Facilities** **Leisure** Green fees include admission to Leeds Castle's Gardens & Attractions. **Conf** Corporate Hospitality Days **Location** M20 junct 8, 4m E of Maidstone on A20 towards Lenham

Hotel ★★★★ 71% Marriott Tudor Park Hotel & Country Club, Ashford Rd, Bearsted, MAIDSTONE
☎ 01622 734334 120 en suite

Marriott Tudor Park Hotel & Country Club Ashford Rd, Bearsted ME14 4NQ

☎ 01622 734334 01622 735360
e-mail: golf.tudorpark@marriotthotels.co.uk
web: www.marriotthotels.com/tdmgs

The course is set in a 220-acre former deer park with the pleasant undulating Kent countryside as a backdrop. The natural features of the land have been incorporated into this picturesque course to form a challenge for those of both high and intermediate standard. The par 5 14th is particularly interesting. It can alter your score dramatically should you gamble with a drive to a narrow fairway. This hole has to be carefully thought out from tee to green depending on the wind direction.

Milgate Course: 18 holes, 6085yds, Par 70, SSS 69, Course record 64.
Club membership 750.
Visitors Mon-Sun & BHs. Booking required. Dress code. **Societies** Phone Golf Events. **Green Fees** phone. **Prof** Nick McNally **Course Designer** Donald Steel **Facilities** **Leisure** hard tennis courts, heated indoor swimming pool, sauna, solarium, gymnasium, steam room & spa bath, golf academy. **Conf** facs Corporate Hospitality Days **Location** M20 junct 8, 1.25m W on A20

Hotel ★★★★ 71% Marriott Tudor Park Hotel & Country Club, Ashford Rd, Bearsted, MAIDSTONE
☎ 01622 734334 120 en suite

NEW ASH GREEN Map 05 TQ66

Redlibbets Manor Ln, West Yoke TN15 7HT

☎ 01474 879190 01474 879290
e-mail: redlibbets@golfandsport.co.uk
web: www.redlibbetsmembers.co.uk

Delightful rolling Kentish course cut through an attractive wooded valley.
18 holes, 6639yds, Par 72, SSS 72, Course record 67.
Club membership 500.
Visitors Mon-Fri except BHs. Dress code. **Societies** Booking required. **Green Fees** £40. **Prof** Ross Taylor **Course Designer** Jonathan Gaunt **Facilities** **Conf** facs Corporate Hospitality Days **Location** off A20, close to Brand's Hatch

RAMSGATE Map 05 TR36

St Augustine's Cottington Rd, Cliffsend CT12 5JN

☎ 01843 590333 01843 590444
e-mail: sagc@ic24.net
web: www.staugustines.8m.com
18 holes, 5254yds, Par 69, SSS 66, Course record 61.
Course Designer Tom Vardon **Location** Off A256 Ramsgate-Sandwich
Phone for further details

Hotel ★★★ 68% Royal Albion Hotel, Albion St, BROADSTAIRS ☎ 01843 868071 19 en suite

ROCHESTER Map 05 TQ76

Rochester & Cobham Park Park Pale ME2 3UL

☎ 01474 823411 01474 824446
e-mail: rcpgc@talk21.com
web: www.rochesterandcobhamgc.co.uk

A first-rate course of challenging dimensions in undulating parkland. All holes differ and each requires accurate drive placing to derive the best advantage. Open Championship regional qualifying course.
18 holes, 6597yds, Par 71, SSS 72, Course record 64.
Club membership 730.
Visitors Mon-Fri except BHs. Handicap certificate. Dress code. **Societies** Booking required. **Green Fees** £47.50 per day, £37.50 per round. **Prof** Iain Higgins **Course Designer** Donald Steel **Facilities** **Conf** Corporate Hospitality Days **Location** 2.5m W on A2

Hotel ★★★★ 74% Bridgewood Manor, Bridgewood Roundabout, Walderslade Woods, CHATHAM
☎ 01634 201333 100 en suite

Continued

Championship Course

Kent

Royal St George's

Sandwich

Map 05 TR35

Consistently ranked among the leading golf courses in the world, Royal St George's occupies a unique place in the history of golf, playing host in 1894 to the first Open Championship outside Scotland. Set among the dunes of Sandwich Bay, the links provide a severe test for the greatest of golfers. Only three Open winners (Bill Rogers in 1981, Greg Norman in 1993 and Ben Curtis in 2003) have managed to under par after 72 holes. The undulating fairways, the borrows on the greens, the strategically placed bunkers, and the prevailing winds that blow on all but the rarest of occasions, these all soon reveal any weakness in the player; there are few over the years who have mastered all the vagaries in one round. It hosted its thirteenth Open Championship in 2003, dramatically won by outsider Ben Curtis.

CT13 9PB
☎ 01304 613090 🖹 01304 611245
e-mail: secretary@royalstgeorges.com
web: www.royalstgeorges.com

18 holes, 7102yds, Par 70, SSS 74, Course record 67.
Club membership 750.

Visitors Mon, Tue, Thu except BHs. Booking required. Handicap certificate. Dress code. **Societies** Booking required. **Green Fees** £150 per 36 holes, £120 per 18 holes. Winter reduced rates. **Prof** A Brooks **Course Designer** Dr Laidlaw Purves **Facilities** ⊗ by arrangement **Conf** Corporate Hospitality Days **Location** 1.5m E of Sandwich. Enter town for golf courses

SANDWICH Map 05 TR35

Prince's Prince's Dr, Sandwich Bay CT13 9QB
☎ 01304 611118 🖷 01304 612000
e-mail: office@princesgolfclub.co.uk
web: www.princesgolfclub.co.uk
With 27 championship holes, Prince's Golf Club has a world-wide reputation as a traditional links of the finest quality and is a venue that provides all that is best in modern links golf. One of only 14 courses to be selected to host the Open Championship.

Dunes: 9 holes, 3425yds, Par 36, SSS 36.
Himalayas: 9 holes, 3163yds, Par 35, SSS 35.
Shore: 9 holes, 3347yds, Par 36, SSS 36.
Club membership 310.
Visitors Mon-Sun & BHs. Booking required. Dress code. **Societies** Booking required. **Green Fees** £90 per 36 holes, £80 per 27 holes, £70 per 18 holes, £100/£90/£80 Sat, Sun & BHs. **Prof** Derek Barbour **Course Designer** Sir Guy Campbell & JSF Morrison **Facilities** by arrangement **Leisure** private beach area. **Conf** facs Corporate Hospitality Days **Location** 2m E via toll road, signs from Sandwich

Hotel ★★★ 71% Dunkerleys Hotel & Restaurant, 19 Beach St, DEAL ☎ 01304 375016 16 en suite

Royal St George's see page 151

Hotel ★★★ 71% Dunkerleys Hotel & Restaurant, 19 Beach St, DEAL ☎ 01304 375016 16 en suite

SEAL Map 05 TR36

Wildernesse Park Ln TN15 0JE
☎ 01732 761199 🖷 01732 763809
e-mail: golf@wildernesse.co.uk
web: www.wildernesse.co.uk
A tight inland course, heavily wooded with tree-lined fairways. Straight driving and attention to the well-placed bunkers is essential. With few slopes and easy walking, it is difficult to beat par.
18 holes, 6501yds, Par 72, SSS 71.
Club membership 720.
Visitors Mon, Thu & Fri except BHs. Booking required Handicap certificate. Dress code. **Societies** Booking required. **Green Fees** £46 per round. **Prof** Craig Walker **Course Designer** Braid (part) **Facilities** **Leisure** hard tennis courts. **Conf** Corporate Hospitality Days

Hotel ★★★ 71% Donnington Manor, London Rd, Dunton Green, SEVENOAKS ☎ 01732 462681 60 en suite

SEVENOAKS Map 05 TQ55

Knole Park Seal Hollow Rd TN15 0HJ
☎ 01732 452150 🖷 01732 463159
e-mail: secretary@knoleparkgolfclub.co.uk
web: www.knoleparkgolfclub.co.uk
The course is laid out within the grounds of the Knole Estate and can rightfully be described as a natural layout. The course designer has used the contours of the land to produce a challenging course in all weather conditions and throughout all seasons. While, for most of the year, it may appear benign, in summer, when the bracken is high, Knole Park represents a considerable challenge but always remains a fair test of golf.

18 holes, 6246yds, Par 70, SSS 70, Course record 62.
Club membership 750.
Visitors Mon-Fri except BHs. Booking required. Handicap certificate. Dress code. **Societies** Booking required. **Green**

Continued

Fees £46 per day, £36 per round. **Prof** Phil Sykes **Course Designer** J Abercromby **Facilities** ⊗ 〽 🏌 ☕ 🍸 🧥 🚘 ✐ **Leisure** squash. **Conf** Corporate Hospitality Days **Location** NE of town centre off B2019

Hotel ★★★ 71% Donnington Manor, London Rd, Dunton Green, SEVENOAKS ☎ 01732 462681 60 en suite

SHEERNESS Map 05 TQ97

Sheerness Power Station Rd ME12 3AE
☎ 01795 662585 🖷 01795 668100
e-mail: thesecretary@sheernessgc.freeserve.co.uk

Semi-links, marshland course, few bunkers, but many ditches and water hazards.

18 holes, 6407yds, Par 71, SSS 70, Course record 66. Club membership 650.

Visitors Mon-Fri except BHs. Sat & Sun pm. Booking required Sat & Sun. Handicap certificate. Dress code. **Societies** Booking required. **Green Fees** £31 per day, £22 per 18 holes. **Prof** L Stanford **Facilities** ⊗ 🏌 ☕ 🍸 🧥 🚘 🛒 ✐ **Location** 1.5m E off A249

Hotel ★★★★ 74% Bridgewood Manor, Bridgewood Roundabout, Walderslade Woods, CHATHAM ☎ 01634 201333 100 en suite

SHOREHAM Map 05 TQ56

Darenth Valley Station Rd TN14 7SA
☎ 01959 522944 🖷 01959 525089
e-mail:darenthvalleygolfcourse@shoreham2000.fsbusiness.co.uk
web: www.darenth-valley.co.uk

18 holes, 6258yds, Par 72, SSS 71, Course record 64.

Location 3m N of Sevenoaks off A225 between Otford & Eynsford

Phone for further details

Hotel ★★★ 71% Donnington Manor, London Rd, Dunton Green, SEVENOAKS ☎ 01732 462681 60 en suite

SITTINGBOURNE Map 05 TQ96

The Oast Golf Centre Church Rd, Tonge ME9 9AR
☎ 01795 473527
e-mail: rmail@oastgolf.co.uk
web: www.oastgolf.co.uk

A par 3 approach course of nine holes with 18 tees augmented by a 17-bay floodlit driving range and a putting green.

9 holes, 1664yds, Par 54, SSS 54.

Visitors contact centre for details. **Societies** Booking required. **Green Fees** £7.50 per 18 holes, £5.50 per 9 holes. Mon-Fri am £5.50, pm £7.50. **Prof** D Chambers **Course Designer** D Chambers **Facilities** 🏌 ☕ 🍸 🚘 ⛳ ✐ 🏌 **Location** 2m NE, A2 between Bapchild

Hotel ★★★★ 74% Bridgewood Manor, Bridgewood Roundabout, Walderslade Woods, CHATHAM ☎ 01634 201333 100 en suite

Sittingbourne & Milton Regis Wormdale, Newington ME9 7PX
☎ 01795 842261 🖷 01795 844117
e-mail: sittingbournegc@btconnect.com
web: www.sittingbournegolfclub.com

A downland course with pleasant vistas and renowned for its greens. There are a few uphill climbs, but the course is far from difficult. The back nine holes are challenging.

18 holes, 6291yds, Par 71, SSS 70, Course record 63. Club membership 715.

Visitors contact club for details **Societies** Booking required. **Green Fees** £40 per 36 holes, £30 per 18 holes. **Prof** John Hearn **Course Designer** Donald Steel **Facilities** ⊗ 〽 by arrangement 🏌 ☕ 🍸 🧥 🚘 ✎ 🛒 ✐ **Conf** Corporate Hospitality Days **Location** Off Chestnut St at Danaway

Hotel ★★★★ 74% Bridgewood Manor, Bridgewood Roundabout, Walderslade Woods, CHATHAM ☎ 01634 201333 100 en suite

Upchurch River Valley Golf Centre Oak Ln, Upchurch ME9 7AY
☎ 01634 379592 🖷 01634 387784

Undulating parkland in picturesque countryside. Testing water hazards on several holes. Excellent winter course. The nine-hole course is ideal for beginners and for those keen to sharpen up their short game.

18 holes, 6237yds, Par 70, SSS 70. Club membership 752.

Visitors Mon-Fri booking required 2 days in advance. Sat & Sun booking required 5 days in advance. **Societies** Booking required. **Green Fees** phone. **Prof** Roger Cornwell **Course Designer** David Smart **Facilities** ⊗ 〽 🏌 ☕ 🍸 🧥 🚘 ✎ 🛒 ✐ 🏌 **Leisure** heated outdoor swimming pool. **Location** A2 between Rainham & Newington

Hotel ★★★ 69% Russell Hotel, 136 Boxley Rd, MAIDSTONE ☎ 01622 692221 42 en suite

SNODLAND Map 05 TQ76

Oastpark Malling Rd ME6 5LG
☎ 01634 242661 🖷 01634 240744

A challenging parkland course for golfers of all abilities. The course has water hazards and orchards.

18 holes, 6298yds, SSS 70. Club membership 60.

Visitors Booking up to 7 days in advance. **Societies** Booking required. **Green Fees** phone. **Prof** David Porthouse **Course Designer** JD Banks **Facilities** 🏌 ☕ 🍸 🧥 🚘 ✐ 🏌 **Location** M20 junct 4

Continued

TENTERDEN Map 05 TQ83

London Beach Hotel & Golf Club Ashford Rd TN30 6HX
01580 766279 01580 763884
e-mail: enquiries@londonbeach.com
web: www.londonbeach.com
Located in a mature parkland setting in the Weald. A test of golf for all abilities of golfer with its rolling fairways and undulating greens.

9 holes, 5860yds, Par 70, SSS 69, Course record 66. Club membership 250.
Visitors Booking required. **Societies** Booking required. **Green Fees** £20 per 18 holes, £18 per 9 holes, £25/£20 Sat, Sun & BHs. **Prof** Mark Chilcott **Course Designer** Golf Landscapes **Facilities** **Leisure** fishing, pitch & putt clay pigeon shooting. **Conf** facs Corporate Hospitality Days **Location** M20 Junct 9, A28 towards Tenterden, hotel on right 1m before Tenterden

Hotel ★★★ 75% London Beach Hotel & Golf Club, Ashford Rd, TENTERDEN 01580 766279 26 en suite

Tenterden Woodchurch Rd TN30 7DR
01580 763987 (sec) 01580 763430
e-mail: enquiries@tenterdengolfclub.co.uk
web: tenterdengolfclub.co.uk
Set in tranquil undulating parkland with beautiful views, the course is challenging with several difficult holes.
18 holes, 6071yds, Par 70, SSS 69, Course record 61. Club membership 600.
Visitors Mon-Sun except BHs. Handicap certificate. Dress code. **Societies** Booking required. **Green Fees** £34 per round, winter £20. **Prof** Kyle Kelsall **Facilities** **Location** 0.75m E on B2067

Hotel ★★★ 75% London Beach Hotel & Golf Club, Ashford Rd, TENTERDEN 01580 766279 26 en suite

TONBRIDGE Map 05 TQ54

Poultwood Higham Ln TN11 9QR
01732 364039 & 366180 01732 353781
web: www.poultwoodgolf.co.uk
There are two public pay and play parkland courses in an idyllic woodland setting. The courses are ecologically designed, over predominantly flat land offering challenging hazards and interesting playing conditions for all standards of golfer.
18 holes, 5524yds, Par 68, SSS 66.
9 holes, 2562yds, Par 28.
Visitors Mon-Sun & BHs. Booking required. Dress code. **Societies** Booking required. **Green Fees** 18 hole course £14.50, £20 Sat, Sun & BHs. 9 hole course £5.50/£7.20. **Prof** Bill Hodkin **Course Designer** Hawtree **Facilities** **Leisure** squash. **Conf** facs Corporate Hospitality Days **Location** Off A227 3m N of Tonbridge

Hotel ★★★ 67% Rose & Crown Hotel, 125 High St, TONBRIDGE 01732 357966 54 en suite

TUNBRIDGE WELLS (ROYAL) Map 05 TQ53

Nevill Benhall Mill Rd TN2 5JW
01892 525818 01892 517861
e-mail: manager@nevillgolfclub.co.uk
web: www.nevillgolfclub.co.uk
The Kent-Sussex border forms the northern perimeter of the course. Open undulating ground, well-wooded with some heather and gorse for the first half. The second nine holes slope away from the clubhouse to a valley where a narrow stream hazards two holes.
18 holes, 6349yds, Par 71, SSS 70, Course record 64. Club membership 800.
Visitors Mon-Fri except BHs. Booking required. Handicap certificate. Dress code. **Societies** Booking required. **Green Fees** £50 per day, £33 per round. **Prof** Paul Huggett **Course Designer** Henry Cotton **Facilities** **Location** S of Tunbridge Wells

Hotel ★★★★ 71% The Spa Hotel, Mount Ephraim, TUNBRIDGE WELLS 01892 520331 69 en suite

Tunbridge Wells Langton Rd TN4 8XH
01892 523034 01892 536918
e-mail: info@tunbridgewellsgolfclub.co.uk
web: www.tunbridgewellsgolfclub.co.uk
Somewhat hilly, well-bunkered parkland course with lake; trees form natural hazards.
9 holes, 4725yds, Par 65, SSS 62, Course record 59. Club membership 470.
Visitors Mon-Sun & BHs. Booking required. Dress code. **Societies** Booking required. **Green Fees** £14 per 18 holes, £10 per 9 holes, £20 per 18 holes, £15 per 9 holes Sat & Sun. **Facilities** **Location** 1m W on A264

Hotel ★★★★ 71% The Spa Hotel, Mount Ephraim, TUNBRIDGE WELLS 01892 520331 69 en suite

WESTERHAM Map 05 TQ45

Park Wood Chestnut Av, Tatsfield TN16 2EG
01959 577744 & 577177 (pro-shop) 01959 572702
e-mail: mail@parkwoodgolf.co.uk
web: www.parkwoodgolf.co.uk
Situated in an Area of Outstanding Natural Beauty, flanked by an ancient woodland with superb views across Kent and Surrey countryside. An undulating course, tree lined and with some interesting water features. Playable in all weather conditions.
18 holes, 6835yds, Par 72, SSS 72, Course record 66. Club membership 500.
Visitors Mon-Fri. After 11am Sat, Sun & BHs. Dress code. **Societies** Booking required. **Green Fees** phone. **Prof** Nick Terry **Facilities** **Conf** facs Corporate Hospitality Days **Location** A25 onto B2024 Croydon Rd & Clarks Ln, at Church Hill junct onto Chestnut Av

Continued

Park Wood

Hotel ★★★ 71% Donnington Manor, London Rd, Dunton Green, SEVENOAKS ☎ 01732 462681 60 en suite

Westerham Valence Park, Brasted Rd TN16 1LJ
☎ 01959 567100 🖷 01959 567101
e-mail: oliver.peel@westerhamgc.co.uk
web: www.westerhamgc.co.uk
Originally forestry land with thousands of mature pines. The storms of 1987 created natural fairways and the mature landscape makes the course both demanding and spectacular. A clubhouse with first-class facilities and magnificent views.

18 holes, 6329yds, Par 72, SSS 72. Club membership 600.
Visitors Mon-Sun & BHs. Booking required. Dress code. **Societies** Booking required. **Green Fees** £32 per round Mon-Thu, £35 Fri, £40 Sat, Sun & BHs. **Prof** J Marshal **Course Designer** D Williams **Facilities** **Leisure** short game practice area. **Conf** facs Corporate Hospitality Days **Location** A25 between Westerham & Brasted

Hotel ★★★ 71% Donnington Manor, London Rd, Dunton Green, SEVENOAKS ☎ 01732 462681 60 en suite

WESTGATE ON SEA Map 05 TR37

Westgate and Birchington 176 Canterbury Rd CT8 8LT
☎ 01843 831115
e-mail: wandbgc@btopenworld.com
A fine blend of inland and seaside holes which provide a good test of the golfer despite the apparently simple appearance of the course.
18 holes, 4926yds, Par 64, SSS 64, Course record 60. Club membership 350.
Visitors Mon-Sun & BHs. Dress code. **Societies** welcome. **Green Fees** £17 per day, £20 Sat, Sun & BHs. **Prof** Roger Game **Facilities** **Conf**

Continued

Corporate Hospitality Days **Location** E of town centre off A28

Hotel ★★★ 68% Royal Albion Hotel, Albion St, BROADSTAIRS ☎ 01843 868071 19 en suite

WEST KINGSDOWN Map 05 TQ56

Woodlands Manor Tinkerpot Ln, Otford TN15 6AB
☎ 01959 523806 🖷 01959 524398
e-mail: info@woodlandsmanorgolf.co.uk
web: www.woodlandsmanorgolf.co.uk
Two nine-hole layouts with views over an area of outstanding natural beauty. The course is challenging but fair with varied and memorable holes of which the 7th, 10th and 18th stand out. Good playing conditions all year round.

18 holes, 6015yds, Par 69, SSS 69, Course record 64. Club membership 600.
Visitors Mon-Sun & BHs. Booking required. Dress code. **Societies** Booking required. **Green Fees** £24 per round, £30 Sat & Sun. **Prof** Philip Womack **Course Designer** Lyons, Coles **Facilities** **Conf** facs Corporate Hospitality Days **Location** A20 through West Kingsdown, right opp Portbello Inn onto School Ln & Tinkerpot Ln, clubhouse left

Hotel Premier Travel Inn Sevenoaks/Maidstone, London Rd, Wrotham Heath, WROTHAM ☎ 08701 977227 40 en suite

WEST MALLING Map 05 TQ65

Kings Hill Fortune Way, Discovery Dr, Kings Hill ME19 4AG
☎ 01732 875040 🖷 01732 875019
e-mail: khatkhgolf@aol.com
web: www.kingshill-golfclub.com
18 holes, 6622yards, Par 72, SSS 72.
Course Designer David Williams Partnership **Location** M20 junct 4, A228 towards Tonbridge
Phone for further details

Hotel Premier Travel Inn Maidstone (Leybourne), Castle Way, LEYBOURNE ☎ 08701 977170 40 en suite

WHITSTABLE Map 05 TR16

Chestfield (Whitstable) 103 Chestfield Rd, Chestfield CT5 3LU
☎ 01227 794411 & 792243 🖷 01227 794454
e-mail: secretary@chestfield-golfclub.co.uk
web: www.chestfield-golfclub.co.uk
Recent changes have been made to this parkland course with undulating fairways and fine views of the sea and countryside. These consist of six new greens and five

Continued

new tees. The clubhouse, dating back to the 15th century, is reputed to the oldest building in the world used for this purpose.
18 holes, 6200yds, Par 70, SSS 70, Course record 66. Club membership 725.
Visitors Mon-Sun & BHs. Booking required. Dress code. **Societies** Booking required. **Green Fees** £36 per day, £29 per round. **Prof** John Brotherton **Course Designer** D Steel, James Braid **Facilities** **Leisure** half-way house providing snacks/refreshments. **Location** 0.5m S by Chestfield Railway Station, off A2990

Hotel Premier Travel Inn Whitstable, Thanet Way, WHITSTABLE 08701 977269 40 en suite

Whitstable & Seasalter Collingwood Rd CT5 1EB

01227 272020 01227 280822
Links course.
9 holes, 5357yds, Par 66, SSS 65, Course record 62. Club membership 350.
Visitors Mon-Sat except BHs. Booking required. Dress code. **Green Fees** £16 per 18 holes, £10 per 9 holes. **Facilities** by arrangement **Location** W of town centre off B2205

Hotel Premier Travel Inn Whitstable, Thanet Way, WHITSTABLE 08701 977269 40 en suite

LANCASHIRE

ACCRINGTON — Map 07 SD72

Accrington & District Devon Av, Oswaldtwistle BB5 4LS

01254 231091 01254 350119
e-mail: info@accrington-golf-club.co.uk
web: www.accrington-golf-club.co.uk
Moorland course with pleasant views of the Pennines and surrounding areas. The course is a real test for even the best amateur golfers and has hosted many county matches and championships over its 100 plus years of history.
18 holes, 6060yds, Par 70, SSS 69, Course record 63. Club membership 600.
Visitors Mon-Fri except BHs. Booking required. Dress code. **Societies** Mon & Fri, booking required. **Green Fees** £27 daily Mon-Thu, £32 Fri. **Prof** Mark Harling **Course Designer** J Braid **Facilities** by arrangement by arrangement **Conf** Corporate Hospitality Days **Location** Between Accrington & Blackburn

Hotel ★★★★ 62% Macdonald Dunkenhalgh Hotel & Spa, Blackburn Rd, Clayton-le-Moors, ACCRINGTON 0870 1942116 61 en suite 119 annexe en suite

Baxenden & District Top o' th' Meadow, Baxenden BB5 2EA

01254 234555
e-mail: baxgolf@hotmail.com
web: www.baxendengolf.co.uk
Moorland course with panoramic views and a long par 3 to start.
9 holes, 5740yds, Par 70, SSS 68, Course record 65. Club membership 340.
Visitors Mon-Sun & BHs. Booking required. Dress code. **Societies** Booking required. **Green Fees** £15 per 18 holes, £25 Sat, Sun & BHs. **Facilities** **Conf** facs Corporate Hospitality Days **Location** 1.5m SE off A680

Continued

Hotel ★★★★ 62% Macdonald Dunkenhalgh Hotel & Spa, Blackburn Rd, Clayton-le-Moors, ACCRINGTON 0870 1942116 61 en suite 119 annexe en suite

Green Haworth Green Haworth BB5 3SL

01254 237580 & 382510 01254 396176
e-mail: golf@greenhaworth.co.uk
web: www.greenhaworthgolfclub.co.uk
Moorland course dominated by quarries and difficult in windy conditions.
9 holes, 5522yds, Par 68, SSS 67, Course record 66. Club membership 250.
Visitors Mon, Tue, Thu & Fri. Booking required. Handicap certificate. Dress code. **Societies** Booking required. **Green Fees** £15 per day. **Facilities** **Conf** Corporate Hospitality Days **Location** 2m S off A680

Hotel ★★★★ 62% Macdonald Dunkenhalgh Hotel & Spa, Blackburn Rd, Clayton-le-Moors, ACCRINGTON 0870 1942116 61 en suite 119 annexe en suite

BACUP — Map 07 SD82

Bacup Maden Rd OL13 8HY

01706 873170 01706 877726
e-mail: secretary@bacupgolfltd.co.uk
Tree-lined moorland course, predominantly flat except climbs to 1st and 10th holes.
9 holes, 6018yds, Par 70, SSS 69. Club membership 350.
Visitors Mon-Sun. Sat & Sun booking required. **Societies** Booking required. **Green Fees** phone. **Facilities** by arrangement by arrangement **Conf** Corporate Hospitality Days **Location** W of town off A671

Hotel ★★★ 72% Rosehill House Hotel, Rosehill Av, BURNLEY 01282 453931 34 en suite

BARNOLDSWICK — Map 07 SD84

Ghyll Skipton Rd BB18 6JH

01282 842466
e-mail: secretary@ghyllgc.freeserve.com
web: www.ghyllgc.co.uk
Excellent parkland course with outstanding views, especially from the 8th tee where you can see the Three Peaks. Testing 8th hole is an uphill par 4. Eleven holes in total, nine in Yorkshire and two in Lancashire.
11 holes, 5790yds, Par 68, SSS 66, Course record 62. Club membership 345.
Visitors Mon, Wed-Sat & BHs. Dress code. **Societies** Booking required. **Green Fees** £15 per day, £20 Sat. **Facilities** **Location** NE of town on B6252

Hotel ★★ 70% Herriots Hotel, Broughton Rd, SKIPTON 01756 792781 23 rms (13 en suite)

BICKERSTAFFE — Map 07 SD40

Mossock Hall Liverpool Rd L39 0EE

01695 421717 01695 424961
18 holes, 6492yards, Par 71, SSS 70, Course record 68.
Course Designer Steve Marnoch **Location** M58 junct 3
Phone for further details

BLACKBURN Map 07 SD62

Blackburn Beardwood Brow BB2 7AX
01254 51122 01254 665578
e-mail: sec@blackburngolfclub.com
web: www.blackburngolfclub.com
Parkland on a high plateau with stream and hills. Superb views of Lancashire coast and the Pennines.
18 holes, 6144yds, Par 71, SSS 70, Course record 62. Club membership 550.
Visitors Mon-Sun & BHs. Booking required Fri-Sun & BHs. Handicap certificate. Dress code. **Societies** Booking required. **Green Fees** £26 per day, £30 Sat & Sun. **Prof** Alan Rodwell **Facilities** **Conf** facs **Location** 1.25m NW of town centre off A677

Hotel ★★ 78% The Millstone at Mellor, Church Ln, Mellor, BLACKBURN 01254 813333 17 en suite 6 annexe en suite

BLACKPOOL Map 07 SD33

Blackpool North Shore Devonshire Rd FY2 0RD
01253 352054 01253 591240
e-mail: office@blackpoolnorthshoregolfclub.com
web: www.bnsgc.com
Undulating parkland.

18 holes, 6432yds, Par 71, SSS 71, Course record 62. Club membership 900.
Visitors Mon-Wed, Fri & Sun except BHs. Booking required. Handicap certificate. Dress code. **Societies** Booking required. **Green Fees** £33 per day, £26 per round, £39/£31 Sun. **Prof** Brendan Ward **Course Designer** H Colt **Facilities** **Conf** Corporate Hospitality Days **Location** on A587 N of town centre

Hotel ★★ 70% Hotel Sheraton, 54-62 Queens Promenade, BLACKPOOL 01253 352723 104 en suite

Blackpool Park North Park Dr FY3 8LS
01253 397916 & 478176 (tee times) 01253 397916
e-mail: secretary@bpgc.org.uk
web: www.bpgc.org.uk
The course, situated in Stanley Park, is municipal. The golf club (Blackpool Park) is private but golfers may use the clubhouse facilities if playing the course. An abundance of grassy pits, ponds and open dykes.
18 holes, 6087yds, Par 70, SSS 70, Course record 64. Club membership 650.
Visitors contact club for details. **Societies** welcome. **Green Fees** £16.50 per round, £19 Sat, Sun & BHs. **Prof** Brian Purdie **Course Designer** A MacKenzie **Facilities** **Location** 1m E of Blackpool Tower

Hotel ★★★ 70% Carousel Hotel, 663-671 New South Prom, BLACKPOOL 01253 402642 92 en suite

De Vere Herons Reach East Park Blackpool FY3 8LL
01253 766156 & 838866 01253 798800
e-mail: dot.kilbride@devere-hotels.com
web: www.deveregolf.co.uk
18 holes, 6628yds, Par 72, SSS 71, Course record 64.
Course Designer Peter Alliss, Clive Clark **Location** Off A587 next to Stanley Park Zoo
Phone for further details

Hotel ★★★★ 68% De Vere Herons' Reach, East Park Dr, BLACKPOOL 01253 838866 172 en suite

BURNLEY Map 07 SD83

Burnley Glen View BB11 3RW
01282 421045 & 451281 01282 451281
e-mail: burnleygolfclub@onthegreen.co.uk
web: www.burnleygolfclub.org.uk
Challenging moorland course with exceptional views.
18 holes, 5939yds, Par 69, SSS 69, Course record 62. Club membership 700.
Visitors Mon-Sun & BHs. Handicap certificate. Dress code. **Societies** Booking required. **Green Fees** £25 per day, £30 Sat, Sun & BHs. **Prof** Matthew Baker **Facilities** **Leisure** snooker table. **Conf** facs Corporate Hospitality Days **Location** S of town off A646

Hotel ★★★ 72% Rosehill House Hotel, Rosehill Av, BURNLEY 01282 453931 34 en suite

Towneley Towneley Park, Todmorden Rd BB11 3ED
01282 438473
18 holes, 5811yds, Par 70, SSS 68, Course record 67.
Location 1m SE of town centre on A671
Phone for further details

Hotel ★★★ 75% Oaks Hotel, Colne Rd, Reedley, BURNLEY 01282 414141 50 en suite

CHORLEY Map 07 SD51

Charnock Richard Preston Rd, Charnock Richard PR7 5LE
01257 470707 01257 791196
e-mail: mail@crgc.co.uk
web: www.charnockrichardgolfclub.co.uk
Flat parkland course with plenty of American-style water hazards. Signature hole the 6th par 5 with an island green.
18 holes, 6239yds, Par 71, SSS 70, Course record 68. Club membership 550.
Visitors Mon-Sun & BHs. Booking required. Dress code. **Societies** Booking required. **Green Fees** £30 per round, £40 Sat & Sun. **Prof** Lee Taylor, Alan Lunt **Course Designer** Martin Turner **Facilities** **Leisure** 9 hole pitch & putt. **Conf** facs Corporate Hospitality Days **Location** On A49, 0.25m from Camelot Theme Park

Hotel ★★★ 68% Park Hall Hotel, Park Hall Rd, Charnock Richard, CHORLEY 01257 455000 56 en suite 84 annexe en suite

Continued

Chorley Hall o' th' Hill, Heath Charnock PR6 9HX
☎ 01257 480263 01257 480722
e-mail: secretary@chorleygolfclub.freeserve.co.uk
web: www.chorleygolfclub.co.uk
A splendid moorland course with plenty of fresh air. The well-sited clubhouse affords some good views of the Lancashire coast and of Angelzarke, a local beauty spot. Beware of the short 3rd hole with its menacing out of bounds.
18 holes, 6269yds, Par 71, SSS 70, Course record 62.
Club membership 550.
Visitors Mon-Fri except BHs. Booking required. **Societies** Tue-Fri. Booking required. **Green Fees** phone. **Prof** Mark Bradley **Course Designer** JA Steer **Facilities** **Location** 2.5m SE on A673

Hotel ★★★ 72% Pines Hotel, 570 Preston Rd, Clayton-Le-Woods, CHORLEY ☎ 01772 338551 37 en suite

Duxbury Jubilee Park Duxbury Hall Rd PR7 4AT
☎ 01257 265380 01257 274500
18 holes, 6390yds, Par 71, SSS 70.
Course Designer Hawtree & Sons **Location** 2.5m S off A6
Phone for further details

Hotel Welcome Lodge Charnock Richard, Welcome Break Service Area, CHORLEY ☎ 01257 791746 100 en suite

Shaw Hill Hotel Golf & Country Club
Preston Rd, Whittle-Le-Woods PR6 7PP
☎ 01257 269221 01257 261223
e-mail: info@shaw-hill.co.uk
web: shaw-hill.co.uk
18 holes, 6246yds, Par 72, SSS 70, Course record 65.
Course Designer Harry Vardon **Location** 1.5m N on A6
Phone for further details

Hotel Shaw Hill Hotel Golf & Country Club, Preston Rd, Whittle-le-Woods, CHORLEY
☎ 01257 269221 & 226820 01257 261223 26 en suite 4 annexe en suite

CLITHEROE Map 07 SD74

Clitheroe Whalley Rd, Pendleton BB7 1PP
☎ 01200 422292 01200 422292
e-mail: secretary@clitheroegolfclub.com
web: www.clitheroegolfclub.com
One of the best inland courses in the country. Clitheroe is a parkland-type course with water hazards and good scenic views, particularly towards Longridge and Pendle Hill.
18 holes, 6326yds, Par 71, SSS 71, Course record 63.
Club membership 700.
Visitors Mon-Fri except BHs. Booking required. Handicap certificate. Dress code. **Societies** Booking required. **Green Fees** Mon-Thu £45 per day, £35 per 18 holes, Fri £45/£38. **Prof** Paul McEvoy **Course Designer** James Braid **Facilities** **Conf** Corporate Hospitality Days **Location** 2m S of Clitheroe

Hotel ★★★ 63% Shireburn Arms Hotel, Whalley Rd, Hurst Green, CLITHEROE ☎ 01254 826518 18 en suite

COLNE Map 07 SD84

Colne Law Farm, Skipton Old Rd BB8 7EB
☎ 01282 863391 01282 870547
9 holes, 6053yds, Par 70, SSS 69, Course record 63.
Location 1m E off A56
Phone for further details

Hotel ★★★ 75% Oaks Hotel, Colne Rd, Reedley, BURNLEY ☎ 01282 414141 50 en suite

DARWEN Map 07 SD62

Darwen Winter Hill BB3 0LB
☎ 01254 701287 (club) & 704367 (office)
01254 773833
e-mail: admin@darwengolfclub.com
First 9 holes on parkland, the second 9 on moorland.
18 holes, 6046yds, Par 71, SSS 71.
Club membership 600.
Visitors Mon, Wed-Fri, Sun except BHs. Booking required. Dress code. **Societies** Booking required. **Green Fees** £25 per round, £30 Sun. **Prof** Wayne Lennon **Facilities** **Conf** facs Corporate Hospitality Days **Location** 1m NW

Hotel Travelodge Blackburn (M65), Darwen Motorway services, DARWEN ☎ 08700 850 950

FLEETWOOD Map 07 SD34

Fleetwood Princes Way FY7 8AF
☎ 01253 873661 & 773573 01253 773573
e-mail: fleetwoodgc@aol.com
web: www.fleetwoodgolfclub.org.uk
Championship length, flat seaside links where the player must always be alert to changes of direction or strength of the wind.

18 holes, 6723yds, Par 72, SSS 72.
Club membership 600.
Visitors contact club for details. Handicap certificate. Dress code. **Societies** Booking required. **Green Fees** phone. **Prof** S McLaughlin **Course Designer** JA Steer **Facilities** **Conf** facs Corporate Hospitality Days **Location** W of town centre

Hotel Premier Travel Inn Blackpool (Bispham), Devonshire Rd, Bispham, BLACKPOOL
☎ 08701 977033 39 en suite

GARSTANG Map 07 SD44

Garstang Country Hotel & Golf Club

Garstang Rd, Bowgreave PR3 1YE
☎ 01995 600100 🖷 01995 600950
e-mail: reception@ghgc.co.uk
web: www.garstanghotelandgolf.co.uk

Fairly flat parkland course following the contours of the Rivers Wyre and Calder and providing a steady test of ability, especially over the longer back nine. Exceptional drainage makes the course playable all year round.

18 holes, 6050yds, Par 68, SSS 68.

Visitors Mon-Sun & BHs. Booking required. Dress code. **Societies** Booking required. **Green Fees** £15 per round, £17 Sat & Sun. **Prof** Robert Head **Course Designer** Richard Bradbeer **Facilities** **Conf** facs Corporate Hospitality Days **Location** 1m S of Garstang on B6430

Hotel ★★★ 70% Garstang Country Hotel & Golf Club, Garstang Rd, Bowgreave, GARSTANG ☎ 01995 600100 32 en suite

GREAT HARWOOD Map 07 SD73

Great Harwood Harwood Bar, Whalley Rd BB6 7TE
☎ 01254 884391

Flat parkland with fine views of the Pendle region.

9 holes, 6404yds, Par 73, SSS 71, Course record 68.
Club membership 400.

Visitors Mon-Sat except BHs. Booking required. Handicap certificate. Dress code. **Societies** Tue-Thu. Booking required in writing. **Green Fees** £20 per day, £26 Sat. **Facilities** **Location** E of town centre on A680

Hotel ★★★★ 62% Macdonald Dunkenhalgh Hotel & Spa, Blackburn Rd, Clayton-le-Moors, ACCRINGTON ☎ 0870 1942116 61 en suite 119 annexe en suite

HASLINGDEN Map 07 SD72

Rossendale Ewood Ln Head BB4 6LH
☎ 01706 831339 (secretary) & 213616 (pro)
🖷 01706 228669
e-mail: rgc@golfers.net
web: www.rossendalegolfclub.co.uk

A surprisingly flat parkland course, situated on a plateau with panoramic views and renowned for excellent greens.

18 holes, 6293yds, Par 72, Course record 64.
Club membership 700.

Visitors Mon-Fri, Sun & BHs. Booking required. Handicap certificate. Dress code. **Societies** Booking

Continued

required. **Green Fees** £25.50, £30.50 Sun. **Prof** Stephen Nicholls **Facilities** **Conf** Corporate Hospitality Days **Location** 0.5m S off A56

Hotel ★★ 78% The Millstone at Mellor, Church Ln, Mellor, BLACKBURN ☎ 01254 813333 17 en suite 6 annexe en suite

HEYSHAM Map 07 SD46

Heysham Trumacar Park, Middleton Rd LA3 3JH
☎ 01524 851011 (sec) & 852000 (pro) 🖷 01524 853030
e-mail: secretary@heyshamgolfclub.co.uk

A seaside parkland course, partly wooded. The 15th is a 459yd par 4 nearly always played into the prevailing south west wind.

18 holes, 5999yds, Par 68, SSS 69.
Club membership 930.

Visitors Mon-Sat, limited availability Sun & BHs. Booking required. Handicap certificate. **Societies** Booking required. **Green Fees** £35 per day, £30 per round, £40 Sat, Sun & BHs. **Prof** Ryan Done **Course Designer** Alex Herd **Facilities** **Leisure** snooker. **Conf** Corporate Hospitality Days **Location** 0.75m S off A589

Hotel ★★★ 65% Clarendon Hotel, 76 Marine Rd West, West End Promenade, MORECAMBE ☎ 01524 410180 29 en suite

KNOTT END-ON-SEA Map 07 SD34

Knott End Wyreside FY6 0AA
☎ 01253 810576 🖷 01253 813446
e-mail: louise@knottendgolfclub.com
web: www.knottendgolfclub.com

Scenic links and parkland course next to the Wyre estuary. The opening five holes run along the river and have spectacular views of the Fylde Coast. Although the course is quite short, the prevailing winds can add to one's score. Over-clubbing can be disastrous with trouble behind most of the smallish and well-guarded greens.

18 holes, 5849yds, Par 69, SSS 68, Course record 63.
Club membership 500.

Visitors Mon-Wed, Sat, Sun & BHs. Thu after 1.30pm. Booking required. Dress code. **Societies** Booking required. **Green Fees** £32 per day, £30 per round, £42/£38 Sat & Sun. **Prof** Paul Walker **Course Designer** Braid **Facilities** **Location** W of village off B5377

Hotel Travelodge Lancaster (M6), White Carr Ln, Bay Horse, FORTON ☎ 08700 850 950 53 en suite

LANCASTER Map 07 SD46

Lancaster Golf Club Ashton Hall, Ashton-with-Stodday LA2 0AJ
☎ 01524 751247 🖷 01524 752742
e-mail: office@lancastergc.co.uk
web: www.lancastergc.co.uk

This parkland course is unusual as it is exposed to winds from the Irish Sea. It is situated on the Lune estuary and has some natural hazards and easy walking. There are several fine holes among woods near the old clubhouse. Fine views towards the Lake District.

18 holes, 6282yds, Par 71, SSS 71, Course record 66.
Club membership 925.

Continued

Visitors Mon-Fri except BHs. Booking required. Handicap certificate. Dress code. **Societies** Booking required. **Green Fees** £45 per day, £38 per round. **Prof** David Sutcliffe **Course Designer** James Braid **Facilities** **Conf** Corporate Hospitality Days **Location** 3m S on A588

Hotel ★★★★ 72% Lancaster House Hotel, Green Ln, Ellel, LANCASTER ☎ 01524 844822 99 en suite

Lansil Caton Rd LA1 3PE
☎ 01524 61233
e-mail: lansilsportsgolfclub@onetel.net
Challenging parkland course.
9 holes, 5540yds, Par 70, SSS 67, Course record 68. Club membership 375.
Visitors Mon-Sat. After 1pm Sun. Booking required. **Societies** Booking required in writing. **Green Fees** phone. **Facilities** by arrangement by arrangement **Location** N of town centre on A683

Hotel ★★★★ 72% Lancaster House Hotel, Green Ln, Ellel, LANCASTER ☎ 01524 844822 99 en suite

LANGHO — Map 07 SD73

Mytton Fold Hotel & Golf Complex
Whalley Rd BB6 8AB
☎ 01254 245392 01254 248119
web: www.myttonfold.co.uk
The course has panoramic views across the Ribble Valley and Pendle Hill. Tight fairways and water hazards are designed to make this a challenging course for any golfer.
18 holes, 6082yds, Par 72, SSS 70, Course record 69. Club membership 450.
Visitors contact hotel for details. **Societies** Booking required. **Green Fees** phone. **Prof** Michael Bardi **Course Designer** Frank Hargreaves **Facilities** **Conf** facs Corporate Hospitality Days **Location** On A59 between Langho & Whalley

Hotel Northcote Manor, Northcote Rd, LANGHO ☎ 01254 240555 14 en suite

LEYLAND — Map 07 SD52

Leyland Wigan Rd PR25 5UD
☎ 01772 436457 01772 435605
e-mail: manager@leylandgolfclub.co.uk
web: www.leylandgolfclub.co.uk
Parkland, fairly flat and usually breezy.
18 holes, 6298yds, Par 70, SSS 70, Course record 67. Club membership 750.
Visitors Mon-Fri except BHs. Booking required. Handicap certificate. Dress code. **Societies** Booking required. **Green Fees** £25 per day. **Prof** Colin Burgess **Facilities** **Conf** facs Corporate Hospitality Days **Location** M6 junct 28, 0.75m

Hotel ★★★ 72% Pines Hotel, 570 Preston Rd, Clayton-Le-Woods, CHORLEY ☎ 01772 338551 37 en suite

LONGRIDGE — Map 07 SD63

Longridge Fell Barn, Jeffrey Hill PR3 2TU
☎ 01772 783291 01772 783022
e-mail: secretary@longridgegolfclub.fsnet.co.uk
web: www.longridgegolfclub.com
One of the oldest clubs in England, which celebrated its 125th anniversary in 2002. A moorland course with panoramic views of the Trough of Bowland, the Fylde coast and Welsh mountains. Small, sloping greens, difficult to read.

18 holes, 5975yds, Par 70, SSS 69, Course record 63. Club membership 600.
Visitors Mon-Fri, Sun & BHs. Booking required. Dress code. **Societies** Booking required. **Green Fees** £35 per day including bar meal, £25 per round Sat & Sun. **Prof** Stephen Taylor **Facilities** **Leisure** 9 hole par 3 course. **Conf** facs Corporate Hospitality Days **Location** 8m NE of Preston off B6243

Hotel ★★★ 63% Shireburn Arms Hotel, Whalley Rd, Hurst Green, CLITHEROE ☎ 01254 826518 18 en suite

LYTHAM ST ANNES — Map 07 SD32

Fairhaven Oakwood Av FY8 4JU
☎ 01253 736741 (secretary) 01253 731461
e-mail: secretary@fairhavengolfclub.co.uk
web: www.fairhavengolfclub.co.uk
A flat, but interesting parkland links course of good standard. There are natural hazards as well as numerous bunkers, and players need to produce particularly accurate second shots. An excellent test of golf for all abilities.
18 holes, 6883yds, Par 74, SSS 73, Course record 64. Club membership 750.
Visitors Mon-Sun & BHs. Booking required. Handicap certificate. Dress code. **Societies** Booking required. **Green Fees** phone. **Prof** Brian Plucknett **Course Designer** JA Steer **Facilities** **Leisure** snooker. **Location** E of town centre off B5261

Hotel ★★★ 69% Bedford Hotel, 307-311 Clifton Dr South, LYTHAM ST ANNES ☎ 01253 724636 45 en suite

Championship Course

Lancashire Royal Lytham & St Annes

Lytham St Annes Map 07 SD32

Founded in 1886, this huge links course can be difficult, especially in windy conditions. Unusually for a championship course, it starts with a par 3, the nearby railway line and red-brick houses are distractions that add to the challenge. The course has hosted 10 Open Championships with some memorable victories: amateur Bobby Jones famously won the first here in 1926; Bobby Charles of New Zealand became the only left-hander to win the title; in 1969 Tony Jacklin helped to revive British golf with his win; and the most recent in 2001 was won by David Duval.

Links Gate FY8 3LQ
☎ 01253 724206 🖹 01253 780946
e-mail: bookings@royallytham.org
web: www.royallytham.org

18 holes, 6882yds, Par 71, SSS 74, Course record 64.
Club membership 850.

Visitors Mon-Fri & Sun. Booking required. Handicap certificate. Dress code. **Societies** Booking required. **Green Fees** £170 per 36 holes, £115 per 18 holes, £170 per 18 holes Sun. **Prof** Eddie Birchenough **Course Designer** George Lowe **Facilities** ⊗ Ⅲ ⛾ ☕ 🍷 ⛨ ⛨ ⛨ ⛨ ⛨ **Leisure** caddies available. **Conf** Corporate Hospitality Days **Location** 0.5m E of St Annes

Lytham Green Drive Ballam Rd FY8 4LE
☎ 01253 737390 🖷 01253 731350
e-mail: sec@lythamgreendrive.co.uk
web: www.lythamgreendrive.co.uk
Green Drive provides a stern but fair challenge for even the most accomplished golfer. Tight fairways, strategically placed hazards and small tricky greens are the trademark of this testing course which meanders through pleasant countryside and is flanked by woods, pastures and meadows. The course demands accuracy in spite of the relatively flat terrain.
18 holes, 6363yds, Par 70, SSS 70, Course record 64. Club membership 700.
Visitors Mon-Fri & BHs. Handicap certificate. Dress code. **Societies** Booking required. **Green Fees** £45 per day, £38 per round. **Prof** Andrew Lancaster **Course Designer** Steer **Facilities** **Conf** Corporate Hospitality Days **Location** E of town centre off B5259

Hotel ★★★ 69% Bedford Hotel, 307-311 Clifton Dr South, LYTHAM ST ANNES ☎ 01253 724636 45 en suite

Royal Lytham & St Annes see page 161

Hotel ★★★★ 70% Clifton Arms Hotel, West Beach, Lytham, LYTHAM ST ANNES ☎ 01253 739898 48 en suite

Hotel ★★★ 69% Chadwick Hotel, South Promenade, LYTHAM ST ANNES ☎ 01253 720061 🖷 01253 714455 75 en suite
See advertisement on this page

Hotel ★★★ 69% Bedford Hotel, 307-311 Clifton Dr South, LYTHAM ST ANNES ☎ 01253 724636 🖷 01253 729244 45 en suite

Hotel ★★★ 68% The Best Western Glendower Hotel, North Promenade, LYTHAM ST ANNES ☎ 01253 723241 🖷 01253 640069 60 en suite

St Annes Old Links Highbury Rd East FY8 2LD
☎ 01253 723597 🖷 01253 781506
e-mail: secretary@stannesoldlinks.com
web: www.stannesoldlinks.com
Seaside links, qualifying course for Open Championship; compact and of very high standard, particularly greens. Windy, very long 5th, 17th and 18th holes. Famous hole: 9th (171yds), par 3. Excellent club facilities.
18 holes, 6684yds, Par 72, SSS 72, Course record 63. Club membership 750.
Visitors Mon-Fri & Sun except BHs. Booking required. Handicap certificate. Dress code. **Societies** Booking required. **Green Fees** Mon-Thur £50 per day, £35 pm. Fri £60/£45. Sun £50 pm. Winter reduced rates. **Prof** DJ Webster **Course Designer** George Lowe **Facilities** **Leisure** snooker room. **Conf** facs Corporate Hospitality Days **Location** N of town centre

St Annes Old Links

Hotel ★★★ 69% Chadwick Hotel, South Promenade, LYTHAM ST ANNES ☎ 01253 720061 75 en suite

MORECAMBE Map 07 SD46

Morecambe Bare LA4 6AJ
☎ 01524 412841 🖷 01524 400088
e-mail: secretary@morecambegolfclub.com
web: www.morecambegolfclub.com
Holiday golf at its most enjoyable. The well-maintained, wind-affected seaside parkland course is not long but full of character. Even so the panoramic

Continued

views of Morecambe Bay, the Lake District and the Pennines make concentration difficult. The 4th is a testing hole.
18 holes, 5750yds, Par 67, SSS 69, Course record 69.
Club membership 850.
Visitors Mon-Sun & BHs, Booking required. Handicap certificate. Dress code. **Societies** Booking required. **Green Fees** phone. **Prof** Simon Fletcher **Course Designer** A MacKenzie **Facilities** **Location** N of town centre on A5105

Hotel ★★★ 63% Elms Hotel, Bare Village, MORECAMBE ☎ 01524 411501 39 en suite

NELSON Map 07 SD83

Marsden Park Townhouse Rd BB9 8DG
☎ 01282 661912
e-mail: martin.robinson@pendleleisuretrust.co.uk
web: www.pendleleisuretrust.co.uk
A semi-parkland course offering panoramic views of surrounding countryside, set in the foothills of Pendle Marsden Park, a testing 18 holes for golfers of all abilities.
18 holes, 5907yds, Par 70, SSS 68, Course record 66.
Club membership 400.
Visitors Mon-Sun & BHs. Booking required Fri-Sun & BHs. **Societies** Tue-Thu. Booking required. **Green Fees** £14 per 18 holes, £11 per 9 holes, £13.50 per 9 holes Sat, Sun & BHs. **Facilities** **Leisure** practice nets. **Conf** facs Corporate Hospitality Days **Location** Off A56 Leeds Rd in town onto Walton Ln to end

Hotel ★★★ 75% Oaks Hotel, Colne Rd, Reedley, BURNLEY ☎ 01282 414141 50 en suite

Nelson King's Causeway, Brierfield BB9 0EU
☎ 01282 611834 01282 611834
Moorland course. Alister MacKenzie, who laid out the course, managed a design that does not include any wearisome climbing and created many interesting holes with wonderful panoramic views of the surrounding Pendle area.
18 holes, 6007yds, Par 70, SSS 69, Course record 64.
Club membership 580.
Visitors Mon-Wed, Fri, Sun & BHs. Booking required. Handicap certificate. Dress code. **Societies** Booking required. **Green Fees** £30 per day, £35 Sun & BHs. **Prof** Neil Reeves **Course Designer** A MacKenzie **Facilities** **Conf** Corporate Hospitality Days **Location** M65 junct 12, A682 to Brierfield, left at lights onto Halifax Rd & King's Causeway

Hotel ★★★ 75% Oaks Hotel, Colne Rd, Reedley, BURNLEY ☎ 01282 414141 50 en suite

ORMSKIRK Map 07 SD40

Hurlston Hall Hurlston Ln, Southport Rd, Scarisbrick L40 8HB
☎ 01704 840400 & 841120 (pro shop) 01704 841404
e-mail: info@hurlstonhall.co.uk
web: www.hurlstonhall.co.uk
Designed by Donald Steel, this gently undulating course offers fine views of the Pennines and Bowland Fells. With generous fairways, large tees and greens, two streams and seven lakes, it provides a good test of golf for players of all standards.
18 holes, 6757yds, Par 72, SSS 72, Course record 66.
Club membership 650.
Visitors Mon, Tue, Thu, Fri & BHs. Booking required. Dress code. **Societies** Booking required. **Green Fees** £35 per 18 holes, £40 Sat & Sun. **Course Designer** Donald Steel **Facilities** **Leisure** heated indoor swimming pool, fishing, gymnasium. **Conf** facs Corporate Hospitality Days **Location** 2m from Ormskirk on A570

Ormskirk Cranes Ln, Lathom L40 5UJ
☎ 01695 572227 01695 572227
e-mail: ormskirk@ukgolfer.org
web: www.ukgolfer.org
Pleasantly secluded, fairly flat parkland with much heath and silver birch. Accuracy from the tees will provide an interesting variety of second shots.
18 holes, 6358yds, Par 70, SSS 71, Course record 63.
Club membership 300.
Visitors Mon, Wed-Fri, Sun & BHs. Tue & Sat pm. Booking required. Dress code. **Societies** Booking required. **Green Fees** £50 per day, £40 per round, £55/£45 Wed, Sat & Sun. **Prof** Jack Hammond **Course Designer** Harold Hilton **Facilities** **Conf** Corporate Hospitality Days **Location** 1.5m NE

PLEASINGTON Map 07 SD62

Pleasington BB2 5JF
☎ 01254 202177 01254 201028
e-mail: secretary-manager@pleasington-golf.co.uk
web: www.pleasington-golf.co.uk
Plunging and rising across lovely parkland and heathland turf, this course tests judgement of distance through the air to greens of widely differing levels. The 11th and 4th are testing holes.
18 holes, 6417yds, Par 70, SSS 70.
Club membership 700.
Visitors Mon, Wed-Fri, Sun & BHs. Booking required. Dress code. **Societies** Booking required. **Green Fees** £45 per round, £50 Sun. **Prof** Ged Furey **Course Designer** George Lowe **Facilities** **Conf** facs Corporate Hospitality Days **Location** M65 junct 3, signed for Blackburn

Hotel ★★ 78% The Millstone at Mellor, Church Ln, Mellor, BLACKBURN ☎ 01254 813333 17 en suite 6 annexe en suite

POULTON-LE-FYLDE Map 07 SD33

Poulton-le-Fylde Breck Rd FY6 7HJ
☎ 01253 892444 & 893150 01253 892444
A pleasant, municipal parkland course suitable for all standards of golfers although emphasis on accuracy is required.
9 holes, 2858yds, Par 35, SSS 34, Course record 66.
Club membership 300.
Visitors Mon-Sun & BHs. Booking required. Dress code. **Societies** Booking required. **Green Fees** £8.50 per 9 holes, £10 Sat & Sun. **Prof** John Greenwood **Course Designer** H Taylor **Facilities** **Location** M55 junct 3, A585 to Poulton, club signed

Hotel ★★ 70% Hotel Sheraton, 54-62 Queens Promenade, BLACKPOOL ☎ 01253 352723 104 en suite

Continued

PRESTON Map 07 SD52

Ashton & Lea Tudor Av, Lea PR4 0XA
☎ 01772 735282 🖹 01772 735762
e-mail: ashtonleagolf@supanet.com
web: www.ukgolfer.org
Fairly flat, well-maintained parkland course with natural water hazards, offering pleasant walks and some testing holes for golfers of all standards. Water comes into play on seven of the last nine holes. The course has three challenging par 3s.
18 holes, 6334yds, Par 71, SSS 70, Course record 65.
Club membership 650.
Visitors Booking required. **Societies** Booking required. **Green Fees** phone. **Prof** M Greenough **Course Designer** J Steer **Facilities** **Leisure** snooker table. **Conf** facs Corporate Hospitality Days **Location** 3m W of Preston on A5085

Fishwick Hall Glenluce Dr, Farringdon Park PR1 5TD
☎ 01772 798300 🖹 01772 704600
e-mail: fishwickhallgolfclub@supanet.com
web: www.fishwickhallgolfclub.co.uk
Meadowland course overlooking River Ribble. Natural hazards.
18 holes, 6045yds, Par 70, SSS 69, Course record 66.
Club membership 650.
Visitors Mon-Sun & BHs. Booking required. Handicap certificate. Dress code. **Societies** Booking required. **Green Fees** £28 per round, £32 Sat & Sun. **Prof** Martin Watson **Facilities** **Conf** Corporate Hospitality Days **Location** M6 junct 31

Hotel ★★★ 67% Macdonald Tickled Trout, Preston New Rd, Samlesbury, PRESTON ☎ 0870 1942120 102 en suite

Ingol Tanterton Hall Rd, Ingol PR2 7BY
☎ 01772 734556 🖹 01772 729815
e-mail: ingol@golfers.net
web: www.ingolgolfclub.co.uk
Championship-designed course with natural water hazards, set in 250 acres of beautiful parkland. A good test for any golfer.

18 holes, 6294yds, Par 72, SSS 70, Course record 68.
Club membership 650.
Visitors Mon-Sun & BHs. Booking required. Dress code. **Societies** Booking required. **Green Fees** phone. **Prof** Ryan Grimshaw **Course Designer** Henry Cotton **Facilities** **Leisure** squash, Snooker & Pool. **Conf** facs **Location** A5085 onto B5411, signs to Ingol

Continued

Hotel Premier Travel Inn Preston East, Bluebell Way, Preston East Link Rd, Fulwood, PRESTON
☎ 08701 977215 65 en suite

Penwortham Blundell Ln, Penwortham PR1 0AX
☎ 01772 744630 🖹 01772 740172
e-mail: penworthamgolfclub@supanet.com
web: www.ukgolfer.org/clubs/penwortham

18 holes, 5877yds, Par 69, SSS 69, Course record 65.
Location 1.5m W of town centre off A59
Phone for further details

Hotel ★★★ 67% Macdonald Tickled Trout, Preston New Rd, Samlesbury, PRESTON ☎ 0870 1942120 102 en suite

Preston Fulwood Hall Ln, Fulwood PR2 8DD
☎ 01772 700011 🖹 01772 794234
e-mail: secretary@prestongolfclub.com
web: www.prestongolfclub.com
Pleasant inland golf at this course set in very agreeable parkland. There is a well-balanced selection of holes, undulating among groups of trees, and not requiring great length.
18 holes, 6312yds, Par 71, SSS 71, Course record 68.
Club membership 800.
Visitors Tue-Thu. Booking required. Handicap certificate. **Societies** Booking required. **Green Fees** phone. **Prof** Andrew Greenbank **Course Designer** James Braid **Facilities** **Conf** facs **Location** 1m N of city centre on A6, right at lights onto Watling St, left onto Fulwood Hall Ln, course 300yds on left

Hotel ★★★★ 68% Preston Marriott Hotel, Garstang Rd, Broughton, PRESTON ☎ 01772 864087 149 en suite

RISHTON Map 07 SD73

Rishton Eachill Links, Hawthorn Dr BB1 4HG
☎ 01254 884442 🖹 01254 887701
e-mail: rishtongc@onetel.net
web: www.rishtongolfclub.co.uk
Undulating moorland course with some interesting holes and fine views of East Lancashire.
Eachill Links: 10 holes, 6097yds, Par 70, SSS 69, Course record 68.
Club membership 270.
Visitors Mon-Fri except BHs. **Societies** Booking required in writing. **Green Fees** phone. **Course Designer** Peter Alliss, Dave Thomas **Facilities** by arrangement **Conf** Corporate Hospitality Days **Location** M65 junct 6/7, 1m. Signed from Station Rd in Rishton

Continued

Hotel ★★★★ 62% Macdonald Dunkenhalgh Hotel & Spa, Blackburn Rd, Clayton-le-Moors, ACCRINGTON ☎ 0870 1942116 61 en suite 119 annexe en suite

SILVERDALE Map 07 SD47

Silverdale Redbridge Ln LA5 0SP
☎ 01524 701300 🖹 01524 702074
e-mail: silverdalegolfclub@ecosse.net
web: silverdalegolfclub.com
Challenging heathland course with rock outcrops, set in an Area of Outstanding Natural Beauty with spectacular views of the Lake District hills and Morecambe Bay. It is a course of two halves, being either open fairways or tight hilly limestone valleys. The 13th hole has been described as one of Britain's 100 extraordinary golf holes.
18 holes, 5526yds, Par 70, SSS 67, Course record 68. Club membership 500.
Visitors Mon-Fri. Booking required Sat, Sun & BHs. Dress code. **Societies** welcome. **Green Fees** £25 per day, £20 per round, £30/£25 Sat & Sun. **Prof** Ryan Grimshaw **Facilities** **Location** Opp Silverdale station Moss RSPB nature reserve

UPHOLLAND Map 07 SD50

Beacon Park Golf & Country Club Beacon Ln WN8 7RU
☎ 01695 622700 🖹 01695 633066/6287100
e-mail: info@beaconparkgolf.com
web: www.beaconparkgolf.com
Undulating or hilly parkland course, designed by Donald Steel, with magnificent view of the Welsh hills. Twenty-four-bay floodlit driving range open 9am-9pm in summer.
18 holes, 6000yds, Par 72, SSS 69, Course record 68. Club membership 250.
Visitors Mon-Sun & BHs. Booking required. Dress code. **Societies** Booking required. **Green Fees** £11 per 18 holes, £15 Sat, Sun & BHs. **Prof** Gary Nelson **Course Designer** Donald Steel **Facilities** by arrangement by arrangement **Conf** Corporate Hospitality Days **Location** M6 junct 26, S of Ashurst Beacon Hill

Dean Wood Lafford Ln WN8 0QZ
☎ 01695 622219 🖹 01695 622245
web: www.deanwoodgolfclub.co.uk
This parkland course has a varied terrain - flat front nine, undulating back nine. Beware the par 4 11th and 17th holes, which have ruined many a card. If there were a prize for the best maintained course in Lancashire, Dean Wood would be a strong contender.
18 holes, 6148yds, Par 71, SSS 70, Course record 65. Club membership 730.
Visitors Mon-Fri. Booking required Tue & Wed. Handicap certificate. Dress code. **Societies** Booking required. **Green Fees** £30 per day. **Prof** Stuart Danchin **Course Designer** James Braid **Facilities** **Conf** Corporate Hospitality Days **Location** M6 junct 26, 1m on A577

WHALLEY Map 07 SD73

Whalley Long Leese Barn, Clerk Hill Rd BB7 9DR
☎ 01254 822236
A parkland course near Pendle Hill, overlooking the Ribble Valley. Superb views. Ninth hole over pond.

Continued

9 holes, 6258yds, Par 72, SSS 71, Course record 69. Club membership 450.
Visitors Mon-Wed, Fri & Sun except BHs. Booking required. Handicap certificate. Dress code. **Societies** Booking required. **Green Fees** £25 per day, £30 Sun. **Prof** Jamie Hunt **Facilities** **Conf** Corporate Hospitality Days **Location** 1m SE off A671

Hotel ★★★★ 62% Clarion Hotel & Suites Foxfields, Whalley Rd, Billington, CLITHEROE ☎ 01254 822556 44 en suite

WHITWORTH Map 07 SD81

Lobden Lobden Moor OL12 8XJ
☎ 01706 343228 & 345598 🖹 01706 343228
Moorland course, with hard walking. Windy with superb views of surrounding hills. Excellent greens.
9 holes, 5697yds, Par 70, SSS 68, Course record 63. Club membership 250.
Visitors contact club for details. Dress code. **Societies** Booking required. **Green Fees** phone. **Facilities** **Location** E of town centre off A671

Hotel ★★★★ 62% Macdonald Norton Grange Hotel, Manchester Rd, Castleton, ROCHDALE ☎ 0870 1942119 51 en suite

WILPSHIRE Map 07 SD63

Wilpshire Whalley Rd BB1 9LF
☎ 01254 248260 🖹 01254 246745
18 holes, 5971yds, Par 69, SSS 69, Course record 62.
Course Designer James Braid **Location** 2m NE of Blackburn, on A666 towards Clitheroe
Phone for further details

Hotel ★★★ 70% Sparth House Hotel, Whalley Rd, Clayton Le Moors, ACCRINGTON ☎ 01254 872263 16 en suite

LEICESTERSHIRE

ASHBY-DE-LA-ZOUCH Map 08 SK31

Willesley Park Measham Rd LE65 2PF
☎ 01530 414596 🖹 01530 564169
e-mail: info@willesleypark.com
web: www.willesleypark.com
18 holes, 6304yds, Par 70, SSS 70, Course record 63.
Course Designer J Braid **Location** SW of town centre on B5006
Phone for further details

BIRSTALL Map 04 SK50

Birstall Station Rd LE4 3BB
☎ 0116 267 4322 🖹 0116 267 4322
e-mail: suechilton@btconnect.com
web: www.birstallgolfclub.co.uk
Parkland with trees, shrubs, ponds and ditches, next to the Great Central Railway Steam Train line.
18 holes, 6213yds, Par 70, SSS 70. Club membership 650.
Visitors Mon-Sun. Booking required. **Societies** Booking required in writing. **Green Fees** phone. **Prof** David Clark **Facilities** **Leisure** billiard room. **Conf** Corporate Hospitality Days **Location** 3m N of Leicester on A6

Continued

Hotel ★★★ 66% Rothley Court, Westfield Ln, ROTHLEY ☎ 0116 237 4141 12 en suite 18 annexe en suite

BOTCHESTON Map 04 SK40

Forest Hill Markfield Ln LE9 9FJ
☎ 01455 824800 📠 01455 828522
Parkland course with many trees, four Par 5s, but no steep gradients.
18 holes, 6126yds, Par 71, SSS 69, Course record 63.
Club membership 700.
Visitors Mon-Fri except BHs. Handicap certificate. Dress code. **Societies** Booking required. **Green Fees** £30 per day, £18 per round. **Prof** Glyn Quilter **Course Designer** Gaunt & Marnoch **Facilities** **Conf** facs

Hotel ★★ 64% Castle Hotel & Restaurant, Main St, KIRBY MUXLOE ☎ 0116 239 5337 22 en suite

COSBY Map 04 SP59

Cosby Chapel Ln, Broughton Rd LE9 1RG
☎ 0116 286 4759 📠 0116 286 4484
e-mail: secretary@cosby-golf-club.co.uk
web: www.cosby-golf-club.co.uk
18 holes, 6410yds, Par 71, SSS 71, Course record 65.
Course Designer Hawtree **Location** M1 junct 21, B4114 to L-turn at BP service station, signed Cosby
Phone for further details

Hotel ★★★★ 74% Sketchley Grange Hotel, Sketchley Ln, Burbage, HINCKLEY ☎ 01455 251133 52 en suite

EAST GOSCOTE Map 08 SK61

Beedles Lake 170 Broome Ln LE7 3WQ
☎ 0116 260 4414 📠 0116 260 4414
e-mail: ian@jelson.co.uk
web: www.beedleslake.co.uk
Fairly flat parkland with easy walking. Ditches, streams and rivers come into play on many holes. Older trees and thousands of newly planted ones give the course a mature feel. Many challenging holes where you can ruin a good score.
18 holes, 6641yds, Par 72, SSS 72, Course record 71.
Club membership 443.
Visitors Mon-Fri. Booking required Sat, Sun & BHs. Dress code. **Societies** Booking required. **Green Fees** £14 per 18 holes, £20 Sat, Sun & BHs. **Prof** Sean Byrne **Course Designer** D Tucker **Facilities** **Leisure** fishing. **Conf** facs Corporate Hospitality Days **Location** Off A607

Hotel ★★★ 66% Rothley Court, Westfield Ln, ROTHLEY ☎ 0116 237 4141 12 en suite 18 annexe en suite

ENDERBY Map 04 SP59

Enderby Mill Ln LE19 4LX
☎ 0116 284 9388 📠 0116 284 9388
A gently undulating nine-hole course at which beginners are especially welcome. The longest hole is the 2nd at 407yds and there are five par 3s.
9 holes, 2856yds, Par 72, SSS 71, Course record 71.
Club membership 150.
Visitors Mon-Sun & BHs. **Societies** welcome. **Green Fees** £8 per 18 holes, £6.50 per 9 holes. **Prof** Chris D'Araujo **Course Designer** David Lowe **Facilities**

Continued

Leisure heated indoor swimming pool, squash, sauna, solarium, gymnasium, indoor bowls snooker badminton. **Location** M1 junct 21, 2m S on Narborough road, right at Toby Carvery rdbt, 0.5m on left, signed

Hotel ★★★ 68% Corus hotel Leicester, Enderby Rd, Blaby, LEICESTER ☎ 0116 278 7898 & 0870 609 6106 📠 0116 278 1974 48 en suite

HINCKLEY Map 04 SP49

Hinckley Leicester Rd LE10 3DR
☎ 01455 615124 & 615014 📠 01455 890841
e-mail: proshop@hinckleygolfclub.com
web: www.hinckleygolfclub.com
Parkland course with a good variety of holes to test all abilities. Water comes into play on a number of holes.
18 holes, 6467yds, Par 71, SSS 71, Course record 65.
Club membership 750.
Visitors Mon-Fri except BHs. Handicap certificate. Dress code. **Societies** Booking required. **Green Fees** £40 per day, £30 per round. **Prof** Richard Jones **Course Designer** Southern Golf Ltd **Facilities** **Leisure** snooker. **Conf** facs Corporate Hospitality Days **Location** 1.5m NE on B4668

Hotel ★★★ 66% Weston Hall Hotel, Weston Ln, Bulkington, NUNEATON ☎ 024 7631 2989 40 en suite

KIBWORTH Map 04 SP69

Kibworth Weir Rd, Beauchamp LE8 0LP
☎ 0116 279 2301 📠 0116 279 6434
e-mail: secretary@kibworthgolfclub.freeserve.co.uk
Easy walking parkland with a brook affecting a number of fairways. Most holes are tightly bunkered.
18 holes, 6354yds, Par 71, SSS 71.
Club membership 700.
Visitors Mon, Wed-Fri except BHs. Handicap certificate. Dress code. **Societies** Booking required. **Green Fees** £35 per day, £27 per round. **Prof** Mike Herbert **Facilities** **Location** S of village off A6

Hotel ★★★ 70% Three Swans Hotel, 21 High St, MARKET HARBOROUGH ☎ 01858 466644 18 en suite 43 annexe en suite

KIRBY MUXLOE Map 04 SK50

Kirby Muxloe Station Rd LE9 2EP
☎ 0116 239 3457 📠 0116 238 8891
e-mail: kirbymuxloegolf@btconnect.com
web: www.kirbymuxloe-golf.co.uk
Pleasant parkland with a lake in front of the 17th green and a short 18th.
18 holes, 6351yds, Par 71, SSS 70, Course record 62.
Club membership 870.
Visitors Mon, Wed-Fri. Booking advised. Handicap certificate. **Societies** Booking advised. **Green Fees** phone. **Prof** Bruce Whipham **Facilities** **Conf** Corporate Hospitality Days **Location** S of village off B5380

Hotel ★★ 64% Castle Hotel & Restaurant, Main St, KIRBY MUXLOE ☎ 0116 239 5337 22 en suite

LEICESTER Map 04 SK50

Humberstone Heights Gypsy Ln LE5 0TB
☎ 0116 276 3680 & 299 5570 (pro) 0116 299 5569
e-mail: hhmgolfclub@freeserve.co.uk
Municipal parkland course with varied layout.
18 holes, 6343yds, Par 70, SSS 70, Course record 66.
Club membership 400.
Visitors Mon-Sun & BHs. Booking required. **Societies** Booking required. **Green Fees** phone. **Prof** Phil Highfield **Course Designer** Hawtry & Sons **Facilities** **Leisure** 9 hole pitch and putt course. **Location** 2.5m NE of city centre

Hotel ★★★ 74% Belmont House Hotel, De Montfort St, LEICESTER ☎ 0116 254 4773 77 en suite

Leicestershire Evington Ln LE5 6DJ
☎ 0116 273 8825 0116 249 8799
e-mail: enquiries@thelgc.co.uk
web: www.thelgc.co.uk
Pleasant undulating parkland.
18 holes, 6134yds, Par 68, SSS 70.
Club membership 800.
Visitors Mon-Fri & Sun. Booking required. Handicap certificate. **Societies** Booking required. **Green Fees** phone. **Prof** Darren Jones **Course Designer** Hawtree **Facilities** **Conf** Corporate Hospitality Days **Location** 2m E of city off A6030

Hotel ★★★ 68% Regency Hotel, 360 London Rd, LEICESTER ☎ 0116 270 9634 32 en suite

Western Scudamore Rd, Braunstone Frith LE3 1UQ
☎ 0116 299 5566 0116 299 5568
18 holes, 6518yds, Par 72, SSS 71.
Location 1.5m W of city centre off A47
Phone for further details

Hotel ★★ 64% Castle Hotel & Restaurant, Main St, KIRBY MUXLOE ☎ 0116 239 5337 22 en suite

LOUGHBOROUGH Map 08 SK51

Longcliffe Snell's Nook Ln, Nanpantan LE11 3YA
☎ 01509 239129 01509 231286
e-mail: longcliffegolf@btconnect.com
web: www.longcliffegolf.co.uk
Course of natural heathland, tree-lined fairways with water in play on the 14th and 15th holes. This course is recognised by the English Golf Championship.

18 holes, 6625yds, Par 72, SSS 73, Course record 65.
Club membership 660.
Visitors Mon-Sun except BHs. Booking required.

Continued

Societies Booking required. Handicap certificate. **Green Fees** phone. **Prof** David Mee **Course Designer** Williamson **Facilities** **Conf** Corporate Hospitality Days **Location** 1.5m from M1 junct 23 off A512

Hotel ★★★ 65% Quality Hotel & Suites Loughborough, New Ashby Rd, LOUGHBOROUGH ☎ 01509 211800 94 en suite

LUTTERWORTH Map 04 SP58

Kilworth Springs South Kilworth Rd, North Kilworth LE17 6HJ
☎ 01858 575082 01858 575078
e-mail: kilworthsprings@ukonline.co.uk
web: www.kilworthsprings.co.uk
An 18-hole course of two loops of nine: the front nine is links style while the back nine is in parkland with four lakes. Greens to USGA specifications.
18 holes, 6543yds, Par 72, SSS 71, Course record 66.
Club membership 850.
Visitors Mon-Sun & BHs. Booking required. Dress code. **Societies** Booking required. **Green Fees** £23 per 18 holes, £26 Sat & Sun. **Prof** Anders Mankert **Course Designer** Ray Baldwin **Facilities** **Conf** Corporate Hospitality Days **Location** M1 junct 20, 4m E A4304 towards Market Harborough between villages of North & South Kilworth

Hotel ★★ 72% The Sun Inn, Main St, MARSTON TRUSSELL ☎ 01858 465531 20 en suite

Lutterworth Rugby Rd LE17 4HN
☎ 01455 552532 01455 553586
Hilly course with the River Swift running through.
18 holes, 6226yds, Par 70, SSS 70.
Club membership 700.
Visitors Mon-Fri. **Societies** Booking required. **Green Fees** phone. **Prof** Roland Tisdall **Facilities** **Conf** Corporate Hospitality Days **Location** M1 junct 20, 0.25m

Hotel ★★★ 68% Corus hotel Rugby, Brownsover Ln, Old Brownsover, RUGBY ☎ 0870 609 6104 01788 546100 01788 579241 27 en suite 20 annexe en suite

MARKET HARBOROUGH Map 04 SP78

Market Harborough Oxendon Rd LE16 8NF
☎ 01858 463684 01858 432906
e-mail: proshop@mhgolf.co.uk
web: www.mhgolf.co.uk
A parkland course close to the town. Undulating and in parts hilly. There are wide-ranging views over the surrounding countryside. Lakes feature on four holes; challenging last three holes.
18 holes, 6086yds, Par 70, SSS 69, Course record 61.
Club membership 650.
Visitors Mon-Fri except BHs. Booking required. Handicap certificate. Dress code. **Societies** Booking required. **Green Fees** £25 per round. **Prof** Frazer Baxter **Course Designer** H Swan **Facilities** **Conf** Corporate Hospitality Days **Location** 1m S on A508

Hotel ★★★ 70% Three Swans Hotel, 21 High St, MARKET HARBOROUGH ☎ 01858 466644 18 en suite 43 annexe en suite

Stoke Albany Ashley Rd, Stoke Albany LE16 8PL
☎ 01858 535208 📠 01858 535505
e-mail: info@stokealbanygolfclub.co.uk
web: www.stokealbanygolfclub.co.uk

A parkland course in the picturesque Welland valley. Affording good views, the course should appeal to the mid-handicap golfer, and provide an interesting test to the more experienced player. There are several water features and the greens are individually contoured, adding to the golfing challenge.

18 holes, 6175yds, Par 71, SSS 70, Course record 65. Club membership 500.

Visitors Mon-Sun & BHs. Booking required. Dress code. **Societies** Booking required. **Green Fees** £17 per 18 holes, £21-£23 Sat, Sun & BHs. **Prof** Adrian Clifford **Course Designer** Hawtree **Facilities** **Conf** facs Corporate Hospitality Days **Location** N off A427 Market Harborough-Corby road, follow Stoke Albany 500yds towards Ashley

Hotel ★★★ 70% Three Swans Hotel, 21 High St, MARKET HARBOROUGH ☎ 01858 466644 18 en suite 43 annexe en suite

MELTON MOWBRAY Map 08 SK71

Melton Mowbray Waltham Rd, Thorpe Arnold LE14 4SD
☎ 01664 562118 📠 01664 562118
e-mail: mmgc@le144sd.fsbusiness.co.uk
web: www.mmgc.org

Easy walking heathland course with undulating fairways. Deceptively challenging.

18 holes, 6222yds, Par 70, SSS 70, Course record 65. Club membership 650.

Visitors Mon-Sun & BHs. Booking required. Dress code. **Societies** Booking required. **Green Fees** £35 per day, £25 per round, £30 per round Sat, Sun & BHs. **Prof** Neil Curtis **Facilities** **Location** 2m NE of Melton Mowbray on A607

Hotel ★★★ 73% Sysonby Knoll Hotel, Asfordby Rd, MELTON MOWBRAY ☎ 01664 563563 23 en suite 7 annexe en suite

Stapleford Park Stapleford LE14 2EF
☎ 01572 787000 📠 01572 787001
e-mail: clubs@stapleford.co.uk
web: www.staplefordpark.com

Set in 500 acres of parkland, lake and woods. Reminiscent of some Scottish links, the course wraps around the heart of the estate in two extended loops. Never more than two holes wide, the whole course is spacious and tranquil. The beauty of the surrounding countryside is the perfect backdrop.

18 holes, 6944yds, Par 73, SSS 73. Club membership 300.

Visitors Mon-Sun & BHs. Booking required. Handicap certificate. Dress code. **Societies** Booking required. **Green Fees** £50-£75 per day seasonal rate. **Prof** Richard Alderson **Course Designer** Donald Steel **Facilities** **Leisure** hard tennis courts, heated indoor swimming pool, fishing, sauna, solarium, gymnasium, shooting, falconry, offroading, horseriding, archery. **Conf** facs Corporate Hospitality Days **Location** 4m E of Melton Mowbray off B676

Hotel ★★★★ Stapleford Park, Stapleford, MELTON MOWBRAY ☎ 01572 787522 44 en suite 8 annexe en suite

OADBY Map 04 SK60

Glen Gorse Glen Rd LE2 4RF
☎ 0116 271 4159 📠 0116 271 4159
e-mail: secretary@gggc.co.uk
web: www.gggc.org

Fairly flat 18-hole parkland course with strategically placed trees encountered on every hole, rewarding the straight hitter. The long approaches and narrow greens require the very best short game. However, a premium is placed on accuracy and length, and no more so than over the closing three holes, considered to be one of the finest finishes in the county.

18 holes, 6648yds, Par 72, SSS 72, Course record 64. Club membership 730.

Visitors Mon-Fri except BHs. Booking required. Handicap certificate. Dress code. **Societies** Booking required. **Green Fees** phone. **Prof** Dominic Fitzpatrick **Facilities** **Leisure** snooker room. **Conf** Corporate Hospitality Days **Location** On A6 between Oadby Glen, 5m S of Leicester

Hotel ★★★ 68% Regency Hotel, 360 London Rd, LEICESTER ☎ 0116 270 9634 32 en suite

Oadby Leicester Rd LE2 4AJ
☎ 0116 270 9052
e-mail: oadbygolf@supanet.com
web: www.oadbygolfclub.co.uk

Flat municipal parkland course.

18 holes, 6376yds, Par 72, SSS 70, Course record 69. Club membership 300.

Visitors Mon-Sun. **Societies** Booking required. **Green Fees** phone. **Prof** Andrew Wells **Facilities** **Leisure** squash, sauna, gymnasium, snooker. **Conf** facs **Location** W of Oadby off A6

Hotel ★★★ 68% Regency Hotel, 360 London Rd, LEICESTER ☎ 0116 270 9634 32 en suite

ROTHLEY Map 08 SK51

Rothley Park Westfield Ln LE7 7LH
☎ 0116 230 2809 📠 0116 230 2809
e-mail: secretary@rothleypark.co.uk
web: www.rothleypark.com

18 holes, 6477yds, Par 71, SSS 71, Course record 67.

Location N of Leicester, W off A6

Phone for further details

Hotel ★★★ 66% Rothley Court, Westfield Ln, ROTHLEY ☎ 0116 237 4141 12 en suite 18 annexe en suite

Continued

SCRAPTOFT Map 04 SK60

Scraptoft Beeby Rd LE7 9SJ
☎ 0116 241 9000 🖷 0116 241 9000
e-mail: secretary@scraptoft-gold.co.uk
A well wooded and beautiful parkland course demanding accuracy.
18 holes, 6166yds, Par 70, SSS 70.
Club membership 650.
Visitors Mon-Fri except BHs. Booking required. Handicap certificate. Dress code. **Societies** welcome. **Green Fees** £40 per day, £30 per round. **Prof** Simon Wood **Facilities** **Location** 1m NE

Hotel ★★★ 74% Belmont House Hotel, De Montfort St, LEICESTER ☎ 0116 254 4773 77 en suite

SEAGRAVE Map 08 SK61

Park Hill Park Hill LE12 7NG
☎ 01509 815454 🖷 01509 816062
e-mail: mail@parkhillgolf.co.uk
web: www.parkhillgolf.co.uk
Nestled in the heart of Leicestershire, overlooking the Charnwood Forest and beyond, Park Hill Golf Club has an 18-hole championship length course that uses the land's natural features to ensure that no two holes are the same. The combination of water features and precisely positioned bunkers provide for a challenging, yet enjoyable course, with excellent playing conditions all year round.
18 holes, 7219yds, Par 73, SSS 75, Course record 71.
Club membership 500.
Visitors Mon-Sun & BHs. Dress code. **Societies** welcome. **Green Fees** £25, £30 Sat, Sun & BHs. **Prof** Matthew Ulyett **Facilities** **Conf** facs Corporate Hospitality Days **Location** 3m N of Leicester off A46, signs to Seagrave

Hotel ★★★ 65% Quality Hotel & Suites Loughborough, New Ashby Rd, LOUGHBOROUGH ☎ 01509 211800 94 en suite

SIX HILLS Map 08 SK62

Six Hills Six Hills Rd LE14 3PR
☎ 01509 881225 🖷 01509 881846
Flat parkland.
18 holes, 5758yds, SSS 69.
Visitors Mon-Fri. Booking required Sat, Sun & BHs. Dress code. **Societies** Booking required Sat & Sun. **Green Fees** phone. **Prof** James Hawley **Facilities** **Location** On B676 between Melton Mowbray & Loughborough

Hotel Travelodge Leicester Thrussington, THRUSSINGTON ☎ 08700 850 950 32 en suite

ULLESTHORPE Map 04 SP58

Ullesthorpe Frolesworth Rd LE17 5BZ
☎ 01455 209023 🖷 01455 202537
e-mail: bookings@ullesthorpecourt.co.uk
web: www.bw-ullesthorpe.co.uk
Set in 120 acres of parkland surrounding a 17th-century manor house, this championship length course can be very demanding and offers a challenge to both beginners and professionals. Excellent leisure facilities. Water plays a part on three holes.

Ullesthorpe

18 holes, 6662yds, Par 72, SSS 72, Course record 67.
Club membership 650.
Visitors Mon-Fri except BHs. Booking required. Dress code. **Societies** Booking required. **Green Fees** £30 per day, £22 per round. **Prof** David Bowring **Facilities** **Leisure** hard tennis courts, heated indoor swimming pool, sauna, solarium, gymnasium. **Conf** facs Corporate Hospitality Days **Location** M1 junct 20, 5m

Hotel ★★★ 70% Ullesthorpe Court Country Hotel & Golf Club, Frolesworth Rd, ULLESTHORPE ☎ 01455 209023 38 en suite

WHETSTONE Map 04 SP59

Whetstone Cambridge Rd, Cosby LE9 1SJ
☎ 0116 286 1424 🖷 0116 286 1424
18 holes, 5795yds, Par 68, SSS 68, Course record 63.
Course Designer E Calloway **Location** 1m S of village
Phone for further details

Hotel ★★★ 68% Corus hotel Leicester, Enderby Rd, Blaby, LEICESTER ☎ 0116 278 7898 & 0870 609 6106 🖷 0116 278 1974 48 en suite

WILSON Map 08 SK42

Breedon Priory Green Ln DE73 1AT
☎ 01332 863081 🖷 01332 865319
web: www.breedongolf.co.uk
18 holes, 5777yds, Par 69, SSS 68, Course record 67.
Course Designer David Snell **Location** Off A453 into Breedon
Phone for further details

Hotel ★★★★ 74% The Priest House on the River, Kings Mills, Castle Donington, ☎ 01332 810649 24 en suite 18 annexe en suite

WOODHOUSE EAVES Map 08 SK51

Charnwood Forest Breakback Ln LE12 8TA
☎ 01509 890259 🖷 01509 890925
e-mail: secretary@charnwoodforestgc.co.uk
web: www.charnwoodforestgc.co.uk
Hilly heathland course with hard walking, but no bunkers. Play is round volcanic rock giving panoramic views over the Charnwood Forest area.
9 holes, 5960yds, Par 69, SSS 69, Course record 64.
Club membership 360.
Visitors Booking required. **Societies** Wed-Fri. Booking required. Mon by arrangement. **Green Fees** phone. **Course Designer** James Braid **Facilities**

Continued

Conf facs Corporate Hospitality Days **Location** M1 junct 22/23, 3m

Hotel ★★★★ 70% Quorn Country Hotel, Charnwood House, 66 Leicester Rd, QUORN ☎ 01509 415050 30 en suite

Lingdale Joe Moore's Ln LE12 8TF
☎ 01509 890703 🖹 01509 890703
18 holes, 6545yds, Par 71, SSS 71, Course record 68.
Course Designer David Tucker **Location** 1.5m S off B5330
Phone for further details

Hotel ★★★★ 70% Quorn Country Hotel, Charnwood House, 66 Leicester Rd, QUORN ☎ 01509 415050 30 en suite

LINCOLNSHIRE

BELTON Map 08 SK93

De Vere Belton Woods Hotel NG32 2LN
☎ 01476 593200 🖹 01476 574547
e-mail: belton.woods@devere-hotels.com
web: www.devereonline.co.uk
Two challenging 18-hole courses, a nine-hole par 3 and a driving range. The Lakes Course has 13 lakes, while The Woodside has the third-longest hole in Europe at 613yds. Many leisure facilities.
The Lakes Course: 18 holes, 6831yds, Par 72, SSS 73, Course record 66.
The Woodside Course: 18 holes, 6623yds, Par 73, SSS 72, Course record 67.
Red Arrows: 9 holes, 1010yds, Par 27, SSS 27.
Club membership 600.
Visitors Booking required except Red Arrows. Dress code. **Societies** Booking required. **Green Fees** phone. **Prof** Steve Sayers **Facilities** ⊗ 🍴 🏨 ☕ 🍷 🚿 🛒 ⛳ 🛏 🚗 🏌 🏌 **Leisure** hard tennis courts, heated indoor swimming pool, squash, fishing, sauna, solarium, gymnasium. **Conf** facs Corporate Hospitality Days **Location** On A607 2m N of Grantham

Hotel ★★★★ 75% De Vere Belton Woods, BELTON ☎ 01476 593200 136 en suite

BLANKNEY Map 08 TF06

Blankney LN4 3AZ
☎ 01526 320202 🖹 01526 322521
web: www.blankneygolf.co.uk
Parkland in pleasant surroundings, with mature trees and testing greens offering a challenging test of golf. Set in the Blankney estate and 2004 was the centenary year.
18 holes, 6634yds, Par 72, SSS 73, Course record 69.
Club membership 700.
Visitors Mon-Sun. Booking required. **Societies** Booking required. **Green Fees** phone. 🚫 **Prof** Graham Bradley **Course Designer** C Sinclair **Facilities** ⊗ 🍴 🏨 ☕ 🍷 🚿 🛒 ⛳ 🏌 🚗 🏌 **Leisure** snooker. **Conf** facs Corporate Hospitality Days **Location** 10m SW on B1188

Hotel ★★★ 72% Branston Hall Hotel, Branston Park, Branston, LINCOLN ☎ 01522 793305 43 en suite 7 annexe en suite

BOSTON Map 08 TF34

Boston Cowbridge, Horncastle Rd PE22 7EL
☎ 01205 350589 🖹 01205 367526
e-mail: steveshaw@bostongc.co.uk
web: www.bostongc.co.uk
Parkland with water coming into play on a number of holes. Renowned for the quality of the greens.
18 holes, 6415yds, Par 72, SSS 71, Course record 67.
Club membership 650.
Visitors Mon, Wed-Fri. Booking required Sat, Sun & BHs. Dress code. **Societies** Booking required. **Green Fees** £30 per day/round. 🚫 **Prof** Nick Hiom **Facilities** ⊗ 🍴 🏨 ☕ 🍷 🚿 🛒 ⛳ 🚗 🏌 🏌 **Conf** Corporate Hospitality Days **Location** 2m N of Boston on B1183

Boston West Golf Centre Hubbert's Bridge PE20 3QX
☎ 01205 290670 🖹 01205 290725
e-mail: info@bostonwestgolfclub.co.uk
web: www.bostonwestgolfclub.co.uk
A well maintained maturing golf course, nestled in the Lincolnshire countryside featuring excellent greens, well positioned lakes and bunkers. Good test of golf for all levels of golfer.

18 holes, 6411yards, Par 72, SSS 71, Course record 63.
Club membership 650.
Visitors Mon-Sun & BHs. Dress code. **Societies** Booking required. **Green Fees** £17 per 18 holes, £10 per 9 holes, £20/£12 Sat, Sun & BHs. **Prof** Simon Collingwood **Course Designer** Michael Zara **Facilities** ⊗ 🍴 🏨 ☕ 🍷 🚿 🛒 ⛳ 🛏 🏌 🚗 🏌 🏌 **Leisure** 6 hole academy course. **Conf** facs Corporate Hospitality Days **Location** 2m W of Boston on A1121-B1192 x-rds

Hotel ★★★ 62% Golf Hotel, The Broadway, WOODHALL SPA ☎ 01526 353535 50 en suite

Kirton Holme Holme Rd, Kirton Holme PE20 1SY
☎ 01205 290669
web: www.kirtonhollmegolfclub.co.uk
A young parkland course designed for mid to high handicappers. It is flat but has 2500 young trees, two natural water courses plus water hazards. The 2nd is a challenging, 386yd par 4 dog-leg.
9 holes, 5778yds, Par 70, SSS 68, Course record 66.
Club membership 320.
Visitors Mon-Sun & BHs. Booking required. Dress code. **Societies** Booking required. **Green Fees** £10 per day, £6 per round, £11/£7 Sat, Sun & BHs. 🚫 **Course Designer** DW Welberry **Facilities** ⊗ 🏨 ☕ 🍷 🚿 ⛳ 🏌 **Conf** Corporate Hospitality Days **Location** 4m W of Boston off A52

BOURNE Map 08 TF02

Toft Hotel Toft PE10 0JT
☎ 01778 590616 🖷 01778 590264

18 holes, 6486yds, Par 72, SSS 71, Course record 63.
Course Designer Roger Fitton **Location** On A6121 Bourne-Stamford road
Phone for further details

Hotel ★★★ 80% The George of Stamford, 71 St Martins, STAMFORD ☎ 01780 750750 & 750700 (Res) 🖷 01780 750701 47 en suite

CLEETHORPES Map 08 TA30

Cleethorpes Kings Rd DN35 0PN
☎ 01472 816110 🖷 01472 814060
e-mail: secretary@cleethorpesgolfclub.co.uk
web: www.cleethorpesgolf club.co.uk
A mature coastal course founded in 1894. Slight undulations give variety but the flat landscape makes for easy walking. The course provides a challenge to all levels of player, especially when the wind blows.

18 holes, 6351yds, Par 70, SSS 70, Course record 65.
Club membership 650.
Visitors Mon-Sun & BHs. Dress code. **Societies** Booking required. **Green Fees** £35 per day, £25 per round, £40/£30 Sat, Sun & BHs. **Prof** Paul Davies **Course Designer** Harry Vardon **Facilities**
Location 2m SE of Cleethorpes near theme park

Hotel ★★★ 71% Kingsway Hotel, Kingsway, CLEETHORPES ☎ 01472 601122 49 en suite

Tetney Station Rd, Tetney DN36 5HY
☎ 01472 211644 🖷 01472 211644
18 holes, 6245yds, Par 71, SSS 69, Course record 65.
Course Designer JS Grant **Location** 1m off A16 Louth-Grimsby road
Phone for further details

Hotel ★★★ 71% Kingsway Hotel, Kingsway, CLEETHORPES ☎ 01472 601122 49 en suite

CROWLE Map 08 SE71

The Lincolnshire DN17 4BU
☎ 01724 711619 🖷 01724 711619
Traditional flat parkland course. Generous greens with discreet use of water and bunkers. Redeveloped greatly in the last few years offering a good test to all standards of golfer.
18 holes, 6283yds, Par 71, SSS 70.
Club membership 420.
Visitors Mon-Fri. Booking required Sat, Sun & BHs. Dress code. **Societies** Booking required. **Green Fees** £16 per round, £13 after 1pm, £22/£15 Sat, Sun & BHs. **Course Designer** Stubley, Byrne **Facilities** **Conf** Corporate Hospitality Days
Location M180 junct 2, 0.5m on Crowle road

Hotel ★★★ 66% Belmont Hotel, Horsefair Green, THORNE ☎ 01405 812320 23 en suite

ELSHAM Map 08 TA01

Elsham Barton Rd DN20 0LS
☎ 01652 680291 (sec) 🖷 01652 680308
e-mail: manager@elshamgolfclub.co.uk
web: www.elshamgolfclub.co.uk
Gently undulating, mature parkland and heathland course in a rural setting with a variety of wildlife, including many pheasants. Each hole is different and has its own challenge. Very secluded with easy walking and a reservoir to maintain irrigation.

18 holes, 6426yds, Par 71, SSS 71.
Club membership 600.
Visitors Mon-Fri except BHs. Booking required. Handicap certificate. Dress code. **Societies** Booking required. **Green Fees** £35 per 36 holes, £26 per 18 holes. **Prof** Stuart Brewer **Course Designer** Various **Facilities** **Conf** facs Corporate Hospitality Days
Location 2m NE of Brigg on B1206

Hotel ★★★ 67% Wortley House Hotel, Rowland Rd, SCUNTHORPE ☎ 01724 842223 38 en suite

If the name of the club appears in italics, details have not been confirmed for this edition of the guide

Continued

GAINSBOROUGH Map 08 SK88

Gainsborough Thonock DN21 1PZ
☎ 01427 613088 📠 01427 810172
e-mail: gainsboroughgc.co.uk
Thonock Park: 18 holes, 6266yds, Par 70, SSS 70, Course record 63.
Karsten Lakes: 18 holes, 6721yds, Par 72, SSS 72, Course record 65.
Course Designer Neil Coles **Location** 1m N off A159. Signed off A631
Phone for further details

Hotel ★★★ 65% The West Retford Hotel, 24 North Rd, RETFORD ☎ 01777 706333 & 0870 609 6162 📠 01777 709951 63 en suite

GEDNEY HILL Map 08 TF31

Gedney Hill West Drove PE12 0NT
☎ 01406 330922 📠 01406 330323
e-mail: n.venters@btinternet.com
Flat parkland course similar to a links course. Made testing by Fen winds and small greens. Also a 10-bay driving range.
18 holes, 5493yds, Par 70, SSS 66, Course record 67.
Club membership 200.
Visitors contact course for details. **Societies** welcome. **Green Fees** phone. **Prof** N Venters **Course Designer** Monkwise Ltd **Facilities** **Location** 5m SE of Spalding

Hotel ★★★ 68% Elme Hall Hotel, Elm High Rd, WISBECH ☎ 01945 475566 7 en suite

GRANTHAM Map 08 SK93

Belton Park Belton Ln, Londonthorpe Rd NG31 9SH
☎ 01476 567399 📠 01476 592078
e-mail: greatgolf@beltonpark
web: www.beltonpark.co.uk
Three nine-hole courses set in classic mature parkland of Lord Brownlow's country seat, Belton House. Gently undulating with streams, ponds, plenty of trees and beautiful scenery, including a deer park. Famous holes: 5th, 12th, 16th and 18th. Combine any of the three courses for a testing 18-hole round.

Brownlow: 18 holes, 6472yds, Par 71, SSS 71, Course record 64.
Ancaster: 18 holes, 6325yds, Par 70, SSS 70.
Belmont: 18 holes, 6075yds, Par 69, SSS 69.
Club membership 850.
Visitors Mon-Fri. Booking required Sat, Sun & BHs. Handicap certificate. Dress code. **Societies** Booking required. **Green Fees** £39 per day, £33 per round, £43/£37 Sat, Sun & BHs. Winter reduced rates. **Prof** Simon Williams **Course Designer** Williamson, Allis **Facilities** **Conf** facs Corporate Hospitality Days **Location** 1.5m NE of Grantham

Hotel ★★★ 70% Kings Hotel, North Pde, GRANTHAM ☎ 01476 590800 21 en suite

Sudbrook Moor Charity St, Carlton Scroop NG32 3AT
☎ 01400 250796
web: www.sudbrookmoor.co.uk
A testing nine-hole parkland and meadowland course in a picturesque valley setting with easy walking.
9 holes, 4811yds, Par 66, SSS 64, Course record 64.
Club membership 600.
Visitors contact club for details. Dress code. **Green Fees** £7-£9 per day, £9-£12 Sat, Sun & BHs. **Prof** Tim Hutton **Course Designer** Tim Hutton **Facilities** **Location** 6m NE of Grantham on A607

Hotel ★★★ 70% Kings Hotel, North Pde, GRANTHAM ☎ 01476 590800 21 en suite

GRIMSBY Map 08 TA21

Grimsby Littlecoates Rd DN34 4LU
☎ 01472 342630 📠 01472 342630
e-mail: secretary@grimsby.fsnet.co.uk
Mature undulating parkland course, not particularly long, but demanding and a good test of golf. The par 3s are all feature holes, not a common feature on most courses. The summer greens are fast and quite small.
18 holes, 6057yds, Par 70, SSS 69, Course record 65.
Club membership 730.
Visitors Booking required. **Societies** Mon & Fri. Booking required with secretary. **Green Fees** phone. **Prof** Richard Smith **Course Designer** Colt **Facilities** **Conf** Corporate Hospitality Days **Location** 1m from A180. 1m from A46

Waltham Windmill Cheapside, Waltham DN37 0HT
☎ 01472 824109 📠 01472 828391
web: www.walthamgolf.co.uk
Nestling in 125 acres of Lincolnshire countryside, the natural springs have been used to great effect giving individuality and challenge to every shot. The course has a mixture of long par 5s and water comes into play on nine holes.
18 holes, 6442yds, Par 71, SSS 71, Course record 66.
Club membership 680.
Visitors Mon-Fri except BHs. Dress code. **Societies** Booking required. **Green Fees** £25 per round, £35 Sat & Sun. Winter reduced rates. **Prof** Steven Bennett **Course Designer** J Payne **Facilities** **Conf** facs Corporate Hospitality Days **Location** 1m off A16

Hotel ★★★ 66% Beeches Hotel, 42 Waltham Rd, Scartho GRIMSBY ☎ 01472 278830 18 en suite

HORNCASTLE Map 08 TF26

Horncastle West Ashby LN9 5PP
☎ 01507 526800
web: www.horncastlegolfclub.com
Parkland course with many water hazards and bunkers; very challenging. There is a 25-bay floodlit driving range.

Continued

18 holes, 5717yds, Par 70, SSS 68, Course record 71.
Club membership 200.
Visitors Mon-Sun & BHs. Booking required. Dress code. **Societies** welcome. **Green Fees** £20 per day, £15 per round. **Prof** EC Wright **Course Designer** EC Wright **Facilities** **Leisure** fishing. **Conf** facs Corporate Hospitality Days **Location** Off A153 at West Ashby

Hotel ★★★ 67% Admiral Rodney Hotel, North St, HORNCASTLE ☎ 01507 523131 31 en suite

See advertisement on page 178

IMMINGHAM Map 08 TA11

Immingham St Andrews Ln, off Church Ln DN40 2EU
☎ 01469 575298 🖷 01469 577636
e-mail: admin@immgc.force9.co.uk
web: www.immgc.com

An excellent, flat parkland course. The natural exaggerated undulations on the fairways form one of the best local examples of medieval strip farming methods. They are natural to the course, particularly on the front nine and require concentration on fairway play. The Lincolnshire drainage channel, which meanders through the course and comes into play on over half of the holes, can catch the unwary golfer.
18 holes, 6215yds, Par 71, SSS 70, Course record 69.
Club membership 700.
Visitors Booking required. **Societies** Booking required. **Green Fees** phone. **Prof** Nick Harding **Course Designer** Hawtree & Son **Facilities** **Conf** facs Corporate Hospitality Days **Location** 7m NW of Grimsby

LACEBY Map 08 TA20

Manor Barton St, Laceby Manor DN37 7LD
☎ 01472 873468 (shop) 🖷 01472 276706
e-mail: judith@manorgolfclub.wanadoo.co.uk
web: www.manorgolf.com

The first seven holes play as a parkland course lined with mature trees. The second nine are more open fairways with water courses running alongside and through the holes. The 16th hole green is surrounded by water. Holes 17 and 18 are tree-lined like the first seven holes.
18 holes, 6354yds, Par 71, SSS 70.
Club membership 550.
Visitors Mon-Sun & BHs. Booking required. **Societies** Booking required. **Green Fees** £20 per round, £23 Sat, Sun & BHs. **Prof** Neil Laybourne **Facilities** **Leisure** fishing. **Conf** facs Corporate Hospitality Days **Location** A18 Laceby-Louth

LINCOLN Map 08 SK97

Canwick Park Canwick Park, Washingborough Rd LN4 1EF
☎ 01522 542912 🖷 01522 526997
e-mail: manager@canwickpark.go-plus.net
web: www.canwickpark.co.uk

Parkland with fine views of Lincoln Cathedral. The 5th and 13th holes are testing par 3s both nearly 200yds in length.
18 holes, 6160yds, Par 70, SSS 69, Course record 65.
Club membership 650.
Visitors Mon-Sun & BHs. Dress code. **Societies** Booking required. **Green Fees** £30 per day, £12 per round. **Prof** S Williamson **Course Designer** Hawtree & Sons **Facilities** **Conf** Corporate Hospitality Days **Location** 1m E of Lincoln

Hotel ★★★ 68% The Lincoln Hotel, Eastgate, LINCOLN ☎ 01522 520348 72 en suite

Carholme Carholme Rd LN1 1SE
☎ 01522 523725 🖷 01522 533733
e-mail: info@carholme-golf-club.co.uk
web: www.carholme-golf-club.co.uk

Parkland where prevailing west winds can add interest. Good views. First hole out of bounds left and right of fairway, pond in front of bunkered green at 5th, lateral water hazards across several fairways.
18 holes, 6215yds, Par 71, SSS 70, Course record 67.
Club membership 500.
Visitors Mon-Sun & BHs. Booking required. Dress code. **Societies** Booking required. **Green Fees** £22 per day, £18 per round. **Course Designer** Willie Park Jnr **Facilities** **Conf** Corporate Hospitality Days **Location** 1m W of city centre on A57

Hotel ★★★ 66% The White Hart, Bailgate, LINCOLN ☎ 01522 526222 48 en suite

LOUTH Map 08 TF38

Kenwick Park Kenwick Park LN11 8NY
☎ 01507 605134 🖷 01507 606556
e-mail: golfatkenwick@nascr.net
web: www.louthnet.com

Situated on the edge of the Lincolnshire Wolds with panoramic views. Course features a mixture of parkland and woodland holes, complemented by a network of lakes.
18 holes, 6782yds, Par 72, SSS 73, Course record 71.
Club membership 520.
Visitors Booking required. **Societies** Booking required. **Green Fees** phone. **Prof** Eric Sharp **Course Designer** Patrick Tallack **Facilities** by arrangement **Conf** Corporate Hospitality Days **Location** 2m S of Louth on A157 (Louth bypass)

Hotel ★★★ 70% Best Western Kenwick Park Hotel, Kenwick Park Estate, LOUTH ☎ 01507 608806 29 en suite 5 annexe en suite

Louth Crowtree Ln LN11 9LJ
☎ 01507 603681 🖹 01507 608501
e-mail: enquiries@louthgolfclub.com
web: www.louthgolfclub.com
Undulating parkland, fine views in an Area of Outstanding Natural Beauty. No winter greens, offering quality golf throughout the year.
18 holes, 6430yds, Par 72, SSS 71, Course record 66. Club membership 700.
Visitors Mon-Fri, Sun & BHs. Booking required. Dress code. **Societies** Booking required. **Green Fees** £30 per day, £24 per round, £36/£30 Sun & BHs. **Prof** A Blundell **Facilities** **Leisure** squash. **Conf** facs Corporate Hospitality Days **Location** W of Louth between A157

Hotel ★★★ 68% Beaumont Hotel, 66 Victoria Rd, LOUTH ☎ 01507 605005 16 en suite

MARKET RASEN Map 08 TF18

Market Rasen & District Legsby Rd LN8 3DZ
☎ 01673 842319
Picturesque, well-wooded heathland course, easy walking, breezy with becks forming natural hazards. Good views of Lincolnshire Wolds.

18 holes, 6239yds, Par 71, SSS 70, Course record 65. Club membership 600.
Visitors Mon-Fri. Booking required. **Societies** Booking required. **Green Fees** phone. **Prof** AM Chester **Course Designer** Hawtree Ltd **Facilities** **Location** 1m E, A46 onto A631

Hotel ★★★ 68% Beaumont Hotel, 66 Victoria Rd, LOUTH ☎ 01507 605005 16 en suite

Market Rasen Race Course (Golf Course)
Legsby Rd LN8 3EA
☎ 01673 843434 🖹 01673 844532
e-mail: marketrasen@rht.net
web: www.marketrasenraces.co.uk
This public course is set within the bounds of Market Rasen race course - the entire racing area is out of bounds. The longest hole is the 4th at 454yds with the race course providing a hazard over the whole length of the drive.
9 holes, 2532yds, Par 32.
Visitors Mon-Sun & BHs. **Societies** welcome. **Green Fees** £6 per 9 holes, £7 Sat, Sun & BHs. **Course Designer** Edward Stenton **Facilities** **Leisure** caravan site. **Conf** facs **Location** 1m E of Market Rasen

Hotel ★★★ 68% Beaumont Hotel, 66 Victoria Rd, LOUTH ☎ 01507 605005 16 en suite

NORMANBY Map 08 SE81

Normanby Hall Normanby Park DN15 9HU
☎ 01724 720226 (pro shop)
18 holes, 6561yds, Par 72, SSS 71, Course record 66.
Course Designer Hawtree & Son **Location** 3m N of Scunthorpe on B1130 next to Normanby Hall
Phone for further details

Hotel ★★★ 67% Wortley House Hotel, Rowland Rd, SCUNTHORPE ☎ 01724 842223 38 en suite

SCUNTHORPE Map 08 SE81

Ashby Decoy Burringham Rd DN17 2AB
☎ 01724 866561 🖹 01724 271708
e-mail: adgc@eurotelbroadband.com
web: www.ashbydecoy.co.uk
Pleasant, flat parkland course to satisfy all tastes, yet test the experienced golfer.
18 holes, 6281yds, Par 71, SSS 71, Course record 66. Club membership 650.
Visitors Mon, Wed-Fri except BHs, Tue after 2pm. Booking required. Handicap certificate. Dress code. **Societies** Booking required. **Green Fees** £27 per day, £22 per round. **Prof** A Miller **Facilities** **Conf** facs Corporate Hospitality Days **Location** 2.5m SW on B1450 near Asda store

Hotel ★★★ 67% Wortley House Hotel, Rowland Rd, SCUNTHORPE ☎ 01724 842223 38 en suite

Forest Pines - Briggate Lodge Inn Hotel
Ermine St, Broughton DN20 0AQ
☎ 01652 650770 🖹 01652 650495
e-mail: enquiries@forestpines.co.uk
web: www.forestpines.co.uk
Set in 185 acres of mature parkland and open heathland and constructed in a similar design to that of Wentworth or Sunningdale, Forest Pines offers three challenging nine-hole courses - Forest, Pines and Beeches. Any combination can be played. Facilities include a 17-bay driving range and a spacious clubhouse.

Forest Course: 9 holes, 3291yds, Par 36, SSS 36.
Pines Course: 9 holes, 3568yds, Par 37, SSS 37.
Beeches: 9 holes, 3291yds, Par 36, SSS 36.
Club membership 330.
Visitors Dress code. **Societies** Booking required. **Green Fees** phone. **Prof** David Edwards **Course Designer** John Morgan **Facilities** **Leisure** heated indoor swimming pool, sauna, solarium, gymnasium. **Conf** facs Corporate Hospitality Days **Location** M180 junct 4, 200yds

Continued

Hotel ★★★★ 75% Forest Pines Hotel, Ermine St, Broughton, SCUNTHORPE ☎ 01652 650770 114 en suite

Grange Park Butterwick Rd, Messingham DN17 3PP
☎ 01724 762945 🖷 01724 762945
e-mail: info@grangepark.com
web: www.grangepark.com
Parkland with challenging water hazards and impressive stone raised teeing areas.
18 holes, 6146yds, Par 70, SSS 69, Course record 64. Club membership 320.
Visitors Mon-Sun & BHs. Dress code. **Societies** Booking required. **Green Fees** £16 per 18 holes, £18 Sat, Sun & BHs. **Prof** Jonathan Drury **Course Designer** R Price **Facilities** **Leisure** hard tennis courts, fishing, par 3 course. **Conf** facs Corporate Hospitality Days **Location** 1.5m W of Messingham towards East Butterwick

Hotel ★★★ 67% Wortley House Hotel, Rowland Rd, SCUNTHORPE ☎ 01724 842223 38 en suite

Holme Hall Holme Ln, Bottesford DN16 3RF
☎ 01724 862078 🖷 01724 862081
e-mail: secretary@holmehallgolf.co.uk
web: www.holmehallgolf.co.uk
Natural heathland course with gorse and heather and sandy subsoil. Easy walking. Tight driving holes and good greens.
18 holes, 6404yds, Par 71, SSS 71, Course record 65. Club membership 650.
Visitors Mon-Fri except BHs. Booking required. Handicap certificate. Dress code. **Societies** Booking required. **Green Fees** £35 per day, £25 per round. **Prof** Richard McKiernan **Facilities** **Conf** Corporate Hospitality Days **Location** M180 junct 4, 4m SE of Scunthorpe

Hotel ★★★ 67% Wortley House Hotel, Rowland Rd, SCUNTHORPE ☎ 01724 842223 38 en suite

SKEGNESS Map 09 TF56

North Shore Hotel & Golf Club
North Shore Rd PE25 1DN
☎ 01754 763298 🖷 01754 761902
e-mail: golf@north-shore.co.uk
web: www.north-shore.co.uk
Part links, part parkland, with two of the nine holes situated next to the sea. A challenging course which starts and finishes outside the hotel bar.

18 holes, 6200yds, Par 71, SSS 71, Course record 68. Club membership 400.
Visitors Mon-Sun & BHs. Booking required. Handicap certificate. Dress code. **Societies** Booking required. **Green Fees** £38 per day, £28 per round, £48/£35 Sat & Sun. **Prof** J Cornelius **Course Designer** James Braid **Facilities** **Leisure** snooker. **Conf** facs Corporate Hospitality Days **Location** 1m N of town centre off A52, opp North Shore Holiday Centre

Hotel ★★ 67% North Shore Hotel & Golf Course, North Shore Rd, SKEGNESS ☎ 01754 763298 33 en suite 3 annexe en suite

Seacroft Drummond Rd, Seacroft PE25 3AU
☎ 01754 763020 🖷 01754 763020
e-mail: enquiries@seacroft-golfclub.co.uk
web: www.seacroft-golfclub.co.uk
A championship seaside links traditionally laid out with tight undulations and hogsback fairways. Adjacent to Gibraltar Point Nature Reserve, overlooking the Wash.

18 holes, 6492yds, Par 71, SSS 71, Course record 65. Club membership 590.
Visitors Mon-Sun & BHs. Booking required. Handicap certificate. Dress code. **Societies** Booking required. **Green Fees** phone. **Prof** Robin Lawie **Course Designer** Tom Dunn, Willie Fernie **Facilities** **Conf** Corporate Hospitality Days **Location** S of town centre towards Gibralter Point Nature Reserve

Hotel ★★★ Crown Hotel, Drummond Rd, SKEGNESS ☎ 01754 610760 29 en suite

SLEAFORD Map 08 TF04

Sleaford Willoughby Rd, Greylees NG34 8PL
☎ 01529 488273 🖷 01529 488644
e-mail: sleafordgolfclub@btinternet.com
web: www.sleafordgolfclub.co.uk
Inland links-type course, moderately wooded and fairly flat with sandy well-draining soil, which supports a variety of trees and shrubs. While the lowest index hole is the awkward dog-leg 4th, the 2nd hole requires two mighty hits to be reached. The feature hole is the 12th, where the green is totally protected by a copse of pine trees. A stream running through the course provides water hazards on several holes.
18 holes, 6503yds, Par 72, SSS 71, Course record 64. Club membership 630.
Visitors Mon-Fri except BHs. Booking required. Handicap certificate. Dress code. **Societies** Booking required. **Green Fees** £32 per day, £25 per round, £36 Sat & Sun. **Prof** James Wilson **Course Designer** T Williamson **Facilities** **Conf** facs Corporate Hospitality Days **Location** 2m W of Sleaford off A153

Hotel ★★★ 70% Kings Hotel, North Pde, GRANTHAM ☎ 01476 590800 21 en suite

Continued

SOUTH KYME Map 08 TF14

South Kyme Skinners Ln LN4 4AT
☎ 01526 861113 🖹 01526 861113
e-mail: southkymegc@hotmail.com
web: www.skgc.co.uk
A challenging fenland course in a tranquil location, described as an inland links with water hazards, trees and fairway hazards.
18 holes, 6482yds, Par 72, SSS 71, Course record 67.
Club membership 470.
Visitors Mon-Sun & BHs. Dress code. **Societies** Booking required. **Green Fees** £20 per round, £10 per 9 holes, £24/£12 Sat, Sun & BHs. **Prof** Peter Chamberlain **Facilities** **Leisure** 6 hole short course. **Conf** Corporate Hospitality Days **Location** Off B1395 into South Kyme

Hotel Travelodge Sleaford, Holdingham, SLEAFORD ☎ 08700 850 950 40 en suite

SPALDING Map 08 TF22

Spalding Surfleet PE11 4EA
☎ 01775 680386 (office) & 680474 (pro) 🖹 01775 680988
e-mail: spaldinggc@btconnect.com
A pretty, well-laid out course in a fenland area. The River Glen runs beside the 1st, 2nd and 4th holes, and ponds and lakes are very much in play on the 9th, 10th and 11th holes. Challenging holes include the river dominated 2nd and the 17th where a good drive is needed for the right hand side of the fairway to leave a challenging second shot to a well protected green, bunkered in front and right with out of bounds on the left.

18 holes, 6478yds, Par 72, SSS 71, Course record 62.
Club membership 750.
Visitors Mon-Sun & BHs. Booking required. Handicap certificate. Dress code. **Societies** Booking required. **Green Fees** £30 per day, £25 per round, £30 per round Sat, Sun & BHs. **Prof** John Spencer, Chris Huggins **Course Designer** Price, Spencer, Ward **Facilities** **Conf** Corporate Hospitality Days **Location** 4m N of Spalding next to A16

Hotel ★★ 70% Cley Hall Hotel, 22 High St, SPALDING ☎ 01775 725157 4 en suite 11 annexe en suite

STAMFORD Map 04 TF00

Burghley Park St Martins PE9 3JX
☎ 01780 753789 🖹 01780 753789
e-mail: burghley.golf@lineone.net
web: www.burghleygolf.org.uk
A compact parkland layout. Tree planting, the introduction of sand and water hazards and the maintenance of fair but punishing rough, have made the course a real challenge. Free draining fairways and greens give first class playing all year.
18 holes, 6236yds, Par 70, SSS 70, Course record 65.
Club membership 775.
Visitors Mon-Fri. Booking required Mon & Fri. Handicap certificate. Dress code. **Societies** Booking required. **Green Fees** £30 per day, £18 twilight (noon winter, 5pm summer). **Prof** Glenn Davies **Facilities** **Conf** Corporate Hospitality Days **Location** 1m S of town on B1081

Hotel ★★★ 80% The George of Stamford, 71 St Martins, STAMFORD ☎ 01780 750750 & 750700 (Res) 🖹 01780 750701 47 en suite

STOKE ROCHFORD Map 08 SK92

Stoke Rochford NG33 5EW
☎ 01476 530275 🖹 01476 530237
web: stokerochfordgolfclub.co.uk
Parkland course designed by C Turner and extended in 1936 to 18 holes by Major Hotchkin.
18 holes, 6252yds, Par 70, SSS 70, Course record 65.
Club membership 525.
Visitors Mon, Tue & Fri except BHs. Booking required. Handicap certificate. Dress code. **Societies** Booking required. **Green Fees** phone. **Prof** Angus Dow **Course Designer** Major Hotchkin **Facilities** **Location** 5m S of Grantham off A1 southbound signed Stoke Rochford, onto A1 northbound, enter club via BP service station

Hotel ★★★ 70% Kings Hotel, North Pde, GRANTHAM ☎ 01476 590800 21 en suite

SUTTON BRIDGE Map 09 TF42

Sutton Bridge New Rd PE12 9RQ
☎ 01406 350323
web: www.club-noticeboard.co.uk/suttonbridge
Established in 1914, the nine holes are played along, over and in a Victorian dock basin which was abandoned as a dock in 1881. The original walls of the dock are still intact and help to make the course one of the most interesting courses in the region. The greens are recognised as among the best in Lincolnshire.
9 holes, 5724yds, Par 70, SSS 68, Course record 64.
Club membership 350.
Visitors Mon-Fri. Dress code. **Societies** Booking required. **Green Fees** Apr-Sep £20 per day, Oct-Mar £15. **Prof** Antony Lowther **Facilities** **Conf** Corporate Hospitality Days **Location** E of village off A17

Hotel Travelodge Kings Lynn Long Sutton, Wisbech Rd, LONG SUTTON ☎ 08700 850 950 40 en suite

Championship Course

Lincolnshire The National Golf Centre

Woodhall Spa Map 08 TF16

The Championship Course at Woodhall Spa, now known as the Hotchkin, is arguably the best inland course in Britain. This classic course has cavernous bunkers and heather-lined fairways. Golf has been played here for over a century and the Hotchkin has hosted most of the top national and international amateur events. The English Golf Union acquired Woodhall Spa in 1995 to create a centre of excellence. A second course, the Bracken, has been built, along with extensive practice facilities including one of Europe's finest short-game practice areas. The English Golf Union actively encourages visits to the National Golf Centre throughout the year, to experience the facilities and to enjoy the unique ambience.

The Broadway LN10 6PU
☎ 01526 352511 🖹 01526 351817
e-mail: booking@englishgolfunion.org
web: www.woodhallspagolf.com

The Hotchkin: 18 holes, 7080yds, Par 73, SSS 75, Course record 66.
The Bracken: 18 holes, 6735yds, Par 72, SSS 74, Course record 68.
Club membership 520.

Visitors Mon-Sun & BHs. Booking required. Handicap certificate. Dress code. **Societies** Booking required. **Green Fees** Hotchkin £100 per day, £65 per round. Bracken £75 per day, £50 round. £90 per day playing both courses. **Prof** A Hare **Course Designer** Col SV Hotchkin **Facilities** ⊗ ⅲ ⊾ ☕ ♀ ⛼ 🏠 ⛟ ⚲ ⊦ **Leisure** pitch & putt 9 hole course. **Conf** facs Corporate Hospitality Days **Location** NE of village off B1191

SUTTON ON SEA Map 09 TF58

Sandilands Roman Bank LN12 2RJ
☎ 01507 441432 📠 01507 441617
Well-manicured links course next to the sea. Renowned for the standard of its greens.
18 holes, 6173yds, Par 70, SSS 68, Course record 64. Club membership 300.
Visitors Mon-Sun & BHs. Booking required. Dress code. **Societies** welcome. **Green Fees** £25 per day, £18 per round, £30/£20 Sat & Sun. Winter reduced rates. **Prof** Simon Sherratt **Facilities** **Leisure** hard and grass tennis courts, gymnasium. **Conf** facs **Location** 1.5m S off A52

Hotel ★★★ 69% The Grange & Links Hotel, Sea Ln, Sandilands, SUTTON-ON-SEA ☎ 01507 441334
23 en suite

TORKSEY Map 08 SK87

Lincoln LN1 2EG
☎ 01427 718721 📠 01427 718721
e-mail: info@lincolngc.co.uk
web: www.lincolngc.co.uk
A mature championship standard course offering a variety of holes, links style to parkland.

18 holes, 6438yds, Par 71, SSS 71, Course record 65. Club membership 750.
Visitors Mon-Sun & BHs. Booking required. Handicap certificate. Dress code. **Societies** Booking required **Green Fees** £40 per day, £32 per round, £50/£40 Sat, Sun & BHs. **Prof** Ashley Carter **Course Designer** JH Taylor **Facilities** **Leisure** 3 hole practice course. **Conf** facs Corporate Hospitality Days **Location** NE of village off A156

Hotel ★★★ 66% The White Hart, Bailgate, LINCOLN
☎ 01522 526222 48 en suite

Millfield Laughterton LN1 2LB
☎ 01427 718255 📠 01427 718473
e-mail: secretary@millfieldgolfclub.fsnet.co.uk
The Millfield: 18 holes, 6004yds, Par 72, SSS 69, Course record 68.
The Grenville Green: 18 holes, 4485yds, Par 65.
Course Designer CW Watson **Location** On A1133 1m N of A57
Phone for further details

Hotel ★★★ 66% The White Hart, Bailgate, LINCOLN
☎ 01522 526222 48 en suite

WOODHALL SPA Map 08 TF16

The National Golf Centre see page 177

Hotel ★★★ 68% Petwood Hotel, Stixwould Rd, WOODHALL SPA ☎ 01526 352411 56 en suite

Hotel ★★★ 62% Golf Hotel, The Broadway, WOODHALL SPA ☎ 01526 353535 📠 01526 353096 50 en suite

Hotel ★★ 65% The Woodhall Spa Hotel, The Broadway, WOODHALL SPA ☎ 01526 353231 📠 01526 352797 25 en suite

See advertisement on page 178

WOODTHORPE Map 09 TF48

Woodthorpe Hall LN13 0DD
☎ 01507 450000 📠 01507 450000
e-mail: secretary@woodthorpehallgolfclub.fsnet.co.uk
web: www.woodthorpehall.co.uk
18 holes, 5140yds, Par 67, SSS 65, Course record 68.
Location 3m N of Alford on B1373
Phone for further details

Hotel ★★★ 69% The Grange & Links Hotel, Sea Ln, Sandilands, SUTTON-ON-SEA ☎ 01507 441334 23 en suite

If the name of the club appears in italics, details have not been confirmed for this edition of the guide

LONDON

Courses that have London postcodes (W1, SW1 etc) are listed here in postcode order commencing East then North, South and West. Courses outside the London postal area, but within Greater London are listed under **Greater London**.

E4 CHINGFORD

Royal Epping Forest Forest Approach, Chingford E4 7AZ
☎ 020 8529 2195 📠 020 8559 4664
e-mail: office@refgc.co.uk
web: www.refgc.co.uk
Woodland course. Red garments must be worn.
18 holes, 6281yds, Par 71, SSS 70, Course record 64. Club membership 400.
Visitors Mon-Sun & BHs. Booking required. Dress code. **Societies** Booking required. **Green Fees** £15, £19 Sat & Sun. **Prof** A Traynor **Course Designer** JG Gibson **Facilities** ⊗ by arrangement by arrangement by arrangement **Conf** facs **Location** 300yds E of Chingford station on Chingford Plain

West Essex Bury Rd, Sewardstonebury, Chingford E4 7QL
☎ 020 8529 7558 📠 020 8524 7870
e-mail: sec@westessexgolfclub.co.uk
web: www.westessexgolfclub.co.uk
Testing parkland course within Epping Forest with spectacular views over Essex and Middlesex. Created by James Braid in 1900 and designed to make full use of the landscape's natural attributes. The front nine is the shorter of the two and provides a test of accuracy with tree-lined fairways that meander through the undulating countryside. The back nine is equally challenging although slightly longer and requiring more long iron play.
18 holes, 6289yds, Par 71, SSS 70, Course record 63. Club membership 710.
Visitors Mon-Fri. Booking required. Handicap certificate. Dress code. **Societies** Booking required. **Green Fees** £45. **Prof** Robert Joyce **Course Designer** James Braid **Facilities** ⊗ **Conf** Corporate Hospitality Days **Location** M25 junct 26, 1.5m N of Chingford station

Hotel ★★★★ 65% Menzies Prince Regent, Manor Rd, WOODFORD BRIDGE ☎ 020 8505 9966 61 en suite

E11 LEYTONSTONE & WANSTEAD

Wanstead Overton Dr, Wanstead E11 2LW
☎ 020 8989 3938 📠 020 8532 9138
e-mail: wgclub@aol.com
web: www.wansteadgolf.org
Flat, picturesque parkland with many trees and shrubs and easy walking. The par 3 16th involves driving across a lake.
18 holes, 6015yds, Par 69, SSS 69, Course record 62. Club membership 600.
Visitors Mon-Fri except BHs. Booking required. Handicap certificate. Dress code. **Societies** Booking required. **Green Fees** £40 per day. **Prof** David Hawkins **Course Designer** James Braid **Facilities** **Leisure** fishing. **Conf** facs Corporate Hospitality Days **Location** Off A12 in Wanstead

N2 East Finchley

Hampstead Winnington Rd N2 0TU
☎ 020 8455 0203 🖹 020 8731 6194
e-mail: golf@hgc.uk.com
Undulating parkland with many mature trees.
9 holes, 5822yds, Par 68, SSS 68, Course record 64.
Club membership 526.
Visitors Mon, Wed-Fri except BHs. Handicap certificate. Dress code. **Green Fees** £30 per 18 holes. **Prof** Peter Brown **Course Designer** Tom Dunn **Facilities** **Location** Off Hampstead Ln

Guest House ♦♦♦♦ Langorf Hotel Apartments, 20 Frognal, Hampstead, LONDON ☎ 020 7794 4483 31 en suite

N6 Highgate

Highgate Denewood Rd N6 4AH
☎ 020 8340 3745 🖹 020 8348 9152
e-mail: nigel@highgategc.co.uk
web: www.highgategc.co.uk
Parkland with fine views over London. The nearest 18-hole course north of the river from Marble Arch. Many interesting holes with a premium on accuracy. The 15th and 16th holes are very demanding par 4s.
18 holes, 5985yds, Par 69, SSS 69, Course record 66.
Club membership 700.
Visitors Mon, Tue, Thu, Fri except BHs. **Societies** Booking required. **Green Fees** phone. **Prof** Robin Turner **Course Designer** Cuthbert Butchart **Facilities** **Conf** facs Corporate Hospitality Days **Location** Off B519 Hampstead Ln

Hotel ★★★★ 73% London Marriott Hotel Regents Park, 128 King Henry's Rd, LONDON ☎ 0870 400 7240 303 en suite

N9 Lower Edmonton

Lee Valley Leisure Lee Valley Leisure Complex, Meridian Way, Edmonton N9 0AS
☎ 020 8803 3611 🖹 020 8884 4975
e-mail: rgarvey@leevalleypark.org.uk
Testing parkland course with a large lake and the river Lea providing natural hazards. Good quality greens all year round.
18 holes, 5204yds, Par 67, SSS 65, Course record 66.
Club membership 200.
Visitors Mon-Fri. Booking required Sat, Sun & BHs. Dress code. **Societies** Booking required. **Green Fees** £13 per 18 holes, £16.50 Sat, Sun & BHs. **Prof** R Gerken **Course Designer** John Jacobs **Facilities**

N14 Southgate

Trent Park Bramley Rd, Oakwood N14 4XS
☎ 020 8367 4653 🖹 0208 366 4581
e-mail: trentpark@americangolf.uk.com
web: americangolf.com
18 holes, 6381yds, Par 70, SSS 69, Course record 64.
Course Designer D McGibbon **Location** Opp Oakwood tube station
Phone for further details

Hotel ★★★★ 73% West Lodge Park Hotel, Cockfosters Rd, HADLEY WOOD ☎ 020 8216 3900 46 en suite 13 annexe en suite

N20 Whetstone

North Middlesex The Manor House, Friern Barnet Ln, Whetstone N20 0NL
☎ 020 8445 1604 & 020 8445 3060 🖹 020 8445 5023
e-mail: office@northmiddlesexgc.co.uk
web: www.northmiddlesexgc.co.uk
18 holes, 5594yds, Par 69, SSS 67, Course record 64.
Course Designer Willie Park Jnr **Location** M25 junct 23, 5m S
Phone for further details

Hotel ★★★ 69% Corus hotel Elstree, Barnet Ln, ELSTREE ☎ 0870 609 6151 47 en suite

South Herts Links Dr, Totteridge N20 8QU
☎ 020 8445 2035 🖹 020 8445 7569
e-mail: secretary@southhertsgolfclub.co.uk
web: www.southhertsgolfclub.co.uk
An open undulating parkland course perhaps most famous for the fact that two of the greatest of all British professionals, Harry Vardon and Dai Rees CBE, were professionals at the club. The course is testing, over rolling fairways, especially in the prevailing south-west wind.
18 holes, 6432yds, Par 72, SSS 71, Course record 63.
Club membership 850.
Visitors Mon-Fri. Booking required. Handicap certificate. Dress code. **Societies** Booking required. **Green Fees** £55 per day, £45 per round. **Prof** Bobby Mitchell **Course Designer** Harry Vardon **Facilities** by arrangement **Conf** Corporate Hospitality Days **Location** 2m E of A1 at Apex Corner

Hotel Innkeeper's Lodge Southgate, 22 The Green, Southgate, LONDON ☎ 020 8447 8022 19 en suite

N21 Winchmore Hill

Bush Hill Park Bush Hill, Winchmore Hill N21 2BU
☎ 020 8360 5738 🖹 020 8360 5583
web: www.bushhillparkgolfclub.co.uk
Pleasant parkland. The holes set a challenge due to the vast array of mature trees, which make it an enjoyable course to play. The course offers all players unlimited opportunities to play a round of golf with a real sense of achievement. Natural obstacles include a large pond and an avenue of trees to thread your drive through.
18 holes, 5809yds, Par 70, SSS 68.
Club membership 700.
Visitors Mon-Fri except BHs. Booking required. Handicap certificate. Dress code. **Societies** Booking required. **Green Fees** £28.50 per day. **Prof** Lee Fickling **Course Designer** Braid **Facilities** **Conf** Corporate Hospitality Days **Location** 1m S of Enfield off A105

Hotel ★★★ 75% Royal Chace Hotel, The Ridgeway, ENFIELD ☎ 020 8884 8181 92 en suite

N22 Wood Green

Muswell Hill Rhodes Av, Wood Green N22 7UT
☎ 020 8888 1764 🖹 020 8889 9380
e-mail: mhgcclubsecretary@btconnect.com
web: www.muswellhillgolf.org.uk
Undulating parkland course with a brook running through the centre, set in 87 acres.

Continued

18 holes, 6438yds, Par 71, SSS 71, Course record 65.
Club membership 560.
Visitors Mon-Sun except BHs. Booking required Fri & Sat. Dress code. **Societies** Booking required. **Green Fees** £30 per round, £35 Sat & Sun. **Prof** David Wilton **Course Designer** Braid, Wilson **Facilities** **Conf** facs Corporate Hospitality Days **Location** Off N Circular Rd near Bounds Green

Hotel ★★★ 66% Days Hotel London North, Welcome Break Service Area, LONDON ☎ 0208 906 7000 200 en suite

NW4 HENDON Map 04 TQ28

The Metro Golf Centre Barnet Copthall Sports Centre, Gt North Way NW4 1PS
☎ 020 8202 1202 020 8203 1203
e-mail: golf@metrogolf.btinternet.com
web: www.metro-golf.co.uk
9 holes, 898yds, Par 27, SSS 27, Course record 24.
Course Designer Cousells **Location** M1 junct 2, off A41/A1, in Barnet Copthall sports complex
Phone for further details

Hotel ★★★★ 73% London Marriott Hotel Regents Park, 128 King Henry's Rd, LONDON ☎ 0870 400 7240 303 en suite

NW7 MILL HILL

Finchley Nether Court, Frith Ln, Mill Hill NW7 1PU
☎ 020 8346 2436 020 8343 4205
e-mail: secretary@finchleygolfclub.co.uk
web: www.finchleygolfclub.co.uk
Compact course with rolling parkland. Tree-lined fairways and heavily contoured greens.

18 holes, 6411yds, Par 72, SSS 71.
Club membership 500.
Visitors Mon-Sun & BHs. Booking required. Handicap certificate. Dress code. **Societies** Booking required. **Green Fees** £40 per day, £30 per 18 holes, £50/£40 Sat, Sun & BHs. **Prof** David Brown **Course Designer** James Braid **Facilities** by arrangement **Conf** facs Corporate Hospitality Days **Location** Near Mill Hill East Tube Station

Hotel ★★★ 69% Corus hotel Elstree, Barnet Ln, ELSTREE ☎ 0870 609 6151 47 en suite

Hendon Ashley Walk, Devonshire Rd, Mill Hill NW7 1DG
☎ 020 8346 6023 020 8343 1974
e-mail: hendongolfclub@globalnet.co.uk
web: www.hendongolfclub.co.uk
Easy walking parkland course with a good variety of trees, and providing testing golf.
18 holes, 6289yds, Par 70, SSS 70, Course record 63.
Club membership 560.
Visitors Mon-Sun & BHs. Booking required. Dress code. **Societies** Booking required. **Green Fees** Summer £35, £40 per round Sat & Sun. Winter £25/£33. **Prof** Matt Deal **Course Designer** HS Colt **Facilities** **Conf** facs Corporate Hospitality Days **Location** M1 junct 2 southbound

Hotel ★★★ 69% Corus hotel Elstree, Barnet Ln, ELSTREE ☎ 0870 609 6151 47 en suite

Mill Hill 100 Barnet Way, Mill Hill NW7 3AL
☎ 020 8959 2339 020 8906 0731
e-mail: haslehurstd@aol.com
Parkland with tree and shrub-lined fairways. Water features strongly on holes 2, 9, 10 and 17.

18 holes, 6247yds, Par 70, SSS 70, Course record 68.
Club membership 550.
Visitors Booking required. **Societies** Booking required. **Green Fees** phone. **Prof** David Beal **Course Designer** J Abercromby, H Colt **Facilities** **Leisure** snooker. **Conf** facs Corporate Hospitality Days **Location** On A1 southbound

Hotel ★★★ 69% Corus hotel Elstree, Barnet Ln, ELSTREE ☎ 0870 609 6151 47 en suite

SE9 ELTHAM

Eltham Warren Bexley Rd, Eltham SE9 2PE
☎ 020 8850 4477
e-mail: secretary@elthamwarren.idps.co.uk
web: www.elthamwarrengolfclub.co.uk
Parkland with narrow fairways, all tree lined, and small greens. The course is bounded by the A210 on one side and Eltham Park on the other.
9 holes, 5874yds, Par 69, SSS 68, Course record 62.
Club membership 440.
Visitors Mon-Fri except BHs. Handicap certificate. Dress code. **Societies** Booking required. **Green Fees** £28 per day. **Prof** Gary Brett **Course Designer** James Braid **Facilities** **Leisure** snooker. **Location** 0.5m from Eltham station on A210

Hotel ★★★ 71% Bromley Court Hotel, Bromley Hill, BROMLEY ☎ 020 8461 8600 114 en suite

Royal Blackheath Court Rd SE9 5AF
☎ 020 8850 1795 020 8859 0150
e-mail: info@rbgc.com
web: www.rbgc.com
A pleasant, parkland course of great character, with many great trees and two ponds. The 18th requires a pitch to the green over a thick clipped hedge, which also crosses the front of the 1st tee. The clubhouse dates from the 17th century, and you may wish to visit the club's fine museum of golf.
18 holes, 6219yds, Par 70, SSS 70, Course record 66. Club membership 720.
Visitors Mon-Fri except BHs. Booking required. Handicap certificate. Dress code. **Societies** Booking required. **Green Fees** £70 per day, £50 per round. **Prof** Richard Harrison **Course Designer** James Braid **Facilities** **Leisure** golf museum. **Conf** facs Corporate Hospitality Days **Location** M25 junct 3, A20 towards London, 2nd lights right, club 500yds on right

Hotel ★★★ 71% Bromley Court Hotel, Bromley Hill, BROMLEY ☎ 020 8461 8600 114 en suite

SE18 Woolwich

Shooters Hill Eaglesfield Rd, Shooters Hill SE18 3DA
☎ 020 8854 6368 020 8854 0469
e-mail: secretary@shootershillgc.co.uk
Hilly and wooded parkland with good views and natural hazards.
18 holes, 5721yds, Par 69, SSS 68, Course record 63. Club membership 900.
Visitors Mon-Fri. Handicap certificate. Dress code. **Societies** Booking required. **Green Fees** £35 per day, £28 per round. **Prof** David Brotherton **Course Designer** Willie Park **Facilities** **Conf** Corporate Hospitality Days **Location** Shooters Hill road from Blackheath

SE21 Dulwich

Dulwich & Sydenham Hill Grange Ln, College Rd SE21 7LH
☎ 020 8693 3961 020 8693 2481
e-mail: secretary@dulwichgolf.co.uk
web: www.dulwichgolf.co.uk
18 holes, 6008yds, Par 69, SSS 69, Course record 63.
Course Designer H Colt
Phone for further details

Hotel ★★★ 71% Bromley Court Hotel, Bromley Hill, BROMLEY ☎ 020 8461 8600 114 en suite

SE28 Woolwich

Thamesview Fairway Dr, Summerton Way, Thamesmead SE28 8PP
☎ 020 8310 7975
e-mail: enquiries@thamesview-golf.fsnet.co.uk
9 holes, 5462yds, Par 70, SSS 66.
Course Designer Heffernan **Location** Off A2 near Woolwich ferry
Phone for further details

SW15 Putney

Richmond Park Roehampton Gate, Priory Ln SW15 5JR
☎ 020 8876 1795 020 8878 1354
e-mail: richmondpark@glendale-services.co.uk
web: www.gcmgolf.com
Two public parkland courses.
Princes Course: 18 holes, 5868yds, Par 69, SSS 67.
Dukes Course: 18 holes, 6036yds, Par 69, SSS 68.
Visitors Mon-Fri. Booking required Sat, Sun & BHs. **Societies** Booking required Sat, Sun & BHs. **Green Fees** £19 per 18 holes, £22 Sat & Sun. **Prof** Stuart Hill & David Bown **Course Designer** Fred Hawtree **Facilities** **Conf** Corporate Hospitality Days **Location** Inside Richmond Park, entrance via Roehampton Gate

Hotel ★★★ 69% The Richmond Hill Hotel, Richmond Hill, RICHMOND UPON THAMES ☎ 020 8940 2247 138 en suite

SW17 Wandsworth

Central London Golf Centre Burntwood Ln, Wandsworth SW17 0AT
☎ 020 8871 2468 020 8874 7447
e-mail: golf@clgc.co.uk
web: www.clgc.co.uk
Attractive flat parkland course in the middle of London. The longest drive is the 430 yard 3rd to one of the course's superb greens. Well placed bunkers trap the careless shot and the course rewards the accurate player.
9 holes, 2277yds, Par 62, SSS 62. Club membership 200.
Visitors Mon-Sun & BHs. Booking required. **Societies** welcome. **Green Fees** phone. **Prof** Jon Woodroffe, Gary Clements **Course Designer** Patrick Tallack **Facilities** **Leisure** short game area. **Conf** facs Corporate Hospitality Days **Location** Between Garatt Ln & Trinity Rd

SW19 Wimbledon

London Scottish Windmill Enclosure, Wimbledon Common SW19 5NQ
☎ 020 8788 0135 & 8789 1207 020 8789 7517
e-mail: secretary.lsgc@virgin.net
web: www.londonscottishgolfclub.co.uk
Heathland course. The original course was seven holes around the windmill, laid out by 'Old' Willie Dunn of Musselburgh. His son, Tom Dunn, was the first professional to the club and laid out the 18-hole course.
18 holes, 5458yds, Par 68, SSS 66, Course record 61. Club membership 300.
Visitors Mon-Fri except BHs. Dress code. **Societies** Booking required. **Green Fees** Mon £18 per day, £12 per round. Tue-Fri £25/£18. **Prof** Steve Barr **Course Designer** Tom Dunn **Facilities**

Hotel Premier Travel Inn London Wimbledon South, Merantum Way, Merton, LONDON POSTAL DISTRICTS ☎ 0870 990 6342

Royal Wimbledon 29 Camp Rd SW19 4UW
☎ 020 8946 2125 020 8944 8652
e-mail: secretary@rwgc.co.uk
web: www.rwgc.co.uk
The third-oldest club in England, established in 1865 and steeped in the history of the game. Mainly heathland with trees and heather, a good test of golf with many fine holes, the 12th being rated as the best.
18 holes, 6350yds, Par 70, SSS 71, Course record 66. Club membership 1050.
Visitors Wed-Thu. Booking required. Handicap certificate. Dress code. **Societies** Booking required. **Green Fees** £95 per day, £70 per round. **Prof** David Jones **Course Designer** H Colt **Facilities** **Conf** Corporate Hospitality Days **Location** 1m from Tibbatt's Corner rdbt on Wimbledon Rd

Hotel Premier Travel Inn London Wimbledon South, Merantum Way, Merton, LONDON POSTAL DISTRICTS ☎ 0870 990 6342

Wimbledon Common 19 Camp Rd SW19 4UW
☎ 020 8946 0294 (pro shop) 020 8947 8697
e-mail: secretary@wcgc.co.uk
web: www.wcgc.co.uk
Quick-drying course on Wimbledon Common. Well wooded, with tight fairways, challenging short holes but no bunkers.
18 holes, 5438yds, Par 68, SSS 66, Course record 63. Club membership 290.
Visitors Mon-Fri except BHs. Dress code. **Societies** Booking required. **Green Fees** £27 per day, £18 per round. **Prof** JS Jukes **Course Designer** Tom & Willie Dunn **Facilities** **Leisure** snooker room. **Conf** facs Corporate Hospitality Days **Location** 0.5m N of Wimbledon Village

Hotel Premier Travel Inn London Wimbledon South, Merantum Way, Merton, LONDON POSTAL DISTRICTS ☎ 0870 990 6342

Wimbledon Park Home Park Rd, Wimbledon SW19 7HR
☎ 020 8946 1250 020 8944 8688
e-mail: secretary@wpgc.co.uk
web: www.wpgc.co.uk
Easy walking parkland. Sheltered lake provides hazard on three holes.

18 holes, 5483yds, Par 66, SSS 66, Course record 59. Club membership 800.
Visitors Mon-Fri except BHs. Handicap certificate. Dress code. **Societies** Booking required. **Green Fees** £50 per round. **Prof** Dean Wingrove **Course Designer** Willie Park Jnr **Facilities** **Leisure** sauna. **Conf** facs Corporate Hospitality Days **Location** 400yds from Wimbledon Park station

Hotel ★★★ 69% The Richmond Hill Hotel, Richmond Hill, RICHMOND UPON THAMES ☎ 020 8940 2247 138 en suite

W7 HANWELL

Brent Valley 138 Church Rd, Hanwell W7 3BE
☎ 020 8567 1287
18 holes, 5426yds, Par 67, SSS 66.
Phone for further details

Hotel ★★★ 65% Best Western Master Robert Hotel, 366 Great West Rd, HOUNSLOW ☎ 020 8570 6261 96 annexe en suite

MERSEYSIDE

BEBINGTON Map 07 SJ38

Brackenwood Brackenwood Golf Course, Bracken Ln CH63 2LY
☎ 0151 608 3093
Municipal parkland course with easy walking, a very testing but fair course in a fine rural setting, usually in very good condition.
18 holes, 6285yds, Par 70, SSS 70, Course record 66. Club membership 320.
Visitors Mon-Fri. Booking required Sat & Sun. **Societies** Booking required. **Green Fees** £11 per round. **Prof** Ken Lamb **Facilities** **Location** M53 junct 4, 0.75m N on B5151

Hotel ★★★★ 70% Thornton Hall Hotel and Health Club, Neston Rd, THORNTON HOUGH ☎ 0151 336 3938 63 en suite

BIRKENHEAD Map 07 SJ38

Arrowe Park Woodchurch CH49 5LW
☎ 0151 677 1527
18 holes, 6435yds, Par 72, SSS 71, Course record 66.
Location M53 junct 3, 1m on A551
Phone for further details

Hotel ★★★ 68% Riverhill Hotel, Talbot Rd, Prenton, BIRKENHEAD ☎ 0151 653 3773 15 en suite

Prenton Golf Links Rd, Prenton CH42 8LW
☎ 0151 609 3426 0151 609 3421
e-mail: info@prentongolfclub.co.uk
web: www.prentongolfclub.co.uk
Parkland with easy walking and views of Welsh hills.
18 holes, 6429yds, Par 71, SSS 71. Club membership 610.
Visitors Mon-Fri, Sun & BHs. Booking required. Handicap certificate. Dress code. **Societies** Booking required. **Green Fees** phone. **Prof** Robin Thompson **Course Designer** James Braid **Facilities** **Location** M53 junct 3, off A552 towards Birkenhead

Hotel ★★★ 68% Riverhill Hotel, Talbot Rd, Prenton, BIRKENHEAD ☎ 0151 653 3773 15 en suite

Wirral Ladies 93 Bidston Rd CH43 6TS
☎ 0151 652 1255 📠 0151 651 3775
e-mail: sue.headford@virgin.net
Compact heathland course with heather and birch, requiring accurate shots.
18 holes, 5185yds, Par 68, SSS 65.
Club membership 590.
Visitors Mon-Sun except BHs. Handicap certificate. Dress code. **Societies** Booking required. **Green Fees** £25.50 per round. **Prof** Angus Law **Facilities** **Leisure** indoor training suite. **Location** W of town centre on B5151

Hotel ★★★ 68% Riverhill Hotel, Talbot Rd, Prenton, BIRKENHEAD ☎ 0151 653 3773 15 en suite

BLUNDELLSANDS Map 07 SJ39

West Lancashire Hall Rd West L23 8SZ
☎ 0151 924 1076 📠 0151 931 4448
e-mail: golf@westlancashiregolf.co.uk
web: www.westlancashiregolf.co.uk
Challenging, traditional links with sandy subsoil overlooking the Mersey estuary. The course provides excellent golf throughout the year. The four short holes are very fine.
18 holes, 6763yds, Par 72, SSS 73, Course record 66.
Club membership 650.
Visitors Mon, Wed-Sun & BHs. Booking required. Dress code. **Societies** Booking required. **Green Fees** £80 per day, £65 per round, £100/£85 Sat & Sun. **Prof** Gary Edge **Course Designer** CK Cotton **Facilities** **Conf** Corporate Hospitality Days **Location** N of village, next to Hall Road station

Hotel ★★★ 66% Tree Tops Country House Restaurant & Hotel, Southport Old Rd, FORMBY ☎ 01704 572430 11 annexe en suite

BOOTLE Map 07 SJ39

Bootle 2 Dunnings Bridge Rd L30 2PP
☎ 0151 928 1371 📠 0151 949 1815
e-mail: bootlegolfcourse@btconnect.com
18 holes, 6362yds, Par 70, SSS 70, Course record 64.
Location 2m NE on A5036
Phone for further details

Hotel Premier Travel Inn Liverpool North, Northern Perimiter Rd, Bootle, LIVERPOOL ☎ 08701 977158 63 en suite

BROMBOROUGH Map 07 SJ38

Bromborough Raby Hall Rd CH63 0NW
☎ 0151 334 2155 📠 0151 334 7300
e-mail: enquiries@bromboroughgolfclub.org.uk
web: www.bromboroughgolfclub.org.uk
18 holes, 6650yds, Par 72, SSS 72, Course record 65.
Course Designer J Hassall **Location** 0.5m W of Station
Phone for further details

Hotel ★★★★ 70% Thornton Hall Hotel and Health Club, Neston Rd, THORNTON HOUGH ☎ 0151 336 3938 63 en suite

CALDY Map 07 SJ28

Caldy Links Hey Rd CH48 1NB
☎ 0151 625 5660 📠 0151 6257394
e-mail: secretarycaldygc@btconnect.com
web: www.caldygolfclub.co.uk
A heathland and clifftop links course situated on the estuary of the River Dee with many of the fairways running parallel to the river. Of championship length, the course offers excellent golf all year, but is subject to variable winds that noticeably alter the day-to-day playing of each hole. There are excellent views of Snowdonia.
18 holes, 6651yds, Par 72, SSS 72, Course record 65.
Club membership 800.
Visitors Mon-Fri. After 3.30pm Tue, after 12.30pm Wed. Booking required. **Societies** Booking required. **Green Fees** phone. **Prof** A Gibbons **Course Designer** J Braid **Facilities** **Conf** Corporate Hospitality Days **Location** Signed from Caldy A540 rdbt to Caldy

Hotel ★★★★ 70% Thornton Hall Hotel and Health Club, Neston Rd, THORNTON HOUGH ☎ 0151 336 3938 63 en suite

EASTHAM Map 07 SJ38

Eastham Lodge 117 Ferry Rd CH62 0AP
☎ 0151 327 3003 📠 0151 327 7574
e-mail: easthamlodge@ukgolfer.org
web: www.ukgolfer.org/clubs/easthamlodge_m.html
A parkland course with many mature trees, recently upgraded to 18 holes. Most holes have a subtle dog-leg to left or right. The 1st hole requires an accurate drive to open up the green which is guarded on the right by a stand of pine trees.
18 holes, 5436yds, Par 68, SSS 68.
Club membership 800.
Visitors Mon-Fri except BHs. Booking required Sat & Sun. Dress code. **Societies** Booking required. **Green Fees** £24.50 per day/round. **Prof** N Sargent **Course Designer** Hawtree, D Hemstock **Facilities** **Leisure** snooker. **Conf** Corporate Hospitality Days **Location** 1.5m N, off A41 to Wirral Metropolitan College Country Park

Hotel ★★★ 69% Quality Hotel Chester, Berwick Rd, Little Sutton, ELLESMERE PORT ☎ 0151 339 5121 75 en suite

FORMBY Map 07 SD30

Formby Golf Rd L37 1LQ
☎ 01704 872164 📠 01704 833028
e-mail: info@formbygolfclub.co.uk
web: www.formbygolfclub.co.uk
Championship seaside links through sandhills and pine trees. Partly sheltered from the wind by high dunes it features firm, springy turf, fast seaside greens and natural sandy bunkers. Well drained it plays well throughout the year.
18 holes, 6701yds, Par 72, SSS 72, Course record 65.
Club membership 700.
Visitors Mon, Tue, Thu-Sun except BHs. Booking required. Handicap certificate. Dress code. **Societies** Booking required. **Green Fees** £90 per day/round, £100

Continued

Championship Course

Merseyside

Royal Liverpool

Hoylake

Map 07 SJ28

Built in 1869 on the site of a former racecourse, this world-famous championship course was one of the first seaside courses to be established in England. In 1921 Hoylake was the scene of the first international match between the US and Britain, now known as the Walker Cup. Over the years, golfing enthusiasts have come to Hoylake to witness 18 amateur championships and 10 Open Championships, which the club hosted again in 2006. Visitors playing on this historic course can expect a challenging match, with crosswinds, deep bunkers and hollows, all set against the backdrop of stunning Welsh hills. Watch out for the 8th hole, which saw the great Bobby Jones take an 8 on this par 5 on the way to his famous Grand Slam in 1930.

Meols Dr CH47 4AL
☎ 0151 632 3101 & 632 3102
🖹 0151 632 6737
e-mail: sec@royal-liverpool-golf.com
web: www.royal-liverpool-golf.com

18 holes, 6240yds, Par 72, SSS 71.
Club membership 650.

Visitors Tue-Fri except BHs. Booking required. Handicap certificate. Dress code. **Societies** Booking required. **Green Fees** £115 per round. **Prof** John Heggarty **Course Designer** R Chambers, G Morris, D Steel **Facilities** ⊗ 🍽 ☕ 🍷 👔 🏠 ⛳ 🛒 🏌 **Conf** Corporate Hospitality Days **Location** SW side of town on A540

Sat & Sun. **Prof** Gary Butler **Course Designer** Park, Colt **Facilities** ⊗ ⅏ ⛳ ☕ 🍷 ⛳ ⛺ ⚲ **Conf** facs Corporate Hospitality Days **Location** N of town next to Freshfield railway station

Formby

Hotel ★★★ 66% Tree Tops Country House Restaurant & Hotel, Southport Old Rd, FORMBY ☎ 01704 572430 11 annexe en suite

Formby Hall Golf & Country Club Southport Old Rd L37 0AB
☎ 01704 875699 📠 01704 832134
e-mail: mark@formby-hall.co.uk
web: www.formbyhallgolfclub.co.uk
A spectacular parkland course with links style bunkers. American style design with water on 16 holes. Generous sized fairways with large undulating greens, many of which are protected by water.
18 holes, 6707yds, Par 72, SSS 73.
Club membership 600.
Visitors Mon-Fri, Sat & Sun pm. Booking required. **Societies** Booking required. **Green Fees** phone. **Prof** David Lloyd **Facilities** ⊗ ⅏ ⛳ ☕ 🍷 ⛳ ⛺ **Leisure** fishing, clay pigeon shooting, paintball. **Conf** facs Corporate Hospitality Days **Location** 0.5m off A565 Formby bypass, opp RAF Woodvale

Hotel ★★★ 66% Tree Tops Country House Restaurant & Hotel, Southport Old Rd, FORMBY ☎ 01704 572430 11 annexe en suite

Formby Ladies Golf Rd L37 1YH
☎ 01704 873493 📠 01704 834654
e-mail: secretary@formbyladiesgolfclub.co.uk
web: www.formbyladiesgolfclub.co.uk
Seaside links - one of the few independent ladies' clubs in the country. The course has contrasting hard-hitting holes in flat country and tricky holes in sandhills and woods.
18 holes, 5374yds, Par 71, SSS 72, Course record 60.
Club membership 570.
Visitors Mon-Wed, Fri-Sun except BHs. Booking required. Handicap certificate. Dress code. **Societies** Booking required. **Green Fees** £45 per day, £50 Sat & Sun. **Prof** Gary Butler **Facilities** ⊗ ⛳ ☕ 🍷 ⛳ ⛺ **Conf** Corporate Hospitality Days **Location** N of town centre

Hotel ★★★ 66% Tree Tops Country House Restaurant & Hotel, Southport Old Rd, FORMBY ☎ 01704 572430 11 annexe en suite

HESWALL Map 07 SJ28

Heswall Cottage Ln CH60 8PB
☎ 0151 342 1237 📠 0151 342 6140
e-mail: dawn@heswallgolfclub.com
web: www.heswallgolfclub.com
Pleasant parkland in soft undulating country overlooking the Dee estuary. There are excellent views of the Welsh hills and coastline, and a good test of golf.
18 holes, 6556yds, Par 72, SSS 72, Course record 62.
Club membership 940.
Visitors Mon, Wed, Fri, Sun except BHs. Booking required. Handicap certificate. Dress code. **Societies** Booking required. **Green Fees** £50, £60 Sun. **Prof** Alan Thompson **Course Designer** MacKenzie, Ebert **Facilities** ⊗ ⛳ ☕ 🍷 ⛳ ⛺ **Conf** Corporate Hospitality Days **Location** 1m S off A540

Hotel ★★★★ 70% Thornton Hall Hotel and Health Club, Neston Rd, THORNTON HOUGH ☎ 0151 336 3938 63 en suite

HOYLAKE Map 07 SJ28

Hoylake Carr Ln, Municipal Links CH47 4BG
☎ 0151 632 2956
18 holes, 6313yds, Par 70, SSS 70, Course record 67.
Course Designer James Braid **Location** SW of town off A540
Phone for further details

Hotel ★★★ 69% Leasowe Castle Hotel, Leasowe Rd, MORETON ☎ 0151 606 9191 47 en suite

Royal Liverpool **see page 185**

Hotel ★★★ 69% Kings Gap Court Hotel, HOYLAKE ☎ 0151 632 2073 30 en suite

Hotel ★★★ 69% Leasowe Castle Hotel, Leasowe Rd, MORETON ☎ 0151 606 9191 📠 0151 678 5551 47 en suite

Hotel ★★★ 68% Riverhill Hotel, Talbot Rd, Prenton, BIRKENHEAD ☎ 0151 653 3773 📠 0151 653 7162 15 en suite

HUYTON Map 07 SJ49

Bowring Roby Rd L36 4HD
☎ 0151 443 & 0424 489 1901
e-mail: bowringpark@knowsley.gov.uk
Bowring Golf Club: 18 holes, 6082yds, Par 70.
Location M62 junct 5, on A5080
Phone for further details

Hotel ⌂ Premier Travel Inn Liverpool (Roby), Roby Rd, Huyton, LIVERPOOL ☎ 0870 9906596 53 en suite

Huyton & Prescot Hurst Park, Huyton Ln L36 1UA
☎ 0151 489 3948 📠 0151 489 0797

18 holes, 5779yds, Par 68, SSS 68, Course record 65.
Location 1.5m NE off B5199
Phone for further details

Hotel Premier Travel Inn Liverpool (Tarbock), Wilson Rd, Tarbock, LIVERPOOL ☎ 08701 977159 40 en suite

LIVERPOOL Map 07 SJ39

Allerton Park Allerton Manor Golf Estate, Allerton Rd L18 3JT
☎ 0151 428 7490 📠 428 7490
Parkland course.
18 holes, 5494yds, Par 67, SSS 66.
Visitors contact club for details. **Societies** Booking required. **Green Fees** £8.50, £9.50 Sat, Sun & BHs. **Prof** Barry Large **Facilities** **Leisure** 9 hole par 3 course. **Location** 5.5m SE of city centre off A562

Hotel ★★★ 68% The Royal Hotel, Marine Ter, Waterloo, LIVERPOOL ☎ 0151 928 2332 25 en suite

The Childwall Naylors Rd, Gateacre L27 2YB
☎ 0151 487 0654 📠 0151 487 0654
e-mail: office@childwallgolfclub.co.uk
web: www.childwallgolfclub.co.uk
Parkland golf is played here over a testing course, where accuracy from the tee is well-rewarded. The course is very popular with visiting societies for the clubhouse has many amenities. Course designed by James Braid.
18 holes, 6425yds, Par 72, SSS 71, Course record 66.
Club membership 650.
Visitors Mon, Wed-Sun except BHs. Booking required. Handicap certificate. Dress code. **Societies** Booking required. **Green Fees** £35, £40 Sat, Sun & BHs. **Prof** Nigel M Parr **Course Designer** James Braid **Facilities** by arrangement **Conf** facs Corporate Hospitality Days **Location** 7m E of city centre off B5178

Hotel Premier Travel Inn Liverpool (Roby), Roby Rd, Huyton, LIVERPOOL ☎ 0870 9906596 53 en suite

Kirkby-Liverpool Municipal Ingoe Ln, Kirkby L32 4SS
☎ 0151 546 5435
18 holes, 6704yds, Par 72, SSS 72, Course record 68.
Location 7.5m NE of city centre on A506
Phone for further details

Hotel ★★★ 68% The Royal Hotel, Marine Ter, Waterloo, LIVERPOOL ☎ 0151 928 2332 25 en suite

Lee Park Childwall Valley Rd L27 3YA
☎ 0151 487 3882 📠 0151 498 4666
e-mail: lee.park@virgin.net
Easy walking parkland with plenty of trees, ponds in places, and nine dog-legs. A test for the short game; being in the right position to attack the pins is a premium.

18 holes, 5959yds, Par 70, SSS 69, Course record 66.
Club membership 600.
Visitors Mon, Thu, Fri except BHs. Dress code. **Societies** Booking required. **Green Fees** £27 per day. **Prof** Chris Crowder **Course Designer** G Cotton **Facilities** **Leisure** snooker room. **Conf** Corporate Hospitality Days **Location** 7m E of city centre off B5178

Hotel Premier Travel Inn Liverpool (Roby), Roby Rd, Huyton, LIVERPOOL ☎ 0870 9906596 53 en suite

West Derby Yew Tree Ln, West Derby L12 9HQ
☎ 0151 254 1034 📠 0151 259 0505
e-mail: pmilne@westderbygc.freeserve.co.uk
A parkland course always in first-class condition, and so giving easy walking. The fairways are well-wooded. Care must be taken on the first nine holes to avoid the brook which guards many of the greens.
18 holes, 6277yds, Par 72, SSS 70, Course record 65.
Club membership 550.
Visitors Mon, Wed-Fri except BHs. Booking required. Dress code. **Societies** Booking required. **Green Fees** £29.50 per day/round. **Prof** Andrew Witherup **Facilities** **Conf** facs Corporate Hospitality Days **Location** 4.5m E of city centre off A57

Hotel ★★★ 68% The Royal Hotel, Marine Ter, Waterloo, LIVERPOOL ☎ 0151 928 2332 25 en suite

Woolton Doe Park, Speke Rd, Woolton L25 7TZ
☎ 0151 486 2298 📠 0151 486 1664
e-mail: golf@wooltongolf.co.uk
web: www.wooltongolf.co.uk
Parkland course providing a good round of golf for all standards. A members-owned course that includes two par 5s and five par 3s.
18 holes, 5717yds, Par 69, SSS 68, Course record 63.
Club membership 600.
Visitors Booking required. **Societies** Booking required. **Green Fees** phone. **Prof** Dave Thompson **Facilities** **Leisure** Indoor teaching unit. **Conf** facs Corporate Hospitality Days **Location** 7m SE of city centre off A562, near Liverpool airport

Hotel ★★★ 68% The Royal Hotel, Marine Ter, Waterloo, LIVERPOOL ☎ 0151 928 2332 25 en suite

Newton-le-Willows Map 07 SJ59

Haydock Park Newton Ln WA12 0HX
☎ 01925 228525 📠 01925 224984
e-mail: secretary@haydockparkgc.co.uk
web: www.haydockparkgc.co.uk
A well-wooded parkland course, close to the well-known racecourse, and always in excellent condition. The pleasant undulating fairways offer some very interesting golf and the 6th, 9th, 11th and 13th holes are particularly testing.
18 holes, 6058yds, Par 70, SSS 69, Course record 65. Club membership 630.
Visitors Mon, Wed-Fri except BHs. Booking required. Handicap certificate. Dress code. **Societies** Booking required. **Green Fees** £35 per day, £30 per round. **Prof** Peter Kenwright **Course Designer** James Braid **Facilities** **Location** 0.75m NE off A49

Hotel ★★ 65% Kirkfield Hotel, 2-4 Church St, NEWTON LE WILLOWS ☎ 01925 228196 17 en suite

Rainhill Map 07 SJ49

Blundells Hill Blundells Ln L35 6NA
☎ 0151 4309551 (secretary) & 4300100 (pro)
📠 0151 4265256
e-mail: information@blundellshill.co.uk
web: www.blundellshill.co.uk
18 holes, 6256yds, Par 71, SSS 70, Course record 69.
Course Designer Steve Marnoch **Location** M62 junct 7, A57 towards Prescot, left after garage, 2nd left onto Blundells Ln
Phone for further details

Hotel Premier Travel Inn Liverpool (Rainhill), 804 Warrington Rd, Rainhill, LIVERPOOL ☎ 0870 9906446 34 en suite

Eccleston Park Rainhill Rd L35 4PG
☎ 0151 493 0033 📠 0151 493 0044
e-mail: eccleston-sales@crown-golf.co.uk
web: www.crown-golf.co.uk
18 holes, 6296yds, Par 70, SSS 72.
Location M62 junct 7, A57 to Prescot, at hump bridge right at lights, course 1m on left
Phone for further details

Hotel Premier Travel Inn Liverpool (Rainhill), 804 Warrington Rd, Rainhill, LIVERPOOL ☎ 0870 9906446 34 en suite

St Helens Map 07 SJ59

Grange Park Prescot Rd WA10 3AD
☎ 01744 26318 📠 01744 26318
e-mail: secretary@grangeparkgolfclub.co.uk
web: www.grangeparkgolfclub.co.uk
Possibly one of the finest tests of inland golf in the northwest, set in 150 acres near the centre of town. While not too long, the contours of the fairways, small greens and penal rough demand the best from players. A wide shot making repertoire is required to gain the best score possible.
18 holes, 6446yds, Par 72, SSS 71, Course record 65. Club membership 730.
Visitors Mon, Wed-Fri, Sun & BHs. Booking required. Handicap certificate. Dress code. **Societies** Booking required. **Green Fees** £30, £35 Sun. **Prof** Paul Roberts **Course Designer** James Braid **Facilities** **Conf** facs Corporate Hospitality Days **Location** 1.5m SW on A58

Hotel ★★ 65% Kirkfield Hotel, 2-4 Church St, NEWTON LE WILLOWS ☎ 01925 228196 17 en suite

Houghwood Golf Billinge Hill, Crank Rd, Crank WA11 8RL
☎ 01744 894444 & 894754 📠 01744 894754
e-mail: houghwoodgolf@btinternet.com
web: www.houghwoodgolfclub.co.uk
From the course's highest point, the 12th tee, there are panoramic views over the Lancashire plain to the Welsh hills. All greens built to USGA specification with a permanent track around the entire course for buggies and trolleys.

18 holes, 6268yds, Par 70, SSS 69, Course record 67. Club membership 680.
Visitors Mon-Sun. Dress code. **Societies** Booking required. **Green Fees** phone. **Prof** Paul Dickenson **Course Designer** Neville Pearson **Facilities** **Leisure** snooker table. **Conf** facs Corporate Hospitality Days **Location** 3.5m N of St Helens off B5205

Hotel Travelodge Haydock St Helens, Piele Rd, HAYDOCK ☎ 08700 850 950 62 en suite

Sherdley Park Sherdley Rd WA9 5DE
☎ 01744 813149 📠 01744 817967
web: www.sthelens.gov.uk
Fairly hilly, challenging, pay and play parkland course with ponds in places. Excellent greens.
18 holes, 5974yds, Par 71, SSS 69.
Visitors Mon-Sun & BHs. Booking required. **Societies** Booking required. **Green Fees** £12 per 18 holes, £14 Sat, Sun & BHs. **Prof** Danny Jones **Course Designer** Peter Parkinson **Facilities** **Location** 2m S of St Helens off A570

Hotel ★★ 65% Kirkfield Hotel, 2-4 Church St, NEWTON LE WILLOWS ☎ 01925 228196 17 en suite

Southport Map 07 SD31

The Hesketh Cockle Dick's Ln, off Cambridge Rd PR9 9QQ
☎ 01704 536897 📠 01704 539250
e-mail: secretary@heskethgolfclub.co.uk
web: www.heskethgolfclub.co.uk
The Hesketh is the oldest of the six clubs in Southport, founded in 1885. Set at the northern end of south-west

Continued

Championship Course

Merseyside

Royal Birkdale

Southport

Map 07 SD31

Founded in 1889, the Royal Birkdale is considered by many to be the ultimate championship venue, having hosted every major event in the game including eight Open Championships, two Ryder Cup matches, the Walker Cup, the Curtis Cup and many amateur events. The 1st hole provides an immediate taste of what is to come, requiring a well-placed drive to avoid a bunker, water hazard and Out of Bounds to leave a reasonably clear view of the green. The 10th, the first of the inward nine is unique in that it is the only hole to display the significant fairway undulations one expects from the classic links course. The 12th is the most spectacular of the short holes on the course, and is considered by Tom Watson to be one of the best par 3s in the world; tucked away in the sand hills it continues to claim its fair share of disasters. The approach on the final hole is arguably the most recognisable in golf with the distinctive clubhouse designed to appear like an ocean cruise liner rising out of the sand hills. It's a par 5 for mere mortals, and played as a par 4 in the Open, but it will provide a memorable finish to any round of golf.

Waterloo Rd, Birkdale PR8 2LX
☎ 01704 567920 🖷 01704 562327
e-mail: secretary@royalbirkdale.com
web: www.royalbirkdale.com

18 holes, 6726yds, Par 72, SSS 73.
Club membership 800.

Visitors Mon-Fri, Sun except BHs. Booking required. Handicap certificate. Dress code. **Societies** Booking required. **Green Fees** May-Sep £150 per round, £175 per round Sun. Oct, Nov £110 per round including soup & sandwiches, £135 Sun. Dec-Feb £80 per round soup & sandwiches, £105 Sun. **Prof** Brian Hodgkinson **Course Designer** Hawtree **Facilities** ⊗ by arrangement **Conf** Corporate Hospitality Days **Location** 1.75m S of town centre on A565

Lancashire's dune system, the course sets a unique challenge with half of the holes threaded through tall dunes while the other holes border the Ribble estuary. The course is next to a renowned bird reserve and across the estuary are fine views of the mountains of Lancashire, Cumbria and Yorkshire. Used as a final qualifying course for the Open Championship.
18 holes, 6655yds, Par 72, SSS 72, Course record 67.
Club membership 600.
Visitors Mon, Wed-Fri, Sun & BHs. Tue & Sat pm. Booking required. Handicap certificate. Dress code. **Societies** welcome. **Green Fees** £60 per day, £50 per round, £60 per round Sat, Sun & BHs. **Prof** Scott Astin **Course Designer** JF Morris **Facilities** **Conf** Corporate Hospitality Days **Location** 1m NE of town centre off A565

Hotel ★★★ 69% Stutelea Hotel & Leisure Club, Alexandra Rd, SOUTHPORT ☎ 01704 544220 22 en suite

Hillside Hastings Rd, Hillside PR8 2LU
☎ 01704 567169 01704 563192
e-mail: secretary@hillside-golfclub.co.uk
web: www.ukgolfer.org
Championship links course with natural hazards open to strong wind.
18 holes, 6850yds, Par 72, SSS 74, Course record 65.
Club membership 700.
Visitors Mon, Wed-Fri & Sun. Booking required. **Societies** Booking required. **Green Fees** phone. **Prof** Brian Seddon **Course Designer** Hawtree, Steel **Facilities** **Conf** Corporate Hospitality Days **Location** 3m S of town centre on A565

Hotel ★★★ 71% Scarisbrick Hotel, Lord St, SOUTHPORT ☎ 01704 543000 88 en suite

Royal Birkdale see page 189

Hotel ★★★ 71% Scarisbrick Hotel, Lord St, SOUTHPORT ☎ 01704 543000 88 en suite

Hotel ★★★ 69% Stutelea Hotel & Leisure Club, Alexandra Rd, SOUTHPORT ☎ 01704 544220 01704 500232 22 en suite

Hotel ★★★ 66% Royal Clifton Hotel, Promenade, SOUTHPORT ☎ 01704 533771 01704 500657 111 en suite

Hotel ★★ 68% Balmoral Lodge Hotel, 41 Queens Rd, SOUTHPORT ☎ 01704 544298 & 530751 01704 501224 15 en suite

Southport & Ainsdale Bradshaws Ln, Ainsdale PR8 3LG
☎ 01704 578000 01704 570896
e-mail: secretary@sandagolfclub.co.uk
web: www.sandagolfclub.co.uk
S and A, as it is known in the north, is another of the fine championship courses for which this part of the country is famed. The club has staged many important events and offers golf of the highest order.
18 holes, 6705yds, Par 72, SSS 73, Course record 62.
Club membership 815.
Visitors Mon-Sun & BHs. Booking required. Handicap certificate. Dress code. **Societies** Booking required. **Green Fees** £65 per 18 holes, £85 per 36 holes, £85 per 18 holes Sat & Sun. **Prof** Jim Payne **Course Designer** James Braid **Facilities** **Conf** facs **Location** 3m S off A565

Hotel ★★★ 66% Royal Clifton Hotel, Promenade, SOUTHPORT ☎ 01704 533771 111 en suite

Southport Municipal Park Rd West PR9 0JR
☎ 01704 535286
18 holes, 6400yds, Par 70, SSS 69, Course record 67.
Location N of town centre off A565
Phone for further details

Hotel ★★★ 66% Royal Clifton Hotel, Promenade, SOUTHPORT ☎ 01704 533771 111 en suite

Southport Old Links Moss Ln, Churchtown PR9 7QS
☎ 01704 228207 01704 505353
e-mail: secretary@solgc.freeserve.co.uk
Seaside course with tree-lined fairways and easy walking. One of the oldest courses in Southport, Harry Vardon won the Leeds Cup here in 1922.
9 holes, 6452yds, Par 72, SSS 71, Course record 68.
Club membership 450.
Visitors Mon, Tue, Thu-Sat except BHs. Handicap certificate. Dress code. **Societies** welcome. **Green Fees** £25 per 18 holes, £30 Sat. **Prof** Gary Copeman **Facilities** **Conf** Corporate Hospitality Days **Location** NW of town centre off A5267

Hotel ★★ 70% Bold Hotel, 585 Lord St, SOUTHPORT ☎ 01704 532578 23 en suite

WALLASEY Map 07 SJ29

Bidston Bidston Link Rd CH44 2HR
☎ 0151 638 3412
Flat, easy walking parkland with westerly winds.
18 holes, 6233yds, Par 70, SSS 70.
Club membership 600.
Visitors Booking required. **Societies** Booking required. **Green Fees** phone. **Prof** Mark Eagle **Facilities** **Location** M53 junct 1, 0.5m W off A551

Hotel ★★★ 69% Leasowe Castle Hotel, Leasowe Rd, MORETON ☎ 0151 606 9191 47 en suite

Leasowe Moreton CH46 3RD
☎ 0151 677 5852 🖷 0151 641 8519
web: www.leasowegolfclub.co.uk
A semi-links, seaside course which has recently undergone landscaping on the first five holes, new mounds removing the former rather flat appearance.
18 holes, 6151yds, Par 71, SSS 70.
Club membership 637.
Visitors Tue, Thu, Fri, Sun except BHs. Booking required. Handicap certificate. Dress code. **Societies** Booking required. **Green Fees** £30.50, £35.50 Sun. **Prof** Andrew Ayre **Course Designer** John Ball Jnr **Facilities** **Conf** Corporate Hospitality Days **Location** M53 junct 1, 2m W on A551

Hotel ★★★ 69% Leasowe Castle Hotel, Leasowe Rd, MORETON ☎ 0151 606 9191 47 en suite

Wallasey Bayswater Rd CH45 8LA
☎ 0151 691 1024 🖷 0151 638 8988
e-mail: wallaseygc@aol.com
web: wallaseygolf.com
A well-established links course, adjacent to the Irish Sea. A true test of golf due in part to the prevailing westerly winds and the natural undulating terrain. Spectacular views across Liverpool Bay and the Welsh hills.
18 holes, 6503yds, Par 72, SSS 72, Course record 65.
Club membership 650.
Visitors Mon-Fri, Sun & BHs. Booking required. Dress code. **Societies** Booking required. **Green Fees** £80 per day, £70 per round, £85/£95 Sun & BHs. **Prof** Mike Adams **Course Designer** Tom Morris **Facilities** by arrangement **Location** N of town centre off A554

Hotel ★★★ 71% Grove House Hotel, Grove Rd, WALLASEY ☎ 0151 639 3947 & 0151 630 4558 🖷 0151 639 0028 14 en suite

Warren Grove Rd CH45 0JA
☎ 0151 639 8323
e-mail: golfer@warrengc.freeserve.co.uk
web: www.warrengc.freeserve.co.uk
Short, undulating links course with first-class greens and prevailing winds off the sea.
9 holes, 5854yds, Par 72, SSS 68, Course record 68.
Club membership 100.
Visitors Mon-Sun. **Societies** Booking required. **Green Fees** phone. **Prof** Mark Eagles **Facilities** **Location** N of town centre off A554

Hotel ★★★ 69% Leasowe Castle Hotel, Leasowe Rd, MORETON ☎ 0151 606 9191 47 en suite

NORFOLK

BARNHAM BROOM — Map 05 TG00

Barnham Broom Hotel, Golf, Conference, Leisure Honingham Rd NR9 4DD
☎ 01603 759552 & 759393 🖷 01603 758224
e-mail: golfmanager@barnham-broom.co.uk
web: www.barnham-broom.co.uk

Continued

Course meanders through the Yare valley, parkland and mature trees. Hill course has wide fairways, heavily guarded greens and spectacular views.
Valley Course: 18 holes, 6483yds, Par 72, SSS 71.
Hill Course: 18 holes, 6495yds, Par 71, SSS 71.
Club membership 500.
Visitors contact club for details. Handicap certificate. Dress code. **Societies** Booking required. **Green Fees** Valley £40, Hill £35. **Prof** Ian Rollett **Course Designer** Frank Pennink **Facilities** **Leisure** hard tennis courts, heated indoor swimming pool, squash, sauna, solarium, gymnasium, 3 academy holes. Golf school. Squash tuition. **Conf** facs Corporate Hospitality Days **Location** Off A47 at Honingham

Hotel ★★★ 75% Barnham Broom Hotel, Golf & Country Club, BARNHAM BROOM ☎ 01603 759393 759522 🖷 01603 758224 52 en suite

BAWBURGH — Map 05 TG10

Bawburgh Glen Lodge, Marlingford Rd NR9 3LU
☎ 01603 740404 🖷 01603 740403
e-mail: info@bawburgh.com
web: www.bawburgh.com
Undulating course, mixture of parkland and heathland. The main feature is a large hollow that meanders down to the River Yare creating many interesting tee and green locations. Excellent 18th hole to finish requiring a long accurate second shot to clear the lake in front of the elevated green.
18 holes, 6209yds, Par 70, SSS 70, Course record 64.
Club membership 650.
Visitors Mon-Sun & BHs. Booking required. Dress code. **Societies** Booking required. **Green Fees** phone. **Prof** Chris Potter **Course Designer** John Barnard **Facilities** **Conf** facs Corporate Hospitality Days **Location** S of Royal Norfolk Showground, off A47 to Bawburgh

Hotel ★★★ 76% Park Farm Hotel, HETHERSETT ☎ 01603 810264 3 en suite 39 annexe en suite

BRANCASTER — Map 09 TF74

Royal West Norfolk PE31 8AX
☎ 01485 210223 🖷 01485 210087
A fine links laid out in grand manner characterised by sleepered greens, superb cross bunkers and salt marshes. The tranquil surroundings include a harbour, the sea, farmland and marshland, inhabited by many rare birds. A great part of the year the club is cut off by tidal flooding that restricts the amount of play.
18 holes, 6428yds, Par 71, SSS 71, Course record 66.
Club membership 871.
Visitors Mon-Fri except BHs. Booking required. Handicap certificate. **Societies** Booking required. **Green Fees** phone. **Prof** S Rayner **Course Designer** Holcombe-Ingleby **Facilities** **Location** Off A149 in Brancaster 1m to seafront

Hotel ★★ 76% The White Horse, BRANCASTER STAITHE ☎ 01485 210262 7 en suite 8 annexe en suite

CROMER Map 09 TG24

Royal Cromer 145 Overstrand Rd NR27 0JH
☎ 01263 512884 01263 512430
e-mail: general.manager@royal-cromer.com
web: www.royalcromergolfclub.com
Challenging course with spectacular views out to sea and overlooking the town. Strong sea breezes affect the clifftop holes, the most famous being the 14th (the Lighthouse) which has a green in the shadow of a lighthouse.
18 holes, 6508yds, Par 72, SSS 72, Course record 67.
Club membership 700.
Visitors Booking required. Handicap certificate. **Societies** Booking required. **Green Fees** phone. **Prof** Lee Patterson **Course Designer** JH Taylor **Facilities** **Conf** Corporate Hospitality Days **Location** 1m E on B1159

Hotel ★★ 73% Red Lion, Brook St, CROMER
☎ 01263 514964 12 en suite

DENVER Map 05 TF60

Ryston Park PE38 0HH
☎ 01366 382133 01366 383834
e-mail: rystonparkgc@fsnet.co.uk
web: www.club-noticeboard.co.uk
Parkland course with two challenging par 4s to open. Water comes into play on holes 5, 6 and 7. The course is well wooded with an abundance of wildlife.
9 holes, 6310yds, Par 70, SSS 70, Course record 66.
Club membership 330.
Visitors Mon-Fri except BHs. Booking required. Handicap certificate. Dress code. **Societies** Booking required. **Green Fees** £30 per day, £20 per round. **Course Designer** James Braid **Facilities** by arrangement **Conf** facs Corporate Hospitality Days **Location** 0.5m S on A10

DEREHAM Map 09 TF91

Dereham Quebec Rd NR19 2DS
☎ 01362 695900 01362 695904
e-mail: derehamgolfclub@dgolfclub.freeserve.co.uk
web: derehamgolfclub.com
9 hole parkland course with 17 tees.
9 holes, 6194yds, Par 71, SSS 70, Course record 64.
Club membership 480.
Visitors contact club for details. Handicap certificate. Dress code. **Societies** Booking required. **Green Fees** £30 per day, £20 per round. **Prof** Neil Allsebrook **Facilities** **Conf** Corporate Hospitality Days **Location** N of town centre off B1110

Hotel ★★★ 75% Barnham Broom Hotel, Golf & Country Club, BARNHAM BROOM ☎ 01603 759393 759522
01603 758224 52 en suite

The Norfolk Golf & Country Club Hingham Rd, Reymerston NR9 4QQ
☎ 01362 850297 01362 850614
e-mail: norfolkgolfsec@ukonline.co.uk
web: www.club-noticeboard.co.uk
The course meanders through more than 200 acres of rolling Norfolk countryside, including ancient ditches, hedges and woodland. Large greens built to USGA specification.

Continued

18 holes, 6609yds, Par 72, SSS 72, Course record 69.
Club membership 500.
Visitors Mon-Sun & BHs. Booking required Mon, Wed, Sat, Sun & BHs. Handicap certificate. Dress code. **Societies** Booking required. **Green Fees** £22, £27 Sat & Sun. **Prof** Tony Varney **Facilities** **Leisure** heated indoor swimming pool, sauna, solarium, gymnasium, pitch & putt. **Conf** facs Corporate Hospitality Days **Location** Off B1135

Hotel ★★★ 75% Barnham Broom Hotel, Golf & Country Club, BARNHAM BROOM ☎ 01603 759393 759522
01603 758224 52 en suite

FAKENHAM Map 09 TF92

Fakenham Gallow Sports Centre, The Race Course NR21 7NY
☎ 01328 863534
9 holes, 6174yds, Par 71, SSS 70, Course record 65.
Course Designer Cotton (UK)
Phone for further details

FRITTON Map 05 TG40

Caldecott Hall Golf & Leisure Caldecott Hall, Beccles Rd NR31 9EY
☎ 01493 488488 01493 488561
e-mail: caldecotthall@supanet
web: www.caldecotthall.co.uk

Main Course: 18 holes, 6685yards, Par 73, SSS 72.
Location On A143
Phone for further details

Hotel ★★★ 73% Caldecott Hall Golf & Leisure, Caldecott Hall, Beccles Rd, FRITTON ☎ 01493 488488 8 en suite

GORLESTON ON SEA Map 05 TG50

Gorleston Warren Rd NR31 6JT
☎ 01493 661911 01493 661911
e-mail: manager@gorlestongolfclub.co.uk
web: www.gorlestongolfclub.co.uk
Clifftop course, the most easterly in the British Isles. One of the outstanding features of the course is the 7th hole, which was rescued from cliff erosion about 20 years ago. The green, only 8yds from the cliff edge, is at the mercy of the prevailing winds and club selection is critical.
18 holes, 6391yds, Par 71, SSS 71, Course record 68.
Club membership 800.
Visitors Mon, Tue & Thu-Sat except BHs. Booking required. Handicap certificate. Dress code. **Societies** Booking required. **Green Fees** £25 per 18 holes, £30 Sat. Day ticket £35. **Prof** Nick Brown **Course Designer** JH Taylor **Facilities** by arrangement

Continued

✐ **Conf** Corporate Hospitality Days **Location** Between Gt Yarmouth & Lowestoft, signed from A12

Hotel ★★★ 77% Cliff Hotel, Cliff Hill, Gorleston, GREAT YARMOUTH ☎ 01493 662179 36 en suite

GREAT YARMOUTH Map 05 TG50

Great Yarmouth & Caister Beach House, Caister-on-Sea NR30 5TD

☎ 01493 728699 🖷 01493 728831
e-mail: office@caistergolf.co.uk
web: www.caistergolf.co.uk

A traditional links-style course played over tight and undulating fairways and partly set amongst sand dunes with gorse and marram grass. Well drained with excellent greens. A challenge for golfers of all abilities.

18 holes, 6330yds, Par 70, SSS 70, Course record 65.
Club membership 720.

Visitors Mon-Fri. Booking required Sat, Sun & BHs. Handicap certificate. Dress code. **Societies** Booking required. **Green Fees** £35 per day, £25 Mon-Fri pm, £45/£30 Sat, Sun & BHs. **Prof** Martyn Clarke **Course Designer** H Colt **Facilities** ⊗ 🍴 🍺 ☕ 🍷 👚 🏪 🏌 ✐ **Leisure** snooker. **Location** 0.5m N off A149, at S end of Caister

Hotel ★★ 69% Burlington Palm Court Hotel, 11 North Dr, GREAT YARMOUTH ☎ 01493 844568 & 842095 🖷 01493 331848 70 en suite

HUNSTANTON Map 09 TF64

Hunstanton Golf Course Rd PE36 6JQ

☎ 01485 532811 🖷 01485 532319
e-mail: hunstanton.golf@eidosnet.co.uk
web: www.hunstantongolfclub.com

A championship links course set among some of the natural golfing country in East Anglia. Keep out of the numerous bunkers and master the fast greens to play to your handicap - then you only have the wind to contend with. Good playing conditions all year round.

18 holes, 6759yds, Par 72, SSS 73.
Club membership 675.

Visitors Mon-Sun except BHs. Booking required. Handicap certificate. Dress code. **Societies** welcome. **Green Fees** £65 per day, £40 after 3pm, £75/£50 Sat & Sun. **Prof** James Dodds **Course Designer** James Braid **Facilities** ⊗ 🍺 ☕ 🍷 👚 🏪 🏌 🛒 🚗 ✐ **Location** Off A149 in Old Hunstanton, signed

Hotel ★★★ 71% Le Strange Arms Hotel, Golf Course Rd, Old Hunstanton, HUNSTANTON ☎ 01485 534411 36 en suite

Searles Leisure Resort South Beach Rd PE36 5BB

☎ 01485 536010 🖷 01485 533815
e-mail: golf@searles.co.uk
web: www.searles.co.uk

This nine-hole par 34 course is designed in a links style and provides generous fairways with good greens. A river runs through the 3rd and 4th holes and the par 5 8th follows the ancient reed bed to finish with the lake-sided par 3 9th in front of the clubhouse. Good views of Hunstanton and the surrounding countryside and a challenge for all standards of golfer.

9 holes, 2773yds, Par 34.
Club membership 200.

Visitors Mon-Sun & BHs. Dress code. **Societies** welcome. **Green Fees** 18 holes £15, 9 holes £9, £16.50/£10 Sat, Sun & BHs. **Prof** Mark Rimmer **Course Designer** Paul Searle **Facilities** ⊗ 🍺 ☕ 🍷 👚 🏪 🏌 🛏 🛒 🚗 ✐ 🏌 **Leisure** hard tennis courts, outdoor and indoor heated swimming pools, fishing, sauna, solarium, gymnasium, bowls green. **Conf** facs Corporate Hospitality Days **Location** A149 N to Hunstanton, 2nd left at rdbt, over minirdbt, 1st left signed Sports and Country Club

Hotel ★★★ 71% Le Strange Arms Hotel, Golf Course Rd, Old Hunstanton, HUNSTANTON ☎ 01485 534411 36 en suite

KING'S LYNN Map 09 TF62

Eagles 39 School Rd, Tilney All Saints PE34 4RS

☎ 01553 827147 🖷 01553 829777
e-mail: shop@eagles-golf-tennis.co.uk
web: www.eagles-golf-tennis.co.uk

Parkland with a variety of trees and shrubs lining the fairways. A large area of water comes into play on several holes.

9 holes, 4284yds, Par 64, SSS 61, Course record 64.
Club membership 200.

Visitors Mon-Sun & BHs. Handicap certificate. Dress code. **Societies** Booking required. **Green Fees** 18 holes £16, 9 holes £11, Sat, Sun & BHs £18/£12. **Prof** Nigel Pickerell **Course Designer** DW Horn **Facilities** ⊗ by arrangement 🍴 🍺 ☕ 🍷 👚 🏪 🏌 ✐ 🏌 **Leisure** hard tennis courts, par 3 course. **Conf** Corporate Hospitality Days **Location** Off A47 at rdbt to Tilney All Saints, between Kings Lynn & Wisbech

Hotel ⌂ Premier Travel Inn King's Lynn, Freebridge Farm, KING'S LYNN ☎ 08701 977149 40 en suite

King's Lynn Castle Rising PE31 6BD
☎ 01553 631654 🖷 01553 631036
e-mail: secretary@kingslynngc.co.uk
web: www.club-noticeboard.co.uk
The course is set among silver birch and fir woodland and benefits, especially in the winter, from well-drained sandy soil.

18 holes, 6609yds, Par 72, SSS 73, Course record 64. Club membership 910.
Visitors Mon-Sun & BHs. Booking required. Handicap certificate. Dress code. **Societies** Booking required. **Green Fees** £45 per day, £50 Sat & Sun. **Prof** John Reynolds **Course Designer** Thomas & Alliss **Facilities** **Leisure** Snooker. **Conf** facs Corporate Hospitality Days **Location** 4m NE off A149

Hotel ★★★ 71% Knights Hill Hotel, Knights Hill Village, South Wootton, KING'S LYNN ☎ 01553 675566 55 en suite 18 annexe en suite

MATTISHALL Map 09 TG01

Mattishall South Green NR20 3JZ
☎ 01362 850111
Mattishall has the distinction of having the longest hole in Norfolk at a very demanding 625yds.
9 holes, 3300mtrs, Par 72, SSS 69. Club membership 120.
Visitors Mon-Fri. Booking required Sat & Sun. Dress code. **Societies** Booking required. **Green Fees** £20 per day, £14 per 18 holes, £10 per 9 holes. **Prof** Gary Polter **Course Designer** B Todd **Facilities** **Location** 0.75m S of Mattishall Church

Hotel ★★★ 75% Barnham Broom Hotel, Golf & Country Club, BARNHAM BROOM ☎ 01603 759393 759522 🖷 01603 758224 52 en suite

MIDDLETON Map 09 TF61

Middleton Hall Hall Orchards PE32 1RH
☎ 01553 841800 & 841801 🖷 01553 841800
e-mail: middleton-hall@btclick.com
web: www.middletonhall.co.uk
Natural undulations and mature specimen trees offer a most attractive environment for golf. The architecturally designed course provides a challenge for the competent golfer; there is also a covered floodlit driving range and practice putting green.
18 holes, 5756yds, Par 71, SSS 68, Course record 70. Club membership 600.
Visitors Mon-Sun except BHs. Dress code. **Societies** Booking required. **Green Fees** £30 per day, £25 per round, £35/£30 Sat, Sun & BHs. **Prof** Steve White **Course Designer** D Scott **Facilities** **Conf** Corporate Hospitality Days **Location** 4m from King's Lynn on A47 towards Norwich

Hotel ★★★ Congham Hall Country House Hotel, Lynn Rd, GRIMSTON ☎ 01485 600250 14 en suite

MUNDESLEY Map 09 TG33

Mundesley Links Rd NR11 8ES
☎ 01263 720279 & 720095 🖷 01263 720279
9 holes, 5377yds, Par 68, SSS 66, Course record 64.
Location W of village off B1159
Phone for further details

Hotel ★★ 73% Red Lion, Brook St, CROMER ☎ 01263 514964 12 en suite

NORWICH Map 05 TG20

Costessey Park Old Costessey NR8 5AL
☎ 01603 746333 & 747085 🖷 01603 746185
e-mail: cpgc@ljgroup.com
web: www.costesseypark.com
The course lies in the gently contoured Tud valley, providing players with a number of holes that bring the river and man-made lakes into play. The 1st hole starts a round with a par 3 that requires an accurate drive across the river, to land the ball on a sculptured green beside a reed fringed lake. To end the round at the 18th hole, you need to make a straight drive past the ruined belfry to allow a second shot back over the river to land the ball on a recessed green.
18 holes, 5881yds, Par 71, SSS 69, Course record 65. Club membership 600.
Visitors Mon-Sun. **Societies** Booking required. **Green Fees** phone. **Prof** Andrew Young **Facilities** **Conf** Corporate Hospitality Days **Location** 4.5m NW of Norwich. A1074 onto Longwater Ln, left onto West End, club on left

Hotel ★★★ 68% Quality Hotel Norwich, 2 Barnard Rd, Bowthorpe, NORWICH ☎ 01603 741161 80 en suite

De Vere Dunston Hall Hotel Ipswich Rd NR14 8PQ
☎ 01508 470444 🖷 01508 471499
e-mail: dhreception@devere-hotels.com
web: www.devereonline.co.uk
Parkland course with water features at many holes. Varied and challenging woodland setting. Floodlit driving range.
18 holes, 6300yds, Par 71, SSS 70, Course record 70.
Visitors Mon-Sun & BHs. Booking required. Dress code. **Societies** Booking required. **Green Fees** from £25. **Prof** Peter Briggs **Course Designer** M Shaw **Facilities** **Leisure** hard tennis courts, heated indoor swimming pool, sauna, solarium, gymnasium. **Conf** facs Corporate Hospitality Days **Location** On A140

Hotel ★★★★ 70% De Vere Dunston Hall, Ipswich Rd, NORWICH ☎ 01508 470444 130 en suite

Eaton Newmarket Rd NR4 6SF
☎ 01603 451686 🖷 01603 457539
e-mail: administrator@eatongc.co.uk
web: www.eatongc.co.uk
An undulating, tree-lined parkland course. Easy opening par 5 followed by an intimidating par 3 that is well bunkered with deep rough on both sides. The

Continued

challenging 17th hole is uphill to a small hidden green and always needs more club than expected.

Eaton

18 holes, 6118yds, Par 70, SSS 70, Course record 64.
Club membership 800.
Visitors Mon-Sun & BHs. Booking required. Handicap certificate. Dress code. **Societies** Booking required. **Green Fees** £35, £45 Sat & Sun. **Prof** Mark Allen **Facilities** ⊗ ♿ ☕ 🍷 ♨ 🏠 ✓ **Location** 1.5m SW of city centre off A11

Hotel ★★★ 76% Park Farm Hotel, HETHERSETT ☎ 01603 810264 3 en suite 39 annexe en suite

Marriott Sprowston Manor Hotel & Country Club Wroxham Rd NR7 8RP

☎ 01603 254290 🖹 01603 788884
e-mail: kieron.tuck@marriotthotels.co.uk
web: www.marriott.co.uk/nwigs

Set in 100 acres of parkland, including an impressive collection of oak trees that provide a backdrop to many holes. The course benefits from USGA specification tees and greens.

18 holes, 6543yds, Par 71, SSS 71, Course record 70.
Club membership 600.
Visitors Mon-Sun. Booking required. **Societies** Booking required. **Green Fees** phone. **Prof** Guy D Ireson **Course Designer** Ross McMurray **Facilities** ⊗ 🍴 ♿ ☕ 🍷 ♨ 🏠 ⛳ 🛏 🔧 🚗 ✓ 🏌 **Leisure** heated indoor swimming pool, sauna, gymnasium. **Conf** facs Corporate Hospitality Days **Location** 4m NE from city centre on A1151

Hotel ★★★★ 75% Marriott Sprowston Manor Hotel & Country Club, Sprowston Park, Wroxham Rd, Sprowston, NORWICH ☎ 01603 410871 94 en suite

Royal Norwich Drayton High Rd, Hellesdon NR6 5AH

☎ 01603 429928 & 408459 🖹 01603 417945
e-mail: mail@royalnorwichgolf.co.uk
web: www.royalnorwichgolf.co.uk

Undulating mature parkland course complimented with gorse. Largely unchanged since the alterations carried out by James Braid in 1924. A challenging test of golf.

18 holes, 6506yds, Par 72, SSS 72, Course record 65.
Club membership 640.
Visitors Mon-Fri except BHs. Booking required. Dress code. **Societies** Booking required. **Green Fees** £40 per day, £25 per round. **Prof** Simon Youd **Course Designer** James Braid **Facilities** ⊗ 🍴 by arrangement ♿ ☕ 🍷 ♨ 🏠 ✓ **Conf** Corporate Hospitality Days **Location** 2.5m NW of city centre on A1067

Hotel ★★★ 68% Quality Hotel Norwich, 2 Barnard Rd, Bowthorpe, NORWICH ☎ 01603 741161 80 en suite

Wensum Valley Hotel, Golf & Country Club Beech Av, Taverham NR8 6HP

☎ 01603 261012 🖹 01603 261664
e-mail: enqs@wensumvalleyhotel.co.uk
web: www.wensumvalleyhotel.co.uk

Two picturesque and contrasting courses set in 350 acres of the attractive Wensum Valley. The Valley course demands length off the tee and skill on the large undulating greens. The Wensum course has smaller, well-protected greens requiring accuracy to score well. Both courses built on free draining soil allowing play in the wettest conditions.

Valley Course: 18 holes, 6223yds, Par 72, SSS 70, Course record 72.
Wensum Course: 18 holes, 6922yds, Par 72, SSS 73, Course record 64.
Club membership 900.
Visitors Mon-Sun & BHs. Booking required. Handicap certificate. Dress code. **Societies** Booking required. **Green Fees** £25 per day inc £7 meal voucher. Twilight £15. **Prof** Darren Game **Course Designer** B Todd **Facilities** ⊗ 🍴 ♿ ☕ 🍷 ♨ 🏠 ⛳ 🛏 🚗 ✓ 🏌 **Leisure** heated indoor swimming pool, fishing, sauna, solarium, gymnasium. **Conf** facs Corporate Hospitality Days **Location** 5m N of Norwich off A1067

Hotel ★★ 67% Wensum Valley Hotel Golf & Country Club, Beech Av, Taverham, NORWICH ☎ 01603 261012 84 en suite

SHERINGHAM Map 09 TG14

Sheringham Weybourne Rd NR26 8HG

☎ 01263 823488 🖹 01263 826129
e-mail: info@sheringhamgolfclub.co.uk
web: www.sheringhamgolfclub.co.uk

The course is laid out along a rolling, gorse-clad cliff top from where the sea is visible on every hole. The par 4 holes are outstanding with a fine view along the cliffs from the 5th tee.

18 holes, 6456yds, Par 70, SSS 71, Course record 64.
Club membership 760.
Visitors Mon-Sun & BHs. Booking required. Handicap certificate. Dress code. **Societies** booking required **Green Fees** phone. 🚭 **Prof** MW Jubb **Course Designer** Tom Dunn **Facilities** ⊗ 🍴 ♿ ☕ 🍷 ♨ 🏠 🚗 ✓ **Conf** Corporate Hospitality Days **Location** W of town centre on A149

Hotel ★★ 72% Beaumaris Hotel, South St, SHERINGHAM ☎ 01263 822370 21 en suite

SWAFFHAM Map 05 TF80

Swaffham Cley Rd PE37 8AE

☎ 01760 721621 (secretary) 🖹 01760 721621
e-mail: swaffamgc@supanet.com
web: www.swaffhamgc.supanet.com

18 holes, 6544yds, Par 71, SSS 71.
Course Designer Jonathan Gaunt **Location** 1.5m SW of town centre
Phone for further details

Hotel ★★★ 66% George Hotel, Station Rd, SWAFFHAM ☎ 01760 721238 29 en suite

THETFORD Map 05 TL88

Feltwell Thor Ave, Feltwell IP26 4AY
☎ 01842 827644 📠 01842 829065
e-mail: secretary@feltwellgolfclub.f9.co.uk
web: www.club-noticeboard.co.uk
In spite of being an inland links, this nine-hole course is still open and windy.
9 holes, 6488yds, Par 72, SSS 71, Course record 71.
Club membership 350.
Visitors contact club for details. Dress code. **Societies** Booking required. **Green Fees** £16 per day, £25 Sat, Sun & BHs. **Prof** Tom Ball **Facilities** **Conf** Corporate Hospitality Days **Location** On B1112 next to RAF Feltwell

Hotel ★★ 66% The Thomas Paine Hotel, White Hart St, THETFORD ☎ 01842 755631 13 en suite

Thetford Brandon Rd IP24 3NE
☎ 01842 752169 📠 01842 766212
e-mail: sally@thetfordgolfclub.co.uk
web: www.club-noticeboard.co.uk
The course has a good pedigree. It was laid out by the fine golfer CH Mayo, later altered by James Braid and then again altered by another famous course designer, Mackenzie Ross. It is a testing heathland course with a particularly stiff finish.
18 holes, 6849yds, Par 72, SSS 73, Course record 66.
Club membership 750.
Visitors Mon-Fri except BHs. Booking required. Handicap certificate. **Societies** Wed-Fri. Booking required. **Green Fees** phone. **Prof** Gary Kitley **Course Designer** James Braid **Facilities** **Leisure** short game area. **Location** 2m W of Thetford on B1107

Hotel ★★ 66% The Thomas Paine Hotel, White Hart St, THETFORD ☎ 01842 755631 13 en suite

WATTON Map 05 TF90

Richmond Park Saham Rd IP25 6EA
☎ 01953 881803 📠 01953 881817
e-mail: info@richmondpark.co.uk
web: www.richmondpark.co.uk
Compact parkland course with mature and young trees set around the Little Wissey river and spread over 100 acres of Norfolk countryside. The river and other water hazards create an interesting but not daunting challenge.

18 holes, 6258yds, Par 71, SSS 70, Course record 69.
Club membership 600.
Visitors Mon-Sun & BHs. Booking required. Dress code. **Societies** Booking required. **Green Fees** £35 per day, £24

Continued

per round, £35 per round Sat & Sun. **Prof** Alan Hemsley **Course Designer** D Jessup, D Scott **Facilities** **Leisure** gymnasium. **Conf** Corporate Hospitality Days **Location** 500yds NW of town centre

Hotel ★★★ 66% George Hotel, Station Rd, SWAFFHAM ☎ 01760 721238 29 en suite

WESTON LONGVILLE Map 09 TG11

Weston Park NR9 5JW
☎ 01603 872363 📠 01603 873040
e-mail: golf@weston-park.co.uk
web: www.weston-park.co.uk
Superb, challenging course, set in 200 acres of magnificent, mature woodland and parkland.
18 holes, 6648yds, Par 72, SSS 72, Course record 68.
Club membership 560.
Visitors Mon-Sun & BHs. Booking required. Handicap certificate. Dress code. **Societies** Booking required. **Green Fees** £45 per day, £36 per 18 holes, £50/£45 Sat & Sun. **Prof** Michael Few **Course Designer** Golf Technology **Facilities** **Leisure** hard tennis courts, croquet lawn. **Conf** facs Corporate Hospitality Days **Location** Brown tourist signs off A1067 or A47

Hotel ★★★ 68% Quality Hotel Norwich, 2 Barnard Rd, Bowthorpe, NORWICH ☎ 01603 741161 80 en suite

WEST RUNTON Map 09 TG14

Links Country Park Hotel & Golf Club
NR27 9QH
☎ 01263 838215 📠 01263 838264
e-mail: proshop@links-hotel.co.uk
web: www.links-hotel.co.uk
Parkland course 500yds from the sea, with superb views overlooking West Runton. The hotel offers extensive leisure facilities.
9 holes, 4842yds, Par 66, SSS 64.
Club membership 250.
Visitors Mon-Sun & BHs. Booking required. Dress code. **Societies** Booking required. **Green Fees** £25 per round, £18 within 4 hours sunset (£15 winter). **Prof** Nick Catchpole **Course Designer** J.H Taylor **Facilities** **Leisure** hard tennis courts, heated indoor swimming pool, sauna, solarium, gymnasium. **Conf** facs Corporate Hospitality Days **Location** S of village off A149

Hotel ★★ 72% Beaumaris Hotel, South St, SHERINGHAM ☎ 01263 822370 21 en suite

If the name of the club appears in italics, details have not been confirmed for this edition of the guide

NORTHAMPTONSHIRE

CHACOMBE Map 04 SP44

Cherwell Edge OX17 2EN
☎ 01295 711591 🖷 01295 713674
e-mail: enquiries@cherwelledgegolfclub.co.uk
web: www.cegc.co.uk
Parkland course over chalk giving good drainage. The back nine is short and tight with mature trees. The front nine is longer and more open. The course is well bunkered with three holes where water can catch the wayward golfer.

Chacombe

18 holes, 6092yds, Par 70, SSS 69, Course record 64. Club membership 500.
Visitors Mon-Sun. Booking required Sat & Sun. Dress code. **Societies** Booking required. **Green Fees** phone. **Prof** Jason Newman **Course Designer** R Davies **Facilities** **Conf** facs Corporate Hospitality Days **Location** M40 junct 11, 0.5m S off B4525, 2m from Banbury

Hotel ★★★ 71% Macdonald Whately Hall, Banbury Cross, BANBURY ☎ 0870 400 8104 69 en suite

COLD ASHBY Map 04 SP67

Cold Ashby Stanford Rd NN6 6EP
☎ 01604 740548 🖷 01604 740548
e-mail: info@coldashbygolfclub.com
web: www.coldashbygolfclub.com
Undulating parkland course, nicely matured, with superb views. The 27 holes consist of three loops of nine, which can be interlinked with each other. All three loops have their own challenge and any combination of two loops will give an excellent course. The start of the Elkington loop offers five holes of scenic beauty and testing golf and the 3rd on the Winwick loop is a 200yd par 3 from a magnificent plateau tee.
Ashby-Elkington: 18 holes, 6308yds, Par 72, SSS 71, Course record 68.
Elkington-Winwick: 18 holes, 6293yds, Par 70, SSS 71, Course record 69.
Winwick-Ashby: 18 holes, 6047yds, Par 70, SSS 70, Course record 65.
Club membership 600.
Visitors Mon-Fri. Booking required Sat, Sun & BHs. Dress code. **Societies** Booking required. **Green Fees** £17 per round, £20 Sat & Sun. **Prof** Shane Rose **Course Designer** David Croxton **Facilities** **Conf** facs Corporate Hospitality Days **Location** M1 junct 18 or A14 junct 1

Hotel Hotel Ibis Rugby East, Parklands, CRICK ☎ 01788 824331 111 en suite

COLLINGTREE Map 04 SP75

Collingtree Park Windingbrook Ln NN4 0XN
☎ 01604 700000 & 701202 🖷 01604 702600
e-mail: info@collingtreeparkgolf.com
web: www.collingtreeparkgolf.com
An 18-hole resort course designed by former US and British Open champion Johnny Miller. The American-style course has water hazards on 10 holes with a spectacular par 5 18th Island Green.

18 holes, 6776yds, Par 72, SSS 72, Course record 66. Club membership 660.
Visitors Mon-Sun & BHs. Booking required. Handicap certificate. Dress code. **Societies** welcome. **Green Fees** phone. **Prof** G Pook, A Carter **Course Designer** Johnny Miller **Facilities** **Leisure** fishing, Golf Academy. **Conf** facs Corporate Hospitality Days **Location** M1 junct 15, on A508 to Northampton

Hotel ★★★★ 70% Northampton Marriott Hotel, Eagle Dr, NORTHAMPTON ☎ 01604 768700 120 en suite

CORBY Map 04 SP88

Corby Public Stamford Rd, Weldon NN17 3JH
☎ 01536 260756 📠 01536 260756
Municipal course laid out on made-up quarry ground and open to prevailing wind.
18 holes, 6677yds, Par 72, SSS 72, Course record 68.
Club membership 600.
Visitors Mon-Sun & BHs. Dress code. **Societies** Booking required. **Green Fees** £12.50 per 18 holes, £17.50 Sat & Sun. **Prof** Jeff Bradbrook **Course Designer** F Hawtree **Facilities** **Location** 4m NE on A43

Inn ♦♦ Raven Hotel, Rockingham Rd, CORBY
☎ 01536 202313 17 rms (5 en suite)

DAVENTRY Map 04 SP56

Daventry & District Norton Rd NN11 5LS
☎ 01327 702829
e-mail: ms@teltec.com
An undulatory course providing panoramic views and whose tight fairways and small fast greens with large burrows provide a good test of golf.
9 holes, 5812yds, Par 69, SSS 68, Course record 62.
Club membership 285.
Visitors Mon-Sat & BHs. Sun pm. Dress code. **Societies** Booking required. **Green Fees** £10 per day. **Facilities** **Conf** facs Corporate Hospitality Days **Location** 0.5m E of Daventry

Hotel ★★★★ 62% The Daventry Hotel, Sedgemoor Way, DAVENTRY ☎ 01327 307000 138 en suite

FARTHINGSTONE Map 04 SP65

Farthingstone Hotel & Golf Course
NN12 8HA
☎ 01327 361291 📠 01327 361645
e-mail: info@farthingstone.co.uk
web: www.farthingstone.co.uk
A mature and challenging course set in picturesque countryside.

18 holes, 6299yds, Par 70, SSS 70, Course record 68.
Club membership 350.
Visitors Booking required. **Societies** Booking required. **Green Fees** phone. **Prof** Luke Brockway **Course Designer** Don Donaldson **Facilities** **Leisure** squash, Snooker room. **Conf** facs Corporate Hospitality Days **Location** M1 junct 16, W near Farthingstone

Hotel Premier Travel Inn Daventry, High St, WEEDON ☎ 0870 9906364 46 en suite

HELLIDON Map 04 SP55

Hellidon Lakes Hotel & Country Club
NN11 6GG
☎ 01327 262550 📠 01327 262559
e-mail: hellidon@marstonhotels.com
web: www.marstonhotels.com
18 holes, 6691yds, Par 72, SSS 72.
Course Designer D Snell **Location** Off A361 into Hellidon, 2nd right
Phone for further details

Hotel ★★★★ 76% Hellidon Lakes, HELLIDON
☎ 01327 262550 110 en suite

KETTERING Map 04 SP87

Kettering Headlands NN15 6XA
☎ 01536 511104 📠 01536 511104
e-mail: secretary@kettering-golf.co.uk
web: www.kettering-golf.co.uk
A mature woodland course with gentle slopes.
18 holes, 6081yds, Par 69, SSS 69, Course record 63.
Club membership 700.
Visitors Mon-Fri except BHs. Booking required. Handicap certificate. Dress code. **Societies** Booking required. **Green Fees** £29 per round. **Prof** Kevin Theobald **Course Designer** Tom Morris **Facilities** **Conf** Corporate Hospitality Days **Location** S of town centre

Hotel ★★★★ 76% Kettering Park Hotel & Spa, Kettering Parkway, KETTERING ☎ 01536 416666 119 en suite

Pytchley Golf Lodge Kettering Rd, Pytchley NN14 1EY
☎ 01536 511527 📠 01536 790266
e-mail: office@golflodge.wanadoo.co.uk
web: www.pytchleygolflodgekettering.co.uk
Academy nine-hole pay and play course, offering a challenge to both experienced and novice players.
9 holes, 2574yards, Par 34, SSS 65, Course record 70.
Club membership 200.
Visitors Mon-Sun & BHs. Booking required (up to 7 days). Dress code. **Societies** Booking required. **Green Fees** £13 per 18 holes, £7 per 9 holes, £17/£9 Sat, Sun & BHs. **Prof** Peter Machin **Course Designer** Roger Griffiths Associates **Facilities** **Location** A14 junct 9, A509 towards Kettering signs

Hotel ★★★★ 76% Kettering Park Hotel & Spa, Kettering Parkway, KETTERING ☎ 01536 416666 119 en suite

NORTHAMPTON Map 04 SP76

Brampton Heath Sandy Ln, Church Brampton NN6 8AX
☎ 01604 843939 📠 01604 843885
e-mail: crose@bhgc.co.uk
web: www.bhgc.co.uk
Appealing to both the novice and experienced golfer, this beautiful, well drained heathland course affords panoramic views over Northampton. It plays like an inland links in the summer - fast running fairways, true rolling greens with the wind always providing a challenge. Excellent play all year round.
18 holes, 6366yds, Par 71, SSS 70, Course record 66.
Club membership 500.
Visitors Mon-Sun & BHs. Booking required. Dress code.

Continue

Societies Booking required. **Green Fees** £17 per round, £11 per 9 holes, £21/£13 Sat, Sun & BHs. **Course Designer** D Snell **Facilities** **Conf** facs Corporate Hospitality Days **Location** Signed off A5199 2m N of Kingsthorpe

Hotel ★★★ 68% Lime Trees Hotel, 8 Langham Place, Barrack Rd, NORTHAMPTON ☎ 01604 632188 20 rms (10 en suite) 7 annexe rms

Delapre Golf Centre Eagle Dr, Nene Valley Way NN4 7DU

☎ 01604 764036 🖷 01604 706378
e-mail: delapre@jbgolf.co.uk
web: www.jackbarker.com

Rolling parkland course, part of a municipal golf complex, which includes two nine-hole par 3 courses, pitch and putt, and a 40-bay floodlit driving range.

The Oaks: 18 holes, 6269yds, Par 70, SSS 70, Course record 66.
Hardingstone Course: 9 holes, 2109yds, Par 32, SSS 32.
Club membership 500.

Visitors Mon-Sun & BHs. Dress code. **Societies** Booking required. **Green Fees** phone. **Prof** John Cuddihy **Course Designer** John Jacobs, John Corby **Facilities** **Leisure** par 3 courses. **Conf** facs Corporate Hospitality Days **Location** M1 junct 15, 3m on A508/A45

Hotel ★★★ 65% Quality Hotel Northampton, Ashley Way, Weston Favell, NORTHAMPTON ☎ 01604 739955 33 en suite 38 annexe en suite

Kingsthorpe Kingsley Rd NN2 7BU

☎ 01604 710610 🖷 01604 710610
e-mail: secretary@kingsthorpe-golf.co.uk
web: www.kingsthorpe-golf.co.uk

A compact, undulating parkland course set within the town boundary. Not a long course but the undulating terrain provides a suitable challenge for golfers of all standards. The 18th hole is claimed to be the longest 400yds in the county when played into wind and is among the finest finishing holes in the area. New clubhouse.

18 holes, 5903yds, Par 69, SSS 69, Course record 63.
Club membership 650.

Visitors Mon-Fri. Booking required. Dress code. **Societies** Booking required. **Green Fees** £30 per day, £25 per round. £20 per round winter. **Prof** Paul Armstrong **Course Designer** Alison, H Colt **Facilities** **Conf** facs Corporate Hospitality Days **Location** N of town centre on A5095 between Kingsthorpe and racecourse

Hotel ★★★ 65% Quality Hotel Northampton, Ashley Way, Weston Favell, NORTHAMPTON ☎ 01604 739955 33 en suite 38 annexe en suite

Northampton Harlestone NN7 4EF

☎ 01604 845155 🖷 01604 820262
e-mail: golf@northamptongolfclub.co.uk
web: www.northamptongolfclub.co.uk

Parkland with water in play on four holes.

18 holes, 6615yds, Par 72, SSS 72, Course record 63.
Club membership 750.

Visitors Mon, Tue, Thu, Fri except BHs. Handicap certificate. Dress code. **Societies** Booking required. **Green Fees** phone. **Prof** Barry Randall **Course Designer** Sinclair Steel **Facilities** by arrangement **Conf** facs Corporate Hospitality Days **Location** NW of town centre on A428

Hotel ★★★ 68% Lime Trees Hotel, 8 Langham Place, Barrack Rd, NORTHAMPTON ☎ 01604 632188 20 rms (10 en suite) 7 annexe rms

Northamptonshire County Golf Ln, Church Brampton NN6 8AZ

☎ 01604 843025 🖷 01604 843463
e-mail: secretary@countrygolfclub.org.uk
web: www.countygolfclub.org

A fine, traditional championship course situated on undulating heathland with areas of gorse, heather and extensive coniferous and deciduous woodland. A river and a railway line pass through the course and there is a great variety of holes.

18 holes, 6505yds, Par 70, SSS 72, Course record 65.
Club membership 750.

Visitors contact club for details. Booking required Wed & Thu. Handicap certificate. Dress code. **Societies** Booking required. **Green Fees** £60 per 36 holes, £50 per 27 holes, £40 per 18 holes. **Prof** Tim Rouse **Course Designer** H Colt **Facilities** **Conf** Corporate Hospitality Days **Location** 5m NW of Northampton off A5199

Hotel ★★★ 65% Quality Hotel Northampton, Ashley Way, Weston Favell, NORTHAMPTON ☎ 01604 739955 33 en suite 38 annexe en suite

Overstone Park Billing Ln NN6 0AS

☎ 01604 647666 🖷 01604 642635
e-mail: enquiries@overstonepark.com
web: www.overstonepark.com

A testing parkland course, gently undulating within panoramic views of local stately home. Excellent drainage and fine greens make the course great all year round. Water comes into play on three holes.

18 holes, 6472yds, Par 72, SSS 72, Course record 69.
Club membership 500.

Visitors Mon-Fri. Booking required Sat, Sun & BHs. Dress code. **Societies** Booking required. **Green Fees** from £26 per round. **Prof** Brain Mudge **Course Designer** Donald Steel **Facilities** **Leisure** hard tennis courts, heated indoor swimming pool, fishing, sauna, solarium, gymnasium. **Conf** facs Corporate Hospitality Days **Location** M1 junct 15, A45 to Billing Aquadrome turn off, course 2m off A5076 Gt Billing Way

Hotel ★★★ 68% Lime Trees Hotel, 8 Langham Place, Barrack Rd, NORTHAMPTON ☎ 01604 632188 20 rms (10 en suite) 7 annexe rms

Continued

OUNDLE Map 04 TL08

Oundle Benefield Rd PE8 4EZ
☎ 01832 273267 📠 01832 273267
e-mail: office@oundlegolfclub.com
web: www.oundlegolfclub.com
Undulating parkland in countryside. Stream running through course in play on nine holes. Small greens demand careful placement from tees and accurate iron play.
18 holes, 6265yds, Par 72, SSS 70, Course record 63.
Club membership 650.
Visitors Mon-Fri. Booking required Sat, Sun & BHs. Handicap certificate. Dress code. **Societies** Booking required. **Green Fees** £34 per day, £25.50 per round, £44 per day/round Sat & Sun. **Prof** Richard Keys **Facilities** **Leisure** Short game practice area. **Conf** facs Corporate Hospitality Days **Location** 1m W on A427

Inn ♦♦ Raven Hotel, Rockingham Rd, CORBY
☎ 01536 202313 17 rms (5 en suite)

STAVERTON Map 04 SP56

Staverton Park Staverton Park NN11 6JT
☎ 01327 302000
18 holes, 6661yds, Par 71, SSS 72, Course record 65.
Course Designer Cmdr John Harris **Location** 0.75m NE on A425
Phone for further details

Hotel ★★★★ 62% The Daventry Hotel, Sedgemoor Way, DAVENTRY ☎ 01327 307000 138 en suite

WELLINGBOROUGH Map 04 SP86

Rushden Kimbolton Rd, Chelveston NN9 6AN
☎ 01933 418511 📠 01933 418511
web: www.rushdengolfclub.org
Undulating parkland with a brook bisecting the course.
10 holes, 6249yds, Par 71, SSS 70, Course record 68.
Club membership 400.
Visitors Mon, Tue, Thu, Fri. Booking required Tue & Fri. Dress code. **Societies** Booking required. **Green Fees** £18. **Facilities** **Location** 6m E of Wellingborough off B645

Hotel Travelodge Wellingborough Rushden, Saunders Lodge, RUSHDEN ☎ 08700 850 950 40 en suite

Wellingborough Great Harrowden Hall NN9 5AD
☎ 01933 677234 📠 01933 679379
e-mail: secretary@wellingboroughgolfclub.com
web: www.wellingboroughgolfclub.org
Undulating parkland with many trees. The 514yd 14th is a testing hole. The clubhouse is a stately home and the 18th is the signature hole.
18 holes, 6651yds, Par 72, SSS 72, Course record 68.
Club membership 820.
Visitors Mon, Wed-Fri except BHs. Dress code. **Societies** Booking required. **Green Fees** £48. **Prof** David Clifford **Course Designer** Hawtree **Facilities** **Leisure** outdoor swimming pool. **Conf** facs Corporate Hospitality Days **Location** 2m N of Wellingborough on A509

Wellingborough

Hotel Travelodge Wellingborough Rushden, Saunders Lodge, RUSHDEN ☎ 08700 850 950 40 en suite

WHITTLEBURY Map 04 SP64

Whittlebury Park Golf & Country Club
NN12 8WP
☎ 01327 850000 📠 01327 850001
e-mail: enquiries@whittlebury.com
web: www.whittlebury.com
The 36 holes incorporate three loops of tournament-standard nines plus a short course. The 1905 course is a reconstruction of the original parkland course built at the turn of the century, the Royal Whittlewood is a lakeland course playing around copses and the Grand Prix, next to Silverstone Circuit, has a strong links feel playing over gently undulating grassland with many challenging features.

Grand Prix: 9 holes, 3339yds, Par 36, SSS 36.
Royal Whittlewood: 9 holes, 3323yds, Par 36, SSS 36.
1905: 9 holes, 3256yds, Par 36, SSS 36.
Club membership 350.
Visitors Mon-Sun & BHs. Booking required. Dress code. **Societies** Booking required. **Green Fees** phone. **Prof** Mark Booth **Course Designer** Cameron Sinclair **Facilities** **Leisure** heated indoor swimming pool, sauna, solarium, shooting, archery, falconry, karting. **Conf** facs Corporate Hospitality Days **Location** M1 junct 15a, on A413 Buckingham Road

Hotel ★★★★ 79% Whittlebury Hall Hotel and Spa, WHITTLEBURY ☎ 01327 857857 211 en suite

Continued

NORTHUMBERLAND

ALLENDALE Map 12 NY85

Allendale High Studdon, Allenheads Rd NE47 9DH
☎ 07005 808246
e-mail: ian@sandhill27.fsnet.co.uk
web: www.allendale-golf.org
Challenging and hilly parkland course set 1000ft above sea level with superb views of Tynedale. New clubhouse.
9 holes, 4541yds, Par 66, SSS 62, Course record 69. Club membership 130.
Visitors Mon-Sat except BHs, Sun after 2pm. **Societies** Booking required. **Green Fees** £12 per day, £15 Sat & Sun. **Facilities** **Conf** Corporate Hospitality Days **Location** 1m S of Allendale on B6295

Hotel ★★★ 68% Beaumont Hotel, Beaumont St, HEXHAM ☎ 01434 602331 25 en suite

ALNMOUTH Map 12 NU21

Alnmouth Foxton Hall NE66 3BE
☎ 01665 830231 01665 830922
e-mail: secretary@alnmouthgolfclub.com
web: www.alnmouthgolfclub.com
The original course, situated on the Northumberland coast, was established in 1869, being the fourth oldest in England. The existing course, created in 1930, provides a testing and enjoyable challenge.

18 holes, 6429yds, Par 71, SSS 71, Course record 64. Club membership 800.
Visitors Mon-Thu, Sun & BHs. Booking required. Handicap certificate. Dress code. **Societies** Booking required. **Green Fees** £40 per day, £30 per round, £35 per round Sun. **Prof** Linzi Hardy **Course Designer** H Colt **Facilities** **Leisure** snooker room. **Conf** Corporate Hospitality Days **Location** 1m NE of Alnmouth

Alnmouth Village Marine Rd NE66 2RZ
☎ 01665 830370
e-mail: golf@alnmouth-village.fsnet.co.uk
web: www.ukgolfer.com
Seaside course with part coastal view.
9 holes, 6090yds, Par 70, SSS 70, Course record 63. Club membership 480.
Visitors Booking required. **Societies** Booking required. **Green Fees** phone. **Course Designer** Mungo Park **Facilities** **Location** E of village

ALNWICK Map 12 NU11

Alnwick Swansfield Park NE66 1AB
☎ 01665 602632
e-mail: mail@alnwickgolfclub.co.uk
A mixture of mature parkland, open grassland and gorse bushes with panoramic views out to sea 5m away. Offers a fair test of golf.
18 holes, 6284yds, Par 70, SSS 70, Course record 66. Club membership 400.
Visitors Mon-Sun & BHs. Booking required. Dress code. **Societies** Booking required. **Green Fees** phone. **Course Designer** Rochester, Rae **Facilities** **Leisure** small practice area. **Location** S of town centre off B6341

Hotel ★★★ 59% White Swan Hotel, Bondgate Within, ALNWICK ☎ 01665 602109 56 en suite

BAMBURGH Map 12 NU13

Bamburgh Castle The Club House, 40 The Wynding NE69 7DE
☎ 01668 214378 (club) & 214321 (sec) 01668 214607
e-mail: bamburghcastlegolfclub@hotmail.com
web: www.bamburghcastlegolfclub.co.uk
Superb coastal course with excellent greens that are both fast and true; natural hazards of heather and whin bushes abound. Magnificent views of the Farne Islands, Holy Island, Lindisfarne Castle, Bamburgh Castle and the Cheviot Hills.
18 holes, 5621yds, Par 68, SSS 67, Course record 64. Club membership 785.
Visitors Mon-Fri & Sun except BHs. Booking required. Dress code. **Societies** Booking required. **Green Fees** £45 per day, £33 per round, £50/£38 Sun. **Course Designer** George Rochester **Facilities** **Conf** Corporate Hospitality Days **Location** 6m E of A1 via B1341 or B1342

Hotel ★★ 69% The Lord Crewe, Front St, BAMBURGH ☎ 01668 214243 18 rms (17 en suite)

BEDLINGTON Map 12 NZ28

Bedlingtonshire Acorn Bank NE22 6AA
☎ 01670 822457 01670 823048
e-mail: secretary@bedlingtongolfclub.com
web: www.bedlingtongolfclub.com
Meadowland and parkland with easy walking. Under certain conditions the wind can be a distinct hazard.

18 holes, 6813yards, Par 73, SSS 73, Course record 64. Club membership 800.
Visitors Mon-Sun & BHs. Booking required. Dress code.

Continued

Societies Booking required. **Green Fees** £35 per day, £22 per round, £36/£28 Sat, Sun & BHs. **Prof** Marcus Webb **Course Designer** Frank Pennink **Facilities** by arrangement **Conf** Corporate Hospitality Days **Location** 1m SW on A1068

BELFORD Map 12 NU13

Belford South Rd NE70 7DP
01668 213232 & 07764 582427 01668 213282
web: www.thebelford.co.uk
A coastal parkland course recently in new ownership. Many new trees have been added and nine new tee boxes, allowing golfers to play each hole from two different angles for a full 18 holes. The course is overlooked by the 18th-century Belford Hall and has fine views of Holy Island.
9 holes, 3227yds, Par 71, SSS 71.
Club membership 200.
Visitors Mon-Sun & BHs. Booking required. **Societies** Booking required. **Green Fees** £19 per 18 holes, £13 per 9 holes, £22/£16 Sat, Sun & BHs. **Prof** Simon Whitaker **Course Designer** Nigel Williams **Facilities** **Conf** Corporate Hospitality Days **Location** Off A1 between Alnwick on Tweed

Hotel Purdy Lodge, Adderstone Services, BELFORD 01668 213000 20 en suite

BELLINGHAM Map 12 NY88

Bellingham Boggle Hole NE48 2DT
01434 220530 (secretary)
e-mail: admin@bellinghamgolfclub.com
web: www.bellinghamgolfclub.com
Rolling parkland with many natural hazards. This highly regarded 18-hole course lies between Hadrian's Wall and the Scottish border. There is a mixture of testing par 3s, long par 5s and tricky par 4s.

18 holes, 6093yds, Par 70, SSS 70, Course record 65.
Club membership 500.
Visitors Mon-Sun & BHs. Dress code. **Societies** Booking required. **Green Fees** £24 per day/round, £29 per round Sat & Sun. **Course Designer** E Johnson, I Wilson **Facilities** **Location** N of village on B6320

If the name of the club appears in italics, details have not been confirmed for this edition of the guide

BERWICK-UPON-TWEED Map 12 NT95

Berwick-upon-Tweed (Goswick) Goswick TD15 2RW
01289 387256 01289 387334
e-mail: goswickgc@btconnect.com
web: www.goswicklinksgc.co.uk
18 holes, 6686yds, Par 72, SSS 72, Course record 69.
Course Designer James Braid **Location** 6m S of Berwick off A1
Phone for further details

Hotel ★★★ 70% Marshall Meadows Country House Hotel, BERWICK-UPON-TWEED 01289 331133 19 en suite

Magdalene Fields Magdalene Fields TD15 1NE
01289 306130 01289 306384
e-mail: mail@magdalene-fields.co.uk
web: www.magdalene-fields.co.uk
Seaside course on a clifftop with natural hazards formed by bays. All holes open to winds. Testing 8th hole over bay (par 3). Scenic views to Holy Island and north to Scotland.
18 holes, 6407yds, Par 72, SSS 71, Course record 65.
Club membership 350.
Visitors Mon-Fri. Booking required Sat, Sun & BHs. Dress code. **Societies** Booking required. **Green Fees** £21 per round, £23 Sat & Sun. **Course Designer** Willie Park **Facilities** **Conf** Corporate Hospitality Days **Location** 0.5m E of town centre

Hotel ★★★ 76% Tillmouth Park Country House Hotel, CORNHILL-ON-TWEED 01890 882255 12 en suite 2 annexe en suite

BLYTH Map 12 NZ38

Blyth New Delaval, Newsham NE24 4DB
01670 540110 (sec) & 356514 (pro) 01670 540134
e-mail: clubmanager@blythgolf.co.uk
web: www.blythgolf.co.uk
Course built over old colliery. Parkland with water hazards. Superb greens.
18 holes, 6456yds, Par 72, SSS 71, Course record 63.
Club membership 860.
Visitors Mon-Sun & BHs. Booking required. Dress code. **Societies** Booking required. **Green Fees** £32 per day, £25 per round, £38/£28 per round Sat & Sun. **Prof** Andrew Brown **Course Designer** Hamilton Stutt **Facilities** **Location** 1m S of town centre

Hotel ★★★ 71% Windsor Hotel, South Pde, WHITLEY BAY 0191 251 8888 69 en suite

CRAMLINGTON Map 12 NZ27

Arcot Hall NE23 7QP
0191 236 2794 0191 217 0370
e-mail: arcothall@tiscali.co.uk
web: www.arcothallgolfclub.com
Wooded parkland, reasonably flat.
18 holes, 6380yds, Par 70, SSS 70, Course record 62.
Club membership 695.
Visitors Mon-Sun & BHs. Dress code. **Societies** Booking required. **Green Fees** £28 per day, £23 after 3pm summer, £32 per round Sat & Sun. **Prof** John Metcalfe **Course Designer** James Braid **Facilities** **Conf** facs **Location** 2m SW off A1

Continued

Hotel Innkeeper's Lodge Cramlington, Blagdon Ln, CRAMLINGTON 01670 736111 18 en suite

EMBLETON Map 12 NU22

Dunstanburgh Castle NE66 3XQ
01665 576562 01665 576562
e-mail: enquiries@dunstanburgh.com
web: www.dunstanburgh.com
Rolling links designed by James Braid, adjacent to the beautiful Embleton Bay. Historic Dunstansburgh Castle is at one end of the course and a National Trust lake and bird sanctuary at the other. Superb views.
18 holes, 6298yds, Par 70, SSS 69, Course record 69.
Club membership 385.
Visitors contact club for details. **Societies** welcome. **Green Fees** £22 per day. £32 per day, £26 per round Sat, Sun & BHs. **Course Designer** James Braid **Facilities** **Conf** facs **Location** 7m NE of Alnwick off A1

Hotel ★★ 72% Dunstanburgh Castle Hotel, EMBLETON 01665 576111 20 en suite

FELTON Map 12 NU10

Burgham Park NE65 8QP
01670 787898 (office) & 787978 (pro shop)
01670 787164
18 holes, 6751yards, Par 72, SSS 72, Course record 67.
Course Designer Andrew Mair **Location** 5m N of Morpeth, 0.5m off A1
Phone for further details

Hotel ★★★ 74% Macdonald Linden Hall, Golf & Country Club, LONGHORSLEY 0870 1942123 50 en suite

GREENHEAD Map 12 NY66

Haltwhistle Wallend Farm CA6 7HN
016977 47367 01434 344311
18 holes, 5522yds, Par 69, SSS 67, Course record 70.
Location N on A69 past Haltwhistle on Gilsland Road
Phone for further details

Hotel ★★★ Farlam Hall Hotel, BRAMPTON 016977 46234 11 en suite 1 annexe en suite

HEXHAM Map 12 NY96

De Vere Slaley Hall, Golf Resort & Spa Slaley NE47 OBX
01434 673154 01434 673152
e-mail: slaley.hall@devere-hotels.com
web: www.deveregolf.co.uk
Measuring 7073yds from the championship tees, this Dave Thomas course incorporates forest, parkland and moorland with an abundance of lakes and streams. The challenging par 4 9th (452yds) is played over water through a narrow avenue of towering trees and dense rhododendrons. The Priestman Course designed by Neil Coles is of equal length and standard as the Hunting Course. Opened in spring 1999, the club is situated in 280 acres on the western side of the estate, giving panoramic views over the Tyne valley.
Hunting Course: 18 holes, 7073yds, Par 72, SSS 74, Course record 65.
Priestman Course: 18 holes, 7010yds, Par 72, SSS 72, Course record 64.
Club membership 350.
Visitors Booking required. **Societies** Booking required. **Green Fees** phone. **Prof** Gordon Robinson **Course Designer** Dave Thomas, Neil Coles **Facilities** **Leisure** heated indoor swimming pool, fishing, sauna, solarium, gymnasium. **Conf** facs **Location** 8m S of Hexham off A68

Hotel ★★★★ 72% De Vere Slaley Hall, Slaley, HEXHAM 01434 673350 139 en suite

Hexham Spital Park NE46 3RZ
01434 603072 01434 601865
e-mail: info@hexhamgolf.co.uk
web: www.hexhamgolf.co.uk
A very pretty, well-drained course with interesting natural contours. Exquisite views from parts of the course of the Tyne valley below. As good a parkland course as any in the north of England.
18 holes, 6294yds, Par 70, SSS 70, Course record 61.
Club membership 700.
Visitors Mon-Sun & BHs. Booking required. Dress code. **Societies** Booking required. **Green Fees** £30 per round, £40 Sat, Sun & BHs. **Prof** Martin Forster **Course Designer** Vardon, Caird **Facilities** **Leisure** squash, squash courts. **Conf** facs Corporate Hospitality Days **Location** 1m NW on B6531

Hotel ★★★ 68% Beaumont Hotel, Beaumont St, HEXHAM 01434 602331 25 en suite

LONGHORSLEY Map 12 NZ19

Linden Hall NE65 8XF
01670 500011 01670 500001
e-mail: golf@lindenhall.co.uk
web: www.lindenhall.co.uk
Set within the picturesque Linden Hall Estate on a mixture of mature woodland and parkland, established lakes and burns provide interesting water features to match the peaceful surroundings. This award-winning course is a pleasure to play for all standards of golfer.

18 holes, 6846yds, Par 72, SSS 73.
Club membership 350.
Visitors Booking required. **Societies** Booking required. **Green Fees** phone. **Prof** David Curry **Course Designer** Jonathan Gaunt **Facilities** **Leisure** hard tennis courts, heated indoor swimming pool, sauna, solarium, gymnasium. **Conf** facs Corporate Hospitality Days **Location** 0.5m N of village off A697

Hotel ★★★ 74% Macdonald Linden Hall, Golf & Country Club, LONGHORSLEY 0870 1942123 50 en suite

Continued

MATFEN Map 12 NZ07

Matfen Hall NE20 0RH
☎ 01661 886400 📠 01661 886055
e-mail: golf@matfenhall.com
web: www.matfenhall.com
18 holes, 6650yds, Par 72, SSS 72, Course record 63.
Course Designer Mair, James, Gaunt **Location** Off B6318
Phone for further details

Hotel ★★★★ 76% Matfen Hall, MATFEN
☎ 01661 886500 855708 📠 01661 886055 53 en suite

MORPETH Map 12 NZ28

Morpeth The Clubhouse NE61 2BT
☎ 01670 504942 📠 01670 504918
18 holes, 6206yds, Par 71, SSS 69, Course record 65.
Course Designer Harry Vardon **Location** S of town centre on A197
Phone for further details

Hotel ★★★ 74% Macdonald Linden Hall, Golf & Country Club, LONGHORSLEY ☎ 0870 1942123 50 en suite

NEWBIGGIN-BY-THE-SEA Map 12 NZ38

Newbiggin-by-the-Sea Prospect Place NE64 6DW
☎ 01670 817344
e-mail: info@newbiggingolfclub.co.uk
web: www.newbiggingolfclub.co.uk
Seaside-links course.
18 holes, 6452yds, Par 72, SSS 71, Course record 65.
Club membership 694.
Visitors Mon-Fri except BHs. Handicap certificate. Dress code. **Societies** Booking required. **Green Fees** £20. **Course Designer** Willie Park **Facilities** **Leisure** snooker. **Conf** facs **Location** N of town centre

Hotel ★★★ 74% Macdonald Linden Hall, Golf & Country Club, LONGHORSLEY ☎ 0870 1942123 50 en suite

PONTELAND Map 12 NZ17

Ponteland 53 Bell Villas NE20 9BD
☎ 01661 822689 📠 01661 860077
e-mail: secretary@thepontelandgolfclub.co.uk
web: www.thepontelandgolfclub.co.uk
Open parkland course offering testing golf and good views.
18 holes, 6524yds, Par 72, SSS 71, Course record 65.
Club membership 720.
Visitors Mon-Fri, Sun & BHs. Booking required. Handicap certificate. Dress code. **Societies** Booking required. **Green Fees** phone. **Prof** Alan Robson-Crosby **Course Designer** Harry Fernie **Facilities** **Conf** Corporate Hospitality Days **Location** 0.5m E on A696

Hotel ★★★ 67% Novotel Newcastle, Ponteland Rd, Kenton, NEWCASTLE UPON TYNE ☎ 0191 214 0303 126 en suite

PRUDHOE Map 12 NZ06

Prudhoe Eastwood Park NE42 5DX
☎ 01661 832466 📠 01661 830710
e-mail: secretary@prudhoegolfclub.co.uk
18 holes, 5812yds, Par 69, SSS 69, Course record 60.
Location E of town centre off A695
Phone for further details

Hotel ★★★ 69% Gibside Hotel, Front St, WHICKHAM
☎ 0191 488 9292 45 en suite

ROTHBURY Map 12 NU00

Rothbury Old Race Course NE65 7TR
☎ 01669 621271
web: www.rothburygolfclub.com
9 holes, 5779yds, Par 68, SSS 67, Course record 65.
Course Designer J Radcliffe **Location** SW of town off B6342
Phone for further details

Hotel ★★★ 74% Macdonald Linden Hall, Golf & Country Club, LONGHORSLEY ☎ 0870 1942123 50 en suite

SEAHOUSES Map 12 NU23

Seahouses Beadnell Rd NE68 7XT
☎ 01665 720794 📠 01665 721994
e-mail: secretary@seahousesgolf.co.uk
web: www.seahousesgolf.co.uk
Typical links course with many hazards, including the famous par 3 10th hole, Logans Loch, water hole. The par 3 15th has been nominated as one of the most difficult holes in the world. Spectacular views of the coastline to the Farne Islands and Lindisfarne.
18 holes, 5542yds, Par 67, SSS 67, Course record 63.
Club membership 550.
Visitors contact club for details. **Societies** welcome. **Green Fees** £27 per day, £20 per round, £32/£27 Sat, Sun & BHs. **Facilities** **Conf** Corporate Hospitality Days **Location** S of village on B1340

Hotel ★★★ 67% Bamburgh Castle Hotel, SEAHOUSES
☎ 01665 720283 20 en suite

STOCKSFIELD Map 12 NZ06

Stocksfield New Ridley Rd NE43 7RE
☎ 01661 843041 📠 01661 843046
e-mail: info@sgcgolf.co.uk
web: www.sgcgolf.co.uk
Challenging course: parkland (nine holes), woodland (nine holes). Some elevated greens, giving fine views, and water hazards.
18 holes, 5991yds, Par 70, SSS 69, Course record 61. Club membership 550.
Visitors Mon, Tue, Thu, Fri, Sun & BHs. Wed pm. Booking required. Dress code. **Societies** Booking required. **Green Fees** £25 per day, £20 per round, £28 Sun & BHs. **Prof** Steven Harrison **Course Designer** Pennick **Facilities** **Leisure** snooker. **Conf** Corporate Hospitality Days **Location** 1.5m S off A695

Hotel ★★★ 68% Beaumont Hotel, Beaumont St, HEXHAM ☎ 01434 602331 25 en suite

SWARLAND Map 12 NU10

Swarland Hall Coast View NE65 9JG
☎ 01670 787010
e-mail: info@swarlandgolf
web: www.swarlandgolf.co.uk
18 holes, 6335yds, Par 72, SSS 72.
Location 1m W of A1
Phone for further details

Hotel ★★★ 74% Macdonald Linden Hall, Golf & Country Club, LONGHORSLEY ☎ 0870 1942123 50 en suite

WOOLER Map 12 NT92

Wooler Dod Law, Doddington NE71 6EA
☎ 01668 282135
web: www.woolergolf.co.uk
9 holes, 6411yds, Par 72, SSS 71, Course record 69.
Location At Doddington on B6525
Phone for further details

Hotel Purdy Lodge, Adderstone Services, BELFORD ☎ 01668 213000 20 en suite

NOTTINGHAMSHIRE

CALVERTON Map 08 SK64

Ramsdale Park Golf Centre Oxton Rd NG14 6NU
☎ 0115 965 5600 📠 0115 965 4105
e-mail: info@ramsdaleparkgc.co.uk
web: www.ramsdaleparkgc.co.uk
The Seely Course is a challenging and comprehensive test for any standard of golf. A relatively flat front nine is followed by an undulating back nine that is renowned as one of the best in the county. The Lee Course is an 18-hole par 3 course which is gaining a similar reputation.
Seely Course: 18 holes, 6546yds, Par 71, SSS 71, Course record 70.
Lee Course: 18 holes, 2844yds, Par 54, SSS 54.
Club membership 400.
Visitors Mon-Sun except BHs. Booking required. Dress code. **Societies** welcome. **Green Fees** £19.50, £25 Sat & Sun. **Prof** Robert Macey **Course Designer** Hawtree **Facilities** **Leisure** fishing. **Conf** facs Corporate Hospitality Days **Location** 8m NE of Nottingham off B6386

Hotel ★★★ 66% Bestwood Lodge, Bestwood Country Park, Arnold, NOTTINGHAM ☎ 0115 920 3011 39 en suite

Springwater Moor Ln NG14 6FZ
☎ 0115 965 2129 (pro shop) & 965 4946
📠 0115 965 4957
e-mail: springwater@rapidial.co.uk
web: www.springwatergolfclub.co.uk
This attractive course set in rolling countryside overlooking the Trent valley, offers an interesting and challenging game of golf to players of all handicaps. The 18th hole is particularly noteworthy, a 183yd par 3 over two ponds

18 holes, 6262yds, Par 71, SSS 71, Course record 68. Club membership 440.
Visitors Mon-Sun & BHs. Booking required. Dress code. **Societies** Booking required. **Green Fees** £22 per round, £27 Sat, Sun & BHs. **Prof** Paul Drew **Course Designer** Neil Footitt, Paul Wharmsby **Facilities** **Leisure** short game academy. **Conf** facs Corporate Hospitality Days **Location** Off A6097 to Calverton, 600yds on left

Hotel ★★★ 67% Westminster Hotel, 312 Mansfield Rd, Carrington, NOTTINGHAM ☎ 0115 955 5000 73 en suite

EAST LEAKE Map 08 SK52

Rushcliffe Stocking Ln LE12 5RL
☎ 01509 852959 📠 01509 852688
e-mail: secretary.rushcliffegc@btopenworld.com
Hilly, tree-lined and picturesque parkland.
Rushcliffe Golf Club: 18 holes, 6013yds, Par 70, SSS 69, Course record 63.
Club membership 750.
Visitors contact club for details. **Societies** Booking

Continued

required. **Green Fees** phone. **Prof** Chris Hall **Facilities** **Location** M1 junct 24

Hotel ★★★ 76% Best Western Yew Lodge Hotel, Packington Hill, Kegworth, ☎ 01509 672518 98 en suite

HUCKNALL Map 08 SK54

Hucknall Golf Centre Wigwam Ln NG15 7TA
☎ 0115 964 2037 📠 0115 964 2724
e-mail: leen@jbgolf.co.uk
web: www.jackbarker.com
A course on two different levels. Upper level has a links feel while the lower level with its ponds, streams and ditches has a parkland feel A relatively short course but still a challenge for all abilities.
18 holes, 6150yds, Par 70, SSS 70.
Club membership 250.
Visitors Mon-Sun & BHs. **Societies** Booking required. **Green Fees** £12.50 per round, £16 Sat & Sun. **Prof** Cyril Jepson **Course Designer** Tom Hodgetts **Facilities** **Conf** facs Corporate Hospitality Days **Location** 0.5m from town centre, signs for railway station, right onto Wigwam Ln

Hotel Premier Travel Inn Nottingham North West, Nottingham Rd, HUCKNALL ☎ 0870 9906518 35 en suite

KEYWORTH Map 08 SK63

Stanton on the Wolds Golf Course Rd, Stanton-on-the-Wolds NG12 5BH
☎ 0115 937 4885 📠 0115 937 1652
e-mail: swgc@zoom.co.uk
Fairly flat parkland with a stream running through four holes. Physically not demanding but challenging to score well.
18 holes, 6369yds, Par 73, SSS 71, Course record 67.
Club membership 705.
Visitors Mon-Fri except BHs. Booking required. Handicap certificate. Dress code. **Societies** Booking required. **Green Fees** £35 per day, £27 per round. **Prof** Nick Hernon **Course Designer** Tom Williamson **Facilities** **Location** E side of village off A606

Hotel Premier Travel Inn Nottingham South, Loughborough Rd, Ruddington, NOTTINGHAM ☎ 0870 9906422 42 en suite

KIRKBY IN ASHFIELD Map 08 SK55

Notts Derby Rd NG17 7QR
☎ 01623 753225 📠 01623 753655
e-mail: nottsgolfclub@hollinwell.fsnet.co.uk
web: www.nottsgolfclub.co.uk
Undulating heathland championship course.
18 holes, 7103yds, Par 72, SSS 75, Course record 64.
Club membership 450.
Visitors Mon-Fri except BHs. Booking required. Handicap certificate. **Societies** Booking required. **Green Fees** phone. **Prof** Mike Bradley **Course Designer** Willie Park **Facilities** **Conf** facs **Location** 2m SE of Mansfield off A611

Hotel ★★★★ 68% Renaissance Derby/Nottingham Hotel, Carter Ln East, SOUTH NORMANTON ☎ 01773 812000 & 0870 4007262 158 en suite

MANSFIELD Map 08 SK56

Sherwood Forest Eakring Rd NG18 3EW
☎ 01623 627403 📠 01623 420412
e-mail: sherwood@forest43.freeserve.co.uk
As the name suggests, the forest is the main feature of this natural heathland course with its heather, silver birch and pine trees. The homeward nine holes are particularly testing. The 11th to the 14th are notable par 4 holes on this well-bunkered course.
18 holes, 6289yds, Par 71, SSS 71.
Club membership 750.
Visitors Mon, Wed-Fri except BHs. Tue pm. Booking required. Handicap certificate. Dress code. **Societies** Booking required. **Green Fees** £70 per day, £50 per round. **Prof** Ken Hall **Course Designer** HS Colt, James Braid **Facilities** **Leisure** snooker. **Conf** facs Corporate Hospitality Days **Location** E of Mansfield

Hotel ★★ 68% Pine Lodge Hotel, 281-283 Nottingham Rd, MANSFIELD ☎ 01623 622308 20 en suite

NEWARK-ON-TRENT Map 08 SK75

Newark Coddington NG24 2QX
☎ 01636 626282 📠 01636 626497
e-mail: secretary@newark-golf-club.co.uk
web: www.newark-golf-club.co.uk
Wooded parkland in a secluded position with easy walking.
18 holes, 6458yds, Par 71, SSS 71, Course record 66.
Club membership 650.
Visitors Mon, Wed-Fri except BHs. Booking required. Handicap certificate. Dress code. **Societies** Booking required. **Green Fees** £33 per day, £27 per round. **Prof** PA Lockley **Course Designer** T Williamson **Facilities** **Leisure** snooker. **Conf** Corporate Hospitality Days **Location** 4m E of Newark on Sleaford road

Hotel ★★★ 71% The Grange Hotel, 73 London Rd, NEWARK ☎ 01636 703399 10 en suite 9 annexe en suite

NOTTINGHAM Map 08 SK53

Beeston Fields Old Dr, Wollaton Rd, Beeston NG9 3DD
☎ 0115 925 7062 📠 0115 925 4280
e-mail: beestonfieldsgolfclub@supanet.com
web: www.bestonfields.co.uk

18 holes, 6402yds, Par 71, SSS 71, Course record 64.
Course Designer Tom Williamson **Location** 400yds SW

Continued

off A52 Nottingham-Derby road
Phone for further details

Hotel Travelodge Nottingham Trowell (M1), TROWELL 08700 850 950 35 en suite

Bulwell Forest Hucknall Rd, Bulwell NG6 9LQ
0115 976 3172 (pro shop) 0115 967 1734
e-mail: david@dnehra.co.uk
Municipal heathland course with many natural hazards. Very tight fairways and subject to wind. Five challenging par 3s. Excellent drainage.
18 holes, 5667yds, Par 68, SSS 67, Course record 62. Club membership 350.
Visitors Booking required with pro shop 1 day in advance. **Societies** Booking required. **Green Fees** phone. **Course Designer** John Doleman **Facilities** **Leisure** hard tennis courts, children's playground. **Location** 4m NW of city on A611

Hotel ★★★ 66% Bestwood Lodge, Bestwood Country Park, Arnold, NOTTINGHAM 0115 920 3011 39 en suite

Chilwell Manor Meadow Ln, Chilwell NG9 5AE
0115 925 8958 0115 922 0575
e-mail: chilwellmanorgolfclub@barbox.net
Flat parkland. Some water, plenty of trees and narrow fairways.
18 holes, 6255yds, Par 70, SSS 71, Course record 66. Club membership 750.
Visitors Mon-Fri. Booking required. Handicap certificate. **Societies** Mon. Booking required. **Green Fees** phone. **Prof** Paul Wilson **Course Designer** Tom Williamson **Facilities** **Location** 4m SW on A6005

Hotel ★★ 60% Europa Hotel, 20-22 Derby Rd, LONG EATON 0115 972 8481 15 en suite

Edwalton Municipal Wellin Ln, Edwalton NG12 4AS
0115 923 4775 0115 923 1647
e-mail: edwalton@glendale-services.co.uk
web: www.glendale-golf.com
Gently sloping nine-hole parkland course. Also a nine-hole par 3 and large practice ground.
9 holes, 3336yds, Par 72, SSS 72, Course record 71. Club membership 536.
Visitors Mon-Sun & BHs. Booking required. **Societies** Booking required. **Green Fees** phone. **Prof** Lee Rawlings **Facilities** by arrangement **Leisure** par 3 course. **Conf** facs Corporate Hospitality Days **Location** S of Nottingham off A606

Hotel Premier Travel Inn Nottingham South, Loughborough Rd, Ruddington, NOTTINGHAM 0870 9906422 42 en suite

Mapperley Central Av, Plains Rd, Mapperley NG3 6RH
0115 955 6673 0115 955 6670
e-mail: house@mapperleygolfclub.org
web: www.mapperleygolfclub.org
Hilly meadowland course but with easy walking.
18 holes, 6307yds, Par 71, SSS 70. Club membership 700.
Visitors Mon, Wed-Fri, Sun & BHs. Booking required. Handicap certificate. Dress code. **Societies** Booking required. **Green Fees** £22.50 per day/round, £27.50 Sun & BHs. **Prof** John Newham **Course Designer** John Mason **Facilities** **Leisure** pool room. **Location** 3m NE of city centre off B684

Hotel Travelodge Nottingham Trowell (M1), TROWELL 08700 850 950 35 en suite

Nottingham City Sandhurst Rd, Bulwell Hall Park NG6 8LF
0115 927 2767 (pro) & 07740 688694
A pleasant municipal parkland course on the city outskirts.
18 holes, 6218yds, Par 69, SSS 70, Course record 63. Club membership 425.
Visitors contact club for details. **Societies** Booking required. **Green Fees** phone. **Prof** Cyril Jepson **Course Designer** H Braid **Facilities** **Conf** facs Corporate Hospitality Days **Location** 4m NW of city centre off A6002

Hotel ★★★ 66% Bestwood Lodge, Bestwood Country Park, Arnold, NOTTINGHAM 0115 920 3011 39 en suite

Wollaton Park Limetree Av, Wollaton Park NG8 1BT
0115 978 7574 0115 970 0736
e-mail: wollatonparkgc@aol.com
web: www.wollatonparkgolfclub.com
A traditional parkland course on slightly undulating land, winding through historic woodland and set in a historic deer park. Fine views of 16th-century Wollaton Hall.
18 holes, 6445yds, Par 71, SSS 71, Course record 64. Club membership 700.
Visitors Mon-Sun & BHs. Dress code. **Societies** Booking required. **Green Fees** £48 per day, £35 per round, £55/£40 Sat, Sun & BHs. **Prof** John Lower **Course Designer** T Williamson **Facilities** **Conf** Corporate Hospitality Days **Location** 2.5m W of city centre off ring road junct A52

Hotel ★★★ 62% Swans Hotel & Restaurant, 84-90 Radcliffe Rd, West Bridgford, NOTTINGHAM 0115 981 4042 30 en suite

OLLERTON Map 08 SK66

Rufford Park Golf & Country Club Rufford Ln, Rufford NG22 9DG
01623 825253 01623 825254
e-mail: enquiries@ruffordpark.co.uk
web: www.ruffordpark.co.uk
Set in the heart of Sherwood Forest, Rufford Park is noted for its picturesque 18 holes with its especially challenging par 3s. From the unique 175yd par 3 17th over water to the riverside 641yd 13th, the course offers everything the golfer needs from beginner to professional.
18 holes, 6368yds, Par 70, SSS 70, Course record 66. Club membership 650.
Visitors Mon-Sun & BHs. Booking required. Dress code. **Societies** Booking required. **Green Fees** Summer £25 per round, £30 Sat & Sun. Winter £20/£25. **Prof** John Vaughan, James Thompson **Course Designer** David

Continued

Hemstock, Ken Brown **Facilities** ⊗ Ⅲ ⛼ ☕ 🍷 ⛳ 🏠 **Conf** facs Corporate Hospitality Days **Location** S of Ollerton, off A614 for Rufford Mill

Hotel ★★★ 65% Clumber Park Hotel, Clumber Park, WORKSOP ☎ 0870 609 6158 48 en suite

OXTON Map 08 SK65

Oakmere Park Oaks Ln NG25 0RH
☎ 0115 965 3545 🖷 0115 965 5628
e-mail: enquiries@oakmerepark.co.uk
web: www.oakmerepark.co.uk
Twenty-seven holes set in rolling heathland in the heart of picturesque Robin Hood country. The par 4 16th and par 5 1st are notable, as are the all weather playing qualities.

Admirals: 18 holes, 6617yds, Par 73, SSS 72, Course record 64.
Commanders: 9 holes, 6407yds, Par 72, SSS 72.
Club membership 900.
Visitors Mon-Sun & BHs. Booking required. Dress code. **Societies** Booking required. **Green Fees** Admirals £20 per round, £28 Sat & Sun. **Prof** Daryl St-John Jones **Course Designer** Frank Pennick **Facilities** ⊗ Ⅲ ⛼ ☕ 🍷 ⛳ 🏠 **Conf** facs Corporate Hospitality Days **Location** 1m NW of Oxton off A6097 or A614

Hotel ★★★ 67% Westminster Hotel, 312 Mansfield Rd, Carrington, NOTTINGHAM ☎ 0115 955 5000 73 en suite

RADCLIFFE ON TRENT Map 08 SK63

Cotgrave Place Golf Club Stragglethorpe, Nr Cotgrave Village NG12 3HB
☎ 0115 933 3344 🖷 0115 933 4567
e-mail: cotgrave@americangolf.com
web: www.americangolf.com
The course offers 36 holes of championship golf. The front nine of the Open course is placed around a beautiful lake, man-made ponds and the Grantham Canal. The back nine is set in magnificent parkland with mature trees and wide fairways. Masters has an opening nine set among hedgerows and coppices. The huge greens with their interesting shapes are a particularly challenging test of nerve. The par 5 17th hole is one of the toughest in the country.
Masters: 18 holes, 5933yds, Par 70, SSS 69, Course record 66.
Open: 18 holes, 6302yds, Par 71, SSS 68, Course record 69.
Club membership 850.
Visitors Booking required. **Societies** Booking required. **Green Fees** phone. **Prof** Robert Smith **Course Designer** Peter Aliss, John Small **Facilities** ⊗ Ⅲ ⛼ ☕ 🍷 ⛳ 🏠 **Conf** Corporate Hospitality Days **Location** 2m SW of Radcliffe off A52

Hotel ★★★ 74% Langar Hall, LANGAR ☎ 01949 860559 12 en suite

Radcliffe on Trent Dewberry Ln, Cropwell Rd NG12 2JH
☎ 0115 933 3000 🖷 0115 911 6991
e-mail: les.wake@radcliffeontrentgc.co.uk
web: www.radcliffeontrentgc.co.uk
Fairly flat, parkland course with three good finishing holes: 16th (423 yds) par 4; 17th (174 yds) through spinney, par 3; 18th (336 yds) dog-leg par 4. Excellent views.
18 holes, 6374yds, Par 70, SSS 71, Course record 64.
Club membership 700.
Visitors Wed. Booking required. Handicap certificate. Dress code. **Societies** Booking required. **Green Fees** £35 per day, £25 per 18 holes. **Prof** Craig George **Course Designer** Tom Williamson **Facilities** ⊗ Ⅲ ⛼ ☕ 🍷 ⛳ 🏠 **Conf** Corporate Hospitality Days **Location** 0.5m SE of town centre off A52

Hotel ★★★ 62% Swans Hotel & Restaurant, 84-90 Radcliffe Rd, West Bridgford, NOTTINGHAM ☎ 0115 981 4042 30 en suite

RETFORD Map 08 SK78

Retford Brecks Rd, Ordsall DN22 7UA
☎ 01777 711188 (secretary) 🖷 01777 710412
18 holes, 6409yds, Par 72, SSS 72, Course record 67.
Course Designer Tom Williamson **Location** 1.5m S A620, between Worksop & Gainsborough
Phone for further details

Hotel ★★★ 65% The West Retford Hotel, 24 North Rd, RETFORD ☎ 01777 706333 & 0870 609 6162 🖷 01777 709951 63 en suite

RUDDINGTON Map 08 SK53

Ruddington Grange Wilford Rd NG11 6NB
☎ 0115 921 1951 (pro shop) & 984 6141
🖷 0115 940 5165
e-mail: info@ruddingtongrange.com
web: www.ruddingtongrange.com
Undulating parkland with many mature trees and water hazards on eight holes. Challenging but fair layout.
18 holes, 6543yds, Par 72, SSS 72, Course record 69.
Club membership 750.
Visitors Booking required. **Societies** Booking required. **Green Fees** phone. **Prof** Robert Simpson **Course Designer** E MacAusland, J Small **Facilities** ⊗ Ⅲ ⛼ ☕ 🍷 ⛳ 🏠 **Conf** facs Corporate Hospitality Days **Location** 1m N of town centre on B680

Hotel ★★★ 62% Swans Hotel & Restaurant, 84-90 Radcliffe Rd, West Bridgford, NOTTINGHAM ☎ 0115 981 4042 30 en suite

Continued

SERLBY Map 08 SK68

Serlby Park DN10 6BA
☎ 01777 818268
e-mail: kjcrook@onetel.com
Peaceful, picturesque setting on well-drained areas of woodland, parkland and farmland on the Serlby Hall Estate. Easy walking.
11 holes, 5404yds, Par 66, SSS 66, Course record 63.
Club membership 250.
Visitors With member only. Handicap certificate. Dress code. **Societies** Booking required. **Green Fees** phone. **Course Designer** Viscount Galway **Facilities** **Location** E of village off A638

Hotel ★★★ 70% Charnwood Hotel, Sheffield Rd, BLYTH ☎ 01909 591610 34 en suite

SOUTHWELL Map 08 SK65

Norwood Park Norwood Park NG25 0PF
☎ 01636 816626
e-mail: mail@norwoodpark.co.uk
web: www.norwoodpark.co.uk
A parkland course that blends perfectly with the historic setting of Norwood Park and highlights its natural features. Built to USGA standards, the course will appeal to all golfers, who will appreciate the well-shaped fairways, large undulating greens, natural and man-made water hazards, and fine views over the surrounding countryside.
18 holes, 6805yds, SSS 72.
Club membership 600.
Visitors Mon-Sun & BHs. Booking required. **Societies** booking required **Green Fees** £18 per 18 holes, £10 per 9 holes, £22/£12 Fri, £26/£15 Sat, Sun & BHs. **Prof** Paul Thornton **Course Designer** Clyde B Johnston **Facilities** **Conf** facs Corporate Hospitality Days **Location** 0.5m N of Southwell on the Kirklington road

Hotel ★★★ 66% Saracens Head Hotel, Market Place, SOUTHWELL ☎ 01636 812701 27 en suite

SUTTON IN ASHFIELD Map 08 SK45

Coxmoor Coxmoor Rd NG17 5LF
☎ 01623 557359 01623 557435
e-mail: coxmoorgc@btconnect.com
web: www.coxmoor.freeuk.com
Undulating moorland and heathland course with easy walking and excellent views. The clubhouse is traditional with a well-equipped games room. The course lies adjacent to Forestry Commission land over which there are several footpaths and extensive views.
18 holes, 6577yds, Par 73, SSS 72, Course record 65.
Club membership 700.
Visitors Mon, Wed-Fri except BHs. Booking required. Handicap certificate. Dress code. **Societies** Booking required. **Green Fees** £55 per day, £40 per round. **Prof** David Ridley **Facilities** **Leisure** snooker. **Conf** Corporate Hospitality Days **Location** 2m SE off A611

Hotel ★★★★ 68% Renaissance Derby/Nottingham Hotel, Carter Ln East, SOUTH NORMANTON
☎ 01773 812000 & 0870 4007262 158 en suite

WORKSOP Map 08 SK57

Bondhay Golf & Country Club Bondhay Ln, Whitwell S80 3EH
☎ 01909 723608 01909 720226
e-mail: enquiries@bondhay.com
web: www.bondhay.com
The wind usually plays quite an active role in making this flat championship course testing. Signature holes are the 10th which requires a second shot over water into a basin of trees; the 11th comes back over the same expanse of water and requires a mid to short iron to a long, narrow green; the 18th is a par 5 with a lake - the dilemma is whether to lay up short or go for the carry. The par 3s are generally island-like in design, requiring accuracy to avoid the many protective bunker features.
Devonshire Course: 18 holes, 6807yds, Par 72, SSS 73, Course record 67.
Club membership 450.
Visitors Mon-Sun & BHs. Booking required. Dress code. **Societies** Booking required. **Green Fees** 18 holes Mon-Tue £16, Wed-Fri £19, Sat-Sun £24. Par 3 Course £5. **Prof** Michael Ramsden **Course Designer** Donald Steel **Facilities** **Leisure** fishing, par 3 family course. **Conf** facs Corporate Hospitality Days **Location** M1 junct 30, 5m W of Worksop off A619

Hotel ★★★ 65% Sitwell Arms Hotel, Station Rd, RENISHAW ☎ 01246 435226 & 01246 437327
01246 433915 29 en suite

College Pines Worksop College Dr S80 3AL
☎ 01909 501431 01909 481227
e-mail: snelljunior@btinternet.com
web: www.collegepinesgolfclub.co.uk
This course was opened in 1994 and the par 73 layout covers 150 acres of well-drained land with heathland characteristics. It is club policy to remain open on full tees and greens all year round.
18 holes, 6801yards, Par 73, SSS 73, Course record 67.
Club membership 500.
Visitors Mon-Sun & BHs. Booking required. Dress code. **Societies** Booking required. **Green Fees** £20 per day, £14 per round, £30/£20 Sat, Sun & BHs. **Prof** Charles Snell **Course Designer** David Snell **Facilities** **Conf** Corporate Hospitality Days **Location** M1 junct 30-31, S of Worksop on B6034 Edwinstowe road

Hotel ★★★ 65% Clumber Park Hotel, Clumber Park, WORKSOP ☎ 0870 609 6158 48 en suite

Kilton Forest Blyth Rd S81 0TL
☎ 01909 486563
18 holes, 6424yds, Par 72, SSS 71, Course record 66.
Location 1m NE of town centre on B6045
Phone for further details

Hotel ★★★ 68% Lion Hotel, 112 Bridge St, WORKSOP
☎ 01909 477925 45 en suite

Lindrick Lindrick Common S81 8BH
☎ 01909 475282 01909 488685
e-mail: lgc@ansbronze.com
web: www.lindrickgolfclub.co.uk
Heathland course with some trees and masses of gorse.
18 holes, 6486yds, Par 71, SSS 71, Course record 63.
Club membership 510.

Continued

Visitors Mon, Wed-Fri, Sun except BHs. Booking required. Handicap certificate. Dress code. **Societies** Booking required. **Green Fees** £65 per day, £50 per 18 holes. Reduced winter rate. **Prof** John R King **Facilities** **Leisure** Buggies for disabled only. **Conf** Corporate Hospitality Days **Location** M1 junct 31, 4m NW of Worksop on A57

Hotel ★★★ 68% Lion Hotel, 112 Bridge St, WORKSOP ☎ 01909 477925 45 en suite

Worksop Windmill Ln S80 2SQ
☎ 01909 477731 📠 01909 530917
e-mail: worksopgolfclub@worksop.co.uk
web: www.worksopgolfclub.com

Adjacent to Clumber Park, this course has heathland terrain, with gorse, broom, oak and birch trees. Fast, true greens, dry all year round.

18 holes, 6660yds, Par 72, SSS 72.
Club membership 600.

Visitors Mon, Wed, Fri-Sun except BHs. Booking required. Handicap certificate. Dress code. **Societies** Booking required. **Green Fees** £48 per 36 holes, £35 per 18 holes. **Prof** K Crossland **Course Designer** Tom Williamson **Facilities** **Leisure** snooker. **Conf** facs Corporate Hospitality Days **Location** A57 ring road onto B6034 to Edwinstowe

Hotel ★★★ 65% Clumber Park Hotel, Clumber Park, WORKSOP ☎ 0870 609 6158 48 en suite

OXFORDSHIRE

ABINGDON — Map 04 SU49

Drayton Park Steventon Rd, Drayton OX14 4LA
☎ 01235 550607 (pro shop) 📠 01235 525731

Set in the heart of Oxfordshire, an 18-hole parkland course designed by Hawtree. Five lakes and sand-based greens.

18 holes, 6030yds, Par 67, SSS 67, Course record 60.
Club membership 500.

Visitors Booking required. Dress code. **Societies** Booking required. **Green Fees** phone. **Prof** Martin Morbey **Course Designer** Hawtree **Facilities** **Leisure** 9 hole par 3 course. **Location** Off A34 at Didcot

Hotel ★★★ 66% Abingdon Four Pillars Hotel, Marcham Rd, ABINGDON ☎ 0800 374 692 & 01235 553456 62 en suite

BANBURY — Map 04 SP44

Banbury Aynho Rd, Adderbury OX17 3NT
☎ 01295 810419 & 812880 📠 01295 810056
e-mail: office@banburygolfcentre.co.uk

Undulating wooded course with water features and USGA specification greens.

Red & Yellow: 18 holes, 6557yds, Par 71, SSS 71.
Yellow & Blue: 18 holes, 6603yds, Par 71, SSS 71.
Red & Blue: 18 holes, 6706yds, Par 72, SSS 72.
Club membership 300.

Visitors Mon-Sun. **Societies** Booking required. **Green Fees** phone. **Prof** Stuart Kier **Course Designer** Reed, Payn **Facilities** **Conf** Corporate Hospitality Days **Location** Off B4100 between Adderbury

Hotel Premier Travel Inn Banbury, Warwick Rd, Warmington, BANBURY ☎ 0870 9906512 39 en suite

Rye Hill Milcombe OX15 4RU
☎ 01295 721818 📠 01295 720089
e-mail: info@ryehill.co.uk
web: www.ryehill.co.uk

Well-drained course, set in 200 acres of rolling countryside, with both parkland and heathland features, including wide fairways, large undulating greens, dramatic lakes, and fine views of the surrounding countryside.

18 holes, 6919yds, Par 72, SSS 73, Course record 62.
Club membership 575.

Visitors Mon-Sun & BHs. **Societies** Booking required. **Green Fees** £40 per day, £25 per round, £55/£32 Sat & Sun. 9 holes £19/£21. **Prof** Tony Pennock **Facilities** by arrangement **Leisure** fishing, pitch & putt course, tri-golf 9 hole family course. **Conf** facs Corporate Hospitality Days **Location** M40 junct 11, A361 towards Chipping Norton, signed 1m out of Bloxham

Hotel ★★★ 69% Wroxton House Hotel, Wroxton St Mary, BANBURY ☎ 01295 730777 32 en suite

BURFORD — Map 04 SP21

Burford Swindon Rd OX18 4JG
☎ 01993 822583 📠 01993 822801
e-mail: secretary@burfordgc.co.uk
web: www.burfordgolfclub.co.uk

Parkland with mature, tree-lined fairways and high quality greens.

18 holes, 6401yds, Par 71, SSS 71, Course record 64.
Club membership 770.

Visitors Mon-Sun except BHs. Dress code. **Societies** Booking required. **Green Fees** £40 per day. **Prof** Michael Ridge **Course Designer** John H Turner **Facilities** **Location** 0.5m S off A361

CHESTERTON — Map 04 SP52

Bicester Golf & Country Club OX26 1TE
☎ 01869 242023 📠 01869 240754
e-mail: bicestergolf@ukonline.co.uk

18 holes, 6600yds, Par 71, SSS 70, Course record 68.

Course Designer R Stagg **Location** 0.5m W off A4095
Phone for further details

Hotel ★★ 72% Jersey Arms Hotel, BICESTER ☎ 01869 343234 6 en suite 14 annexe en suite

CHIPPING NORTON Map 04 SP32

Chipping Norton Southcombe OX7 5QH
☎ 01608 642383 🗎 01608 645422
e-mail: chipping.nortongc@virgin.net
Downland course situated at 244 metres above sea level, its undulations providing a good walk. On a limestone base, the course dries quickly in wet conditions. The opening few holes provide a good test of golf made more difficult when the prevailing wind makes the player use the extremes of the course.

18 holes, 6241yds, Par 71, SSS 70, Course record 62.
Club membership 900.
Visitors contact club for details. **Societies** welcome.
Green Fees £32 per day. **Prof** Neil Rowlands **Facilities** **Location** 1.5m E on A44

Wychwood Lyneham OX7 6QQ
☎ 01993 831841 🗎 01993 831775
e-mail: wychwoodgolfclub@btconnect.com
Wychwood was designed to use the natural features of its location. It is set in 170 acres on the fringe of the Cotswolds and blends superbly with its surroundings. Lakes and streams enhance the challenge of the course with water coming into play on eight of the 18 holes. All greens are sand based, built to USGA specification.
18 holes, 6844yds, Par 72, SSS 72, Course record 67.
Club membership 750.
Visitors Mon-Sun except BHs. Booking required. Dress code. **Societies** Booking required. **Green Fees** £30 per day, £25 per 18 holes, £37/£30 Sat & Sun. **Prof** James Fincher **Facilities** **Leisure** fishing. **Conf** facs Corporate Hospitality Days **Location** Off A361 between Burford & Norton

DIDCOT Map 04 SU59

Hadden Hill Wallingford Rd OX11 9BJ
☎ 01235 510410 🗎 01235 511260
e-mail: info@haddenhillgolf.co.uk
web: www.haddenhillgolf.co.uk
A challenging course on undulating terrain with excellent drainage. Superb greens and fairways.
18 holes, 6563yds, Par 71, SSS 71, Course record 65.
Club membership 400.
Visitors Mon-Sun & BHs. Booking required. Dress code. **Societies** Booking required. **Green Fees** £18 per 18 holes, £11 per 9 holes, £23/£14 Sat & Sun. **Prof** Ian Mitchell **Course Designer** Michael V Morley **Facilities** by arrangement **Leisure** teaching academy. **Conf** Corporate Hospitality Days **Location** A34 Milton interchange, follow A4130, Course located 1m E of Didcot on Wallingford Road

Hotel ★★★ 66% Abingdon Four Pillars Hotel, Marcham Rd, ABINGDON ☎ 0800 374 692 & 01235 553456 🗎 01235 554117 62 en suite

FARINGDON Map 04 SU29

Carswell Carswell SN7 8PU
☎ 01367 870422 🗎 01367 870592
e-mail: info@carswellgolfandcountryclub.co.uk
web: www.carswellgolfandcountryclub.co.uk

18 holes, 6183yds, Par 72, SSS 70.
Course Designer J & E Ely **Location** Off A420
Phone for further details

Hotel ★★★ 70% Sudbury House Hotel & Conference Centre, London St, FARINGDON ☎ 01367 241272 49 en suite

FRILFORD Map 04 SU49

Frilford Heath OX13 5NW
☎ 01865 390864 🗎 01865 390823
e-mail: secretary@frilfordheath.co.uk
web: www.frilfordheath.co.uk
Fifty-four holes in three layouts of differing character. The Green course is a fully mature heathland course of some 6006yds. The Red Course is of championship length at 6884yds with a parkland flavour and a marked degree of challenge. The Blue Course is of modern design, and at 6728yds, it incorporates water hazards and large shallow sand traps.
Red Course: 18 holes, 6884yds, Par 73, SSS 73, Course record 66.
Green Course: 18 holes, 6006yds, Par 69, SSS 69, Course record 67.
Blue Course: 18 holes, 6728yds, Par 72, SSS 72, Course record 63.
Club membership 1300.
Visitors Mon-Sun & BHs. Handicap certificate. Dress code. **Societies** Booking required. **Green Fees** £65 per day, £80 Sat & Sun. **Prof** Derek Craik **Course Designer** J Taylor, D Cotton, S Gidman **Facilities** **Conf** facs Corporate Hospitality Days **Location** 0.5m N of Frilford off A338

Hotel ★★★ 66% Abingdon Four Pillars Hotel, Marcham Rd, ABINGDON ☎ 0800 374 692 & 01235 553456 🗎 01235 554117 62 en suite

Continued

HENLEY-ON-THAMES Map 04 SU78

Badgemore Park Badgemore RG9 4NR
☎ 01491 637300 📠 01491 576899
e-mail: info@badgemorepark.com
web: www.badgemorepark.com
Formerly a country estate, the 120 acres of mature woodland and landscaped park was converted into a golf course 30 years ago. The signature hole of this easy walking course is the 13th, a tough par 3 played across a valley to a narrow raised green.

18 holes, 6129yds, Par 69, SSS 69, Course record 64. Club membership 700.
Visitors Mon-Fri. Booking required Sat, Sun & BHs. Dress code. **Societies** Booking required. **Green Fees** £26 per round, £36 Sat, Sun & BHs. **Prof** Jonathan Dunn **Course Designer** Robert Sandow **Facilities** by arrangement **Conf** facs Corporate Hospitality Days **Location** N from Henley towards Rotherfield Greys, 1.5m on right

Henley Harpsden RG9 4HG
☎ 01491 575742 📠 01491 412179
e-mail: admin@henleygc.com
web: www.henleygc.com
Designed by James Braid in 1907, the course retains many of his classic features, while being a challenge for all golfers even with modern technology. The first four holes are considered the hardest opening holes of any course in Oxfordshire and possibly the UK.
18 holes, 6329yds, Par 70, SSS 70, Course record 62. Club membership 700.
Visitors Mon-Fri. Handicap certificate. Dress code. **Societies** Booking required. **Green Fees** £55 per day, £45 per round, £35 after 4pm. **Prof** Mark Howell **Course Designer** James Braid **Facilities** **Conf** Corporate Hospitality Days **Location** 1.25m S off A4155

HORTON-CUM-STUDLEY Map 04 SP51

Studley Wood The Straight Mile OX33 1BF
☎ 01865 351122 & 351144 📠 01865 351166
e-mail: admin@swgc.co.uk.
web: www.studleywoodgolf.co.uk.
Gently undulating woodland course set in a former deer park. Tranquil setting with an abundance of wildlife. USGA specification tees and greens, with lakes coming into play on nine holes.
18 holes, 6811yds, Par 73, SSS 72, Course record 65. Club membership 700.
Visitors contact club for details. Dress code. **Societies** Booking required. **Green Fees** £36 per round, £46 per round Sat & Sun. **Prof** Tony Williams **Course Designer** Simon Gidman **Facilities** **Leisure** teaching studio with video facilities. **Conf** facs Corporate Hospitality Days **Location** 6m NE of Oxford, off B4027 to Horton

Hotel ★★★★ 70% The Oxford Hotel, Godstow Rd, Wolvercote Roundabout, OXFORD ☎ 01865 489988 168 en suite

KIRTLINGTON Map 04 SP41

Kirtlington OX5 3JY
☎ 01869 351133 📠 01869 351143
e-mail: info@kirtlingtongolfclub.com
web: www.kirtlingtongolfclub.com
An inland links-type course with challenging greens. The course incorporates many natural features and has 102 bunkers and a 110yd par 3 19th when an extra hole is required to determine a winner. The 9 hole course has three par 4's and six par 3's with all year round buggy track.
18 holes, 6107yds, Par 70, SSS 69, Course record 68. Academy Course: 9 holes, 1535yds, Par 30, SSS 53. Club membership 400.
Visitors Mon-Sun & BHs. Booking required. Dress code. **Societies** Booking required. **Green Fees** 18 holes £22, £27 Sat & Sun. 9 holes £10, £12 Sat & Sun. **Prof** Andy Taylor **Course Designer** Graham Webster **Facilities** **Leisure** 9 hole academy course. **Conf** facs Corporate Hospitality Days **Location** M40 junct 9, on A4095 outside Kirtlington

Hotel ★★★ 70% Weston Manor Hotel, WESTON-ON-THE-GREEN ☎ 01869 350621 15 en suite 20 annexe en suite

MILTON COMMON Map 04 SP60

The Oxfordshire Rycote Ln OX9 2PU
☎ 01844 278300 📠 01844 278003
e-mail: info@theoxfordshiregolfclub.com
web: www.theoxfordshiregolfclub.com
Designed by Rees Jones, The Oxfordshire is considered to be one of the most exciting courses in the country. The strategically contoured holes blend naturally into the surrounding countryside to provide a challenging game of golf. With four lakes and 135 bunkers, the course makes full use of the terrain and the natural elements to provide characteristics similar to those of a links course.

18 holes, 7192yds, Par 72, SSS 75, Course record 64. Club membership 456.
Visitors Mon-Sun & BHs. Booking required. Handicap certificate. Dress code. **Societies** Booking required. **Green**

Continued

Continued

Fees Summer £90 per 18 holes, £110 Sat, Sun & BHs. Winter £60/£70. **Prof** Stephen Gibson **Course Designer** Rees Jones **Facilities** ⊗ 𝄃 ♨ ☕ ♀ ⛀ ⌂ ⚐ ⛳ ⛟ ✓ ⛳ **Leisure** Japanese ofuro baths. **Conf** facs Corporate Hospitality Days **Location** M40 junct 7, 1.5m on A329

Hotel ★★★ 74% Spread Eagle Hotel, Cornmarket, THAME ☎ 01844 213661 33 en suite

NUFFIELD Map 04 SU68

Huntercombe RG9 5SL

☎ 01491 641207 🖷 01491 642060
e-mail: office@huntercombegolfclub.co.uk
web: www.huntercombegolfclub.co.uk

This heathland and woodland course overlooks the Oxfordshire plain and has many attractive and interesting fairways and fair true greens. Walking is easy after the 3rd which is a notable hole. The course is subject to wind and grass pot bunkers are interesting hazards.

18 holes, 6271yds, Par 70, SSS 70, Course record 63.
Club membership 800.

Visitors Mon-Sun & BHs. **Societies** Booking required. **Green Fees** £60 per day, £40 per round, £75/£60 per round Sat, Sun & BHs. **Prof** Ian Roberts **Course Designer** Willie Park jnr **Facilities** ⊗ 𝄃 ♨ ☕ ♀ ⛀ ⌂ ⚐ ⛳ ⛟ ✓ ⛳ **Location** Off A4130 at Nuffield

Hotel ★★★ 70% Shillingford Bridge Hotel, Shillingford, WALLINGFORD ☎ 01865 858567 34 en suite 8 annexe en suite

Prices may change during the currency of the guide, always check when booking

OXFORD Map 04 SP50

Hinksey Heights South Hinksey OX1 5AB

☎ 01865 327775 🖷 01865 736930
e-mail: play@oxford-golf.co.uk
web: www.oxford-golf.co.uk

Set in an Area of Outstanding Natural Beauty, overlooking the Dreaming Spires of Oxford and the Thames Valley. The course has a heathland or links feel with several fairways running along the bottom of valleys created by the use of natural and man-made features. Each of the 18 holes is distinctive and there is also a nine-hole par 3 course for golfers of all ages and abilities.

18 holes, 6936yds, Par 74, SSS 73.
Club membership 450.

Visitors Booking required. **Societies** Booking required with professional. **Green Fees** phone. **Prof** Dean Davis **Course Designer** David Heads **Facilities** ⊗ 𝄃 ♨ ☕ ♀ ⛀ ⌂ ⚐ ⛟ ✓ ⛳ **Conf** Corporate Hospitality Days **Location** On A34 Oxford bypass between Abingdon & Oxford Botley junct

Hotel ★★★ 68% Hawkwell House, Church Way, Iffley Village, OXFORD ☎ 01865 749988 66 en suite

North Oxford Banbury Rd OX2 8EZ

☎ 01865 554924 🖷 01865 515921
e-mail: manager@nogc.co.uk
web: www.nogc.co.uk

Gently undulating parkland.

18 holes, 5736yds, Par 67, SSS 67, Course record 62.
Club membership 600.

Visitors Mon-Sun & BHs. **Societies** Booking required. **Green Fees** £25-£38 per day, £20-£30 per round. **Prof** Robert Harris **Facilities** ⊗ 𝄃 ♨ ☕ ♀ ⛀ ⌂ ⚐ ✓ **Conf** Corporate Hospitality Days **Location** 3m N of city centre on A4165

Hotel ★★★★ 70% The Oxford Hotel, Godstow Rd, Wolvercote Roundabout, OXFORD ☎ 01865 489988 168 en suite

Southfield Hill Top Rd OX4 1PF
☎ 01865 242158 📠 01865 250023
e-mail: sgcltd@btopenworld.com
web: www.southfieldgolf.co.uk
Home of the City, University and Ladies Clubs, and well-known to graduates throughout the world. A challenging course, in a varied parkland setting, providing a real test for players.

18 holes, 6325yds, Par 70, SSS 70, Course record 61. Club membership 740.
Visitors Mon-Fri. Booking required Sat, Sun & BHs. Dress code. **Societies** Booking required. **Green Fees** £35 per day/round. **Prof** Tony Rees **Course Designer** H Colt **Facilities** **Conf** Corporate Hospitality Days **Location** 1.5m SE of city centre off B480

Hotel ★★★ 69% Macdonald Eastgate Townhouse, 73 High St, OXFORD ☎ 0870 400 8201 & 01865 248332 📠 01865 791681 63 en suite

SHRIVENHAM Map 04 SU28

Shrivenham Park Penny Hooks Ln SN6 8EX
☎ 01793 783853
web: www.shrivenhampark.com
A flat, mature parkland course with excellent drainage. A good challenge for all standards of golfer.
18 holes, 5769yds, Par 69, SSS 69, Course record 64. Club membership 150.
Visitors Mon-Fri. Booking required Sat, Sun & BHs. Dress code. **Societies** welcome. **Green Fees** £16 per 18 holes £10 per 9 holes, £21/£12 Sat, Sun & BHs. **Prof** Richard Jefferies **Course Designer** Gordon Cox **Facilities** **Conf** Corporate Hospitality Days **Location** 0.5m NE of town centre

Hotel ★★★ 70% Sudbury House Hotel & Conference Centre, London St, FARINGDON ☎ 01367 241272 49 en suite

TADMARTON Map 04 SP33

Tadmarton Heath OX15 5HL
☎ 01608 737278 📠 01608 730548
e-mail: thgc@btinternet.com
web: www.thgc.btinternet.co.uk
A mixture of heath and sandy land on a plateau in the Cotswolds. The course opens gently before reaching the scenic 7th hole across a trout stream close to the clubhouse. The course then progressively tightens

Continued

through the gorse before a challenging 430yd dog-leg completes the round.
18 holes, 5917yds, Par 69, SSS 69, Course record 63. Club membership 650.
Visitors Mon-Wed, Fri-Sun & BHs. Thu pm. Booking required Thu, Sat, Sun & BHs. Handicap certificate. Dress code. **Societies** Booking required. **Green Fees** £45 per day, £40 after 10am. £50 Sat & Sun, £40 pm. **Prof** Tom Jones **Course Designer** Col CK Hutchison **Facilities** by arrangement **Leisure** fishing. **Conf** Corporate Hospitality Days **Location** 1m SW of Lower Tadmarton off B4035, 6m from Banbury

Hotel ★★★ 71% Banbury House, Oxford Rd, BANBURY ☎ 01295 259361 64 en suite

WALLINGFORD Map 04 SU68

The Springs Hotel & Golf Club Wallingford Rd, North Stoke OX10 6BE
☎ 01491 827310 📠 01491 827312
e-mail: proshop@thespringshotel.com
web: www.thespringshotel.com
The 133 acres of parkland are bordered by the River Thames, within which lie three lakes and challenging wetland areas. The course has traditional features like a double green and sleepered bunker with sleepered lake edges of typical American design.

18 holes, 6470yds, Par 72, SSS 71, Course record 67. Club membership 580.
Visitors Mon-Sun & BHs. Handicap certificate. Dress code. **Societies** Booking required. **Green Fees** £29 per 18 holes, £35 Sat, Sun & BHs. **Prof** David Boyce **Course Designer** Brian Hugget **Facilities** **Leisure** heated outdoor swimming pool, fishing, sauna, croquet lawn. **Conf** facs Corporate Hospitality Days **Location** 2m SE of town centre over River Thames

Hotel ★★★ 72% The Springs Hotel & Golf Club, Wallingford Rd, North Stoke, WALLINGFORD ☎ 01491 836687 32 en suite

WATERSTOCK Map 04 SP60

Waterstock Thame Rd OX33 1HT
☎ 01844 338093 📠 01844 338036
e-mail: wgc_oxfordgolf@btinternet.com
web: www.waterstockgolf.co.uk
A 6500yd course designed by Donald Steel with USGA greens and tees fully computer irrigated. Four par 3s facing north, south, east and west. A brook and hidden lake affect six holes, with dog-legs being 4th and 10th holes. Five par 5s on the course, making it a challenge for players of all standards.

Continued

18 holes, 6535yds, Par 72, SSS 72, Course record 69.
Club membership 500.
Visitors Mon-Sun & BHs. Booking required. Dress code. **Societies** Booking required. **Green Fees** £35.50 per day, £21 per round, £16 twilight, £11.50 per 9 holes, £40.50/£26/£17/£14.50 Sat, Sun & BHs. **Prof** Paul Bryant **Course Designer** Donald Steel **Facilities** **Leisure** fishing. **Conf** facs Corporate Hospitality Days **Location** M40 junct 8/8A, E of Oxford near Wheatley

Hotel ★★★ 74% Spread Eagle Hotel, Cornmarket, THAME ☎ 01844 213661 33 en suite

WITNEY Map 04 SP31

Witney Lakes Downs Rd OX29 0SY
☎ 01993 893011 🖹 01993 778866
e-mail: golf@witney-lakes.co.uk
web: www.witney-lakes.co.uk
Five large lakes come into play on eight holes. An excellent test of golf that will use every club in your bag.
18 holes, 6700yds, Par 71, Course record 67.
Club membership 450.
Visitors Mon-Sun & BHs. Dress code. **Societies** Booking required. **Green Fees** £20 per 18 holes, £29 Sat & Sun. **Prof** Adam Souter **Course Designer** Simon Gidman **Facilities** **Leisure** heated indoor swimming pool, sauna, solarium, gymnasium, trim trail. **Conf** facs Corporate Hospitality Days **Location** 2m W of Witney town centre off B4047

Hotel ★★★ 70% Witney Four Pillars Hotel, Ducklington Ln, WITNEY ☎ 0800 374 692 & 01993 779777 🖹 01993 703467 87 en suite

RUTLAND

GREAT CASTERTON Map 04 TF00

Rutland County PE9 4AQ
☎ 01780 460330 🖹 01780 460437
e-mail: info@rutlandcountygolf.co.uk
web: www.rutlandcountygolf.co.uk
Inland links-style course with gently rolling fairways, large tees and greens. Playable all year round due to good drainage.
18 holes, 6425yds, Par 71, SSS 71, Course record 64.
Club membership 740.
Visitors Mon-Sun & BHs. Booking required. Dress code. **Societies** Booking required. **Green Fees** £30 per day, £25 per round, £40/£30 Sat & Sun. **Prof** Ian Melville **Course Designer** Cameron Sinclair **Facilities** **Leisure** Par 3 course. **Conf** facs Corporate Hospitality Days **Location** 2m N of Stamford on A1

Hotel ★★ 68% The White Horse Inn, Main St, EMPINGHAM ☎ 01780 460221 4 en suite 9 annexe en suite

GREETHAM Map 08 SK91

Greetham Valley Wood Ln LE15 7NP
☎ 01780 460444 🖹 01780 460623
e-mail: info@gvgc.co.uk
web: www.gvgc.co.uk
Set in 267 acres, including mature woodland, undulating natural valley, and water hazards. The Lakes course is an excellent test of golf with numerous bunkers. Water plays a big part with four holes over water finishing with the 18th set between two lakes. The Valley course is picturesque with many holes playing across or along the side of North Brook - twelve holes feature water.

Greetham

Lakes: 18 holes, 6779yds, Par 72, SSS 72, Course record 65.
Valley: 18 holes, 5595yds, Par 68, SSS 67, Course record 64.
Club membership 1000.
Visitors Mon-Fri. Booking required Sat, Sun & BHs. Dress code. **Societies** Booking required. **Green Fees** £30 per day, £25 per round, £35/£30 Sat & Sun. **Prof** John Pengelly **Course Designer** FE Hinch, B Stephens **Facilities** **Leisure** fishing, bowls green, 9 hole par 3. **Conf** facs Corporate Hospitality Days **Location** A1 onto B668 Oakham road, course signed

Hotel ★★★ 67% Greetham Valley, Wood Ln, GREETHAM ☎ 01780 460444 35 en suite

KETTON Map 04 SK90

Luffenham Heath PE9 3UU
☎ 01780 720205 🖹 01780 722146
e-mail: jringleby@theluffenhamheathgc.co.uk
web: www.luffenhamheath.co.uk
This undulating heathland course with low bushes, much gorse and many trees, lies in a conservation area for flora and fauna. From the higher part of the course there is a magnificent view across the Chater valley. The course places a premium on accuracy with many demanding driving holes, challenging bunkers and well-guarded greens. The course is not long but there are several outstanding holes.

18 holes, 6315yds, Par 70, SSS 70, Course record 64.
Club membership 550.
Visitors Mon, Wed-Fri. Booking required Sat, Sun & BHs.

Continued

Continued

Handicap certificate. Dress code. **Societies** Booking required. **Green Fees** phone. **Prof** Ian Burnett **Course Designer** James Braid **Facilities** **Conf** Corporate Hospitality Days **Location** 1.5m SW of Ketton on A6121 by Foster's Bridge

Hotel ★★★ 80% The George of Stamford, 71 St Martins, STAMFORD ☎ 01780 750750 & 750700 (Res) 01780 750701 47 en suite

SHROPSHIRE

BRIDGNORTH Map 07 SO79

Bridgnorth Stanley Ln WV16 4SF
☎ 01746 763315 01746 763315
e-mail: secretary.bgc@tiscali.co.uk
web: www.bridgnorthgolfclub.co.uk
Pleasant parkland by the River Severn.
18 holes, 6582yds, Par 73, SSS 72, Course record 68.
Club membership 725.
Visitors Mon.Tue, Thu, Fri & BHs. Handicap certificate. Dress code. **Societies** Booking required. **Green Fees** £31 per day, £25 per round, £41/£31 Sat, Sun & BHs. **Prof** Paul Hinton **Facilities** **Leisure** fishing. **Conf** Corporate Hospitality Days **Location** 1m N off B4373

CHURCH STRETTON Map 07 SO49

Church Stretton Trevor Hill SY6 6JH
☎ 01694 722281 01743 861918
e-mail: secretary@churchstrettongolfclub.co.uk
web: www.churchstrettongolfclub.co.uk
18 holes, 5020yds, Par 66, SSS 65, Course record 63.
Course Designer James Braid **Location** W of town. From Cardington Valley up steep Trevor Hill
Phone for further details

CLEOBURY MORTIMER Map 07 SO67

Cleobury Mortimer Wyre Common DY14 8HQ
☎ 01299 271112 01299 271468
e-mail: secretary@cleoburygolfclub.com
web: www.cleoburygolfclub.com
Well-designed 27-hole parkland course set in undulating countryside with fine views from all holes. An interesting challenge to golfers of all abilities.

Foxes Run: 9 holes, 2980yds, Par 34, SSS 34.
Badgers Sett: 9 holes, 3271yds, Par 36, SSS 36.
Deer Park: 9 holes, 3167yds, Par 35, SSS 35.
Club membership 650.
Visitors Mon-Sun & BHs. Booking required. Dress code.

Continued

Societies Booking required. **Green Fees** £30 per day, £20 per 18 holes, £36/£30 Sat & Sun. **Prof** Jon Jones, Martin Payne **Course Designer** E.G.U **Facilities** **Leisure** fishing, snooker table. **Conf** facs Corporate Hospitality Days **Location** On A4117 1m N of Cleobury Mortimer

Inn ♦♦♦♦ The Crown Inn, Hopton Wafers, CLEOBURY MORTIMER ☎ 01299 270372 7 en suite

LILLESHALL Map 07 SJ71

Lilleshall Hall TF10 9AS
☎ 01952 603840 & 604776 01952 604776
18 holes, 5906yds, Par 68, SSS 68, Course record 65.
Course Designer H Colt **Location** 3m SE
Phone for further details

LUDLOW Map 07 SO57

Ludlow Bromfield SY8 2BT
☎ 01584 856366 01584 856366
e-mail: secretary@ludlowgolfclub.com
web: www.ludlowgolfclub.com
A long-established heathland course in the middle of the racecourse. Very flat, quick drying, with broom and gorse-lined fairways.
18 holes, 6277yds, Par 70, SSS 70, Course record 65.
Club membership 700.
Visitors contact club for details. Handicap certificate. Dress code. **Societies** Booking required. **Green Fees** £28 per round, £35 per day, £35 Sat, Sun & BHs. **Prof** Russell Price **Facilities** **Conf** Corporate Hospitality Days **Location** 1m N of Ludlow off A49

Hotel ★★★ 67% The Feathers Hotel, The Bull Ring, LUDLOW ☎ 01584 875261 40 en suite

Guest House ♦♦♦♦ The Clive Restaurant with Rooms, Bromfield, LUDLOW ☎ 01584 856565 & 856665 01584 856661 15 annexe en suite

MARKET DRAYTON Map 07 SJ63

Market Drayton Sutton Ln TF9 2HX
☎ 01630 652266 01630 656564
e-mail: marketdraytongc@btinternet.com
Undulating parkland course with two steep banks in quiet, picturesque surroundings, providing a good test of golf.
18 holes, 6290yds, Par 71, SSS 71, Course record 67.
Club membership 600.
Visitors Mon, Wed-Fri except BHs. Dress code. **Societies** welcome. **Green Fees** Summer £26 per round. Winter £20. **Prof** Russell Clewes **Facilities**

Continued

Conf Corporate Hospitality Days **Location** 1m S off A41/A529

Hotel ★★★ 72% Goldstone Hall, Goldstone, MARKET DRAYTON ☎ 01630 661202 11 en suite

NEWPORT Map 07 SJ72

Aqualate Golf Centre Stafford Rd TF10 9DB
☎ 01952 811699
A parkland course with gentle gradients and hazards.
9 holes, 5659yds, Par 69, SSS 67, Course record 67.
Club membership 175.
Visitors Booking required. **Societies** Booking required. **Green Fees** phone. **Prof** Kevin Short **Facilities** **Conf** Corporate Hospitality Days **Location** 2m E of town centre on A518, 400yds from junct A41

OSWESTRY Map 07 SJ22

Mile End Mile End, Old Shrewsbury Rd SY11 4JF
☎ 01691 671246 🗎 01691 670580
e-mail: info@mileendgolfclub.co.uk
web: www.mileendgolfclub.co.uk
A gently undulating parkland course covering over 135 acres and including a number of water features, notably the 3rd, 8th and 17th holes, which have greens protected by large pools. The longest hole is the par 5, 542yd 14th, complete with its two tiered green.
18 holes, 6233yds, Par 71, SSS 70, Course record 66.
Club membership 700.
Visitors Mon-Sun & BHs. Booking required. Dress code. **Societies** Booking required. **Green Fees** £16 per round, £25 Sat, Sun & BHs. **Prof** Scott Carpenter **Course Designer** Price, Gough **Facilities** **Conf** Corporate Hospitality Days **Location** 1m SE off A5

Hotel ★★★ 72% Wynnstay Hotel, Church St, OSWESTRY ☎ 01691 655261 29 en suite

Oswestry Aston Park SY11 4JJ
☎ 01691 610535 🗎 01691 610535
e-mail: secretary@oswestrygolfclub.co.uk
web: www.oswestrygolfclub.co.uk
Gently undulating mature parkland course set in splendid Shropshire countryside. Free draining soils make Oswestry an ideal year round test of golf.
18 holes, 6038yds, Par 70, SSS 69, Course record 61.
Club membership 960.
Visitors contact club for details. Handicap certificate. Dress code. **Societies** Booking required. **Green Fees** £33 per day, £27 per round, £36/£31 Sat. **Prof** David Skelton **Course Designer** James Braid **Facilities** **Conf** Corporate Hospitality Days **Location** 2m SE on A5

Hotel ★★★ 72% Wynnstay Hotel, Church St, OSWESTRY ☎ 01691 655261 29 en suite

PANT Map 07 SJ22

Llanymynech SY10 8LB
☎ 01691 830983 & 830542
e-mail: secretary.llanygc@btinternet.com
web: www.llanymynechgolfclub.co.uk
Upland course on the site of a prehistoric hill fort with far-reaching views. With 15 holes in Wales and three in England, drive off in Wales and putt out in England on 4th hole. A quality mature course with a tremendous variety of holes.

Llanymynech

18 holes, 6114yds, Par 70, SSS 69, Course record 64.
Club membership 750.
Visitors Mon-Sun & BHs. Booking required. Dress code. **Societies** Booking required. **Green Fees** £35 per day, £25 per round, £30 Sat, Sun & BHs. **Prof** Andrew P Griffiths **Facilities** **Conf** Corporate Hospitality Days **Location** 6m S of Oswestry, off A483 in Pant at Cross Guns Inn

Hotel ★★★ 72% Wynnstay Hotel, Church St, OSWESTRY ☎ 01691 655261 29 en suite

SHIFNAL Map 07 SJ70

Shifnal Decker Hill TF11 8QL
☎ 01952 460330 🗎 01952 460330
e-mail: secretary@shifnalgolfclub.co.uk
web: www.shifnalgolfclub.co.uk
Well-wooded parkland. Walking is easy and an attractive country mansion serves as the clubhouse.
18 holes, 6468yds, Par 71, SSS 71, Course record 65.
Club membership 700.
Visitors Mon-Wed & Fri except BHs. Booking required. Handicap certificate. Dress code. **Societies** Booking required. **Green Fees** £40 per day, £30 per 18 holes. **Prof** David Ashton **Course Designer** Pennick **Facilities** **Conf** Corporate Hospitality Days **Location** 1m N off B4379

Hotel ★★★★ 66% Park House Hotel, Park St, SHIFNAL ☎ 01952 460128 38 en suite 16 annexe en suite

SHREWSBURY Map 07 SJ41

Arscott Arscott, Pontesbury SY5 0XP
☎ 01743 860114 🗎 01743 860881
e-mail: golf@arscott.dydirect.net
At 111 metres above sea level, the views from Arscott Golf Club of the hills of south Shropshire and Wales are superb. Arscott is set in mature parkland with water features and holes demanding all sorts of club choice. A challenge to all golfers both high and low handicap.
18 holes, 6178yds, Par 70, SSS 69, Course record 66.
Club membership 550.
Visitors Mon-Sun & BHs. Booking required. Dress code. **Societies** Booking required. **Green Fees** £20 per round, £25 Sat, Sun & BHs. **Prof** Glyn Sadd **Course Designer** M Hamer **Facilities** **Leisure** fishing, sports injury treatment, massage. **Conf** facs **Location** Off A488 S of town

Continued

Hotel ★★★ 66% The Lion Hotel, Wyle Cop, SHREWSBURY ☎ 0870 609 6167 59 en suite

Shrewsbury Condover SY5 7BL
☎ 01743 872976 & 872977 (sec) 🖷 01743 874647
e-mail: info@shrewsbury-golf-club.co.uk
Parkland course. First nine flat, second undulating with good views of the Long Mynd. Several holes with water features. Fast putting surfaces.
18 holes, 6300yds, Par 70, SSS 70.
Club membership 872.
Visitors Booking required. Handicap certificate. **Societies** Booking required in writing. **Green Fees** phone. **Prof** Peter Seal **Facilities** **Location** 4m S off A49

Hotel ★★★ 73% Prince Rupert Hotel, Butcher Row, SHREWSBURY ☎ 01743 499955 70 en suite

TELFORD Map 07 SJ60

Shropshire Golf Centre Granville Park, Muxton TF2 8PQ
☎ 01952 677800 🖷 01952 677622
e-mail: sales@theshropshire.co.uk
web: www.theshropshire.co.uk
This 27-hole course is set in rolling countryside. The three loops of nine make the most of the natural undulations and provide a challenge for golfer of all abilities. Ample stretches of water and bullrush lined ditches, wide countered fairways and rolling greens guarded by mature trees, hummocks and vast bunkers. Several elevated tees with spectacular views.

Blue: 9 holes, 3286yds, Par 35, SSS 35.
Silver: 9 holes, 3303yds, Par 36, SSS 36.
Gold: 9 holes, 3334yds, Par 36, SSS 36.
Club membership 320.
Visitors Mon-Sun & BHs. Booking required up to 7 days in advance. Dress code. **Societies** Booking required. **Green Fees** £22 per 27 holes, £15 per 18 holes, £10 per 9 holes, £29/£20/£12 Sat, Sun & BHs. **Prof** Rob Grier **Course Designer** Martin Hawtree **Facilities** **Leisure** par 3 14 hole academy course. **Conf** facs Corporate Hospitality Days **Location** M54/A5 onto B5060 towards Donnington, 3rd exit at Granville rdbt
See advertisement on this page

Telford Golf & Country Club Great Hay Dr, Sutton Heights TF7 4DT
☎ 01952 429977 🖷 01952 586602
18 holes, 6761yds, Par 72, SSS 72, Course record 66.
Course Designer Harris, Griffiths **Location** 4m S of town off A442
Phone for further details

WELLINGTON Map 07 SJ61

Wrekin Ercall Woods, Golf Links Ln TF6 5BX
☎ 01952 244032 🖷 01952 252906
e-mail: wrekingolfclub@btconnect.com
Downland course with some hard walking but superb views.

18 holes, 5570yds, Par 67, SSS 66, Course record 62.
Club membership 675.
Visitors Mon-Sun & BHs. Booking required. Dress code. **Societies** Booking required. **Green Fees** £30 per day, £22 per round, £30 per round Sat, Sun & BHs. **Prof** K Housden **Facilities** **Location** M54 junct 7, 1.25m S off B5061

WESTON-UNDER-REDCASTLE Map 07 SJ52

Hawkstone Park Hotel SY4 5UY
☎ 01939 200611 🖹 01939 200335
e-mail: info@hawkstone.co.uk
web: www.hawkstone.co.uk
The Hawkstone Course plays through the English Heritage designated Grade I landscape of the historic park and follies, providing a beautiful, tranquil yet dramatic back drop to a round of golf. The Windmill Course utilises many American style features and extensive water hazards and is a challenging alternative.

Hawkstone Course: 18 holes, 6491yds, Par 72, SSS 71, Course record 65.
Windmill Course: 18 holes, 6476yds, Par 72, SSS 72, Course record 64.
Academy Course: 6 holes, 741yds, Par 18, SSS 18.
Club membership 650.
Visitors Booking required. **Societies** Booking required. **Green Fees** phone. **Prof** Stuart Leech **Course Designer** J Braid **Facilities** **Leisure** 6 hole, par 3 course, snooker. **Conf** facs Corporate Hospitality Days **Location** Off A49/A442

WHITCHURCH Map 07 SJ54

Hill Valley Terrick Rd SY13 4JZ
☎ 01948 663584 & 667788 🖹 01948 665927
e-mail: info@hillvalley.co.uk
web: www.hill-valley.co.uk
Emerald: 18 holes, 6628yds, Par 73, SSS 72, Course record 64.
Sapphire: 18 holes, 4800yds, Par 66, SSS 64.
Course Designer Peter Alliss, Dave Thomas **Location** 1m N. Follow signs from Bypass
Phone for further details

Hotel ★★ 70% Crown Hotel & Restaurant, High St, NANTWICH ☎ 01270 625283 18 en suite

WORFIELD Map 07 SO79

Chesterton Valley Chesterton WV15 5NX
☎ 01746 783682
Dry course built on sandy soil giving excellent drainage. No temporary greens and no trolley ban.
18 holes, 5938yards, SSS 69.
Club membership 450.
Visitors Mon-Sun & BHs. Booking required. Dress code. **Societies** Booking required. **Green Fees** phone. **Prof** Philip Hinton **Course Designer** Len Vanes **Facilities** **Location** On B4176

Continued

Hotel ★★★ Old Vicarage Hotel, Worfield, BRIDGNORTH ☎ 01746 716497 10 en suite 4 annexe en suite

Worfield Roughton WV15 5HE
☎ 01746 716372 🖹 01746 716302
e-mail: enquiries@worfieldgolf.co.uk
web: www.worfieldgolf.co.uk
A parkland links mix with three large lakes, many bunkers and large trees giving a challenge to golfers. Superb views and drainage which allows play on full greens and tees all year. Water comes into play on four holes, including the short par 4 18th where it lies in front of the green.
18 holes, 6545yds, Par 73, SSS 72, Course record 68.
Club membership 600.
Visitors Mon-Fri & BHs. Sat & Sun pm. Booking required. Dress code. **Societies** Booking required. **Green Fees** £20 per round, £20 Sat & Sun after 1pm. **Prof** Steve Russell **Course Designer** T Williams **Facilities** **Conf** facs Corporate Hospitality Days **Location** 3m W of off A454

Hotel ★★★ Old Vicarage Hotel, Worfield, BRIDGNORTH ☎ 01746 716497 10 en suite 4 annexe en suite

SOMERSET

BACKWELL Map 03 ST46

Tall Pines Cooks Bridle Path, Downside BS48 3DJ
☎ 01275 472076 🖹 01275 474869
e-mail: tallpinesgc@ukonline.co.uk
Parkland with views over the Bristol Channel.
18 holes, 6049yds, Par 70, SSS 70, Course record 65.
Club membership 500.
Visitors contact club for details. **Societies** Sat & Sun. Booking required. **Green Fees** £20 per round. **Prof** Alex Murray **Course Designer** T Murray **Facilities** **Conf** Corporate Hospitality Days **Location** Next to Bristol Airport, 1m off A38/A370

Hotel ★★★ 65% Beachlands Hotel, 17 Uphill Rd North, WESTON-SUPER-MARE ☎ 01934 621401 23 en suite

BATH Map 03 ST76

Bath Sham Castle, North Rd BA2 6JG
☎ 01225 463834 🖹 01225 331027
e-mail: enquiries@bathgolfclub.org.uk
web: www.bathgolfclub.org.uk
Considered to be one of the finest courses in the west, this is the site of Bath's oldest golf club. Situated on high ground overlooking the city and with splendid views over the surrounding countryside. The rocky ground supports good quality turf and there are many good holes. The 17th is a dog-leg right past, or over the corner of an out of bounds wall, and then on to an undulating green.
18 holes, 6442yds, Par 71, SSS 71, Course record 66.
Club membership 750.
Visitors contact club for details. Handicap certificate. Dress code. **Societies** Booking required. **Green Fees** 36 holes £46, 18 holes £38, £42/£50 Sat, Sun & BHs. **Prof** Peter J Hancox **Course Designer** Colt & others **Facilities**

Continued

⊗)ℿ 🍴 ☕ 🍷 🧥 🏠 ⛳ 🏌 ✓ **Conf** Corporate Hospitality Days **Location** 1.5m SE city centre off A36

Hotel ★★★ 72% Macdonald Francis Hotel, Queen Square, BATH ☎ 0870 400 8223 95 en suite

Entry Hill BA2 5NA
☎ 01225 834248
e-mail: timtapley@aol.com
web: www.bathpublicgolf.co.uk

Opened in 1984, this is a short but interesting 9 hole public pay and play facility within a mile of the city centre. With its picturesque settings and stunning views across Bath, the course provides enjoyment for golfers of all standard.

9 holes, 2065yds, Par 33, SSS 30.
Club membership 250.

Visitors Mon-Fri. Booking required Sat, Sun & BHs. **Societies** Booking required. **Green Fees** £18.75 per day, £11.75 per 18 holes, £7.50 per 9 holes. **Prof** Tim Tapley **Facilities** ⊗ 🍴 ☕ 🧥 🏠 ⛳ 🏌 **Location** Off A367

Lansdown Lansdown BA1 9BT
☎ 01225 422138 📠 01225 339252
e-mail: admin@lansdowngolfclub.co.uk
web: www.lansdowngolfclub.co.uk

A flat parkland course situated 800ft above sea level, providing a challenge to both low and high handicap golfers.

18 holes, 6316yds, Par 71, SSS 70, Course record 63.
Club membership 700.

Visitors Booking required. Handicap certificate. **Societies** Booking required. **Green Fees** phone. **Prof** Terry Mercer **Course Designer** CA Whitcombe **Facilities** ⊗)ℿ 🍴 ☕ 🍷 🧥 🏠 🏌 **Conf** facs Corporate Hospitality Days **Location** M4 junct 18, 6m SW by Bath racecourse

Hotel ★★★ 71% Pratt's Hotel, South Pde, BATH ☎ 01225 460441 46 en suite

BRIDGWATER Map 03 ST23

Cannington Cannington Centre for Land Based Studies, Cannington TA5 2LS
☎ 01278 655050 📠 01278 655055
e-mail: macrow@bridgwater.ac.uk
web: www.cannington.ac.uk

Nine-hole links-style course with 18 tees. The 4th hole is a challenging 464 yd par 4, slightly uphill and into the prevailing wind.

9 holes, 6072yds, Par 68, SSS 70, Course record 64.
Club membership 280.

Visitors Mon-Fri. Booking required Sat, Sun & BHs. Dress code. **Societies** Booking required. **Green Fees** 18 holes £14, 9 holes £9.50, £18.50/£12.50 Sat & Sun. 💳 **Prof** Ron Macrow **Course Designer** Martin Hawtree **Facilities** ☕ 🧥 🏠 ⛳ 🏌 ✓ **Location** 4m NW off A39

Hotel ★★ 76% Combe House Hotel, HOLFORD ☎ 01278 741382 17 rms (16 en suite)

BURNHAM-ON-SEA Map 03 ST34

Brean Coast Rd, Brean Sands TA8 2QY
☎ 01278 752111 (pro shop) 📠 01278 752111
e-mail: proshop@brean.com
web: www.breangolfclub.co.uk

18 holes, 5715yds, Par 69, SSS 68, Course record 66.

Course Designer In House **Location** M5 junct 22, 4m on coast road
Phone for further details

Hotel ★★ 70% Batch Country Hotel, Batch Ln, LYMPSHAM ☎ 01934 750371 10 en suite

Burnham & Berrow St Christopher's Way TA8 2PE
☎ 01278 785760 📠 01278 795440
e-mail: secretary@burnhamandberrow.plus.com
web: www.burnhamandberrowgolfclub.co.uk

Natural championship links course with panoramic views of the Somerset hills and the Bristol Channel. A true test of golf suitable only for players with a handicap of 22 or better.

Championship Course: 18 holes, 6383yds, Par 71, SSS 71, Course record 64.
Channel Course: 9 holes, 6120yds, Par 70, SSS 69.
Club membership 900.

Visitors Mon-Fri, Sun & BHs, Sat after 2.30pm. Booking required. Handicap certificate. Dress code. **Societies** welcome. **Green Fees** Championship £60 per day, £48 per round, £60 per round Sat, Sun & BHs. **Prof** Mark Crowther-Smith **Course Designer** H Colt **Facilities** ⊗)ℿ 🍴 ☕ 🍷 🧥 🏠 ⛳ 🛏 🏌 ✓ **Location** 1m N of town on B3140

Continued

Hotel ★★ 68% Battleborough Grange Country Hotel, Bristol Rd - A38, BRENT KNOLL ☎ 01278 760208 21 en suite

Hotel ★★ 72% Woodlands Country House Hotel, Hill Ln, BRENT KNOLL ☎ 01278 760232 9 en suite

CHARD Map 03 ST30

Windwhistle Cricket St Thomas TA20 4DG
☎ 01460 30231 🖷 01460 30055
e-mail: info@windwhistlegolf.co.uk
web: www.windwhistlegolf.co.uk

Parkland course at 735ft above sea level with outstanding views over the Somerset Levels to the Bristol Channel and south Wales.

East/West Course: 18 holes, 6176yds, Par 72, SSS 70, Course record 69.
Club membership 500.

Visitors Mon-Sun & BHs. Booking required. Dress code. **Societies** Booking required. **Green Fees** phone. **Prof** Paul Deeprose **Course Designer** Braid & Taylor, Fisher **Facilities** **Leisure** squash. **Conf** facs Corporate Hospitality Days **Location** 3m E on A30

Hotel ★★★ 68% Shrubbery Hotel, ILMINSTER ☎ 01460 52108 16 en suite

CLEVEDON Map 03 ST47

Clevedon Castle Rd, Walton St Mary BS21 7AA
☎ 01275 874057 🖷 01275 341228
e-mail: secretary@clevedongolfclub.co.uk
web: clevedongolfclub.co.uk

Situated on the cliff overlooking the Severn estuary with distant views of the Welsh coast. Excellent parkland course in first-class condition. Magnificent scenery and some tremendous drop holes.

18 holes, 6557yds, Par 72, SSS 72, Course record 68.
Club membership 750.

Continued

Visitors Mon-Sun & BHs. Booking required. Handicap certificate. Dress code. **Societies** Booking required. **Green Fees** £32 per day, £40 Sat & Sun. **Prof** Robert Scanlan **Course Designer** S Herd **Facilities** **Conf** facs Corporate Hospitality Days **Location** M5 junct 20, 1m NE of town centre

Hotel ★★★ 67% Walton Park Hotel, Wellington Ter, CLEVEDON ☎ 01275 874253 40 en suite

CONGRESBURY Map 03 ST46

Mendip Spring Honeyhall Ln BS49 5JT
☎ 01934 852322 🖷 01934 853021
e-mail: msgc@melhuish9790.fsworld.co.uk
web: www.mendipspring.co.uk

Set in peaceful countryside with the Mendip Hills as a backdrop, this 18-hole course includes lakes and numerous water hazards covering some 12 acres of the course. The 12th is an island green surrounded by water and there are long drives on the 7th and 13th. The nine-hole Lakeside course is easy walking, mainly par 4. Floodlit driving range.

Brinsea Course: 18 holes, 6352yds, Par 71, SSS 70, Course record 64.
Lakeside: 9 holes, 2392yds, Par 34, SSS 66.
Club membership 500.

Visitors Brinsea: booking required, handicap certificate Sat & Sun. Lakeside: Mon-Sun. **Societies** Booking required. **Green Fees** phone. **Prof** John Blackburn & Robert Moss **Facilities** **Conf** facs Corporate Hospitality Days **Location** 2m S between A370

ENMORE Map 03 ST23

Enmore Park TA5 2AN
☎ 01278 672100 (office) & 672102 (pro) 🖷 01278 672101
e-mail: golfclub@enmore.fsnet.co.uk
web: www.enmore-park-gc.co.uk

A parkland course on the foothills of the Quantocks, with water features. Wooded countryside and views of the Mendips; 1st and 10th are testing holes.

18 holes, 6406yds, Par 71, SSS 71, Course record 64.
Club membership 700.

Visitors Mon-Sun & BHs. Booking required. Dress code. **Societies** Booking required. **Green Fees** £32 per round, £42 Sat & Sun. **Prof** Nigel Wixon **Course Designer** Hawtree **Facilities** **Conf** Corporate Hospitality Days **Location** 0.5m E of village, 3.5m SW of Bridgewater

Hotel ★★ 76% Combe House Hotel, HOLFORD ☎ 01278 741382 17 rms (16 en suite)

FARRINGTON GURNEY Map 03 ST65

Farrington Golf & Country Club Marsh Ln BS39 6TS
☎ 01761 451596 Fax 01761 451021
e-mail: info@farringtongolfclub.net
web: www.farringtongolfclub.net
Main Course: 18 holes, 6335yds, Par 72, SSS 71, Course record 66.
Course Designer Peter Thompson **Location** SE of village off A37
Phone for further details

Hotel ★★★ 74% Centurion Hotel, Charlton Ln, MIDSOMER NORTON ☎ 01761 417711 44 en suite

FROME Map 03 ST74

Frome Golf Club Critchill Manor BA11 4LJ
☎ 01373 453410
e-mail: fromegolfclub@yahoo.co.uk
web: www.fromegolfclub.fsnet.co.uk
Attractive parkland course, founded in 1992, situated in a picturesque valley just outside the town, complete with practice areas and a driving range.
18 holes, 5527yds, Par 69, SSS 67, Course record 64. Club membership 420.
Visitors contact club for details. Dress code. **Societies** Booking required. **Green Fees** £25 per day, £21 per 18 holes, £15 per 9 holes, £27/£24.50/£18 Sat, Sun & BHs. **Prof** L Wilkin/T Isaac **Facilities** **Location** 1m SW of town centre

Hotel ★★ 65% The George at Nunney, 11 Church St, NUNNEY ☎ 01373 836458 9 rms (8 en suite)

Orchardleigh BA11 2PH
☎ 01373 454200 Fax 01373 454202
e-mail: secretary@orchardleighgolf.co.uk
web: www.orchardleighgolf.co.uk
An 18-hole parkland course set amid Somerset countryside routed through mature trees with water coming into play on seven holes.
18 holes, 6780yds, Par 72, SSS 73, Course record 67. Club membership 550.
Visitors Mon-Sun & BHs. Booking required. Handicap certificate. Dress code. **Societies** Booking required. **Green Fees** £30 per round, £40 Sat, Sun & BHs. **Prof** Ian Ridsdale **Course Designer** Brian Huggett **Facilities** **Leisure** fishing. **Conf** facs Corporate Hospitality Days **Location** 1m W of Frome on A362

Hotel ★★ 65% The George at Nunney, 11 Church St, NUNNEY ☎ 01373 836458 9 rms (8 en suite)

Booking a tee time is always advisable

GURNEY SLADE Map 03 ST64

Mendip BA3 4UT
☎ 01749 840570 Fax 01749 841439
e-mail: mendipgolfclub@lineone.net
web: www.mendipgolfclub.co.uk
Undulating downland course offering an interesting test of golf on superb fairways and extensive views over the surrounding countryside.
18 holes, 6383yds, Par 71, SSS 71, Course record 65. Club membership 900.
Visitors contact club for details. Handicap certificate. Dress code. **Societies** boooking required. **Green Fees** £27 per round, £38 Sat & Sun. **Prof** Adrian Marsh **Course Designer** CK Cotton **Facilities** **Location** 1.5m S off A37

Hotel ★★★ 74% Centurion Hotel, Charlton Ln, MIDSOMER NORTON ☎ 01761 417711 44 en suite

KEYNSHAM Map 03 ST66

Stockwood Vale Stockwood Ln BS31 2ER
☎ 0117 986 6505 Fax 0117 986 8974
e-mail: stockwoodvalegc@netscapeonline.co.uk
web: www.stockwoodvale.com
18 holes, 6031yds, Par 71, SSS 69.
Location Off Hicks Gate on junct A4
Phone for further details

Guest House ◆◆◆◆ Grasmere Court Hotel, 22-24 Bath Rd, KEYNSHAM ☎ 0117 986 2662 16 en suite

LONG ASHTON Map 03 ST57

Long Ashton The Clubhouse, Clarken Coombe BS41 9DW
☎ 01275 392229 Fax 01275 394395
e-mail: secretary@longashtongolfclub.co.uk
web: www.longashtongolfclub.co.uk
Wooded parkland course with fine turf, wonderful views of Bristol and surrounding areas, and a spacious practice area. Good testing holes, especially the back nine, in prevailing south-west wind. Good drainage ensures pleasant winter golf.

18 holes, 6400yds, Par 71, SSS 71. Club membership 700.
Visitors contact club for details. Dress code. **Societies** Booking required. **Green Fees** £30 per round, £35 Sat & Sun. **Prof** Mike Hart **Course Designer** JH Taylor **Facilities** by arrangement **Conf** Corporate Hospitality Days **Location** 0.5m N on B3128

Hotel ★★★ 68% Corus hotel Bristol, Beggar Bush Ln, Failand, BRISTOL ☎ 0870 609 6144 112 en suite

Woodspring Golf & Country Club Yanley Ln BS41 9LR
☎ 01275 394378 🖷 01275 394473
e-mail: info@woodspring-golf.com
web: www.woodspring-golf.com
Set in 245 acres of undulating Somerset countryside, featuring superb natural water hazards, protected greens and a rising landscape. Designed by Peter Alliss and Clive Clark and laid out by Donald Steel, the course has three individual nine-hole courses, the Avon, Severn and Brunel. The 9th hole on the Brunel Course is a feature hole, with an elevated tee shot over a natural gorge. In undulating hills south of Bristol, long carries to tight fairways, elevated island tees and challenging approaches to greens make the most of the 27 holes.
Avon Course: 9 holes, 2960yds, Par 35, SSS 34.
Brunel Course: 9 holes, 3320yds, Par 37, SSS 35.
Severn Course: 9 holes, 3267yds, Par 36, SSS 35.
Club membership 500.
Visitors Mon-Sun & BHs. Booking required. Dress code. **Societies** Booking required. **Green Fees** £48 per day, £28 per 18 holes, £64/£32 Sat & Sun. **Prof** Kevin Pitts **Course Designer** Clarke, Alliss, Steel **Facilities** **Conf** facs Corporate Hospitality Days **Location** Off A38 Bridgwater Road

Hotel ★★★ 68% Corus hotel Bristol, Beggar Bush Ln, Failand, BRISTOL ☎ 0870 609 6144 112 en suite

MIDSOMER NORTON Map 03 ST65

Fosseway Golf Course Charlton Ln BA3 4BD
☎ 01761 412214 🖷 01761 418357
e-mail: centurion@centurionhotel.co.uk
web: www.centurionhotel.co.uk
Very attractive tree-lined parkland course, not demanding but with lovely views towards the Mendip Hills.
9 holes, 4565yds, Par 67, SSS 61.
Club membership 300.
Visitors Mon-Sun & BHs. **Societies** Booking required. **Green Fees** phone. **Course Designer** CK Cotton, F Pennink **Facilities** **Leisure** heated indoor swimming pool, sauna, gymnasium. **Conf** facs Corporate Hospitality Days **Location** SE of town centre off A367

Hotel ★★★ 74% Centurion Hotel, Charlton Ln, MIDSOMER NORTON ☎ 01761 417711 44 en suite

MINEHEAD Map 03 SS94

Minehead & West Somerset The Warren TA24 5SJ
☎ 01643 702057 🖷 01643 705095
e-mail: secretary@mineheadgolf.co.uk
web: www.mineheadgolf.co.uk
Flat seaside links, very exposed to wind, with good turf set on a shingle bank. The last five holes adjacent to the beach are testing. The 215yd 18th is wedged between the beach and the club buildings and provides a good finish.
18 holes, 6228yds, Par 71, SSS 69, Course record 65.
Club membership 620.
Visitors Mon-Sun & BHs. Booking required. Dress code. **Societies** Booking required. **Green Fees** £35 per day, £40 Sat & Sun. **Prof** Ian Read **Facilities** **Conf** Corporate Hospitality Days **Location** E end of esplanade

Continued

Hotel ★★ Channel House Hotel, Church Path, MINEHEAD ☎ 01643 703229 8 en suite

SALTFORD Map 03 ST66

Saltford Golf Club Ln BS31 3AA
☎ 01225 873513 🖷 01225 873525
Easy walking parkland with panoramic views over the Avon valley. The par 4 2nd and 13th are notable.
18 holes, 6081yds, Par 71, SSS 71.
Club membership 800.
Visitors Booking required. Handicap certificate. **Societies** Booking required. **Green Fees** phone. **Prof** Dudley Millinstead **Course Designer** Harry Vardon **Facilities** **Conf** facs Corporate Hospitality Days **Location** S of village

Hotel ★★★ 79% Hunstrete House Hotel, HUNSTRETE ☎ 01761 490490 25 en suite

SOMERTON Map 03 ST42

Long Sutton Long Sutton TA10 9JU
☎ 01458 241017 🖷 01458 241022
e-mail: reservations@longsuttongolf.com
web: www.longsuttongolf.com
Gentle, undulating, but testing parkland course. Pay and play course.

18 holes, 6369yds, Par 71, SSS 70, Course record 64.
Club membership 750.
Visitors Mon-Sun & BHs. Booking required Fri-Sun & BHs. Dress code. **Societies** welcome. **Green Fees** £30 per day, £20 per 18 holes, £10 per 9 holes, £35/£25/£12.50 Sat & Sun. **Prof** Andrew Hayes **Course Designer** Patrick Dawson **Facilities** **Conf** facs Corporate Hospitality Days **Location** 3.5m E of Langport, 0.5m S of Long Sutton on B3165

Hotel ★★★ 72% The Hollies, Bower Hinton, MARTOCK ☎ 01935 822232 33 annexe en suite

Wheathill Wheathill TA11 7HG
☎ 01963 240667 🖹 01963 240230
e-mail: wheathill@wheathill.fsnet.co.uk
web: www.foremostonline.com/wheathill
A par 68 parkland course with nice views in quiet countryside. It is flat lying with the 13th hole along the river. There is an academy course and a massive practice area.
18 holes, 5839yds, Par 68, SSS 66, Course record 61. Club membership 550.
Visitors Mon-Sun & BHs. Booking required Fri-Sun & BHs. Dress code. **Societies** Booking required. **Green Fees** £17 per round, £22 Sat, Sun & BHs. **Prof** A England **Course Designer** J Pain **Facilities** **Leisure** 8 hole academy course. **Conf** facs Corporate Hospitality Days **Location** 5m E of Somerton off B3153

Hotel ★★★ 57% Wessex Hotel, High St, STREET ☎ 01458 443383 49 en suite

TAUNTON Map 03 ST22

Oake Manor Oake TA4 1BA
☎ 01823 461993 🖹 01823 461995
e-mail: russell@oakemanor.com
web: www.oakemanor.com
A parkland and lakeland course situated in breathtaking Somerset countryside with views of the Quantock, Blackdown and Brendon hills. Ten holes feature water hazards such as lakes, cascades and a trout stream. The 15th hole (par 5, 476yds) is bounded by water all down the left with a carry over another lake on to an island green. The course is challenging yet great fun for all standards of golfer.

18 holes, 6109yds, Par 70, SSS 69, Course record 65. Club membership 600.
Visitors Mon-Sun. Booking required. **Societies** Booking required. **Green Fees** phone. **Prof** R Gardner, J Smallacombe **Course Designer** Adrian Stiff **Facilities** **Leisure** 2 hole academy course, short game area. **Conf** facs Corporate Hospitality Days **Location** M5 junct 26, A38 towards Taunton to Oake

Hotel ★★★ 73% Rumwell Manor Hotel, Rumwell, TAUNTON ☎ 01823 461902 10 en suite 10 annexe en suite

Taunton & Pickeridge Corfe TA3 7BY
☎ 01823 421537 🖹 01823 421742
e-mail: admin@tauntongolf.co.uk
web: www.taunton-golf.co.uk
Downland course established in 1892 with extensive views of the Quantock and Mendip hills. Renowned for its excellent greens.

Continued

18 holes, 6056yds, Par 69, SSS 69, Course record 66. Club membership 800.
Visitors Mon-Fri, Sun except BHs.Handicap certificate. Dress code. **Societies** Booking required. **Green Fees** £32 per day, £26 per round, £40 Sun. **Prof** Simon Stevenson **Facilities** **Conf** facs Corporate Hospitality Days **Location** 4m S off B3170

Hotel ★★★ 73% The Mount Somerset Hotel, Lower Henlade, TAUNTON ☎ 01823 442500 11 en suite

Taunton Vale Creech Heathfield TA3 5EY
☎ 01823 412220 🖹 01823 413583
e-mail: tvgc@easynet.co.uk
web: www.tauntonvalegolf.co.uk
An 18-hole and a nine-hole course in a parkland complex occupying 156 acres in the Vale of Taunton. Floodlit driving range.

Charlton Course: 18 holes, 6163yds, Par 70, SSS 70. Durston Course: 9 holes, 2004yds, Par 32. Club membership 800.
Visitors Mon-Sun & BHs. Booking required. Dress code. **Societies** Booking required. **Green Fees** 18 hole course £20 per round, £25 Sat & Sun. 9 hole course £10 per round, £15 Sat & Sun. **Prof** Martin Keitch **Course Designer** John Payne **Facilities** by arrangement **Conf** facs Corporate Hospitality Days **Location** M5 junct 24 or 25, off A38

Hotel ★★★ 73% The Mount Somerset Hotel, Lower Henlade, TAUNTON ☎ 01823 442500 11 en suite

Vivary Park Municipal Fons George TA1 3JU
☎ 01823 333875 🖹 01823 352713
e-mail: vivary.golf.course@tauntondeane.gov.uk
18 holes, 4620yds, Par 63, SSS 63, Course record 59.
Course Designer WH Fowler **Location** S of town centre off A38
Phone for further details

Hotel ★★★ 67% Corner House Hotel, Park St, TAUNTON ☎ 01823 284683 28 en suite

WEDMORE Map 03 ST4

Isle of Wedmore Lineage BS28 4QT
☎ 01934 712452 (pro shop) 🖹 01934 713554
e-mail: office@wedmoregc.fsnet.co.uk
web: www.wedmoregolfclub.com
Gently undulating course designed to maintain natural environment. Existing woodland and hedgerow enhanced by new planting. Magnificent panoramic views of Cheddar valley and Glastonbury Tor from the back nine. The course design provides two loops of nine holes both starting and finishing at the clubhouse.

Continued

18 holes, 5850yds, Par 70, SSS 69, Course record 67.
Club membership 680.
Visitors Mon-Sun & BHs. Booking required. Dress code. **Societies** Booking required. **Green Fees** £32 per day, £22 per round. Winter reduced rates. **Prof** Graham Coombe **Course Designer** Terry Murray **Facilities** **Leisure** indoor teaching studio & custom fitting centre. **Conf** facs Corporate Hospitality Days **Location** 0.5m N of Wedmore

Hotel ★★★ 74% Swan Hotel, Sadler St, WELLS ☎ 01749 836300 50 en suite

WELLS Map 03 ST54

Wells (Somerset) East Horrington Rd BA5 3DS
☎ 01749 675005 01749 683170
e-mail: secretary@wellsgolfclub99.freeserve.co.uk
web: wellsgolfclub.co.uk
Beautiful wooded course with wonderful views. The prevailing SW wind complicates the 448yd 3rd. Good drainage and paths for trolleys are being constructed all round the course.
18 holes, 6053yds, Par 70, SSS 69, Course record 66.
Club membership 670.
Visitors Mon-Sun & BHs. Handicap certficate Sat & Sun. Dress code. **Societies** Booking required. **Green Fees** £30 per 18 holes, £35 Sat, Sun & BHs. **Prof** Adrian Bishop **Facilities** **Conf** Corporate Hospitality Days **Location** 1.5m E off B3139

Hotel ★★ 70% Ancient Gate House Hotel, 20 Sadler St, WELLS ☎ 01749 672029 9 en suite

Hotel ★★ 72% White Hart Hotel, Sadler St, WELLS ☎ 01749 672056 01749 671074 15 en suite

WESTON-SUPER-MARE Map 03 ST36

Weston-Super-Mare Uphill Rd North BS23 4NQ
☎ 01934 626968 & 633360 (pro) 01934 621360
e-mail: wsmgolfclub@eurotelbroadband.com
web: www.westonsupermaregolfclub.com
A compact and interesting layout with the opening hole adjacent to the beach. The sandy, links-type course is slightly undulating and has beautifully maintained turf and greens. The 15th is a testing 455yd par 4. Superb views across the Bristol Channel to Cardiff.

18 holes, 6245yds, Par 70, SSS 70, Course record 65.
Club membership 750.
Visitors Mon-Sun & BHs. Handicap certificate. Dress code. **Societies** Booking required. **Green Fees** £48 per day, £36 per round. **Prof** Mike Laband **Course Designer** T Dunne, A MacKenzie **Facilities** **Location** S of town centre off A370

Hotel ★★★ 65% Beachlands Hotel, 17 Uphill Rd North, WESTON-SUPER-MARE ☎ 01934 621401 23 en suite

Worlebury Monks Hill BS22 9SX
☎ 01934 625789 01934 621935
e-mail: secretary@worleburygc.co.uk
web: www.worleburygc.co.uk
Parkland course on the ridge of Worlebury Hill, with fairly easy walking and extensive views of the Severn estuary and Wales.
18 holes, 5963yds, Par 70, SSS 68, Course record 66.
Club membership 650.
Visitors Mon-Sun & BHs. Booking required. Handicap certificate. Dress code. **Societies** Booking required. **Green Fees** phone. **Prof** Gary Marks **Course Designer** H Vardon **Facilities** **Location** 2m NE off A370

Hotel ★★★ 65% Beachlands Hotel, 17 Uphill Rd North, WESTON-SUPER-MARE ☎ 01934 621401 23 en suite

YEOVIL Map 03 ST51

Yeovil Sherborne Rd BA21 5BW
☎ 01935 422965 🖹 01935 411283
e-mail: yeovilgolfclub@yeovilgc.fsnet.co.uk
web: yeovilgolfclub.co.uk
On the Old Course the opener lies by the River Yeo before the gentle climb to high downs with good views. The outstanding 14th and 15th holes present a challenge, being below the player with a deep railway cutting on the left of the green. The 1st on the Newton Course is played over the river which then leads to a challenging but scenic course.
Old Course: 18 holes, 6150yds, Par 72, SSS 70, Course record 64.
Newton Course: 9 holes, 4905yds, Par 68, SSS 65, Course record 63.
Club membership 1000.
Visitors contact club for details. **Societies** Booking required. **Green Fees** Old Course Apr-Oct £35, £45 Sat, Sun & BHs. Nov-Mar £25, £30. Newton Course £20. **Prof** Geoff Kite **Course Designer** Fowler & Allison **Facilities** **Location** 1m E on A30

Hotel ★★★ 74% The Yeovil Court Hotel Limited, West Coker Rd, YEOVIL ☎ 01935 863746 18 en suite 12 annexe en suite

STAFFORDSHIRE

BROCTON Map 07 SJ91

Brocton Hall ST17 0TH
☎ 01785 661901 🖹 01785 661591
e-mail: broctonsec@aol.com
web: www.broctonhall.com
Parkland with gentle slopes in places, easy walking.
18 holes, 6064yds, Par 69, SSS 69, Course record 66.
Club membership 665.
Visitors Booking required. **Societies** Booking required. **Green Fees** phone. **Prof** Nevil Bland **Course Designer** Harry Vardon **Facilities** **Leisure** snooker. **Location** NW of village off A34

BURTON UPON TRENT Map 08 SK22

Belmont Tutbury Rd, Needwood DE13 9PH
☎ 01283 814381 🖹 01283 814381
A nine-hole course with five par 4s, the longest hole being 430yds. The course comprises trees, bunkers, some water and great views.
9 holes, 2201yds, Par 32, Course record 31.
Visitors Mon-Sun & BHs. Dress code. **Societies** welcome. **Green Fees** £12 per 18 holes, £7.50 per 9 holes, £15/£9 Sat & Sun. **Prof** R Coy **Facilities** **Leisure** fishing, archery. **Conf** Corporate Hospitality Days **Location** 3m NW of Tutbury, off B5017 towards Tutbury

Hotel ★★ 72% Riverside Hotel, Riverside Dr, Branston, BURTON UPON TRENT ☎ 01283 511234 22 en suite

Branston Burton Rd, Branston DE14 3DP
☎ 01283 512211 🖹 01283 566984
e-mail: sales@branston-golf-club.co.uk
web: www.branston-golf-club.co.uk

18 holes, 6697yds, Par 72, SSS 72, Course record 65.
Course Designer G Ramshall **Location** 1.5m SW on A5121
Phone for further details

Hotel ★★ 72% Riverside Hotel, Riverside Dr, Branston, BURTON UPON TRENT ☎ 01283 511234 22 en suite

Burton upon Trent 43 Ashby Rd East DE15 0PS
☎ 01283 544551 (sec) & 562240 (pro) 🖹 01283 544551
e-mail: Thesecretary@BurtonGolfClub.co.uk
web: www.burtongolfclub.co.uk
Undulating parkland course with notable trees and water features on two holes. Testing par 3s at 10th and 12th.

18 holes, 6579yds, Par 71, SSS 71, Course record 63.
Club membership 650.
Visitors contact club for details. Handicap certificate. Dress code. **Societies** Booking required. **Green Fees** £46 per day, £35 per round, £52/£40 Sat, Sun & BHs. **Prof** Gary Stafford **Course Designer** H Colt **Facilities** **Conf** Corporate Hospitality Days **Location** 3m E of Burton on A511

Guest House ♦♦♦♦ Edgecote Hotel, 179 Ashby Rd, BURTON UPON TRENT ☎ 01283 568966 11 rms (5 en suite)

Craythorne Craythorne Rd, Rolleston on Dove DE13 0AZ
☎ 01283 564329 🖹 01283 511908
e-mail: admin@craythorne.co.uk
web: www.craythorne.co.uk
A relatively short and challenging parkland course with tight fairways and views of the Trent valley. Excellent greens giving all year play. Suits all standards but

Continued

particularly good for society players. The course is now settled and in good condition after major refurbishment.
18 holes, 5645yds, Par 68, SSS 68, Course record 66.
Club membership 500.
Visitors Mon-Sun & BHs. Booking required. Dress code. **Societies** Booking required. **Green Fees** £34 per day, £28 per round. **Prof** Steve Hadfield **Course Designer** AA Wright **Facilities** **Conf** facs Corporate Hospitality Days **Location** Off A38 through Stretton, tourist signs

Guest House ♦♦♦♦ Edgecote Hotel, 179 Ashby Rd, BURTON UPON TRENT ☎ 01283 568966 11 rms (5 en suite)

Hoar Cross Hall Health Spa Resort Hoar Cross DE13 8QS
☎ 01283 575671 🖷 01283 575652
e-mail: info@hoarcross.co.uk
web: www.hoarcross.co.uk
Hoar Cross Hall Health Spa Golf Academy: .
Course Designer Geoffrey Collins
Phone for further details

Hotel Travelodge Rugeley, Western Springs Rd, RUGELEY ☎ 08700 850 950 32 en suite

Cannock Map 07 SJ91

Beau Desert Rugeley Rd, Hazelslade WS12 0PJ
☎ 01543 422626 🖷 01543 451137
e-mail: bdgc@btconnect.com
web: www.bdgc.co.uk
A moorland course with firm and fast fairways and greens, used on many occasions as an Open qualifier course. The course has many varied and testing holes ranging from the 1st over a pit, the 10th over a ravine, to the 18th with a second shot across gorse traversing the fairway.
18 holes, 6310yds, Par 70, SSS 71, Course record 64.
Club membership 650.
Visitors Mon-Sun & BHs. Booking required. Handicap certificate. Dress code. **Societies** Booking required. **Green Fees** £50 per day, £45 per round, £60 Sat, Sun & BHs. **Prof** Barrie Stevens **Course Designer** Herbert Fowler **Facilities** **Conf** facs Corporate Hospitality Days **Location** Off A460 NE of Hednesford

Cannock Park Stafford Rd WS11 2AL
☎ 01543 578850 🖷 01543 578850
e-mail: david.dunk@18global.co.uk
Part of a large leisure centre, this parkland-type course plays alongside Cannock Chase. Severe slopes on some greens. Good drainage, open all year.
18 holes, 5200yds, Par 67, SSS 65.
Club membership 150.
Visitors Mon-Fri. Booking required Sat, Sun & BHs. Dress code. **Societies** Booking required. **Green Fees** £11 per round, £13 Sat & Sun. **Prof** David Dunk **Course Designer** John Mainland **Facilities** **Leisure** hard tennis courts, heated indoor swimming pool, sauna, solarium, gymnasium. **Location** 0.5m N of town centre on A34

Enville Map 07 SO88

Enville Highgate Common DY7 5BN
☎ 01384 872074 (Office) 🖷 01384 873396
e-mail: secretary@envillegolfclub.com
web: www.envillegolfclub.com
Easy walking on two fairly flat woodland and heathland courses.
Highgate Course: 18 holes, 6556yds, Par 72, SSS 72, Course record 65.
Lodge Course: 18 holes, 6290yds, Par 70, SSS 70, Course record 66.
Club membership 900.
Visitors Mon-Fri except BHs. Dress code. **Societies** Booking required. **Green Fees** £50 per day, £40 per 18 holes. **Prof** Sean Power **Facilities** **Conf** Corporate Hospitality Days **Location** 2m NE of Enville off A458

Hotel ★★★★ 68% Mill Hotel & Restaurant, ALVELEY ☎ 01746 780437 41 en suite

Goldenhill Map 07 SJ85

Goldenhill Mobberley Rd ST6 5SS
☎ 01782 787678 🖷 01782 787678
web: www.jackbarker.com
Rolling parkland with two par 3 holes surrounded by water and water in play on six of the back nine holes.
18 holes, 5957yds, Par 71, SSS 69.
Club membership 300.
Visitors Mon-Sun & BHs. **Societies** Booking required. **Green Fees** £8 per round, £12 Sat & Sun. **Facilities** **Location** On A50 4m N of Stoke

Hotel ★★★ 69% Manor House Hotel, Audley Rd, ALSAGER ☎ 01270 884000 57 en suite

Himley Map 07 SO89

Himley Hall Golf Centre Log Cabin, Himley Hall Park DY3 4DF
☎ 01902 895207
Parkland course set in the grounds of Himley Hall Park, with lovely views. Large practice area including a pitch and putt.
9 holes, 6215yds, Par 72, SSS 70, Course record 65.
Club membership 200.
Visitors Sat & Sun booking required. **Societies** Booking required. **Green Fees** phone. **Prof** Mark Sparrow **Course Designer** A Baker **Facilities** **Location** 0.5m E on B4176

Hotel ★★★ 63% The Himley Country Hotel, School Rd, HIMLEY ☎ 0870 609 6112 73 en suite

Leek Map 07 SJ95

Leek Birchall, Cheddleton Rd ST13 5RE
☎ 01538 384779 & 384767 (pro) 🖷 01538 384535
e-mail: secretary@leekgolfclub.fsnet.co.uk
Undulating, challenging, mainly parkland course, reputedly one of the best in the area. In its early years the course was typical moorland with sparse tree growth but its development since the 1960s has produced tree-lined fairways which are much appeciated by golfers for their lush playing qualities.
18 holes, 6218yds, Par 70, SSS 70, Course record 63.
Club membership 825.

Continued

Visitors Booking required with professional. With member after 3pm. **Societies** Booking required with hon secretary. **Green Fees** phone. **Prof** Paul Toyer **Facilities** **Leisure** snooker. **Conf** Corporate Hospitality Days **Location** 0.75m S on A520

Hotel ★★ 70% Three Horseshoes Inn & Restaurant, Buxton Rd, Blackshaw Moor, LEEK ☎ 01538 300296 6 en suite

Westwood (Leek) Newcastle Rd ST13 7AA

☎ 01538 398385 01538 382485

A challenging moorland and parkland course set in beautiful open countryside with an undulating front nine. The back nine is more open and longer with the River Churnet coming into play on several holes.

18 holes, 6207yds, Par 70, SSS 69, Course record 66.
Club membership 700.

Visitors Mon-Fri except BHs. Handicap certificate. Dress code. **Societies** Booking required. **Green Fees** phone. **Prof** Darren Squire **Facilities** **Conf** facs Corporate Hospitality Days **Location** On A53 S of Leek

Hotel ★★ 70% Three Horseshoes Inn & Restaurant, Buxton Rd, Blackshaw Moor, LEEK ☎ 01538 300296 6 en suite

LICHFIELD Map 07 SK10

Seedy Mill Elmhurst WS13 8HE

☎ 01543 417333 01543 418098
e-mail: seedymill.sales@theclubcompany.com
web: www.theclubcompany.com

A 27-hole course in picturesque parkland scenery. Numerous holes crossed by meandering mill streams. Undulating greens defended by hazards lie in wait for the practised approach.

Mill Course: 18 holes, 6042yds, Par 72, SSS 70, Course record 67.
Club membership 1200.

Visitors Booking required no more than 3 days in advance. **Societies** Booking required. **Green Fees** phone. **Prof** Simon Joyce **Course Designer** Hawtree & Son **Facilities** **Leisure** 9 hole par 3 course. **Conf** facs Corporate Hospitality Days **Location** 3m N of Lichfield off B5014

Hotel ★★★ 69% Little Barrow Hotel, 62 Beacon St, LICHFIELD ☎ 01543 414500 32 en suite

Whittington Heath Tamworth Rd WS14 9PW

☎ 01543 432317 01543 433962
e-mail: info@whgcgolf.freeserve.co.uk
web: www.whittingtonheathgc.co.uk

The 18 magnificent holes wind through heathland and trees, presenting a good test for the serious golfer. Leaving the fairway can be severely punished. The dog-legs are most tempting, inviting the golfer to chance his arm. Local knowledge is a definite advantage. Clear views of the famous three spires of Lichfield Cathedral.

18 holes, 6490yds, Par 70, SSS 71, Course record 64.
Club membership 660.

Visitors Mon-Fri except BHs. Booking required. Handicap certificate. Dress code. **Societies** Booking required. **Green Fees** £55 per 36 holes, £48 per 27 holes, £40 per 18 holes. **Prof** Adrian Sadler **Course Designer** Colt **Facilities** **Conf** Corporate Hospitality Days **Location** 2.5m SE on A51

Continued

Hotel ★★★ 69% Little Barrow Hotel, 62 Beacon St, LICHFIELD ☎ 01543 414500 32 en suite

NEWCASTLE-UNDER-LYME Map 07 SJ84

Keele Golf Centre Newcastle Rd, Keele ST5 5AB

☎ 01782 627596 01782 714555
e-mail: jackbarker_keelegolfcentreltd@hotmail.com
web: www.jackbarker.com

Parkland with mature trees and great views of Stoke-on-Trent and the surrounding area.

18 holes, 6396yds, Par 71, SSS 70, Course record 64.
Club membership 400.

Visitors Mon-Sun & BHs. **Societies** welcome. **Green Fees** £10 per round, £12.50 Fri, £15 Sat & Sun. **Course Designer** Hawtree **Facilities** **Location** 2m W on A525 opp Keele University

Hotel ★★ 60% Stop Inn Newcastle-under-Lyme, Liverpool Rd, Cross Heath, NEWCASTLE-UNDER-LYME ☎ 01782 717000 43 rms (42 en suite) 24 annexe en suite

Newcastle-Under-Lyme Whitmore Rd ST5 2QB

☎ 01782 617006 01782 617531
e-mail: info@newcastlegolfclub.co.uk
web: www.newcastlegolfclub.co.uk

Parkland course.

18 holes, 6404yds, Par 72, SSS 71, Course record 66.
Club membership 600.

Visitors Mon, Wed-Fri except BHs. Booking required. Handicap certificate. Dress code. **Societies** Booking required. **Green Fees** £35 per day, £25 per round. **Prof** Paul Symonds **Facilities** **Conf** Corporate Hospitality Days **Location** 1m SW on A5

Hotel ★★ 60% Stop Inn Newcastle-under-Lyme, Liverpool Rd, Cross Heath, NEWCASTLE-UNDER-LYME ☎ 01782 717000 43 rms (42 en suite) 24 annexe en suite

If the name of the club appears in italics, details have not been confirmed for this edition of the guide

Wolstanton Dimsdale Old Hall, Hassam Pde, Wolstanton ST5 9DR
☎ 01782 622413 (sec)
A challenging undulating suburban course incorporating six difficult par 3 holes. The 6th hole (par 3) is 233yds from the Medal Tee.

18 holes, 5533yds, Par 68, SSS 68, Course record 63.
Club membership 700.
Visitors Mon-Fri. Booking required. Handicap certificate. Dress code. **Societies** Booking required. **Green Fees** £27.50 per 18 holes. **Prof** Simon Arnold **Facilities** **Conf** facs Corporate Hospitality Days **Location** 1.5m from town centre. Turn off A34 at McDonalds

Hotel ★★ 60% Stop Inn Newcastle-under-Lyme, Liverpool Rd, Cross Heath, NEWCASTLE-UNDER-LYME ☎ 01782 717000 43 rms (42 en suite) 24 annexe en suite

ONNELEY Map 07 SJ74

Onneley CW3 5QF
☎ 01782 750577 & 846759
e-mail: all@onneleygolf.co.uk
web: www.onneleygolf.co.uk
Parkland having panoramic views to the Welsh hills.
18 holes, 5728yds, Par 70, SSS 68.
Club membership 410.
Visitors Mon-Sat except BHs. Booking required. Dress code. **Societies** Booking required. **Green Fees** £20 per day, £25 per round Sat. **Course Designer** A Benson, G Marks **Facilities** **Location** 2m from Woore on A525

Hotel ★★ 60% Stop Inn Newcastle-under-Lyme, Liverpool Rd, Cross Heath, NEWCASTLE-UNDER-LYME ☎ 01782 717000 43 rms (42 en suite) 24 annexe en suite

PATTINGHAM Map 07 SO89

Patshull Park Hotel Golf & Country Club WV6 7HR
☎ 01902 700100 🖷 01902 700874
e-mail: sales@patshull-park.co.uk
web: www.patshull-park.co.uk
Picturesque course set in 280 acres of glorious 'Capability' Brown landscaped parkland. Designed by John Jacobs, the course meanders alongside trout fishing lakes. Water comes into play alongside the 3rd hole and there is a challenging drive over water on the 13th. Wellingtonia and cedar trees prove an obstacle to wayward drives off several holes. The 12th is the toughest hole on the course and the tee shot is vital, anything wayward and the trees block out the second to the green.

Patshull Park Hotel Golf & Country Club

18 holes, 6400yds, Par 72, SSS 71, Course record 64.
Club membership 360.
Visitors Mon-Sun & BHs, Booking required. Handicap certificate. Dress code. **Societies** Booking required. **Green Fees** £40 per round. **Prof** Richard Bissell **Course Designer** John Jacobs **Facilities** **Leisure** heated indoor swimming pool, fishing, sauna, solarium, gymnasium. **Conf** facs Corporate Hospitality Days **Location** 1.5m W of Pattingham at Pattingham Church take the Patshull Rd, Golf club on right

Hotel ★★★ 69% Patshull Park Hotel Golf & Country Club, Patshull Park, PATTINGHAM ☎ 01902 700100 49 en suite

PENKRIDGE Map 07 SJ91

The Chase Pottal Pool Rd ST19 5RN
☎ 01785 712888 🖷 01785 712191
e-mail: tcgc@crown-golf.co.uk
web: www.crown-golf.co.uk
Parkland course with links characteristics.
18 holes, 6707yds, Par 72, SSS 74.
Club membership 850.
Visitors Booking required. **Societies** Booking required min 4 weeks in advance. **Green Fees** phone. **Prof** Ian Sadler **Facilities** **Conf** facs Corporate Hospitality Days **Location** 2m E off B5012

Hotel ★★★ 66% Quality Hotel Stafford, Pinfold Ln, PENKRIDGE ☎ 01785 712459 47 en suite

PERTON Map 07 SO89

Perton Park Wrottesley Park Rd WV6 7HL
☎ 01902 380103 & 380073 🖷 01902 326219
e-mail: golf@swindonperton.fsbusiness.co.uk
web: www.pertongolfclub.co.uk
Challenging inland links style course set in picturesque Staffordshire countryside.
18 holes, 6520yds, Par 72, SSS 72, Course record 61.
Club membership 500.
Visitors Booking required. **Societies** Booking required. **Green Fees** phone. **Prof** Jeremy Harrold **Facilities** **Leisure** hard tennis courts, bowling greens. **Location** SE of Perton off A454

Continued

RUGELEY Map 07 SK01

St Thomas's Priory Armitage Ln WS15 1ED
☎ 01543 492096 📠 01543 492096
e-mail: rohanlonpro@aol.com
Parkland with undulating fairways. Excellent drainage facilitates golf all year round. A good test of golf for both pro and amateur players.
18 holes, 5969yds, Par 70, SSS 70, Course record 64. Club membership 400.
Visitors Mon-Sun & BHs. Booking required. Dress code. **Societies** Booking required. **Green Fees** £30 per round, £40 Sat & Sun. **Prof** Richard O'Hanlon **Course Designer** P Mulholland **Facilities** **Leisure** fishing. **Conf** facs **Location** A51 onto A513

Hotel Travelodge Rugeley, Western Springs Rd, RUGELEY ☎ 08700 850 950 32 en suite

STAFFORD Map 07 SJ92

Stafford Castle Newport Rd ST16 1BP
☎ 01785 223821 📠 01785 223821
Undulating parkland-type course built around Stafford Castle.
9 holes, 6383yds, Par 71, SSS 70, Course record 68. Club membership 400.
Visitors Mon-Sat except BHs. Booking required. Dress code. **Societies** Booking required. **Green Fees** phone. **Facilities** **Conf** Corporate Hospitality Days **Location** SW of town centre off A518

STOKE-ON-TRENT Map 07 SJ84

Burslem Wood Farm, High Ln, Tunstall ST6 7JT
☎ 01782 837006
On the outskirts of Tunstall, a moorland course with hard walking.
9 holes, 5354yds, Par 66, SSS 66, Course record 66. Club membership 250.
Visitors Mon, Tue, Thu, Fri except BHs. Booking required. Handicap certificate. Dress code. **Societies** Booking required. **Green Fees** phone. **Facilities** by arrangement by arrangement by arrangement **Location** 4m N of city centre on B5049

Hotel ★★★ 64% Quality Hotel, 66 Trinity St, Hanley, STOKE-ON-TRENT ☎ 01782 202361 128 en suite 8 annexe en suite

Greenway Hall Stanley Rd, Stockton Brook ST9 9LJ
☎ 01782 503158 📠 01782 504691
e-mail: greenway@jackbarker.com
web: www.jackbarker.com
Moorland course with fine views of the Pennines.

18 holes, 5678yds, Par 68, SSS 67, Course record 65. Club membership 300.
Visitors contact club for details. Dress code. **Societies** Booking required. **Green Fees** £10, £15 Sat & Sun. **Facilities** **Conf** Corporate Hospitality Days **Location** 5m NE off A53

Hotel ★★★ 64% Quality Hotel, 66 Trinity St, Hanley, STOKE-ON-TRENT ☎ 01782 202361 128 en suite 8 annexe en suite

Trentham 14 Barlaston Old Rd, Trentham ST4 8HB
☎ 01782 658109 📠 01782 644024
e-mail: secretary@trenthamgolf.org
web: www.trenthamgolf.org
Parkland course. The par 3 4th is a testing hole reached through a copse of trees.

18 holes, 6644yds, Par 72, SSS 72, Course record 67. Club membership 600.
Visitors Booking required. **Societies** Booking required. **Green Fees** phone. **Prof** Sandy Wilson **Course Designer** Colt & Alison **Facilities** **Leisure** squash. **Location** Off A5035 in Trentham

Hotel ★★★ 66% Haydon House Hotel, Haydon St, Basford, STOKE-ON-TRENT ☎ 01782 711311 17 en suite 6 annexe en suite

Trentham Park Trentham Park ST4 8AE
☎ 01782 658800 📠 01782 658800
e-mail: trevor-berrisford@barbox.net
18 holes, 6425yds, Par 71, SSS 71, Course record 67.
Location M6 junct 15, 1m E. 3m SW of Stoke off A34
Phone for further details

Hotel ★★★ 66% Haydon House Hotel, Haydon St, Basford, STOKE-ON-TRENT ☎ 01782 711311 17 en suite 6 annexe en suite

STONE Map 07 SJ93

Barlaston Meaford Rd ST15 8UX
☎ 01782 372795 & 372867 📠 01782 372867
e-mail: barlaston.gc@virgin.net
web: www.bgc.everplay.net
Picturesque parkland course designed by Peter Alliss. A number of water features come into play on several holes.
18 holes, 5800yds, Par 69, SSS 68, Course record 65. Club membership 600.
Visitors Mon-Sun & BHs. Booking required. Handicap certificate. Dress code. **Societies** Booking required. **Green Fees** phone. **Prof** Ian Rogers **Course Designer** Peter Alliss **Facilities** **Conf** Corporate Hospitality Days **Location** M6 junct 15, 5m S

Continued

Izaak Walton Eccleshall Rd, Cold Norton ST15 0NS
☎ 01785 760900 (sec) & 760808 (pro)
e-mail: secretary@izaakwaltongolfclub.co.uk
web: www.izaakwaltongolfclub.co.uk
A gently undulating meadowland course with streams and ponds as features.
18 holes, 6325yds, Par 72, SSS 72, Course record 66. Club membership 450.
Visitors Mon-Sun & BHs. Booking required. Dress code. **Societies** Booking required. **Green Fees** £25 per day, £20 per round, £35/£25 Sat, Sun & BHs. **Prof** Paul Brunt **Facilities** **Location** On B5026 between Stone & Eccleshall

Stone Filleybrooks ST15 0NB
☎ 01785 813103
e-mail: enquiries@stonegolfclub.co.uk
web: www.stonegolfclub.co.uk
Nine-hole parkland course with easy walking and 18 different tees.
9 holes, 6299yds, Par 71, SSS 70, Course record 67. Club membership 310.
Visitors Mon-Fri except BHs. Handicap certificate. Dress code. **Societies** Booking required. **Green Fees** £20 per day or round. **Facilities** **Location** 0.5m W on A34

TAMWORTH Map 07 SK20

Drayton Park Drayton Park, Fazeley B78 3TN
☎ 01827 251139 01827 284035
e-mail: draytonparkgc.co.uk
web: www.draytonparkgc.co.uk
18 holes, 6439yds, Par 71, SSS 71, Course record 62.
Course Designer James Braid **Location** 2m S on A4091, next to Drayton Manor Leisure Park
Phone for further details

Hotel ★★★★ 75% De Vere Belfry, WISHAW
☎ 0870 900 0066 324 en suite

Tamworth Municipal Eagle Dr, Amington B77 4EG
☎ 01827 709303 01827 709305
e-mail: david-warburton@tamworth.gov.uk
web: www.tamworth.gov.uk
First-class municipal parkland course and a good test of golf.
18 holes, 6488yds, Par 73, SSS 72, Course record 63. Club membership 460.
Visitors Mon-Sun & BHs. Booking required. **Societies** Booking required. **Green Fees** £17.50 per 18 holes, £9 per 9 holes, £15.50/£10.50 Sat & Sun. **Prof** Wayne Alcock **Course Designer** Hawtree & Son **Facilities** **Conf** facs Corporate Hospitality Days **Location** 2.5m E off B5000

Hotel ★★ 62% Angel Croft Hotel, Beacon St, LICHFIELD
☎ 01543 258737 10 rms (8 en suite) 8 annexe en suite

UTTOXETER Map 07 SK03

Manor Leese Hill, Kingstone ST14 8QT
☎ 01889 563234 01889 563234
e-mail: manorgc@btinternet.com
web: www.manorgolfclub.org.uk
A short but tough course set in the heart of the Staffordshire countryside with fine views of the surrounding area.

Continued

18 holes, 6060yds, Par 71, SSS 69, Course record 67. Club membership 400.
Visitors Mon-Fri. Booking required Sat & Sun. Dress code. **Societies** Booking required. **Green Fees** £18 per day, £28 Sat & Sun. **Prof** Chris Miller **Course Designer** Various **Facilities** **Leisure** fishing. **Conf** Corporate Hospitality Days **Location** 2m from Uttoxeter on A518 towards Stafford

Uttoxeter Wood Ln ST14 8JR
☎ 01889 564884 (pro) & 566552 (office)
01889 567501
web: uttoxetergolfclub.com
18 holes, 5801yds, Par 70, SSS 69, Course record 64.
Course Designer G Rothera **Location** Near A50, 0.5m beyond main entrance to racecourse
Phone for further details

WESTON Map 07 SJ92

Ingestre Park ST18 0RE
☎ 01889 270845 01889 271434
e-mail: office@ingestregolf.co.uk
web: www.ingestregolf.co.uk
Parkland course set in the grounds of Ingestre Hall, former home of the Earl of Shrewsbury, with mature trees and pleasant views.
18 holes, 6352yds, Par 70, SSS 70, Course record 67. Club membership 750.
Visitors Mon-Fri except BHs. Handicap certificate. Dress code. **Societies** Booking required. **Green Fees** £32.50 per day, £28 per round. **Prof** Danny Scullion **Course Designer** Hawtree **Facilities** **Conf** Corporate Hospitality Days **Location** 2m SE off A51

Hotel ★★★ 77% The Swan Hotel, 46 Greengate St, STAFFORD ☎ 01785 258142 31 en suite

WHISTON Map 07 SK04

Whiston Hall Mansion Court Hotel ST10 2HZ
☎ 01538 266260 01538 266820
e-mail: enquiries@whistonhall.com
web: www.whistonhall.com
A challenging 18-hole course in scenic countryside 2m from Alton Towers, incorporating many natural obstacles and providing a test for all golfing abilities.
18 holes, 5742yds, Par 71, SSS 69, Course record 70. Club membership 400.
Visitors Mon-Sun & BHs. **Societies** Booking required. **Green Fees** £10 per round. **Course Designer** T Cooper **Facilities** **Leisure** fishing, snooker. **Conf** facs Corporate Hospitality Days **Location** E of village centre off A52

SUFFOLK

ALDEBURGH Map 05 TM45

Aldeburgh Saxmundham Rd IP15 5PE
☎ 01728 452890 01728 452937
e-mail: info@aldeburghgolfclub.co.uk
web: www.aldeburghgolfclub.co.uk
Good natural drainage provides year round golf in links-type conditions. Accuracy is the first challenge on well-bunkered, gorse-lined holes. Fine views over an Area of Outstanding Natural Beauty.

Continued

18 holes, 6349yds, Par 68, SSS 71, Course record 65.
River Course: 9 holes, 4228yds, Par 64, SSS 61, Course record 62.
Club membership 900.
Visitors contact club for details. Handicap certificate. Dress code. **Societies** Booking required. **Green Fees** £52 per day, £40 pm, £60/£50 Sat & Sun. **Prof** Keith Preston **Course Designer** Thompson, Fernie, Taylor, Park. **Facilities** ⊗ 🍽 ☕ 🍷 ⛺ 🚗 🏌 🚜 🏌 **Location** 1m W on A1094

Hotel ★★★ 78% Wentworth Hotel, Wentworth Rd, ALDEBURGH ☎ 01728 452312 28 en suite 7 annexe en suite
See advertisement on this page

BECCLES Map 05 TM48

Beccles The Common NR34 9YN
☎ 01502 712244 📠 01502 710380
e-mail: becclesgolfclub@aol.com
Commons course with gorse bushes, no water hazards or bunkers.
9 holes, 2779yds, Par 68, SSS 67.
Club membership 50.
Visitors Mon-Sun. **Societies** Booking required. **Green Fees** phone. **Facilities** ☕ 🍷 ⛺ 🏌 **Location** NE of town centre

Hotel ★★★ 72% Hotel Hatfield, The Esplanade, LOWESTOFT ☎ 01502 565337 33 en suite

BUNGAY Map 05 TM38

Bungay & Waveney Valley Outney Common NR35 1DS
☎ 01986 892337 📠 01986 892222
e-mail: golfclub@onetel.com
web: www.club-noticeboard.co.uk
Heathland course, lined with fir trees and gorse. Excellent greens all-year-round, easy walking.
18 holes, 6044yds, Par 69, SSS 69, Course record 64.
Club membership 730.
Visitors Mon-Fri. Booking required. Dress code. **Societies** Booking required. **Green Fees** £36 per day, £26 per round. **Prof** Andrew Collison **Course Designer** James Braid **Facilities** ⊗ 🍴 🍽 ☕ 🍷 ⛺ 🚗 🚜 🏌 **Conf** Corporate Hospitality Days **Location** 0.5m NW on A143 at junct with A144

Hotel ★★★ 72% Hotel Hatfield, The Esplanade, LOWESTOFT ☎ 01502 565337 33 en suite

BURY ST EDMUNDS Map 05 TL86

Bury St Edmunds Tut Hill IP28 6LG
☎ 01284 755979 📠 01284 763288
e-mail: info@burygolf.co.uk
web: www.clubnoticeboard.co.uk/burystedmunds
A mature, undulating course, full of character with some challenging holes. The nine-hole pay and play course consists of five par 3s and four par 4s with modern construction greens.
18 holes, 6675yds, Par 72, SSS 72, Course record 65.
9 holes, 2217yds, Par 62, SSS 62.
Club membership 850.
Visitors 18 hole course Mon-Fri except BHs, 9 hole course Mon-Sun & BHs. Booking required for 18 hole course. Handicap certificate. Dress code. **Societies** Booking required. **Green Fees** 18 hole course £40 per day. 9 hole course £14, £17 Sat & Sun. **Prof** Mark Jillings **Course Designer** Ted Ray **Facilities** ⊗ 🍴 by arrangement 🍽 ☕ 🍷 ⛺ 🚗 🏌 🚜 🏌 **Conf** Corporate Hospitality Days **Location** A14 junct 42, 0.5m NW on B1106

Hotel ★★★ 77% Angel Hotel, Angel Hill, BURY ST EDMUNDS ☎ 01284 714000 76 en suite

Swallow Suffolk Hotel Golf & Country Club Fornham St Genevieve IP28 6JQ
☎ 01284 706801 🖹 01284 706721
e-mail: golfreservations.suffolk@swallowhotels.com
web: www.swallowhotels.com
A classic parkland course with the River Lark running through it. Criss-crossed by ponds and streams with rich fairways. Considerable upgrading of the course in recent years and the three finishing holes are particularly challenging.
The Genevieve Course: 18 holes, 6376yds, Par 72, SSS 71, Course record 69.
Club membership 600.
Visitors Mon-Sun & BHs. Booking required. Dress code. **Societies** Booking required. **Green Fees** £32 per round, £37 Sat, Sun & BHs. £25 Nov-Mar anytime. **Prof** Steve Hall **Facilities** **Leisure** heated indoor swimming pool, sauna, solarium, gymnasium. **Conf** facs Corporate Hospitality Days **Location** Off A14 at Bury St Edmunds, W onto B1106 towards Brandon, club 2.5m on right

Hotel ★★★ 76% Ravenwood Hall Hotel, Rougham, BURY ST EDMUNDS ☎ 01359 270345 7 en suite 7 annexe en suite

CRETINGHAM Map 05 TM26

Cretingham IP13 7BA
☎ 01728 685275 🖹 01728 685488
e-mail: cretinghamgolfclub@hotmail.co.uk
web: www.club-noticeboard.co.uk/cretingham
Parkland course, tree-lined with numerous water features, including the River Deben which runs through part of the course.
18 holes, 4968yds, Par 68, SSS 66.
Club membership 350.
Visitors Mon-Sun & BHs. Booking required. **Societies** Booking required. **Green Fees** phone. **Prof** Neil Jackson, Tim Johnson **Course Designer** J Austin **Facilities** **Leisure** hard tennis courts, outdoor swimming pool, fishing, pitch & putt, 9 hole course. **Conf** Corporate Hospitality Days **Location** NE of village off A1120

Hotel ★★ 69% Cedars Hotel, Needham Rd, STOWMARKET ☎ 01449 612668 25 en suite

FELIXSTOWE Map 05 TM33

Felixstowe Ferry Ferry Rd IP11 9RY
☎ 01394 286834 🖹 01394 273679
e-mail: secretary@felixstowegolf.co.uk
web: www.felixstowegolf.co.uk
An 18-hole seaside links with pleasant views, easy walking. Nine-hole pay and play course, a good test of golf.
Martello Course: 18 holes, 6166yds, Par 72, SSS 70, Course record 66.
Kingsfleet: 9 holes, 2941yds, Par 35, SSS 35.
Club membership 900.
Visitors Mon-Wed & Fri. After 2pm Thu, Sat, Sun & BHs. Booking required. Handicap certificate for 18 hole course. Dress code. **Societies** Booking required. **Green Fees** Martello £35 per day, £25 after 1pm, £40 Sat, Sun & BHs. Kingsfleet £10, £12.50 Sat, Sun & BHs. **Prof** Ian MacPherson **Course Designer** Henry Cotton **Facilities** **Conf** facs Corporate Hospitality Days **Location** NE of town centre, signed from A14

FLEMPTON Map 05 TL86

Flempton IP28 6EQ
☎ 01284 728291 🖹 01284 728468
e-mail: flemptongolfclub@freebie.net
Breckland course with gorse and wooded areas. Very little water but surrounded by woodland and Suffolk Wildlife Trust lakes.
9 holes, 6240yds, Par 70, SSS 70, Course record 67.
Club membership 250.
Visitors Mon-Sun except BHs. Booking required. Handicap certificate. Dress code. **Societies** Small societies only. Booking required in writing. **Green Fees** £35 per day, £30 per 18 holes. **Prof** Chris Aldred **Course Designer** JH Taylor **Facilities** **Location** 0.5m W on A1101

Hotel ★★★ 75% The Best Western Priory Hotel, Milden Hall Rd, BURY ST EDMUNDS ☎ 01284 766181 9 en suite 30 annexe en suite

HALESWORTH Map 05 TM37

Halesworth Bramfield Rd IP19 9XA
☎ 01986 875567 🖹 01986 874565
e-mail: info@halesworthgc.co.uk
web: www.club-noticeboard.co.uk/halesworth
A 27-hole professionally designed parkland complex of one 18-hole membership course and a nine-hole pay and play.
18 holes, 6580yds, Par 72, SSS 72, Course record 71.
9 holes, 2398yds, Par 33, SSS 33.
Club membership 300.
Visitors Mon-Sun. Not Sun am for 18-hole course. Handicap certificate for 18 hole course. **Societies** Booking required. **Green Fees** phone. **Prof** Simon Harrison **Course Designer** JW Johnson **Facilities** **Conf** facs **Location** 0.75m S of town, signed off A144 to Bramfield

Hotel ★★★ 76% Swan Hotel, Market Place, SOUTHWOLD ☎ 01502 722186 25 en suite 17 annexe en suite

HAVERHILL Map 05 TL64

Haverhill Coupals Rd CB9 7UW
☎ 01440 761951 🖹 01440 761951
e-mail: haverhillgolf@coupalsroad.fsnet.co.uk
web: www.club-noticeboard.co.uk
An 18-hole course lying across two valleys in pleasant parkland. The front nine with undulating fairways is complemented by a saucer-shape back nine, bisected by the River Stour, presenting a challenge to golfers of all standards.
18 holes, 5956yds, Par 70, SSS 69, Course record 64.
Club membership 750.
Visitors Mon-Sun & BHs. Dress code. **Societies** Booking required. **Green Fees** phone. **Prof** Nick Duc **Course Designer** P Pilgrem, C Lawrie **Facilities** **Leisure** chipping green. **Conf** facs Corporate Hospitality Days **Location** 1m SE off A1017

HINTLESHAM Map 05 TM04

Hintlesham IP8 3JG
☎ 01473 652761 ▤ 01473 652750
e-mail: office@hintleshamgolfclub.com
web: www.hintleshamgolfclub.com

Magnificent championship length course blending harmoniously with the ancient parkland surrounding the hotel. Opened in 1991 but seeded two years beforehand, this parkland course has reached a level maturity that allows it to be rivalled in the area only by a few ancient courses. The signature holes are the 4th and 17th, both featuring water at very inconvenient interludes.

18 holes, 6638yds, Par 72, SSS 72, Course record 63.
Club membership 470.

Visitors Mon-Sun & BHs. Booking required. Dress code. **Societies** Booking required. **Green Fees** £36 per round, £44 Sat, Sun & BHs. **Prof** Alastair Spink **Course Designer** Hawtree & Sons **Facilities** **Leisure** hard tennis courts, heated outdoor swimming pool, sauna, gymnasium, spa bath. **Conf** Corporate Hospitality Days **Location** In village on A1071

Hotel ★★★★ Hintlesham Hall Hotel, George St, HINTLESHAM ☎ 01473 652334 33 en suite

IPSWICH Map 05 TM14

Alnesbourne Priory Priory Park IP10 0JT
☎ 01473 727393 ▤ 01473 278372
e-mail: golf@priory-park.com
web: www.priory-park.com

A fabulous outlook facing due south across the River Orwell is one of the many good features of this course set in woodland. All holes run among trees with some fairways requiring straight shots. The 8th green is on saltings by the river.

9 holes, 1700yds, Par 29.
Club membership 30.

Visitors Mon, Wed-Sun & BHs. Dress code. **Societies** Booking required. **Green Fees** £10, £15 Sat, Sun & BHs. **Facilities** **Leisure** practice net. **Conf** facs **Location** 3m SE off A14

Hotel ★★★ 71% Courtyard by Marriott Ipswich, The Havens, Ransomes Europark, IPSWICH ☎ 01473 272244 60 en suite

Fynn Valley IP6 9JA
☎ 01473 785267 ▤ 01473 785632
e-mail: enquiries@fynn-valley.co.uk
web: www.fynn-valley.co.uk.

Undulating parkland alongside a protected river valley. The course has matured into an excellent test of golf enhanced by more than 100 bunkers and protected greens that have tricky slopes and contours.

18 holes, 6361yds, Par 70, SSS 71, Course record 65.
Club membership 680.

Visitors Mon-Sun & BHs. Dress code. **Societies** Booking required. **Green Fees** £36 per day, £26 per 18 holes, £40/£32 Sat, Sun & BHs. **Prof** P Wilby, A Lucas & others **Course Designer** Antonio Primavera **Facilities** **Leisure** 9 hole par 3 course, practice bunker. **Conf** facs Corporate Hospitality Days **Location** 2m N of Ipswich on B1077

Hotel ★★★ 65% Novotel Ipswich, Greyfriars Rd, IPSWICH ☎ 01473 232400 100 en suite

Ipswich Purdis Heath IP3 8UQ
☎ 01473 728941 ▤ 01473 715236
e-mail: mail@ipswichgolfclub.com
web: www.ipswichgolfclub.com

Many golfers are surprised when they hear that Ipswich has, at Purdis Heath, a first-class course. In some ways it resembles some of Surrey's better courses; a beautiful heathland course with two lakes and easy walking.

Purdis Heath: 18 holes, 6439yds, Par 71, SSS 71, Course record 64
9 holes, 1930yds, Par 31.
Club membership 865.

Visitors Mon-Sun except BHs. Booking required. Handicap certificate. Dress code. **Societies** Booking required. **Green Fees** 18 hole course £47 per day, £37 per round pm, £52/£42 Sat, Sun & BHs. 9 hole course £16 per day, £12 per round. **Prof** Stephen Whymark **Course Designer** James Braid **Facilities** **Location** 3m E of town centre off A1156

Hotel ★★★ 71% Courtyard by Marriott Ipswich, The Havens, Ransomes Europark, IPSWICH ☎ 01473 272244 60 en suite

Rushmere Rushmere Heath IP4 5QQ
☎ 01473 725648 ▤ 01473 273852
e-mail: rushmeregolfclub@talk21.com
web: www.club-noticeboard.co.uk/rushmere

Heathland course with gorse and prevailing winds. A good test of golf.

18 holes, 6262yds, Par 70, SSS 70, Course record 66.
Club membership 700.

Continued

Visitors Mon-Fri except BHs. Booking required. Handicap required. Dress code. **Societies** Booking required. **Green Fees** £38. **Prof** K Vince **Facilities** ⊗ 〽 ⛾ ☕ ♀ ⛳ 🏠 ✓ **Conf** facs Corporate Hospitality Days **Location** On A1214 Woodbridge road near hospital, signed

Hotel ★★★ 67% The Hotel Elizabeth, Old London Rd, Copdock, IPSWICH ☎ 01473 209988 76 en suite

LOWESTOFT Map 05 TM59

Rookery Park Beccles Rd, Carlton Colville NR33 8HJ
☎ 01502 509190 📠 01502 509191
e-mail: office@rookeryparkgolfclub.co.uk
web: www.club-noticeboard.co.uk
Parkland course with a nine-hole par 3 adjacent.
18 holes, 6714yds, Par 72, SSS 72.
Club membership 1000.
Visitors Mon-Sun & BHs. Booking required. Handicap cerificate. Dress code. **Societies** Booking required. **Green Fees** £29.50, £35 Sat, Sun & BHs. **Prof** Martin Elsworthy **Course Designer** CD Lawrie **Facilities** ⊗ 〽 ⛾ ☕ ♀ ⛳ 🏠 ✓ **Leisure** 9 hole par 3 course. **Location** 3.5m SW of Lowestoft on A146

Hotel ★★★ 72% Hotel Hatfield, The Esplanade, LOWESTOFT ☎ 01502 565337 33 en suite

MILDENHALL Map 05 TL77

West Suffolk Golf Centre New Drove, Beck Row IP28 8DS
☎ 01638 718972 📠 01353 675447
web: www.golfinsuffolk.com
This course has been gradually improved to provide a unique opportunity to play an inland course in all weather conditions. Situated on the edge of the Breckland, the dry nature of the course makes for easy walking with rare flora and fauna.
12 holes, 6461yds, Par 71, SSS 71.
Visitors Mon-Sun & BHs. Dress code. **Societies** Booking required. **Green Fees** £10.50 per day, £14 Sat, Sun & BHs. **Prof** Neil Mitchell **Facilities** ⊗ ⛾ ☕ ♀ ⛳ 🏠 ✓ **Leisure** fishing, pitch and putt practice course. **Conf** Corporate Hospitality Days **Location** A1101 from Mildenhall to Beck Row, 1st left after Beck Row signed to West Row/Golf Centre, 0.5m on right

Hotel ★★★ 67% The Smoke House, Beck Row, MILDENHALL ☎ 01638 713223 94 en suite 2 annexe en suite

NEWMARKET Map 05 TL66

Links Cambridge Rd CB8 0TG
☎ 01638 663000 📠 01638 661476
e-mail: secretary@linksgc.fsbusiness.co.uk
web: www.clubnoticeboard.co.uk/newmarket
Gently undulating parkland.
18 holes, 6582yds, Par 72, SSS 72, Course record 66 or , Par 72.
Club membership 780.
Visitors Mon-Sun & BHs. Booking required. Handicap certificate. Dress code. **Societies** Booking required. **Green Fees** £34 per day, £26 per round, £38/£30 Sat & Sun. **Prof** John Sharkey **Course Designer** Col. Hotchkin **Facilities** ⊗ 〽 ⛾ ☕ ♀ ⛳ 🏠 ✓ **Location** 1m SW on A1034

Hotel ★★★ 69% Heath Court Hotel, Moulton Rd, NEWMARKET ☎ 01638 667171 41 en suite

NEWTON Map 05 TL94

Newton Green Newton Green CO10 0QN
☎ 01787 377217 & 377501 📠 01787 377549
e-mail: info@newtongreengolfclub.co.uk
web: www.newtongreengolfclub.co.uk
Flat 18-hole course with pond. First nine holes are open with bunkers and trees. Second nine holes are tight with ditches and gorse.
18 holes, 5960yds, Par 69, SSS 68.
Club membership 570.
Visitors Mon & Wed-Fri. Tue, Sat, Sun & BHs pm. Booking required Tue. **Societies** Booking required. **Green Fees** £23 per round, £27 Sat & Sun. **Prof** Tim Cooper **Facilities** ⊗ 〽 ⛾ ☕ ♀ ⛳ 🏠 ✓ **Location** W of village on A134

Hotel ★★★ 73% The Bull, Hall St, LONG MELFORD ☎ 01787 378494 25 en suite

RAYDON Map 05 TM03

Brett Vale Noakes Rd IP7 5LR
☎ 01473 310718
e-mail: info@brettvalegolf.com
web: www.brettvalegolf.com
Brett Vale course takes you through a nature reserve and on lakeside walks, affording views over Dedham Vale. The excellent fairways demand an accurate tee and good approach shots; 1, 2, 3, 8, 10 and 15 are all affected by crosswinds, but once in the valley it is much more sheltered. Although only 5864yds the course is testing and interesting at all levels of golf.
18 holes, 5864yds, Par 70, SSS 69, Course record 65.
Club membership 600.
Visitors Mon-Sun & BHs. Booking required. Dress code. **Societies** Booking required. **Green Fees** £22.50 per 18 holes, £28 Sat, Sun & BHs. **Prof** Mark Snow **Course Designer** Howard Swan **Facilities** ⊗ 〽 ⛾ ☕ ♀ ⛳ 🏠 ✓ **Leisure** fishing, gymnasium. **Conf** facs Corporate Hospitality Days **Location** A12 onto B1070 towards Hadleigh, left at Raydon, by water tower

Hotel ★★★ Maison Talbooth, Stratford Rd, DEDHAM ☎ 01206 322367 10 en suite

SOUTHWOLD Map 05 TM57

Southwold The Common IP18 6TB
☎ 01502 723234
Commonland course with fine greens and panoramic views of the sea.
9 holes, 6052yds, Par 70, SSS 69, Course record 67.
Club membership 350.
Visitors Booking required. **Societies** Booking required. **Green Fees** phone. **Prof** Brian Allen **Course Designer** J Braid **Facilities** ⊗ ⛾ ☕ ♀ ⛳ 🏠 ✓ **Conf** Corporate Hospitality Days **Location** S of town off A1095

Hotel ★★★ 76% Swan Hotel, Market Place, SOUTHWOLD ☎ 01502 722186 25 en suite 17 annexe en suite

Continued

STOWMARKET Map 05 TM05

Stowmarket Lower Rd, Onehouse IP14 3DA
☎ 01449 736473 01449 736826
e-mail: mail@stowmarketgc.sagehost.co.uk
web: www.club-noticeboard.co.uk
Parkland course.
18 holes, 6107yds, Par 69, SSS 69, Course record 65. Club membership 630.
Visitors contact club for details. Handicap certificate. Dress code. **Societies** Booking required. **Green Fees** phone. **Prof** Duncan Burl **Facilities** **Conf** Corporate Hospitality Days **Location** 2.5m SW off B1115

Hotel ★★ 69% Cedars Hotel, Needham Rd, STOWMARKET ☎ 01449 612668 25 en suite

STUSTON Map 05 TM17

Diss Stuston IP21 4AA
☎ 01379 641025 01379 644586
e-mail: sec.dissgolf@virgin.net
web: www.club-noticeboard.co.uk
An inland commonland course with the river Waveney coming into play on the 6th hole and having a part parkland, part links feel with small tight greens. Well bunkered with easy walking. Depending on the direction of the wind, the golfer can find the last three holes a pleasure or a pain. The signature hole is the long par 4 13th, a test on any day - the drive must be long to give any chance of reaching the green in two.
18 holes, 6206yds, Par 70, SSS 70, Course record 67. Club membership 750.
Visitors Tue, Thu, Fri & Sun except BHs. Booking required. Handicap certificate. Dress code. **Societies** Booking required. **Green Fees** £36 per day, £28 per 18 holes, £14 per 9 holes. **Prof** NJ Taylor **Facilities** **Leisure** driving nets. **Conf** facs Corporate Hospitality Days **Location** 1.5m SE on B1118

Inn ♦♦♦♦ The White Horse Inn, Stoke Ash, EYE
☎ 01379 678222 7 annexe en suite

THORPENESS Map 05 TM45

Thorpeness Golf Club & Hotel Lakeside Av IP16 4NH
☎ 01728 452176 01728 453868
e-mail: info@thorpeness.co.uk
web: www.thorpeness.co.uk
A 6271yd coastal heathland course, designed in 1923 by James Braid. The quality of his design combined with modern green keeping techniques has resulted in an extremely challenging course for golfers at all levels. It is also one of the driest courses in the region.

Continued

18 holes, 6271yds, Par 69, SSS 71, Course record 66. Club membership 700.
Visitors Mon-Sun & BHs. Booking required. Handicap certificate. Dress code. **Societies** Booking required. **Green Fees** £35 per day/round, £40 Sat, Sun & BHs. £20 after 3pm. **Prof** Frank Hill **Course Designer** James Braid **Facilities** **Leisure** hard and grass tennis courts, fishing, snooker room. **Conf** facs Corporate Hospitality Days **Location** Off A1094 to Aldeburgh, signed

Hotel ★★★ 70% Thorpeness Hotel, Lakeside Av, THORPENESS ☎ 01728 452176 30 annexe en suite

WALDRINGFIELD Map 05 TM24

Waldringfield Heath Newbourne Rd IP12 4PT
☎ 01473 736768 01473 736793
e-mail: patgolf1@aol.com
Easy walking heathland course with long drives on 1st and 13th (590yds) and some ponds.
18 holes, 6057yds, Par 70, SSS 69, Course record 69. Club membership 550.
Visitors Mon-Sun & BHs. Booking required. Dress code. **Societies** Booking required. **Green Fees** £24 per 18 holes, £28 Sat, Sun & BHs. **Prof** Tim Huffer **Course Designer** Phillip Pilgrem **Facilities** **Conf** facs **Location** 1m W of village off A12

Hotel ★★★ 77% Seckford Hall Hotel, WOODBRIDGE ☎ 01394 385678 22 en suite 10 annexe en suite

WOODBRIDGE Map 05 TM24

Best Western Ufford Park Hotel Golf & Leisure Yarmouth Rd, Ufford IP12 1QW
☎ 0844 4773737 0844 4773727
e-mail: mail@uffordpark.co.uk
web: www.uffordpark.co.uk
The 18-hole par 71 course is set in 120 acres of ancient parkland with 12 water features and voted one of the best British winter courses. The course enjoys excellent natural drainage and a large reservoir supplements a spring feed pond to ensure ample water for irrigation. The course is host to the Sky Sports PGA Europro Tour.
18 holes, 6312yds, Par 71, SSS 71, Course record 61. Club membership 350.
Visitors Mon-Sun & BHs. Handicap certificate. Dress code. **Societies** Booking required. **Green Fees** £30 per day, £40 Sat & Sun. **Prof** Stuart Robertson **Course Designer** Phil Pilgrim **Facilities** **Leisure** heated indoor swimming pool, sauna, solarium, gymnasium, golf academy. **Conf** facs Corporate Hospitality Days **Location** A12 onto B1438

Hotel ★★★ 74% Best Western Ufford Park Hotel Golf & Leisure, Yarmouth Rd, Ufford, IPSWICH / WOODBRIDGE ☎ 01394 383555 87 en suite

Seckford Seckford Hall Rd, Great Bealings IP13 6NT
☎ 01394 388000 01394 382818
e-mail: info@seckfordgolf.co.uk
web: www.seckfordgolf.co.uk
A challenging course interspersed with young tree plantations, numerous bunkers, water hazards and undulating fairways, providing a tough test for all levels of golfer. The testing 18th is almost completely surrounded by water.
18 holes, 5303yds, Par 68, SSS 66, Course record 62. Club membership 400.
Visitors Booking required. **Societies** Booking required. **Green Fees** £17 per round, £25 Sat, Sun & BHs. **Prof** Simon Jay **Course Designer** J Johnson **Facilities** **Leisure** heated indoor swimming pool, fishing, gymnasium. **Conf** Corporate Hospitality Days **Location** 1m W of Woodbridge off A12, next to Seckford Hall Hotel

Hotel ★★★ 77% Seckford Hall Hotel, WOODBRIDGE ☎ 01394 385678 22 en suite 10 annexe en suite

Woodbridge Bromeswell Heath IP12 2PF
☎ 01394 382038 01394 382392
e-mail: woodbridgegc@anglianet.co.uk
web: www.woodbridgegolfclub.co.uk
A beautiful course, one of the best in East Anglia. It is situated on high ground and in different seasons presents golfers with a great variety of colour.

Continued

Some say that of the many good holes the 16th is the best.

Main Course: 18 holes, 6299yds, Par 70, SSS 70, Course record 64.
Forest Course: 9 holes, 3191yds, Par 70, SSS 70.
Club membership 700.
Visitors Main Course: Mon-Fri, booking required, handicap certificate. Forest Course: Mon-Sun. **Societies** Booking required. **Green Fees** phone. **Prof** Campbell Elliot **Course Designer** Davie Grant **Facilities** by arrangement **Location** 2.5m NE off A1152
See advertisement on this page.

Hotel ★★★ 77% Seckford Hall Hotel, WOODBRIDGE ☎ 01394 385678 22 en suite 10 annexe en suite

Worlington Map 05 TL67

Royal Worlington & Newmarket IP28 8SD
☎ 01638 712216 & 717787 🖷 01638 717787
web: www.royalworlington.co.uk
Inland links course, renowned as one of the best nine-hole courses in the world. Well drained, giving excellent winter playing conditions.
9 holes, 3123yds, Par 35, SSS 70, Course record 65.
Club membership 325.
Visitors Mon-Fri except BHs. Handicap certificate. Dress code. **Societies** Booking required. **Green Fees** £60 per day. Reductions after 2 pm. **Prof** Steve Barker **Course Designer** Tom Dunn **Facilities** by arrangement **Location** 0.5m SE of Worlington near Mildenhall

Hotel ★★★ 73% Riverside Hotel, Mill St, MILDENHALL ☎ 01638 717274 17 en suite 6 annexe en suite

SURREY

Addlestone Map 04 TQ06

New Zealand Woodham Ln KT15 3QD
☎ 01932 345049 🖷 01932 342891
e-mail: roger.marrett@nzgc.org
18 holes, 6073yds, Par 68, SSS 69, Course record 66.
Course Designer Muir Fergusson, Simpson **Location** 1.5m E of Woking
Phone for further details

Hotel ★★★ 67% The Ship Hotel, Monument Green, WEYBRIDGE ☎ 01932 848364 42 en suite

Ashford Map 04 TQ07

Ashford Manor Fordbridge Rd TW15 3RT
☎ 01784 424644 🖷 01784 424649
e-mail: secretary@ashfordmanorgolfclub.fsnet.co.uk
web: www.amgc.co.uk
Tree-lined parkland course is built on gravel and drains well, never needing temporary tees or greens. A heavy investment in fairway irrigation and an extensive woodland management programme over the past few years have formed a strong future for this course, originally built over a 100 years ago.
18 holes, 6332yds, Par 70, SSS 71, Course record 65.
Club membership 700.
Visitors Mon-Fri except BHs. Booking required. Handicap certificate. Dress code. **Societies** Booking required. **Green Fees** Mon-Fri £50 per day, £40 per round. **Prof** Ian Campbell **Course Designer** Tom Hogg **Facilities** **Conf** Corporate Hospitality Days **Location** 2m E of Staines via A308 Staines bypass

Hotel ★★★ 72% Macdonald Thames Lodge, Thames St, STAINES ☎ 0870 400 8121 & 01784 464433 🖷 01784 454858 78 en suite

Bagshot Map 04 SU96

Pennyhill Park Hotel & The Spa
London Rd GU19 5EU
☎ 01276 471774 🖷 01276 473217
e-mail: enquiries@pennyhillpark.co.uk
web: www.exclusivehotels.co.uk
A nine-hole course set in 11 acres of beautiful parkland. It is challenging to even the most experienced golfer.
9 holes, 2055yds, Par 32, SSS 32.
Club membership 100.
Visitors contact hotel for details. Dress code. **Green Fees** Complimentary for hotel residents/day visitor using hotel facilities. **Facilities** **Leisure** hard tennis courts, outdoor and indoor heated swimming pools, sauna, gymnasium. **Conf** facs **Location** Off A30 between Camberley

Hotel ★★★★★ Pennyhill Park Hotel & The Spa, London Rd, BAGSHOT ☎ 01276 471774 26 en suite 97 annexe en suite

Windlesham Grove End GU19 5HY
☎ 01276 452220 🖷 01276 452290
e-mail: admin@windleshamgolf.com
web: www.windleshamgolf.com
A parkland course with many demanding par 4 holes over 400 yards. Thoughtfully designed by Tommy Horton.
18 holes, 6650yds, Par 72, SSS 72, Course record 69.
Club membership 800.
Visitors Mon-Fri. Sat, Sun & BHs pm. Dress code. **Societies** Booking required. **Green Fees** £25 per round, £35 Sat & Sun. **Prof** Lee Mucklow **Course Designer** Tommy Horton **Facilities** **Conf** facs Corporate Hospitality Days **Location** Junct A30

Hotel ★★★★★ Pennyhill Park Hotel & The Spa, London Rd, BAGSHOT ☎ 01276 471774 26 en suite 97 annexe en suite

Banstead Map 04 TQ25

Banstead Downs Burdon Ln, Belmont, Sutton SM2 7DD
☎ 020 8642 2284 🖷 020 8642 5252
e-mail: secretary@bansteaddowns.com
18 holes, 6194yds, Par 69, SSS 69, Course record 64.
Course Designer JH Taylor, James Braid **Location** M25 junct 8, A217 N for 6m
Phone for further details

Hotel ★★ 62% Thatched House Hotel, 135 Cheam Rd, Sutton ☎ 020 8642 3131 32 rms (29 en suite)

Cuddington Banstead Rd SM7 1RD
☎ 020 8393 0952 🖷 020 8786 7025
e-mail: ds@cuddingtongc.co.uk
Parkland with easy walking and good views. Reputed to have the longest start, over the first three holes, in Surrey.
18 holes, 6614yds, Par 71, SSS 71, Course record 64.
Club membership 694.
Visitors Booking required. Handicap certificate. **Societies** Thu. Booking required. **Green Fees** phone. **Prof** Mark Warner **Course Designer** H Colt **Facilities** **Conf** facs Corporate Hospitality Days **Location** N of Banstead station on A2022

Hotel ★★ 62% Thatched House Hotel, 135 Cheam Rd, Sutton ☎ 020 8642 3131 32 rms (29 en suite)

BLETCHINGLEY Map 05 TQ35

Bletchingley Church Ln RH1 4LP
☎ 01883 744666 🖹 01883 744284
e-mail: info@bletchingleygolf.co.uk
web: www.bletchingleygolf.co.uk
Panoramic views provide the backdrop for this course, constructed on rich sandy loam and playable all year round. The course design has made best use of the interesting and undulating land features with a variety of mixed and mature trees providing essential course definition. A mature stream creates several interesting water features.
18 holes, 6169yds, Par 72, SSS 69.
Club membership 500.
Visitors Mon-Sun & BHs. Booking required. Dress code. **Societies** Booking required. **Green Fees** £32, £45 Sat & Sun. **Prof** Alasdair Dyer **Facilities** by arrangement **Conf** facs Corporate Hospitality Days **Location** A25 onto Church Ln in Bletchingley

Hotel ★★★★ 73% Nutfield Priory, Nutfield, REDHILL ☎ 01737 824400 60 en suite

BRAMLEY Map 04 TQ04

Bramley GU5 0AL
☎ 01483 892696 🖹 01483 894673
e-mail: secretary@bramleygolfclub.co.uk
Parkland course. From the high ground picturesque views of the Wey valley on one side and the Hog's Back. Full on course irrigation system with three reservoirs on the course.
18 holes, 5990yds, Par 69, SSS 68, Course record 61.
Club membership 850.
Visitors Mon-Fri except BHs. Dress code. **Societies** Booking required. **Green Fees** £54 per day, £44 per round. **Prof** Gary Peddie **Course Designer** Charles Mayo, James Braid **Facilities** **Location** 3m S of Guildford on A281

Hotel Innkeeper's Lodge Godalming, Ockford Rd, GODALMING ☎ 01483 419997 19 rms

BROOKWOOD Map 04 SU95

West Hill Bagshot Rd GU24 0BH
☎ 01483 474365 🖹 01483 474252
e-mail: secretary@westhill-golfclub.co.uk
web: www.westhill-golfclub.co.uk
A challenging course with fairways lined with heather and tall pines, one of Surrey's finest courses. Demands every club in the bag to be played.
18 holes, 6343yds, Par 69, SSS 70, Course record 62.
Club membership 500.
Visitors Mon-Fri except BHs. Booking required. Handicap certificate. Dress code. **Societies** Booking required. **Green Fees** £80 per day, £60 per round. Winter reduced rates. **Prof** Guy Shoesmith **Course Designer** C Butchart, W Parke **Facilities** by arrangement **Conf** Corporate Hospitality Days **Location** E of village on A322

Hotel ★★★★★ Pennyhill Park Hotel & The Spa, London Rd, BAGSHOT ☎ 01276 471774 26 en suite 97 annexe en suite

CAMBERLEY Map 04 SU86

Camberley Heath Golf Dr GU15 1JG
☎ 01276 23258 🖹 01276 692505
e-mail: info@camberleyheathgolfclub.co.uk
web: www.camberleyheathgolfclub.co.uk
One of the great heath and heather courses so frequently associated with Surrey. Several very good short holes - especially the 8th. The 10th is a difficult and interesting par 4, as is the 17th, where the drive must be held well to the left as trouble lies to the right. A fairway irrigation system has been installed.

18 holes, 6147yds, Par 72, SSS 70, Course record 65.
Club membership 600.
Visitors Mon-Thu except BHs. Booking required. Handicap certificate. Dress code. **Societies** Booking required. **Green Fees** £74 per 36 holes, £57 per 18 holes. **Prof** Glenn Ralph **Course Designer** Harry S Colt **Facilities** **Conf** facs Corporate Hospitality Days **Location** 1.25m SE of town centre off A325

Hotel ★★★★★ Pennyhill Park Hotel & The Spa, London Rd, BAGSHOT ☎ 01276 471774 26 en suite 97 annexe en suite

Pine Ridge Old Bisley Rd, Frimley GU16 9NX
☎ 01276 675444 & 20770 🖹 01276 678837
e-mail: enquiry@pineridgegolf.co.uk
web: www.pineridgegolf.co.uk
18 holes, 6458yds, Par 72, SSS 71, Course record 65.
Course Designer Clive D Smith **Location** Off B3015, near A30
Phone for further details

Hotel ★★★★ 72% Macdonald Frimley Hall Hotel & Spa, Lime Av, CAMBERLEY ☎ 0870 400 8224 96 en suite

CATERHAM Map 05 TQ35

Surrey National Rook Ln, Chaldon CR3 5AA
☎ 01883 344555 🖹 01883 344422
e-mail: caroline@surreynational.co.uk
web: www.surreynational.co.uk
Opened in April 1999, this American-style course is set in beautiful countryside and features fully irrigated greens and fairways. The setting is dramatic with rolling countryside, thousands of mature trees and water features. The chalk based sub-soil, computerised irrigation and buggy paths combine to make the course enjoyable to play at any time of year.
18 holes, 6612yds, Par 72, SSS 73, Course record 70.
Club membership 750.

Continued

Surrey National

Visitors Mon-Sun & BHs. Booking required. Dress code. **Societies** Booking required **Green Fees** £30 per round, £32 Sat & Sun. **Prof** David Kent, Matthew Stock **Course Designer** David Williams **Facilities** by arrangement **Conf** facs Corporate Hospitality Days **Location** M25 junct 7, A22

CHERTSEY Map 04 TQ06

Laleham Laleham Reach KT16 8RP
☎ 01932 564211 🖹 01932 564448
e-mail: sec@laleham-golf.co.uk
web: www.laleham-golf.co.uk
Well-bunkered parkland and meadowland course. The prevailing wind and strategic placement of hazards makes it a fair but testing challenge. Natural drainage due to the underlying gravel.
18 holes, 6204yds, Par 70, SSS 70.
Club membership 600.
Visitors Mon-Sun except BHs. Dress code. **Societies** welcome. **Green Fees** £30. **Prof** Hogan Stott **Course Designer** Jack White **Facilities** **Conf** facs Corporate Hospitality Days **Location** M25 junct 11, A320 to Thorpe Park rdbt, exit Penton Marina, signed

Hotel ★★★ 72% Macdonald Thames Lodge, Thames St, STAINES ☎ 0870 400 8121 & 01784 464433 🖹 01784 454858 78 en suite

CHIDDINGFOLD Map 04 SU93

Chiddingfold Petworth Rd GU8 4SL
☎ 01428 685888 🖹 01428 685939
e-mail: chiddingfoldgolf@btconnect.com
web: www.chiddingfoldgc.co.uk
With panoramic views across the Surrey hills, this challenging course offers a unique combination of lakes, mature woodland and wildlife.
18 holes, 5568yds, Par 70, SSS 67.
Club membership 250.
Visitors Booking up to 1 week in advance. **Societies** Booking required. **Green Fees** phone. **Prof** John Wells **Course Designer** Jonathan Gaunt **Facilities** **Conf** facs Corporate Hospitality Days **Location** Off A283

Hotel ★★★★ 71% Lythe Hill Hotel & Spa, Petworth Rd, HASLEMERE ☎ 01428 651251 41 en suite

CHIPSTEAD Map 04 TQ25

Chipstead How Ln CR5 3LN
☎ 01737 555781 🖹 01737 555404
e-mail: office@chipsteadgolf.co.uk
web: www.chipsteadgolf.co.uk
Downland course with good views. Testing 18th hole.
18 holes, 5504yds, Par 68, SSS 67, Course record 61.
Club membership 475.
Visitors Mon-Fri except BHs. Dress code. **Societies** Booking required. **Green Fees** £40 per day, £30 per round. **Prof** Gary Torbett **Facilities** **Conf** facs Corporate Hospitality Days **Location** 0.5m N of village

Hotel ★★★★ 69% Selsdon Park Hotel & Golf Course, Addington Rd, Sanderstead, CROYDON ☎ 020 8657 8811 204 en suite

CHOBHAM Map 04 SU96

Chobham Chobham Rd, Knaphill GU21 2TZ
☎ 01276 855584 🖹 01276 855663
e-mail: info@chobhamgolfclub.co.uk
web: www.chobhamgolfclub.co.uk
Designed by Peter Allis and Clive Clark, Chobham course sits among mature oaks and tree nurseries offering tree-lined fairways, together with six man-made lakes.
18 holes, 5959yds, Par 69, SSS 69, Course record 67.
Club membership 750.
Visitors Mon-Thu except BHs. Booking required. Handicap certificate. Dress code. **Societies** Booking required. **Green Fees** phone. **Prof** Tim Coombes **Course Designer** Peter Alliss, Clive Clark **Facilities** by arrangement **Conf** facs Corporate Hospitality Days **Location** on Chobham road between Chobham and Knaphill

Hotel ★★★ 65% Falcon Hotel, 68 Farnborough Rd, FARNBOROUGH ☎ 01252 545378 30 en suite

COBHAM Map 04 TQ16

Silvermere Redhill Rd KT11 1EF
☎ 01932 584300 🖹 01932 584301
e-mail: sales@silvermere-golf.co.uk
web: www.silvermere-golf.co.uk
A mixture of light heathland on the first six holes and parkland on holes 7-16, then two signature water holes at the 17th and 18th, played over the Silvermere Lake.
18 holes, 6430yds, Par 71.
Club membership 600.
Visitors Mon-Sun & BHs. Booking required. Dress code. **Societies** Booking required. **Green Fees** £24 per 18 holes, £37.50 Sat & Sun. **Prof** Doug McClelland **Course Designer** Neil Coles **Facilities** **Leisure** fishing. **Conf** facs Corporate Hospitality Days **Location** 0.5m from M25 junct 10, off A245

Hotel ★★★★ 75% Woodlands Park Hotel, Woodlands Ln, STOKE D'ABERNON ☎ 01372 843933 57 en suite

CRANLEIGH Map 04 TQ03

Cranleigh Golf and Leisure Club Barhatch Ln GU6 7NG
☎ 01483 268855 🖷 01483 267251
e-mail: info@cranleighgolfandleisure.co.uk
web: www.cranleighgolfandleisure.co.uk
Scenic woodland and parkland at the base of the Surrey hills, easy walking. The golfer should not be deceived by the length of the course. Clubhouse in 400-year-old barn.
18 holes, 5263yds, Par 68, SSS 65, Course record 62.
Club membership 1400.
Visitors Mon-Sun & BHs. Booking required. Dress code. **Societies** Booking required. **Green Fees** £38 per day, £30 per round, £33 per round Sat, Sun & BHs. Winter/twilight reduced rates. **Prof** Trevor Longmuir **Facilities** **Leisure** hard tennis courts, heated indoor swimming pool, sauna, solarium, gymnasium, steam room, spa bath. **Conf** Corporate Hospitality Days **Location** 0.5m N of town centre

Hotel ★★★ 61% Gatton Manor Hotel Golf & Country Club, Standon Ln, OCKLEY ☎ 01306 627555 18 en suite

Wildwood Country Club Horsham Rd, Alfold GU6 8JE
☎ 01403 753255 🖷 01403 752005
web: www.wildwoodgolf.co.uk
Parkland with stands of old oaks dominating several holes, a stream fed by a natural spring winds through a series of lakes and ponds. The greens are smooth, undulating and large. The 5th and 16th are the most challenging holes.
18 holes, 6655yds, Par 72, SSS 73, Course record 65.
Club membership 600.
Visitors Mon-Sun & BHs.Booking required. Dress code. **Societies** Booking required. **Green Fees** phone. **Prof** Stephen Plane **Course Designer** Hawtree & Sons **Facilities** **Leisure** gymnasium, Par 3 course. **Conf** facs Corporate Hospitality Days **Location** Off A281 3m SW of Cranleigh

Hotel ★★★ 69% Hurtwood Inn Hotel, Walking Bottom, PEASLAKE ☎ 01306 730851 15 en suite 6 annexe en suite

CROYDON

See Greater London

DORKING Map 04 TQ14

Betchworth Park Reigate Rd RH4 1NZ
☎ 01306 882052 🖷 01306 877462
e-mail: manager@betchworthparkgc.co.uk
web: www.betchworthparkgc.co.uk
Established parkland course with beautiful views, on the southern side of the North Downs near Boxhill.
18 holes, 6307yds, Par 69, SSS 70, Course record 64.
Club membership 725.
Visitors Mon-Fri & Sun. Dress code. **Societies** Booking required. **Green Fees** £37 per day, Sun £50 per round. **Prof** Andy Tocher **Course Designer** Harry Colt **Facilities** **Conf** Corporate Hospitality Days **Location** 1m E of Dorking on A25 towards Reigate

Hotel ★★★ 67% Macdonald White Horse Hotel, High St, DORKING ☎ 0870 400 8282 37 en suite 41 annexe en suite

Dorking Chart Park, Deepdene Av RH5 4BX
☎ 01306 886917
e-mail: info@dorkinggolfclub.co.uk
web: www.dorkinggolfclub.co.uk
Undulating parkland, easy slopes, wind sheltered. Testing holes: 5th Tom's Puddle (par 4); 7th Rest and Be Thankful (par 4); 9th Double Decker (par 4).
9 holes, 5120yds, Par 66, SSS 65, Course record 62.
Club membership 392.
Visitors Tue, Thu & Fri. Mon, Wed, Sat, Sun & BHs pm. Dress code. **Societies** Booking required. **Green Fees** £18 per 18 holes, £12 per 9 holes, £22.50/£18 Sat & Sun. **Prof** Allan Smeal **Course Designer** J Braid & others **Facilities** **Location** 1m S on A24

Hotel ★★★★ 70% Macdonald Burford Bridge Hotel, Burford Bridge, Box Hill, DORKING ☎ 0870 400 8283 57 en suite

EAST HORSLEY Map 04 TQ05

Drift The Drift, Off Forest Rd KT24 5HD
☎ 01483 284641 & 284772 (shop) 🖷 01483 284642
e-mail: info@driftgolfclub.com
web: www.driftgolfclub.com
18 holes, 6425yds, Par 73, SSS 72, Course record 65.
Course Designer Sir Henry Cotton, Robert Sandow **Location** 0.5m N of East Horsley off B2039
Phone for further details

Hotel ★★ 66% Bookham Grange Hotel, Little Bookham Common, Bookham, LEATHERHEAD ☎ 01372 452742 27 en suite

EFFINGHAM Map 04 TQ15

Effingham Guildford Rd KT24 5PZ
☎ 01372 452203 🖷 01372 459959
e-mail: secretary@effinghamgolfclub.com
web: www.effinghamgolfclub.com
Easy-walking downland course laid out on 270 acres with tree-lined fairways. It is one of the longest of the Surrey courses with wide subtle greens that provide a provocative but by no means exhausting challenge. Fine views of the London skyline.
18 holes, 6554yds, Par 71, SSS 71, Course record 64.
Club membership 800.
Visitors Mon-Fri. Handicap certificate. Dress code. **Societies** Booking required. **Green Fees** £60 per day, £50 per round. **Prof** Steve Hoatson **Course Designer** H Colt **Facilities** by arrangement **Leisure** hard tennis courts, snooker table. **Conf** facs Corporate Hospitality Days **Location** W of village on A246

Hotel ★★ 66% Bookham Grange Hotel, Little Bookham Common, Bookham, LEATHERHEAD ☎ 01372 452742 27 en suite

If the name of the club appears in italics, details have not been confirmed for this edition of the guide

ENTON GREEN Map 04 SU94

West Surrey GU8 5AF
☎ 01483 421275 🖹 01483 415419
e-mail: office@wsgc.co.uk
web: www.wsgc.co.uk
A good parkland-type course in rolling, well-wooded setting. Some fairways are tight with straight driving at a premium. The 17th is a testing hole with a long hill walk.
18 holes, 6482yds, Par 71, SSS 71, Course record 65.
Club membership 600.
Visitors Mon-Sun except BHs. Booking required. Handicap certificate. Dress code. **Societies** Booking required. **Green Fees** £60 per day, £40 per round, £70/£50 Sat & Sun. **Prof** Alister Tawse **Course Designer** Herbert Fowler **Facilities** **Leisure** hard tennis courts. **Conf** Corporate Hospitality Days **Location** S of village

Hotel ★★★ 68% Macdonald Bush Hotel, The Borough, FARNHAM ☎ 0870 400 8225 & 01252 715237 🖹 01252 733530 83 en suite

EPSOM Map 04 TQ26

Epsom Longdown Ln South KT17 4JR
☎ 01372 721666 🖹 01372 817183
e-mail: secretary@epsomgolfclub.co.uk
web: www.epsomgolfclub.co.uk
Traditional downland course with many mature trees and fast undulating greens. Thought must be given to every shot to play to one's handicap.
18 holes, 5656yds, Par 69, SSS 67, Course record 63.
Club membership 770.
Visitors Mon, Wed-Fri & BHs. Sat & Sun pm. Booking required. Dress code. **Societies** Booking required. **Green Fees** £24 per round before 2pm, £20 after2pm. **Prof** Ron Goudie **Course Designer** Willie Dunne **Facilities** **Conf** facs Corporate Hospitality Days **Location** SE of town centre on B288

Hotel ★★★★ 75% Woodlands Park Hotel, Woodlands Ln, STOKE D'ABERNON ☎ 01372 843933 57 en suite

Horton Park Golf & Country Club Hook Rd KT19 8QG
☎ 020 8393 8400 & 8394 2626 🖹 020 8394 1369
e-mail: hortonparkgc@aol.com

Millennium: 18 holes, 6257yds, Par 71, SSS 70.
Course Designer Dr Peter Nicholson
Phone for further details

Hotel ★★★★ 75% Woodlands Park Hotel, Woodlands Ln, STOKE D'ABERNON ☎ 01372 843933 57 en suite

ESHER Map 04 TQ16

Moore Place Portsmouth Rd KT10 9LN
☎ 01372 463533
web: www.moore-place.co.uk
Public course on attractive, undulating parkland, laid out some 80 years ago by Harry Vardon. Examples of most of the trees that thrive in the UK are to be found on the course. Testing short holes at 8th and 9th.
9 holes, 2078yds, Par 33, SSS 30, Course record 27.
Club membership 150.
Visitors Mon-Sun. **Societies** Booking required. **Green Fees** phone. **Prof** Nick Gadd **Course Designer** H Vardon, D Allen, N Gadd **Facilities** **Conf** facs **Location** 0.5m from town centre on A307

Hotel ★★★ 67% The Ship Hotel, Monument Green, WEYBRIDGE ☎ 01932 848364 42 en suite

Thames Ditton & Esher Portsmouth Rd KT10 9AL
☎ 020 8398 1551
web: www.tdandegc.co.uk
18 holes, 5149yds, Par 66, SSS 65, Course record 63.
Location 1m NE on A307, next to Marquis of Granby pub
Phone for further details

Hotel Premier Travel Inn Cobham, Portsmouth Rd, Fairmile, COBHAM ☎ 0870 9906358 48 en suite

FARLEIGH Map 05 TQ36

Farleigh Court Old Farleigh Rd CR6 9PX
☎ 01883 627711 🖹 01883 627722
e-mail: fcgc@fbd-uk.u-net.com
web: www.fcg-int.com
Members: 18 holes, 6409yds, Par 72, SSS 71, Course record 67.
Pay & Play: 9 holes, 3281yds, Par 36.
Course Designer John Jacobs **Location** 1.5m from Selsdon
Phone for further details

Hotel ★★★★ 69% Selsdon Park Hotel & Golf Course, Addington Rd, Sanderstead, CROYDON ☎ 020 8657 8811 204 en suite

FARNHAM Map 04 SU84

Blacknest Binsted GU34 4QL
☎ 01420 22888 🖹 01420 22001
Privately owned pay and play golf centre catering for all ages and levels of ability. Facilities include a 15-bay driving range, gymnasium and a challenging 18-hole course featuring water on 14 holes.
18 holes, 5938yds, Par 69, SSS 69, Course record 64.
Club membership 450.
Visitors contact club for details. **Societies** Booking required. **Green Fees** phone. **Prof** Darren Burgess **Course Designer** Nicholson **Facilities** **Leisure** sauna, solarium, gymnasium. **Conf** facs **Location** 5m SW of Farnham off A325

Farnham The Sands GU10 1PX
☎ 01252 782109 🖷 01252 781185
e-mail: info@farnhamgolfclub.com
web: www.farnhamgolfclub.com
A mixture of meadowland and heath with quick drying sandy subsoil. Several of the earlier holes have interesting features.
18 holes, 6447yds, Par 72, SSS 71, Course record 66.
Club membership 700.
Visitors Mon-Fri except BHs. Handicap certificate. Dress code. **Societies** Booking required. **Green Fees** £50 per day, £45 per round. **Prof** Grahame Cowlishaw **Course Designer** Donald Steel **Facilities** by arrangement **Conf** Corporate Hospitality Days **Location** 3m E off A31

Hotel ★★★ 68% Macdonald Bush Hotel, The Borough, FARNHAM ☎ 0870 400 8225 & 01252 715237 🖷 01252 733530 83 en suite

Farnham Park Folly Hill, Farnham Park GU9 0AU
☎ 01252 715216
Pay & Play parkland course in Farnham Park. Challenging and scenic.
9 holes, 1163yds, Par 27, SSS 48, Course record 48.
Club membership 70.
Visitors Mon-Sun & BHs. **Societies** Booking required. **Green Fees** £5.50 per 9 holes, £6.50 Sat & Sun. **Prof** D Bryant, N Ogilvy **Course Designer** Henry Cotton **Facilities** **Location** N of town centre on A287, next to Farnham Castle

Hotel ★★★ 68% Macdonald Bush Hotel, The Borough, FARNHAM ☎ 0870 400 8225 & 01252 715237 🖷 01252 733530 83 en suite

GODALMING Map 04 SU94

Broadwater Park Guildford Rd, Farncombe GU7 3BU
☎ 01483 429955 🖷 01483 429955
A par 3 public course with floodlit driving range.
9 holes, 1287yds, Par 54, SSS 50.
Club membership 160.
Visitors contact club for details. **Societies** welcome. **Green Fees** phone. **Prof** Kevin D Milton, Nick English **Course Designer** Kevin Milton **Facilities** **Conf** Corporate Hospitality Days **Location** NE of Godalming on A3100

Hurtmore Hurtmore Rd, Hurtmore GU7 2RN
☎ 01483 426492 🖷 01483 426121
web: www.hurtmore-golf.co.uk
A Peter Alliss and Clive Clark pay and play course with seven lakes and 85 bunkers. The 15th hole is the longest at 537yds. Played mainly into the wind there are 10 bunkers to negotiate. The 3rd hole at 448yds stroke index 1 is a real test. A dog-leg right around a lake and nine bunkers makes this hole worthy of its stroke index.
18 holes, 5530yds, Par 70, SSS 67, Course record 65.
Club membership 200.
Visitors Mon-Sun & BHs. Dress code. **Societies** Booking required. **Green Fees** £14 per 18 holes, £10 per 9 holes, £20/£12 Sat & Sun. Twilight £10, £12 Sat & Sun. **Prof** Maxine Burton **Course Designer** Peter Alliss, Clive Clark **Facilities** **Leisure** practice nets. **Location** 2m NW of Godalming off A3

GUILDFORD Map 04 SU94

Guildford High Path Rd, Merrow GU1 2HL
☎ 01483 563941 🖷 01483 453228
e-mail: secretary@guildfordgolfclub.co.uk
web: www.guildfordgolfclub.co.uk
The course is on Surrey downland bordered by attractive woodlands. Situated on chalk, it is acknowledged to be one of the best all-weather courses in the area, and the oldest course in Surrey. Although not a long course, the prevailing winds across the open downs make low scoring difficult. It is possible to see four counties on a clear day.

18 holes, 6090yds, Par 69, SSS 69, Course record 64.
Club membership 700.
Visitors Mon, Tue, Thu, Fri except BHs. Wed pm. **Societies** welcome. **Green Fees** £53 per day, £42 per round. **Prof** PG Hollington **Course Designer** JH Taylor, Hawtree **Facilities** **Conf** facs Corporate Hospitality Days **Location** E of town centre off A246

Merrist Wood Coombe Ln, Worplesdon GU3 3PE
☎ 01483 238890 🖷 01483 238896
e-mail: mwgc@merristwood-golfclub.co.uk
web: merristwood-golfclub.co.uk
More parkland than heathland, Merrist Wood has a bit of everything. Water comes into play on five holes, the bunkering is fierce, the greens slope and the back nine has plenty of trees. Two holes stand out especially: the picturesque par 3 11th with a tee shot through the trees and the dastardly par 4 17th, including a 210yd carry over a lake and ditches either side of the green.
18 holes, 6600yds, Par 72, SSS 71, Course record 69.
Club membership 500.
Visitors Mon-Fri. Sat & Sun after 11 am. Booking required. **Societies** Booking required. **Green Fees** phone. **Prof** Greg Brodie **Course Designer** David Williams **Facilities** **Leisure** golf tuition academy. **Conf** facs Corporate Hospitality Days **Location** 3m from Guildford on A323 to Aldershot

Milford Station Ln, Milford GU8 5HS
☎ 01483 419200 🖷 01483 419199
e-mail: milford@crown-golf.co.uk
web: www.crowngolf.com/milford
The design has cleverly incorporated a demanding course within existing woodland and meadow.
18 holes, 5960yds, Par 69, SSS 68, Course record 64.
Club membership 750.
Visitors Mon-Fri. Sat, Sun & BHs pm. Dress code. **Societies** Booking required. **Green Fees** £25 per 18 holes,

Continued

£33 Fri-Sun. **Prof** Paul Creamy **Course Designer** Peter Allis **Facilities** **Conf** facs Corporate Hospitality Days **Location** 6m SW Guildford. Off A3 into Milford, E towards station

Roker Park Rokers Farm, Aldershot Rd GU3 3PB
☎ 01483 236677 01483 232324
A pay and play nine-hole parkland course. A challenging course with two par 5 holes.
9 holes, 3037yds, Par 36, SSS 72.
Club membership 200.
Visitors contact course for details. Dress code. **Societies** Booking required. **Green Fees** £12.50 per day/18 holes, £9 per 9 holes, £17.50/£11.50 Sat, Sun & BHs. **Prof** Adrian Carter **Course Designer** WV Roker **Facilities** **Location** 3m NW of Guildford on A323

HINDHEAD Map 04 SU83

Hindhead Churt Rd GU26 6HX
☎ 01428 604614 01428 608508
e-mail: secretary@the-hindhead-golf-club.co.uk
web: www.hindhead-golfclub.co.uk
A picturesque Surrey heath and heather course. Players must be prepared for some hard walking. The first nine fairways follow narrow valleys requiring straight hitting; the second nine are much less restricted. The 16th looks like a simple par 5 dog-leg but can easily catch out the unwary. The par 4 17th can pull the ball into the left hand rough and the par 4 18th is uphill and often into the prevailing wind. The Open Championship pre-qualifying round is played in July.
18 holes, 6356yds, Par 70, SSS 70, Course record 63.
Club membership 610.
Visitors Mon, Wed-Sun & BHs. Tue pm. Booking required. Handicap certificate. Dress code. **Societies** Booking required. **Green Fees** £60 per day, £50 per round. **Prof** Ian Benson **Course Designer** JH Taylor **Facilities** **Leisure** snooker. **Conf** Corporate Hospitality Days **Location** 1.5m NW of Hindhead on A287

Hotel ★★★★ 71% Lythe Hill Hotel & Spa, Petworth Rd, HASLEMERE ☎ 01428 651251 41 en suite

KINGSWOOD Map 04 TQ25

Kingswood Golf and Country House
Sandy Ln KT20 6NE
☎ 01737 832188 01737 833920
e-mail: sales@kingswood-golf.co.uk
web: www.kingswood-golf.co.uk
Mature parkland course sited on a plateau with delightful views of the Chipstead valley. The course features lush, shaped fairways, testing bunkers positions and true greens. Recent improvements ensure it plays every inch of its 6900yds.
18 holes, 6904yds, Par 72, SSS 73.
Club membership 700.
Visitors Mon-Sun. Booking required. Dress code. **Societies** Booking required. **Green Fees** phone. **Prof** Terry Sims **Course Designer** James Braid **Facilities** **Leisure** squash, 3 snooker tables. **Conf** facs Corporate Hospitality Days **Location** 0.5m S of village off A217

Hotel ★★★ 67% Reigate Manor Hotel, Reigate Hill, REIGATE ☎ 01737 240125 50 en suite

Surrey Downs Outwood Ln KT20 6JS
☎ 01737 839090 01737 839080
e-mail: booking@surreydownsgc.co.uk
18 holes, 6303yards, Par 71, SSS 70, Course record 67.
Course Designer Aliss, Clarke **Location** Off A217 E onto B2032 at Kingswood for 1m, club on right after Eyhurst Park
Phone for further details

Hotel Premier Travel Inn Epsom South, Brighton Rd, Burgh Heath, TADWORTH ☎ 0870 9906442 78 en suite

LEATHERHEAD Map 04 TQ15

Leatherhead Kingston Rd KT22 0EE
☎ 01372 843966 & 843956 01372 842241
e-mail: secretary@lgc-golf.co.uk
web: www.lgc-golf.co.uk
Undulating, 100-year-old parkland course with tree-lined fairways and strategically placed bunkers. Easy walking.
18 holes, 5795yds, Par 70, SSS 68.
Club membership 630.
Visitors Mon, Tue, Thu & Fri except BHs. Booking required. Dress code. **Societies** Booking required. **Green Fees** £38 per round Mon, Tue, £40 Thu, Fri. **Prof** Simon Norman **Facilities** **Conf** facs Corporate Hospitality Days **Location** 0.25m from junct 9 of M25, on A243

Hotel ★★ 66% Bookham Grange Hotel, Little Bookham Common, Bookham, LEATHERHEAD ☎ 01372 452742 27 en suite
See advertisement on page 245

Pachesham Park Golf Complex Oaklawn Rd KT22 0BT
☎ 01372 843453
e-mail: enquiries@pacheshamgolf.co.uk
web: www.pacheshamgolf.co.uk
An undulating parkland course starting with five shorter but tight holes on one side of the road, followed by four longer more open but testing holes to finish.
9 holes, 2805yds, Par 70, SSS 67, Course record 67.
Club membership 150.
Visitors contact centre for details. **Societies** Booking required. **Green Fees** £18 per 18 holes, £10 per 9 holes, £20/£13 Sat, Sun & BHs. **Prof** Philip Taylor **Course Designer** Phil Taylor **Facilities** **Conf** facs Corporate Hospitality Days **Location** M25 junc 9, 0.5m off A244 or A245

Hotel ★★★★ 75% Woodlands Park Hotel, Woodlands Ln, STOKE D'ABERNON ☎ 01372 843933 57 en suite

Tyrrells Wood The Drive KT22 8QP
☎ 01372 376025 🖷 01372 360836
Easy walking parkland.
18 holes, 6282yds, Par 71, SSS 70, Course record 65.
Club membership 700.
Visitors Booking required. **Societies** Booking required. **Green Fees** phone. **Prof** Simon Defoy **Course Designer** James Braid **Facilities** **Conf** facs Corporate Hospitality Days **Location** 2m SE of town off A24

Hotel ★★★★ 70% Macdonald Burford Bridge Hotel, Burford Bridge, Box Hill, DORKING ☎ 0870 400 8283 57 en suite

LIMPSFIELD Map 05 TQ45

Limpsfield Chart Westerham Rd RH8 0SL
☎ 01883 723405 & 722106
Attractive heathland course on National Trust land, easy walking with tree lined fairways.
9 holes, 5718yds, Par 70, SSS 68, Course record 64.
Club membership 300.
Visitors Mon-Fri except BHs. Dress code. **Societies** booking required **Green Fees** phone. **Prof** Mike McLean **Facilities** **Conf** Corporate Hospitality Days **Location** M25 junct 6, 1m E on A25

Hotel ★★★ 71% Donnington Manor, London Rd, Dunton Green, SEVENOAKS ☎ 01732 462681 60 en suite

LINGFIELD Map 05 TQ34

Lingfield Park Lingfield Rd, Racecourse Rd RH7 6PQ
☎ 01342 832659 🖷 01342 836077
e-mail: cmorley@lingfieldpark.co.uk
web: www.lingfieldpark.co.uk
18 holes, 6473yds, Par 71, SSS 72, Course record 65.
Location M25 junct 6, signs to racecourse
Phone for further details

Hotel Premier Travel Inn East Grinstead, London Rd, Felbridge, EAST GRINSTEAD ☎ 08701 977088 41 en suite

NEWDIGATE Map 04 TQ14

Rusper Rusper Rd RH5 5BX
☎ 01293 871871 (shop) 🖷 01293 871456
e-mail: jill@ruspergolfclub.co.uk
web: www.ruspergolfclub.co.uk
The 18-hole course is set in countryside and offers golfers of all abilities a fair and challenging test. After a gentle start the holes wind through picturesque scenery, tree-lined fairways and natural water hazards.
18 holes, 6724yds, Par 72, SSS 72.
Club membership 350.
Visitors Mon-Sun & BHs. Booking required. Dress code. **Societies** Booking required. **Green Fees** £20 per 18 holes, £15 per 9 holes, £25/£18 Sat, Sun & BHs (9 holes pm). **Prof** Janice Arnold **Course Designer** A Blunden **Facilities** **Conf** Corporate Hospitality Days **Location** Off A24 between Newdigate

Hotel ★★★★ 70% Macdonald Burford Bridge Hotel, Burford Bridge, Box Hill, DORKING ☎ 0870 400 8283 57 en suite

OCKLEY Map 04 TQ14

Gatton Manor Hotel Golf & Country Club Standon Ln RH5 5PQ
☎ 01306 627555 🖷 01306 627713
e-mail: gattonmanor@enterprise.net
web: www.gattonmanor.co.uk
A challenging course and delightful Victorian water gardens. No two holes are alike: each one requires the golfer to consider the hazards - lakes, streams and tree-lined fairways.
18 holes, 6629yds, Par 72, SSS 72, Course record 68.
Club membership 300.
Visitors Mon-Sat. Sun pm. Booking up to 10 days in advance. **Societies** Booking required. **Green Fees** phone. **Prof** Rae Sargent **Course Designer** Henry Cotton **Facilities** **Leisure** grass tennis courts, fishing, sauna, solarium, gymnasium. **Conf** facs Corporate Hospitality Days **Location** 1.5m SW off A29

Hotel ★★★ 61% Gatton Manor Hotel Golf & Country Club, Standon Ln, OCKLEY ☎ 01306 627555 18 en suite

OTTERSHAW Map 04 TQ06

Foxhills Club and Resort Stonehill Rd KT16 0EL
☎ 01932 872050 🖷 01932 875200
e-mail: events@foxhills.co.uk
web: www.foxhills.co.uk
The Bernard Hunt Course: 18 holes, 6770yds, Par 73, SSS 72, Course record 65.
Longcross Course: 18 holes, 6453yds, Par 72, SSS 71, Course record 70.

Continued

Course Designer FW Hawtree **Location** 1m NW of Ottershaw
Phone for further details

Hotel ★★★★ 71% Foxhills Club & Resort, Stonehill Rd, OTTERSHAW ☎ 01932 872050 42 en suite

PIRBRIGHT Map 04 SU95

Goal Farm Gole Rd GU24 0PZ
☎ 01483 473183 📠 01483 473205
e-mail: secretary@gfgc.co.uk
web: www.gfgc.co.uk
Beautiful landscaped parkland pay and play course with excellent greens. A range of enjoyable yet demanding holes over trees and over water with plenty of bunkers to swallow up tee shots.
9 holes, 1273yds, Par 54, SSS 48, Course record 50. Club membership 350.
Visitors Mon-Wed, Fri, Sun & BHs. Dress code. **Societies** Booking required. **Green Fees** phone. **Prof** Peter Fuller **Course Designer** Bill Cox **Facilities** **Location** 1.5m NW on B3012

Hotel ★★★ 65% Falcon Hotel, 68 Farnborough Rd, FARNBOROUGH ☎ 01252 545378 30 en suite

PUTTENHAM Map 04 SU94

Puttenham Heath Rd GU3 1AL
☎ 01483 810498 📠 01483 810988
e-mail: enquiries@puttenhamgolfclub.co.uk
web: www.puttenhamgolfclub.co.uk
Mixture of heathland and woodland - undulating layout with stunning views across the Hog's Back and towards the South Downs. Sandy subsoil provides free drainage for year round play.
18 holes, 6220yds, Par 71, SSS 70. Club membership 650.
Visitors Mon-Fri except BHs. Booking required. Dress code. **Societies** Booking required, **Green Fees** £49 per day, £34 per round. **Prof** Dean Lintott **Facilities** by arrangement **Conf** Corporate Hospitality Days **Location** 1m SE on B3000

Hotel ★★★ 68% Macdonald Bush Hotel, The Borough, FARNHAM ☎ 0870 400 8225 & 01252 715237 📠 01252 733530 83 en suite

REDHILL Map 04 TQ25

Redhill & Reigate Clarence Rd, Pendelton Rd RH1 6LB
☎ 01737 244433 📠 01737 242117
e-mail: mail@rrgc.net
web: www.redhillandreigategc.co.uk
Flat picturesque tree-lined course, well over 100 years old.
18 holes, 5272yds, Par 68, SSS 66, Course record 65. Club membership 600.
Visitors Mon-Sun & BHs. Booking required. Dress code. **Societies** Booking required. **Green Fees** £21 per 18 holes, £31 Sat & Sun. **Prof** Warren Pike **Course Designer** James Braid **Facilities** by arrangement **Conf** facs Corporate Hospitality Days **Location** 1m S on A23

Hotel ★★★ 67% Reigate Manor Hotel, Reigate Hill, REIGATE ☎ 01737 240125 50 en suite

REIGATE Map 04 TQ25

Reigate Heath Flanchford Rd RH2 8QR
☎ 01737 242610 & 226793 📠 01737 249226
e-mail: reigateheath@surreygolf.co.uk
web: www.reigateheathgolfclub.co.uk
Gorse, heather, pine and birch trees abound on this popular nine-hole heathland course. The course is short by modern standards but is a good test of golf. Playing 18 holes from nine greens, the second nine is quite different with changes of angle as well as length.
9 holes, 5658yds, Par 67, SSS 67, Course record 65. Club membership 550.
Visitors Mon, Wed-Fri. Handicap certificate. Dress code. **Societies** Booking required. **Green Fees** £33 per round. **Prof** Barry Davies **Facilities** by arrangement **Conf** facs Corporate Hospitality Days **Location** 1.5m W off A25

Hotel ★★★ 67% Reigate Manor Hotel, Reigate Hill, REIGATE ☎ 01737 240125 50 en suite

Reigate Hill Gatton Bottom RH2 0TU
☎ 01737 645577 📠 01737 642650
e-mail: info@reigatehillgolfclub.co.uk
web: www.reigatehillgolfclub.co.uk
18 holes, 6175yds, Par 72, SSS 70, Course record 63.
Course Designer David Williams **Location** M25 junct 8, 1m
Phone for further details

Hotel ★★★ 67% Reigate Manor Hotel, Reigate Hill, REIGATE ☎ 01737 240125 50 en suite

Championship Course

Surrey

Wentworth

Virginia Water

Map 04 TQ06

Wentworth Club, the home of the PGA and World Match Play championships, is a very special venue for any sporting, business or social occasion. The West Course is familiar to millions of television viewers who have followed the championships here. There are two other courses, the East Course and the Edinburgh Course, and a nine-hole par 3 executive course. The courses cross Surrey heathland with woods of pine, oak and birch. The Club is renowned for its fine food, and the health and leisure facilities include a holistic spa, 13 outdoor tennis courts with four different playing surfaces, and a 25-metre indoor pool.

Wentworth Dr GU25 4LS
☎ 01344 842201 🖷 01344 842804
e-mail: reception@wentworthclub.com
web: www.wentworthclub.com

West Course: 18 holes, 7301yds, Par 73, SSS 74, Course record 63.
East Course: 18 holes, 6201yds, Par 68, SSS 70, Course record 62.
Edinburgh Course: 18 holes, 7004yds, Par 72, SSS 74, Course record 67.

Visitors Mon-Fri except BHs. Booking required. Handicap certificate. Dress code. **Societies** Booking required. **Green Fees** West Course £100-£285. Edinburgh Course £80-£160. East Course £75-£130. **Prof** Jason Macniven **Course Designer** Colt, Jacobs, Gallacher, **Player Facilities** **Leisure** hard and grass tennis courts, outdoor and indoor heated swimming pools, fishing, sauna, solarium, gymnasium, spa with 6 treatment rooms. **Conf facs** Corporate Hospitality Days **Location** Main gate directly opposite turning for A329 on main A30

SHEPPERTON Map 04 TQ06

Sunbury Golf Centre Charlton Ln TW17 8QA
☎ 01932 771414 🖷 01932 789300
e-mail: sunbury@crown-golf.co.uk
web: www.crown-golf.co.uk
Twenty-seven holes for all standards of golfer and a 32 bay floodlit driving range. Easy walking.
18 holes, 5103yds, Par 68, SSS 65, Course record 60.
Academy: 9 holes, 2444yds, Par 33, SSS 32.
Club membership 400.
Visitors Mon-Sun & BHs. Booking required. Dress code. **Societies** Booking required. **Green Fees** £18.50 per 18 holes, £10 per 9 holes, £23/£12 Sat & Sun. **Prof** Adrian McColgan **Course Designer** Peter Alliss **Facilities** **Conf** facs Corporate Hospitality Days **Location** M3, junct 1, 1m N off A244

Hotel ★★★ 72% Macdonald Thames Lodge, Thames St, STAINES ☎ 0870 400 8121 & 01784 464433
🖷 01784 454858 78 en suite

SOUTH GODSTONE Map 05 TQ34

Home Park Croydon Barn Ln, Horne RH9 8JP
☎ 01342 844443 🖷 01342 841828
e-mail: info@homepark.co.uk
web: www.homepark.co.uk
Set in attractive Surrey countryside with water coming into play in 5 holes. Relatively flat for easy walking. A different set of tees pose an intriguing second 9 holes.
9 holes, 5436yds, Par 68, SSS 66, Course record 62.
Club membership 350.
Visitors Mon-Fri. Booking required Sat, Sun & BHs. Dress code. **Societies** Booking required. **Green Fees** £15 per 18 holes, £10.50 per 9 holes, £17/£11.50 Sat & Sun. **Prof** Neil Burke **Course Designer** Howard Swan **Facilities** by arrangement **Leisure** caddies available, swing analysis system, teaching academy. **Location** A22, signposted 3m N of East Grinstead

Hotel Premier Travel Inn East Grinstead, London Rd, Felbridge, EAST GRINSTEAD ☎ 08701 977088
41 en suite

SUTTON GREEN Map 04 TQ05

Sutton Green New Ln GU4 7QF
☎ 01483 747898 🖷 01483 750289
e-mail: admin@suttongreengc.co.uk
web: www.suttongreengc.co.uk
Set in the Surrey countryside, a challenging course with many water features. Excellent year round conditions with fairway watering. Many testing holes with water surrounding greens and fairways, making accuracy a premium.
18 holes, 6350yds, Par 71, SSS 70, Course record 64.
Club membership 600.
Visitors contact club for details. Dress code. **Societies** Booking required. **Green Fees** phone. **Prof** Paul Tedder **Course Designer** David Walker, Laura Davies **Facilities** **Conf** facs Corporate Hospitality Days **Location** Off A320 between Woking & Guildford

Hotel ★★★★★ Pennyhill Park Hotel & The Spa, London Rd, BAGSHOT ☎ 01276 471774 26 en suite 97 annexe en suite

TANDRIDGE Map 05 TQ35

Tandridge RH8 9NQ
☎ 01883 712274 🖷 01883 730537
e-mail: secretary@tandridgegolfclub.com
web: www.tandridgegolfclub.com
A parkland course with two loops of nine holes from the clubhouse. The first nine are relatively flat. The second nine undulate with outstanding views of the North Downs.
18 holes, 6277yds, Par 70, SSS 70, Course record 66.
Club membership 750.
Visitors Mon, Wed, Thu except BHs. Booking required. Handicap certificate. Dress code. **Societies** Booking required. **Green Fees** £65 per day, £45 pm. Winter £35 per round. **Prof** Chris Evans **Course Designer** H Colt **Facilities** **Conf** Corporate Hospitality Days **Location** M25 junct 6, 2m SE on A25

Hotel ★★★★ 73% Nutfield Priory, Nutfield, REDHILL
☎ 01737 824400 60 en suite

TILFORD Map 04 SU84

Hankley Common The Club House GU10 2DD
☎ 01252 792493 🖷 01252 795699
web: www.hankley.co.uk
A natural heathland course subject to wind. Greens are first rate. The 18th, a long par 4, is most challenging, the green being beyond a deep chasm which traps any but the perfect second shot. The 7th is a spectacular one-shotter.
18 holes, 6702yds, Par 72, SSS 72, Course record 62.
Club membership 700.
Visitors Mon-Sun except BHs. Booking required. Handicap certificate. Dress code. **Societies** Booking required. **Green Fees** £80 per day, £65 per round, £80 per round Sat & Sun. **Prof** Peter Stow **Course Designer** James Braid **Facilities** **Location** 0.75m SE of Tilford

Hotel ★★★ 68% Macdonald Bush Hotel, The Borough, FARNHAM ☎ 0870 400 8225 & 01252 715237
🖷 01252 733530 83 en suite

VIRGINIA WATER Map 04 TQ06

Wentworth see page 247

Hotel ★★ 72% The Wheatsheaf, London Rd, VIRGINIA WATER ☎ 01344 842057 17 en suite

Hotel ★★★★ 74% Runnymede Hotel & Spa, Windsor Rd EGHAM ☎ 01784 436171 🖷 01784 436340 180 en suite
See advertisement on page 246

Continued

Hotel ★★★★ 70% Macdonald Berystede Hotel & Spa, Bagshot Rd, Sunninghill, ASCOT ☎ 0870 400 8111 ▤ 01344 872301 125 en suite

Hotel ★★★★ The Royal Berkshire Ramada Plaza, London Rd, Sunninghill, ASCOT ☎ 01344 623322 ▤ 01344 627100 63 en suite

WALTON-ON-THAMES Map 04 TQ16

Burhill Burwood Rd KT12 4BL
☎ 01932 227345 ▤ 01932 267159
e-mail: info@burhillgolf-club.co.uk
web: www.burhillgolf-club.co.uk
The Old Course is a mature tree-lined parkland course with some of the finest greens in Surrey. The New Course, opened in 2001, is a modern course built to USGA specifications has many bunkers and water hazards, including the River Mole.
Old Course: 18 holes, 6479yds, Par 70, SSS 71, Course record 65.
New Course: 18 holes, 6597yds, Par 72, SSS 71.
Club membership 1100.
Visitors Mon-Fri except BHs. Booking required. **Societies** Booking required in writing. **Green Fees** phone. **Prof** Ian Partington **Course Designer** Willie Park, Simon Gidman **Facilities** **Conf** facs Corporate Hospitality Days **Location** M25 junct 10 onto A3 towards London, 1st exit Painshill junct

Hotel ★★★ 67% The Ship Hotel, Monument Green, WEYBRIDGE ☎ 01932 848364 42 en suite

WALTON-ON-THE-HILL Map 04 TQ25

Walton Heath **see page 251**

Hotel ★★ 66% Bookham Grange Hotel, Little Bookham Common, Bookham, LEATHERHEAD ☎ 01372 452742 27 en suite

Hotel ★★★ 73% Chalk Lane Hotel, Chalk Ln, Woodcote End, EPSOM ☎ 01372 721179 ▤ 01372 727878 22 en suite

Hotel ★★★ 67% Reigate Manor Hotel, Reigate Hill, REIGATE ☎ 01737 240125 ▤ 01737 223883 50 en suite

Hotel ★★★★ 70% Macdonald Burford Bridge Hotel, Burford Bridge, Box Hill, DORKING ☎ 0870 400 8283 ▤ 01306 880386 57 en suite

Hotel ★★★ 67% Macdonald White Horse Hotel, High St, DORKING ☎ 0870 400 8282 ▤ 01306 887241 37 en suite 41 annexe en suite

WEST BYFLEET Map 04 TQ06

West Byfleet Sheerwater Rd KT14 6AA
☎ 01932 343433 ▤ 01932 340667
e-mail: secretary@wbgc.co.uk
web: www.wbgc.co.uk
An attractive course set against a background of woodland and gorse. The 13th is the famous pond shot with a water hazard and two bunkers fronting the green. No less than six holes of 420yds or more.
18 holes, 6211yds, Par 70, SSS 70.
Club membership 622.
Visitors Mon-Wed, Fr. Booking required with

Continued

professional. **Societies** Booking required. **Green Fees** phone. **Prof** David Regan **Course Designer** CS Butchart **Facilities** **Conf** Corporate Hospitality Days **Location** W of village on A245

WEST CLANDON Map 04 TQ05

Clandon Regis Epsom Rd GU4 7TT
☎ 01483 224888 ▤ 01483 211781
e-mail: office@clandonregis-golfclub.co.uk
web: www.clandonregis-golfclub.co.uk
High quality parkland course with challenging lake holes on the back nine. European Tour specification tees and greens.
18 holes, 6485yds, Par 72, SSS 71, Course record 66.
Club membership 652.
Visitors contact club for details. Dress code. **Societies** Booking required. **Green Fees** £34 per 18 holes, £44 Sat & Sun. **Prof** Steve Lloyd **Course Designer** David Williams **Facilities** **Leisure** sauna. **Conf** facs Corporate Hospitality Days **Location** SE of village off A246

WEST END Map 04 SU96

Windlemere Windlesham Rd GU24 9QL
☎ 01276 858727
A parkland course, undulating in parts with natural water hazards. There is also a floodlit driving range.
9 holes, 2673yds, Par 34, SSS 33, Course record 30.
Visitors contact club for details. **Societies** welcome. **Green Fees** £11 per 9 holes, £12.50 Sat & Sun. **Prof** David Thomas **Course Designer** Clive Smith **Facilities** **Leisure** pool/snooker tables. **Location** N of village at junct A319

Hotel ★★★★★ Pennyhill Park Hotel & The Spa, London Rd, BAGSHOT ☎ 01276 471774 26 en suite 97 annexe en suite

WEYBRIDGE Map 04 TQ06

St George's Hill Golf Club Rd, St George's Hill KT13 0NL
☎ 01932 847758 ▤ 01932 821564
e-mail: admin@stgeorgeshillgolfclub.co.uk
web: www.stgeorgeshillgolfclub.co.uk
Comparable and similar to Wentworth, a feature of this course is the number of long and difficult par 4s. To score well it is necessary to place the drive - and long driving pays handsomely. Walking is hard on this undulating, heavily wooded course with plentiful heather and rhododendrons.
Red & Blue: 18 holes, 6513yds, Par 70, SSS 71, Course record 64.
Green: 9 holes, 2897yds, Par 35.
Club membership 600.
Visitors Wed-Fri except BHs. Booking required. Handicap certificate. Dress code. **Societies** Booking required. **Green Fees** £130 per day, £100 per round. **Prof** AC Rattue **Course Designer** H Colt **Facilities** **Conf** Corporate Hospitality Days **Location** 2m S off B374

Hotel ★★★ 67% The Ship Hotel, Monument Green, WEYBRIDGE ☎ 01932 848364 42 en suite

WOKING Map 04 TQ05

Hoebridge Golf Centre Old Woking Rd GU22 8JH
☎ 01483 722611 🖹 01483 740369
e-mail: info@hoebridgegc.co.uk
web: www.hoebridgegc.co.uk
The setting encompasses 200 acres of mature parkland and includes 3 golf courses containing 45 holes. The Main Course has tree lined fairways, challenging bunkers and fine views. The testing 9 hole Shey Copse is a par 4/par 3 course which winds around the woodland. The Maybury is an 18 holes par 4 course for beginners or golfers wishing to improve their game.

Main Course: 18 holes, 6536yds, Par 72, SSS 71.
Shey Course: 9 holes, 2294yds, Par 33.
Maybury Course: 18 holes, 2181yds, Par 54.
Club membership 1000.
Visitors Mon-Fri. Booking required Sat, Sun & BHs. Dress code. **Societies** Booking required. **Green Fees** Main £22 Mon-Thu, £25 Fri, £29.50 Sat & Sun. Shey £12, £14.50 Sat & Sun. Maybury £9.50, £12 Sat & Sun. **Prof** Russell Covey **Course Designer** John Jacobs **Facilities** **Leisure** sauna, solarium, gymnasium, health & fitness club. **Conf** facs Corporate Hospitality Days **Location** M25 junct 11, follow signs for Old Woking, then Hoebridge

Hotel ★★★★★ Pennyhill Park Hotel & The Spa, London Rd, BAGSHOT ☎ 01276 471774 26 en suite 97 annexe en suite

Pyrford Warren Ln, Pyrford GU22 8XR
☎ 01483 723555 🖹 01483 729777
e-mail: pyrford@americangolf.uk.com
web: www.americangolf.com
18 holes, 6256yds, Par 72, SSS 70, Course record 64.
Course Designer Peter Allis & Clive Clark **Location** Off A3 Ripley to Pyrford
Phone for further details

Hotel ★★★★★ Pennyhill Park Hotel & The Spa, London Rd, BAGSHOT ☎ 01276 471774 26 en suite 97 annexe en suite

Traditions Pyrford Rd, Pyrford GU22 8UE
☎ 01932 350355 🖹 01932 350234
e-mail: traditions@americangolf.uk.com
18 holes, 6304yds, Par 71, SSS 70, Course record 67.
Course Designer Peter Alliss **Location** M25 junct 10, A3, signs to RHS Garden Wisley, through Wisley to Pyford, course 0.5m
Phone for further details

Hotel ★★★★★ Pennyhill Park Hotel & The Spa, London Rd, BAGSHOT ☎ 01276 471774 26 en suite 97 annexe en suite

Woking Pond Rd, Hook Heath GU22 0JZ
☎ 01483 760053 🖹 01483 772441
e-mail: woking.golf@btconnect.com
web: www.wokinggolfclub.co.uk
An 18-hole course on Surrey heathland with few changes from the original course designed in 1892 by Tom Dunn. Bernard Darwin, a past captain and president, has written 'the beauty of Woking is that there is something distinctive about every hole'.
18 holes, 6340yds, Par 70, SSS 70, Course record 65.
Club membership 600.
Visitors Mon-Fri except BHs. Handicap certificate. Dress code. **Societies** Booking required. **Green Fees** phone. **Prof** Carl Bianco **Course Designer** Tom Dunn **Facilities** **Conf** Corporate Hospitality Days **Location** W of town centre in area of St Johns Heath

Hotel ★★★★★ Pennyhill Park Hotel & The Spa, London Rd, BAGSHOT ☎ 01276 471774 26 en suite 97 annexe en suite

Worplesdon Heath House Rd GU22 0RA
☎ 01483 472277
e-mail: office@worplesdongc.co.uk
The scene of the celebrated mixed-foursomes competition. Accurate driving is essential on this heathland course. The short 10th across a lake from tee to green is a notable hole, and the 18th provides a wonderfully challenging par 4 finish.
18 holes, 6431yds, Par 71, SSS 71, Course record 66.
Club membership 610.
Visitors Mon-Fri except BHs. Booking required. Handicap certificate. Dress code. **Societies** Booking required. **Green Fees** £80 per day, £60 per round (winter £35). **Prof** J Christine **Course Designer** J Abercromby **Facilities** **Location** 1.5m N of village off A322

Hotel ★★★★★ Pennyhill Park Hotel & The Spa, London Rd, BAGSHOT ☎ 01276 471774 26 en suite 97 annexe en suite

WOLDINGHAM Map 05 TQ35

North Downs Northdown Rd CR3 7AA
☎ 01883 652057 🖹 01883 652832
e-mail: info@northdownsgolfclub.co.uk
web: www.northdownsgolfclub.co.uk
Parkland course, 850ft above sea level, with several testing holes and magnificent views.
18 holes, 5857yds, Par 69, SSS 68, Course record 64.
Club membership 550.
Visitors Mon-Fri. Booking required for Sat, Sun & BHs. Handicap certificate. Dress code. **Societies** Booking required. **Green Fees** £40 per day, £30 per round. £30 per round Sat & Sun after 3pm summer or pm winter. **Prof** M Homewood **Course Designer** Pennink **Facilities** **Conf** facs Corporate Hospitality Days **Location** 0.75m S of Woldingham

Hotel ★★★ 71% Donnington Manor, London Rd, Dunton Green, SEVENOAKS ☎ 01732 462681 60 en suite

Continued

Championship Course

Surrey

Walton Heath

Walton-on-the-Hill Map 04 TQ25

Walton Heath, a traditional member club, has two extremely challenging courses. Enjoying an enviable international reputation, the club was founded in 1903. It has played host to over 60 major amateur and professional championships, including the 1981 Ryder Cup and five European Open Tournaments (1991, 1989, 1987, 1980 and 1977); among the many prestigious amateur events, Walton Heath hosted the English Amateur in 2002. The Old Course is popular with visitors, while the New Course is very challenging, requiring subtle shots to get the ball near the hole. Straying from the fairway brings gorse, bracken and heather to test the golfer.

Deans Ln, Walton-on-the-Hill KT20 7TP
☎ 01737 812380 🖹 01737 814225
e-mail: secretary@whgc.co.uk
web: www.whgc.co.uk

Old Course: 18 holes, 6836yds, Par 72, SSS 73, Course record 65.
New Course: 18 holes, 6613yds, Par 72, SSS 72, Course record 67.
Club membership 1000.

Visitors Mon-Sun & BHs. Booking required. Dress code. **Societies** Booking required. **Green Fees** £95 9.30-11.30am, £85 after 11.30am, £105 after 11.30am Sat & Sun. **Prof** Ken Macpherson **Course Designer** Herbert Fowler **Facilities** ⊗ ♨ ☕ ♀ ⚐ 🏠 ⛳ ✓ **Conf** Corporate Hospitality Days **Location** SE of village off B2032

Woldingham Halliloo Valley Rd CR3 7HA
☎ 01883 653501 🖷 01883 653502
e-mail: membership@woldingham-golfclub.co.uk
web: www.woldingham-golfclub.co.uk
Located in Halliloo Valley and designed by the American architect Bradford Benz, this pleasant course utilises all the contours and features of the valley.

18 holes, 6393yds, Par 71, SSS 70, Course record 64. Club membership 695.
Visitors Mon-Fri. Booking required Sat, Sun & BHs. Dress code. **Societies** Booking required. **Green Fees** £26 per round, £30 Sat & Sun. **Prof** James Hillen **Course Designer** Bradford Benz **Facilities** **Conf** facs Corporate Hospitality Days **Location** M25 junct 6, A22 N, 1st rdbt onto Woldingham Rd Valley Rd, on left

Hotel ★★★ 71% Donnington Manor, London Rd, Dunton Green, SEVENOAKS ☎ 01732 462681 60 en suite

SUSSEX, EAST

BEXHILL Map 05 TQ70

Cooden Beach Cooden Sea Rd TN39 4TR
☎ 01424 842040 & 843938 (pro shop) 🖷 01424 842040
e-mail: enquiries@coodenbeachgc.com
web: www.coodenbeachgc.com
The course is close by the sea, but is not real links. Despite that, it is dry and plays well throughout the year. There are some excellent holes such as the 4th, played to a built-up green, the short 12th, and three good holes to finish. There are added ponds which make the player think more about tee shots and shots to the green.

18 holes, 6504yds, Par 72, SSS 71, Course record 67. Club membership 850.
Visitors Mon-Fri & BHs. Sat after 1pm, Sun after 11am. Handicap certificate. Dress code. **Societies** Booking

Continued

required. **Green Fees** £43 per day, £37 per round, £46/£49 Sat & Sun. **Prof** Jeffrey Sim **Course Designer** W Herbert Fowler **Facilities** **Leisure** indoor practice facility. **Conf** facs Corporate Hospitality Days **Location** 2m W on A259

Hotel ★★★ 75% Powder Mills Hotel, Powdermill Ln, BATTLE ☎ 01424 775511 30 en suite 10 annexe en suite

Highwoods Ellerslie Ln TN39 4LJ
☎ 01424 212625 🖷 01424 216866
e-mail: highwoods@btconnect.com
web: www.highwoodsgolfclub.co.uk
Undulating parkland with water on six holes.
18 holes, 6218yds, Par 70, SSS 70, Course record 63. Club membership 750.
Visitors Mon-Sat. Booking required. Handicap certificate. **Societies** Booking required. **Green Fees** phone. **Prof** Mike Andrews **Course Designer** JH Taylor **Facilities** **Location** 1.5m NW

Hotel ★★★ 66% Royal Victoria Hotel, Marina, St Leonards-on-Sea, HASTINGS ☎ 01424 445544 50 en suite

BRIGHTON & HOVE Map 04 TQ30

Brighton & Hove Devils Dyke Rd BN1 8YJ
☎ 01273 556482 🖷 01273 554247
e-mail: phil@bhgc68.fsnet.co.uk
web: www.brightonandhovegolfclub.co.uk
Testing nine-hole course with glorious views over the Downs and the sea. Famous drop hole par 3.
9 holes, 5704yds, Par 68, SSS 67, Course record 64. Club membership 380.
Visitors Booking required. **Societies** Booking required with secretary. **Green Fees** phone. **Prof** Phil Bonsall **Course Designer** James Braid **Facilities** **Conf** facs Corporate Hospitality Days **Location** 4m NW of Brighton, 1m from A27 & A23

Hotel ★★★ 69% The Old Tollgate Restaurant & Hotel, The Street, BRAMBER ☎ 01903 879494 10 en suite 20 annexe en suite

Dyke Devils Dyke, Dyke Rd BN1 8YJ
☎ 01273 857296 (office) & 857260 (pro shop)
🖷 01273 857078
e-mail: dykegolfclub@btconnect.com
web: www.thedykegolfclub.co.uk
This downland course has some glorious views both towards the sea and inland. The signature hole on the course is probably the 17th; it is one of those tough par 3s of just over 200yds, and is played across a gully to a high green.
18 holes, 6627yds, Par 72, SSS 72, Course record 66. Club membership 800.
Visitors Mon-Sun & BHs. Dress code. **Societies** welcome. **Green Fees** £28 per round, £35 Sat & Sun. **Prof** Richard Arnold **Course Designer** Fred Hawtree **Facilities** **Conf** Corporate Hospitality Days **Location** 4m N of Brighton, between A23 & A27

Hotel ★★★ 69% The Old Tollgate Restaurant & Hotel, The Street, BRAMBER ☎ 01903 879494 10 en suite 20 annexe en suite

Hollingbury Park Ditchling Rd BN1 7HS
☎ 01273 552010 (sec) 500086 (pro) 🖷 01273 552010/6
e-mail: graemecrompton@sussexgolfcentre.fsnet.co.uk
web: www.hollingburygolfclub.co.uk
Municipal course in hilly situation on the South Downs, overlooking the sea.
18 holes, 6500yds, Par 72, SSS 71, Course record 65.
Club membership 240.
Visitors Booking required. **Societies** Booking required. **Green Fees** £14 per 18 holes, £22 per day, £19 per round Sat & Sun. **Prof** Graeme Crompton **Facilities** **Location** 2m N of town centre

Hotel ★★★ 64% Quality Hotel Brighton, West St, BRIGHTON ☎ 01273 220033 138 en suite

Waterhall Saddlescombe Rd BN1 8YN
☎ 01273 508658
18 holes, 5773yds, Par 69, SSS 68, Course record 66.
Location 2m NE from A27
Phone for further details

Hotel ★★★ 69% The Old Tollgate Restaurant & Hotel, The Street, BRAMBER ☎ 01903 879494 10 en suite 20 annexe en suite

West Hove Church Farm, Hangleton BN3 8AN
☎ 01273 419738 & 413494 (pro) 🖷 01273 439988
e-mail: info@westhovegolf.co.uk
web: www.westhovegolfclub.info
A downland course designed by Hawtree & Sons.
18 holes, 6226yds, Par 71, SSS 70, Course record 62.
Club membership 600.
Visitors Mon-Sun & BHs. Booking required. Dress code. **Societies** Booking required. **Green Fees** £25 per 18 holes. **Prof** Darren Cook **Course Designer** Hawtree & Sons **Facilities** **Conf** facs **Location** Off A27 N of Brighton

Hotel ★★★ 64% The Courtlands, 15-27 The Drive, HOVE ☎ 01273 731055 60 en suite 7 annexe en suite

CROWBOROUGH Map 05 TQ53

Crowborough Beacon Beacon Rd TN6 1UJ
☎ 01892 661511 🖷 01892 611988
e-mail: secretary@cbgc.co.uk
web: www.cbgc.co.uk
Standing some 800ft above sea level, this is a testing heathland course where accuracy off the tee rather than distance is paramount. The Conan Doyle course is an alternative layout played from the blue tees. Panoramic views of the South Downs, Eastbourne and even the sea on a clear day.

Continued

Conan Doyle: 18 holes, 6279yds, Par 71, SSS 70, Course record 66.
Club membership 700.
Visitors Mon-Fri except BHs. Booking required. Handicap certificate. Dress code. **Societies** Booking required. **Green Fees** £50 per round, £60 per day. **Prof** DC Newnham **Facilities** by arrangement **Location** 9m S of Tunbridge Wells on A26

Hotel ★★★★ 71% The Spa Hotel, Mount Ephraim, TUNBRIDGE WELLS ☎ 01892 520331 69 en suite

Dewlands Manor Cottage Hill, Rotherfield TN6 3JN
☎ 01892 852266 🖷 01892 853015
A compact meadowland course built on land surrounding a 15th-century manor. The short par 4 4th can be played by the brave by launching a driver over the trees; the 7th requires accurate driving on a tight fairway; and the final two holes are sweeping par 5s travelling parallel to each other, a small stream guarding the front of the 9th green.
9 holes, 3186yds, Par 36, SSS 70.
Visitors Booking required. **Societies** Booking required. **Green Fees** phone. **Prof** Nick Godin **Course Designer** RM & NM Godin **Facilities** **Leisure** indoor teaching facilities with computer analysis. **Conf** Corporate Hospitality Days **Location** 0.5m S of Rotherfield

Inn ♦♦♦ Plough & Horses Inn, Walshes Rd, CROWBOROUGH ☎ 01892 652614 15 en suite

DITCHLING Map 05 TQ31

Mid Sussex Spatham Ln BN6 8XJ
☎ 01273 846567 🖷 01273 847815
e-mail: admin@midsussexgolfclub.co.uk
web: www.midsussexgolfclub.co.uk
Mature parkland course with many trees, water hazards, strategically placed bunkers and superbly contoured greens. The 14th hole, a spectacular par 5, demands accurate shotmaking to avoid the various hazards along its length.
18 holes, 6462yds, Par 71, SSS 71, Course record 65.
Club membership 650.
Visitors Mon-Fri. Sat, Sun & BHs pm. Dress code. **Societies** Booking required. **Green Fees** £28 per round, £30 Sat & Sun. **Prof** Neil Plimmer **Course Designer** David Williams **Facilities** **Conf** facs Corporate Hospitality Days **Location** 1m E of Ditchling

Hotel ★★★ 75% Shelleys Hotel, High St, LEWES ☎ 01273 472361 19 en suite

EASTBOURNE Map 05 TV69

Eastbourne Downs East Dean Rd BN20 8ES
☎ 01323 720827 🖷 01323 412506
This downland course has spectacular views over the South Downs and Channel. Situated in an Area of Outstanding Natural Beauty 1m behind Beachy Head.
18 holes, 6601yds, Par 72, SSS 72, Course record 69.
Club membership 600.
Visitors Mon-Sun & BHs. Booking required. Handicap certificate Sat & Sun. Dress code. **Societies** Booking required. **Green Fees** £25 per day, £20 per round, £32/£28 Sat, Sun & BHs. **Prof** T Marshall **Course Designer** JH Taylor **Facilities**

Continued

Conf Corporate Hospitality Days **Location** 0.5m W of town centre on A259

Hotel ★★★ 74% Lansdowne Hotel, King Edward's Pde, EASTBOURNE ☎ 01323 725174 101 en suite

Royal Eastbourne Paradise Dr BN20 8BP
☎ 01323 729738 📠 01323 744048
e-mail: sec@regc.co.uk
web: www.regc.co.uk
A famous club which celebrated its centenary in 1987. The course plays longer than it measures. Testing holes are the 8th, a par 3 played to a high green and the 16th, a par 5 righthand dog-leg.
Devonshire Course: 18 holes, 6077yds, Par 70, SSS 69, Course record 62.
Hartington Course: 9 holes, 2147yds, Par 64, SSS 61.
Club membership 800.
Visitors Mon Sun & BHs. Booking required. Handicap certificate. Dress code. **Societies** Booking required. **Green Fees** Devonshire £48 per day, £30 per round, £60/£35 Sat, Sun & BHs. Hartington £18 per day. **Prof** Alan Harrison **Course Designer** Arthur Mayhewe **Facilities** by arrangement **Leisure** snooker table. **Conf** Corporate Hospitality Days **Location** 0.5m W of town centre

Hotel ★★★ 74% Lansdowne Hotel, King Edward's Pde, EASTBOURNE ☎ 01323 725174 101 en suite
See advertisement on this page

Willingdon Southdown Rd, Willingdon BN20 9AA
☎ 01323 410981 📠 01323 411510
e-mail: secretary@willingdongolfclub.co.uk
web: www.willingdongolfclub.co.uk
Unique, hilly downland course set in an oyster-shaped amphitheatre.
18 holes, 6118yds, Par 69, SSS 69.
Club membership 610.
Visitors contact club for details. **Societies** welcome. **Green Fees** £25 per day, £20 per round. **Prof** Troy Moore **Course Designer** J Taylor, A MacKenzie **Facilities** **Location** 0.5m N of town centre off A22

Hotel ★★★ 73% Hydro Hotel, Mount Rd, EASTBOURNE ☎ 01323 720643 84 rms (83 en suite)

FOREST ROW Map 05 TQ43

Royal Ashdown Forest Chapel Ln RH18 5LR
☎ 01342 822018 📠 01342 825211
e-mail: office@royalashdown.co.uk
web: www.royalashdown.co.uk
Old Course is on undulating heathland with no bunkers. Long carries off the tees and magnificent views over the Forest. Not a course for the high handicapper. West Course on natural heathland with no bunkers. Less demanding than Old Course although accuracy is at a premium.
Old Course: 18 holes, 6477yds, Par 72, SSS 71, Course record 67.
West Course: 18 holes, 5606yds, Par 68, SSS 67.
Club membership 450.
Visitors Mon-Sun & BHs. Booking required. Dress code. **Societies** Booking required. **Green Fees** Old Course £50 per round, £70 Sat & Sun. West Course £25 per round, £29 Sat & Sun. **Prof** Martyn Landsborough **Course Designer** Archdeacon Scott **Facilities** **Location** On B2110 in Forest Row

Hotel ★★★★ Ashdown Park Hotel and Country Club, Wych Cross, FOREST ROW ☎ 01342 824988 106 en suite

HAILSHAM Map 05 TQ50

Wellshurst Golf & Country Club North St, Hellingly BN27 4EE
01435 813456 (pro shop) 01435 812444
e-mail: info@wellshurst.com
web: www.wellshurst.com
There are outstanding views of the South Downs and the Weald from this well-manicured, undulating 18-hole course. There are varied features and some water hazards. A practice sand bunker, putting green and driving range are available to improve your golf.
18 holes, 5992yds, Par 70, SSS 68, Course record 64. Club membership 450.
Visitors Mon-Sun & BHs. Dress code. **Societies** Booking required. **Green Fees** £20 per 18 holes, £24 Sat & Sun. **Prof** Mark Jarvis **Course Designer** The Golf Corporation **Facilities** **Leisure** sauna, solarium, gymnasium, spa bath. **Conf** facs Corporate Hospitality Days **Location** 2.5m N off A22 junct at Hailsham, on A267

Hotel ★★ 71% The Olde Forge Hotel & Restaurant, Magham Down, HAILSHAM 01323 842893 7 en suite

HASTINGS & ST LEONARDS Map 05 TQ80

TEN66 Battle Rd TN37 7BP
01424 854243 01424 854244
18 holes, 6248yds, Par 71, SSS 70, Course record 70.
Location 3m N of Hastings on A2100
Phone for further details

Hotel ★★★ 72% Beauport Park Hotel, Battle Rd, HASTINGS 01424 851222 25 en suite

HEATHFIELD Map 05 TQ52

Horam Park Chiddingly Rd, Horam TN21 0JJ
01435 813477 01435 813677
:-mail: angie@horamgolf.freeserve.co.uk
veb: www.horamparkgolf.co.uk
) holes, 6128yds, Par 70, SSS 70, Course record 64.
Course Designer Glen Johnson **Location** Off A267 Hailsham to Heathfield
Phone for further details

Hotel ★★★ 68% Boship Farm Hotel, Lower Dicker, HAILSHAM 01323 844826 47 annexe en suite

HOLTYE Map 05 TQ43

Holtye TN8 7ED
01342 850635 & 850576 01342 850576
-mail: secretary@holtye.com
veb: www.holyte.com
Undulating forest and heathland course with tree-lined fairways providing testing golf. Different tees on the back nine.
holes, 5325yds, Par 66, SSS 66, Course record 62. Club membership 360.
Visitors Mon, Tue, Fri & BHs. Wed, Thu, Sat, Sun pm. Dress code. **Societies** Booking required. **Green Fees** £16 per 18 holes, £10 per 9 holes, £20/£13 Sat & Sun. **Prof** Kevin Hinton **Facilities** **Location** 4m of East Grinstead on A264

Hotel Premier Travel Inn East Grinstead, London Rd, Felbridge, EAST GRINSTEAD 08701 977088 41 en suite

LEWES Map 05 TQ41

Lewes Chapel Hill BN7 2BB
01273 473245 01273 483474
e-mail: secretary@lewesgolfclub.co.uk
web: www.lewesgolfclub.co.uk
Downland course with undulating fairways. Fine views. Proper greens all-year-round.
18 holes, 6190yds, Par 71, SSS 70, Course record 64. Club membership 615.
Visitors Mon-Sun & BHs. Dress code. **Societies** Booking required. **Green Fees** £30 per round, £12.50 Mon, £10 Twilight. **Prof** Paul Dobson **Course Designer** Jack Rowe **Facilities** by arrangement **Location** E of town centre

Hotel ★★★ 71% Deans Place, Seaford Rd, ALFRISTON 01323 870248 36 en suite

NEWHAVEN Map 05 TQ40

Peacehaven Brighton Rd BN9 9UH
01273 512571 01273 512571
e-mail: golf@peacehavengc.freeserve.co.uk
Downland course, sometimes windy. Testing holes: 1st (par 3), 4th (par 4), 9th (par 3). Attractive views over the South Downs, the River Ouse and Newhaven Harbour.
9 holes, 5488yds, Par 70, SSS 66, Course record 65. Club membership 270.
Visitors contact club for details. Dress code. **Societies** Booking required. **Green Fees** £17 per 18 holes, £11 per 9 holes, £23/£15 Sat & Sun. **Prof** Alan Tyson **Course Designer** James Braid **Facilities** **Location** 0.75m W on A259

RYE Map 05 TQ92

Rye New Lydd Rd, Camber TN31 7QS
01797 225241 01797 225460
e-mail: links@ryegolfclub.co.uk
web: www.ryegolfclub.co.uk
Unique links course with superb undulating greens set among ridges of sand dunes alongside Rye Harbour. Fine views over Romney Marsh and towards Fairlight and Dungeness.
Old Course: 18 holes, 6317yds, Par 68, SSS 71, Course record 64.
Jubilee Course: 18 holes, 5848yds, Par 69, SSS 69, Course record 71.
Club membership 1100.
Visitors Mon-Sun & BHs. Booking required. Handicap certificate. Dress code. **Societies** Booking required. **Green Fees** phone. **Prof** Michael Lee **Course Designer** H Colt **Facilities** **Location** 2.75m SE off A259

Continued

SEAFORD Map 05 TV49

Seaford Firle Rd, East Blatchington BN25 2JD
☎ 01323 892442 📠 01323 894113
e-mail: secretary@seafordgolfclub.co.uk
web: www.seafordgolfclub.co.uk
The great JH Taylor did not perhaps design as many courses as his friend and rival, James Braid, but Seaford's original design was Taylor's. It is a splendid downland course with magnificent views and some fine holes.
18 holes, 6546yds, Par 69, SSS 71.
Club membership 600.
Visitors Mon-Sat except BHs. Booking required. Handicap certificate. Dress code. **Societies** Booking required. **Green Fees** Summer £40 per 18 holes, winter £30. **Prof** David Mills, Clay Morris **Course Designer** JH Taylor **Facilities** by arrangement **Conf** Corporate Hospitality Days **Location** Turn inland off A259 at war memorial

Seaford Head Southdown Rd BN25 4JS
☎ 01323 890139 📠 01323 894491
e-mail: fraser1974@mac.com
web: www.seafordheadgolfcourse.co.uk
A links type course situated on the cliff edge giving exception views over the Seven Sisters and coastline. The upper level is reached via a short hole with elevated green - known as the 'Hell Hole' and the 18th Par 5 tee is on the 'Head' being 300 feet above sea level.
18 holes, 5848yds, Par 71, SSS 68, Course record 62.
Club membership 450.
Visitors Mon-Sun & BHs. Booking required. Dress code. **Societies** Booking required. **Green Fees** phone. **Prof** Fraser Morley **Facilities**
Location E of Seaford on A259

Hotel ★★★ 71% Deans Place, Seaford Rd, ALFRISTON
☎ 01323 870248 36 en suite

SEDLESCOMBE Map 05 TQ71

Sedlescombe Kent St TN33 0SD
☎ 01424 871700 📠 01424 871712
e-mail: golf@golfschool.co.uk
web: www.golfschool.co.uk
18 holes, 6269yds, Par 72, SSS 70.
Location 4m N of Hastings on A21
Phone for further details

Hotel ★★★ 70% Brickwall Hotel, The Green, Sedlescombe, BATTLE ☎ 01424 870253 & 870339
📠 01424 870785 25 en suite

TICEHURST Map 05 TQ63

Dale Hill Hotel & Golf Club TN5 7DQ
☎ 01580 200112 📠 01580 201249
e-mail: info@dalehill.co.uk
web: www.dalehill.co.uk
Dale Hill is set in over 350 acres, high on the Weald in an Area of Outstanding Natural Beauty. Offering two 18-hole courses, one of which has been designed by Ian Woosnam to USGA specifications.
Dale Hill: 18 holes, 6106yds, Par 70, SSS 69.
Ian Woosnam: 18 holes, 6512yds, Par 71, SSS 71, Course record 64.
Club membership 850.
Continued

Visitors Mon-Sun & BHs. Dress code. **Societies** welcome. **Green Fees** Dale Hill £25, £35 Sat & Sun. Ian Woosnam (including buggy) £55, £65 Sat & Sun. **Prof** Mark Wood **Course Designer** Ian Woosnam **Facilities** **Leisure** heated indoor swimming pool, sauna, gymnasium. **Conf** facs Corporate Hospitality Days **Location** M25 junct 5, A21 onto B2087, 1m left

Dale Hill Hotel & Golf Club

Hotel ★★★★ 75% Dale Hill Hotel & Golf Club, TICEHURST ☎ 01580 200112 35 en suite

UCKFIELD Map 05 TQ42

East Sussex National see page 257

Hotel ★★★★ 76% Buxted Park Country House Hotel, Buxted, UCKFIELD ☎ 01825 733333 44 en suite

Hotel ★★★ Horsted Place, Little Horsted, UCKFIELD
☎ 01825 750581 📠 01825 750459 17 en suite 3 annexe en suite

Hotel ★★★ Newick Park Hotel & Country Estate, NEWICK ☎ 01825 723633 📠 01825 723969 13 en suite 3 annexe en suite

Piltdown Piltdown TN22 3XB
☎ 01825 722033 📠 01825 724192
e-mail: piltdowngolf@lineone.net
web: www.piltdowngolfclub.co.uk
A relatively short, but difficult heather and gorse course built on Sussex clay. No bunkers, easy walking, fine views.
18 holes, 6076yds, Par 68, SSS 69, Course record 64.
Club membership 400.
Visitors Mon, Wed, Fri, Sat except BHs. Booking required. Handicap certificate. Dress code. **Societies** Booking required. **Green Fees** £50 per day , £34 per round, £27 after 1.30pm, £18 after 4pm. **Prof** Jason Partridge **Facilities**
Location 2m W of Uckfield off A272, club signed

Hotel ★★★ Horsted Place, Little Horsted, UCKFIELD
☎ 01825 750581 17 en suite 3 annexe en suite

Prices may change during the currency of the guide, always check when booking

Championship Course

East Sussex

East Sussex National

Uckfield

Map 05 TQ42

East Sussex National offers two huge courses ideal for big-hitting professionals. The European Open has been staged here and it is home to the European Headquarters of the David Leadbetter Golf Academy, with indoor and outdoor video analysis. Bob Cupp designed the courses using 'bent' grass from tee to green, resulting in an American-style course to test everyone. The greens on both the East and West courses are immaculately maintained. The West Course, with stadium design and chosen for major events, is reserved for members and their guests; visitors are welcome on the East Course, also with stadium design, and which was the venue for the 1993 and 1994 European Open. The entrance seems daunting for first-time visitors, unprepared for the vast car park, huge red-brick clubhouse, and the suspended corridor from the reception through to the well-stocked professional shop.

Little Horsted TN22 5ES
☎ 01825 880088 🖹 01825 880066
e-mail: golf@eastsussexnational.co.uk
web: www.eastsussexnational.co.uk

East Course: 18 holes, 7138yds, Par 72, SSS 74, Course record 63.
West Course: 18 holes, 7154yds, Par 72, SSS 74.
Club membership 650.

Visitors Mon-Sun & BHs. Booking required. Dress code. **Societies** Booking required. **Green Fees** £45 per 18 holes, £50 Sat & Sun. **Prof** Sarah Maclennan, Mike Clark **Course Designer** Bob Cupp **Facilities** **Leisure** hard tennis courts, heated indoor swimming pool, fishing, sauna, solarium, gymnasium, golf academy. **Conf** facs Corporate Hospitality Days **Location** 2m S of Uckfield on A22

SUSSEX, WEST

ANGMERING — Map 04 TQ00

Ham Manor BN16 4JE
☎ 01903 783288 🖷 01903 850886
e-mail: secretary@hammanor.co.uk
web: www.hammanor.co.uk
Two miles from the sea, this parkland course has fine springy turf and provides an interesting test in two loops of nine holes each.
18 holes, 6267yds, Par 70, SSS 70, Course record 64.
Club membership 780.
Visitors Mon-Sun & BHs. Handicap certificate. Dress code. **Societies** welcome. **Green Fees** £35, £50 Sat & Sun. **Prof** Simon Buckley **Course Designer** Harry Colt **Facilities** ⊗ 🍴 🍺 ☕ 🍷 ⛳ 🏠 🛒 ⛳ **Conf** Corporate Hospitality Days **Location** Off A259

Guest House ♦♦♦♦ Kenmore Guest House, Claigmar Rd, RUSTINGTON ☎ 01903 784634 7 rms (6 en suite)

ARUNDEL — Map 04 TQ00

Avisford Park Yapton Ln, Walberton BN18 0LS
☎ 01243 554611 🖷 01243 555580
18 holes, 5703yds, Par 68, SSS 66.
Location Off A27 towards Yapton
Phone for further details

Hotel ★★★ 69% Norfolk Arms Hotel, High St, ARUNDEL ☎ 01903 882101 21 en suite 13 annexe en suite

BOGNOR REGIS — Map 04 SZ99

Bognor Regis Downview Rd, Felpham PO22 8JD
☎ 01243 821929 (secretary) 🖷 01243 860719
e-mail: sec@bognorgoflclub.co.uk
web: www.bognorgolfclub.co.uk
18 holes, 6238yds, Par 70, SSS 70, Course record 64.
Course Designer James Braid **Location** 0.5m N at Felpham lights on A259
Phone for further details

Hotel ★★ 71% Beachcroft Hotel, Clyde Rd, Felpham, BOGNOR REGIS ☎ 01243 827142 35 en suite

BURGESS HILL — Map 04 TQ31

Burgess Hill Cuckfield Rd RH15 8RE
☎ 01444 258585 🖷 01444 247318
e-mail: enquiries@burgesshillgolfcentre.co.uk
Very challenging nine-hole course. Gently undulating layout with trees and water.
9 holes, 1250yds, Par 27.
Visitors Mon-Sun & BHs. **Societies** Booking required. **Green Fees** £10 per 9 holes. **Prof** Mark Collins **Course Designer** Donald Steel **Facilities** ⊗ 🍴 🍺 ☕ 🍷 ⛳ 🏠 ⛳ **Leisure** pitching & chipping green. **Conf** facs Corporate Hospitality Days **Location** N of town on B2036

Hotel ★★ 74% Hilton Park Hotel, Tylers Green, CUCKFIELD ☎ 01444 454555 11 en suite

CHICHESTER — Map 04 SU80

Chichester Hunston Village PO20 1AX
☎ 01243 533833 🖷 01243 539922
e-mail: enquiries@chichestergolf.com
web: www.chichestergolf.co.uk
The front nine has a 601yd par 5 that will challenge the best golfer. This is sandwiched between two formidable par 3s over water. The back nine is more subtle with two par 5s that can be reached in two by the most adventurous and the short but deceptive 15th, framed with 300 Portland stones and surrounded by sand.
Tower Course: 18 holes, 6175yds, Par 72, SSS 69, Course record 67.
Cathedral Course: 18 holes, 6461yds, Par 72, SSS 71, Course record 65.
Club membership 600.
Visitors Mon-Sun & BHs. Booking required. Handicap certificate for Cathedral course. Dress code. **Societies** Booking required. **Green Fees** phone. **Prof** Richard KIrby **Course Designer** Philip Saunders **Facilities** ⊗ 🍴 by arrangement 🍺 ☕ 🍷 ⛳ 🏠 🛒 ⛳ **Leisure** mini golf and par 3 course. **Conf** facs Corporate Hospitality Days **Location** 3m S of Chichester on B2145

Hotel ★★★ 63% The Ship Hotel, North St, CHICHESTER ☎ 01243 778000 36 en suite

COPTHORNE Map 05 TQ33

Copthorne Borers Arms Rd RH10 3LL
☎ 01342 712033 & 712508 🖷 01342 717682
e-mail: info@copthornegolfclub.co.uk
web: www.copthornegolfclub.co.uk
Despite it having been in existence since 1892, this club remains one of the lesser known Sussex courses. It is hard to know why because it is most attractive with plenty of trees and much variety.
18 holes, 6435yds, Par 71, SSS 71, Course record 66.
Club membership 550.
Visitors Mon-Fri except BHs. Handicap certificate. Dress code. **Societies** Booking required. **Green Fees** £36. **Prof** Joe Burrell **Course Designer** James Braid **Facilities** **Location** M23 junct 10, E of village off A264

Hotel ★★★★ 68% Copthorne Hotel London Gatwick, Copthorne Way, COPTHORNE
☎ 01342 348800 & 348888 🖷 01342 348833 227 en suite

Effingham Park The Copthorne Effingham Park, Hotel, West Park Rd RH10 3EU
☎ 01342 716528 🖷 0870 8900 215
web: www.effinghamparkgc.co.uk
Parkland course.

9 holes, 1822yds, Par 30, SSS 57, Course record 28.
Club membership 230.
Visitors contact club for details. **Societies** welcome. **Green Fees** phone. **Prof** Mark Root **Course Designer** Francisco Escario **Facilities** **Leisure** hard tennis courts, heated indoor swimming pool, sauna, solarium, gymnasium. **Conf** facs Corporate Hospitality Days **Location** 2m E on B2028

Hotel ★★★★ 65% Copthorne Hotel and Resort Effingham Park, West Park Rd, COPTHORNE
☎ 01342 714994 122 en suite

CRAWLEY Map 04 TQ23

Cottesmore Buchan Hill, Pease Pottage RH11 9AT
☎ 01293 528256 (reception) & 861777 (shop)
🖷 01293 522819
e-mail: cottesmore@crown-golf.co.uk
Founded in 1974, the Griffin course is a fine test of golfing skill with fairways lined by silver birch, pine, oak and rhododendrons. The natural lakes play a major part in the score. The Phoenix course is easier though still weaving through the same terrain.
Griffin: 18 holes, 6248yds, Par 71, SSS 70, Course record 67.
Phoenix: 18 holes, 5600yds, Par 69, SSS 67.

Continued

Cottesmore

Visitors Mon-Sun & BHs. Griffin course Sat, Sun & BHs pm. Booking required. Dress code. **Societies** Booking required. **Green Fees** Griffin Mon-Thu £29 per round, £34 Fri-Sun. Phoenix £16/£20. **Prof** Calum J Callan **Course Designer** Michael J Rogerson **Facilities** **Leisure** hard tennis courts, heated indoor swimming pool, sauna, solarium, gymnasium. **Conf** facs Corporate Hospitality Days **Location** M23 junct 11, through village of Pease Pottage, 2m on right

Hotel ★★★ Alexander House Hotel & Utopia Spa, East St, TURNERS HILL ☎ 01342 714914 32 en suite

Ifield Golf & Country Club Rusper Rd, Ifield RH11 0LN
☎ 01293 520222 🖷 01293 612973
Parkland course.
18 holes, 6330yds, Par 70, SSS 70, Course record 64.
Club membership 750.
Visitors Mon-Fri. Booking required. **Societies** Booking required. **Green Fees** phone. **Prof** Jonathan Earl **Course Designer** Hawtree & Taylor **Facilities** **Location** 1m W side of town centre off A23

Hotel ★★★ Alexander House Hotel & Utopia Spa, East St, TURNERS HILL ☎ 01342 714914 32 en suite

Tilgate Forest Golf Centre Titmus Dr RH10 5EU
☎ 01293 530103 🖷 01293 523478
e-mail: tilgate@glendale-services.co.uk
Designed by former Ryder Cup players Neil Coles and Brian Huggett, the course has been carefully cut through a silver birch and pine forest. It is possibly one of the most beautiful public courses in the country. The 17th is a treacherous par 5 demanding an uphill third shot to a green surrounded by rhododendrons.
18 holes, 6359yds, Par 71, SSS 70, Course record 69.
Club membership 200.
Visitors Mon-Sun & BHs. Booking required. Dress code. **Societies** Booking required. **Green Fees** 18 hole £17, Fri £20, £23 Sat & Sun. 9 hole £6, £7 Sat & Sun. **Prof** Sean Trussell **Course Designer** Neil Coles, Brian Huggett **Facilities** **Leisure** par 3 nine hole course. **Conf** Corporate Hospitality Days **Location** 2m E of town centre

Hotel ★★★ Alexander House Hotel & Utopia Spa, East St, TURNERS HILL ☎ 01342 714914 32 en suite

EAST GRINSTEAD Map 05 TQ33

Chartham Park Felcourt Rd, Felcourt RH19 2JT
☎ 01342 870340 & 870008 (pro shop) 01342 870719
e-mail: b.smith@clubhaus.com
web: www.clubhaus.com
18 holes, 6680yards, Par 72, SSS 72, Course record 64.
Course Designer Neil Coles **Location** 2m N from town centre towards Felcourt, on right
Phone for further details

Hotel ★★★ Gravetye Manor Hotel, EAST GRINSTEAD ☎ 01342 810567 18 en suite

GOODWOOD Map 04 SU80

Marriott Goodwood Park Hotel & Country Club PO18 0QB
☎ 01243 520117 01243 520120
e-mail: adrian.wratling@marriotthotels.co.uk
web: www.marriotthotels.com
A championship parkland course set within the 12,000-acre Goodwood estate, home to the dukes of Richmond for over 300 years. Fairly generous over the opening holes but gets progressively harder as you approach the turn.

18 holes, 6650yds, Par 72, SSS 71, Course record 64.
Club membership 600.
Visitors Mon-Sun & BHs. Booking required. Dress code. **Societies** Booking required. **Green Fees** £40 per round. **Prof** Christian Fogden **Course Designer** Donald Steele **Facilities** **Leisure** hard tennis courts, heated indoor swimming pool, sauna, solarium, gymnasium. **Conf** facs Corporate Hospitality Days **Location** 3m NE of Chichester in Goodwood House

Hotel ★★★★ 73% Marriott Goodwood Park Hotel & Country Club, GOODWOOD ☎ 0870 400 7225 94 en suite

HASSOCKS Map 04 TQ31

Hassocks London Rd BN6 9NA
☎ 01273 846630 & 846990 01273 846070
e-mail: hassocksgolfclub@btconnect.com
web: www.hassocksgolfclub.co.uk
Set against the backdrop of the South Downs, Hassocks is an 18-hole par 70 course designed and contoured to blend naturally with the surrounding countryside. A friendly and relaxed course, appealing to golfers of all ages and abilities.
18 holes, 5698yds, Par 70, SSS 68, Course record 66.
Club membership 400.
Visitors Mon-Sun & BHs. Booking required. Dress code. **Societies** Booking required. **Green Fees** £18 per 18 holes, £24.50 Sat, Sun & BHs. **Prof** Charles Ledger **Course Designer** Paul Wright **Facilities** **Conf** facs Corporate Hospitality Days **Location** On A273 between Hassocks & Burgess Hill

Hotel ★★★ 62% The Hickstead Hotel, Jobs Ln, Bolney, HICKSTEAD ☎ 01444 248023 49 en suite

HAYWARDS HEATH Map 05 TQ32

Haywards Heath High Beech Ln RH16 1SL
☎ 01444 414457 01444 458319
e-mail: info@haywardsheathgolfclub.co.uk
web: www.haywardsheathgolfclub.co.uk
Pleasant parkland with several challenging par 4s and 3s.
18 holes, 6216yds, Par 71, SSS 70, Course record 65.
Club membership 770.
Visitors Mon-Fri. Sat, Sun & BHs pm. Handicap certificate. Dress code. **Societies** Booking required. **Green Fees** £28 per 18 holes, £40 Sat, Sun & BHs. **Prof** Michael Henning **Course Designer** James Braid **Facilities** **Conf** Corporate Hospitality Days **Location** 1.25m N of Haywards Heath off B2028

Hotel ★★★ 69% The Birch Hotel, Lewes Rd, HAYWARDS HEATH ☎ 01444 451565 51 en suite

Paxhill Park East Mascalls Ln, Lindfield RH16 2QN
☎ 01444 484467 01444 482709
e-mail: mail@paxhill.co.uk
web: www.paxhillpark.co.uk
An easy downland course in two loops of nine in an Area of Outstanding Natural Beauty. Water hazards on 5th, 13th and 14th holes.
18 holes, 5981yds, Par 70, SSS 69, Course record 67.
Club membership 320.
Visitors Mon-Sun & BHs. Booking required. Dress code. **Societies** Bernard Firkins **Green Fees** phone. **Course Designer** P Tallack **Facilities** **Leisure** snooker. **Conf** facs Corporate Hospitality Days **Location** 2m NE of Haywards Heath, E of Lindfield off B2011

Hotel ★★★ 69% The Birch Hotel, Lewes Rd, HAYWARDS HEATH ☎ 01444 451565 51 en suite

HORSHAM Map 04 TQ13

See **Slinfold**

Horsham Worthing Rd RH13 7AX
☎ 01403 271525 01403 274528
e-mail: admin@horshamgolfandfitness.co.uk
9 holes, 4122yds, Par 33, SSS 30, Course record 55.
Location A24 rdbt onto B2237, by garage
Phone for further details

Hotel ★★★★ South Lodge Hotel, Brighton Rd, LOWER BEEDING ☎ 01403 891711 45 en suite

HURSTPIERPOINT Map 04 TQ21

Singing Hills Albourne BN6 9EB
☎ 01273 835353 01273 835444
e-mail: info@singinghills.co.uk
web: www.singinghills.co.uk
Three distinct nines (Lake, River and Valley) can be combined to make a truly varied game. Gently undulating fairways and spectacular waterholes make Singing Hills a test of accurate shotmaking. The

Continued

Continued

opening two holes of the River nine have long drives, while the second hole on the Lake course is an island green where the tee is also protected by two bunkers. The Valley course demands long, accurate tee shots.
Lake: 9 holes, 3253yds, Par 35, SSS 35.
River: 9 holes, 2861yds, Par 34, SSS 34.
Valley: 9 holes, 3362yds, Par 36, SSS 34.
Club membership 410.
Visitors Mon-Sun. Booking required. Dress code. **Societies** Booking required. **Green Fees** phone. **Prof** Wallace Street **Course Designer** MRM Sandow **Facilities** **Conf** facs Corporate Hospitality Days **Location** A23 onto B2117

Hotel ★★★ 62% The Hickstead Hotel, Jobs Ln, Bolney, HICKSTEAD ☎ 01444 248023 49 en suite

LITTLEHAMPTON Map 04 TQ00

Littlehampton 170 Rope Walk, Riverside West BN17 5DL
☎ 01903 717170 01903 726629
e-mail: lgc@talk21.com
web: www.littlehamptongolf.co.uk
A delightful seaside links in an equally delightful setting - and the only links course in the area.
18 holes, 6226yds, Par 70, SSS 70, Course record 64.
Club membership 600.
Visitors Mon-Fri. After 1pm Sat & Sun. Handicap certificate. Dress code. **Societies** welcome. **Green Fees** phone. **Prof** Stuart Fallow **Course Designer** Hawtree **Facilities** **Conf** facs Corporate Hospitality Days **Location** 1m W off A259

Hotel Travelodge Littlehampton Rustington, Worthing Rd, RUSTINGTON ☎ 08700 850 950 36 en suite

LOWER BEEDING Map 04 TQ22

Mannings Heath Hotel Winterpit Ln RH13 6LY
☎ 01403 891191 01403 891499
web: www.manningsheathhotel.com
A nine-hole, 18-tee course with three par 4s set in glorious countryside.
9 holes, 1529yds, Par 31.
Club membership 150.
Visitors contact hotel for details. Dress code. **Societies** welcome. **Green Fees** £7.50 per 18 holes. **Prof** Terry Betts **Facilities** **Leisure** fishing. **Conf** facs Corporate Hospitality Days **Location** Off A281 S of Horsham

Hotel ★★★★ South Lodge Hotel, Brighton Rd, LOWER BEEDING ☎ 01403 891711 45 en suite

MANNINGS HEATH Map 04 TQ22

Mannings Heath Fullers, Hammerpond Rd RH13 6PG
☎ 01403 210228 01403 270974
e-mail: enquiries@manningsheath.com
web: www.manningsheath.com
The Waterfall is a downhill, parkland, part heathland, championship course with streams and trees in abundance. It has three spectacular par 3s but all the holes are memorably unique. The Kingfisher course is a modern design with a lake which comes into play. It is more open and forgiving but not to be underestimated.

Continued

Waterfall: 18 holes, 6483yds, Par 72, SSS 71, Course record 63.
Kingfisher: 18 holes, 6217yds, Par 70, SSS 70, Course record 66.
Club membership 700.
Visitors Mon-Sun & BHs. Booking required Fri-Sun & BHs. Dress code. **Societies** welcome. **Green Fees** Waterfall £63, £73 Sat & Sun. Kingfisher £45/£50. **Prof** Neil Darnell **Course Designer** David Williams **Facilities** **Leisure** hard tennis courts, fishing, sauna, chipping practice area. **Conf** facs Corporate Hospitality Days **Location** Off A281 on N side of village

Hotel ★★★★ South Lodge Hotel, Brighton Rd, LOWER BEEDING ☎ 01403 891711 45 en suite

MIDHURST Map 04 SU82

Cowdray Park Petworth Rd GU29 0BB
☎ 01730 813599 01730 815900
e-mail: enquiries@cowdraygolf.co.uk
web: www.cowdraygolf.co.uk
Undulating parkland with scenic views of the surrounding countryside, including Elizabethan ruins. The course is in a park designed by 'Capability' Brown in the 18th century.

18 holes, 6212yds, Par 70, SSS 70, Course record 65.
Club membership 720.
Visitors Mon-Sun & BHs. Booking required. Dress code. **Societies** Booking required. **Green Fees** £40 per 18 holes. **Prof** Scott Brown **Course Designer** Jack White **Facilities** **Conf** facs Corporate Hospitality Days **Location** 1m E of Midhurst on A272
See advertisement on page 258

PULBOROUGH Map 04 TQ01

West Sussex Golf Club Ln, Wiggonholt RH20 2EN
☎ 01798 872563 01798 872033
e-mail: secretary@westsussexgolf.co.uk
web: www.westsussexgolf.co.uk
An outstanding beautiful heathland course occupying an oasis of sand, heather and pine in the middle of attractive countryside, which is predominantly clay and marsh. The 6th and 13th holes are particularly notable.
18 holes, 6264yds, Par 68, SSS 70, Course record 61.
Club membership 850.
Visitors Mon, Wed, Thu. Tue pm. Sat & Sun by arrangement. Booking required. Handicap certificate. Dress code. **Societies** Booking required. **Green Fees** £80 per 36 holes, £65 per 18 holes, £85/£70 Sat & Sun. **Prof** Tim Packham **Course Designer** Campbell, Hutcheson

Continued

Facilities ⊗ 🍽 ☕ 🍷 ⛳ 🏠 🏌 🚗 ⛳ **Location** 1.5m E of Pulborough off A283

Hotel ★★★ 70% Best Western Roundabout Hotel, Monkmead Ln, WEST CHILTINGTON ☎ 01798 813838 23 en suite

PYECOMBE Map 04 TQ21

Pyecombe Clayton Hill BN45 7FF
☎ 01273 845372 🖷 01273 843338
e-mail: info@pyecombegolfclub.com
web: www.pyecombegolfclub.com
Typical downland course on the inland side of the South Downs with panoramic views of the Weald.
18 holes, 6278yds, Par 71, SSS 70, Course record 65.
Club membership 525.
Visitors Mon-Sun. Dress code. **Societies** Booking required. **Green Fees** £28 per round, £30 per day, £33/£38 Sat & Sun. **Prof** CR White **Course Designer** James Braid **Facilities** ⊗ by arrangement 🍴 by arrangement 🍽 ☕ 🍷 ⛳ 🏠 🏌 ⛳ **Location** E of village on A273

Hotel ★★★ 64% The Courtlands, 15-27 The Drive, HOVE ☎ 01273 731055 60 en suite 7 annexe en suite

SELSEY Map 04 SZ89

Selsey Golf Links Ln PO20 9DR
☎ 01243 608935 🖷 01243 607101
e-mail: secretary@selseygolfclub.co.uk
web: www.selseygolfclub.co.uk
Fairly difficult links type seaside course, exposed to wind and has natural ditches.
9 holes, 5834yds, Par 68, SSS 68, Course record 64.
Club membership 360.
Visitors contact club for details. Handicap certificate. Dress code. **Societies** Booking required. **Green Fees** phone. **Prof** Peter Grindley **Course Designer** JH Taylor **Facilities** ⊗ 🍴 🍽 ☕ 🍷 ⛳ 🏠 ⛳ **Leisure** hard tennis courts. **Location** 1m N off B2145

Hotel ★★★ 63% The Ship Hotel, North St, CHICHESTER ☎ 01243 778000 36 en suite

SLINFOLD Map 04 TQ13

Slinfold Park Golf & Country Club Stane St RH13 7RE
☎ 01403 791555 🖷 01403 791465
e-mail: info@slinfoldpark.co.uk
web: www.slinfoldpark.co.uk

Championship Course: 18 holes, 6407yds, Par 72, SSS 71, Course record 64.
Academy Course: 9 holes, 1315yds, Par 28.

Continued

Course Designer John Fortune **Location** 4m W on A29
Phone for further details

Hotel ★★★ 69% Hurtwood Inn Hotel, Walking Bottom, PEASLAKE ☎ 01306 730851 15 en suite 6 annexe en suite

WEST CHILTINGTON Map 04 TQ01

West Chiltington Broadford Bridge Rd RH20 2YA
☎ 01798 812115 (bookings) & 813574 🖷 01798 812631
e-mail: richard@westchiltgolf.co.uk
web: www.westchiltgolf.co.uk
Set in an area of outstanding natural beauty with panoramic views of the South Downs. The main course has well-drained greens and, although quite short, is in places extremely tight. Three large double greens provide an interesting feature to this course. Also a 9-hole short course.
Windmill: 18 holes, 5866yds, Par 70, SSS 69, Course record 66 or 9 holes, 1360yds, Par 28.
Club membership 500.
Visitors Mon-Sun & BHs. Dress code. **Societies** Booking required. **Green Fees** 18 hole course £25 per round, £15 twilight, Sat & Sun £30 per round. 9 hole course £7.50. **Prof** Lorraine Cousins **Course Designer** Brian Barnes **Facilities** ⊗ 🍽 ☕ 🍷 ⛳ 🏠 🏌 🚗 ⛳ **Conf** facs Corporate Hospitality Days **Location** N of village

Hotel ★★★ 70% Best Western Roundabout Hotel, Monkmead Ln, WEST CHILTINGTON ☎ 01798 813838 23 en suite

WORTHING Map 04 TQ10

Hill Barn Hill Barn Ln BN14 9QF
☎ 01903 237301 🖷 01903 217613
e-mail: info@hillbarngolf.com
Downland course with views of Isle of Wight and Brighton.
18 holes, 6224yds, Par 70, SSS 70.
Club membership 500.
Visitors Mon-Fri. Booking required Sat, Sun & BHs. Dress code. **Societies** Booking required. **Green Fees** £16.50 per 18 holes, £19.50 Sat & Sun. **Prof** Tony Westwood **Course Designer** Fred Hawtree **Facilities** ⊗ 🍴 by arrangement 🍽 ☕ 🍷 ⛳ 🏠 🏌 🚗 ⛳ **Leisure** croquet. **Conf** facs Corporate Hospitality Days **Location** Signed from Grove Lodge rdbt on A24 by Norwich Union

Hotel ★★★ 63% Findon Manor Hotel, High St, Findon, WORTHING ☎ 01903 872733 11 en suite

Worthing Links Rd BN14 9QZ
☎ 01903 260801 🖷 01903 694664
e-mail: enquiries@worthinggolf.com
web: www.worthinggolf.co.uk
The Upper Course, short and tricky with entrancing views, will provide good entertainment. Lower Course is considered to be one of the best downland courses in the country.
Lower Course: 18 holes, 6505yds, Par 71, SSS 71, Course record 62.
Upper Course: 18 holes, 5211yds, Par 66, SSS 65.
Club membership 1200.
Visitors Mon, Thu-Sun & BHs. Booking required. Handicap certificate. Dress code. **Societies** Booking required. **Green Fees** phone. 🚫 **Prof** Stephen Rolley

Continued

Course Designer H Colt **Facilities** ⊗ ⛳ ☕ 🍷 ⛺ 🏠 ⛳ 🚗 ✓ ✓ **Location** N of town centre off A27

Hotel ★★★ 72% Ardington Hotel, Steyne Gardens, WORTHING ☎ 01903 230451 45 en suite

TYNE & WEAR

BACKWORTH Map 12 NZ37

Backworth The Hall NE27 0AH
☎ 0191 268 1048
9 holes, 5930yds, Par 71, SSS 69, Course record 63.
Location W of town on B1322
Phone for further details

Hotel ⌂ Premier Travel Inn Newcastle (Holystone), Holystone Roundabout, NEWCASTLE ☎ 08701 977189 40 en suite

BIRTLEY Map 12 NZ25

Birtley Birtley Ln DH3 2LR
☎ 0191 410 2207
e-mail: birtleygolfclub@aol.com
A nine-hole parkland course. Good test of golf with challenging par 3 and par 4 holes.
9 holes, 5662yds, Par 67, SSS 67, Course record 63.
Club membership 350.
Visitors Mon-Fri except BHs. Dress code. **Societies** Booking required. **Green Fees** £15 per 18 holes. ⊘ **Facilities** by arrangement ☕ ⛺

Hotel ⌂ Travelodge Newcastle South (A1 Northbound), Motorway Service Area, Portobello, BIRTLEY ☎ 08700 850 950 31 en suite

BOLDON Map 12 NZ36

Boldon Dipe Ln, East Boldon NE36 0PQ
☎ 0191 536 5360 & 0191 536 4182 🖷 0191 537 2270
e-mail: info@boldongolfclub.co.uk
web: www.boldongolfclub.co.uk
Parkland links course, easy walking, distant sea views.
18 holes, 6362yds, Par 72, SSS 70, Course record 67.
Club membership 700.
Visitors Mon-Fri. After 2pm Sat, Sun & BHs. **Societies** Booking required. **Green Fees** phone. ⊘ **Course Designer** Harry Varden **Facilities** ⊗ 🍴 ⛳ ☕ 🍷 ⛺ 🏠 ⛳ ✓ 🚗 ✓ ✓ **Leisure** snooker. **Location** S of village off A184

Hotel ★★★ 70% Quality Hotel Sunderland, Witney Way, Boldon, SUNDERLAND ☎ 0191 519 1999 82 en suite

CHOPWELL Map 12 NZ15

Garesfield NE17 7AP
☎ 01207 561309 🖷 01207 561309
e-mail: office@garesfieldgc.fsnet.co.uk
web: www.garesfieldgolf.com
Undulating parkland with good views and picturesque woodland surroundings.
18 holes, 6458yds, Par 72, SSS 70, Course record 68.
Club membership 697.
Visitors Mon-Fri. After 4.30pm Sat & Sun. Booking required. **Societies** Sun. Booking required with secretary. **Green Fees** phone. ⊘ **Prof** David Race **Course Designer** Harry Fernie **Facilities** ⊗ 🍴 ⛳ ☕ 🍷 ⛺ 🏠 ⛳ 🚗 ✓ **Conf** Corporate Hospitality Days **Location** Off B6315 in High Spen at Bute Arms for Chopwell

Hotel ★★★ 64% Quality Hotel Newcastle upon Tyne, Newgate St, NEWCASTLE UPON TYNE ☎ 0191 232 5025 93 en suite

FELLING Map 12 NZ26

Heworth Gingling Gate, Heworth NE10 8XY
☎ 0191 469 4424 🖷 0191 469 9898
Fairly flat parkland.
18 holes, 6422yds, Par 71, SSS 71.
Club membership 800.
Visitors Mon-Fri. Sun after 10am. **Societies** Booking required in writing. **Green Fees** phone. ⊘ **Prof** Adrian Marshall **Facilities** ⊗ 🍴 ⛳ ☕ 🍷 ⛺ 🏠 🚗 ✓ **Conf** facs Corporate Hospitality Days **Location** 0.5m NW of A1(M) junct on A195

Hotel ⌂ Travelodge Newcastle Whitemare Pool, Wardley, Whitemare Pool, WARDLEY ☎ 08700 850 950 71 en suite

GATESHEAD Map 12 NZ26

Ravensworth Angel View, Longbank, Wrekenton NE9 7NE
☎ 0191 487 6014 🖷 0191 487 6014
e-mail: ravensworth.golfclub@virgin.net
web: www.ravensworthgolfclub.co.uk
18 holes, 5966yds, Par 69, SSS 69.
Course Designer JW Fraser **Location** A1(M) onto A167 (Angel of the North) onto A1295 for 300yds
Phone for further details

Hotel ★★★ 71% Eslington Villa Hotel, 8 Station Rd, Low Fell, GATESHEAD ☎ 0191 487 6017 & 420 0666 🖷 0191 420 0667 17 en suite

GOSFORTH Map 12 NZ26

Gosforth Broadway East NE3 5ER
☎ 0191 285 3495 & 285 6710 (catering) 🖷 0191 284 6274
e-mail: gosforth.golf@virgin.net
web: www.gosforthgolfclub.co.uk
Easy walking parkland with natural water hazards.
18 holes, 6024yds, Par 69, SSS 68, Course record 62.
Club membership 500.
Visitors Mon-Sun & BHs. Booking required. Dress code. **Societies** Booking required. **Green Fees** £30 per day, £25 per round, £32/£28 Sat & Sun. **Prof** G Garland **Facilities** ⊗ 🍴 ⛳ ☕ 🍷 ⛺ 🏠 ✓ **Conf** Corporate Hospitality Days **Location** N of town centre off A6125

Hotel ★★★★ 74% Newcastle Marriott Hotel Gosforth Park, High Gosforth Park, Gosforth, NEWCASTLE UPON TYNE ☎ 0191 236 4111 178 en suite

Parklands Gosforth Park Golfing Complex, High Gosforth Park NE3 5HQ
☎ 0191 236 4480 🖷 0191 236 3322
18 holes, 6013yds, Par 71, SSS 69, Course record 66.
Location 3m N at end A1 western bypass
Phone for further details

Hotel ★★★★ 74% Newcastle Marriott Hotel Gosforth Park, High Gosforth Park, Gosforth, NEWCASTLE UPON TYNE ☎ 0191 236 4111 178 en suite

Continued

HOUGHTON-LE-SPRING Map 12 NZ34

Elemore Elemore Ln, Hetton-le-Hole DH5 0QB
☎ 0191 517 3061 🖹 0191 517 3054
Elemore course tests a player's ability in all aspects of the game, with drives over water as well as wedges. The greens are firm all year round and there are well positioned bunkers.
18 holes, 5947yds, Par 69, Course record 68.
Club membership 100.
Visitors Mon-Sun. Booking required. **Societies** Booking required. **Green Fees** phone. **Course Designer** J Gaunt **Facilities** **Location** 4m S of Houghton-le-Spring on A182

Hotel ★★ 67% Chilton Country Pub & Hotel, Black Boy Rd, Chilton Moor, Fencehouses, HOUGHTON-LE-SPRING ☎ 0191 385 2694 25 en suite

Houghton-le-Spring Copt Hill DH5 8LU
☎ 0191 584 1198 & 584 7421 🖹 0191 584 7421
e-mail: houghton.golf@ntlworld.com
web: www.houghtongolfclub.co.uk
Hilly, downland course with natural slope hazards and excellent greens.
18 holes, 6381yds, Par 72, SSS 71, Course record 64.
Club membership 680.
Visitors Mon-Sat & BHs, Sun after 3pm. Booking required. Dress code. **Societies** Booking required. **Green Fees** £25 per 18 holes, £30 Sat, Sun & BHs. **Prof** Kevin Gow **Facilities** **Location** 0.5m E on B1404

Hotel ★★ 67% Chilton Country Pub & Hotel, Black Boy Rd, Chilton Moor, Fencehouses, HOUGHTON-LE-SPRING ☎ 0191 385 2694 25 en suite

NEWCASTLE UPON TYNE Map 12 NZ26

City of Newcastle Three Mile Bridge NE3 2DR
☎ 0191 285 1775 🖹 0191 2840700
e-mail: info@cityofnewcastlegolfclub.com
web: www.cityofnewcastlegolfclub.com
A well-manicured parkland course in the Newcastle suburbs.
18 holes, 6528yds, Par 72, SSS 71, Course record 64.
Club membership 600.
Visitors contact club for details. Dress code. **Societies** Booking required. **Green Fees** £34 per day, £28 per round, £32 Sat & Sun. **Prof** Steve McKenna **Course Designer** Harry Vardon **Facilities** **Conf** Corporate Hospitality Days **Location** 3m N on B1318

Hotel ★★★ 68% The Caledonian Hotel, Newcastle, 64 Osborne Rd, Jesmond, NEWCASTLE UPON TYNE ☎ 0191 281 7881 89 en suite

Newcastle United Ponteland Rd, Cowgate NE5 3JW
☎ 0191 286 9998
e-mail: info@www.nugc.co.uk
web: www.nugc.co.uk
Moorland course with natural hazards.
18 holes, 6617yds, Par 72, SSS 72, Course record 66.
Club membership 650.
Visitors Mon-Fri. **Societies** Booking required. **Green Fees** phone. **Course Designer** Various **Facilities** **Leisure** Snooker table. **Location** 1.25m NW of city centre off A6127

Hotel ★★★ 68% The Caledonian Hotel, Newcastle, 64 Osborne Rd, Jesmond, NEWCASTLE UPON TYNE ☎ 0191 281 7881 89 en suite

Northumberland High Gosforth Park NE3 5HT
☎ 0191 236 2498 🖹 0191 236 2036
e-mail: sec@thengc.co.uk
Predominatly a level heathland style course, the firm, fast greens are a particular feature.
18 holes, 6683yds, Par 72, SSS 72, Course record 65.
Club membership 580.
Visitors Mon-Fri. Booking required Sat, Sun & BHs. Handicap certificate. Dress code. **Societies** Booking required. **Green Fees** £50 per day, £40 per round, £50 per round Sat & Sun. **Course Designer** Colt, Braid **Facilities** **Conf** Corporate Hospitality Days **Location** 4m N of city centre off A1

Hotel ★★★★ 74% Newcastle Marriott Hotel Gosforth Park, High Gosforth Park, Gosforth, NEWCASTLE UPON TYNE ☎ 0191 236 4111 178 en suite

Westerhope Whorlton Grance, Westerhope NE5 1PP
☎ 0191 286 7636 🖹 0191 2146287
e-mail: wgc@btconnect.com
Attractive, easy walking parkland with tree-lined fairways. Good open views towards the airport.
18 holes, 6444yds, Par 72, SSS 71, Course record 64.
Club membership 778.
Visitors Mon-Fri. Booking required. **Societies** Booking required. **Green Fees** phone. **Prof** Nigel Brown **Facilities** **Location** 4.5m NW of city centre off B6324

Hotel ★★★★ 74% Newcastle Marriott Hotel Gosforth Park, High Gosforth Park, Gosforth, NEWCASTLE UPON TYNE ☎ 0191 236 4111 178 en suite

RYTON Map 12 NZ16

Ryton Clara Vale NE40 3TD
☎ 0191 413 3737 🖹 0191 413 1642
e-mail: secretary@rytongolfclub.co.uk
Parkland course.
18 holes, 5950yds, Par 70, SSS 69, Course record 67.
Club membership 600.
Visitors Mon-Fri. **Societies** Booking required. **Green Fees** phone. **Facilities** **Conf** Corporate Hospitality Days **Location** NW of town centre off A695

Hotel ★★★ 69% Gibside Hotel, Front St, WHICKHAM ☎ 0191 488 9292 45 en suite

Tyneside Westfield Ln NE40 3QE
☎ 0191 413 2742 🖹 0191 413 2742
Open, part hilly parkland course with a water hazard.
18 holes, 6009yds, Par 70, SSS 69, Course record 65.
Club membership 641.
Visitors Mon-Fri, Sun & BHs. Booking required. Dress code. **Societies** Booking required. **Green Fees** £30 per day/round. **Prof** Geoff Dixon **Course Designer** H Colt **Facilities** **Conf** Corporate Hospitality Days **Location** NW of town centre off A695

Hotel ★★★ 69% Gibside Hotel, Front St, WHICKHAM ☎ 0191 488 9292 45 en suite

Continued

SOUTH SHIELDS Map 12 NZ36

South Shields Cleadon Hills NE34 8EG
☎ 0191 456 8942 🖷 0191 456 8942
e-mail: thesecretary@south-shields-golf.freeserve.co.uk
web: www.ssgc.co.uk
A slightly undulating downland course on a limestone base ensuring good conditions underfoot. Open to strong winds, the course is testing but fair. There are fine views of the coastline.
18 holes, 6174yds, Par 71, SSS 70, Course record 64. Club membership 700.
Visitors Mon-Sun & BHs. Booking required except Thu. Handicap certificate. Dress code. **Societies** Booking required. **Green Fees** £32-40 per day, £22-28 per round. **Prof** Glyn Jones **Course Designer** MacKenzie, Braid **Facilities** **Conf** facs Corporate Hospitality Days **Location** SE of town centre off A1300

Hotel ★★★ 66% Sea Hotel, Sea Rd, SOUTH SHIELDS ☎ 0191 427 0999 32 en suite

Whitburn Lizard Ln NE34 7AF
☎ 0191 529 4944 (sec) 🖷 0191 529 4944
e-mail: wgsec@ukonline.co.uk
Parkland with sea views. Situated on limestone making it rarely unplayable.
18 holes, 5899yds, Par 70, SSS 68, Course record 67. Club membership 700.
Visitors Mon-Sun & BHs. Booking required Sun & BHs. Handicap certificate. Dress code. **Societies** Booking required. **Green Fees** phone. **Prof** Neil Whinham **Course Designer** Colt, Alison & Morrison **Facilities** **Conf** Corporate Hospitality Days **Location** 2.5m SE off A183

Hotel ★★★★ 69% Sunderland Marriott Hotel, Queen's Pde, Seaburn, SUNDERLAND ☎ 0191 529 2041 82 en suite

SUNDERLAND Map 12 NZ35

Wearside Coxgreen SR4 9JT
☎ 0191 534 2518 🖷 0191 534 6186
web: wearsidegolfclub.com
18 holes, 6373yds, Par 71, SSS 74, Course record 63.
Location 3.5m W off A183
Phone for further details

Hotel ★★★★ 69% Sunderland Marriott Hotel, Queen's Pde, Seaburn, SUNDERLAND ☎ 0191 529 2041 82 en suite

TYNEMOUTH Map 12 NZ36

Tynemouth Spital Dene NE30 2ER
☎ 0191 257 4578 🖷 0191 259 5193
e-mail: secretary@tynemouthgolfclub.com
web: www.tynemouthgolfclub.com
Well-drained parkland course, not physically demanding but providing a strong challenge to both low and high handicap players.
18 holes, 6359yds, Par 70, SSS 70, Course record 66. Club membership 800.
Visitors Mon, Wed-Fri except BHs. Tue pm. Dress code. **Societies** Booking required. **Green Fees** £22.50 per 18 holes, £25 per day. **Prof** JP McKenna **Course Designer** Willie Park **Facilities** **Location** 0.5m W

Continued

Hotel ★★★ 69% Grand Hotel, Grand Pde, TYNEMOUTH ☎ 0191 293 6666 40 en suite 4 annexe en suite

WALLSEND Map 12 NZ26

Wallsend Rheydt Av, Bigges Main NE28 8SU
☎ 0191 262 1973
Parkland course.
18 holes, 6031yds, Par 70, SSS 69, Course record 65. Club membership 655.
Visitors Booking required. **Societies** Booking required. **Green Fees** £15.50 per round, £18.50 Sun. **Prof** Ken Phillips **Course Designer** A Snowball **Facilities** **Location** NW of town centre off A193

Hotel ★★★ 68% The Caledonian Hotel, Newcastle, 64 Osborne Rd, Jesmond, NEWCASTLE UPON TYNE ☎ 0191 281 7881 89 en suite

WASHINGTON Map 12 NZ25

George Washington Golf & Country Club
Stone Cellar Rd, High Usworth NE37 1PH
☎ 0191 4178346 🖷 0191 4151166
e-mail: reservations@georgewashington.co.uk
web: www.georgewashington.co.uk
The course is set in 150 acres of rolling parkland. Wide generous fairways and large greens. Trees feature on most holes, penalising the wayward shot.
18 holes, 6604yds, Par 73, SSS 71, Course record 68. Club membership 550.
Visitors Mon-Sun & BHs. Booking required. Dress code. **Societies** Booking required. **Green Fees** £30 per day, £20 per 18 holes, £35/£25 Sat & Sun. **Prof** Graeme Robinson **Course Designer** Eric Watson **Facilities** **Leisure** heated indoor swimming pool, squash, sauna, solarium, gymnasium, 9 hole par 3 course. **Conf** facs Corporate Hospitality Days **Location** From A195 signed Washington North take last exit on rdbt, then right at mini-rdbt

Hotel ★★★ 68% George Washington Golf & Country Club, Stone Cellar Rd, High Usworth, WASHINGTON ☎ 0191 402 9988 103 en suite

WHICKHAM Map 12 NZ26

Whickham Hollinside Park, Fellside Rd NE16 5BA
☎ 0191 488 1576 🖷 0191 488 1577
e-mail: enquiries@whickhamgolfclub.co.uk
web: www.whickhamgolfclub.co.uk
Undulating parkland in the beautiful Derwent valley. Its undulating fairways and subtly contoured greens create an interesting challenge for players of all abilities.
18 holes, 6542yds, Par 71, SSS 71. Club membership 680.
Visitors Mon-Fri, Sun & BHs. Dress code. **Societies** Booking required. **Green Fees** £25 per day, £20 per round, £27.50/£25 Sun & BHs. **Prof** Simon Williamson **Facilities** **Conf** Corporate Hospitality Days **Location** exit A1 for Whickham. Club is 1m from junct off Front St signed Burnopfield

Hotel ★★★ 69% Gibside Hotel, Front St, WHICKHAM ☎ 0191 488 9292 45 en suite

WHITLEY BAY Map 12 NZ37

Whitley Bay Claremont Rd NE26 3UF
☎ 0191 252 0180 🖷 0191 297 0030
e-mail: secretary@whitleybaygolfclub.co.uk
web: www.whitleybaygolfclub.co.uk
An 18-hole links type course, close to the sea, with a stream running through the undulating terrain.
18 holes, 6579yds, Par 71, SSS 71, Course record 66. Club membership 800.
Visitors Mon, Wed-Fri except BHs. Booking required. Dress code. **Societies** Booking required. **Green Fees** £40 per day, £30 per round. **Prof** Gary Shipley **Facilities** **Location** NW of town centre off A1148

Hotel ★★★ 71% Windsor Hotel, South Pde, WHITLEY BAY ☎ 0191 251 8888 69 en suite

WARWICKSHIRE

ATHERSTONE Map 04 SP39

Atherstone The Outwoods, Coleshill Rd CV9 2RL
☎ 01827 713110 🖷 01827 715686
Scenic parkland course, established in 1894 and laid out on hilly ground. Interesting challenge on every hole.
18 holes, 6006yds, Par 72, SSS 70, Course record 68. Club membership 495.
Visitors Mon-Fri except BHs. Dress code. **Societies** Booking required. **Green Fees** £25 per day/round. **Course Designer** Hawtree & Gaunt Mornoch **Facilities** **Conf** Corporate Hospitality Days **Location** 0.5m S, A5 onto B4116

Hotel Travelodge Tamworth (M42), Green Ln, TAMWORTH ☎ 08700 850 950 & 0800 850950 🖷 01827 260145 62 en suite

BIDFORD-ON-AVON Map 04 SP15

Bidford Grange Stratford Rd B50 4LY
☎ 01789 490319 🖷 01789 490998
web: www.golfinghotel.com
18 holes, 7233yds, Par 72, SSS 74, Course record 66.
Location E of village off B439
Phone for further details

BRANDON Map 04 SP47

City of Coventry-Brandon Wood Brandon Ln, Wolston CV8 3GQ
☎ 024 76543141 🖷 024 76545108
18 holes, 6610yds, Par 72, SSS 71, Course record 68.
Location Off A45 S
Phone for further details

Hotel ★★★★ 67% Macdonald Brandon Hall Hotel & Spa, Main St, BRANDON ☎ 0870 400 8105 60 en suite 60 annexe en suite

COLESHILL Map 04 SP28

Maxstoke Park Castle Ln B46 2RD
☎ 01675 466743 🖷 01675 466185
e-mail: maxstokepark@btinternet.com
Parkland with easy walking. Numerous trees and a lake form natural hazards.
18 holes, 6442yds, Par 71, SSS 71, Course record 64. Club membership 720.
Visitors Mon-Fri except BHs. Booking required Tue & Thu. Handicap certificate. Dress code. **Societies** Booking required. **Green Fees** £30 per 18 holes. **Prof** Neil McEwan **Course Designer** various **Facilities** **Conf** Corporate Hospitality Days **Location** 3m E of Coleshill, off B4114 for Maxstoke

Hotel ★★★ 65% Grimstock Country House Hotel, Gilson Rd, Gilson, COLESHILL ☎ 01675 462121 & 462161 🖷 01675 467646 44 en suite

HENLEY-IN-ARDEN Map 04 SP16

Henley Golf & Country Club Birmingham Rd B95 5QA
☎ 01564 793715 🖷 01564 795754
e-mail: enquiries@henleygcc.co.uk
web: www.henleygcc.co.uk
Attractive course in peaceful rural location which can be played off 4 different tee positions allowing golfers to play the course at varying length to suit different playing and physical abilities.

18 holes, 6933yds, Par 73, SSS 73. Club membership 500.
Visitors Mon-Sun & BHs. Booking required. Dress code. **Societies** welcome. **Green Fees** £40 per day, £27 per round, £47/£34 Sat & Sun. **Prof** Neale Hyde **Course Designer** N Selwyn Smith **Facilities** **Leisure** hard tennis courts, 9 hole par 3 course, beauty salon. **Conf** facs Corporate Hospitality Days **Location** On A3400 just N of Henley-in-Arden

Hotel ★★★ 64% Quality Hotel Redditch, Pool Bank, Southcrest, REDDITCH ☎ 01527 541511 73 en suite

KENILWORTH Map 04 SP27

Kenilworth Crewe Ln CV8 2EA
☎ 01926 858517 🖷 01926 864453
e-mail: secretary@kenilworthgolfclub.co.uk
web: www.kenilworthgolfclub.co.uk
Parkland course in an open hilly location. Club founded in 1889.
18 holes, 6400yds, Par 72, SSS 71, Course record 66. Club membership 755.
Visitors Mon-Sun except BHs. Booking required. Handicap certificate. Dress code. **Societies** Booking required. **Green Fees** £35 per day/round, £45 Sat & Sun. **Prof** Steve Yates **Course Designer** Hawtree **Facilities** **Leisure** Par 3 chipping green. **Conf** facs Corporate Hospitality Days **Location** 0.5m NE

Hotel ★★★★ 64% Chesford Grange Hotel, Chesford Bridge, KENILWORTH ☎ 01926 859331 209 en suite

Continued

LEA MARSTON Map 04 SP29

Lea Marston Hotel & Leisure Complex

Haunch Ln B76 0BY
☎ 01675 470468 ▤ 01675 470871
e-mail: info@leamarstonhotel.co.uk
web: www.leamarstonhotel.co.uk

The Marston Lakes course was opened in April 2001. The layout includes many water and sand hazards through undulating parkland. While short by modern standards, it is a good test for even low handicap players, requiring virtually everything in the bag. Tees and greens have been built to championship course specifications.

Marston Lakes: 9 holes, 2054yds, Par 31, SSS 30. Club membership 330.

Visitors Mon-Sun & BHs. Booking required. Dress code. **Societies** Booking required. **Green Fees** phone. **Prof** Darren Lewis **Course Designer** Contour Golf **Facilities** **Leisure** hard tennis courts, heated indoor swimming pool, sauna, solarium, gymnasium, golf simulator. **Conf** facs Corporate Hospitality Days **Location** M42 junct 9, A4097 towards Kingsbury, 1m right

Hotel ★★★★ 67% Lea Marston Hotel & Leisure Complex, Haunch Ln, LEA MARSTON ☎ 01675 470468 80 en suite

LEAMINGTON SPA Map 04 SP36

Leamington & County Golf Ln, Whitnash CV31 2QA

☎ 01926 425961 ▤ 01926 425961
e-mail: secretary@leamingtongolf.co.uk
web: www.leamingtongolf.co.uk

Undulating parkland with extensive views.

18 holes, 6418yds, Par 72, SSS 71, Course record 65. Club membership 854.

Visitors Mon-Sun & BHs. Handicap certificate. Dress code. **Societies** Booking required. **Green Fees** £35 per round, £40 Sat & Sun. **Prof** Julian Mellor **Course Designer** H Colt **Facilities** **Leisure** snooker. **Conf** Corporate Hospitality Days **Location** S of town centre

Hotel ★★★ 70% Courtyard by Marriott Leamington Spa, Olympus Av, Tachbrook Park, ROYAL LEAMINGTON SPA ☎ 01926 425522 91 en suite

Newbold Comyn Newbold Ter East CV32 4EW

☎ 01926 421157
e-mail: colin@newcomyngc-70.wanadoo.co.uk

Municipal parkland course with a hilly front nine. The par 4 9th is a 467yd testing hole. The back nine is rather flat but include two par 5s. Presently undergoing extensive upgrade.

18 holes, 6315yds, Par 70, SSS 70, Course record 69. Club membership 280.

Visitors Mon-Sun & BHs. Booking required. **Societies** welcome. **Green Fees** 18 holes £10.25, 9 holes £6, £13.50, £10.40 Sat & Sun. **Facilities** **Leisure** heated indoor swimming pool, gymnasium. **Location** 0.75m E of town centre off B4099

Hotel ★★★ 65% Best Western Royal Leamington Hotel, 64 Upper Holly Walk, LEAMINGTON SPA ☎ 01926 883777 32 en suite

LEEK WOOTTON Map 04 SP26

The Warwickshire CV35 7QT

☎ 01926 409409 ▤ 01926 408409
e-mail: ptaylor@theclubcompany.com
web: www.theclubcompany.com

Two courses, the Kings which is an American style course with lots of water and the Earls, which is mainly a woodland course.

Kings: 18 holes, 7000yds, Par 72, SSS 72, Course record 68.
Earls: 18 holes, 7421yds, Par 74, SSS 73, Course record 70.
Club membership 1500.

Visitors Mon-Sun & BHs. Booking required. Handicap certificate. Dress code. **Societies** Booking required. **Green Fees** phone. **Prof** Mark Dulson **Course Designer** Karl Litten **Facilities** **Leisure** heated indoor swimming pool, sauna, solarium, gymnasium, health club. **Conf** facs Corporate Hospitality Days **Location** S of village off A46

Hotel ★★★★ 64% Chesford Grange Hotel, Chesford Bridge, KENILWORTH ☎ 01926 859331 209 en suite

LOWER BRAILES Map 04 SP33

Brailes Sutton Ln OX15 5BB

☎ 01608 685633 ▤ 01608 685205
e-mail: office@brailesgolfclub.co.uk
web: www.brailesgolfclub.co.uk

Undulating meadowland on 105 acres of Cotswold countryside. Sutton Brook passes through the course and must be crossed five times. The par 5 17th offers the most spectacular view of three counties from the tee. Challenging par 3 short holes. Suitable for golfers of all standards.

18 holes, 6304yds, Par 71, SSS 70, Course record 67. Club membership 600.

Visitors Mon-Sun & BHs. Booking required. Handicap certificate. Dress code. **Societies** Booking required. **Green Fees** Summer £35 per day, £25 per round, £35 per round Sat & Sun. Winter £18/£25, £25. **Prof** Mark McGeehan **Course Designer** R Baldwin **Facilities** **Conf** facs Corporate Hospitality Days **Location** S of Lower Brailes off B4035

Inn ♦♦♦♦ The Red Lion, Main St, Long Compton, SHIPSTON ON STOUR ☎ 01608 684221 5 en suite

NUNEATON Map 04 SP39

Nuneaton Golf Dr, Whitestone CV11 6QF
☎ 024 7634 7810 🖷 024 7632 7563
e-mail: nuneatongolfclub@btconnect.com
Undulating parkland and woodland course with silver birch lining the fairways. Easy walking.
18 holes, 6429yds, Par 71, SSS 71.
Club membership 700.
Visitors Mon-Fri. Handicap certificate. **Societies** Bookinf required writing. **Green Fees** phone. **Prof** Craig Phillips **Facilities** **Location** 2m SE off B4114

Hotel ★★★ 66% Weston Hall Hotel, Weston Ln, Bulkington, NUNEATON ☎ 024 7631 2989 40 en suite

Oakridge Arley Ln, Ansley Village CV10 9PH
☎ 01676 541389 & 540542 🖷 01676 542709
e-mail: admin@oakridgegolf.fsnet.co.uk
web: www.oakridgegolf.fsnet.co.uk
The water hazards on the back nine add to the natural beauty of the countryside. The undulating course is affected by winter cross winds on several holes. Overall it will certainly test golfing skills.
18 holes, 6208yds, Par 71, SSS 71.
Club membership 500.
Visitors contact course for details. **Societies** welcome. **Green Fees** £18 per day. **Course Designer** Algy Jayes **Facilities** **Conf** Corporate Hospitality Days **Location** 4m W

Hotel ★★★ 66% Weston Hall Hotel, Weston Ln, Bulkington, NUNEATON ☎ 024 7631 2989 40 en suite

Purley Chase Pipers Ln, Ridge Ln CV10 0RB
☎ 024 7639 3118 🖷 024 7639 8015
e-mail: enquiries@purley-chase.co.uk
web: www.purley-chase.co.uk
18 holes, 6772yds, Par 72, SSS 72, Course record 64.
Location 2m NW off B4114
Phone for further details

Hotel ★★★ 66% Weston Hall Hotel, Weston Ln, Bulkington, NUNEATON ☎ 024 7631 2989 40 en suite

RUGBY Map 04 SP57

Rugby Clifton Rd CV21 3RD
☎ 01788 542306 (sec) & 575134 (pro) 🖷 01788 542306
e-mail: golf@rugbygc.fsnet.co.uk
web: www.warksgolf.co.uk
A short parkland course across the undulating Clifton valley. Clifton brook runs through the lower level of the course and comes into play on seven holes. Accuracy is the prime requirement for a good score.
18 holes, 5457yds, Par 68, SSS 67, Course record 60.
Club membership 700.
Visitors Mon-Fri except BHs. **Societies** Booking required in writing. **Green Fees** phone. **Prof** David Quinn **Facilities** **Leisure** snooker room. **Conf** Corporate Hospitality Days **Location** 1m NE on B5414

Hotel ★★★ 65% Grosvenor Hotel Rugby, 81-87 Clifton Rd, RUGBY ☎ 01788 535686 26 en suite

Whitefields Hotel Golf & Country Club
London Rd, Thurlaston CV23 9LF
☎ 01788 521800 🖷 01788 521695
e-mail: mail@draycotehotel.co.uk
web: www.draycotehotel.co.uk
Whitefields has superb natural drainage. There are many water features and the 13th has a stunning dog-leg 442yd par 4 with a superb view across Draycote Water. The 16th is completely surrounded by water and is particularly difficult.

18 holes, 6289yds, Par 71, SSS 70, Course record 64.
Club membership 400.
Visitors contact course for details. **Societies** Booking required. **Green Fees** £16, £25 Sat & Sun. **Course Designer** Reg Mason **Facilities** **Leisure** gymnasium. **Conf** facs Corporate Hospitality Days **Location** M45 junct 1, 0.5m on A45, on left

Hotel ★★★ 69% The Golden Lion Hotel, Easenhall, RUGBY ☎ 01788 833577 & 832265 🖷 01788 832878 21 en suite

STONELEIGH Map 04 SP37

Stoneleigh Deer Park The Clubhouse, The Old Deer Park, Coventry Rd CV8 3DR
☎ 024 7663 9991 &7663 9912 🖷 024 7651 1533
e-mail: stoneleighdeerpark@ukgateway.net
Parkland course in old deer park with many mature trees. The River Avon meanders through the course and comes into play on four holes. Also a nine-hole par 3 course.
Tantara Course: 18 holes, 6056yds, Par 71, SSS 69, Course record 67.
Avon Course: 9 holes, 1251yds, Par 27.
Club membership 800.
Visitors Mon-Sun & BHs. Booking required. Handicap certificate. Dress code. **Societies** Booking required. **Green Fees** £20, £22 Fri, £30 Sat, Sun & BHs. **Prof** Matt McGuire & Sarah Perkins **Facilities** **Location** 3m NE of Kenilworth

Hotel ★★★★ 62% Macdonald De Montfort Hotel, Abbey End, KENILWORTH ☎ 0870 1942127 108 en suite

STRATFORD-UPON-AVON Map 04 SP25

Ingon Manor Ingon Ln, Snitterfield CV37 0QE
☎ 01789 731857 🖷 01789 731657
e-mail: info@ingonmanor.co.uk
web: www.ingonmanor.co.uk
Nestling in the Welcombe Hills, a short distance from the town. The Manor, dating back to the 14th century, lies within 171 acres of land. The championship course

Continued

Championship Course

Warwickshire The De Vere Belfry

Wishaw Map 07 SP19

The De Vere Belfry is unique as the only venue to have staged the biggest golf event in the world, the Ryder Cup, an unprecedented four times, most recently in 2002. The Brabazon is regarded throughout the world as a great championship course with some of the most demanding holes in golf; the 10th (Ballesteros's Hole) and the 18th, with its dangerous lakes and its amphitheatre around the final green, are remarkable. Or you can pit your wits against a new legend in the making, the PGA National Course, which has won plaudits from near and far. This Dave Thomas and Peter Alliss designed course is already established as one of Britain's leading professional courses. For those who like their golf a little easier or like to get back into the swing gently, the Derby is ideal and can be played by golfers of any standard.

Wishaw B76 9PR
☎ 01675 470301 🖹 01675 470178
e-mail: enquiries@thebelfry.com
web: www.devereonline.co.uk

The Brabazon: 18 holes, 6724yds, Par 72, SSS 71.
PGA National: 18 holes, 6639yds, Par 71, SSS 70.
The Derby: 18 holes, 6057yds, Par 69, SSS 69.
Club membership 450.

Visitors Booking required for non-residents. Handicap certificate. **Societies** Booking required. **Green Fees** Brabazon £140. PGA £75. Derby £40. Winter reduced rates. **Prof** Simon Wordsworth **Course Designer** Dave Thomas, Peter Alliss **Facilities** **Leisure** hard tennis courts, heated indoor swimming pool, squash, sauna, solarium, gymnasium, PGA National Golf Academy. **Conf** facs Corporate Hospitality Days **Location** M42 junct 9, 4m E on A446

is open all year round and has been designed to test all standards of golfers with a variety of challenging holes.
18 holes, 6623yds, Par 72.
Club membership 400.
Visitors Mon-Sun & BHs. Booking required. Dress code. **Societies** welcome. **Green Fees** phone. **Prof** Niel Evans **Facilities** ⊗ ⅏ ℔ ☕ ♀ ⛼ ⌂ ⛟ ✎ ⛍ ✓ ⌠ **Leisure** caddies available. **Conf** facs Corporate Hospitality Days

Menzies Welcombe Hotel Warwick Rd CV37 0NR
☎ 01789 295252 🖹 01789 414666
e-mail: welcombe.golfpro@menzies-hotels.co.uk
web: www.welcombe.co.uk
Wooded parkland course of great character and boasting superb views of the River Avon and Stratford. Set within the hotel's 157-acre estate, it has two lakes and other water features.
18 holes, 6288yds, Par 70, SSS 69, Course record 64.
Club membership 450.
Visitors Booking required. **Societies** Booking required. **Green Fees** phone. **Prof** Matt Nixon **Course Designer** Thomas Macauley **Facilities** ⊗ ⅏ ℔ ☕ ♀ ⛼ ⌂ ⛳ ⛟ ✎ ⛍ ✓ ⌠ **Leisure** hard tennis courts, heated indoor swimming pool, fishing, solarium, gymnasium, golf lessons for individual/groups/company days. **Conf** facs Corporate Hospitality Days **Location** 1.5m NE off A46

Hotel ★★★★ 72% Menzies Welcombe Hotel and Golf Course, Warwick Rd, STRATFORD-UPON-AVON
☎ 01789 295252 73 en suite

Stratford Oaks Bearley Rd, Snitterfield CV37 0EZ
☎ 01789 731980 🖹 01789 731981
e-mail: admin@stratfordoaks.co.uk
web: www.stratfordoaks.co.uk
American-style, level parkland course with some water features designed by Howard Swan.
18 holes, 6135yds, Par 71, SSS 69, Course record 61.
Club membership 700.
Visitors Mon-Sun & BHs. Booking required. Dress code. **Societies** welcome. **Green Fees** £25, £30 Sat & Sun. **Prof** Andrew Dunbar **Course Designer** H Swann **Facilities** ⊗ ⅏ ℔ ☕ ♀ ⛼ ⌂ ⛳ ✓ ⌠ **Leisure** gymnasium, massage and physiotherapy facility. **Conf** Corporate Hospitality Days **Location** 4m N of Stratford-upon-Avon

Hotel ★★★★ 72% Stratford Manor, Warwick Rd, STRATFORD-UPON-AVON ☎ 01789 731173
104 en suite

Stratford-upon-Avon Tiddington Rd CV37 7BA
☎ 01789 205749 🖹 414909
e-mail: sec@stratfordgolf.co.uk
web: www.stratfordgolf.co.uk
Beautiful parkland course. The par 3 16th is tricky and the par 5 17th and 18th provide a tough end.
18 holes, 6311yds, Par 72, SSS 70, Course record 63.
Club membership 750.
Visitors contact club for details. **Societies** welcome. **Green Fees** £50 per day, £40 per 18 holes, £55/£45 Sat & Sun. ⊜ **Prof** D Sutherland **Course Designer** Taylor **Facilities** ⛼ ⌂ ⛳ ✎ ⛍ ✓ **Location** 0.75m E on B4086

Hotel ★★★★ 72% Macdonald Alveston Manor, Clopton Bridge, STRATFORD-UPON-AVON ☎ 0870 400 8181
113 en suite

TANWORTH IN ARDEN Map 07 SP17

Ladbrook Park Poolhead Ln B94 5ED
☎ 01564 742264 🖹 01564 742909
e-mail: secretary@ladbrookparkgolf.co.uk
Parkland course lined with trees.
18 holes, 6427yds, Par 71, SSS 71, Course record 65.
Club membership 700.
Visitors Mon-Fri except BHs. Booking required. Handicap certificate. Dress code. **Societies** Booking required. **Green Fees** £45 per 36 holes, £40 per 28 holes, £35 per 18 holes. **Prof** Richard Mountford **Course Designer** H Colt **Facilities** ⊗ ⅏ ℔ ☕ ♀ ⛼ ⌂ ✓ **Location** M42 junct 3, 2.5m SE

Hotel ★★★ Nuthurst Grange Country House Hotel, Nuthurst Grange Ln, HOCKLEY HEATH
☎ 01564 783972 15 en suite

WARWICK Map 04 SP26

Warwick The Racecourse CV34 6HW
☎ 01926 494316
Easy walking parkland. Driving range with floodlit bays.
9 holes, 2682yds, Par 34, SSS 66, Course record 67.
Club membership 150.
Visitors Mon-Sat & BHs. Sun pm. **Societies** Booking required. **Green Fees** £6.50 per 9 holes, £7 Sat & Sun. ⊜ **Prof** Mario Luca **Course Designer** DG Dunkley **Facilities** ☕ ♀ ⛼ ⌂ ⛳ ✓ ⌠ **Location** W of town centre

Hotel ★★★★ 74% Ardencote Manor Hotel, Country Club & Spa, Lye Green Rd, Claverdon ☎ 01926 843111
75 en suite

WISHAW Map 07 SP19

The De Vere Belfry see page 269

Hotel ★★★★ 75% De Vere Belfry, WISHAW
☎ 0870 900 0066 324 en suite

Hotel ★★★★ 67% Lea Marston Hotel & Leisure Complex, Haunch Ln, LEA MARSTON ☎ 01675 470468
🖹 01675 470871 80 en suite

Hotel ★★★★ 68% Moor Hall Hotel & Spa, Moor Hall Dr Four Oaks, SUTTON COLDFIELD ☎ 0121 308 3751
🖹 0121 308 8974 82 en suite

WEST MIDLANDS

ALDRIDGE Map 07 SK00

Druids Heath Stonnall Rd WS9 8JZ
☎ 01922 455595 (Office) 01922 452887
web: www.druidsheathgc.co.uk
Testing, undulating heathland course. Large greens with subtle slopes.
18 holes, 6661yds, Par 72, SSS 73, Course record 68. Club membership 660.
Visitors Mon-Sun except BHs. After 2pm Sat & Sun. Booking required. **Societies** Booking required. **Green Fees** phone. **Prof** Glenn Williams **Facilities** **Leisure** snooker. **Location** NE of town centre off A454

Hotel ★★★ 77% The Fairlawns at Aldridge, 178 Little Aston Rd, Aldridge, WALSALL ☎ 01922 455122 50 en suite

BIRMINGHAM Map 07 SP08

Alison Nicholas Golf Academy Host Centre, Queslett Park, Great Barr B42 2RG
☎ 0121 360 7600 0121 360 7603
e-mail: info@ the hostcorporation.com
web: www.thehostcorporation.com
9 holes, 905yds, Par 27, SSS 27, Course record 21.
Course Designer Alison Nicholas, Francis Colella
Location M6 junct 7
Phone for further details

Hotel Innkeeper's Lodge Birmingham East, Chester Rd, Streetley, SUTTON COLDFIELD ☎ 0121 353 7785 7 en suite 59 annexe en suite

Brandhall Heron Rd, Oldbury, Warley B68 8AQ
☎ 0121 552 2195
18 holes, 5734yds, Par 70, SSS 68, Course record 66.
Location 5.5m W of Birmingham off A4123
Phone for further details

Cocks Moors Woods Alcester Rd South, Kings Heath B14 4ER
☎ 0121 464 3584 0121 441 1305
Although quite short, this tree-lined parkland course has well-maintained greens and offers a good test of golf.
18 holes, 5769yds, Par 69, SSS 68. Club membership 300.
Visitors Mon-Sun. **Societies** Booking required. **Green Fees** phone. **Prof** Steve Ellis **Facilities** **Leisure** heated indoor swimming pool, solarium, gymnasium. **Location** M42 junct 3, 4m N on A435

Hotel ★★★ 68% Corus hotel Solihull, Stratford Rd, Shirley, SOLIHULL ☎ 0870 609 6133 111 en suite

Edgbaston Church Rd, Edgbaston B15 3TB
☎ 0121 454 1736 0121 454 2395
e-mail: secretary@edgbastongc.co.uk
web: www.edgbastongc.co.uk
Set in 144 acres of woodland, lake and parkland, 2m from the centre of Birmingham, this delightful course utilises the wealth of natural features to provide a series of testing and adventurous holes set in the traditional double loop that starts directly in front of the clubhouse, an imposing Georgian mansion.
18 holes, 6106yds, Par 69, SSS 69, Course record 63. Club membership 970.
Visitors Mon-Fri. Booking required Sat, Sun & BHs. Handicap certificate. Dress code. **Societies** Booking required in writing. **Green Fees** phone. **Prof** Jamie Cundy **Course Designer** H Colt **Facilities** **Conf** facs Corporate Hospitality Days **Location** 2m S of city centre on B4217, off A38

Great Barr Chapel Ln, Great Barr B43 7BA
☎ 0121 358 4376 0121 358 4376
e-mail: info@greatbarrgolfclub.com
Eeasy walking parkland with views of Barr Beacon Park.
18 holes, 6523yds, Par 72, SSS 72, Course record 67. Club membership 600.
Visitors Mon-Sun & BHs. Handicap certificate. Dress code. **Societies** Booking required. **Green Fees** phone. **Prof** Richard Spragg **Facilities** **Location** 6m N of city centre off A 34

Hotel Innkeeper's Lodge Birmingham East, Chester Rd, Streetley, SUTTON COLDFIELD ☎ 0121 353 7785 7 en suite 59 annexe en suite

Handsworth 11 Sunningdale Close, Handsworth Wood B20 1NP
☎ 0121 554 0599 & 554 3387 0121 554 3387
e-mail: info@handsworthgolfclub.net
Undulating parkland with some tight fairways and strategic bunkering with a number of well-placed water features.
18 holes, 6289yds, Par 70, SSS 71, Course record 64. Club membership 730.
Visitors Mon-Fri. Handicap certificate. Dress code. **Societies** Booking required. **Green Fees** £40 per day. **Prof** Lee Bashford **Course Designer** H Colt **Facilities** **Leisure** squash. **Conf** Corporate Hospitality Days **Location** 3.5m NW of city centre off A4040

Hotel Premier Travel Inn West Bromwich, New Gas St, WEST BROMWICH ☎ 08701 977264 40 en suite

Harborne 40 Tennal Rd, Harborne B32 2JE
☎ 0121 427 3058 0121 427 4039
e-mail: harborne@hgolf.fsnet.co.uk
web: www.harbornegolfclub.co.uk
Parkland course in a hilly location, with a brook running through.
18 holes, 6230yds, Par 70, SSS 70, Course record 65. Club membership 600.
Visitors Mon, Wed-Fri except BHs. Booking required. Handicap certificate. Dress code. **Societies** Booking required. **Green Fees** £30 per 36/18 holes. **Prof** Paul Johnson **Course Designer** Harry Colt **Facilities** **Location** 3.5 m SW of city centre off A4040

Harborne Church Farm Vicarage Rd, Harborne B17 0SN
☎ 0121 427 1204 🖹 0121 428 3126
Parkland with two brooks running through. Course is small but tight.
9 holes, 2441yds, Par 66, SSS 64, Course record 62. Club membership 115.
Visitors Mon-Sun & BHs. Booking required. **Societies** Booking required. **Green Fees** £10 per 18 holes, £6.50 per 9 holes, £12/£7.50 Sat & Sun. **Prof** Paul Johnson **Facilities** **Leisure** practice net. **Location** 3.5m SW of city centre off A4040

Hatchford Brook Coventry Rd, Sheldon B26 3PY
☎ 0121 743 9821 🖹 0121 743 3420
e-mail: idt@hbgc.freeserve.co.uk
18 holes, 6155yds, Par 69, SSS 70.
Location 6m E of city centre on A45
Phone for further details

Hotel ★★★ 68% Novotel Birmingham Airport, BIRMINGHAM AIRPORT ☎ 0121 782 7000 & 782 4111 🖹 0121 782 0445 195 en suite

Hilltop Park Ln, Handsworth B21 8LJ
☎ 0121 554 4463
A good test of golf with interesting layout, undulating fairways and large greens, located in the Sandwell Valley conservation area.
18 holes, 6208yds, Par 71, SSS 70, Course record 65. Club membership 400.
Visitors Mon-Sun & BHs. Booking required. **Societies** Booking required. **Green Fees** 18 holes £11, 9 holes £6.50, £13/£7.50 Sat, Sun & BHs. **Prof** Kevin Highfield **Course Designer** Hawtree **Facilities** **Conf** facs Corporate Hospitality Days **Location** M5 junct 1, 1m on A41

Hotel Premier Travel Inn West Bromwich, New Gas St, WEST BROMWICH ☎ 08701 977264 40 en suite

Lickey Hills Rosehill, Rednal B45 8RR
☎ 0121 453 3159 🖹 0121 457 8779
Hilly municipal course overlooking the city, set in National Trust land.
Rose Hill: 18 holes, 5835yds, Par 68, SSS 68. Club membership 300.
Visitors Mon-Sun & BHs. Booking required. Dress code. **Societies** Booking required. **Green Fees** £13 per 18 holes, £7.50 per 9 holes. **Prof** Mark Toombs **Facilities** **Leisure** hard tennis courts. **Conf** facs Corporate Hospitality Days **Location** 10m SW of city centre on B4096

Moseley Springfield Rd, Kings Heath B14 7DX
☎ 0121 444 4957 🖹 0121 441 4662
e-mail: admin@mosgolf.freeserve.co.uk
web: www.moseleygolfclub.co.uk
Parkland with a lake, pond and a stream providing natural hazards. The par 3 4th goes through a cutting in woodland to a tree and garden-lined amphitheatre, and the par 4 5th entails a drive over a lake to a dog-leg fairway.
18 holes, 6300yds, Par 70, SSS 71, Course record 63. Club membership 600.

Moseley

Visitors Mon-Fri except BHs. Booking required. Handicap certificate. Dress code. **Societies** Booking required. **Green Fees** £30 per round. **Prof** Martin Griffin **Course Designer** H Colt with others **Facilities** **Conf** Corporate Hospitality Days **Location** 4m S of city centre on B4146

North Worcestershire Frankley Beeches Rd, Northfield B31 5LP
☎ 0121 475 1047 🖹 0121 476 8681
Designed by James Braid and established in 1907, this is a mature parkland course. Tree plantations rather than heavy rough are the main hazards.
18 holes, 5959yds, Par 69, SSS 68, Course record 64. Club membership 600.
Visitors Mon-Fri except BHs. Booking required. Handicap certificate. Dress code. **Societies** Booking required. **Green Fees** £37 per day, £25 per round. **Prof** Dan Cummins **Course Designer** James Braid **Facilities** **Location** 7m SW of Birmingham city centre, off A38

Warley Woods The Pavilion, Lightswood Hill, Warley B67 5ED
☎ 0121 429 2440 & 686 2619 (secretary)
🖹 0121 434 4430
9 holes, 5346yds, Par 68, SSS 66, Course record 64.
Location 4m W of city centre off A456
Phone for further details

COVENTRY Map 04 SP37

Ansty Golf Centre Brinklow Rd, Ansty CV7 9JH
☎ 024 7662 1341 🖹 024 7660 2568
web: www.coventry.co.uk/ansty/
An 18-hole pay and play parkland course of two nine-hole loops.
18 holes, 6079yds, Par 71, SSS 68, Course record 66. Club membership 230.
Visitors Mon-Sun. **Societies** Booking required. **Green Fees** phone. **Prof** Mark Goodwin **Course Designer** David Morgan **Facilities** **Leisure** par 3 course. **Conf** facs Corporate Hospitality Days **Location** M6/M69 junct 2, 1m

Hotel ★★★ 64% Novotel Coventry, Wilsons Ln, COVENTRY ☎ 024 7636 5000 98 en suite

Continued

Coventry St Martins Rd, Finham Park CV3 6RJ
☎ 024 7641 4152 🖷 024 7669 0131
e-mail: coventrygolfclub@hotmail.com
web: www.coventrygolfcourse.co.uk
The scene of several major professional events, this undulating parkland course has a great deal of quality. More than that, it usually plays its length, and thus scoring is never easy, as many professionals have found to their cost.
18 holes, 6601yds, Par 73, SSS 73, Course record 66.
Club membership 500.
Visitors Mon-Fri except BHs. Handicap certificate. Dress code. **Societies** Wed & Thu. Booking required. **Green Fees** £40 per day. **Prof** Philip Weaver **Course Designer** Vardon Bros, Hawtree **Facilities** **Conf** Corporate Hospitality Days **Location** 3m S of city centre on B4113

Hotel ★★★ Best Western Hylands Hotel, Warwick Rd, COVENTRY ☎ 024 7650 1600 61 en suite

Coventry Hearsall Beechwood Av CV5 6DF
☎ 024 7671 3470 🖷 024 7669 1534
18 holes, 6005yds, Par 70, SSS 69.
Location 1.5m SW of city centre off A429
Phone for further details

Hotel ★★★ Best Western Hylands Hotel, Warwick Rd, COVENTRY ☎ 024 7650 1600 61 en suite

Windmill Village Hotel Golf & Leisure Club Birmingham Rd, Allesley CV5 9AL
☎ 024 7640 4041 🖷 024 7640 4042
e-mail: sales@windmillvillagehotel.co.uk
web: www.windmillvillagehotel.co.uk
An attractive 18-hole course over rolling parkland with plenty of trees and two lakes that demand shots over open water. Four challenging par 5 holes.
18 holes, 5184yds, Par 70, SSS 66, Course record 63.
Club membership 600.
Visitors Mon-Fri. Booking required Sat, Sun & BHs. Dress code. **Societies** Booking required. **Green Fees** phone. **Prof** Robert Hunter **Course Designer** Robert Hunter **Facilities** **Leisure** hard tennis courts, heated indoor swimming pool, sauna, solarium, gymnasium, practice nets. **Conf** facs Corporate Hospitality Days **Location** 3m W of Coventry on A45

Hotel ★★★ 72% Brooklands Grange Hotel & Restaurant, Holyhead Rd, COVENTRY ☎ 024 7660 1601 31 en suite

DUDLEY Map 07 SO99

Dudley Turner's Hill, Rowley Regis, Warley B65 9DP
☎ 01384 233877 🖷 01384 233177
18 holes, 5714yds, Par 69, SSS 68.
Location 2m S of town centre off B4171
Phone for further details

Hotel ★★★ 63% The Himley Country Hotel, School Rd, HIMLEY ☎ 0870 609 6112 73 en suite

Swindon Bridgnorth Rd, Swindon DY3 4PU
☎ 01902 897031 🖷 01902 326219
e-mail: golf@swindonperton.fsbusiness.co.uk
web: www.swindongolfclub.co.uk
Attractive, undulating woodland and parkland with spectacular views.
Old Course: 18 holes, 6121yds, Par 71, SSS 70.
Club membership 700.
Visitors Booking required. **Societies** Booking required.in writing. **Green Fees** phone. **Prof** Phil Lester **Facilities** **Leisure** fishing, Par 3 9-hole course. **Location** 4m W of Dudley on B4176

Hotel ★★★ 63% The Himley Country Hotel, School Rd, HIMLEY ☎ 0870 609 6112 73 en suite

HALESOWEN Map 07 SO98

Halesowen The Leasowes, Leasowes Ln B62 8QF
☎ 0121 501 3606 🖷 0121 501 3606
e-mail: halesowengolfclub@btconnect.com
web: www.halesowengolfclub.com
Parkland course within the only Grade I listed park in the Midlands.
18 holes, 5754yds, Par 69, SSS 69, Course record 64.
Club membership 625.
Visitors Mon-Fri & BHs. Sat & Sun by arrangement. Booking required. Handicap certificate. Dress code. **Societies** Booking required. **Green Fees** £34 per day, £28 per round. **Prof** Jon Nicholas **Facilities** **Conf** Corporate Hospitality Days **Location** M5 junct 3, 1m E, off Manor Ln

KNOWLE Map 07 SP17

Copt Heath 1220 Warwick Rd B93 9LN
☎ 01564 772650 & 731620 🖷 01564 771022/731621
e-mail: golf@copt-heath.co.uk
web: coptheathgolf.co.uk
Flat heathland and parkland course designed by Harry Vardon.
18 holes, 6522yds, Par 71, SSS 71, Course record 64.
Club membership 700.
Visitors Mon, Wed-Fri except BHs. Booking required Sat & Sun. Handicap certificate. Dress code. **Societies** Booking required. **Green Fees** £50 per day, £40 per round, £50 per round Sat & Sun. **Prof** Brian J Barton **Course Designer** H Vardon **Facilities** **Conf** Corporate Hospitality Days **Location** M42 junct 5, 0.5m S on A4141

Hotel ★★★★ 70% Renaissance Solihull Hotel, 651 Warwick Rd, SOLIHULL ☎ 0121 711 3000 179 en suite

MERIDEN Map 04 SP28

Marriott Forest of Arden Golf & Country Club see page 275

Hotel ★★★★ 73% Marriott Forest of Arden Hotel & Country Club, Maxstoke Ln, MERIDEN
☎ 0870 400 7272 214 en suite

Hotel ★★★ 71% Manor Hotel, Main Rd, MERIDEN
☎ 01676 522735 🖷 01676 522186 110 en suite

North Warwickshire Hampton Ln CV7 7LL
☎ 01676 522259 (shop) & 522915 (sec) 01676 523004
9 holes, 6390yds, Par 72, SSS 71, Course record 65.
Location 1m SW on B4102
Phone for further details

Hotel ★★★ 71% Manor Hotel, Main Rd, MERIDEN
☎ 01676 522735 110 en suite

Stonebridge Golf Club Somers Rd CV7 7PL
☎ 01676 522442 01676 522447
e-mail: golf.shop@stonebridgegolf.co.uk
web: www.stonebridgegolf.co.uk
A parkland course set in 170 acres with towering oak trees, lakes, and the River Blythe on its borders.
18 holes, 6240yds, Par 70, SSS 70, Course record 67.
Club membership 400.
Visitors contact club for details. Dress code. **Societies** Booking required. **Green Fees** £19 per 18 holes Mon-Thu, £20 Fri, £25 Sat, Sun & BHs. **Prof** Emma Clifford **Course Designer** Mark Jones **Facilities** **Leisure** fishing, golf academy. **Conf** facs Corporate Hospitality Days **Location** M42 junct 6, 3m

Hotel ★★★ 71% Manor Hotel, Main Rd, MERIDEN
☎ 01676 522735 110 en suite

SEDGLEY Map 07 SO99

Sedgley Golf Centre Sandyfields Rd DY3 3DL
☎ 01902 880503
e-mail: info@sedgleygolf.co.uk
Public pay and play course. Undulating contours and mature trees with extensive views over surrounding countryside.
9 holes, 3147yds, Par 72, SSS 70.
Club membership 100.
Visitors Mon-Sun & BHs. **Societies** Booking required. **Green Fees** £10.50 per 18 holes, £8 per 9 holes. **Prof** Garry Mercer **Course Designer** WG Cox **Facilities** **Location** 0.5m from town centre off A463

Hotel ★★★ 63% The Himley Country Hotel, School Rd, HIMLEY ☎ 0870 609 6112 73 en suite

SOLIHULL Map 07 SP17

Olton Mirfield Rd B91 1JH
☎ 0121 704 1936 0121 711 2010
e-mail: mailbox@oltongolfclub.fsnet.co.uk
web: www.oltongolf.co.uk
Parkland course, over 100 years old, with prevailing south-west wind.
18 holes, 6265yds, Par 69, SSS 70, Course record 63.
Club membership 600.
Visitors Mon, Tue, Thu, Fri except BHs. Handicap certficate. Dress code. **Societies** Booking required. **Green Fees** £50 per 36 holes, £45 per 27 holes, £40 per 18 holes. **Prof** Charles Haynes **Course Designer** JH Taylor **Facilities** **Conf** Corporate Hospitality Days **Location** M42 junct 5, A41 for 1.5m

Hotel ★★★★ 70% Renaissance Solihull Hotel, 651 Warwick Rd, SOLIHULL ☎ 0121 711 3000 179 en suite

Robin Hood St Bernards Rd B92 7DJ
☎ 0121 706 0061 0121 700 7502
e-mail: robin.hood.golf.club@dial.pipex.com
Pleasant parkland with easy walking and good views. Tree-lined fairways and varied holes, culminating in two excellent finishing holes.
18 holes, 6635yds, Par 72, SSS 72, Course record 68.
Club membership 650.
Visitors Mon-Fri except BHs. Handicap certificate. Dress code. **Societies** Booking required. **Green Fees** £30 per day. **Prof** Alan Harvey **Course Designer** H Colt **Facilities** **Conf** Corporate Hospitality Days **Location** 2m W off B4025

Hotel ★★★★ 70% Renaissance Solihull Hotel, 651 Warwick Rd, SOLIHULL ☎ 0121 711 3000 179 en suite

Shirley Stratford Rd, Monkspath, Shirley B90 4EW
☎ 0121 744 6001 0121 746 5645
e-mail: shirleygolfclub@btclick.com
Undulating parkland with water features.
18 holes, 6510yds, Par 72, SSS 71.
Club membership 600.
Visitors Mon-Fri except BHs. Handicap certificate. Dress code. **Societies** Booking required. **Green Fees** phone. **Prof** S Bottrill **Facilities** **Conf** facs Corporate Hospitality Days **Location** M42 junct 4, 0.5m N on A34

Hotel ★★★ 68% Corus hotel Solihull, Stratford Rd, Shirley, SOLIHULL ☎ 0870 609 6133 111 en suite

West Midlands Marsh House Farm Ln, Barston B92 0LB
☎ 01675 444890 01675 444891
e-mail: westmidlandsgc@aol.com
web: www.wmgc.co.uk
Course built to USGA specification with no temporary greens or tees. The 18th hole is a par 3 to an island green totally surrounded by water. A continuous buggy path allows use of buggies all year round.
18 holes, 6624yds, Par 72, SSS 72.
Club membership 750.
Societies Booking required. **Green Fees** phone. **Course Designer** Nigel & Mark Harrhy, David Griffith **Facilities** **Leisure** fishing. **Conf** facs Corporate Hospitality Days **Location** From NEC A45 towards Coventry for 0.5m, onto A452 towards Leamington, club on right

Hotel ★★★ 69% Arden Hotel & Leisure Club, Coventry Rd, Bickenhill, SOLIHULL ☎ 01675 443221 216 en suite

Championship Course

West Midlands Marriott Forest of Arden

Meriden Map 04 SP28

This is one of the finest golf destinations in the UK, with a range of facilities to impress every golfer. The jewel in the crown is the Arden championship parkland course, set in 10,000 acres of the Packington Estate. Designed by Donald Steel, it presents one of the country's most spectacular challenges and has hosted a succession of international tournaments, including the British Masters and English Open. Beware the 18th hole, which is enough to stretch the nerves of any golfer. The shorter Aylesford Course offers a varied and enjoyable challenge, which golfers of all abilities will find rewarding. Golf events are a speciality, and there is a golf academy and extensive leisure facilities.

Maxstoke Ln CV7 7HR
☎ 0870 400 7272 🖹 0870 400 7372
web: www.marriotthotels.com/cvtgs

Arden Course: 18 holes, 6707yds, Par 72, SSS 73, Course record 63.
Aylesford Course: 18 holes, 5801yds, Par 69, SSS 68.
Club membership 800.

Visitors Mon-Sun & BHs. Booking required. Handicap certificate. Dress code. **Societies** Booking required. **Green Fees** Arden £100, £110 Fri-Sun. Aylesford £45/£55. **Prof** Philip Hoye **Course Designer** Donald Steele **Facilities** **Leisure** hard tennis courts, heated indoor swimming pool, fishing, sauna, solarium, gymnasium, croquet lawn, health and beauty salon, steam room, jacuzzi, aerobics studio. **Conf facs** Corporate Hospitality Days **Location** 1m SW on B4102

Widney Manor Saintbury Dr, Widney Manor B91 3SZ
☎ 0121 704 0704 🖷 0121 704 7999
web: www.wmgc.co.uk
Parkland course of medium length, fairly easy walking, it is ideal for beginners and improvers. Other facilities include a driving range, all weather greens built to USGA specification and buggy paths.
18 holes, 5654yards, Par 71, SSS 66.
Club membership 650.
Visitors Booking up to 7 days in advance. **Societies** Booking required. **Green Fees** phone. **Prof** Tim Atkinson **Course Designer** Nigel & Mark Harrhy **Facilities** **Leisure** heated indoor swimming pool, sauna, solarium, gymnasium. **Conf** facs Corporate Hospitality Days **Location** M42 junct 4, signs to Monkspath Manor

Hotel ★★★★ 70% Renaissance Solihull Hotel, 651 Warwick Rd, SOLIHULL ☎ 0121 711 3000 179 en suite

STOURBRIDGE Map 07 SO88

Hagley Golf & Country Club Wassell Grove Ln, Hagley DY9 9JW
☎ 01562 883701 🖷 01562 887518
e-mail: manager@hagleygcc.freeserve.co.uk
web: www.hagleygolfandcountryclub.co.uk
Undulating parkland beneath the Clent Hills. Superb views. Testing 15th, par 5, 559yds, named Monster under Clent Hills.
18 holes, 6353yds, Par 72, SSS 72, Course record 66.
Club membership 700.
Visitors Mon-Fri except BHs. Booking required Wed. Handicap certificate. Dress code. **Societies** Booking required. **Green Fees** £35 per day, £30 per 18 holes. **Prof** Iain Clark **Course Designer** Garratt & Co **Facilities** **Leisure** squash. **Conf** facs Corporate Hospitality Days **Location** 1m E of Hagley off A456. 2m from junct 3 on M5

Hotel Premier Travel Inn Hagley, Birmingham Rd, HAGLEY ☎ 08701 977123 40 en suite

Stourbridge Worcester Ln, Pedmore DY8 2RB
☎ 01384 395566 🖷 01384 444660
e-mail: secretary@stourbridge-golf-club.co.uk
web: www.stourbridge-golf-club.co.uk
Parkland course.
18 holes, 6231yds, Par 70, SSS 69, Course record 67.
Club membership 705.
Visitors contact club for details. **Societies** Booking required. **Green Fees** £30 per 18 holes, £37.50 per day. **Prof** M Male **Facilities** **Conf** Corporate Hospitality Days **Location** 2m S from town centre

Hotel Premier Travel Inn Hagley, Birmingham Rd, HAGLEY ☎ 08701 977123 40 en suite

SUTTON COLDFIELD Map 07 SP19

Boldmere Monmouth Dr B73 6JL
☎ 0121 354 3379 🖷 0121 355 4534
Established municipal course with 10 par 3s and a lake coming into play on the 16th and 18th holes.
18 holes, 4493yds, Par 63, SSS 62, Course record 57.
Club membership 300.
Visitors Booking required. **Societies** Tue-Thu. Booking required in writing. **Green Fees** phone. **Prof** Trevor Short **Facilities** **Location** Next to Sutton Park

Hotel ★★★★ 68% Moor Hall Hotel & Spa, Moor Hall Dr, Four Oaks, SUTTON COLDFIELD ☎ 0121 308 3751 82 en suite

Little Aston Streetly B74 3AN
☎ 0121 353 2942 🖷 0121 580 8387
e-mail: manager@littleastongolf.co.uk
web: www.littleastongolf.co.uk
This parkland course is set in the rolling countryside of the former Little Aston Hall and there is a wide variety of mature trees. There are three par 3 holes and three par 5 holes and although the fairways are not unduly narrow there are rewards for accuracy - especially from the tee. The course features two lakes. At the par 5 12th the lake cuts into the green and at the par 4 17th the lake is also adjacent to the green.
18 holes, 6670yds, Par 72, SSS 73, Course record 63.
Club membership 350.
Visitors Mon-Wed, Fri, Sun & BHs. Booking required. Dress code. **Societies** Booking required. **Green Fees** £85 per day, £65 per round. **Prof** Brian Rimmer **Course Designer** H Vardon **Facilities** **Location** 3.5m NW of Sutton Coldfield off A454

Hotel ★★★★ 68% Moor Hall Hotel & Spa, Moor Hall Dr, Four Oaks, SUTTON COLDFIELD ☎ 0121 308 3751 82 en suite

Moor Hall Moor Hall Dr B75 6LN
☎ 0121 308 6130 🖷 0121 308 9560
e-mail: secretary@moorhallgolfclub.co.uk
Outstanding parkland course with mature trees lining the fairways. The 14th hole is notable and is part of a challenging finish to the round.
18 holes, 6293yds, Par 70, SSS 70, Course record 64.
Club membership 600.
Visitors Mon-Wed. Thu pm. Booking required. Dress code. **Societies** Booking required. **Green Fees** £55 per day, £40 per round. **Prof** Cameron Clark **Course Designer** Hawtree & Taylor **Facilities** **Conf** Corporate Hospitality Days **Location** 2.5m N of town centre off A453

Hotel ★★★★ 68% Moor Hall Hotel & Spa, Moor Hall Dr, Four Oaks, SUTTON COLDFIELD ☎ 0121 308 3751 82 en suite

Pype Hayes Eachel Hurst Rd, Walmley B76 1EP
☎ 0121 351 1014 🖷 0121 313 0206
e-mail: colinmarson@btinternet.com
Attractive, fairly flat course with excellent greens.
18 holes, 5927yds, Par 71, SSS 69, Course record 65.
Club membership 240.
Visitors Mon-Sun & BHs. Booking required. **Societies** booking required **Green Fees** £11 per 18 holes, £13 Sat & Sun. **Prof** Joe Kelly **Course Designer** Bobby Jones **Facilities** **Location** 2.5m S off B4148

Hotel ★★★★ 68% Moor Hall Hotel & Spa, Moor Hall Dr, Four Oaks, SUTTON COLDFIELD ☎ 0121 308 3751 82 en suite

Continued

Sutton Coldfield 110 Thornhill Rd, Streetly B74 3ER
☎ 0121 580 7878 0121 353 5503
e-mail: admin@suttoncoldfieldgc.com
web: www.suttoncoldfieldgc.com
A fine natural, all-weather, heathland course, with tight fairways, gorse, heather and trees. A good challenge for all standards of golfer.
18 holes, 6541yds, Par 72, SSS 71, Course record 65. Club membership 600.
Visitors Mon, Wed-Sun & BHs. Booking required. Dress code. **Societies** Booking required. **Green Fees** £40 per day, £30 per round, £40 per round Sat & Sun. **Prof** Jerry Hayes **Course Designer** A MacKenzie **Facilities** **Conf** facs Corporate Hospitality Days **Location** M6 junct 7, A34 towards Birmingham, 1st lights left onto A4041 Queslett Rd Thornhill Rd, entrance after 4th left

Hotel ★★★★ 68% Moor Hall Hotel & Spa, Moor Hall Dr, Four Oaks, SUTTON COLDFIELD ☎ 0121 308 3751 82 en suite

Walmley Brooks Rd, Wylde Green B72 1HR
☎ 0121 373 0029 0121 377 7272
e-mail: walmleygolfclub@aol.com
web: www.walmleygolfclub.co.uk
Pleasant parkland with many trees. The hazards are not difficult.
18 holes, 6585yds, Par 72, SSS 72, Course record 67. Club membership 700.
Visitors Mon, Wed-Fri except BHs. Booking required. Handicap certificate. Dress code. **Societies** Booking required. **Green Fees** £35 per 18+ holes, £30 per 18 holes. **Prof** CJ Wicketts **Facilities** **Conf** Corporate Hospitality Days **Location** 2m S off A5127

Hotel ★★★★ 68% Moor Hall Hotel & Spa, Moor Hall Dr, Four Oaks, SUTTON COLDFIELD ☎ 0121 308 3751 82 en suite

Wishaw Bulls Ln, Wishaw B76 9QW
☎ 0121 313 2110 0121 351 7498
Parkland with one hill on the course at the 9th and 18th holes. Well drained with irrigation on tees and greens.
18 holes, 5729yards, Par 70, SSS 68, Course record 67. Club membership 338.
Visitors Booking required. **Societies** Booking required. **Green Fees** phone. **Prof** Alan Partridge **Course Designer** R Wallis **Facilities** **Conf** facs Corporate Hospitality Days **Location** W of village off A4097

Hotel ★★★★ 75% De Vere Belfry, WISHAW ☎ 0870 900 0066 324 en suite

WALSALL Map 07 SP09

Bloxwich Stafford Rd, Bloxwich WS3 3PQ
☎ 01922 476593 ext 20 01922 493449
web: www.bloxwichgolfclub.com
Undulating parkland with natural hazards and subject to strong north wind.
18 holes, 6257yds, Par 71, SSS 71, Course record 68. Club membership 680.
Visitors Mon-Fri except BHs. Booking required. Handicap certificate. Dress code. **Societies** Booking required. **Green Fees** phone. **Prof** Richard J Dance **Facilities** **Conf** facs Corporate Hospitality Days **Location** M 6 junct 11/M6 (toll) T7, 3m N of town centre on A34

Hotel ★★★ 77% The Fairlawns at Aldridge, 178 Little Aston Rd, Aldridge, WALSALL ☎ 01922 455122 50 en suite

Calderfields Aldridge Rd WS4 2JS
☎ 01922 632243 01922 640540
e-mail: calderfield@bigfoot.com
web: www.calderfieldsgolf.com
Scenic parkland in peaceful setting, enhanced by a lake and water fountain.
18 holes, 6509yds, Par 73, SSS 71. Club membership 650.
Visitors Mon-Fri. Booking required Sat, Sun & BHs. Dress code. **Societies** Booking required. **Green Fees** £18 per 18 holes, £20 Sat, Sun & BHs. **Prof** Simon Edwin **Course Designer** Roy Winter **Facilities** **Leisure** fishing. **Conf** Corporate Hospitality Days **Location** On A454

Hotel ★★★ 77% The Fairlawns at Aldridge, 178 Little Aston Rd, Aldridge, WALSALL ☎ 01922 455122 50 en suite

Walsall The Broadway WS1 3EY
☎ 01922 613512 01922 616460
e-mail: golfclub@walsallgolf.freeserve.co.uk
web: www.walsallgolfclub.co.uk
18 holes, 6300yds, Par 70, SSS 70, Course record 65.
Course Designer A MacKenzie **Location** 1m S of town centre off A34
Phone for further details

Hotel ★★★ 66% Quality Hotel Birmingham North, Birmingham Rd, WALSALL ☎ 01922 633609 96 en suite

WEST BROMWICH Map 07 SP09

Dartmouth Vale St B71 4DW
☎ 0121 588 5746 & 588 2131
web: dartmouth-golf-club.co.uk
Very tight meadowland course with undulating but easy walking. The 617yd par 5 1st hole is something of a challenge.
9 holes, 6036yds, Par 71, SSS 71, Course record 66. Club membership 250.
Visitors With member Sat & Sun. After 2pm BHs. Booking required with professional. **Societies** Booking required. **Green Fees** phone. **Prof** G Kilmaster **Facilities** **Location** E of town centre off A4041

Hotel ★★★ 68% The Park Inn, Birmingham Rd, WEST BROMWICH ☎ 0121 609 9988 168 en suite

Sandwell Park Birmingham Rd B71 4JJ
☎ 0121 553 4637 📠 0121 525 1651
e-mail: secretary@sandwellparkgolfclub.co.uk
web: www.sandwellparkgolfclub.co.uk
A picturesque course wandering over wooded heathland and utilising natural features. Each hole is entirely separate, shielded from the others by either natural banks or lines of trees. A course that demands careful placing of shots that have been given a great deal of thought. Natural undulating fairways create difficult and testing approach shots to the greens.

18 holes, 6204yds, Par 71, SSS 71, Course record 65. Club membership 550.
Visitors Mon-Fri except BHs. Booking required. Handicap certificate. Dress code. **Societies** Booking required. **Green Fees** £50 per 27/36 holes, £40 per 18 holes. **Prof** Nigel Wylie **Course Designer** HS Colt **Facilities** **Leisure** practice chipping area. **Conf** facs Corporate Hospitality Days **Location** M5 junct 1, 200yds on A41

WOLVERHAMPTON Map 07 SO99

Oxley Park Stafford Rd, Bushbury WV10 6DE
☎ 01902 773989 📠 01902 773981
e-mail: secretary@oxleyparkgolfclub.co.uk
web: www.oxleyparkgolfclub.co.uk
Rolling parkland with trees, bunkers and water hazards.
18 holes, 6226yds, Par 71, SSS 71, Course record 66. Club membership 550.
Visitors contact club for details. **Societies** welcome. **Green Fees** £36 per day, £31 per 18 holes. **Prof** Les Burlison **Course Designer** H Colt **Facilities** by arrangement **Leisure** snooker. **Conf** facs Corporate Hospitality Days **Location** M54 junct 2, 2m S

Penn Penn Common, Penn WV4 5JN
☎ 01902 341142 📠 01902 620504
e-mail: penn-golf.freeserve.co.uk
Heathland course just outside the town.
18 holes, 6487yds, Par 70, SSS 72, Course record 65. Club membership 650.
Visitors Mon-Fri. Handicap certificate. Dress code. **Societies** Booking required. **Green Fees** £28 per 18 holes/£33 per day. **Prof** Guy Dean **Facilities** **Location** SW of town centre off A449

Hotel ★★★ 66% Quality Hotel Wolverhampton, Penn Rd, WOLVERHAMPTON ☎ 01902 429216 66 en suite 26 annexe en suite

South Staffordshire Danescourt Rd, Tettenhall WV6 9BQ
☎ 01902 751065 📠 01902 751159
e-mail: suelebeau@southstaffsgc.co.uk
web: www.southstaffsgc.co.uk
A parkland course.

18 holes, 6513yds, Par 71, SSS 71, Course record 67. Club membership 500.
Visitors Mon, Wed-Fri except BHs. Booking required. Handicap certificate. Dress code. **Societies** Booking required. **Green Fees** £36 per round. **Prof** Peter Baker, Shaun Ball **Course Designer** Harry Vardon **Facilities** **Conf** Corporate Hospitality Days **Location** 3m NW off A41

Three Hammers Short Course Old Stafford Rd, Coven WV10 7PP
☎ 01902 790428
web: www.3hammersgolfcomplex.co.uk
Well maintained short course designed by Henry Cotton and providing a unique challenge to golfers of all standards.
18 holes, 1438yds, Par 54, SSS 54, Course record 43.
Visitors Mon-Sun & BHs. **Societies** Booking required. **Green Fees** £6.50, £7.50 Sat, Sun & BHs. **Prof** Gary Gilligan **Course Designer** Henry Cotton **Facilities** **Conf** facs **Location** M54 junct 2, on A449 N

Wergs Keepers Ln, Tettenhall WV6 8UA
☎ 01902 742225 📠 01902 744748
e-mail: wergs.golfclub@btinternet.com
web: www.wergs.com
Gently undulating parkland with streams and ditches, a mix of evergreen and deciduous trees and large greens.
18 holes, 6250yds, Par 72, SSS 70. Club membership 150.
Visitors Mon-Fri. Booking required Sat, Sun & BHs. Dress code. **Societies** Booking required Sat & Sun. **Green Fees** £17 per day/round, £22 Sat, Sun & BHs. **Prof** Steve Weir **Course Designer** CW Moseley **Facilities** **Location** 3m W of Wolverhampton off A41

WIGHT, ISLE OF

COWES Map 04 SZ49

Cowes Crossfield Av PO31 8HN
☎ 01983 292303 (secretary) 📠 01983 292303
Fairly level, tight parkland course with difficult par 3s and Solent views.
9 holes, 5934yds, Par 70, SSS 68, Course record 66. Club membership 350.
Visitors contact club for details. **Societies** Booking

Continued

required. **Green Fees** £15, £18 Sat & Sun. **Course Designer** Hamilton-Stutt **Facilities** **Location** NW of town centre next to Cowes High School

Hotel ★★★ 68% New Holmwood Hotel, Queens Rd, Egypt Point, COWES ☎ 01983 292508 26 en suite

EAST COWES Map 04 SZ59

Osborne Osborne House Estate PO32 6JX
☎ 01983 295421
e-mail: info@osbornegolfclub.wanadoo.co.uk
web: www.osbornegolfclub.co.uk
Undulating parkland course in the grounds of Osborne House. Quiet and peaceful situation with outstanding views.
9 holes, 6398yds, Par 70, SSS 70, Course record 69.
Club membership 450.
Visitors Mon, Wed-Fri. Tue, Sat & Sun pm. BHs after 11am. Booking required Sat, Sun & BHs. Handicap certificate. Dress code. **Societies** Booking required. **Green Fees** £23, £27 Sat, Sun & BHs. **Facilities** **Leisure** caddies available. **Location** E of town centre off A3021, in Osborne House Estate

Hotel ★★★ 68% New Holmwood Hotel, Queens Rd, Egypt Point, COWES ☎ 01983 292508 26 en suite

FRESHWATER Map 04 SZ38

Freshwater Bay Afton Down PO40 9TZ
☎ 01983 752955 01983 752955
e-mail: tr.fbgc@btopenworld.com
web: www.isle-of-wight.uk.com/golf
18 holes, 5725yds, Par 69, SSS 68.
Course Designer JH Taylor **Location** 0.5m E of village off A3055
Phone for further details

Hotel ★★★ 68% Sentry Mead Hotel, Madeira Rd, TOTLAND BAY ☎ 01983 753212 14 en suite

NEWPORT Map 04 SZ58

Newport St George's Down, Shide PO30 3BA
☎ 01983 525076
e-mail: mail@newportgolfclub.co.uk
web: www.newportgolfclub.co.uk
Challenging nine-hole course with water hazards, dog legs and fine views.
9 holes, 5350yds, Par 68, SSS 66.
Club membership 350.
Visitors Mon-Wed, Fri except BHs. Thu & Sun pm. Booking required. **Societies** Booking required. **Green Fees** £20 per 18 holes, £25 Sat & Sun. **Course Designer** Guy Hunt **Facilities** **Location** 1.5m S off A3020, 200yds past Newport Football Club on left

Hotel ★★★ 68% New Holmwood Hotel, Queens Rd, Egypt Point, COWES ☎ 01983 292508 26 en suite

RYDE Map 04 SZ59

Ryde Binstead Rd PO33 3NF
☎ 01983 614809 01983 567418
e-mail: secretary@rydegolfclub.freeserve.co.uk
web: www.rydegolf.co.uk
9 holes, 5772yds, Par 70, SSS 69.
Course Designer Hamilton-Stutt **Location** 1m W from town centre on A3054
Phone for further details

Hotel ★★★ 65% Yelf's Hotel, Union St, RYDE
☎ 01983 564062 30 en suite

SANDOWN Map 04 SZ58

Shanklin & Sandown The Fairway, Lake PO36 9PR
☎ 01983 403217 (office) & 404424 (pro)
01983 403007 (office)/404424 (pro)
web: www.ssgolfclub.com
An 18-hole county championship course, recognised for its natural heathland beauty, spectacular views and challenging qualities. The course demands respect, with accurate driving and careful club selection the order of the day.
18 holes, 6062yds, Par 70, SSS 69, Course record 63.
Club membership 700.
Visitors Mon-Sun & BHs. Booking required. Handicap certificate. Dress code. **Societies** Booking required. **Green Fees** phone. **Prof** Peter Hammond **Course Designer** Braid **Facilities** **Location** From Sandown towards Shanklin past Heights Leisure Centre, 200yds right into Fairway for 1m

Hotel ★★ 67% Cygnet Hotel, 58 Carter St, SANDOWN
☎ 01983 402930 45 en suite

VENTNOR Map 04 SZ57

Ventnor Steephill Down Rd PO38 1BP
☎ 01983 853326 & 853388 01983 853326
e-mail: secretary@ventnorgolfclub.co.uk
web: www.ventnorgolfclub.co.uk
Downland course subject to wind. Fine seascapes.
12 holes, 5767yds, Par 70, SSS 68, Course record 64.
Club membership 297.
Visitors Mon-Sun except BHs. Dress code. **Societies** Booking required. **Green Fees** £15 per day, £20 Sat, Sun & BHs. **Facilities** **Leisure** practice nets. **Location** 1m NW off B3327, turn at chip shop

Hotel ★★★★ 67% The Royal Hotel, Belgrave Rd, VENTNOR ☎ 01983 852186 55 en suite

WILTSHIRE

BISHOPS CANNINGS Map 04 SU06

North Wilts SN10 2LP
☎ 01380 860627 01380 860877
e-mail: secretary@northwiltsgolf.com
web: northwiltsgolf.com
Established in 1890 and one of the oldest courses in Wiltshire, North Wilts is situated high on the downlands of Wiltshire, with spectacular views over the surrounding countryside. The chalk base allows free draining and the course provides a challenge to golfers of all abilities.
18 holes, 6414yds, Par 71, SSS 71, Course record 65.
Club membership 800.
Visitors Handicap certificate Sat & Sun. **Societies** Booking required. **Green Fees** phone. **Prof** Graham Laing **Course Designer** HS Colt **Facilities** **Conf** Corporate Hospitality Days **Location** 2m NW of Devizes between A4 & A361

Hotel ★★★ 66% Bear Hotel, Market Place, DEVIZES
☎ 01380 722444 24 en suite

Continued

BRADFORD-ON-AVON Map 03 ST86

Cumberwell Park BA15 2PQ
☎ 01225 863322 🖷 01225 868160
e-mail: enquiries@cumberwellpark.com
web: www.cumberwellpark.com
Set within tranquil woodland, parkland, lakes and rolling countryside, this 27-hole course comprises three linked sets of nine holes. A challenge for all levels of golfer.

Parkland: 9 holes, 6405yds, Par 71, SSS 71, Course record 63.
Woodland: 9 holes, 6356yds, Par 72, SSS 70.
Lakeland: 9 holes, 6509, Par 71, SSS 71.
Club membership 1300.
Visitors Mon-Sun & BHs. Booking required. Dress code. **Societies** Booking required. **Green Fees** £40 per 27 holes, £27 per 18 holes, £17 per 9 holes, £50/£33/£23 Sat, Sun & BHs. **Prof** John Jacobs **Course Designer** Adrian Stiff **Facilities** **Conf** facs Corporate Hospitality Days **Location** 1.5m N on A363

Hotel ★★★ 74% Woolley Grange, Woolley Green, BRADFORD-ON-AVON ☎ 01225 864705 14 en suite 12 annexe en suite

CALNE Map 03 ST97

Bowood Golf & Country Club Derry Hill SN11 9PQ
☎ 01249 822228 🖷 01249 822218
e-mail: golfclub@bowood.org
web: www.bowood.org
This Dave Thomas designed course weaves through 200 acres of 'Capability' Brown's mature woodland with cavernous moulded bunkers, skilfully planned hillocks defining the fairways and vast rolling greens. Numerous doglegs, bunkers, tees and lakes will prove a test for any golfer.

18 holes, 6890yds, Par 72, SSS 73, Course record 63.
Club membership 500.

Continued

Visitors Mon-Fri & BHs. Sat & Sun pm. Dress code. **Societies** Booking required. **Green Fees** Mon-Fri £46, Sat & Sun £48. **Prof** John Hansel **Course Designer** Dave Thomas **Facilities** **Leisure** Bowood House and Gardens. **Conf** facs Corporate Hospitality Days **Location** 2.5m W of Calne off A4

Hotel ★★★ 68% Lansdowne Strand Hotel, The Strand, CALNE ☎ 01249 812488 21 en suite 5 annexe en suite

CASTLE COMBE Map 03 ST87

Manor House Hotel & Golf Club SN14 7JW
☎ 01249 782206 🖷 01249 782992
e-mail: enquiries@manorhousegolfclub.com
web: www.exclusivehotels.co.uk
Set in a wonderful location within the wooded estate of the 14th-century Manor House, this course includes five par 5s and some spectacular par 3s. Manicured fairways and hand-cut greens, together with the River Bybrook meandering through the middle make for a picturesque and dramatic course.
18 holes, 6500yds, Par 72.
Club membership 450.
Visitors Mon-Fri. Sat, Sun & BHs pm. Booking required. Handicap certificate. Dress code. **Societies** Booking required. **Green Fees** Summer £75, £90 Fri-Sun. Spring & autumn £65/£80. Winter £40 Mon-Sun. **Prof** Steve Slinger, Peter Green **Course Designer** Peter Alliss, Clive Clark **Facilities** **Leisure** hard tennis courts, heated outdoor swimming pool, fishing, sauna, snooker, croquet. **Conf** facs Corporate Hospitality Days **Location** 5m NW of Chippenham on B4039

Hotel ★★★★ Manor House Hotel and Golf Club, CASTLE COMBE ☎ 01249 782206 22 en suite 26 annexe en suite

CHIPPENHAM Map 03 ST97

Chippenham Malmesbury Rd SN15 5LT
☎ 01249 652040 🖷 01249 446681
e-mail: chippenhamgc@onetel.com
web: www.chippenhamgolfclub.com
Easy walking on downland course. Testing holes at 1st and 15th.
18 holes, 5327yds, Par 69, SSS 66.
Club membership 650.
Visitors Mon-Sun & BHs. Dress code. **Societies** Booking required. **Green Fees** £30 per day, £22 per round, £27 per round Sat, Sun & BHs. **Prof** Bill Creamer **Facilities** **Conf** Corporate Hospitality Days **Location** M4 junct 17, 1m N of Chippenham by A350

Hotel ★★★★ Manor House Hotel and Golf Club, CASTLE COMBE ☎ 01249 782206 22 en suite 26 annexe en suite

If the name of the club appears in italics, details have not been confirmed for this edition of the guide

CRICKLADE Map 04 SU09

Cricklade Hotel & Country Club Common Hill SN6 6HA
☎ 01793 750751 🖷 01793 751767
e-mail: reception@crickladehotel.co.uk
web: www.crickladehotel.co.uk
A challenging nine-hole course with undulating greens and beautiful views. Par 3 6th (128yds) signature hole from an elevated tee to a green protected by a deep pot bunker.

9 holes, 1830yds, Par 62, SSS 58, Course record 59. Club membership 130.
Visitors Mon-Fri except BHs. Dress code. **Societies** Booking required. **Green Fees** £25 per day, £16 per 18 holes. **Prof** Ian Bolt **Course Designer** Ian Bolt, Colin Smith **Facilities** **Leisure** hard tennis courts, heated indoor swimming pool, solarium, gymnasium, snooker, pool, jacuzzi, tennis, steam room. **Conf** facs **Location** On B4040 from Cricklade towards Malmesbury

Hotel ★★★ 72% Cricklade Hotel, Common Hill, CRICKLADE ☎ 01793 750751 25 en suite 21 annexe en suite

ERLESTOKE Map 03 ST95

Erlestoke Sands SN10 5UB
☎ 01380 831069 🖷 01380 831284
e-mail: info@erlestokesands.co.uk
web: www.erlestokesands.co.uk
The course is set on the lower slopes of Salisbury Plain with distant views to the Cotswolds and the Marlborough Downs. The 7th plunges from an elevated three-tiered tee, high in the woods, to a large green with a spectacular backdrop of a meandering river and hills. The course was built to suit every standard of golfer from the novice to the very low handicapper and its two tiers offer lakes and rolling downland.
18 holes, 6406yds, Par 73, SSS 71, Course record 66. Club membership 720.
Visitors Booking required. Dress code. **Societies** Booking required. **Green Fees** phone. **Prof** Michael Waters **Course Designer** Adrian Stiff **Facilities** **Location** On B3098 Devizes-Westbury road

Hotel ★★★ 66% Bear Hotel, Market Place, DEVIZES ☎ 01380 722444 24 en suite

GREAT DURNFORD Map 04 SU13

High Post SP4 6AT
☎ 01722 782356 🖷 01722 782674
e-mail: admin@highpostgolfclub.co.uk
web: www.highpostgolfclub.co.uk
The free-draining, easy walking downland course offers summer tees and greens all year. The opening three holes, usually played with the wind, get you to off to a flying start, but the closing three provide a tough finish. Peter Alliss has rated the 9th among his dream holes. The club welcomes golfers of all abilities.

18 holes, 6305yds, Par 70, SSS 70, Course record 64. Club membership 625.
Visitors Mon-Sun & BHs. Dress code. **Societies** Booking required. **Green Fees** £40 per day, £32 per round, £50/£42 Sat & Sun. **Prof** Tony Isaacs **Course Designer** Hawtree & Ptrs **Facilities** **Conf** facs Corporate Hospitality Days **Location** On A345 between Salisbury & Amesbury

HIGHWORTH Map 04 SU29

Highworth Community Golf Centre Swindon Rd SN6 7SJ
☎ 01793 766014 🖷 01793 766014
9 holes, 3120yds, Par 35, SSS 35, Course record 29.
Course Designer T Watt, B Sandry, D Lang **Location** Off A361 Swindon-Lechlade road
Phone for further details

Hotel ★★★ 70% Sudbury House Hotel & Conference Centre, London St, FARINGDON ☎ 01367 241272 49 en suite

Wrag Barn Golf & Country Club Shrivenham Rd SN6 7QQ
☎ 01793 861327 🖷 01793 861325
e-mail: info@wragbarn.com
web: www.wragbarn.com
A fast maturing parkland course in an Area of Outstanding Natural Beauty with views to the Lambourne Hills and Vale of the White Horse.
18 holes, 6633yds, Par 72, SSS 72, Course record 65. Club membership 750.
Visitors Mon-Fri. Booking required Sat, Sun & BHs. Handicap certificate. Dress code. **Societies** welcome. **Green Fees** phone. **Prof** Barry Loughrey **Course Designer** Hawtree **Facilities** **Conf** facs Corporate Hospitality Days **Location** On B4000 from Highworth, signed

Hotel ★★★ 68% Stanton House Hotel, The Avenue, Stanton Fitzwarren, SWINDON ☎ 01793 861777 84 en suite

KINGSDOWN Map 03 ST86

Kingsdown SN13 8BS
☎ 01225 743472 🖹 01225 743472
e-mail: kingsdowngc@btconnect.com
web: www.kingsdowngolfclub.co.uk
Fairly flat, open downland course with very sparse tree cover but surrounding wood. Many interesting holes with testing features.
18 holes, 6445yds, Par 72, SSS 71, Course record 64. Club membership 650.
Visitors Mon-Fri except BHs. Handicap certificate. Dress code. **Societies** Booking required. **Green Fees** £34 per day. **Prof** Andrew Butler **Facilities** **Location** W of village between Corsham and Bathford

Hotel ★★★★ Lucknam Park, COLERNE
☎ 01225 742777 23 en suite 18 annexe en suite

LANDFORD Map 04 SU21

Hamptworth Golf & Country Club
Hamptworth Rd, Hamptworth SP5 2DU
☎ 01794 390155 🖹 01794 390022
e-mail: info@hamptworthgolf.co.uk
web: www.hamptworthgolf.co.uk
Hamptworth enjoys ancient woodland and an abundance of wildlife in a beautiful setting on the edge of the New Forest. The 14th is one of its most challenging holes with a narrow fairway guarded by established forest oaks. The 2nd is a dog-leg of 543yds and plays differently all year.

18 holes, 6516yds, Par 72, SSS 71, Course record 68. Club membership 750.
Visitors Mon-Sun & BHs. Booking required. Dress code. **Societies** Booking required. **Green Fees** Apr-Sep £30 per round, £40 Sat & Sun. Oct-Mar £20-£25, £30 Sat & Sun. **Prof** M White **Course Designer** Philip Sanders, Brian Pierson **Facilities** **Leisure** hard tennis courts, gymnasium, croquet lawns. **Conf** facs Corporate Hospitality Days **Location** 1.5m W of Landford off B3079

Hotel ★★★ 69% Bartley Lodge, Lyndhurst Rd, CADNAM ☎ 023 8081 2248 31 en suite

MARLBOROUGH Map 04 SU16

Marlborough The Common SN8 1DU
☎ 01672 512147 🖹 01672 513164
e-mail: contactus@marlboroughgolfclub.co.uk
web: www.marlboroughgolfclub.co.uk
Undulating downland course with extensive views over the Og valley and the Marlborough Downs.

Continued

18 holes, 6514yds, Par 72, SSS 71, Course record 61. Club membership 900.
Visitors Mon-Sun & BHs. Handicap certificate Sat & Sun. Dress code. **Societies** Booking required. **Green Fees** £40 per day, £29 per round, £52/£31 Sat & Sun. **Prof** S Amor **Facilities** **Conf** facs Corporate Hospitality Days **Location** N of town centre on A346

Hotel ★★★ 64% The Castle & Ball, High St, MARLBOROUGH ☎ 01672 515201 34 en suite

OGBOURNE ST GEORGE Map 04 SU27

Ogbourne Downs SN8 1TB
☎ 01672 841327 🖹 01672 841101
web: www.ogdgc.co.uk
Downland turf and magnificent greens. Wind and slopes make this one of the most challenging courses in Wiltshire. Extensive views.
18 holes, 6363yds, Par 71, SSS 70, Course record 65. Club membership 800.
Visitors Mon-Fri except BHs. Booking required Wed & Fri. Dress code. **Societies** Booking required. **Green Fees** phone. **Prof** Andrew Kirk **Course Designer** JH Taylor **Facilities** **Location** N of village on A346

Hotel ★★★ 64% The Castle & Ball, High St, MARLBOROUGH ☎ 01672 515201 34 en suite

SALISBURY Map 04 SU12

Salisbury & South Wilts Netherhampton SP2 8PR
☎ 01722 742645 🖹 01722 742676
e-mail: mail@salisburygolf.co.uk
web: www.salisburygolf.co.uk
Gently undulating and well-drained parkland courses in country setting with panoramic views of the cathedral and surrounding countryside. Never easy with six excellent opening holes and four equally testing closing holes.
Main Course: 18 holes, 6485yds, Par 71, SSS 71, Course record 61.
Bibury Course: 9 holes, 2837yds, Par 34.
Club membership 1150.
Visitors Mon-Fri. Booking required Sat, Sun & BHs. Handicap certificate. Dress code. **Societies** Booking required. **Green Fees** Main £32 per day, £26 per 18 holes. Bibury £13 per 18 holes, £10 per 9 holes. **Prof** Geraldine Teschner **Course Designer** JH Taylor, S Gidman **Facilities** **Conf** facs Corporate Hospitality Days **Location** 2m SW of Salisbury on A3094

SWINDON Map 04 SU18

Broome Manor Golf Complex Pipers Way SN3 1RG
☎ 01793 532403 (bookings) 495761 (enquiries)
🖹 01793 433255
Two courses and a 34-bay floodlit driving range. Parkland with water hazards, open fairways and short cut rough. Walking is easy on gentle slopes.
18 holes, 5989yds, Par 71, SSS 70, Course record 61.
9 holes, Par 33.
Club membership 800.
Visitors Mon-Sun & BHs. Booking required. **Societies** welcome. **Green Fees** £26 per 18 holes, £12 per 9 holes. **Prof** Barry Sandry **Course Designer** Hawtree **Facilities**

Continued

Leisure gymnasium. **Conf** facs Corporate Hospitality Days **Location** 1.75m SE of town centre off B4006

Hotel ★★★★ 67% Swindon Marriott Hotel, Pipers Way, SWINDON ☎ 0870 400 7281 156 en suite

TIDWORTH Map 04 SU24

Tidworth Garrison Bulford Rd SP9 7AF
☎ 01980 842301 🖹 01980 842301
e-mail: tidworth@garrison-golfclub.fsnet.co.uk
web: www.tidworthgolfclub.co.uk
A breezy, dry downland course with lovely turf, fine trees and views over Salisbury Plain and the surrounding area. The 4th and 12th holes are notable. The 565yd 14th, going down towards the clubhouse, gives the big hitter a chance to let fly.
18 holes, 6320yds, Par 70, SSS 70, Course record 63. Club membership 750.
Visitors Mon-Thu. Booking required Sat, Sun & BHs. Handicap certificate. Dress code. **Societies** Booking required. **Green Fees** £36 per round/day. **Prof** Terry Gosden **Course Designer** Donald Steel **Facilities** **Location** W of village off A338

Hotel ★★★ 62% Quality Hotel Andover, Micheldever Rd, ANDOVER ☎ 01264 369111 13 en suite 36 annexe en suite

TOLLARD ROYAL Map 03 ST91

Rushmore SP5 5QB
☎ 01725 516326 🖹 01725 516437
e-mail: andrea@rushmoregolfclub.co.uk
web: www.rushmoregolfclub.co.uk
Peaceful and testing parkland course situated on Cranborne Chase with far-reaching views. An undulating course with avenues of trees and well-drained greens. With water on seven out of 18 holes, it will test the most confident of golfers.
18 holes, 6131yds, Par 71, SSS 70. Club membership 679.
Visitors Mon-Sun & BHs. Booking required. Dress code. **Societies** Booking required. **Green Fees** £25 per 18 holes, £30 Sat & Sun. **Prof** Phil Jenkins **Course Designer** David Pottage, John Jacobs Developments **Facilities** by arrangement **Conf** facs Corporate Hospitality Days **Location** N off B3081 between Sixpenny Handley & Tollard Royal

Hotel ★★★ 67% Royal Chase Hotel, Royal Chase Roundabout, SHAFTESBURY ☎ 01747 853355 33 en suite

UPAVON Map 04 SU15

Upavon Douglas Av SN9 6BQ
☎ 01980 630787 & 630281 🖹 01980 635419
e-mail: play@upavongolfclub.co.uk
web: www.upavongolfclub.co.uk
Free-draining course on chalk downland with panoramic views over the Vale of Pewsey and the Alton Barnes White Horse. A fair test of golf with a good mixture of holes including a 602yd par 5 and an excellent finishing hole, a par 3 of 169yds across a valley.
18 holes, 6402yds, Par 71, SSS 71, Course record 69. Club membership 600.
Visitors Mon-Fri. Booking required Sat, Sun & BHs. Dress code. **Societies** Booking required. **Green Fees** £30 per day, £40 Sat & Sun. **Prof** Richard Blake **Course Designer** Richard Blake **Facilities** by arrangement **Location** 1.5m SE of Upavon on A342

Hotel ★★★ 66% Bear Hotel, Market Place, DEVIZES ☎ 01380 722444 24 en suite

WARMINSTER Map 03 ST84

West Wilts Elm Hill BA12 0AU
☎ 01985 213133 🖹 01985 219809
e-mail: sec@westwiltsgolfclub.co.uk
web: www.westwiltsgolfclub.co.uk
A hilltop chalk downland course among the Wiltshire downs. Free draining, short, but a very good test of accurate iron play. Excellent fairways and greens all year round.
18 holes, 5754yds, Par 70, SSS 68, Course record 60. Club membership 570.
Visitors Mon-Fri, Sun & BHs. Booking required Sun. Handicap certificate. Dress code. **Societies** Booking required. **Green Fees** £30 per day/round, £35 Sun & BHs. **Prof** Rob Morris **Course Designer** JH Taylor **Facilities** **Location** N of town centre off A350

Hotel ★★★★ 79% Bishopstrow House, WARMINSTER ☎ 01985 212312 32 en suite

WOOTTON BASSETT Map 04 SU08

Brinkworth Longmans Farm, Brinkworth SN15 5DG
☎ 01666 510277
18 holes, 5884yds, Par 70, SSS 70.
Course Designer Jullian Sheppard **Location** Off B4042 between Malmesbury & Wootton Bassett
Phone for further details

Hotel ★★★ 67% Marsh Farm Hotel, Coped Hall, WOOTTON BASSETT ☎ 01793 848044 11 en suite 39 annexe en suite

Wiltshire Vastern SN4 7PB
☎ 01793 849999 🖹 01793 849988
e-mail: thelodge@the-wiltshire.co.uk
web: www.the-wiltshire.co.uk
A Peter Alliss and Clive Clark design set in rolling Wiltshire downland. A number of lakes add a challenge for both low and high handicappers.
18 holes, 6519yds, Par 72, SSS 72, Course record 67. Club membership 800.
Visitors contact club for details. Dress code. **Societies** Booking required. **Green Fees** £25 per 18 holes, £35 Sat, Sun & BHs. **Course Designer** Peter Allis & Clive Clark **Facilities** **Leisure** heated indoor swimming pool, sauna, solarium, gymnasium, creche, jacuzzi. **Conf** facs Corporate Hospitality Days **Location** Off A3102 SW of Wootton Bassett

Hotel ★★★ 69% The Wiltshire Hotel & Country Club, WOOTTON BASSETT ☎ 01793 849999 58 en suite

Continued

WORCESTERSHIRE

ALVECHURCH Map 07 SP07

Kings Norton Brockhill Ln, Weatheroak B48 7ED
☎ 01564 826706 & 826789 🖷 01564 826955
e-mail: info@kingsnortongolfclub.co.uk
web: www.kingsnortongolfclub.co.uk
Parkland with water hazards. A 27-hole championship venue playing as three combinations of nine holes.
Weatheroak: 18 holes, 6748yds, Par 72, SSS 72, Course record 65.
Brockhill: 18 holes, 6648yds, Par 72, SSS 72.
Wythall: 18 holes, 6612yds, Par 72, SSS 72.
Club membership 1000.
Visitors Mon-Fri except BHs. Handicap certificate. Dress code. **Societies** Booking required. **Green Fees** phone. **Prof** Kevin Hayward **Course Designer** F Hawtree **Facilities** **Leisure** par 3 course. **Conf** facs Corporate Hospitality Days **Location** M42 junct 3, off A435

Hotel ★★★★ 66% The Bromsgrove Hotel, Kidderminster Rd, BROMSGROVE ☎ 01527 576600 109 en suite

BEWDLEY Map 07 SO77

Little Lakes Golf and Country Club
Lye Head DY12 2UZ
☎ 01299 266385 🖷 01299 266398
e-mail: mark.laing@littlelakes.co.uk
web: www.little-lakes.co.uk
A pleasant undulating 18-hole parkland course. A challenging test of golf with stunning views of the Worcestershire countryside. Well acclaimed for the use of natural features.

18 holes, 6298yds, Par 71, SSS 70, Course record 68.
Club membership 475.
Visitors Mon-Sun & BHs. Booking required. Dress code. **Societies** Booking required. **Green Fees** £19, £24 Sat & Sun. **Prof** Mark A Laing **Course Designer** M Laing **Facilities** by arrangement by arrangement by arrangement by arrangement **Leisure** hard tennis courts, heated outdoor swimming pool, fishing. **Conf** facs **Location** 2.25m W of Bewdley off A456

Wharton Park Longbank DY12 2QW
☎ 01299 405163 🖷 01299 405121
e-mail: enquiries@whartonpark.co.uk
web: www.whartonpark.co.uk
An 18-hole championship-standard course set in 200 acres of beautiful Worcestershire countryside, with stunning views. Some long par 5s such as the 9th (594yds) as well as superb par 3 holes at 3rd, 10th and 15th make this a very challenging course.

Wharton Park

18 holes, 6435yds, Par 72, SSS 71, Course record 66.
Club membership 500.
Visitors contact club for details. Dress code. **Societies** Booking required. **Green Fees** phone. **Prof** Angus Hoare **Course Designer** Howard Swan **Facilities** **Conf** facs Corporate Hospitality Days **Location** Off A456 Bewdley bypass

BISHAMPTON Map 03 SO95

Vale Golf Club Hill Furze Rd WR10 2LZ
☎ 01386 462781 🖷 01386 462597
e-mail: vale-sales@crown-golf.co.uk
web: www.crown-golf.co.uk
This course offers an American-style layout, with large greens, trees and bunkers and several water hazards. Its rolling fairways provide a testing round, as well as superb views of the Malvern Hills. Picturesque and peaceful.
International Course: 18 holes, 7174yds, Par 74, SSS 74, Course record 67.
Lenches Course: 9 holes, 5518yds, Par 70, SSS 66.
Club membership 800.
Visitors Mon-Sun & BHs. Booking required Dress code. **Societies** Booking required. **Green Fees** International £28 per round, £40 Sat & Sun. Lenches 9 holes £11, £12. **Prof** Richard Jenkins **Course Designer** Bob Sandow **Facilities** **Conf** facs Corporate Hospitality Days **Location** Signed off A44

Hotel ★★★ 72% Salford Hall Hotel, ABBOT'S SALFORD ☎ 01386 871300 & 0800 212671 🖷 01386 871301 14 en suite 19 annexe en suite

BROADWAY Map 04 SP03

Broadway Willersey Hill WR12 7LG
☎ 01386 853683 🖷 01386 858643
e-mail: secretary@broadwaygolfclub.co.uk
web: www.broadwaygolfclub.co.uk
At the edge of the Cotswolds this downland course lies at an altitude of 900ft above sea level, with extensive views. Natural contours and man-made hazards mean that drives have to be placed, approaches carefully judged and the greens expertly read.
18 holes, 6228yds, Par 72, SSS 70, Course record 66.
Club membership 850.
Visitors Not Sat Apr-Sep before 3pm. Booking required. **Societies** Wed-Fri. Booking required. **Green Fees** phone. **Prof** Martyn Freeman **Course Designer** James Braid **Facilities** **Conf** facs Corporate Hospitality Days **Location** 1.5m E on A44

Continued

Continued

Hotel ★★★ 79% Dormy House Hotel, Willersey Hill, BROADWAY ☎ 01386 852711 25 en suite 22 annexe en suite

Guest House ♦♦♦♦ Leasow House, Laverton Meadows, BROADWAY ☎ 01386 584526 📠 01386 584596 5 en suite 2 annexe en suite

BROMSGROVE Map 07 SO97

Blackwell Agmore Rd, Blackwell B60 1PY

☎ 0121 445 1994 📠 0121 445 4911
e-mail: info@blackwellgolfclub.com
web: www.blackwellgolfclub.co.uk

Mature undulating parkland course over a 110 years old, with a variety of trees. Laid out in two nine-hole loops.

18 holes, 6080yds, Par 70, SSS 71, Course record 61.
Club membership 355.

Visitors Mon, Wed-Fri except BHs. Tue pm. Handicap certificate. Dress code. **Societies** Booking required. **Green Fees** £65 per 18 holes, £75 per 27/36 holes. **Prof** Finlay Clark **Course Designer** Herbert Fowler, Tom Simpson **Facilities** by arrangement **Conf** Corporate Hospitality Days **Location** 2.5m NE of Bromsgrove off B4096

Guest House ♦♦♦♦ Amberley, Aqueduct Ln, ALVECHURCH ☎ 0121 445 6526 & 07854 496006

Bromsgrove Golf Centre Stratford Rd B60 1LD

☎ 01527 575886 & 570505 📠 01527 570964
e-mail: enquiries@bromsgrovegolfcentre.com
web: www.bromsgrovegolfcentre.com

This gently undulating course with superb views over Worcestershire is not to be underestimated. Creative landscaping and a selection of well-defined bunkers ensure that the course delivers a uniquely satisfying experience through a variety of challenging, yet enjoyable, holes.

Continued

Bromsgrove Golf Centre

18 holes, 5969yds, Par 68, SSS 69.
Club membership 900.

Visitors Mon-Sun + BHs. Booking required Fri-Sun & BHs. Dress code. **Societies** Booking required. **Green Fees** £19.40 per 18 holes, £25 Sat & Sun. Discount scheme available. **Prof** Graeme Long, Danny Wall **Course Designer** Hawtree & Son **Facilities** **Conf** facs Corporate Hospitality Days **Location** 1m from town centre at junct A38A448, signed

Hotel ★★★★ 66% The Bromsgrove Hotel, Kidderminster Rd, BROMSGROVE ☎ 01527 576600 109 en suite

DROITWICH Map 03 SO86

Droitwich Golf & Country Club Ford Ln WR9 0BQ

☎ 01905 774344 📠 01905 797290
e-mail: droitwich-golf-club@tiscali.co.uk

Undulating wooded parkland with scenic views from the highest points.

18 holes, 5976yds, Par 70, SSS 69, Course record 62.
Club membership 732.

Visitors Mon-Fri except BHs. Handicap certificate. Dress code. **Societies** Booking required. **Green Fees** £30 per day, £25 per round. **Course Designer** J Braid, G Franks **Facilities** **Leisure** snooker. **Conf** Corporate Hospitality Days **Location** M5 junct 5, off A38 at Droitwich opposite Chateau Impney Hotel

Hotel ★★★★ 67% Chateau Impney Hotel, DROITWICH SPA ☎ 01905 774411 67 en suite 53 annexe en suite

Gaudet Luce Middle Ln, Hadzor WR9 7DP

☎ 01905 796375 📠 01905 797245
e-mail: info@gaudet-luce.co.uk
web: www.gaudet-luce.co.uk

18 holes, 6040yds, Par 70, SSS 68.

Course Designer MA Laing **Location** M5 junct 5, left at Tagwell Rd onto Middle Ln, 1st driveway on left
Phone for further details

Hotel ★★★★ 67% Chateau Impney Hotel, DROITWICH SPA ☎ 01905 774411 67 en suite 53 annexe en suite

Ombersley Bishops Wood Rd, Lineholt, Ombersley WR9 0LE

☎ 01905 620747 📠 01905 620047
e-mail: enquiries@ombersleygolfclub
web: www.ombersleygolfclub.co.uk

Undulating course in beautiful countryside high above the edge of the Severn valley. Covered driving range and putting green.

Continued

18 holes, 6139yds, Par 72, SSS 69, Course record 67.
Club membership 750.
Visitors Mon-Sun & BHs. Booking required. Dress code. **Societies** Booking required. **Green Fees** £18.95 per 18 holes, £11.40 per 9 holes, £26.90/£16.20 Sat, Sun & BHs. **Prof** Glenister, Woodman, Garbett **Course Designer** David Morgan **Facilities** **Leisure** chipping green & practice bunker. **Conf** facs Corporate Hospitality Days **Location** 3m W of Droitwich off A449. At Mitre Oak pub A4025 to Stourport, signed 400yds on left

Hotel ★★★★ 62% Raven Hotel, Victoria Square, DROITWICH SPA ☎ 01905 772224 72 en suite

FLADBURY Map 03 SO94

Evesham Craycombe Links, Old Worcester Rd WR10 2QS

☎ 01386 860395 🖷 01386 861356
e-mail: eveshamgolfclub@talk21.com
web: eveshamgolf.com
9 holes, 6415yds, Par 72, Course record 65.
Location 0.75m N on A4538
Phone for further details

Hotel ★★★ 77% The Evesham Hotel, Coopers Ln, Off Waterside, EVESHAM
☎ 01386 765566 & 0800 716969 (Res) 🖷 01386 765443
39 en suite 1 annexe en suite

HOLLYWOOD Map 07 SP07

Gay Hill Hollywood Ln B47 5PP

☎ 0121 430 8544 & 474 6001 (pro) 🖷 0121 436 7796
e-mail: secretary@ghgc.org.uk
web: www.ghgc.org.uk
Parkland with some 10,000 trees and a brook running through.
18 holes, 6406yds, Par 72, SSS 72, Course record 64.
Club membership 700.
Visitors Mon-Sun except BHs. Booking required. Handicap certificate. Dress code. **Societies** Booking required. **Green Fees** £32 per day. **Prof** Chris Harrison **Facilities** **Location** N of village

Hotel ★★★ 68% Corus hotel Solihull, Stratford Rd, Shirley, SOLIHULL ☎ 0870 609 6133 111 en suite

KIDDERMINSTER Map 07 SO87

Churchill and Blakedown Churchill Ln, Blakedown DY10 3NB

☎ 01562 700018 🖷 0871 242 2049
e-mail: cbgolfclub@tiscali.co.uk
Mature hilly course, playable all year round, with good views.
9 holes, 6488yds, Par 72, SSS 71.
Club membership 410.
Visitors Tue, Wed, Fri & BHs. Booking required. Handicap certificate. Dress code. **Societies** Booking required. **Green Fees** £25. **Prof** G Wright **Facilities** **Conf** Corporate Hospitality Days **Location** W of village off A456

Hotel ★★★★ 68% Stone Manor Hotel, Stone, KIDDERMINSTER ☎ 01562 777555 52 en suite 5 annexe en suite

Habberley Low Trimpley DY11 5RF

☎ 01562 745756 🖷 01562 745756
Very hilly, wooded parkland.
9 holes, 5401yds, Par 69, Course record 62.
Club membership 122.
Visitors Mon-Fri except BHs. Handicap certificate. Dress code. **Societies** Booking required. **Green Fees** Summer £15 per day. Winter £10. **Facilities** **Location** 2m NW of Kidderminster

Hotel ★★★★ 68% Stone Manor Hotel, Stone, KIDDERMINSTER ☎ 01562 777555 52 en suite 5 annexe en suite

Kidderminster Russell Rd DY10 3HT

☎ 01562 822303 🖷 01562 827866
e-mail: info@kidderminstergolfclub.com
web: www.kidderminstergolfclub.com
Pleasant wooded parkland course, mainly flat, but a good test of golf for all levels of player. Two small lakes add to the challenge.

18 holes, 6422yds, Par 72, SSS 71, Course record 65.
Club membership 860.
Visitors Mon-Fri except BHs. Booking required. Handicap certificate. Dress code. **Societies** Booking required. **Green Fees** £35 per day/round. **Prof** Pat Smith **Facilities** **Conf** facs Corporate Hospitality Days **Location** 0.5m SE of town centre, signed off A449

Hotel ★★★★ 68% Stone Manor Hotel, Stone, KIDDERMINSTER ☎ 01562 777555 52 en suite 5 annexe en suite

Wyre Forest Zortech Av DY11 7EX

☎ 01299 822682 🖷 01299 879433
e-mail: chris@wyreforestgolf.com
web: www.wyreforestgolf.co.uk
Making full use of the existing contours, this interesting and challenging course is bounded by woodland and gives extensive views over the surrounding area. Well drained fairways and greens give an inland links style.
18 holes, 5790yds, Par 70, SSS 68, Course record 68.
Club membership 397.
Visitors Mon-Fri. Booking required Sat, Sun & BHs. Dress code. **Societies** Booking required. **Green Fees** £15 per 18 holes, £20 Sat & Sun. **Prof** Chris Botterill **Facilities** **Conf** Corporate Hospitality Days **Location** On A451 between Kidderminster & Stourport

Hotel ★★★★ 73% Menzies Stourport Manor, Hartlebury Rd, STOURPORT-ON-SEVERN ☎ 01299 289955 68 en suite

MALVERN WELLS Map 03 SO74

Worcestershire Wood Farm, Wood Farm Rd WR14 4PP
01684 575992 01684 893334
e-mail: secretary@theworcestershiregolfclub.co.uk
web: www.theworcestershiregolfclub.co.uk

Fairly easy walking on windy downland course with trees, ditches and other natural hazards. Outstanding views of the Malvern Hills and the Severn valley. The 17th hole (par 5) is approached over small lake.

18 holes, 6500yds, Par 71, SSS 72.
Club membership 750.

Visitors contact club for details. **Societies** welcome. **Green Fees** £35 per day, £28 per round, £40/£34 Sat, Sun & BHs. **Prof** Richard Lewis **Course Designer** JH Taylor **Facilities** **Leisure** indoor teaching facility. **Conf** Corporate Hospitality Days **Location** 2m S of Gt Malvern on B4209

Hotel ★★★ 74% The Cottage in the Wood Hotel and Restaurant, Holywell Rd, Malvern Wells, MALVERN 01684 575859 8 en suite 23 annexe en suite

REDDITCH Map 07 SP06

Abbey Hotel Golf & Country Club Dagnell End Rd, Hither Green Ln B98 9BE
01527 406600 & 406500 01527 406514
e-mail: info@theabbeyhotel.co.uk
web: www.theabbeyhotel.co.uk

Parkland with rolling fairways with trees and lakes on several holes. Recent course improvements have resulted in a course which requires more thought than before. Pure putting surfaces are a worthy reward for some solid iron play, allowing the golfer to make the most of a birdie.

18 holes, 6561yds, Par 72, SSS 72.
Club membership 397.

Visitors Mon-Sun & BHs. Booking required. Dress code. **Societies** Booking required. **Green Fees** £21 per round, £28 Fri-Sun & BHs. **Prof** R Davies **Course Designer** Donald Steele **Facilities** **Leisure** heated indoor swimming pool, fishing, sauna, solarium, gymnasium. **Conf** facs Corporate Hospitality Days **Location** A441 N from town, onto B4101 signed Beoley, right onto Hither Green Ln

Hotel ★★★★ 67% The Abbey Hotel Golf & Country Club, Hither Green Ln, Dagnell End Rd, Bordesley, REDDITCH 01527 406600 72 en suite

Pitcheroak Plymouth Rd B97 4PB
01527 541054 01527 65216

Woodland course, hilly in places. There is also a putting green and a practice ground.

9 holes, 4561yds, Par 65, SSS 62.
Club membership 150.

Visitors Mon-Fri. Booking required Sat, Sun & BHs. **Societies** Booking required. **Green Fees** £10.75 per 18 holes, £8.30 per 9 holes, £12.40/£9.10 Sat, Sun & BHs. **Prof** David Stewart **Facilities** **Location** SW of town centre off A448

Hotel ★★★ 64% Quality Hotel Redditch, Pool Bank, Southcrest, REDDITCH 01527 541511 73 en suite

Continued

Redditch Lower Grinsty, Green Ln, Callow Hill B97 5PJ
☎ 01527 543079 (sec) 01527 547413
e-mail: redditchgolfclub@btconnect.com
web: www.redditchgolfclub.com
Parkland with many tree-lined fairways, excellent greens, and a particularly tough finish. The par 3s are all long and demanding.
18 holes, 6671yds, Par 72, SSS 72, Course record 68.
Club membership 650.
Visitors Mon-Fri except BHs. Dress code. **Societies** Booking required in writing to secretary. **Green Fees** £35 per round, £45 per day. **Prof** David Down **Course Designer** F Pennick **Facilities** **Location** 2m SW

Hotel ★★★ 64% Quality Hotel Redditch, Pool Bank, Southcrest, REDDITCH ☎ 01527 541511 73 en suite

TENBURY WELLS Map 07 SO56

Cadmore Lodge Hotel & Country Club St Michaels, Berrington Green WR15 8TQ
☎ 01584 810044 01584 810044
e-mail: info@cadmorelodge.demon.co.uk
web: www.cadmorelodge.demon.co.uk
9 holes, 5132yds, Par 68, SSS 65.
Location A4112 from Tenbury to Leominster, 2m right for Berrington, 0.75m on left
Phone for further details

Hotel ★★ 67% Cadmore Lodge Hotel & Country Club, Berrington Green, St Michaels, TENBURY WELLS ☎ 01584 810044 15 rms (14 en suite)

WORCESTER Map 03 SO85

Bank House Hotel Golf & Country Club Bransford WR6 5JD
☎ 01886 833545 01886 832461
e-mail: info@bransfordgolfclub.co.uk
web: www.bankhousehotel.co.uk
The Bransford Course is a Florida-style course with fairways weaving between water courses, 13 lakes and sculpted mounds with colourful plant displays. The 6204yd course has dog-legs, island greens and tight fairways to challenge all standards of player. The 10th, 16th and 18th (The Devil's Elbow) are particularly tricky.

Bransford Course: 18 holes, 6204yds, Par 72, SSS 71, Course record 65.
Club membership 380.
Visitors After 9.30am. Booking required. **Societies** Booking required. **Green Fees** phone. **Prof** Scott Fordyce **Course Designer** Bob Sandow **Facilities** **Leisure** outdoor swimming pool, sauna, solarium, gymnasium, spa pool, vertical sunbed. **Conf** facs Corporate Hospitality Days **Location** M5 junct 7, A4103 3m S of Worcester

Continued

Perdiswell Park Bilford Rd WR3 8DX
☎ 01905 754668 & 457189
Set in 85 acres of attractive parkland and suitable for all levels of golfer.
18 holes, 5297yds, Par 68, SSS 66.
Club membership 285.
Visitors Mon-Sun & BHs. Dress code. **Societies** welcome. **Green Fees** £10.50 per 18 holes, £7 per 9 holes, £14.25/£9 Sat & Sun. **Prof** Mark Woodward **Facilities** **Leisure** gymnasium. **Conf** facs Corporate Hospitality Days **Location** N of city centre off A30

Hotel ★★★ 74% Pear Tree Inn & Country Hotel, Smite, WORCESTER ☎ 01905 756565 24 en suite

Worcester Golf & Country Club Boughton Park WR2 4EZ
☎ 01905 422555 01905 749090
e-mail: worcestergcc@btconnect.com
web: www.worcestergcc.co.uk
Fine parkland course with many trees, lakes and views of the Malvern Hills.
18 holes, 6251yds, Par 70, SSS 70, Course record 64.
Club membership 1050.
Visitors Mon-Fri except BHs. Booking required. Handicap certificate. Dress code. **Societies** Booking required. **Green Fees** £40 per day, £30 per round. **Prof** Graham Farr **Course Designer** A MacKenzie **Facilities** by arrangement by arrangement **Leisure** hard and grass tennis courts, squash. **Conf** facs Corporate Hospitality Days **Location** 1.5m from city centre on A4103

WYTHALL Map 07 SP07

Fulford Heath Tanners Green Ln B47 6BH
☎ 01564 824758 01564 822629
e-mail: secretary@fulfordheath.co.uk
web: www.fulfordheath.co.uk
A mature parkland course encompassing two classic par 3s. The 11th, a mere 149yds, shoots from an elevated tee through a channel of trees to a well-protected green. The 16th, a 166yd par 3, elevated green, demands a 140yd carry over an imposing lake.
18 holes, 5959yds, Par 70, SSS 69.
Club membership 750.
Visitors Mon-Fri except BHs. Booking required. Handicap certificate. Dress code. **Societies** Booking required. **Green Fees** £35 per day/round. **Prof** Richard Dunbar **Course Designer** Braid, Hawtree **Facilities** **Conf** Corporate Hospitality Days **Location** 1m SE off A435

Hotel ★★★★ 70% Renaissance Solihull Hotel, 651 Warwick Rd, SOLIHULL ☎ 0121 711 3000 179 en suite

YORKSHIRE, EAST RIDING OF

ALLENTHORPE Map 08 SE85

Allerthorpe Park Allerthorpe Park YO42 4RL
☎ 01759 306686 01759 304308
e-mail: allerthorpepark@aol.com
A picturesque parkland course, maintained to a high standard, with many interesting features, including a meandering beck and the 18th hole over the lake.
18 holes, 6430yds, Par 70, SSS 70, Course record 67.
Club membership 550.
Visitors Booking required. **Societies** Booking required. **Green Fees** phone. **Prof** James Calam **Course Designer** JG Hatcliffe & Partners **Facilities** by arrangement **Conf** facs Corporate Hospitality Days **Location** 2m SW of Pocklington off A1079

Hotel ★★ 64% Feathers Hotel, 56 Market Place, POCKLINGTON ☎ 01759 303155 10 en suite 6 annexe en suite

AUGHTON Map 08 SE73

Oaks Aughton Common YO42 4PW
☎ 01757 288577 01757 288232
e-mail: info@theoaksgolfclub.co.uk
web: www.theoaksgolfclub.co.uk
The course is built in harmony with its natural wooded parkland setting, near to the Derwent Ings. The wide green fairways blend and bend with the gentle countryside. Seven lakes come into play.
18 holes, 6792yds, Par 72, SSS 72, Course record 65.
Club membership 700.
Visitors Mon-Fri & BHs. Booking required. Handicap certificate. Dress code. **Societies** Booking required. **Green Fees** £35 per day, £25.per round. **Prof** Graham Walker **Course Designer** Julian Covey **Facilities** **Leisure** heated indoor swimming pool, sauna, solarium, gymnasium, 2 self-catering cottages with own putting greens. **Conf** facs Corporate Hospitality Days **Location** 1m N of Bubwith on B1228

Hotel ★★★ 74% The Parsonage Country House Hotel, York Rd, ESCRICK ☎ 01904 728111 12 en suite 36 annexe en suite

BEVERLEY Map 08 TA03

Beverley & East Riding The Westwood HU17 8RG
☎ 01482 868757 01482 868757
e-mail: golf@beverleyandeastridinggolfclub.karoo.co.uk
Picturesque parkland with some hard walking and natural hazards - trees and gorse bushes. Only two fairways adjoin. Cattle (spring to autumn) and horse-riders are occasional early morning hazards.
Westwood: 18 holes, 6127yds, Par 69, SSS 69, Course record 64.
Club membership 530.
Visitors Mon-Sun & BHs. Booking required. Dress code. **Societies** Booking required. **Green Fees** £22 per day, £17 per round, £29/£24 Sat & Sun. **Prof** Alex Ashby **Facilities** **Location** 1m SW on B1230

BRANDESBURTON Map 08 TA14

Hainsworth Park Burton Holme YO25 8RT
☎ 01964 542362
18 holes, 6362yds, Par 71, SSS 71.
Location SW of village on A165
Phone for further details

Hotel ★★ 69% Burton Lodge Hotel, BRANDESBURTON ☎ 01964 542847 7 en suite 2 annexe en suite

BRIDLINGTON Map 08 TA16

Bridlington Belvedere Rd YO15 3NA
☎ 01262 606367 01262 606367
e-mail: enquiries@bridlingtongolfclub.co.uk
web: www.bridlingtongolfclub.co.uk
Parkland alongside Bridlington Bay, with tree-lined fairways and six ponds, comprising two loops of 9 holes. Excellent putting surfaces.
18 holes, 6638yds, Par 72, SSS 72, Course record 66.
Club membership 600.
Visitors Mon-Sun & BHs. Booking required. Handicap certificate. Dress code. **Societies** Booking required. **Green Fees** Sun-Thu £32 per day, £26 per round, Fri £36/£30, £40/£32 Sat. **Prof** Anthony Howarth **Course Designer** James Braid **Facilities** **Leisure** snooker. **Conf** Corporate Hospitality Days **Location** 1m S off A165

Hotel ★★★ 70% Revelstoke Hotel, 1-3 Flamborough Rd, BRIDLINGTON ☎ 01262 672362 26 en suite

Bridlington Links Flamborough Rd, Marton YO15 1DW
☎ 01262 401584 01262 401702
Main: 18 holes, 6719yds, Par 72, SSS 72, Course record 70.
Course Designer Swan **Location** On B1255 between Bridlington
Phone for further details

Hotel ★★★ 69% Expanse Hotel, North Marine Dr, BRIDLINGTON ☎ 01262 675347 48 en suite

BROUGH Map 08 SE92

Brough Cave Rd HU15 1HB
☎ 01482 667291 01482 669873
e-mail: gt@brough-golfclub.co.uk
web: www.brough-golfclub.co.uk
Parkland course, where accurate positioning of the tee ball is required for good scoring. Testing for the scratch player without being too difficult for the higher handicap.
18 holes, 6067yds, Par 68, SSS 69, Course record 62.
Club membership 680.
Visitors Mon, Tue, Thu, Fri except BHs. Booking required. Handicap certificate. Dress code. **Societies** Booking required. **Green Fees** £50 per day, £35 per round, £70/£55 Sat, Sun & BHs. **Prof** Gordon Townhill **Facilities** **Conf** Corporate Hospitality Days **Location** 8m W of Hull off A63

COTTINGHAM Map 08 TA03

Cottingham Parks Golf & Country Club
Woodhill Way HU16 5RZ
☎ 01482 846030 📠 01482 845932
e-mail: jane.wiles@cottinghamparks.co.uk
web: www.cottinghamparks.co.uk
Gently undulating parkland course incorporating many natural features, including lateral water hazards, several ponds on the approach to greens, and rolling fairways.

18 holes, 6453yds, Par 72, SSS 71, Course record 66. Club membership 600.
Visitors Mon-Sun & BHs. Booking required. Handicap certificate. Dress code. **Societies** Booking required. **Green Fees** £20 per round, £28 Sat, Sun & BHs. **Prof** Chris Gray **Course Designer** Terry Litten **Facilities** **Leisure** heated indoor swimming pool, sauna, solarium, gymnasium, Jacuzzi Remedial masseur. **Conf** facs Corporate Hospitality Days **Location** A164 onto B1233 towards Cottingham, 100yds left onto Woodhill Way

Hotel ★★ 66% The Rowley Manor Hotel, Rowley Rd, LITTLE WEIGHTON ☎ 01482 848248 16 en suite

DRIFFIELD (GREAT) Map 08 TA05

Driffield Sunderlandwick YO25 9AD
☎ 01377 253116 📠 01377 240599
e-mail: info@diffieldgolfclub.co.uk
web: www.driffieldgolf.co.uk
An easy walking, mature parkland course set within the beautiful Sunderlandwick Estate, including numerous water features, one of which is a renowned trout stream.
18 holes, 6215yds, Par 70, SSS 69, Course record 65. Club membership 693.
Visitors Mon, Wed-Sun & BHs. Tue pm. Booking required. Handicap certificate. Dress code. **Societies** Booking required. **Green Fees** £35 per day, £26 per round, £45/£35 Sat & Sun. **Prof** Kenton Wright **Facilities** **Leisure** fishing. **Conf** facs Corporate Hospitality Days **Location** 0.5m S off A164

Hotel ★★★ 73% Bell Hotel, 46 Market Place, DRIFFIELD ☎ 01377 256661 16 en suite

FLAMBOROUGH Map 08 TA27

Flamborough Head Lighthouse Rd YO15 1AR
☎ 01262 850333 📠 01262 850279
e-mail: secretary@flamboroughheadgolfclub.co.uk
web: www.flamboroughheadgolfclub.co.uk
Undulating cliff top links type course on the Flamborough headland.
18 holes, 6189yds, Par 71, SSS 69, Course record 71. Club membership 500.
Visitors Mon-Sun & BHs. Booking required Wed, Sat, Sun & BHs. Dress code. **Societies** Booking required. **Green Fees** £25 per day, £20 per round, £32/£27 Sat, Sun & BHs. **Prof** Paul Harrison **Facilities** **Location** 2m E off B1259

Hotel ★★ 72% North Star Hotel, North Marine Dr, FLAMBOROUGH ☎ 01262 850379 7 en suite

HESSLE Map 08 TA02

Hessle Westfield Rd, Raywell HU16 5YL
☎ 01482 650171 & 650190 (pro) 📠 01482 652679
e-mail: secretary@hessle-golf-club.co.uk
web: www.hessle-golf-club.co.uk
Well-wooded downland course with easy walking. The greens, conforming to USGA specification, are large and undulating with excellent drainage, enabling play throughout the year.
18 holes, 6608yds, Par 72, SSS 72, Course record 65. Club membership 720.
Visitors Mon-Sun & BHs. Booking required. Dress code. **Societies** Booking required. **Green Fees** £34 per day, £26 per round, £35 per round Sat & Sun. **Prof** Grahame Fieldsend **Course Designer** D Thomas, P Allis **Facilities** **Conf** facs Corporate Hospitality Days **Location** 3m SW of Cottingham

HORNSEA Map 08 TA14

Hornsea Rolston Rd HU18 1XG
☎ 01964 532020 📠 01964 532080
e-mail: hornseagolfclub@aol.com
web: www.hornseagolfclub.co.uk
Easy walking parkland course renowned for the quality of its greens.
18 holes, 6685yds, Par 72, SSS 72, Course record 66. Club membership 600.
Visitors Mon-Fri. Booking required Sat, Sun & BHs. Dress code. **Societies** welcome. **Green Fees** £40 per day, £30 per round. **Prof** Stretton Wright **Course Designer** Herd, A MacKenzie, J Braid **Facilities** by arrangement **Conf** Corporate Hospitality Days **Location** 1m S on B1242, signs for Hornsea Freeport

HOWDEN Map 08 SE72

Boothferry Park Spaldington Ln DN14 7NG
☎ 01430 430364 📠 01430 430567
Pleasant, meadowland course in the Vale of York with interesting natural dykes, creating challenges on some holes. The par 5 9th is a test for any golfer with its dyke coming into play on the tee shot, second shot and approach.
18 holes, 6651yds, Par 73, SSS 72, Course record 64. Eagles: 9 holes, 2700yds, Par 29, SSS 30. Club membership 250.

Continued

Visitors Mon-Fri. Booking required Sat, Sun & BHs. Dress code. **Societies** Booking required. **Green Fees** 18 holes £15, £11 per 9 holes, £18/£13 Sat & Sun. Eagles £8 per 18 holes, £5 per 9 holes. **Prof** Matthew Rumble **Course Designer** Donald Steel **Facilities** **Conf** Corporate Hospitality Days **Location** M62 junct 37, 2.5m N of Howden off B1228

Hotel Premier Travel Inn Goole, Rawcliffe Rd, Airmyn, GOOLE ☎ 08701 977 031 79 en suite

KINGSTON UPON HULL Map 08 TA02

Ganstead Park Longdales Ln, Coniston HU11 4LB
☎ 01482 817754 📠 01482 817754
e-mail: secretary@gansteadpark.co.uk
web: www.gansteadpark.co.uk
Easy walking parkland with water features.
18 holes, 6801yds, Par 72, SSS 73, Course record 62.
Club membership 500.
Visitors Mon-Sun except BHs. Booking required. Handicap certificate. Dress code. **Societies** Booking required. **Green Fees** £27 per day, £18 per round. **Prof** Michael J Smee **Course Designer** P Green **Facilities** **Conf** Corporate Hospitality Days **Location** A165 Hull exit, pass Ganstead right onto B1238 to Bilton, course on right

Hotel ★★★ 67% Quality Hotel Royal Hull, 170 Ferensway, HULL ☎ 01482 325087 155 en suite

Hull The Hall, 27 Packman Ln HU10 7TJ
☎ 01482 658919 📠 01482 658919
e-mail: info.hullgolfclub@virgin.net
web: hullgolfclub.com
Attractive mature parkland course.
18 holes, 6262yds, Par 70, SSS 70, Course record 64.
Club membership 768.
Visitors Mon, Tue, Thu-Sun & BHs. Booking required. Handicap certificate. Dress code. **Societies** Booking required. **Green Fees** Dec-Feb £21 per day/round. Mar-Nov £32 per day, £26.50 per round. **Prof** David Jagger **Course Designer** James Braid **Facilities** **Leisure** snooker. **Conf** Corporate Hospitality Days **Location** 5m W of city off A164

Hotel ★★★ 73% Willerby Manor Hotel, Well Ln, WILLERBY ☎ 01482 652616 51 en suite

Springhead Park Willerby Rd HU5 5JE
☎ 01482 656309
Municipal parkland course with tight, undulating tree-lined fairways.
18 holes, 6402yds, Par 71, SSS 71.
Club membership 200.
Visitors Mon-Sat. Booking required. **Societies** Booking required. **Green Fees** phone. **Facilities** **Conf** Corporate Hospitality Days **Location** 5m W off A164

Hotel ★★★ 73% Willerby Manor Hotel, Well Ln, WILLERBY ☎ 01482 652616 51 en suite

Sutton Park Salthouse Rd HU8 9HF
☎ 01482 374242 📠 01482 701428
18 holes, 6251yds, Par 70, SSS 69, Course record 67.
Location 3m NE on B1237, off A165
Phone for further details

Hotel ★★★ 67% Quality Hotel Royal Hull, 170 Ferensway, HULL ☎ 01482 325087 155 en suite

POCKLINGTON Map 08 SE84

Kilnwick Percy Kilnwick Percy YO42 1UF
☎ 01759 303090 📠 01759 303090
e-mail: aaronpheasant@easy.com
web: kilnwickpercygolfclub.co.uk
This parkland course on the edge of the Wolds above Pocklington combines a good walk with interesting golf. Undulating fairways, mature trees, water hazards and breathtaking views from every hole.
18 holes, 6218yards, Par 70, SSS 70, Course record 66.
Club membership 450.
Visitors Mon-Sun & BHs. Dress code. **Societies** Booking required. **Green Fees** £18 per 18 holes, £12 per 9 holes, £20/£14 Sat, Sun & BHs. **Prof** Aaron Pheasant **Course Designer** John Day **Facilities** **Conf** Corporate Hospitality Days **Location** 1m E of Pocklington off B1246

Hotel ★★ 64% Feathers Hotel, 56 Market Place, POCKLINGTON ☎ 01759 303155 10 en suite 6 annexe en suite

SOUTH CAVE Map 08 SE93

Cave Castle Hotel & Country Club Church Hill, South Cave HU15 2EU
☎ 01430 426262 & 426259 📠 01430 421118
e-mail: admin@cavecastlegolf.co.uk
web: www.cavecastlegolf.co.uk
Undulating meadow and parkland at the foot of the Wolds, with superb views.
18 holes, 6524yds, Par 72, SSS 71, Course record 68.
Club membership 410.
Visitors Mon-Sun & BHs. Booking required. Dress code. **Societies** Booking required. **Green Fees** phone. **Prof** Stephen MacKinder **Course Designer** N Freling **Facilities** **Leisure** heated indoor swimming pool, sauna, solarium, gymnasium. **Conf** facs Corporate Hospitality Days **Location** 1m from A63

WITHERNSEA Map 08 TA32

Withernsea Chesnut Av HU19 2PG
☎ 01964 612078 & 612258 📠 01964 612078
e-mail: golf@withernseagolfclub.fsnet.co.uk
Exposed seaside links with narrow, undulating fairways, bunkers and small greens.
9 holes, 6207yds, Par 72, SSS 69.
Club membership 250.
Visitors Mon-Fri. Booking required Sat & Sun. Dress code. **Societies** Booking required **Green Fees** £15 per 18 holes/per day. **Facilities** **Leisure** senior/junior coaching. **Conf** facs Corporate Hospitality Days **Location** S of town centre off A1033, signed from Victoria Av

Hotel ★★★ 67% Quality Hotel Royal Hull, 170 Ferensway, HULL ☎ 01482 325087 155 en suite

YORKSHIRE, NORTH

ALDWARK Map 08 SE46

Aldwark Manor YO61 1UF
☎ 01347 838353 📠 01347 833991
An easy walking, scenic 18-hole parkland course with holes both sides of the River Ure. The course surrounds the Victorian Aldwark Manor Golf Hotel.
18 holes, 6187yds, Par 72, SSS 70, Course record 67. Club membership 400.
Visitors Mon-Sun & BHs. Booking required. Dress code. **Societies** Booking required. **Green Fees** £35 per day, £25 per round, £40/£30 Sat, Sun & BHs. **Facilities** **Leisure** heated indoor swimming pool, fishing, sauna, gymnasium. **Conf** facs Corporate Hospitality Days **Location** 5m SE of Boroughbridge off A1

Hotel ★★★★ 77% Aldwark Manor, ALDWARK
☎ 01347 838146 60 en suite

BEDALE Map 08 SE28

Bedale Leyburn Rd DL8 1EZ
☎ 01677 422451 (sec) 📠 01677 427143
e-mail: bedalegolfclub@aol.com
web: www.bedalegolfclub.com
One of North Yorkshire's most picturesque and interesting courses. The 18-hole course is in parkland with mature trees, water hazards and strategically placed bunkers. Easy walking, no heavy climbs.

18 holes, 6610yds, Par 72, SSS 72, Course record 68. Club membership 600.
Visitors Booking required. Dress code. **Societies** Booking required. **Green Fees** £32 per day, £26 per round, £40/£35 Sat & Sun. **Prof** Tony Johnson **Course Designer** Hawtree **Facilities** **Conf** Corporate Hospitality Days **Location** A1 onto A684 at Leeming Bar to Bedale

Hotel ★ 69% Buck Inn, THORNTON WATLASS
☎ 01677 422461 7 rms (5 en suite)

BENTHAM Map 07 SD66

Bentham Robin Ln LA2 7AG
☎ 01524 62455
e-mail: secretary@benthamgolfclub.co.uk
web: www.benthamgolfclub.co.uk
Moorland course with glorious views and excellent greens.
18 holes, 6005yds, Par 71, SSS 69, Course record 69. Club membership 600.
Visitors Booking required. **Societies** Booking required.

Continued

Green Fees phone. **Prof** Alan Watson **Facilities** **Conf** Corporate Hospitality Days **Location** N side of High Bentham

CATTERICK GARRISON Map 08 SE29

Catterick Leyburn Rd DL9 3QE
☎ 01748 833268 📠 01748 833268
e-mail: grant@catterickgolfclub.co.uk
web: www.catterickgolfclub.co.uk
18 holes, 6329yds, Par 71, SSS 71, Course record 64.
Course Designer Arthur Day **Location** 0.5m W of Catterick Garrison
Phone for further details

Hotel ★★★ 66% King's Head Hotel, Market Place, RICHMOND ☎ 01748 850220 26 en suite 4 annexe en suite

COPMANTHORPE Map 08 SE54

Pike Hills Tadcaster Rd YO23 3UW
☎ 01904 700797 📠 01904 700797
e-mail: thesecretary@pikehills.fsnet.co.uk
web: www.pikehillsgolfclub.com
Parkland course surrounding a nature reserve. Level terrain.
18 holes, 6146yds, Par 71, SSS 70, Course record 63. Club membership 750.
Visitors Mon-Fri. Booking required. Handicap certificate. Dress code. **Societies** Booking required. **Green Fees** phone. **Prof** Ian Gradwell **Facilities** **Conf** facs Corporate Hospitality Days **Location** 3m SW of York on A64

Hotel ★★★★ 70% York Marriott Hotel, Tadcaster Rd, YORK ☎ 01904 701000 151 en suite

EASINGWOLD Map 08 SE56

Easingwold Stillington Rd YO61 3ET
☎ 01347 821964 (pro) & 822474 (sec) 📠 01347 822474
e-mail: brian@easingwold-golf-club.fsnet.co.uk
web: www.easingwold-golf-club.co.uk
Parkland with easy walking. Trees are a major feature and on six holes water hazards come into play.
18 holes, 6559yds, Par 74, SSS 72. Club membership 750.
Visitors Mon-Fri. Booking required. Handicap certificate. Dress code. **Societies** Booking required. **Green Fees** £35 per day, £28 per round. **Prof** John Hughes **Course Designer** Hawtree **Facilities** **Conf** Corporate Hospitality Days **Location** 1m S of Easingwold

Hotel ★★ 72% George Hotel, Market Place, EASINGWOLD ☎ 01347 821698 15 en suite

FILEY Map 08 TA18

Filey West Av YO14 9BQ
☎ 01723 513293 📠 01723 514952
e-mail: secretary@fileygolfclub.wanadoo.co.uk
web: www.fileygolfclub.com
Links and parkland course with good views. Stream runs through course. Testing 9th and 13th holes.
18 holes, 6112yds, Par 70, SSS 69, Course record 64
9 holes, 1513yds, Par 30.
Club membership 900.
Visitors Mon-Sun & BHs. Handicap certificate. Dress code. **Societies** Booking required. **Green Fees** £30 per day

Continued

Sat & Sun £35 per round. **Prof** Gary Hutchinson **Course Designer** Braid **Facilities** **Location** 0.5m S of Filey

Hotel ★★ 69% Wrangham House Hotel, 10 Stonegate, HUNMANBY ☎ 01723 891333 8 en suite 4 annexe en suite

GANTON Map 08 SE97

Ganton YO12 4PA
☎ 01944 710329 01944 710922
e-mail: secretary@gantongolfclub.com
web: www.gantongolfclub.com

Championship course, heathland, gorse-lined fairways and heavily bunkered; variable winds. The opening holes make full use of the contours of the land and the approach to the second demands the finest touch. The 4th is considered one of the best holes on the outward half with its shot across a valley to a plateau green, the surrounding gorse punishing anything less than a perfect shot. The finest hole is possibly the 18th, requiring an accurately placed drive to give a clear shot to the sloping, well-bunkered green.

18 holes, 6734yds, Par 72, SSS 73, Course record 65. Club membership 500.

Visitors Booking required. Handicap certificate. Dress code. **Societies** Booking required. **Green Fees** £70 per day/round, £80 Sat, Sun & BHs. **Prof** Gary Brown **Course Designer** Dunn, Vardon, Braid, Colt **Facilities** **Conf** Corporate Hospitality Days **Location** N of village off A64

Hotel ★★★ 65% East Ayton Lodge Country House, Moor Ln, Forge Valley, East Ayton, SCARBOROUGH ☎ 01723 864227 10 en suite 20 annexe en suite

HARROGATE Map 08 SE35

Harrogate Forest Ln Head, Starbeck HG2 7TF
☎ 01423 862999 01423 860073
e-mail: hon.secretary@harrogate-gc.co.uk
web: www.harrogate-gc.co.uk

Course on fairly flat terrain with MacKenzie-style greens and tree-lined fairways. While not a long course, the layout penalises the golfer who strays off the fairway. Subtly placed bunkers and copses of trees require the golfer to adopt careful thought and accuracy if par is be bettered. The last six holes include five par 4s, of which four exceed 400yds.

18 holes, 6241yds, Par 69, SSS 70, Course record 63. Club membership 700.

Visitors Mon, Wed-Fri, Sun & BHs. Tue pm. Handicap certificate. Dress code. **Societies** Booking required. **Green Fees** £40 per day, £35 per round, £45 Sat & Sun. **Prof** Paul Johnson **Course Designer** Sandy Herd **Facilities** **Leisure** snooker. **Conf** Corporate Hospitality Days **Location** 2.25m N on A59

Hotel ★★★ 74% Grants Hotel, 3-13 Swan Rd, HARROGATE ☎ 01423 560666 42 en suite

Oakdale Oakdale Glen HG1 2LN
☎ 01423 567162 01423 536030
e-mail: sec@oakdale-golfclub.com
web: www.oakdale-golfclub.com

A pleasant, undulating parkland course which

Continued

provides a good test of golf for the low handicap player without intimidating the less proficient. A special feature is an attractive stream which comes in to play on four holes. Excellent views from the clubhouse with good facilities.

18 holes, 6456yds, Par 71, SSS 71, Course record 61. Club membership 1034.

Visitors Mon-Sun & BHs. Handicap certificate. Dress code. **Societies** Booking required. **Green Fees** £46 per 27 holes, £39 per round, £55 per round Sat, Sun & BHs. **Prof** Clive Dell **Course Designer** A MacKenzie **Facilities** **Conf** Corporate Hospitality Days **Location** N of town centre off A61

Hotel ★★★ 74% Grants Hotel, 3-13 Swan Rd, HARROGATE ☎ 01423 560666 42 en suite

Rudding Park Hotel & Golf Rudding Park, Follifoot HG3 1JH
☎ 01423 872100 01423 873011
e-mail: sales@ruddingpark.com
web: www.ruddingpark.com

Running through Rudding Park's mature parkland, originally designed as a deer park. Water comes into play on seven holes, while trees are present on all fairways.

18 holes, 6883yds, Par 72, SSS 73, Course record 65. Club membership 700.

Visitors Mon-Sun & BHs. Booking required. Dress code. Handicap certificate. **Societies** Booking required. **Green Fees** Mon-Thu £32 per 18 holes, £37.50 Fri-Sun. **Prof** Moore, Hobkinson, Fountain **Course Designer** Martin

Continued

Hawtree **Facilities** ⊗ ꟾ 🍽 ☕ 🍷 ⛳ 🏠 🏌 ⛱ 🚗 🛒 🏌 **Conf** facs Corporate Hospitality Days **Location** 2m SE of Harrogate town centre, off A658, brown tourist signs

Rudding Park Hotel & Golf

Hotel ★★★★ Rudding Park Hotel & Golf, Rudding Park, Follifoot, HARROGATE ☎ 01423 871350 49 en suite

See advertisement on page 293

KIRKBYMOORSIDE Map 08 SE68

Kirkbymoorside Manor Vale YO62 6EG
☎ 01751 430402 🖷 01751 433190
e-mail: enqs@kirkbymoorsidegolf.co.uk
web: www.kirkbymoorsidegolf.co.uk

Hilly parkland with narrow fairways, gorse and hawthorn bushes. Beautiful views.

18 holes, 6207yds, Par 69, SSS 69, Course record 65.
Club membership 650.

Visitors Mon-Sun & BHs. Booking required. Dress code. **Societies** Booking required. **Green Fees** £22 per round, £28 per day, £32 Sat, Sun & BHs. **Prof** John Hinchliffe **Facilities** ⊗ ꟾ 🍽 ☕ 🍷 ⛳ 🏠 🏌 🚗 🛒 **Conf** Corporate Hospitality Days **Location** N of village

Hotel ★★ 68% George & Dragon Hotel, 17 Market Place, KIRKBYMOORSIDE ☎ 01751 433334 12 en suite 7 annexe en suite

KNARESBOROUGH Map 08 SE35

Knaresborough Boroughbridge Rd HG5 0QQ
☎ 01423 862690 🖷 01423 869345
e-mail: knaresboroughgolfclub@btopenworld.com
web: theknaresboroughgolfclub.co.uk

Pleasant and well-presented parkland course in a rural setting. The first 11 holes are tree-lined and are constantly changing direction around the clubhouse. The closing holes head out overlooking the old quarry with fine views.

18 holes, 6864yds, Par 72, SSS 72.
Club membership 840.

Visitors Mon-Sun & BHs. Handicap certificate. Dress code. **Societies** Booking required. **Green Fees** £40 per day, £30 per round, £35 per round Sat & Sun. ⊘ **Prof** Gary J Vickers **Course Designer** Hawtree **Facilities** ⊗ ꟾ 🍽 ☕ 🍷 ⛳ 🏠 🛒 **Conf** Corporate Hospitality Days **Location** 1.25m N on A6055

Hotel ★★★ 70% Dower House Hotel, Bond End, KNARESBOROUGH ☎ 01423 863302 28 en suite 3 annexe en suite

MALTON Map 08 SE77

Malton & Norton Welham Park, Norton YO17 9QE
☎ 01653 697912 🖷 01653 697912
e-mail: maltonandnorton@btconnect.com
web: www.maltonandnortongolfclub.co.uk

Parkland course, consisting of three nine-hole loops, with panoramic views of the moors. Very testing 1st hole (564yd dog-leg, left) on the Welham Course.

Welham Course: 18 holes, 6456yds, Par 72, SSS 71, Course record 66.
Park Course: 18 holes, 6251yds, Par 72, SSS 70, Course record 67.
Derwent Course: 18 holes, 6295yds, Par 72, SSS 70, Course record 66.
Club membership 880.

Visitors Mon-Sun & BHs. Handicap certificate. Dress code. **Societies** Booking required. **Green Fees** £27 per round/day, £32 Sat, Sun & BHs. **Prof** S Robinson **Facilities** ⊗ ꟾ 🍽 ☕ 🍷 ⛳ 🏠 🛒 🏌 **Conf** Corporate Hospitality Days **Location** 0.75m from Malton

Hotel ★★★ 73% Burythorpe House Hotel, Burythorpe, MALTON ☎ 01653 658200 11 en suite 5 annexe en suite

MASHAM Map 08 SE28

Masham Burnholme, Swinton Rd HG4 4HT
☎ 01765 688054 & 689379 🖷 01765 688054

Flat parkland crossed by River Burn, which comes into play on six holes.

9 holes, 6068yds, Par 70, SSS 69, Course record 70.
Club membership 290.

Visitors Mon-Fri. **Societies** Booking required. **Green Fees** £20 per day, £17 per round. ⊘ **Facilities** ⊗ by arrangement ꟾ by arrangement 🍽 by arrangement ☕ by arrangement 🍷 ⛳ **Location** SW of Masham centre off A6108

Hotel ★ 69% Buck Inn, THORNTON WATLASS ☎ 01677 422461 7 rms (5 en suite)

MIDDLESBROUGH Map 08 NZ41

Middlesbrough Brass Castle Ln, Marton TS8 9EE
☎ 01642 311515 🖷 01642 319607
e-mail: enquiries@middlesbroughgolfclub.co.uk
web: www.middlesbroughgolfclub.co.uk

Undulating wooded parkland affected by the wind. Testing 6th, 8th and 12th holes.

18 holes, 6278yds, Par 70, SSS 70, Course record 63.
Club membership 1004.

Visitors Mon, Wed-Fri, Sun. **Societies** Mon, Wed-Fri. Booking required. **Green Fees** phone. ⊘ **Prof** Don Jones **Course Designer** Baird **Facilities** ⊗ ꟾ 🍽 ☕ 🍷 ⛳ 🏠 🏌 🚗 🛒 **Leisure** snooker table. **Conf** facs Corporate Hospitality Days **Location** 4m S off A172

Hotel ★★★ 73% Parkmore Hotel & Leisure Park, 636 Yarm Rd, Eaglescliffe, STOCKTON-ON-TEES ☎ 01642 786815 55 en suite

Middlesbrough Municipal Ladgate Ln TS5 7YZ
☎ 01642 315533 🖷 01642 300726

18 holes, 6333yds, Par 71, SSS 70, Course record 67.
Course Designer Shuttleworth **Location** 2m S of Middlesbrough on the A174
Phone for further details

Hotel ★★★ 73% Parkmore Hotel & Leisure Park, 636 Yarm Rd, Eaglescliffe, STOCKTON-ON-TEES ☎ 01642 786815 55 en suite

NORTHALLERTON Map 08 SE39

Romanby Yafforth Rd DL7 0PE
☎ 01609 778855 🖷 01609 779084
e-mail: grant@romanby.com
web: www.romanbygolf.co.uk
Set in natural undulating terrain with the River Wiske meandering through the course, it offers a testing round of golf for all abilities. In addition to the river, two lakes come into play on the 2nd, 5th and 11th holes. A 12-bay floodlit driving range.
18 holes, 6663yds, Par 72, SSS 72, Course record 72.
Club membership 635.
Visitors Mon-Sun & BHs. Dress code. **Societies** Booking required with Mark Boersma 01609 778855. **Green Fees** £25 per 18 holes, £30 Sat & Sun. **Prof** Richard Wood **Course Designer** Will Adamson **Facilities** **Leisure** 6 hole par 3 academy course. **Conf** facs Corporate Hospitality Days **Location** 1m W of Northallerton on B6271

PANNAL Map 08 SE35

Pannal Follifoot Rd HG3 1ES
☎ 01423 872628 🖷 01423 870043
e-mail: secretary@pannalgc.co.uk
web: www.pannalgc.co.uk
Fine championship course. Moorland turf but well-wooded with trees closely involved with play. Excellent views enhance the course.
18 holes, 6622yds, Par 72, SSS 72, Course record 62.
Club membership 780.
Visitors Mon, Sun & BHs. Booking required. Dress code. **Societies** Booking required. **Green Fees** £55 per day, £45 per round, £60 per round Sat & Sun. **Prof** David Padgett **Course Designer** Sandy Herd **Facilities** **Leisure** snooker. **Conf** Corporate Hospitality Days **Location** E of village off A61

RAVENSCAR Map 08 NZ90

Raven Hall Hotel Golf Course YO13 0ET
☎ 01723 870353 🖷 01723 870072
e-mail: enquiries@ravenhall.co.uk
web: www.ravenhall.co.uk
Opened by the Earl of Cranbrook in 1898, this nine-hole clifftop course is sloping and with good quality small greens. Because of its clifftop position it is subject to strong winds which make it great fun to play, especially the 6th hole.
9 holes, 1894yds, Par 32, SSS 32.
Club membership 120.
Visitors Mon-Sun & BHs. **Societies** Booking required. **Green Fees** £8 per round. **Facilities** **Leisure** hard tennis courts, heated indoor plus outdoor swimming pool, sauna, gymnasium, snooker, croquet, bowls. **Conf** facs Corporate Hospitality Days **Location** A171 from Scarborough towards Whitby, through Cloughton, right to Ravenscar, hotel on clifftop

Hotel ★★★ 67% Raven Hall Country House Hotel, RAVENSCAR ☎ 01723 870353 52 en suite

REDCAR Map 08 NZ62

Cleveland Majuba Rd TS10 5BJ
☎ 01642 471798 🖷 01642 471798
e-mail: secretary@clevelandgolfclub.co.uk
web: www.clevelandgolfclub.co.uk
18 holes, 6696yds, Par 72, SSS 72, Course record 67.
Course Designer Donald Steel (new holes) **Location** 8m E of Middlesborough, at N end of Redcar
Phone for further details

Hotel ★★★ 66% Rushpool Hall Hotel, Saltburn Ln, SALTBURN-BY-THE-SEA ☎ 01287 624111 21 en suite

Wilton Wilton TS10 4QY
☎ 01642 465265 (secretary) 🖷 01642 465463
e-mail: secretary@wiltongolfclub.co.uk
web: www.wiltongolfclub.co.uk
Parkland with some fine views and an abundance of trees and shrubs.
18 holes, 6540yds, Par 70, SSS 69, Course record 64.
Club membership 730.
Visitors After 10am Mon-Fri & Sun. Booking required. **Societies** Booking required. **Green Fees** phone. **Prof** PD Smillie **Facilities** by arrangement **Leisure** snooker. **Conf** Corporate Hospitality Days **Location** 3m W of Redcar on A174

Hotel ★★★ 66% Rushpool Hall Hotel, Saltburn Ln, SALTBURN-BY-THE-SEA ☎ 01287 624111 21 en suite

RICHMOND Map 07 NZ10

Richmond Bend Hagg DL10 5EX
☎ 01748 823231 (secretary) 🖷 01748 821709
Undulating parkland. Ideal to play 27 holes, not too testing but very interesting.
18 holes, 6073yds, Par 71, SSS 69, Course record 63.
Club membership 600.
Visitors Mon-Sat. After 3.30pm Sun. **Societies** Booking required. **Green Fees** phone. **Prof** Paul Jackson **Course Designer** F Pennink **Facilities** **Conf** facs **Location** 0.75m N

Continued

Hotel ★★★ 66% King's Head Hotel, Market Place, RICHMOND ☎ 01748 850220 26 en suite 4 annexe en suite

RIPON Map 08 SE37

Ripon City Palace Rd HG4 3HH

☎ 01765 603640 🖷 01765 692880
e-mail: office@ripongolf.com
web: www.ripongolf.com

Moderate walking on undulating parkland course; two testing par 3s at 5th and 14th.

18 holes, 6084yds, Par 70, SSS 69, Course record 66.
Club membership 750.

Visitors Mon-Sun & BHs. Booking required Sat, Sun & BHs. Dress code. **Societies** Booking required. **Green Fees** phone. **Prof** ST Davis **Course Designer** H Varden **Facilities** **Location** 1m NW on A6108

Hotel ★★★ 69% Ripon Spa Hotel, Park St, RIPON ☎ 01765 602172 40 en suite

SALTBURN-BY-THE-SEA Map 08 NZ62

Hunley Hall Golf Club & Hotel Ings Ln, Brotton TS12 2QQ

☎ 01287 676216 🖷 01287 678250
e-mail: enquiries@hunleyhall.co.uk
web: www.hunleyhall.co.uk

A picturesque 27-hole coastal course with panoramic views of the countryside and coastline, providing a good test of golf and a rewarding game for all.

Morgans: 18 holes, 6872yds, Par 73, SSS 73, Course record 63.
Millennium: 18 holes, 5945yds, Par 68, SSS 68, Course record 67.
Jubilee: 18 holes, 6289yds, Par 71, SSS 70, Course record 65.
Club membership 600.

Visitors Mon-Sun & BHs. Booking required. Dress code. **Societies** Booking required. **Green Fees** £25 per day, £35 Sat, Sun & BHs. **Prof** Andrew Brook **Course Designer** John Morgan **Facilities** **Conf** facs Corporate Hospitality Days **Location** Off A174 in Brotton onto St Margarets Way, 700yds to club

Hotel ★★ 67% Hunley Hall Golf Club & Hotel, Ings Ln, Brotton, SALTBURN ☎ 01287 676216 8 en suite

Saltburn by the Sea Hob Hill, Guisborough Rd TS12 1NJ

☎ 01287 622812 🖷 01287 625988
e-mail: info@saltburngolf.co.uk
web: www.saltburngolf.co.uk

Undulating meadowland course surrounded by woodland. Particularly attractive in autumn. There are fine views of the Cleveland Hills and of Tees Bay.

18 holes, 5846yds, Par 70, SSS 68, Course record 62.
Club membership 900.

Visitors Mon-Fri & Sun. Handicap certificate. Dress code. **Societies** Booking required. **Green Fees** £27 per day, £31 Sat & Sun. **Prof** Paul Bolton **Course Designer** J Braid **Facilities** **Leisure** 2 snooker tables. **Conf** Corporate Hospitality Days **Location** 0.5m S from Saltburn

Hotel ★★★ 66% Rushpool Hall Hotel, Saltburn Ln, SALTBURN-BY-THE-SEA ☎ 01287 624111 21 en suite

SCARBOROUGH Map 08 TA08

Scarborough North Cliff North Cliff Av YO12 6PP

☎ 01723 355397 🖷 01723 362134
e-mail: info@northcliffgolfclub.co.uk
web: www.northcliffgolfclub.co.uk

Seaside course beginning on clifftop overlooking North Bay and castle winding inland through parkland with stunning views of the North Yorkshire Moors.

18 holes, 6425yds, Par 71, SSS 71, Course record 66.
Club membership 895.

Visitors Booking required. Handicap certificate. Dress code. **Societies** Booking required with secretary for parties of 8-40. **Green Fees** £39 per day, £33 per round, £45/£40 Fri-Sun & BHs. **Prof** Simon N Deller **Course Designer** James Braid **Facilities** **Conf** Corporate Hospitality Days **Location** 2m N of town centre off A165

Hotel ★★★ 66% Esplanade Hotel, Belmont Rd, SCARBOROUGH ☎ 01723 360382 73 en suite

Scarborough South Cliff Deepdale Av YO11 2UE

☎ 01723 374737 🖷 01723 374737
e-mail: clubsecretary.sscgc@virgin.net
web: www.scarboroughgolfclub.co.uk

Parkland and seaside course which falls into two parts, divided from one another by the main road from Scarborough to Filey. On the seaward side of the road lie holes 4 to 10. On the landward side the first three holes and the last eight are laid out along the bottom of a rolling valley, stretching southwards into the hills.

18 holes, 6405yds, Par 72, SSS 71, Course record 68.
Club membership 560.

Visitors Mon-Fri. Sun & BHs. Booking required. Dress code. **Societies** Booking required with secretary. **Green Fees** £35 per day/round, £40 Fri-Sun & BHs. **Prof** Tony Skingle **Course Designer** A MacKenzie **Facilities** **Location** 1m S on A165

Hotel ★★ 66% Bradley Court Hotel, Filey Rd, South Cliff, SCARBOROUGH ☎ 01723 360476 40 en suite

SELBY Map 08 SE63

Selby Mill Ln, Brayton YO8 9LD
☎ 01757 228622 🖷 01757 228622
e-mail: selbygolfclub@hotmail.com
web: www.selbygolfclub.co.uk
Mainly flat, links-type course; prevailing south-west wind. Testing holes including the 3rd, 7th and 16th.
18 holes, 6374yds, Par 71, SSS 71, Course record 68.
Club membership 840.
Visitors Mon, Wed-Fri. Booking required. Handicap certificate. Dress code. **Societies** Mon-Fri. Booking required. **Green Fees** £37 per day, £32 per round. **Prof** Nick Ludwell **Course Designer** J Taylor & Hawtree **Facilities** **Location** Off A63 Selby bypass

Hotel ★★★ 74% Monk Fryston Hall Hotel, MONK FRYSTON ☎ 01977 682369 29 en suite

SETTLE Map 07 SD86

Settle Buckhaw Brow, Giggleswick BD24 0DH
☎ 01729 825288 🖷 01729 825288 & 823727 (sec)
web: settlegolfclub.com
Picturesque parkland with a stream affecting play on four holes.
9 holes, 6200yds, Par 72, SSS 70.
Club membership 380.
Visitors Mon-Sun & BHs. Booking required Sat & Sun. Dress code. **Societies** Booking required. **Green Fees** £17 per round. **Course Designer** Tom Vardon **Facilities** **Location** 1m W of Settle on Kendal Rd

SKIPTON Map 07 SD95

Skipton Short Lee Ln BD23 3LF
☎ 01756 795657 🖷 01756 796665
e-mail: enquiries@skiptongolfclub.co.uk
web: www.skiptongolfclub.co.uk
Undulating parkland with some water hazards and panoramic views.
18 holes, 6049yds, Par 70, SSS 69, Course record 66.
Club membership 800.
Visitors Mon-Sun & BHs. Booking required. Dress code. **Societies** Booking required. **Green Fees** £30 per day, £24 per 18 holes, £26 Sat & Sun. **Prof** Peter Robinson **Facilities** **Leisure** snooker. **Conf** Corporate Hospitality Days **Location** 1m N of Skipton on A59

Hotel ★★★ The Devonshire Arms Country House Hotel & Spa, BOLTON ABBEY ☎ 01756 710441 & 718111 🖷 01756 710564 40 en suite

TADCASTER Map 08 SE44

Scathingwell Scarthingwell LS24 9PF
☎ 01937 557864 (pro) 557878 (club) 🖷 01937 557909
Testing water hazards and well-placed bunkers and trees provide a challenging test of golf for all handicaps at this scenic parkland course. Easy walking.
18 holes, 6771yds, Par 72, SSS 72.
Club membership 500.
Visitors Mon-Fri, Sun & BHs. Booking required. Dress code. **Societies** Booking required. **Green Fees** phone. **Prof** Steve Footman **Facilities** **Conf** Corporate Hospitality Days **Location** 4m S of Tadcaster on A162 Tadcaster-Ferrybridge road

Hotel ★★★ 77% Hazlewood Castle, Paradise Ln, Hazlewood, TADCASTER ☎ 01937 535353 9 en suite 12 annexe en suite

THIRSK Map 08 SE48

Thirsk & Northallerton Thornton-le-Street YO7 4AB
☎ 01845 522170 & 525115 🖷 01845 525115
e-mail: secretary@tngc.co.uk
web: www.tngc.co.uk
The course has good views of the nearby Hambleton Hills to the east and Wensleydale to the west. Testing course, mainly flat.
18 holes, 6495yds, Par 72, SSS 71, Course record 66.
Club membership 500.
Visitors With member Sun. Booking required. Handicap certificate. Dress code. **Societies** Booking required. **Green Fees** £30 per day, £24 per round, £40/£30 Sat & Sun. **Prof** Robert Garner **Course Designer** ADAS **Facilities** **Location** 2m N on A168

Hotel ★★ 75% Golden Fleece Hotel, 42 Market Place, THIRSK ☎ 01845 523108 23 en suite

WHITBY Map 08 NZ81

Whitby Low Straggleton, Sandsend Rd YO21 3SR
☎ 01947 600660 🖷 01947 600660
e-mail: whitby_golf_club@compuserve.com
web: www.whitbygolfclub.co.uk
Seaside course with four holes along clifftops and over ravines. Good views and a fresh sea breeze.
18 holes, 6003yds, Par 70, Course record 65.
Club membership 500.
Visitors Mon-Sun & BHs. Booking required. Handicap certificate. Dress code. **Societies** Booking required in writing. **Green Fees** £25 per day, £31 Sat & Sun. **Prof** Tony Mason **Facilities** **Location** 1.5m NW on A174

Hotel ★★ 70% White House Hotel, Upgang Ln, West Cliff, WHITBY ☎ 01947 600469 11 en suite 5 annexe en suite

YORK Map 08 SE65

Forest of Galtres Moorlands Rd, Skelton YO32 2RF
☎ 01904 766198 🖷 01904 769400
e-mail: secretary@forestofgaltres.co.uk
web: www.forestofgaltres.co.uk
Level parkland in the heart of the ancient Forest of Galtres, with mature oak trees and interesting water features coming into play on the 6th, 14th and 17th holes. Views of York Minster.
18 holes, 6534yds, Par 72, SSS 71, Course record 67. Club membership 450.
Visitors Mon-Sun & BHs. Booking required. Dress code. **Societies** Mon-Fri & Sun. Booking required. **Green Fees** £30 per day, £25 per round, £40/£30 Sat, Sun & BHs. **Prof** Phil Bradley **Course Designer** Simon Gidman **Facilities** by arrangement **Location** 0.5m from the York ring road B1237, just off A19 Thirsk road through the village of Skelton

Hotel ★★ 70% Beechwood Close Hotel, 19 Shipton Rd, Clifton, YORK ☎ 01904 658378 & 627093 🖷 01904 647124 14 en suite

Forest Park Stockton-on-the-Forest YO32 9UW
☎ 01904 400425 & 400688 🖷 01904 400717
e-mail: admin@forestparkgolfclub.co.uk
web: www.forestparkgolfclub.co.uk
Flat parkland 27-hole course with large greens and narrow tree-lined fairways. The Old Foss beck meanders through the course, creating a natural hazard on many holes.
Old Foss Course: 18 holes, 6673yds, Par 71, SSS 72, Course record 66.
The West Course: 9 holes, 3186yds, Par 35, SSS 70. Club membership 600.
Visitors Mon-Sun & BHs. Booking required. Dress code. **Societies** Booking required. **Green Fees** 18 holes £25, Sat & Sun £30. 9 holes £10, Sat & Sun £12. **Prof** Mark Winterburn **Facilities** **Conf** Corporate Hospitality Days **Location** 4m NE of York off A64 York bypass

Hotel ★★ 67% Jacobean Lodge Hotel, Plainville Ln, Wigginton, YORK ☎ 01904 762749 8 en suite

Fulford Heslington Ln YO10 5DY
☎ 01904 413579 🖷 01904 416918
e-mail: info@fulfordgolfclub.co.uk
web: www.fulfordgolfclub.co.uk
A flat, parkland and heathland course well-known for the superb quality of its turf, particularly the greens, and now famous as the venue for some of the best golf tournaments in the British Isles in past years.

Continued

18 holes, 6775yds, Par 72, SSS 72, Course record 62. Club membership 775.
Visitors Mon, Tue pm, Wed-Sun. Booking required. **Societies** Mon, Tue pm, Wed-Sun. Booking required with manager. **Green Fees** phone. **Prof** Martin Brown **Course Designer** C MacKenzie **Facilities** **Conf** Corporate Hospitality Days **Location** 2m S of York off A19

Hotel ★★★★ 70% York Marriott Hotel, Tadcaster Rd, YORK ☎ 01904 701000 151 en suite

Hotel ★★★ 71% York Pavilion Hotel, 45 Main St, Fulford, YORK ☎ 01904 622099 🖷 01904 626939 57 en suite

Heworth Muncaster House, Muncastergate YO31 9JY
☎ 01904 422389 🖷 01904 426156
e-mail: golf@heworth-gc.fsnet.co.uk
web: www.heworth-gc.co.uk
A 12-hole parkland course, easy walking. Holes 3 to 7 and 9 played twice from different tees.
12 holes, 6105yds, Par 69, SSS 69, Course record 68. Club membership 550.
Visitors Mon-Sun & BHs. Dress code. **Societies** Booking required. **Green Fees** £20 per day, £15 per round, £25/£20 Sat, Sun & BHs. **Prof** Stephen Burdett **Course Designer** B Cheal **Facilities** by arrangement **Conf** Corporate Hospitality Days **Location** 1.5m NE of city centre on A1036

Hotel ★★★ 70% Monkbar Hotel, Monkbar, YORK ☎ 01904 638086 99 en suite

Swallow Hall Crockey Hill YO19 4SG
☎ 01904 448889 🖷 01904 448219
e-mail: jtscores@hotmail.com
web: www.swallowhall.co.uk
A small 18-hole, par 3 course with three par 4s. Attached to a caravan park and holiday cottages.
18 holes, 3600yds, Par 57, SSS 56, Course record 58. Club membership 100.
Visitors Mon-Sun & BHs. **Societies** Booking required. **Green Fees** £12 per round, £14 Sat & Sun. **Course Designer** Brian Henry **Facilities** **Leisure** hard tennis courts, fishing. **Conf** facs Corporate Hospitality Days **Location** Off A19 signed Wheldrake

Hotel ★★★ 71% York Pavilion Hotel, 45 Main St, Fulford, YORK ☎ 01904 622099 57 en suite

York Lords Moor Ln, Strensall YO32 5XF
☎ 01904 491840 (sec) 490304 (pro) 🖹 01904 491852
e-mail: secretary@yorkgolfclub.co.uk
web: www.yorkgolfclub.co.uk
A pleasant, well-designed, heathland course with easy walking. The course is of good length but is flat so not too tiring. The course is well bunkered with excellent greens and there are two testing pond holes.
18 holes, 6301yds, Par 70, SSS 70, Course record 66. Club membership 750.
Visitors Mon-Fri except BHs. Dress code. Booking required. **Societies** Booking required. **Green Fees** £30 per 36 holes, £42 per 27 holes, £36 per 18 holes, Sat & Sun £47 per 27 holes, £43 per 18 holes. **Prof** AP Hoyles **Course Designer** JH Taylor **Facilities** **Location** 6m NE of York, E of Strensall

Hotel ★★★ 77% Dean Court Hotel, Duncombe Place, YORK ☎ 01904 625082 37 en suite

YORKSHIRE, SOUTH

BARNSLEY Map 08 SE30

Barnsley Wakefield Rd, Staincross S75 6JZ
☎ 01226 382856 🖹 01226 382856
e-mail: barnsleygolfclub@hotmail.com
Undulating municipal parkland course with easy walking apart from last 4 holes. Testing 8th and 18th holes.
18 holes, 5951yds, Par 69, SSS 69, Course record 64. Club membership 450.
Visitors Booking required. **Societies** Booking required. **Green Fees** phone. **Prof** Shaun Wyke **Facilities** by arrangement by arrangement by arrangement **Location** 3m N on A61

Hotel ★★★ 75% Ardsley House Hotel & Health Club, Doncaster Rd, Ardsley, BARNSLEY ☎ 01226 309955 75 en suite

Sandhill Middlecliffe Ln, Little Houghton S72 0HW
☎ 01226 753444 🖹 01226 753444
web: www.sandhillgolfclub.co.uk
Attractive, easy walking parkland with views of the surrounding countryside. The course has now almost reached full maturity and is both rewarding and challenging to the club member. The 4th hole poses a challenge, having a deep bunker directly in front of the green.
18 holes, 6257yds, Par 71, SSS 70, Course record 69. Club membership 450.
Visitors Mon-Sun & BHs. Booking required. **Societies** Booking required. **Green Fees** £15 per round, £20 Sat & Sun. **Course Designer** John Royston **Facilities** **Location** 5m E of Barnsley off A635

Hotel ★★★ 75% Ardsley House Hotel & Health Club, Doncaster Rd, Ardsley, BARNSLEY ☎ 01226 309955 75 en suite

BAWTRY Map 08 SK69

Bawtry Cross Ln, Austerfield DN10 6RF
☎ 01302 710841
web: www.bawtrygolfclub.co.uk
Championship moorland course featuring the 618yd 7th and the Postage Stamp 8th. Well drained and easy walking with attached driving range.
18 holes, 6994yds, Par 73, SSS 73, Course record 67. Club membership 600.
Visitors Booking required Sat & Sun. **Societies** Sat & Sun pm. Booking required. **Green Fees** phone. **Prof** Darran Roberts **Facilities** **Conf** Corporate Hospitality Days **Location** 2m from Bawtry on A614

Hotel ★★★★ 70% Mount Pleasant Hotel, Great North Rd, ☎ 01302 868696 & 868219 🖹 01302 865130 57 en suite

CONISBROUGH Map 08 SK59

Crookhill Park Municipal Carr Ln DN12 2AH
☎ 01709 862979 🖹 01709 866455
Naturally sloping parkland with many holes featuring tight dog-legs and small, undulating greens. The signature hole (11th) involves a fearsome tee shot over a ditch onto a sloping fairway and final shot to an elevated green surrounded by tall trees and deep bunkers.
18 holes, 5849yds, Par 70, SSS 68, Course record 64. Club membership 350.
Visitors Booking required. **Societies** Booking required. **Green Fees** phone. **Prof** Richard Swaine **Facilities** **Location** 1.5m SE on B6094

Hotel ★★ 64% Pastures Hotel, Pastures Rd, MEXBOROUGH ☎ 01709 577707 29 en suite

DONCASTER Map 08 SE50

Doncaster 278 Bawtry Rd, Bessacarr DN4 7PD
☎ 01302 865632 🖹 01302 865994
e-mail: doncastergolf@aol.com
web: www.doncastergolfclub.org.uk
18 holes, 6220yds, Par 69, SSS 70, Course record 66.
Course Designer A MacKenzie, F Hawtree **Location** 4m SE on A638
Phone for further details

Hotel ★★★★ 70% Mount Pleasant Hotel, Great North Rd, ☎ 01302 868696 & 868219 🖹 01302 865130 57 en suite

Doncaster Town Moor Bawtry Rd, Belle Vue DN4 5HU
☎ 01302 535286 (pro shop) & 533167 (bar)
🖹 01302 533778
e-mail: dtmgc@btconnect.com
Easy walking, but testing, heathland course with good true greens. Notable hole is 11th (par 4), 464yds. Situated in centre of racecourse.
18 holes, 6072yds, Par 69, SSS 69, Course record 63. Club membership 520.
Visitors Mon-Sat. Sun pm. Booking required. **Societies** Booking required. **Green Fees** £20 per round, £22 Sat & Sun. **Prof** Steven Shaw **Facilities** **Conf** Corporate Hospitality Days **Location** 1.5m E at racecourse on A638

Hotel Campanile, Doncaster Leisure Park, Bawtry Rd, DONCASTER ☎ 01302 370770 50 en suite

Continued

Owston Park Owston Ln, Owston DN6 8EF
☎ 01302 330821
e-mail: will@owstonpark.fsnet.co.uk
9 holes, 2866yds, Par 35, SSS 70.
Course Designer M Parker **Location** 5m N of Doncaster off A19
Phone for further details

Hotel ★★★ 68% Danum Hotel, High St, DONCASTER
☎ 01302 342261 66 en suite

Thornhurst Park Holme Ln, Owston DN5 0LR
☎ 01302 337799 🖹 01302 721495
e-mail: info@thornhurst.co.uk
web: www.thornhurst.co.uk
Surrounded by Owston Wood, this scenic parkland course has numerous strategically placed bunkers, and a lake comes into play at the 7th and 8th holes.
18 holes, 6490yds, Par 72, SSS 72, Course record 72. Club membership 160.
Visitors Mon-Sun & BHs. Booking required Fri-Sun & BHs. Dress code. **Societies** Booking required. **Green Fees** £12 per 18 holes, £7 per 9 holes, £14/£8 Sat, Sun & BHs. **Prof** Kevin Pearce **Facilities** **Conf** facs Corporate Hospitality Days **Location** On A19 between Bentley & Askern

Hotel ★★★ 68% Danum Hotel, High St, DONCASTER
☎ 01302 342261 66 en suite

Wheatley Armthorpe Rd DN2 5QB
☎ 01302 831655 🖹 01302 812736
18 holes, 6405yds, Par 71, SSS 71, Course record 64.
Course Designer George Duncan **Location** NE of town centre off A18
Phone for further details

Hotel ★★★ 69% Regent Hotel, Regent Square, DONCASTER ☎ 01302 364180 52 en suite

HATFIELD Map 08 SE60

Kings Wood Thorne Rd DN7 6EP
☎ 01405 741343
A flat course with ditches that come into play on several holes, especially on the testing back nine. Notable holes are the 12th par 4, 16th and par 5 18th. Water is a prominent feature with several large lakes strategically placed.
18 holes, 6002yds, Par 70, SSS 69, Course record 67. Club membership 100.
Visitors Booking required. **Societies** Booking required. **Green Fees** £7.50 per 18 holes, £4.50 per 9 holes, £8.50/£5 Sat, Sun & BHs. **Prof** Mark Cunningham **Course Designer** John Hunt **Facilities** **Location** M180 junct 1, A614 towards Thorne, onto A1146 towards Hatfield for 0.8m

Hotel ★★★ 66% Belmont Hotel, Horsefair Green, THORNE ☎ 01405 812320 23 en suite

HICKLETON Map 08 SE40

Hickleton Lidgett Ln DN5 7BE
☎ 01709 896081 🖹 01709 896083
e-mail: hickleton@hickletongolfclub.freeserve.co.uk
web: www.hickletongolf.co.uk
Undulating, picturesque parkland course designed by Neil Coles and Brian Huggett offering a good test of golf and fine views of the eastern Pennines.
18 holes, 6434yds, Par 71, SSS 71, Course record 64. Club membership 625.
Visitors Mon-Fri. Booking required. Dress code. **Societies** Booking required. **Green Fees** £30 per day, £25 per round, £30 per round Sat, Sun & BHs. **Prof** Paul J Audsley **Course Designer** Huggett, Coles **Facilities** **Conf** facs Corporate Hospitality Days **Location** A1(M) junct 37, 3m W off A635

Hotel ★★★ 68% Danum Hotel, High St, DONCASTER
☎ 01302 342261 66 en suite

HIGH GREEN Map 08 SK39

Tankersley Park S35 4LG
☎ 0114 246 8247 🖹 0114 245 7818
e-mail: secretary@tpgc.freeserve.co.uk
Rolling parkland course that demands accuracy rather than length. Lush fairways. The 18th hole considered to be one of the best last hole tests in Yorkshire.
18 holes, 6244yds, Par 70, SSS 70, Course record 64. Club membership 634.
Visitors Mon-Fri & BHs. Handicap certificate. Dress code. Booking required. **Societies** Booking required in writing. **Green Fees** £36 per day, £27 per round, £36 per round Sat & Sun. **Prof** Ian Kirk **Course Designer** Hawtree **Facilities** **Conf** Corporate Hospitality Days **Location** A61/M1 onto A616 Stocksbridge bypass

Hotel ★★★★ 75% Tankersley Manor, Church Ln, TANKERSLEY ☎ 01226 744700 99 en suite

RAWMARSH Map 08 SK49

Wath Abdy Ln S62 7SJ
☎ 01709 878609 🖹 01709 877097
e-mail: golf@wathgolfclub.co.uk
Parkland course, not easy in spite of its length. Testing course with narrow fairways and small greens. Many dikes crisscross fairways, making playing for position paramount. Strategically placed copses reward the golfer who is straight off the tee. Playing over a pond into a prevailing wind on the 12th hole to a postage stamp size green, will test the most accomplished player.
18 holes, 6123yds, Par 70, SSS 69, Course record 65. Club membership 650.
Visitors Mon-Fri. Booking required. Handicap certificate. Dress code. **Societies** Booking required. **Green Fees** £30 per day, £25 per round. **Prof** Chris Bassett **Facilities** **Conf** facs Corporate Hospitality Days **Location** 2m N of Rotherham on B6089

Hotel ★★★ 65% Carlton Park Hotel, 102-104 Moorgate Rd, ROTHERHAM ☎ 01709 849955 80 en suite

ROTHERHAM Map 08 SK49

Grange Park Upper Wortley Rd S61 2SJ
☎ 01709 559497
e-mail: crowncourt@bun.com
18 holes, 6421yds, Par 71, SSS 71, Course record 65.
Course Designer Fred Hawtree **Location** 3m NW off A629
Phone for further details

Hotel ★★★★ 75% Tankersley Manor, Church Ln, TANKERSLEY ☎ 01226 744700 99 en suite

Phoenix Pavilion Ln, Brinsworth S60 5PA
☎ 01709 363864 & 382624 01709 363788
Undulating meadowland course with variable wind.
18 holes, 6182yds, Par 71, SSS 70, Course record 65.
Club membership 930.
Visitors Booking required. Handicap certificate. Dress code. **Societies** Booking required. **Green Fees** Summer £25 per day, £19 per round, £33/£25 Sat, Sun & BHs. Winter £16 per round/day, £22 Sat, Sun & BHs. **Prof** M Roberts **Course Designer** CK Cotton **Facilities** **Leisure** hard tennis courts, squash, fishing, gymnasium. **Conf** facs Corporate Hospitality Days **Location** SW of Rotherham off A630

Hotel ★★★ 65% Carlton Park Hotel, 102-104 Moorgate Rd, ROTHERHAM ☎ 01709 849955 80 en suite

Rotherham Golf Club Ltd Thrybergh Park, Doncaster Rd, Thrybergh S65 4NU
☎ 01709 859500 01709 859517
18 holes, 6324yds, Par 70, SSS 70, Course record 65.
Location 3.5m E on A630
Phone for further details

Hotel ★★★ 69% Best Western Elton Hotel, Main St, Bramley, ROTHERHAM ☎ 01709 545681 13 en suite 16 annexe en suite

Sitwell Park Shrogswood Rd S60 4BY
☎ 01709 541046 01709 703637
e-mail: secretary@sitwellgolf.co.uk
Undulating parkland.
18 holes, 5960yds, Par 71, SSS 69.
Club membership 450.
Visitors Mon-Fri & Sun. Booking required. Handicap certificate. Dress code. **Societies** Booking required. **Green Fees** £34 per day, £26 per round, £40/£32 Sun. **Prof** Nic Taylor **Course Designer** A MacKenzie **Facilities** **Conf** Corporate Hospitality Days **Location** 2m SE of Rotherham centre off A631

Hotel ★★★★ 64% Hellaby Hall Hotel, Old Hellaby Ln, Hellaby, ROTHERHAM ☎ 01709 702701 90 en suite

SHEFFIELD Map 08 SK38

Abbeydale Twentywell Ln, Dore S17 4QA
☎ 0114 236 0763 0114 236 0762
e-mail: abbeygolf@compuserve.com
web: www.abbeydalegolf.co.uk
18 holes, 6261yds, Par 71, SSS 71, Course record 64.
Course Designer Herbert Fowler **Location** 4m SW of city off A621
Phone for further details

Hotel ★★★ 72% The Beauchief Hotel, 161 Abbeydale Rd South, SHEFFIELD ☎ 0114 262 0500 50 en suite

Beauchief Public Abbey Ln S8 0DB
☎ 0114 236 7274
18 holes, 5469yds, Par 67, SSS 66, Course record 65.
Location 4m SW of city off A621
Phone for further details

Hotel ★★★ 72% The Beauchief Hotel, 161 Abbeydale Rd South, SHEFFIELD ☎ 0114 262 0500 50 en suite

Birley Wood Birley Ln S12 3BP
☎ 0114 264 7262
e-mail: birley@sivltd.com
web: www.birleywood.com
Undulating meadowland course with well-varied features, easy walking and good views. Practice range and putting green.
Fairway course: 18 holes, 5734yds, Par 69, SSS 67, Course record 64.
Birley Course: 18 holes, 5037, Par 66, SSS 65.
Club membership 278.
Visitors Mon-Sun & BHs. **Societies** Booking required. **Green Fees** £13 per 18 holes, £8.40 per 9 holes. **Prof** Peter Ball **Facilities** **Location** 4.5m SE of city off A616

Hotel ★★★ 66% Mosborough Hall Hotel, High St, Mosborough, SHEFFIELD ☎ 0114 248 4353 52 en suite

Concord Park Shiregreen Ln S5 6AE
☎ 0114 257 7378
Hilly municipal parkland course with some fairways wood-flanked, good views, often windy. Seven par 3 holes.
18 holes, 4872yds, Par 67, SSS 64, Course record 57.
Club membership 150.
Visitors Booking required. **Societies** Pay & play. **Green Fees** phone. **Prof** W Allcroft **Facilities** **Leisure** hard tennis courts, heated indoor swimming pool, squash, gymnasium. **Conf** Corporate Hospitality Days **Location** 3.5m N of city on B6086, off A6135

Hotel Premier Travel Inn Sheffield (Meadowhall), Sheffield Rd, Meadowhall, SHEFFIELD ☎ 0870 9906440 103 en suite

Dore & Totley Bradway Rd, Bradway S17 4QR
☎ 0114 2366 844 0114 2366 844
e-mail: dtgc@lineone.net
web: www.doreandtotleygolf.co.uk
18 holes, 6265yds, Par 70, SSS 70, Course record 65.
Location 7m S of city on B6054, off A61
Phone for further details

Hotel ★★★ 72% The Beauchief Hotel, 161 Abbeydale Rd South, SHEFFIELD ☎ 0114 262 0500 50 en suite

Prices may change during the currency of the guide, always check when booking

Hallamshire Golf Club Ltd Sandygate S10 4LA
☎ 0114 230 2153 Fax 0114 230 5413
e-mail: secretary@hallamshiregolfclub.co.uk
web: www.hallamshiregolfclub.co.uk
Situated on a shelf of land at a height of 850ft. Magnificent views to the west. Moorland turf, long carries over ravine and small and quick greens.
18 holes, 6346yds, Par 71, SSS 71, Course record 65. Club membership 600.
Visitors Mon-Fri. Booking required. Handicap certificate. Dress code. **Societies** Booking required. **Green Fees** £45 per day/round, £60 Sat, Sun & BHs. **Prof** GR Tickell **Course Designer** Various **Facilities** **Conf** Corporate Hospitality Days **Location** Off A57 at Crosspool onto Sandygate Rd, clubhouse 0.75m on right

Hotel ★★★★ 71% Marriott Sheffield, Kenwood Rd, SHEFFIELD ☎ 0870 400 7261 114 en suite

Hillsborough Worrall Rd S6 4BE
☎ 0114 234 9151 (sec) Fax 0114 229 4105
e-mail: admin@hillsboroughgolfclub.co.uk
web: www.hillsboroughgolfclub.co.uk
Beautiful moorland and woodland course 500ft above sea level, reasonable walking. Challenging first four holes into a prevailing wind and a tight, testing 14th hole.
18 holes, 6345yards, Par 71, SSS 70, Course record 63. Club membership 650.
Visitors Mon-Fri & Sun. Booking required. Dress code. **Societies** Booking required. **Green Fees** phone. **Prof** Lewis Horsman **Facilities** **Location** 3m NW of city off A616

Hotel ★★★★ 75% Tankersley Manor, Church Ln, TANKERSLEY ☎ 01226 744700 99 en suite

Lees Hall Hemsworth Rd, Norton S8 8LL
☎ 0114 250 7868
18 holes, 6171yds, Par 71, SSS 70, Course record 63.
Location 3.5m S of city off A6102
Phone for further details

Hotel ★★★★ 71% Marriott Sheffield, Kenwood Rd, SHEFFIELD ☎ 0870 400 7261 114 en suite

Rother Valley Golf Centre Mansfield Rd, Wales Bar S26 5PQ
☎ 0114 247 3000 Fax 0114 247 6000
e-mail: rother-jackbarker@btinternet.com
web: www.jackbarker.com
The challenging Blue Monster parkland course features a variety of water hazards. Notable holes include the 7th, with its island green fronted by water and dominated by bunkers to the rear. Lookout for the water on the par 5 18th.
18 holes, 6602yds, Par 72, SSS 72, Course record 70. Club membership 500.
Visitors Mon-Sun & BHs. Booking required Fri-Sun & BHs. Dress code. **Societies** Booking required. **Green Fees** £15 per 18 holes Mon-Thu, £17 Fri, £19.50 Sat & Sun. **Prof** Jason Ripley **Course Designer** Michael Shattock & Mark Roe **Facilities** **Location** M1 junct 31, signs to Rother Valley Country Park

Hotel ★★★ 66% Mosborough Hall Hotel, High St, Mosborough, SHEFFIELD ☎ 0114 248 4353 52 en suite

Tinsley Park Municipal Golf High Hazels Park, Darnall S9 4PE
☎ 0114 244 8974
e-mail: tinsleyparkgc@hotmail.com
Undulating parkland with plenty of trees and rough. Easy walking. The signature hole is the par 3 17th.
18 holes, 6064yds, Par 70, SSS 68, Course record 66. Club membership 150.
Visitors Mon-Sun & BHs. **Societies** Booking required. **Green Fees** £10.40 per round, £13 Sat & Sun. **Prof** W Yellott **Facilities** by arrangement **Leisure** hard tennis courts. **Location** 4m E of city off A630

Hotel ★★★ 66% Mosborough Hall Hotel, High St, Mosborough, SHEFFIELD ☎ 0114 248 4353 52 en suite

SILKSTONE — Map 08 SE20

Silkstone Field Head, Elmhirst Ln S75 4LD
☎ 01226 790328 Fax 01226 794902
Parkland and downland course, fine views over the Pennines. Testing golf.
18 holes, 6069yds, Par 70, SSS 70, Course record 64. Club membership 530.
Visitors Mon-Fri. Booking required. Dress code. **Societies** Booking required. **Green Fees** £26 per round, £34 per day. **Prof** Kevin Guy **Facilities** **Conf** Corporate Hospitality Days **Location** 1m E off A628

Hotel ★★★ 75% Ardsley House Hotel & Health Club, Doncaster Rd, Ardsley, BARNSLEY ☎ 01226 309955 75 en suite

STOCKSBRIDGE — Map 08 SK29

Stocksbridge & District Royd Ln, Deepcar S36 2RZ
☎ 0114 288 2003 (office) Fax 0114 283 1460
e-mail: secretary@stocksbridgeanddistrictgolfclub.com
web: www.stocksbridgeanddistrictgolfclub.com
18 holes, 5200yds, Par 65, SSS 65, Course record 60.
Course Designer Dave Thomas **Location** S of town centre
Phone for further details

Hotel ★★★ 71% Whitley Hall Hotel, Elliott Ln, Grenoside, SHEFFIELD ☎ 0114 245 4444 20 en suite

THORNE — Map 08 SE61

Thorne Kirton Ln DN8 5RJ
☎ 01405 812084 Fax 01405 741899
Picturesque parkland with 6000 newly planted trees. Water hazards on 11th, 14th and 18th holes.
18 holes, 5366yds, Par 68, SSS 66, Course record 62. Club membership 300.
Visitors Mon-Sun & BHs. **Societies** Booking required. **Green Fees** £10, £12 Sat & Sun. **Prof** Edward Highfield **Course Designer** RD Highfield **Facilities** **Conf** facs Corporate Hospitality Days **Location** M180 Junct 1, A614 into Thorne, left onto Kirton Ln

Hotel ★★★ 66% Belmont Hotel, Horsefair Green, THORNE ☎ 01405 812320 23 en suite

WORTLEY Map 08 SK39

Wortley Hermit Hill Ln S35 7DF
☎ 0114 288 8469 🖷 0114 288 8488
e-mail: wortley.golfclub@btconnect.com

18 holes, 6028yds, Par 69, SSS 68, Course record 62.
Location 0.5m NE of village off A629
Phone for further details

Hotel ★★★ 71% Whitley Hall Hotel, Elliott Ln, Grenoside, SHEFFIELD ☎ 0114 245 4444 20 en suite

YORKSHIRE, WEST

ADDINGHAM Map 07 SE04

Bracken Ghyll Skipton Rd LS29 0SL
☎ 01943 831207 🖷 01943 839453
e-mail: office@brackenghyll.co.uk
web: www.brackenghyll.co.uk
On the edge of the Yorkshire Dales, the course commands superb views over Ilkley Moor and the Wharfe valley. The demanding 18-hole layout is a test of both golfing ability and sensible course management.
18 holes, 5600yds, Par 69, SSS 67, Course record 69.
Club membership 350.
Visitors Mon-Sun& BHs. Booking required. Dress code. **Societies** Booking required. **Green Fees** £15 per 18 holes, £18 Sat, Sun & BHs. **Prof** John Hammond **Facilities** **Conf** Corporate Hospitality Days **Location** Off A65 between Ilkley and Skipton

Hotel ★★★ 76% Rombalds Hotel & Restaurant, 11 West View, Wells Rd, ILKLEY ☎ 01943 603201 15 en suite

ALWOODLEY Map 08 SE24

Alwoodley Wigton Ln LS17 8SA
☎ 0113 268 1680 🖷 0113 293 9458
e-mail: alwoodley@btconnect.com
web: www.alwoodley.co.uk
Natural moorland course with heather, whins and shrubs. Plentifully and cunningly bunkered with undulating and interesting greens.

18 holes, 6666yds, Par 72, SSS 72.
Club membership 460.
Visitors Mon-Sun except BHs. Booking required. Dress code. **Societies** Booking required.i **Green Fees** £70 per day/round (£85 weekends). £35 after 4pm. Winter reduced rates. **Prof** John R Green **Course Designer** A MacKenzie **Facilities** **Conf** Corporate Hospitality Days **Location** 5m N off A61

BAILDON Map 07 SE13

Baildon Moorgate BD17 5PP
☎ 01274 584266
web: www.baildongolfclub.com
Moorland course set out in links style with the outward front nine looping back to clubhouse. Panoramic views with testing short holes in prevailing winds. The 2nd hole has been described as one of Britain's scariest.

18 holes, 6225yds, Par 70, SSS 70, Course record 63.
Club membership 750.
Visitors Mon-Fri, Sun & BHs. Booking required Tue. Dress code. **Societies** Booking required. **Green Fees** 18 holes £26 (weekends £30). **Prof** Richard Masters **Course Designer** Tom MorrisJames Braid **Facilities** **Leisure** snooker tables. **Conf** facs **Location** 3m N of Bradford off A6038 at Shipley

Hotel ★★★★ 70% Marriott Hollins Hall Hotel & Country Club, Hollins Hill, Baildon, SHIPLEY ☎ 0870 400 7227 122 en suite

If the name of the club appears in italics, details have not been confirmed for this edition of the guide

BINGLEY Map 07 SE13

Bingley St Ives Golf Club House, St Ives Estate, Harden BD16 1AT
☎ 01274 562436 01274 511788
e-mail: secretary@bingleystivesgc.co.uk
web: www.bingleystivesgc.co.uk
Parkland and moorland course.
18 holes, 6485yds, Par 71, SSS 71, Course record 69.
Club membership 450.
Visitors contact club for details. Handicap certificate. Dress code. **Societies** Booking required. **Green Fees** Phone. **Prof** Ray Firth **Course Designer** A MacKenzie **Facilities** **Conf** facs Corporate Hospitality Days **Location** 0.75m W off B6429

Hotel ★★ 67% Dalesgate Hotel, 406 Skipton Rd, Utley, KEIGHLEY ☎ 01535 664930 20 en suite

Shipley Beckfoot Ln BD16 1LX
☎ 01274 568652 (Secretary) 01274 567739
e-mail: office@shipleygc.co.uk
web: www.shipleygc.co.uk
Well-established parkland course, founded in 1922, featuring six good par 3s.
18 holes, 6235yds, Par 71, SSS 70, Course record 65.
Club membership 600.
Visitors Mon, Wed-Fri, Sun & BHs. Tue pm only. Booking required. Dress code. **Societies** Booking required. **Green Fees** £39 per day, £33 per round, £49/£40 Sun & BHs. **Prof** J R Parry **Course Designer** Colt, Allison, MacKenzie, Braid **Facilities** **Conf** facs Corporate Hospitality Days **Location** 6m N of Bradford on A650

Hotel ★★ 67% Dalesgate Hotel, 406 Skipton Rd, Utley, KEIGHLEY ☎ 01535 664930 20 en suite

BRADFORD Map 07 SE13

Bradford Moor Scarr Hall, Pollard Ln BD2 4RW
☎ 01274 771716 & 771693
Moorland course with tricky undulating greens.
9 holes, 5900yds, Par 70, SSS 68, Course record 65.
Club membership 330.
Visitors Mon-Fr & BHs. Booking required BHs. Dress code. **Societies** Booking required. **Green Fees** £12 weekdays only. **Facilities** **Location** 2m NE of city centre off A658

Hotel ★★★ 71% Midland Hotel, Forster Square, BRADFORD ☎ 01274 735735 90 en suite

Clayton Thornton View Rd, Clayton BD14 6JX
☎ 01274 880047
Parkland course, difficult in windy conditions.
9 holes, 6300yds, Par 72, SSS 72.
Club membership 250.
Visitors Mon-Fri & BHs. Dress code. **Societies** Booking required. **Green Fees** £17 per 18 holes, £9 per 9 holes. **Facilities** **Conf** Corporate Hospitality Days **Location** 2.5m SW of city centre on A647

Hotel ★★★ 64% Novotel Bradford, 6 Roydsdale Way, BRADFORD ☎ 01274 683683 119 en suite

East Bierley South View Rd, East Bierley BD4 6PP
☎ 01274 681023 01274 683666
e-mail: rjwelch@hotmail.com
Hilly moorland course with narrow fairways. Two par 3 holes over 200yds.
9 holes, 4700yds, Par 64, SSS 63, Course record 59.
Club membership 300.
Visitors Mon-Sat & BHs. Dress code. **Societies** welcome. **Green Fees** terms on application. **Prof** J. Whittom **Facilities** **Location** 4m SE of city centre off A650

Hotel ★★★ 64% Novotel Bradford, 6 Roydsdale Way, BRADFORD ☎ 01274 683683 119 en suite

Headley Headley Ln, Thornton BD13 3LX
☎ 01274 833481 01274 833481
e-mail: honsec-hgc@yahoo.com
9 holes, 4864yds, Par 65, SSS 65, Course record 57.
Location 4m W of city centre off B6145 at Thornton
Telephone for further details

Hotel ★★★ 71% Midland Hotel, Forster Square, BRADFORD ☎ 01274 735735 90 en suite

Queensbury Brighouse Rd, Queensbury BD13 1QF
☎ 01274 882155 & 816864 01274 882155
e-mail: queensburygolf@supanet.com
Undulating woodland and parkland.
9 holes, 5024yds, Par 66, SSS 65, Course record 59.
Club membership 350.
Visitors Mon-Fri & BHs. Booking required BHs. Dress code. **Societies** Booking required. **Green Fees** Phone. **Prof** David Delaney **Course Designer** Jonathan Gaunt **Facilities** **Conf** Corporate Hospitality Days **Location** 4m from Bradford on A647

Hotel ★★★ 71% Midland Hotel, Forster Square, BRADFORD ☎ 01274 735735 90 en suite

South Bradford Pearson Rd, Odsal BD6 1BH
☎ 01274 673346 (pro shop) & 679195 01274 690643
Hilly course with good greens, trees and ditches. Interesting short 2nd hole (par 3) 200yds, well-bunkered and played from an elevated tee.
9 holes, 6068yds, Par 70, SSS 68, Course record 65.
Club membership 300.
Visitors Mon-Sun & BHs. Booking required. Dress code. **Societies** Booking required. **Green Fees** Phone. **Prof** Paul Cooke **Facilities** by arrangement **Location** 2m S of city centre off A638

Hotel ★★★ 64% Novotel Bradford, 6 Roydsdale Way, BRADFORD ☎ 01274 683683 119 en suite

West Bowling Newall Hall, Rooley Ln BD5 8LB
☎ 01274 393207 (office) & 728036 (pro)
🖹 01274 393207
18 holes, 5769yds, Par 69, SSS 67, Course record 65.
Location Junct M606
Telephone for further details

Hotel ★★★ 67% Cedar Court Hotel, Mayo Av, Off Rooley Ln, BRADFORD ☎ 01274 406606 131 en suite

West Bradford Chellow Grange Rd, Haworth Rd BD9 6NP
☎ 01274 542767 🖹 01274 482079
e-mail: secretary @westbradfordgolfclub.co.uk
web: www.westbradfordgolfclub.co.uk
Parkland course, not of great length by modern standards, but provides a good test for golfers of all abilities with its undulating terrain, tree-lined fairways and demanding par 3 holes.
18 holes, 5738yds, Par 69, SSS 68, Course record 63.
Club membership 440.
Visitors Mon-Sun & BHs. Booking required. Dress code. **Societies** Booking required. **Green Fees** £30 per day/round. **Prof** Nigel M Barber **Facilities** **Leisure** snooker room. **Conf** facs Corporate Hospitality Days **Location** 3.5 m W of city centre off B6144

Hotel ★★★★ 70% Marriott Hollins Hall Hotel & Country Club, Hollins Hill, Baildon, SHIPLEY ☎ 0870 400 7227 122 en suite

BRIGHOUSE Map 07 SE12

Willow Valley Highmoor Ln, Clifton HD6 4JB
☎ 01274 878624
e-mail: golf@wvgc.co.uk
web: www.wvgc.co.uk
A championship length 18-hole course offering a unique golfing experience, featuring island greens, shaped fairways and bunkers, and multiple teeing areas. The nine-hole course offers an exciting challenge to less experienced golfers and a new 18 hole course, Pine Valley, open Spring 2006, is suitable for golfers of all abilities.

Willow Valley: 18 holes, 6496yds, Par 72, SSS 74, Course record 69.
Pine Valley: 18 holes, 5250yds, Par 67.
Fountain Ridge: 9 holes, 2039, Par 62, SSS 60.
Club membership 350.
Visitors may play Mon-Sun & BHs. Dress code. **Societies** Booking required. **Green Fees** Willow Valley £25 per round (£35 Sat, Sun & BHs), Pine Valley £14 per round (£16 Sat, Sun & BHs), Fountain Ridge per round £7.50 (£9 Sat, Sun & BHs). **Prof** Julian Haworth **Course Designer** Jonathan Gaunt **Facilities** by arrangement **Leisure** 3 hole floodlit academy course. **Conf** Corporate Hospitality Days **Location** M62 junct 25, A644 towards Brighouse, right at rdbt onto A643, course 2m on right

Continued

Hotel ★★★ 66% Healds Hall Hotel, Leeds Rd, Liversedge, DEWSBURY ☎ 01924 409112 24 en suite

CLECKHEATON Map 08 SE12

Cleckheaton & District Bradford Rd BD19 6BU
☎ 01274 851266 🖹 01274 871382
e-mail: info@cleckheatongolf.fsnet.co.uk
web: www.cleckheatongolfclub.fsnet.co.uk
Parkland with gentle hills and easy walking. Feature holes: 5th, 16th and 17th.
18 holes, 5706yds, Par 70, SSS 68, Course record 61.
Club membership 550.
Visitors Mon-Sat. Booking required Sun. **Societies** Booking required. **Green Fees** Phone. **Prof** Mike Ingham **Course Designer** A MacKenzie **Facilities** **Location** M62 junct 26, towards Oakenshaw, 100yds on left, signed Low Moor

Hotel ★★★ 71% Gomersal Park Hotel, Moor Ln, GOMERSAL ☎ 01274 869386 100 en suite

DEWSBURY Map 08 SE22

Hanging Heaton White Cross Rd WF12 7DT
☎ 01924 461606 🖹 01924 430100
e-mail: ken.wood@hhgc.org
web: www.h.h.gc.org.uk
Arable land, easy walking, fine views. Testing 4th hole (par 3).
9 holes, 5836yds, Par 69, SSS 68.
Club membership 500.
Visitors Mon-Fri except BHs. Booking required. **Societies** Booking required. **Green Fees** £17 per round. **Prof** Gareth Moore **Facilities** by arrangement by arrangement by arrangement **Conf** facs Corporate Hospitality Days **Location** 0.75m NE off A653

Hotel ★★★ 66% Healds Hall Hotel, Leeds Rd, Liversedge, DEWSBURY ☎ 01924 409112 24 en suite

ELLAND Map 07 SE12

Elland Hammerstone, Leach Ln HX5 0TA
☎ 01422 372505 & 374886 (pro)
Nine-hole parkland course played off 18 tees.
9 holes, 5498yds, Par 66, SSS 67, Course record 65.
Club membership 450.
Visitors Mon-Sun. **Societies** Booking required. **Green Fees** Phone. **Prof** N Krzywicki **Facilities** **Location** M62 junct 24, signs to Blackley

FENAY BRIDGE Map 08 SE11

Woodsome Hall HD8 0LQ
☎ 01484 602739 01484 608260
e-mail: thesecretary@woodsome.co.uk
web: www.woodsomehall.co.uk
A parkland course with good views and a historic clubhouse.

18 holes, 6096yds, Par 70, SSS 69, Course record 67.
Club membership 800.
Visitors Mon-Sun & BHs. Booking required Tue, Sat & Sun. Handicap certificate. Dress code. **Societies** Booking required. **Green Fees** Phone. **Prof** M Higginbotton **Facilities** **Location** 1.5m SW off A629

Hotel ★★★ 69% Bagden Hall, Wakefield Rd, Scissett, HUDDERSFIELD ☎ 01484 865330 16 en suite

GARFORTH Map 08 SE43

Garforth Long Ln LS25 2DS
☎ 0113 286 2021 0113 286 3308
e-mail: garforthgcltd@lineone.net
web: www.garforthgolfclub.co.uk
Gently undulating parkland with fine views and easy walking.
18 holes, 6304yds, Par 70, SSS 70, Course record 64.
Club membership 600.
Visitors Mon-Fri except BHs. Booking required. Dress code. **Societies** Booking required. **Green Fees** Mon-Fri £36 per round/£42 per day. **Prof** Ken Findlater **Course Designer** A MacKenzie **Facilities** **Conf** Corporate Hospitality Days **Location** 6m E of Leeds, next to A1/M1 link road

Hotel ★★★ 73% Milford Hotel, A1 Great North Rd, Peckfield, LEEDS ☎ 01977 681800 46 en suite

GUISELEY Map 08 SE14

Bradford (Hawksworth) Hawksworth Ln LS20 8NP
☎ 01943 875570 01943 875570
web: www.bradfordgolfclub.co.uk
Set in undulating countryside, the course is a moorland links laid out on the southern slope of a wooded ridge about 650ft above sea level. The spacious greens with their subtle borrows, together with some tough and uncompromising par 4s make this a challenging course. The testing par 4 10th and the par 3 14th require accurate shots to well-protected greens.
Hawksworth: 18 holes, 6303yds, Par 71, SSS 71, Course record 65.
Club membership 650.
Visitors Handicap certificate and contact in advance. May not play Sat. **Societies** Booking required. **Green Fees** Phone. **Prof** Sydney Weldon **Course Designer** W H Fowler **Facilities** **Conf** Corporate Hospitality Days **Location** SW of town centre off A6038

Hotel ★★★★ 70% Marriott Hollins Hall Hotel & Country Club, Hollins Hill, Baildon, SHIPLEY ☎ 0870 400 7227 122 en suite

HALIFAX Map 07 SE02

Halifax Union Ln, Ogden HX2 8XR
☎ 01422 244171
e-mail: halifax.golfclub@virgin.net
web: www.halifaxgolfclub.co.uk
Moorland course crossed by streams, natural hazards and offering fine views of wildlife and the surroundings. Testing 172-yd 17th (par 3).
18 holes, 6037yds, Par 70, SSS 69, Course record 65.
Club membership 700.
Visitors Tue-Fri. Booking required Sat, Sun & BHs. Dress code. **Societies** Booking required. **Green Fees** Phone. **Prof** Michael Allison **Course Designer** A Herd, J Braid **Facilities** **Conf** facs Corporate Hospitality Days **Location** 4m from Halifax on A629 Halifax-Keighley road

Hotel ★★★ 72% Holdsworth House Hotel, Holdsworth, HALIFAX ☎ 01422 240024 40 en suite

Lightcliffe Knowle Top Rd, Lightcliffe HX3 8SW
☎ 01422 202459 204081
A parkland course where positioning of the drive is as important as length. Signature hole is a dog-leg with the second shot over a deep ravine.
9 holes, 5388 metres, Par 68, SSS 68.
Club membership 460.
Visitors Mon, Tue, Thu, Fri, Sun & BHs. Handicap certificate. Dress code. **Societies** welcome. **Green Fees** £18 per 18 holes, £22 Sun. **Prof** Robert Tickle **Facilities** **Location** 3.5m E of Halifax on A58

Hotel ★★★ 72% Holdsworth House Hotel, Holdsworth, HALIFAX ☎ 01422 240024 40 en suite

West End Paddock Ln, Highroad Well HX2 0NT
☎ 01422 341878 01422 341878
e-mail: westendgc@btinternet.com
web: www.westendgc.co.uk
Semi-moorland course. Tree lined. Two ponds.
18 holes, 5951yds, Par 69, SSS 69, Course record 62.
Club membership 560.
Visitors Mon, Wed-Fri, Sun & BHs. Booking required Sun & BHs. Dress code. **Societies** Booking required. **Green Fees** £15 per round. **Prof** David Rishworth **Facilities** **Conf** Corporate Hospitality Days **Location** W of town centre off A646

Hotel ★★★ 72% Holdsworth House Hotel, Holdsworth, HALIFAX ☎ 01422 240024 40 en suite

HEBDEN BRIDGE Map 07 SD92

Hebden Bridge Great Mount, Wadsworth HX7 8PH
☎ 01422 842896 & 842732
Moorland course with splendid views.
9 holes, 5242yds, Par 68, SSS 67, Course record 61.
Club membership 300.
Visitors Mon-Fr, Sun except BHs. Booking required Tue, Thu & Sun. Handicap certificate. Dress code. **Societies** Booking required. **Green Fees** £12 per 18 holes (£15 weekends). **Facilities** **Location** 1.5m E off A6033

Hotel ★★ 71% Old White Lion Hotel, Main St, HAWORTH ☎ 01535 642313 15 en suite

HOLYWELL GREEN Map 07 SE01

Halifax Bradley Hall HX4 9AN
☎ 01422 374108
18 holes, 6138yds, Par 70, SSS 70, Course record 65.
Location S on A6112
Telephone for further details

HUDDERSFIELD Map 07 SE11

Bagden Hall Hotel & Golf Course Wakefield Rd, Scissett HD8 9LE
☎ 01484 865330 01484 861001
e-mail: info@bagdenhallhotel.co.uk
web: www.bagdenhallhotel.co.uk.demon.co.uk.
Well maintained tree-lined course set in idyllic surroundings and offering a challenging test of golf for all levels of handicap. Lake guarded greens require pin-point accuracy.
9 holes, 3002yds, Par 56, SSS 55, Course record 60.
Visitors Mon-Sun & BHs. Dress code. **Societies** welcome. **Green Fees** £10 per 18 holes (£13 weekends). **Course Designer** F O'Donnell, R Braithwaite **Facilities** **Conf** facs Corporate Hospitality Days **Location** A636 Wakefield-Denby Dale

Hotel ★★★ 69% Bagden Hall, Wakefield Rd, Scissett, HUDDERSFIELD ☎ 01484 865330 16 en suite

Bradley Park Off Bradley Rd HD2 1PZ
☎ 01484 223772 01484 451613
e-mail: parnellreilly@tinyworld.co.uk
Parkland course, challenging with good mix of long and short holes. Also 14-bay floodlit driving range and a nine-hole par 3 course, ideal for beginners. Superb views.
18 holes, 6284yds, Par 70, SSS 70, Course record 65.
Club membership 300.
Visitors Mon-Sun except BHs Booking Sat, Sun & BHs. **Societies** Booking required. **Green Fees** £15.50 (£17.50 weekends). **Prof** Parnell E Reilly **Course Designer** Cotton, Pennick, Lowire & Ptnrs **Facilities** **Leisure** 9 hole par 3 course. **Conf** facs Corporate Hospitality Days **Location** M62 junct 25, 2.5m

Hotel ★★★★ 61% Cedar Court Hotel, Ainley Top, HUDDERSFIELD ☎ 01422 375431 114 en suite

Crosland Heath Felk Stile Rd, Crosland Heath HD4 7AF
☎ 01484 653216 01484 461079
web: www.croslandheath.co.uk
Moorland course with fine views over valley.
18 holes, 6087yds, Par 71, SSS 69.
Club membership 650.
Visitors Mon, Tue, Thu & Sat except BHs. Booking required Handicap certificate. Dress code. **Societies** Booking required. **Green Fees** Phone. **Prof** John Eyre **Course Designer** A MacKenzie **Facilities** **Conf** facs Corporate Hospitality Days **Location** SW off A62

Hotel ★★★ 66% Pennine Manor Hotel, Nettleton Hill Rd, Scapegoat Hill, HUDDERSFIELD ☎ 01484 642368 30 en suite

Huddersfield Fixby Hall, Lightridge Rd, Fixby HD2 2EP
☎ 01484 426203 01484 424623
e-mail: secretary@huddersfield-golf.co.uk
web: www.huddersfield-golf.co.uk
A testing heathland course of championship standard laid out in 1891.
18 holes, 6466yds, Par 71, SSS 71, Course record 63.
Club membership 760.
Visitors Mon-Sun & BHs. Booking required. Handicap certificate. Dress code. **Societies** Booking required. **Green Fees** £47 per day, £37 per round (£57/£47 Sat, Sun & BHs). **Prof** Paul Carman **Facilities** **Conf** facs Corporate Hospitality Days **Location** 2m N off A641

Hotel ★★★★ 61% Cedar Court Hotel, Ainley Top, HUDDERSFIELD ☎ 01422 375431 114 en suite

Longley Park Maple St, Off Somerset Rd HD5 9AX
☎ 01484 422304
Lowland course, surrounded by mature woodland.
9 holes, 5212yds, Par 66, SSS 66, Course record 61.
Club membership 440.
Visitors Mon, Tue, Fri & BHs. Booking required. Dress code. **Societies** Booking required. **Green Fees** Phone. **Prof** Nick Leeming **Facilities** **Conf** facs Corporate Hospitality Days **Location** 0.5m SE of town centre off A629

Hotel ★★★★ 61% Cedar Court Hotel, Ainley Top, HUDDERSFIELD ☎ 01422 375431 114 en suite

Continued

ILKLEY Map 07 SE14

Ben Rhydding High Wood, Ben Rhydding LS29 8SB
☎ 01943 608759
e-mail: secretary@benrhyddinggc.freeserve.co.uk
Moorland and parkland with splendid views over the Wharfe valley. A compact but testing course.
9 holes, 4611yds, Par 65, SSS 63, Course record 64.
Club membership 250.
Visitors Mon, Tue, Thu, Fri except BHs. Wed & Sat pm only, Sun after 3pm. Handicap certificate. Dress code. **Societies** Booking required **Green Fees** £15 per round (£20 Sat, Sun & BHs). **Course Designer** William Dell **Facilities** **Location** SE of town centre. Off Wheatley Ln onto Wheatley Grove, left onto High Wood, clubhouse on left

Hotel ★★★ 76% Rombalds Hotel & Restaurant, 11 West View, Wells Rd, ILKLEY ☎ 01943 603201 15 en suite

Ilkley Nesfield Rd, Myddleton LS29 0BE
☎ 01943 600214 01943 816130
e-mail: honsec@ilkleygolfclub.co.uk
web: www.ikleygolfclub.co.uk
A beautiful parkland course in Wharfedale. The Wharfe is a hazard on the first seven holes - in fact, the 3rd is laid out entirely on an island in the river.
18 holes, 5953yds, Par 69, SSS 70, Course record 64.
Club membership 450.
Visitors Mon-Sun & BHs. Booking required. Handicap certificate. Dress code. **Societies** Booking required. **Green Fees** £42 (£50 weekends). **Prof** John L Hammond **Course Designer** A MacKenzie **Facilities** **Leisure** fishing. **Conf** facs Corporate Hospitality Days **Location** W side of town centre off A65

Hotel ★★★ 76% Rombalds Hotel & Restaurant, 11 West View, Wells Rd, ILKLEY ☎ 01943 603201 15 en suite

KEIGHLEY Map 07 SE04

Branshaw Branshaw Moor, Oakworth BD22 7ES
☎ 01535 643235 (sec) 01535 648011
e-mail: branshaw@golfclub.fslife.co.uk
Picturesque moorland course with fairly narrow fairways and good greens. Extensive views.
18 holes, 5823yds, Par 69, SSS 68, Course record 64.
Club membership 500.
Visitors Booking required. **Societies** apply in writing to Professional. **Green Fees** Phone. **Prof** Simon Jowitt **Course Designer** James Braid **Facilities** **Conf** Corporate Hospitality Days **Location** 2m SW on B6149, signed Oakworth

Hotel ★★ 67% Dalesgate Hotel, 406 Skipton Rd, Utley, KEIGHLEY ☎ 01535 664930 20 en suite

Keighley Howden Park, Utley BD20 6DH
☎ 01535 604778 01535 604778
e-mail: manager@keighleygolfclub.com
web: www.keighleygolfclub.com
Parkland course is good quality and has great views down the Aire valley. The 17th hole has been described as 'one of the most difficult and dangerous holes in Yorkshire golf'. The club celebrated its centenary in 2004.
18 holes, 6141yds, Par 69, SSS 70, Course record 64.
Club membership 650.

Continued

Visitors Mon-Fri, Sun & BHs. Booking required. Handicap certificate. Dress code. **Societies** Booking required. **Green Fees** £42 per day, £35 per round (£47/£39 Sat, Sun & BHs). **Prof** Andrew Rhodes **Course Designer** Henry Smith **Facilities** **Leisure** Snooker table. **Conf** facs Corporate Hospitality Days **Location** 1m NW of town centre off B6265, turn N at Roebuck pub

Hotel ★★ 67% Dalesgate Hotel, 406 Skipton Rd, Utley, KEIGHLEY ☎ 01535 664930 20 en suite

LEEDS Map 08 SE33

Brandon Hollywell Ln, Shadwell LS17 8EZ
☎ 0113 273 7471
An 18-hole links type course enjoying varying degrees of rough, water and sand hazards.
18 holes, 4000yds, Par 63.
Visitors Mon-Sun & BHs. Booking required. Dress code. **Societies** Booking required. **Green Fees** £8 per 18 holes (£9 Sat, Sun & BHs). **Prof** Carl Robinson **Course Designer** William Binner **Facilities** **Location** Off A58 into Shadwell, onto Main St, right at Red Lion pub

Hotel ★★★ 74% Haley's Hotel & Restaurant, Shire Oak Rd, Headingley, LEEDS ☎ 0113 278 4446 22 en suite 6 annexe en suite

Cookridge Hall Golf & Country Club
Cookridge Ln LS16 7NL
☎ 0113 2300641 0113 203 0198
e-mail: info@cookridgehall.co.uk
web: www.cookridgehall.co.uk
American-style course designed by Karl Litten. Expect plenty of water hazards, tees for all standards. Large bunkers and fairways between mounds and young trees.
18 holes, 6788yds, Par 72, SSS 72, Course record 72.
Club membership 570.
Visitors Mon-Sun & BHs. Booking required. Dress code. **Societies** welcome. **Green Fees** £12 (£25 Sat, Sun & BHs) **Prof** Mark Pinkett **Course Designer** Karl Liiten **Facilities** **Leisure** chipping and practice bunker. **Conf** Corporate Hospitality Days **Location** 6m NW of Leeds, off A660

Hotel ★★★ 74% Haley's Hotel & Restaurant, Shire Oak Rd, Headingley, LEEDS ☎ 0113 278 4446 22 en suite 6 annexe en suite

De Vere Oulton Hall Rothwell Ln, Oulton LS26 8HN
☎ 0113 282 3152 0113 282 6290
27-hole championship-length course. Major refurbishment underway to include a luxury clubhouse and state of the art golf academy.
Hall Course: 9 holes, 3300yds, Par 36, SSS 36.
Park Course: 18 holes, 6428yds, Par 71, SSS 71.
Club membership 200.
Visitors Mon-Sun & BHs. Booking required. Handicap certificate. Dress code. **Societies** Booking required **Green Fees** Park 36.50 per 18 holes (£50 weekends). Hall £15 pe 9 holes (£12 weekends). **Prof** Keith Pickard **Course Designer** Dave Thomas **Facilities** **Leisure** heated indoor swimming pool, sauna, solarium, gymnasium. **Conf** Corporate Hospitality Days **Location** M62 junct 30

Continue

Hotel ★★★★★ 64% De Vere Oulton Hall, Rothwell Ln, Oulton, LEEDS ☎ 0113 282 1000 152 en suite

Gotts Park Armley Ridge Rd LS12 2QX
☎ 0113 231 1896 & 2562994
e-mail: maurice.gl@sagainternet.co.uk
18 holes, 4960yds, Par 65, SSS 64, Course record 63.
Location 3m W of city centre off A647
Telephone for further details

Hotel ★★★★ 68% Queens Hotel, City Square, LEEDS ☎ 0113 243 1323 217 en suite

Headingley Back Church Ln, Adel LS16 8DW
☎ 0113 267 9573 🖷 0113 281 7334
e-mail: manager@headingleygolfclub.co.uk
web: www.headingleygolfclub.co.uk
An undulating course with a wealth of natural features offering fine views from higher ground. Its most striking hazard is the famous ravine at the 18th. Leeds's oldest course, founded in 1892.
18 holes, 6608yds, Par 71, SSS 72.
Club membership 700.
Visitors Mon-Sun & BHs. Booking required except BHs. Handicap certificate. Dress code. **Societies** Booking required. **Green Fees** £45 per day, £36 per round (£45 per day/round weekends). **Prof** Neil M Harvey **Course Designer** A MacKenzie **Facilities** **Conf** Corporate Hospitality Days **Location** 5.5m N of city centre. A660 to Skipton, right at lights junct Farrar Ln & Church Ln, follow Eccup signs

Hotel Premier Travel Inn Leeds/Bradford Airport, Victoria Av, Yeadon, LEEDS ☎ 08701 977153 40 en suite

Horsforth Layton Rise, Layton Rd, Horsforth LS18 5EX
☎ 0113 258 6819 🖷 0113 258 9336
e-mail: secretary@horsforthgolfclubltd.co.uk
web: www.horsforthgolfclubltd.co.uk
Moorland and parkland course combining devilish short holes with some more substantial challenges. Extensive views across Leeds and on a clear day York Minster can be seen from the 14th tee.
18 holes, 6243yds, Par 71, SSS 70, Course record 65.
Club membership 750.
Visitors Mon-Fri, Sun except BHs. Booking required. Handicap certificate. Dress code. **Societies** Booking required. **Green Fees** £30 per round (£36 Sat, Sun & BHs). **Prof** Dean Stokes, Simon Booth **Course Designer** A MacKenzie **Facilities** **Conf** facs Corporate Hospitality Days **Location** 6.5m NW of city centre off A65

Hotel Travelodge Leeds Bradford Airport, White House Ln, LEEDS ☎ 0113 250 3996 48 en suite

Leeds Elmete Ln LS8 2LJ
☎ 0113 265 8775 🖷 0113 232 3369
e-mail: leedsgccobble@btconnect.com
web: leedsgolfclub.com
18 holes, 6097yds, Par 69, SSS 69, Course record 63.
Location 5m NE of city centre on A6120, off A58
Telephone for further details

Hotel ★★★ 74% Haley's Hotel & Restaurant, Shire Oak Rd, Headingley, LEEDS ☎ 0113 278 4446 22 en suite 6 annexe en suite

Leeds Golf Centre Wike Ridge Ln, Shadwell LS17 9JW
☎ 0113 288 6000 🖷 0113 288 6185
e-mail: info@leedsgolfcentre.com
web: www.leedsgolfcentre.com
Wike Ridge Course: 18 holes, 6482yds, Par 72, SSS 71.
Oaks: 12 holes, 1610yds, Par 36.
Course Designer Donald Steel **Location** 5m N, A58, course on N side of Shadwell
Telephone for further details

Hotel ★★★ 74% Haley's Hotel & Restaurant, Shire Oak Rd, Headingley, LEEDS ☎ 0113 278 4446 22 en suite 6 annexe en suite

Middleton Park Municipal Middleton Park, Middleton LS10 3TN
☎ 0113 270 0449 🖷 0113 270 0449
e-mail: lynn@ratcliffel.fsnet.co.uk
18 holes, 5263yds, Par 68, SSS 66, Course record 63.
Location 3m S off A653
Telephone for further details

Hotel ★★★★ 68% Queens Hotel, City Square, LEEDS ☎ 0113 243 1323 217 en suite

Moor Allerton Coal Rd, Wike LS17 9NH
☎ 0113 266 1154 🖷 0113 237 1124
e-mail: info@magc.co.uk
web: www.magc.co.uk
The Moor Allerton Club, established in 1923, has 27 holes set in 220 acres of undulating parkland, with testing water hazards and magnificent views extending across the Vale of York. The championship course was designed by Robert Trent Jones, the famous American course architect, and provides a challenge to both high and low handicapped golfers.
Lakes Course: 18 holes, 6470yds, Par 71, SSS 72.
Blackmoor Course: 18 holes, 6673yds, Par 71, SSS 73.
High Course: 18 holes, 6841yds, Par 72, SSS 74.
Club membership 500.
Visitors Booking required. **Societies** Booking required. **Green Fees** not confirmed. **Prof** Richard Lane **Course Designer** Robert Trent Jones **Facilities** **Leisure** sauna. **Conf** facs Corporate Hospitality Days **Location** 5.5m N of city centre on A61

Continued

Moortown Harrogate Rd, Alwoodley LS17 7DB
☎ 0113 268 6521 🖷 0113 268 0986
e-mail: secretary@moortown-gc.co.uk
web: www.moortown-gc.co.uk
Championship course, tough but fair. Springy moorland turf, natural hazards of heather, gorse and streams, cunningly placed bunkers and immaculate greens. No winter tees or greens. Original home of Ryder Cup in 1929.
18 holes, 6757yds, Par 72, SSS 73, Course record 64.
Club membership 585.
Visitors Mon-Sun & BHs. Booking required. Dress code. **Societies** Booking required. **Green Fees** £75 per day, £65 per round. Winter reduced rates. **Prof** Martin Heggie **Course Designer** A MacKenzie **Facilities** **Conf** facs Corporate Hospitality Days **Location** 6m N of city centre on A61

Roundhay Park Ln LS8 2EJ
☎ 0113 266 2695 & 266 4225
Attractive municipal parkland course, natural hazards, easy walking.
9 holes, 5223yds, Par 70, SSS 65, Course record 61.
Club membership 240.
Visitors Mon-Sun & BHs. Booking required. Dress code. **Societies** Booking required. **Green Fees** Phone. **Prof** James Pape **Facilities** **Location** 4m NE of city centre off A58

Hotel ★★★ 74% Haley's Hotel & Restaurant, Shire Oak Rd, Headingley, LEEDS ☎ 0113 278 4446 22 en suite 6 annexe en suite

Sand Moor Alwoodley Ln LS17 7DJ
☎ 0113 268 5180 🖷 0113 266 1105
e-mail: ian.kerr@sandmoorgolf.co.uk
web: www.sandmoorgolf.co.uk
A beautiful, inland course situated next to Eccup reservoir on the north side of Leeds. It has been described as the finest example of golfing paradise being created out of a barren moor. With magnificent views of the surrounding countryside, the course has sandy soil and drains exceptionally well.
18 holes, 6414yds, Par 71, SSS 71, Course record 63.
Club membership 600.
Visitors Mon-Fri, Sun except BHs. Booking required. Handicap certificate. Dress code. **Societies** Booking required. **Green Fees** £50 per day, £40 per round (£50 per round weekends). **Prof** Frank Houlgate **Course Designer** A MacKenzie **Facilities** **Conf** Corporate Hospitality Days **Location** 5m N of city centre off A61

Hotel ★★★★ 64% Cedar Court Hotel, Denby Dale Rd, WAKEFIELD ☎ 01924 276310 150 en suite

South Leeds Gipsy Ln, Beeston LS11 5TU
☎ 0113 277 1676 (office)
e-mail: sec@slgc.freeserve.co.uk
web: www.southleedsgolfclub.co.uk
Hard-walking parkland, windy but good views. The small undulating greens are a very good test of putting.
18 holes, 5865yds, Par 69, SSS 68, Course record 63.
Club membership 400.
Visitors Mon-Fri. Booking required. **Societies** Booking required **Green Fees** Phone. **Prof** Laurie Turner **Course Designer** A MacKenzie **Facilities** **Conf** Corporate Hospitality Days **Location** 3m S of city centre off A653

Hotel ★★★★ 68% Queens Hotel, City Square, LEEDS ☎ 0113 243 1323 217 en suite

Temple Newsam Temple-Newsam Rd LS15 0LN
☎ 0113 264 7362
web: www.templenewsamgolfcourse.co.uk
Two parkland courses. Testing long 13th (563yds) on second course.
Lord Irwin: 18 holes, 6460yds, Par 68, SSS 71, Course record 66.
Lady Dorothy: 18 holes, 6299yds, Par 70, SSS 70, Course record 67.
Club membership 520.
Visitors booking required for Sat, Sun & BHs, **Societies** Booking required. **Green Fees** Phone. **Prof** Adrian Newboult **Facilities** by arrangement **Conf** facs Corporate Hospitality Days **Location** 3.5m E of city centre off A63

Hotel ★★★ 74% Haley's Hotel & Restaurant, Shire Oak Rd, Headingley, LEEDS ☎ 0113 278 4446 22 en suite 6 annexe en suite

MARSDEN Map 07 SE01

Marsden Mount Rd, Hemplow HD7 6NN
☎ 01484 844253
Moorland course with good views, natural hazards, windy.
9 holes, 5702yds, Par 68, SSS 68, Course record 64.
Club membership 280.
Visitors Mon, Wed-Fri & BHs. Booking required. Handicap certificate. Dress code. **Societies** Booking required. **Green Fees** £15 per round (£20 BHs). **Course Designer** A MacKenzie **Facilities** **Leisure** tennis courts. **Location** S side off A62

Hotel ★★ 67% Old Bridge Hotel, HOLMFIRTH ☎ 01484 681212 20 en suite

MELTHAM Map 07 SE01

Meltham Thick Hollins Hall HD9 4DQ
☎ 01484 850227 (office) & 851521 (pro) 🖷 01484 850227
e-mail: melthamgolf@supanet.com
web: www.meltham-golf.co.uk
Parkland with good views. Testing 548yd 13th hole (par 5).
18 holes, 6139yds, Par 71, SSS 70.
Club membership 756.
Visitors Mon, Tue, Thu, Fri, Sun. **Societies** Booking required. **Green Fees** not confirmed. **Prof** Paul Davies **Course Designer** Alex Herd **Facilities** **Location** 0.5m E of Meltham on B6107

Hotel ★★ 75% Hey Green Country House Hotel, Waters Rd, MARSDEN ☎ 01484 844235 12 en suite

Continued

MIRFIELD Map 08 SE21

Dewsbury District Sands Ln WF14 8HJ
☎ 01924 492399 & 496030 🖷 01924 492399
e-mail: dewsbury.golf@btconnect.com
web: www.dewsburygolf.co.uk
Moorland or parkland terrain with panoramic views. Ponds in middle of 3rd fairway, left of 5th green and 17th green. A challenging test of golf.
18 holes, 6360yds, Par 71, SSS 71, Course record 64. Club membership 700.
Visitors Mon-Sun & BHs. Booking required. **Societies** Booking required. **Green Fees** £28 per day, £22 per round (£17.50 weekend after 3pm). **Prof** Nigel P Hirst **Course Designer** Old Tom Morris, Peter Alliss **Facilities** by arrangement **Leisure** snooker tables. **Conf** facs Corporate Hospitality Days **Location** M62 junct 25, 6m off A644

Hotel ★★★ 66% Healds Hall Hotel, Leeds Rd, Liversedge, DEWSBURY ☎ 01924 409112 24 en suite

MORLEY Map 08 SE22

Howley Hall Scotchman Ln LS27 0NX
☎ 01924 350100 🖷 01924 350104
e-mail: office@howleyhall.co.uk
web: www.howleyhall.co.uk
Easy walking parkland with superb views of the Pennines and the Calder valley.
18 holes, 6092yds, Par 71, SSS 69, Course record 66. Club membership 700.
Visitors Mon-Fr, Sun & BHs. Dress code. **Societies** Booking required. **Green Fees** £36 per day, £30 per round (£40 Sat, Sun & BHs). **Prof** Gary Watkinson **Course Designer** A MacKenzie **Facilities** by arrangement **Conf** facs Corporate Hospitality Days **Location** 1.5m S on B6123

Hotel ★★ 70% Alder House Hotel, Towngate Rd, Healey Ln, BATLEY ☎ 01924 444777 20 en suite

OSSETT Map 08 SE22

Low Laithes Parkmill Ln, Flushdyke WF5 9AP
☎ 01924 274667 & 266067 🖷 01924 266067
Testing parkland course.
18 holes, 6463yds, Par 72, SSS 71, Course record 65. Club membership 600.
Visitors contact club for details. Dress code. **Societies** Booking required. **Green Fees** £25 per day, £22 per round (£36 Sat, Sun & BHs). **Prof** Paul Browning **Course Designer** A MacKenzie **Facilities** **Conf** Corporate Hospitality Days **Location** M1 junct 40, 0.5m on Dewsbury road, signed

Hotel ★★★ 67% Heath Cottage Hotel & Restaurant, Wakefield Rd, DEWSBURY ☎ 01924 465399 22 en suite annexe en suite

OTLEY Map 08 SE24

Otley Off West Busk Ln LS21 3NG
☎ 01943 465329 🖷 01943 850387
e-mail: office@otley-golfclub.co.uk
web: www.otley-golfclub.co.uk
An expansive course with magnificent views across Wharfedale. It is well wooded with streams crossing the fairway. The 4th is a fine hole which generally needs two woods to reach the plateau green. The 17th is a good short hole. A test of golf as opposed to stamina.
18 holes, 6237yds, Par 70, SSS 70, Course record 62. Club membership 700.
Visitors Mon, Wed-Fri except BHs. Handicap certificate. Dress code. **Societies** Booking required. **Green Fees** £38 per day, £32 per 18/27 holes (£45/£38 Sat, Sun & BHs). **Prof** Steven Tomkinson **Facilities** **Leisure** practice bunker. **Conf** facs Corporate Hospitality Days **Location** 1m W of Otley off A6038

Hotel Premier Travel Inn Leeds/Bradford Airport, Victoria Av, Yeadon, LEEDS ☎ 08701 977153 40 en suite

OUTLANE Map 07 SE01

Outlane Slack Ln, Off New Hey Rd HD3 3FQ
☎ 01422 374762 🖷 01422 311789
web: www.outlanegolfclub.ltd.uk
An 18-hole moorland course with undulating fairways. Four par 3 holes with an 8th hole of 249yds and a 15th regarded as the hardest par 3 in Yorkshire. The three par 5s may be reachable on a good day in two strokes but in adverse conditions will take more than three. Smaller than average greens on some holes, which makes for accurate second shots.
18 holes, 6015yds, Par 71, SSS 69, Course record 67. Club membership 600.
Visitors Tue-Fri, Sun except BHs. Booking required. Dress code. **Societies** Booking required. **Green Fees** Phone. **Prof** David Chapman **Facilities** **Location** M62 junct 23, A640 New Hey Rd through Outlane

Hotel ★★★ 64% The Old Golf House Hotel, New Hey Rd, Outlane, HUDDERSFIELD ☎ 0870 609 6128 52 en suite

PONTEFRACT Map 08 SE42

Mid Yorkshire Havercroft Ln, Darrington WF8 3BP
☎ 01977 704522 🖷 01977 600823
e-mail: linda_midyorksgc@btconnect.com
web: www.midyorkshiregolfclub.com

18 holes, 6500yds, Par 72, SSS 71, Course record 68.
Course Designer Steve Marnoch **Location** On A1 0.5m S junct A1/M62
Telephone for further details

Hotel ★★★ 75% Wentbridge House Hotel, Wentbridge, PONTEFRACT ☎ 01977 620444 14 en suite 4 annexe en suite

Pontefract & District Park Ln WF8 4QS
☎ 01977 792241 🖷 01977 792241
e-mail: manager@pdgc.co.uk
web: www.pdgc.co.uk
Undulating parkland course, some elevated tees.
18 holes, 6227yds, Par 72, SSS 70.
Club membership 800.
Visitors Mon, Tue, Thu-Sun except BHs. Booking required Sat & Sun. Handicap certificate. Dress code. **Societies** Booking required. **Green Fees** £30 per day, £25 per round.(£32 per round/day Sat, Sun & BHs). **Prof** Nick Newman **Course Designer** A MacKenzie **Facilities** **Location** W of Pontefract. A639 onto B6134, club 1m on right

Hotel ★★★ 75% Wentbridge House Hotel, Wentbridge, PONTEFRACT ☎ 01977 620444 14 en suite 4 annexe en suite

PUDSEY Map 08 SE23

Calverley Golf Club Woodhall Ln LS28 5QY
☎ 0113 256 9244 🖷 0113 256 4362
e-mail: golf@cgc1.freeserve.co.uk
Gently undulating parkland. The small greens require accurate approach shots.

18 holes, 5590yds, Par 68, SSS 67, Course record 62.
9 holes, 3000yds, Par 36.
Club membership 535.
Visitors Mon-Fri. Sat, Sun & BHs after 1pm. Booking required. Handicap certificate. Dress code. **Societies** Booking required. **Green Fees** Phone. **Prof** Neil Wendel-Jones **Facilities** **Conf** Corporate Hospitality Days **Location** Signed Calverley from A647

Hotel Travelodge Bradford, 1 Mid Point, Dick Ln, PUDSEY ☎ 08700 850 950 48 en suite

Fulneck LS28 8NT
☎ 0113 256 5191
9 holes, 5456yds, Par 66, SSS 67, Course record 65.
Location Pudsey, between Leeds
Telephone for further details

Hotel ★★★ 64% Novotel Bradford, 6 Roydsdale Way, BRADFORD ☎ 01274 683683 119 en suite

Woodhall Hills Calverley LS28 5UN
☎ 0113 255 4594 🖷 0113 255 4594
e-mail: whhgc@tiscali.co.uk
Meadowland course, recently redeveloped with an improved layout and open ditches around the course. A challenging opening hole, a good variety of par 3s and testing holes at the 6th and 11th.

Continued

18 holes, 6184yds, Par 71, SSS 70, Course record 64.
Club membership 550.
Visitors Mon-Fri, Sun & BHs. Dress code. **Societies** Booking required. **Green Fees** £24 per round (£29 weekends). Twilight weekends £12. **Prof** Warren Lockett **Facilities** **Conf** facs Corporate Hospitality Days **Location** 1m NW off A647

Hotel Travelodge Bradford, 1 Mid Point, Dick Ln, PUDSEY ☎ 08700 850 950 48 en suite

RIDDLESDEN Map 07 SE04

Riddlesden Howden Rough BD20 5QN
☎ 01535 602148
Undulating moorland course with prevailing west winds and beautiful views. Nine par 3 holes and spectacular 6th and 15th holes played over old quarry sites.
18 holes, 4295yds, Par 63, SSS 61, Course record 59.
Club membership 300.
Visitors Mon-Sun & BHs. **Societies** Booking required. **Green Fees** £16 per day/round (£21 weekends). **Facilities** **Conf** Corporate Hospitality Days **Location** 1m NW

Hotel ★★ 67% Dalesgate Hotel, 406 Skipton Rd, Utley, KEIGHLEY ☎ 01535 664930 20 en suite

SCARCROFT Map 08 SE34

Scarcroft Syke Ln LS14 3BQ
☎ 0113 289 2311 🖷 0113 289 3835
e-mail: secretary@scarcroftgolfclub.com
web: www.scarcroftgolfclub.com
Undulating parkland course with prevailing west wind and easy walking.
18 holes, 6426yds, Par 71, SSS 69.
Club membership 667.
Visitors contact club for details. **Societies** Booking required. **Green Fees** terms on application. **Prof** Darren Tear **Course Designer** Charles Mackenzie **Facilities** **Conf** facs **Location** 0.5m N of village off A58

SHIPLEY Map 07 SE13

Marriott Hollins Hall Hotel & Country Club Hollins Hill, Otley Rd BD17 7QW
☎ 01274 534212 🖷 01274 534220
e-mail: golfsales.hollinshall@marriotthotels.co.uk
web: www.marriotthotels.co.uk/lbags
Set in 200 acres of natural heathland amongst the beautiful Yorkshire moors and dales. The 6671 yard course offers multiple teeing areas which challenge any standard of golfer and is majestic, challenging and classically designed in the spirit of the game.

Continued

18 holes, 6671yds, Par 71, SSS 71, Course record 65.
Club membership 350.
Visitors Booking required. Handicap certificate required weekends. **Societies** Booking required. 01274 534273 **Green Fees** £55 per day, £40 per round (£75/£50 Fri-Sun, incl BHs). **Prof** Brian Rumney **Course Designer** Ross McMurray **Facilities** **Leisure** heated indoor swimming pool, sauna, solarium, gymnasium. **Conf** facs Corporate Hospitality Days **Location** 3m N on the A6038

Hotel ★★★★ 70% Marriott Hollins Hall Hotel & Country Club, Hollins Hill, Baildon, SHIPLEY ☎ 0870 400 7227 122 en suite

Northcliffe High Bank Ln BD18 4LJ
☎ 01274 596731 🖹 01274 584148
e-mail: northcliffegc@hotmail.com
web: www.northcliffegolfclubshipley.co.uk
Parkland with magnificent views of moors. Testing 1st hole, dog-leg left over a ravine. The 18th hole is one of the most picturesque and difficult par 3s in the country, with a green 100feet below the tee and protected by bunkers, water and trees.
18 holes, 6104yds, Par 71, SSS 70, Course record 64.
Club membership 700.
Visitors Mon-Fri, Sun & BHs. Booking required. Handicap certificate. Dress code. **Societies** Booking required. **Green Fees** £30 per day, £25 per round (£30 per round Sat, Sun & BHs). **Prof** M Hillas **Course Designer** James Braid **Facilities** **Conf** Corporate Hospitality Days **Location** 1.25m SW of Shipley, off A650

Hotel ★★★★ 70% Marriott Hollins Hall Hotel & Country Club, Hollins Hill, Baildon, SHIPLEY ☎ 0870 400 7227 122 en suite

SILSDEN Map 07 SE04

Silsden Brunthwaite Ln, Brunthwaite BD20 0ND
☎ 01535 652998 🖹 01535 654273
e-mail: info@silsdengolfclub.co.uk
web: www.silsdengolfclub.co.uk
Tight downland course which can be windy. Good views of the Aire valley.
18 holes, 5062yds, Par 67, SSS 64, Course record 62.
Club membership 350.
Visitors Booking required Sat & Sun. **Societies** Booking required. **Green Fees** Phone. **Facilities** **Conf** facs **Location** E of town off Howden Rd onto Hawber Ln

Hotel ★★ 67% Dalesgate Hotel, 406 Skipton Rd, Utley, KEIGHLEY ☎ 01535 664930 20 en suite

SOWERBY Map 07 SE02

Ryburn The Shaw, Norland HX6 3QP
☎ 01422 831355
Moorland course, easy walking. Panoramic views of the Ryburn and Calder valleys.
9 holes, 5127yds, Par 66, SSS 65, Course record 64.
Club membership 300.
Visitors Mon-Fri except BHs. Booking required. Handicap certificate. Dress code. **Societies** Booking required. **Green Fees** £20. **Facilities** **Conf** Corporate Hospitality Days **Location** 1m S of Sowerby Bridge off A58

TODMORDEN Map 07 SD92

Todmorden Rive Rocks, Cross Stone Rd OL14 8RD
☎ 01706 812986 🖹 01706 812986
A tough but fair moorland course with spectacular scenery.
9 holes, 5874yds, Par 68, SSS 68, Course record 67.
Club membership 240.
Visitors Mon, Tue, Wed Fri & BHs. Restricted Thu & Sat. Dress code. **Societies** Booking required. **Green Fees** £15 per day (Sat, Sun & BHs £20). **Facilities** **Conf** Corporate Hospitality Days **Location** NE off A646

Hotel ★★★ 72% Holdsworth House Hotel, Holdsworth, HALIFAX ☎ 01422 240024 40 en suite

WAKEFIELD Map 08 SE32

City of Wakefield Horbury Rd WF2 8QS
☎ 01924 360282
18 holes, 6319yds, Par 72, SSS 70, Course record 64.
Course Designer J S F Morrison **Location** 1.5m W of city centre on A642
Telephone for further details

Hotel ★★★ 75% Waterton Park Hotel, Walton Hall, The Balk, Walton, WAKEFIELD ☎ 01924 257911 & 249800 🖹 01924 259686 25 en suite 43 annexe en suite

Lofthouse Hill Leeds Rd WF3 3LR
☎ 01924 823703 🖹 01924 823703
e-mail: lofthousehillgolfclub@fsmail.net
web: www.lofthousehillgolfclub.co.uk
New parkland course.
18 holes, 5988yds, Par 70, SSS 69.
Visitors Mon-Sun & BHs. Booking required. Handicap certificate. Dress code. **Societies** Booking required. **Green Fees** £12 per 18 holes. **Prof** Simon Hotham, Derek Johnson **Facilities** **Conf** facs Corporate Hospitality Days **Location** 2m from Wakefield off A61

Hotel ★★★ 75% Waterton Park Hotel, Walton Hall, The Balk, Walton, WAKEFIELD ☎ 01924 257911 & 249800 🖹 01924 259686 25 en suite 43 annexe en suite

Normanton Hatfield Hall, Aberford Rd WF3 4JP
☎ 01924 377943 🖹 01924 200777
web: normantongolf.co.uk
18 holes, 6205yds, Par 72, SSS 71.
Location M62 junct 30, A642 towards Wakefield, 2m on right
Telephone for further details

Hotel U Chasley Hotel, Queen St, WAKEFIELD ☎ 01924 372111 64 en suite

Painthorpe House Painthorpe Ln, Painthorpe, Crigglestone WF4 3HE
☎ 01924 254737 & 255083 🖹 01924 252022
Undulating meadowland course, easy walking.
9 holes, 4544yds, Par 62, SSS 62, Course record 63.
Club membership 100.
Visitors Mon-Sat & BHs. Sun after 1.30pm **Societies** Booking required. **Green Fees** £7 for 18 holes (£8 weekends). **Facilities** **Leisure** bowling green. **Location** 2m S off A636

Hotel ★★★★ 64% Cedar Court Hotel, Denby Dale Rd, WAKEFIELD ☎ 01924 276310 150 en suite

Wakefield Woodthorpe Ln, Sandal WF2 6JH
☎ 01924 258778 (sec) 01924 242752
Well-sheltered meadowland and parkland with easy walking and good views.
18 holes, 6653yds, Par 72, SSS 72, Course record 67. Club membership 540.
Visitors Mon-Sun & BHs. Booking required. Dress code. **Societies** Booking required. **Green Fees** Phone. **Prof** Ian M Wright **Course Designer** A MacKenzie, S Herd **Facilities** **Conf** Corporate Hospitality Days **Location** 3m S of Wakefield, off A61

Hotel ★★★ 69% Hotel St Pierre, Barnsley Rd, Newmillerdam, WAKEFIELD ☎ 01924 255596 54 en suite

WETHERBY Map 08 SE44

Wetherby Linton Ln LS22 4JF
☎ 01937 580089 01937 581915
e-mail: info@wetherbygolfclub.co.uk
web: www.wetherbygolfclub.co.uk
A medium length parkland course renowned for its lush fairways. Particularly memorable holes are the 7th, a par 4 which follows the sweeping bend of the River Wharfe, and the 14th (the quarry hole), an intimidating par 3.
18 holes, 6213yds, Par 71, SSS 70, Course record 63. Club membership 950.
Visitors Mon-Fri, Sun except BHs. Booking required. Handicap certificate. Dress code. **Societies** Booking required. **Green Fees** £39 per day, £32 per round (£44 per day/round). **Prof** Mark Daubney **Facilities** **Conf** facs Corporate Hospitality Days **Location** 1m W off A661

Hotel ★★★★ 78% Wood Hall Hotel, Trip Ln, Linton, WETHERBY ☎ 01937 587271 14 en suite 30 annexe en suite

WIKE Map 08 SE34

The Village Golf Course Backstone Gill Ln LS17 9JU
☎ 0113 273 7471 & 07759012364
A nine-hole pay and play course in an elevated position enjoying long panoramic views. The holes are par 3, 4 and 5s and include water hazards and shaped large greens. There are now three extra optional holes (no extra charge), all par 3s over water.
12 holes, 5780yds, Par 75, SSS 68, Course record 66.
Visitors Mon-Sun & BHs. Booking required. Dress code. **Societies** Booking required. **Green Fees** 18 holes £10 (weekends £12); 12 holes £7 (£8). **Prof** Deborah Snowden **Course Designer** William Binner **Facilities** **Leisure** fishing. **Conf** facs Corporate Hospitality Days **Location** Signed, 1m off A61, 2m off A58

Hotel ★★★ 68% Jurys Inn Leeds, Kendell St, Brewery Place, Brewery Wharf, LEEDS ☎ 0113 283 8800 248 en suite

WOOLLEY Map 08 SE31

Woolley Park New Rd WF4 2JS
☎ 01226 380144 01226 390295
web: www.woolleyparkgolfclub.co.uk
A demanding course set in a mature wooded parkland. With many water features in play and undulating greens, the course offers a challenge to all golfers.
18 holes, 6636yds, Par 71, SSS 72.
Visitors Mon-Sun & BHs. Booking required. Dress code. **Societies** Booking required. **Green Fees** £18.50 per 18 holes (£25 weekends). **Prof** Jon Baldwin **Course Designer** M Shattock **Facilities** **Conf** Corporate Hospitality Days **Location** M1 junct 38, off A61 between Wakefield

Hotel ★★★★ 64% Cedar Court Hotel, Denby Dale Rd, WAKEFIELD ☎ 01924 276310 150 en suite

CHANNEL ISLANDS

ALDERNEY

ALDERNEY Map 16

Alderney Route des Carrieres GY9 3YD
☎ 01481 822835
Undulating seaside course with sea on all sides, offering magnificent views from its high tees and greens.
9 holes, 5006yds, Par 64, SSS 65, Course record 65. Club membership 400.
Visitors Mon-Fri. After 10am Sat & Sun. Booking required. **Societies** Booking required. **Green Fees** not confirmed. **Facilities** by arrangement **Location** 1m E of St Annes

GUERNSEY

L'ANCRESSE VALE Map 16

Royal Guernsey GY3 5BY
☎ 01481 246523 01481 243960
e-mail: bobby@rggc.fsnet.co.uk
web: www.royalguernseygolfclub.com
Not quite as old as its neighbour Royal Jersey, Royal Guernsey is a sporting course which was redesigned after World War II by Mackenzie Ross, who has many fine courses to his credit. It is a pleasant links, well-maintained, and administered by the States of Guernsey. The 8th hole, a good par 4, requires an accurate second shot to the green set among the gorse and thick rough. The 18th, with lively views, needs a strong shot to reach the green well down below. The course is windy, with hard walking.
18 holes, 6215yds, Par 70, SSS 70, Course record 64. Club membership 934.
Visitors must have a handicap certificate; may not play on Thu, Sat afternoons & Sun. **Green Fees** Phone. **Prof** Norman Wood **Course Designer** Mackenzie Ross **Facilities** **Location** 3m N of St Peter Port

Hotel ★★★★ 67% St Pierre Park Hotel, Rohais, ST PETER PORT ☎ 01481 728282 131 en suite

CASTEL Map 16

La Grande Mare Golf & Country Club
Vazon Bay GY5 7LL
☎ 01481 253544 01481 255197
e-mail: golf@lagrandemare.com
web: www.lgm.guernsey.net
This hotel and golf complex is set in over 120 acres of grounds. The Hawtree designed parkland course opened in 1994 and was originally designed around 14 holes with four double greens. Water hazards on 15 holes.
18 holes, 4755yards, Par 64, SSS 64, Course record 65. Club membership 800.
Visitors Mon-Sun & BHs. Booking required. Dress code. **Societies** Booking required. **Green Fees** £33 per 18 holes (£38 weekends). **Prof** Matt Groves **Course Designer** Hawtree **Facilities** **Leisure** hard tennis courts, outdoor and indoor heated swimming pools, fishing, sauna, gymnasium, sports massage. **Conf** facs Corporate Hospitality Days

Hotel ★★★ 67% Hotel Hougue du Pommier, Hougue du Pommier Rd, CATEL ☎ 01481 256531 37 en suite 6 annexe en suite

ST PETER PORT Map 16

St Pierre Park Golf Club Rohais GY1 1FD
☎ 01481 728282 01481 712041
e-mail: stppark@itl.net
web: www.stpierrepark.co.uk
Par 3 parkland course with delightful setting, with lakes, streams and many tricky holes.
9 holes, 2610yds, Par 54, SSS 50, Course record 52. Club membership 200.
Visitors Mon-Sun & BHs. Dress code. **Societies** welcome. **Green Fees** from £20 per 18 holes, from £15 per 9 holes. **Prof** Roy Corbet **Course Designer** Jacklin **Facilities** **Leisure** hard tennis courts, heated indoor swimming pool, sauna, solarium, gymnasium. **Conf** facs **Location** 1m W off Rohais Rd

Hotel ★★★★ 67% St Pierre Park Hotel, Rohais, ST PETER PORT ☎ 01481 728282 131 en suite

JERSEY

GROUVILLE Map 16

Royal Jersey Le Chemin au Greves JE3 9BD
☎ 01534 854416 01534 854684
e-mail: thesecretary@royaljersey.com
web: www.royaljersey.com
18 holes, 6100yds, Par 70, SSS 70, Course record 63.
Location 4m E of St Helier off coast road
Telephone for further details

Hotel ★★★ 69% Old Court House Hotel, GOREY ☎ 01534 854444 58 en suite

LA MOYE Map 16

La Moye La Route Orange JE3 8GQ
☎ 01534 743401 01534 747289
e-mail: secretary@lamoyegolfclub.co.uk
web: www.lamoyegolfclub.co.uk
Seaside championship links course (venue for the Jersey Seniors Open) situated in an exposed position on the south western corner of the island overlooking St Ouen's Bay. Offers spectacular views, two start points, full course all year - no temporary greens.
18 holes, 6664yds, Par 72, SSS 73, Course record 65. Club membership 1300.
Visitors Mon-Sun & BHs. Booking required. Handicap certificate. Dress code. **Societies** Booking required. **Green Fees** 18 holes £55 (Sat, Sun & BHs £60). **Prof** Mike Deeley **Course Designer** James Braid **Facilities** **Location** W of village off A13

Hotel ★★★★ The Atlantic Hotel, Le Mont de la Pulente, ST BRELADE ☎ 01534 744101 50 en suite

ST CLEMENT Map 16

St Clement Jersey Recreation Grounds JE2 6PN
☎ 01534 721938 01534 721012
Very tight moorland course. Impossible to play to scratch. Suitable for middle to high handicaps.
9 holes, 2244yds, Par 30, SSS 31, Course record 30. Club membership 500.
Visitors Mon-Sun except BHs. Booking required Sat & Sun. **Green Fees** £20 per day/round, £12 per 9 holes. **Prof** Lee Elstone **Facilities** **Leisure** hard tennis courts, squash, bowls. **Location** E of St Helier on A5

Hotel ★★★★ Longueville Manor Hotel, ST SAVIOUR ☎ 01534 725501 29 en suite 1 annexe en suite

ST OUEN Map 16

Les Mielles Golf & Country Club JE3 7FQ
☎ 01534 482787 01534 485414
e-mail: enquiry@lesmielles.co.je
web: www.lesmielles.com
Challenging championship course with bent grass greens, dwarf rye fairways and picturesque ponds situated in the Island's largest conservation area within St Ouen's Bay.

18 holes, 5261yds, Par 70, SSS 68, Course record 65. Club membership 1500.
Visitors contact club for details. **Societies** Booking required. **Green Fees** terms on application. **Prof** W Osmand, L Cummins, A Jones **Course Designer** J Le

Continued

Brun, R Whitehead **Facilities** **Leisure** Laser clay pigeon shooting, 'Breakers' realistic golf course. **Conf** facs Corporate Hospitality Days **Location** Centre of St Ouen's Bay

Hotel ★★★★ 78% Hotel L'Horizon, St Brelade's Bay, ST BRELADE ☎ 01534 743101 106 en suite

ISLE OF MAN

CASTLETOWN Map 06 SC26

Castletown Golf Links Fort Island, Derbyhaven IM9 1UA
☎ 01624 822220 📠 01624 829661
e-mail: 1sttee@manx.net
web: www.golfiom.com
Set on the Langness peninsula, this superb championship course is surrounded on three sides by the sea, and holds many surprises from its Championship tees.

18 holes, 6707yds, Par 72, SSS 72, Course record 64. Club membership 500.
Visitors Mon-Sun & BHs. Booking required. Handicap certificate. Dress code. **Societies** welcome. **Green Fees** £50 Mon-Thu (£55 Fri-Sun & BHs). **Prof** Michael Brookes **Course Designer** McKenzie Ross, Old Tom Morris **Facilities** **Leisure** heated indoor swimming pool, sauna, snooker. **Conf** Corporate Hospitality Days

Hotel ★★ 67% Falcon's Nest, The Promenade, PORT ERIN ☎ 01624 834077 35 en suite

DOUGLAS Map 06 SC37

Douglas Pulrose Park IM2 1AE
☎ 01624 675952
e-mail: mug@hotmail.co.uk
Hilly, parkland and moorland course under the control of Douglas Corporation.
18 holes, 5937yds, Par 69, SSS 69, Course record 62. Club membership 330.
Visitors Mon-Sun & BHs. Booking required Sat, Sun & BHs. **Societies** Booking required. **Green Fees** £11 per day (£16 weekends). **Prof** Mike Vipond **Course Designer** A MacKenzie **Facilities** **Conf** Corporate Hospitality Days **Location** 1m from Douglas on Castletown road on Pulrose Estate

Hotel ★★★ 70% The Empress Hotel, Central Promenade, DOUGLAS ☎ 01624 661155 102 en suite

Mount Murray Hotel & Country Club
Mount Murray, Santon IM4 2HT
☎ 01624 661111 📠 01624 611116
e-mail: hotel@mountmurray.com
web: www.mountmurray.com
A challenging course with many natural features, lakes, streams etc. Five par 5s, six par 3s and the rest par 4. Fine views over the whole island.

18 holes, 6361yds, Par 71, SSS 71, Course record 66. Club membership 378.
Visitors Mon-Sun & BHs. Booking required Sat, Sun & BHs. Dress code. **Societies** Booking required. **Green Fees** £25 per round (£30 weekends). **Prof** Andrew Dyson **Course Designer** Bingley Sports Research **Facilities** **Leisure** hard tennis courts, heated indoor swimming pool, squash, sauna, solarium, gymnasium. **Conf** facs Corporate Hospitality Days **Location** 5m from Douglas towards airport

Hotel ★★★★ 70% Mount Murray Hotel & Country Club, Santon, DOUGLAS ☎ 01624 695315 90 en suite

ONCHAN Map 06 SC47

King Edward Bay Golf & Country Club
Howstrake, Groudle Rd IM3 2JR
☎ 01624 672709 620430
e-mail: mail@kebgc.com
web: kebgc.com
18 holes, 5492yds, Par 67, SSS 65, Course record 58.
Course Designer Tom Morris **Location** E of town off A1
Telephone for further details

PEEL Map 06 SC28

Peel Rheast Ln IM5 1BG
☎ 01624 842227 & 843456 📠 01624 843456
e-mail: lcullen@peelgolfclub.idps.co.uk
web: www.geocities.com/peelgc
Moorland course, with natural hazards and easy walking. Good views. The drop down to the 12th and climb back up to the 13th interrupt an otherwise fairly level course. The long, dog-legged 11th hole is an outstanding par 4, where the gorse must be carried to get a good second shot to the green. Most notable of th short holes are the 10th and 17th where an errant tee shot finds bunker, gorse or thick rough.
18 holes, 5850yds, Par 69, SSS 69, Course record 64. Club membership 856.
Visitors Mon-Wed, Fri, Sun & BHs. Thu pm only. Booking required. Handicap certificate. Dress code. **Societies** welcome. **Green Fees** £20 per day (£30 Sat, Su & BHs). **Prof** Paul O'Reilly **Course Designer** James Braide **Facilities** **Leisure** snooker. **Conf**

Continu

Corporate Hospitality Days **Location** SE of town centre on A1

Hotel ★★★ 70% The Empress Hotel, Central Promenade, DOUGLAS ☎ 01624 661155 102 en suite

PORT ERIN Map 06 SC16

Rowany Rowany Dr IM9 6LN
☎ 01624 834108 or 834072 🖹 01624 834072
e-mail: rowany@iommail.net
Undulating seaside course with testing later holes, which cut through gorse and rough. However, those familiar with this course maintain that the 7th and 12th holes are the most challenging.
18 holes, 5840yds, Par 70, SSS 69, Course record 62. Club membership 500.
Visitors contact club for details. **Societies** welcome. **Green Fees** Phone. **Course Designer** G Lowe **Facilities** **Conf** Corporate Hospitality Days **Location** N of village off A32

Hotel ★★★ 67% Ocean Castle Hotel, The Promenade, PORT ERIN ☎ 01624 836399 40 en suite

PORT ST MARY Map 06 SC26

Port St Mary Kallow Point Rd
☎ 01624 834932
Slightly hilly course with beautiful scenic views over Port St Mary and the Irish Sea.

Continued

9 holes, 5702yds, Par 68, SSS 68, Course record 62. Club membership 324.
Visitors contact club for details. **Societies** welcome. **Green Fees** Phone. **Course Designer** George Duncan **Facilities** **Leisure** hard tennis courts, Croquet lawn. **Conf** Corporate Hospitality Days **Location** Signed entering Port St Mary, one-way system, 2nd left to end , 1st right

Hotel ★★★ 67% Ocean Castle Hotel, The Promenade, PORT ERIN ☎ 01624 836399 40 en suite

RAMSEY Map 06 SC49

Ramsey Brookfield IM8 2AH
☎ 01624 812244 🖹 01624 815833
e-mail: ramseygolfclub@manx.net
web: www.ramseygolfclub.com
Parkland with easy walking and good views. Windy. Testing holes: 1st, par 5; 18th, par 3.
18 holes, 5960yds, Par 70, SSS 69, Course record 63. Club membership 1000.
Visitors After 10am Mon-Fri. Booking required. **Societies** Booking required. **Green Fees** Phone. **Prof** Andrew Dyson **Course Designer** James Braid **Facilities** by arrangement **Conf** Corporate Hospitality Days **Location** SW of town centre

Hotel ★★★ 70% The Empress Hotel, Central Promenade, DOUGLAS ☎ 01624 661155 102 en suite

Scotland

ABERDEEN CITY

ABERDEEN Map 15 NJ90

Auchmill Bonnyview Rd, West Heatheryfold AB16 7FQ
☎ 01224 714577 🖹 01224 648693
18 holes, 5123 metres, Par 70, SSS 67, Course record 67.
Course Designer Neil Coles, Brian Hugget **Location** Outskirts Aberdeen, A96 Aberdeen-Inverness
Telephone for further details

Hotel ★★★ 70% The Craighaar Hotel, Waterton Rd, Bucksburn, ABERDEEN ☎ 01224 712275 55 en suite

Balnagask St Fitticks Rd AB11 3QT
☎ 01224 876407 🖹 01224 648693
18 holes, 5986yds, Par 70, SSS 69.
Location 2m E of city centre
Telephone for further details

Hotel ★★★ 68% Maryculter House Hotel, South Deeside Rd, Maryculter, ABERDEEN ☎ 01224 732124 23 en suite

Craibstone Golf Centre Craibstone Estate, Bucksburn AB21 9YA
☎ 01224 716777 711012 🖹 01224 711298
e-mail: craibstonegolf@sac.co.uk
This parkland course is a fair and enjoyable test for all golfers. The course rewards accuracy off the tee, with the difficult 11th, 12th and 13th holes, and true and fast greens.
18 holes, 5757yards, Par 69, SSS 69, Course record 66.
Club membership 425.
Visitors Booking required up to 7 days in advance. **Societies** Booking required. **Green Fees** Phone. **Prof** Iain Buchan **Facilities** **Leisure** sauna, gymnasium, floodlit astroturf sports area. **Conf** facs **Location** NW of city off A96 Aberdeen-Inverness road. A96 through Bucksburn. Before next rdbt left signed Forrit Brae. At top of road club signed

Hotel ★★★★ 67% Aberdeen Marriott Hotel, Overton Circle, Dyce, ABERDEEN ☎ 01224 770011 155 en suite

Deeside Golf Rd, Bieldside AB15 9DL
☎ 01224 869457 🖹 01224 861800
e-mail: admin@deesidegolfclub.com
web: www.deesidegolfclub.com
An interesting riverside course with several tree-lined fairways. A stream comes into play at nine of the 18 holes on the main course. In recent years major reconstruction work has taken place to provide a testing course in which only five of the original holes are virtually unchanged. These include the 15th (the old 6th) which bears the name of James Braid who advised the club during previous course alterations. Various water features are incorporated into the course including pools at the 4th, 10th and 17th.
Haughton: 18 holes, 6286yds, Par 70, SSS 71, Course record 65.
Blairs: 9 holes, 5042yds, Par 68, SSS 64.
Club membership 1000.
Visitors Mon-Sun & BHs. Booking required. Handicap certificate. Dress code. **Societies** Booking required. **Green Fees** Phone. **Prof** Frank J Coutts **Course Designer** Archie Simpson **Facilities** **Conf** Corporate Hospitality Days **Location** 3m W of city centre off A93

Continued

Hotel ★★★★ 73% Macdonald Ardoe House, South Deeside Rd, Blairs, ABERDEEN ☎ 0870 194 2104 109 en suite

Hazelhead Hazlehead Av AB15 8BD
☎ 01224 321830 🖹 01224 810452
e-mail: golf@aberdeencity.gov.uk
web: www.aberdeencity.gov.uk
Three picturesque courses and a pitch and putt course which provide a true test of golfing skills with gorse and woodlands being a hazard for any wayward shots.
No 1 Course: 18 holes, 6224yds, Par 70, SSS 70.
No 2 Course: 18 holes, 5764yds, Par 67, SSS 67.
Visitors Mon-Sun & BHs. Dress code. **Societies** Booking required. **Green Fees** Phone. **Prof** C Nelson **Facilities** **Leisure** 9 hole pitch & putt course. **Location** 4m W of city centre off A944

Hotel ★★★★ 73% Macdonald Ardoe House, South Deeside Rd, Blairs, ABERDEEN ☎ 0870 194 2104 109 en suite

Kings Links AB24 1RZ
☎ 01224 632269 🖹 01224 648693
18 holes, 6384yds, Par 72, SSS 71.
Location 0.75m NE of city centre
Telephone for further details

Murcar Links Bridge of Don AB23 8BD
☎ 01224 704354 🖹 01224 704354
e-mail: golf@murcar.co.uk
web: www.murcar.co.uk
Seaside links course with a prevailing south-west wind. Its main attraction is the challenge of playing round and between gorse, heather and sand dunes. The additional hazards of burns and out of bounds give any golfer a testing round of golf.

18 holes, 6500yds, Par 71, SSS 72, Course record 64.
Strabathie: 9 holes, 2680yds, Par 35, SSS 35.
Club membership 650.
Visitors Mon-Sun & BHs. Booking required. Dress code. **Societies** Booking required. **Green Fees** £80 per day, £60 per round, £90/£70 Sat, Sun & BHs. Strabathie £35 per day, £14 per 9 holes (£44/£22 Sat, Sun & BHs). **Prof** Gary Forbes **Course Designer** A Simpson, J Braid, G Webster **Facilities** **Location** 5m NE of city centre off A90

Hotel ★★★ 70% The Craighaar Hotel, Waterton Rd, Bucksburn, ABERDEEN ☎ 01224 712275 55 en suite

Royal Aberdeen Links Rd, Balgownie, Bridge of Don AB23 8AT
☎ 01224 702571 🖹 01224 826591
e-mail: admin@royalaberdeengolf.com
web: www.royalaberdeengolf.com
Championship links course with undulating dunes. Windy, easy walking.
Balgownie Course: 18 holes, 6504yds, Par 71, SSS 71, Course record 63.
Silverburn Course: 18 holes, 4066yds, Par 60, SSS 60.
Club membership 500.
Visitors Mon-Sun & BHs. Booking required. Handicap certificate. Dress code. **Societies** Booking required. **Green Fees** £80 per round (weekends £95). **Prof** Ronnie MacAskill **Course Designer** Baird & Simpson **Facilities** **Location** 2.5m N of city centre off A92

Westhill Westhill Heights, Westhill AB32 6RY
☎ 01224 740159 🖹 01224 749124
e-mail: westhillgolfclub@btinternet.com
web: www.westhillgolfclub.co.uk
A challenging parkland course.
18 holes, 5921yds, Par 69, SSS 69, Course record 65.
Club membership 808.
Visitors Mon-Sun & BHs. Booking required. Dress code. **Societies** Booking required. **Green Fees** £16 per round (£22 weekends). **Prof** George Bruce **Course Designer** Charles Lawrie **Facilities** **Leisure** Snooker table. **Conf** facs Corporate Hospitality Days **Location** 7m NW of city centre off A944

PETERCULTER Map 15 NJ80

Peterculter Oldtown, Burnside Rd AB14 0LN
☎ 01224 734994 (shop) & 735245 (office)
🖹 01224 735580
e-mail: info@petercultergolfclub.co.uk
web: www.petercultergolfclub.co.uk
Surrounded by wonderful scenery and bordered by the River Dee, a variety of birds, deer and foxes may be seen on the course, which also has superb views up the Dee Valley.
18 holes, 6219yds, Par 71, SSS 70, Course record 64.
Club membership 1035.
Visitors contact club for details. Dress code. **Societies** Booking required. **Green Fees** £24 per round/£32 per day (weekend £30/£38). **Prof** Dean Vannet **Course Designer** Greens of Scotland **Facilities** **Location** On A93

If the name of the club appears in italics, details have not been confirmed for this edition of the guide

ABERDEENSHIRE

ABOYNE Map 15 NO59

Aboyne Formaston Park AB34 5HP
☎ 013398 86328 🖹 013398 87592
e-mail: aboynegolfclub@btconnect.com
web: www.aboynegolfclub.co.uk
Beautiful parkland with outstanding views. Two lochs on course.
18 holes, 5963yds, Par 68, SSS 69, Course record 62.
Club membership 970.
Visitors Mon-Sun & BHs. Booking required. Handicap certificate. Dress code. **Societies** Booking required. **Green Fees** £22 per round/£30 per day (weekend £25/£35). **Prof** Stephen Moir **Facilities** **Location** E side of village, N of A93

Hotel ★★ 73% Loch Kinord Hotel, Ballater Rd, Dinnet, BALLATER ☎ 013398 85229 21 rms (19 en suite)

ALFORD Map 15 NJ51

Alford Montgarrie Rd AB33 8AE
☎ 019755 62178 🖹 019755 64910
e-mail: info@alford-golf-club.co.uk
web: golf.alford.co.uk
Flat parkland in scenic countryside. The course is challenging, testing golfers of all skills and abilities. Divided into sections by a road, a narrow-gauge railway and a burn.
18 holes, 5483yds, Par 69, SSS 65, Course record 64.
Club membership 800.
Visitors Mon-Sun & BHs. Booking required Sat & Sun. **Societies** Booking required. **Green Fees** £20 per round, £25 per day (weekends £25/£30). **Facilities** **Conf** Corporate Hospitality Days **Location** In village centre on A944

Hotel ★★ 63% Gordon Arms Hotel, The Square, HUNTLY ☎ 01466 792288 13 en suite

AUCHENBLAE Map 15 NO77

Auchenblae AB30 1WQ
☎ 01561 320002
Short but demanding course set in spectacular scenery and renowned for its excellent greens. A mixture of short and long holes, small and large greens add to the challenge and enjoyment of the course.
9 holes, 2217yds, Par 32, SSS 61, Course record 60.
Club membership 500.
Visitors Mon-Sun & BHs. **Societies** Booking required. **Green Fees** £10 per day (£12 weekends). **Course Designer** Robin Hiseman **Facilities** **Leisure** hard tennis courts. **Location** 10m S of Laurencekirk off A90

BALLATER Map 15 NO39

Ballater Victoria Rd AB35 5QX
☎ 013397 55567
e-mail: sec@ballatergolfclub.co.uk
web: www.ballatergolfclub.co.uk
Heather covered course with testing long holes and beautiful scenery.
18 holes, 5638yds, Par 67, SSS 67, Course record 62.
Club membership 750.

Continued

Visitors Mon-Sun & BHs. Booking required. Dress code. **Societies** Booking required. **Green Fees** £24 per round (weekend £28). **Prof** Bill Yule **Facilities** **Leisure** hard tennis courts, fishing, snooker. **Conf** Corporate Hospitality Days **Location** W side of town

Hotel ★★ 73% Loch Kinord Hotel, Ballater Rd, Dinnet, BALLATER ☎ 013398 85229 21 rms (19 en suite)

BALMEDIE Map 15 NJ91

East Aberdeenshire Golf Centre Millden AB23 8YY
☎ 01358 742111 🖹 01358 742123
e-mail: info@eagolf.com
web: www.eagolf.com

Designed as two loops of nine holes each, starting and finishing outside the clubhouse. Skilful use of 130 acres of rolling Buchan farmland has resulted in a challenging course of 6276yds in length. Even in the short history of the course, the par 3 holes have gained the reputation of being equal to any in the north of Scotland.

18 holes, 6276yards, Par 71, SSS 71, Course record 69. Club membership 400.

Visitors Booking required. **Societies** Booking required. **Green Fees** Phone. **Prof** Ian Bratton **Course Designer** Ian Cresswell **Facilities** **Conf** facs Corporate Hospitality Days

BANCHORY Map 15 NO69

Banchory Kinneskie Rd AB31 5TA
☎ 01330 822365 🖹 01330 822491
e-mail: info@banchorygolfclub.co.uk
web: www.banchorygolfclub.co.uk

Sheltered parkland beside the River Dee, with easy walking and woodland scenery. Testing 12th and 13th holes.

18 holes, 5801yds, Par 69, SSS 68, Course record 63. Club membership 975.

Visitors Booking required Sat & Sun. Dress code. **Societies** Booking required. **Green Fees** £24 per round (£30 weekends). **Prof** David Naylor **Facilities** **Location** A93, 300yds from W end of High St

Hotel ★★★ 74% Banchory Lodge Hotel, BANCHORY ☎ 01330 822625 22 en suite

Inchmarlo Golf Club Inchmarlo AB31 4BQ
☎ 01330 826422 🖹 01330 826425
e-mail: info@inchmarlo.com
web: www.inchmarlo.com

The Laird's is laid out on the gentle parkland slopes of the Inchmarlo Estate and the designer has taken advantage of the natural contours of the land and its many mature trees. The nine-hole facility is a tricky and testing course with ponds, meadering burns and dry stone wall combined with the more traditional bunkers to test the skill of even the most accomplished player.

Laird's Course: 18 holes, 6218yards, Par 71, SSS 71, Course record 66.
9 hole course: 9 holes, 2150yards, Par 32, SSS 31.
Club membership 900.

Visitors Mon-Sun & BHs. Booking required. Dress code. **Societies** Booking required. **Green Fees** Laird's £30 per round (£35 weekends). 9 hole course £16 per 18 holes, £11 per 9 holes (£18/£12 weekends). **Prof** Patrick Lovie **Course Designer** Graeme Webster **Facilities** **Conf** facs Corporate Hospitality Days **Location** 0.5m from A93 Aberdeen-Braemar road

BANFF Map 15 NJ66

Duff House Royal The Barnyards AB45 3SX
☎ 01261 812062 🖹 01261 812224
e-mail: duff_house_royal@btinternet.com
web: www.theduffhouseroyalgolfclub.co.uk

Well-manicured flat parkland, bounded by woodlands and the River Deveron. Well bunkered and renowned for its large, two-tier greens. The river is a hazard for those who wander off the tee at the 7th, 16th and 17th holes.

18 holes, 6161yds, Par 68, SSS 70, Course record 62. Club membership 1000.

Visitors Mon-Sun. Booking required. Handicap certificate. Dress code. **Societies** Booking required. **Green Fees** £31 per day, £25 per round (£37/£32 weekends). **Prof** Gary Holland **Course Designer** A MacKenzie **Facilities** **Conf** Corporate Hospitality Days **Location** 0.5m S on A98

Hotel ★★★ 71% Banff Springs Hotel, Golden Knowes Rd, BANFF ☎ 01261 812881 31 en suite

BRAEMAR Map 15 NO19

Braemar Cluniebank Rd AB35 5XX
☎ 013397 41618 🖹 013397 41400
e-mail: colin.mcintosh4@virgin.net

Flat course, set amid beautiful countryside on Royal Deeside, with River Clunie running through several holes. The 2nd hole is one of the most testing in the area.

18 holes, 5000yds, Par 65, SSS 64, Course record 59. Club membership 450.

Visitors Mon-Sun & BHs. Booking required. Dress code. **Societies** Booking required. **Green Fees** £20 per round, £25 per day (weekend £25/£30). **Course Designer** Joe Anderson **Facilities** **Location** 0.5m S

CRUDEN BAY Map 15 NK03

Cruden Bay Aulton Rd AB42 0NN
☎ 01779 812285 🖹 01779 812945
e-mail: cbaygc@aol.com
web: www.crudenbaygolfclub.co.uk
A typical links course which epitomises the old fashioned style of rugged links golf. The drives require accuracy with bunkers and protecting greens, blind holes and undulating greens. The 10th provides a panoramic view of half the back nine down at beach level, and to the east can be seen the outline of the spectacular ruin of Slains Castle featured in Bram Stoker's Dracula. The figure eight design of the course is quite unusual.
Main Course: 18 holes, 6395yds, Par 70, SSS 72, Course record 65.
St Olaf Course: 9 holes, 5106yds, Par 64, SSS 65.
Club membership 1100.
Visitors Mon-Sun & BHs. Booking required. Handicap certificate. Dress code. **Societies** Booking required. **Green Fees** £60 per round, £80 per day (weekend £70 per round). **Prof** Robbie Stewart **Course Designer** Thomas Simpson **Facilities** **Conf** Corporate Hospitality Days **Location** SW side of village on A975

Hotel ★★ 66% Red House Hotel, Aulton Rd, CRUDEN BAY ☎ 01779 812215 6 rms (5 en suite)

ELLON Map 15 NJ93

McDonald Hospital Rd AB41 9AW
☎ 01358 720576 🖹 01358 720001
e-mail: mcdonald.golf@virgin.net
Tight, parkland course with streams.
18 holes, 5986yds, Par 70, SSS 70, Course record 62.
Club membership 710.
Visitors Mon-Sun & BHs. Booking required Sat-Sun & BHs. Dress code. **Societies** Booking required. **Green Fees** £22 per round, £30 per day (weekend £27/£35). **Prof** Ronnie Urquhart **Facilities** **Conf** Corporate Hospitality Days **Location** 0.25m N on A948

FRASERBURGH Map 15 NJ96

Fraserburgh AB43 8TL
☎ 01346 516616 🖹 01346 516616
e-mail: fburghgolf@aol.com
web: www.fraserburghgolfclub.net
Corbie: 18 holes, 6308yds, Par 70, SSS 71, Course record 63.
Rosehill: 9 holes, 2416yds, Par 66, SSS 63.
Course Designer James Braid **Location** 1m SE on B9033
Telephone for further details

HUNTLY Map 15 NJ53

Huntly Cooper Park AB54 4SH
☎ 01466 792643 🖹 01466 792643
e-mail: huntlygc1@tiscali.co.uk
Parkland between the rivers Deveron and Bogie.
18 holes, 5399yds, Par 67, SSS 66.
Club membership 700.
Visitors Mon-Sun & BHs. Booking required. **Societies** Booking required. **Green Fees** £21per day, £16 per round (£27/£20 weekends). **Facilities** **Location** N side of Huntly, turn off A96 at bypass rdbt

Hotel ★★ 63% Gordon Arms Hotel, The Square, HUNTLY ☎ 01466 792288 13 en suite

INSCH Map 15 NJ62

Insch Golf Ter AB52 6JY
☎ 01464 820363 🖹 01464 820363
e-mail: inschgolf@tiscali.co.uk
web: www.insch4golf.com
A challenging 18-hole course, a mixture of flat undulating parkland, with trees, stream and pond. The most challenging hole of the course is the 9th, a testing par 5 of 536yds requiring long and accurate play. This follows the par 3 8th, a hole which demands a well-positioned tee shot played over a large water hazard to a long narrow green. Although a relatively short course, the natural woodland, water hazards and large contoured greens require accurate play.

18 holes, 5350yds, Par 69, SSS 67.
Club membership 400.
Visitors Mon-Sun & BHs. **Societies** Booking required. **Green Fees** £16 per day (£22 weekends) reductions during winter. **Course Designer** Greens of Scotland **Facilities** by arrangement by arrangement **Conf** Corporate Hospitality Days **Location** A96

INVERALLOCHY Map 15 NK06

Inverallochy Whitelink AB43 8XY
☎ 01346 582000
Seaside links course with natural hazards, tricky par 3s and easy walking.
18 holes, 5351yds, Par 67, SSS 66, Course record 57.
Club membership 600.
Visitors Mon-Sun & BHs. Booking required Sat & Sun. **Societies** Booking required. **Green Fees** Mon-Fri £25 per day, £17 per round; Sat & Sun £30/£20. **Facilities** **Leisure** Bowling green. **Location** E side of village off B9107

INVERURIE Map 15 NJ72

Inverurie Davah Wood AB51 5JB
☎ 01467 624080 🖹 01467 672869
e-mail: administrator@inveruriegc.co.uk
web: www.inveruriegc.co.uk
Parkland course, part of which is through a wood.
18 holes, 5711yds, Par 69, SSS 68, Course record 63.
Club membership 750.
Visitors Mon-Sun & BHs. Booking required. Dress code. **Societies** Booking required. **Green Fees** £24 per day, £20 per round (£30/£24 weekends). **Prof** John Logue **Facilities** **Location** Off Blackhall rdbt off A96 bypass

Continued

KEMNAY Map 15 NJ71

Kemnay Monymusk Rd AB51 5RA
☎ 01467 642225 (shop) 01467 643746
e-mail: administrator@kemnaygolfclub.co.uk
web: www.kemnaygolfclub.co.uk
Parkland with stunning views, incorporating tree-lined and open fairways, and a stream crossing four holes. The course is not physically demanding but a challenge is presented to every level of golfer due to the diverse characteristics of each hole.
18 holes, 6362yds, Par 71, SSS 71, Course record 66. Club membership 800.
Visitors contact club for details. **Societies** welcome. **Green Fees** £26 per day, £20 per round (£30/£24 weekends). **Prof** Ronnie McDonald **Course Designer** Greens of Scotland **Facilities** **Conf** Corporate Hospitality Days **Location** W side of village on B993

KINTORE Map 15 NJ71

Kintore Balbithan AB51 0UR
☎ 01467 632631 01467 632995
e-mail: kintoregolfclub@lineone.net
web: www.kintoregolfclub.net
The course covers a large area of ground, from the Don Basin near the clubhouse, to mature woodland at the far perimeter. The 1st is one of the toughest opening holes in the North East, and the 7th requires an accurate drive followed by a second shot over a burn which runs diagonally across the front of the green. The 11th is the longest hole on the course, made longer by the fact that it slopes upwards all the way to the green. The final holes are short, relatively hilly and quite tricky but offer spectacular views to the Bennachie and Grampian hills.
18 holes, 6019yds, Par 70, SSS 69, Course record 62. Club membership 700.
Visitors Mon-Sun & BHs. Booking required. Dress code **Societies** Booking required. **Green Fees** Phone. **Facilities** **Conf** Corporate Hospitality Days **Location** 1m from village centre on B977

MACDUFF Map 15 NJ76

Royal Tarlair Buchan St AB44 1TA
☎ 01261 832897 01261 833455
e-mail: info@royaltarlair.co.uk
web: www.royaltarlair.co.uk
Seaside clifftop course. Testing 13th, Clivet (par 3).
18 holes, 5866yds, Par 71, SSS 68, Course record 62. Club membership 350.
Visitors Mon-Sun & BHs. Booking required Sat & Sun. **Societies** Booking required. **Green Fees** £15 per round, £20 per day (weekends £18/£22). **Facilities** **Conf** Corporate Hospitality Days **Location** 0.75m E off A98

Hotel ★★★ 71% Banff Springs Hotel, Golden Knowes Rd, BANFF ☎ 01261 812881 31 en suite

MINTLAW Map 15 NJ94

Longside West End, Longside AB42 4XJ
☎ 01779 821558 01779 821564
Flat parkland course with a river winding through, providing a challenging course which requires accurate play.
18 holes, 5225yds, Par 66, SSS 66, Course record 64. Club membership 700.
Visitors Mon-Sun & BHs. Booking required. Handicap certificate. **Societies** Booking required. **Green Fees** £16 per day, £12 per round (£22/£18 Sun). **Facilities** **Location** 4m W of Peterhead on New Pitsligo road

Hotel ★★★ 66% Palace Hotel, Prince St, PETERHEAD ☎ 01779 474821 64 en suite

NEWBURGH Map 15 NJ92

Newburgh on Ythan Beach Rd AB41 6BE
☎ 01358 789058 01358 788104
e-mail: secretary@newburgh-on-ythan.co.uk
web: www.newburgh-on-ythan.co.uk
18 holes, 6162yds, Par 72, SSS 71, Course record 68.
Location 10m N of Aberdeen on A975
Telephone for further details

NEWMACHAR Map 15 NJ81

Newmachar Swailend AB21 7UU
☎ 01651 863002 01651 863055
e-mail: info@newmachargolfclub.co.uk
web: www.newmachargolfclub.co.uk
Hawkshill is a championship-standard parkland course designed by Dave Thomas. Several lakes affect five of the holes and there are well-developed birch and Scots pine trees. Swailend is a parkland course, also designed by Dave Thomas and opened in 1997. It provides a test all of its own with some well-positioned bunkering and testing greens.
Hawkshill Course: 18 holes, 6659yds, Par 72, SSS 74, Course record 67.
Swailend Course: 18 holes, 6388yds, Par 72, SSS 71, Course record 67.
Club membership 900.
Visitors Mon-Sun & BHs. Booking required. Handicap certificate. Dress code. **Societies** Booking required. **Green Fees** Phone. **Prof** Gordon Simpson **Course Designer** Dave Thomas/Peter Allis **Facilities** **Location** 2m N of Dyce, off A947

OLDMELDRUM Map 15 NJ82

Old Meldrum Kirk Brae AB51 0DJ
☎ 01651 872648 01651 872896
e-mail: admin@oldmeldrumgolf.co.uk
web: www.oldmeldrumgolf.co.uk
Parkland with tree-lined fairways and superb views. Challenging 196yd, par 3 11th over two ponds to a green surrounded by bunkers.
18 holes, 5988yds, Par 70, SSS 69, Course record 66. Club membership 850.
Visitors contact club for details. **Societies** Booking required. **Green Fees** £22 per round (weekend £26). **Prof** Hamish Love **Course Designer** Various **Facilities** **Location** E side of village off A947

PETERHEAD Map 15 NK14

Peterhead Craigewan Links, Riverside Dr AB42 1LT
☎ 01779 472149 & 480725 🖹 01779 480725
e-mail: phdgc@freenetname.co.uk
web: www.peterheadgolfclub.co.uk
The Old Course is a natural links course bounded by the sea and the River Ugie. Varying conditions of play depending on wind and weather. The New Course is more of a parkland course.
Old Course: 18 holes, 6173yds, Par 70, SSS 71, Course record 64.
New Course: 9 holes, 2228yds, Par 31.
Club membership 650.
Visitors Mon-Fri & Sun. Booking required. **Societies** Apply in writing. **Green Fees** Phone. **Course Designer** W Park/L Auchterconie/J Braid **Facilities** **Location** N side of town centre off A90

PORTLETHEN Map 15 NO99

Portlethen Badentoy Rd AB12 4YA
☎ 01224 782575 & 781090 🖹 01224 783383
e-mail: info@portlethengc.fsnet.co.uk
Set in pleasant parkland, this new course features mature trees and a stream which affects a number of holes.
18 holes, 6707yds, Par 72, SSS 72, Course record 63.
Club membership 1200.
Visitors may not play Sat. Contact in advance. **Societies** apply in advance. **Green Fees** Phone. **Prof** Muriel Thomson **Course Designer** Cameron Sinclair **Facilities** **Conf** facs **Location** Off A90 S of Aberdeen

STONEHAVEN Map 15 NO88

Stonehaven Cowie AB39 3RH
☎ 01569 762124 🖹 01569 765973
e-mail: stonehaven.golfclub@virgin.net
Challenging meadowland course overlooking sea with three gullies and splendid views.
18 holes, 5103yds, Par 66, SSS 65, Course record 61.
Club membership 850.
Visitors Mon-Fri, Sun & BHs. Booking required. Handicap certificate. Dress code. **Societies** welcome. **Green Fees** £19 per round/£25 per day (weekend £25/£30). **Course Designer** C Simpson **Facilities** **Leisure** snooker. **Location** 1m N off A92

TARLAND Map 15 NJ40

Tarland Aberdeen Rd AB34 4TB
☎ 013398 81000 🖹 013398 81000
e-mail: telward@aol.com
Difficult upland course, but easy walking. Some spectacular holes, mainly 4th (par 4) and 5th (par 3) and fine scenery. A challenge to golfers of all abilities.
9 holes, 5888yds, Par 67, SSS 68, Course record 65.
Club membership 325.
Visitors Mon-Sun & BHs. Dress code **Societies** Booking required. **Green Fees** £16 per day (£21 weekends). **Course Designer** Tom Morris **Facilities** **Conf** Corporate Hospitality Days **Location** E side of village off B9119

Hotel ★★ 73% Loch Kinord Hotel, Ballater Rd, Dinnet, BALLATER ☎ 013398 85229 21 rms (19 en suite)

TORPHINS Map 15 NJ60

Torphins Bog Rd AB31 4JU
☎ 013398 82115 & 82402 (Sec) 🖹 013398 82402
e-mail: stuart@macgregor5.fsnet.co.uk
Heathland and parkland course built on a hill with views of the Cairngorms.
9 holes, 4800yds, Par 64, SSS 64, Course record 59.
Club membership 380.
Visitors Mon-Sun & BHs. Booking required Sat-Sun & BHs. **Societies** Booking required. **Green Fees** £13 per day (£14 weekends). £7 per 9 holes. **Facilities** **Location** 0.25m W of village off A980

TURRIFF Map 15 NJ75

Turriff Rosehall AB53 4HD
☎ 01888 562982 🖹 01888 568050
e-mail: grace@turriffgolf.sol.co.uk
web: www.turriffgolfclub.com
An inland course with tight fairways, well-paced greens and well-sighted bunkers to test all golfers. The par 5 12th hole sets a challenge for the longest driver while the short par 3 4th, with its green protected by bunkers is a challenge in its own right.

18 holes, 5664yds, Par 68, SSS 68.
Club membership 650.
Visitors Mon-Sun & BHs. Handicap certificate. Dress code. **Societies** Booking required. **Green Fees** £26 per day £22 per day (£32/£26 weekends & holidays). **Prof** Crai Mackie **Facilities** **Conf** Corporate Hospitality Days **Location** 1m W off B9024

Hotel ★★★ 71% Banff Springs Hotel, Golden Knowes Rd, BANFF ☎ 01261 812881 31 en suite

ANGUS

ARBROATH Map 12 NO64

Arbroath Elliot DD11 2PE
☎ 01241 875837 🖹 01241 875837
e-mail: arbroathgolf@btinternet.com
A typical links layout, predominately flat, with the prevailing south westerly wind facing for the first seve holes, making a big difference to how certain holes play When the wind is in a northerly direction the back nin holes are very tough. The greens are well protected by deep riveted pot bunkers. Fast tricky greens make for difficult putting.
18 holes, 6185yds, Par 70, SSS 69, Course record 64.
Club membership 550.
Visitors may play Mon-Sun & BHs. Advance booking required. Dress code. **Societies** Booking required. **Green**

Continu

Angus

Carnoustie Golf Links

Carnoustie

Map 12 NO53

This Championship Course has been voted the top course in Britain by many golfing greats and described as Scotland's ultimate golfing challenge. The course developed from origins in the 1560s; James Braid added new bunkers, greens and tees in the 1920s. The Open Championship first came to the course in 1931 and Carnoustie hosted the Scottish Open in 1995 and 1996, and was the venue for the 1999 Open Championship and will stage the Championship in 2007. The Burnside Course (6028yds) is enclosed on three sides by the Championship Course and has been used for Open Championship qualifying rounds. The Buddon Course (5420yds) has been extensively remodelled, making it ideal for mid to high handicappers.

Links Pde DD7 7JE
☎ 01241 853789 bookings 🖹 01241 852720
e-mail: golf@carnoustiegolflinks.co.uk
web: www.carnoustiegolflinks.co.uk

Championship: 18 holes, 6941yds, Par 72, SSS 75, Course record 64.
Burnside: 18 holes, 6028yds, Par 68, SSS 70.
Buddon Links: 18 holes, 5420yds, Par 66, SSS 67.

Visitors Mon-Sun & BHs. Booking required. Handicap certificate. Dress code. **Societies** Booking required. **Green Fees** Phone. **Prof** Colin Sinclair **Course Designer** James Braid **Facilities** ⊗ ✉ ⊾ ☕ ♀ ⚠ ☖ ⚲ ⛟ ✓ ⚲ **Leisure** heated indoor swimming pool, sauna, solarium, gymnasium. **Location** SW of town centre off A930

Fees £25 per day, £20 per round (£35/£25 Sat, Sun & BHs). **Prof** Lindsay Ewart **Course Designer** Braid **Facilities** **Location** 2m SW on A92

Letham Grange Golf Ltd Colliston DD11 4RL
☎ 01241 890373 01241 890725
e-mail: lethamgrangegolf@yahoo.co.uk
Often referred to as the 'Augusta of Scotland', the Old Course provides championship standards in spectacular surroundings with attractive lochs and burns. The Glens Course is less arduous and shorter using many natural features of the estate.
Old Course: 18 holes, 6632yds, Par 73, SSS 73, Course record 67.
Glens Course: 18 holes, 5528yds, Par 68, SSS 68, Course record 60.
Club membership 600.
Visitors Mon-Sun & BHs. Booking required. Dress code. **Societies** Booking required. **Green Fees** Old £40 (£45 weekends). Glens £22 (£27 weekends). **Course Designer** G K Smith/Donald Steel **Facilities** **Conf** facs Corporate Hospitality Days **Location** 4m N on A933

BARRY Map 12 NO53

Panmure Burnside Rd DD7 7RT
☎ 01241 855120 01241 859737
e-mail: secretary@panmuregolfclub.co.uk
web: www.panmuregolfclub.co.uk
A nerve-testing, adventurous course which opens quietly and builds its challenge amongst the sandhills further out. The course is used for Open championship final qualifying rounds.
18 holes, 6317yds, Par 70, SSS 71, Course record 62.
Club membership 700.
Visitors Mon-Fri, Sun & BHs. Dress code. **Societies** Booking required. **Green Fees** £75 per day, £55 per round. **Prof** Neil Mackintosh **Facilities** **Conf** Corporate Hospitality Days **Location** S side of village off A930

Hotel Premier Travel Inn Dundee East, 115-117 Lawers Dr, Panmurefield Village, BROUGHTY FERRY
☎ 0870 9906324 60 en suite

BRECHIN Map 15 NO56

Brechin Trinity DD9 7PD
☎ 01356 622383 & 625270 01356 625270
e-mail: brechingolfclub@tiscali.co.uk
web: www.brechingolfclub.co.uk
Rolling parkland with easy walking and good views of the Grampian mountains. Set among many tree-lined fairways with excellent greens and lush green fairways. A wide variation of holes with dog legs, long par 3s, tricky par 4s and reachable in two par 5s, where the longer hitters can take a more challenging tee shot.
18 holes, 6092yds, Par 72, SSS 70, Course record 66.
Club membership 850.
Visitors Mon-Sun & BHs. Booking required. Dress code. **Societies** Booking required. **Green Fees** £33 per day, £25 pe round (£40/£30 weekends). **Prof** Stephen Rennie **Course Designer** James Braid (partly) **Facilities** **Leisure** squash. **Conf** Corporate Hospitality Days **Location** 1m N on B966

Hotel ★★★ 65% Glenesk Hotel, High St, EDZELL
☎ 01356 648319 24 en suite

CARNOUSTIE Map 12 NO53

Carnoustie Golf Links see page 325

EDZELL Map 15 NO66

Edzell High St DD9 7TF
☎ 01356 647283 (Secretary) 01356 648094
e-mail: secretary@edzellgolfclub.net
web: www.edzellgolfclub.net
This delightful, gentle, flat course is situated in the foothills of the Highlands and provides good golf as well as conveying a feeling of peace and quiet to everyone who plays here. The village of Edzell is one of the most picturesque in Scotland.
18 holes, 6367yds, Par 71, SSS 71, Course record 62.
West Water: 9 holes, 2057yds, Par 32, SSS 31.
Club membership 855.
Visitors Mon-Sun & BHs. Booking required. Handicap certificate. Dress code. **Societies** Booking required. **Green Fees** £45 per day, £33 per round (£56/£40 weekends). West Water £15 per 18 holes, £12 per 9 holes. **Prof** A J Webster **Course Designer** Bob Simpson **Facilities** **Location** On B966, S end of Edzell

Hotel ★★★ 65% Glenesk Hotel, High St, EDZELL
☎ 01356 648319 24 en suite

FORFAR Map 15 NO45

Forfar Cunninghill, Arbroath Rd DD8 2RL
☎ 01307 463773 01307 468495
e-mail: forfargolfclub@uku.co.uk
web: forfargolfclub.com
18 holes, 6066yds, Par 69, SSS 70, Course record 61.
Course Designer James Braid **Location** 1.5m E of Forfar on A932
Telephone for further details

Hotel ★★★ Castleton House Hotel, Castleton of Eassie, GLAMIS ☎ 01307 840340 6 en suite

KIRRIEMUIR Map 15 NO35

Kirriemuir Shielhill Rd, Northmuir DD8 4LN
☎ 01575 573317 01575 574608
e-mail: kirriemuirgolfclub@fsmail.net
Parkland and heathland course set at the foot of the Angus glens, with good view.
18 holes, 5553yds, Par 68, SSS 67, Course record 62.
Club membership 750.
Visitors Mon-Sun & BHs. Booking required. Dress code. **Societies** Booking required. **Green Fees** £29 per day, £22 per round (£40/£30 weekends). **Prof** Karyn Dallas **Course Designer** James Braid **Facilities** **Location** 1m N off B955

Hotel ★★★ Castleton House Hotel, Castleton of Eassie, GLAMIS ☎ 01307 840340 6 en suite

MONIFIETH Map 12 NO43

Monifieth Princes St DD5 4AW
☎ 01382 532767 (Medal) & 532967 (Ashludie)
01382 535816
The chief of the two courses at Monifieth is the Medal Course. It has been one of the qualifying venues for the Open Championship on more than one occasion. A

Continued

seaside links, but divided from the sand dunes by a railway which provides the principal hazard for the first few holes. The 10th hole is outstanding, the 17th is excellent and there is a delightful finishing hole. The other course here is the Ashludie, and both are played over by a number of clubs who share the links.

Monifieth

Medal Course: 18 holes, 6655yds, Par 71, SSS 72, Course record 63.
Ashludie Course: 18 holes, 5123yds, Par 68, SSS 66.
Club membership 1750.

Visitors Mon-Sun & BHs. Booking required. Handicap certificate. Dress code. **Societies** Booking required. **Green Fees** Medal £39 per round (£49 weekends). Ashludie £19 per round (£23 weekends). **Prof** Ian McLeod **Facilities** **Location** NE side of town on A930

Hotel Premier Travel Inn Dundee East, 115-117 Lawers Dr, Panmurefield Village, BROUGHTY FERRY ☎ 0870 9906324 60 en suite

MONTROSE Map 15 NO75

Montrose Golf Links Traill Dr DD10 8SW
☎ 01674 672932 Fax 01674 671800
e-mail: secretary@montroselinks.co.uk
web: www.montroselinks.co.uk

The links at Montrose like many others in Scotland are on commonland and are shared by three clubs. The Medal Course at Montrose - the fifth oldest in the world - is typical of Scottish links, with narrow, undulating fairways and problems from the first hole to the last. The Broomfield course is flatter and easier.

Medal Course: 18 holes, 6544yds, Par 71, SSS 72, Course record 63.
Broomfield Course: 18 holes, 4830yds, Par 66, SSS 63.
Club membership 1300.

Visitors Mon-Sun & BHs. Booking required. Handicap certificate. Dress code. **Societies** Booking required. **Green** Continued

Fees Medal £50 per day, £40 per round (£58/£44 weekends). Broomfield £18 per round (£20 weekends). **Prof** Jason J Boyd **Course Designer** W Park/Tom Morris **Facilities** **Location** NE side of town off A92

Hotel ★★★ 74% Best Western Links Hotel, Mid Links, MONTROSE ☎ 01674 671000 25 en suite

ARGYLL & BUTE

CARDROSS Map 10 NS37

Cardross Main Rd G82 5LB
☎ 01389 841754 Fax 01389 842162
e-mail: golf@cardross.com
web: www.cardross.com

Undulating, testing parkland course with good views.
18 holes, 6469yds, Par 71, SSS 72, Course record 64.
Club membership 800.

Visitors Mon-Sun. Booking required. Dress code. **Societies** Booking required. **Green Fees** £35 per round/£50 per day. Winter reduced rates. **Prof** Robert Farrell **Course Designer** James Braid **Facilities** by arrangement **Conf** Corporate Hospitality Days **Location** In village centre on A814

Hotel ★★★★★ 70% De Vere Cameron House, BALLOCH ☎ 01389 755565 96 en suite

CARRADALE Map 10 NR83

Carradale The Arch PA28 6QT
☎ 01583 431321
Pleasant seaside course built on a promontory overlooking the Isle of Arran. Natural terrain and small greens are the most difficult natural hazards. Described as the most sporting nine-hole course in Scotland. Testing 7th hole (240yds), par 3.
9 holes, 2358yds, Par 65, SSS 64, Course record 62.
Club membership 246.
Visitors Mon-Sun & BHs. **Societies** Booking required. **Green Fees** £15 per day. **Facilities** **Location** S side of village, on B842

DALMALLY Map 10 NN12

Dalmally Old Saw Mill PA33 1AE
☎ 01866 822708
e-mail: golfclub@lock-awe.com
web: www.loch-awe.com/golfclub/default.htm
A nine-hole flat parkland course bounded by the River Orchy and surrounded by mountains. Many water hazards and bunkers.
9 holes, 2257yds, Par 64, SSS 63, Course record 64.
Club membership 130.
Visitors Mon-Fri & BHs. **Societies** welcome. **Green Fees** £12 per day/round. **Course Designer** MacFarlane Barrow Co **Facilities** **Location** On A85, 1.5m W of Dalmally

Hotel ★★★ 68% Loch Fyne Hotel & Leisure Club, INVERARAY ☎ 0870 950 6270 78 en suite

DUNOON Map 10 NS17

Cowal Ardenslate Rd PA23 8LT
☎ 01369 705673 🖷 01369 705673
e-mail: secretary@cowalgolfclub.com
web: www.cowalgolfclub.com
Moorland course. Panoramic views of the Clyde estuary and surrounding hills.

18 holes, 6063yds, Par 70, SSS 70, Course record 63.
Club membership 900.
Visitors Booking required. **Societies** Booking required. **Green Fees** Phone. **Prof** Russell Weir **Course Designer** James Braid **Facilities** **Location** 1m N

Hotel ★★ 66% Selborne Hotel, Clyde St, West Bay, DUNOON ☎ 01369 702761 98 en suite

ERISKA Map 10 NM94

Isle of Eriska PA37 1SD
☎ 01631 720371 🖷 01631 720531
e-mail: gc@eriska-hotel.co.uk
web: www.eriska-hotel.co.uk
This remote and most beautiful six-hole course, set around the owners' hotel, is gradually being upgraded to a testing nine-hole challenge, complete with stunning views. The signature 5th hole provides a 140yd carry to a green on a hill surrounded by rocks and bunkers.
6 holes, 1588yds, Par 22.
Club membership 40.
Visitors Mon-Sun & BHs. Booking required. Dress code. **Green Fees** £10 per day. **Course Designer** H Swan **Facilities** **Leisure** hard tennis courts, heated indoor swimming pool, sauna, gymnasium. **Location** A828 Connel-Fort William, signed 4m N of Benderloch

Hotel ★★★★ Isle of Eriska, Eriska, Ledaig, BY OBAN ☎ 01631 720371 17 en suite

GIGHA ISLAND Map 10 NR64

Isle of Gigha PA41 7AA
☎ 01583 505242 🖷 01583 505244
A nine-hole course with scenic views of the Sound of Gigha and Kintyre. Ideal for the keen or occasional golfer.
9 holes, 5042yds, Par 66, SSS 65.
Club membership 40.
Visitors Mon-Sun & BHs. Booking required. **Societies** welcome. **Green Fees** £10 per day/round. **Course Designer** Members **Facilities** **Location** Near ferry landing

HELENSBURGH Map 10 NS28

Helensburgh 25 East Abercromby St G84 9HZ
☎ 01436 674173 🖷 01436 671170
e-mail: thesecretary@helensburghgolfclub.org.uk
web: www.helensburghgolfclub.org.uk
Testing moorland course with superb views of Loch Lomond and River Clyde.
18 holes, 6104yds, Par 69, SSS 70, Course record 62.
Club membership 875.
Visitors Mon-Fri, Sun & BHs. Booking required. Handicap certificate. Dress code. **Societies** Booking required. **Green Fees** £40 per day, £30 per round. **Prof** Fraser Hall **Course Designer** Old Tom Morris **Facilities** **Conf** Corporate Hospitality Days **Location** NE side of town off B832

Hotel ★★★★★ 70% De Vere Cameron House, BALLOCH ☎ 01389 755565 96 en suite

INNELLAN Map 10 NS17

Innellan Knockamillie Rd PA23 7SG
☎ 01369 830242 & 702573
Situated above the village of Innellan, this undulating hilltop, parkland course has extensive views of the Firth of Clyde.
9 holes, 4683yds, Par 64, SSS 64, Course record 63.
Club membership 199.
Visitors Mon-Sat & BHs. **Societies** Welcome. **Green Fees** £13 per day. £10 per round. (£15 at weekends) per 9 holes. **Facilities** **Location** 4m S of Dunoon

Continued

Hotel ★★ 75% Royal Marine Hotel, Hunters Quay, DUNOON ☎ 01369 705810 31 en suite 10 annexe en suite

INVERARAY Map 10 NN00

Inveraray North Cromalt PA32 8XT
☎ 01499 302116
Testing parkland course with beautiful views overlooking Loch Fyne.
9 holes, 5628yds, Par 70, SSS 69, Course record 69. Club membership 160.
Visitors Mon-Sun & BHs. Sun only. Contact club for details. **Societies** welcome. **Green Fees** £15 per day per 18 holes. **Facilities** **Location** 1m S of Inveraray

Hotel ★★★ 68% Loch Fyne Hotel & Leisure Club, INVERARAY ☎ 0870 950 6270 78 en suite

LOCHGILPHEAD Map 10 NR88

Lochgilphead Blarbuie Rd PA31 8LE
☎ 01546 602340 510383

9 holes, 2242yds, Par 64, SSS 63, Course record 58.
Course Designer Dr I McCamond **Location** Next to hospital, signed from village
Telephone for further details

MACHRIHANISH Map 10 NR62

Machrihanish PA28 6PT
☎ 01586 810213 🖹 01586 810221
e-mail: secretary@machgolf.com
web: www.machgolf.com
Magnificent natural links of championship status. The 1st hole is the famous drive across the Atlantic. Sandy soil allows for play all year round. Large greens, easy walking, windy. Fishing.
18 holes, 6225yds, Par 70, SSS 71. Club membership 1400.
Visitors contact club for details. Dress code. **Societies** Booking required. **Green Fees** Sun-Fri £40 per round/£60 per day. Sat £50/£75. 9 hole course £12 per day. **Prof** Ken Campbell **Course Designer** Tom Morris **Facilities** **Location** 5m W of Campbeltown on B843

OBAN Map 10 NM83

Glencruitten Glencruitten Rd PA34 4PU
☎ 01631 564604
e-mail: info@obangolf.com
web: www.obangolf.com
There is plenty of space and considerable variety of hole on this downland course - popular with holidaymakers. In a beautiful, isolated situation, the course is hilly and testing, particularly the 1st and 12th (par 4s) and 10th and 17th (par 3s).
18 holes, 4452yds, Par 61, SSS 63, Course record 55. Club membership 500.
Visitors Mon-Sat & BHs. Dress code. **Societies** Booking required. **Green Fees** Mon-Fri £25 per day. Weekends £30 per day. **Course Designer** James Braid **Facilities** **Location** NE side of town centre off A816

Hotel ★★★ 72% Manor House Hotel, Gallanach Rd, OBAN ☎ 01631 562087 11 en suite

SOUTHEND Map 10 NR60

Dunaverty PA28 6RW
☎ 01586 830677 🖹 01586 830677
e-mail: dunavertygc@aol.com
18 holes, 4799yds, Par 66, SSS 63, Course record 58.
Location 10m S of Campbeltown on B842
Telephone for further details

TARBERT Map 10 NR86

Tarbert PA29 6XX
☎ 01546 606896
Hilly parkland with views over West Loch Tarbert.
9 holes, 4460yds, Par 66, SSS 63, Course record 62. Club membership 90.
Visitors Mon-Sun & BHs. **Societies** Booking required. **Green Fees** £10 per round, £20 per day. **Location** N1m W on B8024

TIGHNABRUAICH Map 10 NR97

Kyles of Bute PA212AB
☎ 01700 811603
Moorland course which is hilly and exposed. Fine mountain and sea views. Heather, whin and burns provide heavy penalties for inaccuracy. Wild life abounds.
9 holes, 4778yds, Par 66, SSS 64, Course record 62. Club membership 150.
Visitors Mon-Sun & BHs. Sun only. **Societies** Booking required. **Green Fees** £10 per day/round per 9 holes. **Facilities** **Location** 1.25m S off B8000

Hotel ★★ 81% The Royal at Tighnabruaich, Shore Rd, TIGHNABRUAICH ☎ 01700 811239 11 en suite

CITY OF EDINBURGH

EDINBURGH Map 11 NT27

Baberton 50 Baberton Av, Juniper Green EH14 5DU
☎ 0131 453 4911 🖹 0131 453 4678
e-mail: manager@baberton.co.uk
web: www.baberton.co.uk
Parkland course offering the golfer a variety of interesting and challenging holes. The outward half

Continued

follows the boundary of the course and presents some demanding par 3 and 4 holes over the undulating terrain. The inward half has some longer, equally challenging holes contained within the course and presents some majestic views of the Pentland Hills and the Edinburgh skyline.
18 holes, 6129yds, Par 69, SSS 70, Course record 64. Club membership 900.
Visitors Mon-Sun & BHs. Dress code. **Societies** Booking required. **Green Fees** £37 per day, £27 per round (£40/£30 weekends). **Prof** Ken Kelly **Course Designer** Willie Park Jnr **Facilities** **Leisure** Snooker. **Conf** Corporate Hospitality Days **Location** 5m W of city centre off A70

Hotel ★★★★ 69% Edinburgh Marriott Hotel, 111 Glasgow Rd, EDINBURGH ☎ 0870 400 7293 & 0131 334 9191 Fax 0870 400 7393 245 en suite

Braid Hills Braid Hills Approach EH10 6JZ
☎ 0131 447 6666 Fax 0131 651 2299
e-mail: golf@edinburghleisure.co.uk
web: www.edinburghleisure.co.uk
Course No 1: 18 holes, 5345yds, Par 70, SSS 66.
Course Designer Peter McEwan & Bob Ferguson
Location 2.5m S of city centre off A702
Telephone for further details

Hotel ★★★ 70% Braid Hills Hotel, 134 Braid Rd, EDINBURGH ☎ 0131 447 8888 67 en suite
See advertisement on this page

Bruntsfield Links Golfing Society 32 Barnton Av EH4 6JH
☎ 0131 336 1479 Fax 0131 336 5538
e-mail: secretary@bruntsfield.sol.co.uk
web: www.sol.co.uk/b/bruntsfieldlinks
Mature parkland course with magnificent views over the Firth of Forth and to the west. Greens and fairways are generally immaculate. Challenging for all categories of handicap.
18 holes, 6428yds, Par 71, SSS 71, Course record 64. Club membership 1180.
Visitors Mon-Sun & BHs. Booking required. Handicap certificate. Dress code. **Societies** Booking required. **Green Fees** £75 per day, £52 per round (£80/£60 weekends). **Prof** Brian Mackenzie **Course Designer** Willie Park Jr, A Mackenzle, Hawtree **Facilities** **Conf** Corporate Hospitality Days **Location** 4m NW of city centre off A90

Hotel ★★★★ 70% Menzies Belford Hotel, 69 Belford Rd, EDINBURGH ☎ 0131 332 2545 146 en suite

Carrick Knowe Carrick Knowe, Glendevon Park EH12 5UZ
☎ 0131 337 1096 Fax 0131 651 2299
e-mail: golf@edinburghleisure.co.uk
18 holes, 5697yds, Par 70, SSS 69.
Location 3m W of city centre, S of A8
Telephone for further details

Craigentinny Fillyside Rd EH7 6RG
☎ 0131 554 7501 Fax 0131 651 2299
e-mail: golf@edinburghleisure.co.uk
An interesting mix of holes on an undulating parkland layout. From some tricky par 3s to some testing par 4s, this relatively short course will suit all abilities. The greens are surrounded by some awkward bunkers, requiring a great deal of forethought and an amount of accuracy to make par. The dog-leg 414yd par 4 10th requires a long tee shot to beyond the trees and an equally long second to the front of the green.
18 holes, 5205yds, Par 67, SSS 65, Course record 62.
Visitors Mon-Sun & BHs. Booking required. **Societies** Booking required. **Green Fees** £13 per round (£15 weekends & BHs). **Prof** Steve Craig **Facilities** **Location** NE side of city, between Leith & Portobello

Hotel ★★★ 69% Kings Manor, 100 Milton Rd East, EDINBURGH ☎ 0131 669 0444 & 468 8003 Fax 0131 669 6650 67 en suite

Craigmillar Park 1 Observatory Rd EH9 3HG
☎ 0131 667 0047 🖹 0131 662 8091
e-mail: secretary@craigmillarpark.co.uk
web: www.craigmillarpark.co.uk
Parkland with good views.
18 holes, 5851yds, Par 70, SSS 69, Course record 63.
Club membership 750.
Visitors Mon-Fri. Sun after 2.30pm. Booking required. **Societies** Booking required in writing. **Green Fees** Phone. **Prof** Scott Gourlay **Course Designer** James Braid **Facilities** **Location** 2m S of city centre off A7

Hotel ★★★ 70% Braid Hills Hotel, 134 Braid Rd, EDINBURGH ☎ 0131 447 8888 67 en suite

Duddingston Duddingston Rd West EH15 3QD
☎ 0131 661 4301 🖹 0131 661 4301
e-mail: generalmanager@duddingston-golf-club.com
web: www.duddingston-golf-club.com
Easy walking parkland with a burn as a natural hazard. Testing 11th hole.
18 holes, 6473yds, Par 72, SSS 72, Course record 63.
Club membership 700.
Visitors limited availability at weekends - booking advised. **Societies** Mon, Tue & Thu. Booking required. **Green Fees** Phone. **Prof** Alastair McLean **Course Designer** Willie Park Jnr **Facilities** **Conf** facs Corporate Hospitality Days **Location** 2.5m SE of city centre off A1

Hotel ★★★ 69% Kings Manor, 100 Milton Rd East, EDINBURGH ☎ 0131 669 0444 & 468 8003 🖹 0131 669 6650 67 en suite

Kingsknowe 326 Lanark Rd EH14 2JD
☎ 0131 441 1145 (Secretary) 🖹 0131 441 2079
e-mail: louis@kingsknowe.com
web: www.kingsknowe.com
Picturesque parkland course set amid gently rolling hills. This course provides a varied and interesting challenge for all levels of golfers.

18 holes, 5981yds, Par 69, SSS 69, Course record 63.
Club membership 930.
Visitors Mon-Fri & BHs. Booking required. Dress code. **Societies** Booking required. **Green Fees** £30 per day, £25 per round (£35 per round weekends after 3pm). **Prof** Chris Morris **Course Designer** A Herd/James Braid **Facilities** **Leisure** Indoor teaching/practice facility. **Conf** Corporate Hospitality Days **Location** 4m SW of city centre on A70

Hotel ★★★ 76% Best Western Bruntsfield Hotel, 69/74 Bruntsfield Place, EDINBURGH ☎ 0131 229 1393 71 en suite

Liberton 297 Gilmerton Rd EH16 5UJ
☎ 0131 664 3009 (sec) 🖹 0131 666 0853
e-mail: info@libertongc.co.uk
web: www.libertongc.co.uk
Undulating, wooded parkland.
18 holes, 5344yds, Par 67, SSS 66, Course record 62.
Club membership 846.
Visitors contact club for details. Dress code. **Societies** Booking required. **Green Fees** £25 per round/£30 two rounds (weekends £30 per round). **Prof** Iain Seath **Facilities** **Conf** facs Corporate Hospitality Days **Location** 3m SE of city centre on A7

Hotel ★★★ 75% Dalhousie Castle and Aqueous Spa, Bonnyrigg, EDINBURGH ☎ 01875 820153 27 en suite 6 annexe en suite

Lothianburn 106A Biggar Rd, Fairmilehead EH10 7DU
☎ 0131 445 2288 🖹 0131 445 5067
e-mail: info@lothianburngc.co.uk
web: www.lothianburngc.co.uk
Situated to the south-west of Edinburgh, on the slopes of the Pentland Hills, the course rises from the clubhouse some 300ft to its highest point at the 13th green. There is only one real climb of note, after playing the 2nd shot to the 9th green. The course is noted for its excellent greens, and challenging holes include the 5th, where one drives for position in order to pitch at almost right angles to a plateau green; and the 14th, longest hole on the course, three-quarters of which is downhill with out of bounds on both sides of the fairway.
18 holes, 5662yds, Par 71, SSS 69, Course record 64.
Club membership 850.
Visitors Mon-Fri. Booking required. Dress code. **Societies** Booking required. **Green Fees** £19 per round. **Prof** Kurt Mungall **Course Designer** J Braid (re-designed 1928) **Facilities** **Location** 4.5m S of city centre on A702

Hotel ★★★ 70% Braid Hills Hotel, 134 Braid Rd, EDINBURGH ☎ 0131 447 8888 67 en suite

Marriott Dalmahoy Hotel Golf & Country Club **see page 333**

Hotel ★★★★ 72% Marriott Dalmahoy Hotel & Country Club, Kirknewton, EDINBURGH ☎ 0870 400 7299 43 en suite 172 annexe en suite

Hotel ★★★★ 72% Macdonald Houstoun House, UPHALL ☎ 0870 1942107 🖹 01506 854220 24 en suite 47 annexe en suite

Hotel ★★★★ 69% Edinburgh Marriott Hotel, 111 Glasgow Rd, EDINBURGH ☎ 0870 400 7293 & 0131 334 9191 🖹 0870 400 7393 245 en suite

Merchants of Edinburgh 10 Craighill Gardens EH10 5PY
☎ 0131 447 1219 🖹 0131 446 9833
e-mail: admin@merchantsgolf.com
web: www.merchantsgolf.com
18 holes, 4889yds, Par 65, SSS 64, Course record 59.
Course Designer Ben Sayers **Location** 2m SW of city centre off A702
Telephone for further details

Hotel ★★★ 70% Braid Hills Hotel, 134 Braid Rd, EDINBURGH ☎ 0131 447 8888 67 en suite

Mortonhall 231 Braid Rd EH10 6PB
☎ 0131 447 6974 🖹 0131 447 8712
e-mail: clubhouse@mortonhallgc.co.uk
web: www.mortonhallgc.co.uk
18 holes, 6502yds, Par 72, SSS 72, Course record 66.
Course Designer James Braid/F Hawtree **Location** 3m S of city centre off A702
Telephone for further details

Hotel ★★★ 70% Braid Hills Hotel, 134 Braid Rd, EDINBURGH ☎ 0131 447 8888 67 en suite

Murrayfield 43 Murrayfield Rd EH12 6EU
☎ 0131 337 3478 🖹 0131 313 0721
e-mail: marjorie@murrayfieldgolfclub.ltd.uk
Parkland on the side of Corstorphine Hill, with fine views.
18 holes, 5725yds, Par 70, SSS 69.
Club membership 815.
Visitors Mon-Fri. Booking required. Handicap certificate. Dress code. **Societies** Booking required. **Green Fees** £35 per round/£45 per day. **Prof** K. Stevenson **Facilities** **Location** 2m W of city centre off A8

Portobello Stanley St EH15 1JJ
☎ 0131 669 4361 & 557 5457 (bookings)
🖹 0131 557 5170
9 holes, 2252yds, Par 32, SSS 32.
Location 3m E of city centre off A1
Telephone for further details

Hotel ★★★ 69% Kings Manor, 100 Milton Rd East, EDINBURGH ☎ 0131 669 0444 & 468 8003
🖹 0131 669 6650 67 en suite

Prestonfield 6 Priestfield Rd North EH16 5HS
☎ 0131 667 9665 🖹 0131 667 9665
e-mail: generalmanager@prestonfieldgolfclub.co.uk
web: www.prestonfieldgolfclub.co.uk
Parkland with beautiful views.
18 holes, 6212yds, Par 70, SSS 70, Course record 66.
Club membership 850.
Visitors May not play Sat before 10.30am or between 12pm-1.30pm & Sun before 11.30am. **Societies** Booking required. **Green Fees** Phone. **Prof** Gavin Cook **Course Designer** James Braid **Facilities** **Conf** facs Corporate Hospitality Days **Location** 1.5m S of city centre off A68

Hotel ★★★★ Prestonfield, Priestfield Rd, EDINBURGH ☎ 0131 225 7800 24 en suite

Ravelston 24 Ravelston Dykes Rd EH4 3NZ
☎ 0131 315 2486 🖹 0131 315 2486
Parkland on the north-east side of Corstorphine Hill, overlooking the Firth of Forth.
9 holes, 5230yds, Par 66, SSS 66, Course record 64.
Club membership 610.
Visitors Mon-Fri. Handicap certificate. Dress code. **Green Fees** Phone. **Course Designer** James Braid **Facilities** **Location** 3m W of city centre off A90

Hotel ★★★★ 69% Edinburgh Marriott Hotel, 111 Glasgow Rd, EDINBURGH
☎ 0870 400 7293 & 0131 334 9191 🖹 0870 400 7393
245 en suite

Royal Burgess 181 Whitehouse Rd, Barnton EH4 6BU
☎ 0131 339 2075 🖹 0131 339 3712
e-mail: secretary@royalburgess.co.uk
web: www.royalburgess.co.uk
No mention of golf clubs would be complete without the Royal Burgess, which was instituted in 1735 and is the oldest golfing society in the world. Its course is a pleasant parkland, and one with a great deal of variety. A club which anyone interested in the history of the game should visit.
18 holes, 6111yds, Par 68, SSS 69.
Club membership 635.
Visitors Mon-Sun & BHs. Booking advisable. Handicap certificate. Dress code. **Societies** Booking required. **Green Fees** Phone. **Prof** Steven Brian **Course Designer** Tom Morris **Facilities** **Conf** Corporate Hospitality Days **Location** 5m W of city centre off A90

Hotel ★★★★ 70% Menzies Belford Hotel, 69 Belford Rd, EDINBURGH ☎ 0131 332 2545 146 en suite

Silverknowes Silverknowes, Parkway EH4 5ET
☎ 0131 336 3843 🖹 0131 651 2299
e-mail: golf@edinburghleisure.co.uk
web: www.edinburghleisure.co.uk
Public links course on coast overlooking the Firth of Forth with magnificent views, generous fairways and expansive greens. The 601yd 18th will be a final test that will make or break your game. The ball needs to be kept low against the prevailing westerlies.
18 holes, 6070yds, Par 71, SSS 70.
Visitors Mon-Sun & BHs. **Societies** Booking required. **Green Fees** Mon-Fri £9-£14. Weekends & BHs £12-£17. **Facilities** **Location** 4m NW of city centre, easy access from city bypass

Hotel ★★★★ 70% Menzies Belford Hotel, 69 Belford Rd, EDINBURGH ☎ 0131 332 2545 146 en suite

Swanston 111 Swanston Rd, Fairmilehead EH10 7DS
☎ 0131 445 2239 🖹 0131 445 2239
18 holes, 5024yds, Par 66, SSS 65, Course record 63.
Course Designer Herbert More **Location** 4m S of city centre off B701
Telephone for further details

Hotel ★★★ 70% Braid Hills Hotel, 134 Braid Rd, EDINBURGH ☎ 0131 447 8888 67 en suite

City of Edinburgh Marriott Dalmahoy Hotel

Edinburgh Map 11 NT27

The Championship East Course has hosted many major events including the Solheim Cup and the PGA Championship of Scotland. The course has long sweeping fairways and generous greens protected by strategic bunkers. Many of the long par 4 holes offer a serious challenge to any golfer. The signature 18th hole has the green set in front of Dalmahoy's historic hotel with a testing approach over a wide ravine. The shorter West Course offers a different test with tighter fairways requiring more accuracy from the tee. The finishing holes incorporate the Golgar burn meandering through the fairway to create a tough finish.

Kirknewton EH27 8EB
☎ 0131 335 1845 📠 0131 335 1433
e-mail: mhrs.golf@marriotthotels.com
web: www.marriott.com/edigs

East Course: 18 holes, 7055yds, Par 73, SSS 75, Course record 70.
West Course: 18 holes, 5168yds, Par 68, SSS 66, Course record 60.

Visitors Mon-Sun & BHs. Booking required. Handicap certificate. Dress code. **Societies** Booking required. **Green Fees** East £65 per 18 holes (£80 Sat, Sun & BHs). West £40 (£45 Sat, Sun & BHs). Winter reduced rates. **Prof** Scott Dixon/David MacMullen **Course Designer** James Braid **Facilities** **Leisure** hard tennis courts, heated indoor swimming pool, sauna, solarium, gymnasium, fitness studio, golf academy, health salon. **Conf facs** Corporate Hospitality Days **Location** 7m W of city on A71

Torphin Hill Torphin Rd, Colinton EH13 0PG
☎ 0131 441 1100 🖷 0131 441 7166
e-mail: torphinhillgc@btconnect.com
web: www.torphinhillgc.co.uk
Beautiful hillside, heathland course, with fine views of Edinburgh and the Forth Estuary. From 600 to 700ft above sea level with 14 holes set on a relatively flat plateau.
18 holes, 5285yds, Par 68, SSS 67, Course record 64.
Club membership 550.
Visitors Mon-Fri & BHs. Booking required. Sat-Sun & BHs only. Dress code. **Societies** Booking required. **Green Fees** Mon-Fri £20 per day, £15 per round. Sat-Sun £20 per round. **Prof** Jamie Browne **Facilities** **Conf** Corporate Hospitality Days **Location** 5m SW of city centre S of A720

Hotel ★★★ 70% Braid Hills Hotel, 134 Braid Rd, EDINBURGH ☎ 0131 447 8888 67 en suite

Turnhouse 154 Turnhouse Rd EH12 0AD
☎ 0131 339 1014
e-mail: secretary@turnhousegc.com
web: www.turnhousegc.com
Challenging tree-lined course with numerous par 4s in excess of 400yds. Large sloping greens give a real challenge and the golfer is virtually guaranteed to use all the clubs in the bag.
18 holes, 6171yds, Par 69, SSS 70, Course record 62.
Club membership 800.
Visitors Mon-Sun & BHs. Dress code. **Societies** Booking required. **Green Fees** £30 per day (£38 per day, £25 per 18 holes weekends). **Prof** John Murray **Course Designer** J Braid **Facilities** **Conf** facs Corporate Hospitality Days **Location** 6m W of city centre N of A8

Hotel ★★★★ 69% Edinburgh Marriott Hotel, 111 Glasgow Rd, EDINBURGH
☎ 0870 400 7293 & 0131 334 9191 🖷 0870 400 7393
245 en suite

RATHO Map 11 NT17

Ratho Park EH28 8NX
☎ 0131 335 0068 & 335 0069 🖷 0131 333 1752
e-mail: secretary@rathoparkgolfclub.co.uk
web: www.rathoparkgolfclub.com
Easy walking parkland, with a converted mansion as the clubhouse.
18 holes, 5960yds, Par 69, SSS 68, Course record 62.
Club membership 850.
Visitors Mon-Sun & BHs. Booking required. Handicap certificate. Dress code. **Societies** welcome. **Green Fees** £37 per day, £27 per round (£37 per round weekends). **Prof** Alan Pate **Course Designer** James Braid **Facilities** **Conf** Corporate Hospitality Days **Location** 0.75m E, N of A71

Hotel ★★★★ 78% Norton House Hotel & Restaurant, Ingliston, EDINBURGH ☎ 0131 333 1275 47 en suite

SOUTH QUEENSFERRY Map 11 NT17

Dundas Parks Dundas Estate EH30 9SS
☎ 0131 331 4252
e-mail: cmkwood@btinternet.com
Parkland course situated on the estate of Dundas Castle, with excellent views. For 18 holes, the nine are played twice.
9 holes, 6056yds, Par 70, SSS 69, Course record 62.
Club membership 500.
Visitors Mon-Fri & BHs. Booking required. Dress code. **Societies** Booking required. **Green Fees** £15. **Facilities** **Location** 0.5m S on A8000

Hotel Premier Travel Inn (South Queensferry), Builyeon Rd, SOUTH QUEENSFERRY ☎ 08701 977094 46 en suite

CITY OF GLASGOW

GLASGOW Map 11 NS56

Alexandra Alexandra Park, Alexandra Pde G31 8SE
☎ 0141 556 1294
Hilly parkland with some woodland. Many bunkers and a barrier of trees between 1st and 9th fairway. Work has been in progress to improve the fairways.
9 holes, 2800yds, Par 31, Course record 25.
Club membership 85.
Visitors Mon-Sun & BHs. Booking required. **Societies** Welcome. **Green Fees** £3.60. **Course Designer** G McArthur **Facilities** **Leisure** bowling green. **Location** 2m E of city centre off M8/A8

Cowglen Barrhead Rd G43 1AU
☎ 0141 632 0556 🖷 01505 503000
e-mail: r.jamieson-accountants@rsmail.net
Undulating and challenging parkland course with good views over the Clyde valley to the Campsie Hills. Club and line selection is most important on many holes due to the strategic placing of copses on the course.

18 holes, 6053yds, Par 70, SSS 69, Course record 64.
Club membership 805.
Visitors Mon, Wed & Thu. Booking required. Handicap certificate. **Societies** must be booked in writing. **Green Fees** Phone. **Prof** Simon Payne **Course Designer** David Adams/James Braid **Facilities** **Conf** facs Corporate Hospitality Days **Location** M77 S from Glasgow, Pollok/Barrhead slip road, left at lights club 0.5m right

Hotel Travelodge Glasgow Paisley Road, 251 Paisley Rd, GLASGOW ☎ 08700 850 950 75 en suite

Haggs Castle 70 Dumbreck Rd, Dumbreck G41 4SN
☎ 0141 427 1157 🖷 0141 427 1157
e-mail: secretary@haggscastlegolfclub.com
web: www.haggscastlegolfclub.com
Wooded, parkland course where Scottish National Championships and the Glasgow and Scottish Open have been held.

Continued

18 holes, 6426yds, Par 72, SSS 71, Course record 63. Club membership 900.
Visitors Mon-Fri. Booking required. Handicap certificate. Dress code. **Societies** Booking required. **Green Fees** £40 per round, £50 per day. **Prof** Campbell Elliott **Course Designer** James Braid **Facilities** **Conf** Corporate Hospitality Days **Location** M77 junct 1, 2.5m SW of city centre

Kirkhill Greenless Rd, Cambuslang G72 8YN
☎ 0141 641 8499 🖹 0141 641 8499
e-mail: carol.downes@virgin.net
web: www.kirkhillgolfclub.org.uk
Meadowland course designed by James Braid.
18 holes, 6030yds, Par 70, SSS 70, Course record 63. Club membership 650.
Visitors Mon-Fri. Booking required. Handicap certificate. Dress code. **Societies** Booking required. **Green Fees** Phone. **Prof** Duncan Williamson **Course Designer** J Braid **Facilities** **Location** 5m SE of city centre off A749

Hotel ★★★ 68% Bothwell Bridge Hotel, 89 Main St, BOTHWELL ☎ 01698 852246 90 en suite

Knightswood Lincoln Av G13 5QZ
☎ 0141 959 6358
9 holes, 5586yds, Par 68, SSS 67.
Location 4m W of city centre off A82
Telephone for further details

Lethamhill 1240 Cumbernauld Rd, Millerston G33 1AH
☎ 0141 770 6220 & 0141 770 7135 🖹 1041 770 0520
18 holes, 5859yds, Par 70, SSS 69.
Location 3m NE of city centre on A80
Telephone for further details

Hotel ★★★★ 73% Millennium Hotel Glasgow, George Square, GLASGOW ☎ 0141 332 6711 117 en suite

Linn Park Simshill Rd G44 5EP
☎ 0141 633 0377
18 holes, 4952yds, Par 65, SSS 65, Course record 61.
Location 4m S of city centre off B766
Telephone for further details

Pollok 90 Barrhead Rd G43 1BG
☎ 0141 632 4351 🖹 0141 649 1398
e-mail: secretary@pollokgolf.com
web: www.pollokgolf.com
Parkland with woods and river. Gentle walking until the 18th hole.
18 holes, 6358yds, Par 71, SSS 71, Course record 62. Club membership 620.
Visitors contact club for details. **Societies** Booking required. **Green Fees** £50 per round weekdays. **Course Designer** J Douglas & A MacKenzie **Facilities** **Conf** facs **Location** M77 junct 2, S to A762 Barrhead Rd, 1m E

Hotel The Ewington, Balmoral Ter, 132 Queens Dr, Queens Park, GLASGOW ☎ 0141 423 1152 43 en suite

Williamwood Clarkston Rd G44 3YR
☎ 0141 637 1783 🖹 0141 571 0166
Undulating parkland with mature woods.
18 holes, 5878yds, Par 68, SSS 69, Course record 61. Club membership 800.
Visitors Mon-Fri. Booking required. **Societies** midweek bookings only, apply in writing to secretary. **Green Fees** Phone. **Prof** Stewart Marshall **Course Designer** James Braid **Facilities** **Location** 5m S of city centre on B767

Continued

CLACKMANNANSHIRE

ALLOA Map 11 NS89

Alloa Schawpark, Sauchie FK10 3AX
☎ 01259 724476 🖹 01259 724476
e-mail: davidherd@btinternet.com
web: alloagolfpage.co.uk
Set in 150 acres of rolling parkland beneath the Ochil Hills, this course will challenge the best golfers while offering great enjoyment to the average player. The challenging finishing holes, 15th to 18th, consist of two long par 3s split by two long and demanding par 4s which will test any golfer's ability. Privacy provided by mature tree-lined fairways.
18 holes, 6229yds, Par 69, SSS 71, Course record 63. Club membership 910.
Visitors Mon-Fri, Sun & BHs. Booking required. Dress code. **Societies** Booking required. **Green Fees** Mon-Fri £28 per 18 holes & £38 per 36 holes; Sun £34 per 18 holes. **Prof** David Herd **Course Designer** James Braid **Facilities** **Conf** Corporate Hospitality Days **Location** 1.5m NE on A908

Braehead Cambus FK10 2NT
☎ 01259 725766 🖹 01259 214070
e-mail: braehead.gc@btinternet.com
web: www.braehead.gc@btinternet.com
Attractive parkland at the foot of the Ochil Hills, having spectacular views.
18 holes, 6053yds, Par 70, SSS 69, Course record 64. Club membership 800.
Visitors Mon-Sun & BHs. Handicap certificate. Dress code. **Societies** Booking required. **Green Fees** £32 per day, £24 per round (£40/£32 weekends). **Prof** Jamie Stevenson **Course Designer** Robert Tait **Facilities** **Conf** Corporate Hospitality Days **Location** 1m W on A907

ALVA Map 11 NS89

Alva Beauclerc St FK12 5LD
☎ 01259 760431
e-mail: alva@alvagolfclub.wanadoo.com
web: www.alvagolfclub.com
A nine-hole course at the foot of the Ochil Hills which gives it its characteristic sloping fairways and fast greens.
9 holes, 2423yds, Par 66, SSS 64, Course record 63. Club membership 318.
Visitors Booking required. **Societies** apply in writing or telephone in advance. **Green Fees** Phone. **Facilities** **Location** 7m from Stirling, A91 Stirling-St Andrews

Hotel ★★★ 68% Royal Hotel, Henderson St, BRIDGE OF ALLAN ☎ 01786 832284 32 en suite

DOLLAR Map 11 NS99

Dollar Brewlands House FK14 7EA
01259 742400 01259 743497
e-mail: info@dollargolfclub.com
web: www.dollargolfclub.com
Compact hillside course with magnificent views along the Ochil Hills.
18 holes, 5242yds, Par 69, SSS 66, Course record 60.
Club membership 450.
Visitors Mon-Sun & BHs. Booking required. Dress code. **Societies** Booking required. **Green Fees** Phone. **Course Designer** Ben Sayers **Facilities** **Leisure** snooker table. **Conf** Corporate Hospitality Days **Location** 0.5m N off A91

Hotel ★★★ 68% Royal Hotel, Henderson St, BRIDGE OF ALLAN 01786 832284 32 en suite

MUCKHART Map 11 NO00

Muckhart FK14 7JH
01259 781423 & 781493 01259 781544
e-mail: enquiries@muckhartgolf.com
web: www.muckhartgolf.com
Scenic heathland and downland course comprising 27 holes in three combinations of nine, all of which start and finish close to the clubhouse. Each of the nine holes requires a different approach, demanding tactical awareness and a skilful touch with all the clubs in the bag. There are superb views from the course's many vantage points, including the aptly named 5th Top of the World'.
Cowden: 9 holes, 3251yds, Par 36.
Naemoor Course: 9 holes, 3234yards, SSS 36.
Arndean: 9 holes, 2835yds, Par 35.
Club membership 750.
Visitors Booking required. Dress code. **Societies** Booking by arrangement. **Green Fees** Phone. **Prof** Keith Salmoni **Facilities** **Location** S of village between A91

Hotel ★★ 72% Castle Campbell Hotel, 11 Bridge St, DOLLAR 01259 742519 8 en suite

TILLICOULTRY Map 11 NS99

Tillicoultry Alva Rd FK13 6BL
01259 750124 01259 750124
e-mail: miket@tillygc.freeserve.co.uk
Parkland at foot of the Ochil Hills. Some hard walking but fine views.
9 holes, 5004 metres, Par 68, SSS 67, Course record 64.
Club membership 400.
Visitors Mon-Sun & BHs. Booking required Sat & Sun. Dress code. **Societies** welcome. **Green Fees** £12 per 18 holes (£17 Sat, Sun & BHs). **Facilities** **Conf** Corporate Hospitality Days **Location** A91, 9m E of Stirling

Hotel ★★★ 68% Royal Hotel, Henderson St, BRIDGE OF ALLAN 01786 832284 32 en suite

DUMFRIES & GALLOWAY

CASTLE DOUGLAS Map 11 NX76

Castle Douglas Abercromby Rd DG7 1BA
01556 502801 & 502509 01556 502509
e-mail: cdgolfclub@aol.com
2006 saw the layout of a new testing parkland course, featuring the region's longest par 5, the 603yd 6th hole.
9 holes, 6254yds, Par 70, SSS 70, Course record 61.
Club membership 320.
Visitors may play Mon-Sun & BHs. **Societies** apply by writing to secretary. **Green Fees** £15 per round/day. **Facilities** **Leisure** pool table. **Conf** Corporate Hospitality Days **Location** 0.5m from town centre on A713 Abercrombie road

Hotel ★★ 67% Imperial Hotel, 35 King St, CASTLE DOUGLAS 01556 502086 12 en suite

COLVEND Map 11 NX85

Colvend Sandyhills DG5 4PY
01556 630398 01556 630495
e-mail: thesecretary@colvendgolfclub.co.uk
web: www.colvendgolfclub.co.uk
Picturesque and challenging course on the Solway coast. Superb views.
18 holes, 5250yds, Par 68, SSS 67, Course record 64.
Club membership 490.
Visitors contact club for details. **Societies** welcome. **Green Fees** £30 per day, £25 per round. **Course Designer** Allis & Thomas **Facilities** **Location** 6m SE from Dalbeattie on A710

CUMMERTREES Map 11 NY16

Powfoot DG12 5QE
01461 204100 01461204111
e-mail: par71@powfootgolfclub.fsnet.co.uk
web: www.powfootgolfclub.com
This British Championship course is on the Solway Firth, playing at this delightfully compact semi-links seaside course is a scenic treat. Lovely holes include the 2nd, the 8th and the 11th, also 9th with second world war bomb crater.
18 holes, 6283yds, Par 69, SSS 69, Course record 63.
Club membership 950.
Visitors Mon-Sun & BHs. Booking required. Handicap certificate. Dress code. **Societies** Booking required. **Green Fees** £44 per day, £33 per round, £55/£39 Sat & Sun. **Course Designer** J Braid **Facilities** **Location** 0.5m off B724

Hotel ★★★ 68% Hetland Hall Hotel, CARRUTHERSTOWN 01387 840201 14 en suite 15 annexe en suite

DALBEATTIE Map 11 NX86

Dalbeattie 19 Maxwell Park DG5 4LR
☎ 01556 610666 Fax 01556 612247
e-mail: ocm@associates-ltd.fsnet.co.uk
web: dalbeattiegc.co.uk
This nine-hole course provides an excellent challenge for golfers of all abilities. There are a few gentle slopes to negotiate but compensated by fine views along the Urr Valley. The 363yd 4th hole is a memorable par 4, with views across to the Lake District.
9 holes, 5710yds, Par 68, SSS 68.
Club membership 250.
Visitors Mon-Sun & BHs. Dress code. **Societies** Booking required. **Green Fees** £18 per 18 holes. **Course Designer** Bryan C Moor **Facilities** **Location** Signed off B794. Access by Maxwell Park

DUMFRIES Map 11 NX97

Dumfries & County Nunfield, Edinburgh Rd DG1 1JX
☎ 01387 253585 Fax 01387 253585
e-mail: dumfriesc@aol.com
web: thecounty.org.uk
Parkland alongside the River Nith, with views of the Queensberry Hills. Greens built to USPGA specifications. Nature trails link the fairways.

Nunfield: 18 holes, 5918yds, Par 69, SSS 69, Course record 61.
Club membership 800.
Visitors Mon-Fri, Sun & BHs. Booking required. Dress code. **Societies** Booking required. **Green Fees** £40 per 36 holes, £35 per 27 holes, £30 per round (£45/£40/£35 Sun & BHs). **Prof** Stuart Syme **Course Designer** William Fernie **Facilities** **Conf** Corporate Hospitality Days **Location** 1m NE of Dumfries on A701

Hotel ★★★ 69% Cairndale Hotel & Leisure Club, English St, DUMFRIES ☎ 01387 254111 91 en suite

Dumfries & Galloway 2 Laurieston Av DG2 7NY
☎ 01387 263848 Fax 01387 263848
e-mail: info@dandggolfclub.co.uk
web: www.dandggolfclub.co.uk
Attractive parkland course, a good test of golf but not physically demanding.
18 holes, 6309yds, Par 70, SSS 71.
Club membership 800.
Visitors Mon-Fri & Sun. Booking required. Handicap certificate. Dress code. **Societies** Booking required. **Green Fees** £35 per day, £28 per round weekdays, (weekend £40/£30). **Prof** Joe Fergusson **Course Designer** W

Continued

Fernie **Facilities**
Location W of town centre on A780

Hotel ★★★ 69% Station Hotel, 49 Lovers Walk, DUMFRIES ☎ 01387 254316 32 en suite

Pines Golf Centre Lockerbie Rd DG1 3PF
☎ 01387 247444 Fax 01387 249600
e-mail: admin@pinesgolf.com
web: www.pinesgolf.com
A mixture of parkland and woodland with numerous water features and dog-legs. Excellent greens.
18 holes, 5604yds, Par 68, SSS 68, Course record 66.
Club membership 280.
Visitors Mon-Sun & BHs. **Societies** Booking required. **Green Fees** £24 per day, £20 per round. **Prof** Brian Gemmell/Bruce Gray **Course Designer** Duncan Gray **Facilities** **Conf** Corporate Hospitality Days **Location** Off A701 Lockerbie Rd, beside A75 Dumfries bypass

Hotel ★★★ 69% Cairndale Hotel & Leisure Club, English St, DUMFRIES ☎ 01387 254111 91 en suite

GATEHOUSE OF FLEET Map 11 NX55

Gatehouse Laurieston Rd DG7 2BE
☎ 01644 450260 Fax 01644 450260
e-mail: gatehousegolf@sagainternet.co.uk
9 holes, 2521yds, Par 66, SSS 66, Course record 62.
Course Designer Tom Fernie **Location** 0.25m N of town
Telephone for further details

Continued

Hotel ★★★★ 73% Cally Palace Hotel, GATEHOUSE OF FLEET ☎ 01557 814341 55 en suite
See advertisement on previous page

GLENLUCE Map 10 NX15

Wigtownshire County Mains of Park DG8 0NN
☎ 01581 300420 🖷 01581 300420
e-mail: enquiries@wigtownshirecountygolfclub.com
web: www.wigtownshirecountygolfclub.com
Seaside links course on the shores of Luce Bay, easy walking but affected by winds. The 12th hole, a dog-leg with out of bounds to the right, is named after the course's designer, Gordon Cunningham.
18 holes, 5904yds, Par 70, SSS 69, Course record 63. Club membership 450.
Visitors Mon-Sun & BHs. Booking required. Dress code. **Societies** Booking required. **Green Fees** £31 per day, £24 per round per 18 holes (£33/£26 weekends). **Course Designer** W Gordon Cunningham **Facilities** **Conf** Corporate Hospitality Days **Location** 1.5m W off A75 on Luce Bay

Hotel ★★★★ 68% North West Castle Hotel, STRANRAER ☎ 01776 704413 70 en suite 2 annexe en suite

GRETNA Map 11 NY36

Gretna Kirtle View DG16 5HD
☎ 01461 338464 🖷 01461 337362
A nice parkland course on gentle hills. It offers a good test of skill.
9 holes, 3214yds, Par 72, SSS 71, Course record 71. Club membership 200.
Visitors Mon-Sun & BHs. **Societies** Booking required. **Green Fees** Phone. **Prof** Mr Gareth Dick **Course Designer** N Williams **Facilities** **Conf** facs **Location** 0.5m W of Gretna on B721, signed

Hotel ★★★ 67% Garden House Hotel, Sarkfoot Rd, GRETNA ☎ 01461 337621 38 en suite

KIRKCUDBRIGHT Map 11 NX65

Brighouse Bay Brighouse Bay, Borgue DG6 4TS
☎ 01557 870409 🖷 01557 870409
e-mail: leisureclub@brighouse-bay.co.uk
web: www.gillespie-leisure.co.uk
18 holes, 6366yds, Par 73, SSS 73.
Course Designer D Gray **Location** 3m S of Borgue off B727
Telephone for further details

Hotel ★★ 67% Arden House Hotel, Tongland Rd, KIRKCUDBRIGHT ☎ 01557 330544 9 rms (8 en suite)

Kirkcudbright Stirling Crescent DG6 4EZ
☎ 01557 330314 🖷 01557 330314
e-mail: david@kirkcudbrightgolf.co.uk
web: kirkcudbrightgolf.co.uk
Hilly parkland with good views over the harbour town of Kirkcudbright and the Dee estuary.
18 holes, 5739yds, Par 69, SSS 69, Course record 63. Club membership 500.
Visitors Mon-Sun & BHs. Booking required. Handicap certificate. Dress code. **Societies** Booking required. **Green Fees** £27 per day, £22 per round. **Course Designer** E. Shamash **Facilities**
Location NE side of town off A711

Hotel ★★ 67% Arden House Hotel, Tongland Rd, KIRKCUDBRIGHT ☎ 01557 330544 9 rms (8 en suite)

LANGHOLM Map 11 NY38

Langholm Whitaside DG13 0JR
☎ 07724 875151
e-mail: golf@langholmgolfclub.co.uk
web: www.langholmgolgclub.co.uk
Hillside course with fine views, easy to medium walking.
9 holes, 6180yds, Par 70, SSS 69, Course record 65. Club membership 200.
Visitors contact club for details. Dress code. **Societies** Booking required. **Green Fees** Phone. **Facilities** by arrangement by arrangement by arrangement
Location E side of village off A7

LOCHMABEN Map 11 NY08

Lochmaben Castlehillgate DG11 1NT
☎ 01387 810552
e-mail: lgc@naims.co.uk
web: www.lochmabengolf.co.uk
Attractive parkland surrounding Kirk Loch. Excellent views from this well-maintained course.
18 holes, 5890yds, Par 70, SSS 69, Course record 60. Club membership 850.
Visitors Mon- Sun & BHs. Booking required. Handicap certificate. Dress code. **Societies** welcome. **Green Fees** £35 per day, £28 per round (£40/£30 weekends). **Course Designer** James Braid **Facilities**
Leisure fishing. **Conf** Corporate Hospitality Days **Location** 4m from Lockerbie on A74. S side of village off A709

Hotel ★★★ 74% The Dryfesdale Country House Hotel, Dryfebridge, LOCKERBIE ☎ 01576 202427 16 en suite

LOCKERBIE Map 11 NY18

Lockerbie Corrie Rd DG11 2ND
☎ 01576 203363 🖷 01576 203363
e-mail: enquiries@lockerbiegolf.com
web: www.lockerbiegolf.com
Parkland course with fine views and featuring the only pond hole in Dumfriesshire. Pond comes into play at 3 holes.
18 holes, 5614yds, Par 68, SSS 67, Course record 64. Club membership 620.
Visitors Mon-Sun & BHs. Booking required. Dress code. **Societies** Booking required. **Green Fees** £22 per 18 holes (£24 weekends). **Course Designer** James Braid **Facilities** **Conf** Corporate Hospitality Days **Location** E side of town centre off B7068

Hotel ★★★ 74% The Dryfesdale Country House Hotel, Dryfebridge, LOCKERBIE ☎ 01576 202427 16 en suite

MOFFAT Map 11 NT00

Moffat Coatshill DG10 9SB
☎ 01683 220020 01683 221802
e-mail: bookings@moffatgolfclub.co.uk
web: www.moffatgolfclub.co.uk
Scenic moorland course overlooking the town, with panoramic views of southern uplands.
18 holes, 5259yds, Par 69, SSS 67, Course record 60.
Club membership 350.
Visitors Booking required. **Societies** Booking required. **Green Fees** Phone. **Course Designer** Ben Sayers **Facilities** **Leisure** snooker. **Conf** Corporate Hospitality Days **Location** A74(M) junct 15 onto A701 to Moffat, course signed on left after 30mph sign

Hotel ★★★ 69% Moffat House Hotel, High St, MOFFAT ☎ 01683 220039 20 en suite

MONREITH Map 10 NX34

St Medan DG8 8NJ
☎ 01988 700358
Scotland's most southerly course. This links nestles in Monreith Bay with panoramic views across to the Isle of Man. The testing nine-hole course is a challenge to both high and low handicaps.
9 holes, 4520yds, Par 64, SSS 64, Course record 60.
Club membership 300.
Visitors Mon-Sun & BHs. **Societies** welcome. **Green Fees** £24 per day, £15 per 18 holes, £10 per 9 holes. **Course Designer** James Braid **Facilities** **Location** 3m S of Port William off A747

NEW GALLOWAY Map 11 NX67

New Galloway High St DG7 3RN
☎ 01644 420737 & 450685 01644 450685
web: www.nggc.com
Set on the edge of the Galloway Hills and overlooking Loch Ken, the course has excellent tees, no bunkers and first class greens. The course rises through the first two fairways to a plateau with all round views that many think unsurpassed.
9 holes, 5006yds, Par 68, SSS 67, Course record 64.
Club membership 250.
Visitors Mon-Sun. **Societies** contact club for details. **Green Fees** £18 per day. **Course Designer** James Braid **Facilities** **Conf** Corporate Hospitality Days **Location** S side of town on A762

Hotel ★★ 67% Imperial Hotel, 35 King St, CASTLE DOUGLAS ☎ 01556 502086 12 en suite

NEWTON STEWART Map 10 NX46

Newton Stewart Kirroughtree Av, Minnigaff DG8 6PF
☎ 01671 402172 01671 402172
e-mail: newtonstewartgc@btconnect.com
web: www.newtonstewartgolfclub.com
A parkland course in a picturesque setting. A good test for all standards of golfer with a variety of shots required. Many mature trees on the course and the five short holes have interesting features.
18 holes, 5903yds, Par 69, SSS 70, Course record 66.
Club membership 380.
Visitors Mon-Sun & BHs. Booking required. Dress code. **Societies** Booking required. **Green Fees** £25 per round (£28 Sat, Sun & BHs). **Facilities** **Location** 0.5m N of town centre off A75

Hotel ★★★ Kirroughtree House, Minnigaff, NEWTON STEWART ☎ 01671 402141 17 en suite

PORTPATRICK Map 10 NX05

Lagganmore Hotel DG9 9AB
☎ 01776 810499
e-mail: lagganmoregolf@aol.com
web: www.lagganmoregolf.co.uk
Parkland and heath course with many water features. The signature hole is the 7th, considered the best in the county.
18 holes, 5698yds, Par 69, SSS 68, Course record 66.
Club membership 50.
Visitors Mon-Sun & BHs. Booking required Sat. **Societies** Booking required. **Green Fees** £25 per day, £15 per 18 holes (£30/£20 weekends). **Course Designer** Stephen Hornby **Facilities** **Conf** facs Corporate Hospitality Days **Location** on A77

Hotel ★★★ 74% Fernhill Hotel, Heugh Rd, PORTPATRICK ☎ 01776 810220 27 en suite 9 annexe en suite

Portpatrick Golf Course Rd DG9 8TB
☎ 01776 810273 01776 810811
e-mail: enquiries@portpatrickgolfclub.com
web: www.portpatrickgolfclub.com
Seaside links-type course, set on cliffs overlooking the Irish Sea, with magnificent views.
Dunskey Course: 18 holes, 5908yds, Par 70, SSS 69, Course record 63.
Dinvin Course: 9 holes, 1504yds, Par 27, SSS 27, Course record 23.
Club membership 750.
Visitors Mon-Sun & BHs. Booking required. Handicap certificate. Dress code. **Societies** Booking required. **Green Fees** £40 per day, £30 per round (£45/£35 weekends). **Prof** Ivan Lee **Course Designer** Charles Hunter **Facilities** **Location** Entering village fork right at war memorial, signed 300yds

Hotel ★★★ 74% Fernhill Hotel, Heugh Rd, PORTPATRICK ☎ 01776 810220 27 en suite 9 annexe en suite

Continued

SANQUHAR Map 11 NS70

Sanquhar Euchan Golf Course, Blackaddie Rd DG4 6JZ
☎ 01659 50577
e-mail: tich@rossirence.fsnet.co.uk
Easy walking parkland, fine views. A good test for all standards of golfer.
9 holes, 5594yds, Par 70, SSS 68, Course record 66. Club membership 200.
Visitors Mon-Sun & BHs. Dress code. **Societies** welcome. **Green Fees** £10 per day (£12 weekends). **Course Designer** Willie Fernie **Facilities** **Leisure** snooker, pool. **Conf** Corporate Hospitality Days **Location** 0.5m SW off A76

SOUTHERNESS Map 11 NX95

Southerness DG2 8AZ
☎ 01387 880677 01387 880644
e-mail: admin@southernessgc.sol.co.uk
web: www.southernessgolfclub.com
Natural links, championship course with panoramic views. Heather and bracken abound.
18 holes, 6105yds, Par 69, SSS 70, Course record 64. Club membership 830.
Visitors Mon-Sun & BHs. Booking required. Handicap certificate. Dress code. **Societies** Booking required. **Green Fees** £60 per day, £45 per round (£70/£55 weekends). **Course Designer** Mackenzie Ross **Facilities** **Location** 3.5m S of Kirkbean off A710

STRANRAER Map 10 NX06

Stranraer Creachmore DG9 0LF
☎ 01776 870245 01776 870445
e-mail: stranraergolf@btclick.com
web: www.stranraergolfclub.net
Parkland with beautiful views over Loch Ryan to Ailsa Craig, Arran and beyond. Several notable holes including the 3rd, where a winding burn is crossed three times to a green set between a large bunker and a steep bank sloping down to the burn; the scenic 5th with spectacular views; the 11th requiring a demanding tee shot with trees and out of bounds to the left, then a steep rise to a very fast green. The 15th is a difficult par 3 where accuracy is paramount with ground sloping away either side of the green.
18 holes, 6308yds, Par 70, SSS 72, Course record 66. Club membership 700.
Visitors Mon-Sun except BHs. Dress code **Societies** welcome. **Green Fees** £26 per 18 holes (£31 weekends). **Course Designer** James Braid **Facilities** **Location** 2.5m NW on A718 from Stranraer

Hotel ★★★★ 68% North West Castle Hotel, STRANRAER ☎ 01776 704413 70 en suite 2 annexe en suite

THORNHILL Map 11 NX89

Thornhill Blacknest DG3 5DW
☎ 01848 331779 & 330546
e-mail: thornhillgc@fsmail.net
Moorland and parkland with fine views of the southern uplands.
18 holes, 6085yds, Par 71, SSS 70, Course record 67. Club membership 560.
Visitors Mon-Sun & BHs. Booking required. Dress code. **Societies** Booking required. **Green Fees** £34 per day, £24 per round (weekends £40/£30). **Course Designer** Willie Fernie **Facilities** **Location** 1m E of town off A76

Hotel ★★ 75% Trigony House Hotel, Closeburn, THORNHILL ☎ 01848 331211 8 en suite

WIGTOWN Map 10 NX45

Wigtown & Bladnoch Lightlands Ter DG8 9DY
☎ 01988 403354
Slightly hilly parkland with fine views over Wigtown Bay to the Galloway Hills.
9 holes, 5462yds, Par 68, SSS 67, Course record 62. Club membership 150.
Visitors Mon-Sun & BHs. Booking required Sat-Sun. **Societies** Booking required. **Green Fees** £17 for 18 holes/£12 for 9 holes. **Course Designer** W Muir **Facilities** **Location** SW on A714

Hotel ★★★ Kirroughtree House, Minnigaff, NEWTON STEWART ☎ 01671 402141 17 en suite

DUNDEE CITY

DUNDEE Map 11 NO43

Ballumbie Castle 2 Old Quarry Rd DD4 0SY
☎ 01382 730026 (club) & 770028 (pro) 01382 730008
e-mail: ballumbie2000@yahoo.com
web: www.ballumbiecastlegolfclub.com
Parkland/heathland course built in 2000. No two holes go in the same direction and every golf club is required. Water comes into play on 4 holes.
18 holes, 6127yds, Par 69, SSS 70, Course record 65. Club membership 550.
Visitors Mon-Sun & BHs. Booking required. Dress code. **Societies** Booking required. **Green Fees** £25 per 18 holes. **Prof** Lee Sutherland **Facilities** **Conf** Corporate Hospitality Days **Location** NE outskirts of town, signed off A90

Hotel Premier Travel Inn Dundee East, 115-117 Lawers Dr, Panmurefield Village, BROUGHTY FERRY ☎ 0870 9906324 60 en suite

Caird Park Mains Loan DD4 9BX
☎ 01382 438871 01382 433211
e-mail: la.bookings@dundeecity.gov.uk
web: www.dundeecity.gov.uk/golf
A pay and play course situated in extensive parkland in the heart of Carnoustie countryside. A reasonably easy start belies the difficulty of the middle section (holes 7-13) and the back nine cross the Gelly Burn four times.
18 holes, 6280yds, Par 72, SSS 69, Course record 65. Club membership 1800.
Visitors Mon-Sun & BHs. Booking required Sat-Sun. Dress code. **Societies** Booking required. **Green Fees** £20 Mon-Fri (£25 weekends). **Prof** J Black **Facilities** **Leisure** sports stadium. **Location** Off A90 Kingsway onto Forfar Rd, left onto Claverhouse Rd, 1st left into Caird Park

Hotel ★★★★ 76% Apex City Quay Hotel & Spa, 1 West Victoria Dock Rd, DUNDEE
☎ 01382 202404 & 0845 365 0000 01382 201401
153 en suite

Continued

Camperdown Camperdown Park, Coupar Angus Rd DD2 4TF
01382 431820 01382 433486
web: www.dundeecity.gov.uk
18 holes, 6548yds, Par 71, SSS 72.
Location A90 Kingsway onto A923 Coupar Angus Rd into Camperdown Park
Telephone for further details

Downfield Turnberry Av DD2 3QP
01382 825595 01382 813111
e-mail: downfieldgc@aol.com
web: www.downfieldgolf.co.uk
A 2007 Open Qualifying venue. A course with championship credentials providing an enjoyable test for all golfers.
18 holes, 6803yds, Par 73, SSS 73, Course record 65.
Club membership 750.
Visitors Mon-Fri, Sun & BHs. Booking required. Dress code. **Societies** Booking required. **Green Fees** £45 per 18 holes, £54 per 36 holes. **Prof** Kenny Hutton **Course Designer** James Braid **Facilities** **Leisure** snooker room. **Conf** Corporate Hospitality Days **Location** N of city centre, signed at junct A90

EAST AYRSHIRE

GALSTON Map 11 NS53

Loudoun Edinburgh Rd KA4 8PA
01563 821993 01563 820011
e-mail: secy@loudoungowfclub.co.uk
web: www.loudoungowfclub.co.uk
Pleasant, fairly flat parkland with many mature trees, in the Irvine valley. Excellent test of golf skills without being too strenuous.
18 holes, 6005yds, Par 68, SSS 69, Course record 60.
Club membership 850.
Visitors Mon-Fri. Booking required. Handicap certificate. Dress code **Societies** Booking required. **Green Fees** £35 per day, £25 per 18 holes. **Facilities** **Conf** Corporate Hospitality Days **Location** NE side of town on A71

Hotel ★★★ 74% Strathaven Hotel, Hamilton Rd, STRATHAVEN 01357 521778 22 en suite

KILMARNOCK Map 10 NS43

Annanhill Irvine Rd KA1 2RT
01563 521644 & 521512
Municipal, tree-lined parkland course.
18 holes, 6269yds, Par 71, SSS 70, Course record 66.
Club membership 274.
Visitors Mon-Sun & BHs. Booking required. **Societies** Booking required. **Green Fees** Phone. **Course Designer** Jack McLean **Facilities** **Location** 1m N on B7081

Hotel Premier Travel Inn Kilmarnock, Annadale, KILMARNOCK 08701 977148 40 en suite

Caprington Ayr Rd KA1 4UW
01563 523702 & 521915 (Gen Enq)
18 holes, 5810yds, Par 68, SSS 68.
Location 1.5m S on B7038
Telephone for further details

Hotel Travelodge Kilmarnock, Kilmarnock By Pass, KILMARNOCK 08700 850 950 40 en suite

MAUCHLINE Map 11 NS42

Ballochmyle Catrine Rd KA5 6LE
01290 550469 01290 553657
e-mail: secretary@ballochmylegolf.wanadoo.co.uk
Parkland course.
18 holes, 5972yds, Par 70, SSS 69, Course record 64.
Club membership 730.
Visitors Mon-Fri, Sun & BHs. Dress code. **Societies** Booking required. **Green Fees** £20 18 holes, £30 36 holes (weekends £25/£35). **Facilities** **Leisure** snooker. **Location** 1m SE on B705

Hotel Travelodge Kilmarnock, Kilmarnock By Pass, KILMARNOCK 08700 850 950 40 en suite

NEW CUMNOCK Map 11 NS61

New Cumnock Lochhill, Cumnock Rd KA18 4PN
01290 338848
9 holes, 5176yds, Par 68, SSS 68, Course record 63.
Course Designer Willie Fernie **Location** 0.75m N on A76
Telephone for further details

PATNA Map 10 NS41

Doon Valley Hillside Park KA6 7JT
01292 531607
Established parkland course located on an undulating hillside.
9 holes, 5886yds, Par 70, SSS 70, Course record 56.
Club membership 100.
Visitors Mon-Sun & BHs. Booking required Sat-Sun. Dress code. **Societies** Booking required. **Green Fees** £14 per 18 holes. **Facilities** **Leisure** fishing, fitness and games hall nearby. **Location** 10m S of Ayr on the A713

Hotel ★★ Ladyburn, MAYBOLE 01655 740585 5 en suite

EAST DUNBARTONSHIRE

BALMORE Map 11 NS57

Balmore Golf Course Rd G64 4AW
01360 620284 01360 622742
e-mail: balmoregolf@btconnect.com
web: www.balmoregolfclub.co.uk
Parkland with fine views. Greens to USGA standards.
18 holes, 5530yds, Par 66, SSS 67, Course record 61.
Club membership 700.
Visitors Mon-Fri. Booking required. Dress code. **Societies** Booking required. **Green Fees** £40 per day, £30 per round. **Course Designer** Harry Vardon **Facilities** **Location** N off A807

Hotel Premier Travel Inn Glasgow (Bearsden), Milngavie Rd, BEARSDEN 0870 9906532 61 en suite

BEARSDEN Map 11 NS57

Bearsden Thorn Rd G61 4BP
☎ 0141 586 5300
e-mail: secretary@bearsdengolfclub.com
web: www.bearsdengolfclub.com
Parkland course with 16 greens and 11 teeing grounds. Easy walking and views of city and the Campsie Hills.
9 holes, 6014yds, Par 68, SSS 69, Course record 64.
Club membership 560.
Visitors Mon-Sun. Booking required. Handicap certificate. Dress code. **Societies** Booking required. **Green Fees** terms on application. **Facilities** **Location** 1m W off A809

Hotel Premier Travel Inn Glasgow (Bearsden), Milngavie Rd, BEARSDEN ☎ 0870 9906532 61 en suite

Douglas Park Hillfoot G61 2TJ
☎ 0141 942 2220 (Clubhouse) 0141 942 0985
e-mail: secretary@douglasparkgolfclub.co.uk
web: www.douglasparkgolfclub.co.uk
Parkland course with a variety of holes.
18 holes, 5962yds, Par 69, SSS 69, Course record 64.
Club membership 960.
Visitors Mon-Thu, Sat-Sun & BHs. Booking required. Dress Code. **Societies** Booking required. **Green Fees** £31 per day, £23 per round (£30 per round wknds/BHs). **Prof** David Scott **Course Designer** Willie Fernie **Facilities** **Location** E side of town on A81

Hotel Premier Travel Inn Glasgow (Bearsden), Milngavie Rd, BEARSDEN ☎ 0870 9906532 61 en suite

Glasgow Killermont G61 2TW
☎ 0141 942 2011 0141 942 0770
e-mail: secretary@glasgow-golf.com
One of the finest parkland courses in Scotland.
Killermont: 18 holes, 5968yds, Par 70, SSS 69.
Club membership 800.
Visitors Mon-Fri. Booking required. Handicap certificate. Dress code. **Societies** welcome. **Green Fees** £70 per day, £55 per round. **Prof** J Steven **Course Designer** Tom Morris Snr **Facilities** **Conf** Corporate Hospitality Days **Location** SE side off A81

Windyhill Baljaffray Rd G61 4QQ
☎ 0141 942 2349 0141 942 5874
e-mail: secretary@windyhill.co.uk
web: www.windyhill.co.uk
Interesting parkland and moorland course with panoramic views of Glasgow and beyond; testing 12th hole.
18 holes, 6254yds, Par 71, SSS 70, Course record 64.
Club membership 800.
Visitors Mon-Fri. Booking required. Handicap certificate. Dress code. **Societies** Booking required. **Green Fees** £25 per round/£35 per day. **Prof** Chris Duffy **Course Designer** James Braid **Facilities** **Location** 2m NW off B8050, 1.5m from Bearsden cross, just off Drymen road

Hotel Premier Travel Inn Glasgow (Bearsden), Milngavie Rd, BEARSDEN ☎ 0870 9906532 61 en suite

BISHOPBRIGGS Map 11 NS67

Bishopbriggs Brackenbrae Rd G64 2DX
☎ 0141 772 1810 & 772 8938 0141 762 2532
e-mail: secretarybgc@yahoo.co.uk
web: www.bishopbriggsgolfclub.com
18 holes, 6041yds, Par 69, SSS 69, Course record 63.
Course Designer James Braid **Location** 0.5m NW off A803
Telephone for further details

Hotel ★★★★ 70% Glasgow Marriott Hotel, 500 Argyle St, Anderston, GLASGOW ☎ 0870 400 7230 300 en suite

Cawder Cadder Rd G64 3QD
☎ 0141 761 1281 0141 761 1285
e-mail: secretary@cawdergolfclub.org.uk
web: www.cawdergolfclub.org.uk
Two parkland courses: Cawder Course is hilly, with the 5th, 9th, 10th and 11th testing holes; Keir Course is flat.
Cawder Course: 18 holes, 6295yds, Par 70, SSS 71, Course record 63.
Keir Course: 18 holes, 5877yds, Par 68, SSS 68.
Club membership 1150.
Visitors must contact in advance & may play on weekdays only. **Societies** Booking required. **Green Fees** Phone. **Prof** Ken Stevely **Course Designer** James Braid **Facilities** **Conf** Corporate Hospitality Days **Location** 5 m NE off A803

Hotel ★★★★ 70% Glasgow Marriott Hotel, 500 Argyle St, Anderston, GLASGOW ☎ 0870 400 7230 300 en suite

Littlehill Auchinairn Rd G64 1UT
☎ 0141 772 1916
18 holes, 6240yds, Par 70, SSS 70.
Location 3m NE of Glasgow city centre on A803
Telephone for further details

Hotel ★★★★ 70% Glasgow Marriott Hotel, 500 Argyle St, Anderston, GLASGOW ☎ 0870 400 7230 300 en suite

KIRKINTILLOCH Map 11 NS67

Hayston Campsie Rd G66 1RN
☎ 0141 776 1244 0141 776 9030
e-mail: secretary@haystongolf.com
web: www.haystongolf.com
An undulating, tree-lined course with a sandy subsoil.
18 holes, 6042yds, Par 70, SSS 70, Course record 60.
Club membership 800.
Societies Booking required. **Green Fees** Phone. **Prof** Steven Barnett **Course Designer** James Braid **Facilities** **Location** 1m NW off A803

Hotel ★★★★ The Westerwood Hotel, 1 St Andrews Dr, Westerwood, CUMBERNAULD ☎ 01236 457171 100 en suite

Kirkintilloch Todhill, Campsie Rd G66 1RN
☎ 0141 776 1256 & 775 2387 0141 775 2424
e-mail: secretary@kirkintillochgolfclub.co.uk
web: www.kirkintillochgolfclub.co.uk
Rolling parkland in the foothills of the Campsie Fells. The course was extended some years ago giving testing but enjoyable holes over the whole 18.

Continu

18 holes, 5860yds, Par 70, SSS 69, Course record 64. Club membership 650.
Visitors Mon-Wed & Fri. Booking required. Handicap :ertificate. Dress code. **Societies** Booking required. **Green Fees** £30 per 36 holes, £20 per 18 holes. **Prof** Jamie Good **Course Designer** James Braid **Facilities** **Conf** facs Corporate Hospitality Days **Location** m NW off A803

Hotel ★★★★ The Westerwood Hotel, 1 St Andrews Dr, Westerwood, CUMBERNAULD ☎ 01236 457171 00 en suite

LENNOXTOWN Map 11 NS67

Campsie Crow Rd G66 7HX
☎ 01360 310244 01360 310244
-mail: campsiegolfclub@aol.com
veb: www.campsiegolfclub.org.uk
Scenic hillside course.
'8 holes, 5507yds, Par 70, SSS 68, Course record 69. Club membership 620.
Visitors Booking required. **Societies** written application. **Green Fees** Phone. **Prof** Mark Brennan **Course Designer** W Auchterlonie **Facilities** **Conf** Corporate Hospitality Days **Location** 0.5m N on 3822

Hotel ★★★★ The Westerwood Hotel, 1 St Andrews Dr, Westerwood, CUMBERNAULD ☎ 01236 457171 00 en suite

LENZIE Map 11 NS67

Lenzie 19 Crosshill Rd G66 5DA
☎ 0141 776 1535 & 812 3018
0141 777 7748 or 0141 812 3018
-mail: scottdavidson@lenziegolfclub.demon.co.uk
veb: www.lenziegolfclub.co.uk
The course is parkland and prominent features include he old beech trees, which line some of the fairways ogether with thorn hedges and shallow ditches. Extensive larch and fir plantations have also been reated. The course is relatively flat apart from a steep ill to the green at the 5th hole.
8 holes, 5984yds, Par 69, SSS 69, Course record 64. lub membership 890.
Visitors must contact in advance. **Societies** Booking quired. **Green Fees** Phone. **Prof** Jim McCallum **Facilities** **Conf** facs **Location** N Glasgow, M80 exit Kirkintilloch

Hotel ★★★★ The Westerwood Hotel, 1 St Andrews Dr, Westerwood, CUMBERNAULD ☎ 01236 457171 0 en suite

MILNGAVIE Map 11 NS57

Clober Craigton Rd G62 7HP
☎ 0141 956 1685 0141 955 1416
mail: clobergolfclub@btopenworld.com
eb: www.clober.co.uk
hort parkland course that requires skill in chipping ith eight par 3s. Testing 5th hole, par 3 with out of ounds left and right and a burn in front of the tee.
holes, 4824yds, Par 66, SSS 65, Course record 61. ub membership 600.
Visitors Mon-Fri. Booking required. Handicap certificate. Dress code. **Societies** Booking required. **Green Fees** £22 per round, £30 per day, **Prof** J McFadyen **Facilities** **Location** NW side of town

Hotel Premier Travel Inn Glasgow (Milngavie), 103 Main St, MILNGAVIE ☎ 08701 977112 60 en suite

Esporta, Dougalston Strathblane Rd G62 8HJ
☎ 0141 955 2404 0141 955 2406
e-mail: hilda.everett@esporta.com
A course of tremendous character set in 300 acres of beautiful woodland dotted with drumlins, lakes and criss-crossed by streams and ditches. The course makes excellent use of the natural features to create mature, tree-lined fairways. The course is currently being upgraded to improve drainage and introduce three new holes as well as clearing shrubbery to widen some others.
18 holes, 6120yds, Par 70, SSS 71, Course record 65. Club membership 800.
Visitors Mon-Fri, Sat-Sun by arrangement. Booking required. Handicap certificate. Dress code. **Societies** Booking required. **Green Fees** Phone. **Prof** Craig Everett **Course Designer** Commander Harris **Facilities** **Leisure** hard tennis courts, heated indoor swimming pool, sauna, solarium, gymnasium. **Conf** Corporate Hospitality Days **Location** NE side of town on A81

Hotel Premier Travel Inn Glasgow (Milngavie), 103 Main St, MILNGAVIE ☎ 08701 977112 60 en suite

Hilton Park Auldmarroch Estate, Stockiemuir Rd G62 7HB
☎ 0141 956 4657 0141 956 4657
e-mail: info@hiltonparkgolfclub.fsnet.co.uk
web: www.hiltonpark.co.uk
Moorland courses set amid magnificent scenery.
Hilton Course: 18 holes, 6054yds, Par 70, SSS 70, Course record 65.
Allander Course: 18 holes, 5487yards, Par 69, SSS 67, Course record 65.
Club membership 1200.
Visitors must contact in advance but may not play at weekends. **Societies** Booking required. **Green Fees** Phone. **Prof** W McCondichie **Course Designer** James Braid **Facilities** **Location** 3m NW of Milngavie, on A809

Hotel Premier Travel Inn Glasgow (Milngavie), 103 Main St, MILNGAVIE ☎ 08701 977112 60 en suite

Milngavie Laighpark G62 8EP
☎ 0141 956 1619 0141 956 4252
18 holes, 5818yds, Par 68, SSS 68, Course record 59.
Course Designer The Auchterlonie Brothers **Location** 1.25m N
Telephone for further details

Hotel Premier Travel Inn Glasgow (Milngavie), 103 Main St, MILNGAVIE ☎ 08701 977112 60 en suite

Continued

EAST LOTHIAN

ABERLADY Map 12 NT47

Kilspindie EH32 0QD
☎ 01875 870358 📠 01875 870358
e-mail: kilspindie@btconnect.com
web: golfeastlothian.com
Traditional Scottish seaside links, short but good challenge of golf and well-bunkered. Situated on the shores of the River Forth with panoramic views.
18 holes, 5480yds, Par 69, SSS 66, Course record 59. Club membership 800.
Visitors Mon-Sun & BHs. Booking required. Dress code. **Societies** Booking required. **Green Fees** £47.50 per day, £32 per round (£57.50/£40 weekends). **Prof** Graham J Sked **Course Designer** Various **Facilities** **Conf** Corporate Hospitality Days **Location** N side of village off A198. Private access at E end of Aberlady

Hotel ★★★ Greywalls Hotel, Muirfield, GULLANE ☎ 01620 842144 17 en suite 6 annexe en suite

Luffness New EH32 0QA
☎ 01620 843336 📠 01620 842933
e-mail: secretary@luffnessnew.com
Links course, national final qualifying course for the Open Championship.
18 holes, 6122yds, Par 69, SSS 70, Course record 63. Club membership 750.
Visitors Mon-Fri & BHs. Booking required. Handicap certificate. Dress code. **Societies** Booking required. **Green Fees** £85 per day, £60 per round. **Course Designer** Tom Morris **Facilities** **Location** 1m E Aberlady on A198

Hotel ★★★ Greywalls Hotel, Muirfield, GULLANE ☎ 01620 842144 17 en suite 6 annexe en suite

DUNBAR Map 12 NT67

Dunbar East Links EH42 1LL
☎ 01368 862317 📠 01368 865202
e-mail: secretary@dunbargolfclub.sol.co.uk
web: www.dunbar-golfclub.co.uk
Another of Scotland's old links. It is said that it was some Dunbar members who first took the game of golf to the north of England. A natural links course on a narrow strip of land, following the contours of the sea shore. There is a wall bordering one side and the shore on the other side making this quite a challenging course for all levels of player. The wind, if blowing from the sea, is a problem.
18 holes, 6406yds, Par 71, SSS 71, Course record 64. Club membership 1000.
Visitors Fri-Wed & BHs. Booking required. Dress code. **Societies** Booking required. **Green Fees** £45 per round/£60 per day (weekend £60/£80). **Prof** Jacky Montgomery **Course Designer** Tom Morris **Facilities** **Location** 0.5m E off A1087

Winterfield North Rd EH42 1AU
☎ 01368 863562
e-mail: kevinphillips@tiscali.co.uk
web: myweb.tiscali.co.uk/kevinphillips
Seaside course with superb views.
18 holes, 5155yds, Par 65, SSS 64, Course record 61. Club membership 350.
Visitors Mon-Sun & BHs. Booking required Sat-Sun. Dress code. **Societies** Booking required. **Green Fees** £18 per round, £25 per day (weekends £20/£32). **Prof** Kevin Phillips **Facilities** **Location** W side of town off A1087

GIFFORD Map 12 NT56

Castle Park Castlemains EH41 4PL
☎ 01620 810733 📠 01620 810691
e-mail: castleparkgolf@hotmail.com
web: www.castleparkgolfclub.co.uk
Naturally undulating parkland course in beautiful setting with much wild life. Wide rolling fairways on the first nine with tantalising water and dyke hazards. The mature back nine is shorter but full of hidden surprises requiring good golfing strategy as you pass Yester Castle.
18 holes, 6126yds, Par 72, SSS 70, Course record 71. Club membership 400.
Visitors Mon-Sun & BHs. Booking required. Dress code. **Societies** Booking required. **Green Fees** £20 (£28 weekends). **Prof** Derek Small **Course Designer** Archie Baird **Facilities** **Conf** Corporate Hospitality Days **Location** off B6355, 2m S of Gifford

Guest House ♦♦♦♦♦ Kippielaw Farmhouse, EAST LINTON ☎ 01620 860368 2 rms (1 en suite)

Gifford Edinburgh Rd EH41 4JE
☎ 01620 810267
e-mail: thesecretary@giffordgolfclub.fsnet.co.uk
web: www.giffordgolfclub.com
Parkland with easy walking.
9 holes, 6057yds, Par 71, SSS 69. Club membership 600.
Visitors Booking required. **Societies** Booking required. **Green Fees** Phone. **Facilities** **Location** 1m SW off B6355

GULLANE Map 12 NT48

Gullane West Links Rd EH31 2BB
☎ 01620 842255 📠 01620 842327
e-mail: bookings@gullanegolfclub.com
web: www.gullanegolfclub.com
Gullane is a delightful village and one of Scotland's great golf centres. The game has been played on the 3 links courses for over 300 years and was formed in 1882. The first tee of the Championship No 1 course (a Final Qualifier when The Open is played at Muirfield) is literally in the village and the three courses stretch out along the coast line. All have magnificent views ov[er] the Firth of the Fourth, standing on the highest point a[t] the 7th Tee is reported as one of the 'finest views in golf'.

Continu[ed]

Championship Course

East Lothian

(Honourable Company of Edinburgh Golfers) Muirfield

Gullane

Map 12 NT48

The course at Muirfield was designed by Old Tom Morris in 1891 and is generally considered to be one of the top ten courses in the world. The club itself has an excellent pedigree: it was founded in 1744, making it just 10 years older than the Royal and Ancient but not as old as Royal Blackheath. Muirfield has staged some outstanding Open championships. Perhaps one of the most memorable was in 1972 when Lee Trevino, the defending champion, seemed to be losing his grip until a spectacular shot brought him back to beat Tony Jacklin, who subsequently never won another Open.

Muirfield EH31 2EG
☎ 01620 842123 🖹 01620 842977
e-mail: hceg@muirfield.org.uk
web: www.muirfield.org.uk

18 holes, 6601yds, Par 70, SSS 73, Course record 63.
Club membership 700.

Visitors Tue & Thu. Booking required. Handicap certificate. Dress code. **Societies** Booking required. **Green Fees** £170 per 36 holes, £135 per 18 holes. **Course Designer** Harry Colt **Facilities** ⊗ by arrangement ☕ 🍷 ⛢ 🚿 ✐ **Location** NE of village

Course No 1: 18 holes, 6466yds, Par 71, SSS 72, Course record 65.
Course No 2: 18 holes, 6244yds, Par 71, SSS 71, Course record 64.
Course No 3: 18 holes, 5252yds, Par 68, SSS 66.
Club membership 1200.
Visitors Mon-Sun & BHs. Booking required. Dress code. **Societies** Booking required. **Green Fees** £85 per round (weekends £100). **Prof** Alasdair Good **Course Designer** Various **Facilities** ⊗ **Leisure** golf museum. **Conf** facs Corporate Hospitality Days **Location** W end of village on A198

Hotel ★★★ Greywalls Hotel, Muirfield, GULLANE ☎ 01620 842144 17 en suite 6 annexe en suite

Muirfield - Honourable Company of Edinburgh Golfers see page 345

Hotel ★★★ Greywalls Hotel, Muirfield, GULLANE ☎ 01620 842144 17 en suite 6 annexe en suite

Hotel ★★★ 72% The Open Arms Hotel, DIRLETON ☎ 01620 850241 🖷 01620 850570 10 en suite

Hotel U Macdonald Marine Hotel, Cromwell Rd, NORTH BERWICK ☎ 0870 400 8129 🖷 01620 894480 84 en suite

Hotel ★★ 68% Nether Abbey Hotel, 20 Dirleton Av, NORTH BERWICK ☎ 01620 892802 🖷 01620 895298 13 en suite

HADDINGTON Map 12 NT57

Haddington Amisfield Park EH41 4PT
☎ 01620 822727 & 823627 🖷 01620 826580
e-mail: info@haddingtongolf.co.uk
web: www.haddingtongolf.co.uk
A slightly undulating parkland course within the grounds of a former country estate beside the River Tyne. New ponds and bunkers have been constructed to improve the course even more.
18 holes, 6335yds, Par 71, SSS 71, Course record 65.
Club membership 850.
Visitors Mon-Sun & BHs. Booking required. Dress code. **Societies** Booking required. **Green Fees** £34 per day, £22 per round (£44/£32 weekends). **Prof** John Sandilands **Facilities** ⊗ **Leisure** driving net, practice bunker. **Conf** facs Corporate Hospitality Days **Location** E side of town centre

Hotel ★★★ Greywalls Hotel, Muirfield, GULLANE ☎ 01620 842144 17 en suite 6 annexe en suite

LONGNIDDRY Map 12 NT47

Longniddry Links Rd EH32 0NL
☎ 01875 852141 🖷 01875 853371
e-mail: secretary@longniddrygolfclub.co.uk
web: www.longniddrygolfclub.co.uk
Undulating seaside links and partial parkland course with no par 5s. One of the numerous courses which stretch east from Edinburgh to Dunbar. The inward half is more open than the wooded outward half, but can be difficult in prevailing west wind.
18 holes, 6260yds, Par 68, SSS 70, Course record 63.
Club membership 1100.

Continued

Visitors Mon-Sun & BHs. Booking required. Dress code. **Societies** Booking required. **Green Fees** £55 per day, £37.50 per round (weekends £48 per round). **Prof** John Gray **Course Designer** H S Colt **Facilities** ⊗ **Conf** Corporate Hospitality Days **Location** N side of village off A198

Hotel ★★★ Greywalls Hotel, Muirfield, GULLANE ☎ 01620 842144 17 en suite 6 annexe en suite

MUSSELBURGH Map 11 NT37

Musselburgh Monktonhall EH21 6SA
☎ 0131 665 2005 🖷 0131 665 4435
e-mail: secretary@themusselburghgolfclub.com
web: www.themusselburghgolfclub.com
Testing parkland course with natural hazards including trees and a burn; easy walking.
18 holes, 6725yds, Par 71, SSS 72, Course record 65.
Club membership 1000.
Visitors Mon-Fri, Sun & BHs. Booking required. Dress Code. **Societies** welcome. **Green Fees** £45 per day, £35 per round (£50/£40 weekends). **Prof** Fraser Mann **Course Designer** James Braid **Facilities** ⊗ **Conf** Corporate Hospitality Days **Location** 1m S on B6415

Hotel Premier Travel Inn Edinburgh (Inveresk), Carberry Rd, Inveresk, Musselburgh, EDINBURGH ☎ 08701 977092 40 en suite

Musselburgh Links, The Old Golf Course
10 Balcarres Rd EH21 7SD
☎ 0131 665 5438 (starter) 665 6981 (clubhouse)
🖷 0131 665 5438
e-mail: info@musselburgholdlinks.co.uk
web: www.musselburgholdlinks.co.uk
A delightful nine-hole links course weaving in and out of the famous Musselburgh Race Course. This course is steeped in the history and tradition of golf. Mary Queen of Scots reputedly played golf at the old course in 1567, but documentary evidence dates back to 1672. The 1st hole is a par 3 and the next three holes play eastward from the grandstand at the racecourse. The course turns north-west towards the sea then west for the last four holes. Designed by nature and defined over the centuries by generations of golfers, the course has many natural features and hazards.
9 holes, 2874yds, Par 34, SSS 34, Course record 29.
Club membership 300.
Visitors contact club for details. **Societies** welcome. **Green Fees** £9 per 9 holes, £18 per 18 holes (£9.50/£19 weekends). **Facilities** **Conf** facs **Location** 1m E of town off A1

Hotel Premier Travel Inn Edinburgh (Inveresk), Carberry Rd, Inveresk, Musselburgh, EDINBURGH ☎ 08701 977092 40 en suite

NORTH BERWICK Map 12 NT58

Glen East Links, Tantallon Ter EH39 4LE
☎ 01620 892726 🖷 01620 895447
e-mail: secretary@glengolfclub.co.uk
web: www.glengolfclub.co.uk
A popular course with a good variety of holes including the famous 13th, par 3 Sea Hole. The views of the town, the Firth of Forth and the Bass Rock are breathtaking.

Continued

18 holes, 6243yds, Par 70, SSS 70, Course record 67. Club membership 650.
Visitors Mon-Sun & BHs. Booking required. Dress code. **Societies** Booking required. **Green Fees** £54 per day, £34 per round (weekends £67/£47). **Course Designer** Ben Sayers/James Braid **Facilities** **Conf** facs Corporate Hospitality Days **Location** A1 onto A198 to North Berwick. Right at seabird centre sea-wall road

Hotel ★★ 68% Nether Abbey Hotel, 20 Dirleton Av, NORTH BERWICK ☎ 01620 892802 13 en suite

North Berwick Beach Rd EH39 4BB
☎ 01620 892135 🖷 01620 893274
e-mail: secretary@northberwickgolfclub.com
web: www.northberwickgolfclub.com
Another of East Lothian's famous courses, the links at North Berwick is still popular. A classic championship links, it has many hazards including the beach, streams, bunkers, light rough and low walls. The great hole on the course is the 15th, the famous Redan.
West Links: 18 holes, 6420yds, Par 71, SSS 72, Course record 63.
Club membership 730.
Visitors Mon-Sun & BHs. Booking required. Handicap certificate. Dress code. **Societies** Booking required. **Green Fees** £80 per day, £60 per round (£75 weekends). **Prof** D Huish **Facilities** **Conf** Corporate Hospitality Days **Location** W side of town on A198

Hotel Macdonald Marine Hotel, Cromwell Rd, NORTH BERWICK ☎ 0870 400 8129 84 en suite

Whitekirk Whitekirk EH39 5PR
☎ 01620 870300 🖷 01620 870330
e-mail: countryclub@whitekirk.com
web: www.whitekirk.com
Scenic coastal course with lush green fairways, gorse covered rocky banks and stunning views. Natural water hazards and strong sea breezes make this well-designed course a good test of golf.
18 holes, 6526yds, Par 72, SSS 72, Course record 64. Club membership 400.
Visitors Mon-Sun & BHs. Booking required. Dress code. **Societies** Booking required. **Green Fees** £28 per round, £40 per day (weekend £38/£55). **Prof** Paul Wardell **Course Designer** Cameron Sinclair **Facilities** **Leisure** indoor swimming pool, sauna, solarium, gymnasium, health spa. **Conf** facs Corporate Hospitality Days **Location** 3m off A1 Edinburgh-Berwick-upon-Tweed, A198 North Berwick

Hotel ★★ 68% Nether Abbey Hotel, 20 Dirleton Av, NORTH BERWICK ☎ 01620 892802 13 en suite

PRESTONPANS Map 11 NT37

Royal Musselburgh Prestongrange House EH32 9RP
☎ 01875 810276 🖷 01875 810276
e-mail: royalmusselburgh@btinternet.com
web: www.royalmusselburgh.co.uk
Tree-lined parkland course overlooking Firth of Forth. Well maintained and providing an excellent challenge. The final third of the course can make or break a score. The tough four hole stretches from the long par 4 13th including The Gully, a par 3 14th where to be short is to court disaster, followed by the par 4 15th huddled tight beside trees to the left. A precision drive is required to find the rollercoaster fairway and from there a long iron or fairway wood is played over an uphill approach to a tilting green.

Royal Musselburgh

18 holes, 6237yds, Par 70, SSS 70, Course record 64. Club membership 1000.
Visitors Booking required. **Societies** Booking required. **Green Fees** Phone. **Prof** John Henderson **Course Designer** James Braid **Facilities** **Conf** facs Corporate Hospitality Days **Location** W of town centre on B1361 to North Berwick

Hotel Premier Travel Inn Edinburgh (Inveresk), Carberry Rd, Inveresk, Musselburgh, EDINBURGH ☎ 08701 977092 40 en suite

Continued

EAST RENFREWSHIRE

BARRHEAD Map 11 NS45

Fereneze Fereneze Av G78 1HJ
☎ 0141 880 7058 🖷 0141 881 7149
e-mail: ferenezegc@lineone.net
web: www.ferenezegolf.ic24.net
18 holes, 5962yds, Par 71, SSS 69, Course record 66.
Location NW side of town off B774
Telephone for further details

Hotel ★★ 74% Uplawmoor Hotel, Neilston Rd, UPLAWMOOR ☎ 01505 850565 14 en suite

CLARKSTON Map 11 NS55

Cathcart Castle Mearns Rd G76 7YL
☎ 0141 638 9449 🖷 0141 638 1201
18 holes, 5832yds, Par 68, SSS 68.
Location 0.75m SW off A726
Telephone for further details

Hotel Premier Travel Inn Glasgow East Kilbride West, Eaglesham Rd, EAST KILBRIDE ☎ 0870 9906542 40 en suite

EAGLESHAM Map 11 NS55

Bonnyton Kirktonmoor Rd G76 0QA
☎ 01355 302781 🖷 01355 303151
Dramatic moorland course offering spectacular views of beautiful countryside as far as snow-capped Ben Lomond. Tree-lined fairways, plateau greens, natural burns and well-situated bunkers and a unique variety of holes offer golfers both challenge and reward.
18 holes, 6255yds, Par 72, SSS 71.
Club membership 960.
Visitors Mon & Thu. Booking required. Dress code. **Societies** Booking required. **Green Fees** £40 per round. **Prof** Kendal McWade **Facilities** **Location** 0.25m SW off B764

NEWTON MEARNS Map 11 NS55

East Renfrewshire Pilmuir G77 6RT
☎ 01355 500256 🖷 01355 500323
e-mail: secretary@eastrengolfclub.co.uk
web: www.eastrengolfclub.co.uk
Undulating moorland with loch; prevailing south-west wind. Extensive views of Glasgow and the southern Highlands.
18 holes, 6097yds, Par 70, SSS 70, Course record 63.
Club membership 900.
Visitors Mon-Sun & BHs. Booking required. Handicap certificate. Dress code. **Societies** Booking required. **Green Fees** £40 per round/£50 per day (weekends £50/£60). **Prof** Stewart Russell **Course Designer** James Braid **Facilities** **Conf** Corporate Hospitality Days **Location** 3m SW of Newton Mearns on A77, junct 5

Hotel ★★ 74% Uplawmoor Hotel, Neilston Rd, UPLAWMOOR ☎ 01505 850565 14 en suite

Eastwood Muirshield, Loganswell G77 6RX
☎ 01355 500280 🖷 01355 500333
e-mail: eastwoodgolfclub@btconnect.com
web: www.eastwoodgolfclub.co.uk
An undulating moorland course situated in a scenic setting. Originally built in 1937, the course was redesigned in 2003. The greens are now of modern design, built to USGA specification.
18 holes, 6071yds, Par 70, SSS 70.
Club membership 900.
Visitors contact club for details. Dress code. **Societies** Booking required. **Green Fees** £40 per day, £30 per round. **Prof** Iain J Darroch **Course Designer** Graeme J. Webster/Theodore Moone **Facilities** **Location** 2.5m S of Newton Mearns, on A77

Hotel ★★ 74% Uplawmoor Hotel, Neilston Rd, UPLAWMOOR ☎ 01505 850565 14 en suite

UPLAWMOOR Map 10 NS45

Caldwell G78 4AU
☎ 01505 850366 (Secretary) & 850616 (Pro)
🖷 01505 850604
e-mail: caldwellgolfclub@aol.com
web: www.caldwellgolfclub.i8.co
Parkland course.
18 holes, 6294yds, Par 71, SSS 71, Course record 62.
Club membership 600.
Visitors Mon-Fri. Booking required. Handicap certificate. Dress code **Societies** Booking required. **Green Fees** £25 per round, £35 per day. **Prof** Stephen Forbes **Course Designer** W. Fernie **Facilities** **Conf** Corporate Hospitality Days **Location** 5m SW of Barrhead on A736 Irvine road

Hotel ★★ 74% Uplawmoor Hotel, Neilston Rd, UPLAWMOOR ☎ 01505 850565 14 en suite

FALKIRK

FALKIRK Map 11 NS88

Falkirk Carmuirs, 136 Stirling Rd, Camelon FK2 7YP
☎ 01324 611061 (club) 🖷 01324 639573 (Sec)
e-mail: falkirkgolfclub@btconnect.com
web: www.falkirkcarmuirsgolfclub.co.uk
Parkland with gorse and streams.
18 holes, 6230yds, Par 71, SSS 70, Course record 65.
Club membership 800.
Visitors Sun-Fri & BHs. Dress code. **Societies** Booking required. **Green Fees** £30 per day, £20 per round (£40/£30 Sun). **Prof** Stewart Craig **Course Designer** James Braid **Facilities** **Conf** Corporate Hospitality Days **Location** 1.5m W on A9

Hotel ★★★★ 69% Macdonald Inchyra Grange Hotel, Grange Rd, POLMONT ☎ 0870 1942115 103 en suite

LARBERT Map 11 NS88

Falkirk Tryst 86 Burnhead Rd FK5 4BD
☎ 01324 562054 🖷 01324 562054
e-mail: falkirktrystgc@tiscali.co.uk
Links-type course, fairly level with trees and broom, well-bunkered. Winds can affect play.
18 holes, 6053yds, Par 70, SSS 69, Course record 62.
Club membership 850.
Visitors Sun-Fri & BHs. Booking required. Dress code.

Continue

Societies Booking required. **Green Fees** £30 per day, £24 per round (£30 per round on Sun pm). **Prof** Steven Dunsmore **Facilities** **Location** On A88 between A9

Hotel ★★★★ 69% Macdonald Inchyra Grange Hotel, Grange Rd, POLMONT ☎ 0870 1942115 103 en suite

Glenbervie Stirling Rd FK5 4SJ
☎ 01324 562605 🖹 01324 551054
e-mail: secretary@glenberviegolfclub.com
web: www.glenberviegolfclub.com
Parkland with good views of the Ochil Hills.
18 holes, 6438yds, Par 71, SSS 71, Course record 64.
Club membership 600.
Visitors Mon to Fri till 4pm. **Societies** Tue & Thu only. Apply in writing. **Green Fees** Phone. **Prof** David Ross **Course Designer** James Braid **Facilities** **Conf** facs Corporate Hospitality Days **Location** 2m NW on A9

Hotel ★★★★ 69% Macdonald Inchyra Grange Hotel, Grange Rd, POLMONT ☎ 0870 1942115 103 en suite

POLMONT Map 11 NS97

Grangemouth Polmont Hill FK2 0YE
☎ 01324 503840 🖹 01324 503841
e-mail: greg.mcfarlane@falkirk.gov.uk
Windy parkland. Testing holes: 3rd, 4th (par 4s); 5th (par 5); 7th (par 3) 216yds over reservoir (elevated green); 8th, 9th, 18th (par 4s).
18 holes, 6314yds, Par 71, SSS 71, Course record 65.
Club membership 800.
Visitors Mon-Sun & BHs. Dress code. **Societies** Booking required. **Green Fees** £15 per round (£19 weekends). **Prof** Greg McFarlane **Facilities** **Location** M9 junct 4, 0.5m N

Hotel ★★★★ 69% Macdonald Inchyra Grange Hotel, Grange Rd, POLMONT ☎ 0870 1942115 103 en suite

Polmont Manuelrigg, Maddiston FK2 0LS
☎ 01324 711277 🖹 01324 712504
e-mail: polmontgolfclub@btconnect.com
Hilly parkland with small greens protected by bunkers. Views of the River Forth and the Ochil Hills.
9 holes, 3073yds, Par 72, SSS 69, Course record 66.
Club membership 300.
Visitors Sun-Fri & BHs. Dress code. **Societies** welcome. **Green Fees** £10 per round (weekends £15). **Facilities** by arrangement by arrangement by arrangement **Conf** facs **Location** A805 from Falkirk, 1st right after fire brigade headquarters

Hotel ★★★★ 69% Macdonald Inchyra Grange Hotel, Grange Rd, POLMONT ☎ 0870 1942115 103 en suite

FIFE

ABERDOUR Map 11 NT18

Aberdour Seaside Place KY3 0TX
☎ 01383 860080 🖹 01383 860050
e-mail: aberdourgc@aol.com
web: www.aberdourgolfclub.co.uk
Parkland with lovely views over Firth of Forth.

Aberdour

18 holes, 5460yds, Par 67, SSS 66, Course record 59.
Club membership 800.
Visitors Sun-Fri & BHs. Booking required. Dress code. **Societies** Booking required. **Green Fees** £30 per day, £22 per round (£35 per day/round Sun). **Prof** David Gemmell **Facilities** **Location** S side of village

ANSTRUTHER Map 12 NO50

Anstruther Marsfield, Shore Rd KY10 3DZ
☎ 01333 310956 🖹 01333 310956
web: anstruthergolf.co.uk
A tricky links course with some outstanding views of the river Forth. The nine holes consist of four par 4s and five par 3s. The 5th hole is rated one of the hardest par 3s anywhere, measuring 235yds from the medal tees.
9 holes, 2249yds, Par 62, SSS 63, Course record 60.
Club membership 550.
Visitors Mon-Sun & BHs. Booking required Sat-Sun & BHs. Dress code. **Societies** Booking required. **Green Fees** £18 per 18 holes, £12 per 9 holes (£20/£14 weekends). **Course Designer** Tom Morris **Facilities** **Location** Turn right at Craw's Hotel, SW off A917

Hotel ★★ 66% Balcomie Links Hotel, Balcomie Rd, CRAIL ☎ 01333 450237 15 rms (13 en suite)

BURNTISLAND Map 11 NT28

Burntisland Golf House Club Dodhead, Kirkcaldy Rd KY3 9LQ
☎ 01592 874093 (Manager) 🖹 01592 873247
e-mail: wktbghc@aol.com
web: www.burntislandgolfhouseclub.co.uk
A lush, testing course offering magnificent views over the Forth estuary.

18 holes, 5965yds, Par 70, SSS 70, Course record 62.
Club membership 800.

Continued

Visitors Mon-Sun & BHs. Booking required. Handicap certificate. Dress code. **Societies** Booking required. **Green Fees** £35 per day, £25 per round (£42/£35 weekends). **Prof** Paul Wytrazek **Course Designer** Willie Park Jnr **Facilities** **Conf** facs Corporate Hospitality Days **Location** 1m E on B923

Hotel ★★ 68% Inchview Hotel, 65-69 Kinghorn Rd, BURNTISLAND ☎ 01592 872239 16 en suite

COLINSBURGH Map 12 NO40

Charleton Charleton KY9 1HG
☎ 01333 340249 01333 340583
e-mail: bonde@charleton.co.uk
web: www.charleton.co.uk
18 holes, 6216yds, Par 72, SSS 70.
Course Designer J Salvesen **Location** Off B942, NW of Colinsburgh
Telephone for further details

The Inn at Lathones, Largoward, ST ANDREWS ☎ 01334 840494 13 annexe en suite

COWDENBEATH Map 11 NT19

Cowdenbeath Seco Place KY4 8PD
☎ 01383 511918
A parkland-based 18 hole golf course.
Dora Course: 18 holes, 6300yds, Par 71, SSS 71, Course record 64.
Club membership 250.
Visitors Mon-Sun & BHs. Booking required. Dress code. **Societies** Booking required. **Green Fees** £15 per round (£20 weekends). **Facilities**
Location Off A92 into Cowdenbeath, 2nd right signed

CRAIL Map 12 NO60

Crail Golfing Society Balcomie Clubhouse, Fifeness KY10 3XN
☎ 01333 450686 & 450960 01333 450416
e-mail: info@crailgolfingsociety.co.uk
web: www.crailgolfingsociety.co.uk
Perched on the edge of the North Sea, the Crail Golfing Society's courses at Balcomie are picturesque and sporting. Crail Golfing Society began its life in 1786 and the course is highly thought of by students of the game both for its testing holes and the standard of its greens. Craighead Links has panoramic seascape and country views. With wide sweeping fairways and USGA specification greens it is a testing but fair challenge.
Balcomie Links: 18 holes, 5922yds, Par 69, SSS 70, Course record 62.
Craighead Links: 18 holes, 6700yds, Par 72, SSS 74, Course record 69.
Club membership 1600.
Visitors contact club for details. **Societies** Booking required. **Green Fees** per day: Balcomie/Balcomie £65, Craighead/Balcomie £55; per round £40 (weekends £78/£68/£50). **Prof** Graeme Lennie **Course Designer** Tom Morris **Facilities**
Location 2m NE off A917

Hotel ★★ 66% Balcomie Links Hotel, Balcomie Rd, CRAIL ☎ 01333 450237 15 rms (13 en suite)

CUPAR Map 11 NO31

Cupar Hilltarvit KY15 5JT
☎ 01334 653549 01334 653549
e-mail: cupargc@fsmail.net
web: www.cupargolfclub.co.uk
Hilly parkland with fine views over north-east Fife. The 5th/14th hole is most difficult - uphill into the prevailing wind. Said to be the oldest nine-hole club in the UK.
9 holes, 5153yds, Par 68, SSS 66, Course record 61.
Club membership 400.
Visitors Mon-Sun & BHs. Booking required Sat-Sun & BHs. Dress code. **Societies** Booking required. **Green Fees** £20 per day. **Course Designer** Allan Robertson **Facilities** **Location** 0.75m S off A92

Elmwood Stratheden KY15 5RS
☎ 01334 658780 01334 658781
e-mail: clubhouse@elmwood.co.uk
web: www.elmwoodgc.co.uk
A parkland course set in a rural location, offering fine views of the Lomond Hills to the west and the Tarvit Hills to the east.
18 holes, 5653yds, Par 70, SSS 68.
Club membership 750.
Visitors Mon-Sun & BHs. Booking required. Dress code. **Societies** Booking required. **Green Fees** £20 per round (£24 weekends & BHs). **Prof** Graeme McDowall **Course Designer** John Salveson **Facilities** **Conf** facs Corporate Hospitality Days **Location** M90 junct 8, A91 to St Andrews, 0.5m before Cupar. At Wisemans Dairy right, right at next junct, course 400yds on left

DUNFERMLINE Map 11 NT08

Canmore Venturefair Av KY12 0PE
☎ 01383 724969 01383 731649
e-mail: canmoregolfclub@aol.com
web: www.canmoregolf.co.uk
Parkland course with excellent turf, moderate in length but a good test of accuracy demanding a good short game. Ideal for 36-hole play, and suitable for all ages.
18 holes, 5376yds, Par 67, SSS 66, Course record 61.
Club membership 650.
Visitors contact club for more details. Dress code. **Societies** Booking required. **Green Fees** £26 per day, £20 per round (£25/£35 weekends). **Prof** Daryn Cochrane **Course Designer** Ben Sayers & others **Facilities** **Location** 1m N on A823

Hotel ★★★ 75% Best Western Keavil House Hotel, Crossford, DUNFERMLINE ☎ 01383 736258 47 en suite

Dunfermline Pitfirrane, Crossford KY12 8QW
☎ 01383 723534 & 729061 01383 723547
e-mail: secretary@dunfermlinegolfclub.com
web: www.dunfermlinegolfclub.com
Gently undulating parkland course with interesting contours. Five par 5s, five par 3s. No water hazards. Centre of the course is a disused walled garden, which is a haven for wildlife.
18 holes, 6121yds, Par 72, SSS 70, Course record 65.
Club membership 720.
Visitors Sun-Fri & BHs. Booking required. Dress code. **Societies** Booking required. **Green Fees** £28 per round, £40 per day (Sun £35 per round). **Prof** Chris Nugent

Continued

Course Designer J R Stutt **Facilities** ⊗ 🍴 🛏 ☕ 🍸 👤 🏠 🏌 🚗 🛒 ✓ **Location** 2m W of Dunfermline on A994

Hotel ★★★ 75% Best Western Keavil House Hotel, Crossford, DUNFERMLINE ☎ 01383 736258 47 en suite

Forrester Park Pitdinnie Rd, Cairneyhill KY12 8RF
☎ 01383 880505 📠 01383 882505
e-mail: forresterpark@aol.com
web: www.forresterparkresort.com
Set in the heart of 350 acres of parkland on what was originally the Keavil Estate. Ponds and streams come into play on 9 holes and all greens have been constructed to USGA specifications.
18 holes, 7000yds, Par 72, SSS 74, Course record 69. Club membership 700.
Visitors Mon-Sun & BHs. Booking required Sat, Sun & BHs. Dress code. **Societies** welcome. **Green Fees** £35 per 18 holes (£45 weekends). **Prof** R Forrester **Facilities** ⊗ 🍴 🛏 ☕ 🍸 👤 🏠 🏌 🚗 🛒 ✓ **Location** 2.5m W of Dunfermline in village of Cairneyhill

Hotel ★★★ 75% Best Western Keavil House Hotel, Crossford, DUNFERMLINE ☎ 01383 736258 47 en suite

Pitreavie Queensferry Rd KY11 8PR
☎ 01383 722591 📠 01383 722592
e-mail: secpdgc@btconnect.com
Picturesque woodland course with panoramic view of the Forth valley. Testing golf.
18 holes, 6086yds, Par 70, SSS 69, Course record 64. Club membership 700.
Visitors contact club for details. Dress code. **Societies** Booking required. **Green Fees** £34 per day, £24 per round (£40/£28 weekends). **Prof** Paul Brookes **Course Designer** A MacKenzie **Facilities** ⊗ 🍴 🛏 ☕ 🍸 👤 🏠 🏌 ✓ **Conf** Corporate Hospitality Days **Location** SE side of town on A823

ELIE — Map 12 NO40

Golf House Club KY9 1AS
☎ 01333 330301 📠 01333 330895
e-mail: secretary@golfhouseclub.org
web: www.golfhouseclub.org
One of Scotland's most delightful holiday courses with panoramic views over the Firth of Forth. Some of the holes out towards the rocky coastline are splendid. This is the course which has produced many good professionals, including James Braid.
18 holes, 6273yds, Par 70, SSS 70, Course record 62. Club membership 600.
Visitors Mon-Sun & BHs. Booking required. Handicap certificate. Dress code. **Societies** Booking required. **Green Fees** £75 per day, £55 per round (£85/£65 weekends). **Prof** Ian Muir **Facilities** ⊗ 🍴 🛏 ☕ 🍸 👤 🏠 🏌 ✓ **Leisure** hard tennis courts. **Location** W side of village off A917

The Inn at Lathones, Largoward, ST ANDREWS ☎ 01334 840494 13 annexe en suite

FALKLAND — Map 11 NO20

Falkland The Myre KY15 7AA
☎ 01337 857404
9 holes, 4988yds, Par 67, SSS 65, Course record 62.
Location N side of town on A912
Telephone for further details

GLENROTHES — Map 11 NO20

Glenrothes Golf Course Rd KY6 2LA
☎ 01592 754561
18 holes, 6444yds, Par 71, SSS 71, Course record 67.
Course Designer J R Stutt **Location** W side of town off B921
Telephone for further details

Hotel ★★★★ Balbirnie House, Balbirnie Park, MARKINCH ☎ 01592 610066 30 en suite

KINCARDINE — Map 11 NS98

Tulliallan Alloa Rd FK10 4BB
☎ 01259 730798 📠 01259 733950
e-mail: tulliallangolf@btconnect.com
web: www.tulliallangolf.co.uk
Pleasant parkland with scenic views of the Ochil Hills and the River Forth. A burn meanders through the course, which combined with maturing trees make this a challenging test of golf. The course is renowned for it's true greens.
18 holes, 5965yds, Par 69, SSS 69, Course record 63. Club membership 700.
Visitors Sun-Fri & BHs. Booking required. Handicap certificate. Dress code. **Societies** Booking required. **Green Fees** £35 per day, £20 per round (£42/£35 weekends). **Prof** Steven Kelly **Facilities** ⊗ 🍴 🛏 ☕ 🍸 👤 🏠 🏌 ✓ **Conf** facs Corporate Hospitality Days **Location** 1m NW on A977

Hotel Premier Travel Inn Falkirk North, Bowtrees Farm, KINCARDINE BRIDGE ☎ 08701 977099 40 en suite

KINGHORN — Map 11 NT28

Kinghorn Macduff Cres KY3 9RE
☎ 01592 890345 & 890978
Municipal course, 300ft above sea level with views over the Firth of Forth and the North Sea. Undulating and quite testing.
18 holes, 5269yds, Par 65, SSS 67, Course record 62. Club membership 190.
Visitors Mon-Sun. Booking required. Dress code. **Societies** Booking required. **Green Fees** £15 per round, £25 per day (weekend £20/£35). **Course Designer** Tom Morris **Facilities** ☕ 🍸 👤 **Location** S side of town on A921

Hotel ★★★ 67% Dean Park Hotel, Chapel Level, KIRKCALDY ☎ 01592 261635 34 en suite 12 annexe en suite

KIRKCALDY — Map 11 NT29

Dunnikier Park Dunnikier Way KY1 3LP
☎ 01592 261599 📠 01592 642541
e-mail: dunnikierparkgolfclub@btinternet.com
Parkland, rolling fairways, not heavily bunkered, views of the Firth of Forth.
18 holes, 6036 metres, Par 72, SSS 72, Course record 65. Club membership 700.
Visitors Mon-Sun & BHs. Booking required. Dress code. **Societies** Booking required. **Green Fees** Phone. **Prof** Gregor Whyte **Course Designer** R Stutt **Facilities** ⊗ 🍴 🛏 ☕ 🍸 👤 🏠 🚗 ✓ **Location** 2m N on B981, next to Kirkcaldy High School

Continued

Hotel ★★★ 67% Dean Park Hotel, Chapel Level, KIRKCALDY ☎ 01592 261635 34 en suite 12 annexe en suite

Kirkcaldy Balwearie Rd KY2 5LT
☎ 01592 205240 & 203258 (Pro Shop) 🖹 01592 205240
e-mail: enquiries@kirkcaldygolfclub.co.uk
web: kirkcaldygolfclub.co.uk
A challenging parkland course in countryside, with beautiful views. A burn meanders by five holes. The club celebrated its centenary in 2004.
18 holes, 6086yds, Par 71, SSS 69, Course record 65. Club membership 892.
Visitors Mon-Sun & BHs. Booking required. Dress code. **Societies** welcome. **Green Fees** £34 per day, £28 per round (weekends £42/£34). **Prof** Anthony Caira **Course Designer** Tom Morris **Facilities** **Conf** facs Corporate Hospitality Days **Location** SW side of town off A910

Hotel ★★★ 67% Dean Park Hotel, Chapel Level, KIRKCALDY ☎ 01592 261635 34 en suite 12 annexe en suite

LADYBANK Map 11 NO30

Ladybank Annsmuir KY15 7RA
☎ 01337 830814 🖹 01337 831505
e-mail: info@ladybankgolf.co.uk
web: www.ladybankgolf.co.uk
Picturesque classic heathland course of championship status set among heather, Scots pines and silver birch and comprising two loops of nine holes. The drive at the dog-leg 3rd and 9th holes requires extreme care as do the 15th and 16th on the back nine. The greens are compact and approach shots require precision to find the putting surface.

18 holes, 6601yds, Par 71, SSS 72, Course record 63. Club membership 1000.
Visitors Booking required. **Societies** Booking required. **Green Fees** Phone. **Prof** Sandy Smith **Course Designer** Tom Morris **Facilities** **Conf** facs Corporate Hospitality Days **Location** N of town off A92

Hotel ★★★ 61% Fernie Castle, Letham, CUPAR ☎ 01337 810381 20 en suite

LESLIE Map 11 NO20

Leslie Balsillie Laws KY6 3EZ
☎ 01592 620040
9 holes, 4686yds, Par 63, SSS 64, Course record 63.
Course Designer Tom Morris **Location** N side of town off A911
Telephone for further details

Hotel ★★ 77% Rescobie House Hotel & Restaurant, 6 Valley Dr, Leslie, GLENROTHES ☎ 01592 749555 10 en suite

LEUCHARS Map 12 NO42

Drumoig Hotel & Golf Course Drumoig KY16 0BE
☎ 01382 541800 🖹 01382 542211
e-mail: drumoig@sol.co.uk
web: www.drumoigleisure.com
A developing but challenging young championship course. Set in a parkland environment, the course is links-like in places. Features include Whinstone Quarries and views over to St Andrews and Carnoustie. Water features are demanding, especially on the 9th where the fairway runs between Drumoig's two tiny lochs.
18 holes, 6835yds, Par 72, SSS 73, Course record 67. Club membership 350.
Visitors advisable to telephone in advance. **Societies** Booking required. **Green Fees** Phone. **Facilities** **Leisure** Scottish National Golf Centre in grounds. **Conf** facs Corporate Hospitality Days **Location** On A914 between St Andrews & Dundee

Hotel ★★★ Rufflets Country House & Garden Restaurant, Strathkinness Low Rd, ST ANDREWS ☎ 01334 472594 19 en suite 5 annexe en suite

St Michaels KY16 0DX
☎ 01334 839365 🖹 01334 838789
e-mail: honsec@stmichaelsgolf.co.uk
web: www.stmichaelsgolf.co.uk
Parkland with open views over Fife and Tayside. The undulating course weaves its way through tree plantations. The short par 4 17th, parallel to the railway and over a pond to a stepped green, poses an interesting challenge.
18 holes, 5802yds, Par 70, SSS 68, Course record 66. Club membership 650.
Visitors Not Sun am. **Societies** Apply in writing. **Green Fees** Phone. **Facilities** by arrangement **Location** NW side of village on A919

LEVEN Map 11 NO30

Leven Links The Promenade KY8 4HS
☎ 01333 428859 & 421390 🖹 01333 428859
e-mail: secretary@leven-links.com
web: www.leven-links.com
Leven has the classic ingredients which make up a golf links in Scotland; undulating fairways with hills and hollows, out of bounds and a burn or stream. Turning into the prevailing west wind at the 13th leaves the golfer with a lot of work to do before one of the finest finishing holes in golf. A top class championship links course used for Open final qualifying stages, it has fine views over Largo Bay.

Continued

Leven Links

18 holes, 6506yds, Par 71, SSS 70, Course record 61.
Club membership 1000.
Visitors Sun-Fri & BHs. Dress code. **Societies** Booking required. **Green Fees** £55 per day, £40 per round (weekends £65/£50). **Course Designer** Tom Morris **Facilities**

Scoonie North Links KY8 4SP
☎ 01333 307007 & 423437 (Starter) 01333 307008
e-mail: manager@scooniegolfclub.com
web: www.scooniegolfclub.com
A pleasant inland links course suitable for all ages.
18 holes, 5494 metres, Par 67, SSS 66, Course record 62.
Club membership 200.
Visitors contact club for details. **Societies** welcome. **Green Fees** Summer £17 per day, £11 per round (£21/£15 weekends). Winter £12 per day, £7 per round (£14/£8 weekends). **Facilities**

LOCHGELLY Map 11 NT19

Lochgelly Cartmore Rd KY5 9PB
☎ 01592 780174
Easy walking parkland, often windy.
18 holes, 5491yds, Par 68, SSS 67, Course record 62.
Club membership 300.
Visitors Mon-Sun & BHs. Booking required Sat-Sun. Handicap certificate. Dress code. **Societies** Booking required. **Green Fees** Phone. **Prof** Martin Goldie **Course Designer** Ian Marchbanks **Facilities** **Location** W side of town off A910

Hotel ★★★ 67% Dean Park Hotel, Chapel Level, KIRKCALDY ☎ 01592 261635 34 en suite 12 annexe en suite

Lochore Meadows Lochore Meadows Country Park, Crosshill, Lochgelly KY5 8BA
☎ 01592 414300 01592 414345
e-mail: info@lochore-meadows.co.uk
web: www.lochore-meadows.co.uk
Lochside course with a stream running through it and woodland nearby. Country park offers many leisure facilities.
9 holes, 3207yds, Par 72, SSS 71.
Club membership 240.
Visitors Mon-Sun & BHs. Booking required. Dress code. **Societies** Booking required. **Green Fees** £12 per round (weekends £15). **Facilities** **Leisure** fishing, outdoor education centre, childrens play park. **Conf** facs **Location** 0.5m W off B920

Hotel ★★★ 75% Green Hotel, 2 The Muirs, KINROSS ☎ 01577 863467 46 en suite

LUNDIN LINKS Map 12 NO40

Lundin Golf Rd KY8 6BA
☎ 01333 320202 01333 329743
e-mail: secretary@lundingolfclub.co.uk
web: www.lundingolfclub.co.uk
The Leven Links and the course of the Lundin Club adjoin each other. The course is part seaside and part inland. The holes are excellent but those which can be described as seaside holes have a very different nature from the inland style ones. The par 3 14th looks seawards across the Firth of Forth, a 177 yard downhill hole played from an elevated tee to a well bunkered green below. The old railway line defines out of bounds at several holes. A number of burns snake across the fairways.
18 holes, 6371yds, Par 71, SSS 71, Course record 63.
Club membership 895.
Visitors Mon-Sun & BHs. Booking required. Dress code. **Societies** Booking required. **Green Fees** £60 per day, £45 per round. (£50 per round weekends). **Prof** David Webster **Course Designer** James Braid **Facilities** **Location** W side of village off A915

Lundin Ladies Woodielea Rd KY8 6AR
☎ 01333 320832 & 320022
e-mail: secretary@lundinladies.co.uk
web: www.lundinladies.co.uk
Short, lowland course with Bronze Age standing stones on the second fairway and coastal views.
9 holes, 2365yds, Par 68, SSS 68, Course record 64.
Club membership 350.
Visitors Mon-Sun. Booking required Wed. **Societies** Booking required. **Green Fees** Phone. **Course Designer** James Braid **Facilities** **Location** W side of village off A915

MARKINCH Map 11 NO20

Balbirnie Park Balbirnie Park KY7 6NR
☎ 01592 612095 & 752006 (tee times)
01592 612383/752006
e-mail: craigfdonnelly@aol.com
web: www.balbirniegolf.com
Set in the magnificent Balbirnie Park, a fine example of the best in traditional parkland design, with natural contours the inspiration behind the layout. A course that will suit all standards of golfers.

18 holes, 6214yds, Par 71, SSS 71, Course record 62.
Club membership 900.
Visitors Mon-Sun & BHs. Booking required. **Societies** Booking required. **Green Fees** £35 per round, £45 per day (weekends £40/£55). **Prof** Craig Donnelly **Course**

Designer Fraser Middleton **Facilities** **Conf** facs Corporate Hospitality Days **Location** 2m E of Glenrothes, off A92

Hotel ★★★★ Balbirnie House, Balbirnie Park, MARKINCH ☎ 01592 610066 30 en suite

ST ANDREWS Map 12 NO51

British Golf Museum

☎ 01334 460046 (situated opposite Royal & Ancient Golf Club)

The museum which tells the history of golf from its origins to the present day, is of interest to golfers and non-golfers alike. Themed galleries and interactive displays explore the history of the major championships and the lives of the famous players, and trace the development of golfing equipment. An audio-visual theatre shows historic golfing moments.

Open Mar-Oct, Mon-Sat 9.30am-5.30pm, Sun 10-5. Nov-Mar, Mon-Sun 10-4. **Admission** Phone.

Dukes Course Craigtoun KY16 8NS

☎ 01334 474371 01334 479456

e-mail: reservations@oldcoursehotel.co.uk

web: www.oldcoursehotel.co.uk

Now owned and managed by the Old Course Hotel, with a spectacular setting above St Andrews. Blending the characteristics of a links course with an inland course, Duke's offers rolling fairways, undulating greens and a testing woodland section, and magnificent views over St Andrews Bay towards Carnoustie. Five separate tees at every hole and buggy paths running throughout the course.

18 holes, 6749yds, Par 71, SSS 73, Course record 67. Club membership 500.

Visitors Mon-Sun & BHs. Booking required. Dress code **Societies** Booking required. **Green Fees** From £95 per 18 holes. **Prof** Ron Walker **Course Designer** Tim Liddy **Facilities** **Leisure** heated indoor swimming pool, sauna, solarium, gymnasium, computer swing analyses. **Conf** facs Corporate Hospitality Days **Location** A91 to St Andrews, turn off for Strathkiness

Hotel ★★★★★ The Old Course Hotel, Golf Resort & Spa, ST ANDREWS ☎ 01334 474371 146 en suite

St Andrews Links see page 355

Hotel ★★★★★ The Old Course Hotel, Golf Resort & Spa, ST ANDREWS ☎ 01334 474371 146 en suite

Hotel ★★★ St Andrews Golf Hotel, 40 The Scores, ST ANDREWS ☎ 01334 472611 01334 472188 21 en suite

Hotel ★★★ Rufflets Country House & Garden Restaurant, Strathkinness Low Rd, ST ANDREWS ☎ 01334 472594 01334 478703 19 en suite 5 annexe en suite

Hotel ★★★★★ 71% St Andrews Bay Golf Resort & Spa, St Andrews ☎ 01334 837000 01334 471115 209 en suite 8 annexe en suite

Hotel ★★★★ 71% Macdonald Rusacks Hotel, Pilmour Links, ST ANDREWS ☎ 0870 400 8128 01334 477896 68 en suite

Hotel ★★★ 71% Scores Hotel, 76 The Scores, ST ANDREWS ☎ 01334 472451 01334 473947 30 en suite

St Andrews Bay Golf Resort & Spa KY16 8PN

☎ 01334 837000 01334 471115

e-mail: info@standrewsbay.com

web: www.standrewsbay.com

The Torrance course is a traditional Scottish layout, which works its way around the hotel before bursting open to reveal a cross section of the remaining 12 holes, which wind down towards the coastal edge. The Devlin is a stunning clifftop course with unique characteristics and requiring a well-devised strategy of play. One of the longest courses in the UK.

Torrance: 18 holes, 7037yds, Par 72, SSS 74.
Devlin: 18 holes, 7049yds, Par 72, SSS 74.

Visitors must book in advance. **Societies** telephone or e-mail in advance. **Green Fees** Phone. **Prof** John Kerr **Course Designer** Sam Torrance/Gene Sarazen **Facilities** **Leisure** heated indoor swimming pool, sauna, solarium, gymnasium. **Conf** facs Corporate Hospitality Days

Hotel ★★★★★ 71% St Andrews Bay Golf Resort & Spa, St Andrews ☎ 01334 837000 209 en suite 8 annexe en suite

Championship Course

St Andrews Links

Fife

St Andrews | Map 12 NO51

Golf was first played here around 1400 and the Old Course is acknowledged worldwide as the home of golf. The Old Course has played host to the greatest golfers in the world and many of golf's most dramatic moments. The New Course (6604yds) was opened in 1895, having been laid out by Old Tom Morris. The Jubilee was opened in 1897, and is 6805yds long from the medal tees. A shorter version of the Jubilee Course is also available, known as the Bronze Course, measuring 5674yds. There is no handicap limit for the shorter course and it is best for lower and middle-handicap golfers. The Eden opened in 1914 and is recommended for middle to high handicap golfers. The Strathtyrum has a shorter, less testing layout, best for high handicap golfers. The nine-hole Balgrove Course, upgraded and re-opened in 1993, is best for beginners and children. The facilities and courses here make this the largest golf complex in Europe.

Pilmour House KY16 9SF
☎ 01334 466666 🖹 01334 479555
e-mail: linkstrust@standrews.org.uk
web: www.standrews.org.uk

Old Course: 18 holes, 6609yds, Par 72, SSS 72, Course record 62.
New Course: 18 holes, 6604yds, Par 71, SSS 73.
Jubilee Course: 18 holes, 6742yds, Par 72, SSS 73, Course record 63.
Eden Course: 18 holes, 6112yds, Par 70, SSS 70.
Strathtyrum Course: 18 holes, 5094yds, Par 69, SSS 69.
Balgove Course: 9 holes, 1530yds, Par 30, SSS 30.

Visitors Old Course: contact course for booking details. Handicap certificate required. Other courses: 1 month advance booking required New/ Jubilee/Eden/Strath. **Societies** Booking required. **Green Fees** Old £59-£120 according to season. New £28-£57. Jubilee £28-£57. Eden £17-£34. Strathtyrum £11-£23. Balgrove £7-£10. **Prof** Steve North **Facilities** **Conf** Corporate Hospitality Days **Location** Off A91

Saline Map 11 NT09

Saline Kinneddar Hill KY12 9LT
☎ 01383 852591 🖹 01383 853517
e-mail: saline-golf-club@supanet.com
web: www.saline-golf-club.co.uk
Hillside parkland course with excellent turf and panoramic view of the Forth Valley.
9 holes, 5302yds, Par 68, SSS 66, Course record 62.
Club membership 330.
Visitors Mon-Fri & BHs. Booking required. Dress code. **Societies** Booking required. **Green Fees** £11 per day (£14 weekends). **Facilities** **Location** M90 junct 4, 0.5m E at junct B913

Tayport Map 12 NO42

Scotscraig Golf Rd DD6 9DZ
☎ 01382 552515 🖹 01382 553130
e-mail: scotscraig@scottishgolf.com
web: www.scotscraiggolfclub.com
Combined with heather and rolling fairways, the course is part heathland, part links, with the greens being renowned for being fast and true.
18 holes, 6550yds, Par 71, SSS 72, Course record 62.
Club membership 900.
Visitors Mon-Sun & BHs. Booking required. Dress code. **Societies** Booking required. **Green Fees** £60 per day, £45 per round (weekends £60/£50). **Prof** John Kelly **Course Designer** James Braid **Facilities** **Conf** Corporate Hospitality Days **Location** S side of village off B945

Hotel ★★★ 64% Sandford Country House Hotel, Newton Hill, Wormit, DUNDEE ☎ 01382 541802 16 en suite

Thornton Map 11 NT29

Thornton Station Rd KY1 4DW
☎ 01592 771111 🖹 01592 774955
e-mail: thorntongolf@btconnect.com
web: www.thorntongolfclubfife.co.uk
A relatively flat, lightly tree-lined parkland course, bounded on three sides by a river that comes into play at holes 14 to 16.
18 holes, 6170yds, Par 70, SSS 69, Course record 61.
Club membership 700.
Visitors Mon-Sun & BHs. Booking required. Dress code. **Societies** Booking required. **Green Fees** £35 per day, £25 per round (£50/£35 Fri-Sun). **Facilities** **Location** 1m E of town off A92

Hotel ★★★★ Balbirnie House, Balbirnie Park, MARKINCH ☎ 01592 610066 30 en suite

HIGHLAND

Alness Map 14 NH66

Alness Ardross Rd IV17 0QA
☎ 01349 883877
e-mail: info@alness-golfclub.co.uk
web: www.alness-golfclub.co.uk
A testing, parkland course with beautiful views over the Cromarty Firth and the Black Isle. It is located on the north west edge of the village of Alness and four holes run parallel to the gorge of the River Averon. Golfers of all abilities will find the course interesting and challenging. A particular test of skill is required at the 14th hole where the tee is located far above the green which lies beside the gorge at a distance of 406yds.
18 holes, 4886yds, Par 67, SSS 64, Course record 62.
Club membership 350.
Visitors Mon-Sun & BHs. **Societies** welcome. **Green Fees** £23 (£28 weekends). **Prof** Gary Lister **Facilities** **Leisure** fishing. **Conf** facs Corporate Hospitality Days **Location** 0.5m N off A9

Arisaig Map 13 NM68

Traigh Traigh PH39 4NT
☎ 01687 450337 🖹 01678 450293
web: www.traighgolf.co.uk
According to at least one newspaper Traigh is 'probably the most beautifully sited nine-hole golf course in the world'. True or not, Traigh lies alongside sandy beaches with views to Skye and the Inner Hebrides. The feature of the course is a line of grassy hills, originally sand dunes, that rise to some 60ft, and provide a challenge to the keenest golfer.
9 holes, 2456yds, Par 68, SSS 65, Course record 67.
Club membership 150.
Visitors Mon-Sun & BHs (Apr-Oct). **Societies** Booking required. **Green Fees** £16 per day. **Course Designer** John Salvesen 1994 **Facilities** **Location** A830 to Arisaig, signed onto B8008, 2m N of Arisaig

Aviemore Map 14 NH81

Spey Valley Aviemore Highland Resort PH22 1PJ
☎ 01479 815100 🖹 01479 812128
e-mail: fraser.cromarty@macdonald-hotels.co.uk
web: www.speyvalleygolf.com
Opened in Spring 2006 with a total length of 7200 yards and featuring one of the longest par 5 holes in the country, Creag Eabraich, which measures 641 yards from the championship tee. Situated beneath the Cairngorm Mountains with breathtaking views.
18 holes, 7153yds, Par 72.
Club membership 300.
Visitors Mon-Sun & BHs. Booking required. Handicap certificate. Dress code. **Societies** Booking required. **Green Fees** Phone. **Facilities** **Conf** facs Corporate Hospitality Days **Location** leave A9 signposted Aviemore on B970. Follow road to village then turn off for Dalfaber and follow signs for golf course.

Guest House ♦♦♦♦ Ravenscraig Guest House, Grampian Rd, AVIEMORE ☎ 01479 810278 6 en suite 6 annexe en suite

Boat Of Garten Map 14 NH91

Boat of Garten PH24 3BQ
☎ 01479 831282 🖹 01479 831523
e-mail: boatgolf@enterprise.net
web: www.boatgolf.com
This heathland course was cut out from a silver birch forest though the fairways are adequately wide. There are natural hazards of broom and heather, good views and walking is easy. A round provides great variety.
18 holes, 5876yds, Par 70, SSS 69, Course record 67.
Club membership 650.
Visitors Mon-Sun & BHs. Booking required. Handicap certificate. Dress code. **Societies** Booking required. **Green**

Continued

Fees £41 per day, £31 per round (£46/£36 weekends). **Course Designer** James Braid **Facilities** ⊗)|| 🍽 ☕ 🍸 👔 🏠 ⛳ 🚗 🏌 ✈ **Leisure** hard tennis courts. **Conf** Corporate Hospitality Days **Location** E side of village

Boat of Garten

Hotel ★★★ 76% Boat Hotel, BOAT OF GARTEN ☎ 01479 831258 & 831696 📠 01479 831414 22 en suite

BONAR BRIDGE Map 14 NH69

Bonar Bridge-Ardgay Migdale Rd IV24 3EJ
☎ 01863 766750 (Sec) & 766199 (Clubhouse)
e-mail: bonarardgaygolf@aol.com

Wooded moorland course with picturesque views of hills and loch.

9 holes, 5162yds, Par 68, SSS 65.
Club membership 250.

Visitors Mon-Sun & BHs **Societies** Booking required. **Green Fees** £15 per day. **Course Designer** Various **Facilities** ⊗ 🍽 ☕ 👔 ⛳ ✈ **Location** 0.5m E

Guest House ♦♦♦ Kyle House, Dornoch Rd, BONAR BRIDGE ☎ 01863 766360 6 rms (3 en suite)

BRORA Map 14 NC90

Brora Golf Rd KW9 6QS
☎ 01408 621417 📠 01408 622157
e-mail: secretary@broragolf.co.uk
web: www.broragolf.co.uk

Typical seaside links with little rough and fine views. Some testing holes including the 17th Tarbatness, so called because of the lighthouse which gives the line; the elevated tee is one of the best driving holes in Scotland.

18 holes, 6110yds, Par 69, SSS 70, Course record 61.
Club membership 704.

Visitors advisable to book in advance May-Oct. **Societies** advisable to book in advance. **Green Fees** Phone. **Course Designer** James Braid **Facilities** ⊗)|| 🍽 ☕ 🍸 👔 🏠 ⛳ 🚗 🏌 ✈ **Location** E side of village, signs to Beach Car Park

CARRBRIDGE Map 14 NH92

Carrbridge Inverness Rd PH23 3AU
☎ 0844 414 1415
e-mail: katie@carrbridgegolf.co.uk
web: www.carrbridgegolf.com

Challenging part-parkland, part-moorland course with magnificent views of the Cairngorms.

9 holes, 5402yds, Par 71, SSS 68, Course record 63.
Club membership 550.

Visitors Mon-Sun & BHs. Booking required. Dress code. **Societies** Booking required. **Green Fees** Phone. **Facilities** ⊗)|| by arrangement 🍽 ☕ 👔 🏠 ⛳ ✈ **Location** N side of village

Continued

Hotel ★★★ 69% Dalrachney Lodge Hotel, CARRBRIDGE ☎ 01479 841252 11 en suite

DORNOCH Map 14 NH78

Royal Dornoch Golf Rd IV25 3LW
☎ 01862 810219 ext.185 📠 01862 810792
e-mail: bookings@royaldornoch.com
web: www.royaldornoch.com

The championship course was recently rated 15th among the world's top courses and is a links of rare subtlety. It appears amicable but proves very challenging in play with stiff breezes and tight lies. The 18-hole Struie links course provides, in a gentler style, an enjoyable test of a golfer's accuracy for players of all abilities.

Continued

Championship: 18 holes, 6514yds, Par 70, SSS 73.
Struie Course: 18 holes, 6276yds, Par 72, SSS 70.
Club membership 1700.
Visitors Mon-Sun & BHs. Booking required. Handicap certificate. **Societies** Booking required. **Green Fees** Championship £75 per round (£85 weekends). Struie £45 per day, £35 per round. **Prof** A Skinner **Course Designer** Tom Morris **Facilities** **Leisure** hard tennis courts. **Conf** Corporate Hospitality Days **Location** E side of town
See advertisement on previous page

Durness — Map 14 NC46

Durness Balnakeil IV27 4PG
☎ 01971 511364 📠 01971 511321
e-mail: lucy@durnessgolfclub.org
web: www.durnessgolfclub.org
A nine-hole course set in tremendous scenery overlooking Balnakeil Bay. Part links and part inland with water hazards. Off alternative tees for second nine holes giving surprising variety. Tremendous last hole played over a deep gully to the green over 100yds away.
9 holes, 5555yds, Par 70, SSS 67, Course record 69.
Club membership 150.
Visitors Mon-Sun & BHs **Societies** Booking required. **Green Fees** £15 per day, £10 after 5pm. **Course Designer** F Keith **Facilities** **Leisure** fishing. **Conf** Corporate Hospitality Days **Location** 1m W of village overlooking Balnakeil Bay

Guest House ♦♦♦♦ Port-Na-Con House, Loch Eriboll, LAIRG ☎ 01971 511367 3 rms (1 en suite)

Fort Augustus — Map 14 NH30

Fort Augustus Markethill PH32 4DP
☎ 01320 366660 & 366758
web: www.fagc.com
Moorland course, with narrow fairways and good views. Bordered by the tree-lined Caledonian Canal to the north and heather clad hills to the south.
9 holes, 5379yds, Par 67, SSS 67, Course record 67.
Club membership 170.
Visitors contact club for details. **Societies** welcome. **Green Fees** £15 per day, £12 per round. **Course Designer** Colt **Facilities** **Location** 1m SW on A82

Fortrose — Map 14 NH75

Fortrose & Rosemarkie Ness Rd East IV10 8SE
☎ 01381 620529 📠 01381 621328
e-mail: secretary@fortrosegolfclub.co.uk
web: www.fortrosegolfclub.co.uk

18 holes, 5883yds, Par 71, SSS 69, Course record 63.

Continued

Course Designer James Braid **Location** A9 N over Kessock Bridge, signs to Munlochy
Telephone for further details

Hotel ★★★★ 69% Inverness Marriott Hotel, Culcabock Rd, INVERNESS ☎ 01463 237166 76 en suite 6 annexe en suite

Fort William — Map 14 NN17

Fort William Torlundy PH33 6SN
☎ 01397 704464
web: www.fortwilliamgolf.co.uk
Spectacular moorland location looking onto the north face of Ben Nevis.
18 holes, 6217yds, Par 72, SSS 71, Course record 67.
Club membership 420.
Visitors Mon-Sun & BHs. Booking required. Dress code. **Societies** Booking required. **Green Fees** £25 per round. **Course Designer** Hamilton Stutt **Facilities** **Location** 3m NE on A82

Hotel ★★★ 75% Moorings Hotel, Banavie, FORT WILLIAM ☎ 01397 772797 28 en suite

Gairloch — Map 14 NG87

Gairloch IV21 2BE
☎ 01445 712407 📠 01445 712865
e-mail: secretary@gairlochgc.freeserve.co.uk
web: www.gairlochgolfclub.co.uk
Fine seaside links course running along Gairloch Sands with good views over the sea to Skye. In windy conditions each hole is affected. Founded in 1898, the course, although short is challenging for all golfers.
9 holes, 4108yds, Par 62, SSS 62, Course record 64.
Club membership 275.
Visitors Mon-Sun & BHs. Booking required. Dress code. **Societies** Booking required. **Green Fees** Phone. **Course Designer** Capt Burgess **Facilities** **Conf** Corporate Hospitality Days **Location** 1m S on A832

Golspie — Map 14 NH89

Golspie Ferry Rd KW10 6ST
☎ 01408 633266 📠 01408 633393
e-mail: info@golspie-golf-club.co.uk
web: www-golspie-golf-club.co.uk
Founded in 1889 and redesigned in 1926 by James Braid, Golspie's seaside course offers easy walking and natural hazards including beach heather and whins. Spectacular scenery.
18 holes, 5980yds, Par 68, SSS 68, Course record 64.
Club membership 300.
Visitors Mon-Sun & BHs. Booking required. **Societies** Booking required. **Green Fees** £40 per day, £25 per round. **Course Designer** James Braid **Facilities** **Location** 0.5m S off A9

Grantown-on-Spey — Map 14 NJ02

Craggan Craggan PH26 3NT
☎ 01479 873283 📠 01479 872325
e-mail: fhglaing@btopenworld.com
web: www.cragganforleisure.co.uk
A golf course in miniature set in stunning scenery on the edge of the Cairngorms National Park.
18 holes, 2400yds, Par 54, SSS 54, Course record 52.
Club membership 400.

Continued

Visitors Mon-Sun & BHs. **Societies** welcome. **Green Fees** £17.50 per day, £12.50 per round. **Course Designer** Bill Mitchel **Facilities** ⊗ ⛳ ☕ 🍸 🏠 ⛳ ✓ **Leisure** fishing, biking. **Location** off A95, 1m S of Grantown-on-Spey

Hotel ★★ 79% Culdearn House, Woodlands Ter, GRANTOWN ON SPEY ☎ 01479 872106 7 en suite

Grantown-on-Spey Golf Course Rd PH26 3HY
☎ 01479 872079 📠 01479 873725
e-mail: secretary@grantownonspeygolfclub.co.uk
web: www.grantownonspeygolfclub.co.uk
Parkland and woodland course. Part easy walking, remainder hilly. The 7th to 13th holes really sort out the golfers.

18 holes, 5710yds, Par 70, SSS 68, Course record 60. Club membership 800.
Visitors advisable to contact in advance. No visitors before 10am weekends. **Societies** Apply in advance to secretary. **Green Fees** Phone. **Course Designer** A Brown/W Park/J Braid **Facilities** ⊗ 🍴 by arrangement ⛳ ☕ 🍸 ⛳ 🏠 ⛳ ⛳ ⛳ ✓ **Location** NE side of town centre

Hotel ★★ 79% Culdearn House, Woodlands Ter, GRANTOWN ON SPEY ☎ 01479 872106 7 en suite

HELMSDALE Map 14 ND01

Helmsdale Golf Rd KW8 6JA
☎ 01431 821063
9 holes, 1860yds, Par 62, SSS 61.
Location NW side of town on A896
Telephone for further details

INVERGORDON Map 14 NH76

Invergordon King George St IV18 0BD
☎ 01349 852715 📠 01349 852715
e-mail: invergordongolf@tiscali.co.uk
web: www.invergordongolf.co.uk
Fairly easy but windy 18-hole parkland course, with woodland, wide fairways and good views over Cromarty Firth. Very good greens and a fair challenge, especially if the wind is from the west. Four par 3s and one par 5.
18 holes, 6030yds, Par 69, SSS 69, Course record 63. Club membership 240.
Visitors Mon-Sun & BHs. Booking required Tue, Thu, Sat-Sun. **Societies** Booking required. **Green Fees** £25 per day, £20 per round. **Course Designer** A Rae **Facilities** ⊗ ⛳ ☕ 🍸 ⛳ ⛳ ✓ **Location** W side of town centre on B817

INVERNESS Map 14 NH64

Inverness Culcabock IV2 3XQ
☎ 01463 239882 📠 01463 240616
e-mail: igc@freeuk.com
web: www.invernessgolfclub.co.uk
Fairly flat parkland. A burn runs through and alongside several of the holes, and also acts as a lateral water hazard and out of bounds elsewhere. Considered short by modern day standards, it is an excellent test of golf rewarding straight drives and accurate iron play to well-manicured greens.

18 holes, 6256yds, Par 69, SSS 70, Course record 64. Club membership 1182.
Visitors Mon-Fri, Sun & BHs. Booking required. Handicap certificate. Dress code. **Societies** Booking required. **Green Fees** £48 per day, £35 per round. **Prof** Alistair P Thomson **Course Designer** J Fraser/G Smith **Facilities** ⊗ 🍴 ⛳ ☕ 🍸 ⛳ 🏠 ⛳ ✓ **Conf** Corporate Hospitality Days **Location** 1m E of town centre on Culcabock Rd

Hotel ★★★★ 69% Inverness Marriott Hotel, Culcabock Rd, INVERNESS ☎ 01463 237166 76 en suite 6 annexe en suite

Loch Ness Fairways, Castle Heather IV2 6AA
☎ 01463 713335 📠 01463 712695
e-mail: info@golflochness.com
web: www.golflochness.com
Course with two 18 hole options and a 9 hole family course with seven par 3's and two par 4's and small undulating greens and deep bunkers to test short game skills. The New and Old courses combine several holes giving a great variety from the 550 yard 2nd hole to the 76 yard hole called Chance which is played over a deep gully.

Loch Ness Golf Course (Old): 18 holes, 6772yds, Par 73, SSS 72, Course record 67.
New Course: 18 holes, 5907yds, Par 70, SSS 69, Course record 68.

Continued

Wee Course: 9 holes, 1442yds, Par 29.
Club membership 500.
Visitors Mon-Sun & BHs. Dress code. **Societies** Booking required. **Green Fees** £40-£50 per day, £25-£35 per round. Wee course £10. **Prof** Martin Piggot **Course Designer** Caddies **Facilities** **Leisure** indoor bowls, petanque. **Conf** facs Corporate Hospitality Days **Location** SW outskirts of Inverness, along bypass

Hotel ★★★ 63% Loch Ness House Hotel, Glenurquhart Rd, INVERNESS ☎ 01463 231248 21 en suite

Torvean Glenurquhart Rd IV3 8JN
☎ 01463 711434 (Starter) & 225651 (Office)
01463 711417
e-mail: info@torveangolfclub.com
web: www.torveangolfclub.co.uk
Public parkland course, easy walking, good views. One of the longest par 5s in the north at 565yds. Three ponds come into play at the 8th, 15th and 17th holes.
18 holes, 5754yds, Par 69, SSS 68, Course record 64.
Club membership 950.
Visitors Mon-Sun & BHs. Booking required Sat & Sun. Dress code. **Societies** Booking required. **Green Fees** £24 per 18 holes (£26.50 weekends). **Course Designer** Hamilton **Facilities** **Conf** Corporate Hospitality Days **Location** 1.5m SW on A82

Hotel ★★★ 63% Loch Ness House Hotel, Glenurquhart Rd, INVERNESS ☎ 01463 231248 21 en suite

KINGUSSIE Map 14 NH70

Kingussie Gynack Rd PH21 1LR
☎ 01540 661600 01540 662066
e-mail: sec@kingussie-golf.co.uk
web: www.kingussie-golf.co.uk
Upland course with natural hazards and magnificent views. Stands about 1000ft above sea level at its highest point, and the River Gynack, which runs through the course, comes into play on five holes. Golf has been played here for over 100years and some tight fairways and deceptive par threes make the course a challenge for all golfers.
18 holes, 5500yds, Par 67, SSS 68, Course record 61.
Club membership 650.
Visitors Mon-Sun & BHs. Booking required. **Societies** Booking required. **Green Fees** £23 per round/£30 per day (weekends £26/£32). **Course Designer** Vardon **Facilities** **Location** 0.25m N off A86

The Cross at Kingussie, Tweed Mill Brae, Ardbroilach Rd, KINGUSSIE ☎ 01540 661166 8 en suite

LOCHCARRON Map 14 NG83

Lochcarron IV54 8YS
☎ 01599 577219
e-mail: mail@lochcarrongolf.co.uk
web: www.lochcarrongolf.co.uk
Seaside links course with some parkland with an interesting 1st hole. A short course but great accuracy is required.
9 holes, 3575yds, Par 60, SSS 60, Course record 58.
Club membership 130.
Visitors Mon-Sun & BHs. **Societies** Booking required. **Green Fees** £14 per day/ £55 per week. **Facilities** **Location** 1m E of Lochcarron by A896

LYBSTER Map 15 ND23

Lybster Main St KW3 6AE
☎ 01593 721486 & 721316
web: www.lybstergolfclub.co.uk
Picturesque, short heathland course, easy walking.
9 holes, 1896yds, Par 62, SSS 61, Course record 57.
Club membership 140.
Visitors no restrictions. **Societies** Booking required. **Green Fees** Phone. **Facilities** **Location** E side of village

Hotel ★★ 72% Mackay's Hotel, Union St, WICK ☎ 01955 602323 27 rms (19 en suite)

MUIR OF ORD Map 14 NH55

Muir of Ord Great North Rd IV6 7SX
☎ 01463 870825 01463 871867
e-mail: muirgolf@supanet.com-email
web: www.golfhighland.co.uk
Long-established (1875) heathland course with tight fairways and easy walking. Testing par 3 13th, Castle Hill.
18 holes, 5596yds, Par 68, SSS 68, Course record 61.
Club membership 750.
Visitors contact club for details. **Societies** Booking required Sat & Sun. **Green Fees** £18 per round/£22 per day (weekends £25/£30). **Course Designer** James Braid **Facilities** by arrangement by arrangement by arrangement **Conf** Corporate Hospitality Days **Location** S side of village on A862

Hotel ★★★ 72% Priory Hotel, The Square, BEAULY ☎ 01463 782309 34 en suite

NAIRN Map 14 NH85

Nairn Seabank Rd IV12 4HB
☎ 01667 453208 01667 456328
e-mail: secretary@nairngolfclub.co.uk
web: www.nairngolfclub.co.uk
18 holes, 6430yds, Par 71, SSS 73, Course record 64.
Newton: 9 holes, 3542yds, Par 58, SSS 57.
Course Designer A Simpson/Old Tom Morris/James Braid
Location 16m E of Inverness on A96
Telephone for further details

Nairn Dunbar Lochloy Rd IV12 5AE
☎ 01667 452741 01667 456897
e-mail: secretary@nairndunbar.com
web: www.nairndunbar.com
Links course with sea views and testing gorse and whin-lined fairways. Testing hole: Long Peter (527yds).
18 holes, 6765yds, Par 72, SSS 74, Course record 64.
Club membership 1200.
Visitors Booking required. **Societies** Booking required. **Green Fees** Phone. **Prof** David Torrance **Facilities** **Conf** facs Corporate Hospitality Days **Location** E side of town off A96

Hotel ★★ 58% Alton Burn Hotel, Alton Burn Rd, NAIRN ☎ 01667 452051 & 453325 01667 456697 23 en suite

NETHY BRIDGE Map 14 NJ02

Abernethy PH25 3EB

☎ 01479 821305 🖹 01479 821305
e-mail: info@abernethygolfclub.com
web: www.abernethygolfclub.com

Traditional Highland course built on moorland surrounded by pine trees and offering a great variety of shot making for the low handicapped or casual visitor. The 2nd hole, although very short is played across bogland and a B road to a two-tiered green. The small and fast greens are the most undulating and tricky in the valley. The Abernethy forest lies on the boundary and from many parts of the course there are splendid views of Strathspey.

9 holes, 2551yds, Par 66, SSS 66.
Club membership 400.

Visitors Mon-Sun & BHs. **Societies** welcome. **Green Fees** Weekdays £17, weekends £19. **Facilities** **Location** N side of village on B970

Hotel ★★★ 71% Muckrach Lodge Hotel, Dulnain Bridge, GRANTOWN-ON-SPEY ☎ 01479 851257 10 en suite 4 annexe en suite

NEWTONMORE Map 14 NN79

Newtonmore Golf Course Rd PH20 1AT

☎ 01540 673878 🖹 01540 670147
e-mail: secretary@newtonmoregolf.com
web: www.newtonmoregolf.com

18 holes, 6031yds, Par 70, SSS 69, Course record 64.

Location E side of town off A9
Telephone for further details

Hotel ★★ 68% The Scot House Hotel, Newtonmore Rd, KINGUSSIE ☎ 01540 661351 9 en suite

REAY Map 14 NC96

Reay KW14 7RE

☎ 01847 811288 🖹 01847 894189
e-mail: info@reaygolfclub.co.uk
web: www.reaygolfclub.co.uk

Picturesque seaside links with natural hazards, following the contours of Sandside Bay. Most northerly 18-hole links on the British mainland. The 581yd par 5 4th hole Sahara requires a solid tee shot and fairway wood to set up an approach to a sheltered green protected by a burn. The 196yd par 3 7th Pilkington is a beautiful short hole played across Reay burn to a raised green. The two-tiered 18th protected by its greenside bunkers provides a formidable finishing hole. Unique feature in that it opens and closes with a par 3 and the sea is visible from every hole. An excellent natural seaside links.

18 holes, 5831yds, Par 69, SSS 69, Course record 64.
Club membership 250.

Visitors Mon-Sun & BHs. **Societies** Booking required. **Green Fees** £20 per day/round. **Course Designer** Braid **Facilities** by arrangement by arrangement by arrangement **Leisure** see web site. **Conf** Corporate Hospitality Days **Location** 11m W of Thurso on A836

STRATHPEFFER Map 14 NH45

Strathpeffer Spa IV14 9AS

☎ 01997 421219 & 421011 🖹 01997 421011
e-mail: mail@strathpeffergolf.co.uk
web: www.strathpeffergolf.co.uk

Beautiful, testing upland course in this historic village. Many natural hazards mean only three sand bunkers on the course and the course's claim to fame is the 1st hole which features the longest drop from tee to green in Scotland. Stunning views.

18 holes, 4792yds, Par 65, SSS 64, Course record 60.
Club membership 400.

Visitors Mon-Sun & BHs. Booking required. Dress code. **Societies** Booking required. **Green Fees** £25 per day, £20 per round per 18 holes. **Course Designer** Willie Park/Tom Morris **Facilities** **Location** 0.25m N of village off A834, signed

Hotel ★★★ 67% Achilty Hotel, CONTIN ☎ 01997 421355 9 en suite 2 annexe en suite

TAIN Map 14 NH78

Tain Chapel Rd IV19 1JE

☎ 01862 892314 🖹 01862 892099
e-mail: info@tain-golfclub.co.uk
web: www.tain-golfclub.co.uk

Links course with river affecting three holes; easy walking, fine views.

18 holes, 6404yds, Par 70, SSS 71, Course record 68.
Club membership 600.

Visitors Mon-Sun & BHs. Contact club for details. **Societies** Booking required. **Green Fees** £45 per day, £40 per round (£55/£45 weekends). **Course Designer** Old Tom Morris **Facilities** **Leisure** Practice net. **Conf** Corporate Hospitality Days **Location** E side of town centre off B9174

If the name of the club appears in italics, details have not been confirmed for this edition of the guide

THURSO Map 15 ND16

Thurso Newlands of Geise KW14 7XD
☎ 01847 893807
web: europgolf.com
Parkland course, windy, but with fine views of Dunnet Head and the Orkney Islands. Tree-lined fairways but 4th and 16th holes are testing into the prevailing wind. The 13th is a short par 4 but has a testing drive over a burn with heather on left and punishing rough on right.

18 holes, 5853yds, Par 69, SSS 69, Course record 63. Club membership 320.
Visitors contact club for details. **Societies** Booking required. **Green Fees** £20 per day. **Course Designer** W S Stewart **Facilities** **Location** 2m SW of Thurso on B874

ULLAPOOL Map 14 NH19

Ullapool The Clubhouse, North Rd, Morefield IV26 2TH
☎ 01854 613323
web: www.ullapool-golf.co.uk
Seaside/parkland course with fine views.
9 holes, 5281yds, Par 70, SSS 67, Course record 68. Club membership 210.
Visitors Mon-Fri & BHs. **Societies** Booking required. **Green Fees** £18 per day, £15 per 9 holes. **Facilities** **Conf** Corporate Hospitality Days

WICK Map 15 ND35

Wick Reiss KW1 4RW
☎ 01955 602726
e-mail: wickgolfclub@hotmail.com
web: www.wickgolfclub.fsnet.co.uk/
Typical seaside links course, fairly flat, easy walking. Nine holes straight out and straight back. Normally breezy.
18 holes, 6123yds, Par 69, SSS 71, Course record 63. Club membership 352.
Visitors Mon-Sun & BHs. **Societies** welcome. **Green Fees** £25 per day. **Course Designer** James Braid **Facilities** **Conf** Corporate Hospitality Days **Location** 3.5m N off A9

Hotel ★★ 72% Mackay's Hotel, Union St, WICK
☎ 01955 602323 27 rms (19 en suite)

INVERCLYDE

GOUROCK Map 10 NS27

Gourock Cowal View PA19 1HD
☎ 01475 631001 & 636834 (pro) 🖹 01475 638307
e-mail: adt@gourockgolfclub.freeserve.co.uk
18 holes, 6408yds, Par 73, SSS 72, Course record 64.
Course Designer J Braid/H Cotton **Location** SW side of town off A770
Telephone for further details

Hotel Premier Travel Inn Greenock, 1-3 James Watt Way, GREENOCK ☎ 08701 977120 40 en suite

GREENOCK Map 10 NS27

Greenock Forsyth St PA16 8RE
☎ 01475 720793 🖹 01475 791912
Testing moorland course with panoramic views of Clyde Estuary.
18 holes, 5838yds, Par 69, SSS 69. Club membership 700.
Visitors Mon-Sun & BHs. Booking required. Handicap certificate. Dress code. **Societies** Booking required. **Green Fees** Phone. **Course Designer** James Braid **Facilities** **Location** SW side of town off A770

Hotel Premier Travel Inn Greenock, 1-3 James Watt Way, GREENOCK ☎ 08701 977120 40 en suite

Greenock Whinhill Beith Rd PA16 9LN
☎ 01475 724694 evenings & weekends only
Picturesque heathland public course.
18 holes, 5504yds, Par 68, SSS 68, Course record 64. Club membership 200.
Visitors Contact club for details. **Green Fees** Phone. **Course Designer** William Fernie **Facilities** **Location** 1.5m SW off B7054

KILMACOLM Map 10 NS36

Kilmacolm Porterfield Rd PA13 4PD
☎ 01505 872139 🖹 01505 874007
e-mail: secretary@kilmacolmgolf.com
web: www.kilmacolmgolf.sagehost.co.uk
Moorland course, easy walking, fine views. Testing 7th, 13th and 14th holes.
18 holes, 5961yds, Par 69, SSS 69, Course record 64. Club membership 850.
Visitors must contact in advance, visitors welcome Monday-Friday **Societies** apply in writing. **Green Fees** Phone. **Prof** Iain Nicholson **Course Designer** Willie Campbell **Facilities** **Location** SE side of town off A761

Hotel Gleddoch House Hotel, LANGBANK
☎ 01475 540711 62 en suite

PORT GLASGOW Map 10 NS37

Port Glasgow Devol Rd PA14 5XE
☎ 01475 704181 & 791214 (Sec)
18 holes, 5712yds, Par 68, SSS 68.
Location 1m S
Telephone for further details

Hotel Gleddoch House Hotel, LANGBANK
☎ 01475 540711 62 en suite

MIDLOTHIAN

BONNYRIGG Map 11 NT36

Broomieknowe 36 Golf Course Rd EH19 2HZ
☎ 0131 663 9317 0131 663 2152
e-mail: administrator@broomieknowe.com
web: www.bromieknowe.com
Easy walking mature parkland course laid out by Ben Sayers and extended by James Braid. Elevated site with excellent views.
18 holes, 6150yds, Par 70, SSS 70, Course record 65.
Club membership 900.
Visitors Mon-Sun & BHs. Handicap certificate. Dress code. **Societies** Booking required. **Green Fees** Phone. **Prof** Mark Patchett **Course Designer** Ben Sayers/Hawtree **Facilities** **Conf** Corporate Hospitality Days **Location** 0.5m NE off B704

Hotel ★★★ 75% Dalhousie Castle and Aqueous Spa, Bonnyrigg, EDINBURGH ☎ 01875 820153 27 en suite 6 annexe en suite

DALKEITH Map 11 NT36

Newbattle Abbey Rd EH22 3AD
☎ 0131 663 2123 & 0131 663 1819 0131 654 1810
e-mail: mail@newbattlegolfclub.com
web: www.newbattlegolfclub.com
Gently undulating parkland course, dissected by the South Esk river and surrounded by woods.
18 holes, 6025yds, Par 69, SSS 69, Course record 61.
Club membership 700.
Visitors Mon-Fri. Dress code. **Societies** Booking required. **Green Fees** £35 per day, £25 per round. **Prof** Scott McDonald **Course Designer** S Colt **Facilities** **Conf** Corporate Hospitality Days **Location** SW side of town off A68

Hotel ★★★ 75% Dalhousie Castle and Aqueous Spa, Bonnyrigg, EDINBURGH ☎ 01875 820153 27 en suite 6 annexe en suite

GOREBRIDGE Map 11 NT36

Vogrie Vogrie Estate Country Park EH23 4NU
☎ 01875 821716 01875 823958
e-mail: ritchie.fraser@midlothian.gov.uk
web: www.midlothian.gov.uk
A 9-hole municipal course located within a country park. The wide fairways are particularly suited to beginners.
9 holes, 2530yds, Par 33.
Visitors Mon-Fri & BHs. Booking advised Sat, Sun & BHs. **Green Fees** not confirmed. **Facilities** **Location** Off B6372

LASSWADE Map 11 NT36

Kings Acre EH18 1AU
☎ 0131 663 3456 0131 663 7076
e-mail: info@kings-acregolf.com
web: www.kings-acregolf.com
Parkland course set in countryside location and making excellent use of the natural contours of the land with strategically placed water hazards and over 50 bunkers leading to large undulating greens. The naturally sandy based soil ensures excellent play all year.
18 holes, 6031yds, Par 70, SSS 68.
Club membership 300.
Visitors Mon-Sun & BHs. Dress code. **Societies** welcome. **Green Fees** £34 per day, £24 per 18 holes (£46/£32 weekends). **Prof** Alan Murdoch **Course Designer** Graeme Webster **Facilities** **Conf** facs Corporate Hospitality Days **Location** off A720, City of Edinburgh bypass road

Hotel ★★★ 71% Melville Castle Hotel, Melville Gate, Gilmerton Rd, EDINBURGH ☎ 0131 654 0088 32 en suite

PENICUIK Map 11 NT25

Glencorse Milton Bridge EH26 0RD
☎ 01968 677189 & 676481 01968 674399
e-mail: glencorsegc@btconnect.com
web: www.glencorsegolfclub.com
Picturesque parkland with a burn affecting 10 holes. Testing 5th hole (237yds) par 3.
18 holes, 5217yds, Par 64, SSS 66, Course record 60.
Club membership 700.
Visitors Mon-Fri, Sun pm & BHs. Booking required. Dress code. **Societies** Booking required. **Green Fees** £32 per day, £25 per round. **Prof** Cliffe Jones **Course Designer** Willie Park **Facilities** **Location** 9m S of Edinburgh on A701 Peebles Road

Inn ♦♦♦ Olde Original Rosslyn Inn, 4 Main St, ROSLIN ☎ 0131 440 2384 6 en suite

MORAY

BALLINDALLOCH Map 15 NJ12

Ballindalloch Castle Lagmore AB37 9AA
☎ 01807 500305 01807 500226
e-mail: golf@ballindallochcastle.co.uk
Course nestling among mature trees on the banks of the river Avon with fine views of the surrounding hills and woods.
9 holes, 6495yds, Par 72, SSS 71, Course record 64.
Visitors Mon-Sun & BHs. **Societies** welcome. **Green Fees** £20 per 18 holes, £15 per 9 holes. **Course Designer** Donald Steel **Facilities** **Conf** Corporate Hospitality Days **Location** off A95 13 NE of Grantown-on-Spey

BUCKIE Map 15 NJ46

Buckpool Barhill Rd, Buckpool AB56 1DU
☎ 01542 832236 01542 832236
e-mail: golf@buckpoolgolf.com
web: www.buckpoolgolf.com
Links course with superlative view over Moray Firth, easy walking.
18 holes, 6097yds, Par 70, SSS 69, Course record 63.
Club membership 430.
Visitors Apply in advance. **Societies** apply in advance. **Green Fees** Phone. **Course Designer** J H Taylor **Facilities** **Leisure** squash, snooker. **Location** Off A98

Hotel ★★★ 67% The Seafield Hotel, Seafield St, CULLEN ☎ 01542 840791 19 en suite

Continued

Strathlene Buckie Portessie AB56 2DJ
☎ 01542 831798 Fax 01542 831798
e-mail: strathgolf@ukonline.co.uk
web: www.strathlenegolfclub.co.uk
Raised seaside links course with magnificent view. A special feature of the course is approach shots to raised greens (holes 4, 5, 6 and 13).
18 holes, 5980yds, Par 69, SSS 69, Course record 65.
Visitors Mon-Sun & BHs. Dress code. **Societies** Booking required. **Green Fees** Weekdays £21 per day, £16 per round (weekends £27/£20). **Course Designer** George Smith **Facilities** **Conf** Corporate Hospitality Days **Location** 2m E of Buckie on A942

Hotel ★★★ 67% The Seafield Hotel, Seafield St, CULLEN ☎ 01542 840791 19 en suite

CULLEN Map 15 NJ56

Cullen The Links AB56 4WB
☎ 01542 840685
e-mail: cullengolfclub@btinternet.com
web: www.cullen-golf-club.co.uk
Interesting links on three levels with rocks and ravines offering some challenging holes. Spectacular scenery.
18 holes, 4610yds, Par 63, SSS 62, Course record 55.
Club membership 400.
Visitors Mon-Sun & BHs. Booking required. **Societies** Booking required. **Green Fees** Mon-Fri £17 per round. **Course Designer** Tom Morris/Charlie Neaves **Facilities** **Conf** Corporate Hospitality Days **Location** 0.5m W off A98

Hotel ★★★ 67% The Seafield Hotel, Seafield St, CULLEN ☎ 01542 840791 19 en suite

DUFFTOWN Map 15 NJ34

Dufftown Tomintoul Rd AB55 4BS
☎ 01340 820325 Fax 01340 820325
e-mail: admin_dufftowngolfclub@yahoo.com
web: www.dufftowngolfclub.com
A short and undulating inland course with spectacular views. The tee of the highest hole, the 9th, is over 1200ft above sea level.
18 holes, 5308yds, Par 67, SSS 67, Course record 64.
Club membership 350.
Visitors Mon-Sat & BHs. Booking required. **Societies** welcome. **Green Fees** £15 per round/£20 per day. **Course Designer** Members **Facilities** by arrangement by arrangement by arrangement by arrangement **Conf** facs Corporate Hospitality Days **Location** 0.75m SW off B9009

Hotel ★★★ 79% Craigellachie Hotel, CRAIGELLACHIE ☎ 01340 881204 25 en suite

ELGIN Map 15 NJ26

Elgin Hardhillock, Birnie Rd, New Elgin IV30 8SX
☎ 01343 542338 Fax 01343 542341
e-mail: secretary@elgingolfclub.com
web: www.elgingolfclub.com
Possibly the finest inland course in the north of Scotland, with undulating greens and compact holes that demand the highest accuracy. There are 13 par 4s and one par 5 hole on its parkland layout, eight of the par 4s being over 400yds long.

Continued

Hardhillock: 18 holes, 6416yds, Par 68, SSS 69, Course record 63.
Club membership 1000.
Visitors Mon-Sun & BHs. Booking required. Handicap certificate. Dress code. **Societies** Booking required. **Green Fees** £43 per day, £33 per round (weekends £45/£35). **Prof** Kevin Stables **Course Designer** John Macpherson **Facilities** **Conf** facs **Location** 1m S on A941

Hotel ★★★ 74% Mansion House Hotel, The Haugh, ELGIN ☎ 01343 548811 23 en suite

FORRES Map 14 NJ05

Forres Muiryshade IV36 2RD
☎ 01309 672250 Fax 01309 672250
e-mail: sandy@forresgolf.demon.co.uk
web: www.forresgolf.demon.co.uk
An all-year parkland course laid on light, well-drained soil in wooded countryside. Walking is easy despite some hilly holes. A test for the best golfers.
18 holes, 6240yds, Par 70, SSS 70, Course record 60.
Club membership 1000.
Visitors Mon-Sun & BHs. Booking advisable. Dress code. **Societies** Booking required. **Green Fees** £26 per round, £34 per day. **Prof** Sandy Aird **Course Designer** James Braid/Willie Park **Facilities** **Conf** Corporate Hospitality Days **Location** SE side of town centre off B9010

Hotel ★★★ 68% Ramnee Hotel, Victoria Rd, FORRES ☎ 01309 672410 20 en suite

GARMOUTH Map 15 NJ36

Garmouth & Kingston Spey St IV32 7NJ
☎ 01343 870388 Fax 01343 870388
e-mail: garmouthgolfclub@aol.com
Flat seaside course with several parkland holes and tidal waters. The 8th hole measures only 328yds from the medal tee but the fairway is bounded by a ditch on either side, the left hand one being out of bounds for the entire length of the hole. The par 5 17th Whinny Side has gorse bordering on both sides of the fairway which can be intimidating to any level of golfer.
18 holes, 5545yds, Par 69, SSS 67.
Club membership 500.
Visitors contact club for details. **Societies** Booking required. **Green Fees** £25 per day, £20 per round (£28/£25 weekends). **Course Designer** George Smith **Facilities** by arrangement by arrangement **Conf** Corporate Hospitality Days **Location** In village on B9015

Hotel ★★★ 74% Mansion House Hotel, The Haugh, ELGIN ☎ 01343 548811 23 en suite

HOPEMAN Map 15 NJ16

Hopeman Clubhouse IV30 5YA
☎ 01343 830578 Fax 01343 830152
e-mail: hopemangc@aol.com
web: www.hopeman-golf-club.co.uk
Links-type course with beautiful views over the Moray Firth. The 12th hole, called the Priescach, is a short hole with a drop of 100ft from tee to green. It can require anything from a wedge to a wood depending on the wind.

Continued

18 holes, 5624yds, Par 68, SSS 67.
Club membership 700.
Visitors Booking required. **Societies** contact in advance. **Green Fees** Phone. **Facilities** **Location** E side of village off B9040

Hotel ★★★ 74% Mansion House Hotel, The Haugh, ELGIN ☎ 01343 548811 23 en suite

KEITH Map 15 NJ45

Keith Fife Park AB55 5DF
☎ 01542 882469 🖷 01542 888176
e-mail: secretary@keithgolfclub.org.uk
web: www.keithgolfclub.org.uk
Parkland course, with natural hazards over first 9 holes. Testing 7th hole, 232 yds, par 3.
18 holes, 5767yds, Par 69, SSS 68, Course record 65.
Club membership 500.
Visitors Mon-Sun & BHs. **Societies** Booking required. **Green Fees** £15 per day, £12 per round (£20/£15 weekends). **Course Designer** Roy Phimister **Facilities** **Location** NW of town centre, A96 onto B9014 right

Hotel ★★★ 79% Craigellachie Hotel, CRAIGELLACHIE ☎ 01340 881204 25 en suite

LOSSIEMOUTH Map 15 NJ27

Moray Stotfield Rd IV31 6QS
☎ 01343 812018 🖷 01343 815102
e-mail: secretary@moraygolf.co.uk
web: www.moraygolf.co.uk
Two fine Scottish Championship links courses, known as Old and New (Moray), and situated on the Moray Firth where the weather is unusually mild.
Old Course: 18 holes, 6643yds, Par 71, SSS 73, Course record 65.
New Course: 18 holes, 6004yds, Par 69, SSS 69, Course record 62.
Club membership 1550.
Visitors Mon-Sun & BHs. Handicap certificate. Dress code. **Societies** Booking required. **Green Fees** Phone. **Prof** Alistair Thomson **Course Designer** Tom Morris & Henry Cotton **Facilities** **Conf** Corporate Hospitality Days **Location** N side of town

Hotel ★★★ 74% Mansion House Hotel, The Haugh, ELGIN ☎ 01343 548811 23 en suite

ROTHES Map 15 NJ24

Rothes Blackhall AB38 7AN
☎ 01340 831443 (evenings) 🖷 01340 831443
e-mail: rothesgolfclub@netscapeonline.co.uk
9 holes, 4972yds, Par 68, SSS 64.
Course Designer John Souter **Location** SW of town centre
Telephone for further details

Hotel ★★★ 79% Craigellachie Hotel, CRAIGELLACHIE ☎ 01340 881204 25 en suite

SPEY BAY Map 15 NJ36

Spey Bay IV32 7PJ
☎ 01343 820424 🖷 01343 829282
e-mail: info@speybay.com
web: www.speybay.com
Picturesque, undulating links with a long beach on one side. The fairways are lined with swathes of gorse and heather while shingle and beach form a border at some holes. Each hole requires a good deal of thought from the tee and a deft touch around the greens.
18 holes, 6182yds, Par 70, SSS 70, Course record 65.
Club membership 350.
Visitors Booking required. **Societies** book by telephone. **Green Fees** Phone. **Course Designer** Ben Sayers **Facilities** **Conf** facs Corporate Hospitality Days **Location** 4.5m N of Fochabers on B9104

NORTH AYRSHIRE

BEITH Map 10 NS35

Beith Threepwood Rd KA15 2JR
☎ 01505 503166 & 506814 🖷 01505 506814
e-mail: beith_secretary@btconnect.com
web: www.beithgolfclub.co.uk
Hilly course, with panoramic views over seven counties.
18 holes, 5616yds, Par 68, SSS 68.
Club membership 487.
Visitors Mon-Sun & BHs. Booking required Sat, Sun & BHs. Handicap certificate. Dress code. **Societies** Booking required. **Green Fees** £20 per round/£28 per day (weekend £25 per round). **Course Designer** Members **Facilities** **Location** 1st left on Beith bypass, S on A737

Guest House ♦♦♦♦ Whin Park, 16 Douglas St, LARGS ☎ 01475 673437 5 en suite

GREAT CUMBRAE ISLAND (MILLPORT) Map 10 NS15

Millport Golf Rd KA28 OHB
☎ 01475 530305 (Prof) 🖷 01475 530306
e-mail: secretary@millportgolfclub.co.uk
web: www.millportgolfclub.co.uk
18 holes, 5828yds, Par 68, SSS 69, Course record 64.
Course Designer James Braid **Location** 4m from ferry slip
Telephone for further details

Hotel ★★ 69% Willowbank Hotel, 96 Greenock Rd, LARGS ☎ 01475 672311 & 675435 🖷 01475 689027 30 en suite

IRVINE Map 10 NS34

Glasgow Gailes KA11 5AE
☎ 0141 942 2011 🖷 0141 942 0770
e-mail: secretary@glasgow-golf.com
web: www.glasgowgailes-golf.com
A lovely seaside links. The turf of the fairways and all the greens is truly glorious and provides tireless play. Established in 1882, this is a qualifying course for the Open Championship.
18 holes, 6535yds, Par 71, SSS 72, Course record 63.
Club membership 1200.

Continued

Visitors Mon-Sun & BHs. Booking required. Contact club for details. **Societies** Booking required. **Green Fees** £75 per day, £60 per round (£65 per round weekends). **Prof** J Steven **Course Designer** W Park Jnr **Facilities** by arrangement **Conf** Corporate Hospitality Days **Location** Off A78 at Newhouse junct, S of Irvine

Hotel ★★★ 69% Montgreenan Mansion House Hotel, Montgreenan Estate, KILWINNING ☎ 01294 850005 21 en suite

Irvine Bogside KA12 8SN
☎ 01294 275979 01294 278209
e-mail: secretary@theirvinegolfclub.co.uk
web: www.theirvinegolfclub.co.uk
Testing links course; only two short holes.
18 holes, 6400yds, Par 71, SSS 73, Course record 65. Club membership 450.
Societies are welcome weekdays and pm weekends, telephone in advance. **Green Fees** Phone. **Prof** Jim McKinnon **Course Designer** James Braid **Facilities** **Location** N side of town off A737

Hotel ★★★ 69% Montgreenan Mansion House Hotel, Montgreenan Estate, KILWINNING ☎ 01294 850005 21 en suite

Irvine Ravenspark 13 Kidsneuk Ln KA12 8SR
☎ 01294 271293
e-mail: secretary@irgc.co.uk
web: www.irgc.co.uk
18 holes, 6457yds, Par 71, SSS 71, Course record 65.
Location N side of town on A737
Telephone for further details

Hotel ★★★ 69% Montgreenan Mansion House Hotel, Montgreenan Estate, KILWINNING ☎ 01294 850005 21 en suite

Western Gailes Gailes by Irvine KA11 5AE
☎ 01294 311649 01294 312312
e-mail: enquiries@westerngailes.com
web: www.westerngailes.com
A magnificent seaside links with glorious turf and wonderful greens. The view is open across the Firth of Clyde to the neighbouring islands. It is a well-balanced course crossed by three burns. There are two par 5s, the 6th and 14th, and the 11th is a testing 445yd par 4 dog-leg.
18 holes, 6639yds, Par 71, SSS 74, Course record 65.
Visitors Mon, Wed, Fri & Sun pm. Booking required. Dress code. **Societies** Booking required. **Green Fees** £100 per 18 holes, £150 per 36 holes (both including lunch). £110 Sun (no lunch). **Facilities** by arrangement **Conf** Corporate Hospitality Days **Location** 2m S off A737

Hotel ★★★ 69% Montgreenan Mansion House Hotel, Montgreenan Estate, KILWINNING ☎ 01294 850005 21 en suite

KILBIRNIE Map 10 NS35

Kilbirnie Place Largs Rd KA25 7AT
☎ 01505 684444 & 683398
e-mail: kilbirnie.golfclub@tiscali.co.uk
Easy walking parkland. The fairways are generally narrow and burns come into play on five holes.
18 holes, 5543yds, Par 69, SSS 67, Course record 65. Club membership 578.
Visitors Sun-Fri. Contact in advance. **Societies** Booking required. **Green Fees** Phone. **Facilities** **Conf** Corporate Hospitality Days **Location** 1m W from Kilbirnie Cross on A760

Hotel ★★ 69% Willowbank Hotel, 96 Greenock Rd, LARGS ☎ 01475 672311 & 675435 01475 689027 30 en suite

LARGS Map 10 NS25

Largs Irvine Rd KA30 8EU
☎ 01475 673594 01475 673594
e-mail: secretary@largsgolfclub.co.uk
web: www.largsgolfclub.co.uk
A parkland, tree-lined course with views to the Clyde coast and the Arran Isles.
18 holes, 6140yds, Par 70, SSS 71, Course record 63. Club membership 850.
Visitors Booking required. **Societies** apply in writing. **Green Fees** Phone. **Prof** Kenneth Docherty **Course Designer** H Stutt **Facilities** **Location** 1m S of town centre on A78

Hotel ★★ 69% Willowbank Hotel, 96 Greenock Rd, LARGS ☎ 01475 672311 & 675435 01475 689027 30 en suite

Routenburn Routenburn Rd KA30 8QA
☎ 01475 673230 & 686475 01475 687240
Heathland course with fine views over the Firth of Clyde.
18 holes, 5675yds, Par 68, SSS 68, Course record 63. Club membership 300.
Visitors Mon-Sun. Booking required. **Societies** Booking required. **Green Fees** Phone. **Prof** J Grieg McQueen **Course Designer** J Braid **Facilities** **Conf** Corporate Hospitality Days **Location** 1m N off A78

Hotel ★★ 69% Willowbank Hotel, 96 Greenock Rd, LARGS ☎ 01475 672311 & 675435 01475 689027 30 en suite

SKELMORLIE Map 10 NS16

Skelmorlie Beithglass PA17 5ES
☎ 01475 520152 01475 521902
e-mail: sec@skelmorliegolf.co.uk
web: www.skelmorliegolf.co.uk
Parkland and moorland course with magnificent views over the Firth of Clyde.
18 holes, 5030yds, Par 65, SSS 65, Course record 63. Club membership 450.
Visitors no visitors before 3pm Sat. **Societies** apply by telephone. **Green Fees** Phone. **Course Designer** James Braid **Facilities** by arrangement by arrangement by arrangement **Leisure** fishing. **Location** E side of village off A78

Continued

Hotel ★★ 69% Willowbank Hotel, 96 Greenock Rd, LARGS ☎ 01475 672311 & 675435 📠 01475 689027 30 en suite

STEVENSTON Map 10 NS24

Ardeer Greenhead KA20 4LB
☎ 01294 464542 & 465316 📠 01294 465316
e-mail: peewee_watson@lineone.net
web: www.ardeergolfclub.co.uk
Parkland with natural hazards, including several water features.
18 holes, 6401yds, Par 72, SSS 71, Course record 66.
Club membership 650.
Visitors may not play Sat. Must contact in advance. **Societies** must contact in advance. **Green Fees** Phone. **Course Designer** Stutt **Facilities** **Leisure** snooker. **Conf** facs Corporate Hospitality Days **Location** 0.5m N off A78

Hotel ★★★ 69% Montgreenan Mansion House Hotel, Montgreenan Estate, KILWINNING ☎ 01294 850005 21 en suite

WEST KILBRIDE Map 10 NS24

West Kilbride 33-35 Fullerton Dr, Seamill KA23 9HT
☎ 01294 823911 📠 01294 829573
e-mail: golf@westkilbridegolfclub.com
web: www.westkilbridegolfclub.com
Seaside links course on the Firth of Clyde, with fine views of Isle of Arran from every hole.
18 holes, 5974yds, Par 70, SSS 70, Course record 63.
Club membership 840.
Visitors Mon-Fri. Booking required. Handicap certificate. Dress code. **Societies** Booking required. **Green Fees** Phone. **Prof** Graham Ross **Course Designer** James Braid **Facilities** **Location** W side of town off A78

Hotel ★★ 69% Willowbank Hotel, 96 Greenock Rd, LARGS ☎ 01475 672311 & 675435 📠 01475 689027 30 en suite

NORTH LANARKSHIRE

AIRDRIE Map 11 NS76

Airdrie Rochsoles ML6 0PQ
☎ 01236 762195
e-mail: airdriegolfclub@virgin.net
Picturesque parkland course with good views.
18 holes, 6004yds, Par 69, SSS 68, Course record 61.
Club membership 450.
Visitors Mon, Wed-Fri, Sun & BHs. Booking required. Dress code. **Societies** Booking required. **Green Fees** £25 per day, £15 per round. **Prof** S McLean **Course Designer** J Braid **Facilities** **Location** 1m N on B802

Hotel ★★★★ The Westerwood Hotel, 1 St Andrews Dr, Westerwood, CUMBERNAULD ☎ 01236 457171 100 en suite

Easter Moffat Mansion House, Station Rd, Plains ML6 8NP
☎ 01236 842878 📠 01236 842904
e-mail: secretary@emgc.org.uk
A challenging moorland and parkland course which enjoys good views of the Campsie and Ochil hills. Although fairways are generous, accurate placement from the tee is essential on most holes. The signature hole on the course, the 18th is a truly memorable par 3, played from an elevated tee, to a receptive green in front of the clubhouse.
18 holes, 6221yds, Par 72, SSS 70, Course record 66.
Club membership 500.
Visitors Mon-Fri. Booking required. Dress code. **Societies** Booking required. **Green Fees** £33 per day, £22 per round. **Prof** Graham King **Facilities** **Location** 2m E of Airdrie on A89

Hotel ★★★★ The Westerwood Hotel, 1 St Andrews Dr, Westerwood, CUMBERNAULD ☎ 01236 457171 100 en suite

BELLSHILL Map 11 NS76

Bellshill Community Rd, Orbiston ML4 2RZ
☎ 01698 745124 📠 01698 292576
e-mail: info@bellshillgolfclub.com
Tree-lined 18 holes situated in the heart of Lanarkshire near Strathclyde Park. First opened for play in 1905 and extended in 1970. The 2nd hole has recently been redesigned by Mark James and Andrew Mair. The first five holes are extremely demanding but are followed by the gentler birdie alley where shots can be recovered. The signature hole is the 17th, a par 3 which involves a tricky tee shot from an elevated tee to a small well-bunkered green with out of bounds on the right.
18 holes, 6272yds, Par 70, SSS 69.
Club membership 700.
Visitors Mon-Fri. Booking required. Dress code. **Societies** Booking required. **Green Fees** Summer £32 per day, £20 per round. Winter reduced rates. **Facilities** **Location** 1m SE off A721

Hotel Premier Travel Inn Glasgow (Bellshill), Belziehill Farm, New Edinburgh Rd, BELLSHILL ☎ 08701 977106 40 en suite

COATBRIDGE Map 11 NS76

Drumpellier Drumpellier Av ML5 1RX
☎ 01236 424139 📠 01236 428723
e-mail: administrator@drumpelliergc.freeserve.co.uk
web: www.drumpellier.com
Parkland with rolling fairways and fast greens.

Continued

18 holes, 6227yds, Par 71, SSS 70, Course record 62.
Club membership 827.
Visitors Mon-fri. Booking required. Handicap certificate. Dress code. **Societies** Booking required. **Green Fees** £40 per day, £30 per round. **Prof** Jaimie Carver **Course Designer** W Fernie **Facilities** **Conf** facs Corporate Hospitality Days **Location** 0.75m W off A89

Hotel ★★★ 68% Bothwell Bridge Hotel, 89 Main St, BOTHWELL ☎ 01698 852246 90 en suite

CUMBERNAULD Map 11 NS77

Dullatur 1A Glen Douglas Dr G68 0DW
☎ 01236 723230 🖹 01236 727271
e-mail: graeme.campbell@dullaturgolf.com
web: www.dullaturgolf.com
Dullatur Carrickstone is a parkland course, with natural hazards and wind. Dullatur Antonine, designed by Dave Thomas, is a modern course.
Carrickstone: 18 holes, 6204yds, Par 70, SSS 70, Course record 68.
Antonine: 18 holes, 5875yds, Par 69, SSS 68.
Club membership 700.
Visitors telephone for availability. **Societies** Booking required. **Green Fees** £30 per day, £20 per 18 holes (£35/£25 weekends). **Prof** Duncan Sinclair **Course Designer** James Braid **Facilities** **Leisure** hard tennis courts, sauna, solarium, gymnasium, bowling green. **Conf** Corporate Hospitality Days **Location** 1.5m N of A80 at Cumbernauld

Hotel ★★★★ The Westerwood Hotel, 1 St Andrews Dr, Westerwood, CUMBERNAULD ☎ 01236 457171 100 en suite

Palacerigg Palacerigg Country Park G67 3HU
☎ 01236 734969 & 721461 🖹 01236 721461
e-mail: palacerigg-golfclub@lineone.net
web: www.palacerigggolfclub.co.uk
Well-wooded parkland course set in Palacerigg Country Park, with good views to the Campsie Hills.
18 holes, 6444yds, Par 72, SSS 71, Course record 65.
Club membership 300.
Visitors Mon-Fri & BHs. Booking required. **Societies** Booking required. **Green Fees** £8 per round/£12 per day (weekend £10 per round). **Course Designer** Henry Cotton **Facilities** **Conf** Corporate Hospitality Days **Location** 2m S of Cumbernauld on Palacerigg road off Lenziemill road B8054

Hotel ★★★★ The Westerwood Hotel, 1 St Andrews Dr, Westerwood, CUMBERNAULD ☎ 01236 457171 100 en suite

Westerwood Hotel 1 St Andrews Dr, Westerwood G68 0EW
☎ 01236 725281 🖹 01236 738478
e-mail: alantait@morton-hotels.com
web: www.morton-hotels.com
Undulating parkland and woodland course designed by Dave Thomas and Seve Ballasteros. Holes meander through silver birch, firs, heaths and heather, and the spectacular 15th, The Waterfall, has its green set against a 40ft rockface. Buggie track.
18 holes, 6557yds, Par 72, SSS 72, Course record 65.
Club membership 400.

Westerwood Hotel

Visitors Mon-Sun & BHs. Booking required. Dress code. **Societies** Booking required. **Green Fees** Apr-Oct £29.50 (£32 weekends) per 18 holes. Nov-Mar £15. **Prof** Alan Tait **Course Designer** Seve Ballesteros/Dave Thomas **Facilities** **Leisure** hard tennis courts, heated indoor swimming pool, sauna, gymnasium, Beauty salon. **Conf** facs Corporate Hospitality Days **Location** By A80, 14m from Glasgow

Hotel ★★★★ The Westerwood Hotel, 1 St Andrews Dr, Westerwood, CUMBERNAULD ☎ 01236 457171 100 en suite

GARTCOSH Map 11 NS66

Mount Ellen Johnston Rd G69 8EY
☎ 01236 872277 🖹 01236 872249
Downland course with 73 bunkers. Testing 10th (Bedlay), 156yds, par 3.
18 holes, 5525yds, Par 68, SSS 67, Course record 67.
Club membership 500.
Visitors Mon-Fri. Must contact in advance. **Societies** Booking required. **Green Fees** Phone. **Prof** Iain Bilsborough **Facilities** **Location** 0.75m N off A752

Hotel ★★★★ 73% Millennium Hotel Glasgow, George Square, GLASGOW ☎ 0141 332 6711 117 en suite

KILSYTH Map 11 NS77

Kilsyth Lennox Tak Ma Doon Rd G65 0RS
☎ 01236 824115 🖹 01236 823089
18 holes, 5912yds, Par 70, SSS 70, Course record 66.
Location N side of town off A803
Telephone for further details

Hotel ★★★★ The Westerwood Hotel, 1 St Andrews Dr, Westerwood, CUMBERNAULD ☎ 01236 457171 100 en suite

MOTHERWELL Map 11 NS75

Colville Park New Jerviston House, Jerviston Estate, Merry St ML1 4UG
☎ 01698 265779 (pro) 🖹 01698 230418
18 holes, 6250yds, Par 71, SSS 70, Course record 63.
Course Designer James Braid **Location** 1.25m NE of Motherwell town centre on A723
Telephone for further details

Hotel ★★★ 68% Bothwell Bridge Hotel, 89 Main St, BOTHWELL ☎ 01698 852246 90 en suite

Continued

MUIRHEAD Map 11 NS66

Crow Wood Garnkirk House, Cumbernauld Rd G69 9JF
☎ 0141 779 1943 🖷 0141 779 9148
e-mail: crowwood@golfclub.fsbusiness.co.uk
web: www.golfagent.co.uk
18 holes, 6261yds, Par 71, SSS 71, Course record 62.
Course Designer James Braid **Location** Off A80 to Stirling, between Stepps & Muirhead
Telephone for further details

Hotel ★★★ 75% Malmaison, 278 West George St, GLASGOW ☎ 0141 572 1000 72 en suite

SHOTTS Map 11 NS86

Shotts Blairhead ML7 5BJ
☎ 01501 822658 🖷 01501 822650
18 holes, 6205yds, Par 70, SSS 70, Course record 63.
Course Designer James Braid **Location** 2m from M8 off Benhar Road
Telephone for further details

Hotel ★★★ 68% The Hilcroft Hotel, East Main St, WHITBURN ☎ 01501 740818 32 en suite

WISHAW Map 11 NS75

Wishaw 55 Cleland Rd ML2 7PH
☎ 01698 372869 (club house) & 357480 (admin)
🖷 01698 356930
e-mail: jwdouglas@btconnect.com
web: www.wishawgolfclub.com
Parkland with many tree-lined fairways. Bunkers protect 17 of the 18 greens.
18 holes, 5999yds, Par 69, SSS 69, Course record 62.
Club membership 984.
Visitors Mon-Fri, Sun & BHs. Dress code. **Societies** Booking required. **Green Fees** £24 per round, £34 per day (Sun £28/£38). **Prof** Stuart Adair **Course Designer** James Braid **Facilities** **Location** NW side of town off A721

Hotel ★★★ 72% Popinjay Hotel, Lanark Rd, ROSEBANK ☎ 01555 860441 38 en suite

PERTH & KINROSS

ABERFELDY Map 14 NN84

Aberfeldy Taybridge Rd PH15 2BH
☎ 01887 820535 🖷 01887 820535
e-mail: abergc@tiscali.com.uk
web: www.aberfeldygolf.co.uk
Founded in 1895, this flat, parkland course is situated by the River Tay near the famous Wade Bridge and Black Watch Monument, and enjoys some splendid scenery. The new layout will test the keen golfer.
18 holes, 5283yds, Par 68, SSS 66, Course record 67.
Club membership 250.
Visitors Mon-Fri. Dress code. **Societies** Booking required. **Green Fees** Phone. **Course Designer** Soutars **Facilities** **Location** N side of town centre

ALYTH Map 15 NO24

Alyth Pitcrocknie PH11 8HF
☎ 01828 632268 🖷 01828 633491
e-mail: enquiries@alythgolfclub.co.uk
web: www.alythgolfclub.co.uk
Windy, heathland course with easy walking.
18 holes, 6205yds, Par 71, SSS 71, Course record 64.
Club membership 1000.
Visitors Booking advisable, handicap certificate required. Dress code. **Societies** must telephone in advance. **Green Fees** Phone. **Prof** Tom Melville **Course Designer** James Braid **Facilities** **Conf** facs **Location** 1m E on B954

Hotel ★★★ 64% Angus Hotel, Wellmeadow, BLAIRGOWRIE ☎ 01250 872455 81 en suite

Strathmore Golf Centre Leroch PH11 8NZ
☎ 01828 633322 🖷 01828 633533
e-mail: enquiries@strathmoregolf.com
web: www.strathmoregolf.com
The Rannaleroch Course is set on rolling parkland and heath with splendid views over Strathmore. The course is laid out in two loops of nine, which both start and finish at the clubhouse. It is generous off the tee but beware of the udulating, links-style greens. Among the challenging holes is the 480yd 5th with a 180yd carry over water from a high tee position. The nine-hole Leitfie Links has been specially designed with beginners, juniors and older golfers in mind.
Rannaleroch Course: 18 holes, 6454yds, Par 72, SSS 72, Course record 67.
Leitfie Links: 9 holes, 1719yds, Par 29, SSS 29.
Club membership 450.
Visitors Contact club for details. **Societies** booking preferable. **Green Fees** £26 per round (weekends £32). Leitfie £10 per round (weekend £11). **Prof** Andy Lamb **Course Designer** John Salvesen **Facilities** **Conf** Corporate Hospitality Days **Location** 2m SE of Alyth, B954 at Meigle onto A926, signed from Blairgowrie

Hotel ★★★ 64% Angus Hotel, Wellmeadow, BLAIRGOWRIE ☎ 01250 872455 81 en suite

AUCHTERARDER Map 11 NN91

Auchterarder Orchil Rd PH3 1LS
☎ 01764 662804 (sec) 🖷 01764 664423 (sec)
e-mail: secretary@auchterardergolf.co.uk
web: www.auchterardergolf.co.uk
Flat parkland course, part woodland with pine, larch and silver birch. It may be short but tricky with cunning dog-legs and guarded greens that require accuracy rather than sheer power. The 14th Punchbowl hole is perhaps the trickiest. A blind tee shot needs to be hit accurately over the left edge of the cross bunker to a long and narrow green - miss and you face a difficult downhill chip shot from deep rough.
18 holes, 5775yds, Par 69, SSS 68, Course record 61.
Club membership 820.
Visitors Mon-Sun & BHs. Booking required. Handicap certificate. Dress code. **Societies** Booking required. **Green Fees** £25 per round/£35 per day (weekends £30/£45). **Prof** Gavin Baxter **Course Designer** Ben Sayers **Facilities** **Conf** Corporate Hospitality Days **Location** 0.75m SW on A824

Continued

Hotel ★★ 77% Cairn Lodge, Orchil Rd, AUCHTERARDER ☎ 01764 662634 🖷 01764 662866 10 en suite

Gleneagles Hotel see page 371

Hotel ★★★★★ The Gleneagles Hotel, AUCHTERARDER ☎ 01764 662231 269 en suite

BLAIR ATHOLL — Map 14 NN86

Blair Atholl Invertilt Rd PH18 5TG
☎ 01796 481407 🖷 01796 481292
Easy walking parkland with a river alongside three holes.
9 holes, 5816yds, Par 70, SSS 68, Course record 65.
Club membership 425.
Visitors contact club for details. **Societies** Booking required. **Green Fees** £20 per day (£22 weekends). **Course Designer** Tom Morriss **Facilities** **Location** 0.5m S off B8079

Hotel ★★ 74% Atholl Arms Hotel, Old North Rd, BLAIR ATHOLL ☎ 01796 481205 30 en suite

BLAIRGOWRIE — Map 15 NO14

Blairgowrie Golf Course Rd, Rosemount PH10 6LG
☎ 01250 872622 🖷 01250 875451
e-mail: office@theblairgowriegolfclub.co.uk
web: www.theblairgowriegolfclub.co.uk
Two 18-hole championship heathland/woodland courses, also a nine-hole course.

Rosemount Course: 18 holes, 6590yds, Par 72, SSS 72, Course record 64.
Lansdowne Course: 18 holes, 6834yds, Par 72, SSS 73, Course record 66.
Wee Course: 9 holes, 2352yds, Par 32.
Club membership 1724.
Visitors Mon-Sun & BHs. Booking required. Handicap certificate. Dress code. **Societies** Booking required. **Green Fees** Rosemount £75 per round. Lansdowne £65 per round. Wee £30 day ticket. **Prof** Charles Dernie **Course Designer** J Braid/P Allis/D Thomas/Old Tom Morris **Facilities** **Conf** Corporate Hospitality Days **Location** Off A93 Rosemount

Hotel ★★★ 64% Angus Hotel, Wellmeadow, BLAIRGOWRIE ☎ 01250 872455 81 en suite

COMRIE — Map 11 NN72

Comrie Laggan Braes PH6 2LR
☎ 01764 670055
e-mail: enquiries@comriegolf.co.uk
web: www.comriegolf.co.uk
Scenic highland course with two tricky par 3 holes.
9 holes, 6040yds, Par 70, SSS 70, Course record 62.
Club membership 350.
Visitors Booking required. **Societies** Booking required. **Green Fees** Phone. **Course Designer** Col. Williamson **Facilities** **Location** E side of village off A85

Hotel ★★★ 68% The Four Seasons Hotel, Loch Earn, ST FILLANS ☎ 01764 685333 12 en suite 6 annexe en suite

CRIEFF — Map 11 NN82

Crieff Ferntower, Perth Rd PH7 3LR
☎ 01764 652909 🖷 01764 655096
e-mail: bookings@crieffgolf.co.uk
web: www.crieffgolf.co.uk
Set in dramatic countryside, Crieff Golf Club was established in 1891. The Ferntower championship course has magnificent views over the Strathearn valley and offers all golfers an enjoyable round. The short nine-hole Dornoch course, which incorporates some of the James Braid designed holes from the original 18 holes, provides an interesting challenge for juniors, beginners and others short of time.

Ferntower Course: 18 holes, 6474yds, Par 71, SSS 72, Course record 64.
Dornock Course: 9 holes, 2372yds, Par 32, SSS 63.
Club membership 720.
Visitors Mon-Sun & BHs. Booking required. Handicap certificate. Dress code. **Societies** Booking required. **Green Fees** Ferntower, weekday per round: Mar-Apr £25, May & Oct £29, Jun-Sep £32 (weekends £32/£36/£40). Dornock £12 for 9 holes, £16 for 18 holes. **Prof** David Murchie **Course Designer** James Braid **Facilities** **Conf** Corporate Hospitality Days **Location** 0.5m NE on A85

Hotel ★★★ 73% Royal Hotel, Melville Square, COMRIE ☎ 01764 679200 11 en suite

Championship Course

Perth & Kinross

Gleneagles Hotel

Auchterarder

Map 11 NN91

The PGA Centenary Course, designed by Jack Nicklaus and James Braid, and launched in style in May 1993, has an American-Scottish layout with many water hazards, elevated tees and raised contoured greens. It is the selected venue for the Ryder Cup 2014. It has a five-tier tee structure, making it both the longest and shortest playable course at the resort, as well as the most accommodating to all standards of golfer. The King's Course, with its abundance of heather, gorse, raised greens and plateau tees, is set within the valley of Strathearn with the Grampian mountains spectacularly in view to the north. The shorter Queen's Course, with fairways lined with Scots pines and water hazards, is set within a softer landscape and is considered an easier test of golf. You can improve your game at the golf academy at Gleneagles, where the philosophy is that golf should be fun and fun in golf comes from playing better. A complete corporate golf package is available.

PH3 1NF
☎ 01764 662231 🖹 01764 662134
e-mail: resort.sales@gleneagles.com
web: www.gleneagles.com

King's Course: 18 holes, 6471yds, Par 70, SSS 73, Course record 60.
Queen's Course: 18 holes, 5965yds, Par 68, SSS 70, Course record 62.
PGA Centenary Course: 18 holes, 6551yds, Par 72, SSS 73, Course record 63.

Visitors Booking required. **Societies** Booking required. **Green Fees** May-Sept £115 up to 3pm, £75 after 3pm, £40 after 5pm. Reduced rates rest of the year. **Prof** Russell Smith **Course Designer** James Braid/Jack Nicklaus **Facilities** **Leisure** hard and grass tennis courts, outdoor and indoor heated swimming pools, squash, fishing, sauna, solarium, gymnasium, golf academy, horse riding, shooting, falconry, off road driving. **Conf facs** Corporate Hospitality Days **Location** 2m SW off A823

DUNKELD Map 11 NO04

Dunkeld & Birnam Fungarth PH8 0ES

01350 727524 01350 728660
e-mail: secretary-dunkeld@tiscali.co.uk
web: dunkfeldandbirnamgolfclub.co.uk

Interesting and challenging course with spectacular views of the surrounding countryside. The original nine-hole heathland course is now augmented by an additional nine holes of parkland character close to the Loch of the Lowes.

18 holes, 5511yds, Par 70, SSS 67, Course record 63.
Club membership 600.

Visitors Mon-Sun & BHs. Booking required. Dress code. **Societies** Booking required. **Green Fees** Phone. **Course Designer** D A Tod **Facilities** **Conf** Corporate Hospitality Days **Location** 1m N of village on A923

Hotel ★★★ Kinnaird, Kinnaird Estate, DUNKELD 01796 482440 9 en suite

DUNNING Map 11 NO01

Dunning Rollo Park PH2 0QX

01764 684747

A pleasant parkland course with some testing holes, complicated by the burn which is a feature of four of the nine holes.

9 holes, 4836yds, Par 66, SSS 63, Course record 62.
Club membership 580.

Visitors Mon-Sun & BHs. Booking required. Dress code. **Societies** Booking required. **Green Fees** £16 per 18 holes, 9 holes £10, weekends £17. **Facilities** **Location** 1.5m off A9, 4m N of Auchterarder on B9146

Hotel ★★★ 67% Lovat Hotel, 90 Glasgow Rd, PERTH 01738 636555 30 en suite

Whitemoss Whitemoss Rd PH2 0QX

01738 730300 01738 730490
e-mail: info@whitemossgolf.com
web: www.whitemossgolf.com

18 holes, 5595yds, Par 68, SSS 68, Course record 63.

Course Designer Whitemoss Leisure **Location** Off A9 at Whitemoss Rd junct, 3m N of Gleneagles
Telephone for further details

Hotel ★★ 77% Cairn Lodge, Orchil Rd, AUCHTERARDER 01764 662634 10 en suite

GLENSHEE (SPITTAL OF) Map 15 NO17

Dalmunzie Dalmunzie Estate PH10 7QE

01250 885226
e-mail: enquiries@dalmunziecottages.com
web: www.dalmunziecottages.com

Well-maintained Highland course with difficult walking. Testing short course with small but good greens. One of the highest courses in Britain at 1200ft.

9 holes, 2099yds, Par 30, SSS 30.
Club membership 91.

Visitors Mon-Sun. Booking required. **Societies** Booking required. **Green Fees** £13 per day. **Course Designer** Alistair Campbell **Facilities** **Leisure** hard tennis courts, fishing, mountain bikes. **Conf** facs Corporate Hospitality Days **Location** 2m NW of Spittal of Glenshee

Hotel ★★ 74% Dalmunzie House Hotel, SPITTAL OF GLENSHEE 01250 885224 19 rms (16 en suite)

KENMORE Map 14 NN74

Kenmore PH15 2HN

01887 830226 01887 830775
e-mail: golf@taymouth.co.uk
web: www.taymouth.co.uk

Testing course in mildly undulating natural terrain. Beautiful views in tranquil setting by Loch Tay. The par 5 4th is 560yds and only one of the par 4s, the 2nd, is under 400yds - hitting from the tee out of a mound of trees down a snaking banking fairway which encourages the ball to stay on the fairway. The slightly elevated green is surrounded by banks to help hold the ball on the green. The fairways are generous and the rough short, which tends to encourage an unhindered round.

9 holes, 6052yds, Par 70, SSS 69, Course record 67.
Club membership 200.

Visitors contact club for details. **Societies** Booking required. **Green Fees** £35 per day, £25 per 18 holes, £17 per 9 holes (£30/£20/£15 weekends). **Course Designer** Robin Menzies **Facilities** **Leisure** fishing. **Location** On A827, beside Kenmore Bridge

Hotel ★★★ 67% Kenmore Hotel, The Square, KENMORE 01887 830205 27 en suite 13 annexe en suite

Taymouth Castle Taymouth Castle Estate PH15 2NT

01887 830228 01887 830830
e-mail: taymouth@fishingnet.com
web: www.fishingnet.com/taymouth

18 holes, 6066yds, Par 69, SSS 69, Course record 62.

Course Designer James Braid **Location** 1m E on A827, 5m W of Aberfeldy
Telephone for further details

Hotel ★★★ 67% Kenmore Hotel, The Square, KENMORE 01887 830205 27 en suite 13 annexe en suite

KINROSS Map 11 NO10

Kinross The Green Hotel, 2 The Muirs KY13 8AS
☎ 01577 863407 🖷 01577 863180
e-mail: golf@green-hotel.com
web: www.green-hotel.com

Two interesting and picturesque parkland courses, with easy walking. Many of the fairways are bounded by trees and plantations. A number of holes Course have views over Loch Leven to the hills beyond. The more challenging of the two is the Montgomery which has recently been enhanced by the addition of a new pond in front of the 11th green and 19 extra bunkers. The Bruce is slightly shorter but still provides a stern test of golf with notable features being the 6th Pond Hole and the run of four par 5's in six holes on the front nine.

Bruce: 18 holes, 6231yds, Par 73, SSS 71.
Montgomery: 18 holes, 6452yds, Par 71, SSS 72.
Club membership 600.

Visitors Mon-Sun & BHs. Booking required. Dress code. **Societies** Booking required. **Green Fees** The Bruce £35 per day, £25 per round (£45/£35 weekends); The Montgomery £45 per day, £30 per round (£45/£55 weekends). **Prof** Stuart Geraghty **Course Designer** Sir David Montgomery **Facilities** **Leisure** hard tennis courts, heated indoor swimming pool, squash, fishing, sauna, solarium, gymnasium, 4 sheet curling rink, croquet. **Conf** facs Corporate Hospitality Days **Location** NE side of town on B996

Hotel ★★★ 75% Green Hotel, 2 The Muirs, KINROSS ☎ 01577 863467 46 en suite
See advertisement on this page

MILNATHORT Map 11 NO10

Milnathort South St KY13 9XA
☎ 01577 864069
e-mail: milnathortgolf@ukgateway.net

Undulating inland course with lush fairways and excellent greens for most of the year. Strategically placed copses require accurate tee shots. Different tees and greens for some holes will make for more interesting play.

9 holes, 5969yds, Par 71, SSS 69, Course record 62.
Club membership 575.

Visitors Mon-Fri & Sun. Dress code. **Societies** Booking required. **Green Fees** Weekdays £22 per day, £15 per round (weekends £25/£17). **Facilities** by arrangement **Location** S side of town on A922

Hotel ★★★ 75% Green Hotel, 2 The Muirs, KINROSS ☎ 01577 863467 46 en suite

MUTHILL Map 11 NN81

Muthill Peat Rd PH5 2DA
☎ 01764 681523 🖷 01764 681557
e-mail: muthillgolfclub@lineone.net
web: muthillgolfclub.co.uk

A nine-hole course that, although short, requires accurate shot making to match the SSS. The three par 3s are all challenging holes with the 9th, a 205yd shot to a small well-bunkered green making a fitting end to nine holes characterised by great views and springy well-maintained fairways.

9 holes, 4700yds, Par 66, SSS 63, Course record 62.
Club membership 285.

Visitors Mon-Sun & BHs. Booking required. Dress code. **Societies** Booking required. **Green Fees** £15 per day, £10 per 9 holes (£18 Sat, Sun & BHs)). **Course Designer** Members **Facilities** **Location** W side of village off A822

Hotel ★★ 77% Cairn Lodge, Orchil Rd, AUCHTERARDER ☎ 01764 662634 10 en suite

PERTH Map 11 NO12

Craigie Hill Cherrybank PH2 0NE
☎ 01738 622644 (pro) 🖷 01738 620829
e-mail: golf@craigiehill.com
web: www.craigiehill.scottishgolf.com

Slightly hilly, heathland course. Panoramic views of Perth and the surrounding hills.

18 holes, 5386yds, Par 66, SSS 67, Course record 60.
Club membership 600.

Continued

Visitors Mon-Fri, Sun & BHs. Booking required. Dress code. **Societies** Booking required. **Green Fees** £30 per day, £20 per round (£30/£25 weekends) per 18 holes. **Prof** Kris Esson **Course Designer** Fernie/Anderson **Facilities** **Conf** facs Corporate Hospitality Days **Location** 1m SW of city centre off A952

Hotel ★★★ 67% Best Western Queens Hotel, Leonard St, PERTH ☎ 01738 442222 50 en suite

King James VI Moncreiffe Island PH2 8NR

☎ 01738 445132 (Secretary) & 632460 (Pro)
01738 445132
e-mail: info@kingjamesvi.co.uk
web: www.kingjamesvi.co.uk

Parkland course on island in the River Tay. Easy walking.

18 holes, 6038yds, Par 70, SSS 69, Course record 62. Club membership 650.

Visitors Mon-Sun & BHs. Booking required. Handicap certificate. **Societies** Booking required. **Green Fees** Phone. **Prof** Andrew Crerar **Course Designer** Tom Morris **Facilities** **Location** SE side of city centre

Hotel ★★★ 67% Best Western Queens Hotel, Leonard St, PERTH ☎ 01738 442222 50 en suite

Murrayshall House Hotel Murrayshall, Scone PH2 7PH

☎ 01738 552784 & 551171 01738 552595
e-mail: info@murrayshall.com
web: www.murrayshall.com

Murrayshall Course: 18 holes, 6441yds, Par 73, SSS 72.
Lyndoch Course: 18 holes, 5800yds, Par 69.

Course Designer Hamilton Stutt **Location** E side of village off A94

See advertisement on this page

Hotel ★★★ 75% Murrayshall House Hotel & Golf Course, New Scone, PERTH ☎ 01738 551171 27 en suite 14 annexe en suite

North Inch North Inch, off Hay St PH1 5PH

☎ 01738 636481
e-mail: es@pkc.gov.uk

18 holes, 5442yds, Par 68, SSS 66, Course record 62.

Course Designer Tom Morris **Location** N of City

Telephone for further details

Hotel ★★★ 67% Best Western Queens Hotel, Leonard St, PERTH ☎ 01738 442222 50 en suite

PITLOCHRY Map 14 NN95

Pitlochry Golf Course Rd PH16 5QY

☎ 01796 472792 01796 473947
e-mail: pro@pitlochrygolf.co.uk
web: www.pitlochrygolf.co.uk

A varied and interesting heathland course with fine views and posing many problems. Its SSS permits few errors in its achievement.

18 holes, 5670yds, Par 69, SSS 69, Course record 63. Club membership 400.

Societies Booking required. **Green Fees** £36 per day, £26 per round (£45/£35 weekends). **Prof** Mark Pirie **Course Designer** Willy Fernie **Facilities** **Location** Off A924 onto Larchwood Rd

Hotel ★★ 72% Moulin Hotel, 11-13 Kirkmichael Rd, Moulin, PITLOCHRY ☎ 01796 472196 15 en suite

St Fillans Map 11 NN62

St Fillans South Loch Earn Rd PH6 2NJ
☎ 01764 685312 🖷 01764 685312
web: www.stfillans-golf.com
Fairly flat, beautiful parkland course. Beside the river Earn and set amongst the Perthshire hills. Wonderfully rich in flora, animal and bird life. Easy to play but hard to score.
9 holes, 6054yds, Par 69, SSS 69, Course record 73. Club membership 400.
Visitors Mon-Sun & BHs. Booking advised. Dress code. **Societies** welcome. **Green Fees** Phone. **Course Designer** W Auchterlonie **Facilities** **Location** E side of village off A85

Hotel ★★★ 68% The Four Seasons Hotel, Loch Earn, ST FILLANS ☎ 01764 685333 12 en suite 6 annexe en suite

Strathtay Map 14 NN95

Strathtay Lyon Cottage PH9 0PG
☎ 01887 840373 🖷 01887 840777
e-mail: aivr@aol.com
Very attractive Highland course in a charming location. Steep in places but with fine views of surrounding hills and the Tay valley.
9 holes, 4082yds, Par 63, SSS 62, Course record 61. Club membership 212.
Visitors Mon-Sun & BHs. **Societies** welcome. **Green Fees** £12 per day (£15 Sat, Sun & BHs). **Facilities** **Location** E of village centre off A827

RENFREWSHIRE

Bishopton Map 10 NS47

rskine PA7 5PH
☎ 01505 862108 🖷 01505 862302
-mail: peter@erskinegc.wanadoo.co.uk
'arkland on the south bank of the River Clyde, with iews of the hills beyond.
8 holes, 6372yds, Par 71, SSS 71. 'lub membership 800.
'isitors Mon-Fri & BHs. Dress code. **Societies** Booking equired. **Green Fees** £31 per round, £42 per day. **Prof** eter Thomson **Facilities** **.ocation** 0.75 NE off B815

Bridge Of Weir Map 10 NS36

)ld Course Ranfurly Ranfurly Place PA11 3DE
☎ 01505 613612 🖷 01505 613214
-mail: secretary@oldranfurly.com
eb: www.oldranfurly.com
par 70 course that is both fun and challenging to play. rom the higher, moorland part of the course the River lyde comes into view and makes a spectacular backdrop, ith Ben Lomond and the Campsie Fells in the distance.
8 holes, 6061yds, Par 70, SSS 70, Course record 63. lub membership 819.
isitors Mon-Fri. Booking required. Handicap certificate. ress code. **Societies** Booking required. **Green Fees** £35 r day, £25 per round. **Prof** Grant Miller **Course esigner** W Park **Facilities** **Conf** orporate Hospitality Days **Location** 6m S of Glasgow irport

Ranfurly Castle The Clubhouse, Golf Rd PA11 3HN
☎ 01505 612609 🖷 01505 610406
e-mail: secretary@ranfurlycastlegolfclub.co.uk
web: www.ranfurlycastlegolfclub.co.uk
A picturesque, highly challenging 240-acre moorland course.
18 holes, 6261yds, Par 70, SSS 71, Course record 65. Club membership 825.
Visitors Mon-Fri. Booking required. Dress code. **Societies** Booking required. **Green Fees** £30 per round, £40 per day. **Prof** Tom Eckford **Course Designer** A Kirkcaldy/W Auchterlonie **Facilities** **Location** 5m NW of Johnstone

Hotel Premier Travel Inn Glasgow (Paisley), Phoenix Retail Park, PAISLEY ☎ 08701 977113 40 en suite

Johnstone Map 10 NS46

Cochrane Castle Scott Av, Craigston PA5 0HF
☎ 01505 328465 🖷 01505 325338
web: www.cochranecastle.scottishgolf.com
Fairly hilly parkland, wooded with two small streams running through.
18 holes, 6194yds, Par 71, SSS 71, Course record 63. Club membership 721.
Visitors Mon-Fri. Booking required. Handicap certificate. Dress code. **Societies** Booking required. **Green Fees** £30 per day, £22 per round. **Prof** Alan J Logan **Course Designer** J Hunter **Facilities** **Location** 1m from town centre, off Beith Rd

Elderslie 63 Main Rd, Elderslie PA5 9AZ
☎ 01505 323956 🖷 01505 340346
e-mail: eldersliegolfclub@btconnect.com
web: www.eldersliegolfclub.net
Undulating parkland with good views.
18 holes, 6175yds, Par 70, SSS 70, Course record 61. Club membership 940.
Visitors Mon-Fri. Booking required. Dress code. **Societies** Booking required. **Green Fees** £28 per round, £47.50 per day. **Prof** Richard Bowman **Course Designer** J Braid **Facilities** **Leisure** snooker & pool tables. **Conf** facs Corporate Hospitality Days **Location** E side of town on A737

Langbank Map 10 NS37

Gleddoch Golf and Country Club PA14 6YE
☎ 01475 540304 🖷 01475 540201
e-mail: golf@gleddochhouse.co.uk
web: www.gleddochhouse.co.uk
18 holes, 6330yds, Par 71, SSS 71, Course record 64.
Course Designer Hamilton Strutt **Location** B789-Old Greenock Road
Telephone for further details

Hotel Gleddoch House Hotel, LANGBANK
☎ 01475 540711 62 en suite

Lochwinnoch Map 10 NS35

Lochwinnoch Burnfoot Rd PA12 4AN
☎ 01505 842153 & 01505 843029 🖷 01505 843668
18 holes, 6243yds, Par 71, SSS 71, Course record 63.
Location W side of town off A760
Telephone for further details

Guest House ♦♦♦♦♦ East Lochhead, Largs Rd, LOCHWINNOCH ☎ 01505 842610 & 07785 565131 🖷 01505 842610 3 en suite

PAISLEY Map 11 NS46

Barshaw Barshaw Park PA1 3TJ
☎ 0141 889 2908
18 holes, 5703yds, Par 68, SSS 67, Course record 63.
Course Designer J R Stutt **Location** 1m E off A737
Telephone for further details

Hotel ★★★ 71% Glynhill Hotel & Leisure Club, Paisley Rd, RENFREW ☎ 0141 886 5555 145 en suite

Paisley Braehead Rd PA2 8TZ
☎ 0141 884 3903 884 2292 📠 0141 884 3903
e-mail: paisleygolfclub@btconnect.com
web: www.paisleygolfclub.co.uk
Moorland course with good views which suits all handicaps. The course has been designed in two loops of nine holes. Holes feature trees and gorse.
18 holes, 6466yds, Par 71, SSS 72, Course record 64. Club membership 810.
Visitors Mon-Fri. Booking required. Handicap certificate. Dress code. **Societies** Booking required. **Green Fees** £40 per day, £30 per round. **Prof** Gordon Stewart **Course Designer** John Stutt **Facilities** **Conf** facs **Location** Exit M8 junct 27, Renfrew Rd and continue through lights. Left at Causeyside St, right at Jet filling station, left at rdbt, at top of hill

Hotel ★★★ 71% Glynhill Hotel & Leisure Club, Paisley Rd, RENFREW ☎ 0141 886 5555 145 en suite

Ralston Strathmore Av, Ralston PA1 3DT
☎ 0141 882 1349 📠 0141 883 9837
e-mail: thesecretary@ralstongolf.co.uk
web: www.ralstongolfclub.co.uk
Parkland course.
18 holes, 6071yds, Par 70, SSS 69, Course record 62. Club membership 750.
Visitors Mon-Fri & BHs. Booking required. Dress code. **Societies** Booking required. **Green Fees** £42 per day, £27 per round. **Prof** Colin Munro **Course Designer** J Braid **Facilities** **Conf** facs Corporate Hospitality Days **Location** 2m E of Paisley town centre on A761

Hotel Premier Travel Inn Glasgow (Paisley), Phoenix Retail Park, PAISLEY ☎ 08701 977113 40 en suite

RENFREW Map 11 NS46

Renfrew Blythswood Estate, Inchinnan Rd PA4 9EG
☎ 0141 886 6692 📠 0141 886 1808
e-mail: secretary@renfrew.scottishgolf.com
web: www.renfrew.scottishgolf.com
A tree-lined parkland course.
18 holes, 6818yds, Par 72, SSS 73, Course record 65. Club membership 800.
Visitors Mon-Tue & Thu. Booking required. Dress code. **Societies** Booking required. **Green Fees** £40 per day, £30 per round. **Course Designer** Commander Harris **Facilities** **Location** 0.75m W off A8

Hotel ★★★ 71% Glynhill Hotel & Leisure Club, Paisley Rd, RENFREW ☎ 0141 886 5555 145 en suite

SCOTTISH BORDERS

ASHKIRK Map 12 NT52

Woll New Woll Estate TD7 4PE
☎ 01750 32711
e-mail: wollgolf@btinternet.com
web: www.wollgolf.co.uk
Flat parkland course with mature trees and a natural burn and ponds. The course is gentle but testing for all standards of golfer. Set in outstanding countryside in the Ale valley.
18 holes, 6051yds, Par 70, SSS 69.
Visitors Mon-Sun & BHs. Booking required. Dress code. **Societies** Booking required. **Green Fees** £30 per day, £24 per round. **Prof** Murray Cleghorn **Course Designer** Alec Cleghorn **Facilities** **Conf** facs Corporate Hospitality Days **Location** off A7 at village of Ashkirk

COLDSTREAM Map 12 NT83

Hirsel Kelso Rd TD12 4NJ
☎ 01890 882678 & 882233 📠 01890 882233
e-mail: bookings@hirselgc.co.uk
web: www.hirselgc.co.uk
A beautifully situated parkland course set in the Hirsel Estate, with panoramic views of the Cheviot Hills. Each hole offers a different challenge especially the 7th, a 170yd par 3 demanding accuracy of flight and length from the tee to ensure achieving a par.
18 holes, 6111yds, Par 70, SSS 70, Course record 65. Club membership 680.
Visitors contact club for details. **Societies** Booking required. **Green Fees** £28 per day (£34 weekends). **Facilities** **Conf** Corporate Hospitality Days **Location** On A697 at W end of Coldstream

Hotel ★★★ 71% Ednam House Hotel, Bridge St, KELSO ☎ 01573 224168 30 en suite

The Wheatsheaf at Swinton, Main St, SWINTON ☎ 01890 860257 📠 01890 860688 7 en suite
See advertisement on page 377

DUNS Map 12 NT75

Duns Hardens Rd TD11 3NR
☎ 01361 882194 📠 01361 883599
e-mail: secretary@dunsgolfclub.com
web: www.dunsgolfclub.com
18 holes, 6209yds, Par 70, SSS 70, Course record 67.
Course Designer A H Scott **Location** 1m W off A6105
Telephone for further details

Continu

Hotel ★★★ 70% Marshall Meadows Country House Hotel, BERWICK-UPON-TWEED ☎ 01289 331133 19 en suite

EYEMOUTH Map 12 NT96

Eyemouth Gunsgreen Hill TD14 5SF
☎ 01890 750551 (clubhouse) & 750004 (Pro shop)
e-mail: eyemouth@gxn.co.uk
web: www.eyegolfclub.co.uk

A superb course set on the coast, containing interesting and challenging holes, in particular the intimidating 6th hole, a formidable par 3 across a vast gully with the waves crashing below and leaving little room for error. The clubhouse overlooks the picturesque fishing village of Eyemouth and provides panoramic views over the course and the North Sea.

18 holes, 6520yds, Par 72, SSS 72, Course record 66. Club membership 400.

Visitors Mon-Sun & BHs. Dress code. **Societies** welcome. **Green Fees** £30 per day, £25 per round (£35/£30 weekends). **Prof** Paul Terras, Tony McLeman **Course Designer** J R Bain **Facilities** **Conf** Corporate Hospitality Days **Location** E side of town, 8m N of Berwick and 2m off A1

Hotel ★★★ 70% Marshall Meadows Country House Hotel, BERWICK-UPON-TWEED ☎ 01289 331133 19 en suite

GALASHIELS Map 12 NT43

Galashiels Ladhope Recreation Ground TD1 2NJ
☎ 01896 753724
e-mail: secretary@galashiels-golfclub.co.uk
web: www.galashiels-golfclub.co.uk

Hillside course, superb views from the top; 10th hole very steep.

18 holes, 5185yds, Par 67, SSS 66, Course record 61. Club membership 311.

Visitors contact club for details. **Societies** Booking required. **Green Fees** £12 per 9 holes, £20 per 18 holes (£15/£28 weekends). **Course Designer** James Braid **Facilities** by arrangement by arrangement by arrangement by arrangement **Location** N side of town centre off A7

Hotel ★★★ 67% Kingsknowes Hotel, Selkirk Rd, GALASHIELS ☎ 01896 758375 12 en suite

Torwoodlee Edinburgh Rd TD1 2NE
☎ 01896 752260 🖷 01896 752306
e-mail: thesecretary@torwoodleegolfclub.org.uk
web: torwoodleegolfclub.org.uk

A picturesque course flanked by the River Gala and set among a mix of mature woodland and rolling parkland.

18 holes, 6021yds, Par 69, SSS 70, Course record 64. Club membership 550.

Visitors restricted Thu & Sat. **Societies** letter to secretary. **Green Fees** Phone. **Course Designer** Willie Park **Facilities** **Location** 1.75m NW off A7

Hotel ★★★ 67% Kingsknowes Hotel, Selkirk Rd, GALASHIELS ☎ 01896 758375 12 en suite

HAWICK Map 12 NT51

Hawick Vertish Hill TD9 0NY
☎ 01450 372293
e-mail: thesecretary@hawickgolfclub.fsnet.co.uk
web: www.hawickgolfclub.com

Hill course with good views.

18 holes, 5933yds, Par 68, SSS 69, Course record 63. Club membership 600.

Visitors contact club for details. Handicap certificate. Dress code. **Societies** Booking required. **Green Fees** £35 per day, £28 per round. **Facilities** **Conf** Corporate Hospitality Days **Location** SW side of town

INNERLEITHEN Map 11 NT33

Innerleithen Leithen Water, Leithen Rd EH44 6NL
☎ 01896 830951

Moorland course, with easy walking. Burns and rivers are natural hazards. Testing 5th hole (100yds) par 3.

9 holes, 6066yds, Par 70, SSS 69, Course record 65. Club membership 280.

Visitors contact club for details. **Societies** welcome. **Green Fees** £20 per 18 holes, £10 per 9 holes, £30 per day. **Course Designer** Willie Park **Facilities** **Conf** Corporate Hospitality Days **Location** 1.5m N on B709

Hotel ★★★★ 70% Peebles Hotel Hydro, PEEBLES ☎ 01721 720602 128 en suite

JEDBURGH Map 12 NT62

Jedburgh Dunion Rd TD8 6TA
☎ 01835 863587
web: www.tweeddalepress.co.uk/jedburghgolfclub.htlm
9 holes, 5760yds, Par 68, SSS 67, Course record 62.
Course Designer William Park **Location** 1m W on B6358
Telephone for further details

KELSO Map 12 NT73

Kelso Racecourse Rd TD5 7SL
☎ 01573 223009 🖹 01573 228490
18 holes, 6046yds, Par 70, SSS 69, Course record 64.
Course Designer James Braid **Location** N side of town centre off B6461
Telephone for further details

Hotel ★★★ 68% Cross Keys Hotel, 36-37 The Square, KELSO ☎ 01573 223303 27 en suite

Roxburghe Heiton TD5 8JZ
☎ 01573 450331 🖹 01573 450611
e-mail: hotel@roxburghe.net
web: www.roxburghe.net
An exceptional parkland layout designed by Dave Thomas and opened in 1997. Surrounded by natural woodland on the banks of the River Teviot. Owned by the Duke of Roxburghe, this course has numerous bunkers, wide rolling and sloping fairways and strategically placed water features. The signature hole is the 14th.
18 holes, 6925yds, Par 72, SSS 74, Course record 66. Club membership 300.
Visitors Mon-Sun & BHs. Booking required. Handicap certificate. Dress code. **Societies** Booking required. **Green Fees** £80 per day, £60 per round. **Prof** Craig Montgomerie **Course Designer** Dave Thomas **Facilities** **Leisure** fishing, Clay pigeon shooting, falconry, archery, mountain bikes. **Conf** facs Corporate Hospitality Days **Location** 2m W of Kelso on A698

Hotel ★★★ 76% The Roxburghe Hotel & Golf Course, Heiton, KELSO ☎ 01573 450331 16 en suite 6 annexe en suite

LAUDER Map 12 NT54

Lauder Galashiels Rd TD2 6RS
☎ 01578 722240 🖹 01578 722526
e-mail: laudergc@aol.com
web: www.laudergolfclub.org.uk
Inland course and practice area on gently sloping hill with stunning views of the Lauderdale district. The signature holes are The Wood, a dog-leg par 4 played round the corner of a wood which is itself out of bounds, and The Quarry, a 150yd par 3 played over several old quarry holes into a bowl shaped green.
9 holes, 6050yds, Par 72, SSS 69, Course record 66. Club membership 260.
Visitors Mon-Sun & BHs. Booking required. Dress code. **Societies** Booking required. **Green Fees** £15 per day/round. **Course Designer** Willie Park Jnr **Facilities** **Conf** Corporate Hospitality Days **Location** Off A68, 0.5m from Lauder

Hotel ★★ 68% Lauderdale Hotel, 1 Edinburgh Rd, LAUDER ☎ 01578 722231 10 en suite

MELROSE Map 12 NT53

Melrose Dingleton TD6 9HS
☎ 01896 822855
Undulating tree-lined fairways with spendid views. Many bunkers.
9 holes, 5562yds, Par 70, SSS 68, Course record 61. Club membership 380.
Visitors Mon-Fri & BHs. Booking required Tue & Sat-Sun. Dress code. **Societies** welcome. **Green Fees** £20 per 18 holes. **Course Designer** James Braid **Facilities** **Location** S side of town centre on B6359

Hotel ★★★ 71% Burt's Hotel, Market Square, MELROSE ☎ 01896 822285 20 en suite

MINTO Map 12 NT52

Minto TD9 8SH
☎ 01450 870220 🖹 01450 870126
e-mail: pat@mintogolfclub.freeserve.co.uk
web: mintogolf.co.uk
Pleasant, undulating parkland, featuring mature trees and panoramic views of the border country. Short but quite testing course.
18 holes, 5542yds, Par 69, SSS 67, Course record 63. Club membership 500.
Visitors Mon-Sun & BHs. Booking required. Dress code. **Societies** Booking required. **Green Fees** £30 per day, £27 per round (£38/£32 Sat, Sun & BHs). **Course Designer** Thomas Telford **Facilities** **Conf** Corporate Hospitality Days **Location** 5m NE from Hawick off B6405

NEWCASTLETON Map 12 NY48

Newcastleton Holm Hill TD9 0QD
☎ 01387 375608
Hilly course with scenic views over the Liddesdale valley and Newcastleton.
9 holes, 5491yds, Par 69, SSS 70, Course record 67. Club membership 100.
Visitors Mon-Sun & BHs. Booking required Sat-Sun. Dress code. **Societies** Booking required. **Green Fees** £10 per day/round. **Course Designer** J Shade **Facilities** **Leisure** fishing. **Location** W side of village

Hotel ★★★ 67% Garden House Hotel, Sarkfoot Rd, GRETNA ☎ 01461 337621 38 en suite

Continued

PEEBLES Map 11 NT24

Macdonald Cardrona Hotel, Golf & Country Club Cardrona EH45 6LZ
☎ 01896 833600 🖷 01896 831166
e-mail: golf.cardrona@macdonald-hotels.co.uk
web: www.macdonaldhotels.co.uk
Opened for play in 2001 and already a settled and inspiring test. The terrain is a mixture of parkland, heathland and woodland with an additional 20,000 trees planted. The USPGA specification greens are mostly raised and mildly contoured with no two being the same shape.
18 holes, 6856yds, Par 72, SSS 74, Course record 64.
Club membership 200.
Visitors Mon-Sun & BHs. Booking required. Dress code. **Societies** Booking required. **Green Fees** £67.50 per day, £45 per round. **Prof** Ross Harrower **Course Designer** Dave Thomas **Facilities** **Leisure** heated indoor swimming pool, fishing, sauna, solarium, gymnasium. **Conf** facs Corporate Hospitality Days **Location** off A72, 3m S of Peebles

Hotel ★★★★ 74% Macdonald Cardrona Hotel Golf & Country Club, Cardrona Mains, PEEBLES
☎ 0870 1942114 100 en suite

Peebles Kirkland St EH45 8EU
☎ 01721 720197 🖷 01721 724441
e-mail: secretary@peeblesgolfclub.co.uk
web: peeblesgolfclub.co.uk
This parkland course is one of the most picturesque courses in Scotland, shadowed by the rolling border hills and Tweed valley and set high above the town. The tough opening holes are balanced by a more generous stretch through to the 14th hole but from here the closing five prove a challenging test.
18 holes, 5729yds, Par 70, SSS 70, Course record 63.
Club membership 750.
Visitors Sun-Fri & BHs. Booking required Sun. Handicap certificate. Dress code. **Societies** Booking required. **Green Fees** £38 per round/£50 per day. **Prof** Craig Imlah **Course Designer** H S Colt **Facilities** **Location** W side of town centre off A72

Hotel ★★★★ 70% Peebles Hotel Hydro, PEEBLES
☎ 01721 720602 128 en suite

ST BOSWELLS Map 12 NT53

St Boswells Braeheads TD6 0DE
☎ 01835 823527
Attractive, easy walking parkland by the River Tweed.
9 holes, 5274yds, Par 68, SSS 66.
Club membership 320.
Visitors Mon-Sun & BHs. **Societies** welcome. **Green Fees** £20 per round, £12 per 9 holes. **Course Designer** W Park **Facilities** **Location** 500yds off A68 east end of village

Hotel ★★★ 74% Dryburgh Abbey Hotel, ST BOSWELLS
☎ 01835 822261 37 en suite 1 annexe en suite

SELKIRK Map 12 NT42

Selkirk Selkirk Hill TD7 4NW
☎ 01750 20621
e-mail: secretary@selkirkgolfclub.co.uk
Pleasant moorland course with gorse and heather, set around Selkirk Hill. A testing course for all golfers. Unrivalled views.
9 holes, 5620yds, Par 68, SSS 68, Course record 61.
Club membership 300.
Visitors Mon-Fri & BHs. Booking required Sat-Sun. Handicap certificate. Dress code. **Societies** Booking required. **Green Fees** £22 per 18 holes, £11 per 9 holes. **Facilities** **Location** 1m S on A7

Hotel ★★★ 71% Burt's Hotel, Market Square, MELROSE ☎ 01896 822285 20 en suite

WEST LINTON Map 11 NT15

Rutherford Castle Golf Club EH46 7AS
☎ 01968 661 233 🖷 01968 661 233
e-mail: info@ruth-castlegc.co.uk
web: www.ruth-castlegc.co.uk
Undulating parkland set beneath the Pentland Hills. The many challenging holes are a good test for the better player while offering great enjoyment to the average player.
18 holes, 6525yds, Par 72, SSS 71.
Club membership 120.
Visitors Booking required. **Green Fees** Phone. **Course Designer** Bryan Moore **Facilities** **Location** On A702 towards Carlisle

Hotel ★★★★ 70% Peebles Hotel Hydro, PEEBLES
☎ 01721 720602 128 en suite

West Linton EH46 7HN
☎ 01968 660256 & 660970 🖷 01968 660970
e-mail: secretarywlgc@btinternet.com
web: www.wlgc.co.uk
Moorland course with beautiful views of Pentland Hills. This well-maintained course offers a fine challenge to all golfers with ample fairways and interesting layouts. The wildlife and natural scenery give added enjoyment.
18 holes, 6132yds, Par 69, SSS 70, Course record 63.
Club membership 1000.
Visitors Mon-Fri, Sat-Sun pm only & BHs. Booking required Fri-Sun & BHs. Dress code. **Societies** Booking required. **Green Fees** £40 per day, £30 per round (£40 per round weekends). **Prof** Ian Wright **Course Designer** Millar/Braid/Fraser **Facilities** **Conf** Corporate Hospitality Days **Location** NW side of village off A702

Hotel ★★★★ 70% Peebles Hotel Hydro, PEEBLES
☎ 01721 720602 128 en suite

SOUTH AYRSHIRE

AYR Map 10 NS32

Belleisle Belleisle Park KA7 4DU
☎ 01292 441258 🖷 01292 442632
e-mail: belleisle.golf@south-ayrshire.gov.uk
web: www.golfsouthayrshire.com
Parkland course with beautiful sea views. First-class conditions.
Belleisle Course: 18 holes, 6431yds, Par 71, SSS 72, Course record 63.
Seafield Course: 18 holes, 5498yds, Par 68, SSS 67.
Visitors Mon-Sun & BHs. Booking required. Dress code. **Societies** Booking required. **Green Fees** Belleisle £25 (£31 weekends). Seafield £17.50 (£20 weekends). **Prof** David

Continued

Gemmell **Course Designer** James Braid **Facilities** ⊗ 🍴 🍽 ☕ 🍷 👕 🏪 ⛳ 🛏 🔧 **Conf** facs **Location** 2m S of Ayr on A719

Hotel ★★★ 71% Savoy Park Hotel, 16 Racecourse Rd, AYR ☎ 01292 266112 15 en suite

Dalmilling Westwood Av KA8 0QY

☎ 01292 263893 📠 01292 610543

Meadowland course, with easy walking. Tributaries of the River Ayr add interest to early holes.

18 holes, 5724yds, Par 69, SSS 68, Course record 61.

Club membership 260.

Visitors Mon-Sun & BHs. Booking required. Dress code. **Societies** Booking required. **Green Fees** £14 per round, £20 per day (weekends £17.50/£25). **Prof** Philip Cheyney **Facilities** 👕 🏪 ⛳ 🔧 **Location** 1.5m E of town centre off A77

Hotel ★★★★ 74% Fairfield House Hotel, 12 Fairfield Rd, AYR ☎ 01292 267461 40 en suite 4 annexe en suite

BARASSIE Map 10 NS33

Kilmarnock (Barassie) 29 Hillhouse Rd KA10 6SY

☎ 01292 313920 📠 01292 318300

e-mail: secretarykbgc@lineone.net

web: www.kbgc.co.uk

The club now has a 27-hole layout. Magnificent seaside links, relatively flat with much heather and small, undulating greens.

18 holes, 6817yds, Par 72, SSS 74, Course record 63.

9 hole course: 9 holes, 2888yds, Par 34.

Club membership 600.

Visitors Mon-Tue, Thu-Fri & Sun. Booking required. Dress code. **Societies** Booking required. **Green Fees** £65 for up to 36 holes. **Prof** Gregor Howie **Course Designer** Theodore Moone **Facilities** ⊗ 🍴 🍽 ☕ 🍷 👕 🏪 🚗 🔧 **Location** E side of village on B746, 2m N of Troon

Hotel ★★★★ 69% Marine Hotel, Crosbie Rd, TROON ☎ 01292 314444 90 en suite

GIRVAN Map 10 NX19

Brunston Castle Golf Course Rd, Dailly KA26 9GD

☎ 01465 811471 📠 01465 811545

e-mail: golf@brunstoncastle.co.uk

web: www.brunstoncastle.co.uk

Burns: 18 holes, 6662yds, Par 72, SSS 72, Course record 63.

Course Designer Donald Steel **Location** 5m E of Girvan

Telephone for further details

Hotel ★★★ 75% Malin Court, TURNBERRY ☎ 01655 331457 18 en suite

Girvan Golf Course Rd KA26 9HW

☎ 01465 714346 📠 01465 714272

18 holes, 5098yds, Par 64, SSS 65, Course record 61.

Course Designer D Kinnell/J Braid **Location** N side of town off A77

Telephone for further details

Hotel ★★★ 75% Malin Court, TURNBERRY ☎ 01655 331457 18 en suite

MAYBOLE Map 10 NS20

Maybole Municipal Memorial Park KA19 7DX

☎ 01655 889770

9 holes, 2635yds, Par 33, SSS 65, Course record 64.

Location Off A77 S of town

Telephone for further details

Hotel ★★ Ladyburn, MAYBOLE ☎ 01655 740585 5 en suite

PRESTWICK Map 10 NS32

Prestwick 2 Links Rd KA9 1QG

☎ 01292 477404 📠 01292 477255

e-mail: bookings@prestwickgc.co.uk

web: www.prestwickgc.co.uk

Seaside links with natural hazards, tight fairways and difficult fast undulating greens.

18 holes, 6544yds, Par 71, SSS 73, Course record 67.

Club membership 575.

Visitors Sun-Fri & BHs. Booking required. Handicap certificate. Dress code. **Societies** Booking required. **Green Fees** £105 per round, £160 per day (Sun £135 per round). **Prof** D A Fleming **Course Designer** Tom Morris **Facilities** ⊗ 🍽 ☕ 🍷 👕 🏪 ⛳ 🔧 **Conf** Corporate Hospitality Days **Location** In town centre off A79

Hotel ★★★ 70% Parkstone Hotel, Esplanade, PRESTWICK ☎ 01292 477286 30 en suite

Prestwick St Cuthbert East Rd KA9 2SX

☎ 01292 477101 📠 01292 671730

e-mail: secretary@stcuthbert.co.uk

web: www.stcuthbert.co.uk

Parkland with easy walking and natural hazards. Sometimes windy. Tree-lined fairways and well bunkered.

18 holes, 6470yds, Par 71, SSS 71, Course record 64.

Club membership 880.

Visitors Mon-Fri. Booking required. Dress code. **Societies** Booking required. **Green Fees** £45 per day. **Course Designer** Stutt & Co **Facilities** ⊗ 🍴 🍽 ☕ 🍷 👕 🔧 **Conf** Corporate Hospitality Days **Location** 0.5m E of town centre off A77

Hotel ★★★ 70% Parkstone Hotel, Esplanade, PRESTWICK ☎ 01292 477286 30 en suite

Prestwick St Nicholas Grangemuir Rd KA9 1SN

☎ 01292 477608 📠 01292 473900

e-mail: secretary@prestwickstnicholas.com

web: www.prestwickstnicholas.com

Classic seaside links course with views across the Firth of Clyde to the Isle of Arran to the west and Ailsa Craig to the south.

18 holes, 5952yds, Par 69, SSS 69, Course record 63.

Club membership 750.

Visitors Sun-Fri & BHs. Dress code. **Societies** Booking required. **Green Fees** £65 per day, £55 per round (£60 per round Sun). **Course Designer** Charles Hunter **Facilities** ⊗ 🍴 🍽 ☕ 🍷 👕 🏪 ⛳ 🔧 **Location** S side of town off A79

Hotel ★★★ 70% Parkstone Hotel, Esplanade, PRESTWICK ☎ 01292 477286 30 en suite

Championship Course

South Ayrshire

Royal Troon

Troon

Map 10 NS33

Troon was founded in 1878 with just five holes on linksland. In its first decade it grew from five holes to six, then 12, and finally 18 holes. It became Royal Troon in 1978 on its 100th anniversary. Royal Troon's reputation is based on its combination of rough and sandy hills, bunkers, and a severity of finish that has diminished the championship hopes of many. The most successful players have relied on an equal blend of finesse and power. The British Open Championship has been played at Troon eight times - in 1923, 1950, 1962, 1973, 1982, 1989, 1997, and lastly in 2004 when it hosted the 133rd tournament. It has the shortest hole of courses hosting the Open. Ten new bunkers and four new tees were added after the 1997 competition. It is recommended that you apply to the course in advance for full visitor information.

Craigend Rd KA10 6EP
☎ 01292 311555 🗎 01292 318204
e-mail: bookings@royaltroon.com
web: www.royaltroon.com

Old Course: 18 holes, 6641yds, Par 71, SSS 73, Course record 64.
Portland: 18 holes, 6289yds, Par 71, SSS 71, Course record 65.
Craigend: 9 holes.
Club membership 800.

Visitors Mon-Tue & Thu. Booking required. Handicap certificate. Dress code. Societies welcome. **Green Fees** £210 per day including coffee/lunch, 1 round over Old & 1 round over Portland. **Prof** R B Anderson **Course Designer** C Hunter/G Strath/W Fernie **Facilities** **Location** S of town on B749. 5m from Prestwick airport

TROON Map 10 NS33

Royal Troon see page 381

Hotel ★★★★ 69% Marine Hotel, Crosbie Rd, TROON ☎ 01292 314444 90 en suite

Hotel ★★★ Lochgreen House Hotel, Monktonhill Rd, Southwood, TROON ☎ 01292 313343 01292 318661 32 en suite 8 annexe en suite

Hotel ★★★ 75% Piersland House Hotel, Craigend Rd, TROON ☎ 01292 314747 01292 315613 15 en suite 15 annexe en suite

Troon Municipal Harling Dr KA10 6NE
☎ 01292 312464 01292 312578
e-mail: troongolf@south-ayrshire.gov.uk
web: www.golfsouthayshire.com
Three links courses, two of championship standard.
Lochgreen Course: 18 holes, 6820yds, Par 74, SSS 73.
Darley Course: 18 holes, 6360yds, Par 71, SSS 63.
Fullarton Course: 18 holes, 4870yds, Par 66, SSS 64.
Visitors Mon-Sun & BHs. Booking required. Dress code. **Societies** Booking required. **Green Fees** Lochgreen £25 (£31 weekend). Darley £19.50 (£24 weekend). Fullarton £14 (£17.50 weekends). **Prof** Gordon McKinlay **Facilities** **Location** 100yds from railway station

Hotel ★★★★ 69% Marine Hotel, Crosbie Rd, TROON ☎ 01292 314444 90 en suite

TURNBERRY Map 10 NS20

Westin Turnberry Resort see page 383

Hotel ★★★★★ The Westin Turnberry Resort, TURNBERRY ☎ 01655 331000 132 en suite 89 annexe en suite

Hotel ★★★ 75% Malin Court, TURNBERRY ☎ 01655 331457 01655 331072 18 en suite

Hotel ★★ Ladyburn, MAYBOLE ☎ 01655 740585 01655 740580 5 en suite

SOUTH LANARKSHIRE

BIGGAR Map 11 NT03

Biggar The Park, Broughton Rd ML12 6AH
☎ 01899 220618 (club) & 220319 (course)
18 holes, 5600yds, Par 68, SSS 67, Course record 61.
Course Designer W Park Jnr **Location** S side of town
Telephone for further details

Hotel ★★★ 73% Shieldhill Castle, Quothquan, BIGGAR ☎ 01899 220035 16 en suite

BOTHWELL Map 11 NS75

Bothwell Castle Uddingston Rpad G71 8TD
☎ 01698 801971 & 801972 01698 801971
Flattish tree-lined parkland course in a residential area.
18 holes, 6220yds, Par 70, SSS 70, Course record 62.
Club membership 1000.
Visitors Mon-Fri. Booking required. Dress code. **Societies** welcome. **Green Fees** £38 per day, £28 per round. **Prof** Alan McCloskey **Facilities** **Conf** Corporate Hospitality Days **Location** NW of village off B7071

Hotel ★★★ 68% Bothwell Bridge Hotel, 89 Main St, BOTHWELL ☎ 01698 852246 90 en suite

BURNSIDE Map 11 NS65

Blairbeth Fernbrae Av, Fernhill G73 4SF
☎ 0141 634 3355 & 634 3325
e-mail: bgc1910@yahoo.co.uk
web: www.blairbethgc.fsnet.co.uk
Parkland with some small elevated greens and views over Glasgow and the Clyde valley.
18 holes, 5537yds, Par 70, SSS 68, Course record 63.
Club membership 480.
Visitors Mon-Sun & BHs. Booking required Sat-Sun & BHs. Dress code. **Societies** welcome. **Green Fees** £28 per day, £22 per round. **Facilities** **Conf** Corporate Hospitality Days **Location** 2m S of Rutherglen off Burnside Rd

Cathkin Braes Cathkin Rd G73 4SE
☎ 0141 634 6605 0141 630 9186
e-mail: golf@cathkinbraes.freeserve.co.uk
web: www.cathkinbraesgolfclub.co.uk
Moorland course, 600ft above sea level but relatively flat with a prevailing westerly wind and views over Glasgow. A small loch hazard at 5th hole. Very strong finishing holes.
18 holes, 6200yds, Par 71, SSS 71, Course record 62.
Club membership 920.
Visitors Mon-Fri. Booking required. **Societies** Booking required. **Green Fees** £33 per round/£43 per day. **Prof** Stephen Bree **Course Designer** James Braid **Facilities** **Conf** Corporate Hospitality Days **Location** 1m S on B759

CARLUKE Map 11 NS85

Carluke Mauldslie Rd, Hallcraig ML8 5HG
☎ 01555 770574 & 771070
e-mail: admin.carlukegolf@supanet.com
18 holes, 5853yds, Par 70, SSS 68, Course record 63.
Location 1m W off A73
Telephone for further details

Hotel ★★★ 72% Popinjay Hotel, Lanark Rd, ROSEBANK ☎ 01555 860441 38 en suite

CARNWATH Map 11 NS94

Carnwath 1 Main St ML11 8JX
☎ 01555 840251 01555 841070
e-mail: carnwathgc@hotmail.co.uk
web: www.carnwathgc.co.uk
Picturesque parkland, slightly hilly, panoramic views. The small greens call for accuracy.
18 holes, 5222yds, Par 66, SSS 66, Course record 63.
Club membership 586.
Visitors Sun-Fri & BHs. Booking required Sun-Mon, Wed-Fri, & BHs. Dress code. **Societies** welcome. **Green Fees** £30 per day, £18 per round (£36/£24 Sun). **Facilities** **Location** W side of village on A70

Hotel ★★★ 60% Cartland Bridge Hotel, Glasgow Rd, LANARK ☎ 01555 664426 20 rms (18 en suite)

Continued

South Ayrshire Westin Turnberry Resort

Turnberry Map 10 NS20

For thousands of players of all nationalities, Turnberry is one of the finest of all golf destinations, where some of the most remarkable moments in Open history have taken place. The legendary Ailsa Course is complemented by the new highly acclaimed Kintyre Course, while the nine-hole Arran Course, created by Donald Steel and Colin Montgomerie, has similar challenges such as undulating greens, tight tee shots, pot bunkers and thick Scottish rough. With the famous hotel on the left and the magnificent Ailsa Craig away to the right, there are few vistas in world golf to match the 1st tee here. To help you prepare for your game the Colin Montgomerie Links Golf Academy, alongside the luxurious and extensive clubhouse, was opened in April 2000; it features 12 driving bays, four short-game bays, two dedicated teaching rooms and a group teaching room.

KA26 9LT
☎ 01655 331000 🖷 01655 331069
e-mail: turnberry@westin.com
web: www.westin.com/turnberry

Ailsa Course: 18 holes, 6440yds, Par 69, SSS 72, Course record 63.
Kintyre Course: 18 holes, 6376yds, Par 71, SSS 72, Course record 63.
Arran Course: 9 holes, 1996, Par 31, SSS 31.

Visitors Mon-Sun & BHs. Booking required. Dress code. **Societies** Booking required. **Green Fees** Ailsa £150 per round (£190 weekends). Kintyre £120 per 18 holes. **Prof** Paul Burley **Course Designer** Mackenzie Ross, Donald Steel **Facilities** **Leisure** hard tennis courts, heated indoor swimming pool, fishing, sauna, solarium, gymnasium, Colin Montgomerie Links Golf Academy. **Conf** Corporate Hospitality Days **Location** 15m SW of Ayr on A77

EAST KILBRIDE Map 11 NS65

East Kilbride Chapelside Rd, Nerston G74 4PF
☎ 01355 247728
18 holes, 6419yds, Par 71, SSS 71, Course record 64.
Location 0.5m N off A749
Telephone for further details

Torrance House Calderglen Country Park, Strathaven Rd G75 0QZ
☎ 01355 248638 📠 01355 570916
18 holes, 6476yds, Par 72, SSS 69, Course record 71.
Course Designer Hawtree & Son **Location** 1.5m SE of East Kilbride on A726
Telephone for further details

HAMILTON Map 11 NS75

Hamilton Carlisle Rd, Ferniegair ML3 7UE
☎ 01698 282872 📠 01698 204650
e-mail: secretary@hamiltongolfclub.co.uk
Beautiful parkland.
18 holes, 6498yds, Par 70, SSS 70, Course record 62.
Visitors contact club for details. **Societies** welcome.
Green Fees Phone. **Prof** Derek Wright **Course Designer** James Braid **Facilities** **Location** 1.5m SE on A72

Hotel Premier Travel Inn Glasgow (Hamilton), Hamilton Motorway Service Area, HAMILTON
☎ 08701 977124 36 en suite

Strathclyde Park Mote Hill ML3 6BY
☎ 01698 429350
Municipal wooded parkland course with views of the Strathclyde Park sailing loch. Surrounded by a nature reserve and Hamilton racecourse.
9 holes, 3113yds, Par 36, SSS 70, Course record 68.
Club membership 120.
Visitors Mon-Sun & BHs. Booking required. Dress code.
Societies Booking required. **Green Fees** £3.40 per 9 holes. **Prof** William Walker **Facilities**
Location N side of town off B7071

Hotel Premier Travel Inn Glasgow (Hamilton), Hamilton Motorway Service Area, HAMILTON
☎ 08701 977124 36 en suite

LANARK Map 11 NS84

Lanark The Moor, Whitelees Rd ML11 7RX
☎ 01555 663219 & 661456 📠 01555 663219
e-mail: lanarkgolfclub@supanet.com
web: www.lanarkgolfclub.co.uk
Lanark is renowned for its smooth fast greens, natural moorland fairways and beautiful scenery. The course is built on a substrate of glacial sands, providing a unique feeling of tackling a links course at 600ft above sea level. The par of 70 can be a real test when the prevailing wind blows.
Old Course: 18 holes, 6306yds, Par 70, SSS 71, Course record 62.
Wee Course: 9 holes, 1489yds, Par 28.
Club membership 880.
Visitors Mon-Fri. Booking required. Dress code. **Societies** Booking required. **Green Fees** £45 per day, £35 per round. Wee Course, £8 per day. **Prof** Alan White **Course Designer** Tom Morris **Facilities**

Continued

Conf Corporate Hospitality Days **Location** E side of town centre off A73

Hotel ★★★ 60% Cartland Bridge Hotel, Glasgow Rd, LANARK ☎ 01555 664426 20 rms (18 en suite)

LARKHALL Map 11 NS75

Larkhall Burnhead Rd ML9 3AA
☎ 01698 889597
9 holes, 6234yds, Par 70, SSS 70, Course record 69.
Location E side of town on B7019
Telephone for further details

Hotel ★★★ 72% Popinjay Hotel, Lanark Rd, ROSEBANK ☎ 01555 860441 38 en suite

LEADHILLS Map 11 NS81

Leadhills 51 Main St ML12 6XP
☎ 01659 74456
e-mail: harry@glenfranka.fsnet.co.uk
A testing, hilly course. At 1500ft above sea level it is the highest golf course in Scotland.
9 holes, 4354yds, Par 66, SSS 64.
Club membership 80.
Visitors Mon-Sun & BHs. **Societies** Booking required, weekends only. **Green Fees** £10 per day. **Location** E side of village off B797

LESMAHAGOW Map 11 NS83

Holland Bush Acretophead ML11 0JS
☎ 01555 893484 & 893646 📠 01555 893984
e-mail: mail@hollandbushgolfclub.co.uk
web: www.hollandbushgolfclub.co.uk
18 holes, 6246yds, Par 71, SSS 70, Course record 63.
Course Designer J Lawson/K Pate **Location** 3m S of Lesmahagow on Coalburn Rd
Telephone for further details

Hotel ★★★ 74% Strathaven Hotel, Hamilton Rd, STRATHAVEN ☎ 01357 521778 22 en suite

RIGSIDE Map 11 NS83

Douglas Water Ayr Rd ML11 9NP
☎ 01555 880361 📠 01555 880361
A 9-hole course with good variety and some hills and spectacular views. An interesting course with a challenging longest hole of 564 yards but, overall, not too testing for average golfers.
9 holes, 5890yds, Par 72, SSS 69, Course record 63.
Club membership 150.
Visitors Sun-Fri & BHs. **Societies** Booking required.
Green Fees £8per day (£10 weekends). **Facilities** **Location** On A70

Hotel ★★★ 60% Cartland Bridge Hotel, Glasgow Rd, LANARK ☎ 01555 664426 20 rms (18 en suite)

STRATHAVEN Map 11 NS74

Strathaven Glasgow Rd ML10 6NL
☎ 01357 520421 📠 01357 520539
e-mail: info@strathavengc.com
web: www.strathavengc.com
Gently undulating, tree-lined, championship parkland course with views over the town and the Avon valley.

Continued

18 holes, 6250yds, Par 71, SSS 71, Course record 65.
Club membership 1050.
Visitors Mon-Fri. Booking required Tue. Handicap certificate. Dress code. **Societies** Booking required. **Green Fees** £39 per day, £29 per round. **Prof** Stuart Kerr **Course Designer** Willie Fernie/J Stutt **Facilities** **Conf** facs **Location** NE side of town on A726

Hotel ★★★ 74% Strathaven Hotel, Hamilton Rd, STRATHAVEN ☎ 01357 521778 22 en suite

UDDINGSTON Map 11 NS66

Calderbraes 57 Roundknowe Rd G71 7TS
☎ 01698 813425
Parkland with good views of Clyde valley. Testing 4th hole (par 4), hard uphill.
9 holes, 5046yds, Par 66, SSS 67, Course record 65.
Club membership 230.
Visitors Mon-Fri & BHs. Dress code. **Societies** Booking required. **Green Fees** £12 per day. **Facilities** **Location** 1.5m NW off A74

Hotel ★★★ 68% Bothwell Bridge Hotel, 89 Main St, BOTHWELL ☎ 01698 852246 90 en suite

STIRLING

ABERFOYLE Map 11 NN50

Aberfoyle Braeval FK8 3UY
☎ 01877 382493
Scenic heathland course with mountain views.
18 holes, 5210yds, Par 66, SSS 66, Course record 64.
Club membership 665.
Visitors Mon-Sun & BHs. Booking required Sat-Sun. Handicap certificate. **Societies** welcome. **Green Fees** £18 per round, £24 per day (£24/30 weekends). **Facilities** **Location** 1m E on A81

Hotel ★★★★ 66% Macdonald Forest Hills Hotel & Resort, Kinlochard, ABERFOYLE ☎ 0870 1942105 54 en suite

BANNOCKBURN Map 11 NS89

Brucefields Family Golfing Centre Pirnhall Rd FK7 8EH
☎ 01786 818184 🖷 01786 817770
e-mail: christine_frost@brucefields.co.uk
Gently rolling parkland with fine views. Most holes can be played without too much difficulty with the exception of the 2nd which is a long and tricky par 4 and the 6th, a par 3 which requires exact club selection and a straight shot.
Main Course: 9 holes, 2513yds, Par 68, SSS 68, Course record 66.
Club membership 300.
Visitors Mon-Sun & BHs. Booking advised. Dress code. **Societies** welcome. **Green Fees** £17 per 18 holes, £10 per 9 holes (£19/£11 weekends). **Prof** Gregor Monks **Course Designer** Souters Sportsturf **Facilities** **Leisure** golf academy, par 3 9 hole course. **Conf** facs Corporate Hospitality Days **Location** M80/M9 junct 9, A91, 1st left signed

BRIDGE OF ALLAN Map 11 NS79

Bridge of Allan Sunnylaw FK9 4LY
☎ 01786 832332
Very hilly parkland with good views of Stirling Castle and beyond to the Trossachs. Testing par 3 1st hole, 221yds uphill, with a 6ft wall 25yds before green.
9 holes, 4932yds, Par 66, SSS 66, Course record 59.
Club membership 400.
Visitors Mon-Fri. Dress code. **Societies** Booking required. **Green Fees** Phone. **Course Designer** Tom Morris **Facilities** **Location** 0.5m N off A9

Hotel ★★★ 68% Royal Hotel, Henderson St, BRIDGE OF ALLAN ☎ 01786 832284 32 en suite

CALLANDER Map 11 NN60

Callander Aveland Rd FK17 8EN
☎ 01877 330090 & 330975 🖷 01877 330062
e-mail: callandergc@nextcall.net
web: www.callandergolfclub.co.uk
Challenging parkland course with tight fairways and a number of interesting holes. Designed by Tom Morris Snr and overlooked by the Trossachs.
18 holes, 5151yds, Par 66, SSS 65, Course record 61.
Club membership 600.
Visitors Mon-Sun & BHs. Dress code. **Societies** Booking required. **Green Fees** £22 per round/£30 per day (weekends £30/£40). **Prof** Allan Martin **Course Designer** Morris/Fernie **Facilities** **Conf** Corporate Hospitality Days **Location** E side of town off A84

Hotel ★★★ 77% Roman Camp Country House Hotel, CALLANDER ☎ 01877 330003 14 en suite

DRYMEN Map 11 NS48

Buchanan Castle G63 0HY
☎ 01360 660307 🖷 01360 660993
e-mail: buchanancastle@sol.co.uk
web: www.buchanancastlegolfclub.com
Easy walking parkland with and good views. A quiet and relaxed place to play golf, with views of the old castle. Owned by the Duke of Montrose.
18 holes, 6059yds, Par 70, SSS 69.
Club membership 830.
Visitors Booking required. **Societies** Booking required. **Green Fees** Phone. **Prof** Keith Baxter **Course Designer** James Braid **Facilities** **Conf** facs Corporate Hospitality Days **Location** 1m W

Hotel ★★★ 68% Winnock Hotel, The Square, DRYMEN ☎ 01360 660245 48 en suite

Strathendrick G63 0AA
☎ 01360 660695
e-mail: melvinquyn@hotmail.com
Hillside course with breathtaking views of the Campsie and Luss Hills and Ben Lomond. Mainly natural hazards with few bunkers. Greens are comparatively small but in immaculate condition.
9 holes, 4982yards, Par 66, SSS 64, Course record 60.
Club membership 470.
Visitors Mon-Fri & BHs. **Societies** Booking required. **Green Fees** £18 per day, £15 per 18 holes, £10 per 9 holes. **Facilities** **Leisure** hard tennis courts, driving net. **Location** 0.5m S of Drymen via access lane E of A811

Hotel ★★★★★ 70% De Vere Cameron House, BALLOCH ☎ 01389 755565 96 en suite

DUNBLANE Map 11 NN70

Dunblane New Golf Club Perth Rd FK15 0LJ
☎ 01786 821521 01786 825066
e-mail: secretary@dngc.co.uk
web: www.dngc.co.uk
Well-maintained parkland course. Testing par 3 holes.
18 holes, 5930yds, Par 69, SSS 69.
Club membership 1000.
Visitors Sun-Mon, Wed-Fri & BHs. Booking required. Dress code. **Societies** Booking required. **Green Fees** £40 per day, £30 per round. **Prof** Bob Jamieson **Course Designer** James Braid **Facilities** **Conf** facs Corporate Hospitality Days **Location** Off fourways rdbt in town centre

Hotel ★★★ Cromlix House Hotel, Kinbuck, Nr DUNBLANE ☎ 01786 822125 14 en suite

KILLIN Map 11 NN53

Killin FK21 8TX
☎ 01567 820312 & 07795 483107 01567 820312
e-mail: info@killingolfclub.co.uk
web: www.killingolfclub.co.uk
Parkland course at the west end of Loch Tay with outstanding views. Challenging nine-hole course with 14 different tees.

9 holes, 2600yds, Par 66, SSS 65, Course record 61.
Club membership 250.
Visitors contact club for details. Dress code. **Societies** Booking required. **Green Fees** Phone. **Course Designer** John Duncan/J Braid **Facilities** **Conf** Corporate Hospitality Days **Location** 0.5m N of village centre on A827

Guest House ♦♦♦♦ Fairview House, Main St, KILLIN ☎ 01567 820667 6 en suite

STIRLING Map 11 NS79

Stirling Queens Rd FK8 3AA
☎ 01786 464098 01786 460090
e-mail: enquiries@stirlinggolfclub.tv
web: www.stirlinggolfclub.com
Undulating parkland with magnificent views of Stirling Castle and the Grampian Mountains. Testing 15th, Cotton's Fancy, 384yds (par 4).
18 holes, 6438yds, Par 72, SSS 71, Course record 64.
Club membership 1100.
Visitors Sun-Fri & BHs. Booking required. Dress code. **Societies** welcome. **Green Fees** £45 per day, £30 per round. **Prof** Ian Collins **Course Designer** Henry Cotton **Facilities** **Conf** Corporate Hospitality Days **Location** W side of town on B8051

WEST DUNBARTONSHIRE

BALLOCH Map 10 NS48

De Vere Cameron House Hotel Loch Lomond G83 8QZ
☎ 01389 755565
e-mail: stewart.smith@cameronhouse.co.uk
The 18-hole The Carrick on Loch Lomond course opens spring 2007.

Carrick on Loch Lomond: 18 holes, 7200yds, Par 71.
Wee Demon: 9 holes, 3200yds, Par 32.
Club membership 250.
Visitors Mon-Sun & BHs. Booking required. Handicap certificate (Carrick course). **Societies** Booking required. **Green Fees** Carrick £95 per round. Wee Demon £18 per day. **Prof** Stewart Smith **Facilities** **Leisure** hard tennis courts, heated indoor swimming pool, squash, fishing, sauna, solarium, gymnasium. **Conf** facs Corporate Hospitality Days **Location** M8 (W) junct 30 for Erskine Bridge, then A82 for Crainlarich. Course adjacent 1m past Balloch roundabout

Hotel ★★★★★ 70% De Vere Cameron House, BALLOCH ☎ 01389 755565 96 en suite

BONHILL Map 10 NS37

Vale of Leven North Field Rd G83 9ET
☎ 01389 752351 🖹 0870 749 8950
e-mail: rbarclay@volgc.org
web: www.volgc.org
Moorland course, tricky with many natural hazards - gorse, burns, trees. Overlooks Loch Lomond.
18 holes, 5277yds, Par 67, SSS 67, Course record 63.
Club membership 750.
Visitors Mon-Fri, Sun & BHs. Booking required Fri, Sun & BHs. Dress code. **Societies** Booking required. **Green Fees** £30 per day, £20 per round (£37.50/£25 Sun). **Prof** Barry Campbell **Facilities** **Conf** facs Corporate Hospitality Days **Location** E side of town off A813

Hotel ★★★★★ 70% De Vere Cameron House, BALLOCH ☎ 01389 755565 96 en suite

CLYDEBANK Map 11 NS56

Clydebank & District Glasgow Rd, Hardgate G81 5QY
☎ 01389 383831 & 383833 🖹 01389 383831
An undulating parkland course established in 1905, overlooking Clydebank.
18 holes, 5823yds, Par 68, SSS 68, Course record 64.
Club membership 889.
Visitors Mon-Fri. Booking required. Handicap certificate. Dress code. **Societies** Booking required. **Green Fees** Phone. **Prof** A Waugh **Course Designer** Members **Facilities** **Location** 2m E of Erskine Bridge

Hotel Premier Travel Inn Glasgow (Bearsden), Milngavie Rd, BEARSDEN ☎ 0870 9906532 61 en suite

Clydebank Municipal Overtoun Rd, Dalmuir G81 3RE
☎ 0141 952 6372
18 holes, 5349yds, Par 67, SSS 66, Course record 63.
Location 2m NW of town centre
Telephone for further details

Hotel ★★★★ 74% Beardmore Hotel, Beardmore St, CLYDEBANK ☎ 0141 951 6000 166 en suite

DUMBARTON Map 10 NS37

Dumbarton Broadmeadow G82 2BQ
☎ 01389 732830 & 765995 🖹 01389 765995
Flat parkland.
18 holes, 6017yds, Par 71, SSS 69, Course record 64.
Club membership 800.
Visitors Mon-Fri. Booking required. Dress code. **Societies** Booking required. **Green Fees** £30 per day, £20 per round. **Prof** David Muir **Facilities** **Conf** Corporate Hospitality Days **Location** 0.25m N off A814

Guest House ♦♦♦♦♦ Kirkton House, Darleith Rd, CARDROSS ☎ 01389 841951 6 en suite

WEST LOTHIAN

BATHGATE Map 11 NS96

Bathgate Edinburgh Rd EH48 1BA
☎ 01506 630553 & 652232/630505 🖹 01506 636775
e-mail: bathgate.golfclub@lineone.net
web: www.bathgategolfclub.visps.com
Moorland course. Easy walking. Testing 11th hole, par 3.
18 holes, 6328yds, Par 71, SSS 71, Course record 58.
Club membership 900.
Visitors Mon-Sat. Dress code. **Societies** Booking required. **Green Fees** £25 per day, £20 per round (£35/£25 Sat). **Prof** Sandy Strachan **Course Designer** W Park **Facilities** **Conf** Corporate Hospitality Days **Location** E side of town off A89

Hotel ★★★ 68% The Hilcroft Hotel, East Main St, WHITBURN ☎ 01501 740818 32 en suite

BROXBURN Map 11 NT07

Niddry Castle Castle Rd, Winchburgh EH52 6RQ
☎ 01506 891097 🖹 01506 891097
An 18-hole parkland course, requiring accurate golf to score well.
18 holes, 5914yds, Par 70, SSS 69, Course record 63.
Club membership 600.
Visitors Mon-Wed & Fri. Booking required. Dress code. **Societies** Booking required. **Green Fees** Phone. **Course Designer** A Scott **Facilities** **Conf** Corporate Hospitality Days **Location** 9m W of Edinburgh on B9080

Hotel ★★★★ 72% Macdonald Houstoun House, UPHALL ☎ 0870 1942107 24 en suite 47 annexe en suite

FAULDHOUSE Map 11 NS96

Greenburn 6 Greenburn Rd EH47 9HJ
☎ 01501 770292 🖹 01501 772615
e-mail: administrator@greenburngolfclub.freeserve.co.uk
web: www.greenburngolfclub.co.uk
A testing course, with a mixture of parkland and moorland. Water features on 14 of the 18 holes, with a burn crossing most of the holes on the back 9.
18 holes, 6067yds, Par 71, SSS 70, Course record 65.
Club membership 900.
Visitors Mon-Sun. Booking required Wed, Sat-Sun. Dress code. **Societies** Booking required. **Green Fees** £26 per day, £19 per round (weekends £32/£25). **Prof** Scott Catlin **Facilities** **Location** 3m SW of Whitburn

Hotel ★★★ 68% The Hilcroft Hotel, East Main St, WHITBURN ☎ 01501 740818 32 en suite

LINLITHGOW Map 11 NS97

Linlithgow Braehead EH49 6QF
☎ 01506 844356 (Pro) 🖹 01506 842764
e-mail: info@linlithgowgolf.co.uk
web: www.linlithgowgolf.co.uk
A short but testing undulating parkland course with panoramic views of the Forth valley.
18 holes, 5800yds, Par 70, SSS 68, Course record 64.
Club membership 450.

Continued

Visitors Mon-Tue, Thu, Fri am, Sun & BHs. Dress code. **Societies** welcome. **Green Fees** £35 per day, £25 per round (£40/£30 Sun). **Prof** Steven Rosie **Course Designer** R Simpson of Carnoustie **Facilities** **Conf** Corporate Hospitality Days **Location** 1m S off A706

Hotel ★★★★ 69% Macdonald Inchyra Grange Hotel, Grange Rd, POLMONT ☎ 0870 1942115 103 en suite

West Lothian Airngath Hill EH49 7RH
☎ 01506 825060 01506 826462
web: www.thewestlothiangolfclub.co.uk
18 holes, 6249yds, Par 71, SSS 70.
Course Designer Fraser Middleton **Location** 1m N off A706
Telephone for further details

Hotel ★★★★ 69% Macdonald Inchyra Grange Hotel, Grange Rd, POLMONT ☎ 0870 1942115 103 en suite

LIVINGSTON Map 11 NT06

Deer Park Golf & Country Club Golf Course Rd EH54 8AB
☎ 01506 446699 01506 435608
e-mail: deerpark@muir-group.co.uk
web: www.deer-park.co.uk
Long testing course, fairly flat, championship standard.
18 holes, 6690yds, Par 72, SSS 72, Course record 65.
Visitors Booking required. Dress code. **Societies** telephone or write **Green Fees** Phone. **Prof** Brian Dunbar **Course Designer** Alliss/Thomas **Facilities** **Leisure** heated indoor swimming pool, squash, sauna, solarium, gymnasium, snooker table, ten pin bowling. **Conf** facs Corporate Hospitality Days **Location** M8 junct 3, to N side of town

Hotel Premier Travel Inn Livingston (Nr Edinburgh), Deer Park Av, Knightsridge, LIVINGSTON
☎ 08701 977161 83 en suite

Pumpherston Drumshoreland Rd, Pumpherston EH53 0LH
☎ 01506 433336 & 433337 (pro) 01506 438250
e-mail: sheena.corner@tiscali.co.uk
web: www.pumpherstongolfclub.co.uk
Undulating, well-bunkered parkland course with very testing 2nd and 15th holes. The course has water features at five holes and has won several environmental awards. Panoramic views of Edinburgh and the Pentland Hills.
18 holes, 6006yds, Par 70, SSS 72.
Club membership 800.
Visitors Mon-Sun & BHs. Dress code. **Societies** Booking required. **Green Fees** Phone. **Prof** Richard Fyvie **Course Designer** G Webster **Facilities** by arrangement **Leisure** Pool table. **Location** 1m E of Livingston off B8046

Hotel Premier Travel Inn Livingston (Nr Edinburgh), Deer Park Av, Knightsridge, LIVINGSTON
☎ 08701 977161 83 en suite

UPHALL Map 11 NT07

Uphall EH52 6JT
☎ 01506 856404 01506 855358
e-mail: uphallgolfclub@businessunmetered.com
A windy parkland course with easy walking.
18 holes, 5588yds, Par 69, SSS 67, Course record 61.
Club membership 650.
Visitors must contact in advance, restricted weekends. **Societies** Booking required. **Green Fees** Phone. **Prof** Gordon Law **Facilities** **Location** W side of village on A899

Hotel ★★★★ 72% Macdonald Houstoun House, UPHALL ☎ 0870 1942107 24 en suite 47 annexe en suite

WEST CALDER Map 11 NT06

Harburn EH55 8RS
☎ 01506 871131 & 871256 01506 870286
e-mail: info@harburngolfclub.co.uk
web: www.harburngolfclub.co.uk
Parkland with a variety of beech, oak and pine trees. The 11th and 12th holes were extended in 2004. Fine views of the Pentlands

18 holes, 6125yds, Par 71, SSS 70, Course record 64.
Club membership 870.
Visitors Mon-Sun & BHs. Booking required. Handicap certificate. Dress code. **Societies** Booking required. **Green Fees** £30 per day, £25 per 18 holes (Fri £35/£30, Sat-Sun £40/£35). **Prof** Stephen Mills **Facilities** **Conf** facs Corporate Hospitality Days **Location** 2m S of West Calder on B7008

Hotel ★★★ 68% The Hilcroft Hotel, East Main St, WHITBURN ☎ 01501 740818 32 en suite

WHITBURN Map 11 NS96

Polkemmet Country Park EH47 0AD
☎ 01501 743905 01506 846256
e-mail: mail@beecraigs.com
web: www.beecraigs.com
Public parkland course surrounded by mature woodland and rhododendron bushes and bisected by a river. Interesting and demanding last hole.
9 holes, 2946 metres, Par 37.
Visitors Mon-Sun & BHs. **Societies** Booking required. **Green Fees** 9 holes £5.40; 18 holes £9.10 (weekends and BHs £6.35/£10.75). **Facilities** **Leisure** bowling green. **Location** 2m W of Whitburn on B7066

Hotel ★★★ 68% The Hilcroft Hotel, East Main St, WHITBURN ☎ 01501 740818 32 en suite

ARRAN, ISLE OF

BLACKWATERFOOT Map 10 NR92

Shiskine Shore Rd KA27 8HA
☎ 01770 860226 🖷 01770 860205
e-mail: info@shiskinegolf.com
web: www.shiskinegolf.com
Unique 12-hole links course with gorgeous outlook to the Mull of Kintyre. The course is crossed by two burns and includes the longest par 5 on the island at 509yds. There are several blind holes at which various signals indicate when the green is clear and it is safe to play.
12 holes, 2990yds, Par 42, SSS 42, Course record 38. Club membership 670.
Visitors Mon-Sun & BHs. Booking required. Handicap certificate. **Societies** Booking required. **Green Fees** £28 per day, £16 per round (£33/£20 Sat, Sun & BHs). **Course Designer** Fernie of Troon **Facilities** by arrangement **Leisure** hard tennis courts, bowling green, golf practice nets. **Conf** Corporate Hospitality Days **Location** W side of village off A841

Hotel ★★ Kilmichael Country House Hotel, Glen Cloy, BRODICK ☎ 01770 302219 4 en suite 3 annexe en suite

BRODICK Map 10 NS03

Brodick KA27 8DL
☎ 01770 302349 🖷 01770 302349
e-mail: info@brodickgolfclub.org
web: www.brodickgolfclub.org
18 holes, 4747yds, Par 65, SSS 64, Course record 60.
Location N side of village, 0.5m N of Brodick Ferry Terminal
Telephone for further details

Hotel ★★★ 77% Auchrannie House Hotel, BRODICK ☎ 01770 302234 28 en suite

LAMLASH Map 10 NS03

Lamlash KA27 8JU
☎ 01770 600296 🖷 01770 600296
e-mail: lamlashgolfclub@connectfree.co.uk
web: www.lamlashgolfclub.co.uk
Undulating heathland course with magnificent views of the mountains and sea.
18 holes, 4510yds, Par 64, SSS 64, Course record 58. Club membership 480.
Visitors Mon-Sun & BHs. Booking required. **Societies** Booking required. **Green Fees** Phone. **Course Designer** Auchterlonie **Facilities** **Location** 0.75m N of Lamlash on A841

Hotel ★★★ 77% Auchrannie House Hotel, BRODICK ☎ 01770 302234 28 en suite

LOCHRANZA Map 10 NR95

Lochranza KA27 8HL
☎ 01770 830273 🖷 01770 830600
e-mail: office@lochgolf.demon.co.uk
web: www.lochranzagolf.com
This course is mainly on the level, set amid spectacular scenery where the fairways are grazed by wild red deer, while overhead buzzards and golden eagles may be seen. There are water hazards including the river which is lined by mature trees. The final three holes, nicknamed the Bermuda Triangle, provide an absorbing finish right to the 18th hole - a 530yd dogleg through trees and over the river. The large greens, six single and six double, are played off 18 tees.
18 holes, 5033 metres, Par 70, SSS 67, Course record 72.
Visitors Mon-Sun & BHs. Contact club for details. **Societies** welcome. **Green Fees** £16 per 18 holes, £10 per 9 holes, £21 per day. **Course Designer** re laid 1991 I Robertson **Facilities** **Location** In Lochranza village

Hotel ★★ Kilmichael Country House Hotel, Glen Cloy, BRODICK ☎ 01770 302219 4 en suite 3 annexe en suite

MACHRIE Map 10 NR83

Machrie Bay KA27 8DZ
☎ 01770 840259 🖷 01770 840266
e-mail: office@dougarie.com
web: www.dougarie.com
Fairly flat seaside course. Designed at the start of the 20th century by William Fernie.
9 holes, 4556yds, Par 66, SSS 63, Course record 63. Club membership 350.
Visitors Mon-Sun & BHs. **Societies** Booking required. **Green Fees** £14 per day. **Course Designer** W Fernie **Facilities** **Leisure** hard tennis courts. **Location** 9m W of Brodick via String Rd

Hotel ★★ Kilmichael Country House Hotel, Glen Cloy, BRODICK ☎ 01770 302219 4 en suite 3 annexe en suite

SANNOX Map 10 NS04

Corrie KA27 8JD
☎ 01770 810223 & 810606
A heathland course on the coast with beautiful mountain scenery. An upward climb to 6th hole then a descent from the 7th. All these holes are subject to strong winds in bad weather.
9 holes, 1948yds, Par 62, SSS 61, Course record 56. Club membership 300.
Visitors Mon-Fri, Sun & BHs. **Societies** Booking required. **Green Fees** £14 per day/round. **Facilities** **Location** 6m N of A841

Hotel ★★★ 77% Auchrannie House Hotel, BRODICK ☎ 01770 302234 28 en suite

WHITING BAY Map 10 NS02

Whiting Bay KA27 8QT
☎ 01770 700487
Heathland course.
18 holes, 4405yds, Par 63, SSS 63, Course record 59. Club membership 350.
Visitors Mon-Fri & BHs. Booking required Sat, Sun & BHs. Contact club for details. **Societies** welcome. **Green Fees** £20 per day, £19 per round. **Facilities** **Location** NW side of village off A841

Hotel ★★ Kilmichael Country House Hotel, Glen Cloy, BRODICK ☎ 01770 302219 4 en suite 3 annexe en suite

Continued

BUTE, ISLE OF

KINGARTH Map 10 NS05

Bute St Ninians, 32 Marine Place, Ardbeg, Rothesay PA20 0LF
☎ 01700 502158
e-mail: info@butegolfclub.com
web: www.butegolfclub.com
Flat seaside course with good fenced greens and fine views over the Sound of Bute to Isle of Arran. Challenging par 3 along sea.
9 holes, 2361 metres, Par 68, SSS 64, Course record 61. Club membership 250.
Visitors Mon-Sun & BHs. Sat after 11.30am. **Societies** Booking required. **Green Fees** £10 per day. **Facilities** **Location** 6m from Rothesay pier on A845

Hotel ★★ 81% The Royal at Tighnabruaich, Shore Rd, TIGHNABRUAICH ☎ 01700 811239 11 en suite

PORT BANNATYNE Map 10 NS06

Port Bannatyne Bannatyne Mains Rd PA20 0PH
☎ 01700 505142
e-mail: macleodbute@btopenworld.com
web: www.geocities.com/~golftraveler/
Seaside hill course with panoramic views. Almost unique in having 13 holes, with the first five being played again before a separate 18th. Difficult 4th (par 3).
13 holes, 5085yds, Par 68, SSS 65, Course record 63. Club membership 150.
Visitors Mon-Sat & BHs. Dress code. **Societies** Booking required. **Green Fees** Mon-Fri £13 per day. £10 per round. Sat & Sun £16 per day. £13 per round. **Course Designer** Peter Morrison **Facilities** **Location** W side of village off A886

Hotel ★★ 81% The Royal at Tighnabruaich, Shore Rd, TIGHNABRUAICH ☎ 01700 811239 11 en suite

ROTHESAY Map 10 NS06

Rothesay Canada Hill PA20 9HN
☎ 01700 503554 📠 01700 503554
e-mail: thepro@rothesaygolfclub.com
web: www.rothesaygolfclub.com
18 holes, 5419yds, Par 69, SSS 66, Course record 62.
Course Designer James Braid & Ben Sayers **Location** 500yds SE from main ferry terminal
Telephone for further details

Hotel ★★ 81% The Royal at Tighnabruaich, Shore Rd, TIGHNABRUAICH ☎ 01700 811239 11 en suite

COLONSAY, ISLE OF

SCALASAIG Map 10 NR39

Colonsay Machrins Farm PA61 7YR
☎ 01951 200290 📠 01951 200290
Traditional links course on natural machair (hard wearing short grass), challenging, primitive.
18 holes, 4775yds, Par 72, SSS 72. Club membership 200.
Visitors Mon-Sun & BHs. Handicap certificate. **Societies** Booking required. **Green Fees** Phone. **Facilities** **Location** 2m W on A870

ISLAY, ISLE OF

PORT ELLEN Map 10 NR34

Machrie Hotel Machrie PA42 7AN
☎ 01496 302310 📠 01496 302404
e-mail: machrie@machrie.com
web: www.machrie.com
Championship links course opened in 1891, where golf's first £100 Open Championship was played in 1901. Fine turf and many blind holes. Par 4.
18 holes, 6226yds, Par 71, SSS 71, Course record 66. Club membership 340.
Visitors no restrictions. **Societies** apply in writing or telephone. **Green Fees** Phone. **Course Designer** W Campbell **Facilities** **Leisure** fishing, snooker, table tennis. **Conf** facs **Location** 4m N off A846

Inn ♦♦♦♦♦ The Harbour Inn and Restaurant, BOWMORE ☎ 01496 810330 7 en suite

LEWIS, ISLE OF

STORNOWAY Map 13 NB43

Stornoway Lady Lever Park HS2 0XP
☎ 01851 702240
e-mail: admin@stornowaygolfclub.co.uk
web: www.stornowaygolfclub.co.uk
A short but tricky undulating parkland course set in the grounds of Lews Castle with fine views over the Minch to the mainland. The terrain is peat based and there has been substantial investment in drainage works.
18 holes, 5252yds, Par 68, SSS 67, Course record 61. Club membership 500.
Visitors Mon-Sat & BHs. Booking required Sat. **Societies** Booking required. **Green Fees** £20 per round/day. **Course Designer** J & R Stutt **Facilities** by arrangement by arrangement **Conf** facs **Location** 0.5m from town centre off A857

MULL, ISLE OF

CRAIGNURE Map 10 NM73

Craignure Scallastle PA65 6BA
☎ 01680 300402 📠 01680 300402
e-mail: mullair@btinternet.com
9 holes, 5357yds, Par 69, SSS 66, Course record 72.
Location 1.5m N of Craignure A849
Telephone for further details

Continued

TOBERMORY Map 13 NM55

Tobermory PA75 6PG
☎ 01688 302338 🖷 01688 302140
e-mail: enquiries@tobermorygolfclub.com
web: www.tobermorygolfclub.com
A beautifully maintained hilltop course with superb views over the Sound of Mull. Testing 7th hole (par 3). Often described as the best nine-hole course in Scotland.
9 holes, 4890yds, Par 64, SSS 64, Course record 65. Club membership 150.
Visitors Booking required. **Societies** preferable to contact in advance. **Green Fees** Phone. **Course Designer** David Adams **Facilities** **Location** 0.5m N off A848

ORKNEY

KIRKWALL Map 16 HY41

Orkney Grainbank KW15 1RB
☎ 01856 872457
e-mail: les@orkneygolfclub.co.uk
web: www.orkneygolfclub.co.uk
Open parkland course with few hazards and superb views over Kirkwall and islands. Very exposed to the elements which can make play tough.
18 holes, 5411yds, Par 70, SSS 67, Course record 63. Club membership 350.
Visitors Mon-Sun & BHs. Booking required Sat-Sun. **Societies** Booking required. **Green Fees** £20 per day. **Facilities** **Conf** Corporate Hospitality Days **Location** 0.5m W off A965

STROMNESS Map 16 HY20

Stromness Ness KW16 3DW
☎ 01856 850772
e-mail: sgc@stromnessgc.co.uk
web: www.stromnessgc.co.uk
Testing parkland and seaside course with easy walking. Magnificent views of Scapa Flow.
18 holes, 4762yds, Par 65, SSS 64, Course record 61. Club membership 350.
Visitors Mon-Sun & BHs. **Societies** welcome. **Green Fees** £20 per day. **Facilities** **Leisure** hard tennis courts, Bowling. **Location** S side of town centre off A965

SHETLAND

LERWICK Map 16 HU44

Shetland PO Box 18, Dale ZE2 9SB
☎ 01595 840369 🖷 840369
e-mail: shetlandgolfclub@btopenworld.com
web: www.shetlandgolfclub.co.uk
Challenging moorland course, hard walking. A burn runs the full length of the course and provides a natural hazard. Testing holes include the 3rd (par 4), 5th (par 4).
Dale Course: 18 holes, 5562yds, Par 68, SSS 68. Club membership 430.
Visitors Booking required. **Societies** Booking required. **Green Fees** Phone. **Course Designer** Fraser Middleton **Facilities** **Conf** facs Corporate Hospitality Days **Location** 4m N on A970

Hotel ★★★ 68% Lerwick Hotel, 15 South Rd, LERWICK ☎ 01595 692166 34 en suite

WHALSAY, ISLAND OF Map 16 HU56

Whalsay Skaw Taing ZE2 9AA
☎ 01806 566450 566705
The most northerly golf course in Britain, with a large part of it running round the coastline, offering spectacular holes in an exposed but highly scenic setting. There are no cut fairways as yet, these are defined by marker posts, with preferred lies in operation all year round.
18 holes, 6140yds, Par 71, SSS 69, Course record 69. Club membership 205.
Visitors Booking required. **Societies** Booking required. **Green Fees** Phone. **Facilities** by arrangement **Location** Whalsay Island & Portree

SKYE, ISLE OF

SCONSER Map 13 NG53

Isle of Skye IV48 8TD
☎ 01478 650414
e-mail: info@isleofskyegolfclub.co.uk
web: www.isleofskyegolfclub.co.uk
Seaside course with spectacular views; nine holes with 18 tees. Suitable for golfers of all abilities.
18 holes, 4677yds, Par 66, SSS 64, Course record 62. Club membership 270.
Visitors Booking required. **Societies** Booking required. **Green Fees** Phone. **Facilities** **Location** On A87 between Broadford & Portree

Hotel ★★ 73% Rosedale Hotel, Beaumont Crescent, PORTREE ☎ 01478 613131 18 en suite

SOUTH UIST

ASKERNISH Map 13 NF72

Askernish Lochboisdale PA81 5SY
☎ 01878 700298
e-mail: askernish.golf.club@cwcom.net
18 holes, 5042yds, Par 68, SSS 67, Course record 64.
Course Designer Tom Morris **Location** 5m NW of Lochboisdale off A865
Telephone for further details

Continued

Wales

ANGLESEY, ISLE OF

AMLWCH Map 06 SH49

Bull Bay LL68 9RY
01407 830960 01407 832612
e-mail: secretary@bullbaygolf.freeserve.co.uk
web: ww.bullbaygc.co.uk
Wales's northernmost course, Bull Bay is a pleasant coastal, heathland course with natural rock, gorse and wind hazards. Views from several tees across the Irish Sea to the Isle of Man, and across Anglesey to Snowdonia.
18 holes, 6217yds, Par 70, SSS 70, Course record 60. Club membership 700.
Visitors Mon-Sun & BHs. Booking required. Handicap certificate. Dress code. **Societies** welcome. **Green Fees** £30 per day, £27 per round (£36/£33 weekends, no day ticket on Sat). **Prof** John Burns **Course Designer** W H Fowler **Facilities** **Conf** Corporate Hospitality Days **Location** 1m W of Amlwch on A5025

Hotel ★★ 70% Lastra Farm Hotel, Penrhyd, AMLWCH 01407 830906 5 en suite 3 annexe en suite

BEAUMARIS Map 06 SH67

Baron Hill LL58 8YW
01248 810231 01248 810231
e-mail: golf@baronhill.co.uk
web: www.baronhill.co.uk
Undulating course with natural hazards of rock and gorse. Testing 3rd and 4th holes (par 4s). Hole 5/14 plays into the prevailing wind with an elevated tee across two streams. The hole is between two gorse covered mounds.
9 holes, 5572yds, Par 68, SSS 68, Course record 65. Club membership 350.
Visitors Mon-Sat & BHs. Booking required. Dress code. **Societies** Booking required. **Green Fees** £15 per day. **Course Designer** R Dawson **Facilities** **Conf** Corporate Hospitality Days **Location** A545 from Menai Bridge to Beaumaris, course signed on approach to town

Hotel ★★ 76% Ye Olde Bulls Head Inn, Castle St, BEAUMARIS 01248 810329 12 en suite 1 annexe en suite

Princes Henllys Hall LL58 8HU
01248 811717 01248 811511
e-mail: henllys@hpbsite.com
18 holes, 6062yards.
Course Designer Roger Jones **Location** A545 through Beaumaris, 0.25m Henllys Hall signed on left
Telephone for further details

Hotel ★★ 76% Ye Olde Bulls Head Inn, Castle St, BEAUMARIS 01248 810329 12 en suite 1 annexe en suite

HOLYHEAD Map 06 SH28

Holyhead Lon Garreg Fawr, Trearddur Bay LL65 2YL
01407 763279 01407 763279
e-mail: mqrsec@aol.com
web: www.holyheadgolfclub.co.uk
Treeless, undulating seaside course which provides a

Continued

varied and testing game, particularly in a south wind. The fairways are bordered by gorse, heather and rugged outcrops of rock. Accuracy from most tees is paramount as there are 43 fairway and greenside bunkers and lakes. Designed by James Braid.
18 holes, 6058yds, Par 70, SSS 70, Course record 64. Club membership 1350.
Visitors must contact in advance. **Societies** Booking required. **Green Fees** Phone. **Prof** Stephen Elliot **Course Designer** James Braid **Facilities** **Location** A55 to rdbt at Holyhead, left onto B4545 to Trearddur Bay 1m

Hotel ★★★ 73% Trearddur Bay Hotel, TREARDDUR BAY 01407 860301 34 en suite 6 annexe en suite

RHOSNEIGR Map 06 SH37

Anglesey Station Rd LL64 5QX
01407 811127 & 811202 01407 811127
e-mail: info@theangleseygolfclub.com
web: www.theangleseygolfclub.co.uk
An interesting 18-hole links course set among sand dunes and heather, renowned for its excellent greens and numerous streams. The whole course has an abundance of wildlife and is an important conservation area.
18 holes, 6330yds, Par 70, SSS 71, Course record 64. Club membership 500.
Visitors Booking required. Dress code. **Societies** telephone & confirm in writing. **Green Fees** Phone. **Prof** Mr Matthew Parry **Course Designer** H Hilton **Facilities** **Location** NE side of village on A4080

Hotel ★★★ 73% Trearddur Bay Hotel, TREARDDUR BAY 01407 860301 34 en suite 6 annexe en suite

BLAENAU GWENT

NANTYGLO Map 03 SO11

West Monmouthshire Golf Rd, Winchestown NP23 4QT
01495 310233
e-mail: care@westmongolfclub.co.uk
web: www.westmongolfclub.co.uk
Established in 1906, this mountain and heathland course was officially designated by the Guinness Book of Records in 1994 as being the highest above sea level, with the 14th tee at a height of 1513ft. The course has plenty of picturesque views, hard walking and natural hazards. Testing 3rd hole, par 5, and 7th hole, par 4.
18 holes, 6300yds, Par 71, SSS 69, Course record 65. Club membership 350.
Visitors contact club for details. Dress code. **Societies** Booking required. **Green Fees** £12 per day (£15 weekends). **Course Designer** Ben Sayers **Facilities** **Conf** facs Corporate Hospitality Days **Location** 0.25m W off A467

Hotel ★★ 72% Llanwenarth Hotel & Riverside Restaurant, Brecon Rd, ABERGAVENNY 01873 810550 17 en suite

TREDEGAR Map 03 SO10

Tredegar and Rhymney Cwmtysswg, Rhymney NP2 3BQ
☎ 01685 840743 (club) 07761 005184 (sec)
e-mail: golfclub@tredegarandrhymney.fsnet.co.uk
Mountain course with lovely views. The course has now been developed into an 18-hole course with easy walking.
18 holes, 6250yds, Par 67, SSS 67, Course record 68.
Club membership 194.
Visitors Mon-Sun & BHs. Booking required Sun. Dress code. **Societies** Booking required. **Green Fees** £10 per day. **Facilities** **Conf** Corporate Hospitality Days **Location** 1.75m SW on B4256

Hotel Tregenna Hotel, Park Ter, MERTHYR TYDFIL ☎ 01685 723627 382055 01685 721951 21 en suite

BRIDGEND

BRIDGEND Map 03 SS97

Coed-Y-Mwstwr The Clubhouse, Coychurch CF35 6AF
☎ 01656 864934 01656 864934
e-mail: secretary@coed-y-mwstwr.co.uk
web: www.coed-y-mwstwr.co.uk
Challenging holes on this course include the par 3 11th (180yds) involving a drive across a pond and the par 4 5th (448yds) which is subject to strong prevailing winds. Previously 12 holes but extended to 18 holes during 2005.
18 holes, 5463yds, Par 69, SSS 68.
Club membership 300.
Visitors Sun-Fri & BHs. Booking required. Handicap certificate. Dress code. **Societies** Booking required. **Green Fees** £20 per 18 holes (£25 Sun & BHs). **Course Designer** Chapman/Warren **Facilities** **Conf** facs Corporate Hospitality Days **Location** M4 junct 35, A473 into Coychurch, course 1m N

Hotel ★★★★ 68% Coed-Y-Mwstwr Hotel, Coychurch, BRIDGEND ☎ 01656 860621 28 en suite

Southerndown Ogmore By Sea CF32 0QP
☎ 01656 880476 01656 880317
e-mail: southerndowngolf@btconnect.com
web: www.southerndowngolfclub.co.uk
Downland-links championship course with rolling fairways and fast greens. Golfers who successfully negotiate the four par 3s still face a testing finish with three of the last four holes played into the prevailing wind. The par 3 5th is played across a valley and the 18th, with its split-level fairway, is a demanding finishing hole. Superb views.
18 holes, 6449yds, Par 70, SSS 72, Course record 64.
Club membership 710.
Visitors Mon-Sun & BHs. Booking required. Handicap certificate. Dress code. **Societies** Booking required. **Green Fees** £45 per 18 holes £55 per 36 holes (£65 weekends). **Prof** D G McMonagle **Course Designer** W Park/W Fernie & others **Facilities** **Location** 3m SW of Bridgend on B4524

Hotel ★★★ 69% Heronston Hotel, Ewenny Rd, BRIDGEND ☎ 01656 668811 & 666087 01656 767391 69 en suite 6 annexe en suite

MAESTEG Map 03 SS89

Maesteg Mount Pleasant, Neath Rd CF34 9PR
☎ 01656 734106 01656 731822
e-mail: ijm@fsmail.net
web: www.maesteg-golf.co.uk
Reasonably flat hill-top course with scenic views.
18 holes, 5929yds, Par 70, SSS 69, Course record 69.
Club membership 789.
Visitors Handicap certificate. **Societies** apply in writing. **Green Fees** Phone. **Course Designer** James Braid **Facilities** **Conf** facs **Location** 0.5m W off B4282

Hotel ★★★ 68% Aberavon Beach Hotel, PORT TALBOT ☎ 01639 884949 52 en suite

PENCOED Map 03 SS98

St Mary's Hotel Golf & Country Club St Mary Hill CF35 5EA
☎ 01656 868900 01656 863400
St Mary's Course: 18 holes, 5291yds, Par 69, SSS 66, Course record 65.
Sevenoaks Course: 12 holes, 3125yds, Par 35.
Course Designer Peter Johnson **Location** M4 junct 35, 5m
Telephone for further details

Hotel ★★★ 70% St Mary's Hotel & Country Club, St Marys Golf Club, PENCOED ☎ 01656 861100 & 860280 01656 863400 24 en suite

PORTHCAWL Map 03 SS87

Royal Porthcawl Rest Bay CF36 3UW
☎ 01656 782251 01656 771687
e-mail: royalporthcawl@btconnect.com
web: www.royalporthcawl.com
One of the great links courses, Royal Porthcawl is unique in that the sea is in full view from every single hole. The course enjoys a substantial reputation with heather, broom, gorse and a challenging wind demanding a player's full skill and attention.
18 holes, 6440yds, Par 72, SSS 73.
Club membership 800.
Visitors Tue, Thu & Fri. Booking required. Handicap certificate. Dress code. **Societies** Booking required. **Green Fees** £120 per day, £80 per round (£150/£100 weekends). **Prof** Peter Evans **Course Designer** Ramsey Hunter **Facilities** **Location** M4 junct 37, proceed to Rest Bay

Hotel ★★★ 65% Seabank Hotel, The Promenade, PORTHCAWL ☎ 01656 782261 67 en suite

PYLE Map 03 SS88

Pyle & Kenfig Waun-Y-Mer CF33 4PU
☎ 01656 783093 01656 772822
e-mail: secretary@pandkgolfclub.co.uk
web: www.pandkgolfclub.co.uk
Links and downland course, with dunes. Easy walking.
18 holes, 6776yds, Par 71, SSS 73, Course record 61.
Club membership 950.
Visitors Mon-Fri, Sun in summer & BHs. Booking required. Handicap certificate. Dress code. **Societies** Booking required. **Green Fees** £50 per day (£70 Sun) max 27 holes. **Prof** Robert Evans **Course Designer** Colt

Continued

Facilities ⊗)Ⅲ ⛳ ☕ 🍸 ⛹ 🏨 ⛳ ✓ ⚑ **Location** M4 junct 37, S side of Pyle off A4229

Hotel ★★★ 65% Seabank Hotel, The Promenade, PORTHCAWL ☎ 01656 782261 67 en suite

CAERPHILLY

BARGOED Map 03 ST19

Bargoed Heolddu CF81 9GF
☎ 01443 836179 🖷 01143 830608
18 holes, 6049yds, Par 70, SSS 70, Course record 64.
Location NW side of town
Telephone for further details

Hotel ★★★ 68% Maes Manor Hotel, BLACKWOOD ☎ 01495 220011 13 en suite 14 annexe en suite

BLACKWOOD Map 03 ST19

Blackwood Cwmgelli NP12 1BR
☎ 01495 222121 (Office) & 223152 (Club)
Heathland course with sand bunkers. Undulating, with hard walking. Testing 2nd hole par 4. Good views.
9 holes, 5332yds, Par 67, Course record 62.
Club membership 310.
Visitors Mon-Fri. Handicap certificate. **Societies** by arrangement for members of a recognised golf club. **Green Fees** Phone. **Facilities** ⊗ ⛳ ☕ 🍸 ⛹ **Location** 0.25m N of Blackwood, off A4048

Hotel ★★★ 68% Maes Manor Hotel, BLACKWOOD ☎ 01495 220011 13 en suite 14 annexe en suite

CAERPHILLY Map 03 ST18

Caerphilly Pencapel, Mountain Rd CF83 1HJ
☎ 029 20883481 & 20863441 🖷 029 20863441
18 holes, 5732yds, Par 71, SSS 69.
Location 0.5m S on A469
Telephone for further details

Hotel ★★★ 71% Manor Parc Country Hotel & Restaurant, Thornhill Rd, Thornhill, CARDIFF ☎ 029 2069 3723 21 en suite

Mountain Lakes & Castell Heights
Blaengwynlais CF83 1NG
☎ 029 20861128 & 20886666 🖷 029 20863243
e-mail: sales@golfclub.co.uk
web: www.golfclub.co.uk
The nine-hole Castell Heights course within the Mountain Lakes complex was established in 1982 on a 45-acre site. In 1988 a further 18-hole course, Mountain Lakes was designed by Bob Sandow to take advantage of 160 acres of mountain heathland, combining both mountain-top golf and parkland. Most holes are tree-lined and there are 20 lakes as hazards. Host to major PGA tournaments.
Mountain Lakes Course: 18 holes, 6046 metres, Par 74, SSS 73, Course record 69.
Castell Heights Course: 9 holes, 2751 metres, Par 35, SSS 32, Course record 32.
Club membership 500.
Visitors contact club for details. **Societies** welcome. **Green Fees** Phone. **Prof** Sion Bebb **Course Designer** Bob Sandow **Facilities** ⛹ 🏨 ⛳ ⛳ 🚗 ✓ ⚑ **Conf** facs Corporate Hospitality Days **Location** M4 junct 32, near Black Cock Inn, Caerphilly Mountain

Hotel ★★★ 71% Manor Parc Country Hotel & Restaurant, Thornhill Rd, Thornhill, CARDIFF ☎ 029 2069 3723 21 en suite

MAESYCWMMER Map 03 ST19

Bryn Meadows Golf & Country Hotel Mr G Mayo CF82 7FN
☎ 01495 225590 or 224103 🖷 01495 228272
e-mail: information@brynmeadows.co.uk
18 holes, 6132yds, Par 72, SSS 69, Course record 68.
Course Designer Mayo/Jeffries **Location** On A4048 Blackwood-Ystrad Mynach road
Telephone for further details

Hotel ★★★ 68% Maes Manor Hotel, BLACKWOOD ☎ 01495 220011 13 en suite 14 annexe en suite

NELSON Map 03 ST19

Whitehall The Pavilion CF46 6ST
☎ 01443 740245
e-mail: m.wilde001@tiscali.co.uk
Hilltop course. Testing 4th hole (225yds) par 3, and 6th hole (402yds) par 4. Pleasant views.
9 holes, 5666yds, Par 69, SSS 68, Course record 63.
Club membership 300.
Visitors Mon-Sat & BHs. Booking required Sat & BHs. Handicap certificate. Dress code. **Societies** Booking required. **Green Fees** £10 per 18 holes. **Facilities** ⊗)Ⅲ ⛳ ☕ 🍸 ⛹ **Leisure** snooker. **Conf** facs Corporate Hospitality Days **Location** 1m SW of Nelson off A4054

Hotel ★★★ 71% Llechwen Hall Hotel, Llanfabon, PONTYPRIDD ☎ 01443 742050 & 743020 🖷 01443 742189 12 en suite 8 annexe en suite

OAKDALE Map 03 ST19

Oakdale Llwynon Ln NP12 0NF
☎ 01495 220044 & 220440
A challenging parkland course for players of all abilities. Well-maintained mature greens.
9 holes, 1344yds, Par 28, Course record 27.
Visitors no restrictions pay & play. **Societies** Booking required. **Green Fees** Phone. **Course Designer** Ian Goodenough **Facilities** ⛳ ☕ 🍸 ⛹ 🏨 ⛳ 🚗 ✓ ⚑ **Leisure** fishing, Snooker tables. **Location** Off B4251 at Oakdale

Hotel ★★★ 68% Maes Manor Hotel, BLACKWOOD ☎ 01495 220011 13 en suite 14 annexe en suite

CARDIFF

CARDIFF Map 03 ST17

Cardiff Sherborne Av, Cyncoed CF23 6SJ
☎ 029 20753320 🖷 029 20680011
e-mail: cardiff.golfclub@virgin.net
web: www.cardiffgc.co.uk
Parkland where trees form natural hazards. Interesting variety of holes, mostly bunkered. A stream flows through course and comes into play on nine separate holes.

Continued

18 holes, 6099yds, Par 70, SSS 70, Course record 66.
Club membership 900.
Visitors Mon-Sun & BHs. Booking required Fri & Sat. Handicap certificate. Dress code. **Societies** Booking required. **Green Fees** Phone. **Prof** Terry Hanson **Facilities** **Leisure** snooker. **Conf** facs Corporate Hospitality Days **Location** 3m N of city centre

Hotel Hotel Ibis Cardiff Gate, Malthouse Av, Cardiff Gate Business Park, Pontprennau, CARDIFF
029 2073 3222 78 en suite

Cottrell Park
Cottrell Park, St Nicholas CF5 6JY
01446 781781 01446 781187
e-mail: admin@golfwithus.com
web: www.golfwithus.com
Two well-designed courses, opened in 1996, set in historic parkland which was landscaped 200 years ago and offers spectacular views, especially from the Button course. An enjoyable yet testing game of golf for players of all abilities.

Mackintosh: 18 holes, 6110yds, Par 72, SSS 70, Course record 66.
Button: 18 holes, 6156yds, Par 71, SSS 68.
Club membership 1470.
Visitors Mon-Sun & BHs. Booking required Fri-Sun & BHs. Dress code. **Societies** Booking required. **Green Fees** £25 per 18 holes (£35 Fri-Sun). **Prof** Steve Birch **Course Designer** MRM Sandow **Facilities** **Conf** facs Corporate Hospitality Days **Location** 6.5m W of Cardiff off A48, NW of St Nicholas

Hotel ★★★★ 68% Copthorne Hotel Cardiff-Caerdydd, Copthorne Way, Culverhouse Cross, CARDIFF
029 2059 9100 135 en suite

Llanishen
Cwm Lisvane CF4 9UD
029 20755078 029 20755078
e-mail: secretary.llanishen@virgin.net
Picturesque sloping course overlooking England & the Bristol Channel.
18 holes, 5338yds, Par 68, SSS 67, Course record 63.
Club membership 900.
Visitors Sun-Tue, Thu-Fri & BHs. Booking required. Handicap certificate. Dress code. **Societies** Booking required. **Green Fees** Phone. **Prof** Adrian Jones **Facilities** **Conf** facs **Location** 5m N of city off A469

Hotel ★★★ 66% Quality Hotel & Suites Cardiff, Merthyr Rd, Tongwynlais, CARDIFF 029 2052 9988
95 en suite

Peterstone
Peterstone, Wentloog CF3 2TN
01633 680009 01633 680563
e-mail: peterstone_lakes@yahoo.com
web: www.peterstonelakes.com
Parkland course with abundant water features and several long drives (15th, 601yds).
18 holes, 6555yds, Par 72.
Club membership 600.
Visitors contact club for details. Dress code. **Societies** welcome. **Green Fees** £19 (Mon-Tue), £21 (Wed-Fri), £29 (weekends) per round. Reductions in winter. **Prof** Paul Glyn **Course Designer** Bob Sandow **Facilities** **Conf** facs **Location** 3m from Castleton off A48

Radyr
The Clubhouse, Drysgol Rd, Radyr CF15 8BS
029 20842408 029 20843914
e-mail: manager@radyrgolf.co.uk
web: www.radyrgolf.co.uk
Parkland course that celebrated its centenary in 2002. Good views. Venue for many county and national championships.
18 holes, 6078yds, Par 69, SSS 70, Course record 62.
Club membership 935.
Visitors Booking required. **Societies** Booking required. **Green Fees** Phone. **Prof** Simon Swales **Course Designer** Colt **Facilities** **Leisure** Table tennis. **Conf** facs Corporate Hospitality Days **Location** M4 junct 32, 4.5m NW of city off A4119

Hotel ★★★ 71% Manor Parc Country Hotel & Restaurant, Thornhill Rd, Thornhill, CARDIFF 029 2069 3723
21 en suite

St Mellons
St Mellons CF3 2XS
01633 680408 01633 681219
e-mail: stmellons@golf2003.fsnet.co.uk
web: www.stmellonsgolfclub.co.uk
Opened in 1936, St Mellons is a parkland course on the eastern edge of Cardiff. The course is laid out in the shape of a clover leaf and provides one of the best tests of golf in south Wales. The course comprises three par 5s, five par 3s and 10 par 4s. The par 3s will make or break your card but the two finishing par 4 holes are absolutely superb.
18 holes, 6275yds, Par 70, SSS 70, Course record 63.
Club membership 700.
Visitors Mon-Tue, Thu & Fri am only. Booking required. Handicap certificate. Dress code. **Societies** Booking required. **Green Fees** £32 per round, £40 per day. **Prof** Barry Thomas **Course Designer** Colt & Morrison **Facilities** **Conf** Corporate Hospitality Days **Location** M4 junct 30, 2m E off A48

Whitchurch
Pantmawr Rd, Whitchurch CF14 7TD
029 20620985 029 20529860
e-mail: secretary@whitchurchcardiffgolfclub.com
This undulating parkland course is an urban oasis and offers panoramic views of the city. It is an easy walk and always in good condition with excellent drainage and smooth, quick greens.
18 holes, 6258yds, Par 71, SSS 71, Course record 62.
Club membership 750.
Visitors Mon-Fri. Booking required. Handicap certificate.

Continued

Dress code. **Societies** Booking required. **Green Fees** £40 per day (£45 per round weekends). **Prof** Rhys Davies **Course Designer** F Johns **Facilities** **Conf** Corporate Hospitality Days **Location** M4 junct 32, 0.5m S on A470

Hotel ★★★ 71% Manor Parc Country Hotel & Restaurant, Thornhill Rd, Thornhill, CARDIFF ☎ 029 2069 3723 21 en suite

CREIGIAU (CREIYIAU) Map 03 ST08

Creigiau Llantwit Rd CF15 9NN
☎ 029 20890263 📠 20890706
e-mail: manager@creigiaugolf.co.uk
web: www.creigiaugolf.co.uk
Downland course, with small greens and many interesting water hazards.
18 holes, 6063yds, Par 71, SSS 70.
Club membership 800.
Visitors Mon, Wed-Fri. Booking required. Handicap certificate. Dress code. **Societies** Booking required. **Green Fees** £35 per day. **Prof** Iain Luntz **Facilities** **Location** 6m NW of Cardiff on A4119

Hotel ★★★★ 67% Miskin Manor Country Hotel, Pendoylan Rd, MISKIN ☎ 01443 224204 34 en suite 9 annexe en suite

CARMARTHENSHIRE

AMMANFORD Map 03 SN61

Glynhir Glynhir Rd, Llandybie SA18 2TF
☎ 01269 851365 📠 01269 851365
e-mail: glynhir.golfclub@virgin.net
18 holes, 5917yds, Par 69, SSS 70, Course record 66.
Course Designer F Hawtree **Location** 2m N of Ammanford
Telephone for further details

Hotel ★★ 69% Mill at Glynhir, Glynhir Rd, Llandybie, AMMANFORD ☎ 01269 850672 7 en suite 3 annexe en suite

BURRY PORT Map 02 SN40

Ashburnham Cliffe Ter SA16 0HN
☎ 01554 832269 & 833846
18 holes, 6916yds, Par 72, SSS 74, Course record 70.
Course Designer J H Taylor **Location** W of town centre on B4311
Telephone for further details

Hotel ★★ 70% Ashburnham Hotel, Ashburnham Rd, Pembrey, LLANELLI ☎ 01554 834343 & 834455 📠 01554 834483 13 en suite

CARMARTHEN Map 02 SN42

Carmarthen Blaenycoed Rd SA33 6EH
☎ 01267 281588 📠 01267 281493
e-mail: carmarthengolfc@aol.com
web: www.carmarthengolfclub.com
A well-maintained heathland course with tricky greens. Magnificent clubhouse and scenery.
18 holes, 6245yds, Par 71, SSS 71, Course record 66.
Club membership 600.
Visitors Mon-Sun & BHs. Booking required. Dress code. **Societies** Booking required. **Green Fees** £20 (£25 weekends). **Prof** Jon Hartley **Course Designer** J H Taylor **Facilities** **Conf** facs Corporate Hospitality Days **Location** 4m N of town

Hotel ★★ 70% Falcon Hotel, Lammas St, CARMARTHEN ☎ 01267 234959 & 237152 📠 01267 221277 16 en suite

Derllys Court Llysonnen Rd SA33 5DT
☎ 01267 211575 📠 01267 211575
e-mail: derllys@hotmail.com
web: www.derllyscourtgolfclub.com
The back and front halves provide an interesting contrast. The greens on the front 9 are extremely undulating as opposed to the relatively flat greens of the back 9. Water hazards and bunkers come into play providing an interesting challenge. Fine views.
18 holes, 5847yds, Par 70, SSS 68, Course record 69.
Club membership 30.
Visitors Mon-Sun & BHs. Dress code. **Societies** Booking required. **Green Fees** Phone. **Course Designer** Peter Johnson/Stuart Finney **Facilities** **Conf** Corporate Hospitality Days **Location** Off A40 between Carmarthen & St Clears

Hotel ★★ 70% Falcon Hotel, Lammas St, CARMARTHEN ☎ 01267 234959 & 237152 📠 01267 221277 16 en suite

GARNANT Map 03 SN71

Garnant Park Dinefwr Rd SA18 1NP
☎ 01269 823365
web: www.parcgarnantgolf.co.uk
Superb setting in the Brecon Beacons, designed to high standards for all abilities of golfer.
18 holes, 6670yds, Par 72, SSS 72, Course record 69.
Club membership 400.
Visitors Mon-Sun & BHs. Booking required Sat, Sun & BHs. Dress code. **Societies** Booking required. **Green Fees** £15 (£20 Sat, Sun & BHs). **Prof** Gethin Collins **Course Designer** Roger Jones **Facilities** **Leisure** par 3 course. **Conf** facs Corporate Hospitality Days **Location** M4 junct48, off A474 in village of Garnant, signed

Hotel ★★ 69% Mill at Glynhir, Glynhir Rd, Llandybie, AMMANFORD ☎ 01269 850672 7 en suite 3 annexe en suite

KIDWELLY Map 02 SN40

Glyn Abbey Trimsaran SA17 4LB
☎ 01554 810278 🖹 01554 810889
e-mail: course-enquiries@glynabbey.co.uk
web: www.glynabbey.co.uk
Beautiful parkland course with spectacular views of the Gwendraeth valley, set in 200 acres with mature wooded backdrops. USGA greens and tees.
18 holes, 6173yds, Par 70, SSS 70, Course record 70.
Club membership 420.
Visitors contact club for details. Dress code. **Societies** Booking required. **Green Fees** £17 per round (£22.50 weekends & BHs). **Prof** Darren Griffiths **Course Designer** Hawtree **Facilities** **Leisure** solarium, gymnasium. **Conf** facs Corporate Hospitality Days **Location** E of Kidwelly on B4317 between Trimsaran & Carway

Hotel ★★ 70% Ashburnham Hotel, Ashburnham Rd, Pembrey, LLANELLI ☎ 01554 834343 & 834455 🖹 01554 834483 13 en suite

LLANELLI Map 03 SN50

Machynys Peninsula Golf & Country Club Nicklaus Av, Machynys SA15 2DG
☎ 01554 744888 🖹 01554 744680
e-mail: info@machynys.com
web: www.machynys.com
A picturesque course with stunning views over Carmarthen Bay and the Gower Peninsula and including 25 acres of salt and fresh water lakes. The most challenging and interesting holes are the 4th, 5th, 16th and 18th. The 16th is a par 4 played across a lake and the view of the bay from the green is spectacular.
18 holes, 7051yds, Par 72, SSS 75.
Club membership 400.
Visitors Mon-Sun & BHs. Booking required. Handicap certificate. Dress code. **Societies** Booking required. **Green Fees** £30 per 18 holes (£40 Fri-Sun). **Prof** M Reed/J Peters/G Lewis **Course Designer** Gary Nicklaus **Facilities** **Leisure** sauna, gymnasium, health spa. **Conf** facs Corporate Hospitality Days **Location** M4 junct 47/48, follow directions for Llanelli. Take B4034 to Machynys, golf club on left

Hotel ★★ 64% Hotel Miramar, 158 Station Rd, LLANELLI ☎ 01554 754726 12 en suite

RHOS Map 02 SN44

Saron Saron, Penwern SA44 5EL
☎ 01559 370705
e-mail: c9mbl@sarongolf.freeserve.co.uk
web: www.saron-golf.com
Set in 50 acres of mature parkland with large trees and magnificent Teifi valley views. Numerous water hazards and bunkers.
9 holes, 2400yds, Par 32, Course record 34.
Visitors Mon-Sun & BHs. **Societies** welcome. **Green Fees** £11 per 18 holes, £8 per 9 holes. **Course Designer** Adas **Facilities** **Location** Off A484 at Saron, between Carmarthen & Newcastle Emlyn

CEREDIGION

ABERYSTWYTH Map 06 SN58

Aberystwyth Brynymor Rd SY23 2HY
☎ 01970 615104 🖹 01970 626622
e-mail: aberystwythgolf@talk21.com
web: www.aberystwythgolfclub.com
Undulating meadowland course. Testing holes: 16th (The Loop), par 3; 17th, par 4; 18th, par 3. Good views over Cardigan Bay.
18 holes, 5801yds, Par 70, SSS 69.
Club membership 400.
Visitors Mon-Sun & BHs. Booking required. Dress code. **Societies** Booking required. **Green Fees** £25 per round (£30 weekends & BHs). **Prof** Jim McLeod **Course Designer** Harry Vardon **Facilities** **Conf** facs **Location** N side of town

Hotel ★★★ 67% Belle Vue Royal Hotel, Marine Ter, ABERYSTWYTH ☎ 01970 617558 37 rms (34 en suite)

BORTH Map 06 SN69

Borth & Ynyslas SY24 5JS
☎ 01970 871202 🖹 01970 871202
e-mail: secretary@borthgolf.co.uk
web: www.borthgolf.co.uk
Traditional championship links course with superb scenery. Provides a true test of golf for all standards of player.
18 holes, 6116yds, Par 70, SSS 70, Course record 61.
Club membership 550.
Visitors Mon-Sun & BHs. Handicap certificate. Dress code. **Societies** Booking required. **Green Fees** winter £23 per round, summer £34. **Prof** J G Lewis **Course Designer** Harry Colt **Facilities** by arrangement **Conf** Corporate Hospitality Days **Location** 0.5m N on B4353

Hotel ★★★ Ynyshir Hall, EGLWYSFACH ☎ 01654 781209 781268 🖹 01654 781366 7 en suite 2 annexe en suite

CARDIGAN Map 02 SN14

Cardigan Gwbert-on-Sea SA43 1PR
☎ 01239 621775 & 612035 🖹 01239 621775
e-mail: golf@cardigan.fsnet.co.uk
web: www.cardigangolf.co.uk
A links course, very dry in winter, with wide fairways, light rough and gorse. Every hole overlooks the sea.
18 holes, 6687yds, Par 72, SSS 73, Course record 68.
Club membership 600.
Visitors Mon-Sun & BHs. Booking required. Dress code. **Societies** Booking required. **Green Fees** £27.50 per day (£35 weekends & BHs). **Prof** Colin Parsons **Course Designer** Grant/Hawtree **Facilities** **Leisure** squash. **Location** 3m N off A487

Hotel ★★★ 67% The Cliff Hotel, GWBERT-ON-SEA ☎ 01239 613241 50 en suite 20 annexe en suite

Gwbert on Sea Map 02 SN15

Cliff Hotel SA43 1PP
☎ 01239 613241 🖷 01239 615391
e-mail: reservations@cliffhotel.com
This is a short course with two par 4s and the remainder are challenging par 3s. Particularly interesting holes are played across the sea on to a small island.

9 holes, 1545yds, Par 29.
Visitors Mon-Sun & BHs. **Societies** Booking required. **Green Fees** from £7. **Facilities** **Leisure** heated outdoor swimming pool, fishing, sauna, gymnasium. **Conf** facs Corporate Hospitality Days **Location** 3m N 0f Cardigan off B4548

Hotel ★★★ 67% The Cliff Hotel, GWBERT-ON-SEA ☎ 01239 613241 50 en suite 20 annexe en suite

Llangybi Map 02 SN65

Cilgwyn SA48 8NN
☎ 01570 493286
9 holes, 5309yds, Par 68, SSS 66, Course record 66.
Course Designer Sandor **Location** 5m N of Lampeter on A485
Telephone for further details

Hotel ★★★ 74% Falcondale Mansion, LAMPETER ☎ 01570 422910 20 en suite

Llanrhystud Map 06 SN56

Penrhos Golf & Country Club SY23 5AY
☎ 01974 202999 🖷 01974 202100
e-mail: info@penrhosgolf.co.uk
web: www.penrhosgolf.co.uk
Beautifully scenic course incorporating lakes and spectacular coastal and inland views.
Championship: 18 holes, 6641yds, Par 72, SSS 73, Course record 71.
Academy: 9 holes, 1827yds, Par 31.
Club membership 300.
Visitors Mon-Sun & BHs. Booking required. Dress code. **Societies** Booking required. **Green Fees** Main £25 Academy £5 (weekends & BHs £35/£5). **Prof** Paul Diamond **Course Designer** Jim Walters **Facilities** **Leisure** hard tennis courts, heated indoor swimming pool, sauna, solarium, gymnasium, bowling green. **Conf** facs Corporate Hospitality Days **Location** A487 onto B4337 in Llanrhystud, course 0.25m on left

Hotel ★★★ 76% Conrah Hotel, Ffosrhydygaled, Chancery, ABERYSTWYTH ☎ 01970 617941 11 en suite 6 annexe en suite

CONWY

Abergele Map 06 SH97

Abergele Tan-y-Gopa Rd LL22 8DS
☎ 01745 824034 🖷 01745 824772
e-mail: secretary@abergelegolfclub.co.uk
web: abergelegolfclub.co.uk
A beautiful parkland course with views of the Irish Sea and Gwyrch Castle. There are splendid finishing holes: a testing par 5 16th; a 185yd 17th to an elevated green; and a superb par 5 18th with out of bounds just behind the green.
18 holes, 6520yds, Par 72, SSS 71, Course record 66.
Club membership 1250.
Visitors Sun-Fri & BHs. Booking required. Handicap certificate. Dress code. **Societies** Booking required. **Green Fees** £30 (£35 weekends). **Prof** Iain R Runcie **Course Designer** Hawtree **Facilities** **Conf** facs **Location** 0.5m W off A547

Hotel ★★★ 67% Kinmel Manor Hotel, St George's Rd, ABERGELE ☎ 01745 832014 51 en suite

Betws-y-Coed Map 06 SH75

Betws-y-Coed LL24 0AL
☎ 01690 710556
e-mail: info@golf-betws-y-coed.co.uk
web: www.golf-betws-y-coed.co.uk
Attractive flat meadowland course set between two rivers in Snowdonia National Park, known as the Jewel of the Nines.
9 holes, 4998yds, Par 64, SSS 64, Course record 63.
Club membership 300.
Visitors Mon-Sun. Booking required Tue-Wed & Sat-Sun. Handicap certificate. Dress code. **Societies** Booking required. **Green Fees** Summer £16 per 18 holes (£21 weekends). **Facilities** **Location** NE side of village off A5

Hotel ★★★ 71% The Royal Oak Hotel, Holyhead Rd, BETWS-Y-COED ☎ 01690 710219 27 en suite

Colwyn Bay Map 06 SH87

Old Colwyn Woodland Av, Old Colwyn LL29 9NL
☎ 01492 515581
web: www.oldcolwyngolfclub.co.uk
Hilly, meadowland course with sheep and cattle grazing on parts.
9 holes, 5243yds, Par 68, SSS 66, Course record 62.
Club membership 276.
Visitors welcome ex Sat. Contact in advance. **Societies** must contact in advance by telephone. **Green Fees** Phone. **Course Designer** James Braid **Facilities** **Location** E of town centre on B5383

Hotel ★★★ 68% Hopeside Hotel, 63-67 Princes Dr, West End, COLWYN BAY ☎ 01492 533244 16 en suite

CONWY Map 06 SH77

Conwy (Caernarvonshire) Beacons Way, Morfa LL32 8ER
☎ 01492 592423 🖷 01492 593363
e-mail: secretary@conwygolfclub.co.uk
web: www.conwygolfclub.co.uk
Founded in 1890, Conwy has hosted national and international championships since 1898. Set among sand hills, possessing true links greens and a profusion of gorse on the latter holes, especially the 16th, 17th and 18th. This course provides the visitor with real golfing enjoyment in stunning scenery.
18 holes, 6647yds, Par 72, SSS 72, Course record 64. Club membership 1050.
Visitors Mon-Sun & BHs. Booking required. Handicap certificate. Dress code. **Societies** Booking required. **Green Fees** £43 per day, £38 per round (£48/£42 weekends & BHs). **Prof** Peter Lees **Facilities** **Leisure** snooker tables. **Location** 1m W of town centre on A55

Hotel ★★★ 72% Castle Hotel Conwy, High St, CONWY ☎ 01492 582800 28 en suite

North Wales 72 Bryniau Rd, West Shore LL30 2DZ
☎ 01492 875325 🖷 01492 873355
e-mail: golf@nwgc.freeserve.co.uk
web: www.northwalesgolfclub.co.uk
Challenging seaside links with superb views of Anglesey and Snowdonia. It possesses hillocky fairways, awkward stances and the occasional blind shot. Heather and gorse lurk beyond the fairways and several of the greens are defended by deep bunkers. The first outstanding hole is the 5th, a par 5 that dog-legs into the wind along a rollercoasting, bottleneck fairway. Best par 4s include the 8th, played through a narrow valley menaced by a railway line and the beach and the 11th, which runs uphill into the wind and where the beach again threatens. The finest par 3 is the 16th, with a bunker to the left of a partially hidden, bowl-shape green.
18 holes, 6287yds, Par 71, SSS 71, Course record 66. Club membership 670.
Visitors Mon-Sun & BHs. Booking required. Dress code. **Societies** Booking required. **Green Fees** £30 per round, after 4pm £15, Mon & Wed pm £20 (£40 weekends and BHs). **Prof** Richard Bradbury **Course Designer** Tancred Cummins **Facilities** **Leisure** snooker. **Location** W side of town on A546

Hotel ★★ St Tudno Hotel and Restaurant, The Promenade, LLANDUDNO ☎ 01492 874411 19 en suite

LLANDUDNO Map 06 SH78

Llandudno (Maesdu) Hospital Rd LL30 1HU
☎ 01492 876450 🖷 01492 876450
e-mail: george@maesdugolfclub.freeserve.co.uk
Part links, part parkland, this championship course starts and finishes on one side of the main road, the remaining holes, more seaside in nature, being played on the other side. The holes are pleasantly undulating and present a pretty picture when the gorse is in bloom. Often windy, this varied and testing course is not for beginners.
18 holes, 6545yds, Par 72, SSS 72, Course record 62. Club membership 1120.
Visitors must book in advance. **Societies** must apply in advance to secretary. **Green Fees** Phone. **Prof** Simon Boulden **Facilities** **Leisure** snooker. **Location** S of town centre on A546

Hotel ★★★ 74% Imperial Hotel, The Promenade, LLANDUDNO ☎ 01492 877466 100 en suite

Rhos-on-Sea Penryhn Bay LL30 3PU
☎ 01492 548115 (Prof) & 549641 (clubhouse)
🖷 01492 549100

18 holes, 6064yds, Par 69, SSS 69, Course record 68.
Course Designer J J Simpson **Location** 0.5m W of Llandudno off A55
See advertisement on page 401

Hotel ★★★ 68% Hopeside Hotel, 63-67 Princes Dr, West End, COLWYN BAY ☎ 01492 533244 16 en suite

LLANFAIRFECHAN Map 06 SH67

Llanfairfechan Llannerch Rd LL33 0ES
☎ 01248 680144 & 680524
Hillside course with panoramic views of coast. All holes par but 7 over 200 yds.
9 holes, 3119yds, Par 54, SSS 57, Course record 53. Club membership 191.
Visitors Mon-Sun & BHs. Booking required Sat-Sun & BHs. Handicap certificate. Dress code. **Societies** Booking required. **Green Fees** £10 per day. **Facilities** **Conf** Corporate Hospitality Days **Location** W side of town on A55

PENMAENMAWR Map 06 SH77

Penmaenmawr Conway Old Rd LL34 6RD
☎ 01492 623330 Fax 01492 622105
e-mail: clubhouse@pengolfclub.co.uk
web: www.pengolf.co.uk
Hilly course with magnificent views across the bay to Llandudno and Anglesey. Drystone wall hazards.
9 holes, 5350yds, Par 67, SSS 66, Course record 62. Club membership 600.
Visitors Mon-Sun & BHs. Booking required Sat-Sun & BHs. Handicap certificate. Dress code. **Societies** Booking required. **Green Fees** £15 per day (£20 Sat, Sun & BHs). **Facilities** **Location** 1.5m NE off A55

Hotel ★★★ 72% Castle Hotel Conwy, High St, CONWY
☎ 01492 582800 28 en suite

Prices may change during the currency of the guide, always check when booking

DENBIGHSHIRE

BODELWYDDAN Map 06 SJ07

Kimnel Park LL18 5SR
☎ 01745 833548 Fax 01745 833544
Kimnel Park Golf Course: 9 holes, 3100, Par 58, SSS 58.
Telephone for further details

DENBIGH Map 06 SJ06

Bryn Morfydd Hotel Llanrhaedr LL16 4NP
☎ 01745 589090 Fax 01745 589093
e-mail: reception@brynmorfyddhotelgolf.co.uk
web: www.byrnmorfyddhotelgolf.co.uk
Dukes Course: 18 holes, 5650yds, Par 70, SSS 67, Course record 74.
Duchess Course: 9 holes, 2098yds, Par 27.
Course Designer Peter Allis **Location** On A525 between Denbigh & Ruthin
Telephone for further details

Hotel ★★★ 70% Ruthin Castle, RUTHIN
☎ 01824 702664 58 en suite

Denbigh Henllan Rd LL16 5AA
☎ 01745 814159 Fax 01745 814888
e-mail: denbighgolfclub@aol.com
web: www.denbighgolfclub.co.uk
Parkland course, giving a testing and varied game. Good views.
18 holes, 5712yds, Par 69, SSS 68, Course record 64. Club membership 725.
Visitors contact club for details. Handicap certificate. Dress code. **Societies** Booking required. **Green Fees** £24 per 18 holes, £30 per 36 holes (£30/£35 weekends). **Prof** Mike Jones **Course Designer** John Stockton **Facilities** **Conf** Corporate Hospitality Days **Location** 1.5m NW on B5382

LLANGOLLEN Map 07 SJ24

Vale of Llangollen Holyhead Rd LL20 7PR
☎ 01978 860906
Parkland in superb scenery by the River Dee.
18 holes, 6705yds, Par 72, SSS 73, Course record 66. Club membership 800.
Visitors contact club for details. Handicap certificate. Dress code. **Societies** Booking required. **Green Fees** £30 per round (£35 weekends). **Prof** David Vaughan **Facilities** **Location** 1.5m E on A5

PRESTATYN Map 06 SJ08

Prestatyn Marine Rd East LL19 7HS
☎ 01745 854320 Fax 01745 854320
e-mail: prestatyngcmanager@freenet.co.uk
web: www.prestatyngc.co.uk
Set besides rolling sand dunes and only a few hundred yards from the sea, this course enjoys a temperate climate and its seaside location ensures that golfers can play on superb greens all year round. Some holes of note are the par 5 3rd with out of bounds on the left dog-leg followed by the Ridge, a par 4 of 468yds normally played with the prevailing wind. The pretty 9th is surrounded by a moat where birdies and double bogies are common followed by the challenging par 4 450yd 10th.

Continued

Prestatyn

18 holes, 6568yds, Par 72, SSS 72, Course record 65.
Club membership 673.
Visitors Sun-Fri & BHs. Handicap certificate. Dress code. **Societies** welcome. **Green Fees** £25 per round (£30 Sun). **Prof** David Ames **Course Designer** S Collins **Facilities** **Leisure** snooker. **Conf** Corporate Hospitality Days **Location** 0.5m N off A548

Guesthouse ♦♦♦♦ Barratt's at Ty'N Rhyl, Ty'N Rhyl, 167 Vale Rd, RHYL ☎ 01745 344138 & 0773 095 4994 01745 344138 3 en suite

St Melyd The Paddock, Meliden Rd LL19 8NB
☎ 01745 854405 01745 856908
e-mail: info@stmelydgolf.co.uk
web: www.stmelydgolf.co.uk
Parkland with good views of mountains and the Irish Sea. Testing 1st hole (423yds) par 4. 18 tees.
9 holes, 5829yds, Par 68, SSS 68, Course record 65.
Club membership 400.
Visitors advisable to telephone in advance. Restrictions Thu & Sat. **Societies** must telephone in advance. **Green Fees** Phone. **Prof** Andrew Barnett **Facilities** **Leisure** snooker. **Conf** Corporate Hospitality Days **Location** 0.5m S on A547

RHUDDLAN Map 06 SJ07

Rhuddlan Meliden Rd LL18 6LB
☎ 01745 590217 (sec) & 590898 (pro) 01745 590472
e-mail: secretary@rhuddlangolfclub.co.uk
web: www.rhuddlangolfclub.co.uk
Attractive, gently undulating parkland with good views. Well bunkered with trees and water hazards. The 476yd 8th and 431yd 11th require both length and accuracy.
18 holes, 6471yds, Par 71, SSS 71, Course record 66.
Club membership 1060.
Visitors Mon, Wed-Sat & BHs. Booking required. Dress code. **Societies** Booking required. **Green Fees** £30 per day, £25 per round (£30 per round Sat). **Prof** Andrew Carr **Course Designer** Hawtree & Son **Facilities** **Conf** Corporate Hospitality Days **Location** E side of town on A547

Hotel ★★★ 67% Kinmel Manor Hotel, St George's Rd, ABERGELE ☎ 01745 832014 51 en suite

RHYL Map 06 SJ08

Rhyl Coast Rd LL18 3RE
☎ 01745 353171 01745 360007
e-mail: rhylgolfclub@112.com
web: www.rhylgolfclub.co.uk
Flat links course with challenging holes.
9 holes, 6220yds, Par 71, SSS 70, Course record 64.
Club membership 500.
Visitors Sun-Fri & BHs. Dress code. **Societies** Booking required. **Green Fees** £15 per round (£20 weekends). **Prof** John Stubbs **Course Designer** James Braid **Facilities** by arrangement **Conf** Corporate Hospitality Days **Location** 1m E on A548

Guesthouse ♦♦♦♦ Barratt's at Ty'N Rhyl, Ty'N Rhyl, 167 Vale Rd, RHYL ☎ 01745 344138 & 0773 095 4994 01745 344138 3 en suite

RUTHIN Map 06 SJ15

Ruthin-Pwllglas Pwllglas LL15 2PE
☎ 01824 702296 & 702383
100 year old course established 1905. Hilly parkland with panoramic views. Stiff climb to 3rd and 9th holes. At 600ft above sea level, the 355yd 5th hole is the highest point at Pwliglas. When the seventh is played the second time - as the 16th - the tee is from a spectacular sheer rock face.
18 holes, 5362yds, Par 66, SSS 66.
Club membership 380.
Visitors Mon-Sun & BHs. Dress code. **Societies** welcome. **Green Fees** £16 per day (£22 weekends and BHs). **Prof** M Jones **Course Designer** Dai Rees **Facilities** **Conf** Corporate Hospitality Days **Location** 2.5m S off A494

Hotel ★★★ 70% Ruthin Castle, RUTHIN
☎ 01824 702664 58 en suite

ST ASAPH Map 06 SJ07

Llannerch Park North Wales Golf Range, Llannerch Park LL17 0BD
☎ 01745 730805
e-mail: steve@parkgolf.co.uk
web: www.parkgolf.co.uk
Mainly flat parkland with one dog-leg hole. Fine views towards the Clwydian Range.
9 holes, 1587yds, Par 30, Course record 27.
Visitors Mon-Sun & BHs. **Societies** welcome. **Green Fees** £4 per 9 holes. **Prof** Andrew Barnett **Course Designer** B Williams **Facilities** **Leisure** fishing. **Location** 200yds S off A525

Hotel ★★ 67% Plas Elwy Hotel & Restaurant, The Roe, ST ASAPH ☎ 01745 582263 & 582089 01745 583864 7 en suite 6 annexe en suite

FLINTSHIRE

BRYNFORD Map 07 SJ17

Holywell Brynford CH8 8LQ
☎ 01352 713937 & 710040 01352 713937
e-mail: holywell_golf_club@lineone.net
Links type course on well-drained mountain turf, with bracken and gorse flanking undulating fairways. 720ft above sea level.

Continued

18 holes, 6100yds, Par 70, SSS 70, Course record 67.
Club membership 505.
Visitors Sun-Fri & BHs. Booking required. Dress code. **Societies** Booking required. **Green Fees** £20 per round (£25 weekends & BHs). **Prof** Matt Parsley **Facilities** **Location** 1.25m SW off B5121

Hotel ★★ 70% Stamford Gate Hotel, Halkyn Rd, HOLYWELL ☎ 01352 712942 12 en suite

FLINT Map 07 SJ27

Flint Cornist Park CH6 5HJ
☎ 01352 735645
e-mail: paulm@jearrinsurance.co.uk
Parkland incorporating woods and streams. Excellent views of Dee estuary and the Welsh hills.
9 holes, 6984yds, Par 70, SSS 69, Course record 65.
Club membership 200.
Visitors Mon-Sat & BHs. Booking required. Handicap certificate. Dress code. **Societies** Booking required. **Green Fees** £12 per day, £10 per 18 holes, £5 per 9 holes. **Course Designer** H G Griffith **Facilities** **Location** 1m W of Flint, signs for Cornist Hall Golf Club

Hotel ★★★ 66% Mountain Park Hotel, Northop Rd, Flint Mountain, FLINT ☎ 01352 736000 & 730972 🖷 01352 736010 21 annexe en suite

HAWARDEN Map 07 SJ36

Hawarden Groomsdale Ln CH5 3EH
☎ 01244 531447 & 520809 🖷 01244 536901
e-mail: secretary@hawardengolfclub.co.uk
Parkland course with comfortable walking and good views.
18 holes, 5842yds, Par 69, SSS 69.
Club membership 750.
Visitors Sun-Fri & BHs. Booking required. Handicap certificate. Dress code. **Societies** Booking required. **Green Fees** £20 (£25 Sun). **Prof** Alex Rowland **Facilities** **Location** W side of town off B5125

Hotel ★★ 70% The Gateway To Wales Hotel, Welsh Rd, Sealand, Deeside, CHESTER ☎ 01244 830332 39 en suite

MOLD Map 07 SJ26

Old Padeswood Station Ln, Padeswood CH7 4JL
☎ 01244 547401 & 547701 🖷 01244 545082
web: www.oldpadeswoodgolfclub.co.uk
Situated in the beautiful Alyn valley, part bounded by the River Alyn, this challenging course suits all categories of golfers. Nine holes are flat and nine are gently undulating. The signature hole is the 18th, a par 3 that needs a carry to the green as a valley waits below.
18 holes, 6685yds, Par 72, SSS 72, Course record 66.
Club membership 600.
Visitors Mon-Sun & BHs. Booking required. Dress code. **Societies** Booking required. **Green Fees** £25 per round (£30 Sat, Sun & BHs). **Prof** Tony Davies **Course Designer** Jeffries **Facilities** **Conf** facs Corporate Hospitality Days **Location** 3m SE off A5118

Hotel ★★★ 68% Beaufort Park Hotel, Alltami Rd, New Brighton, MOLD ☎ 01352 758646 106 en suite

Padeswood & Buckley The Caia, Station Ln, Padeswood CH7 4JD
☎ 01244 550537 🖷 01244 541600
e-mail: admin@padeswoodgolf.plus.com
Bounded by the banks of the River Alyn, gently undulating parkland with natural hazards and good views of the Welsh hills.
18 holes, 6042yds, Par 70, SSS 69.
Club membership 800.
Visitors Mon-Fri. Dress code. **Societies** Booking required. **Green Fees** £25 per round weekdays. **Prof** David Ashton **Course Designer** Williams Partnership **Facilities** **Leisure** snooker tables. **Conf** Corporate Hospitality Days **Location** 3m SE off A5118

Hotel ★★★ 68% Beaufort Park Hotel, Alltami Rd, New Brighton, MOLD ☎ 01352 758646 106 en suite

NORTHOP Map 07 SJ26

Northop Golf & Country Club CH7 6WA
☎ 01352 840440 🖷 01352 840445

18 holes, 6750yds, Par 72, SSS 73, Course record 64.
Course Designer John Jacobs **Location** 150yds from Connahs Quay turning on A55
Telephone for further details

Hotel ★★★★ 70% De Vere St David's Park, St Davids Park, EWLOE ☎ 01244 520800 145 en suite

PANTYMWYN Map 07 SJ16

Mold Cilcain Rd CH7 5EH
☎ 01352 741513 🖷 01352 741517
e-mail: info@moldgolfclub.co.uk
web: www.moldgolfclub.co.uk
Meadowland course with some hard walking and natural hazards. Fine views.
18 holes, 5512yds, Par 67, SSS 67, Course record 63.
Club membership 700.
Visitors contact in advance. Restricted play at weekends **Societies** Booking required. **Green Fees** Phone. **Prof** Mark Jordan **Course Designer** Hawtree **Facilities** **Conf** facs **Location** E side of village

Hotel ★★★ 68% Beaufort Park Hotel, Alltami Rd, New Brighton, MOLD ☎ 01352 758646 106 en suite

WHITFORD

Pennant Park CH8 9EP
☎ 01745 563000
e-mail: enquiries@pennant-park.co.uk
web: www.pennant-park.co.uk
Parkland course set in rolling countryside with fine quality greens and spectacular views.
18 holes, 6059yds, Par 70, SSS 70, Course record 69. Club membership 175.
Visitors Mon-Sun & BHs. Booking required. Dress code. **Societies** Booking required. **Green Fees** £20 per round (£25 weekends). **Course Designer** Roger Jones **Facilities** **Conf** Corporate Hospitality Days **Location** from Chester take A55 towards Holyhead. Exit at junct 32 to Holywell, follow signs for Pennant Park

Hotel ★★ 70% Stamford Gate Hotel, Halkyn Rd, HOLYWELL ☎ 01352 712942 12 en suite

GWYNEDD

ABERDYFI Map 06 SN69

Aberdovey see page 405

Hotel ★★★ 75% Trefeddian Hotel, ABERDYFI ☎ 01654 767213 59 en suite

Hotel ★★ 76% Penhelig Arms Hotel Restaurant, ABERDYFI ☎ 01654 767215 🖹 01654 767690 10 en suite 5 annexe en suite

Hotel ★★ 69% Dovey Inn, Seaview Ter, ABERDOVEY ☎ 01654 767332 🖹 01654 767996 8 en suite

ABERSOCH Map 06 SH32

Abersoch LL53 7EY
☎ 01758 712622 (shop) 712636 (office) 🖹 01758 712777
e-mail: admin@abersochgolf.co.uk
web: www.abersochgolf.co.uk

18 holes, 5819yds, Par 69, SSS 68, Course record 66.
Course Designer Harry Vardon **Location** S side of village
See advertisement on this page

Hotel ★★ 75% Neigwl Hotel, Lon Sarn Bach, ABERSOCH ☎ 01758 712363 9 en suite

BALA Map 06 SH93

Bala Penlan LL23 7YD
☎ 01678 520359 & 521361 🖹 01678 521361
e-mail: balagolfclub@one-tel.com
Upland course with natural hazards. All holes except first and last affected by wind. First hole is a most challenging par 3. Irrigated greens and spectacular views of surrounding countryside.
10 holes, 4962yds, Par 66, SSS 64, Course record 64. Club membership 229.
Visitors Mon-Sun & BHs. Booking required Sat-Sun & BHs. **Societies** Booking required. **Green Fees** £15 (£20 weekends & BHs). **Prof** A R Davies **Course Designer** Syd Collins **Facilities** by arrangement **Location** 0.5m SW off A494

Hotel ★★ 65% Plas Coch Hotel, High St, BALA ☎ 01678 520309 10 en suite

BANGOR Map 06 SH57

St Deiniol Penybryn LL57 1PX
☎ 01248 353098 🖹 01248 370792
e-mail: secretary@stdeiniol.fsbusiness.co.uk
web. www.st-deiniol.co.uk
Elevated parkland course with panoramic views of Snowdonia, the Menai Strait and Anglesey. Designed by James Braid in 1906 this course is a test test of accuracy and course management. The 3rd has a narrow driving area and a shot to an elevated green. The 4th, one of six par 3s, provides a choice of pitching the green or utilising the contours, making it one of the most difficult holes on the course. The 13th, a dog-leg par 4,

Continued

Gwynedd

Aberdovey

Aberdyfi

Map 06 SN69

Golf was first played at Aberdovey in 1886, with the club founded six years later. The links has since developed into one of the finest championship courses in Wales. The club has hosted many prestigious events over the years, and is popular with golfing societies and clubs who regularly return here. Golfers can enjoy spectacular views and easy walking alongside the dunes of this characteristic seaside links. Fine holes include the 3rd, the 11th, and a good short hole at the 12th. The late Bernard Darwin, a former president and captain of the club, was a golf correspondent for the Times. Many of his writings feature the course, which he referred to as, 'the course that my soul loves best of all the courses in the world'; Darwin was a major contributor to its success. He would easily recognise the course today. In 1995 the old clubhouse was destroyed by fire, and rebuilt with the help of a National Lottery grant. The fine new clubhouse was opened by HRH the Duke of York in 1998.

LL35 0RT
☎ 01654 767493 🖹 01654 767027
web: www.aberdoveygolf.co.uk

18 holes, 6454yds, Par 71, SSS 72, Course record 66.
Club membership 1000.

Visitors Mon-Sun. Booking required. Handicap certificate. Dress code. **Societies** Booking required. **Green Fees** £50 per day, £40 per round (£60/£45 weekends). **Prof** John Davies **Course Designer** J Braid **Facilities** ⊗ ⅢI ℔ ☕ 🍷 ⛺ 🏠 ✈ 🚗 ✓ **Leisure** snooker. **Conf facs** **Location** 0.5m W on A493

is the last hole of the course's own Amen Corner with its out of bounds to the right and left. Centenary in 2006.
18 holes, 5421yds, Par 68, SSS 67, Course record 61.
Club membership 300.
Visitors Mon-Sun & BHs. Booking required. Dress code **Societies** Booking required. **Green Fees** £20 per day (£25 weekends & BHs). **Course Designer** James Braid **Facilities** **Location** A55 junct 11, E of town centre off A5122

CAERNARFON Map 06 SH46

Caernarfon Llanfaglan LL54 5RP
☎ 01286 673783 & 678359 (pro) 01286 672535
e-mail: caerngc@talk21.com
web: www.caernarfongolfclub.co.uk
Parkland with gentle gradients. Immaculately kept course with excellent greens and tree-lined fairways.
18 holes, 5941yds, Par 69, SSS 68, Course record 63.
Club membership 660.
Visitors Mon-Sun & BHs. Booking required. Handicap certificate. Dress code. **Societies** Booking required. **Green Fees** £30 per day, £25 per round (£30 per round weekends). **Prof** Aled Owen **Facilities** **Conf** Corporate Hospitality Days **Location** 1.75m SW

Hotel ★★★ 71% Celtic Royal Hotel, Bangor St, CAERNARFON ☎ 01286 674477 110 en suite

CRICCIETH Map 06 SH43

Criccieth Ednyfed Hill LL52 0PH
☎ 01766 522154
e-mail: aaguide@cricciethgolfclub.co.uk
web: www.criccieth golf club.co.uk
Hilly course on high ground, with generous fairways and natural hazards. The 16th tee has panoramic views in all directions.
18 holes, 5787yds, Par 69, SSS 68.
Club membership 200.
Visitors Mon-Sun & BHs. Booking required. **Societies** Booking required. **Green Fees** £20 per day May-Sep (£15 all other times). **Facilities** **Location** 1m NE

Hotel ★★★ 77% Bron Eifion Country House Hotel, CRICCIETH ☎ 01766 522385 19 en suite

DOLGELLAU Map 06 SH71

Dolgellau Hengwrt Estate, Pencefn Rd LL40 2ES
☎ 01341 422603 01341 422603
e-mail: dolgellaugolfclub@hengwrt.fsnet.co.uk
9 holes, 4671yds, Par 66, SSS 63, Course record 62.
Course Designer Jack Jones **Location** 0.5m N, near Town Bridge
Telephone for further details

Hotel ★★★ 74% Plas Dolmelynllyn, Ganllwyd, DOLGELLAU ☎ 01341 440273 10 en suite

FFESTINIOG Map 06 SH93

Ffestiniog Y Cefn LL41 4LS
☎ 01766 762637
e-mail: info@ffestinioggolf.org
web: www.ffestiniog.org
Moorland course set in Snowdonia National Park.
9 holes, 4570yds, Par 68, SSS 66.
Club membership 150.
Visitors Mon-Sat. Booking required Sun & BHs. Dress code. **Societies** Booking required. **Green Fees** £10 per day. **Facilities** **Location** 1m E of Ffestiniog on B4391

Hotel ★★ Maes y Neuadd Country House Hotel, TALSARNAU ☎ 01766 780200 16 en suite

HARLECH Map 06 SH53

Royal St Davids LL46 2UB
☎ 01766 780361 01766 781110
e-mail: secretary@royalstdavids.co.uk
web: www.royalstdavids.co.uk
Championship links with easy walking. Natural hazards demand strength and accuracy. Under the gaze of Harlech Castle, with a magnificent backdrop of the Snowdonia mountains.

18 holes, 6263yds, Par 69, SSS 71.
Club membership 900.
Visitors Mon-Sun & BHs. Booking required. Handicap certificate. Dress code. **Societies** welcome. **Green Fees** £52 per day, £42 per round, £26 after 3pm (£62/£52 weekends & BHs, £32 after 3pm). Winter reduced rates. **Prof** John Barnett **Course Designer** Harold Finch-Hatton **Facilities** **Conf** facs Corporate Hospitality Days **Location** W side of town on A496

Hotel ★★ 64% Ty Mawr Hotel, LLANBEDR
☎ 01341 241440 10 en suite

MORFA NEFYN Map 06 SH24

Nefyn & District LL53 6DA
01758 720966 01758 720476
e-mail: nefyngolf@tesco.net
web: nefyn-golf-club.com
A 27-hole course played as two separate 18s, Nefyn is a cliff-top links where you never lose sight of the sea. A well-maintained course which will be a very tough test for the serious golfer, but still user friendly for the casual visitor. Every hole has a different challenge and the old 13th fairway is some 30yds across from sea to sea. The course has the bonus of a pub on the beach roughly halfway round for those whose golf may need some bolstering.
Old Course: 18 holes, 6201yds, Par 71, SSS 71, Course record 67.
New Course: 18 holes, 6317yds, Par 71, SSS 71, Course record 66.
Club membership 800.
Visitors Mon-Sun & BHs. Booking required. Handicap certificate. Dress code. **Societies** Booking required. **Prof** John Froom **Course Designer** James Braid **Facilities** **Conf** facs **Location** 0.75m NW

Hotel ★★★ 75% Porth Tocyn Hotel, Bwlch Tocyn, ABERSOCH 01758 713303 17 en suite

PORTHMADOG Map 06 SH53

Porthmadog Morfa Bychan LL49 9UU
01766 514124 01766 514124
e-mail: secretary@porthmadog-golf-club.co.uk
web: www.porthmadog-golf-club-co.uk
Seaside links, very interesting but with easy walking and good views.
18 holes, 6322yds, Par 71, SSS 71.
Club membership 1000.
Visitors Mon-Sun & BHs. Booking required. Handicap certificate. Dress code. **Societies** Booking required. **Green Fees** £30 per round £37 per day (weekends £35/£42). **Prof** Peter L Bright **Course Designer** James Braid **Facilities** **Leisure** snooker. **Conf** Corporate Hospitality Days **Location** 1.5m SW of Porthmadog

Hotel ★★★ 77% Bron Eifion Country House Hotel, CRICCIETH 01766 522385 19 en suite

PWLLHELI Map 06 SH33

Pwllheli Golf Rd LL53 5PS
01758 701644 01758 701644
e-mail: admin@pwllheligolfclub.co.uk
web: www.pwllheligolfclub.co.uk
Easy walking on flat seaside course, 9 holes links, 9 holes parkland. Outstanding views of Snowdon, Cader Idris and Cardigan Bay.
18 holes, 6091yds, Par 69, SSS 70, Course record 66.
Club membership 880.
Visitors Mon-Sun & BHs. Booking required. Handicap certificate. Dress code. **Societies** Booking required. **Green Fees** £30 per day (£35 weekends & BHs). **Prof** Stuart Pilkington **Course Designer** Tom Morris **Facilities** **Conf** Corporate Hospitality Days **Location** 0.5m SW off A497

Hotel ★★★ 75% Porth Tocyn Hotel, Bwlch Tocyn, ABERSOCH 01758 713303 17 en suite

MERTHYR TYDFIL

MERTHYR TYDFIL Map 03 SO00

Merthyr Tydfil Cilsanws Mountain, Cefn Coed CF48 2NT
01685 723308
Mountain-top course in the Brecon Beacons National Park with beautiful views of the surrounding area. The course plays longer than its card length and requires accuracy off the tee.
18 holes, 5625yds, Par 69, SSS 68, Course record 65.
Club membership 160.
Visitors Mon-Sat & BHs. Dress code. **Societies** Booking required. **Green Fees** £10 per day (£15 Sat, Sun & BHs). **Course Designer** V Price/R Mathias **Facilities** by arrangement by arrangement by arrangement by arrangement **Location** Off A470 at Cefn Coed

Hotel ★★★ 75% Nant Ddu Lodge, Bistro & Spa, Cwm Taf, Nant Ddu, MERTHYR TYDFIL 01685 379111 27 en suite 4 annexe en suite

Morlais Castle Pant, Dowlais CF48 2UY
01685 722822 01685 388555
e-mail: morlaiscastlegolfclub@uk2.net
web: www.morlaiscastle-golfclub.com
Beautiful moorland course with excellent views of the Brecon Beacons and surrounding countryside. The interesting layout makes for a testing game.
18 holes, 6320yds, Par 71, SSS 71, Course record 64.
Club membership 600.
Visitors Mon-Fri, Sun & BHs. Booking required. Dress code. **Societies** Booking required. **Green Fees** Phone. **Prof** H Jarrett **Course Designer** James Braid **Facilities** **Conf** facs Corporate Hospitality Days **Location** 2.5m N off A465. Follow signs for Mountain Railway. Course entrance opposite railway car park

Hotel ★★★ 75% Nant Ddu Lodge, Bistro & Spa, Cwm Taf, Nant Ddu, MERTHYR TYDFIL 01685 379111 27 en suite 4 annexe en suite

MONMOUTHSHIRE

ABERGAVENNY Map 03 SO21

Monmouthshire Gypsy Ln, LLanfoist NP7 9HE
01873 852606 01873 850470
e-mail: secretary@mgcabergavenny.fsnet.co.uk
web: www.themonmouthshiregolfclub.com
This parkland course is very picturesque, with the beautifully wooded River Usk running alongside. There are a number of par 3 holes and a testing par 4 at the 15th.
18 holes, 5806yds, Par 70, SSS 69, Course record 65.
Club membership 650.
Visitors Mon-Fri. Booking required Mon & Fri. Handicap certificate. Dress code. **Societies** Booking required. **Green Fees** Phone. **Prof** B Edwards **Course Designer** James Braid **Facilities** by arrangement **Location** 2m S off B4269

Hotel ★★ 72% Llanwenarth Hotel & Riverside Restaurant, Brecon Rd, ABERGAVENNY 01873 810550 17 en suite

Continued

Guest House ♦♦♦♦♦ Glangrwyney Court, CRICKHOWELL ☎ 01873 811288 🖷 01873 810317 5 rms (4 en suite)
See advertisement on this page

Wernddu Golf Centre Old Ross Rd NP7 8NG
☎ 01873 856223 🖷 01873 852177
e-mail: info@wernddu-golf-club.co.uk
web: www.wernddu-golf-club.co.uk
A parkland course with magnificent views, wind hazards on several holes in certain conditions, and water hazards on four holes. This gently undulating course has a long front nine and a shorter back nine, while the final hole, a par 3, is an outstanding finish.
18 holes, 5572yds, Par 69, SSS 67, Course record 63.
Club membership 550.
Visitors Mon-Sun & BHs. Booking required. Dress code. **Societies** Booking required. **Green Fees** £18 per 18 holes. **Prof** Tina Tetley **Course Designer** G Watkins **Facilities** **Leisure** fishing, 9 hole pitch & putt course. **Location** 1.5m NE on B4521

Continued

Hotel ★★★ 70% Llansantffraed Court Hotel, Llanvihangel Gobion, ABERGAVENNY ☎ 01873 840678 21 en suite

BETTWS NEWYDD Map 03 SO30

Alice Springs Kemeys Commander NP15 1JY
☎ 01873 880708 🖷 01873 881381
e-mail: alice@springs18.fsnet.co.uk
web: www.alicespringsgolfclub.co.uk
Two 18-hole undulating parkland courses set back to back with magnificent views of the Usk Valley. The Monow course has testing 7th and 15th holes.

Monow Course: 18 holes, 5544yds, Par 69, SSS 69.
Usk Course: 18 holes, 5934, Par 70, SSS 70.
Club membership 450.
Visitors Mon-Sun & BHs. Booking required. Sat, Sun & BHs. Dress code. **Societies** Booking required. **Green Fees** Phone. **Prof** Stuart Steel **Course Designer** Keith R Morgan **Facilities** **Conf** facs Corporate Hospitality Days **Location** N of Usk on B4598

Hotel ★★★ 67% Three Salmons Hotel, Porthycarne St, USK ☎ 01291 672133 10 en suite 14 annexe en suite

CAERWENT Map 03 ST49

Dewstow NP26 5AH
☎ 01291 430444 🖷 01291 425816
e-mail: info@dewstow.com
web: www.dewstow.co.uk
Two picturesque parkland courses with easy walking and spectacular views over the Severn estuary towards Bristol. Testing holes include the par 3 7th, Valley Course, which is approached over water, some 50ft lower than the tee, and the par 4 15th, Park Course, which has a 50ft totem pole in the middle of the fairway, a unique feature. There is also a 26-bay floodlit driving range.
Valley Course: 18 holes, 6110yds, Par 72, SSS 70, Course record 64.
Park Course: 18 holes, 6226yds, Par 69, SSS 69, Course record 67.
Club membership 950.
Visitors Booking required. **Societies** Booking required. **Green Fees** Phone. **Prof** Jonathan Skuse **Facilities** **Conf** facs Corporate Hospitality Days **Location** 0.5m S of Caerwent

Hotel ⌂ Travelodge Magor Newport, Magor Service Area, MAGOR ☎ 08700 850 950 43 en suite

Championship Course

Monmouthshire

Marriott St Pierre Hotel

Chepstow

Map 03 ST59

Set in 400 acres of beautiful parkland, Marriott St Pierre offers two 18-hole courses. The Old Course is one of the finest in the country and has played host to many major championships. The par 3 18th is famous for its tee shot over the lake to an elevated green. The Mathern has its own challenges and is highly enjoyable for golfers of all abilities. The hotel has teaching professionals as well as hire of clubs and equipment.

St Pierre Park NP16 6YA
☎ 01291 625261 🖹 01291 627977
e-mail: golf.stpierre@marriotthotels.co.uk
web: marriott.com/cwlgs

Old Course: 18 holes, 6733yds, Par 71, SSS 72, Course record 64.
Mathern Course: 18 holes, 5732yds, Par 68, SSS 67.
Club membership 800.

Visitors Booking required (up to 10 days weekdays, 48hrs weekends). **Societies** Booking required. **Green Fees** Phone. **Prof** Craig Dun **Course Designer** H Cotton **Facilities** **Leisure** hard tennis courts, heated indoor swimming pool, fishing, sauna, solarium, gymnasium, steam room, health & beauty suite, chipping green. **Conf facs** Corporate Hospitality Days **Location** M48 junct 2, A466 towards Chepstow, onto A48 towards Caldicot

CHEPSTOW Map 03 ST59

Marriott St Pierre Hotel Country Club
see page 409

Hotel ★★★★ 71% Marriott St Pierre Hotel & Country Club, St Pierre Park, CHEPSTOW ☎ 01291 625261 148 en suite

Hotel ★★★ 66% The Chepstow Hotel, Newport Rd, CHEPSTOW ☎ 01291 626261 & 0845 6588700 📠 01291 626263 31 en suite

Hotel ★★ 68% Castle View Hotel, 16 Bridge St, CHEPSTOW ☎ 01291 620349 📠 01291 627397 9 en suite 4 annexe en suite

MONMOUTH Map 03 SO51

Monmouth Leasbrook Ln NP25 3SN
☎ 01600 712212 (clubhouse) 📠 01600 772399
e-mail: sec.mongc@barbox.net
web: ww.monmouthgolfclub.co.uk
Parkland on high undulating land with beautiful views. The 8th hole, Cresta Run, is renowned as one of Britain's most extraordinary golf holes.

18 holes, 5698yds, Par 69, SSS 69, Course record 67. Club membership 500.
Visitors Mon-Sun & BHs. Booking required. Dress code. **Societies** Booking required. **Green Fees** £30 per day (£34 weekends) £23 per round (£27 weekends). **Prof** Mike Waldron **Course Designer** George Walden **Facilities** ⊗ 🍴 🍺 ☕ 🍷 ⛳ 🏠 🏌 🚗 🛒 🏌 **Conf** Corporate Hospitality Days **Location** Turn into Leasbrook Lane, 150 yds past Dixon rdbt on Monmouth to Ross on Wye dual carriageway. Club 0.5m up lane on right

Rolls of Monmouth The Hendre NP25 5HG
☎ 01600 715353 📠 01600 713115
e-mail: sandra@therollsgolfclub.co.uk
web: www.therollsgolfclub.co.uk
A hilly and challenging parkland course encompassing several lakes and ponds and surrounded by woodland. Set within a beautiful private estate complete with listed mansion and panoramic views towards the Black Mountains. The short 4th has a lake beyond the green and both the 17th and 18th holes are magnificent holes with which to end your round.
18 holes, 6733yds, Par 72, SSS 73, Course record 69. Club membership 160.
Visitors Mon-Sun & BHs. Booking required. Dress code. **Societies** Booking required. **Green Fees** £40 per day (weekends £44) (Mon special, £38 for round + lunch). **Facilities** ⊗ 🍴 🍺 ☕ 🍷 ⛳ 🏠 🏌 🚗 🏌 **Location** 4m W on B4233

RAGLAN Map 03 SO40

Raglan Parc Parc Lodge, Station Rd NP5 2ER
☎ 01291 690077
18 holes, 6604yds, Par 72, SSS 73, Course record 67.
Location Off junct A449
Telephone for further details

Hotel ★★★ 70% Llansantffraed Court Hotel, Llanvihangel Gobion, ABERGAVENNY
☎ 01873 840678 21 en suite

NEATH PORT TALBOT

GLYNNEATH Map 03 SN80

Glynneath Pen-y-graig, Pontneathvaughan SA11 5UH
☎ 01639 720452 & 720872 📠 01639 720452
e-mail: enquiries@glynneathgolfclub.co.uk
web: www.glynneathgolfclub.co.uk
Attractive hillside golf overlooking the Vale of Neath in the foothills of the Brecon Beacons National Park. Reasonably level parkland and wooded course.
18 holes, 6211yds, Par 71, SSS 70, Course record 69. Club membership 603.
Visitors Mon-Sun & BHs. Booking required Sat & Sun. Dress code. **Societies** Booking required. **Green Fees** £16 per day (£22 Sat, Sun & BHs). £11 Monday. **Prof** Shane McMenamin **Course Designer** Cotton/Pennick/Lawrie/Williams **Facilities** ⊗ 🍴 🍺 ☕ 🍷 ⛳ 🏠 🏌 🛒 🚗 🏌 **Leisure** Snooker. **Conf** facs Corporate Hospitality Days **Location** 2m NE of Glynneath on B4242 then take Pontneath Vaughan Rd

Hotel ★★★ 66% Castle Hotel, The Parade, NEATH
☎ 01639 641119 & 643581 📠 01639 641624 29 en suite

MARGAM Map 03 SS78

Lakeside Water St SA13 2PA
☎ 01639 899959
web: www.lakesidegolf.co.uk
A parkland course with bunkers and natural hazards. Eight par 4's and ten par 3's.
18 holes, 4550yds, Par 63, SSS 63, Course record 65. Club membership 250.
Visitors Mon-Sun & BHs. **Societies** Booking required. **Green Fees** £14 per 18 holes. **Prof** Mathew Wootton

Continued

Course Designer Matthew Wootton **Facilities** **Conf** Corporate Hospitality Days **Location** M4 junct 38, off B4283

Hotel ★★★ 68% Aberavon Beach Hotel, PORT TALBOT
01639 884949 52 en suite

NEATH Map 03 SS79

Earlswood Jersey Marine SA10 6JP
01792 321578
Earlswood is a hillside course offering spectacular scenic views over Swansea Bay. The terrain is gently undulating downs with natural hazards and is designed to appeal to both the new and the experienced golfer.
18 holes, 5084yds, Par 68, SSS 68.
Visitors no restrictions. **Societies** advisable to contact in advance. **Green Fees** Phone. **Prof** Mike Day **Course Designer** Gorvett Estates **Facilities** **Location** 4m E of Swansea, off A483

Hotel ★★★ 66% Castle Hotel, The Parade, NEATH
01639 641119 & 643581 01639 641624 29 en suite

Neath Cadoxton SA10 8AH
01639 643615 (clubhouse) & 632759 01639 632759
e-mail: neathgolf@btconnect.com
web: www.neathgolfclub.com
Mountain course, with spectacular views of the Brecon Beacons to the north and the Bristol Channel to the south.

18 holes, 6490yds, Par 72, SSS 72, Course record 66. Club membership 700.
Visitors Mon-Sun. Booking required. Handicap certificate. Dress code. **Societies** Booking required. **Green Fees** Apr-Sep £25 weekdays, £30 weekends; Oct & Mar £17, Nov & Feb £15, Dec & Jan £11. **Prof** R Bennett **Course Designer** James Braid **Facilities** **Leisure** snooker. **Conf** Corporate Hospitality Days **Location** 2m NE off A4230

Hotel ★★★ 66% Castle Hotel, The Parade, NEATH
01639 641119 & 643581 01639 641624 29 en suite

Swansea Bay Jersey Marine SA10 6JP
01792 812198 & 814153
Fairly level seaside links with part dunes.
18 holes, 6605yds, Par 72, SSS 71, Course record 69. Club membership 500.
Visitors Booking required. **Societies** Booking required. **Green Fees** Phone. **Prof** Mike Day **Facilities** **Location** M4 junct 42, onto A483, 1st right onto B4290 towards Jersey Marine, 1st right to clubhouse

Hotel ★★★ 68% Aberavon Beach Hotel, PORT TALBOT
01639 884949 52 en suite

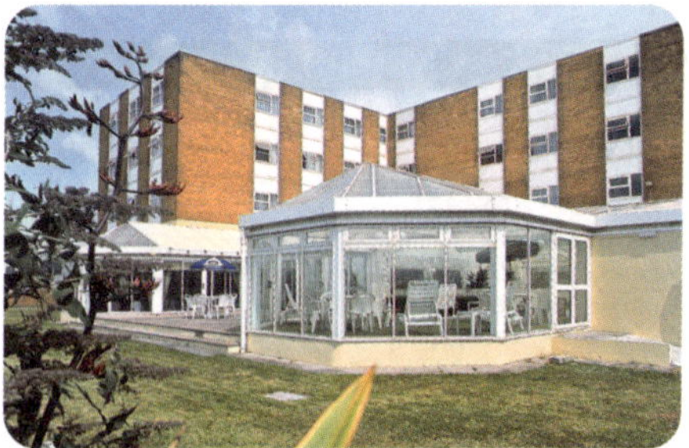

PONTARDAWE Map 03 SN70

Pontardawe Cefn Llan SA8 4SH
01792 863118 01792 830041
e-mail: pontardawe@btopenworld.com
web: pontardawegc.co.uk
Meadowland course situated on plateau 600ft above sea level with good views of the Bristol Channel and the Brecon Beacons.
18 holes, 6101yds, Par 70, SSS 70, Course record 64. Club membership 500.
Visitors Mon-Fri. Handicap certificate. Dress code. **Societies** Booking required. **Green Fees** £20 per day. **Prof** Gary Hopkins **Facilities** **Leisure** snooker & pool rooms. **Conf** Corporate Hospitality Days **Location** M4 junct 45, off A4067 N of town centre

Hotel ★★★ 66% Castle Hotel, The Parade, NEATH
01639 641119 & 643581 01639 641624 29 en suite

PORT TALBOT Map 03 SS78

British Steel Port Talbot Sports & Social Club, Margam SA13 2NF
01639 791938
e-mail: tony.edwards@ntlworld.com
9 holes, 4726yds, Par 62, SSS 63, Course record 60.
Location M4 junct 40
Telephone for further details

Hotel ★★★ 68% Aberavon Beach Hotel, PORT TALBOT
01639 884949 52 en suite

YSTRADGYNLAIS Map 03 SN71

Palleg Lower Cwmtwrch SA9 2QQ
01639 842193 01639 845661
e-mail: palleggolf-club.freeserve.co.uk
web: www.palleg-golf.co.uk
Meadowland course with fine views. An attractive ravine runs through the back nine holes.
18 holes, 5902yds, Par 72, SSS 72. Club membership 300.
Visitors Mon-Sun & BHs. Booking required. Dress code. **Societies** Booking required. **Green Fees** £20 per day, £12 per round. **Prof** Graham Coombe **Facilities** **Leisure** practice nets. **Conf** facs Corporate Hospitality Days **Location** M4 junct 45, A4067 towards Brecon, at 6th rdbt (Powys sign) left to Cwmtwrch, right at minirdbt, up hill onto Palleg Rd, 1m on left

Continued

Continued

Hotel ★★★ 66% Castle Hotel, The Parade, NEATH
☎ 01639 641119 & 643581 📠 01639 641624 29 en suite

NEWPORT

CAERLEON Map 03 ST39

Caerleon NP6 1AY
☎ 01633 420342 📠 01633 420342
9 holes, 2900yds, Par 34, SSS 34, Course record 29.
Course Designer Steel **Location** M4 junct 24, B4236 to Caerleon, 1st left after Priory Hotel, follow road to bottom
Telephone for further details

Hotel ★★★★★ 71% The Celtic Manor Resort, Coldra Woods, NEWPORT ☎ 01633 413000 330 en suite

LLANWERN Map 03 ST38

Llanwern Tennyson Av NP18 2DY
☎ 01633 412029 (sec) & 413233 (pro) 📠 01633 412029
e-mail: llanwerngolfclub@btconnect.com
web: www.llanwerngolfclub.co.uk
Established in 1928, a mature, parkland course in a picturesque village setting.
18 holes, 6177yds, Par 70, SSS 69, Course record 66.
Club membership 650.
Visitors Mon-Sat & BHs. Contact club for details. Handicap certificate. Dress code. **Societies** Booking required. **Green Fees** Weekdays £35 (£40 weekends) per day, £25/£30 per round per 18 holes. **Prof** Stephen Price **Facilities** ⊗)𝕀𝕀 ⛾ ☕ 🍸 ⛾ 🏠 ⛾ ⛾ **Conf** Corporate Hospitality Days **Location** 0.5m S off A455, signed

Hotel ★★★★★ 71% The Celtic Manor Resort, Coldra Woods, NEWPORT ☎ 01633 413000 330 en suite

NEWPORT Map 03 ST38

Celtic Manor Resort see page 413

Hotel ★★★★★ 71% The Celtic Manor Resort, Coldra Woods, NEWPORT ☎ 01633 413000 330 en suite

Hotel ★★★ 68% Newport Lodge Hotel, Bryn Bevan, Brynglas Rd, NEWPORT ☎ 01633 821818
📠 01633 856360 27 en suite

Hotel ★★★ 66% The Kings Hotel, High St, NEWPORT
☎ 01633 842020 📠 01633 244667 61 en suite

Newport Great Oak, Rogerstone NP10 9FX
☎ 01633 892643 📠 01633 896676
e-mail: newportgolfclub.gwent@euphony.net
web: newportgolfclub.org.uk
18 holes, 6460yds, Par 72, SSS 71, Course record 63.
Course Designer W Fernie **Location** M4 junct 27, 1m NW on B4591
Telephone for further details

Hotel ★★★★★ 71% The Celtic Manor Resort, Coldra Woods, NEWPORT ☎ 01633 413000 330 en suite

Parc Church Ln, Coedkernew NP10 8TU
☎ 01633 680933 📠 01633 681011
e-mail: enquiries@parcgolf.co.uk
web: www.parcgolf.co.uk
A challenging but enjoyable 18-hole course with water hazards and accompanying wildlife. The 38-bay driving range is floodlit until 10pm.
18 holes, 5619yds, Par 70, SSS 68, Course record 66.
Club membership 400.
Visitors Mon-Sun & BHs. Booking required. Dress code. **Societies** Booking required. **Green Fees** Weekdays £15 (Sat, Sun & BHs £20). **Prof** M Phillips/R Dinsdale/J Wills **Course Designer** B Thomas/T F Hicks **Facilities** ⊗)𝕀𝕀 ⛾ ☕ 🍸 ⛾ 🏠 ⛾ ⛾ ⛾ ⛾ ⛾ **Leisure** 9 hole astra turf short course. **Conf** facs Corporate Hospitality Days **Location** 3m SW of Newport, off A48

Hotel ★★★ 66% The Kings Hotel, High St, NEWPORT
☎ 01633 842020 61 en suite

Tredegar Park Parc-y-Brain Rd, Rogerstone NP10 9TG
☎ 01633 894433 📠 01633 897152
e-mail: tpgc@btinternet.com
18 holes, 6150yds, Par 72, SSS 72.
Course Designer R Sandow **Location** M4 junct 27, B4591 N, club signed
Telephone for further details

Hotel ★★★ 66% The Kings Hotel, High St, NEWPORT
☎ 01633 842020 61 en suite

PEMBROKESHIRE

HAVERFORDWEST Map 02 SM91

Haverfordwest Arnolds Down SA61 2XQ
☎ 01437 764523 & 768409 📠 01437 764143
e-mail: haverwestgolf@lineone.net
web: www.hwestgolf.homestead.com
18 holes, 5966yds, Par 70, SSS 69, Course record 63.
Location 1m E on A40
Telephone for further details

Hotel ★★ 68% Hotel Mariners, Mariners Square, HAVERFORDWEST ☎ 01437 763353 28 en suite

LETTERSTON Map 02 SM92

Priskilly Forest Castlemorris SA62 5EH
☎ 01348 840276 📠 01348 840276
e-mail: jevans@priskilly-forest.co.uk
web: www.priskilly-forest.co.uk
Challenging parkland course with panoramic views and a stunning 18th hole. Immaculate greens and fairways surrounded by rhododendrons, established shrubs and trees. Testing lies.
9 holes, 5874yds, Par 70, SSS 68, Course record 73.
Club membership 180.
Visitors Mon-Sun & BHs. Booking required BHs. Dress code. **Societies** welcome. **Green Fees** £24 per day, £20 per 18 holes, £14 for 9 holes. **Prof** S Parsons **Course Designer** J Walters **Facilities** ⊗)𝕀𝕀 ⛾ ☕ 🍸 ⛾ 🏠 ⛾ ⛾ ⛾ ⛾ ⛾ **Leisure** fishing. **Conf** facs Corporate Hospitality Days **Location** Off B4331 between Letterston

Hotel ★★ 75% Wolfscastle Country Hotel, WOLF'S CASTLE ☎ 01437 741688 & 741225 📠 01437 741383 20 en suite 4 annexe en suite

Championship Course

Newport

Celtic Manor Resort

Newport Map 03 ST38

This resort has quickly become a world-renowned venue for golf, set in 1400 acres of beautiful, unspoiled parkland at the southern gateway to Wales. Boasting three championship courses, Celtic Manor offers a challenge for all levels of play, complemented by a golf school and one of the largest clubhouses in Europe, as well as extensive leisure facilities. In 2010, The Celtic Manor Resort will host the 38th Ryder Cup on the world's first ever course to be specifically designed for this prestigious tournament. The new course, scheduled to open in spring 2007, will feature nine holes from the original Wentwood Hills course and nine spectacular new holes in the valley of the River Usk.

Coldra Woods NP18 1HQ
☎ 01633 413000 🖷 01633 410269
e-mail: golf@celtic-manor.com
web: www.celtic-manor.com

Roman Road: 18 holes, 6030yds, Par 70, SSS 72, Course record 63.
Coldra Woods: 18 holes, 3539yds, Par 59, SSS 61.
Wentwood Hills: 18 holes, 6211yds, Par 71, SSS 75, Course record 61.
Club membership 580.

Visitors Mon-Sun & BHs. Booking required. Dress code. **Societies** Booking required. **Green Fees** Apr-Oct: Wentworth Hills £60, Roman Road £60, Coldra Woods £25. **Prof** Kevin Carpenter **Course Designer** Robert Trent Jones **Facilities** **Leisure** hard tennis courts, heated indoor swimming pool, fishing, sauna, solarium, gymnasium, Health spa, Golf Academy with 18 hole course, Shooting school. **Conf facs** Corporate Hospitality Days **Location** M4 junct 24, B4237 towards Newport, 300yds right

MILFORD HAVEN Map 02 SM90

Milford Haven Woodbine House, Hubberston SA73 3RX
☎ 01646 697762 📠 01646 697870
e-mail: enquiries@mhgc.co.uk
web: www.mhgc.co.uk
18 holes, 6030yds, Par 71, SSS 70, Course record 64.
Location 1.5m W of Milford Haven
Telephone for further details

Hotel ★★★ 67% Cleddau Bridge Hotel, Essex Rd, PEMBROKE DOCK ☎ 01646 685961 24 en suite

NEWPORT (PEMBROKESHIRE) Map 02 SN03

Newport (Pemb) The Golf Club SA42 0NR
☎ 01239 820244 📠 01239 820085
e-mail: newportgc@lineone.net
web: www.newportgc.sagenet.co.uk
9 holes, 5815yds, Par 70, SSS 68, Course record 64.
Course Designer James Baird **Location** 1.25m N
Telephone for further details

Hotel ★★ 69% Trewern Arms, NEVERN
☎ 01239 820395 10 en suite

PEMBROKE DOCK Map 02 SM90

South Pembrokeshire Military Rd SA72 6SE
☎ 01646 621453 & 682442 📠 01646 621453
18 holes, 6100yds, Par 71, SSS 70, Course record 65.
Course Designer Committee **Location** SW of town centre off B4322
Telephone for further details

Hotel ★★ 65% Old Kings Arms, Main St, PEMBROKE
☎ 01646 683611 18 en suite

ST DAVID'S Map 02 SM72

St David's City Whitesands Bay SA62 6HR
☎ 01437 720572 & 721751
9 holes, 6117yds, Par 70, SSS 70, Course record 68.
Location 2m W overlooking Whitesands Bay
Telephone for further details

Hotel ★★★ 77% Warpool Court Hotel, ST DAVID S
☎ 01437 720300 25 en suite

TENBY Map 02 SN10

Tenby The Burrows SA70 7NP
☎ 01834 844447 & 842978 📠 01834 842978
e-mail: tenbygolfclub@uku.co.uk
web: www.tenbygolf.co.uk
The oldest club in Wales, this fine seaside links, with sea views and natural hazards, provides good golf all the year round.
18 holes, 6224yds, Par 69, SSS 71, Course record 65.
Club membership 800.
Visitors Mon-Sun & BHs. Booking required. Handicap certificate. Dress code. **Societies** Booking required. **Green Fees** Phone. **Prof** Mark Hawkey **Course Designer** James Braid **Facilities** **Conf** Corporate Hospitality Days **Location** Near railway station

Hotel ★★★ 75% Atlantic Hotel, The Esplanade, TENBY
☎ 01834 842881 & 844176 📠 01834 842881 ex 256
42 en suite

Trefloyne Golf, Bar & Restaurant Trefloyne Park, Penally SA70 7RG
☎ 01834 842165 📠 01834 844288
e-mail: enquiries@trefloyne
web: www.trefloyne.com
Idyllic parkland course with backdrop of mature mixed woodlands and distant views of Tenby, Carmarthen Bay and Caldey Island. Opened in 1996, natural features and hazards such as the Old Quarry make for exciting and challenging golf.
18 holes, 6635yds, Par 71, SSS 73.
Club membership 400.
Visitors Mon-Sun & BHs. Booking required Sat, Sun & BHs. Dress code. **Societies** Booking required. **Green Fees** £26 per day. **Prof** Steven Laidler **Course Designer** F H Gillman **Facilities** **Leisure** lessons by PGA Professional. **Conf** facs Corporate Hospitality Days **Location** In Trefloyne Park, just W of Tenby

Hotel ★★★ 70% Fourcroft Hotel, North Beach, TENBY
☎ 01834 842886 40 en suite

POWYS

BRECON Map 03 SO02

Brecon Newton Park LD3 8PA
☎ 01874 622004
Easy walking parkland. Natural hazards include two rivers on the boundary. Good river and mountain scenery.
9 holes, 5476yds, Par 68, SSS 66, Course record 63.
Club membership 360.
Visitors Mon-Sun & BHs. Contact club for details. Handicap certificate. Dress code. **Societies** Booking required. **Green Fees** £12 per day/per round (£15 Sat, Sun & BHs). **Course Designer** James Braid **Facilities** **Conf** Corporate Hospitality Days
Location 0.75m W of town centre on A40

Cradoc Penoyre Park, Cradoc LD3 9LP
☎ 01874 623658 📠 01874 611711
e-mail: secretary@cradoc.co.uk
web: www.cradoc.co.uk
Parkland with wooded areas, ponds and spectacular views over the Brecon Beacons. Challenging golf. New course layout in 2005 included two new holes.

18 holes, 6188yds, Par 71, SSS 71, Course record 65.
Club membership 700.
Visitors Mon-Sun & BHs. Booking advised. Handicap certificate. Dress code. **Societies** welcome. **Green Fees** £26 per day (£32 Sat, Sun & BHs). **Prof** Richard Davies

Continued

Course Designer C K Cotton **Facilities** **Location** 2m N of Brecon off B4520

Builth Wells Map 03 SO05

Builth Wells Golf Links Rd LD2 3NF
01982 553296 01982 551064
e-mail: info@builthwellsgolf.co.uk
web: www.buithwellsgolf.co.uk
Well-guarded greens and a stream running through the centre of the course add interest to this 18-hole undulating parkland course. The clubhouse is a converted 16th-century Welsh longhouse.
18 holes, 5424yds, Par 66, SSS 67, Course record 62.
Club membership 380.
Visitors Mon-Sun & BHs. Booking required. Handicap certificate. Dress code. **Societies** Booking required. **Green Fees** £27 per day, £21 per round (£30/£25 Sat, Sun & BHs). **Prof** Simon Edwards **Facilities** **Conf** Corporate Hospitality Days **Location** N of A483

Hotel ★★★ 70% Caer Beris Manor Hotel, BUILTH WELLS 01982 552601 23 en suite

Hotel ★★ 70% Lasswade Country House Hotel, Station Rd, LLANWRTYD WELLS 01591 610515 01591 610611 8 en suite

Knighton Map 07 SO27

Knighton Ffrydd Wood LD7 1DG
01547 528046 (Sec) & 528646
Upland course with some hard walking. Fine views over the England border.
9 holes, 5362yds, Par 68, SSS 66, Course record 65.
Club membership 150.
Visitors Mon-Sat. Contact club for details. Dress code. **Societies** welcome. **Green Fees** £10 per day (£15 Sat, Sun & BHs). **Course Designer** Harry Vardon **Facilities** by arrangement by arrangement **Location** 0.5m S off B4355

Hotel ★★ 80% Milebrook House Hotel, Milebrook, KNIGHTON 01547 528632 10 en suite

Llandrindod Wells Map 03 SO06

Llandrindod Wells The Clubhouse LD1 5NY
01597 823873 (sec) 01597 823873
-mail: secretary@lwgc.co.uk
veb: www.lwgc.co.uk
An upland links course, designed by Harry Vardon, with easy walking and panoramic views.
8 holes, 5759yds, Par 69, SSS 69, Course record 65.
lub membership 465.
isitors Mon-Sun & BHs. Booking required. Dress code. **ocieties** Booking required. **Green Fees** £22 per round/£31 er day (Sat, Sun & BHs £28/£35). **Prof** Philip Davies **ourse Designer** H Vardon **Facilities** **Conf** facs Corporate Hospitality Days **ocation** 1m SE off A483

Hotel ★★★ 74% The Metropole, Temple St, LANDRINDOD WELLS 01597 823700 120 en suite

Llangattock Map 03 SO21

Old Rectory NP8 1PH
01873 810373 018373 810373
9 holes, 2200yds, Par 54, SSS 59, Course record 53.
Location SW of village
Telephone for further details

Hotel ★★★ 72% Gliffaes Hotel Ltd, CRICKHOWELL 01874 730371 19 en suite 3 annexe en suite

Llanidloes Map 06 SN98

St Idloes Penrallt SY18 6LG
01686 412559
Hill-course, slightly undulating but walking is easy. Good views, partly lined with trees. Sand and grass bunkers.
9 holes, 5540yds, Par 66, SSS 66, Course record 61.
Club membership 339.
Visitors Mon-Sat & BHs. **Societies** Booking required. **Green Fees** £20 day rate, £15 per 18 hole, £10 per 9 hole. **Facilities** by arrangement by arrangement **Conf** facs **Location** 1m N off B4569

Guesthouse ♦♦♦♦ Old Vicarage, LLANGURIG 01686 440280 4 en suite

Machynlleth Map 06 SH70

Machynlleth SY20 8UH
01654 702000 01654 702928
Lowland course with mostly natural hazards.
9 holes, 5726yds, Par 68, SSS 68, Course record 65.
Club membership 200.
Visitors Mon-Sun & BHs. Dress code. **Societies** Booking required. **Green Fees** £18 per day. **Course Designer** James Braid **Facilities** **Location** 0.5m E off A489

Hotel ★★ 70% Wynnstay Hotel, Maengwyn St, MACHYNLLETH 01654 702941 23 en suite

Newtown Map 06 SO19

St Giles Pool Rd SY16 3AJ
01686 625844 01686 625844
e-mail: stgilesgolf@tiscali.co.uk
Inland country course with easy walking. Testing 2nd hole, par 3, and 4th hole, par 4. River Severn skirts four holes.
9 holes, 6012yds, Par 70, SSS 70, Course record 67.
Club membership 350.
Visitors Contact club for details. Dress code. **Societies** Booking required. **Green Fees** £15 per round. **Prof** D P Owen **Facilities** by arrangement by arrangement by arrangement by arrangement **Location** 0.5m NE on A483

Hotel ★★ 70% Wynnstay Hotel, Maengwyn St, MACHYNLLETH 01654 702941 23 en suite

WELSHPOOL Map 07 SJ20

Welshpool Golfa Hill SY21 9AQ
☎ 01938 850249 🖹 01938 850249
e-mail: welshpool.golfclub@virgin.net
web: www.welshpoolgolfclub.co.uk
Undulating, hilly, heathland course with bracing air. Testing holes are 2nd (par 5), 14th (par 3), 17th (par 3) and a memorable 18th.
18 holes, 5716yds, Par 71, SSS 68, Course record 68.
Club membership 400.
Visitors Mon-Sun & BHs. Booking required Sat, Sun & BHs. **Societies** Booking required. **Green Fees** £15.50 per day (£25.50 weekends) **Prof** Bob Barlow **Course Designer** James Braid **Facilities** **Conf** Corporate Hospitality Days **Location** 3m W off A458

Hotel ★★★ 68% Royal Oak Hotel, The Cross, WELSHPOOL ☎ 01938 552217 25 en suite

RHONDDA CYNON TAFF

ABERDARE Map 03 SO00

Aberdare Abernant CF44 0RY
☎ 01685 872797 🖹 01685 872797
e-mail: sec-age@tiscali.co.uk
Mountain course with parkland features overlooking the Brecon Beacons. Tree-lined with many mature oaks.
18 holes, 5875yds, Par 69, SSS 69, Course record 64.
Club membership 550.
Visitors Mon-Sun & BHs. Handicap certificate. Dress code. **Societies** Booking required. **Green Fees** £17 (Sat, Sun & BHs £21). **Prof** A Palmer **Facilities** **Leisure** 3 practice nets. **Conf** facs Corporate Hospitality Days **Location** 1m NE of town centre. Past hospital, 400yds on right

Hotel Tregenna Hotel, Park Ter, MERTHYR TYDFIL ☎ 01685 723627 382055 🖹 01685 721951 21 en suite

MOUNTAIN ASH Map 03 ST09

Mountain Ash Cefnpennar CF45 4DT
☎ 01443 479459 🖹 01443 479628
e-mail: geoff@magc.fsnet.co.uk
web: www.mountainash.co.uk
Mountain moorland course with panoramic views of the Brecon Beacons. Not long but testing and demands accuracy from the opening hole, a 390yd par 4 that rises up halfway down its length with woodland on the left and out of bounds on the right. The 10th hole is the highest point, hitting from an elevated platform with woodland on the left below. The 18th is a dramatic finale in the form of a 510yd, par 5, with a carry over gorse, a ditch crossing the fairway and bunkers and sand traps protecting the green.
18 holes, 5553yds, Par 69, SSS 67, Course record 60.
Club membership 560.
Visitors contact in advance for details. **Societies** must contact in writing. **Green Fees** Phone. **Prof** Darren Clark **Facilities** **Conf** facs **Location** 1m NW off A4059

Hotel Tregenna Hotel, Park Ter, MERTHYR TYDFIL ☎ 01685 723627 382055 🖹 01685 721951 21 en suite

PENRHYS Map 03 ST09

Rhondda Golf Club House CF43 3PW
☎ 01443 441384 🖹 01443 441384
e-mail: rhondda@btinternet.com
Mountain course with good views.
18 holes, 6205yds, Par 70, SSS 71, Course record 67.
Club membership 600.
Visitors Mon-Fri. Booking required. Handicap certificate. Dress code. **Societies** Booking required. **Green Fees** Weekdays £20, weekends £25 (summer), £10/£15 (winter). **Facilities** by arrangement by arrangement **Conf** facs **Location** 0.5m W off B4512

Hotel ★★★ 67% Heritage Park Hotel, Coed Cae Rd, Trehafod, PONTYPRIDD ☎ 01443 687057 44 en suite

PONTYPRIDD Map 03 ST08

Pontypridd Ty Gwyn Rd CF37 4DJ
☎ 01443 409904 🖹 01443 491622
Well-wooded mountain course with springy turf. Good views of the Rhondda Valley and coast.
18 holes, 5721yds, Par 69, SSS 68, Course record 65.
Club membership 850.
Visitors must contact in advance. Must play with member on Sat, Sun & BHs. Must have a handicap certificate. **Societies** Must contact in advance. **Green Fees** Phone. **Prof** Wade Walters **Facilities** **Location** E of town centre off A470

Hotel ★★★ 67% Heritage Park Hotel, Coed Cae Rd, Trehafod, PONTYPRIDD ☎ 01443 687057 44 en suite

TALBOT GREEN Map 03 ST08

Llantrisant & Pontyclun Off Ely Valley Rd CF72 8AL
☎ 01443 228169 🖹 01443 224601
e-mail: lpgc@barbox.net
Scenic, undulating parkland.
18 holes, 5328yds, Par 68, SSS 66.
Club membership 600.
Visitors Mon-Sun except BHs. Booking required Fri, Sat, Sun. Handicap certificate. Dress code. **Societies** Booking required. **Green Fees** £20 per day (£25 weekends). **Prof** Steve Hurley & Matt Vanstone **Facilities** **Conf** Corporate Hospitality Days **Location** M4 junct 34, A4119 to Llantrisant, over 1st rdbt, left at 2nd lights to Talbot Green, right at minirdbt, club 50yds on lef

Hotel ★★★★ 67% Miskin Manor Country Hotel, Pendoylan Rd, MISKIN ☎ 01443 224204 34 en suite 9 annexe en suite

If the name of the club appears in italics, details have not been confirmed for this edition of the guide

SWANSEA

CLYDACH Map 03 SN60

Inco SA6 5QR
☎ 01792 842929
e-mail: secretaryinco.golf@amserve.com
Flat meadowland course bordered by meandering River Tawe and the Swansea valley. Recently completed an ambitious development programme.
18 holes, 6064yds, Par 70, SSS 69.
Club membership 450.
Visitors Mon-Sun & BHs. Contact club for details. Dress code. **Societies** Booking required. **Green Fees** £18 per round (£23 weekend). **Facilities** **Leisure** outdoor bowling green. **Conf** Corporate Hospitality Days **Location** M4 junct 25, 1.5m NE on A4067

Hotel Premier Travel Inn Swansea North, Upper Fforest Way, Morriston, SWANSEA ☎ 08701 977246 40 en suite

PONTLLIW Map 02 SS69

Allt-y-Graban Allt-y-Grabam Rd SA4 1DT
☎ 01792 885757
9 holes, 2210yds, Par 66, SSS 66, Course record 63.
Course Designer F G Thomas **Location** M4 junct 47, A48 towards Pontardulais, left after Glamorgan Arms
Telephone for further details

Hotel Travelodge Swansea (M4), Penllergaer, SWANSEA ☎ 08700 850 950 50 en suite

SOUTHGATE Map 02 SS58

Pennard 2 Southgate Rd SA3 2BT
☎ 01792 233131 & 233451 01792 234797
e-mail: sec@pennardgolfclub.com
web: www.pennardgolfclub.com
Undulating, cliff-top seaside links with good coastal views. At first sight it can be intimidating with steep hills that make club selection important - there are a few blind shots to contend with. The difficulties are not insurmountable unless the wind begins to blow in calm weather. Greens are slick and firm all year.
18 holes, 6265yds, Par 71, SSS 72, Course record 69.
Club membership 1020.
Visitors Mon & Wed-Sun. Handicap certificate. Dress code. **Societies** Booking required. **Green Fees** £40 per 18 holes (£50 Sat, Sun & BHs). **Prof** M V Bennett **Course Designer** James Braid **Facilities** **Location** 8m W of Swansea by A4067 and B4436

Hotel ★★★ Fairyhill, REYNOLDSTON
☎ 01792 390139 8 en suite

SWANSEA Map 03 SS69

Clyne 120 Owls Lodge Ln, The Mayals, Blackpyl SA3 5DP
☎ 01792 401989 01792 401078
e-mail: clynegolfclub@supanet.com
web: www.clynegolfclub.com
Challenging moorland course with excellent greens and scenic views of Swansea Bay and the Gower. Many natural hazards with a large number of bunkers and gorse and bracken in profusion.
18 holes, 6334yds, Par 70, SSS 72, Course record 64.
Club membership 900.
Visitors Mon-Sun & BHs. Contact club for details. Handicap certificate. Dress code. **Societies** Booking required. **Green Fees** £28 per round (£36 Sat, Sun & BHs). **Prof** Jonathan Clewett **Course Designer** H S Colt & Harries **Facilities**
Leisure chipping green, driving nets, indoor practice net. **Location** 3.5m SW on B4436

Hotel ★★★ 68% Aberavon Beach Hotel, PORT TALBOT
☎ 01639 884949 01639 897885 52 en suite

Langland Bay Langland Bay SA3 4QR
☎ 01792 361721 01792 361082
e-mail: info@langlandbaygolfclub.com
web: www.langlandbaygolfclub.com
Parkland situated on cliff tops and land between Caswell and Langland Bay. The par 4 6th is an uphill dog-leg open to the wind, and the par 3 16th (151yds) is aptly named Death or Glory.

18 holes, 5857yds, Par 70, SSS 70, Course record 63.
Club membership 850.
Visitors Contact club for details. Handicap certificate. Dress code. **Societies** Booking required. **Green Fees** £40 weekdays, £50 Sat, Sun & BHs. **Prof** Mark Evans **Facilities** **Location** 6m SW off B4593

Hotel ★★★ 62% St Anne's Hotel, Western Ln, MUMBLES ☎ 01792 369147 33 en suite

Morriston 160 Clasemont Rd SA6 6AJ
☎ 01792 796528 01792 796528
e-mail: morristongolf@btconnect.com
18 holes, 5891yds, Par 68, SSS 68, Course record 61.
Location M4 junct 46, 1m E on A48
Telephone for further details

Hotel Premier Travel Inn Swansea North, Upper Fforest Way, Morriston, SWANSEA ☎ 08701 977246 40 en suite

Continued

THREE CROSSES Map 02 SS59

Gower Cefn Goleu SA4 3HS
☎ 01792 872480 01792 872480
e-mail: info@gowergolf.co.uk
web: www.gowergolf.co.uk
Set in attractive rolling countryside, this Donald Steel designed course provides good strategic hazards, including trees, water and bunkers. Outstanding views and a challenging game of golf.
18 holes, 6441yds, Par 71, SSS 72, Course record 67. Club membership 400.
Visitors Mon-Sun & BHs. Booking required Fri-Sun. Handicap certificate. Dress code. **Societies** Booking required. **Green Fees** Mon-Thu £24 per 18 holes, Fri £25 (£32 weekends). **Prof** Alan Williamson **Course Designer** Donald Steel **Facilities** **Conf** facs Corporate Hospitality Days **Location** Off A4118 Swansea to Gower, signed from Three Crosses

Hotel ★★ 72% Beaumont Hotel, 72-73 Walter Rd, SWANSEA ☎ 01792 643956 16 en suite

UPPER KILLAY Map 02 SS59

Fairwood Park Fairwood SA2 7JN
☎ 01792 297849 01792 297849
e-mail: info@fairwoodpark.com
web: www.fairwoodpark.com
Parkland championship course on the beautiful Gower peninsula.
18 holes, 6650yds, Par 73, SSS 73, Course record 68. Club membership 500.
Visitors Mon-Sun & BHs. Booking required. Dress code. **Societies** Booking required. **Green Fees** Mon-Thu £20 per 18 holes, Fri-Sun £25 per 18 holes. **Prof** Gary Hughes **Course Designer** Hawtree **Facilities** **Conf** Corporate Hospitality Days **Location** 1.5m S off A4118

Hotel ★★ 71% Windsor Lodge Hotel & Restaurant, Mount Pleasant, SWANSEA ☎ 01792 642158 & 652744 01792 648996 19 en suite

TORFAEN

CWMBRAN Map 03 ST29

Green Meadow Golf & Country Club
Treherbert Rd, Croesyceiliog NP44 2BZ
☎ 01633 869321 & 862626 01633 868430
e-mail: info@greenmeadowgolf.com
web: www.greenmeadowgolf.com
Undulating parkland with panoramic views. Tree-lined fairways, water hazards and pot bunkers. The greens are excellent and are playable all year round.
18 holes, 6029yds, Par 70, SSS 70, Course record 64. Club membership 400.
Visitors Mon-Fri & BHs. Weekends after 11am. Booking required Sat & Sun. Dress code. **Societies** Booking required. **Green Fees** £19 per round Tues-Fri, £16 Mon, £23 Sat, Sun & BHs. **Prof** Dave Woodman **Course Designer** Peter Richardson **Facilities** **Leisure** hard tennis courts, sauna, gymnasium. **Conf** facs Corporate Hospitality Days **Location** NE of town off A4042
See advertisement on this page

Green Meadow Golf & Country Club

Hotel ★★★★ 66% Parkway Hotel, Cwmbran Dr, CWMBRAN ☎ 01633 871199 70 en suite

Pontnewydd Maesgwyn Farm, Upper Cwmbran NP44 1AB
☎ 01633 482170 01633 838598
e-mail: ct.phillips@virgin.net
Mountainside course with hard walking. Good views across the Severn estuary.
18 holes, 5278yds, Par 68, SSS 67, Course record 61. Club membership 502.
Visitors contact club for details. **Green Fees** £15 per round. **Facilities** **Location** N of town centre

Hotel ★★★★ 66% Parkway Hotel, Cwmbran Dr, CWMBRAN ☎ 01633 871199 70 en suite

Continued

PONTYPOOL Map 03 SO20

Pontypool Lasgarn Ln, Trevethin NP4 8TR
☎ 01495 763655 🖹 01495 755564
e-mail: pontypoolgolf@btconnect.com
web: pontypoolgolf.co.uk
Undulating mountain course with magnificent views of the Bristol Channel.
18 holes, 5963yds, Par 69, SSS 69, Course record 64.
Club membership 638.
Visitors Mon-Fri. Booking required. Handicap certificate. Dress code. **Societies** welcome. **Green Fees** Phone. **Prof** Neil Matthews **Facilities** **Leisure** indoor teaching academy with video analysis. **Conf** Corporate Hospitality Days **Location** 1.5m N off A4043

Hotel ★★ 69% Mill at Glynhir, Glynhir Rd, Llandybie, AMMANFORD ☎ 01269 850672 7 en suite 3 annexe en suite

Woodlake Park Golf & Country Club
Glascoed NP4 0TE
☎ 01291 673933 🖹 01291 673811
e-mail: golf@woodlake.co.uk
web: www.woodlake.co.uk
Undulating parkland with magnificent views over the Llandegfedd Reservoir. Superb greens constructed to USGA specification. Holes 4, 7 and 16 are par 3s, which are particularly challenging. Holes 6 and 17 are long par 4s, which can be wind affected.
18 holes, 6278yds, Par 71, SSS 72, Course record 67.
Club membership 500.
Visitors Mon-Sun & BHs. Booking required. Handicap certificate. Dress code. **Societies** Booking required. **Green Fees** Mon-Thu £30 per day (Fri, Sat, Sun & BHs £40); Mon-Thu £25 per 18 holes (Fri, Sat, Sun & BHs £30). **Prof** Leon Lancey **Facilities** **Leisure** fishing. **Conf** facs Corporate Hospitality Days **Location** Overlooking Llandegfedd Reservoir

Hotel ★★ 69% Mill at Glynhir, Glynhir Rd, Llandybie, AMMANFORD ☎ 01269 850672 7 en suite 3 annexe en suite

VALE OF GLAMORGAN

BARRY Map 03 ST16

Brynhill Port Rd CF62 8PN
☎ 01446 720277 🖹 01446 740422
e-mail: postbox@brynhillgolfclub.co.uk
web: www.brynhillgolfclub.co.uk
Meadowland course with some hard walking. Prevailing west wind.
18 holes, 6516yds, Par 72, SSS 71.
Club membership 750.
Visitors Mon-Sat & BHs. Handicap certificate. Dress code. **Societies** Booking required. **Green Fees** £25 per round. **Prof** Duncan Prior **Facilities** **Location** 1.25m N on B4050

Hotel ★★★ 69% Mount Sorrel Hotel, Porthkerry Rd, BARRY ☎ 01446 740069 42 en suite

RAF St Athan Clive Rd, St Athan CF62 4JD
☎ 01446 751043 🖹 01446 751862
Parkland affected by strong winds straight from the sea. Further interest is added by this being a very tight course with lots of trees. Beware of low-flying RAF jets.
9 holes, 6480yds, Par 72, SSS 72.
Club membership 450.
Visitors Mon-Sat. Booking required Fri & Sat. Handicap certificate. Dress code. **Societies** welcome. **Green Fees** £15 per day (weekend £20). **Course Designer** the members **Facilities** **Location** Between Barry & Llantwit Major

Hotel ★★★ 74% Egerton Grey Country House Hotel, Porthkerry, BARRY ☎ 01446 711666 10 en suite

St Andrews Major Argae Ln, Coldbrook Rd East, Cadoxton CF63 1BL
☎ 01446 722227 🖹 01446 748953
e-mail: standrewsmajor@hotmail.co.uk
web: www.standrewsmajorgolfclub.co.uk
A scenic 18-hole parkland course, suitable for all standards of golfer. The greens are designed to US specifications. The course provides excellent challenges to all levels of golfers without being physically exerting.
18 holes, 5300yds, Par 69, SSS 70.
Club membership 400.
Visitors Mon-Sun & BHs. Booking required. Dress code. **Societies** welcome. **Green Fees** £16 per round (weekends £18). **Prof** Iestyn Taylor **Course Designer** Richard Hurd **Facilities** **Conf** facs Corporate Hospitality Days **Location** 1.5m NE of Barry off A4231

Hotel ★★★ 74% Egerton Grey Country House Hotel, Porthkerry, BARRY ☎ 01446 711666 10 en suite

DINAS POWYS Map 03 ST17

Dinas Powis High Walls Av CF64 4AJ
☎ 029 2051 2727 🖹 029 2051 2727
18 holes, 5486yds, Par 67, SSS 67, Course record 60.
Location NW side of village
Telephone for further details

Hotel ★★★ 69% Mount Sorrel Hotel, Porthkerry Rd, BARRY ☎ 01446 740069 42 en suite

HENSOL Map 03 ST07

Vale Hotel Golf & Spa Resort Hensol Park CF72 8JY
☎ 01443 665899 🖹 01443 222220
e-mail: golf@vale-hotel.com
web: www.vale-hotel.com
Lake: 18 holes, 6426yds, Par 72, SSS 71.
Hensol: 9 holes, 3115yds, Par 72, SSS 71.
Course Designer Peter Johnson **Location** M4 junct 34
Telephone for further details

Hotel ★★★★ 73% Vale Hotel Golf & Spa Resort, Hensol Park, HENSOL ☎ 01443 667800 29 en suite 114 annexe en suite

PENARTH Map 03 ST17

Glamorganshire Lavernock Rd CF64 5UP
☎ 029 20701185 029 20701185
e-mail: glamgolf@btconnect.com
web: www.glamorganshiregolfclub.co.uk
Parkland overlooking the Bristol Channel.
18 holes, 6184yds, Par 70, SSS 70, Course record 64. Club membership 1000.
Visitors Mon, Wed-Fri & Sun. Booking required. Handicap certificate. Dress code. **Societies** Booking required. **Green Fees** £38 per day (£40 Sat, Sun & BHs). **Prof** Andrew Kerr-Smith **Course Designer** James Braid **Facilities** **Location** S of town centre on B4267

Hotel ★★★ 69% Mount Sorrel Hotel, Porthkerry Rd, BARRY ☎ 01446 740069 42 en suite

WENVOE Map 03 ST17

Wenvoe Castle CF5 6BE
☎ 029 20594371
18 holes, 6422yds, Par 72, SSS 71, Course record 64.
Location 1m S off A4050
Telephone for further details

Hotel ★★★ 74% Egerton Grey Country House Hotel, Porthkerry, BARRY ☎ 01446 711666 10 en suite

WREXHAM

CHIRK Map 07 SJ23

Chirk Golf Club LL14 5AD
☎ 01691 774407 01691 773878
e-mail: chirkjackbarker@btinternet.com
web: www.jackbarker.com
Overlooked by the National Trust's Chirk Castle, a championship-standard 18-hole course with a 664yd par 5 at the 9th - one of the longest in Europe. Also a nine-hole course, driving range and golf academy.
Chirk: 18 holes, 7045yds, Par 72, SSS 73, Course record 69.
Club membership 300.
Visitors Mon-Sun & BHs. Booking required. **Societies** Booking required. **Green Fees** Mon-Thurs £14, Fri £16, Sat & Sun £18 per round. **Prof** M Maddison **Facilities** **Leisure** 9 hole par 3 course. **Conf** facs **Location** 1m NW of Chirk, near Chirk Castle

EYTON Map 07 SJ34

Plassey LL13 0SP
☎ 01978 780020 01978 781397
web: www.plasseygolf.co.uk
Picturesque nine-hole course in undulating parkland.
9 holes, 4962yds, Par 66, SSS 64, Course record 62. Club membership 222.
Visitors Booking required. **Societies** Booking required. **Green Fees** Phone. **Prof** Simon Ward **Course Designer** Welsh Golf Union **Facilities** **Location** 4m S of Wrexham off B5426, signed

Hotel ★★★ 68% Cross Lanes Hotel & Restaurant, Cross Lanes, Bangor Rd, Marchwiel, WREXHAM
☎ 01978 780555 16 en suite

RUABON Map 07 SJ34

Penycae Ruabon Rd, Penycae LL14 1TP
☎ 01978 810108
9 holes, 2140yds, Par 64, SSS 62, Course record 62.
Course Designer John Day **Location** 1m off A5
Telephone for further details

WREXHAM Map 07 SJ35

Clays Bryn Estyn Rd, Llan-y-Pwll LL13 9UB
☎ 01978 661406 01978 661406
e-mail: claysgolf@claysgolf.co.uk
web: www.claysgolf.co.uk
Gently undulating parkland course in countryside with views of the Welsh mountains. Noted for its difficult par 3s.
18 holes, 6010yds, Par 69, SSS 69, Course record 62. Club membership 420.
Visitors Contact club for details. **Societies** welcome. **Green Fees** £19 per 18 holes (£25 weekends). **Prof** David Larvin **Course Designer** R D Jones **Facilities** **Conf** Corporate Hospitality Days **Location** Off A534

Hotel ★★★ 67% Llwyn Onn Hall Hotel, Cefn Rd, WREXHAM ☎ 01978 261225 13 en suite

Wrexham Holt Rd LL13 9SB
☎ 01978 364268 01978 364268
e-mail: info@wrexhamgolfclub.co.uk
web: www.wrexhamgolfclub.co.uk
Inland, sandy course with easy walking. Testing dog-leg 7th hole (par 4), and short 14th hole (par 3) with full carry to green.
18 holes, 6233yds, Par 70, SSS 70, Course record 64. Club membership 680.
Visitors Mon, Wed-Fri. Handicap certificate. Dress code. **Societies** Booking required. **Green Fees** Phone. **Prof** Paul Williams **Course Designer** James Braid **Facilities** **Location** 2m NE on A534

Hotel ★★★ 67% Llwyn Onn Hall Hotel, Cefn Rd, WREXHAM ☎ 01978 261225 13 en suite

Ireland

NORTHERN IRELAND

CO ANTRIM

ANTRIM Map 01 D5

Massereene 51 Lough Rd BT41 4DQ
☎ 028 9442 8096 📠 028 9448 7661
e-mail: info@massereene.com
web: www.massereene.com
The first nine holes are parkland, while the second, adjacent to the shore of Lough Neagh, have more of a links character with sandy ground.
18 holes, 6602yds, Par 72, SSS 72, Course record 63.
Club membership 969.
Visitors Mon-Sun & BHs. Booking required. Handicap certificate. Dress code. **Societies** Booking required. **Green Fees** £25 weekdays. £30 weekends. **Prof** Jim Smyth **Course Designer** F Hawtree/H Swan **Facilities** **Conf** facs Corporate Hospitality Days **Location** 1m SW of town

BALLYCASTLE Map 01 D6

Ballycastle Cushendall Rd BT54 6QP
☎ 028 2076 2536 📠 028 2076 9909
e-mail: info@ballycastlegolfclub.com
web: www.ballycastlegolfclub.com
An unusual mixture of terrain beside the sea, lying at the foot of one of the nine glens of Antrim, with magnificent views from all parts. The first five holes are parkland with natural hazards; the middle holes are links type and the rest on adjacent upland. Accurate iron play is essential for good scoring while the undulating greens will test putting skills.
18 holes, 5927 metres, Par 71, SSS 70, Course record 64.
Club membership 825.
Visitors Mon-Sun & BHs. Booking required. Dress code. **Societies** Booking required. **Green Fees** £25 per round (£35 Sat, Sun & BHs). **Prof** Ian McLaughlin **Facilities** **Conf** facs Corporate Hospitality Days **Location** Between Portrush & Cushendall (A2)

BALLYCLARE Map 01 D5

Ballyclare 23 Springdale Rd BT39 9JW
☎ 028 9332 2696 📠 028 9332 2696
e-mail: ballyclaregolfclub@supanet
web: www.ballyclaregolfclub.com
Parkland with lots of trees and shrubs, and water hazards provided by the river, streams and lakes. The long 3rd hole is played from an elevated tee across a lake to a curving fairway lined with mature trees,
18 holes, 5745 metres, Par 71, SSS 71, Course record 66.
Club membership 580.
Visitors must contact in advance. **Societies** Booking required. **Green Fees** Phone. **Prof** Alan Johnston **Course Designer** T McCauley **Facilities** **Conf** Corporate Hospitality Days **Location** 1.5m N of Ballyclare

Greenacres 153 Ballyrobert Rd BT39 9RT
☎ 028 9335 4111 📠 028 9335 4166
Designed and built into the rolling countryside, and with the addition of lakes at five of the holes, provides a challenge for both the seasoned golfer and the higher-handicapped player.

Continued

18 holes, 6031yds, Par 71, SSS 69.
Club membership 520.
Visitors Mon-Fri, Sun & BHs. Dress code **Societies** Booking required. **Green Fees** Mon-Thurs £16, Fri £20, Sat & Sun £22. **Facilities** **Conf** facs Corporate Hospitality Days **Location** 12m from Belfast city centre

BALLYGALLY Map 01 D5

Cairndhu 192 Coast Rd BT40 2QG
☎ 028 2858 3954 📠 028 2858 3324
e-mail: cairndhugc@btconnect.com
Built on a hilly headland, this course is both testing and scenic, with wonderful coastal views. The par 3 second hole can require anything from a 9 to a 3 iron depending on the wind, while the 3rd has a carry of 165 metres over a headland to the fairway. The 10th, 11th and 12th holes constitute Cairndhu's Amen Corner, feared and respected by any standard of golfer.
18 holes, 5611 metres, Par 70, SSS 69, Course record 64.
Club membership 905.
Visitors Mon-Fri , Sun & BHs. Booking required. Handicap certificate. Dress code. **Societies** Booking required **Green Fees** £20 per 18 holes (£25 Sun). **Prof** Stephen Hood **Course Designer** Mr Morrison **Facilities** **Conf** facs **Location** 4m N of Larne on coast road

Guest House ♦♦♦♦ Manor Guest House, 23 Older Fleet Rd, Harbour Highway, LARNE ☎ 028 2827 3305
8 en suite

BALLYMENA Map 01 D5

Ballymena 128 Raceview Rd BT42 4HY
☎ 028 2586 1487 📠 028 2586 1487
18 holes, 5299 metres, Par 68, SSS 67, Course record 62.
Location 2m E on A42
Telephone for further details

Galgorm Castle Golf & Country Club
Galgorm Rd BT42 1HL
☎ 028 2564 6161 📠 028 2565 1151
e-mail: golf@galgormcastle.co.uk
web: www.galgormcastle.com
An 18-hole USGA championship course set in 220 acres of mature parkland in the grounds of one of Ireland's most historic castles. The course is bordered by two rivers which come into play and includes five lakes. A course of outstanding beauty offering a challenge to both the novice and low handicapped golfer.

18 holes, 6736yds, Par 72, SSS 72, Course record 67.
Club membership 450.
Visitors Mon-Sun. Booking required Sat. Dress code.

Continued

Societies Booking required. **Green Fees** £28 (weekends £32). **Prof** Phil Collins **Course Designer** Simon Gidman **Facilities** **Leisure** fishing, PGA staffed Academy. **Conf** facs Corporate Hospitality Days **Location** 1m S of Ballymena on A42

BALLYMONEY Map 01 D6

Gracehill 141 Ballinlea Rd, Stranocum BT53 8PX
☎ 028 2075 1209 028 2075 1074
e-mail: info@gracehillgolfclub.co.uk
web: www.gracehillgolfclub.co.uk
Challenging parkland course with some holes played over water and many mature trees coming into play.
18 holes, 6553yds, Par 72, SSS 73, Course record 69.
Club membership 400.
Visitors Mon-Sun & BHs. Booking required Sat-Sun & BHs. Dress code. **Societies** Booking required. **Green Fees** £25 midweek. £30 weekend. **Course Designer** Frank Ainsworth **Facilities** **Conf** facs Corporate Hospitality Days **Location** M2 N from Belfast, onto A26 N to Ballymoney, signs for Coleraine. At Ballymoney bypass onto B147/A2 to Sranocum/Ballintoy

CARRICKFERGUS Map 01 D5

Carrickfergus 35 North Rd BT38 8LP
☎ 028 9336 3713 028 9336 3023
e-mail: carrickfergusgc@btconnect.com
Parkland course, fairly level but nevertheless demanding, with a notorious water hazard at the 1st. Well-maintained, with an interesting in-course riverway and fine views across Belfast Lough.
18 holes, 5768yds, Par 68, SSS 68.
Club membership 850.
Visitors Mon-Fri, Sun & BHs. Booking required. Dress code. **Societies** Booking required. **Green Fees** £12-£19 weekdays. £15-£25 weekends & BHs. **Prof** Gary Mercer **Facilities** **Conf** facs Corporate Hospitality Days **Location** 9m NE of Belfast on A2

Hotel ★★ 66% Dobbins Inn Hotel, 6-8 High St, CARRICKFERGUS ☎ 028 9335 1905 15 en suite

Greenisland 156 Upper Rd, Greenisland BT38 8RW
☎ 028 9086 2236
A parkland course nestling at the foot of Knockagh Hill, with scenic views over Belfast Lough.
9 holes, 6045yds, Par 71, SSS 69.
Club membership 660.
Visitors Contact club for details. **Societies** welcome. **Green Fees** £12 (£18 weekends). **Facilities** **Location** N of Belfast, close to Carrickfergus

Hotel ★★ 66% Dobbins Inn Hotel, 6-8 High St, CARRICKFERGUS ☎ 028 9335 1905 15 en suite

CUSHENDALL Map 01 D6

Cushendall 21 Shore Rd BT44 0NG
☎ 028 2177 1318
e-mail: cushendallgolfclub@hotmail.com
Scenic course with spectacular views over the Sea of Moyle and Red Bay to the Mull of Kintyre. The River Dall winds through the course, coming into play in seven of the nine holes. This demands a premium on accuracy rather than length. The signature hole is the par 3 2nd, requiring a tee shot across the river to a plateau green with a steep slope in front and out of bounds behind.
9 holes, 4386 metres, Par 66, SSS 63, Course record 59.
Club membership 834.

Continued

Visitors Mon-Wed, Fri & BHs. Booking required BHs. Handicap certificate. Dress code. **Societies** Booking required. **Green Fees** £13 per day (£18 BHs). **Course Designer** D Delargy **Facilities** **Location** In Cushendall beside beach on Antrim coast road

Guest House ♦♦♦♦ The Villa Farm House, 185 Torr Rd, CUSHENDUN ☎ 028 2176 1252 3 en suite

LARNE Map 01 D5

Larne 54 Ferris Bay Rd, Islandmagee BT40 3RT
☎ 028 9338 2228 028 9338 2088
e-mail: info@larnegolfclub.co.uk
web: www.larnegolfclub.co.uk
An exposed part links, part heathland course offering a good test, particularly on the last three holes along the sea shore.
9 holes, 6686yds, Par 70, SSS 70, Course record 64.
Club membership 430.
Visitors Contact club for details. **Societies** welcome. **Green Fees** £10 per day (Sat, Sun & BHs £18). **Course Designer** G L Bailie **Facilities** **Location** 6m N of Whitehead on Browns Bay road

Guest House ♦♦♦♦ Drumkeerin, 201A Torr Rd, CUSHENDUN ☎ 028 2176 1554 3 en suite

LISBURN Map 01 D5

Aberdelghy Bell's Ln, Lambeg BT27 4QH
☎ 028 92662738 028 92603432
e-mail: info@mmsportsgolf.com
web: mmsportsgolf.com
18 holes, 4139 metres, Par 66, SSS 62, Course record 64.
Course Designer Alec Blair **Location** 1.5m N of Lisburn off A1
Telephone for further details

Hotel ★★★ 71% Malone Lodge Hotel, 60 Eglantine Av, BELFAST ☎ 028 9038 8000 51 en suite

Lisburn 68 Eglantine Rd BT27 5RQ
☎ 028 9267 7216 028 9260 3608
e-mail: lisburngolfclub@aol.com
web: www.lisburngolfclub.com
18 holes, 6647yds, Par 72, SSS 72, Course record 67.
Course Designer Hawtree **Location** 2m from town on A1
Telephone for further details

Hotel ★★★ 71% Malone Lodge Hotel, 60 Eglantine Av, BELFAST ☎ 028 9038 8000 51 en suite

MAZE Map 01 D5

Down Royal Park Dunygarton Rd BT27 5RT
☎ 028 92621339 028 92621339
Down Royal Park Course: 18 holes, 6824yds, Par 72, SSS 72, Course record 69.
Valley Course: 9 holes, 2019, Par 33.
Location Inside Down Royal Race Course
Telephone for further details

Hotel ★★★ 71% Malone Lodge Hotel, 60 Eglantine Av, BELFAST ☎ 028 9038 8000 51 en suite

NEWTOWNABBEY Map 01 D5

Ballyearl Golf & Leisure Centre 585 Doagh Rd, Mossley BT36 5RZ
☎ 028 9084 8287 028 9084 4896
9 holes, 2520yds, Par 27.
Course Designer V Lathery
Telephone for further details

Mallusk Antrim Rd BT36
☎ 028 90843799
9 holes, 4444yds, Par 62, SSS 62, Course record 62.
Course Designer David Fitzgerald
Telephone for further details

PORTBALLINTRAE Map 01 C6

Bushfoot 50 Bushfoot Rd, Portballintrae BT57 8RR
☎ 028 2073 1317 028 2073 1852
e-mail: bushfootgolfclub@btconnect.com
A seaside links course with superb views in an area of outstanding beauty. A challenging par 3 7th is ringed by bunkers with out of bounds beyond, while the 3rd has a blind approach. Also a putting green and pitch and putt course.
9 holes, 6075yds, Par 70, SSS 68, Course record 68.
Club membership 850.
Visitors Mon, Wed-Fri, Sun & BHs. Contact club for details. **Societies** Booking required. **Green Fees** £16 weekdays. £20 Sun & BHs. **Facilities** **Location** Off Ballaghmore road

PORTRUSH Map 01 C6

Royal Portrush **see page 425**

WHITEHEAD Map 01 D5

Bentra Municipal Slaughterford Rd BT38 9TG
☎ 028 9337 8996
9 holes, 2885 metres, Par 37, SSS 35.
Location 6m from Carrickfergus
Telephone for further details

Hotel ★★ 66% Dobbins Inn Hotel, 6-8 High St, CARRICKFERGUS ☎ 028 9335 1905 15 en suite

Whitehead McCrae's Brae BT38 9NZ
☎ 028 9337 0820 & 9337 0822 028 9337 0825
e-mail: robin@whiteheadgc.fsnet.co.uk
Undulating parkland course with magnificent sea views.
18 holes, 5952yds, Par 70, SSS 69, Course record 65.
Club membership 962.
Visitors Mon-Fri, Sun & BHs. Booking required. Dress code. **Societies** Booking required. **Green Fees** £18 per round weekdays. £22 Sun & BHs. **Prof** Colin Farr **Course Designer** A B Armstrong **Facilities** **Conf** facs Corporate Hospitality Days
Location 1m from town

Hotel ★★ 66% Dobbins Inn Hotel, 6-8 High St, CARRICKFERGUS ☎ 028 9335 1905 15 en suite

CO ARMAGH

ARMAGH Map 01 C5

County Armagh The Demesne, Newry Rd BT60 1EN
☎ 028 3752 5861 & 3752 8768 028 3752 5861
e-mail: june@golfarmagh.co.uk
web: www.golfarmagh.co.uk
18 holes, 6212yds, Par 70, SSS 69, Course record 63.
Location On Newry Rd
Telephone for further details

Hotel The Cohannon Inn & Autolodge, 212 Ballynakilly Rd, DUNGANNON ☎ 028 8772 4488 42 en suite

CULLYHANNA Map 01 C5

Ashfield 44 Creggandufff Rd BT35 0JJ
☎ 028 3086 8611
18 holes, 5840yds, Par 69.
Course Designer Frank Ainsworth
Telephone for further details

Hotel ★★ 67% Enniskeen House Hotel, 98 Bryansford Rd, NEWCASTLE ☎ 028 4372 2392 12 en suite

LURGAN Map 01 D5

Craigavon Golf & Ski Centre Turmoyra Ln, Silverwood BT66 6NG
☎ 028 3832 6606 028 3834 7272
e-mail: geoffcoupland@craigavon.gov.uk
18 holes, 6496yds, Par 72, SSS 72.
Location 2m N at Silverwood off M1
Telephone for further details

Lurgan The Demesne BT67 9BN
☎ 028 3832 2087 028 3831 6166
e-mail: lurgangolfclub@btconnect.com
web: www.lurgangolfclub.co.uk
Testing parkland course bordering Lurgan Park Lake with a need for accurate shots. Drains well in wet weather and suits a long straight hitter.
18 holes, 6257yds, Par 70, SSS 70, Course record 66.
Club membership 903.
Visitors Mon-Tue, Thu-Fri, Sun & BHs. Booking required. Dress code. **Societies** Booking required. **Green Fees** £17 weekdays. £22 Sun & BHs. **Prof** Des Paul **Course Designer** A Pennink **Facilities** **Conf** facs Corporate Hospitality Days **Location** 0.5m from town centre near Lurgan Park

Continued

Championship Course

Co Antrim

Royal Portrush

Portrush

Map 01 C6

This course, designed by Harry S Colt, is considered to be among the best six in the UK. Founded in 1888, it was the venue of the first professional golf event in Ireland, held in 1895, when Sandy Herd beat Harry Vardon in the final. Royal Portrush is spectacular and breathtaking, one of the tightest driving courses known to golfers. On a clear day there's a fine view of Islay and the Paps of Jura from the 3rd tee, and the Giant's Causeway from the 5th. While the greens have to be 'read' from the start, there are fairways up and down valleys, and holes called Calamity Corner and Purgatory (for good reason). The 2nd hole, Giant's Grave, is 509yds, but the 17th is even longer.

Dunluce Rd BT56 8JQ
☎ 028 7082 2311 🖹 028 7082 3139
e-mail: info@royalportrushgolfclub.com
web: www.royalportrushgolfclub.com

Dunluce: 18 holes, 6641yds, Par 72, SSS 73.
Valley: 18 holes, 6054yds, Par 70, SSS 72.
Club membership 1300.

Visitors Mon-Sun & BHs. Handicap certificate. Dress code. **Societies** Booking required. **Green Fees** Dunluce £105 per round, £120 weekends. Valley £35 per round, £40 weekends. **Prof** Gary McNeill **Course Designer** Harry Colt **Facilities** **Location** 0.8km from Portrush on Bushmills road

PORTADOWN Map 01 D5

Portadown 192 Gilford Rd BT63 5LF
☎ 028 3835 5356 Fax 028 3839 1394
e-mail: portadown.gc@btconnect.com
web: www.portadowngolfclub.co.uk
Well-wooded parkland on the banks of the River Bann, which is one of the water hazards.
18 holes, 6130yds, Par 70, SSS 69, Course record 65. Club membership 800.
Visitors Mon-Sun & BHs. Booking required. Dress code. **Societies** Booking required. **Green Fees** £18 weekdays. £22 weekends & BHs. **Prof** Paul Stevenson **Facilities** **Leisure** squash. **Conf** facs Corporate Hospitality Days **Location** SE via A59

Hotel The Cohannon Inn & Autolodge, 212 Ballynakilly Rd, DUNGANNON ☎ 028 8772 4488 42 en suite

TANDRAGEE Map 01 D5

Tandragee Markethill Rd BT62 2ER
☎ 028 3884 1272 Fax 028 3884 0664
e-mail: office@tandragee.co.uk
web: www.tandragee.co.uk
Pleasant parkland course, the signature hole is the demanding par 3 16th known as 'The Quarry Hole'; the real strength of Tandragee is in the short holes.
18 holes, 5747 metres, Par 71, SSS 70, Course record 65. Club membership 1018.
Visitors Mon-Fri, Sun & BHs. Contact club for details. Dress code. **Societies** Booking required. **Green Fees** £15 per round (£20 weekends). **Prof** Dympna Keenan **Course Designer** John Stone **Facilities** **Leisure** sauna, gymnasium, snooker. **Conf** facs **Location** On B3 from Tandragee towards Markethill

CO BELFAST

BELFAST Map 01 D5

See also **The Royal Belfast, Holywood, Co Down**.

Balmoral 518 Lisburn Rd BT9 6GX
☎ 028 9038 1514 Fax 028 9066 6759
e-mail: enquiries@balmoralgolf.com
web: www.balmoralgolf.com
Parkland course in the suburbs of south Belfast. An enjoyable challenge for golfers of all levels.
18 holes, 6276yds, Par 69, SSS 70, Course record 64. Club membership 912.
Visitors may not play Sat or Sun before 2.30pm. **Societies** Mon & Thu. Must contact in advance. **Green Fees** Phone. **Prof** Geoff Bleakley **Facilities** **Leisure** snooker. **Conf** facs Corporate Hospitality Days **Location** 2m S next to Kings Hall

Hotel ★★★ 71% Malone Lodge Hotel, 60 Eglantine Av, BELFAST ☎ 028 9038 8000 51 en suite

Cliftonville 44 Westland Rd BT14 6NII
☎ 028 9074 4158 & 9022 8585
web: www.cliftonvillegolfclub.com
9 holes, 6242yds, Par 70, SSS 70, Course record 65.
Location Between Cavehill Rd & Cliftonville Circus
Telephone for further details

Hotel ★★★ 66% Jurys Inn Belfast, Fisherwick Place, Great Victoria St, BELFAST ☎ 028 9053 3500 190 en suite

Dunmurry 91 Dunmurry Ln, Dunmurry BT17 9JS
☎ 028 9061 0834 Fax 028 9060 2540
e-mail: dunmurrygc@hotmail.com
web: www.dunmurrygolfclub.co.uk
18 holes, 6096yds, Par 70, SSS 69, Course record 65.
Telephone for further details

Hotel ★★★ 71% Malone Lodge Hotel, 60 Eglantine Av, BELFAST ☎ 028 9038 8000 51 en suite

Fortwilliam Downview Ave BT15 4EZ
☎ 028 9037 0770 (Office) & 9077 0980 (Pro)
Fax 028 9078 1891
e-mail: admin@fortwilliam.co.uk
web: www.fortwilliam.co.uk
Parkland course in most attractive surroundings. The course is bisected by a lane.
18 holes, 6030yds, Par 70, SSS 68, Course record 65. Club membership 1000.
Visitors Mon-Fri, Sun & BHs. Booking required. Handicap certificate. Dress code. **Societies** Booking required. **Green Fees** £22 (£29 Sun). **Prof** Peter Hanna **Facilities** **Conf** facs **Location** Off Antrim road

Hotel ★★★ 66% Jurys Inn Belfast, Fisherwick Place, Great Victoria St, BELFAST ☎ 028 9053 3500 190 en suite

Malone 240 Upper Malone Rd, Dunmurry BT17 9LB
☎ 028 9061 2758 (Office) & 9061 4917 (Pro)
Fax 028 9043 1394
e-mail: manager@malonegolfclub.co.uk
web: www.malonegolfclub.co.uk
Two parkland courses, extremely attractive with a large lake, mature trees and flowering shrubs and bordered by the River Lagan. Very well maintained and offering a challenging round.

Main Course: 18 holes, 6706yds, Par 71, SSS 72. Edenderry: 9 holes, 6320yds, Par 72, SSS 70. Club membership 1450.
Visitors Mon, Wed-Fri, Sun & BHs. Booking required. Dress code. **Societies** Booking required. **Green Fees** Main £55 per day (£60 Sun). Edenderry £20 per day (£25 Sun). **Prof** Michael McGee **Course Designer** C K Cotton **Facilities** **Leisure** fishing, Outdoor bowling green. **Conf** Corporate Hospitality Days **Location** 4.5m S opposite Lady Dixon Park

Hotel ★★★ 71% Malone Lodge Hotel, 60 Eglantine Av, BELFAST ☎ 028 9038 8000 51 en suite

Mount Ober Golf & Country Club
24 Ballymaconaghy Rd BT8 6SB
☎ 028 9040 1811 & 9079 5666 🖹 028 9070 5862
web: www.mountober.com
Inland parkland course which is a great test of golf for all handicaps.
18 holes, 5281yds, Par 67, SSS 66, Course record 67.
Club membership 400.
Visitors Mon-Fri, Sun & BHs. Dress code. **Societies** Booking required. **Green Fees** £16 per 18 holes (Sun £18). **Prof** Wesley Ramsay **Facilities** **Leisure** American billiards & snooker. **Conf** facs Corporate Hospitality Days **Location** Off Saintfield Rd

Hotel ★★★ 70% The Crescent Townhouse, 13 Lower Crescent, BELFAST ☎ 028 9032 3349 17 en suite

Ormeau 50 Park Rd BT7 2FX
☎ 028 9064 0700 🖹 028 9064 6250
e-mail: ormeau.golfclub@virgin.net
Nine hole parkland course which provides a challenge for low and high handicap golfers, good shots being rewarded and those that stray offline receiving due punishment. The long par 4 5th hole has an intimidating out of bounds on the right and a narrow sloping green, well protected by trees and bunkers. Two long par 3 holes each demand an accurate drive and when playing the 3rd and 12th holes, visitors are advised to look for the Fairy Tree which graces the middle of the fairway. Club folklore states that if a golfer hits this tree he should apologise to the fairies or his game will suffer!
9 holes, 2688yds, Par 68, SSS 66.
Club membership 520.
Visitors Mon, Wed-Fri, Sun & BHs. Booking required Fri, Sun & BHs. Dress code. **Societies** Booking required. **Green Fees** £12-£18 weekdays. £14-£20 Sun. **Prof** Mr Stephen Rourke **Facilities** **Location** S of city centre between Ravenhill & Ormeau roads

Hotel ★★★ 70% The Crescent Townhouse, 13 Lower Crescent, BELFAST ☎ 028 9032 3349 17 en suite

Shandon Park 73 Shandon Park BT5 6NY
☎ 028 90805030
e-mail: shandonpark@btconnect.com
Fairly level parkland offering a pleasant challenge.
18 holes, 6261yds, Par 70, SSS 70.
Club membership 1100.
Visitors Mon, Thu, Fri, Sun & BHs. Booking required. Handicap certificate. Dress code. **Societies** Booking required. **Green Fees** £22 per round (£27 Sun). **Prof** Barry Wilson **Facilities** **Conf** facs Corporate Hospitality Days **Location** Off Knock road

Hotel ★★★ 70% The Crescent Townhouse, 13 Lower Crescent, BELFAST ☎ 028 9032 3349 17 en suite

DUNDONALD Map 01 D5

Knock Summerfield BT16 2QX
☎ 028 9048 3251 🖹 028 9048 7277
18 holes, 6435yds, Par 70, SSS 71, Course record 66.
Course Designer Colt, Allison & MacKenzie **Location** 5m E of Belfast
Telephone for further details

Hotel ★★★ 78% The Old Inn, 15 Main St, CRAWFORDSBURN ☎ 028 9185 3255 31 en suite 1 annexe en suite

NEWTOWNBREDA Map 01 D5

The Belvoir Park 73 Church Rd BT8 7AN
☎ 028 90491693 🖹 028 90646113
web: www.belvoirparkgolfclub.com
18 holes, 6516yds, Par 71, SSS 71, Course record 65.
Course Designer H Holt **Location** 2m from city centre off Saintfield-Newcastle road
Telephone for further details

Hotel ★★★ 78% Clandeboye Lodge Hotel, 10 Estate Rd, Clandeboye, BANGOR ☎ 028 9185 2500 43 en suite

CO DOWN

ARDGLASS Map 01 D5

Ardglass Castle Place BT30 7TP
☎ 028 44841219 🖹 028 44841841
e-mail: info@ardglassgolfclub.com
web: www.ardglassgolfclub.com
A scenic clifftop seaside course with championship standard greens. The first five holes, with the Irish Sea and cliffs tight to the left, should be treated with respect as anything resembling a hook will meet with disaster. The 2nd hole is a daunting par 3. The tee shot must carry a cliff and canyon - meanwhile the superb views of the Mountains of Mourne should not be missed.
18 holes, 5498 metres, Par 70, SSS 69, Course record 65.
Club membership 900.
Visitors must contact in advance. **Societies** must contact in advance. **Green Fees** Phone. **Prof** Philip Farrell **Course Designer** David Jones **Facilities** **Conf** facs **Location** 7m from Downpatrick on B1

Hotel ★★ 67% Enniskeen House Hotel, 98 Bryansford Rd, NEWCASTLE ☎ 028 4372 2392 12 en suite

ARDMILLAN Map 01 D5

Mahee Island 14 Mahee Island, Comber BT23 6EP
☎ 028 9754 1234
e-mail: mahee_gents@hotmail.com
An undulating parkland course, almost surrounded by water, with magnificent views of Strangford Lough and its islands, with Scrabo Tower in the background. The greens are small and tricky to play.
9 holes, 5822yds, Par 71, SSS 70, Course record 66.
Club membership 600.
Visitors Mon-Fri, Sun & BHs. Dress code **Societies** Booking required. **Green Fees** £12 (Sun & BHs £17). **Course Designer** Mr Robinson **Facilities** by arrangement by arrangement by arrangement **Location** Off Comber-Killyleagh road 0.5m from Comber

Hotel ★★★ 78% Clandeboye Lodge Hotel, 10 Estate Rd, Clandeboye, BANGOR ☎ 028 9185 2500 43 en suite

Continued

BALLYNAHINCH Map 01 D5

Spa 20 Grove Rd BT24 8PN
☎ 028 97562365 Fax 028 97564158
e-mail: spagolfclub@btconnect.com
web: www.yearofsport.com

Parkland course with tree-lined fairways and scenic views of the Mourne Mountains. A long and demanding course and feature holes include the par 3 2nd and 405yd par 4 11th.

18 holes, 6003 metres, Par 72, SSS 72, Course record 66. Club membership 871.

Visitors Mon-Fri, Sun & BHs. Booking required Mon, Tue & Sun. Dress code. **Societies** Booking required. **Green Fees** £18 per round (£23 Sun & BHs). **Course Designer** F Ainsworth **Facilities** **Leisure** gymnasium, outdoor bowls. **Conf** facs Corporate Hospitality Days **Location** 1m S

Hotel ★★ 67% Enniskeen House Hotel, 98 Bryansford Rd, NEWCASTLE ☎ 028 4372 2392 12 en suite

BANBRIDGE Map 01 D5

Banbridge 116 Huntly Rd BT32 3UR
☎ 028 40662211 Fax 028 40669400
e-mail: banbridgegolf@btconnect.com
web: www.banbridge-golf.freeserve.co.uk

A mature parkland course with excellent views of the Mourne mountains. The holes are not long, but are tricky. Signature holes are the 6th with its menacing pond and the par 3 10th where playing for a safe 4 is usually the best option.

18 holes, 5003 metres, Par 69, SSS 67, Course record 61. Club membership 800.

Visitors Mon-Sun & BHs. Booking required Sat, Sun & BHs. Dress code. **Societies** welcome. **Green Fees** £17 (£22 weekends). **Course Designer** F Ainsworth **Facilities** **Location** 0.5m along Huntly Rd

BANGOR Map 01 D5

Bangor Broadway BT20 4RH
☎ 028 9127 0922 Fax 028 9145 3394
e-mail: admin@bangorgolfclubni.co.uk
web: www.bangorgolfclubni.co.uk

Undulating parkland course in the town. It is well maintained and pleasant and offers a challenging round, particularly at the 5th. Scenic views to Scotland on a clear day.

18 holes, 6410yds, Par 71, SSS 71, Course record 62. Club membership 1147.

Visitors Mon, Wed-Fri & Sun except BHs. Handicap certificate. Dress code. **Societies** welcome. **Green Fees** Phone. **Prof** Michael Bannon **Course Designer** James Braid **Facilities** **Conf** Corporate Hospitality Days **Location** 1m from town centre, 300yds off Donaghadee Rd

Hotel ★★★ 66% Royal Hotel, Seafront, BANGOR ☎ 028 9127 1866 50 en suite

Blackwood Golf Centre 150 Crawfordsburn Rd, Clandeboye BT19 1GB
☎ 028 9185 2706 Fax 028 9185 3785
web: www.blackwoodgolf.co.uk

The golf centre is a pay and play development with a computerised booking system for the 18-hole championship-standard Hamilton Course. The course is built on mature woodland with man-made lakes that come into play on five holes. The Temple course is an 18-hole par 3 course with holes ranging from the 75yd 1st to the 185yd 10th, which has a lake on the right of the green. Banked by gorse with streams crossing throughout, this par 3 course is no pushover.

Hamilton Course: 18 holes, 6392yds, Par 71, SSS 70, Course record 62.
Temple Course: 18 holes, 2492yds, Par 54.

Visitors Mon-Sun & BHs. Dress code. **Societies** Booking required. **Green Fees** Phone. **Prof** Debbie Hanna **Course Designer** Simon Gidman **Facilities** **Location** 2m from Bangor off A2 to Belfast

Hotel ★★★ 78% Clandeboye Lodge Hotel, 10 Estate Rd, Clandeboye, BANGOR ☎ 028 9185 2500 43 en suite

Carnalea Station Rd BT19 1EZ
☎ 028 9127 0368 Fax 028 9127 3989

A scenic course on the shores of Belfast Lough.

18 holes, 5647yds, Par 69, SSS 67, Course record 63. Club membership 1354.

Visitors Mon-Fri, Sun except BHs. Dress code. **Societies** Booking required. **Green Fees** £16.50 (£21 Sun). **Prof** Tom Loughran **Facilities** **Location** 2m W next to railway station

Hotel ★★★ 78% The Old Inn, 15 Main St, CRAWFORDSBURN ☎ 028 9185 3255 31 en suite 1 annexe en suite

Clandeboye Tower Rd, Conlig, Newtownards BT23 3PN
☎ 028 9127 1767 Fax 028 9147 3711
e-mail: cgc-ni@btconnect.com
web: www.cgc-ni.com

Parkland and heathland courses. The Dufferin is the championship course and offers a tough challenge demanding extreme accuracy, with gorse, bracken and strategically placed trees that flank every hole. Errors will be punished. The Ava compliments the Dufferin perfectly. Accuracy is the key on this course with small targets and demanding tee shots. Outstanding panoramic views.

Dufferin Course: 18 holes, 6559yds, Par 71, SSS 71.
Ava Course: 18 holes, 5755yds, Par 70, SSS 68.
Club membership 1450.

Visitors must contact in advance, weekends after 2.30pm. **Societies** Mon-Wed & Fri. Must contact in advance. **Green Fees** Phone. **Prof** Peter Gregory **Course Designer** Von Limburger/Allis/Thomas **Facilities** **Leisure** snooker, table tennis, indoor bowls. **Conf** facs Corporate Hospitality Days **Location** 2m S on A1 between Bangor & Newtownards

Continued

Continued

Hotel ★★★ 66% Royal Hotel, Seafront, BANGOR
☎ 028 9127 1866 50 en suite

Helen's Bay Golf Rd, Helen's Bay BT19 1TL
☎ 028 91852815 & 91852601 🖷 028 91852660
e-mail: mail@helensbaygc.com
A parkland course on the shores of Belfast Lough with panoramic views along the Antrim coast. The 4th hole par 3 is particularly challenging as the green is screened by high trees.
9 holes, 5644yds, Par 68, SSS 67, Course record 67. Club membership 750.
Visitors contact club for details. **Societies** Booking required. **Green Fees** £17 per 18 holes (Mon-Thu) £20 (Fri-Sun & BHs). **Facilities**
Location A2 from Belfast

Hotel ★★★ 78% The Old Inn, 15 Main St, CRAWFORDSBURN ☎ 028 9185 3255 31 en suite 1 annexe en suite

CARRYDUFF Map 01 D5

Rockmount 28 Drumalig Rd, Carryduff BT8 8EQ
☎ 028 9081 2279 🖷 020 9081 5851
e-mail: rockmountgc@btconnect.com
web: www.rockmountgolfclub.co.uk
A cleverly designed course incorporating natural features with water coming into play as streams with a lake at the 11th and 14th.
18 holes, 6373yds, Par 71, SSS 71, Course record 68. Club membership 750.
Visitors Mon-Fri, Sun & BHs. Dress code. **Societies** welcome. **Green Fees** £24 (£28 Sun). **Course Designer** Robert Patterson **Facilities** **Conf** Corporate Hospitality Days **Location** 10m S of Belfast

CLOUGHEY Map 01 D5

Kirkistown Castle 142 Main Rd, Cloughey BT22 1JA
☎ 028 4277 1233 🖷 028 4277 1699
e-mail: kirkistown@supanet.com
web: www.links.golfkirkistown.com
A seaside part-links, designed by James Braid, popular with visiting golfers because of its quiet location. The course is exceptionally dry and remains open when others in the area have to close. The short but treacherous par 4 15th hole was known as Braid's Hole. The 2nd and 10th holes are long par 4s with elevated greens, which are a feature of the course. The 10th is particularly distinctive with a long drive and a slight dog-leg to a raised green with a gorse covered motte waiting for the wayward approach shot. It has the reputation of being one of the hardest par 4s in Ireland.
18 holes, 6167yds, Par 69, SSS 70, Course record 65. Club membership 1012.
Visitors must contact in advance, restricted weekends. **Societies** Booking required. **Green Fees** Phone. **Prof** Richard Whitford **Course Designer** James Braid **Facilities** **Leisure** snooker room. **Conf** Corporate Hospitality Days **Location** 16m from Newtownards on A2

Hotel ★★★ 78% The Old Inn, 15 Main St, CRAWFORDSBURN ☎ 028 9185 3255 31 en suite 1 annexe en suite

DONAGHADEE Map 01 D5

Donaghadee Warren Rd BT21 0PQ
☎ 028 9188 3624 🖷 028 9188 8891
e-mail: deegolf@freenet.co.uk
18 holes, 5616 metres, Par 71, SSS 69, Course record 64.
Location 5m S of Bangor on Coast Rd
Telephone for further details

Hotel ★★★ 78% The Old Inn, 15 Main St, CRAWFORDSBURN ☎ 028 9185 3255 31 en suite 1 annexe en suite

DOWNPATRICK Map 01 D5

Bright Castle 14 Coniamstown Rd, Bright BT30 8LU
☎ 028 44841319
18 holes, 7300yds, Par 74, SSS 74, Course record 69.
Course Designer Mr Ennis Snr **Location** 5m S
Telephone for further details

Hotel ★★ 67% Enniskeen House Hotel, 98 Bryansford Rd, NEWCASTLE ☎ 028 4372 2392 12 en suite

Downpatrick 43 Saul Rd BT30 6PA
☎ 028 44615947 🖷 028 44617502
e-mail: info@downpatrickgolfclub.org.com
web: www.downpatrickgolfclub.org.com
18 holes, 6100yds, Par 70, SSS 69, Course record 66.
Course Designer Hawtree & Son **Location** 1.5m from town centre
Telephone for further details

Hotel ★★ 67% Enniskeen House Hotel, 98 Bryansford Rd, NEWCASTLE ☎ 028 4372 2392 12 en suite

HOLYWOOD Map 01 D5

Holywood Nuns Walk, Demesne Rd BT18 9LE
☎ 028 90423135 🖷 028 90425040
e-mail: mail@holywoodgolfclub.co.uk
web: www.holywoodgolfclub.co.uk
18 holes, 5480 metres, Par 69, SSS 68, Course record 64.
Location Off Bangor dual carriageway, behind Holywood
Telephone for further details

Hotel ★★★ 78% The Old Inn, 15 Main St, CRAWFORDSBURN ☎ 028 9185 3255 31 en suite 1 annexe en suite

The Royal Belfast Station Rd, Craigavad BT18 0BP
☎ 028 9042 8165 🖷 028 9042 1404
e-mail: royalbelfastgc@btclick.com
web: www.royalbelfast.com
On the shores of Belfast Lough, this attractive course consists of wooded parkland on undulating terrain which provides a pleasant, challenging game.
18 holes, 6185yds, Par 70, SSS 69. Club membership 1200.
Visitors Booking required. **Societies** must contact in writing/by telephone. **Green Fees** Phone. **Prof** Chris Spence **Course Designer** H C Colt **Facilities** **Leisure** hard tennis courts, squash. **Conf** Corporate Hospitality Days **Location** 2m E on A2

Hotel ★★★ 78% The Old Inn, 15 Main St, CRAWFORDSBURN ☎ 028 9185 3255 31 en suite 1 annexe en suite

KILKEEL Map 01 D5

Kilkeel Mourne Park BT34 4LB
☎ 028 4176 5095 🖹 028 4176 5579
e-mail: kilkeelgolfclub@gmail.com
Picturesquely situated at the foot of the Mourne Mountains. Eleven holes have tree-lined fairways with the remainder in open parkland. The 13th hole is testing and a well-positioned tee shot is essential.
18 holes, 6579yds, Par 72, SSS 72, Course record 67. Club membership 750.
Visitors Mon-Fri, Sun & BHs. Booking required Sun & BHs. Handicap certificate. Dress code. **Societies** Booking required. **Green Fees** £23 per 18 holes (£28 Sun). **Course Designer** Babington/Hackett **Facilities** **Conf** facs Corporate Hospitality Days **Location** 3m from Kilkeel on Newry road

Hotel ★★ 67% Enniskeen House Hotel, 98 Bryansford Rd, NEWCASTLE ☎ 028 4372 2392 12 en suite

KILLYLEAGH Map 01 D5

Ringdufferin Golf Course 31 Ringdufferin Rd, Toye BT30 9PH
☎ 028 44828812 🖹 028 44828812
18 holes, 4652 metres, Par 68, SSS 66.
Course Designer Frank Ainsworth **Location** 2m N of Killyleagh
Telephone for further details

MAGHERALIN Map 01 D5

Edenmore Edenmore House, 70 Drumnabreeze Rd BT67 0RH
☎ 028 9261 1310 🖹 028 9261 3310
e-mail: edenmoregc@aol.com
web: www.edenmore.com
18 holes, 6244yds, Par 71, SSS 70, Course record 70.
Course Designer F Ainsworth **Location** M1 Moira exit, through Moira towards Lurgan. Turn off in Magheralin signed
Telephone for further details

Hotel ★★★ 78% The Old Inn, 15 Main St, CRAWFORDSBURN ☎ 028 9185 3255 31 en suite 1 annexe en suite

NEWCASTLE Map 01 D5

Royal County Down **see page 431**

Hotel ★★ 67% Enniskeen House Hotel, 98 Bryansford Rd, NEWCASTLE ☎ 028 4372 2392 12 en suite

NEWRY Map 01 D5

Newry 11 Forkhill Rd BT35 8LZ
☎ 028 30263871 🖹 028 30263871
18 holes, 3000 metres, Par 53, SSS 52, Course record 51.
Course Designer Michael Heaney **Location** 1m from Newry off Dublin road
Telephone for further details

Hotel ★★ 67% Enniskeen House Hotel, 98 Bryansford Rd, NEWCASTLE ☎ 028 4372 2392 12 en suite

NEWTOWNARDS Map 01 D5

Scrabo 233 Scrabo Rd BT23 4SL
☎ 028 9181 2355 🖹 028 9182 2919
e-mail: admin.scrabogc@btconnect.com
web: www.scrabo-golf-club.org
Hilly and picturesque, this heathland course stands on a 150-metre hill with rocky outcrops. Accuracy is important. Fine views.
18 holes, 5722 metres, Par 71, SSS 71, Course record 65. Club membership 1002.
Visitors may not play on Sat. Contact in advance. **Societies** Booking required. **Green Fees** Phone. **Prof** Paul McCrystal **Facilities** **Location** Outskirts of Newtownards on Ards peninsula, signs for Scrabo Country Park

Hotel ★★★ 78% Clandeboye Lodge Hotel, 10 Estate Rd, Clandeboye, BANGOR ☎ 028 9185 2500 43 en suite

WARRENPOINT Map 01 D5

Warrenpoint Lower Dromore Rd BT34 3LN
☎ 028 4175 3695 🖹 028 4175 2918
e-mail: office@warrenpointgolf.com
web: www.warrenpointgolf.com
Parkland course with marvellous views and a need for accurate shots.
18 holes, 6108yds, Par 71, SSS 70, Course record 61. Club membership 1460.
Visitors Mon, Thu, Fri, Sun & BHs. Booking required. Handicap certificate. Dress code. **Societies** Booking required. **Green Fees** £25 per 18 holes (£30 Sun & BHs). **Prof** Nigel Shaw **Course Designer** Tom Craddock/Pat Ruddy **Facilities** **Leisure** 9 hole par 3 academy course. **Conf** facs Corporate Hospitality Days **Location** 1m W

Hotel ★★ 67% Enniskeen House Hotel, 98 Bryansford Rd, NEWCASTLE ☎ 028 4372 2392 12 en suite

CO FERMANAGH

ENNISKILLEN Map 01 C5

Ashwoods Golf Centre Sligo Rd BT74 7JY
☎ 028 66325321 & 66322908 🖹 028 66329411
14 holes, 1930yds, Par 42.
Course Designer P Loughran **Location** 1.5m W of Enniskillen on Sligo road
Telephone for further details

Hotel ★★★★ 74% Killyhevlin Hotel, ENNISKILLEN ☎ 028 6632 3481 70 en suite

Castle Hume Castle Hume, Belleek Rd BT93 7ED
☎ 028 6632 7077 🖹 028 6632 7076
e-mail: info@castlehumegolf.com
web: www.castlehumegolf.com
Castle Hume is a particularly scenic and challenging course. Set in undulating parkland with large rolling greens, rivers, lakes and water hazards all in play on a championship standard course.
18 holes, 5770 metres, Par 72, SSS 70, Course record 69. Club membership 350.
Visitors Mon-Sun & BHs. Booking required Wed, Sat & Sun. Dress code. **Societies** Booking required. **Green Fees** £25 per 18 holes (£30 Sat, Sun & BHs). **Prof** Shaun

Continued

Championship Course

Co Down

Royal County Down

Newcastle

Map 01 D5

The Championship Course is consistently rated among the world's top ten courses. Laid out beneath the imperious Mourne Mountains, the course has a magnificent setting as it stretches out along the shores of Dundrum Bay. As well as being one of the most-beautiful courses, it is also one of the most challenging, with great swathes of heather and gorse lining fairways that tumble beneath vast sand hills, and wild tussock-faced bunkers defending small, subtly contoured greens. The Annesley Links offers a less formidable yet extremely characterful game, played against the same incomparable backdrop. Recently substantially revised under the direction of Donald Steel, the course begins quite benignly before charging headlong into the dunes. Several charming and one or two teasing holes have been carved out amid the gorse, heather and bracken.

36 Golf Links Rd BT33 0AN
☎ 028 43723314 🖹 028 43726281
e-mail: golf@royalcountydown.org
web: www.royalcountydown.org

Championship Course: 18 holes, 7181yds, Par 71, SSS 74, Course record 66.
Annesley: 18 holes, 4681yds, Par 66, SSS 63.
Club membership 450.

Visitors Mon, Tue, Thu, Fri, Sun & BHs. Booking required. Dress code. **Societies** Booking required. **Green Fees** Championship £125 weekdays, £110 afternoon (£140 Sun). **Prof** Kevan Whitson **Course Designer** Tom Morris **Facilities** ⊗ by arrangement by arrangement **Location** N of town centre off A2

Donnelly **Course Designer** B Browne **Facilities** ⊗) ⊩ ⊡ ☕ 🍷 ⚲ ⌂ ⛳ ✎ 🛒 🏌 **Leisure** fishing. **Conf** facs Corporate Hospitality Days **Location** 4m from Enniskillen on A46 Belleek-Donegal road

Hotel ★★★★ 74% Killyhevlin Hotel, ENNISKILLEN ☎ 028 6632 3481 70 en suite

Enniskillen Castlecoole BT74 6HZ
☎ 028 6632 5250 🖹 028 6632 5250
e-mail: enniskillengolfclub@mail.com
web: www.enniskillengolfclub.com
Tree lined parkland course offering panoramic views of Enniskillen town and the surrounding lakeland area. Situated beside the National Trust's Castlecoole Estate.
18 holes, 6230yds, Par 71, SSS 69, Course record 67.
Club membership 550.
Visitors Mon-Sun & BHs. Booking required Tue, Sat & Sun. Dress code. **Societies** Booking required. **Green Fees** £18 per day (£22 weekends). **Facilities** ⊗ by arrangement) by arrangement ⊡ by arrangement ☕ 🍷 ⚲ ⛳ 🛒 🏌 **Conf** facs Corporate Hospitality Days **Location** 1m E of town centre

Hotel ★★★★ 74% Killyhevlin Hotel, ENNISKILLEN ☎ 028 6632 3481 70 en suite

CO LONDONDERRY

AGHADOWEY Map 01 C6

Brown Trout Golf & Country Inn
209 Agivey Rd BT51 4AD
☎ 028 7086 8209 🖹 028 7086 8878
e-mail: bill@browntroutinn.com
web: www.browntroutinn.com
A challenging course with two par 5s. During the course of the nine holes, players have to negotiate water seven times and all the fairways are lined with densely packed fir trees.
9 holes, 5510yds, Par 70, SSS 68, Course record 64.
Club membership 100.
Visitors Mon-Sun & BHs. Booking required Sat & Sun. **Societies** Booking required. **Green Fees** £10 (£15 weekends). **Prof** Ken Revie **Course Designer** Bill O'Hara Snr **Facilities** ⊗) ⊡ ☕ 🍷 ⚲ ⛳ 🛏 🏌 **Leisure** fishing, gymnasium. **Location** Junct A54 , 7m S of Coleraine

Hotel ★★ 71% Brown Trout Golf & Country Inn, 209 Agivey Rd, AGHADOWEY ☎ 028 7086 8209 15 en suite

Prices may change during the currency of the guide, always check when booking

CASTLEDAWSON Map 01 C5

Moyola Park 15 Curran Rd BT45 8DG
☎ 028 7946 8468 & 7946 8830 (Prof) 🖹 028 7946 8626
e-mail: moyolapark@btconnect.com
web: www.moyolapark.com
Parkland championship course with some difficult shots, calling for length and accuracy. The Moyola River provides a water hazard at the 8th. Newly designed par 3 17th demands good shot placement to a green on an island in the Moyola river, when players' capabilities will be tested by the undulating green.
18 holes, 6519yds, Par 71, SSS 71, Course record 67.
Club membership 1000.
Visitors Booking required. Dress code. **Societies** must contact in advance, preferably in writing **Green Fees** Phone. **Prof** Bob Cockcroft **Course Designer** Don Patterson **Facilities** ⊗) ⊡ ☕ 🍷 ⚲ ⌂ 🛒 🏌 **Conf** facs Corporate Hospitality Days **Location** Club signed

CASTLEROCK Map 01 C6

Castlerock 65 Circular Rd BT51 4TJ
☎ 028 7084 8314 🖹 028 7084 9440
e-mail: info@castlerockgc.co.uk
web: www.castlerockgc.co.uk
A most exhilarating course with three superb par 4s, four testing short holes and five par 5s. After an uphill start, the hazards are many, including the river and a railway, and both judgement and accuracy are called for. The signature hole is the 4th, Leg of Mutton. A challenge in calm weather, any trouble from the elements will test your golf to the limits.
Mussenden Course: 18 holes, 6499yds, Par 73, SSS 71, Course record 64.
Bann Course: 9 holes, 2938yds, Par 34, SSS 33, Course record 60.
Club membership 1250.
Visitors Mon-Sun & BHs. Booking required. Dress code. **Societies** Booking required. **Green Fees** £50 per day (£70 per round Sat, Sun & BHs). **Prof** Ian Blair **Course Designer** Ben Sayers **Facilities** ⊗) ⊡ ☕ 🍷 ⚲ ⌂ ⛳ ✎ 🛒 🏌 **Conf** Corporate Hospitality Days **Location** 6m from Coleraine on A2

Guest House ♦♦♦♦♦ Greenhill House, 24 Greenhill Rd, Aghadowey, COLERAINE ☎ 028 7086 8241 6 en suite

KILREA Map 01 C5

Kilrea 47a Lisnagrot Rd BT51 5TB
☎ 028 2954 0044
Inland course, winner of an environmental award. Course development completed spring 2005.
9 holes, 5578yds, Par 68, SSS 68, Course record 66.
Club membership 300.
Visitors Mon-Sun & BHs. Booking required Tue, Wed & Sat. Dress code. **Societies** Booking required. **Green Fees** £15 per 18 holes. ⊘ **Facilities** ⊗) ⊡ ☕ 🍷 ⚲

Hotel ★★ 71% Brown Trout Golf & Country Inn, 209 Agivey Rd, AGHADOWEY ☎ 028 7086 8209 15 en suite

LIMAVADY Map 01 C6

Benone 53 Benone Ave BT49 0LQ
☎ 028 77750555 🖹 028 77750919
Beside a beach, a delightful mix of parkland quite testing for the short game. Nestling at the foot of the Binevenagh mountains with picturesque views.

9 holes, 1459yds, Par 27.
Club membership 100.
Visitors Mon-Sun & BHs. Booking required Etr, Jul, Aug & BHs, **Societies** Booking required. **Green Fees** £6.25 per day (£7.20 Sat, Sun & BHs). **Facilities** **Leisure** hard tennis courts, heated outdoor swimming pool. **Location** Between Coleraine & Limavady on A2

Radisson SAS Roe Park Hotel & Golf Resort Roe Park BT49 9LB
☎ 028 7772 2222 🖹 028 7772 2313
e-mail: sales@radissonroepark.com
web: www.radissonroepark.com
A parkland course opened in 1992 on an historic Georgian estate. The course surrounds the original buildings and a driving range has been created in the old walled garden. Final holes 15-18 are particularly memorable with water, trees and out-of-bounds to provide a testing finish.
18 holes, 6318yds, Par 70, SSS 70, Course record 67.
Club membership 600.
Visitors Mon-Sun & BHs. Booking required. Dress code. **Societies** Booking required. **Green Fees** £25 per round (£30 Sat, Sun & BHs). **Prof** Shaun Devenney **Course Designer** Frank Ainsworth **Facilities** **Leisure** heated indoor swimming pool, fishing, sauna, solarium, gymnasium, indoor golf academy. **Conf** facs Corporate Hospitality Days **Location** Just outside Limavady on A2 Ballykelly-Londonderry road

Hotel ★★★★ 70% Radisson SAS Roe Park Resort, LIMAVADY ☎ 028 7772 2222 118 en suite

LONDONDERRY Map 01 C5

City of Derry 49 Victoria Rd BT47 2PU
☎ 028 71346369 🖹 028 71310008
e-mail: cityofderry@aol.com
Prehen Course: 18 holes, 6406yds, Par 71, SSS 71, Course record 68.
Dunhugh Course: 9 holes, 2354yds, Par 66, SSS 66.
Location 2m S
Telephone for further details

Hotel ★★★ 73% Beech Hill Country House Hotel, 32 Ardmore Rd, LONDONDERRY ☎ 028 7134 9279 17 en suite 10 annexe en suite

Foyle International Golf Centre 12 Alder Rd BT48 8DB
☎ 028 7135 2222 🖹 028 7135 3967
e-mail: mail@foylegolf.club24.co.uk
web: www.foylegolfcentre.co.uk
Foyle International has a championship course, a nine-hole par 3 course and a driving range. It is a fine test of golf with water coming into play on the 3rd, 10th and 11th holes. The 6th green overlooks the Amelia Earhart centre.
Earhart: 18 holes, 6643yds, Par 71, SSS 71, Course record 70.
Club membership 320.
Visitors Mon-Sun & BHs. Booking required. Dress code. **Societies** Booking required. **Green Fees** £14 (£17 weekends). **Prof** Kieran McLaughlin **Course Designer** Frank Ainsworth **Facilities** **Leisure** 9 hole par 3 course . **Conf** facs Corporate Hospitality Days **Location** 1.5m from Foyle Bridge towards Moville

PORTSTEWART Map 01 C6

Portstewart 117 Strand Rd BT55 7PG
☎ 028 70832015 & 70833839 🖷 028 70834097
e-mail: bill@portstewartgc.co.uk
web: www.portstewartgc.co.uk
Three links courses with spectacular views, offering a testing round on the Strand course in particular with every shot in the bag required.
Strand Course: 18 holes, 6784yds, Par 72, SSS 72, Course record 67.
Old Course: 18 holes, 4733yds, Par 64, SSS 62.
Riverside: 9 holes, 2622yds, Par 32.
Club membership 1666.
Visitors Mon-Sun & BHs. Booking required. Handicap certificate. Dress code. **Societies** Booking required **Green Fees** Strand £70 per round, £90 per day (£50 weekends). Old £10 (£15 weekends). Riverside £20 (£25 weekends). **Prof** Alan Hunter **Course Designer** Des Giffin **Facilities** **Conf** facs

CO TYRONE

COOKSTOWN Map 01 C5

Killymoon 200 Killymoon Rd BT80 8TW
☎ 028 8676 3762 & 8676 2254 🖷 028 8676 3762
e-mail: killymoongolf@btconnect.com
web: www.killymoongolfclub.com
Parkland course on elevated, well-drained land. The signature hole is the aptly named 6th hole - the Giant's Grave. Accuracy is paramount here and a daunting tee shot into a narrow-necked fairway will challenge even the most seasoned golfer. The enclosing influence of the trees continues the whole way to the green.
18 holes, 6202yds, Par 70, SSS 69, Course record 64.
Club membership 950.
Visitors Mon-Fri, Sun & BHs. Dress code. **Societies** Booking required. **Green Fees** Mon (except BHs) £15 per 18 holes; Tues-Fri £21; Sat-Sun £26. **Prof** Gary Chambers **Course Designer** John Nash **Facilities** **Leisure** snooker & pool. **Conf** facs Corporate Hospitality Days

Guest House ♦♦♦♦♦ Grange Lodge, 7 Grange Rd, DUNGANNON ☎ 028 8778 4212 5 en suite

DUNGANNON Map 01 C5

Dungannon 34 Springfield Ln BT70 1QX
☎ 028 8772 2098 🖷 028 8772 7338
e-mail: info@dungannongolfclub.com
web: www.dungannongolfclub.com
Parkland course with five par 3s and tree-lined fairways.
18 holes, 6046yds, Par 72, SSS 69, Course record 62.
Club membership 1100.
Visitors contact club for details. **Societies** welcome. **Green Fees** £18 per 18 holes (£22 weekends). **Prof** Vivian Teague **Course Designer** Sam Bacon **Facilities** **Location** 0.5m outside town on Donaghmore road

Hotel The Cohannon Inn & Autolodge, 212 Ballynakilly Rd, DUNGANNON ☎ 028 8772 4488 42 en suite

FINTONA Map 01 C5

Fintona Ecclesville Demesne, 1 Kiln St BT78 2BJ
☎ 028 82841480 & 82840777 (office) 🖷 028 82841480
Attractive nine-hole parkland course with a notable water hazard - a trout stream that meanders through the course causing many problems for badly executed shots.
9 holes, 5765 metres, Par 72, SSS 70.
Club membership 400.
Visitors Contact in advance at weekends. **Societies** Apply in writing well in advance. **Green Fees** Phone. **Prof** Paul Leonard **Facilities** by arrangement by arrangement by arrangement **Location** 8m S of Omagh

Hotel ★★ 64% Mahons Hotel, Mill St, IRVINESTOWN
☎ 028 6862 1656 & 6862 1657 🖷 028 6862 8344
24 en suite

NEWTOWNSTEWART Map 01 C5

Newtownstewart 38 Golf Course Rd BT78 4HU
☎ 028 8166 1466 🖷 028 8166 2506
e-mail: newtown.stewart@lineone.net
web: www.globalgolf/newtownstewart.com
Parkland course bisected by a stream. Deer and pheasant are present on the course.
18 holes, 5818yds, Par 70, SSS 69, Course record 65.
Club membership 550.
Visitors Mon-Sun & BHs. Booking required Wed, Sat, Sun & BHs. Dress code. **Societies** Booking required. **Green Fees** £17 per 18 holes (£25 Sat, Sun & BHs). **Course Designer** Frank Pennick **Facilities** **Leisure** snooker. **Conf** facs Corporate Hospitality Days **Location** 2m SW on B84

OMAGH Map 01 C5

Omagh 83a Dublin Rd BT78 1HQ
☎ 028 82243160 🖷 028 82243160
18 holes, 5683 metres, Par 71, SSS 70.
Course Designer Dun Patterson **Location** S outskirts of town
Telephone for further details

STRABANE Map 01 C5

Strabane Ballycolman Rd BT82 9HY
☎ 028 7138 2271 & 7138 2007 🖷 028 7188 6514
e-mail: strabanegc@btconnect.com
Testing parkland course alongside the River Mourne.
18 holes, 5537 metres, Par 69, SSS 69, Course record 62.
Club membership 650.
Visitors by arrangement, may not play Tue & Sat **Societies** must telephone in advance. **Green Fees** Phone. **Course Designer** Eddie Hackett/P Jones **Facilities** **Conf** facs **Location** 1m from Strabane on Dublin road

REPUBLIC OF IRELAND

CO CARLOW

BORRIS Map 01 C3

Borris Deerpark
☎ 059 9773310 🖷 059 9773750
e-mail: borrisgolfclub@eircom.net
Testing parkland course with tree-lined fairways situated within the McMorrough Kavanagh Estate at the foot of Mount Leinster. Modern sand based greens.
9 holes, 5680 metres, Par 70, SSS 69, Course record 66. Club membership 718.
Visitors advisable to contact in advance, weekends with member only. **Societies** applications in writing. **Green Fees** Phone. **Facilities**

Hotel ★★★★ Mount Juliet Conrad Hotel, THOMASTOWN ☎ 056 777 3000 32 en suite 27 annexe en suite

CARLOW Map 01 C3

Carlow Deerpark
☎ 059 9131695 🖷 059 9140065
e-mail: carlowgolfclub@eircom.net
web: www.carlowgolfclub.com
Created in 1922 to a design by Cecil Barcroft, this testing and enjoyable course is set in a wild deer park, with beautiful dry terrain and a varied character. With sandy subsoil, the course is playable all year round. There are water hazards at the 2nd, 10th and 11th and only two par 5s, both offering genuine birdie opportunities.
18 holes, 5974 metres, Par 70, SSS 71, Course record 63. Club membership 1200.
Visitors Mon-Sat except BHs. Booking required. Handicap certificate. Dress code. **Societies** Booking required. **Green Fees** €50 per round (€60 Sat). **Prof** Andrew Gilbert **Course Designer** Cecil Barcroft/Tom Simpson **Facilities** **Location** 3km N of Carlow on N9

Hotel ★★★ 71% Seven Oaks Hotel, Athy Rd, CARLOW ☎ 059 913 1308 59 en suite

TULLOW Map 01 C3

Mount Wolseley Hotel, Spa, Golf & Country Club
☎ 059 9151674 🖷 059 9152123
e-mail: billy.murray@hilton.com
web: www.hilton.co.uk/mountwolseley
A magnificent setting, a few hundred yards from the banks of the River Slaney with its mature trees and lakes set against the backdrop of the East Carlow and Wicklow mountains. With wide landing areas the only concession for demanding approach shots to almost every green. There is water in play on 11 holes, with the 11th an all-water carry off the tee of 207yds. The 18th is a fine finishing hole - a fairway lined with mature oak trees, then a second shot uphill across a water hazard to a green.
18 holes, 6582 metres, Par 72, SSS 70, Course record 68. Club membership 350.
Visitors Mon-Sun & BHs. Handicap certificate. Dress code. **Societies** Booking required. **Green Fees** €60 (weekends €80). **Course Designer** Christy O'Connor Jnr **Facilities** **Leisure** hard tennis courts, heated indoor swimming pool, sauna, solarium, gymnasium, treatment rooms. **Conf** facs Corporate Hospitality Days **Location** 1.6km from Tullow centre

Hotel ★★★ 71% Seven Oaks Hotel, Athy Rd, CARLOW ☎ 059 913 1308 59 en suite

CO CAVAN

BALLYCONNELL Map 01 C4

Slieve Russell Hotel Golf & Country Club
☎ 049 9525090 🖷 049 9526640
e-mail: slieve-russell@quinn-hotels.com
web: www.quinnhotels.com
An 18-hole course opened in 1992 and rapidly establishing itself as one of the finest parkland courses in the country. The complex incorporates a nine-hole par 3 course and driving range. On the main course, the 2nd plays across water while the 16th has water surrounding the green. The course finishes with a 519yd, par 5 18th.
18 holes, 6048 metres, Par 72, SSS 72, Course record 65. Club membership 400.
Visitors Book in advance for Sat. Telephone in advance. **Societies** write or telephone in advance **Green Fees** Phone. **Prof** Liam McCool **Course Designer** Paddy Merrigan **Facilities** **Leisure** hard tennis courts, heated indoor swimming pool, sauna, solarium, gymnasium, New spa for 2005. **Conf** facs Corporate Hospitality Days **Location** 4km E of Ballyconnell

Hotel ★★★★ 70% Slieve Russell Hotel Golf and Country Club, BALLYCONNELL ☎ 049 9526444 219 en suite

BELTURBET Map 01 C4

Belturbet Erne Hill
☎ 049 9522287 & 9524044
Beautifully maintained parkland course with elevated greens on most holes. The 7th hole is a stern test for any golfer.
9 holes, 5011 metres, Par 68, SSS 65, Course record 64. Club membership 200.
Visitors welcome **Societies** must contact secretary in advance. **Green Fees** Phone. **Course Designer** Eddie Hackett **Facilities** **Location** 0.8km N of town off N3

Hotel ★★★★ 70% Slieve Russell Hotel Golf and Country Club, BALLYCONNELL ☎ 049 9526444 219 en suite

BLACKLION Map 01 C5

Blacklion Toam
☎ 072 53024 & 53418 🖷 072 53418
9 holes, 5614 metres, Par 72, SSS 69.
Course Designer Eddie Hackett
Telephone for further details

Hotel ★★★ 72% Sligo Park Hotel, Pearse Rd, SLIGO ☎ 071 9190400 138 en suite

Continued

CAVAN Map 01 C4

County Cavan Drumelis
☎ 049 4331541 & 049 4371313 📠 049 31541
e-mail: info@cavangolf.ie
web: www.cavangolf.ie
18 holes, 5634 metres, Par 70, SSS 69, Course record 64.
Course Designer Eddie Hackett **Location** On road towards Killeshandra
Telephone for further details

Hotel ★★★ 67% Kilmore Hotel, Dublin Rd, CAVAN
☎ 049 4332288 39 en suite

VIRGINIA Map 01 C4

Virginia
☎ 049 47235 & 48066
9 holes, 4139 metres, Par 64, SSS 62, Course record 57.
Location By Lough Ramor
Telephone for further details

Hotel ★★ 67% The Park Hotel, Virginia Park, VIRGINIA
☎ 049 8546100 26 en suite

CO CLARE

BODYKE Map 01 B3

East Clare
☎ 061 921322 📠 061 921717
e-mail: eastclaregolfclub@eircon.net
web: www.eastclare.com
An 18-hole championship course designed by Arthur Spring beside Lough Derg, with natural trees and water on well-drained land. Set on 150 acres of rolling quiet countryside with superb views of East Clare.
18 holes, 5415 metres, Par 71, SSS 71.
Club membership 813.
Visitors Booking required. **Societies** apply in writing, deposit required. **Green Fees** Phone. **Course Designer** Dr Arthur Spring **Facilities** ⊗ 🍴 🍷 ☕ 🏌 ⛳

Hotel ★★★ 67% Temple Gate Hotel, The Square, ENNIS
☎ 065 6823300 70 en suite

ENNIS Map 01 B3

Ennis Drumbiggle
☎ 065 6824074 & 6865415 📠 065 6841848
e-mail: info@ennisgolfclub.com
web: www.ennisgolfclub.com
On rolling hills, this immaculately manicured course presents an excellent challenge to both casual visitors and aspiring scratch golfers, with tree-lined fairways and well-protected greens.
18 holes, 5612 metres, Par 70, SSS 69, Course record 65.
Club membership 1370.
Visitors Mon-Sat & BHs. Booking required. Handicap certificate. **Societies** Booking required. **Green Fees** €35 (Sat, Sun & BHs €40). **Facilities** ⊗ 🍴 by arrangement **Conf** Corporate Hospitality Days
Location Signed near town

Hotel ★★★ 67% Temple Gate Hotel, The Square, ENNIS
☎ 065 6823300 70 en suite

Woodstock Golf and Country Club
Shanaway Rd
☎ 065 6829463 & 6842406 📠 065 6820304
e-mail: woodstock.ennis@eircon.net
18 holes, 5864 metres, Par 71, SSS 71.
Course Designer Arthur Spring **Location** Off N85
Telephone for further details

Hotel ★★★ 67% Temple Gate Hotel, The Square, ENNIS
☎ 065 6823300 70 en suite

KILKEE Map 01 B3

Kilkee East End
☎ 065 9056048 📠 065 9656977
e-mail: kilkeegolfclub@eircom.net
web: www.kilkeegolfclub.ie
Well-established course on the cliffs of Kilkee Bay. Mature championship course with a great variety of challenges - seaside holes, clifftop holes and holes that feature well-positioned water hazards. The spectacular 3rd hole hugs the cliff top. The ever present Atlantic breeze provides golfers with a real test.
18 holes, 5555 metres, Par 70, SSS 69, Course record 68.
Club membership 770.
Visitors Mon-Sun & BHs. Booking required Sat, Sun & BHs. Dress code. **Societies** Booking required. **Green Fees** Sep-Jun €25 (weekends €30), Jul-Aug €30/€35. **Course Designer** Eddie Hackett **Facilities** ⊗ 🍴 🍷 ☕ 🏌 ⛳

Hotel ★★ 64% Halpin's Townhouse Hotel, Erin St, KILKEE ☎ 065 9056032 12 en suite

KILRUSH Map 01 B3

Kilrush Parknamoney
☎ 065 9051138 📠 065 9052633
e-mail: info@kilrushgolfclub.com
web: www.kilrushgolfclub.com
18 holes, 5474 metres, Par 70, SSS 70, Course record 68.
Course Designer Arthur Spring **Location** 0.8km from Kilrush towards Ennis
Telephone for further details

Hotel ★★ 64% Halpin's Townhouse Hotel, Erin St, KILKEE ☎ 065 9056032 12 en suite

LAHINCH Map 01 B3

Lahinch
☎ 065 708 1592 📠 065 708 1592
e-mail: info@lahinchgolf.com
web: www.lahinchgolf.com
Old Course: 18 holes, 6123 metres, Par 72, SSS 73.
Castle Course: 18 holes, 5115 metres, Par 70, SSS 70.
Course Designer A MacKenzie **Location** 3km W of Ennisstymon on N67
Telephone for further details

Hotel Kincora Country House & Gallery Restaurant, LISDOONVARNA ☎ 065 7074300 14 en suite

MILLTOWN MALBAY Map 01 B3

Spanish Point
☎ 065 7084198 📠 065 7084263
e-mail: dkfitzgerald@tinet.ie
web: spanish-point.com

Continued

9 holes, 4600 metres, Par 64, SSS 63, Course record 59.
Location 3km SW of Miltown Malbay on N67
Telephone for further details

Hotel ★★ 64% Halpin's Townhouse Hotel, Erin St, KILKEE ☎ 065 9056032 12 en suite

NEWMARKET-ON-FERGUS Map 01 B3

Dromoland Golf & Country Club

☎ 061 368444 & 368144 🖹 061 363355/368498
e-mail: golf@dromoland.ie
web: www.dromolandgolf.com

Set in 81 hectares of parkland, the course is enhanced by numerous trees and a lake. Three holes are played around the lake which is in front of the castle.

18 holes, 6264 metres, Par 72, SSS 72, Course record 65. Club membership 500.
Visitors must contact in advance. **Societies** contact in writing. **Green Fees** Phone. **Prof** David Foley **Course Designer** Ron Kirby & J. B. Carr **Facilities** **Leisure** hard tennis courts, heated indoor swimming pool, fishing, sauna, solarium, gymnasium. **Conf** facs Corporate Hospitality Days **Location** 3km N on Limerick-Galway road
See advertisement on this page

Hotel ★★★★★ Dromoland Castle Hotel, NEWMARKET-ON-FERGUS ☎ 061 368144 100 en suite

SHANNON AIRPORT Map 01 B3

Shannon

☎ 061 471849 🖹 061 471507
e-mail: shannongolfclub@eircom.net

18 holes, 6285 metres, Par 72, SSS 74, Course record 65.
Course Designer John Harris **Location** 3km from Shannon Airport
Telephone for further details

Hotel ★★★ 67% Bunratty Shannon Shamrock Hotel, BUNRATTY ☎ 061 361177 115 en suite

CO CORK

BANDON Map 01 B2

Bandon Castlebernard

☎ 023 41111 🖹 023 44690
e-mail: bandongolfclub@eircom.net

Lovely parkland in pleasant countryside. Hazards of water, sand and trees. The course has recently been extended around the picturesque ruin of Castle Barnard.

Continued

18 holes, 5854 metres, Par 71, SSS 71. Club membership 900.
Visitors Must contact in advance. **Societies** must apply in writing or telephone well in advance. **Green Fees** Phone. **Prof** Paddy O'Boyle **Facilities** **Leisure** hard tennis courts, caddies available.
Location 2.5km W

Hotel ★★★ 63% Innishannon House Hotel, INNISHANNON ☎ 021 4775121 12 en suite

BANTRY Map 01 B2

Bantry Bay Donemark

☎ 027 50579 🖹 027 53790
e-mail: info@bantrygolf.com
web: www.bantrygolf.com

Designed by Christy O'Connor Jnr and extended in 1997 to 18 holes, this challenging and rewarding course is idyllically set at the head of Bantry Bay. Testing holes include the par 5 of 487 metres and the little par 3 of 127 metres where accuracy is all-important.

18 holes, 6117 metres, Par 71, SSS 72, Course record 71. Club membership 600.
Visitors Mon-Sun & BHs. Booking required. **Societies** Booking required. **Green Fees** €40 per 18 holes (€45 weekends), reductions in winter. **Course Designer** Christy O'Connor Jnr/Eddie Hackett **Facilities** **Conf** facs Corporate Hospitality Days
Location 3km N of town on N71

Hotel ★★★ 64% Westlodge Hotel, BANTRY ☎ 027 50360 90 en suite

BLACKROCK Map 01 B2

Mahon Clover Hill
☎ 021 4294280
18 holes, 4862 metres, Par 70, SSS 67, Course record 64.
Course Designer Eddie Hackett
Telephone for further details

Hotel ★★★★ 72% Rochestown Park Hotel, Rochestown Rd, Douglas, CORK ☎ 021 4890800 160 en suite

BLARNEY Map 01 B2

Muskerry Carrigrohane
☎ 021 4385297 🖹 021 4516860
e-mail: muskgc@eircom.net
web: www.muskerrygolfclub.com
An adventurous game is guaranteed at this course, with its wooded hillsides and the meandering Shournagh River coming into play at a number of holes. The 15th is a notable hole - not long, but very deep - and after that all you need to do to get back to the clubhouse is stay out of the water.
18 holes, 5520 metres, Par 71, SSS 70.
Club membership 851.
Visitors Mon, Tue, Fri except BHs.Wed am only, Thu, Sat, Sun pm only. Booking required. Handicap certificate. Dress code. **Societies** Booking required. **Green Fees** €40 per round (€50 weekends). **Prof** W M Lehane **Course Designer** A MacKenzie **Facilities** ⊗ ⛳ ☕ 🍷 ⛓ 🏠 🚩 ✓ **Location** 4km W of Blarney

Hotel ★★★ 67% Blarney Castle Hotel, The Village Green, Blarney ☎ 021 4385116 13 en suite

CARRIGALINE Map 01 B2

Fernhill Hotel & Golf Club
☎ 021 4372226 🖹 021 4371011
e-mail: fernhill@iol.ie
web: www.fernhillgolfhotel.com

Continued

18 holes, 5000 metres, Par 69, SSS 68.
Course Designer M L Bowes **Location** 3km from Ringaskiddy
Telephone for further details

Hotel ★★★★ 72% Rochestown Park Hotel, Rochestown Rd, Douglas, CORK ☎ 021 4890800 160 en suite

CASTLETOWNBERE (CASTLETOWN BEARHAVEN) Map 01 A2

Berehaven Millcove
☎ 027 70700 🖹 027 71957
9 holes, 2624 metres, Par 68, SSS 67, Course record 63.
Course Designer Royal Navy **Location** 3km E from Castletownbere on R572
Telephone for further details

Hotel ★★★ Sea View House Hotel, BALLYLICKEY ☎ 027 50073 & 50462 🖹 027 51555 25 en suite

CHARLEVILLE Map 01 B2

Charleville
☎ 063 81257 & 81515 🖹 063 81274
e-mail: charlevillegolf@eircom.net
web: www.charlevillegolf.com

West Course: 18 holes, 5680 metres, Par 71, SSS 69, Course record 65.
East Course: 9 holes, 6128 metres, Par 72, SSS 72.
Course Designer Eddie Connaughton **Location** 3km W of town centre
Telephone for further details

Hotel ★★★ Longueville House Hotel, MALLOW ☎ 022 47156 & 47306 🖹 022 47459 20 en suite

CLONAKILTY Map 01 B2

Dunmore Dunmore, Muckross
☎ 023 33352
9 holes, 4082 metres, Par 64, SSS 61, Course record 57.
Course Designer E Hackett **Location** 5.5km S of Clonakilty
Telephone for further details

Hotel ★★★★ 75% Inchydoney Island Lodge & Spa, CLONAKILTY ☎ 023 33143 67 en suite

CORK Map 01 B2

Cork Little Island
☎ 021 4353451 🖹 021 4353410
e-mail: corkgolfclub@eircom.net
web: www.corkgolfclub.ie
This championship-standard course is kept in superb condition and is playable all year round. Memorable

Continued

and distinctive features include holes at the water's edge and in a disused quarry. The 4th hole is considered to be among the most attractive and testing holes in Irish golf.

Cork

18 holes, 5910 metres, Par 72, SSS 72, Course record 67. Club membership 750.

Visitors Mon-Wed, Fri-Sun except BHs. Booking required. Handicap certificate. Dress code. **Societies** Booking required. **Green Fees** €85 (€95 weekends). **Prof** Peter Hickey **Course Designer** A MacKenzie **Facilities** **Conf** Corporate Hospitality Days **Location** 8km E of Cork on N25

Fota Island Carrigtwohill

☎ 021 4883700 021 4883713
e-mail: reservations@fotaisland.ie
web: www.fotaisland.ie

Set in the heart of a 780-acre island in Cork Harbour. The course is routed among mature woodlands with occasional views of the harbour. The traditional design features pot bunkers and undulating putting surfaces. A new hotel and spa opened in 2006 with a new 9 holes.

18 holes, 6334 metres, Par 71, SSS 71, Course record 63. Club membership 600.

Visitors advisable to contact in advance. Dress code. **Societies** Booking required. **Green Fees** €65-€110. **Prof** Kevin Morris **Course Designer** Jeff Howes **Facilities** **Leisure** heated indoor swimming pool, sauna, gymnasium, spa treatments. **Conf** facs Corporate Hospitality Days **Location** E of Cork. N25 exit for Cobh, 500 metres on right

Hotel ★★★ 73% Midleton Park Hotel & Spa, MIDLETON ☎ 021 4631767 40 en suite

The Ted McCarthy Municipal Golf Course

Blackrock
☎ 021 4292543 021 4292604
e-mail: mahon-golf@leisureworldcork.com

Municipal course which stretches alongside the river estuary, with some holes across water.

18 holes, 5033 metres, Par 70, SSS 66, Course record 65. Club membership 400.

Visitors Mon-Sun & BHs. Booking required. **Societies** Booking required. **Green Fees** €24 per day (€27 Sat, Sun & BHs). **Course Designer** E Hackett **Facilities** **Location** 3km from city centre

Hotel ★★★★ 71% Silver Springs Moran Hotel, Tivoli, CORK ☎ 021 4507533 109 en suite

DONERAILE — Map 01 B2

Doneraile

☎ 022 24137 & 24379

9 holes, 5055 metres, Par 68, SSS 67, Course record 61.

Location N of town centre
Telephone for further details

Hotel ★★★ 65% Springfort Hall Country House Hotel, MALLOW ☎ 022 21278 49 en suite

DOUGLAS Map 01 B2

Douglas

☎ 021 4895297 🖷 021 4895297
e-mail: admin@douglasgolfclub.ie
web: www.douglasgolfclub.ie

Well-maintained, very flat parkland course with panoramic views from the clubhouse.

18 holes, 5607 metres, Par 72, SSS 69.
Club membership 900.

Visitors Mon, Thu-Sun except BHs. Booking required. Handicap certificate. Dress code. **Societies** Booking required. **Green Fees** €45 per round (€50 Sat, Sun & BHs). **Prof** Gary Nicholson **Course Designer** Peter McEvoy **Facilities** **Location** 6km E of Cork

Hotel ★★★★ 72% Rochestown Park Hotel, Rochestown Rd, Douglas, CORK ☎ 021 4890800 160 en suite

FERMOY Map 01 B2

Fermoy Corrin Cross

☎ 025 32694 (office) & 31472 (shop) 🖷 025 33072
e-mail: fermoygolfclub@eircom.net

A mature 18-hole heathland course facing the slopes of Corrin Hill and set in a profusion of natural heather and gorse and bisected by a road. The course commands panoramic views over the plains of East Cork.

18 holes, 5596 metres, Par 70, SSS 69, Course record 66.
Club membership 820.

Visitors Tue-Fri. Sat-Sun & BHs after 3pm. Booking required Wed, Fri-Sun. Dress code. **Societies** Booking required. **Green Fees** €20 (€30 Sat, Sun & BHs). **Prof** Brian Moriarty **Course Designer** John Harris **Facilities** **Location** 'S of town off N8, signed'

Hotel ★★★ Longueville House Hotel, MALLOW ☎ 022 47156 & 47306 🖷 022 47459 20 en suite

GLENGARRIFF Map 01 B2

Glengarriff

☎ 027 63150 🖷 027 63575

Course is surrounded by one of the remaining ancient oak forests of Ireland. The course is set amid mountain scenery of breathtaking beauty, overlooking world renowned Garnish Island and Bantry Bay.

9 holes, 2042 metres, Par 66, SSS 62.
Club membership 300.

Visitors Mon-Sun. Booking required Sat-Sun & BHs. Dress code. **Societies** welcome. **Green Fees** €25. **Facilities** **Location** On N71

Hotel ★★★ 64% Westlodge Hotel, BANTRY ☎ 027 50360 90 en suite

KANTURK Map 01 B2

Kanturk Fairyhill

☎ 029 50534 🖷 029 20951

18 holes, 5721 metres, Par 71, SSS 69, Course record 68.

Course Designer Richard Barry **Location** 1.6km SW of Kanturk

Telephone for further details

KINSALE Map 01 B2

Kinsale Farrangalway

☎ 021 4774722 🖷 021 4773114
e-mail: office@kinsalegolf.com
web: www.kinsalegolf.com

Set in farmland surrounded by rolling countryside. A stiff yet fair challenge to be enjoyed by all standards of golfers.

Farrangalway: 18 holes, 6043 metres, Par 71, SSS 71, Course record 70.
Ringenane: 9 holes, 4856 metres, Par 70, SSS 68.
Club membership 800.

Visitors Mon-Sun & BHs. Booking required Sat-Sun & BHs. Dress code. **Societies** Booking required. **Green Fees** €35 (€40 Fri-Sun). **Prof** Ger Broderick **Course Designer** Jack Kenneally **Facilities** **Location** Farrangalway N off R607. Ringenane N off R600

Hotel ★★★ 71% Trident Hotel, Worlds End, KINSALE ☎ 021 4779300 75 en suite

Old Head

☎ 021 4778444 🖷 021 4778022
e-mail: info@oldheadgolf.ie
web: www.oldheadgolflinks.com

Spectacular location on a promontory jutting out into the Atlantic. As well as bringing the sea and cliffs into play, you have to contend with strong prevailing winds - a fine test for serious golfers.

18 holes, 6675metres, Par 72, SSS 73.
Club membership 350.

Visitors Mon-Sun & BHs. Booking required. Handicap certificate. Dress code. **Societies** Booking required. **Green Fees** 18 holes €275; 36 holes €450/€475. **Prof** Danny Brassil **Course Designer** R Kirby/J Carr/P Merrigan/E Hackett **Facilities** **Conf** Corporate Hospitality Days **Location** On R600 towards Cork, signed

Hotel ★★★ 73% Actons Hotel, Pier Rd, KINSALE ☎ 021 4772135 76 en suite

LITTLE ISLAND Map 01 B2

Harbour Point Clash Rd

☎ 021 4353094 🖷 021 4354408
e-mail: hpoint@iol.ie

18 holes, 5883 metres, Par 72, SSS 71, Course record 71.

Course Designer Patrick Merrigan **Location** 8km E of Cork on Rosslare road

Telephone for further details

Hotel ★★★★ 71% Silver Springs Moran Hotel, Tivoli, CORK ☎ 021 4507533 109 en suite

Macroom Map 01 B2

Macroom Lackaduve
☎ 026 41072 & 42615 📠 026 41391
e-mail: mcroomgc@iol.ie
A particularly scenic parkland course located on undulating ground along the banks of the River Sullane. Bunkers and mature trees make a variable and testing course and the 12th has a 73-metre carry over the river to the green.

18 holes, 5574 metres, Par 72, SSS 70, Course record 67. Club membership 725.
Visitors booking essential for at all times **Societies** Booking required. **Green Fees** Phone. **Course Designer** Jack Kenneally/Eddie Hackett **Facilities** **Location** Through castle entrance in town square

Hotel ★★★ 74% Castle Hotel, Main St, MACROOM
☎ 026 41074 60 en suite

Mallow Map 01 B2

Mallow Ballyellis
☎ 022 21145 📠 022 42501
e-mail: golfmall@gofree.indigo.ie
Mallow Golf Club was established in the late 19th century. A well-wooded parkland course overlooking the Blackwater Valley, Mallow is straightforward, but no less of a challenge for it. The front nine is by far the longer, but the back nine is demanding in its call for accuracy and the par 3 18th provides a tough finish.

18 holes, 5769 metres, Par 72, SSS 71, Course record 67. Club membership 1250.
Visitors must contact in advance. **Societies** apply in advance. **Green Fees** Phone. **Prof** Sean Conway **Course Designer** D W Wishart **Facilities** **Leisure** hard tennis courts, squash. **Location** 1.6km of Mallow

Hotel ★★★ Longueville House Hotel, MALLOW
☎ 022 47156 & 47306 📠 022 47459 20 en suite

Midleton Map 01 C2

East Cork Gortacrue
☎ 021 4631687 & 4631273 📠 021 4613695
e-mail: eastcorkgolfclub@eircom.net
web: eastcorkgolfclub.com
A well-wooded course calling for accuracy of shots.
18 holes, 5152 metres, Par 69, SSS 66, Course record 64. Club membership 820.
Visitors may not play Sun mornings. **Societies** must telephone. **Green Fees** Phone. **Prof** Don MacFarlane **Course Designer** E Hackett **Facilities** **Location** 3km N of Midleton on A626

Hotel ★★★ 73% Midleton Park Hotel & Spa, MIDLETON ☎ 021 4631767 40 en suite

Water Rock Water Rock
☎ 021 4613499
e-mail: waterrock@eircom.net
web: www.waterrockgolfcourse.com
A pay and play parkland course on the banks of the Owencurra river, employing international standards and construction including mildly contoured sand based greens. The course comprises five par 3s and three par 5s in two loops. The signature hole is known as Swan Lake, the 240yd 12th par 3, plays over water to a contoured green.
18 holes, 6223yds, Par 70.
Visitors advance booking advisable. **Societies** welcome all year, may book by telephone. **Green Fees** Phone. **Course Designer** Patrick Merrilas **Facilities** **Location** Next to N25 on outskirts of Midleton

Hotel ★★★ 73% Midleton Park Hotel & Spa, MIDLETON ☎ 021 4631767 40 en suite

Mitchelstown Map 01 B2

Mitchelstown Limerick Rd
☎ 025 24072 & 087 2650110
e-mail: info@mitchelstown-golf.com
web: www.mitchelstown-golf.com
Attractive, gently undulating parkland course set in the Golden Vale, noted for the quality of the greens, the magnificent views of the Galtee Mountains and its friendly atmosphere. Strategically placed sand bunkers will need accurate play. The course offers woodland and water in a undulating parkland setting.
18 holes, 5493 metres, Par 71, SSS 70. Club membership 600.
Visitors Booking required. **Societies** Booking required. **Green Fees** Phone. **Course Designer** David Jones **Facilities** **Location** 1km from Mitchelstown

Hotel ★★★ Longueville House Hotel, MALLOW
☎ 022 47156 & 47306 📠 022 47459 20 en suite

MONKSTOWN Map 01 B2

Monkstown Parkgariffe, Monkstown
☎ 021 4841376 🖷 021 4841722
e-mail: office@monkstowngolfclub.com
web: www.monkstowngolfclub.com
Undulating parkland with five tough finishing holes.

18 holes, 5441 metres, Par 70, SSS 68, Course record 66.
Club membership 960.
Visitors Thu-Mon. Dress code. **Societies** welcome. **Green Fees** €43 per day (weekend €50). **Prof** Batt Murphy **Course Designer** Peter O'Hare & Tom Carey **Facilities** ⊗ 🍴 🍽 ☕ 🍷 ⛳ 🏠 🏌 🏌 🛒 🏌 ⛳ **Conf** Corporate Hospitality Days **Location** 0.8km SE of Monkstown

Hotel ★★★★ 67% Carrigaline Court Hotel, CARRIGALINE ☎ 021 4852100 91 en suite

OVENS Map 01 B2

Lee Valley Golf & Country Club Clashanure
☎ 021 7331721 🖷 021 7331695
e-mail: leevalleygolfclub@eircom.net
web: www.golfclubireland.com or www.leevalleygcc.ie
18 holes, 5883 metres, Par 72, SSS 70, Course record 62.
Course Designer Christy O'Connor **Location** Off N22
Telephone for further details

Hotel ★★★ 74% Castle Hotel, Main St, MACROOM
☎ 026 41074 60 en suite

SKIBBEREEN Map 01 B2

Skibbereen & West Carbery Licknavar
☎ 028 21227 🖷 028 22994
e-mail: bookings@skibbgolf.com
web: www.skibbgolf.com
18 holes, 5490 metres, Par 71, SSS 69, Course record 66.
Course Designer Jack Kenneally **Location** 1.6km SW on R595
Telephone for further details

Hotel ★★★ 67% Baltimore Harbour Hotel & Leisure Cntr, BALTIMORE ☎ 028 20361 64 en suite

YOUGHAL Map 01 C2

Youghal Knockaverry
☎ 024 92787 & 92861 🖷 024 92641
e-mail: youghalgolfclub@eircom.ie
web: www.youghalgolf.com
For many years the host of various Golfing Union championships, Youghal offers a good test of golf and is well maintained for year-round play. The Parkland

Continued

course has recently been extended with the addition of two new holes. There are panoramic views of Youghal Bay and the Blackwater estuary.
18 holes, 6175 metres, Par 72, SSS 72, Course record 68.
Club membership 1050.
Visitors Thu-Tue. Booking required. Handicap certificate. Dress code. **Societies** Booking required. **Green Fees** €32 per round (€42 weekends). **Prof** Liam Burns **Course Designer** Jeff Howes Golf Design **Facilities** ⊗ 🍴 🍽 ☕ 🍷 ⛳ 🏠 🏌 🛒 🏌 **Conf** Corporate Hospitality Days
Location Off N25

CO DONEGAL

BALLYBOFEY Map 01 C5

Ballybofey & Stranorlar Stranorlar
☎ 074 9131093 🖷 074 9130158
A most scenic course incorporating pleasant valleys backed by mountains with three of its holes bordered by a lake. There are three par 3s on the first nine and two on the second. The most difficult hole is the long uphill par 4 16th. The only par 5 is the 7th.
18 holes, 5366 metres, Par 68, SSS 68, Course record 64.
Club membership 648.
Visitors may play on weekdays. Advisable to book in advance **Societies** Booking required. **Green Fees** Phone. **Course Designer** P C Carr **Facilities** ⊗ 🍴 🍽 ☕ 🍷 ⛳ 🏠 🏌 🏌 🏌 **Conf** facs Corporate Hospitality Days **Location** 0.4km E of Stranorlar

BALLYLIFFIN Map 01 C6

Ballyliffin Clonmany
☎ 074 9376119 🖷 074 9376672
e-mail: info@ballyliffingolfclub.com
web: www.ballyliffingolfclub.com
The Old course is a links course with rolling fairways, surrounded by rolling hills and bounded on one side by the ocean. The 18-hole Glashedy course offers a modern championship test.
Old Links: 18 holes, 6039 metres, Par 71, SSS 72, Course record 65.
Glashedy Links: 18 holes, 6524 metres, Par 72, SSS 74, Course record 68.
Club membership 1400.
Visitors Mon-Sun & BHs. Booking required. Handicap certificate. Dress code. **Societies** Booking required. **Green Fees** Old Links: €60 (€65 weekends); Glashedy:€70 (€80 weekends). **Prof** John P Dolan **Course Designer** Nick Faldo/Tom Craddock/Pat Ruddy **Facilities** ⊗ 🍴 🍽 ☕ 🍷 ⛳ 🏠 🏌 🏌 🛒 🏌 ⛳ **Conf** facs Corporate Hospitality Days **Location** Off R238

Guest House ♦♦♦♦ Mount Royd Country Home, CARRIGANS ☎ 074 914 0163 4 en suite

BUNCRANA Map 01 C6

Buncrana Municipal Railway Rd, Ballymacarry
☎ 07493 62279 & 0749320749
e-mail: buncranagc@eircom.net
A nine-hole course with a very challenging par 3 3rd hole with all carry out of bounds on either side. Situated on the banks of The White Strand, overlooking the beautiful Lough Swilly. The 9 hole course offers a challenge to golfers of all ability.

Continued

9 holes, 1943 metres, Par 62, SSS 60, Course record 59. Club membership 200.
Visitors Mon-Sun & BHs. Booking required Sat-Sun & BHs. Handicap certificate. **Societies** Booking required. **Green Fees** €13 per round. **Prof** Jim Doherty **Facilities** **Conf** facs

Guest House ♦♦♦♦ Mount Royd Country Home, CARRIGANS ☎ 074 914 0163 4 en suite

North West Lisfannon, Fahan, Buncrana
☎ 074 9361715 074 9363284
e-mail: nwgc@tinet.ie
A traditional links course on gently rolling sandy terrain with some long par 4s. Good judgement is required on the approaches and the course offers a satisfying test coupled with undemanding walking.
18 holes, 5457 metres, Par 70, SSS 70, Course record 64. Club membership 580.
Visitors contact in advance. **Societies** Booking required. **Green Fees** Phone. **Prof** Seamus McBriarty **Course Designer** Thompson Davy **Facilities** **Location** 1.6km S of Buncrana on R238

Guest House ♦♦♦♦ Mount Royd Country Home, CARRIGANS ☎ 074 914 0163 4 en suite

BUNDORAN Map 01 B5

Bundoran
☎ 071 9841302 071 9842014
e-mail: bundorangolfclub@eircom.net
web: www.bundorangolfclub.com
This popular course, acknowledged as one of the best in the country, runs along the high cliffs above Bundoran beach and has a difficult par of 70. Designed by Harry Vardon, it offers a challenging game of golf in beautiful surroundings and has been the venue for a number of Irish golf championships.
18 holes, 5688 metres, Par 70, SSS 70, Course record 67. Club membership 770.
Visitors Mon-Sun & BHs. Booking required. Handicap certificate. Dress code. **Societies** welcome. **Green Fees** €45 per round (weekend €55). **Prof** David T Robinson **Course Designer** Harry Vardon **Facilities** **Conf** Corporate Hospitality Days **Location** Off Main St onto Sligo-Derry road

Hotel ★★★ 79% Sand House Hotel, ROSSNOWLAGH ☎ 071 985 1777 55 en suite

CRUIT ISLAND (AN CHRUIT) Map 01 B5

Cruit Island Kincasslagh
☎ 074 9543296 074 9548028
9 holes, 4833 metres, Par 68, SSS 66, Course record 62.
Course Designer Michael Doherty **Location** 8km N of Dungloe
Telephone for further details

Hotel ★★★ 68% Arnold's Hotel, DUNFANAGHY ☎ 074 913 6208 30 en suite

DUNFANAGHY Map 01 C6

Dunfanaghy Kill
☎ 074 9136335 074 9136684
e-mail: dunfanaghygolf@eircom.net
web: www.dunfanaghygolfclub.com
Overlooking Sheephaven Bay, the course has a flat central area with three difficult streams to negotiate. At the Port-na-Blagh end there are five marvellous holes, including one across the beach, while at the Horn Head end, the last five holes are a test for any golfer.
18 holes, 5247 metres, Par 68, SSS 66, Course record 63. Club membership 335.
Visitors Mon-Sun & BHs. Booking required Wed, Fri-Sun & BHs. **Societies** Booking required. **Green Fees** €30 (€40 weekend). **Course Designer** Harry Vardon **Facilities** **Conf** facs **Location** 30m W of Letterkenny

Hotel ★★★ 68% Arnold's Hotel, DUNFANAGHY ☎ 074 913 6208 30 en suite

GREENCASTLE Map 01 C6

Greencastle Geencastle
☎ 074 9381013 074 9381015
e-mail: info@greencastlegolfclub.net
web: www.greencastlegolfclub.net
18 holes, 5118 metres, Par 69, SSS 67, Course record 65.
Course Designer E Hackett
Telephone for further details

GWEEDORE (GAOTH DOBHAIR) Map 01 B6

Gweedore Derrybeg
☎ 075 31140
With breath taking scenery, this 9-hole links course provides plenty of challenge with two subtle par 3s and the par 5 5th/14th at 556yards into the prevailing west wind is a monster.
9 holes, 5670 metres, Par 71, SSS 69. Club membership 175.
Visitors Mon-Tue, Thu-Sat. Handicap certificate. **Societies** welcome. **Green Fees** €20. **Facilities**

LETTERKENNY Map 01 C5

Letterkenny Barnhill
☎ 074 9121150 074 9121175
18 holes, 5705 metres, Par 70, SSS 71, Course record 65.
Course Designer Eddie Hacket **Location** 3km NE of town on R245
Telephone for further details

MOVILLE Map 01 C6

Redcastle Redcastle
☎ 074 9382073 074 9382214
e-mail: redcastle.hotel@oceanfree.net
web: redcastlehotel.com
9 holes, 2813 metres, Par 36.
Location 6km SW on R238
Telephone for further details

NARIN (NARAN) Map 01 B5

Narin & Portnoo
☎ 074 9545107 🖹 074 9545994
e-mail: narinportnoo@eircom.net
web: www.narinportnoogolfclub.ie
Seaside links with every hole presenting its own special feature, the signature hole being the chasm-crossing 8th. One of the few natural links layouts remaining, with undulating fairways and greens. Fine views of Gweebarra Bay are visible from the course with an adjacent award winning beach. The links will test a player's iron play, with raised greens a common feature.
18 holes, 5322 metres, Par 69, SSS 68, Course record 63.
Club membership 150.
Visitors contact in advance for weekend. **Societies** telephone or email in advance. **Green Fees** Phone. **Course Designer** Leo Wallace/Hugh McNeill **Facilities** **Leisure** Blue Flag beach 200 metres. **Location** Off R261

PORTSALON Map 01 C6

Portsalon
☎ 074 9159459 🖹 074 9159919
e-mail: portsalongolfclub@eircom.net
Another course blessed by nature. The golden beaches of Ballymastocker Bay lie at one end, while the beauty of Lough Swilly and the Inishowen Peninsula beyond is a distracting but pleasant feature to the west. Situated on the Fanad Peninsula, this lovely links course provides untiring holiday golf at its best.
18 holes, 6185 metres, Par 72, SSS 72, Course record 71.
Club membership 500.
Visitors Mon-Sun & BHs. Booking required. Handicap certificate. Dress code. **Societies** Booking required. **Green Fees** €35 (€40 Sat, Sun & BHs). **Course Designer** Pat Ruddy **Facilities** by arrangement by arrangement **Conf** Corporate Hospitality Days **Location** Off R246

Hotel ★★★ 75% Fort Royal Hotel, Fort Royal, RATHMULLAN ☎ 074 9158100 11 en suite 4 annexe en suite

RATHMULLAN Map 01 C6

Otway Saltpans
☎ 074 58319
e-mail: otway_golf_club@iolfree.ie
One of the oldest courses in Ireland, created in 1861 by British military personnel as a recreational facility.
9 holes, 3872 metres, Par 64, SSS 60, Course record 60.
Club membership 112.
Visitors Mon-Sun & BHs. Booking required Sat. Dress code. **Societies** Booking required. **Green Fees** €15 per day (€20 weekends). **Facilities** **Conf** Corporate Hospitality Days **Location** In Rathmullan left at Mace convenience store for Knockalla coast road, 3km signed

Guest House ♦♦♦♦ Ballyraine Guest House, Ramelton Rd, LETTERKENNY ☎ 074 912 4460 & 912 0851 🖹 074 912 0851 8 en suite

ROSEPENNA (MACHAIR LOISCTHE) Map 01 C6

Rosapenna Downings
☎ 074 9155301 🖹 074 9155128
e-mail: rosapenna@tinet.ie
web: www.rosapenna.ie
Dramatic links course offering a challenging round. Originally designed by Tom Morris and later modified by James Braid and Harry Vardon, it includes features such as bunkers in mid-fairway. The best part of the links runs in the low valley along the ocean.
Old Tom Morris: 18 holes, 5734 metres, Par 70, SSS 71.
Sandy Hills Links: 18 holes, 5812 metres, Par 71.
Club membership 400.
Visitors no restrictions. **Societies** Booking required. **Green Fees** Phone. **Prof** Brian Patterson **Course Designer** Old Tom Morris **Facilities** **Leisure** hard tennis courts, heated indoor swimming pool. **Conf** facs **Location** NE of village off R248

Hotel ★★★ 68% Arnold's Hotel, DUNFANAGHY ☎ 074 913 6208 30 en suite

CO DUBLIN

BALBRIGGAN Map 01 D4

Balbriggan Blackhall
☎ 01 8412229 🖹 01 8413927
e-mail: balbriggangolfclub@eircom.net
web: www.balbriggangolfclub.com
A parkland course with great variations and good views of the Mourne and Cooley mountains.
18 holes, 5922 metres, Par 71, SSS 71.
Club membership 650.
Visitors must contact in advance. With member only at weekends. **Societies** must apply in writing. **Green Fees** Phone. **Prof** Nigel Howley **Course Designer** Paramoir **Facilities** **Location** 1km S of Balbriggan on N1

Hotel ★★★ 67% Boyne Valley Hotel & Country Club, Stameen, Dublin Rd, DROGHEDA ☎ 041 9837737 73 en suite

BALLYBOUGHAL Map 01 D4

Hollywood Lakes
☎ 01 8433406 🖹 01 8433002
e-mail: hollywoodlakesgc@eircom.net
web: www.hollywoodlakesgolfclub.com
A parkland course opened in 1992 with large USGA-type, sand-based greens and tees. There are water features on seven holes. The front nine requires accuracy while the second nine includes a 581-metre par 5.

Hollywood Lakes

18 holes, 6246 metres, Par 72, SSS 72, Course record 67. Club membership 780.
Visitors welcome Mon-Fri but may only play weekends from 2pm. **Societies** Booking required. **Green Fees** Phone. **Prof** Sid Baldwin **Course Designer** Mel Flanagan **Facilities** **Location** N of village on R108

Hotel ★★★ 71% Marine Hotel, Sutton Cross, DUBLIN 13 ☎ 01 8390000 48 en suite

BRITTAS Map 01 D4

Slade Valley Lynch Park
☎ 01 4582183 & 4582739 ▤ 01 4582784
18 holes, 5388 metres, Par 69, SSS 68, Course record 65.
Course Designer W Sullivan & D O Brien **Location** Off N81
Telephone for further details

CASTLEKNOCK Map 01 D4

Elm Green
☎ 01 8200797 ▤ 01 8226662
e-mail: elmgreen@golfdublin.com
web: www.golfdublin.com
18 holes, 5300 metres, Par 71, SSS 66, Course record 65.
Course Designer Eddie Hackett **Location** Off N3
Telephone for further details

Hotel ★★★ 70% Finnstown Country House Hotel, Newcastle Rd, Lucan, DUBLIN ☎ 01 6010700 25 en suite 28 annexe en suite

Luttrellstown Castle Dublin15
☎ 01 8089988 ▤ 01 8089989
e-mail: golf@luttrellstown.ie
web: www.luttrellstown.ie
Set in the grounds of the magnificent 560-acre Luttrellstown Castle estate, this championship course has recently been re-designed to enhance the golfing experience. The new layout will respect and retain the integrity of the mature and ancient parkland. The course is renowned for the quality of its greens and facilities.

18 holes, 6378 metres, Par 72, SSS 73, Course record 66. Club membership 400.
Visitors Mon-Sun & BHs. Booking required. Dress code. **Societies** Booking required. **Green Fees** Phone. **Prof** Edward Doyle **Course Designer** Donald Steele & Tom Mackenzie **Facilities** **Leisure** fishing, clay shooting. **Conf** facs Corporate Hospitality Days **Location** W of town off R121

Hotel ★★★ 70% Finnstown Country House Hotel, Newcastle Rd, Lucan, DUBLIN ☎ 01 6010700 25 en suite 28 annexe en suite

CLOGHRAN Map 01 D4

Forrest Little
☎ 01 8401183 & 8401763 ▤ 01 8908499
e-mail: margarey@forrestlittle.ie
web: www.forrestlittle.ie
A well-manicured and mature parkland with many water features, large sand based greens and undulating fairways, playable all year.
18 holes, 5902 metres, Par 71, SSS 72, Course record 68. Club membership 1000.
Visitors Mon-Fri. Handicap certificate. Dress code. **Societies** Booking required. **Green Fees** €50 per 18 holes. **Prof** Tony Judd **Course Designer** Mr Hawtree snr **Facilities** **Location** N of Dublin Airport off R132

Hotel ★★★ 71% Marine Hotel, Sutton Cross, DUBLIN 13 ☎ 01 8390000 48 en suite

DONABATE Map 01 D4

Balcarrick Corballis
☎ 01 8436957 ▤ 01 8436228
e-mail: balcarr@iol.ie
web: www.balcarrickgolfclub.com
Splendid 18-hole semi-links course with many challenging holes, located close to the sea. A strong prevailing wind often plays a big part on every hole and many of the par 3s are fronted by water.
18 holes, 6273 metres, Par 73, SSS 71. Club membership 750.
Visitors must contact in advance. **Societies** Booking required. **Green Fees** Phone. **Prof** Stephen Rayfus **Course Designer** Barry Langan **Facilities** **Location** Off R126

Hotel ★★★ 68% Deer Park Hotel, Golf & Spa, HOWTH ☎ 01 8322624 80 en suite

Donabate Balcarrick
☎ 01 8436346 ▤ 01 8434488
e-mail: info@donabategolfclub.com
27 holes, 6068 metres, Par 72, SSS 73, Course record 66.
Course Designer Pat Suttle **Location** E of town off R126
Telephone for further details

Hotel ★★★ 68% Deer Park Hotel, Golf & Spa, HOWTH ☎ 01 8322624 80 en suite

Continued

Island Corballis
☎ 01 8436205 📠 01 8436860
e-mail: info@theislandgolfclub.com
web: www.theislandgolfclub.com
An old links course surrounded by the Irish Sea, Donabate beach and the Broadmeadow estuary, nestling between the highest sand dunes of any links course in Ireland. The rugged beauty cannot fail to impress. An Irish qualifying course for the Open Championship from 2005.

18 holes, 6206 metres, Par 71, SSS 63.
Club membership 1020.
Visitors must contact in advance. **Societies** Booking required. **Green Fees** Phone. **Prof** Kevin Kelliher **Course Designer** Martin Hawtree **Facilities** **Conf** facs Corporate Hospitality Days **Location** Off R126

Hotel ★★★ 68% Deer Park Hotel, Golf & Spa, HOWTH ☎ 01 8322624 80 en suite

Turvey Golf Hotel Turvey Av
☎ 01 8435169 📠 01 8435179
e-mail: turveygc@eircom.net
A mature parkland course with oak trees over 220 years old. A test of golf for all levels of golfer.
18 holes, 6068 metres, Par 71, SSS 72.
Club membership 500.
Visitors Mon-Fri & BHs, Sat-Sun after 1pm only. Bookng required Sat-Sun & BHs. Dress code. **Societies** Booking required. **Green Fees** €30 per 18 holes, €15 per 9 holes (€35/€20 weekends). **Course Designer** P McGurk **Facilities** **Conf** facs Corporate Hospitality Days **Location** M1, 1st junct N after Dublin airport, 1m Turvey signed on right

Hotel ★★★ 68% Deer Park Hotel, Golf & Spa, HOWTH ☎ 01 8322624 80 en suite

DUBLIN Map 01 D4

The Carrickmines Carrickmines
☎ 01 2955972
Meadowland and partly hilly gorseland course.
9 holes, 5554 metres, Par 71, SSS 69.
Club membership 600.
Visitors Mon, Tue, Thu, Fri & Sun. Handicap certificate. Dress code. **Green Fees** Phone. **Facilities** **Location** 11km SE of city centre off N11

Hotel ★★★ 68% The Gresham Royal Marine Hotel, Marine Rd, DUN LAOGHAIRE ☎ 01 2801911 103 en suite

Castle Woodside Dr, Rathfarnham
☎ 01 4904207 📠 01 4920264
e-mail: office@castlegc.ie
web: www.castlegc.ie
A tight, tree-lined parkland course which is very highly regarded by all who play there.
18 holes, 5732 metres, Par 71, SSS 66, Course record 63.
Club membership 1350.
Visitors Mon, Thu, Fri & Sun. Booking required. Handicap certificate. Dress code. **Societies** Booking required. **Green Fees** €80 per 18 holes. **Prof** David Kinsella **Course Designer** Harry Colt **Facilities** **Location** Off Dodder Park Rd

Hotel ★★★★ 73% Jurys Hotel and Towers, Pembroke Rd, Ballsbridge, DUBLIN 4 ☎ 01 660 5000 303 en suite

Clontarf Donnycarney House, Malahide Rd
☎ 01 8331892 & 8331520 📠 01 8331933
e-mail: info.cgc@indigo.ie
web: clontarfgolfclub.ie
The nearest golf course to Dublin city, with a historic building as a clubhouse, Clontarf is a parkland type course bordered on one side by a railway line. Although a relatively short course, its narrow fairways and punitive rough call for accuracy off the tee and will test players' golfing skill. There are several challenging holes including the 12th, which involves playing over a pond and a quarry.

18 holes, 5317 metres, Par 69, SSS 68, Course record 64.
Club membership 1150.
Visitors Mon-Sun & BHs. Booking required. Dress code. **Societies** Booking required. **Green Fees** €50 per round (€60 weekends). **Prof** Mark Callan **Course Designer** Harry Colt **Facilities** **Leisure** bowling green, snooker room, golf teaching by pro. **Conf** facs Corporate Hospitality Days **Location** 4km NE of city centre via Fairview

Corrstown Corrstown, Kilsallaghan
☎ 01 8640533 & 8640534 📠 01 8640537
e-mail: info@corrstowngolfclub.com
web: www.corrstowngolfclub.com
The 18-hole course has a small river meandering through, coming into play at several holes culminating in a challenging island green finish. Orchard course has mature trees and rolling pastureland offering golfers a relaxing enjoyable game.
River Course: 18 holes, 6077 metres, Par 72, SSS 71, Course record 69.
Orchard Course: 9 holes, 2792 metres, Par 35, SSS 69.
Club membership 1050.

Continued

Visitors Mon-Sun & BHs. Booking required. Dress code. **Societies** Booking required. **Green Fees** £50 per 18 holes (£60 weekends). Orchard course £25 (£30 weekends). **Prof** Pat Gittens **Course Designer** Eddie Connaughton **Facilities** ⊗ 𝍗 ⛾ ☕ 🍷 ⛽ 🏠 **Location** 10km N of city centre via St Margarets

Edmondstown Edmondstown Rd, Edmondstown

☎ 01 4931082 & 4932461 📠 01 4933152
e-mail: info@edmondstowngolfclub.ie
web: www.edmondstowngolfclub.ie

A popular and testing parkland course situated at the foot of the Dublin Mountains in the suburbs of the city. Now completely renovated and redesigned. All greens are now sand based to the highest standard. An attractive stream flows in front of the 4th and 6th greens calling for an accurate approach shot. The par 3 17th will test the best golfers and the 5th and 12th require thoughtful club selection to the green.

18 holes, 6111 metres, Par 71, SSS 73, Course record 66. Club membership 750.

Visitors Mon, Thu, Fri, Sat am & BHs. Booking required. Dress code. **Societies** Booking required. **Green Fees** €55 per round (€65 weekends). **Prof** Gareth McShea **Course Designer** McEvoy/Cooke **Facilities** ⊗ **Conf** facs Corporate Hospitality Days **Location** M50 junct 12

Hotel ★★★ 70% Jurys Montrose Hotel, Stillorgan Rd, DUBLIN ☎ 01 2693311 178 en suite

Elm Park Golf & Sports Club Nutley House, Nutley Ln, Donnybrook

☎ 01 2693438 📠 01 2694505
e-mail: office@elmparkgolfclub.ie
web: www.elmparkgolfclub.ie

Interesting parkland course requiring a degree of accuracy, particularly as half of the holes involve crossing the stream.

18 holes, 5380 metres, Par 69, SSS 69, Course record 64. Club membership 1900.

Visitors must contact in advance. **Societies** apply in advance. **Green Fees** Phone. **Prof** Seamus Green **Course Designer** Paytrick Merrigan **Facilities** ⊗ **Leisure** hard and grass tennis courts. **Location** 3km SE of city centre off N11

Hotel ★★★★ 73% Jurys Hotel and Towers, Pembroke Rd, Ballsbridge, DUBLIN 4 ☎ 01 660 5000 303 en suite

Grange Rathfarnham

☎ 01 4932889

18 holes, 5517 metres, Par 68, SSS 69.

Location 10km S of city centre
Telephone for further details

Hotel ★★★ 70% Jurys Montrose Hotel, Stillorgan Rd, DUBLIN ☎ 01 2693311 178 en suite

Hollystown Hollystown

☎ 01 8207444 📠 01 8207447
e-mail: info@hollystown.com
web: www.hollystown.com

Set in the Dublin countryside, this mature parkland course incorporates the natural features of trees, lakes and streams. Three loops of nine holes provide three distinctly different 18-hole combinations, each offering a unique challenge to all golfing standards.

Red/Yellow: 18 holes, 5829yds, Par 70, SSS 69.
Yellow/Blue: 18 holes, 6216yds, Par 71, SSS 69.
Blue/Red: 18 holes, 6201yds, Par 71, SSS 69.
Club membership 690.

Visitors no restrictions **Societies** contact in advance. **Green Fees** Phone. **Prof** Joe Murray **Course Designer** Eddie Hackett **Facilities** ⊗ **Conf** facs Corporate Hospitality Days **Location** 8m off N3 Dublin-Cavan road at Mulhuddart or off the N2 Dublin-Ashbourne road at Ward

Hotel ⌂ Travelodge Dublin Castleknock, Auburn Av Roundabout, Navan Rd, ☎ 08700 850 950 100 en suite

Continued

Howth St Fintan's, Carrickbrack Rd, Sutton
☎ 01 8323055 🖹 01 8321793
e-mail: secretary@howthgolfclub.ie
web: www.howthgolfclub.ie
18 holes, 5618 metres, Par 72, SSS 69.
Course Designer James Braid **Location** 14.5km NE of city
Telephone for further details

Hotel ★★★ 71% Marine Hotel, Sutton Cross, DUBLIN 13
☎ 01 8390000 48 en suite

Milltown Lower Churchtown Rd
☎ 01 4976090 🖹 01 4976008
e-mail: info@milltowngolfclub.ie
web: www.milltowngolfclub.ie.
Level parkland three miles from Dublin City Centre.
18 holes, 5638 metres, Par 71, SSS 69, Course record 64.
Club membership 1400.
Visitors Mon, Thu & Fri. Booking required. Handicap certificate. Dress code. **Societies** Booking required. **Green Fees** €80 per 18 holes. **Prof** John Harnett **Course Designer** Freddie Davis **Facilities**

Hotel ★★★★ 73% Jurys Hotel and Towers, Pembroke Rd, Ballsbridge, DUBLIN 4 ☎ 01 660 5000 303 en suite

Newlands Clondalkin
☎ 01 4593157 & 4593498 🖹 01 4593498
Mature parkland course offering a testing game.
18 holes, 5714 metres, Par 71, SSS 70.
Club membership 1000.
Visitors must contact in advance and may play Mon, Thu, Fri and Wed mornings. **Societies** must contact in writing. **Green Fees** Phone. **Prof** Karl O'Donnell **Course Designer** James Braid **Facilities**

Hotel ★★★ 70% Lynch Green Isle Hotel, Naas Rd, Newlands Cross, Naas Rd, DUBLIN 22 ☎ 01 4593406 240 en suite

Open Golf Centre Newton House, St Margaret's
☎ 01 8640324 🖹 01 8341400
e-mail: rwwright@iol.ie
Yellow & Red Course: 18 holes, 5462 metres, Par 71, SSS 69, Course record 66.
Blue Course: 9 holes, 2267 metres, Par 31.
Course Designer M Hawtree **Location** Next to Dublin Airport
Telephone for further details

Hotel ★★★ 71% Marine Hotel, Sutton Cross, DUBLIN 13
☎ 01 8390000 48 en suite

Rathfarnham Newtown
☎ 01 4931201 & 4931561 🖹 01 4931561
e-mail: rgc@oceanfree.net
Parkland course designed by John Jacobs in 1962.
14 holes, 5815 metres, Par 71, SSS 70, Course record 69.
Club membership 685.
Visitors Mon, Wed-Fri. Booking required. Dress code. **Societies** Booking required. **Green Fees** €40 per 18 holes. **Prof** Brian O'Hara **Course Designer** John Jacobs **Facilities** **Location** 5km S of city centre off N81

Hotel ★★★★ 73% Jurys Hotel and Towers, Pembroke Rd, Ballsbridge, DUBLIN 4 ☎ 01 660 5000 303 en suite

Royal Dublin North Bull Island Reserve, Dollymount
☎ 01 8336346 🖹 01 8336504
e-mail: jlambe@theroyaldublingolfclub.com
web: www.theroyaldublingolfclub.com
A popular course with visitors, for its design subtleties, the condition of the links and the friendly atmosphere. Founded in 1885, the club moved to its present site in 1889 and received its Royal designation in 1891. A notable former club professional was Christy O'Connor, who was appointed in 1959 and immediately made his name. Along with its many notable holes, Royal Dublin has a fine and testing finish. The 18th is a sharp dog-leg par 4, with out of bounds along the right-hand side. The decision to try the long carry over the 'garden' is one many visitors have regretted.
18 holes, 6002 metres, Par 72, SSS 71, Course record 63.
Club membership 1250.
Visitors Mon-Tue & Thu-Sun. Booking required. Handicap certificate. Dress code. **Societies** Booking required. **Green Fees** €150 (€170 weekends). **Prof** Leonard Owens **Course Designer** H S Colt **Facilities** **Conf** facs Corporate Hospitality Days **Location** 5.5km NE of city centre

Hotel ★★★ 61% Longfield's Hotel, Fitzwilliam St Lower, DUBLIN 2 ☎ 01 6761367 26 en suite

St Margaret's Golf & Country Club
St Margaret's
☎ 01 8640400 🖹 01 8640408
e-mail: reservations@stmargaretsgolf.com
web: www.stmargaretsgolf.com
A championship standard course which measures nearly 7,000 yards off the back tees, but flexible teeing offers a fairer challenge to the middle and high handicap golfer. The modern design makes wide use of water hazards and mounding. The par 5 8th hole is set to become notorious - featuring lakes to the left and right of the tee and a third lake in front of the green. Ryder Cup player, Sam Torrance, has described the 18th as 'possibly the strongest and most exciting in the world'.
18 holes, 6325 metres, Par 73, SSS 73, Course record 69.
Club membership 260.
Visitors Mon-Sun & BHs. Booking required. Dress code. **Societies** Booking required. **Green Fees** fr €40. **Prof** John Kelly **Course Designer** Craddock/Ruddy **Facilities** **Location** 9km N of city centre off R122

Hotel ★★★ 71% Marine Hotel, Sutton Cross, DUBLIN 13
☎ 01 8390000 48 en suite

Stackstown Kellystown Rd, Rathfarnham
☎ 01 4942338 & 4941993 🖹 01 4933934
e-mail: stackstowngc@eircom.net
web: stackstowngolfclub.ie
Pleasant course in the foothills of the Dublin mountains affording breathtaking views of Dublin city and bay. Mature woodland borders every hole and premium is placed on accuracy off the tee. In 1999 the course was remodelled and the mountain streams which run through the course were harnessed to bring them into play and provide attractive on-course water features.
18 holes, 5625 metres, Par 72, SSS 72, Course record 68.
Club membership 1092.

Continued

Visitors preferred Mon, Thu-Fri & Sun pm. **Societies** Booking required. **Green Fees** Phone. **Prof** Michael Kavanagh **Course Designer** Shaftrey **Facilities** **Conf** facs Corporate Hospitality Days **Location** 9km S of city centre. M50 junct 13, signs for Rathfarnham, 3rd lights left for Leopardstown, next lights follow road under M50, club 300 metres

Hotel ★★★ 70% Jurys Montrose Hotel, Stillorgan Rd, DUBLIN ☎ 01 2693311 178 en suite

DUN LAOGHAIRE Map 01 D4

Dun Laoghaire Eglinton Park, Tivoli Rd
☎ 01 2803916 📠 01 2804868
e-mail: dlgc@iol.ie
web: www.dunlaoghairegolfclub.ie
18 holes, 5313 metres, Par 69, SSS 68, Course record 63.
Course Designer Harry Colt **Location** 1.2km from town centre port
Telephone for further details

Hotel ★★★ 68% The Gresham Royal Marine Hotel, Marine Rd, DUN LAOGHAIRE ☎ 01 2801911 103 en suite

HOWTH Map 01 D4

Deer Park Hotel, Golf & Spa D13
☎ 01 8322624 📠 01 8392405
e-mail: sales@deerpark.iol.ie
web: www.deerpark-hotel.ie
Claiming to be Ireland's largest golf-hotel complex, Deer Park offers a challenge to all levels of golfer. Spectacular scenery within the parkland setting surrounding Howth Castle.

t Fintans: 9 holes, 3084 metres, Par 37.
eer Park: 18 holes, 6245 metres, Par 72.
race O'Malley: 9 holes, 2862 metres, Par 35.
hort Course: 12 holes, 1655 metres, Par 36.
lub membership 350.
isitors no restrictions. **Societies** must contact by lephone. **Green Fees** Phone. **Course Designer** Fred awtree **Facilities** **Leisure** ard tennis courts, heated indoor swimming pool, sauna. **onf** facs Corporate Hospitality Days **Location** 14.5km E of city centre, off coast road 0.8km before Howth arbour
e advertisement on page 447

otel ★★★ 68% Deer Park Hotel, Golf & Spa, HOWTH ☎ 01 8322624 80 en suite

KILLINEY Map 01 D4

Killiney Ballinclea Rd
☎ 01 2852823 📠 01 2852861
e-mail: killineygolfclub@eircom.net
The course is on the side of Killiney Hill with picturesque views of south Dublin and the Wicklow Mountains.
9 holes, 5655 metres, Par 70, SSS 70.
Club membership 450.
Visitors welcome Mon, Wed, Fri & Sun pm. **Societies** Apply in writing. **Green Fees** Phone. **Prof** P O'Boyle **Facilities** **Conf** facs

Hotel ★★★★ 69% Fitzpatrick Castle Hotel, KILLINEY ☎ 01 2305400 113 en suite

LUCAN Map 01 D4

Hermitage Ballydowd
☎ 01 6268491 📠 01 6238881
e-mail: hermitagegolf@eircom.net
web: www.hermitagegolf.ie
Part level, part undulating course bordered by the River Liffey and offering some surprises.
18 holes, 6034 metres, Par 71, SSS 71.
Club membership 1100.
Visitors Mon & Thu-Fri. Booking required. Dress code. **Societies** Booking required. **Green Fees** €80 per 18 holes. **Prof** Simon Byrne **Course Designer** J McKenna **Facilities** **Location** On N4

Hotel ★★★ 70% Finnstown Country House Hotel, Newcastle Rd, Lucan, DUBLIN ☎ 01 6010700 25 en suite 28 annexe en suite

Lucan Celbridge Rd
☎ 01 6282106 📠 01 6282929
e-mail: luncangolf@eircom.net
web: lucangolfclub.ie
Founded in 1897 as a nine-hole course and extended to 18 holes in 1988, Lucan involves playing over a lane which bisects the 1st and 7th holes. The front nine is undulating while the back nine is flatter and features water hazards and a 531-metre par 5 18th hole.
18 holes, 5958 metres, Par 71, SSS 71, Course record 67.
Club membership 920.
Visitors Mon-Tue & Fri. Dress code. **Societies** Booking required. **Green Fees** €45. **Course Designer** Eddie Hackett **Facilities** **Location** W of town towards Celbridge

Hotel ★★★ 64% Lucan Spa Hotel, LUCAN ☎ 01 6280494 71 rms (61 en suite)

MALAHIDE Map 01 D4

Malahide Beechwood, The Grange
☎ 01 8461611 🖹 01 8461270
e-mail: malgc@clubi.ie
web: www.malahidegolfclub.ie

Main Course: 18 holes, 6066 metres, Par 71.
Course Designer E Hackett **Location** 1.6km from R106 coast road at Portmarnock
Telephone for further details

Hotel ★★★★ Portmarnock Hotel & Golf Links, Strand Rd, PORTMARNOCK ☎ 01 8460611 98 en suite

PORTMARNOCK Map 01 D4

Portmarnock **see page 451**

Hotel ★★★★ Portmarnock Hotel & Golf Links, Strand Rd, PORTMARNOCK ☎ 01 8460611 98 en suite

Portmarnock Hotel & Golf Links Strand Rd
☎ 01 8460611 🖹 01 8462442
e-mail: golfres@portmarnock.com
web: www.portmarnock.com
This links course makes full use of the dunes and natural terrain to provide an authentic links layout. The elevated tees and greens, blind approaches and doglegs - not to mention sea breezes, will keep the golfer thinking through every round. Gently undulating fairways leading to large fast greens must be negotiated through 98 strategically placed bunkers, while hillocks, wild grasses and gorse await wayward shots.
18 holes, 5992 metres, Par 71, SSS 72, Course record 67.
Visitors Mon-Sun & BHs. Dress code. **Societies** Booking required. **Green Fees** €125 per round. **Course Designer** Bernhard Langer **Facilities** **Leisure** sauna, gymnasium. **Conf** facs Corporate Hospitality Days

Hotel ★★★★ Portmarnock Hotel & Golf Links, Strand Rd, PORTMARNOCK ☎ 01 8460611 98 en suite

RATHCOOLE Map 01 D4

Beech Park Johnstown
☎ 01 4580522 🖹 01 4588365
e-mail: info@beechpark.ie
web: www.beechpark.ie
Undulating flat parkland course with heavily wooded fairways. Famous for its Amen Corner (holes 10 to 13).
Beech Park: 18 holes, 5753 metres, Par 72, SSS 70, Course record 67.
Club membership 1038.
Visitors Mon & Thu-Fri. Booking required. Dress code. **Societies** Booking required. **Green Fees** €40 per 18 holes. **Prof** Zak Rouiller **Course Designer** Eddie Hackett **Facilities** **Conf** Corporate Hospitality Days **Location** From N7, take exit signed Rathcoole North. Follow local signs.

Hotel ★★★ 70% Finnstown Country House Hotel, Newcastle Rd, Lucan, DUBLIN ☎ 01 6010700 25 en suite 28 annexe en suite

RUSH Map 01 D4

Rush
☎ 01 8438177 (office) & 8437548 (club) 🖹 01 8438177
e-mail: info@rushgolfclub.com
Seaside borders three fairways on this links course. There are 28 bunkers and undulating fairways to add to the challenge of the variable and strong winds that blow at all times and change with the tides. There are no easy holes.
9 holes, 5598 metres, Par 70, SSS 69.
Club membership 500.
Visitors Mon-Fri. Booking required. Dress code. **Societies** Booking required. **Green Fees** €32 per 18 holes. **Facilities** **Location** SW of town

Redbank House & Restaurant, 5-7 Church St, SKERRIES ☎ 01 8491005 8490439 7 en suite 5 annexe en suite

SAGGART Map 01 D4

City West Hotel & Golf Resort
☎ 01 4010500 & 4010878 (shop) 🖹 01 4588565
e-mail: info@citywest-hotel.iol.ie
web: citywesthotel.com
Championship: 18 holes, 5774 metres, Par 70, SSS 70, Course record 65.
Executive: 18 holes, 4713 metres, Par 65, SSS 69.
Course Designer Christy O'Connor Jnr **Location** Off N7 S to village
Telephone for further details

Hotel ★★★ 66% Bewley's Hotel Newlands Cross, Newlands Cross, Naas Rd, DUBLIN 22 ☎ 01 4640140 258 en suite

SKERRIES Map 01 D4

Skerries Hacketstown
☎ 01 8491567 🖹 01 8491591
e-mail: skerriesgolfclub@eircom.net
web: www.skerriesgolfclub.ie
Tree-lined parkland course on gently rolling countryside, with sea views from some holes. The 1st and 18th are particularly challenging.
18 holes, 6081 metres, Par 73, SSS 72, Course record 67.
Club membership 800.
Visitors must contact in advance but may not play at weekends. **Societies** must contact in writing. **Green Fees** Phone. **Prof** Jimmy Kinsella **Facilities** **Location** S of town off R127

Hotel ★★★ 67% Boyne Valley Hotel & Country Club, Stameen, Dublin Rd, DROGHEDA ☎ 041 9837737 73 en suite

Continued

Co Dublin

Portmarnock

Portmarnock

Map 01 D4

Universally acknowledged as one of the truly great links courses, Portmarnock has hosted many great events from the British Amateur Championships of 1949 and the Canada Cup in 1960, to 12 stagings of the revised Irish Open. Founded in 1894, the serpentine championship course offers a classic challenge: surrounded by water on three sides, no two successive holes play in the same direction. Unlike many courses that play nine out and nine home, Portmarnock demands a continual awareness of wind direction. Extraordinary holes include the 14th, which Henry Cotton regarded as the best hole in golf; the 15th, which Arnold Palmer regards as the best par 3 in the world; and the 5th, regarded as the best on the course by the late Harry Bradshaw. Bradshaw was for 40 years Portmarnock's golf professional and runner-up to AD Locke in the 1949 British Open, playing his ball from an empty bottle of stout.

☎ 01 8462968 🗎 01 8462601
e-mail: emer@portmarnockgolfclub.ie
web: www.portmarnockgolfclub.ie

Old Course: 18 holes, 6567 metres, Par 72, SSS 73.
New Course: 9 holes, 3082 metres, Par 37.
Club membership 1100.

Visitors Booking required. Handicap certificate. Dress code. Societies Booking required. Green Fees Phone. Prof Joey Purcell Course Designer W Pickeman Facilities by arrangement Location S of town off R106

SWORDS Map 01 D4

Swords Open Golf Course Balheary Av, Swords
☎ 01 8409819 & 8901030 📠 01 8409819
e-mail: info@swordsopengolfcourse.com
web: www.swordsopengolfcourse.com
Parkland beside the River Broadmeadow, in countryside 16km from Dublin.
18 holes, 5612 metres, Par 70, SSS 70, Course record 73.
Club membership 475.
Visitors Mon-Sun & BHs. Booking required. Dress code. **Societies** Booking required. **Green Fees** €18 per 18 holes (€25 weekends). **Course Designer** T Halpin **Facilities** **Location** N of town centre

TALLAGHT Map 01 D4

Dublin City Ballinascorney
☎ 01 4516430 📠 01 4598445
e-mail: info@dublincitygolf.com
web: www.dublincitygolf.com
Set in the valley of Glenasmole, this very scenic course offers a variety of terrain, where every hole is different, many would be considered feature holes.
18 holes, 5061 metres, Par 69, SSS 67, Course record 63.
Club membership 500.
Visitors Mon-Sun & BHs. Booking required. Dress code. **Societies** Booking required. **Green Fees** €25 (€38 weekends & BHs). **Course Designer** Eddie Hackett **Facilities** **Conf** facs **Location** 12km SW of city centre on R114

Hotel ★★★ 70% Lynch Green Isle Hotel, Naas Rd, Newlands Cross, Naas Rd, DUBLIN 22 ☎ 01 4593406 240 en suite

CO GALWAY

BALLINASLOE Map 01 B4

Ballinasloe Rosglos
☎ 090 9642126 📠 090 9642538
e-mail: ballinasloegolfclub@eircom.net
web: ballinasloegolfclub.com

18 holes, 5865 metres, Par 72, SSS 70, Course record 69.
Course Designer E Hackett/E Connaughton **Location** 3km S on R355
Telephone for further details

BALLYCONNEELY Map 01 A4

Connemara
☎ 095 23502 & 23602 📠 095 23662
e-mail: links@iol.ie
web: www.connemaragolflinks.com
This championship links course has a spectacular setting by the Atlantic Ocean, with the Twelve Bens Mountains in the background. Established in 1973, it is a tough challenge, due in no small part to its exposed location, with the back nine the equal of any in the world. The last six holes are exceptionally long and offer a great challenge to golfers of all abilities. When the wind blows, club selection is crucial. Notable holes are the 13th (200yd par 3), the long par 5 14th, the 15th with a green nestling in the hills, the 16th guarded by water and the 17th and 18th, both par 5s over 500yds long.

Championship: 18 holes, 6095 metres, Par 72, SSS 73, Course record 64.
New: 9 holes, 2754 metres, Par 35.
Club membership 970.
Visitors Mon-Sun & BHs. **Societies** Booking required. **Green Fees** Mon-Thu €60 per round; Fri-Sun €65. **Prof** Hugh O'Neill **Course Designer** Eddie Hackett **Facilities** **Conf** Corporate Hospitality Days **Location** W of village off R342

Hotel ★★★★ 71% Abbeyglen Castle Hotel, Sky Rd, CLIFDEN ☎ 095 21201 45 en suite

BEARNA Map 01 B3

Bearna Golf and Country Club Corboley
☎ 091 592677 📠 091 592674
e-mail: info@bearnagolfclub.com
web: www.bearnagolfclub.com

Set amid the beautiful landscape of the west of Ireland and enjoying commanding views of Galway Bay, the

Continu

course covers more than 100 hectares. This has resulted in generously proportioned fairways, many elevated tees and some splendid carries. Water comes into play at thirteen holes and the final four holes provide a memorable finish. Lakes on 6th, 7th and 10th holes.
18 holes, 5746 metres, Par 72, SSS 72, Course record 68. Club membership 600.
Visitors Mon-Sun & BHs. Dress code. **Societies** welcome. **Green Fees** €35 per round Mon-Thu (€40 Fri, €50 Sat-Sun & BHs). **Prof** Declan Cunningham **Course Designer** Robert J Brown **Facilities** **Conf** facs **Location** 3.5km N of Bearna, off R336

Hotel ★★★★ 70% Galway Bay Hotel Conference & Leisure Centre, The Promenade, Salthill, GALWAY ☎ 091 520520 153 en suite

GALWAY Map 01 B4

Galway Blackrock, Salthill
☎ 091 522033 091 529783
e-mail: galwaygolf@eircom.net
web: galwaygolf.com
Designed by Alister MacKenzie, this course is inland by nature, although some of the fairways run close to the ocean. The terrain is of gently sloping hillocks with plenty of trees and furze bushes to catch out the unwary. Although not a long course it continues to delight visiting golfers.
18 holes, 5995 metres, Par 70, SSS 71, Course record 67. Club membership 1238.
Visitors Mon, Wed-Sat & BHs. Booking required. Handicap certificate. Dress code. **Societies** Booking required. **Green Fees** €50 per round Mon-Fri (€60 weekends). **Prof** Don Wallace **Course Designer** A MacKenzie **Facilities** **Conf** Corporate Hospitality Days **Location** 3km W in Salthill

Glenlo Abbey Bushypark
☎ 091 526666 091 527800
e-mail: glenlo@iol.ie
web: www.glenlo.com
9 holes, 6009 metres, Par 71, SSS 71.
Course Designer Jeff Howes **Location** 4km NW off N59
Telephone for further details

Hotel ★★★★ 78% Glenlo Abbey Hotel, Bushypark, GALWAY ☎ 091 526666 46 en suite

If the name of the club appears in italics, details have not been confirmed for this edition of the guide

GORT Map 01 B3

Gort Castlequarter
☎ 091 632244 091 632387
e-mail: info@gortgolf.com
web: www.gortgolf.com

Set in 65 hectares of picturesque parkland. The 515-metre 9th and the 472-metre 17th are played into a prevailing wind and the par 4 dog-leg 7th will test the best.
18 holes, 5705 metres, Par 71, SSS 69. Club membership 1060.
Visitors Mon-Sun & BHs. Booking required Sat-Sun & BHs. Dress code. **Societies** Booking required. **Green Fees** €25 per day (€30 weekends). **Course Designer** Christy O'Connor Jnr **Facilities**

LOUGHREA Map 01 B3

Loughrea Bullaun Rd, Graigue
☎ 091 841049 091 847472
e-mail: loughreagolfclub@eircom.net
An excellent parkland course with good greens and extended in 1992 to 18-holes. The course has an unusual feature in that it incorporates a historic souterrain (underground shelter/food store).
18 holes, 5825 metres, Par 69, SSS 67, Course record 68. Club membership 700.
Visitors Mon-Sun & BHs. Booking required Fri-Sun & BHs. Dress code. **Societies** Booking required. **Green Fees** €25 per day. **Course Designer** Eddie Hackett **Facilities** **Location** Follow signs from bypass for Mountbellew/New Inn. 1.5m N of town.

MOUNTBELLEW Map 01 B4

Mountbellew Ballinasloe
☎ 0905 79259 0905 79274
9 holes, 5143 metres, Par 69, SSS 66, Course record 63.
Location Off N63
Telephone for further details

ORANMORE Map 01 B3

Athenry Palmerstown
☎ 091 794466 091 794971
e-mail: athenrygc@eircom.net
web: athenrygolfclub.net
A mixture of parkland and heathland built on a limestone base against the backdrop of a large pine forest. The par 3 holes are notable with a feature hole at the 12th - from an elevated tee played between beech and pine trees.
18 holes, 5687 metres, Par 70, SSS 70, Course record 67. Club membership 1000.

Continued

Visitors Mon-Sat & BHs. Booking required Wed, Fri-Sat & BHs. Dress code. **Societies** Booking required. **Green Fees** Apr-Sep: €35 per day Mon-Thu (€40 Fri-Sun). Oct-Mar €25 (weekends €28). **Prof** Raymond Ryan **Course Designer** Eddie Hackett **Facilities** **Conf** Corporate Hospitality Days **Location** 6km E on R348

Galway Bay Golf Resort Renville
☎ 091 790711 091 792510
e-mail: info@galwaybaygolfresort.com
web: www.galwaybaygolfresort.com
A championship golf course surrounded on three sides by the Atlantic Ocean and featuring water hazards on a number of holes. Each hole has its own characteristics made more obvious by the everchanging seaside winds. The design of the course highlights and preserves the ancient historic features of the Renville Peninsula. The spectacular setting and distractingly beautiful and cleverly designed mix of holes presents a real golfing challenge, demanding total concentration.
18 holes, 6533 metres, Par 72, SSS 73, Course record 68. Club membership 280.
Visitors contact club for details. **Societies** Booking required. **Green Fees** Mon-Thur €55 per round (Fri-Sun & BHs €70). **Prof** Eugene O'Connor **Course Designer** Christy O'Connor Jnr **Facilities** **Leisure** sauna. **Conf** Corporate Hospitality Days **Location** 5km SW of village

OUGHTERARD Map 01 B4

Oughterard
☎ 091 552131 091 552377
e-mail: golfough@iol.ie
18 holes, 6090 metres, Par 70, SSS 69, Course record 67.
Course Designer P Merrigan **Location** 1km SE of town on N59
Telephone for further details

Hotel ★★★ Lough Inagh Lodge Hotel, Inagh Valley, RECESS ☎ 095 34706 & 34694 095 34708 12 en suite

PORTUMNA Map 01 B3

Portumna
☎ 090 9741059 090 9741798
e-mail: portumnagc@eircom.net
18 holes, 6225 metres, Par 72, SSS 72.
Course Designer E Connaughton **Location** 4km W of town on R352
Telephone for further details

RENVYLE Map 01 A4

Renvyle House Hotel
☎ 095 43511 095 43515
e-mail: renvyle@iol.ie
web: www.renvyle.com
Pebble Beach: 9 holes, 3200 metres, Par 36, Course record 34.
Location Renvyle 6km off N59, course NW of village
Telephone for further details

Hotel ★★★ 70% Renvyle House Hotel, RENVYLE
☎ 095 43511 68 en suite

TUAM Map 01 B4

Tuam Barnacurragh
☎ 093 28993 093 26003
18 holes, 5513 metres, Par 72, SSS 69.
Course Designer Eddie Hackett **Location** 1km S of town on R347
Telephone for further details

CO KERRY

BALLYBUNION Map 01 A3

Ballybunion **see page 455**

Guest House ♦♦♦♦♦ Cashen Course House, Golf Links Rd, Ballybunion ☎ 068 27351 9 en suite

BALLYFERRITER (BAILE AN FHEIRTEARAIGH) Map 01 A2

Dingle Links
☎ 066 9156255 066 9156409
e-mail: dinglegc@iol.ie
web: www.dinglelinks.com
This most westerly course in Europe has a magnificent scenic location. It is a traditional links course with beautiful turf, many bunkers, a stream that comes into play on 14 holes and, usually, a prevailing wind.

18 holes, 6126 metres, Par 72, SSS 71, Course record 72. Club membership 432.
Visitors Mon-Sun & BHs. Booking required. Handicap certificate. Dress code. **Societies** Booking required. **Green Fees** Nov-Feb €40 per 18 holes (weekends €40); Mar, Apr, Oct €50 (€60); May-Sep €65 (€75). **Course Designer** Hackett/O'Connor Jnr **Facilities** **Leisure** buggies for hire May-Oct. **Location** 2.5km NW of village off R559

Guesthouse ♦♦♦♦♦ Gormans Clifftop House & Restaurant, Glaise Bheag, Ballydavid, DINGLE
☎ 066 9155162 9 en suite

CASTLEGREGORY Map 01 A2

Castlegregory Stradbally
☎ 066 7139444 066 7139958
e-mail: castlegregorygolf@oceanfree.net
web: www.castlegregorygolfclub.com
A links course sandwiched between the sea and a freshwater lake and mountains on two sides. The 3rd hole is visually superb with a 334-metre drive into the wind.

Continued

Championship Course

Ballybunion

Co Kerry

Ballybunion

Map 01 A3

Having excellent links, Ballybunion is recognised for its fine development of the natural terrain. Mr Murphy built the Old Course in 1906. With large sand dunes and an Atlantic backdrop, Ballybunion offers the golfer an exciting round of golf in a scenic location. But be warned, the Old course is difficult to play in the wind. President Clinton played Ballybunion on his historic visit to Ireland in 1998. Although overshadowed by the Old Course, the Cashen Course designed by Robert Trent Jones is also world class, characterised by narrow fairways, small greens and large dunes.

Sandhill Rd
☎ 068 27146 📠 068 27387
e-mail: bbgolfgc@ioe.ie
web: www.ballybuniongolfclub.ie

Old Course: 18 holes, 6083 metres, Par 71, SSS 72, Course record 67.
Cashen: 18 holes, Par 72, SSS 71, Course record 69.
Club membership 1500.

Visitors contact club for details.Handicap certificate. Dress code. Societies welcome. Green Fees Old Course: €150 per round: Cashen Course:€110 per round. Both courses €200. Prof Brian O'Callaghan Course Designer Simpson Facilities Leisure sauna. Location 2km S of town

9 holes, 2569 metres, Par 68, SSS 68, Course record 67. Club membership 426.
Visitors Mon-Sun. Booking required Sat & Sun. **Societies** Booking required. **Green Fees** €30 per 18 holes, €20 per 9 holes. **Course Designer** Dr Arthur Spring **Facilities** **Leisure** fishing. **Location** 3km W of town near Stradbally

Hotel ★★★ 68% Abbey Gate Hotel, Maine St, TRALEE ☎ 066 7129888 100 en suite

GLENBEIGH Map 01 A2

Dooks
☎ 066 9768205 📠 066 9768476
e-mail: office@dooks.com
web: dooks.com
Long-established course on the shore between the Kerry mountains and Dingle Bay. Sand dunes are a feature (the name Dooks is a derivation of the Gaelic word for sand bank) and the course offers a fine challenge in a superb Ring of Kerry location. Recently redesigned by Martin Hantree.
18 holes, 5944 metres, Par 71, SSS 70. Club membership 1000.
Visitors Mon-Sat & BHs. Booking required. Dress code. **Societies** Booking required. **Green Fees** €70 per 18 holes. **Course Designer** Martin Hawtree **Facilities** **Conf** Corporate Hospitality Days **Location** NE of village off on N70

Hotel ★★★ 70% Gleneagle Hotel, Muckeoss Rd, KILLARNEY ☎ 064 36000 250 en suite

KENMARE Map 01 B2

Ring of Kerry Golf & Country Club Templenoe
☎ 064 42000 📠 064 42533
e-mail: reservations@ringofkerrygolf.com
web: www.ringofkerrygolf.com
A world class golf facility with spectacular views across Kenmare Bay. Opened in 1998, the club has gone from strength to strength and is fast becoming a must-play course for golfers visiting the area. Every hole is memorable.

18 holes, 5788 metres, Par 72, SSS 73, Course record 68. Club membership 250.
Visitors Mon-Sun & BHs. Booking required Sat-Sun & BHs. Handicap certificate. Dress code. **Societies** Booking required. **Green Fees** €70 per round; €110 per 36 holes (€80/€120 weekends). **Prof** Adrian Whitehead **Course Designer** Eddie Hackett **Facilities** **Conf** facs Corporate Hospitality Days **Location** 6.5km W of Kenmare

Continued

Hotel ★★★★ Sheen Falls Lodge, KENMARE ☎ 064 41600 66 en suite

KILLARNEY Map 01 B2

Beaufort Churchtown, Beaufort
☎ 064 44440 📠 064 44752
e-mail: beaufortgc@eircom.net
web: www.beaufortgolfclub.com
A championship-standard parkland course designed by Dr Arthur Spring. This course is in the centre of south-west Ireland's golfing mecca. Ruins of a medieval castle dominate the back nine and the whole course is overlooked by the MacGillycuddy Reeks. The par 3 8th and par 4 11th are two of the most memorable holes.

18 holes, 6035 metres, Par 71, SSS 72, Course record 68. Club membership 350.
Visitors Mon-Sun & BHs. Booking required Fri-Sun & BHs. Dress code. **Societies** Booking required. **Green Fees** €50 (€60 weekends). **Prof** Keith Coveney **Course Designer** Arthur Spring **Facilities** **Conf** Corporate Hospitality Days **Location** 11km W of Killarney off N72

Hotel ★★★ 69% Castlerosse Hotel, KILLARNEY ☎ 064 31144 121 en suite

Castlerosse Hotel
☎ 064 31144 📠 064 31031
e-mail: res@castlerosse.ie
web: www.castlerosse.com
Set in mature parkland, the course commands stunning views and has fully irrigated USGA standard greens plus a practice green.
9 holes, 2761 metres, Par 36. Club membership 70.
Visitors Mon-Sun & BHs. Handicap certificate. **Societies** Booking required. **Green Fees** €28 for 18 holes, €17 for 9 holes. **Course Designer** H Wallace **Facilities** **Leisure** hard tennis courts, heated indoor swimming pool, sauna, gymnasium. **Conf** facs

Hotel ★★★ 69% Castlerosse Hotel, KILLARNEY ☎ 064 31144 121 en suite

Killarney Golf & Fishing Club Mahony's Point
☎ 064 31034 📠 064 33065
e-mail: reservations@killarney-golf.com
web: www.killarney-golf.com
The three courses are lakeside with tree-lined fairways; many bunkers and small lakes provide no mean challenge. Mahoney's Point Course has a particularly

Continued

testing par 5, 4, 3 finish and the courses call for great skill from the tee. Killarney has been the venue for many important events and is a favourite of many famous golfers.
Mahony's Point: 18 holes, 5826 metres, Par 72, SSS 72, Course record 64.
Killeen: 18 holes, 6001 metres, Par 72, SSS 72, Course record 68.
Lackabane: 18 holes, 6011 metres, Par 72, SSS 72.
Club membership 1600.
Visitors Mon-Sun & BHs. Booking required. Handicap certificate. Dress code. **Societies** Booking required. **Green Fees** per 18 holes: Mahony's Point €100, Killeen €120, Lackabane €80. **Prof** Tony Coveney **Course Designer** H Longhurst/Sir Guy Campbell **Facilities** ⊗ 𝍖 ⛳ ☕ 🍸 🏌 🏠 🏌 ✈ 🚗 ✈ **Leisure** sauna, gymnasium. **Conf** Corporate Hospitality Days **Location** 3.5km W on N72

Hotel ★★★★★ Aghadoe Heights Hotel, KILLARNEY ☎ 064 31766 73 en suite

KILLORGLIN Map 01 A2

Killorglin Stealroe
☎ 066 9761979 📠 066 9761437
e-mail: kilgolf@iol.ie
A parkland course designed by Eddie Hackett as a challenging but fair test of golf, surrounded by magnificent views.
18 holes, 5941 metres, Par 72, SSS 71, Course record 68.
Club membership 510.
Visitors Booking required. **Societies** Booking required. **Green Fees** Phone. **Prof** Hugh Duggan **Course Designer** Eddie Hackett **Facilities** ⊗ 𝍖 ⛳ ☕ 🍸 🏌 🏠 🏌 ✈ 🚗 ✈ **Leisure** fishing. **Location** 3km NE on N70

Guest House ♦♦♦♦ The Grove Lodge, Killarney Rd, KILLORGLIN ☎ 066 9761157 & 08720 73238 📠 066 9762330 10 en suite

PARKNASILLA Map 01 A2

Parknasilla
☎ 064 45122 📠 064 45323

9 holes, 5400 metres, Par 70, SSS 69.
Course Designer Arthur Spring **Location** Near village off N70
Telephone for further details

Hotel ★★★★ 75% Great Southern Hotel, PARKNASILLA ☎ 064 45122 24 en suite 59 annexe en suite

TRALEE Map 01 A2

Tralee West Barrow
☎ 066 7136379 📠 066 7136008
e-mail: info@traleegolfclub.com
web: www.traleegolfclub.com
The first Arnold Palmer designed course in Europe, this magnificent 18-hole links is set in spectacular scenery on the Barrow peninsula, surrounded on three sides by the sea. Perhaps the most memorable hole is the par 4 17th which plays from a high tee, across a deep gorge to a green perched high against a backdrop of mountains. The back nine is very difficult and challenging. Not suitable for beginners.
18 holes, 5970 metres, Par 71, SSS 71, Course record 66.
Club membership 1306.
Visitors Booking required. Handicap certificate. **Societies** weekdays only; must contact in writing. **Green Fees** Phone. **Prof** David Power **Course Designer** Arnold Palmer **Facilities** ⊗ 𝍖 ⛳ ☕ 🍸 🏌 🏠 🏌 ✈ **Location** 13km NW of Tralee off R558

Hotel ★★★★ 70% Meadowlands Hotel, Oakpark, TRALEE ☎ 066 7180444 58 en suite

WATERVILLE (AN COIREÁN) Map 01 A2

Waterville House & Golf Links
☎ 066 9474102 📠 066 9474482
e-mail: wvgolf@iol.ie
web: www.watervillegolflink.ie
18 holes, 6072 metres, Par 72, SSS 72, Course record 65.
Course Designer Eddie Hackett/Tom Fazio **Location** 0.5km from Waterville on N70
Telephone for further details

Hotel ★★★ 66% Derrynane Hotel, CAHERDANIEL ☎ 066 9475136 73 en suite

CO KILDARE

ATHY Map 01 C3

Athy Geraldine
☎ 059 8631729 📠 059 8634710
e-mail: info@athygolfclub.com
web: www.athygolfclub.com
The course was upgraded in 2003 to include new tees, new bunkers, a new par 5 with a lake feature and trees have been planted to create a more exacting course. The last five holes are now more demanding and the 16th and 17th are considered to be among the most difficult consecutive par 4s found anywhere. The 18th is a testing finishing hole with bunkers off the tee and also for the next two shots.
18 holes, 5921 metres, Par 72, SSS 71.
Club membership 800.
Visitors Booking required. **Societies** Booking required. **Green Fees** Phone. **Course Designer** Jeff Howes **Facilities** ⊗ 𝍖 by arrangement ⛳ ☕ 🍸 🏌 ✈ 🚗 ✈ **Conf** facs Corporate Hospitality Days **Location** 1.6km NE of town on N78

Guest House ♦♦♦♦♦ Coursetown Country House, Stradbally Rd, ATHY ☎ 059 8631101 5 en suite

CARBURY Map 01 C4

Highfield Highfield House

☎ 046 9731021 🖷 046 9731021
e-mail: highfieldgolf@eircom.ie
web: www.highfield-golf.ie

Relatively flat parkland with interesting undulations, enhanced by the fast stream that runs through many holes. The 4th dog-legs over the lake, the 7th is a great par 5 with a challenging green, the 10th par 3 is over rushes onto a plateau green (out of bounds on left). The 1st tee is situated on top of the new cedar log clubhouse, which provides a spectacular starting point.

18 holes, 5493 metres, Par 70, SSS 69.
Club membership 500.

Visitors Mon-Sun & BHs. Booking required Fri-Sun & BHs. Dress code. **Societies** Booking required. **Green Fees** Mon-Fri €20-£30 per day (€30-€40 weekends). **Prof** Conor Devery **Course Designer** Alan Duggan **Facilities** **Conf** facs Corporate Hospitality Days **Location** 4.5km NW of village off R402

Hotel ★★★★ 72% Keadeen Hotel, NEWBRIDGE
☎ 045 431666 75 en suite

CASTLEDERMOT Map 01 C3

Kilkea Castle

☎ 0503 45555 🖷 0503 45505
e-mail: kilkeagolfclub@eircom.net
web: www.kilkeacastlehotelgolf.com
18 holes, 6200 metres, Par 71, SSS 71.
Telephone for further details

Hotel ★★★ 71% Seven Oaks Hotel, Athy Rd, CARLOW
☎ 059 913 1308 59 en suite

DONADEA Map 01 C4

Knockanally Golf & Country Club

☎ 045 869322 🖷 045 869322
e-mail: golf@knockanally.com
web: www.knockanally.com

Home of the Irish International Professional Matchplay championship, this parkland course is set in a former estate, with a Palladian-style clubhouse.

18 holes, 5930 metres, Par 72, SSS 72, Course record 66.
Club membership 500.

Visitors Mon-Sun & BHs. Booking required Sat & Sun. Dress code. **Societies** Booking required. **Green Fees** €35 per round (€50 weekends). **Prof** Martin Darcy **Course Designer** Noel Lyons **Facilities** **Leisure** fishing. **Conf** Corporate Hospitality Days **Location** 6km NW of village off M4

Hotel ★★★ 67% The Hamlet Court Hotel, Johnstownbridge, ENFIELD ☎ 046 954 1200 30 en suite
See advertisement on page 466

KILDARE Map 01 C3

Cill Dara Cill Dara, Little Curragh

☎ 045 521295 & 521433
e-mail: cilldaragolfclub@ireland.com
9 holes, 5852 metres, Par 71, SSS 70, Course record 64.
Location 1.6km E of town
Telephone for further details

Hotel ★★★★ 72% Keadeen Hotel, NEWBRIDGE
☎ 045 431666 75 en suite

The Curragh Curragh

☎ 045 441238 & 441714 🖷 045 441714
18 holes, 6035 metres, Par 72, SSS 71, Course record 63.
Location E of town off R413
Telephone for further details

Hotel ★★★★ 72% Keadeen Hotel, NEWBRIDGE
☎ 045 431666 75 en suite

KILL Map 01 D4

Killeen

☎ 045 866003 🖷 045 875881
e-mail: admin@killeengc.ie
18 holes, 5561 metres, Par 71, SSS 71, Course record 70.
Course Designer Pat Ruddy/M Kelly **Location** Signed off N7 at Kill
Telephone for further details

Hotel U Barberstown Castle, STRAFFAN ☎ 01 6288157 59 en suite

MAYNOOTH Map 01 D4

Carton House

☎ 01 5052000 🖷 01 6286555
e-mail: reservations@cartonhouse.com
web: www.cartonhouse.com

The O'Meara is a parkland course surrounded by the ancient specimen trees of this fine estate. Feature holes include the 14th, 15th and 16th - a pair of par 3s wrapped around a par 5 crossing the loops of the river Rye. The Montgomerie plays like a links course with bunker hazards and a prevailing wind. The fairways run firm and fast and the bunker complexes demand strategic and shot making excellence and the ground game is always in play.

O'Meara: 18 holes, 6042 metres, Par 72, SSS 72.
Montgomerie: 18 holes, 6237 metres, Par 72, SSS 73, Course record 68.
Club membership 600.

Visitors Mon-Sun & BHs. Booking required. Handicap certificate. Dress code. **Societies** Booking required. **Green Fees** Apr: €85 per round , May-Oct: €115 per round (€95/€135 Fri-Sun). **Prof** Francis Howley **Course Designer** O'Meara/Lobb & Montgomerie/Edy **Facilities** **Leisure** fishing, sauna, solarium, gymnasium. **Conf** facs Corporate Hospitality Days **Location** N4 W from Dublin, exit Leixlip West, signed

The K Club

Co Kildare

Straffan

Map 01 D4

The K Club was the venue for the Ryder Cup in 2006, the first time that Ireland has hosted the event. The course reflects the personality of its architect, Arnold Palmer, covering 220 acres of Kildare woodland, with 14 man-made lakes and the River Liffey providing the water hazards. From the instant you arrive at the 1st tee, you are enveloped by a unique atmosphere: the courses are both cavalier and charismatic. The Palmer Course is one of Europe's most spectacular courses, charming, enticing, and invariably bringing out the very best in your game. The best way to describe the Smurfit Course is that of an inland links, but its attributes do not stop there. The course has many dramatic landscapes with dunes moulding throughout, while some 14 acres of water have been worked in to the design, especially through the final holes 13-18; a watery grave awaits many on the home stretch. The course is entirely different from the Palmer Course located just across the River Liffey.

☎ 01 6017300 📠 01 6017399
e-mail: golf@kclub.ie
web: www.kclub.ie

Palmer Course: 18 holes, 6526 metres, Par 74, SSS 72, Course record 65.
Smurfit Course: 18 holes, 6636 metres, Par 72, SSS 72.
Club membership 540.

Visitors Booking required. **Societies** Booking required. **Green Fees** Palmer €350, Smurfit €130. Winter reduced rates. **Prof** John McHenry/Peter O'Hagan **Course Designer** Arnold Palmer **Facilities** **Leisure** heated indoor swimming pool, fishing, sauna, solarium, gymnasium. **Conf facs** Corporate Hospitality Days **Location** W of village off R403

NAAS Map 01 D4

Craddockstown Blessington Rd
☎ 045 897610 🖹 045 896968
e-mail: gaynolan@craddockstown.com
web: www.craddockstown.com
A parkland course with easy walking. A major redevelopment was completed in 2004 with new tee boxes, 2 new greens, many water features, fairway improvements and the redevelopment of all greenside bunkers.
18 holes, 5748 metres, Par 72, SSS 72, Course record 66. Club membership 800.
Visitors Mon-Tue, Thu-Fri & Sun. Booking required. Dress code. **Societies** Booking required. **Green Fees** Mon-Thu €40, Fri €45, Sat-Sun & BHs €50. **Course Designer** A Spring & R Jones **Facilities** **Conf** facs Corporate Hospitality Days **Location** SE of town off R410

Hotel ★★★ 59% Ambassador Hotel, KILL
☎ 045 877064 36 en suite

Naas Kerdiffstown
☎ 045 897509 & 874644 🖹 045 896109
e-mail: naasgolfclubisdn@eircom.net
web: naasgolfclub.com
Recent completed renovations have made this course a truly unique challenge with water hazards, bunkers and sand-based greens. The par 3 17th hole is now one of the most challenging tee shots where a round of golf can be won or lost.
18 holes, 5663 metres, Par 71, SSS 69, Course record 65. Club membership 1200.
Visitors Mon, Wed, Fri-Sat & BHs. Booking required Sat. Dress code. **Societies** Booking required. **Green Fees** €40 (€45 weekends & bank holiday). **Course Designer** E Hackett/A Spring/J Howes **Facilities** **Location** NE of town, off N7 onto Johnstown-Sallins road

STRAFFAN Map 01 D4

Castlewarden
☎ 01 4589254 & 4589838 🖹 01 4588972
e-mail: info@castlewardengolfclub.com
web: www.castlewardengolfclub.com
18 holes, 5940 metres, Par 72, SSS 70.
Course Designer Tommy Halpin **Location** 6km S of village off N7
Telephone for further details

Hotel ★★★ 59% Ambassador Hotel, KILL
☎ 045 877064 36 en suite

The K Club **see page 459**

Hotel ★★★★★ The K Club, STRAFFAN
☎ 01 6017200 69 en suite 10 annexe en suite

CO KILKENNY

CALLAN Map 01 C3

Callan Geraldine
☎ 056 25136 & 25949 🖹 056 55155
e-mail: info@callangolfclub.com
web: www.callangolfclub.com
18 holes, 5872 metres, Par 72, SSS 70, Course record 66.
Course Designer B Moore/J Power **Location** 1.6km SE of village on R699
Telephone for further details

Hotel ★★★ 75% Newpark Hotel, KILKENNY
☎ 056 776 0500 130 en suite

KILKENNY Map 01 C3

Kilkenny Glendine
☎ 056 7765400 🖹 056 7723593
e-mail: enquiries@kilkennygolfclub.com
web: www.kilkennygolfclub.com
18 holes, 5925 metres, Par 71, SSS 70, Course record 68.
Location 1.6km N of town on N77
Telephone for further details

Hotel ★★★ 67% Langtons Hotel, 69 John St, KILKENNY ☎ 056 776 5133 552 1728 🖹 056 776 3693 14 en suite 16 annexe en suite

THOMASTOWN Map 01 C3

Mount Juliet Hotel & Golf Club **see page 461**

Hotel ★★★★ Mount Juliet Conrad Hotel, THOMASTOWN ☎ 056 777 3000 32 en suite 27 annexe en suite

Hotel ★★★★ 71% Kilkenny River Court Hotel, The Bridge, John St, KILKENNY ☎ 056 772 3388 🖹 056 772 3389 90 en suite

Hotel ★★★ 75% Newpark Hotel, KILKENNY
☎ 056 776 0500 🖹 056 776 0555 130 en suite

Hotel ★★★ 67% Langtons Hotel, 69 John St, KILKENNY ☎ 056 776 5133 552 1728 🖹 056 776 3693 14 en suite 16 annexe en suite

CO LAOIS

ABBEYLEIX Map 01 C3

Abbeyleix Rathmoyle
☎ 00353 31450 🖹 0502 30108
e-mail: info@abbeyleixgolfclub.ie
web: www.abbeyleixgolfclub.ie
A pleasant, parkland 18-hole course. Undulating with water features at five holes.
18 holes, 5557 metres, Par 72, SSS 70. Club membership 470.
Visitors Mon-Sun. Booking required Sat-Sun. **Societies** Booking required. **Green Fees** €25 per round (€30 weekends). **Course Designer** Mel Flanagan **Facilities** **Location** 0.6km from Abbeyleix on Ballyroan road

Hotel ★★★ 75% Newpark Hotel, KILKENNY
☎ 056 776 0500 130 en suite

MOUNTRATH Map 01 C3

Mountrath Knockanina
☎ 0502 32558 & 32643 (office) 🖹 0502 32643
e-mail: info@mountrathgolfclub.ie
web: www.mountrathgolfclub.ie
A picturesque course at the foot of the Slieve Bloom Mountains in central Ireland. The 18-hole course has

Continued

Championship Course

Mount Juliet Hotel

Co Kilkenny

Thomastown

Map 01 C3

Venue for the American Express Championship in 2002 and 2004, Mount Juliet's superb 18-hole course was designed by Jack Nicklaus. It has also hosted many prestigious events including the Irish Open on three occasions. The course has a cleverly concealed drainage and irrigation system, perfect even when inclement weather would otherwise halt play. It takes advantage of the estate's mature landscape to provide a world-class 72-par challenge for professionals and high-handicap golfers alike. A unique three-hole golfing academy has been added to allow novice and experienced players ample opportunity to improve their game, while a new 18-hole putting course provides an extra dimension of golfing pleasure and is the venue for the National Putting Championship.

☎ 056 7773064 📠 056 7773078
e-mail: golfinfo@mountjuliet.ie
web: www.mountjuliet.com

18 holes, 6639 metres, Par 72, SSS 75, Course record 62.
Club membership 500.

Visitors Mon-Sun & BHs. Booking required Sat-Sun. Dress code. **Societies** Booking required. **Green Fees** from €75 in winter to €160 weekend summer. **Prof** Sean Cotter **Course Designer** Jack Nicklaus **Facilities** **Leisure** hard tennis courts, heated indoor swimming pool, fishing, sauna, solarium, gymnasium, Archery/clay shooting/equestrian. **Conf** facs Corporate Hospitality Days **Location** 4km S of town off N9

fine fairways and well-bunkered greens, the River Nore flows through the course.
18 holes, 5732 metres, Par 71, SSS 70, Course record 68. Club membership 600.
Visitors Mon-Sun & BHs. Booking required Sat-Sun & BHs. **Societies** Booking required. **Green Fees** 18 holes €25 (weekends €30). **Facilities** by arrangement by arrangement **Location** 2.5km SW of town off N7

Hotel ★★★★ 72% Keadeen Hotel, NEWBRIDGE
☎ 045 431666 75 en suite

PORTARLINGTON Map 01 C3

Portarlington Garryhinch
☎ 0502 23115 0502 23044
e-mail: portalingtongc@eircom.net
web: www.portalingtongolf.com
Lovely parkland course designed around a pine forest. It is bounded on the 16th and 17th by the River Barrow which makes the back 9 very challenging.
18 holes, 5723 metres, Par 71, SSS 70, Course record 66. Club membership 700.
Visitors contact club for details. **Societies** welcome. **Green Fees** €20 per round (€25 weekends). **Course Designer** Eddie Hackett **Facilities** **Conf** Corporate Hospitality Days **Location** 6.5km SW of town on R423

Hotel ★★★★ 72% Keadeen Hotel, NEWBRIDGE
☎ 045 431666 75 en suite

PORTLAOISE Map 01 C3

The Heath
☎ 0502 46533 & 46045 (office) 0502 46866
e-mail: info@theheathgc.ie
web: www.theheathgc.ie
Course noted for its rough heather and gorze furze and scenic views of the rolling hills of Co Laois. Remarkably dry conditions all year round.
18 holes, 5857 metres, Par 71, SSS 70, Course record 67. Club membership 950.
Visitors Mon-Sat. Booking required. **Societies** Booking required. **Green Fees** €20 per round (€30 weekends). **Prof** Mark O'Boyle **Course Designer** Jeff Howes **Facilities** **Location** 6.5km N on N7

Hotel ★★★★ 72% Keadeen Hotel, NEWBRIDGE
☎ 045 431666 75 en suite

RATHDOWNEY Map 01 C3

Rathdowney
☎ 0505 46170 0505 46065
e-mail: rathdowneygolf@eircom.net
web: rathdowneygolfclub.com
An 18-hole parkland course, with undulating terrain. The 17th hole is a tricky par 3, 12th and 15th are particularly tough par 4s and the 6th is a challenging par 5 (503 metres) into the prevailing wind. A good test for golfers of all abilities.
18 holes, 5894 metres, Par 71, SSS 70, Course record 67. Club membership 500.
Visitors Mon-Sun & BHs. Booking required Fri-Sun & BHs. Dress code. **Societies** Booking required. **Green Fees** €25. **Course Designer** Eddie Hackett **Facilities** **Conf** Corporate Hospitality Days **Location** 0.8km SE, Johnstown signs from town square

Continued

Hotel ★★★ 75% Newpark Hotel, KILKENNY
☎ 056 776 0500 130 en suite

CO LEITRIM

BALLINAMORE Map 01 C4

Ballinamore
☎ 071 9644346
A very dry and very testing nine-hole parkland course along the Ballinamore-Ballyconnell Canal. Not busy on weekdays which makes it ideal for high handicap golfers, while at the same time it tests the ability of even a scratch golfer.
9 holes, 5194 metres, Par 70, SSS 68, Course record 66. Club membership 300.
Visitors contact club for details. Booking required Sat-Sun & BHs. **Societies** welcome. **Green Fees** €20 per day. **Course Designer** A Spring **Facilities** **Leisure** fishing. **Location** 3km W of town along Shannon-Erne canal

Hotel ★★★★ 70% Slieve Russell Hotel Golf and Country Club, BALLYCONNELL ☎ 049 9526444 219 en suite

CARRICK-ON-SHANNON Map 01 C4

Carrick-on-Shannon Woodbrook
☎ 071 9667015 071 9667015
e-mail: ckgc@eircom.net
9 holes, 5545 metres, Par 70, SSS 68.
Course Designer Eddie Hackett **Location** 6.5km W of town on N4
Telephone for further details

Hotel ★★★★ 70% Slieve Russell Hotel Golf and Country Club, BALLYCONNELL ☎ 049 9526444 219 en suite

CO LIMERICK

ADARE Map 01 B3

Adare Manor
☎ 061 396204 061 396800
e-mail: info@adaremanorgolfclub.com
web: www.adaremanorgolfclub.com
18 holes, 5304 metres, Par 69, SSS 69, Course record 63.
Course Designer Ben Sayers/Eddie Hackett **Location** NE of town off N21
Telephone for further details

Hotel ★★★★ 72% Dunraven Arms Hotel, ADARE
☎ 061 396633 75 en suite

LIMERICK Map 01 B3

Castletroy Castletroy
☎ 061 335753 & 335261 061 335373
e-mail: cgc@iol.ie
web: www.castletroygolfclub.com
Parkland course with out of bounds on the left of the first two holes. The long par 5 10th features a narrow entrance to a green guarded by a stream. The par 3 13th has a panoramic view of the course and the surrounding countryside from the tee. The 18th is a daunting finish, along a valley with the ground rising towards the green, which is protected on both sides by bunkers.

Continued

18 holes, 5854 metres, Par 71, SSS 70, Course record 65. Club membership 1062.
Visitors must contact in advance & have handicap certificate but may not play Sun. **Societies** apply in writing. **Green Fees** not confirmed. **Course Designer** Eddie Connaughton **Facilities** **Conf** Corporate Hospitality Days **Location** 5km E of city centre

Hotel ★★★★ 72% Castletroy Park Hotel, Dublin Rd, LIMERICK ☎ 061 335566 107 en suite

Limerick Ballyclough
☎ 061 415146 🖷 061 319219
e-mail: pat.murray@limerickgc.com
web: www.limerickgc.com
Tree-lined parkland course. The club is the only Irish winner of the European Cup Winners Team Championship.
18 holes, 5938 metres, Par 72, SSS 71, Course record 63. Club membership 1500.
Visitors Mon, Wed-Sun & BHs. Booking required Mon-Sun & BHs. Handicap certificate. Dress code. **Societies** Booking required. **Green Fees** €50 Mon-Thu (€70 Fri-Sun & BHs). **Prof** Lee Harrington/Denise Mullew **Course Designer** A MacKenzie **Facilities** **Conf** Corporate Hospitality Days **Location** 5km S on R511

Limerick County Golf & Country Club
Ballyneety
☎ 061 351881 🖷 061 351384
e-mail: lcgolf@ioi.ie
web: www.limerickcounty.com
Limerick County was designed by Des Smyth and presents beautifully because of the strategic location of the main features. It stretches over undulating terrain with one elevated section providing views of the surrounding countryside. It features over 70 bunkers with six lakes and several unique design features.
18 holes, 5876 metres, Par 72, SSS 71, Course record 70. Club membership 800.
Visitors Mon-Sun & BHs. Booking required Fri-Sun & BHs. Dress code. **Societies** Booking required. **Green Fees** €40 per round. **Prof** Donal McSweeney **Course Designer** Des Smyth **Facilities** **Conf** facs Corporate Hospitality Days **Location** 8km SE of city on R512

Hotel ★★★ 67% Hotel Greenhills, Caherdavin, LIMERICK ☎ 061 453033 18 rms (13 en suite)

NEWCASTLE WEST Map 01 B3

Killeline Cork Rd
☎ 069 61600 🖷 069 77428
e-mail: killeline@eircom.net
web: www.killeline.com
18 holes, 6100 metres, Par 72, SSS 68.
Location 0.4km off N21
Telephone for further details

Hotel ★★★★ 72% Dunraven Arms Hotel, ADARE ☎ 061 396633 75 en suite

Newcastle West Ardagh
☎ 069 76500 🖷 069 76511
e-mail: ncwgolf@eircom.net

18 holes, 5615 metres, Par 71, SSS 72, Course record 67.
Course Designer Dr Arthur Spring **Location** 3.5km off N21
Telephone for further details

Hotel ★★★★ 72% Dunraven Arms Hotel, ADARE ☎ 061 396633 75 en suite

CO LONGFORD

LONGFORD Map 01 C4

County Longford Glack, Dublin Rd
☎ 043 46310 🖷 043 47082
e-mail: colonggolf@eircom.net
A lovely 18-hole parkland course with lots of trees.
18 holes, 5766 metres, Par 72, Course record 71. Club membership 819.
Visitors Mon-Sun & BHs. Booking required. **Societies** Booking required. **Green Fees** €30 per round (€35 Sat, Sun & BHs). **Course Designer** Irish Golf Design **Facilities** **Location** E of town

Hotel ★★★ 71% Abbey Hotel, Galway Rd, ROSCOMMON ☎ 090 662 6240 50 en suite

CO LOUTH

ARDEE Map 01 D4

Ardee Townparks
☎ 041 6853227 🖷 041 6856137
e-mail: ardeegolfclub@eircom.net
web: www.ardeegolfclub.com
Pleasant parkland with mature trees and natural water features. The 13th hole, a par 3 over water, is the main feature of the course.
18 holes, 5934 metres, Par 71, SSS 72, Course record 64. Club membership 680.
Visitors contact club for details. Dress code. **Societies** Booking required. **Green Fees** €35 per 18 holes (€50 Sat). **Prof** Scott Kirkpatrick **Course Designer** Eddie Hackett & Declan Branigan **Facilities** **Conf** Corporate Hospitality Days **Location** N33 to Ardee, 400 metres from Fair Green

Hotel ★★★★ 71% Ballymascanlon House Hotel, DUNDALK ☎ 042 9358200 90 en suite

BALTRAY Map 01 D4

County Louth
☎ 041 9881530 041 9881531
e-mail: reservations@countylouthgolfclub.com
web: www.countylouthgolfclub.com
Generally held to have the best greens in Ireland, this links course was designed by Tom Simpson to have well-guarded and attractive greens without being overly dependant on bunkers. It provides a good test for the modern champion, notably as the annual venue for the East of Ireland Amateur Open.
18 holes, 6102 metres, Par 72, SSS 72, Course record 64. Club membership 1342.
Visitors must contact in advance. **Societies** by arrangement. **Green Fees** Phone. **Prof** Paddy McGuirk **Course Designer** Tom Simpson **Facilities** **Leisure** hard tennis courts. **Location** 8km NE of Drogheda

DUNDALK Map 01 D4

Ballymascanlon House Hotel
☎ 042 9358200 042 9371598
e-mail: info@ballymascanlon.com
web: www.ballymascanlon.com
A testing 18-hole parkland course with numerous water hazards and two difficult holes through woodland, this very scenic course is set at the edge of the Cooley Mountains.

18 holes, 5073 metres, Par 68, SSS 66.
Visitors Mon-Sun & BHs. Booking required Fri-Sun & BHs. Dress code. **Societies** Booking required. **Green Fees** Phone. **Course Designer** Craddock/Ruddy **Facilities** **Leisure** hard tennis courts, heated indoor swimming pool, sauna, gymnasium. **Conf** facs Corporate Hospitality Days **Location** 5km NE of town on R173

Hotel ★★★★ 71% Ballymascanlon House Hotel, DUNDALK ☎ 042 9358200 90 en suite

Dundalk Blackrock
☎ 042 9321731 042 9322022
e-mail: manager@dundalkgolfclub.ie
web: www.dundalkgolfclub.ie
A championship course with fine mountain and sea views.
18 holes, 6028 metres, Par 72, SSS 71. Club membership 1500.
Visitors must contact in advance and may not play Tue or Sun. **Societies** must apply in writing. **Green Fees** Phone. **Prof** Leslie Walker **Facilities** **Leisure** sauna. **Conf** Corporate Hospitality Days **Location** 4km S of town on R172 coast road

Continued

Hotel ★★★★ 71% Ballymascanlon House Hotel, DUNDALK ☎ 042 9358200 90 en suite

Killin Park Killin Park
☎ 042 9339303 042 9320848
e-mail: johnfmcann@eircom.net
Opened in 1991 and designed by Eddie Hackett, this undulating 18-hole parkland course has mature woodland and river features. It provides challenging golf and breathtaking scenery. Bordered on the north side by Killin Wood and on the south by the Castletown River.
18 holes, 4840 metres, Par 69, SSS 65, Course record 65. Club membership 300.
Visitors Mon-Sun & BHs. Booking required Sat-Sun & BHs. Dress code. **Societies** Booking required. **Green Fees** €22 per 18 holes (€27 Sat, Sun & BHs). **Prof** Stephen Hoey **Course Designer** Eddie Hackett **Facilities** by arrangement **Location** 4.5km NW of village off N53

Hotel ★★★★ 71% Ballymascanlon House Hotel, DUNDALK ☎ 042 9358200 90 en suite

GREENORE Map 01 D4

Greenore
☎ 042 9373212 & 9373678 042 9383898
e-mail: greenoregolfclub@eircom.net
web: www.greenoregolf.com
Situated amid beautiful scenery on the shores of Carlingford Lough, with views of the Mourne Mountains. The pine trees here are an unusual feature on a part-links course. There are quite a number of water facilities, tight fairways and very good greens.
18 holes, 6078 metres, Par 71, SSS 73, Course record 69. Club membership 1035.
Visitors Mon-Sun & BHs. Booking required. Dress code. **Societies** welcome. **Green Fees** €35 per round (€50 Sat, Sun & BHs). **Prof** Mr Robert Giles **Course Designer** Eddie Hackett **Facilities** **Leisure** Golf lessons available on request but must be pre booked. **Conf** Corporate Hospitality Days **Location** Near village off R175

Hotel ★★★★ 71% Ballymascanlon House Hotel, DUNDALK ☎ 042 9358200 90 en suite

TERMONFECKIN Map 01 D4

Seapoint
☎ 041 9822333 041 9822331
e-mail: golflinks@seepoint.ie
web: www.seapointgolfclub.com
A premier championship links course with a particularly interesting 17th hole.
18 holes, 6470 metres, Par 72, SSS 74. Club membership 580.
Visitors phone in advance for restrictions. **Societies** Booking required. **Green Fees** Phone. **Prof** David Carroll **Course Designer** Des Smyth **Facilities** **Location** 6.5km NE of Drogheda

Hotel ★★★ 67% Boyne Valley Hotel & Country Club, Stameen, Dublin Rd, DROGHEDA ☎ 041 9837737 73 en suite

CO MAYO

BALLINA Map 01 B4

Ballina Mossgrove, Shanaghy
☎ 096 21050 🖹 096 21718
e-mail: ballinagc@eircom.net
Undulating but mostly flat inland course.
18 holes, 5581 metres, Par 71, SSS 69, Course record 69. Club membership 520.
Visitors Mon-Sun & BHs. Booking required. Handicap certificate. Dress code. **Societies** Booking required. **Green Fees** Phone. **Prof** Eddie Tracey **Course Designer** E Hackett **Facilities** **Location** 1.5km W of town on R294

BALLINROBE Map 01 B4

Ballinrobe Cloonacastle
☎ 094 9541118 🖹 094 9541889
e-mail: info@ballinrobegolfclub.com
web: ballinrobegolfclub.com
A championship parkland 18-hole course, set in the mature woodlands of a historic estate at Cloonacastle. The layout of the course incorporates seven man-made lakes with the River Robe flowing at the back of the 3rd and 5th greens. Ballinrobe is full of character, typified by the 19th-century residence now used as the clubhouse.
18 holes, 6334 metres, Par 73, SSS 72, Course record 67. Club membership 650.
Visitors Mon-Sat & BHs. Booking required. Dress code. **Societies** Booking required. **Green Fees** €28 (€33 Sat). **Prof** Courtney Cougar **Course Designer** Eddie Hackett **Facilities** **Conf** facs Corporate Hospitality Days **Location** NE of town on R331

BALLYHAUNIS Map 01 B4

Ballyhaunis Coolnaha
☎ 0907 30014 🖹 094 81829
e-mail: tmack@tinet.ie
9 holes, 5413 metres, Par 70, SSS 68, Course record 68.
Location 5km N on N83
Telephone for further details

BELMULLET (BÉAL AN MHUIRTHEAD) Map 01 A5

Carne Carne
☎ 097 82292 🖹 097 81477
e-mail: carngolf@iol.ie
web: www.carnegolflinks.com
A wild tumultuous roller-coaster landscape, which has been shaped into an inspirational links course by Eddie Hackett.

18 holes, 6119 metres, Par 72, SSS 72, Course record 66. Club membership 460.
Visitors Booking required. **Societies** Booking required. **Green Fees** Phone. **Course Designer** Eddie Hackett **Facilities** **Location** 3km W of town off R313

CASTLEBAR Map 01 B4

Castlebar Hawthorn Av, Rocklands
☎ 094 21649 🖹 094 26088
e-mail: info@castlebargolfclub.ie
web: www.castlebargolfclub.ie
Course opened September 2000. Fast greens with severe borrows. Accuracy is essential from the tee on most holes. Long difficult course from blue (championship) tees.
18 holes, 5698 metres, Par 71, SSS 70. Club membership 650.
Visitors Mon-Sat & BHs. Booking required. Dress code. **Societies** Booking required. **Green Fees** €25 per day (€32 Fri, Sat & Sun). **Prof** David McQuillan **Course Designer** Peter McEvoy **Facilities** **Location** 1.6km SE of town off N84

Hotel ★★ 64% Welcome Inn Hotel, CASTLEBAR
☎ 094 902 2288 & 902 2054 🖹 094 902 1766 40 en suite

CLAREMORRIS Map 01 B4

Claremorris Castlemacgarrett
☎ 094 93 71527 🖹 094 93 72919
e-mail: info@claremorrisgolfclub.com
web: www.claremorrisgolfclub.com
A 18-hole parkland course designed by Tom Craddock, designer of Druids Glen. It consists of many eye-catching water features, bunkers, trees and wooded backgrounds. The feature hole is the short par 4 14th with its island green.
18 holes, 6600 metres, Par 73, SSS 70, Course record 68. Club membership 600.
Visitors Mon-Sat & BHs. Booking required Thu, Sat & BHs. Dress code. **Societies** Booking required. **Green Fees** Oct-Mar €26, €32 per round; Apr-Sep €32/€40. **Course Designer** Tom Craddock **Facilities** **Location** 2km S of town on N17

Hotel ★★★ 64% Belmont Hotel, KNOCK
☎ 094 094 938 8122 63 en suite

KEEL Map 01 A4

Achill Achill Island, Westport
☎ 098 43456
e-mail: achillgolfclub@eircom.net
Seaside links in a scenic location by the Atlantic Ocean.
9 holes, 2723 metres, Par 70, SSS 66, Course record 69. Club membership 240.
Visitors welcome but cannot play on some Sundays **Societies** must write or telephone in advance. **Green Fees** Phone. **Course Designer** Paddy Skirrit **Facilities** **Location** E of Keel on R319

Hotel ★★★ 78% Hotel Westport Conference & Leisure Centre, Newport Rd, WESTPORT ☎ 098 25122 129 en suite

Continued

SWINFORD Map 01 B4

Swinford Brabazon Park
☎ 094 92 51378 🖷 094 92 51378
e-mail: sheetsjj@eircom.net
web: www.swinfordgolf.com
Pleasant parkland with good views of the beautiful surrounding countryside. Tough par 3s.
9 holes, 5542 metres, Par 70, SSS 68.
Club membership 300.
Visitors Mon-Sun & BHs. **Societies** Booking required. **Green Fees** €20 per day. **Facilities** **Location** S of town on R320

Hotel ★★ 64% Welcome Inn Hotel, CASTLEBAR ☎ 094 902 2288 & 902 2054 🖷 094 902 1766 40 en suite

WESTPORT Map 01 B4

Westport Carrowholly
☎ 098 28262 & 27070 🖷 098 27217
e-mail: wpgolf@eircom.net
web: www.golfwestport.com
This is a beautiful course with wonderful views of Clew Bay, with its 365 islands, and the holy mountain called Croagh Patrick, famous for the annual pilgrimage to its summit. Golfers indulge in a different kind of penance on this challenging course with many memorable holes. Perhaps the most exciting is the par 5 15th, 580yds long and featuring a long carry from the tee over an inlet of Clew Bay.
18 holes, 6096 metres, Par 73, SSS 71, Course record 61.
Club membership 600.
Visitors Mon-Sun & BHs. Booking required Fri-Sun & BHs. Dress code. **Societies** Booking required. **Green Fees** €38/€45 per round (weekends €42/€55). **Prof** Alex Mealia **Course Designer** Fred Hawtree **Facilities** **Conf** Corporate Hospitality Days **Location** 4km from town off N59

Hotel ★★★ 78% Hotel Westport Conference & Leisure Centre, Newport Rd, WESTPORT ☎ 098 25122 129 en suite

Where to stay, where to eat?
Visit www.theAA.com

CO MEATH

BETTYSTOWN Map 01 D4

Laytown & Bettystown
☎ 041 9827170 🖷 041 28506
e-mail: links@landb.ie
web: www.landb.ie
A very competitive and trying links course.
18 holes, 5652 metres, Par 71, SSS 70, Course record 65.
Club membership 950.
Visitors contact club for details. Handicap certificate. Dress code. **Societies** Booking required. **Green Fees** €60 per 18 holes (€75 Sat, Sun & BHs). **Prof** Robert J Browne **Facilities** **Leisure** hard tennis courts. **Location** N of village on R150

DUNSHAUGHLIN Map 01 D4

Black Bush Thomastown
☎ 01 8250021 🖷 01 8250400
e-mail: info@blackbushgolfclub.ie
web: www.blackbushgolfclub.ie
Three 9-hole courses, giving three possible 18-hole combinations, set in lovely parkland, with a lake providing a hazard at the 1st. Recently added creeks, trees and bunkers make for challenging and accurate shot-making.
Black Bush:18 holes, 6337 metres, Par 73, SSS 72.
Agore: 18 holes, 6033 metres, Par 71, SSS 69.
Thomastown: 18 holes, 5882 metres, Par 70, SSS 68.
Club membership 950.

Continued

Visitors contact club for details. **Societies** welcome. **Green Fees** €20 per 18 holes (€25 Sat, Sun & BHs). **Prof** Shane O'Grady **Course Designer** Bobby Browne **Facilities** **Location** 2.5km E of village on R125

Black Bush

Hotel ★★★ 70% Finnstown Country House Hotel, Newcastle Rd, Lucan, DUBLIN ☎ 01 6010700 25 en suite 28 annexe en suite

KELLS Map 01 C4

Headfort

☎ 046 9240146 📠 046 9249282
e-mail: info@headfortgolfclub.ie
web: www.headfortgolfclub.ie

Headfort Old Course is a delightful parkland course which is regarded as one of the best of its kind in Ireland. There are ample opportunities for birdies, but even if these are not achieved, provides a challenging test. The New Course is a modern course which criss-crosses the Blackwater river, making use of two islands.

Old Course: 18 holes, 5973 metres, Par 72, SSS 71.
New Course: 18 holes, 6164 metres, Par 72, SSS 74.
Club membership 1608.

Visitors Mon-Sun & BHs. **Societies** Booking required. **Green Fees** Old Course: €45 per round (€50 Fri-Sun). New Course; €60 per round (€65 Fri-Sun). **Prof** Brendan McGovern **Course Designer** Christy O'Connor jnr **Facilities** **Location** 0.8km E of village on N3

KILCOCK Map 01 C4

Kilcock Gallow

☎ 01 6287592 📠 01 6287283
e-mail: kilcockgolfclub@eircom.net
web: www.kilcockgolfclub.com

A parkland course with generous fairways, manicured greens and light rough only.

18 holes, 5775 metres, Par 72, SSS 70, Course record 69.
Club membership 700.

Visitors Mon-Fri. Booking required. Dress code. **Societies** Booking required. **Green Fees** €25 per 18 holes Mon-Thu (€32 Fri). **Course Designer** Eddie Hackett **Facilities** **Location** "M4 exit Kilcock, course 3km "

Hotel ★★★ 64% Lucan Spa Hotel, LUCAN ☎ 01 6280494 71 rms (61 en suite)

NAVAN Map 01 C4

Royal Tara Bellinter

☎ 046 25508 & 25244 📠 046 25508
e-mail: info@royaltaragolfclub.com
web: royaltaragolfclub.com

New Course: 18 holes, 5757 metres, Par 71, SSS 70.
Bellinter Nine: 9 holes, 2911 metres, Par 35, SSS 35.

Course Designer Des Smyth **Location** 10km from town on N3

Telephone for further details

TRIM Map 01 C4

County Meath Newtownmoynagh
☎ 046 31463 📠 046 37554
18 holes, 6720 metres, Par 73, SSS 72, Course record 68.
Course Designer Eddie Hackett/Tom Craddock **Location** 5km SW of town on R160
Telephone for further details

CO MONAGHAN

CARRICKMACROSS Map 01 C4

Mannan Castle Donaghmoyne
☎ 042 9663308 📠 042 9663308
e-mail: mannancastlegc@eircom.net
Parkland and picturesque, the course features the par 3 2nd to an island green. The short par 4 12th through the woods and the 14th to 18th, all crossing water at least once. A test of golf for both amateur and professional.
18 holes, 5944 metres, Par 70, SSS 69.
Club membership 700.
Visitors Booking required. **Societies** apply in writing to the secretary. **Green Fees** Phone. **Course Designer** F Ainsworth **Facilities** **Location** 6.5km N of town

Hotel ★★★★ 71% Ballymascanlon House Hotel, DUNDALK ☎ 042 9358200 90 en suite

Nuremore
☎ 042 9671368 📠 042 9661853
e-mail: nuremore@eircom.net
web: www.nuremore-hotel.ie

18 holes, 6400yds, Par 71, SSS 69, Course record 64.
Course Designer Eddie Hackett **Location** 1.6km SE of town on N2
Telephone for further details

Hotel ★★★★ 73% Nuremore Hotel, CARRICKMACROSS ☎ 042 9661438 72 en suite

CASTLEBLAYNEY Map 01 C4

Castleblayney Onomy
☎ 042 9740451 📠 042 9740451
e-mail: rayker@eircom.com
9 holes, 4918 metres, Par 68, SSS 66, Course record 65.
Course Designer Bobby Browne **Location** In town on Hope Castle Estate
Telephone for further details

Hotel ★★★★ 71% Ballymascanlon House Hotel, DUNDALK ☎ 042 9358200 90 en suite

CLONES Map 01 C5

Clones Hilton Park
☎ 047 56017 & 56913 📠 047 56913
e-mail: clonesgolfclub@eircom.net
web: clonesgolf.com
A parkland course set in drumlin country and renowned for the quality of the greens and the wildlife. Due to a limestone belt, the course is very dry and playable all year.
18 holes, 5549 metres, Par 69, SSS 69, Course record 62.
Club membership 450.
Visitors must contact in advance. **Societies** Booking required. **Green Fees** Phone. **Course Designer** Dr Arthur Spring **Facilities** **Conf** Corporate Hospitality Days **Location** 5km S of town on R212

Hotel Hillgrove Hotel, Old Armagh Rd, MONAGHAN ☎ 047 4781288 44 en suite

MONAGHAN Map 01 C5

Rossmore Rossmore Park, Cootehill Rd
☎ 047 71222
e-mail: golffees@hotmail.com
An undulating, 18-hole parkland course in beautiful countryside.
18 holes, 5590 metres, Par 70, SSS 69, Course record 68.
Club membership 650.
Visitors Mon-Sun & BHs. Booking required Sat-Sun & BHs. Dress code. **Societies** Booking required. **Green Fees** €30 per round (€40 Sat, Sun & BHs). **Prof** Ciaran Smyth **Course Designer** Des Smyth **Facilities** **Leisure** snooker. **Conf** Corporate Hospitality Days **Location** 3km S of town on R188

Hotel Hillgrove Hotel, Old Armagh Rd, MONAGHAN ☎ 047 4781288 44 en suite

CO OFFALY

BIRR Map 01 C3

Birr The Glenns
☎ 0509 20082 📠 0509 22155
e-mail: birrgolfclub@eircom.net
web: www.globalgolf.com
The course has been laid out over undulating parkland utilising the natural contours of the land, which were created during the ice age. The sandy subsoil means that the course is playable all year round.
18 holes, 5700 metres, Par 70, SSS 70, Course record 62.
Club membership 800.
Visitors contact in advance. **Societies** advance contact to secretary. **Green Fees** Phone. **Course Designer** Eddie Connaughton **Facilities** **Location** 3km N of town on R439

DAINGEAN Map 01 C4

Castle Barna
☎ 057 9353384 📠 057 9353077
e-mail: info@castlebarna.ie
web: www.castlebarna.ie
Parkland beside the Grand Canal. Many mature trees, natural streams and the naturally undulating landscape provide a great challenge for golfers of all abilities.

Continue

18 holes, 5798 metres, Par 72, SSS 69, Course record 66. Club membership 600.
Visitors Mon-Sun & BHs. Booking required Sat-Sun & BHs. Dress code. **Societies** Booking required. **Green Fees** €20 per round (€30 Sat, Sun & BHs). **Course Designer** Alan Duggan/Kieran Monahan **Facilities** by arrangement by arrangement **Conf** Corporate Hospitality Days **Location** 11km off N6 Dublin-Galway road at Tyrellspass

EDENDERRY Map 01 C4

Edenderry
☎ 046 9731072 046 9733911
e-mail: enquiries@edenderrygolfclub.com
web: www.edenderrygolfclub.com
A most friendly club which offers a relaxing game in pleasant surroundings.
18 holes, 6029 metres, Par 72, SSS 72, Course record 66. Club membership 900.
Visitors Mon-Wed & Fri. Booking required. Dress code. **Societies** Booking required. **Green Fees** €30 (€35 weekends). **Course Designer** Havers/Hackett **Facilities** **Conf** facs Corporate Hospitality Days **Location** 1.2km outside Edenderry on Dublin route

TULLAMORE Map 01 C4

Esker Hills
☎ 0506 55999 0506 55021
e-mail: info@eskerhillsgolf.com
web: www.eskerhillsgolf.com
Esker Hills is built on a landscape of plateaux, sweeping valleys and natural lakes created by the retreating glaciers of the ice age 10,000 years ago. In a unique setting with 18 challenging holes, no two of which are remotely alike. A parkland course with a links feel and sand-based greens.
18 holes, 6051 metres, Par 71, SSS 71, Course record 65. Club membership 280.
Visitors Mon-Sun & BHs. Booking required. **Societies** Booking required. **Green Fees** £35 (£48 Sat, Sun & BHs. **Course Designer** Christy O'Connor jnr **Facilities** **Location** 4.8km from Tullamore off N80 Tullamore to Clara road

Tullamore Brookfield
☎ 0506 21439 0506 41806
e-mail: tullamoregolfclub@eircom.net
web: www.tullamoregolfclub.ie
Course set in mature parkland of oak, beech and chestnut. The original design was by James Braid and this has been radically altered to meet the highest standards of the modern game, with new sand-based undulating greens, lakes, bunkering, mounding and more trees.
18 holes, 5666 metres, Par 70, SSS 71, Course record 68. Club membership 1000.
Visitors must contact in advance, restricted on Tue & at weekends. **Societies** Booking required. **Green Fees** Phone. **Prof** Donagh McArdle **Course Designer** James Braid/Paddy Merrigam **Facilities** **Location** 4km SW of town on R421

Hotel ★★★ 70% Hodson Bay Hotel, Hodson Bay, ATHLONE ☎ 090 6442000 133 en suite

CO ROSCOMMON

ATHLONE Map 01 C4

Athlone Hodson Bay
☎ 090 6492073 090 6494080
e-mail: athlonegolfclub@eircom.net
A picturesque course with a panoramic view of Lough Ree. Overall, it is a tight, difficult course with some outstanding holes and is noted for its magnificent greens. Many championships have taken place here.
18 holes, 5854 metres, Par 71, SSS 71, Course record 66. Club membership 1250.
Visitors Mon-Sat & BHs. Booking required. Handicap certificate. Dress code. **Societies** welcome. **Green Fees** €30 per round (€35 Sat, Sun & BHs). **Prof** Kevin Grealy **Course Designer** J McAllister **Facilities** **Location** 6.5km from town beside Lough Ree

Hotel ★★★ 70% Hodson Bay Hotel, Hodson Bay, ATHLONE ☎ 090 6442000 133 en suite

BALLAGHADERREEN Map 01 B4

Ballaghaderreen
☎ 094 9860295
Mature nine-hole course with an abundance of trees. Accuracy off the tee is vital for a good score. Small protected greens require a good short-iron plan. The par 3, 5th hole at 178yds has ruined many a good score.
9 holes, 5237 metres, Par 70, SSS 67, Course record 68. Club membership 400.
Visitors Mon-Sun & BHs. **Societies** Booking required. **Green Fees** €15 per day. **Course Designer** Paddy Skerritt **Facilities** **Location** 3.5km S of town

BOYLE Map 01 B4

Boyle Roscommon Rd
☎ 071 9662594
9 holes, 5324 metres, Par 67, SSS 66, Course record 65.
Course Designer E Hackett **Location** 3km S off N61
Telephone for further details

CASTLEREA Map 01 B4

Castlerea Clonalis
☎ 094 9620068
The clubhouse is virtually at the centre of Castlerea course with seven tees visible. A pleasant parkland course incorporating part of the River Francis.
9 holes, 4974 metres, Par 68, SSS 66, Course record 62. Club membership 837.

Continued

Visitors welcome, but Sunday by arrangement only. **Societies** contact for details. **Green Fees** Phone. **Facilities** **Location** Near town centre on N60

Hotel ★★★ 71% Abbey Hotel, Galway Rd, ROSCOMMON ☎ 090 662 6240 50 en suite

ROSCOMMON Map 01 B4

Roscommon Mote Park
☎ 090 6626382 090 6626043
e-mail: rosegolfclub@eircom.net
web: www.golfclubireland.com/roscommon
Located on the rolling pastures of the Mote Park estate. Numerous water hazards, notably on the tricky 13th, multi-tiered greens and an excellent irrigation to give an all-weather surface.
18 holes, 6290 metres, Par 72, SSS 70.
Club membership 700.
Visitors contact club for details. **Societies** welcome. **Green Fees** €30 (€35 weekends). **Course Designer** E Connaughton **Facilities** **Location** 0.8km S of town

Hotel ★★★ 71% Abbey Hotel, Galway Rd, ROSCOMMON ☎ 090 662 6240 50 en suite

STROKESTOWN Map 01 C4

Strokestown Bumlin
☎ 071 9633528
Picturesque nine-hole course set in parkland with fine views.
9 holes, 2615 metres, Par 68.
Club membership 250.
Visitors Mon-Sat. Booking required Sat, Sun & BHs. Dress code. **Societies** Booking required. **Green Fees** €15 per 18 holes. **Course Designer** Mel Flanagan **Facilities** **Location** 2.5km SW of village off R368

Hotel ★★★ 71% Abbey Hotel, Galway Rd, ROSCOMMON ☎ 090 662 6240 50 en suite

CO SLIGO

BALLYMOTE Map 01 B4

Ballymote Ballinascarrow
☎ 071 9183089 071 9189210
e-mail: jocon@iol.ie
web: www.ballymotegolfclub.com
9 holes, 5302 metres, Par 70, SSS 68.
Course Designer Eddie Hacket/Mel Flanagan **Location** 1.5km from town centre
Telephone for further details

Hotel ★★★ 72% Sligo Park Hotel, Pearse Rd, SLIGO ☎ 071 9190400 138 en suite

INISHCRONE Map 01 B5

Enniscrone
☎ 096 36297 096 36657
e-mail: enniscronegolf@eircom.net
web: www.enniscronegolf.com
27 holes, 6125 metres, Par 73, SSS 72, Course record 70.
Course Designer E Hackett/Donald Steel **Location** 0.8km S of village
Telephone for further details

SLIGO Map 01 B5

County Sligo Rosses Point
☎ 071 9177134 or 9177186 071 9177460
e-mail: cosligo@iol.ie
web: countysligogolfclub.ie
Now considered to be one of the top links courses in Ireland, County Sligo is host to a number of competitions, including the West of Ireland championships and internationals. Set in an elevated position on cliffs above three large beaches, the prevailing winds provide an additional challenge. Tom Watson described it as 'a magnificent links, particularly the stretch of holes from the 14th to the 17th'.
18 holes, 6043 metres, Par 71, SSS 72, Course record 67.
Bomore: 9 holes, 2785 metres, Par 35, SSS 69.
Club membership 1250.
Visitors Mon-Sun & BHs. Booking required. Handicap certificate. Dress code. **Societies** Booking required. **Green Fees** Championship Course:€70 per 18 holes Mon-Thur (€85 Fri-Sun & BHs). **Prof** Jim Robinson **Course Designer** Harry Colt **Facilities** **Conf** facs Corporate Hospitality Days **Location** N of town off N15

Strandhill Strandhill
☎ 071 91 68188 071 91 68811
e-mail: strandhillgc.eircom.net
18 holes, 5516 metres, Par 69, SSS 68.
Location 8km W of town off R292
Telephone for further details

Hotel ★★★ 72% Sligo Park Hotel, Pearse Rd, SLIGO ☎ 071 9190400 138 en suite

TOBERCURRY Map 01 B4

Tobercurry
☎ 071 85849
e-mail: contacttubbercurry@eircom.net
web: www.tubbercurrygolfclub.com
9 holes, 5490 metres, Par 70, SSS 69, Course record 65.
Course Designer Eddie Hackett **Location** 0.4km from town centre
Telephone for further details

CO TIPPERARY

CAHIR Map 01 C3

Cahir Park Kilcommon
☎ 052 41474 052 42717
e-mail: management@cahirparkgolfclub.com
web: www.cahirparkgolfclub.com
Parkland dissected by the River Suir, which adds a challenge to the par 4 8th and par 3 16th. Water in play on seven holes.
18 holes, 5806 metres, Par 71, SSS 71, Course record 66.
Club membership 750.
Visitors Mon-Fri. Contact club for details. Dress code. **Societies** Booking required. **Green Fees** €30 (€35 weekends). **Course Designer** Eddie Hackett **Facilities** **Location** 1.6km SW of town centre on R668

CARRICK-ON-SUIR Map 01 C2

Carrick-on-Suir Garvonne
☎ 051 640047 🖹 051 640558
e-mail: cosgc@eircom.net
18 holes, 6061 metres, Par 72, SSS 71, Course record 69.
Course Designer Eddie Hackett **Location** 3km SW of town
Telephone for further details

Hotel ★★★ 75% Hotel Minella, CLONMEL
☎ 052 22388 70 en suite

CLONMEL Map 01 C2

Clonmel Lyreanearla, Mountain Rd
☎ 052 24050 🖹 052 83349
e-mail: cgc@indigo.ie
web: clonmelgolfclub.com
Set in the scenic, wooded slopes of the Comeragh Mountains, this is a testing course with lots of open space and plenty of interesting features. It provides an enjoyable round in exceptionally tranquil surroundings.
18 holes, 5804 metres, Par 72, SSS 71.
Club membership 850.
Visitors Mon-Sun & BHs. Booking required Wed, Sat & Sun. Handicap certificate. Dress code. **Societies** Booking required. **Green Fees** Weekdays €25 per round per 18 holes, (Sat, Sun & BHs €35). **Prof** Robert Hayes **Course Designer** Eddie Hackett **Facilities** ⊗ by arrangement **Location** 5km from Clonmel off N24

Hotel ★★★ 75% Hotel Minella, CLONMEL
☎ 052 22388 70 en suite

MONARD Map 01 B3

Ramada Hotel Ballykisteen, Limerick Junction
☎ 062 33333 🖹 062 31555
web: www.ramadaireland.com
Set in emerald green countryside just two miles from Tipperary. The course, with landscaped surroundings against a backdrop of mountains, lakes and streams, offers an excellent challenge for the champion golfer. The use of forward tees provide a course that is playable and enjoyable for the average golfer.
18 holes, 6186 metres, Par 72, SSS 72.
Club membership 350.
Visitors Mon-Sun & BHs. Booking required. Dress code. **Societies** Booking required. **Green Fees** Apr-Oct €50 weekdays (€60 weekends), Nov-Mar €30/€40. **Prof** James Harris **Course Designer** Des Smith **Facilities** ⊗ **Leisure** tennis courts, indoor swimming pool, sauna, gymnasium. **Conf** facs **Location** 1.6km SE of village on N24 towards Tipperary

Guest House ♦♦♦ Ach-na-Sheen Guesthouse, Clonmel Rd, TIPPERARY ☎ 062 51298 8 en suite

NENAGH Map 01 B3

Nenagh Beechwood
☎ 067 31476 🖹 067 34808
e-mail: nenaghgolfclub@eircom.net
web: www.nenaghgolfclub.com
The sand-based greens guarded by intimidating bunkers are a challenge for even the most fastidious putters. Excellent drainage and firm surfaces allow play all year round.
18 holes, 6009 metres, Par 72, SSS 72, Course record 71.
Club membership 1100.
Visitors Contact club for details. Handicap certificate. Dress code. **Societies** Booking required. **Green Fees** €30 per 18 holes. **Prof** Robert Kelly **Course Designer** Patrick Merrigan **Facilities** ⊗ by arrangement by arrangement **Location** 5km NE of town on R491

Guest House ♦♦♦♦ Ashley Park House, NENAGH
☎ 067 38223 & 38013 🖹 067 38013 5 en suite

ROSCREA Map 01 C3

Roscrea Golf Club Derryvale
☎ 0505 21130 🖹 0505 23410
Course situated on the eastern side of Roscrea in the shadows of the Slieve Bloom Mountains. A special feature of the course is the variety of the par 3 holes, most noteworthy of which is the 165-metre 4th, which is played almost entirely over a lake. It is widely recognised that the finishing six holes will prove a worthy challenge to even the best players. The most famous hole on the course in the 5th, referred to locally as the Burma Road, a par 5 of over 457 metres with the fairway lined with trees and out of bounds on the left side.
18 holes, 5809 metres, Par 71, SSS 70, Course record 66.
Club membership 600.
Visitors Mon-Sun & BHs. Booking required Sat-Sun & BH's. Dress code. **Societies** Booking required at weekends. **Green Fees** €25 (€30 weekends). **Course Designer** A Spring **Facilities** ⊗ **Conf** Corporate Hospitality Days **Location** E of town on N7

TEMPLEMORE Map 01 C3

Templemore Manna South
☎ 0504 31400 & 32923 🖹 0504 35450
Parkland with many mature and some newly planted trees, which provide a pleasant test without being too difficult. The course is undergoing changes with three new holes being brought into play.
9 holes, 5443 metres, Par 70, SSS 69, Course record 68.
Club membership 330.
Visitors Booking required. **Societies** Booking required. **Green Fees** Phone. **Facilities** ⊗ **Leisure** hard tennis courts. **Location** 0.8km S of town on N62

THURLES Map 01 C3

Thurles Turtulla
☎ 0504 21983 & 24599 🖹 0504 24647
18 holes, 5904 metres, Par 72, SSS 71, Course record 67.
Course Designer Mr J McMlister **Location** 1.6km S of town on N62
Telephone for further details

Guest House ♦♦♦ Ach-na-Sheen Guesthouse, Clonmel Rd, TIPPERARY ☎ 062 51298 8 en suite

Continued

TIPPERARY Map 01 C3

County Tipperary Golf & Country Club

Dundrum House Hotel, Dundrum
☎ 062 71717 🖷 062 71718
e-mail: dundrumh@id.ie
web: www.dundrumhousehotel.com
18 holes, 6447 metres, Par 72, SSS 72, Course record 70.
Course Designer Philip Walton **Location** 12km NE of town on R505
Telephone for further details

Guest House ♦♦♦ Ach-na-Sheen Guesthouse, Clonmel Rd, TIPPERARY ☎ 062 51298 8 en suite

Tipperary Rathanny

☎ 062 51119 🖷 062 51119
e-mail: tipperarygolfclub@eircom.net
18 holes, 5761 metres, Par 71, SSS 71, Course record 66.
Location 1.6km S of town on R664
Telephone for further details

Guest House ♦♦♦ Ach-na-Sheen Guesthouse, Clonmel Rd, TIPPERARY ☎ 062 51298 8 en suite

CO WATERFORD

DUNGARVAN Map 01 C2

Dungarvan Knocknagranagh

☎ 058 41605 & 43310 🖷 058 44113
e-mail: dungarvangc@eircom.net
web: www.dungarvangolfclub.com
A championship-standard course beside Dungarvan Bay, with seven lakes and hazards placed to challenge all levels of golfer. The greens are considered to be among the best in Ireland.
18 holes, 5998 metres, Par 72, SSS 71, Course record 66.
Club membership 900.
Visitors contact club for details. **Societies** welcome. **Green Fees** €31 (Sat, Sun & BHs €42). **Prof** David Hayes **Course Designer** Moss Fives **Facilities** **Leisure** snooker. **Location** Off N25

Hotel ★★★ 60% Lawlors Hotel, DUNGARVAN
☎ 058 41122 & 41056 🖷 058 41000 89 en suite

Gold Coast Golf & Leisure Ballinacourty

☎ 058 44055 🖷 058 44055
e-mail: info@goldcoastgolfclub.com
web: www.goldcoastclub.com
Parkland beside the Atlantic Ocean with unrivalled views of Dungarvan Bay. The mature tree-lined fairways of the old course are tastefully integrated with the long and challenging newer holes to create a superb course.
18 holes, 6171 metres, Par 72, SSS 72, Course record 70.
Club membership 600.
Visitors contact club for details. Booking required. Dress code. **Societies** Booking required. **Green Fees** €35 per 18 holes (€45 weekends). **Course Designer** Maurice Fives **Facilities** **Leisure** hard tennis courts, heated indoor swimming pool, sauna, gymnasium. **Conf** facs Corporate Hospitality Days **Location** 3km N of town off N25

Hotel ★★★ 60% Lawlors Hotel, DUNGARVAN
☎ 058 41122 & 41056 🖷 058 41000 89 en suite

West Waterford

☎ 058 43216 & 41475 🖷 058 44343
e-mail: info@westwaterfordgolf.com
web: westwaterfordgolf.com
Designed by Eddie Hackett, the course is on 150 acres of rolling parkland by the Brickey River with a backdrop of the Comeragh Mountains, Knockmealdowns and Drum Hills. The first nine holes are laid out on a large plateau featuring a stream which comes into play at the 3rd and 4th holes. The river at the southern boundary affects several later holes.
18 holes, 6137 metres, Par 72, SSS 72, Course record 70.
Club membership 400.
Visitors Mon-Sun & BHs. Booking required Sat-Sun & BHs. Dress code. **Societies** Booking required. **Green Fees** €32 per 18 holes (€44 Sat, Sun & BHs). **Course Designer** Eddie Hackett **Facilities** **Leisure** hard tennis courts. **Conf** Corporate Hospitality Days **Location** 5km W of town off N25

Hotel ★★★ 60% Lawlors Hotel, DUNGARVAN
☎ 058 41122 & 41056 🖷 058 41000 89 en suite

DUNMORE EAST Map 01 C2

Dunmore East

☎ 051 383151 🖷 051 383151
e-mail: dunmoregolf@eircom.net
web: www.dunmore-golf.com

18 holes, 5400 metres, Par 72, SSS 69, Course record 65.
Course Designer W H Jones **Location** Into Dunmore East left after fuel station, left at Strand Inn right
Telephone for further details

Hotel ★★★ 65% Majestic Hotel, TRAMORE
☎ 051 381761 60 en suite

LISMORE Map 01 C2

Lismore Ballyin

☎ 058 54026 🖷 058 53338
e-mail: moynihan@eircom.net
web: www.lismoregolf.org
Picturesque, tree-dotted, sloping, nine-hole parkland course on the banks of the Blackwater River.
9 holes, 2748 metres, Par 69, SSS 68.
Club membership 400.
Visitors Mon-Sun & BHs. Booking required Wed, Sat-Sun. Dress code. **Societies** Booking required. **Green Fees** €20 per 18 holes. **Course Designer** Eddie Hackett **Facilities** **Location** 1.6km W of town on R666

Hotel ★★★ 60% Lawlors Hotel, DUNGARVAN
☎ 058 41122 & 41056 🖷 058 41000 89 en suite

TRAMORE Map 01 C2

Tramore Newtown Hill
☎ 051 386170 🖷 051 390961
e-mail: tragolf@iol.ie
web: www.tramoregolfclub.com
18 holes, 5918 metres, Par 72, SSS 72, Course record 65.
Course Designer Capt H C Tippet **Location** 0.8km W of town on R675 coast road
Telephone for further details

Hotel ★★★ 65% Majestic Hotel, TRAMORE
☎ 051 381761 60 en suite

WATERFORD Map 01 C2

Faithlegg Faithlegg
☎ 051 382000 & 086 3840215 🖷 051 382010
e-mail: golf@faithlegg.com
web: www.faithlegg.com
Set on the banks of the River Suir, the course has been integrated into a landscape textured with mature trees, flowing parkland and five lakes. Length is not the main defence, rather the greens provide a test for all levels making a good score a true reflection of good golf. Long par 3's and tricky to mange par 4's provide a challenge while reachable par 5's may allow you to reclaim a shot or two.
18 holes, 6629yds, Par 72, SSS 72, Course record 69. Club membership 620.
Visitors Mon-Sun & BHs. Booking required Fri-Sun & BHs. Handicap certificate. Dress code. **Societies** Booking required. **Green Fees** Mon-Thu €49; Sat-Sun €61. **Prof** Darragh Tighe & Ryan Hault **Course Designer** Patrick Merrigan **Facilities** **Leisure** hard tennis courts, heated indoor swimming pool, fishing, sauna, solarium, gymnasium, full P.G.A. club repair & custom fitting service available, coaching specialists. **Conf** facs **Location** 9km E of town off R684 towards Cheekpoint

Waterford Newrath
☎ 051 876748 🖷 051 853405
e-mail: info@waterfordgolfclub.com
web: www.waterfordgolfclub.com
One of the finest inland courses in Ireland. This is exemplified by the spectacular closing stretch, in particular the downhill 18th with its elevated tee, a wonderful viewpoint and a narrow gorse lined fairway demanding a very accurate tee shot.
18 holes, 5722 metres, Par 71, SSS 70, Course record 64. Club membership 1102.
Visitors must contact in advance. **Societies** must apply in writing. **Green Fees** Phone. **Course Designer** W Park/J Braid **Facilities** **Location** 1.6km N of town on N77

Waterford Castle The Island, Ballinakill
☎ 051 871633 🖷 051 871634
e-mail: golf@waterfordcastle.com
web: www.waterfordcastle.com/golf
A unique 130-hectare island course in the River Suir and accessed by private ferry. The course has four water features on the 2nd, 3rd, 4th and 16th holes with a Swilken Bridge on the 3rd hole. Two of the more challenging holes are the par 4s at the 9th and 12th, the 9th being a 379-metre uphill, dog-leg right. The 417-

Continued

metre 12th is a fine test of accuracy and distance. The views from the course are superb.
18 holes, 6231 metres, Par 72, SSS 71, Course record 70. Club membership 770.
Visitors Mon-Sun & BHs. Booking required Fri-Sun & BHs. Dress code. **Societies** Booking required. **Green Fees** Winter €45-€50; Summer €50-€60. **Course Designer** Des Smyth **Facilities** **Leisure** hard tennis courts. **Conf** facs Corporate Hospitality Days **Location** 3km E of town via private ferry

Hotel ★★★★ Waterford Castle Hotel, The Island, WATERFORD ☎ 051 878203 19 en suite

CO WESTMEATH

ATHLONE Map 01 C4

Glasson Golf Hotel Glasson
☎ 090 6485120 🖷 090 6485444
e-mail: info@glassongolf.ie
web: www.glassongolf.ie
Opened in 1993, the course has a reputation for being one of the most challenging and scenic courses in Ireland. Designed by Christy O'Connor Jnr it is reputedly his best yet. Surrounded on three sides by Lough Ree the views from everywhere on the course are breathtaking.
18 holes, 6100 metres, Par 72, SSS 72, Course record 65. Club membership 220.
Visitors Mon-Sun & BHs. Booking required. Dress code. **Societies** Booking required. **Green Fees** €60 (Mon-Thur); €65 (Fri & Sun); €75 (Sat) per round. **Course Designer** Christy O'Connor Jnr **Facilities** **Leisure** sauna, gymnasium, chipping green, hot tub, steam room. **Conf** facs Corporate Hospitality Days **Location** 10km N of town on N55

Hotel ★★★ 70% Hodson Bay Hotel, Hodson Bay, ATHLONE ☎ 090 6442000 133 en suite

DELVIN Map 01 C4

Delvin Castle Clonyn
☎ 044 64315 & 64671 🖷 044 64315
18 holes, 5800 metres, Par 70, SSS 68.
Course Designer John Day **Location** On N52
Telephone for further details

MOATE Map 01 C4

Moate
☎ 090 6481271 🖷 090 6482645
web: www.moategolfclub.ie
Parkland with trees, lakes and many bunkers.
18 holes, 5742 metres, Par 72, SSS 70, Course record 67. Club membership 650.
Visitors welcome, advisable to telephone in advance. **Societies** Booking required. **Green Fees** Phone. **Prof** Paul Power **Course Designer** B Browne **Facilities** **Location** 1.6km N of town

Hotel ★★★ 70% Hodson Bay Hotel, Hodson Bay, ATHLONE ☎ 090 6442000 133 en suite

Mount Temple Mount Temple Village
☎ 090 6481841 6481957 🖷 090 6481957
e-mail: mttemple@iol.ie
web: www.mounttemplegolfclub.com
A traditionally built, championship course with unique links-type greens and natural undulating fairways. A challenge for all levels of golfers and all year golfing available.
18 holes, 6020 metres, Par 72, SSS 72, Course record 71. Club membership 250.
Visitors Mon-Sun & BHs. Booking required Sat-Sun & BHs. Dress code. **Societies** Booking required. **Green Fees** €30 per round (€35 weekends & public holidays). **Prof** David Keenan **Course Designer** Michael Dolan **Facilities** **Conf** Corporate Hospitality Days **Location** 5km NW of town to Temple Mount

Hotel ★★★ 70% Hodson Bay Hotel, Hodson Bay, ATHLONE ☎ 090 6442000 133 en suite

MULLINGAR Map 01 C4

Mullingar
☎ 044 48366 🖷 044 41499

18 holes, 5858 metres, Par 72, SSS 71, Course record 63.
Course Designer James Braid **Location** 5km S of town on N52
Telephone for further details

Hotel ★★★★ 67% Mullingar Park Hotel, Dublin Rd, MULLINGAR ☎ 044 44446 37500 🖷 044 35937 95 en suite

CO WEXFORD

ENNISCORTHY Map 01 D3

Enniscorthy Knockmarshall
☎ 054 33191 🖷 054 37367
18 holes, 6115 metres, Par 72, SSS 72.
Course Designer Eddie Hackett **Location** 1.6km W of town on N30
Telephone for further details

GOREY Map 01 D3

Courtown Kiltennel
☎ 055 25166 🖷 055 25553
e-mail: courtown@iol.ie
web: www.courtowngolfclub.com
18 holes, 5898 metres, Par 71, SSS 71, Course record 65.
Course Designer Harris & Associates **Location** 5km SE of town off R742
Telephone for further details

Hotel ★★★★ 67% Ashdown Park Hotel, The Coach Rd, GOREY TOWN ☎ 055 80500 80 en suite

NEW ROSS Map 01 C3

New Ross Tinneranny
☎ 051 421433 🖷 051 420098
This well-kept parkland course has an attractive backdrop of hills and mountains. Straight hitting and careful placing of shots is very important, especially on the 2nd, 6th, 10th and 15th, all of which are challenging holes.
18 holes, 5259 metres, Par 70, SSS 70. Club membership 700.
Visitors welcome, booking required for weekend play. **Societies** apply to secretary/manager. **Green Fees** Phone. **Course Designer** Des Smith **Facilities** **Location** 5km from town

ROSSLARE Map 01 D2

Rosslare Rosslare Strand
☎ 053 32203 🖷 053 32263
e-mail: office@rosslare.com
web: www.rosslaregolf.com
This traditional links course is within minutes of the ferry terminal at Rosslare. Many of the greens are sunken and are always in beautiful condition, but the semi-blind approaches are among features of this course which provide a healthy challenge. Celebrated 100 years of golf in 2005.

Continued

Old Course: 18 holes, 6042 metres, Par 72, SSS 72, Course record 66.
Burrow: 12 holes, 3617 metres, Par 46.
Club membership 1000.
Visitors Booking required. **Societies** Booking required. **Green Fees** Phone. **Prof** Johnny Young **Course Designer** Hawtree/Taylor **Facilities** **Leisure** sauna. **Conf** Corporate Hospitality Days **Location** N of Rosslare village

Hotel ★★★★ Kelly's Resort Hotel, ROSSLARE ☎ 053 32114 118 annexe en suite

St Helen's Bay Golf & Country Club
St Helens, Kilrane
☎ 053 33234 053 33803
e-mail: sthelens@iol.ie
web: www.sthelensbay.com
27 holes, 5813 metres, Par 72, SSS 72, Course record 69.
Course Designer Philip Walton **Location** SE of Rosslare Harbour off N25
Telephone for further details

Hotel ★★★★ 72% Ferrycarrig Hotel, Ferrycarrig Bridge, WEXFORD ☎ 053 20999 102 en suite

WEXFORD Map 01 D3

Wexford Mulgannon
☎ 053 42238 053 42243
e-mail: info@wexfordgolfclub.ie
web: www.wexfordgolfclub.ie
Parkland with panoramic view of the Wexford coastline and mountains.
18 holes, 5578 metres, Par 72, SSS 70.
Club membership 800.
Visitors must contact in advance but may not play Thu & Sundays. **Societies** must contact in writing. **Green Fees** Phone. **Prof** LIam Bowler **Facilities**

Hotel ★★★ 74% Talbot Hotel Conference & Leisure Centre, The Quay, WEXFORD ☎ 053 22566 & 55559 053 23377 109 en suite

CO WICKLOW

ARKLOW Map 01 D3

Arklow Abbeylands
☎ 0402 32492 0402 91604
e-mail: arklowgolflinks@eircom.net
Scenic links course.
18 holes, 5802 metres, Par 69, SSS 68, Course record 64.
Club membership 780.
Visitors Mon-Sat. Booking required. Handicap certificate. Dress code. **Societies** Booking required. **Green Fees** €40. **Course Designer** Hawtree & Taylor **Facilities** **Location** 0.8km E of town centre

Hotel ★★★ Marlfield House Hotel, GOREY ☎ 055 21124 20 en suite

BALTINGLASS Map 01 D3

Baltinglass Dublin Rd
☎ 059 6481350 059 6481842
e-mail: baltinglassgc@eircom.net
18 holes, 5912 metres, Par 71, SSS 71, Course record 68.
Course Designer Lionel Hewston **Location** 500 metres N of village
Telephone for further details

Hotel ★★★ 71% Seven Oaks Hotel, Athy Rd, CARLOW ☎ 059 913 1308 59 en suite

BLAINROE Map 01 D3

Blainroe
☎ 0404 68168 0404 69369
e-mail: blainroegolfclub@eircom.net
web: www.blainroe.com
Parkland course overlooking the east coast, a challenge to golfers of all abilities. Some holes are situated right on the coast and two notable holes are the 14th, played over the sea from a cliff promontory, and the par 3 15th over a lake.
18 holes, 6175 metres, Par 72, SSS 72, Course record 71.
Club membership 1140.
Visitors must contact in advance. **Societies** must telephone in advance. **Green Fees** Phone. **Prof** John McDonald **Course Designer** Fred Hawtree **Facilities** **Conf** Corporate Hospitality Days **Location** 5km SE of Wicklow on R750 coast road

Farmhouse ♦♦♦♦ Kilpatrick House, Redcross, WICKLOW ☎ 0404 47137 & 087 6358325 0404 47866 4 rms (3 en suite)

BLESSINGTON Map 01 D3

Tulfarris House Hotel & Country Club
☎ 045 867644 & 867600 045 867000
e-mail: info@tulfarris.com
web: www.tulfarris.com
Designed by Paddy Merrigan, this course is on the Blessington lakeshore with the Wicklow Mountains as a backdrop. The use of the natural landscape is evident throughout the whole course, the variety of trees guarding fairways and green approaches.
18 holes, 6507 metres, Par 72, SSS 74, Course record 68.
Club membership 255.
Visitors Booking required Sat-Sun. **Societies** Booking required. **Green Fees** €80 per round (€100 weekends). **Prof** Stephen Brown **Course Designer** Patrick Merrigan **Facilities** **Leisure** hard tennis courts, fishing, gymnasium. **Conf** facs Corporate Hospitality Days **Location** 3.5km from village off N81

BRAY Map 01 D4

Bray Greystones Rd
☎ 01 2763200 01 2763262
e-mail: braygolfclub@eircom.net
web: www.braygolfclub.com
A USGA standard parkland course of nearly 81 hectares, combining stunning scenery with a classic layout. The 11th par 4 signature hole provides a fine view of the coastline.

Continued

18 holes, 5990 metres, Par 71, SSS 72, Course record 66. Club membership 784.
Visitors Mon, Thu-Fri (Sat 10:30-12). Booking required. Dress code. **Societies** Booking required. **Green Fees** €50 per 18 holes (€60 weekends). **Prof** Ciaran Carroll **Course Designer** Smyth/Brannigan **Facilities** **Conf** facs Corporate Hospitality Days **Location** Near town off R761

Hotel ★★★ 65% Royal Hotel & Leisure Centre, Main St, BRAY ☎ 01 2862935 98 en suite

Old Conna Ferndale Rd

☎ 01 2826055 & 2826766 📠 01 2825611
e-mail: info@oldconna.com
Parkland course set in wooded terrain with panoramic views of the Irish Sea and the Wicklow mountains.
18 holes, 5989 metres, Par 72, SSS 72, Course record 68. Club membership 1000.
Visitors Mon-Fri. Booking required. Dress code. **Societies** Booking required. **Green Fees** €50 per round (weekends €65). **Prof** Michael Langford **Course Designer** Eddie Hackett **Facilities** **Conf** facs Corporate Hospitality Days **Location** 3.5km from town centre

Hotel ★★★ 65% Royal Hotel & Leisure Centre, Main St, BRAY ☎ 01 2862935 98 en suite

Woodbrook Dublin Rd

☎ 01 2824799 📠 01 2821950
e-mail: golf@woodbrook.ie
web: www.woodbrook.ie
Perched on top of 30-metre seacliffs, the course has recently been redesigned with 18 new sand-based, bent-grass greens of varying sculpture and built to USGA specification. Cunning placement of fairway and greenside bunkers call for shot making virtuosity of the highest calibre.
18 holes, 6017 metres, Par 72, SSS 71, Course record 65. Club membership 1200.
Visitors Mon, Thu-Fri. Booking required. Handicap certificate. Dress code. **Societies** Booking required. **Green Fees** €95 per 18 holes (€100 Sat, Sun & BHs). **Prof** Billy Kinsella **Course Designer** Peter McEvoy **Facilities** **Location** On N11

Hotel ★★★ 65% Royal Hotel & Leisure Centre, Main St, BRAY ☎ 01 2862935 98 en suite

BRITTAS BAY Map 01 D3

The European Club

☎ 0404 47415 📠 0404 47449
e-mail: info@europeanclub.com
web: www.theeuropeanclub.com
A links course that runs through a large dunes system. Since it was opened in 1992 it is rapidly gaining recognition as one of Irelands best courses. Notable holes include the 7th, 13th and 14th.
20 holes, 6737 metres, Par 71, SSS 73, Course record 67. Club membership 100.
Visitors Mon-Sun & BHs. Booking required. Dress code. **Societies** welcome. **Green Fees** €80 per round Nov-Mar; €150 Apr-Oct. **Course Designer** Pat Ruddy **Facilities** **Conf** Corporate Hospitality Days **Location** 1.6km from Brittas Bay

Farmhouse ♦♦♦♦ Kilpatrick House, Redcross, WICKLOW ☎ 0404 47137 & 087 6358325 📠 0404 47866 4 rms (3 en suite)

DELGANY Map 01 D3

Delgany

☎ 01 2874536 📠 01 2873977
e-mail: delganygolf@eircom.net
web: www.delganygolfclub.com
Undulating parkland amid beautiful scenery. Remodelled in 2002 with sand-based greens and tees to USGA specifications.
18 holes, 5473 metres, Par 69, SSS 68. Club membership 1070.
Visitors may play Mon, Thu & Fri. Contact in advance. **Societies** contact in advance. **Green Fees** Phone. **Prof** Gavin Kavanagh **Course Designer** H Vardon **Facilities** **Location** 1.2km from village off N11

Hotel ★★★★ 64% Glenview Hotel, Glen O' the Downs, DELGANY ☎ 01 2873399 70 en suite

Glen of the Downs Coolnaskeagh

☎ 01 2876240 📠 01 2870063
e-mail: info@glenofthedowns.com
web: www.glenofthedowns.com
A parkland course that plays much like a links course with sand-based greens and tees. Among its features is a five-tier double green, which is shared by the 8th and 10th holes. Sandwiched in between is a fine par 5, the 9th, which measures 500yds off the back.
18 holes, 5468 metres, Par 71, SSS 70, Course record 68. Club membership 650.
Visitors may play Mon-Sun & BHs. Advance booking required. Dress code. **Societies** Booking required. **Green Fees** from €35-€85. **Course Designer** Peter McEvoy **Facilities** **Conf** facs Corporate Hospitality Days **Location** off N11 southbound, 4m from Bray

Hotel ★★★★ 64% Glenview Hotel, Glen O' the Downs, DELGANY ☎ 01 2873399 70 en suite

DUNLAVIN Map 01 D3

Rathsallagh

☎ 045 403316 📠 045 403295
e-mail: info@rathsallagh.com
web: www.rathsallagh.com
Designed by Peter McEvoy and Christy O'Connor Jnr, this is a spectacular course which will test the pro's without intimidating the club golfer. Set in 252 acres of lush parkland with thousands of mature trees, natural water hazards and gently rolling landscape. The greens are of high quality, in design, construction and condition.

Continued

Druids Glen

Co Wicklow

Kilcoole

Map 01 D3

Druid's Glen from the 1st tee to the 18th green creates an exceptional golfing experience, with its distinguished surroundings and spectacular views. This masterpiece of inspired planning and golfing architecture was designed by Tom Craddock and Pat Ruddy. It is the culmination of years of preparation, creating a unique inland course that challenges and satisfies in equal parts. Special features include an island green on the 17th hole and a Celtic Cross on the 12th. Druid's Glen hosted the Murphy's Irish Open in 1996, 1997, 1998 and for an unprecedented fourth time in 1999. In 2000 Druid's Glen won the title of European Golf Course of the Year and in 2002 it hosted the Seve Trophy. The world's top professionals and club golfers alike continue to enjoy the challenge here. A variety of teeing positions are available and there is a practice area, including three full-length academy holes. Individual and corporate members enjoy generous reserved tee times; visitors are very welcome but it is recommended that you book well in advance.

Newtownmountkennedy
☎ 01 2873600 🖹 01 2873699
e-mail: info@druidsglen.ie
web: www.druidsglen.ie

18 holes, 5987 metres, Par 71, SSS 73, Course record 62.
Club membership 219.

Visitors Booking required. **Societies** Booking required. **Green Fees** Phone. **Prof** George Henry **Course Designer** Tom Craddock/Pat Ruddy **Facilities** **Leisure** heated indoor swimming pool, sauna, gymnasium. **Location** S of village on R761

Rathsallagh

18 holes, 6324 metres, Par 72, SSS 74, Course record 68. Club membership 410.

Visitors Mon-Sun & BHs. Booking required. Dress code. **Societies** Booking required. **Green Fees** €60 per round (€75 Fri-Sat & BHs). Reduced rates for hotel residents;. **Prof** Brendan McDaid **Course Designer** McEvoy/O'Connor **Facilities** **Leisure** hard tennis courts, sauna, private jacuzzi/steam room, croquet lawn, walled garden. **Conf** facs Corporate Hospitality Days **Location** SW of village off N9

Guest House ♦♦♦♦♦ Rathsallagh House, DUNLAVIN ☎ 045 403112 29 en suite

ENNISKERRY Map 01 D4

Powerscourt Powerscourt Estate

☎ 01 2046033 🖷 01 2761303
e-mail: golfclub@powerscourt.ie
web: www.powerscourt.ie

A free-draining course with links characteristics. This championship course with top quality tees and exceptional tiered greens, is set in some of Ireland's most beautiful parkland. The course has an abundance of mature trees and natural features, with stunning views of the sea and the Sugarloaf mountain.

East Course: 18 holes, 5930 metres, Par 72, SSS 72.
West Course: 18 holes, 5906 metres, Par 72, SSS 72.
Club membership 980.

Visitors Mon-Sun & BHs. Booking required. Handicap certificate. Dress code. **Societies** Booking required. **Green Fees** Phone. **Prof** Paul Thompson **Course Designer** Peter McEvoy & David McClaykind **Facilities** **Conf** facs Corporate Hospitality Days **Location** 19km S of Dublin off N11 to Enniskerry, signs for Powerscourt Estate

Hotel ★★★ 65% Royal Hotel & Leisure Centre, Main St, BRAY ☎ 01 2862935 98 en suite

GREYSTONES Map 01 D3

Charlesland Golf & Country Club Hotel

☎ 01 2874350 & 2878200 🖷 01 2874360
e-mail: teetimes@charlesland.com
web: www.charlesland.com

Championship length, par 72 course with a double dog-leg at the 9th and 18th. Water hazards at the 3rd and 11th.

18 holes, 5963 metres, Par 72, SSS 72.

Visitors contact club for details. Dress code. **Societies** Booking required. **Green Fees** €32 Mon-Thu (€45 Fri-Sun). **Prof** Peter Duignan **Course Designer** Eddie Hackett **Facilities** **Conf** facs **Location** 1.6km S of town on R762

Hotel ★★★★ 64% Glenview Hotel, Glen O' the Downs, DELGANY ☎ 01 2873399 70 en suite

Greystones

☎ 01 2874136 🖷 01 2873749
e-mail: secretary@greystonesgc.com
web: www.greystonesgc.com

18 holes, 5322 metres, Par 69, SSS 68.

Course Designer P Merrigan
Telephone for further details

Hotel ★★★★ 64% Glenview Hotel, Glen O' the Downs, DELGANY ☎ 01 2873399 70 en suite

Kilcoole Map 01 D3

Druids Glen Golf Club see page 477

Hotel ★★★★★ 72% Marriott Druids Glen Hotel & Country Club, NEWTOWNMOUNTKENNEDY ☎ 01 2870800 148 en suite

Hotel ★★★ 68% Hunter's Hotel, RATHNEW ☎ 0404 40106 🖷 0404 40338 16 en suite

Hotel ★★★★ 64% Glenview Hotel, Glen O' the Downs, DELGANY ☎ 01 2873399 🖷 01 2877511 70 en suite

Kilcoole

☎ 01 2872066 🖷 01 2010497
e-mail: adminkg@eircom.net
web: www.kilcoolegolfclub.com
Beautifully manicured nine holes with water features on five holes. The course is dry and flat with sand based greens and the Sugarloaf Mountain in the background provides a pleasing view. Near the sea but well protected by tree lined fairways.
9 holes, 5506 metres, Par 70, SSS 69, Course record 66. Club membership 600.
Visitors Mon-Sun & BHs. Booking required. Dress code. **Societies** Booking required. **Green Fees** €25. **Facilities** **Conf** facs Corporate Hospitality Days **Location** S of village on R761

Hotel ★★★★ 64% Glenview Hotel, Glen O' the Downs, DELGANY ☎ 01 2873399 70 en suite

Rathdrum Map 01 D3

Glenmalure Greenane

☎ 0404 46679 🖷 0404 46783
e-mail: golf@glenmalure-golf.ie
web: www.glenmalure-golf.ie
18 holes, 4846 metres, Par 71, SSS 67, Course record 71.
Course Designer P Suttle **Location** 3km W of town
Telephone for further details

Hotel ★★★ 67% Woodenbridge Hotel, WOODEN BRIDGE ☎ 0402 35146 23 en suite

Roundwood Map 01 D3

Roundwood Newtown, Mountkennedy

☎ 01 2818488 & 2802555 🖷 01 2843642
e-mail: rwood@indigo.ie
web: www.globalgolf.com
18 holes, 6113 metres, Par 72, SSS 72.
Location 4km NE of village on R765
Telephone for further details'

Hotel ★★★ 65% The Glendalough Hotel, GLENDALOUGH ☎ 0404 45135 44 en suite

Shillelagh Map 01 D3

Coollattin Coollattin

☎ 055 29125 🖷 055 29125
18 holes, 5622 metres, Par 70, SSS 68, Course record 70.
Course Designer Peter McEvoy
Telephone for further details

Hotel ★★★ Marlfield House Hotel, GOREY ☎ 055 21124 20 en suite

Wicklow Map 01 D3

Wicklow Dunbur Rd

☎ 0404 67379 🖷 64756
e-mail: info@wicklowgolfclub.ie
web: www.wicklowgolfclub.ie
Situated on the cliffs overlooking Wicklow Bay, this course provides a challenging test of golf, each hole having individual features. Spectacular views of the coastline from every hole.

18 holes, 5437 metres, Par 71, SSS 70. Club membership 700.
Visitors Mon-Sat. Booking required. Dress code. **Societies** Booking required. **Green Fees** €40 per round. **Prof** Darren McLoughlin **Course Designer** Craddock & Ruddy **Facilities** **Location** SE of town centre

Farmhouse ♦♦♦♦ Kilpatrick House, Redcross, WICKLOW ☎ 0404 47137 & 087 6358325 🖷 0404 47866 4 rms (3 en suite)

Woodenbridge Map 01 D3

Woodenbridge Woodenbridge, Arklow

☎ 0402 35202 🖷 0402 35754
e-mail: wgc@eircom.net
web: www.globalgolf.com
18 holes, 5852 metres, Par 71, SSS 70, Course record 71.
Course Designer Patrick Merrigan **Location** N of village
Telephone for further details

Hotel ★★★ 67% Woodenbridge Hotel, WOODEN BRIDGE ☎ 0402 35146 23 en suite

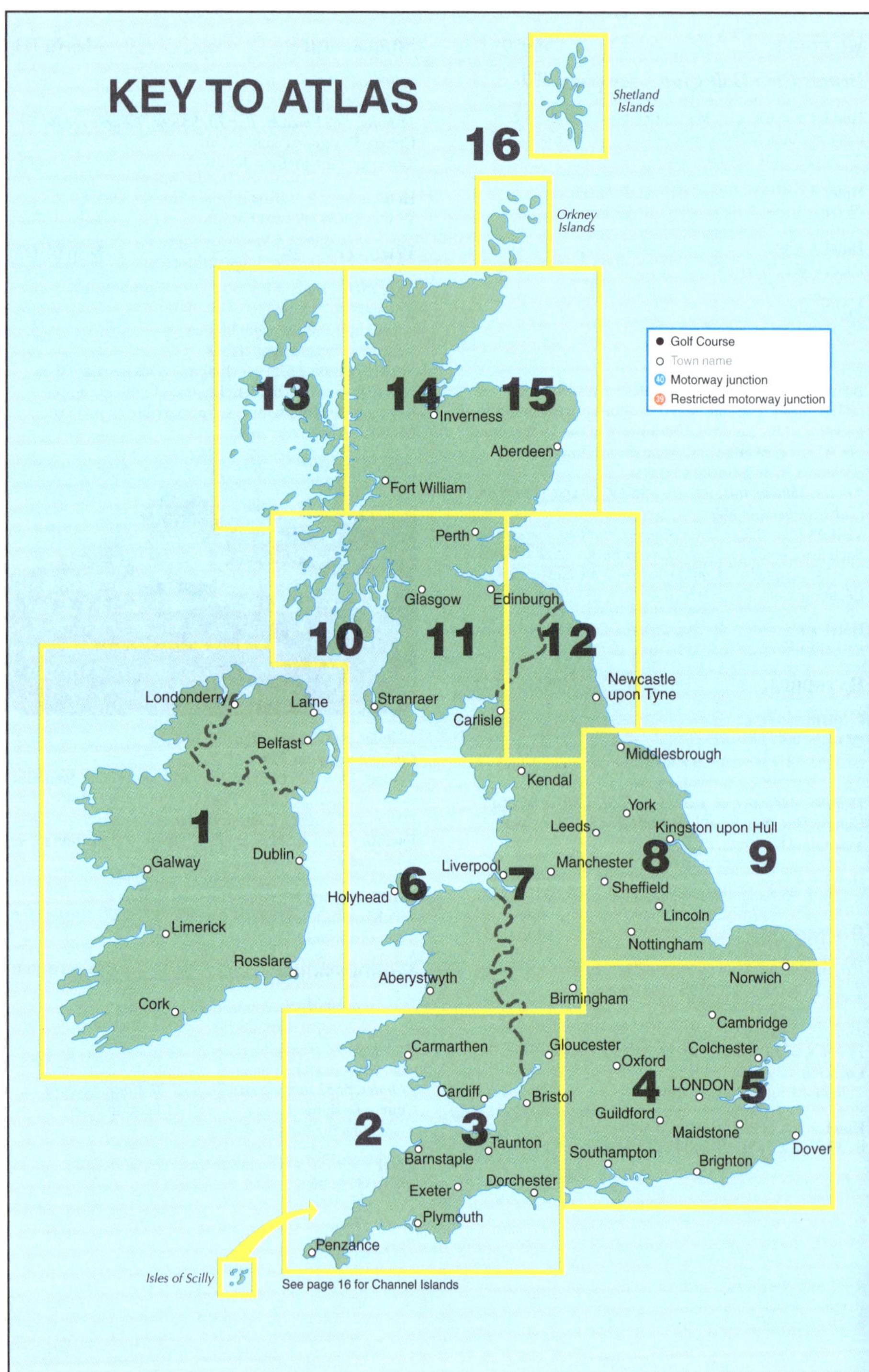
KEY TO ATLAS
Shetland Islands
16
Orkney Islands
Golf Course
Town name
Motorway junction
Restricted motorway junction
13
14
15
Inverness
Aberdeen
Fort William
Perth
Glasgow
Edinburgh
10
11
12
Londonderry
Larne
Belfast
Stranraer
Carlisle
Newcastle upon Tyne
Middlesbrough
Kendal
York
Leeds
Kingston upon Hull
1
Galway
Dublin
Liverpool
Manchester
8
9
Holyhead
6
7
Sheffield
Lincoln
Limerick
Nottingham
Rosslare
Aberystwyth
Norwich
Cork
Birmingham
Cambridge
Carmarthen
Gloucester
Colchester
Oxford
Cardiff
Bristol
4
LONDON
5
Guildford
2
3
Taunton
Maidstone
Barnstaple
Southampton
Dover
Brighton
Exeter
Dorchester
Plymouth
Penzance
Isles of Scilly
See page 16 for Channel Islands

1
A
B
C
D
6
5
4
3
2
1
Rathlin Island
Ballyliffin
Machair Loiscthe (Rosepenna)
Portsalon
Greencastle
Portrush
Portballintrae
Ballycastle
Portstewart
Cushendall
Moville
Castlerock
Ballymoney
Gaoth Dobhair (Gweedore)
Dunfanaghy
Rathmullan
Buncrana
Limavady
Aghadowey
An Chruit (Cruit Island)
Letterkenny
LONDONDERRY
Kilrea
Ballymena
M2
Ballygally
Larne
Carrickfergus
Naran
Ballybofey
Strabane
Castledawson
Newtownabbey
Whitehead
Ballyclare
Holywood
Bangor
Donaghadee
Antrim
Dundonald
Newtownards
Newtownbreda
Ardmillan
Donegal
Newtonstewart
Cookstown
BELFAST
Lisburn
Maze
Carryduff
Omagh
Dungannon
Lurgan
M1
Killyleagh
Cloughey
Portadown
Tandragee
Ballynahinch
Fintona
Bundoran
Armagh
Magheralin
Downpatrick
Ardglass
Enniskillen
Banbridge
Sligo
Blacklion
Monaghan
Newry
Newcastle
Warrenpoint
Béal an Mhuirthead (Belmullet)
Inishcrone
Belturbet
Clones
Cullyhanna
Kilkeel
Greenore
Ballina
Ballymote
Ballyconnell
Castleblayney
Achill Island
Tobercurry
Boyle
Ballinamore
Carrickmacross
Dundalk
Carrick-on-Shannon
Cavan
Ardee
Termonfeckin
Keel
Castlebar
Swinford
Ballaghaderreen
Virginia
Baltray
Clare Island
Westport
Ballyhaunis
Strokestown
Kells
Drogheda
Bettystown
Toll
Castlerea
Inishturk
Claremorris
Longford
Delvin
Navan
Balbriggan
Skerries
Dunshaughlin
Inishbofin
Ballinrobe
Roscommon
Rush
Renvyle
Tuam
Mullingar
Trim
Malahide
Mountbellew
Maynooth
Portmarnock
Kilcock
M4
M50
DUBLIN
Ballyconneely
Athlone
Moate
Donadea
Oughterard
Ballinasloe
Daingean
Carbury
Dun Laoghaire
GALWAY
Oranmore
Tullamore
Edenderry
Killiney
Naas
Bray
Gorumna Island
Bearna (Barna)
Loughrea
Birr
Portarlington
Kildare
M9
M11
Greystones
Delgany
Portumna
Portlaoise
Athy
Dunlavin
Kilcoole
Inishmore
Gort
Mountrath
Rathdrum
Wicklow
Roscrea
Abbeyleix
Castledermot
Baltinglass
Blainroe
Lahinch
Bodyke
Carlow
Woodenbridge
Brittas Bay
Arklow
Milltown Malbay
Ennis
Nenagh
Rathdowney
Tullow
Newmarket-on-Fergus
Templemore
Shillelagh
Gorey
Kilkee
Thurles
Kilkenny
Borris
Shannon Airport
LIMERICK
Kilrush
Thomastown
Enniscorthy
Adare
Monard
Callan
Ballybunion
Newcastle West
Tipperary
Cahir
Carrick-on-Suir
Wexford
Clonmel
New Ross
Rosslare
Charleville
Mitchelstown
Castlegregory
Tralee
Doneraile
WATERFORD
Baile an Fheirtearaigh (Ballyferriter)
Kanturk
Fermoy
Lismore
Tramore
Dunmore East
Killorglin
Mallow
An Daingean (Dingle)
Killarney
Glenbeigh
Youghal
Dungarvan
Blarney
Midleton
Macroom
CORK
Parknasilla
Kenmare
Ovens
Little Island
Douglas
Blackrock
Monkstown
An Coireán (Waterville)
Glengarriff
Bandon
Carrigaline
Bantry
Kinsale
Dursey Island
Castletown Bearhaven
Skibbereen
Clonakilty
Clear Island
1 Ballyboghil
2 Donabate
3 Swords
4 Cloghran
5 Castleknock
6 Lucan
7 Straffan
8 Rathcoole
9 Kill
10 Brittas
11 Saggart
12 Tallaght
13 Enniskerry
14 Roundwood
15 Blessington
Golf Course
Town name
0 20 40 miles
0 20 40 60 kilometres

For continuation pages refer to numbered arrows

3
HEREFORDSHIRE
WORCESTERSHIRE
WARWICKSHIRE
POWYS
GLOUCESTERSHIRE
MONMOUTHSHIRE
WILTSHIRE
SOMERSET
DORSET
Bristol Channel
Lyme Bay
Brecon Beacons
Exmoor
Salisbury Plain
New Forest
Chesil Beach
Portland Bill
Prawle Point
HEREFORD
WORCESTER
GLOUCESTER
CHELTENHAM
BRISTOL
BATH
CARDIFF
NEWPORT
SWINDON
SALISBURY
EXETER
TORQUAY
BOURNEMOUTH
SO
SP
ST
SU
SY
SZ
0
10
20 miles
0
10
20
30 kilometres

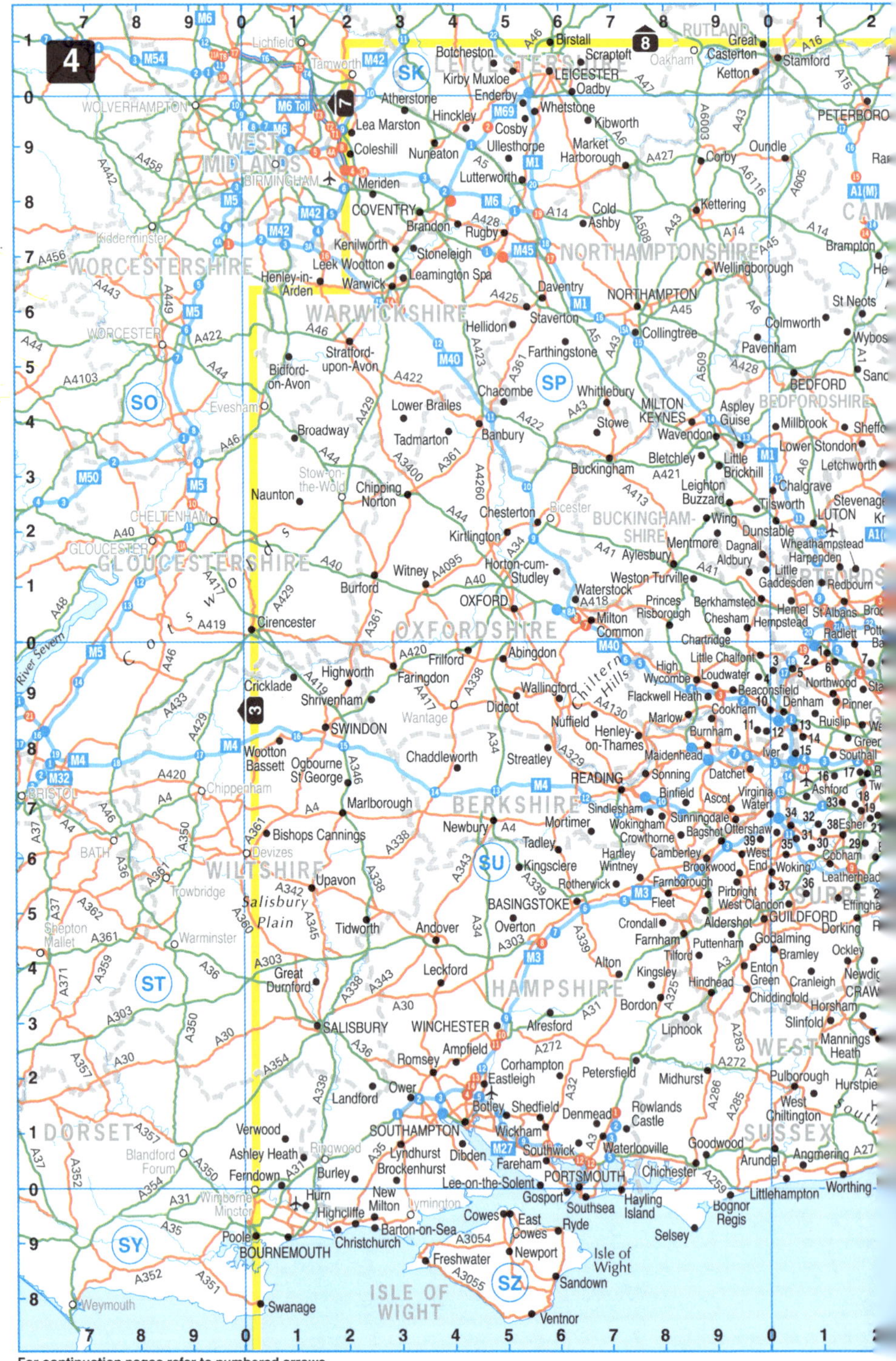

For continuation pages refer to numbered arrows

5
TF
TG
TL
TM
TQ
TR
TV
NORFOLK
SUFFOLK
ESSEX
KENT
EAST SUSSEX
GREAT YARMOUTH
Gorleston on Sea
NORWICH
Barnham Broom
Bawburgh
Swaffham
Downham Market
Watton
Denver
March
Fritton
LOWESTOFT
Bungay
Beccles
Thetford
Diss
Ely
Mildenhall
Worlington
Halesworth
Southwold
Stuston
Flempton
Bury St Edmunds
Longstanton
Girton
Newmarket
CAMBRIDGE
Cretingham
Thorpeness
Aldeburgh
Stowmarket
Woodbridge
Waldringfield
Orford Ness
Haverhill
Hintlesham
IPSWICH
Saffron Walden
Sudbury
Newton
Raydon
Felixstowe
Gosfield
Earls Colne
Harwich
The Naze
Braintree
COLCHESTER
Frinton-on-Sea
Bishop's Stortford
Sawbridgeworth
Witham
Tolleshunt Knights
Clacton-on-Sea
Woodham Walter
Maldon
Harlow
CHELMSFORD
Toot Hill
Purleigh
Theydon Bois
Abridge
Stapleford Abbotts
Stock
Billericay
Burnham-on-Crouch
Canewdon
Foulness Island
Chigwell Row
Chigwell
Brentwood
Ingrave
Rochford
Romford
Basildon
Benfleet
SOUTHEND-ON-SEA
Upminster
Ilford
Bulphan
Orsett
Stanford le Hope
Canvey Island
R Thames
Barnehurst
South Ockendon
Sheerness
Isle of Sheppey
Herne Bay
Westgate on Sea
MARGATE
Broadstairs
Ramsgate
Dartford
Gravesend
Hoo
Sidcup
New Ash Green
Rochester
Gillingham
Bromley
Eynsford
Ash
Whitstable
Sittingbourne
Orpington
West Kingsdown
Snodland
Addington
Faversham
CANTERBURY
Sandwich
Biggin Hill
Shoreham
North Downs
MAIDSTONE
Bearsted
Sevenoaks
Borough Green
West Malling
Deal
Limpsfield
Hildenborough
Edenbridge
Tonbridge
Chart Sutton
Barham
Kingsdown
Hever
TUNBRIDGE WELLS
Headcorn
CHANNEL TUNNEL TERMINAL
Ashford
Dover
Holtye
Brenchley
Biddenden
Folkestone
Lamberhurst
Cranbrook
Tenterden
Hythe
Crowborough
Ticehurst
Hawkhurst
Strait of Dover
Littlestone
Heathfield
Sedlescombe
Uckfield
Lydd
Rye
Dungeness
Hailsham
HASTINGS
Bexhill
Seaford
EASTBOURNE
Beachy Head
1 – Aldenham
2 – Watford
3 – Rickmansworth
4 – Chalfont St Giles
5 – Chorleywood
6 – Bushey
7 – Elstree
8 – Hadley Wood
9 – Enfield
10 – Gerrards Cross
11 – Stoke Poges
12 – Wexham Street
13 – Uxbridge
14 – Hillingdon
15 – West Drayton
16 – Hounslow
17 – Isleworth
18 – Hampton Wick
19 – Kingston upon Thames
20 – New Malden
21 – Surbiton
22 – Carshalton
23 – Croydon
24 – Coulsdon
25 – Chipstead
26 – Kingswood
27 – Walton-on-the-Hill
28 – Banstead
29 – Chessington
30 – Weybridge
31 – Addlestone
32 – Walton-on-Thames
33 – Hampton
34 – Chertsey
35 – West Byfleet
36 – East Horsley
37 – Sutton Green
38 – Shepperton
39 – Chobham
40 – Caterham
41 – Downe
42 – Halstead
43 – Addington
44 – Farleigh
45 – Woldingham
46 – Westerham
47 – Bletchingley
48 – Tandridge
49 – South Godstone
Golf Course
Town name
0 10 20 miles
0 10 20 30 kilometres

For continuation pages refer to numbered arrows

7
NY
NZ
SD
SE
SJ
SK
SO
SP
12
8
4
3
Richmond
Scotch Corner
North York Moors
Northallerton
Bowness-on-Windermere
Kendal
CUMBRIA
Sedbergh
THE PENNINES
Hawes
Leyburn
Yorkshire Dales
NORTH YORKSHIRE
Thirsk
Ulverston
Grange-over-Sands
Silverdale
Kirkby Lonsdale
BARROW-IN-FURNESS
Bentham
Ripon
Malton
Morecambe
Heysham
LANCASTER
Settle
Harrogate
Knott End-on-Sea
Fleetwood
Skipton
Addingham
Ilkley
YORK
Garstang
LANCASHIRE
Barnoldswick
Silsden
Keighley
Riddlesden
Baildon
Clitheroe
Longridge
Whalley
Colne
Nelson
Bingley
Shipley
LEEDS
Selby
Langho
Great Harwood
Wilpshire
Rishton
Burnley
BRADFORD
PRESTON
Blackburn
Accrington
Hebden Bridge
Halifax
WEST YORKSHIRE
Pleasington
Bacup
Todmorden
Sowerby
Brighouse
Goole
Leyland
Darwen
Haslingden
Holywell Green
Elland
Wakefield
Chorley
Whitworth
Littleborough
Outlane
Huddersfield
Southport
Westhoughton
Rochdale
Milnrow
Marsden
Ormskirk
Standish
Bolton
Bury
Meltham
Formby
Shevington
Whitefield
Middleton
Oldham
Barnsley
Up Holland
Wigan
Kearsley
Walkden
Prestwich
Uppermill
Hindley
Swinton
Failsworth
DONCASTER
Bickerstaffe
Ashton-in-Makerfield
Worsley
MANCHESTER
Ashton-under-Lyne
SOUTH YORKSHIRE
Bootle
Newton-le-Willows
Stalybridge
Wallasey
St Helens
Urmston
Hyde
Denton
Glossop
LIVERPOOL
Winwick
Flixton
Sale
Romiley
Huyton
Rainhill
Lymm
Gatley
Stockport
Cheadle
Mellor
Hazel Grove
SHEFFIELD
Birkenhead
Bebington
Warrington
Altrincham
Bramhall
New Mills
Widnes
Bromborough
Runcorn
Antrobus
Wilmslow
Poynton
Disley
Chapel-en-le-Frith
Peak District
Eastham
Ellesmere Port
Frodsham
Sutton Weaver
Knutsford
Alderley Edge
Prestbury
Flint
Helsby
Sandiway
Macclesfield
Buxton
Chesterfield
CHESTER
Delamere
CHESHIRE
Hawarden
Oscroft
Winsford
Mold
Tarporley
Sandbach
Congleton
DERBYSHIRE
NOTTINGHAMSHIRE
FLINTS
Aldersey Green
Crewe
Alsager
Leek
WREXHAM
Nantwich
Goldenhill
STOKE-ON-TRENT
Newcastle-under-Lyme
Whiston
Ashbourne
Ruabon
Eyton
Onneley
NOTTINGHAM
Chirk
Whitchurch
Stone
Uttoxeter
DERBY
Market Drayton
Weston-under-Redcastle
STAFFORDSHIRE
Weston
Burton upon Trent
Pant
STAFFORD
Newport
Brocton
Loughborough
Lilleshall
Rugeley
SHREWSBURY
Wellington
Penkridge
Cannock
Lichfield
Welshpool
Shifnal
LEICESTERSHIRE
Oakham
TELFORD
Tamworth
LEICESTER
Pattingham
WOLVERHAMPTON
Aldridge
Church Stretton
Worfield
Perton
Walsall
Sutton Coldfield
Bridgnorth
Sedgley
West Bromwich
Wishaw
Nuneaton
Himley
Enville
Dudley
BIRMINGHAM
WEST MIDLANDS
SHROPSHIRE
Stourbridge
Halesowen
Solihull
Cleobury Mortimer
Kidderminster
Hollywood
Knowle
COVENTRY
Wythall
Rugby
Ludlow
Tenbury Wells
Bewdley
Bromsgrove
Alvechurch
Tanworth in Arden
Redditch
M6
M55
M65
M61
M66
M62
M58
M53
M56
M60
M621
M18
M181
M180
M1
A1(M)
M42
M54
M6 Toll
M69
M5
M45
M40

For continuation pages refer to numbered arrows

9
rn Head
Mablethorpe
Sutton on Sea
Woodthorpe
A52
Skegness
TF
TG
The Wash
Brancaster
Hunstanton
A149
Sheringham
West Runton
Cromer
Mundesley
A148
Fakenham
North Walsham
Aylsham
A140
KING'S LYNN
A17
NORFOLK
A1067
A149
Middleton
A1065
Dereham
A47
Weston Longville
A1151
The Broads
Swaffham
Mattishall
NORWICH
GREAT YARMOUTH
Wisbech
A10
5
0 10 20 miles
0 10 20 30 kilometres
Golf Course
Town name

For continuation pages refer to numbered arrows

PERTH AND KINROSS
DUNDEE CITY
FIFE
NORTH SEA
Firth of Forth
Firth of Tay
EDINBURGH
EAST LOTHIAN
MIDLOTHIAN
FALKIRK
SOUTH LANARKSHIRE
BORDERS (SCOTTISH)
DUMFRIES AND GALLOWAY
NORTHUMBERLAND
CUMBRIA
DURHAM
Southern Uplands
Lammermuir Hills
The Cheviot Hills
Solway Firth
Lake District
1 – Burnside
2 – Uddingston
3 – Bishopbriggs
4 – Dumbarton
5 – Langbank
DUNDEE
PERTH
Arbroath
St Andrews
St Andrews Bay
Fife Ness
Anstruther
Isle of May
Cupar
Ladybank
Falkland
Milnathort
Kinross
Leslie
Markinch
Leven
Glenrothes
Thornton
Lochgelly
Cowdenbeath
Kirkcaldy
Kinghorn
Burntisland
Aberdour
Dunfermline
Saline
Kincardine
Dollar
Tillicoultry
Alva
Alloa
Muckhart
STIRLING
Bridge of Allan
Bannockburn
Dunblane
Callander
Dunning
Auchterarder
Crieff
Muthill
Comrie
St Fillans
Killin
Dunkeld
North Berwick
Haddington
Prestonpans
Musselburgh
Dalkeith
Lasswade
Bonnyrigg
Gorebridge
Penicuik
South Queensferry
Linlithgow
Uphall
Broxburn
Ratho
Livingston
West Calder
Bathgate
Whitburn
Fauldhouse
Shotts
Polmont
Falkirk
Larbert
Kilsyth
Lennoxtown
Balmore
Kirkintilloch
Cumbernauld
Lenzie
Muirhead
Gartcosh
Airdrie
Coatbridge
GLASGOW
Bellshill
Motherwell
Wishaw
Clarkston
Bothwell
Hamilton
East Kilbride
Larkhall
Carluke
Lanark
Strathaven
Lesmahagow
Carnwath
West Linton
Biggar
Rigside
Peebles
Innerleithen
Galashiels
Kelso
Coldstream
Berwick-upon-Tweed
Holy Island
St Abb's Head
Jedburgh
Hawick
Alnwick
Leadhills
Sanquhar
New Cumnock
Moffat
Thornhill
Lochmaben
Lockerbie
Langholm
Dumfries
Cummertrees
Annan
Gretna
CARLISLE
Castle Douglas
Dalbeattie
Gatehouse of Fleet
Colvend
Southerness
Kirkcudbright
Abbey Head
Silloth
Wigton
Maryport
Cockermouth
Workington
Whitehaven
St Bees Head
St Bees
Keswick
Penrith
Brough
Alston
Hexham
Consett
Morpeth
NN
NO
NT
NS
NY

For continuation pages refer to numbered arrows

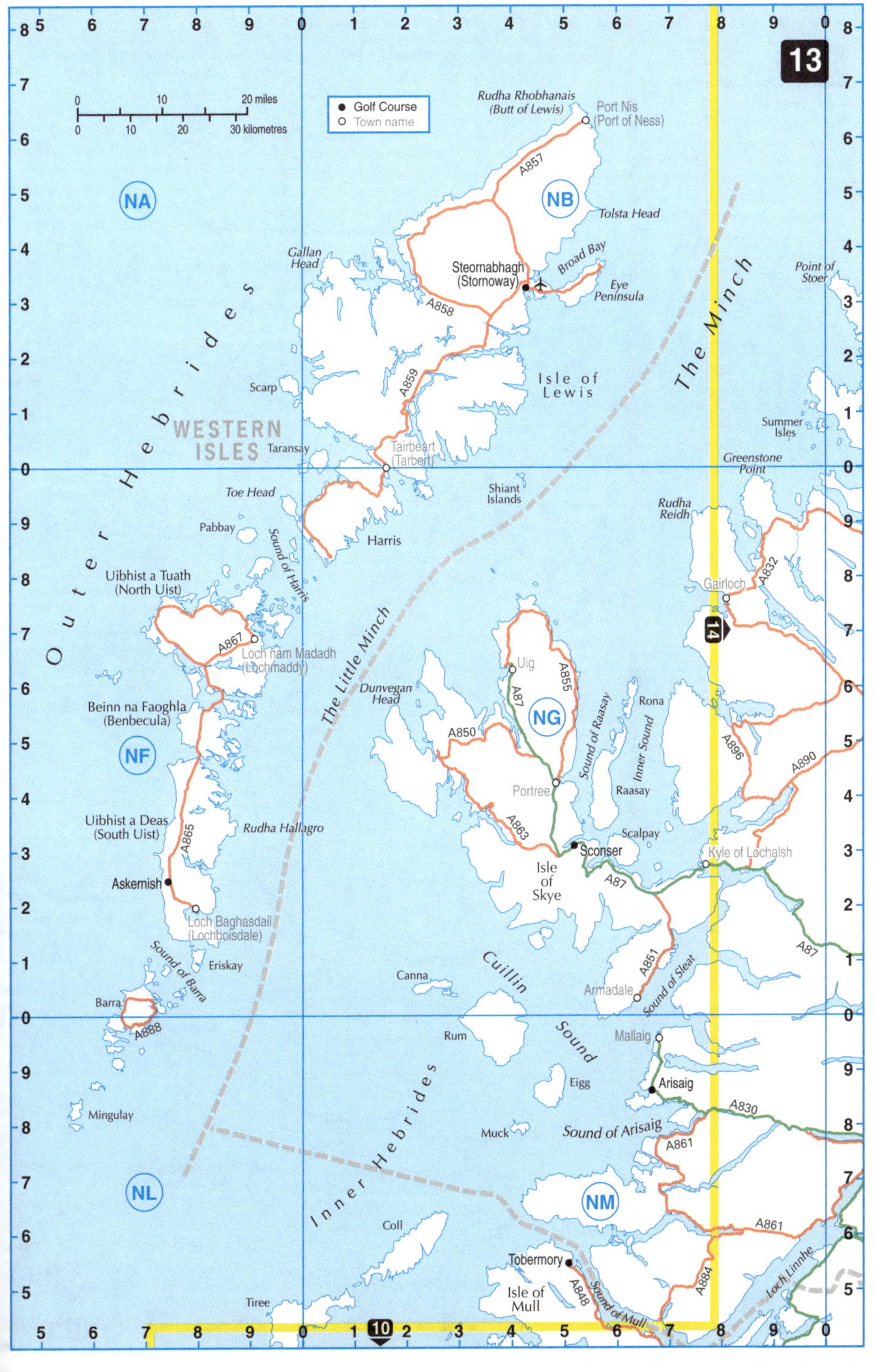
13
0 10 20 miles
0 10 20 30 kilometres
Golf Course
Town name
NA
NB
NF
NG
NL
NM
Rudha Rhobhanais (Butt of Lewis)
Port Nis (Port of Ness)
A857
Tolsta Head
Gallan Head
Steornabhagh (Stornoway)
Broad Bay
Eye Peninsula
A858
A859
Scarp
Isle of Lewis
The Minch
Point of Stoer
Summer Isles
Greenstone Point
Outer Hebrides
WESTERN ISLES
Taransay
Tairbeart (Tarbert)
Toe Head
Shiant Islands
Rudha Reidh
Pabbay
Sound of Harris
Harris
Uibhist a Tuath (North Uist)
Gairloch
A832
14
A867
Loch nam Madadh (Lochmaddy)
The Little Minch
Uig
A855
A87
Dunvegan Head
Beinn na Faoghla (Benbecula)
Rona
A850
Sound of Raasay
Inner Sound
A896
A890
Portree
Raasay
Uibhist a Deas (South Uist)
A865
Rudha Hallagro
A863
Scalpay
Sconser
Kyle of Lochalsh
Askernish
Isle of Skye
Loch Baghasdail (Lochboisdale)
Sound of Barra
Eriskay
Canna
Cuillin Sound
A851
Sound of Sleat
Armadale
Barra
A888
Rum
Mallaig
Eigg
Arisaig
A830
Mingulay
Muck
Sound of Arisaig
A861
Inner Hebrides
Coll
Tobermory
A884
Loch Linnhe
Isle of Mull
A848
Sound of Mull
Tiree
10

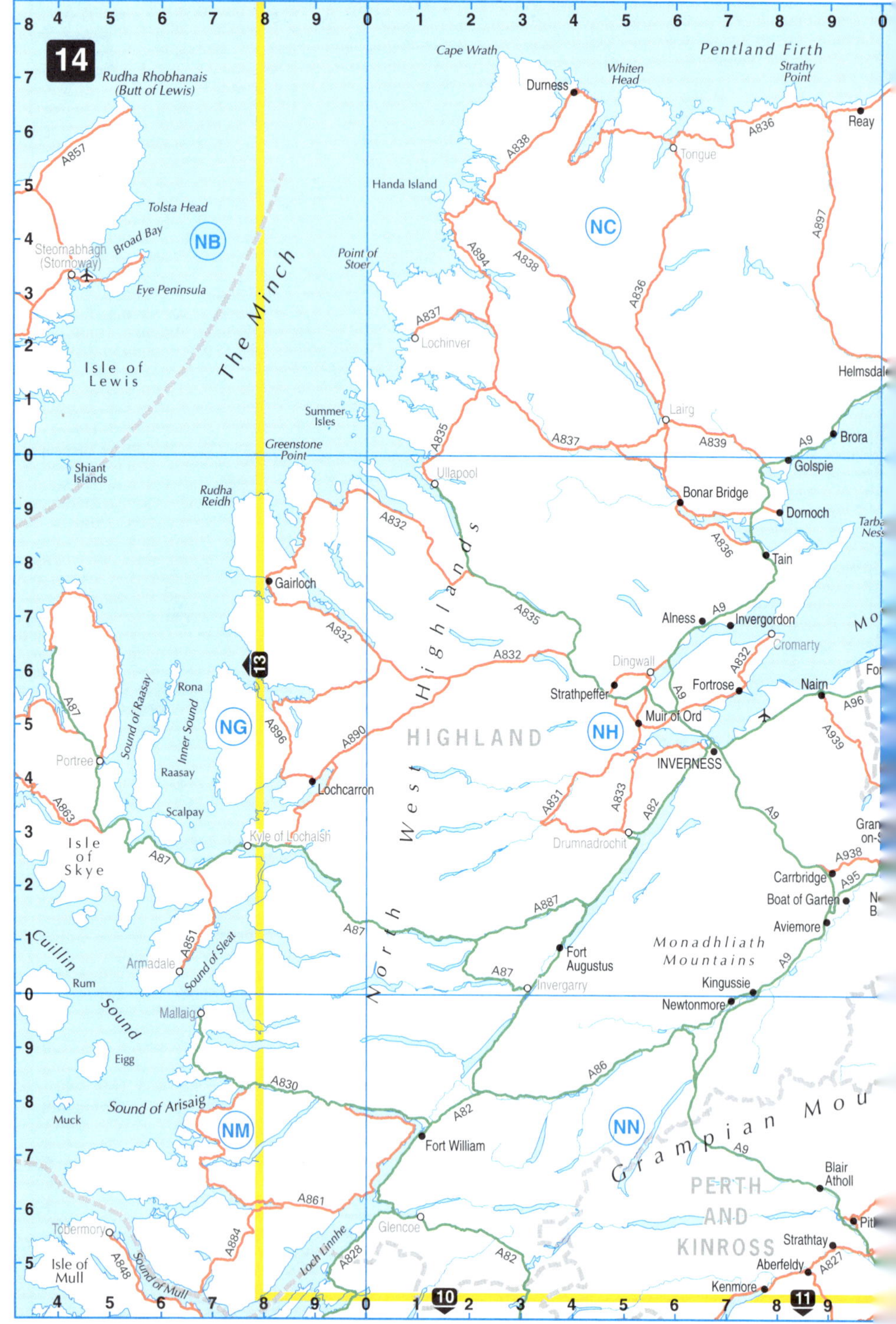

For continuation pages refer to numbered arrows

Island of Stroma
Duncansby Head
John o'Groats
Thurso
Noss Head
Wick
Lybster
ND
NJ
NK
NO
Lossiemouth
Garmouth
Spey Bay
Buckie
Cullen
Banff
Macduff
Fraserburgh
Inverallochy
Elgin
Keith
Rothes
Turriff
Mintlaw
Peterhead
Dufftown
Huntly
Ballindalloch
Cruden Bay
Ellon
Oldmeldrum
Insch
Inverurie
Newburgh
Newmachar
Balmedie
Tomintoul
ABERDEENSHIRE
Alford
Kemnay
Kintore
ABERDEEN CITY
ABERDEEN
Tarland
Torphins
Peterculter
Aboyne
Ballater
Banchory
Portlethen
Stonehaven
Auchenblae
Edzell
ANGUS
Brechin
Montrose
Kirriemuir
Alyth
Forfar
Lunan Bay
Golf Course
Town name
0 10 20 miles
0 10 20 30 kilometres
12

16

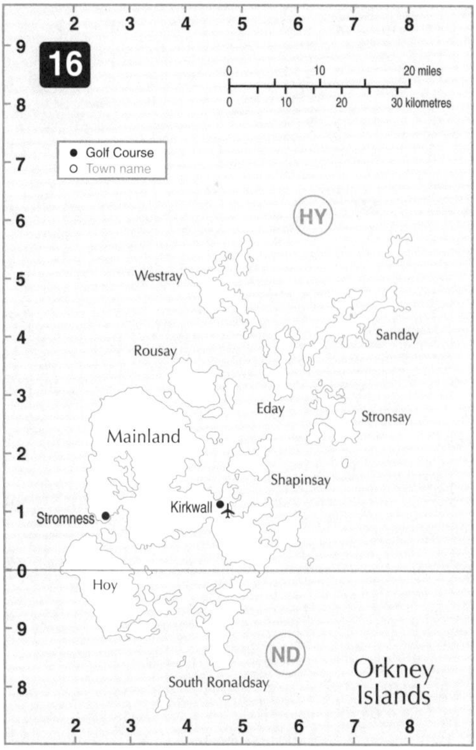

0 10 20 miles
0 10 20 30 kilometres

● Golf Course
○ Town name

HY
Westray
Rousay
Sanday
Eday
Stronsay
Mainland
Shapinsay
Kirkwall
Stromness
Hoy
ND
South Ronaldsay

Orkney Islands

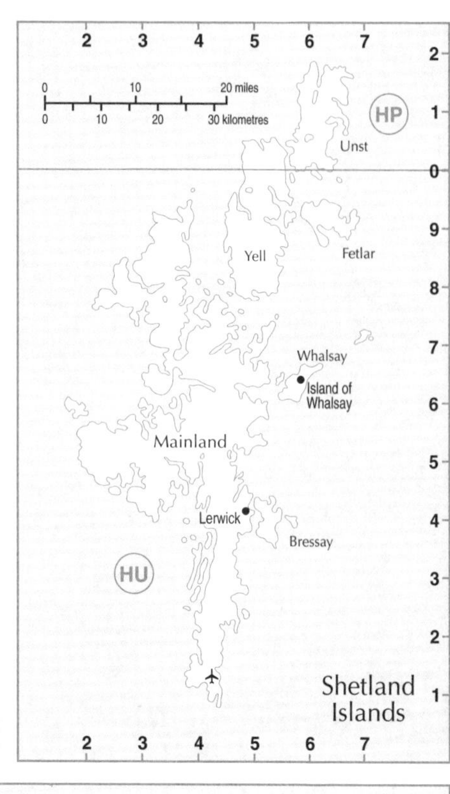

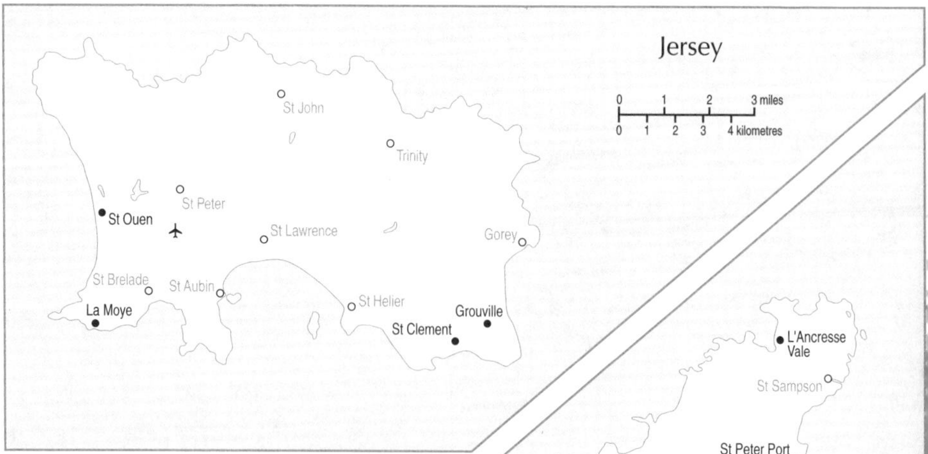

Jersey

0 1 2 3 miles
0 1 2 3 4 kilometres

St John
Trinity
St Peter
St Ouen
St Lawrence
Gorey
St Brelade
St Aubin
St Helier
La Moye
Grouville
St Clement

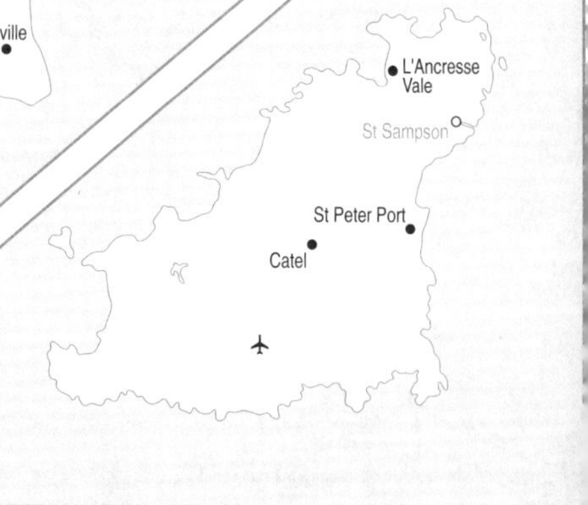

L'Ancresse Vale
St Sampson
St Peter Port
Catel

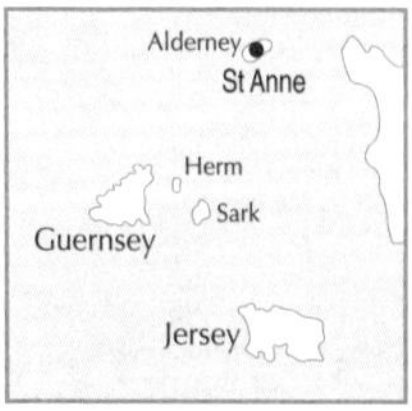

Guernsey

0 1 2 3 miles
0 1 2 3 4 kilometres

Alderney
St Anne
Herm
Sark
Guernsey
Jersey

Index

A

Abbeyleix 460
Aberdare 416
Aberdeen 319
ABERDEEN CITY 319
ABERDEENSHIRE 320
Aberdour 349
Aberdyfi 404
Aberfeldy 369
Aberfoyle 385
Abergavenny 407
Abergele 399
Aberlady 344
Abersoch 404
Aberystwyth 398
Abingdon 210
Aboyne 320
Abridge 87
Accrington 156
Adare 462
Addingham 303
Addington 102
Addington 143
Addlestone 238
Aghadowey 432
Airdrie 367
Aldbury 134
Aldeburgh 231
Aldenham 134
Alderley Edge 41
ALDERNEY 314
Alderney 314
Aldersey Green 41
Aldershot 123
Aldridge 271
ldwark 292
lford 320
lfreton 63
llendale 201
llenthorpe 289
lloa 335
lmondsbury 97
lness 356
lnmouth 201
lnwick 201
lsager 41
lston 58
lton 123
ltrincham 113
lva 335
lvechurch 284
lwoodley 303
lyth 369
mlwch 393
mmanford 397
mpfield 123
Ancresse Vale, Guernsey 314
ndover 123
NGLESEY, ISLE OF 393
ngmering 258
NGUS 324
nstruther 349
NTRIM 422
ntrim 422
Antrobus 42
Appleby-in-Westmorland 58
Arbroath 324
Ardee 463
Ardglass 427
Ardmillan 427
ARGYLL & BUTE 327
Arisaig 356
Arklow 475
ARMAGH 424
Armagh 424
ARRAN, ISLE OF 389
Arundel 258
Ascot 24
Ash 143
Ashbourne 63
Ashby-de-la-Zouch 165
Ashford 238
Ashford 144
Ashkirk 376
Ashley Heath 77
Ashton-in-Makerfield 113
Ashton-under-Lyne 114
Askam-in-Furness 59
Askernish 391
Aspley Guise 21
Atherstone 266
Athlone 473
Athlone 469
Athy 457
Auchenblae 320
Auchterarder 369
Aughton 289
Aviemore 356
Axmouth 68
Aylesbury 31
Ayr 379

B

Backwell 219
Backworth 263
Bacup 156
Bagshot 238
Baildon 303
Bakewell 64
Bala 404
Balbriggan 444
Ballaghaderreen 469
Ballater 320
Ballina 465
Ballinamore 462
Ballinasloe 452
Ballindalloch 363
Ballinrobe 465
Balloch 386
Ballybofey 442
Ballyboughal 444
Ballybunion 454
Ballycastle 422
Ballyclare 422
Ballyconneely 452
Ballyconnell 435
Ballyferriter (Baile An Fheirtearaigh) 454
Ballygally 422
Ballyhaunis 465
Ballyliffin 442
Ballymena 422
Ballymoney 423
Ballymote 470
Ballynahinch 428
Balmedie 321
Balmore 341
Baltinglass 475
Baltray 464
Bamburgh 201
Bamford 64
Banbridge 428
Banbury 210
Banchory 321
Bandon 437
Banff 321
Bangor 428
Bangor 404
Bannockburn 385
Banstead 238
Bantry 437
Bar Hill 38
Barassie 380
Bargoed 395
Barham 144
Barnard Castle 82
Barnehurst 103
Barnet 103
Barnham Broom 191
Barnoldswick 156
Barnsley 299
Barrhead 348
Barrow-in-Furness 59
Barry 419
Barry 326
Barton-on-Sea 124
Basildon 88
Basingstoke 124
Bath 219
Bathgate 387
Bawburgh 191
Bawtry 299
Beaconsfield 31
Beaminster 77
Beamish 83
Bearna 452
Bearsden 342
Bearsted 144
Beaumaris 393
Bebington 183
Beccles 232
Beckenham 104
Bedale 292
Bedford 21
BEDFORDSHIRE 21
Bedlington 201
Beith 365
Belchalwell 77
BELFAST 426
Belfast 426
Belford 202
Bellingham 202
Bellshill 367

Belmullet
(Béal An Mhuirthead) 465
Belton 170
Belturbet 435
Benfleet 88
Bentham 292
Bere Regis 78
Berkhamsted 135
BERKSHIRE 24
Berwick-upon-Tweed 202
Bettws Newydd 408
Bettystown 466
Betws-y-Coed 399
Beverley 289
Bewdley 284
Bexhill 252
Bexleyheath 104
Bickerstaffe 156
Biddenden 144
Bidford-on-Avon 266
Bigbury-on-Sea 68
Biggar 382
Biggin Hill 104
Billericay 88
Billingham 83
Binfield 25
Bingley 304
Birkenhead 183
Birmingham 271
Birr 468
Birstall 165
Birtley 263
Bishampton 284
Bishop Auckland 83
Bishop's Stortford 135
Bishopbriggs 342
Bishops Cannings 279
Bishopton 375
Blackawton 68
Blackburn 157
Blacklion 435
Blackpool 157
Blackrock 438
Blackwaterfoot 389
Blackwood 395
BLAENAU GWENT 393
Blainroe 475
Blair Atholl 370
Blairgowrie 370
Blandford Forum 78
Blankney 170
Blarney 438
Blessington 475
Bletchingley 239
Bletchley 31
Blundellsands 184
Blyth 202
Boat Of Garten 356
Bodelwyddan 401
Bodenham 132
Bodmin 49
Bodyke 436
Bognor Regis 258
Boldon 263
Bolton 114
Bonar Bridge 357
Bonhill 387
Bonnyrigg 363
Bootle 184
Bordon 124
Borough Green 144
Borris 435
Borth 398
Boston 170
Botcheston 166
Bothwell 382
Botley 124
Bourn 38
Bourne 171
Bournemouth 78
Bowness-on-Windermere 59
Boyle 469
Bradford 304
Bradford-on-Avon 280
Braemar 321
Braintree 88
Bramhall 115
Bramley 239
Brampton 38
Brampton 59
Brancaster 191
Brandesburton 289
Brandon 266
Bray 475
Breadsall 64
Brechin 326
Brecon 414
Brenchley 144
Brentwood 88
Brickendon 135
Bridge of Allan 385
Bridge of Weir 375
BRIDGEND 394
Bridgend 394
Bridgnorth 216
Bridgwater 220
Bridlington 289
Bridport 79
Brighouse 305
Brighton & Hove 252
BRISTOL 28
Bristol 28
Brittas 445
Brittas Bay 476
Broadstairs 145
Broadstone 79
Broadway 284
Brockenhurst 125
Brocton 226
Brodick 389
Bromborough 184
Bromley 104
Bromsgrove 285
Brookmans Park 135
Brookwood 239
Brora 357
Brough 289
Broxbourne 136
Broxburn 387
Brynford 402
Buckie 363
Buckingham 32
BUCKINGHAMSHIRE 31
Bude 49
Budleigh Salterton 68
Budock Vean 50
Builth Wells 415
Bulphan 89
Buncrana 442
Bundoran 443
Bungay 232
Buntingford 136
Burford 210
Burgess Hill 258
Burley 125
Burnham 32
Burnham-on-Crouch 89
Burnham-on-Sea 220
Burnley 157
Burnopfield 83
Burnside 382
Burntisland 349
Burry Port 397
Burton upon Trent 226
Bury 115
Bury St Edmunds 232
Bushey 136
BUTE, ISLE OF 390
Buxton 64

C

Caerleon 412
Caernarfon 406
CAERPHILLY 395
Caerphilly 395
Caerwent 408
Cahir 470
Caldy 184
Callan 460
Callander 385
Calne 280
Calverton 205
Camberley 239
Camborne 50
Cambridge 38
CAMBRIDGESHIRE 38
Camelford 50
Canewdon 89
Cannock 227
Canterbury 145
Canvey Island 89
Carbury 458
CARDIFF 395
Cardiff 39
Cardigan 39
Cardross 32
Carlisle 6
CARLOW 43
Carlow 43
Carluke 38
Carlyon Bay 5
Carmarthen 39
CARMARTHENSHIRE 39
Carnoustie 32
Carnwath 38
Carradale 32
Carrbridge 35
Carrick-on-Shannon 46
Carrick-on-Suir 47
Carrickfergus 42
Carrickmacross 46
Carrigaline 43
Carryduff 42
Carshalton 10

Castel 315
Castle Combe 280
Castle Douglas 336
Castlebar 465
Castleblayney 468
Castledawson 432
Castledermot 458
Castlegregory 454
Castleknock 445
Castlerea 469
Castlerock 432
Castletown 316
Castletownbere
(Castletown Bearhaven) 438
Caterham 239
Catterick Garrison 292
CAVAN 435
Cavan 436
CEREDIGION 398
Chacombe 197
Chaddleworth 25
Chalfont St Giles 32
Chalgrave 21
Chapel-en-le-Frith 64
Chard 221
Charleville 438
Chart Sutton 145
Chartridge 32
Cheadle 116
Chelmsford 89
Cheltenham 97
Chepstow 410
Chertsey 240
Chesham 32
CHESHIRE 41
Cheshunt 136
Chessington 104
Chester 42
Chester-le-Street 83
Chesterfield 65
Chesterton 210
Chichester 258
Chiddingfold 240
Chigwell 90
Chigwell Row 91
Chingford
179
Chippenham 280
Chipping Norton 211
Chipping Sodbury 97
Chipstead 240
Chirk 420
Chislehurst 105
Chittlehamholt 69
Chobham 240
Chopwell 263
Chorley 157
Chorleywood 136
Christchurch 79
Christow 69
Chulmleigh 69
Church Stretton 216
Churston Ferrers 69
Cirencester 98
CITY OF EDINBURGH 329
CITY OF GLASGOW 334
CLACKMANNANSHIRE 335
Clacton-on-Sea 91
CLARE 436
Claremorris 465
Clarkston 348
Cleckheaton 305
Cleethorpes 171
Cleeve Hill 98
Cleobury Mortimer 216
Clevedon 221
Clifford 132
Clitheroe 158
Cloghran 445
Clonakilty 438
Clones 468
Clonmel 471
Cloughey 429
Clydach 417
Clydebank 387
DURHAM, CO 82
Coalpit Heath 98
Coatbridge 367
Cobham 240
Cockermouth 60
Codnor 65
Codrington 98
Colchester 91
Cold Ashby 197
Coldstream 376
Coleford 98
Coleshill 266
Colinsburgh 350
Collingtree 197
Colmworth 22
Colne 158
COLONSAY, ISLE OF 390
Colvend 336
Colwyn Bay 399
Comrie 370
Congleton 43
Congresbury 221
Conisbrough 299
Consett 84
Constantine Bay 51
CONWY 399
Conwy 400
Cookham 25
Cookstown 434
Copmanthorpe 292
Copthorne 259
Corby 198
Corhampton 125
CORK 437
Cork 438
CORNWALL &
ISLES OF SCILLY 49
Cosby 166
Cottingham 290
Coulsdon 105
Coventry 272
Cowdenbeath 350
Cowes 278
Craignure 390
Crail 350
Cramlington 202
Cranbrook 145
Cranleigh 241
Crawley 259
Crediton 69
Creigiau (Creiyiau) 397
Cretingham 233
Crewe 43
Criccieth 406
Cricklade 281
Crieff 370
Cromer 192
Crondall 125
Crook 84
Crosby-on-Eden 61
Crowborough 253
Crowle 171
Crowthorne 25
Croydon 241
Croydon 105
Cruden Bay 322
Cruit Island (An Chruit) 443
Cullen 364
Cullompton 70
Cullyhanna 424
Cumbernauld 368
CUMBRIA 58
Cummertrees 336
Cupar 350
Cushendall 423
Cwmbran 418

D

Dagnall 33
Daingean 468
Dalbeattie 337
Dalkeith 363
Dalmally 328
Darlington 84
Dartford 145
Darwen 158
Datchet 25
Daventry 198
Dawlish Warren 70
Deal 146
Delamere 43
Delgany 476
Delvin 473
Denbigh 401
DENBIGHSHIRE 401
Denham 33
Denmead 125
Denton 116
Denver 192
Derby 65
DERBYSHIRE 63
Dereham 192
DEVON 68
Dewsbury 305
Dibden 126
Didcot 211
Dinas Powys 419
Disley 43
Ditchling 253
Dolgellau 406
Dollar 336
Donabate 445
Donadea 458
Donaghadee 429
Doncaster 299
DONEGAL 442
Doneraile 439
Dorchester 79
Dorking 241

Dornoch 357
DORSET 77
Douglas 440
Douglas 316
DOWN 427
Downe 106
Downpatrick 429
Down St Mary 70
Driffield (Great) 290
Droitwich 285
Dronfield 66
Drymen 385
DUBLIN 444
Dublin 446
Dudley 273
Duffield 66
Dufftown 364
Dulwich 182
Dumbarton 387
Dumfries 337
DUMFRIES & GALLOWAY 336
Dun Laoghaire 449
Dunbar 344
Dunblane 386
Dundalk 464
Dundee 340
DUNDEE CITY 340
Dundonald 427
Dunfanaghy 443
Dunfermline 350
Dungannon 434
Dungarvan 472
Dunkeld 372
Dunlavin 476
Dunmore East 472
Dunning 372
Dunoon 328
Duns 376
Dunshaughlin 466
Dunstable 22
Durham 85
Durness 358
Dursley 99
Dymock 99

E

Eaglescliffe 86
Eaglesham 348
Earls Colne 92
Easingwold 292
EAST AYRSHIRE 341
Eastbourne 253
East Cowes 279
EAST DUNBARTONSHIRE 341
East Finchley 180
East Goscote 166
East Grinstead 260
Eastham 184
East Horsley 241
East Kilbride 384
East Leake 205
Eastleigh 126
EAST LOTHIAN 344
EAST RENFREWSHIRE 348
Edenbridge 146
Edenderry 469
Edinburgh 329
Edzell 326
Effingham 241
Elgin 364
Elie 351
Elland 306
Ellesmere Port 44
Ellon 322
Elsham 171
Elstree 137
Eltham 181
Ely 38
Embleton 203
Enderby 166
Enfield 106
Enmore 221
Ennis 436
Enniscorthy 474
Enniskerry 478
Enniskillen 430
Enton Green 242
Enville 227
Epping 92
Epsom 242
Eriska 328
Erlestoke 281
Esher 242
Essendon 137
ESSEX 87
Exeter 70
Eyemouth 377
Eynsford 146
Eyton 420

F

Failsworth 116
Fakenham 192
FALKIRK 348
Falkirk 348
Falkland 351
Falmouth 51
Fareham 126
Faringdon 211
Farleigh 242
Farnborough 126
Farnham 242
Farrington Gurney 222
Farthingstone 198
Fauldhouse 387
Faversham 146
Felixstowe 233
Felling 263
Felton 203
Fenay Bridge 306
FERMANAGH 430
Fermoy 440
Ferndown 79
Ffestiniog 406
FIFE 349
Filey 292
Fintona 434
Flackwell Heath 33
Fladbury 286
Flamborough 290
Fleet 126
Fleetwood 158
Flempton 233
Flint 403
FLINTSHIRE 402
Flixton 116
Folkestone 146
Forest Row 254
Forfar 326
Formby 184
Forres 364
Fort Augustus 358
Fort William 358
Fortrose 358
Fraserburgh 322
Freshwater 279
Frilford 211
Frinton-on-Sea 92
Fritton 192
Frodsham 44
Frome 222

G

Gainsborough 172
Gairloch 358
Galashiels 377
Galston 341
GALWAY 452
Galway 453
Ganton 293
Garforth 306
Garmouth 364
Garnant 397
Garstang 159
Gartcosh 368
Gatehouse of Fleet 337
Gateshead 263
Gatley 116
Gedney Hill 172
Gerrards Cross 33
Gifford 344
Gigha Island 328
Gillingham 147
Girton 39
Girvan 38
Glasgow 33
Glenbeigh 45
Glengarriff 44
Glenluce 33
Glenrothes 35
Glenshee (Spittal of) 37
Glossop 6
Gloucester 9
GLOUCESTERSHIRE 9
Glynneath 41
Godalming 24
Goldenhill 22
Golspie 35
Goodwood 26
Gorebridge 36
Gorey 47
Gorleston on Sea 19
Gort 45
Gosfield 9
Gosforth 26
Gosport 12
Gourock 36
Grange-over-Sands 6
Grantham 17
Grantown-on-Spey 35
Graveley 13
Gravesend 14
Great Casterton 21

Great Cumbrae Island (Millport) 365
Great Durnford 281
Great Harwood 159
Great Yarmouth 193
GREATER LONDON 102
GREATER MANCHESTER 113
Greencastle 443
Greenford 106
Greenhead 203
Greenock 362
Greenore 464
Greetham 215
Gretna 338
Greystones 478
Grimsby 172
Grouville 315
GUERNSEY 314
Guildford 243
Guiseley 306
Gullane 344
Gurney Slade 222
Gwbert on Sea 399
Gweedore (Gaoth Dobhair) 443
GWYNEDD 404

H

Haddington 346
Hadley Wood 107
Hailsham 255
Halesowen 273
Halesworth 233
Halifax 306
Halstead 147
Halstock 80
Hamilton 384
HAMPSHIRE 123
Hampton 107
Hampton Wick 107
Hanwell 183
Harlech 406
Harlow 93
Harpenden 137
Harrogate 293
Hartlepool 86
Hartley Wintney 127
Harwich 93
Haslingden 159
Hassocks 260
Hastings & St Leonards 255
Hatfield 300
Haverfordwest 412
Haverhill 233
Hawarden 403
Hawick 377
Hawkhurst 147
Hayling Island 127
Haywards Heath 260
Hazel Grove 116
Headcorn 147
Heathfield 255
Hebden Bridge 307
Helensburgh 328
Hellidon 198
Helmsdale 359
Helsby 44
Hemel Hempstead 137
Hemingford Abbots 39
Hendon 181
Henley-in-Arden 266
Henley-on-Thames 212
Hensol 419
Hereford 133
HEREFORDSHIRE 132
Herne Bay 148
HERTFORDSHIRE 134
Hessle 290
Heswall 186
Hever 148
Hexham 203
Heysham 159
Hickleton 300
High Bickington 71
High Green 300
High Wycombe 33
Highcliffe 80
Highgate 180
HIGHLAND 356
Highworth 281
Hildenborough 148
Hillingdon 107
Himley 227
Hinckley 166
Hindhead 244
Hindley 116
Hintlesham 234
Hollywood 286
Holsworthy 72
Holtye 255
Holyhead 393
Holywell Bay 52
Holywell Green 307
Holywood 429
Honiton 72
Hoo 148
Hopeman 364
Horncastle 172
Hornsea 290
Horsham 260
Horsley 66
Horton-cum-Studley 212
Houghton-le-Spring 264
Hounslow 108
Howden 290
Howth 449
Hoylake 186
Hucknall 206
Huddersfield 307
Hunstanton 193
Huntly 322
Hurn 80
Hurstpierpoint 260
Huyton 186
Hyde 116
Hythe 148

I

Ilford 108
Ilfracombe 72
Ilkley 308
Immingham 173
Ingrave 93
Inishcrone 470
Innellan 328
Innerleithen 377
Insch 322
Inverallochy 322
Inveraray 329
INVERCLYDE 362
Invergordon 359
Inverness 359
Inverurie 322
Ipplepen 72
Ipswich 234
Irvine 365
ISLAY, ISLE OF 390
ISLE OF WIGHT 278
Isleworth 108
Iver 33
Ivybridge 72

J

Jedburgh 378
JERSEY 315
Johnstone 375

K

Kanturk 440
Kearsley 117
Kedleston 66
Keel 465
Keighley 308
Keith 365
Kells 467
Kelso 378
Kemnay 323
Kendal 61
Kenilworth 266
Kenmare 456
Kenmore 372
KENT 143
KERRY 454
Keswick 61
Kettering 198
Ketton 215
Keynsham 222
Keyworth 206
Kibworth 166
Kidderminster 286
Kidwelly 398
Kilbirnie 366
Kilcock 467
Kilcoole 479
KILDARE 457
Kildare 458
Kilkee 436
Kilkeel 430
KILKENNY 460
Kilkenny 460
Kill 458
Killarney 456
Killin 386
Killiney 449
Killorglin 457
Killyleagh 430
Kilmacolm 362
Kilmarnock 341
Kilrea 432
Kilrush 436
Kilsyth 368
Kincardine 351
King's Lynn 193
Kingarth 390
Kinghorn 351

Kingsclere 127
Kingsdown 282
Kingsdown 148
Kingsley 128
Kingston upon Hull 291
Kingston upon Thames 108
Kingswood 244
Kington 133
Kingussie 360
Kinross 373
Kinsale 440
Kintore 323
Kirby Muxloe 166
Kirkby in Ashfield 206
Kirkby Lonsdale 61
Kirkbymoorside 294
Kirkcaldy 351
Kirkcudbright 338
Kirkintilloch 342
Kirkwall 391
Kirriemuir 326
Kirtlington 212
Knaresborough 294
Knebworth 138
Knighton 415
Knott End-on-Sea 159
Knowle 273
Knutsford 44

L

Laceby 173
Ladybank 352
Lahinch 436
Lamberhurst 149
Lamlash 389
Lanark 384
LANCASHIRE 156
Lancaster 159
Landford 282
Langbank 375
Langho 160
Langholm 338
LAOIS 460
Larbert 348
Largs 366
Larkhall 384
Larne 423
Lasswade 363
Lauder 378
Launceston 52
Lea Marston 267
Leadhills 384
Leamington Spa 267
Leatherhead 244
Leckford 128
Lee-on-the-Solent 128
Leeds 308
Leek 227
Leek Wootton 267
Leicester 167
LEICESTERSHIRE 165
Leighton Buzzard 22
LEITRIM 462
Lelant 52
Lennoxtown 343
Lenzie 343
Leominster 133
Lerwick 391
Leslie 352
Lesmahagow 384
Letchworth 138
Letterkenny 443
Letterston 412
Leuchars 352
Leven 352
Lewes 255
LEWIS, ISLE OF 390
Leyland 160
Leytonstone & Wanstead 179
Lichfield 228
Lilleshall 216
Limavady 433
LIMERICK 462
Limerick 462
Limpsfield 245
Lincoln 173
LINCOLNSHIRE 170
Lingfield 245
Linlithgow 387
Liphook 128
Lisburn 423
Lismore 472
Little Brickhill 34
Little Chalfont 34
Little Gaddesden 138
Little Island 440
Littleborough 117
Littlehampton 261
Littlestone 149
Liverpool 187
Livingston 388
Llandrindod Wells 415
Llandudno 400
Llanelli 398
Llanfairfechan 400
Llangattock 415
Llangollen 401
Llangybi 399
Llanidloes 415
Llanrhystud 399
Llanwern 412
Lochcarron 360
Lochgelly 353
Lochgilphead 329
Lochmaben 338
Lochranza 389
Lochwinnoch 375
Lockerbie 338
LONDON 179
LONDONDERRY 432
Londonderry 433
Long Ashton 222
Long Eaton 67
LONGFORD 463
Longford 463
Longhorsley 203
Longniddry 346
Longridge 160
Longstanton 39
Looe 52
Lossiemouth 365
Lostwithiel 53
Loudwater 34
Loughborough 167
Loughrea 453
Loughton 93
LOUTH 463
Louth 173
Lower Beeding 261
Lower Brailes 267
Lower Edmonton 180
Lower Stondon 22
Lowestoft 235
Lucan 449
Ludlow 216
Lundin Links 353
Lurgan 424
Luton 23
Lutterworth 167
Lybster 360
Lydd 149
Lydney 100
Lyme Regis 81
Lymm 45
Lyndhurst 128
Lytchett Matravers 81
Lytham St Annes 160

M

Macclesfield 45
Macduff 323
Machrie 389
Machrihanish 329
Machynlleth 415
Macroom 441
Maesteg 394
Maesycwmmer 395
Magheralin 430
Maidenhead 26
Maidstone 149
Malahide 450
Maldon 94
Mallow 441
Malton 294
Malvern Wells 287
Manchester 117
Mannings Heath 261
Mansfield 206
March 39
Margam 410
Market Drayton 216
Market Harborough 167
Market Rasen 174
Markinch 353
Marlborough 28
Marlow 36
Marsden 31
Maryport 6
Masham 29
Matfen 20
Matlock 6
Mattishall 19
Mauchline 34
Mawgan Porth 5
Mawnan Smith 5
Maybole 38
Maynooth 45
MAYO 46
Maze 42
MEATH 46
Meldreth 3
Mellor 11
Melrose 37

Meltham 310
Melton Mowbray 168
Mentmore 36
Meriden 273
MERSEYSIDE 183
MERTHYR TYDFIL 407
Merthyr Tydfil 407
Mickleover 67
Middlesbrough 294
Middleton 118
Middleton 194
Middleton St George 86
Midhurst 261
Midleton 441
MIDLOTHIAN 363
Midsomer Norton 223
Mildenhall 235
Milford Haven 414
Mill Hill 181
Millbrook 23
Milltown Malbay 436
Milnathort 373
Milngavie 343
Milnrow 119
Milton Common 212
Milton Keynes 36
Minchinhampton 100
Minehead 223
Mintlaw 323
Minto 378
Mirfield 311
Mitcham 108
Mitchelstown 441
Moate 473
Moffat 339
Mold 403
MONAGHAN 468
Monaghan 468
Monard 471
Monifieth 326
Monkstown 442
Monmouth 410
MONMOUTHSHIRE 407
Monreith 339
Montrose 327
MORAY 363
Morecambe 162
Moretonhampstead 72
Morfa Nefyn 407
Morley 311
Morley 67
Morpeth 204
Mortehoe 73
Mortimer 26
Motherwell 368
Mountain Ash 416
Mountbellew 453
Mountrath 460
Moville 443
La Moye, Jersey 315
Much Hadham 138
Muckhart 336
Muir Of Ord 360
Muirhead 369
MULL, ISLE OF 390
Mullingar 474
Mullion 54
Mundesley 194
Musselburgh 346
Muthill 373

N

Naas 460
Nairn 360
Nantwich 45
Nantyglo 393
Narin (Naran) 444
Naunton 100
Navan 467
Neath 411
NEATH PORT TALBOT 410
Nelson 395
Nelson 163
Nenagh 471
Nethy Bridge 361
New Alresford 129
Newark-on-Trent 206
New Ash Green 150
Newbiggin-by-the-Sea 204
Newburgh 323
Newbury 26
Newcastle 430
Newcastleton 378
Newcastle upon Tyne 264
Newcastle-under-Lyme 228
Newcastle West 463
New Cumnock 341
Newdigate 245
New Galloway 339
Newhaven 255
Newmachar 323
New Malden 109
Newmarket 235
Newmarket-on-Fergus 437
New Mills 67
New Milton 129
NEWPORT 412
Newport (Newport) 412
Newport (Isle of Wight) 279
Newport (Shropshire) 217
Newport (Pembrokeshire) 414
Newquay 54
New Ross 474
Newry 430
Newton 235
Newton Abbot 73
Newton Aycliffe 86
Newton-le-Willows 188
Newton Mearns 348
Newton Stewart 339
Newtonmore 361
Newtown 415
Newtownabbey 424
Newtownards 430
Newtownbreda 427
Newtownstewart 434
NORFOLK 191
Normanby 174
Northallerton 295
Northampton 198
NORTHAMPTONSHIRE 197
NORTH AYRSHIRE 365
North Berwick 346
NORTH LANARKSHIRE 367
Northop 403
NORTHUMBERLAND 201
Northwood 109
Norwich 194
Nottingham 206
NOTTINGHAMSHIRE 205
Nuffield 213
Nuneaton 268

O

Oadby 168
Oakdale 395
Oban 329
Ockley 245
OFFALY 468
Ogbourne St George 282
Okehampton 73
Oldham 119
Oldmeldrum 323
Ollerton 207
Omagh 434
Onchan 316
Onneley 229
Oranmore 453
ORKNEY 391
Ormskirk 163
Orpington 109
Orsett 94
Oscroft 46
Ossett 311
Oswestry 217
Otley 311
Ottershaw 245
Oughterard 454
Oundle 200
Outlane 311
Ovens 442
Overton 129
Ower 129
Oxford 213
OXFORDSHIRE 210
Oxton 208

P

Padstow 54
Painswick 100
Paisley 376
Pannal 295
Pant 217
Pantymwyn 403
Parknasilla 457
Patna 341
Pattingham 229
Pavenham 23
Peebles 379
Peel 316
Pembroke Dock 414
PEMBROKESHIRE 412
Penarth 420
Pencoed 394
Penicuik 363
Penkridge 229
Penmaenmawr 401
Penrhys 416
Penrith 62
Perranporth 54
Perth 373
PERTH & KINROSS 369
Perton 229
Peterborough 39

Peterculter 320
Peterhead 324
Petersfield 129
Pidley 40
Pinner 110
Pirbright 246
Pitlochry 374
Pleasington 163
Plymouth 73
Pocklington 291
Polmont 349
Pontardawe 411
Pontefract 311
Ponteland 204
Pontlliw 417
Pontypool 419
Pontypridd 416
Poole 81
Portadown 426
Portarlington 462
Portballintrae 424
Port Bannatyne 390
Port Ellen 390
Port Erin 317
Port Glasgow 362
Porthcawl 394
Porthmadog 407
Portlaoise 462
Portlethen 324
Portmarnock 450
Portpatrick 339
Portrush 424
Port St Mary 317
Portsalon 444
Portsmouth 130
Portstewart 434
Port Talbot 411
Portumna 454
Portwrinkle 55
Potters Bar 139
Poulton-le-Fylde 163
POWYS 414
Poynton 46
Praa Sands 55
Prestatyn 401
Prestbury 46
Preston 164
Prestonpans 347
Prestwich 119
Prestwick 380
Princes Risborough 36
Prudhoe 204
Pudsey 312
Pulborough 261
Purleigh 94
Purley 110
Putney 182
Puttenham 246
Pwllheli 407
Pyecombe 262
Pyle 394

R

Radcliffe on Trent 208
Radlett 139
Raglan 410
Rainhill 188
Ramsey (Cambridgeshire) 40
Ramsey (Isle of Man) 317
Ramsgate 150
Rathcoole 450
Rathdowney 462
Rathdrum 479
Rathmullan 444
Ratho 334
Ravenscar 295
Rawmarsh 300
Raydon 235
Reading 27
Reay 361
Redbourn 139
Redcar 295
Redditch 287
Redhill 246
Reigate 246
Renfrew 376
RENFREWSHIRE 375
Renishaw 67
Renvyle 454
Retford 208
RHONDDA CYNON TAFF 416
Rhos 398
Rhosneigr 393
Rhuddlan 402
Rhyl 402
Richmond (North Yorkshire) 295
Richmond (Greater London) 110
Rickmansworth 139
Riddlesden 312
Rigside 384
Ripon 296
Rishton 164
Risley 67
Rochdale 119
Rochester 150
Rochford 94
Rock 55
Romford 110
Romiley 120
Romsey 130
ROSCOMMON 469
Roscommon 470
Roscrea 471
Rosepenna (Machair Loiscthe) 444
Ross-on-Wye 134
Rosslare 474
Rothbury 204
Rotherham 301
Rotherwick 130
Rothes 365
Rothesay 390
Rothley 168
Roundwood 479
Rowland's Castle 130
Royston 139
Ruabon 420
Ruddington 208
Rugby 268
Rugeley 230
Ruislip 111
Runcorn 46
Rush 450
Ruthin 402
RUTLAND 215
Ryde 279
Rye 255
Ryton 264

S

Saffron Walden 94
Saggart 450
St Albans 140
St Andrews 354
St Asaph 402
St Austell 55
St Bees 62
St Boswells 379
St Clement 315
St David's 414
St Fillans 375
St Helens 188
St Ives (Cornwall) 56
St Ives (Cambridgeshire) 40
St Just (near Land's End) 56
St Mellion 56
St Minver 56
St Neots 40
St Ouen 315
St Peter Port 315
Sale 120
Saline 356
Salisbury 282
Saltash 56
Saltburn-by-the-Sea 296
Saltford 223
Sandbach 46
Sandiway 46
Sandown 279
Sandwich 152
Sandy 23
Sannox 389
Sanquhar 340
Saunton 75
Sawbridgeworth 142
Scalasaig 390
Scarborough 296
Scarcroft 312
Sconser 391
SCOTTISH BORDERS 376
Scraptoft 169
Scunthorpe 174
Seaford 256
Seagrave 169
Seaham 86
Seahouses 204
Seal 15
Seascale 6
Seaton Carew 8
Sedbergh 6
Sedgefield 8
Sedgley 27
Sedlescombe 25
Selby 29
Selkirk 37
Selsey 26
Serlby 20
Settle 29
Sevenoaks 15
Shannon Airport 43
Shedfield 13
Sheerness 15
Sheffield 30
Shefford 2

Shepperton 248
Sherborne 81
Sheringham 195
SHETLAND 391
Shevington 120
Shifnal 217
Shillelagh 479
Shipley 312
Shirland 67
Shoreham 153
Shotts 369
Shrewsbury 217
Shrivenham 214
SHROPSHIRE 216
Sidcup 111
Sidmouth 75
Silecroft 63
Silkstone 302
Silloth 63
Silsden 313
Silverdale 165
Sindlesham 27
Sittingbourne 153
Six Hills 169
Skegness 175
Skelmorlie 366
Skerries 450
Skibbereen 442
Skipton 297
SKYE, ISLE OF 391
Sleaford 175
SLIGO 470
Sligo 470
Slinfold 262
Snodland 153
Solihull 274
SOMERSET 219
Somerton 223
Sonning 28
Southall 111
Southampton 131
SOUTH AYRSHIRE 379
South Brent 75
South Cave 291
South Godstone 248
Southend 329
Southend-on-Sea 95
Southerness 340
Southgate (London) 180
Southgate (Swansea) 417
South Kyme 176
SOUTH LANARKSHIRE 382
South Ockendon 95
Southport 188
South Queensferry 334
South Shields 265
SOUTH UIST 391
Southwell 209
Southwick 131
Southwold 235
Sowerby 313
Spalding 176
Sparkwell 75
Spey Bay 365
Stafford 230
STAFFORDSHIRE 226
Stalybridge 120
Stamford 176
Standish 120
Stanford le Hope 95
Stanley 87
Stanmore 111
Stanstead Abbotts 142
Stanton by Dale 68
Stapleford Abbotts 95
Staverton 200
Stevenage 142
Stevenston 367
STIRLING 385
Stirling 386
Stock 95
Stockport 120
Stocksbridge 302
Stocksfield 205
Stockton-on-Tees 87
Stoke-on-Trent 230
Stoke Poges 37
Stoke Rochford 176
Stone 230
Stonehaven 324
Stoneleigh 268
Stornoway 390
Stourbridge 276
Stowe 37
Stowmarket 236
Strabane 434
Straffan 460
Stranraer 340
Stratford-upon-Avon 268
Strathaven 384
Strathpeffer 361
Strathtay 375
Streatley 28
Strokestown 470
Stromness 391
Sturminster Marshall 81
Stuston 236
SUFFOLK 231
Sunderland 265
Sunningdale 28
Surbiton 112
SURREY 238
SUSSEX, EAST 252
SUSSEX, WEST 258
Sutton Bridge 176
Sutton Coldfield 276
Sutton Green 248
Sutton in Ashfield 209
Sutton On Sea 178
Sutton Weaver 47
Swaffham 195
Swanage 82
SWANSEA 417
Swansea 417
Swarland 205
Swindon 282
Swinford 466
Swinton 121
Swords 452

T

Tadcaster 297
Tadley 131
Tadmarton 214
Tain 361
Talbot Green 416
Tallaght 452
Tamworth 231
Tandragee 426
Tandridge 248
Tanworth in Arden 270
Tarbert 329
Tarland 324
Tarporley 47
Taunton 224
Tavistock 75
Tayport 356
Tedburn St Mary 75
Teignmouth 76
Telford 218
Templemore 471
Tenbury Wells 288
Tenby 414
Tenterden 154
Termonfeckin 464
Tewkesbury 100
Thetford 196
Theydon Bois 95
Thirsk 297
Thomastown 460
Thornbury 102
Thorne 302
Thorney 41
Thornhill 340
Thornton 356
Thorpeness 236
Three Crosses 418
Thurles 471
Thurlestone 76
Thurso 362
Ticehurst 256
Tidworth 283
Tighnabruaich 329
Tilford 248
Tillicoultry 336
Tilsworth 23
TIPPERARY 470
Tipperary 472
Tiverton 76
Tobercurry 470
Tobermory 391
Todmorden 313
Toft 41
Tollard Royal 283
Tolleshunt Knights 96
Tonbridge 154
Toot Hill 96
TORFAEN 418
Torksey 178
Torphins 324
Torquay 76
Torrington (Great) 76
Tralee 457
Tramore 473
Tredegar 394
Trim 468
Troon 382
Truro 58
Tuam 454
Tullamore 469
Tullow 435
Tunbridge Wells (Royal) 154
Turnberry 382
Turriff 324

Twickenham 112
TYNE & WEAR 263
Tynemouth 265
TYRONE 434

U

Uckfield 256
Uddingston 385
Ullapool 362
Ullesthorpe 169
Ulverston 63
Unstone 68
Upavon 283
Uphall 388
Upholland 165
Uplawmoor 348
Upminster 112
Upper Killay 418
Uppermill 121
Upper Sapey 134
Urmston 122
Uttoxeter 231
Uxbridge 112

V

VALE OF GLAMORGAN 419
Ventnor 279
Verwood 82
Virginia 436
Virginia Water 248

W

Wadebridge 58
Wakefield 313
Waldringfield 236
Walkden 122
Wallasey 190
Wallingford 214
Wallsend 265
Walsall 277
Walton-on-Thames 249
Walton-on-the-Hill 249
Wandsworth 182
Ware 142
Wareham 82
Warminster 283
Warrenpoint 430
Warrington 47
Warwick 270
WARWICKSHIRE 266
Washington 265
WATERFORD 472
Waterford 473
Waterlooville 131
Waterstock 214
Waterville (An Coireán) 457
Watford 143
Watton 196
Wavendon 37
Wedmore 224
Wellingborough 200
Wellington 218
Wells 225
Welshpool 416
Welwyn Garden City 143
Wembley 113
Wenvoe 420
West Bromwich 277
West Byfleet 249
West Calder 388
West Chiltington 262
West Clandon 249
West Drayton 113
WEST DUNBARTONSHIRE 386
West End 249
Westerham 154
Westgate on Sea 155
Westhoughton 122
West Kilbride 367
West Kingsdown 155
West Linton 379
WEST LOTHIAN 387
West Malling 155
WESTMEATH 473
WEST MIDLANDS 271
Weston 231
Westonbirt 102
Weston Longville 196
Weston Turville 37
Weston-Super-Mare 225
Weston-under-Redcastle 219
Westport 466
West Runton 196
Westward Ho! 76
Wetherby 314
WEXFORD 474
Wexford 475
Wexham Street 37
Weybridge 249
Weymouth 82
Whalley 165
Whalsay, Island Of 391
Wheathampstead 143
Whetstone (London) 180
Whetstone (Leicestershire) 169
Whickham 265
Whiston 231
Whitburn 388
Whitby 297
Whitchurch 219
Whitefield 122
Whitehead 424
Whitford 404
Whiting Bay 389
Whitley Bay 266
Whitstable 155
Whittlebury 200
Whitworth 165
Wick (Gloucestershire) 102
Wick (Highland) 362
Wickham 132
WICKLOW 475
Wicklow 479
Widnes 48
Wigan 122
Wigtown 340
Wike 314
Wilmslow 48
Wilpshire 165
Wilson 169
WILTSHIRE 279
Wimbledon 182
Wimborne 82
Winchester 132
Winchmore Hill 180
Windermere 63
Wing 38
Winsford 49
Winwick 49
Wishaw (Warwickshire) 270
Wishaw (North Lanarkshire) 369
Witham 96
Withernsea 291
Witney 215
Woking 250
Wokingham 28
Woldingham 250
Wolverhampton 278
Woodbridge 236
Woodenbridge 479
Woodford Green 113
Wood Green 180
Woodhall Spa 178
Woodham Walter 96
Woodhouse Eaves 169
Woodthorpe 179
Wooler 205
Woolfardisworthy 77
Woolley 314
Woolwich (SE18) 182
Woolwich (SE28) 182
Wootton Bassett 283
Worcester 288
WORCESTERSHIRE 284
Worfield 219
Workington 63
Worksop 209
Worlington 238
Wormsley 134
Worsley 12
Worthing 26
Wortley 30
Wotton-under-edge 10
WREXHAM 42
Wrexham 42
Wyboston 2
Wythall 28

Y

Yelverton 7
Yeovil 22
York 29
YORKSHIRE, EAST RIDING OF 28
YORKSHIRE, NORTH 29
YORKSHIRE, SOUTH 29
YORKSHIRE, WEST 30
Youghal 44
Ystradgynlais 41

- Notes -

- Notes -

- Notes -

NEED A HANDICAP?
* Calculate your handicap online
* Track & store your scores
* Analyse your total game
onpar-golf.com

GOLF PRODUCTS